Official
WORLD SERIES RECORDS

1984 EDITION

Editor/World Series Records
CRAIG CARTER

President-Chief Executive Officer
RICHARD WATERS

Editor
DICK KAEGEL

Director of Books and Periodicals
RON SMITH

Published by

The Sporting News
1212 North Lindbergh Boulevard
P.O. Box 56 — St. Louis, MO 63166

Copyright © 1984
The Sporting News Publishing Company
a Times Mirror company

IMPORTANT NOTICE

The World Series Records is protected by copyright. All information, in the form presented here, except playing statistics, was compiled by the publishers and proof is available.
Information from the World Series Records must not be used elsewhere without special written permission, and then only with full credit to the World Series Records, published by THE SPORTING NEWS, St. Louis, Missouri.

ISBN 0-89204-173-0   ISSN 0078-3900

Table of Contents

1984 World Series	3-20
1903 Through 1983 World Series	21-304
Year-by-Year Results	305
Player Eligibles	306-321
Team Won-Lost Breakdown	323-325
World Series Standings	325
Tie Games	326
Shutout Games	326-327
.400 Hitters	327-378
Year-by-Year Batting Leaders	329-331
Extra-Inning Games	331
Year-by-Year Club Batting	332-334
Year-by-Year Club Fielding	334-336
Home Runs	336-339
Attendance	339
Individual Batting, Base Running Records	340-354
Club Batting, Base Running Records	354-372
Individual Fielding Records	372-387
Club Fielding Records	387-393
Individual Pitching Records	393-401
Club Pitching Records	401-402
General Records	402-409
Managers	409-410
Umpires	411-412

World Series MVP Alan Trammell gets a big welcome at home plate from Tiger teammate Kirk Gibson after hitting the first of his two home runs in a Game 4 victory over San Diego. Gibson followed Trammell's lead and blasted two homers in Detroit's Series-clinching victory the next day.

—Photo by J. B. Forbes

World Series 1984

The Year of the Tiger

By DAVE NIGHTINGALE
National Correspondent

Deacon Jones, the San Diego Padres' batting instructor, leaned against the side of the batting cage at San Diego Jack Murphy Stadium on October 9 and scratched the thinning follicles on his scalp.

"Can you believe it? Can you believe it?" he kept repeating before the opening game of the 81st World Series. "After what this team did in Chicago (two quick losses to open the National League Championship Series), can you believe that we're really here in the World Series?"

Somebody should have pinched the rest of the Padres, who appeared equally shell-shocked by their sudden conquest of the Cubs, because before they knew it, their postseason competition against the Detroit Tigers was over.

It was over, mercifully, in five games. That was one game more than many prognosticators had expected it would take the Tigers to dispense with the Padres. After a 35-5 start, 104 regular-season victories and a sweep of the Kansas City Royals in the American League playoffs, the Tigers had "Destiny's Darling" written all over them —especially since the National League's team of destiny, the Cubs, had bitten the dust.

It was bad enough that the Padres had to face what was, arguably, the best team baseball had seen in some time. But San Diego Manager Dick Williams also was forced to deal with a short deck. Kevin McReynolds, his talented center fielder, went down with a fractured wrist during the N.L. playoffs.

McReynolds' loss alone didn't cost San Diego the Series. But it did have a domino effect on the rest of the squad.

For instance, Williams had no legitimate replacements available when rookie left fielder Carmelo Martinez started sour (1 for 13 in the first four games) or when utility outfielder Bobby Brown, pressed into a starting center-field role, stayed sour (1 for 15).

Detroit's Jack Morris, the best starting pitcher in the 1984 World Series, leaves the mound after his opening-game victory over the Padres.

Even Detroit Manager Sparky Anderson, who became the first skipper in baseball history to win world titles in both leagues (he won two in Cincinnati), felt compassion for the losers.

No, make that pity.

"Look," Anderson said, "for starters, we have the best team in baseball, and that's all there is to it. For San Diego to have to face us at less than full strength, well, it just wasn't fair!"

In winning the best-of-seven Series with two games to spare, the Tigers boasted this stacked deck:

• The best starting pitcher—Jack Morris, who came up with a pair of complete-game performances and had two victories and a 2.00 earned-run average to show for it.

• The best everyday player—shortstop Alan Trammell, who played well in the field, had two hits in each of the first three games and had three hits, four runs batted in and two homers in the fourth game, all of which earned him Most Valuable Player honors. And he did all this despite a right shoulder and a left knee in need of surgery.

• The best one-game performance—by Kirk Gibson, who drove in five runs with a pair of homers in the final contest and scored the actual go-ahead run on a sacrifice fly to an infielder. He also led all Series basestealers with three.

Beyond that, don't forget the offensive and defensive contributions of second baseman Lou Whitaker; the rifle arm and occasional power of catcher Lance Parrish; the clutch hitting of Larry Herndon; the wondrous glove of center fielder Chet Lemon, and the ever-consistent relief work of "Senor Smoke" and "Senor Save"—Aurelio Lopez and Willie Hernandez, respectively.

Considering the season-long track records of the aforementioned, none of their efforts in the Series could have been termed "unexpected."

So, in attempting to counter such derring-do, the Padres knew they had little margin for error. In poker parlance, they had to draw at least three "wild cards" in order to come up with four of a kind (as in victories).

Preferably, these three wild cards:

• Consistent on-base efforts from both Alan Wiggins and major league batting champion Tony Gwynn, the No. 1 and No. 2 hitters in the order.

• Exceptional RBI production from Steve Garvey, Graig Nettles and Terry Kennedy, the heart of the batting order.

• Reasonably strong showings from their four listed starting pitchers.

Sorry to say, there wasn't a joker in the bunch.

Wiggins performed admirably, hitting .364 in the five games, but Gwynn's bat was silent (1 for 9) in the last two games, when it was needed most.

The Garvey-Nettles-Kennedy troika drove home an average of only 1.4 runs per game and combined for only a .216 batting average (11 for 51).

The San Diego starting pitchers—Mark Thurmond (twice), Ed Whitson, Tim Lollar and Eric Show—probably would have preferred to remain anonymous, considering their performances. Pseudonyms such as Groucho, Zeppo, Harpo and Chico were quite appropriate.

The starters lasted a total of 10⅓ innings over five games. They gave up 25 hits, 16 earned runs and eight walks and had a combined ERA of 13.94. Only one of them (Thurmond, Game 1) lasted as long as five innings. Show (Game 4) failed to finish the third inning. Lollar (Game 3) couldn't make it through the second. Whitson (Game 2) was shelled out in the first, throwing just 17 pitches to seven batters. But even that effort was better than Thurmond's in Game 5. The second time around against the Tigers, Thurmond faced only six batters, and he, too, didn't survive the opening stanza.

Considering these major shortcomings, it was a tribute to the Padres that their four losses came by only one, two, three and four runs.

It could have been worse. Far worse.

It should have been worse. Far worse.

And it would have been worse, except for these three reasons:

• The San Diego relievers were absolutely magnificent. Andy Hawkins, Craig Lefferts, Dave Dravecky and Greg Harris allowed only one run and 12 hits in 28 innings of relief. As a result, the Tigers actually wound up with four fewer hits than the Padres, 40 to 44, and with a lower team batting average, .253 to .265. (The Tigers batted .455 against the Padres' starters.) Only Goose Gossage, San Diego's Mr. Bullpen, was something of a disappointment with a 13.50 ERA. (In fairness to the Goose, he wasn't all that bad: Three of the four runs scored against him came on one errant pitch to Gibson in Game 5.)

• The designated hitter rule was in effect. On offense, it permitted Williams to use Kurt Bevacqua (.412 average and four RBIs in the Series) instead of a non-hitting pitcher. Dirty Kurt easily bettered his four Detroit peers (Barbaro Garbey, John Grubb, Rusty Kuntz and Howard Johnson), who managed a composite .059 average (1 for 17) with one RBI. On defense, the DH meant that Williams didn't have to think twice about yanking his woebegone starters before they dug themselves even deeper holes than their daily six-foot pits.

• The Tigers spent nearly the entire Series searching for their "killer instinct," as Anderson called it. "The guys on the bench knew we didn't have it—not until the last game anyway," the manager said. "I really

The pivotal play in Game 1 occurred in the seventh inning when San Diego's Kurt Bevacqua was cut down at third while trying to stretch a double into a triple.

wanted us to cut loose, for one game anyway, so that we could show people around the country just how good this team really is. The only time we came close, the only time that maybe we looked like the 'real' Detroit Tigers, was in the last game."

The "imitation" Detroit Tigers did just fine, Sparky.

GAME ONE

Site: San Diego Jack Murphy Stadium, San Diego.
Date: October 9.
Score: Tigers 3, Padres 2.
Heroes: Jack Morris, Lou Whitaker, Larry Herndon.

Prior to postseason play, much ado had been made about the quintessential San Diego baseball fan. Was he (or she), indeed, nothing more than a wimp? A wine-sipper? A quiche-eater? A front-runner? All of the above?

During the previous week's National League Championship Series, though, the Padres' faithful had proved one thing: They at least were a *loud* bunch of quiche-eating, wine-sipping, front-running wimps.

They were so loud, in fact, during the Padres' three straight playoff victories over the Chicago Cubs that Manager Dick Williams and first baseman Steve Garvey, among others, were quick to honor the San Diego fans with the ultimate accolade: the collective title of "10th man" for the Padres.

To hear Detroit second baseman Lou Whitaker tell it, though, Padre followers—inadvertently—were the 10th man for the Tigers in Game 1 of the World Series.

"I couldn't have made that play without them, and I want to thank them for their help," said Whitaker, referring to his seventh-inning relay that cut off a San Diego threat and enabled starting pitcher Jack Morris and the Tigers to post a 3-2 victory.

Morris, who became the first man ever to pitch a complete World Series game for

When Padres starter Ed Whitson was knocked out early by the Tigers in Game 2, Andy Hawkins (above) came on to shut the door.

Manager Sparky Anderson, was clinging to that same 3-2 lead in the top of the seventh when he faced leadoff man Kurt Bevacqua, the Padres' designated hitter.

Bevacqua laced into an outside fastball and sent it screaming into the right-field corner for extra bases. Kirk Gibson ran down the ball in the bullpen and fired to Whitaker, the middle man, who was standing in short right field. Bevacqua, meanwhile, rambled around second, stumbled briefly, then continued toward third.

"I wasn't sure whether or not he was going for a triple because I had my back to the play," the second baseman said.

If Whitaker had been forced to turn and look for the runner, Bevacqua might have made it to third—with none out. "But then I heard the crowd roar, and I knew he was going for it," Whitaker said. "So I didn't hesitate; I just took Kirk's relay and turned and threw."

Whitaker's relay beat the runner to the bag, and Bevacqua didn't help matters by attempting his head-first slide prematurely. Bevacqua, in fact, never did reach third as Marty Castillo slapped the tag on his back.

One of baseball's oldest rules is that you don't make the first out of an inning at either third base or home plate. Bevacqua violated it. "How did I feel? I felt as helpless as the people on the Titanic," he said.

Said Williams: "I know Kurt broke a rule, but he does make it to third if he doesn't stumble."

That play wasn't the only break Detroit got on defense.

The Tigers had taken a quick 1-0 first-inning lead on a double by Whitaker and Alan Trammell's single. But in the bottom half of the inning, Terry Kennedy doubled to score Garvey and Graig Nettles, both of whom had singled. Nursing a 2-1 lead, the Padres then threatened to blow the game wide open in the third when Alan Wiggins (infield single) and Tony Gwynn (walk) reached second and first, respectively, with nobody out.

That brought to the plate the ever-dangerous Garvey, hero of the National League playoffs. Both runners were on the move as Morris delivered the 2-0 pitch. Wiggins clearly had third base stolen, but Garvey tried to punch the ball through the right-side hole left by Whitaker, who was moving to cover second. Instead, he hit it up the middle and right to Whitaker, who was in perfect position to turn a double play and blunt the threat.

"They could have taken us out of the game right there," Anderson said.

Larry Herndon, the silent one—he had stopped talking to the media after Anderson made him a platoon player—gave Detroit a 3-2 lead in the fifth when he followed Lance Parrish's two-out double with a sharp opposite-field home run off San Diego starter Mark Thurmond. But San Diego was back to challenge Morris again when Nettles and Kennedy opened the sixth inning with back-to-back singles. Unfortunately for the Padres, though, it was the last time in the inning they were able to lay a bat on the big righthander.

Bobby Brown faked a bunt and took the pitch for ball one. He swung at the second pitch and fouled it off. He squared to bunt again—and missed.

At this point, Morris, who had been known to coast when his team was leading, took the bull by the horns and blazed a third strike past not only Brown but also Carmelo Martinez and Garry Templeton. Inning over, threat removed.

"When Brown didn't get the bunt down, that was the turning point to me," Whitaker said.

Williams agreed. "Morris was practically

San Diego's Kurt Bevacqua, the goat in Game 1, got his revenge in Game 2 by hitting a three-run, game-winning homer.

unhittable after that," he said.

Morris, who finished with nine strikeouts, said he didn't know whether he started throwing the ball any harder in the San Diego sixth, but he conceded, "I did put more effort into my pitching at that point."

Anderson, the winning manager for a 12th straight time in postseason play (eight at Cincinnati in 1975 and '76, plus three over Kansas City in the 1984 American League playoffs), saluted that extra effort.

"I was ready to hook Morris in the sixth," said Anderson, the original Captain Hook. "If he had put one more man on base that inning, he'd have been gone—and we'd have lost the game."

GAME TWO

Site: San Diego Jack Murphy Stadium, San Diego.
Date: October 10.
Score: Padres 5, Tigers 3.
Heroes: Kurt Bevacqua, Andy Hawkins, Craig Lefferts.

One of the beauties of baseball, as opposed to, say, football, is the scheduling.

If you blow it in football, you have to hang your head and wear your hair shirt and your goat horns for a full week—until someone else inherits them.

In baseball, though, redemption can be almost instantaneous. You can go from the outhouse to the penthouse in less time than it takes for the sun to rise the next morning, set in the evening and rise again.

Just ask San Diego's Kurt Bevacqua.

Bevacqua, though, is the kind of guy you might tend to associate more with one of the heavens' lunar bodies than with Old Sol.

This is a guy who once caught five baseballs that were dropped, at 110 mph, from the 325-foot Imperial Tower Building in San Diego as part of a charity stunt. This is a guy who, in his own words, "will do anything to get my name in the paper."

So, under a full San Diego moon, Bevacqua hit the three-run homer that beat Detroit, 5-3, in Game 2 and put the Padres back into Series contention.

And as 57,911 fans and a national television audience looked on, the man they call Dirty Kurt did a 360-degree midair pirouette before reaching first base, clapped his hands and then raised his fist into the air on his way to second base and blew a kiss to his wife in the stands as he headed for a high-five reception at home plate.

Funny how quickly those delirious fans forgot about Bevacqua's baserunning gaffe of a day earlier. (San Diego Manager Dick Williams had an even shorter memory. Instead of chastising his 37-year-old journeyman for his Game 1 blunder, he moved Bevacqua from the No. 9 slot to the No. 6 spot in the Padre batting order for Game 2.)

One journalist with a master's degree in cliches asked Bevacqua after the game if Kurt knew the ball was gone as soon as he hit it.

"Hey, I only hit one other homer this year," said Bevacqua, who had hit only 23 major league homers entering 1984. "How the hell could I tell?"

Another journalist with a master's degree in psyche-probing asked Bevacqua if the homer was a "blow for the little man" or a "message" to all marginally talented athletes that perseverance conquers adversity.

"All I know," said Bevacqua, his dark eyes flashing, "is that I had three hits in a World Series game. The bottom line, and nothing else, is that I had one helluva night."

So, too, did San Diego's Andy Hawkins, a blond, soft-spoken, mainly anonymous, 24-year-old relief pitcher from Bruceville, Tex., population 5,000. ("It's 5,000, that is, if you count the pigs, the cows and the dogs," Hawkins said.)

The righthanded reliever, who said a visit to the spotlight is kind of awkward because "it usually means one of our starters is having a rough time," faced only 16 men in $5\frac{1}{3}$ innings out of the bullpen to become the pitching beneficiary of Bevacqua's homer.

San Diego starter Ed Whitson was long gone by that time.

Whitson did retire two men with the 17 pitches he was allowed to throw, but he gave up hits to the five other Tigers he faced. He was behind 1-0 after three pitches, which were drilled for consecutive singles by Lou Whitaker, Alan Trammell and Kirk Gibson. And he was behind 3-0 after 11 pitches because of Lance Parrish's sacrifice fly and Darrell Evans' run-scoring single. Designated hitter John Grubb also singled off Whitson.

But then Hawkins, despite having pitched $2\frac{2}{3}$ innings the night before, ventured forth to slam the door on the Tigers.

Hawkins attributed his success to a correction in his pitching delivery, a correction he had had plenty of time to make as a member of the Padre bullpen corps after being demoted from the team's starting rotation earlier in the season.

"I cut down my motion on the backswing," he explained, "and this helped me start throwing lower strikes, and it helped me get my breaking ball over the plate. The rap against me in the past, I guess, was that I was afraid to challenge hitters, that I wasn't aggressive enough, that I'd pitch for the corners. Well, I want to say that I wasn't afraid to throw strikes earlier this year. It was just that I was so erratic, I couldn't throw strikes."

With the Tiger offense spinning in neutral—Detroit managed only two more hits over the last $8\frac{1}{3}$ innings—the Padres crept

The Tigers continued their early scoring rampage in Game 3 with four second-inning runs. Lou Whitaker (above) scored one on Alan Trammell's double.

back into contention. They scored a run in the bottom of the first on a sacrifice fly by Graig Nettles and another in the fourth when Bevacqua and Garry Templeton singled and Bobby Brown grounded into a forceout, scoring Bevacqua.

Trailing 3-2, the Padres caught a huge break when Terry Kennedy's low line drive took an explosive hop into second baseman Lou Whitaker's chest in the fifth. Instead of becoming an inning-ending double play, Kennedy's hit gave the Padres two baserunners—and the table was set for Bevacqua's game-winning homer.

Hawkins gave up only one hit in his stint, a bloop single by Gibson (who later was erased in a double play) that left fielder Carmelo Martinez should have caught. He was relieved in the seventh by Craig Lefferts, a lefthanded screwballer who struck out half of the 10 batters he faced in the last three innings.

Observers of the previous week's National League Championship Series couldn't help but notice the similarities between this contest and Game 5 of the playoffs—when the Chicago Cubs took a quick 3-0 lead, only to be stopped cold by the San Diego bullpen; when a hard grounder by the Padres' Tony Gwynn took a bad hop on Cubs second baseman Ryne Sandberg and went from a seeming double-play ball to a two-run double.

"I never saw middle relief carry a team like this in postseason play," Williams gushed. "Our bullpen has been positively brilliant."

GAME THREE

Site: Tiger Stadium, Detroit.
Date: October 12.
Score: Tigers 5, Padres 2.
Heroes: Marty Castillo, Chet Lemon, Milt Wilcox.

Twenty-four autumns ago, when he was all of 3 years old, Marty Castillo had been a bad boy, so his parents punished him by telling him to go into his father's closet and not come out until they gave him permission.

Permission was soon granted.

Marty, you see, was carrying this cigarette lighter in his pocket. (Doesn't every 3-year-old carry a cigarette lighter?) And he brought a little light into the closet darkness by torching his father's clothes.

"When I was that age, I wanted to be a fireman," Castillo recalled. "I guess I figured that if I started a fire, I would get to see some fire trucks."

He saw plenty of them: Casa Castillo burned to the ground.

In Game 3 of the World Series, the San Diego Padres were wishing that Castillo, now a sometimes third baseman, sometimes catcher for the Detroit Tigers, had chosen to follow his boyhood dreams.

Maybe he had, in a manner of speaking. The third baseman extinguished a potential San Diego threat with a fine defensive play in the fourth inning, knocking down a hard-hit grounder and crawling to the base ahead of the sliding Kurt Bevacqua for a key forceout. But 1½ innings earlier, Cas-

The big blow for the Tigers in Game 3 was Marty Castillo's two-run second-inning homer.

tillo had reverted to the arsonous tendencies of his youth by igniting, however briefly, a Detroit offense that had long been simmering but was yet to explode. Castillo scorched the Padres with a two-run, upper-deck home run, only the seventh homer of his major league playing days, to start the Tigers down the path to a 5-2 victory.

The contest was scoreless in the bottom of the second with two outs and Chet Lemon on base when San Diego starter Tim Lollar sailed a 1-2 fastball (it was supposed to be a waste pitch) across the letters to Castillo, the No. 9 hitter in the Detroit batting order.

"That was the kind of pitch that a hitter is supposed to hit out of the park," Castillo said. "Even me."

Lollar was so unnerved by Castillo's blast that he then issued a walk to Lou Whitaker, a run-scoring double to Alan Trammell, a walk to Kirk Gibson and an infield hit to Lance Parrish. And with that, the San Diego starting (and losing) pitcher went the way of all of his Padre peers—to an early shower. The fourth and final run of the inning came on Greg Booker's bases-loaded walk to Larry Herndon.

"Castillo's homer hurt; anytime the Number 9 hitter gets a homer it hurts," San Diego Manager Dick Williams said. "But Trammell's hit was the killer. If we get out of the inning after giving up only two runs, we're still in the game."

Whatever that "game" might have been. It sure didn't look much like baseball.

The Tigers managed only one run and three hits against the Padres' bullpen over the last six innings. But it's kind of hard to get hits when you don't see any strikes. Few were thrown.

In all, San Diego pitchers walked 11 Detroit batters (matching a World Series record) and hit another. After Booker was pulled for loading the bases on three walks in the third, Gibson took a slider from reliever Greg Harris on his toe to force home the final Tiger run.

The plethora of free transportation and the dearth of Detroit hitting led to the Tigers stranding 14 runners, which equaled another Series record. And the 24-man left-on-base total for both clubs in the contest equaled nothing; it *was* an outright post-season futility mark.

"The game wasn't very pretty," Williams conceded in a burst of understatement.

The chief benefactor of the Padres' ineptness was Detroit starter Milt Wilcox, who scattered seven hits in six innings to earn the victory. He allowed just one run, that coming on hits by Alan Wiggins and Tony Gwynn and an infield grounder by Steve Garvey in the third. Still, Wilcox had to be one of the most "invisible" heroes in Series annals. He emerged from the dugout for only about three minutes out of every 30 because the San Diego pitchers were taking forever to complete their appointed rounds.

The length of the tedious contest—3 hours, 11 minutes—had a numbing effect on the brains of fans and participants alike. For instance, Detroit Manager Sparky Anderson kept insisting that the Padres, on a couple of occasions, were "only one hit away" from tying the score when, in fact, the potential tying run for San Diego never got any closer than the on-deck circle after the Tigers had moved ahead, 5-1.

Only one play, in the seventh inning, saved the fans from having to set alarm clocks to know when the game was over. That play was a real firecracker.

San Diego scored its second (and last) run in the seventh against Tigers reliever Bill Scherrer when, with one out, Gwynn beat out an infield grounder, took third on Garvey's double to left and scored on Graig Nettles' warning-track sacrifice fly. Anderson then summoned lefthander Willie Hernandez to face Padres slugger Terry Kennedy.

Game 4 hero Alan Trammell watches the flight of his first-inning home run, the first of two he hit in the game.

Kennedy promptly drilled a ball toward the deepest recesses of center field. Lemon was off at the crack of the bat, head down. "All I could consider was the general direction of the ball, and I tried to go that way," Lemon said. He finally stopped and looked up—to his right. The ball, finally returning from orbit about 20 feet short of the "440" painted on the outfield fence, was coming down—to his left. But it was within range, and Lemon hauled it in for the third out.

Visions of Willie Mays and Vic Wertz began dancing in the heads of Series observers.

"Aw, it was a routine catch," Anderson said. "It didn't excite me that much. I've seen Chet make a lot of those. I've seen him do better."

Said Lemon: "I don't want to sound like I'm patting myself on the back, but if he thought it was 'routine,' I sure didn't."

GAME FOUR

Site: Tiger Stadium, Detroit.
Date: October 13.
Score: Tigers 4, Padres 2.
Heroes: Alan Trammell, Jack Morris.

After three tries in 1984, San Diego pitcher Eric Show knew one thing: He was yet to find, in postseason play, a major league ball park that could contain his mistakes.

Not Wrigley Field. In Game 1 of the National League Championship Series in Chicago, Show gave up three home runs in four innings of work as the Padres lost, 13-0.

Not San Diego Jack Murphy Stadium. In Game 5 of the N.L. playoffs, Show surrendered two more homers but was replaced before the game got too far out of hand, and the Padres came back to win the deciding game, 6-3.

Not Tiger Stadium. In Game 4 of the World Series, Show offered two gopher balls to Detroit shortstop Alan Trammell, who connected in the first and third innings for two-run homers and provided the Tigers with all the offense they needed to win, 4-2.

The question was why. Why couldn't Show keep the baseball inside the fences? He did, for the most part, during the regular season; only 18 times in 206⅔ innings were batters facing Show treated to home run trots. But in just eight innings of postseason competition, the beleaguered right-hander served up seven homers and 11 earned runs, giving him an earned-run average of 12.38, compared with his regular-season ERA of 3.40.

San Diego Manager Dick Williams couldn't understand it. "Eric was a steady pitcher all year.... Frankly, what has happened to him in postseason play is baffling to me," he said.

The last person who was baffled in Tiger Stadium that day was Trammell. After collecting two hits in each of the first three games of the Series, Trammell added a single to his two home run shots and raised his Series batting average to .563 (9 for 16) and his runs-batted-in total to six. His performance in Game 4 was the icing on the cake as he wrapped up World Series Most Valuable Player honors.

Considering the strain Trammell was under, his exploits were all the more incredible.

Trammell, to use the hackneyed professional parlance, had "played hurt" all year for the Tigers. He was hobbled by torn ligaments in his left knee, an injury that occurred when he took a head-over-high-heels tumble while portraying Frankenstein's monster at a 1983 Halloween party. He also was suffering from a sore right shoulder, which he treated all season long with more ice than a Waldorf Astoria chef would use in a career's worth of shrimp cocktails.

"I've been with him in the locker room; I know all about his leg and his shoulder," teammate Kirk Gibson said. "He is pure guts and competitive ability."

The night before Game 4, Trammell was told by doctors that the knee, and possibly the shoulder, would require surgery as soon after the Series as possible. (He later underwent both operations.) It was not a message that generally would ease one's peace of mind.

Then, on the morning of Game 4, the shortstop arrived at Tiger Stadium with the keys to the family van in his pocket. His wife, Barbara, was soon to call the Tigers' clubhouse and ask her husband just how he thought she could drive a house full of relatives to the game when he had the car keys. Again, it was not a message that would relax a person's nerves. "Barbara was mad as hell," he noted.

But in the bottom of the first inning, with Lou Whitaker on base because of Alan Wiggins' error, Trammell drilled a fastball into the left-field lower deck for a 2-0 Tiger lead. Terry Kennedy halved the Padres' deficit with a solo homer in the top of the second, but in the third, Whitaker singled and went to second when outfielder Tony Gwynn misplayed the ball for an error, and Trammell then walloped a hanging slider from Show into the left-field upper deck for a 4-1 Detroit lead. That's the way it stood until the ninth when Morris uncorked a two-out, two-strike wild pitch with Kennedy at bat to allow Steve Garvey to score a harmless final run for San Diego.

"I was in a daze when I circled the bases after the second homer," Trammell said. "I didn't jump up and down because that's not me. I may agitate in the clubhouse, but I don't show up my opponents. That's not my

The Padres were denied in the first inning of Game 5 when Detroit catcher Lance Parrish lunged to tag out a sliding Alan Wiggins, who tried to score on an infield grounder.

style."

Trammell, who was 6 for 7 when Whitaker was on base ahead of him through Game 4, was quick to credit the Tigers' leadoff man for much of his success. "Our situation is just like with Wiggins and Gwynn on the Padres," he said. "Gwynn led the majors in hitting (.351 average), and I'd like to see his average for times at bat when Wiggins was on base ahead of him. I'll bet it was even higher."

After Show left for the showers with two outs in the third inning, Game 4 settled down to an even match: Morris vs. the San Diego bullpen. Padre relievers Dave Dravecky, Craig Lefferts and Goose Gossage held the Tigers to three hits and no runs while running the bullpen's Series mop-up numbers to one run and nine hits in 24 innings for a 0.38 ERA.

"I wish we had been able to get some more runs," Detroit Manager Sparky Anderson said. "But frankly, I wasn't all that worried. When Jack is in top form, as he was today, a couple of runs is all he needs."

Said Morris: "My forkball was working for me, so I felt pretty comfortable out there. Kennedy's homer in the second didn't bother me, but when Kurt (Bevacqua) got a good swing (for a double after Kennedy's blast), it kind of woke me up."

Morris faced only 26 batters—three over the minimum—after Bevacqua's double and used only 98 pitches to dispatch the Padres for his second straight complete-game Series victory.

Say good night, Jack.

GAME FIVE

Site: Tiger Stadium, Detroit.
Date: October 14.
Score: Tigers 8, Padres 4.
Heroes: Kirk Gibson, Aurelio Lopez.

This is the story of a head-to-head battle between two mighty foes—and not just the Detroit Tigers and the San Diego Padres.

It is the story of a World Series confrontation between two very strong-willed and highly talented athletes, one of whom, obviously, was destined to lose.

It is the story of Detroit's Kirk Gibson vs. San Diego's Goose Gossage—fastball hitter vs. fastball pitcher.

It is the story, in microcosm, of the entire 1984 Series.

San Diego relief ace Goose Gossage walks dejectedly from the mound after failing to hold the Tigers in Game 5.

Gibson, a former All-America football player at Michigan State University, once was hailed by his manager, Sparky Anderson, as "the next Mickey Mantle." The comparison nearly destroyed him mentally as he failed, under the pressure of high expectations, to produce stunning numbers. For almost four years, the only similarity between Gibson and Mantle was that they were injury-prone. But Gibson came of age in 1984, hitting .282 with 27 home runs, 91 runs batted in and 29 stolen bases during the regular season.

Gossage, a major leaguer at age 20, long has been considered baseball's premier power reliever. "If I get my fastball over the plate, the batter has some chance," he has often said. "But if I get Number 2 (the curveball) over when he's looking for heat, well, it's see ya later."

That Gibson and Gossage would clash in Game 5 was a foregone conclusion: San Diego starting pitchers in the first four games averaged only 7.5 outs per game before being handed the proverbial cake of soap.

That Gibson and Gossage would clash with Game 5 on the line was something that only the gods of the diamond could decide.

Gibson didn't look as if he was ready to clash with anyone entering Game 5. He was hitting a mediocre .214 in Series play thus far, and his pregame performance in the batting cage showed no indications of imminent improvement.

"I was terrible in batting practice," Gibson said. "But I went over to (coach) Alex Grammas and said, 'Greek, I guarantee you there's going to be some thunder in this bat tonight.'"

The thunder came faster than lightning.

In the first inning, Gibson cracked a two-run homer off San Diego starter Mark Thurmond for a 2-0 Detroit lead. After facing three more batters, all of whom singled, Thurmond was relieved by Andy Hawkins with Detroit ahead, 3-0.

The Padres battled back, scoring a run in the third inning on an RBI single by Steve Garvey and two more in the fourth (chasing Detroit starter Dan Petry) on a sacrifice fly by Bobby Brown and a run-scoring single by Alan Wiggins. The score remained tied, 3-3, until the Tigers regained the lead—for good—in the fifth, thanks to Gibson's legs.

Gibson led off with a single to left and took second on Lance Parrish's warning-track fly ball to left. When Larry Herndon walked, Craig Lefferts, the Padres' lefty screwballer, was summoned to replace Hawkins. And Lefferts promptly walked Chet Lemon to load the bases.

Pinch-hitter Rusty Kuntz then launched a high pop-up to short right field. Outfielder Tony Gwynn had plenty of time to make the catch and fire the ball to home plate, but he lost sight of the ball and second baseman Wiggins had to backpedal to make an over-the-shoulder catch. Despite the shallow depth of the pop-up, Gibson tagged up and raced home, beating Wiggins' off-balance throw, which reached the plate on seven bounces.

Armed with a 4-3 lead, Detroit reliever Aurelio (Senor Smoke) Lopez took charge, retiring all seven batters he faced (including one in the fifth inning) and fanning four of them. Lopez, the eventual winner, enjoyed some added protection when Parrish greeted Gossage with a bases-empty home run to give Detroit a 5-3 edge after seven innings.

But a homer by Kurt Bevacqua off the Tigers' Willie (Senor Save) Hernandez in the top of the eighth trimmed the lead to 5-4. The stage was set for the final Gibson-Gossage confrontation.

Marty Castillo drew a walk from Gossage to open the Detroit eighth and made it safely to second when shortstop Garry

Detroit's Kirk Gibson lets his emotions go after hitting his second home run of Game 5.

The celebration got into full swing after Detroit relief ace Willie Hernandez (right, hugging catcher Lance Parrish) recorded the final out of the 1984 World Series.

Templeton was standing off the bag as he took third baseman Graig Nettles' throw on Lou Whitaker's sacrifice bunt. Alan Trammell then moved both runners along with another bunt.

With Gibson coming to the plate, Gossage's next move appeared obvious: Walk Gibson intentionally, thus loading the bases and setting up a double-play situation for the next batter (Parrish).

It was obvious to Anderson, who held up four fingers to Gibson, indicating that free transportation was expected. "They're gonna put you on," the Detroit skipper shouted.

And it was obvious to San Diego Manager Dick Williams, who also held up four fingers, signalling Gossage to walk Gibson.

It was not obvious, however, to either Gibson or Gossage.

"I faced him (Gossage) in my first big-league time at bat (in September of 1979, when Gossage was pitching for the New York Yankees)," Gibson said. "I fouled off a couple of his pitches then, but he eventually struck me out. . . . I didn't expect to be walked (in this Game 5 situation)."

Gossage also remembered 1979. And he yelled toward the San Diego dugout. The words were lost in the Tiger Stadium din, but Padres pitching coach Norm Sherry didn't figure the Goose was flapping his lips for the fun of it. "I think he wants to talk to you, Dick," Sherry said to Williams. "I really don't think he wants to give Gibson a walk."

Williams trudged toward the mound and learned the truth of Sherry's words. He acquiesced. Even if you're a manager with the strongest of wills, how do you tell your best relief pitcher that he can't strike out a guy when the pitcher says he can?

Meanwhile, Gibson turned toward the Tigers' dugout and held up all 10 fingers for Anderson to see. "I bet him 10 bucks that Gossage would pitch to me—*and* that I would hit the ball out of the park," Gibson said.

Gossage's first pitch to Gibson was a fastball at the knees, a bit inside. The next pitch was right down the middle, and Gibson blasted it into the right-field upper deck to win his $10 bet.

"I challenged him and I lost," said Gossage, who was not charged with the loss (Hawkins was) despite giving up half of the Tigers' runs. "So, that makes me dog meat.

"Today, anyway."

Said Gibson: "When the chips are down, I want to be the guy they count on. The game was becoming a nail-biter—at least it was until I was able to put 'em away."

For 1984, anyway.

The box scores:

Tuesday, October 9—At San Diego

Detroit (A.L.)	AB.	R.	H.	O.	A.	E.
Whitaker, 2b	4	1	1	3	3	0
Trammell, ss	5	0	2	0	2	0
Gibson, rf	4	0	0	1	1	0
Parrish, c	3	1	2	9	1	0
Herndon, lf	3	1	2	1	0	0
Garbey, dh	4	0	0	0	0	0
Lemon, cf	4	0	1	2	0	0
Evans, 1b	3	0	0	4	1	0
cBergman, 1b	0	0	0	3	0	0
Castillo, 3b	2	0	0	1	0	0
bGrubb	0	0	0	0	0	0
dBrookens, 3b	1	0	0	0	2	0
Morris, p	0	0	0	3	0	0
Totals	33	3	8	27	10	0

San Diego (N.L.)	AB.	R.	H.	O.	A.	E.
Wiggins, 2b	4	0	1	1	2	0
Gwynn, rf	2	0	1	3	0	0
Garvey, 1b	4	1	1	9	2	0
Nettles, 3b	2	1	2	3	1	0
aSalazar, 3b	1	0	0	0	0	0
Kennedy, c	4	0	2	3	0	0
Brown, cf	4	0	0	3	0	0
Martinez, lf	4	0	0	3	0	1
Templeton, ss	4	0	0	2	2	0
Bevacqua, dh	3	0	1	0	0	0
Thurmond, p	0	0	0	0	2	0
Hawkins, p	0	0	0	0	1	0
Dravecky, p	0	0	0	0	0	0
Totals	32	2	8	27	10	1

Detroit .... 1 0 0   0 2 0   0 0 0—3
San Diego ...... 2 0 0   0 0 0   0 0 0—2

Detroit	IP.	H.	R.	ER.	BB.	SO.
Morris (W)	9	8	2	2	3	9

San Diego	IP.	H.	R.	ER.	BB.	SO.
Thurmond (L)	5	7	3	3	3	2
Hawkins	2⅔	1	0	0	3	0
Dravecky	1⅓	0	0	0	0	1

Bases on balls—Off Morris 3 (Gwynn 2, Nettles), off Thurmond 3 (Parrish, Castillo, Gibson), off Hawkins 3 (Whitaker, Herndon, Evans).

Strikeouts—By Morris 9 (Wiggins, Garvey, Kennedy, Brown 2, Martinez, 2, Templeton 2), by Thurmond 2 (Gibson, Garbey), by Dravecky 1 (Whitaker).

Game-winning RBI—Herndon.

aRan for Nettles in sixth. bAnnounced as pinch-hitter for Castillo in eighth. cRan for Evans in eighth. dFlied out for Grubb in eighth. Runs batted in—Trammell, Herndon 2, Kennedy 2. Two-base hits—Whitaker, Kennedy, Parrish, Bevacqua. Home run—Herndon. Stolen bases—Trammell, Gwynn. Caught stealing—Trammell, Gibson, Gwynn. Double plays—Whitaker and Evans; Garvey unassisted. Left on bases—Detroit 9, San Diego 6. Umpires—Harvey (N.L.) plate, Barnett (A.L.) first, Froemming (N.L.) second, Garcia (A.L.) third, Runge (N.L.) left, Reilly (A.L.) right. Time—3:18. Attendance—57,908.

Wednesday, October 10—At San Diego

Detroit (A.L.)	AB.	R.	H.	O.	A.	E.
Whitaker, 2b	4	1	1	2	1	0
Trammell, ss	4	1	2	3	2	1
Gibson, rf	4	1	2	1	0	2
Parrish, c	3	0	0	3	2	0
Evans, 3b-1b	4	0	1	4	1	0
Jones, lf	2	0	0	2	0	0
aHerndon, lf	2	0	0	0	0	0
Grubb, dh	2	0	1	0	0	0
bKuntz	1	0	0	0	0	0
Lemon, cf	3	0	0	5	0	0
Bergman, 1b	2	0	0	4	1	0
cBrookens, 3b	1	0	0	0	1	0
Petry, p	0	0	0	0	1	0
Lopez, p	0	0	0	0	0	0
Scherrer, p	0	0	0	0	1	0
Bair, p	0	0	0	0	0	0
Hernandez, p	0	0	0	0	0	0
Totals	32	3	7	24	10	3

San Diego (N.L.)	AB.	R.	H.	O.	A.	E.
Wiggins, 2b	5	1	3	2	1	0
Gwynn, rf	3	0	1	2	1	0
Garvey, 1b	3	0	0	7	0	0
Nettles, 3b	1	1	0	1	4	0
Kennedy, c	4	1	1	9	0	0
Bevacqua, dh	4	2	3	0	0	0
Martinez, lf	3	0	0	1	0	0
Templeton, ss	4	0	3	4	0	0
Brown, cf	3	0	0	0	0	0
Salazar, cf	1	0	0	1	0	0
Whitson, p	0	0	0	0	0	0
Hawkins, p	0	0	0	0	0	0
Lefferts, p	0	0	0	0	0	0
Totals	31	5	11	27	6	0

Detroit .... 3 0 0   0 0 0   0 0 0—3
San Diego ...... 1 0 0   1 3 0   0 0 *—5

Detroit	IP.	H.	R.	ER.	BB.	SO.
Petry (L)	4⅓	8	5	5	3	2
Lopez	⅔	1	0	0	1	0
Scherrer	1⅓	2	0	0	0	0
Bair	⅔	0	0	0	0	1
Hernandez	1	0	0	0	0	0

San Diego	IP.	H.	R.	ER.	BB.	SO.
Whitson	⅔	5	3	3	0	0
Hawkins (W)	5⅓	1	0	0	0	3
Lefferts (S)	3	1	0	0	0	5

Bases on balls—Off Petry 3 (Gwynn, Nettles 2), off Lopez 1 (Martinez).

Strikeouts—By Petry 2 (Brown, Martinez), by Bair 1 (Martinez), by Hawkins 3 (Trammell 2, Whitaker), by Lefferts 5 (Kuntz, Brookens, Gibson, Parrish, Evans).

Game-winning RBI—Bevacqua.

aFlied out for Jones in seventh. bStruck out for Grubb in seventh. cStruck out for Bergman in eighth. Runs batted in—Gibson, Parrish, Evans, Nettles, Bevacqua 3, Brown. Home run—Bevacqua. Stolen base—Gibson. Caught stealing—Wiggins, Gwynn, Bevacqua. Sacrifice hit—Garvey. Sacrifice flies—Parrish, Nettles. Balk—Petry. Double plays—Gwynn and Garvey; Parrish and Whitaker. Left on bases—Detroit 3, San Diego 8. Umpires—Barnett (A.L.) plate, Froemming (N.L.) first, Garcia (A.L.) second, Runge (N.L.) third, Reilly (A.L.) left, Harvey (N.L.) right. Time—2:44. Attendance—57,911.

Friday, October 12—At Detroit

San Diego (N.L.)	AB.	R.	H.	O.	A.	E.
Wiggins, 2b	5	1	2	4	1	0
Gwynn, rf	5	1	2	2	0	0
Garvey, 1b	5	0	1	7	0	0
Nettles, 3b	2	0	0	0	2	0
Kennedy, c	3	0	0	5	0	0
Bevacqua, dh	4	0	1	0	0	0
Martinez, lf	4	0	1	0	0	0
Templeton, ss	4	0	2	1	3	0
Brown, cf	3	0	0	5	0	0
aSalazar	1	0	1	0	0	0
Lollar, p	0	0	0	0	0	0
Booker, p	0	0	0	0	1	0
Harris, p	0	0	0	0	0	0
Totals	36	2	10	24	7	0

Detroit (A.L.)	AB.	R.	H.	O.	A.	E.
Whitaker, 2b	3	1	0	3	4	0
Trammell, ss	3	1	2	3	1	0
Gibson, rf	2	0	0	1	0	0
Parrish, c	3	0	1	6	0	0
Herndon, lf	4	0	1	1	0	0
Garbey, dh	5	0	0	0	0	0
Lemon, cf	5	1	2	4	0	0
Evans, 1b	2	1	0	3	1	0
Bergman, 1b	0	0	0	3	0	0
Castillo, 3b	4	1	1	2	2	0
Wilcox, p	0	0	0	1	1	0
Scherrer, p	0	0	0	0	0	0
Hernandez, p	0	0	0	0	0	0
Totals	31	5	7	27	9	0

San Diego .... 0 0 1 0 0 0 1 0 0—2
Detroit .... 0 4 1 0 0 0 0 0 *—5

San Diego	IP.	H.	R.	ER.	BB.	SO.
Lollar (L)	1⅔	4	4	4	4	0
Booker	1	0	1	1	4	0
Harris	5⅓	3	0	0	3	5

Detroit	IP.	H.	R.	ER.	BB.	SO.
Wilcox (W)	6	7	1	1	2	4
Scherrer	⅔	2	1	1	0	0
Hernandez (S)	2⅓	1	0	0	0	0

Bases on balls—Off Lollar 4 (Trammell, Parrish, Whitaker, Gibson), off Booker 4 (Herndon, Evans, Whitaker, Trammell), off Harris 3 (Evans, Gibson, Parrish), off Wilcox 2 (Nettles, Kennedy).

Strikeouts—By Harris 5 (Lemon, Whitaker 2, Garbey, Evans), by Wilcox 4 (Garvey, Martinez 2, Gwynn).

Game-winning RBI—Castillo.

aSingled for Brown in ninth. Runs batted in—Garvey, Nettles, Trammell, Gibson, Herndon, Castillo 2. Two-base hits—Wiggins, Trammell, Garvey. Home run—Castillo. Stolen base—Gibson. Sacrifice fly—Nettles. Hit by pitcher—By Harris (Gibson). Wild pitch—Lollar. Left on bases—San Diego 10, Detroit 14. Umpires—Froemming (N.L.) plate, Garcia (A.L.) first, Runge (N.L.) second, Reilly (A.L.) third, Harvey (N.L.) left, Barnett (A.L.) right. Time—3:11. Attendance—51,970.

Saturday, October 13—At Detroit

San Diego (N.L.)	AB.	R.	H.	O.	A.	E.
Wiggins, 2b	3	0	0	2	2	1
dSummers	1	0	0	0	0	0
Roenicke, lf	0	0	0	0	0	0
Gwynn, rf	4	0	1	1	0	1
Garvey, 1b	4	1	1	8	0	0
Nettles, 3b	4	0	0	1	4	0
Kennedy, c	4	1	1	8	1	0
Bevacqua, dh	3	0	1	0	0	0
Martinez, lf	2	0	0	1	0	0
cFlannery, 2b	1	0	1	1	0	0
Templeton, ss	3	0	0	0	3	0
Brown, cf	3	0	0	2	0	0
Show, p	0	0	0	0	0	0
Dravecky, p	0	0	0	0	0	0
Lefferts, p	0	0	0	0	0	0
Gossage, p	0	0	0	0	0	0
Totals	32	2	5	24	10	2

Detroit (A.L.)	AB.	R.	H.	O.	A.	E.
Whitaker, 2b	4	2	2	3	7	0
Trammell, ss	4	2	3	2	1	0
Gibson, rf	4	0	1	1	0	0
Parrish, c	4	0	0	4	0	0
Evans, 3b	2	0	0	1	1	0
Brookens, 3b	1	0	0	0	0	0
Grubb, dh	1	0	0	0	0	0
aGarbey, dh	2	0	0	0	0	0
Jones, lf	1	0	0	1	0	0
bHerndon, lf	2	0	1	0	0	0
Lemon, cf	2	0	0	2	0	0
Bergman, 1b	3	0	0	11	2	0
Morris, p	0	0	0	2	1	0
Totals	30	4	7	27	12	0

San Diego .... 0 1 0 0 0 0 0 0 1—2
Detroit .... 2 0 2 0 0 0 0 0 *—4

San Diego	IP.	H.	R.	ER.	BB.	SO.
Show (L)	2⅔	4	4	3	1	2
Dravecky	3⅓	3	0	0	1	4
Lefferts	1	0	0	0	0	0
Gossage	1	0	0	0	0	0

Detroit	IP.	H.	R.	ER.	BB.	SO.
Morris (W)	9	5	2	2	0	4

Bases on balls—Off Show 1 (Evans), off Dravecky 1 (Lemon).

Strikeouts—By Show 2 (Jones, Lemon), by Dravecky 4 (Herndon, Bergman, Gibson, Evans), by Morris 4 (Martinez, Templeton, Bevacqua, Summers).

Game-winning RBI—Trammell.

aHit into forceout for Grubb in third. bStruck out for Jones in fourth. cSingled for Martinez in eighth. dStruck out for Wiggins in eighth. Runs batted in—Kennedy, Trammell 4. Two-base hits—Bevacqua, Whitaker, Garvey. Home runs—Trammell 2, Kennedy. Stolen bases—Gibson, Lemon. Caught stealing—Lemon. Wild pitches—Morris 2. Double plays—Kennedy and Nettles; Templeton, Wiggins and Garvey. Left on bases—San Diego 3, Detroit 4. Umpires—Garcia (A.L.) plate, Runge (N.L.) first, Reilly (A.L.) second, Harvey (N.L.) third, Barnett (A.L.) left, Froemming (N.L.) right. Time—2:20. Attendance—52,130.

Detroit Manager Sparky Anderson (left) and President Jim Campbell had an uncomfortable conversation with President Ronald Reagan in the triumphant Tigers' locker room.

Sunday, October 14—At Detroit

San Diego (N.L.)	AB.	R.	H.	O.	A.	E.
Wiggins, 2b	5	0	2	4	0	1
Gwynn, rf	5	0	0	4	0	0
Garvey, 1b	4	0	1	3	1	0
Nettles, 3b	3	0	1	2	1	0
Kennedy, c	4	0	0	5	1	0
Bevacqua, dh	3	2	1	0	0	0
Martinez, lf	4	0	2	2	0	0
dSalazar, cf	0	0	0	0	0	0
Templeton, ss	4	1	1	1	3	0
Brown, cf-lf	2	1	1	3	0	0
eBochy	1	0	1	0	0	0
fRoenicke	0	0	0	0	0	0
Thurmond, p	0	0	0	0	0	0
Hawkins, p	0	0	0	0	0	0
Lefferts, p	0	0	0	0	0	0
Gossage, p	0	0	0	0	1	0
Totals	35	4	10	24	7	1

Detroit (A.L.)	AB.	R.	H.	O.	A.	E.
Whitaker, 2b	3	1	1	4	3	0
Trammell, ss	4	1	0	0	3	0
Gibson, rf	4	3	3	1	0	0
Parrish, c	5	2	2	8	0	1
Herndon, lf	4	0	1	4	0	0
Lemon, cf	3	0	2	2	0	0
Garbey, dh	1	0	0	0	0	0
aGrubb	0	0	0	0	0	0
bKuntz	0	0	0	0	0	0
cJohnson	1	0	0	0	0	0
Evans, 1b	4	0	0	6	1	0
Bergman, 1b	0	0	0	1	1	0
Castillo, 3b	3	1	2	0	1	0
Petry, p	0	0	0	1	0	0
Scherrer, p	0	0	0	0	1	0
Lopez, p	0	0	0	0	0	0
Hernandez, p	0	0	0	0	1	0
Totals	32	8	11	27	11	1

San Diego	0	0	1	2	0	0	0	1	0—4
Detroit	3	0	0	0	1	0	1	3	*—8

San Diego	IP.	H.	R.	ER.	BB.	SO.
Thurmond	⅓	5	3	3	0	0
Hawkins (L)	4	2	1	1	3	1
Lefferts	2	1	0	0	1	2
Gossage	1⅔	3	4	4	1	2

Detroit	IP.	H.	R.	ER.	BB.	SO.
Petry	3⅔	6	3	3	2	2
Scherrer	1	1	0	0	0	0
Lopez (W)	2⅓	0	0	0	0	4
Hernandez (S)	2	3	1	1	0	0

Bases on balls—Off Hawkins 3 (Gibson, Whitaker, Herndon), off Lefferts 1 (Lemon), off Gossage 1 (Castillo), off Petry 2 (Nettles, Bevacqua).

Strikeouts—By Hawkins 1 (Castillo), by Lefferts 2 (Evans, Gibson), by Gossage 2 (Parrish, Herndon), by Petry 2 (Gwynn, Martinez), by Lopez 4 (Bevacqua, Martinez, Brown, Wiggins).

Game-winning RBI—Kuntz.

aHit by pitch for Garbey in fourth. bHit sacrifice fly for Grubb in fifth. cReached first base on error for Kuntz in seventh. dRan for Martinez in eighth. eSingled for Brown in ninth. fRan for Bochy in ninth. Runs batted in—Wiggins, Garvey, Bevacqua, Brown, Gibson 5, Parrish, Lemon, Kuntz. Two-base hit—Templeton. Home runs—Gibson 2, Parrish, Bevacqua. Stolen bases—Wiggins, Parrish, Lemon. Caught stealing—Herndon, Salazar. Sacrifice hits—Whitaker, Trammell. Sacrifice flies—Brown, Kuntz. Hit by pitcher—By Hawkins (Grubb). Wild pitch—Hawkins. Double play—Garvey and Templeton. Left on bases—San Diego 7, Detroit 9. Umpires—Runge (N.L.) plate, Reilly (A.L.) first, Harvey (N.L.) second, Barnett (A.L.) third, Froemming (N.L.) left, Garcia (A.L.) right. Time—2:55. Attendance—51,901.

COMPOSITE BATTING AVERAGES
Detroit Tigers

Player-Position	G.	AB.	R.	H.	2B.	3B.	HR.	RBI.	BA.
Trammell, ss	5	20	5	9	1	0	2	6	.450
Gibson, rf	5	18	4	6	0	0	2	7	.333
Herndon, lf-ph	5	15	1	5	0	0	1	3	.333
Castillo, 3b	3	9	2	3	0	0	1	2	.333
Grubb, ph-dh	4	3	0	1	0	0	0	0	.333
Lemon, cf	5	17	1	5	0	0	0	1	.294
Parrish, c	5	18	3	5	1	0	1	2	.278
Whitaker, 2b	5	18	6	5	2	0	0	0	.278
Evans, 1b-3b	5	15	1	1	0	0	0	1	.067
Bair, p	1	0	0	0	0	0	0	0	.000
Hernandez, p	3	0	0	0	0	0	0	0	.000
Lopez, p	2	0	0	0	0	0	0	0	.000
Morris, p	2	0	0	0	0	0	0	0	.000
Petry, p	2	0	0	0	0	0	0	0	.000
Scherrer, p	3	0	0	0	0	0	0	0	.000
Wilcox, p	1	0	0	0	0	0	0	0	.000
Johnson, ph	1	1	0	0	0	0	0	0	.000
Kuntz, ph	2	1	0	0	0	0	0	1	.000
Brookens, ph-3b	3	2	0	0	0	0	0	0	.000
Jones, lf	2	3	0	0	0	0	0	0	.000
Bergman, pr-1b	5	5	0	0	0	0	0	0	.000
Garbey, dh-ph	4	12	0	0	0	0	0	0	.000
Totals	5	158	23	40	4	0	7	23	.253

San Diego Padres

Player-Position	G.	AB.	R.	H.	2B.	3B.	HR.	RBI.	BA.
Bochy, ph	1	1	0	1	0	0	0	0	1.000
Flannery, ph-2b	1	1	0	1	0	0	0	0	1.000
Bevacqua, dh	5	17	4	7	2	0	2	4	.412
Wiggins, 2b	5	22	2	8	1	0	0	1	.364
S'zar, pr-3b-cf-ph	4	3	0	1	0	0	0	0	.333
Templeton, ss	5	19	1	6	1	0	0	0	.316
Gwynn, rf	5	19	1	5	0	0	0	0	.263
Nettles, 3b	5	12	2	3	0	0	0	2	.250
Kennedy, c	5	19	2	4	1	0	1	3	.211
Garvey, 1b	5	20	2	4	2	0	0	2	.200
Martinez, lf	5	17	0	3	0	0	0	0	.176
Brown, cf-lf	5	15	1	1	0	0	0	2	.067
Booker, p	1	0	0	0	0	0	0	0	.000
Dravecky, p	2	0	0	0	0	0	0	0	.000
Gossage, p	2	0	0	0	0	0	0	0	.000
Harris, p	1	0	0	0	0	0	0	0	.000
Hawkins, p	3	0	0	0	0	0	0	0	.000
Lefferts, p	3	0	0	0	0	0	0	0	.000
Lollar, p	1	0	0	0	0	0	0	0	.000
Roenicke, lf-pr	2	0	0	0	0	0	0	0	.000
Show, p	1	0	0	0	0	0	0	0	.000
Thurmond, p	2	0	0	0	0	0	0	0	.000
Whitson, p	1	0	0	0	0	0	0	0	.000
Summers, ph	1	1	0	0	0	0	0	0	.000
Totals	5	166	15	44	7	0	3	14	.265

COMPOSITE PITCHING AVERAGES
Detroit Tigers

Pitcher	G.	IP.	H.	R.	E.	BB.	SO.	W.	L.	ERA.
Lopez	2	3	1	0	0	1	4	1	0	0.00
Bair	1	⅔	1	0	0	1	0	0	0	0.00
Wilcox	1	6	7	1	1	2	4	1	0	1.50
Hernandez	3	5⅓	4	1	1	0	3	0	0	1.69
Morris	2	18	13	4	4	3	13	2	0	2.00
Scherrer	3	3	5	1	1	0	0	0	0	3.00
Petry	2	8	14	8	8	5	4	0	1	9.00
Totals	5	44	44	15	15	11	26	4	1	3.07

San Diego Padres

Pitcher	G.	IP.	H.	R.	E.	BB.	SO.	W.	L.	ERA.
Lefferts	3	6	2	0	0	1	7	0	0	0.00
Harris	1	5⅓	3	0	0	3	5	0	0	0.00
Dravecky	2	4⅔	3	0	0	1	6	0	0	0.00
Hawkins	3	12	4	1	1	6	4	1	1	0.75
Booker	1	1	0	1	1	0	0	0	0	9.00
Thurmond	2	5⅓	12	6	6	3	2	0	1	10.13
Show	1	2⅔	4	4	3	1	2	0	1	10.13
Gossage	2	2⅔	3	4	4	1	2	0	0	13.50
Lollar	1	1⅔	4	4	4	4	0	0	1	21.60
Whitson	1	⅔	5	3	3	0	0	0	0	40.50
Totals	5	42	40	23	22	24	27	1	4	4.71

World Series Box Scores
1903 Through 1983

SERIES OF 1903

	W.	L.	Pct.
Boston A. L.	5	3	.625
Pittsburgh N. L.	3	5	.375

The first modern World Series in 1903 was personally arranged by the presidents of the Boston and Pittsburgh clubs when it became apparent in August that those two teams would win the American and National League pennants. Nine games were agreed upon, with the clubs dividing the gate receipts equally and each making its own arrangements with its players. The Boston club was at a disadvantage because its contracts expired September 30, while those of the Pittsburgh Pirates ran until October 15, and the Boston players demanded and received the lion's share of the club's receipts, each getting $1,182 and the owner $6,699.56. Pittsburgh players, though defeated, fared considerably better, as President Barney Dreyfuss tossed in his share, and each man received $1,316.25, in addition to his salary in full. The Series netted approximately $50,000.

The Red Sox won the Series, five games to three, making one of the greatest comebacks in the long history of the event. They were trailing, three games to one, after four contests, and then won the Series by sweeping over the Pirates in four consecutive victories.

Both clubs captured their league pennants by comfortable margins. Boston, managed by Jimmy Collins, won by 14½ games over the Athletics and the Pirates by six and one-half games over the Giants. However, Manager Fred Clarke of the Pittsburgh club was handicapped, having only one winning pitcher, Deacon Phillippe, the other famous Pirate hurling headliner, Jack Chesbro, having jumped to the American League the winter before. Boston eventually won because of Collins' two aces, Bill Dinneen and Cy Young. Pitchers in those days were worked much more often than they are today, but the fact that the Series was stretched through 13 days made it possible for Phillippe to pitch five complete games and Dinneen four and Young three for Boston. Cy relieved early in a fourth contest.

Dinneen, later an American League umpire, was the outstanding hero of his league's first World Series victory, winning three games, two of them shutouts, while losing one. In the second game, he held the Pirates to three hits and fanned 11. Young won two and lost one, while Phillippe, after winning the first, third and fourth games for the only victories for Barney Dreyfuss' Pirates, dropped the seventh and eighth clashes. Jimmy Sebring, who led the Series batters with .367, had the distinction of hitting Young for a homer in the first game, the first four-bagger of the many hit in the history of the Classic. It was the only round-tripper hit by Pittsburgh. Pat Dougherty clouted two for Boston, both coming in the second game, won by the Hub team, 3 to 0.

Honus Wagner, Pittsburgh's immortal shortstop and the National League batting champion that year with a mark of .355, was handcuffed, getting only six hits in the eight games for an average of .222. The box scores:

Thursday, October 1—At Boston

Pittsburgh (N.L.)	AB.	R.	H.	O.	A.	E.
Beaumont, cf	5	1	0	3	0	0
Clarke, lf	5	0	2	4	0	0
Leach, 3b	5	1	4	0	1	1
Wagner, ss	3	1	1	1	2	1
Bransfield, 1b	5	2	1	7	0	0
Ritchey, 2b	4	1	0	1	2	0
Sebring, rf	5	1	3	1	0	0
Phelps, c	4	0	1	10	0	0
Phillippe, p	4	0	0	0	2	0
Totals	40	7	12	27	7	2

Boston (A.L.)	AB.	R.	H.	O.	A.	E.
Dougherty, lf	4	0	0	1	1	0
Collins, 3b	4	0	0	2	3	0
Stahl, cf	4	0	1	2	0	0
Freeman, rf	4	2	2	2	0	0
Parent, ss	4	1	2	4	4	0
LaChance, 1b	4	0	0	8	0	0
Ferris, 2b	3	0	1	2	4	2
Criger, c	3	0	0	6	1	2
aO'Brien	1	0	0	0	0	0
Young, p	3	0	0	0	1	0
bFarrell	1	0	0	0	0	0
Totals	35	3	6	27	14	4

Pittsburgh .... 4 0 1 1 0 0 1 0 0—7
Boston .... 0 0 0 0 0 0 2 0 1—3

aStruck out for Criger in ninth. bGrounded out for Young in ninth. Three-base hits—Freeman, Parent, Leach 2, Bransfield. Home run—Sebring. Runs batted in—Sebring 4, Leach, Wagner, LaChance 2, Parent. Stolen bases—Wagner, Bransfield, Ritchey. Left on bases—Boston 6, Pittsburgh 9. Earned runs—Boston 2, Pittsburgh 3. Bases on balls—Off Young 3. Struck out—By Young 5, by Phillippe 10. Hit by pitcher—by Phillippe (Ferris). Passed ball—Criger. Umpires—O'Day (N.L.) and Connolly (A.L.). Time—1:55. Attendance—16,242.

Friday, October 2—At Boston

Pittsburgh (N.L.)	AB.	R.	H.	O.	A.	E.
Beaumont, cf	3	0	0	3	0	0
Clarke, lf	3	0	1	3	0	0
Leach, 3b	3	0	0	0	2	0
Wagner, ss	3	0	0	3	3	0
Bransfield, 1b	3	0	0	9	1	0
Ritchey, 2b	3	0	1	3	3	0
Sebring, rf	3	0	1	1	0	0
Smith, c	3	0	0	2	1	1
Leever, p	0	0	0	0	0	0

1903 WORLD SERIES

	AB.	R.	H.	O.	A.	E.
Veil, p	2	0	0	0	0	1
aPhelps	1	0	0	0	0	0
Totals	27	0	3	24	10	2

Boston (A.L.)	AB.	R.	H.	O.	A.	E.
Dougherty, lf	4	2	3	0	1	0
Collins, 3b	4	0	1	1	1	0
Stahl, cf	4	1	1	1	0	0
Freeman, rf	4	0	2	0	0	0
Parent, ss	3	0	1	3	3	0
LaChance, 1b	2	0	0	8	1	0
Ferris, 2b	4	0	0	3	0	0
Criger, c	3	0	0	11	0	0
Dinneen, p	2	0	1	0	3	0
Totals	30	3	9	27	9	0

Pittsburgh .... 0 0 0 0 0 0 0 0 0—0
Boston .... 2 0 0 0 0 1 0 0 *—3

aStruck out for Veil in ninth. Two-base hit—Stahl. Home runs—Dougherty 2. Runs batted in—Dougherty 2, Freeman. Sacrifice hits—LaChance, Dinneen. Stolen bases—Collins 2. Double plays—Ferris, unassisted; Ritchey, Wagner and Bransfield; Wagner, Ritchey and Bransfield. Left on bases—Boston 11, Pittsburgh 2. Earned runs—Boston 3. Bases on balls—Off Dinneen 2, off Leever 1, off Veil 4. Struck out—By Dinneen 11, by Veil 1. Hit by pitcher—By Veil (Dougherty). Hits—Off Leever 3 in 1 inning, off Veil 6 in 7 innings. Loser—Leever. Umpires—O'Day (N.L.) and Connolly (A.L.). Time—1:47. Attendance—9,415.

Saturday, October 3—At Boston

Pittsburgh (N.L.)	AB.	R.	H.	O.	A.	E.
Beaumont, cf	4	1	0	1	0	0
Clarke, lf	4	0	1	0	0	0
Leach, 3b	4	1	1	0	1	0
Wagner, ss	3	1	1	0	7	0
Bransfield, 1b	3	0	0	15	0	0
Ritchey, 2b	4	1	1	2	2	0
Sebring, rf	3	0	1	4	0	0
Phelps, c	4	0	2	5	1	0
Phillippe, p	4	0	0	0	4	0
Totals	33	4	7	27	15	0

Boston (A.L.)	AB.	R.	H.	O.	A.	E.
Dougherty, lf	4	0	0	1	1	0
Collins, 3b	4	2	2	2	6	1
Stahl, cf	3	0	1	2	0	0
Freeman, rf	3	0	0	1	0	0
Parent, ss	4	0	0	0	7	0
LaChance, 1b	3	0	1	15	0	0
Ferris, 2b	4	0	0	2	2	0
Criger, c	3	0	0	4	1	0
Hughes, p	0	0	0	0	0	0
Young, p	3	0	0	0	2	1
Totals	31	2	4	27	19	2

Pittsburgh .... 0 1 2 0 0 0 0 1 0—4
Boston .... 0 0 0 1 0 0 0 1 0—2

Two-base hits—Collins, LaChance, Clarke, Ritchey, Wagner, Phelps 2. Runs batted in—Leach, Ritchey, Sebring, Phelps, Stahl, Parent. Sacrifice hit—Bransfield. Stolen base—Leach. Double play—Dougherty and Collins. Left on bases—Boston 5, Pittsburgh 6. Earned runs—Pittsburgh 3, Boston 2. Bases on balls—Off Hughes 2, off Phillippe 3. Struck out—By Phillippe 5, by Young 2. Hit by pitched ball—By Young (Wagner). Hits—Off Hughes 4 in 2 innings (pitched to three batters in third), off Young 3 in 7 innings. Passed ball—Criger. Loser—Hughes. Umpires—O'Day (N.L.) and Connolly (A.L.). Time—1:50. Attendance—18,801.

Tuesday, October 6—At Pittsburgh

Boston (A.L.)	AB.	R.	H.	O.	A.	E.
Dougherty, lf	4	0	0	3	0	1
Collins, 3b	4	1	1	1	2	0
Stahl, cf	4	1	2	3	1	0
Freeman, rf	4	0	1	0	0	0
Parent, ss	4	1	1	1	3	0
LaChance, 1b	4	1	2	6	0	0
Ferris, 2b	4	0	1	2	0	0
Criger, c	3	0	1	8	1	0
aFarrell	1	0	0	0	0	0
Dinneen, p	3	0	0	0	1	0
bO'Brien	1	0	0	0	0	0
Totals	36	4	9	24	8	1

Pittsburgh (N.L.)	AB.	R.	H.	O.	A.	E.
Beaumont, cf	4	2	3	3	0	0
Clarke, lf	4	1	1	1	0	0
Leach, 3b	4	1	2	2	5	0
Wagner, ss	4	0	3	1	1	0
Bransfield, 1b	4	0	1	9	1	1
Ritchey, 2b	3	0	0	5	5	0
Sebring, rf	4	0	0	1	0	0
Phelps, c	4	0	1	4	0	0
Phillippe, p	3	1	1	1	1	0
Totals	34	5	12	27	13	1

Boston .... 0 0 0 0 1 0 0 0 3—4
Pittsburgh .... 1 0 0 0 1 0 3 0 *—5

aFlied out for Criger in ninth, Parent scoring after the catch. bFlied out for Dinneen in ninth. Three-base hits—Beaumont, Leach. Runs batted in—Leach 3, Wagner, Bransfield, Freeman, Criger, Farrell, Parent. Stolen base—Wagner. Double plays—Ritchey and Bransfield; Criger and Parent. Left on bases—Boston 5, Pittsburgh 6. Earned runs—Pittsburgh 5, Boston 4. Struck out—By Phillippe 1, by Dinneen 7. Bases on balls—Off Dinneen 1. Umpires—O'Day (N.L.) and Connolly (A.L.). Time—1:30. Attendance—7,600.

Wednesday, October 7—At Pittsburgh

Boston (A.L.)	AB.	R.	H.	O.	A.	E.
Dougherty, lf	6	0	3	3	0	0
Collins, 3b	6	0	2	0	4	0
Stahl, cf	5	2	1	2	0	0
Freeman, rf	4	2	2	2	0	0
Parent, ss	5	1	2	1	4	1
LaChance, 1b	4	2	1	13	0	1
Ferris, 2b	5	2	1	1	3	0
Criger, c	3	1	0	5	0	0
Young, p	5	1	2	0	2	0
Totals	43	11	14	27	13	2

Pittsburgh (N.L.)	AB.	R.	H.	O.	A.	E.
Beaumont, cf	4	1	1	0	0	0
Clarke, lf	4	1	0	3	0	1
Leach, 3b	4	0	2	2	1	1
Wagner, ss	4	0	0	1	3	2
Bransfield, 1b	4	0	0	9	1	0
Ritchey, 2b	4	0	1	1	4	0
Sebring, rf	4	0	1	2	0	0
Phelps, c	3	0	0	9	0	0
Kennedy, p	2	0	1	0	1	0
Thompson, p	1	0	0	0	1	0
Totals	34	2	6	27	11	4

Boston .... 0 0 0 0 0 6 4 1 0—11
Pittsburgh .... 0 0 0 0 2 0 0 0 0— 2

Two-base hit—Kennedy. Three-base hits—Leach, Dougherty 2, Collins, Stahl, Young. Runs batted in—Leach 2, Dougherty 3, Young 3, Freeman, LaChance, Ferris 2. Sacrifice hits—Phelps, Criger. Stolen bases—Collins, Stahl. Left on bases—Boston 9, Pittsburgh 6. Earned runs—Boston 5.

Struck out—By Kennedy 3, by Thompson 1, by Young 4. Bases on balls—Off Kennedy 3. Hits—Off Kennedy 11 in 7 innings, off Thompson 3 in 2 innings. Loser—Kennedy. Umpires—Connolly (A.L.) and O'Day (N.L.). Time—2:00. Attendance—12,322.

Thursday, October 8—At Pittsburgh

Boston (A.L.)	AB.	R.	H.	O.	A.	E.
Dougherty, lf	3	1	1	1	0	0
Collins, 3b	5	1	1	1	2	0
Stahl, cf	5	1	2	2	0	0
Freeman, rf	5	0	0	1	0	0
Parent, ss	4	2	1	5	2	0
LaChance, 1b	4	0	1	9	2	0
Ferris, 2b	4	0	2	1	3	0
Criger, c	4	0	1	6	0	1
Dinneen, p	4	1	1	1	2	0
Totals	38	6	10	27	11	1

Pittsburgh (N.L.)	AB.	R.	H.	O.	A.	E.
Beaumont, cf	5	1	4	5	0	0
Clarke, lf	5	0	2	2	0	0
Leach, 3b	5	0	0	1	2	2
Wagner, ss	3	0	0	2	5	1
Bransfield, 1b	3	0	1	11	0	0
Ritchey, 2b	3	0	0	1	3	0
Sebring, rf	4	1	2	2	0	0
Phelps, c	4	1	1	3	0	0
Leever, p	4	0	0	0	2	0
Totals	36	3	10	27	12	3

Boston .... 0 0 3 0 2 0 1 0 0—6
Pittsburgh .... 0 0 0 0 0 0 3 0 0—3

Two-base hits—Clarke, LaChance. Three-base hits—Stahl, Parent. Stolen bases—Beaumont 2, Clarke, Leach, Stahl. Runs batted in—Beaumont 2, Leach, Collins, Stahl, Freeman, LaChance, Ferris. Double plays—Ritchey, Wagner and Bransfield; Parent and LaChance. Left on bases—Boston 8, Pittsburgh 9. Earned runs—Boston 5, Pittsburgh 3. Struck out—By Leever 2, by Dinneen 3. Bases on balls—Off Leever 2, off Dinneen 3. Hit by pitched ball—By Leever (Parent). Umpires—O'Day (N.L.) and Connolly (A.L.) Time—2:02. Attendance—11,556.

Saturday, October 10—At Pittsburgh

Boston (A.L.)	AB.	R.	H.	O.	A.	E.
Dougherty, lf	5	0	1	3	0	0
Collins, 3b	5	1	0	2	2	1
Stahl, cf	4	1	2	0	0	0
Freeman, rf	4	1	1	0	0	0
Parent, ss	4	2	2	3	6	1
LaChance, 1b	3	1	0	11	0	2
Ferris, 2b	3	1	2	4	4	0
Criger, c	4	0	2	6	2	0
Young, p	4	0	1	0	2	0
Totals	36	7	11	27	16	4

Pittsburgh (N.L.)	AB.	R.	H.	O.	A.	E.
Beaumont, cf	5	0	1	2	0	0
Clarke, lf	5	1	1	1	0	0
Leach, 3b	5	0	0	0	1	0
Wagner, ss	3	0	0	2	6	1
Bransfield, 1b	4	1	3	13	2	0
Ritchey, 2b	4	0	0	5	8	0
Sebring, rf	4	1	2	1	0	0
Phelps, c	3	0	1	2	3	1
Phillippe, p	4	0	2	1	0	1
Totals	37	3	10	27	20	3

Boston .... 2 0 0 2 0 2 0 1 0—7
Pittsburgh .... 0 0 0 0 1 0 1 0 0—3

Three-base hits—Clarke, Bransfield, Collins, Stahl, Freeman, Parent, Ferris. Runs batted in— Wagner, Ritchey, Phillippe, Criger 3, Stahl, Parent. Sacrifice hits—Wagner, LaChance, Ferris. Double plays—Ritchey, Wagner and Bransfield; Ferris and LaChance. Left on bases—Boston 4, Pittsburgh 9. Earned runs—Pittsburgh 2, Boston 5. Struck out—By Phillippe 2, by Young 6. Bases on balls—Off Young 1. Wild pitch—Phillippe. Umpires—Connolly (A.L.) and O'Day (N.L.). Time—1:45. Attendance—17,038.

Tuesday, October 13—At Boston

Pittsburgh (N.L.)	AB.	R.	H.	O.	A.	E.
Beaumont, cf	4	0	0	5	0	0
Clarke, lf	4	0	1	3	0	0
Leach, 3b	3	0	0	0	3	0
Wagner, ss	4	0	1	3	0	1
Bransfield, 1b	3	0	0	7	1	1
Ritchey, 2b	2	0	0	2	1	0
Sebring, rf	3	0	1	1	1	0
Phelps, c	3	0	0	3	0	1
Phillippe, p	3	0	1	0	2	0
Totals	29	0	4	24	8	3

Boston (A.L.)	AB.	R.	H.	O.	A.	E.
Dougherty, lf	4	0	0	3	0	0
Collins, 3b	4	0	1	0	2	0
Stahl, cf	4	0	0	2	0	0
Freeman, rf	4	1	1	2	0	0
Parent, ss	4	1	0	1	1	0
LaChance, 1b	3	1	1	11	0	0
Ferris, 2b	4	0	2	0	3	0
Criger, c	3	0	2	8	3	0
Dinneen, p	3	0	1	0	3	0
Totals	33	3	8	27	12	0

Pittsburgh .... 0 0 0 0 0 0 0 0 0—0
Boston .... 0 0 0 2 0 1 0 0 *—3

Three-base hits—Freeman, LaChance, Sebring. Runs batted in—Ferris 3. Sacrifice hit—LaChance. Stolen base—Wagner. Double play—Criger and LaChance. Left on bases—Boston 7, Pittsburgh 4. Earned runs—Boston 3. Struck out—By Dinneen 7, by Phillippe 2. Bases on balls—Off Dinneen 2. Umpires—O'Day (N.L.) and Connolly (A.L.). Time—1:35. Attendance—7,455.

COMPOSITE BATTING AVERAGES

Boston Red Sox

Player-Position	G.	AB.	R.	H.	2B.	3B.	HR.	RBI.	BA.
Stahl, cf	8	33	6	10	1	3	0	3	.303
Ferris, 2b	8	31	3	9	0	1	0	6	.290
Freeman, rf	8	32	6	9	0	3	0	4	.281
Parent, ss	8	32	8	9	0	3	0	4	.281
Collins, 3b	8	36	5	9	1	2	0	1	.250
Dinneen, p	4	12	1	3	0	0	0	0	.250
Dougherty, lf	8	34	3	8	0	2	2	5	.235
Criger, c	8	26	1	6	0	0	0	4	.231
LaChance, 1b	8	27	5	6	2	1	0	4	.222
Young, p	4	15	1	2	0	1	0	3	.133
Farrell, ph	2	2	0	0	0	0	0	1	.000
O'Brien, ph	2	2	0	0	0	0	0	0	.000
Hughes, p	1	0	0	0	0	0	0	0	.000
Totals	8	282	39	71	4	16	2	35	.252

Pittsburgh Pirates

Player-Position	G.	AB.	R.	H.	2B.	3B.	HR.	RBI.	BA.
Kennedy, p	1	2	0	1	1	0	0	0	.500
Sebring, rf	8	30	3	11	0	1	1	5	.367
Leach, 3b	8	33	3	9	0	4	0	8	.273
Beaumont, cf	8	34	6	9	0	1	0	2	.265
Clarke, lf	8	34	3	9	2	1	0	0	.265
Phelps, ph-c	8	26	1	6	2	0	0	1	.231
Wagner, ss	8	27	2	6	1	0	0	3	.222
Phillippe, p	5	18	1	4	0	0	0	1	.222
Bransfield, 1b	8	29	3	6	0	2	0	1	.207
Ritchey, 2b	8	27	2	3	0	0	2	0	.111
Leever, p	2	4	0	0	0	0	0	0	.000
Smith, c	1	3	0	0	0	0	0	0	.000
Thompson, p	1	1	0	0	0	0	0	0	.000
Veil, p	1	2	0	0	0	0	0	0	.000
Totals	8	270	24	64	7	9	1	23	.237

COMPOSITE PITCHING AVERAGES
Boston Red Sox

Pitcher	G.	IP.	H.	R.	E.	SO.	BB.	W.	L.	ERA.
Young	4	34	31	13	6	17	4	2	1	1.59
Dinneen	4	35	29	8	8	28	8	3	1	2.06
Hughes	1	2	4	3	2	0	2	0	1	9.00
Totals	8	71	64	24	16	45	14	5	3	2.03

Pittsburgh Pirates

Pitcher	G.	IP.	H.	R.	E.	SO.	BB.	W.	L.	ERA.
Veil	1	7	6	1	1	1	4	0	0	1.29
Phillippe	5	44	38	19	16	20	3	3	2	3.27
Thompson	1	2	3	1	1	1	0	0	0	4.50
Kennedy	1	7	11	10	4	3	3	0	1	5.14
Leever	2	10	13	8	7	2	3	0	2	6.30
Totals	8	70	71	39	29	27	13	3	5	3.73

SERIES OF 1905

	W.	L.	Pct.
New York N. L.	4	1	.800
Philadelphia A. L.	1	4	.200

The two runners-up of 1903, the Giants and Athletics, clashed in the 1905 Series, the first played under the John T. Brush rules governing such championship classics. It was the first of three sets played between the Giants and Athletics, the first of nine Series for John McGraw, famous manager of the New Yorkers, and the first of eight for Connie Mack, his illustrious rival. The National League gained its first victory from its young opponent, four games to one, all of the contests being shutouts.

The Athletics received a terrific blow in the last fortnight of the championship season when Rube Waddell, their famous southpaw hurler, injured his left shoulder during some horseplay with his teammate, Andy Coakley. His absence from the Series proved not only a severe blow to the Athletics, but also a distinct disappointment to the great American public. For weeks there had been much speculation as to what would happen when Rube met the great young righthander of the Giants, Christy Mathewson. Both had brilliant records; Matty won 31 games that season and lost only nine, striking out 206 batsmen. The great Rube won 26, lost 11, and struck out 286.

What would have happened had Mack been able to pitch Waddell against Mathewson never will be known, but Connie had no one to compete with Matty's magic. Matty, famous Big Six, not only defeated the Athletics three times within a period of six days, but made each a shutout, giving up four, four and six hits, respectively. He walked only one man and whiffed 18 in his three games and defeated each of Mack's starters, Eddie Plank, Andy Coakley and Chief Bender. Iron Man Joe McGinnity won the other game for the Giants, a 1 to 0 pitching duel over Plank in the fourth game. Bender scored Mack's lone victory, a 3 to 0 shutout over McGinnity and Leon Ames in the second game. In the Indian's second appearance, he lost the fifth and last game to Mathewson, 2 to 0, though giving up one less hit than McGraw's aceMfive against six. However, Bender walked three, and the passes led to both of the Giants' tallies.

The batting was light, the Giants hitting only .209 against .161 for their opponents. Mike Donlin of the Giants set the pace with .316. There were no home runs, but the Polo Grounders stole 11 bases to two for Philadelphia, getting five in Mathewson's 9 to 0 victory over Coakley in the third game. The box scores:

Monday, October 9—At Philadelphia

New York (N.L.)	AB.	R.	H.	O.	A.	E.
Bresnahan, c	3	1	1	6	1	0
Browne, rf	5	0	0	1	0	0
Donlin, cf	5	1	2	1	0	1
McGann, 1b	3	0	1	14	0	0
Mertes, lf	4	0	1	0	0	0
Dahlen, ss	4	0	0	3	5	0
Devlin, 3b	4	0	1	0	5	0
Gilbert, 2b	4	1	3	2	4	0
Mathewson, p	3	0	1	0	3	0
Totals	35	3	10	27	18	1

Phila'phia (A.L.)	AB.	R.	H.	O.	A.	E.
Hartsel, lf	4	0	1	1	0	0
Lord, cf	4	0	0	2	0	0
Davis, 1b	4	0	1	14	0	0
L. Cross, 3b	4	0	0	0	2	0
Seybold, rf	3	0	0	0	0	0
Murphy, 2b	3	0	1	2	3	0
M. Cross, ss	3	0	0	3	7	0
Schreckengost, c	3	0	1	5	1	0
Plank, p	3	0	0	0	1	0
Totals	31	0	4	27	14	0

New York .... 0 0 0   0 2 0   0 0 1—3
Philadelphia ...... 0 0 0   0 0 0   0 0 0—0

Two-base hits—McGann, Mertes, Schreckengost, Murphy, Davis. Runs batted in—Bresnahan, Donlin, Mertes. Sacrifice hit—Mathewson. Stolen bases—Devlin, Gilbert, Bresnahan, Donlin. Double play—Dahlen and McGann. Earned runs—New York 2. Left on bases—New York 9, Philadelphia 4. Struck out—By Mathewson 6, by Plank 5. Bases on balls—Off Plank 2. Hit by pitched ball—By Plank (Bresnahan). Umpires—Sheridan (A.L.) and O'Day (N.L.). Time—1:46. Attendance—17,955.

Tuesday, October 10—At New York

Phila'phia (A.L.)	AB.	R.	H.	O.	A.	E.
Hartsel, lf	4	1	2	0	0	0
Lord, cf	4	0	2	2	1	0
Davis, 1b	4	0	0	8	0	0
L. Cross, 3b	3	0	0	1	1	0
Seybold, rf	4	0	0	1	0	0
Murphy, 2b	4	0	1	0	3	1
M. Cross, ss	4	0	0	4	1	1
Schreckengost, c	4	2	1	10	2	0
Bender, p	2	0	0	1	0	0
Totals	33	3	6	27	8	2

New York (N.L.)	AB.	R.	H.	O.	A.	E.
Bresnahan, c	4	0	1	3	1	0
Browne, rf	4	0	0	2	0	0
Donlin, cf	4	0	2	4	1	0
McGann, 1b	3	0	0	12	0	1
Mertes, lf	4	0	0	1	0	0
Dahlen, ss	3	0	0	1	6	0

1905 WORLD SERIES

	AB	R	H	O	A	E
Devlin, 3b	3	0	1	2	1	1
Gilbert, 2b	3	0	0	3	4	1
McGinnity, p	2	0	0	0	2	0
aStrang	1	0	0	0	0	0
Ames, p	0	0	0	0	1	0
Totals	31	0	4	27	17	2

| Philadelphia | 0 0 1 | 0 0 0 | 0 2 0—3 |
| New York | 0 0 0 | 0 0 0 | 0 0 0—0 |

aStruck out for McGinnity in eighth. Two-base hits—Bresnahan, Donlin, Hartsel. Runs batted in—Lord 2. Sacrifice hit—Bender. Stolen bases—Dahlen, Devlin. Earned runs—None. Left on bases—New York 7, Philadelphia 5. Struck out—By McGinnity 2, by Ames 1, by Bender 9. Bases on balls—Off Ames 1, off Bender 3. Hits—Off McGinnity 5 in 8 innings, off Ames, 1 in 1 inning. Losing pitcher—McGinnity. Umpires—O'Day (N.L.) and Sheridan (A.L.). Time—1:51. Attendance—24,992.

Thursday, Oct. 12—At Philadelphia

New York (N.L.)	AB	R	H	O	A	E
Bresnahan, c	3	2	0	8	3	0
Browne, rf	5	2	1	0	0	0
Donlin, cf	3	3	2	4	0	0
McGann, 1b	5	1	3	9	1	0
Mertes, lf	3	0	1	1	0	0
Dahlen, ss	3	1	0	2	1	0
Devlin, 3b	4	0	1	0	6	1
Gilbert, 2b	4	0	0	2	0	0
Mathewson, p	4	0	1	1	2	0
Totals	34	9	9	27	13	1

Phila'phia (A.L.)	AB	R	H	O	A	E
Hartsel, lf	4	0	0	2	0	1
Lord, cf	4	0	0	2	0	0
Davis, 1b	4	0	1	10	0	0
L. Cross, 3b	4	0	0	1	2	1
Seybold, rf	3	0	1	1	1	0
Murphy, 2b	3	0	0	2	2	3
M. Cross, ss	3	0	1	4	2	0
Schreckengost, c	2	0	0	2	1	0
Powers, c	1	0	0	2	3	0
Coakley, p	2	0	0	0	2	0
Totals	30	0	4	27	12	5

| New York | 2 0 0 | 0 5 0 | 0 0 2—9 |
| Philadelphia | 0 0 0 | 0 0 0 | 0 0 0—0 |

Two-base hit—McGann. Runs batted in—McGann 4, Mertes 2, Dahlen, Devlin. Stolen bases—Browne 2, Donlin, Dahlen, Devlin, Hartsel. Double plays—Coakley, Schreckengost and Davis; Seybold and Davis. Earned runs—None. Left on bases—New York 4, Philadelphia 5. Struck out—By Mathewson 8, by Coakley 2. Bases on balls—Off Mathewson 1, off Coakley 5. Hit by pitched ball—By Mathewson (Coakley), by Coakley (Bresnahan). Umpires—Sheridan (A.L.) and O'Day (N.L.). Time—1:55. Attendance—10,991.

Friday, October 13—At New York

Phila'phia (A.L.)	AB	R	H	O	A	E
Hartsel, lf	1	0	0	2	0	0
Lord, cf	4	0	0	2	0	0
Davis, 1b	4	0	1	8	1	0
L. Cross, 3b	4	0	1	2	1	1
Seybold, rf	3	0	0	3	0	0
Murphy, 2b	3	0	1	0	4	0
M. Cross, ss	4	0	1	0	0	1
Powers, c	3	0	0	6	0	0
aHoffman	1	0	0	0	0	0
Plank, p	3	0	1	1	5	0
Totals	30	0	5	24	8	2

New York (N.L.)	AB	R	H	O	A	E
Bresnahan, c	2	0	1	5	0	0
Browne, rf	4	0	2	0	0	0
Donlin, cf	3	0	0	6	0	1
McGann, 1b	3	0	0	10	0	0
Mertes, lf	4	1	0	1	0	0
Dahlen, ss	3	0	0	1	2	0
Devlin, 3b	3	0	1	4	1	0
Gilbert, 2b	3	0	0	0	3	0
McGinnity, p	3	0	0	0	4	0
Totals	28	1	4	27	10	1

| Philadelphia | 0 0 0 | 0 0 0 | 0 0 0—0 |
| New York | 0 0 0 | 1 0 0 | 0 0 *—1 |

aStruck out for Powers in ninth. Run batted in—None (scored on Cross' error). Two-base hit—Devlin. Sacrifice hits—Donlin, McGann, Hartsel, Murphy. Stolen base—Hartsel. Earned runs—None. Left on bases—Philadelphia 8, New York 7. Struck out—By McGinnity 4, by Plank 6. Bases on balls—Off McGinnity 3, off Plank 2. Wild pitch—Plank. Umpires—O'Day (N.L.) and Sheridan (A.L.). Time—1:55. Attendance—13,598.

Saturday, October 14—At New York

Phila'phia (A.L.)	AB	R	H	O	A	E
Hartsel, lf	4	0	2	4	1	0
Lord, cf	4	0	0	3	0	0
Davis, 1b	4	0	1	10	0	0
L. Cross, 3b	4	0	0	1	2	0
Seybold, rf	3	0	1	0	0	0
Murphy, 2b	3	0	0	0	1	0
M. Cross, ss	3	0	1	1	3	0
Powers, c	3	0	1	5	1	0
Bender, p	3	0	0	0	6	0
Totals	31	0	6	24	14	0

New York (N.L.)	AB	R	H	O	A	E
Bresnahan, c	4	0	2	5	2	0
Browne, rf	4	0	1	0	0	0
Donlin, cf	4	0	0	1	0	0
McGann, 1b	3	0	0	12	1	0
Mertes, lf	2	1	1	1	0	0
Dahlen, ss	2	0	0	3	5	0
Devlin, 3b	2	0	0	1	4	0
Gilbert, 2b	3	0	1	3	5	0
Mathewson, p	1	1	0	1	3	1
Totals	25	2	5	27	20	1

| Philadelphia | 0 0 0 | 0 0 0 | 0 0 0—0 |
| New York | 0 0 0 | 0 1 0 | 0 1 *—2 |

Two-base hits—Bresnahan, Powers. Runs batted in—Browne, Gilbert. Sacrifice hits—Devlin, Mathewson. Double play—Dahlen and McGann. Earned runs—New York 2. Left on bases—Philadelphia 4, New York 4. Struck out—By Mathewson 4, by Bender 4. Bases on balls—Off Bender 3. Umpires—Sheridan (A.L.) and O'Day (N.L.). Time—1:35. Attendance—24,187.

COMPOSITE BATTING AVERAGES
New York Giants

Player-Position	G	AB	R	H	2B	3B	HR	RBI	BA
Donlin, cf	5	19	4	6	1	0	0	1	.316
Bresnahan, c	5	16	3	5	2	0	0	0	.313
Devlin, 3b	5	16	0	4	1	0	0	1	.250
Mathewson, p	3	8	1	2	0	0	0	0	.250
McGann, 1b	5	17	1	4	2	0	0	4	.235
Gilbert, 2b	5	17	1	4	0	0	0	1	.235
Browne, rf	5	22	2	4	0	0	0	1	.182
Mertes, lf	5	17	2	3	1	0	0	3	.176
Dahlen, ss	5	15	1	0	0	0	0	1	.000
McGinnity, p	2	5	0	0	0	0	0	0	.000
Strang, ph	1	1	0	0	0	0	0	0	.000
Ames, p	1	0	0	0	0	0	0	0	.000
Totals	5	153	15	32	7	0	0	13	.209

1906 WORLD SERIES

Philadelphia Athletics

Player-Position	G.	AB.	R.	H.	2B.	3B.	HR.	RBI.	BA.
Hartsel, lf	5	17	1	5	1	0	0	0	.294
Schreckengost, c	3	9	2	2	1	0	0	0	.222
Davis, 1b	5	20	0	4	1	0	0	0	.200
Murphy, 2b	5	16	0	3	1	0	0	0	.188
M. Cross, ss	5	17	0	3	0	0	0	0	.176
Plank, p	2	6	0	1	0	0	0	0	.167
Powers, c	3	7	0	1	1	0	0	0	.143
Seybold, rf	5	16	0	2	0	0	0	0	.125
L. Cross, 3b	5	19	0	2	0	0	0	0	.105
Lord, cf	5	20	0	2	0	0	0	2	.100
Bender, p	2	5	0	0	0	0	0	0	.000
Coakley, p	1	2	0	0	0	0	0	0	.000
Hoffman, ph	1	1	0	0	0	0	0	0	.000
Totals	5	155	3	25	5	0	0	2	.161

COMPOSITE PITCHING AVERAGES

New York Giants

Pitcher	G.	IP.	H.	R.	E.	BB.	SO.	W.	L.	ERA.
Mathewson	3	27	14	0	0	18	1	3	0	0.00
McGinnity	2	17	10	3	0	6	3	1	1	0.00
Ames	1	1	1	0	0	1	1	0	0	0.00
Totals	5	45	25	3	0	25	5	4	1	0.00

Philadelphia Athletics

Pitcher	G.	IP.	H.	R.	E.	BB.	SO.	W.	L.	ERA.
Coakley	1	9	9	9	0	2	5	0	1	0.00
Plank	2	17	14	4	2	11	4	0	2	1.06
Bender	2	17	9	2	2	13	6	1	1	1.06
Totals	5	43	32	15	4	26	15	1	4	0.84

SERIES OF 1906

	W.	L.	Pct.
Chicago A. L.	4	2	.667
Chicago N. L.	2	4	.333

One of the greatest of all World Series upsets was the victory of the White Sox over the Cubs in the all-Chicago Series of 1906. The Cubs, led by Frank Chance, had established a major league record by winning 116 games; they finished 20 games ahead of the second-place Giants. The White Sox, called the Hitless Wonders because of a team batting average of .228, the lowest in their loop, won the American League pennant by three games from the New York Highlanders largely as the result of an August winning streak of 19 straight.

However, Fielder Jones, the White Sox manager, had a fine pitching staff, with Big Ed Walsh and Frank Owen and a pair of great southpaws, Nick Altrock and Georgetown Doc White, the anchors of the corps, and they triumphed over Chance's equally famous staff built around Mordecai (Miner) Brown, Ed Reulbach, Orval Overall and Jack Pfiester. Though a three-to-one underdog in the betting, the White Sox won the Series, four games to two, by scoring 8 to 6 and 8 to 3 victories in the last two clashes.

The hero for the Chicago Americans was a utility infielder, George Rohe. He went to third base when George Davis, veteran shortstop of the White Sox, was injured before the Series, the regular third baseman, Lee Tannehill, moving over to short. Rohe tied Jiggs Donahue, White Sox first baseman, for Series batting leadership with a mark of .333. George hit two historic triples which enabled the White Sox to win the first and third games by scores of 2 to 1 and 3 to 0. Chided by Jones, his manager, for failing to hit, Frank Isbell, White Sox second baseman, broke out with four doubles in the fifth game.

Pitching highlighted the Series, especially in the early games, and the winning White Sox hit only .198 against .196 for the Cubs. Reulbach pitched a one-hitter in the second game, while Walsh and Brown hurled successive two-hit shutouts in the third and fourth clashes, respectively. In scoring his victory, Walsh fanned 12 against nine for Pfiester, his lefthanded opponent. In the fourth game, which Altrock lost to Brown, 1 to 0, the White Sox southpaw had three putouts and eight assists. The box scores:

Tuesday, Oct. 9—At West Side Grounds

White Sox (A.L.)	AB.	R.	H.	O.	A.	E.
Hahn, rf	3	0	0	1	0	0
Jones, cf	4	1	1	3	0	0
Isbell, 2b	4	0	1	0	1	1
Rohe, 3b	4	1	1	1	2	0
Donahue, 1b	4	0	0	12	2	0
Dougherty, lf	3	0	0	1	0	0
Sullivan, c	3	0	0	5	2	0
Tannehill, ss	3	0	0	1	4	0
Altrock, p	2	0	1	3	3	0
Totals	30	2	4	27	14	1

Cubs (N.L.)	AB.	R.	H.	O.	A.	E.
Hofman, cf	3	0	0	1	1	0
Sheckard, lf	3	0	0	1	0	0
aMoran	1	0	0	0	0	0
Schulte, rf	4	0	1	1	0	0
Chance, 1b	4	0	1	11	0	0
Steinfeldt, 3b	4	0	0	0	2	0
Tinker, ss	3	0	0	2	3	0
Evers, 2b	3	0	0	1	3	0
Kling, c	2	1	1	9	1	1
Brown, p	2	0	1	1	6	1
Totals	29	1	4	27	16	2

White Sox .... 0 0 0 0 1 1 0 0 0—2
Cubs .... 0 0 0 0 0 1 0 0 0—1

aFlied out for Sheckard in ninth. Three-base hit—Rohe. Run batted in—Isbell. Sacrifice hits—Hahn, Hofman, Brown. Stolen bases—Isbell, Dougherty. Earned runs—Cubs 1, White Sox 0. Left on bases—Cubs 4, White Sox 3. Struck out—By Brown 7, by Altrock 3. Bases on balls—Off Brown 1, off Altrock 1. Wild pitches—Brown, Altrock. Passed balls—Kling 2. Umpires—Johnstone (N.L.) and O'Loughlin (A.L.). Time—1:45. Attendance—12,693.

Wed., Oct. 10—At South Side Park

Cubs (N.L.)	AB.	R.	H.	O.	A.	E.
Hofman, cf	4	0	2	2	0	0
Sheckard, lf	4	0	0	3	1	0
Schulte, rf	4	0	1	1	0	0
Chance, 1b	5	2	2	12	0	0
Steinfeldt, 3b	3	1	3	0	2	0
Tinker, ss	3	3	2	0	3	1
Evers, 2b	4	1	1	4	6	1
Kling, c	2	0	1	5	1	0
Reulbach, p	3	0	0	0	2	0
Totals	32	7	10	27	15	2

1906 WORLD SERIES

White Sox (A.L.)	AB.	R.	H.	O.	A.	E.
Hahn, rf	3	0	0	0	0	0
Jones, cf	3	0	0	1	0	0
Isbell, 2b	4	0	0	6	2	1
Rohe, 3b	2	0	0	0	3	0
Donahue, 1b	3	0	1	10	1	0
Dougherty, lf	2	1	0	1	0	0
Sullivan, c	4	0	0	8	2	1
Tannehill, ss	3	0	0	0	3	0
White, p	0	0	0	0	1	0
aTowne	1	0	0	0	0	0
Owen, p	2	0	0	1	4	0
Totals	27	1	1	27	16	2

Cubs.............. 0 3 1 0 0 1 0 2 0—7
White Sox...... 0 0 0 0 1 0 0 0 0—1

aFlied out for White in third. Two-base hit—Kling. Runs batted in—Hofman, Steinfeldt, Tinker, Reulbach. Sacrifice hits—Sheckard, Steinfeldt, Reulbach. Stolen bases—Hofman, Chance 2, Tinker, Evers. Double plays—Sheckard and Kling; Evers and Chance. Earned runs—Cubs 2, White Sox 0. Left on bases—Cubs 6, White Sox 6. Struck out—By Reulbach 3, by White 1, by Owen 2. Bases on balls—Off Reulbach 6, off White 2, off Owens 3. Hit by pitcher—By Reulbach (Rohe). Wild pitches—Reulbach, Owens. Hits—Off White 4 in 3 innings, off Owens 6 in 6 innings. Losing pitcher—White. Umpires—O'Loughlin (A.L.) and Johnstone (N.L.). Time—1:58. Attendance—12,595.

Thursday, Oct. 11—At West Side Grounds

White Sox (A.L.)	AB.	R.	H.	O.	A.	E.
Hahn, rf	2	0	0	0	0	0
aO'Neill, rf	1	1	0	1	0	0
Jones, cf	4	0	0	1	0	0
Isbell, 2b	4	0	0	1	4	1
Rohe, 3b	3	0	1	0	1	0
Donahue, 1b	3	0	2	14	0	0
Dougherty, lf	4	0	0	0	0	0
Sullivan, c	3	0	0	10	2	0
Tannehill, ss	3	1	1	0	5	0
Walsh, p	2	1	0	0	3	0
Totals	29	3	4	27	15	1

Cubs (N.L.)	AB.	R.	H.	O.	A.	E.
Hofman, cf	4	0	1	1	0	0
Sheckard, lf	4	0	0	2	0	0
Schulte, rf	4	0	1	1	0	0
Chance, 1b	2	0	0	7	1	0
Steinfeldt, 3b	3	0	0	1	2	0
Tinker, ss	3	0	0	3	2	1
Evers, 2b	3	0	0	1	2	0
Kling, c	3	0	0	11	3	0
Pfiester, p	2	0	0	0	2	1
bGessler	1	0	0	0	0	0
Totals	29	0	2	27	12	2

White Sox......... 0 0 0 0 0 3 0 0 0—3
Cubs.................. 0 0 0 0 0 0 0 0 0—0

aRan for Hahn in sixth. bReached first on error for Pfiester in ninth. Two-base hit—Schulte. Three-base hits—Donahue, Rohe. Runs batted in—Rohe 3. Sacrifice hits—Donahue, Sullivan. Stolen base—Rohe. Earned runs—White Sox 3, Cubs 0. Left on bases—Cubs 3, White Sox 4. Struck out—By Pfiester 9, by Walsh 12. Bases on balls—Off Pfiester 2, off Walsh 1. Hit by pitcher—By Pfiester (Hahn). Wild pitch—Walsh. Umpires—Johnstone (N.L.) and O'Loughlin (A.L.). Time—2:10. Attendance—13,667.

Friday, Oct. 12—At South Side Park

Cubs (N.L.)	AB.	R.	H.	O.	A.	E.
Hofman, cf	4	0	2	1	0	0
Sheckard, lf	3	0	0	1	0	0
Schulte, rf	4	0	0	1	0	0
Chance, 1b	4	1	2	13	1	0
Steinfeldt, 3b	2	0	1	1	1	1
Tinker, ss	1	0	0	1	4	0
Evers, 2b	3	0	1	2	4	0
Kling, c	3	0	0	6	3	0
Brown, p	3	0	1	1	5	0
Totals	27	1	7	27	18	1

White Sox (A.L.)	AB.	R.	H.	O.	A.	E.
Hahn, rf	4	0	1	1	0	0
Jones, cf	3	0	0	0	0	0
Isbell, 2b	4	0	0	1	3	0
Rohe, 3b	3	0	0	0	4	0
Donahue, 1b	1	0	0	13	2	0
Dougherty, lf	3	0	1	2	0	0
Davis, ss	3	0	0	4	2	1
Sullivan, c	3	0	0	3	1	0
Altrock, p	2	0	0	3	8	0
aMcFarland	1	0	0	0	0	0
Totals	27	0	2	27	20	1

Cubs.............. 0 0 0 0 0 0 1 0 0—1
White Sox...... 0 0 0 0 0 0 0 0 0—0

aGrounded out for Altrock in ninth. Run batted in—Evers. Two-base hits—Donahue, Steinfeldt 2, Tinker 3. Stolen base—Sheckard. Double plays—Kling and Evers; Altrock, Donahue and Sullivan. Earned runs—Cubs 1, White Sox 0. Left on bases—Cubs 5, White Sox 3. Struck out—By Brown 5, by Altrock 2. Bases on balls—Off Brown 2, off Altrock 1. Passed ball—Kling. Umpires—O'Loughlin (A.L.) and Johnstone (N.L.). Time—1:36. Attendance—18,385.

Saturday, Oct. 13—At West Side Grounds

White Sox (A.L.)	AB.	R.	H.	O.	A.	E.
Hahn, rf	5	2	1	1	0	0
Jones, cf	4	1	1	1	0	0
Isbell, 2b	5	3	4	2	2	2
Davis, ss	5	2	2	2	8	1
Rohe, 3b	4	0	3	0	2	2
Donahue, 1b	3	0	1	15	2	0
Dougherty, lf	5	0	0	0	0	0
Sullivan, c	4	0	0	6	2	0
Walsh, p	2	0	0	0	2	1
White, p	0	0	0	0	0	0
Totals	37	8	12	27	18	6

Cubs (N.L.)	AB.	R.	H.	O.	A.	E.
Hofman, cf	3	2	1	2	0	0
Sheckard, lf	4	0	0	1	0	0
Schulte, rf	5	1	3	2	1	0
Chance, 1b	4	0	1	8	0	0
Steinfeldt, 3b	5	1	1	1	2	0
Tinker, ss	4	1	0	2	2	0
Evers, 2b	3	0	0	2	5	0
aMoran	1	0	0	0	0	0
Kling, c	3	0	0	9	0	0
Reulbach, p	0	0	0	0	2	0
Pfiester, p	0	0	0	0	0	0
Overall, p	2	1	0	0	1	0
Totals	34	6	6	27	13	0

White Sox......... 1 0 2 4 0 1 0 0 0—8
Cubs.................. 3 0 0 1 0 2 0 0 0—6

aForced runner for Evers in ninth. Two-base hits—Isbell 4, Rohe, Davis 2, Donahue, Chance, Schulte, Steinfeldt. Runs batted in—Schulte 2, Steinfeldt, Davis 3, Isbell 2, Rohe, Donahue. Sacrifice hits—Jones, Sheckard, Reulbach. Stolen bases—Dougherty, Davis, Tinker, Evers. Double play—

Schulte, Evers and Kling. Earned runs—White Sox 8, Cubs 3. Left on bases—Cubs 10, White Sox 8. Struck out—By Reulbach 1, by Pfiester 2, by Overall 5, by Walsh 5. Bases on balls—Off Reulbach 2, off Pfiester 1, off Walsh 5, off Overall 1, off White 1. Hit by pitcher—By Pfiester (Donahue), by Walsh (Chance). Wild pitch—Overall. Passed ball—Sullivan. Hits—off Reulbach 5 in 2 innings (pitched to 2 batters in third), off Pfiester 3 in 1⅓ innings (pitched to 5 batters in fourth), off Overall 4 in 5⅔ innings, off Walsh 5 in 6 innings, off White 1 in 3 innings. Winner—Walsh. Loser—Pfiester. Umpires—Johnstone (N.L.), O'Loughlin (A.L.). Time—2:40. Attendance—23,257.

Sunday, Oct. 14—At South Side Park

Cubs (N.L.)	AB.	R.	H.	O.	A.	E.
Hofman, cf	5	1	2	3	0	0
Sheckard, lf	3	0	0	2	0	0
Schulte, rf	5	0	1	0	0	0
Chance, 1b	2	0	0	9	0	0
Steinfeldt, 3b	3	0	0	0	0	0
Tinker, ss	4	0	1	2	6	0
Evers, 2b	4	1	1	2	0	0
Kling, c	4	1	1	6	2	0
Brown, p	1	0	0	0	1	0
Overall, p	2	0	1	0	1	0
aGessler	0	0	0	0	0	0
Totals	33	3	7	24	10	0

White Sox (A.L.)	AB.	R.	H.	O.	A.	E.
Hahn, rf	5	2	4	0	0	0
Jones, cf	3	2	0	3	0	0
Isbell, 2b	5	1	3	1	4	0
Davis, ss	5	2	2	1	4	0
Rohe, 3b	5	1	2	3	4	1
Donahue, 1b	4	0	2	15	1	1
Dougherty, lf	3	0	1	0	0	1
Sullivan, c	4	0	0	3	1	0
White, p	3	0	0	1	2	0
Totals	37	8	14	27	16	3

Cubs..................... 1 0 0   0 1 0   0 0 1—3
White Sox .... 3 4 0   0 0 0   0 1 *—8

aBatted for Overall in ninth. Two-base hits—Schulte, Overall, Evers, Davis, Donahue. Runs batted in—Donahue 3, Davis 3, Isbell, Dougherty, Hofman, Schulte, Sheckard. Sacrifice hits—Sheckard, Jones. Stolen base—Rohe. Double play—Davis and Donahue. Earned runs—White Sox 8, Cubs 3. Left on bases—White Sox 9, Cubs 9. Struck out—By Overall 3, by White 2. Bases on balls—Off Brown 1, off Overall 2, off White 4. Hit by pitcher—By White (Chance). Hits—Off Brown 8 in 1⅔ innings, off Overall 6 in 6⅓ innings. Loser—Brown. Umpires—O'Loughlin (A.L.), Johnstone (N.L.). Time—1:55. Attendance—19,249.

COMPOSITE BATTING AVERAGES
Chicago White Sox

Player-Position	G.	AB.	R.	H.	2B.	3B.	HR.	RBI.	BA.
Rohe, 3b	6	21	2	7	1	2	0	4	.333
Donahue, 1b	6	18	0	6	2	1	0	4	.333
Isbell, 2b	6	26	4	8	4	0	0	4	.308
Davis, ss	3	13	4	4	3	0	0	6	.308
Hahn, rf	6	22	4	6	0	0	0	0	.273
Altrock, p	2	4	0	1	0	0	0	0	.250
Tannehill, ss	3	9	1	1	0	0	0	0	.111
Dougherty, lf	6	20	1	2	0	0	0	1	.100
Jones, cf	6	21	4	2	0	0	0	0	.095
Sullivan, c	6	21	0	0	0	0	0	0	.000
White, p	3	3	0	0	0	0	0	0	.000
Walsh, p	2	4	1	0	0	0	0	0	.000
Towne, ph	1	1	0	0	0	0	0	0	.000
Owen, p	1	2	0	0	0	0	0	0	.000
O'Neill, ph	1	1	1	0	0	0	0	0	.000
McFarland, ph	1	1	0	0	0	0	0	0	.000
Totals	6	187	22	37	10	3	0	19	.198

Chicago Cubs

Player-Position	G.	AB.	R.	H.	2B.	3B.	HR.	RBI.	BA.
Brown, p	3	6	0	2	0	0	0	0	.333
Hofman, cf	6	23	3	7	1	0	0	2	.304
Schulte, rf	6	26	1	7	3	0	0	3	.269
Overall, p	2	4	1	1	1	0	0	0	.250
Steinfeldt, 3b	6	20	2	5	1	0	0	2	.250
Chance, 1b	6	21	3	5	1	0	0	0	.238
Kling, c	6	17	2	3	1	0	0	0	.176
Tinker, ss	6	18	4	3	0	0	0	1	.167
Evers, 2b	6	20	2	3	1	0	0	1	.150
Sheckard, lf	6	21	0	0	0	0	0	1	.000
Moran, ph	2	2	0	0	0	0	0	0	.000
Reulbach, p	2	3	0	0	0	0	0	1	.000
Pfiester, p	2	2	0	0	0	0	0	0	.000
Gessler, ph	2	1	0	0	0	0	0	0	.000
Totals	6	184	18	36	9	0	0	11	.196

COMPOSITE PITCHING AVERAGES
Chicago White Sox

Pitcher	G.	IP.	H.	R.	E.	SO.	BB.	W.	L.	ERA.
Altrock	2	18	11	2	2	5	2	1	1	1.00
Walsh	2	15	7	6	3	17	6	2	0	1.80
White	3	15	12	7	3	0	3	1	1	1.80
Owen	1	6	6	3	2	2	3	0	0	3.00
Totals	6	54	36	18	10	27	18	4	2	1.67

Chicago Cubs

Pitcher	G.	IP.	H.	R.	E.	SO.	BB.	W.	L.	ERA.
Overall	2	12	10	2	2	8	3	0	0	1.50
Reulbach	2	11	6	4	3	4	8	1	0	2.45
Brown	3	19⅔	14	9	7	12	4	1	2	3.20
Pfiester	2	10⅓	7	7	7	11	3	0	2	6.10
Totals	6	53	37	22	19	35	18	2	4	3.23

SERIES OF 1907

	W.	L.	T.	Pct.
Chicago N. L.	4	0	1	1.000
Detroit A. L.	0	4	1	.000

Rallying from their humiliating defeat of the previous year, Frank Chance's Cubs swept into their own in 1907, defeating Hugh Jennings' Detroit Tigers four straight after the first game resulted in a 12-inning, 3 to 3 tie, the contest being called because of darkness. Chance's club again won the pennant in a breeze, topping Pittsburgh by 17½ games, while the Tigers were a tired team, having nosed out the Athletics by a slim six-point margin in a tough autumn drive.

This Series saw the great Cub pitching staff at its best, with the Bengals becoming weaker and weaker as the battling progressed. After scoring three runs off Orval Overall and Ed Reulbach in the first game, Detroit then registered one run in each the second, third and fourth games off Jack Pfiester, Reulbach and Overall, respectively. Then Miner Brown wound it up with a 2 to 0, seven-hit shutout.

Bill Donovan, Jennings' pitching headliner, had a particular piece of misfortune in the first game, the failure of Charlie Schmidt, his catcher, to hold a third strike in the ninth costing the big righthander a 3 to 2 victory. The pitch would have retired the side and ended the game, but Schmidt's bobble enabled the tying run to come in from third. The miscue also gave a decided blow to the Tiger morale.

However, the Cubs clearly deserved their

victory, outhitting the Tigers, .257 to .208, with Harry Steinfeldt, the Chicago third baseman, hitting .471 and Johnny Evers, the team's fiery second sacker, .350. Only Claude Rossman of the American leaguers could fathom the Cub pitching, the bulky first baseman hitting .400. Ty Cobb, young American League batting champion, was held to a meek .200, while Sam Crawford, his slugging associate, hit only .238.

The Cubs also ran the Tigers ragged, stealing 18 bases, six of them by Jimmy Slagle, center fielder and leadoff man. In desperation, Jennings put in a rookie, Jimmy Archer, his third-string receiver, to catch George Mullin in the fifth and last game. Chicago stole four bases on Jimmy, who in later years was to become one of baseball's foremost throwing catchers. The box scores:

Tuesday, October 8—At Chicago

Detroit (A.L.)	AB.	R.	H.	O.	A.	E.
Jones, lf	5	1	3	3	1	0
Schaefer, 2b	6	1	1	7	4	0
Crawford, cf	5	1	3	1	0	0
Cobb, rf	5	0	0	0	0	0
Rossman, 1b	4	0	0	9	3	0
Coughlin, 3b	5	0	0	1	0	1
Schmidt, c	5	0	2	12	3	2
O'Leary, ss	4	0	0	0	3	0
Donovan, p	5	0	0	3	2	0
Totals	44	3	9	36	16	3

Chicago (N.L.)	AB.	R.	H.	O.	A.	E.
Slagle, cf	6	0	2	2	0	0
Sheckard, lf	5	0	1	2	0	0
Chance, 1b	4	2	1	15	0	0
Steinfeldt, 3b	3	1	1	2	2	0
Kling, c	4	0	2	7	4	1
Evers, 2b-ss	4	0	2	3	2	2
Schulte, rf	5	0	1	2	0	1
Tinker, ss	3	0	0	3	6	1
aHoward	1	0	0	0	0	0
Zimmermann, 2b	1	0	0	0	1	0
Overall, p	3	0	0	0	3	0
bMoran	0	0	0	0	0	0
Reulbach, p	2	0	0	0	0	0
Totals	41	3	10	36	18	5

Detroit .... 0 0 0   0 0 0   0 3 0   0 0 0—3
Chicago .... 0 0 0   1 0 0   0 0 2   0 0 0—3

(Game called at end of 12th inning on account of darkness.)

aStruck out for Tinker in ninth, but reached first on missed third strike. bBatted for Overall in ninth, but side retired before his time at bat was completed. Runs batted in—Crawford 2, Rossman, Kling, Schulte. Sacrifice hits—Steinfeldt, Evers, O'Leary. Stolen bases—Slagle 2, Sheckard, Howard, Chance, Steinfeldt, Evers, Jones 2, Schaefer, Rossman. Double plays—Evers and Tinker; Schaefer and Rossman. Earned runs—Detroit 1, Chicago 1. Left on bases—Chicago 9, Detroit 8. Struck out—By Overall 5, by Reulbach 2, by Donovan 12. Missed-third strike—Schmidt. Bases on balls—Off Overall 2, off Donovan 3. Hit by pitcher—By Donovan (Sheckard, Steinfeldt). Hits—Off Overall 9 in 9 innings, off Reulbach 0 in 3 innings. Umpires—O'Day (N.L.), and Sheridan (A.L.). Time—2:40. Attendance—24,377.

Wednesday, October 9—At Chicago

Detroit (A.L.)	AB.	R.	H.	O.	A.	E.
Jones, lf	4	0	2	1	0	0
Schaefer, 2b	4	0	1	2	3	0
Crawford, cf	4	0	0	1	1	0
Cobb, rf	3	0	1	0	0	0
Rossman, 1b	4	1	3	12	1	0
Coughlin, 3b	4	0	0	2	1	0
Payne, c	4	0	1	5	1	1
O'Leary, ss	2	0	1	0	6	0
Mullin, p	3	0	0	1	2	0
Totals	32	1	9	24	15	1

Chicago (N.L.)	AB.	R.	H.	O.	A.	E.
Slagle, cf	3	1	2	3	0	0
Sheckard, lf	3	0	1	2	0	0
Chance, 1b	3	0	1	6	0	0
Steinfeldt, 3b	3	0	0	3	1	0
Kling, c	4	1	1	5	4	0
Evers, 2b	4	0	2	2	0	0
Schulte, rf	4	0	1	1	1	0
Tinker, ss	2	1	1	5	4	1
Pfiester, p	2	0	0	0	0	0
Totals	28	3	9	27	10	1

Detroit .... 0 1 0   0 0 0   0 0 0—1
Chicago .... 0 1 0   2 0 0   0 0 *—3

Two-base hit—Sheckard. Three-base hit—Rossman. Runs batted in—Slagle, Sheckard, Tinker, Payne. Sacrifice hits—Sheckard, Pfiester. Stolen bases—Slagle 2, Chance, Tinker, Evers. Double plays—Tinker and Chance 2; Crawford and Schaefer. Earned runs—Chicago 3, Detroit 1. Left on bases—Chicago 7, Detroit 6. Struck out—By Mullin 5, by Pfiester 3. Bases on balls—Off Mullin 3, off Pfiester 1. Hit by pitcher—By Mullin (Steinfeldt), by Pfiester (Cobb). Passed ball—Kling. Umpires—Sheridan (A.L.) and O'Day (N.L.). Time—2:13. Attendance—21,901.

Thursday, October 10—At Chicago

Detroit (A.L.)	AB.	R.	H.	O.	A.	E.
Jones, lf	3	0	0	2	0	1
Schaefer, 2b	4	0	1	0	3	0
Crawford, cf	4	0	1	3	1	0
Cobb, rf	4	0	1	1	0	0
Rossman, 1b	4	0	2	9	0	0
Coughlin, 3b	3	0	0	4	1	0
Schmidt, c	3	0	0	1	2	0
O'Leary, ss	4	0	0	3	4	0
Siever, p	1	0	0	1	0	0
Killian, p	2	1	1	0	0	0
Totals	32	1	6	24	11	1

Chicago (N.L.)	AB.	R.	H.	O.	A.	E.
Slagle, cf	4	0	0	3	0	0
Sheckard, lf	4	0	1	4	0	0
Chance, 1b	4	1	1	12	1	0
Steinfeldt, 3b	3	1	2	0	2	0
Kling, c	3	1	1	2	0	0
Evers, 2b	4	0	3	3	2	1
Schulte, rf	4	1	1	0	0	0
Tinker, ss	4	1	0	2	7	0
Reulbach, p	3	0	1	1	2	0
Totals	33	5	10	27	14	1

Detroit .... 0 0 0   0 0 1   0 0 0—1
Chicago .... 0 1 0   3 1 0   0 0 *—5

Two-base hits—Sheckard, Chance, Evers 2, Steinfeldt. Runs batted in—Steinfeldt, Evers, Schulte, Reulbach, Crawford. Sacrifice hit—Kling. Double plays—Tinker, unassisted; Steinfeldt, Evers and Chance. Earned runs—Chicago 3, Detroit 1. Left on bases—Detroit 7, Chicago 6. Struck out—By Reulbach 2, by

Siever 1, by Killian 1. Bases on balls—Off Reulbach 3, off Killian 1. Hits—Off Siever 7 in 4 innings, off Killian 3 in 4 innings. Losing pitcher—Siever. Umpires—O'Day (N.L.) and Sheridan (A.L.). Time—1:35. Attendance—13,114.

base hit—Steinfeldt. Runs batted in—Slagle, Steinfeldt. Stolen bases—Slagle, Tinker, Evers, Schulte, Jones, Rossman, Coughlin. Earned runs—Chicago 1, Detroit 0. Left on bases—Chicago 8, Detroit 7. Struck out—By Brown 4, by Mullin 2. Bases on balls—Off Brown 1, off Mullin 3. Umpires—O'Day (N.L.) and Sheridan (A.L.). Time—1:42. Attendance—7,370.

Friday, October 11—At Detroit

Chicago (N.L.)	AB.	R.	H.	O.	A.	E.
Slagle, cf	5	1	1	2	0	1
Sheckard, lf	5	0	2	1	0	0
Chance, 1b	3	0	0	11	0	0
Steinfeldt, 3b	4	0	2	3	2	0
Kling, c	4	0	0	6	0	0
Evers, 2b	4	1	0	0	2	0
Schulte, rf	3	2	1	2	1	0
Tinker, ss	1	2	0	2	3	1
Overall, p	2	0	1	0	3	0
Totals	31	6	7	27	11	2

Detroit (A.L.)	AB.	R.	H.	O.	A.	E.
Jones, lf	2	0	0	3	0	0
Schaefer, 2b	3	0	0	2	3	0
Crawford, cf	4	0	0	2	0	0
Cobb, rf	4	1	1	4	0	0
Rossman, 1b	4	0	1	9	0	0
Coughlin, 3b	4	0	3	3	1	0
Schmidt, c	3	0	0	3	4	0
O'Leary, ss	4	0	0	3	2	0
Donovan, p	3	0	0	0	1	0
Totals	31	1	5	27	11	2

Chicago .... 0 0 0   0 2 0   3 0 1—6
Detroit .... 0 0 0   1 0 0   0 0 0—1

Three-base hit—Cobb. Runs batted in—Overall 2, Slagle 2, Sheckard, Rossman. Sacrifice hits—Tinker 2, Overall 2, Jones, Schaefer. Stolen bases—Slagle, Chance. Double play—Tinker, unassisted. Earned runs—Chicago 3, Detroit 1. Left on bases—Detroit 7, Chicago 5. Struck out—By Overall 6, by Donovan 4. Bases on balls—Off Overall 2, off Donovan 2. Hit by pitcher—By Donovan (Chance). Umpires—Sheridan (A.L.) and O'Day (N.L.). Time—1:45. Attendance—11,306.

Saturday, October 12—At Detroit

Chicago (N.L.)	AB.	R.	H.	O.	A.	E.
Slagle, cf	4	1	1	3	0	0
Sheckard, lf	4	0	0	1	0	0
Howard, 1b	4	0	1	10	1	0
Steinfeldt, 3b	4	0	3	2	0	0
Kling, c	4	0	0	5	1	0
Evers, 2b	4	1	0	1	6	0
Schulte, rf	4	0	1	1	0	1
Tinker, ss	3	0	1	3	3	0
Brown, p	3	0	0	1	1	0
Totals	34	2	7	27	12	1

Detroit (A.L.)	AB.	R.	H.	O.	A.	E.
Jones, lf	3	0	1	1	1	0
Schaefer, 2b	4	0	0	1	8	0
Crawford, cf	4	0	1	0	0	0
Cobb, rf	4	0	1	4	0	0
Rossman, 1b	4	0	2	13	0	1
aPayne	0	0	0	0	0	0
Coughlin, 3b	4	0	2	1	2	1
Archer, c	3	0	0	4	1	0
bSchmidt	1	0	0	0	0	0
O'Leary, ss	3	0	0	3	3	0
Mullin, p	3	0	0	0	2	0
Totals	33	0	7	27	17	2

Chicago .... 1 1 0   0 0 0   0 0 0—2
Detroit .... 0 0 0   0 0 0   0 0 0—0

aRan for Rossman in ninth. bFlied out for Archer in ninth. Two-base hit—Crawford. Three-

COMPOSITE BATTING AVERAGES
Chicago Cubs

Player-Position	G.	AB.	R.	H.	2B.	3B.	HR.	RBI.	BA.
Steinfeldt, 3b	5	17	2	8	1	0	2	.471
Evers, 2b-ss	5	20	2	7	2	0	0	1	.350
Slagle, cf	5	22	3	6	0	0	0	4	.273
Schulte, rf	5	20	3	5	0	0	0	2	.250
Sheckard, lf	5	21	0	5	2	0	0	2	.238
Chance, 1b	5	14	3	3	1	0	0	0	.214
Kling, c	5	19	2	4	0	0	0	1	.211
Howard, ph-1b	2	5	0	1	0	0	0	0	.200
Overall, p	2	5	0	1	0	0	0	2	.200
Reulbach, p	2	5	0	1	0	0	0	1	.200
Tinker, ss	5	13	4	2	0	0	0	0	.154
Zimmerman, 2b	1	1	0	0	0	0	0	0	.000
Moran, ph	1	0	0	0	0	0	0	0	.000
Pfiester, p	1	2	0	0	0	0	0	0	.000
Brown, p	1	3	0	0	0	0	0	0	.000
Totals	5	167	19	43	6	1	0	16	.257

Detroit Tigers

Player-Position	G.	AB.	R.	H.	2B.	3B.	HR.	RBI.	BA.
Killian, p	1	2	1	1	0	0	0	0	.500
Rossman, 1b	5	20	1	8	0	1	0	2	.400
Jones, lf	5	17	1	6	0	0	0	0	.353
Coughlin, 3b	5	20	0	5	0	0	0	0	.250
Payne, c-pr	2	4	0	1	0	0	0	0	.250
Crawford, cf	5	21	1	5	1	0	0	3	.238
Cobb, rf	5	20	1	4	0	1	0	0	.200
Schmidt, c-ph	4	12	0	2	0	0	0	0	.167
Schaefer, 2b	5	21	1	3	0	0	0	0	.143
O'Leary, ss	5	17	0	1	0	0	0	0	.059
Donovan, p	2	8	0	0	0	0	0	0	.000
Mullin, p	2	6	0	0	0	0	0	0	.000
Siever, p	1	1	0	0	0	0	0	0	.000
Archer, c	1	3	0	0	0	0	0	0	.000
Totals	5	172	6	36	1	2	0	6	.209

COMPOSITE PITCHING AVERAGES
Chicago Cubs

Pitcher	G.	IP.	H.	R.	E.	BB.	SO.	W.	L.	ERA.
Brown	1	9	7	0	0	4	1	1	0	0.00
Reulbach	2	12	6	1	1	4	3	1	0	0.75
Overall	2	18	14	4	2	11	4	1	0	1.00
Pfiester	1	9	9	1	1	3	1	1	0	1.00
Totals	5	48	36	6	4	22	9	4	0	0.75

Detroit Tigers

Pitcher	G.	IP.	H.	R.	E.	BB.	SO.	W.	L.	ERA.
Donovan	2	21	17	9	4	16	5	0	1	1.71
Mullin	2	17	16	5	4	7	6	0	2	2.11
Killian	1	4	3	1	1	1	1	0	0	2.25
Siever	1	4	7	4	2	1	0	0	1	4.50
Totals	5	46	43	19	11	25	12	0	4	2.15

SERIES OF 1908

	W.	L.	Pct.
Chicago N. L.	4	1	.800
Detroit A. L.	1	4	.200

History repeated itself when the Cubs again bowled over the Tigers in 1908. This time the American Leaguers bagged one victory, giving them only one triumph and a tie for the two sets of games. The Series was a repetition of 1907 in several respects. After showing some offensive strength in the early games, scoring 15 runs in the first three encounters, the Tigers bowed out in two buckets of whitewash, being blanked

1908 WORLD SERIES

with four hits by Miner Brown in the fourth game and with three by Orval Overall in the fifth. By that time Detroit was pretty well disgusted, a crowd of only 6,210, the smallest in modern World Series history, seeing the windup contest at Bennett Park.

The Cubs, in gaining their third straight pennant, finished just one game ahead of the Giants, winning the flag by defeating John McGraw's club in a replay of the Merkle game the day after the regular season ended. Detroit also had to go to its last game, a victory over the White Sox, before clinching the American League championship.

The Cubs again clearly excelled Hugh Jennings' team in the Series, their batting margin this time being .293 to .203. Where Harry Steinfeldt and Johnny Evers were the batting leaders the year before, Frank Chance showed the way for his team, with the high average of .421, with Frank Schulte behind him at .389. Evers again had a great Series, hitting .350. On the American League side, young Ty Cobb, in his second year as his league's batting champion, did much better; he hit .368 and stole two bases.

The opening game of the Series, at Detroit, was played under adverse weather conditions with rain falling all during the contest. The Cubs, who routed Ed Killian with four runs in the third inning, held a 5 to 1 lead going into the last half of the seventh, when the Tigers bared their claws, ripping into Ed Reulbach for three runs and then chasing Overall during a two-run rally in the eighth to go ahead, 6 to 5. Seemingly beaten, the Cubs came to life in the ninth with six consecutive hits off Eddie Summers in a thrilling five-run rally that resulted in a 10 to 6 victory.

Bill Donovan pitched almost perfect ball against Overall for seven innings of the second game, but in the eighth, Circus Solly Hofman scratched a hit and a wind-swept homer by Joe Tinker then paved the way for a six-run Cub outburst to defeat the Tigers, 6 to 1.

George Mullin posted Detroit's only victory in the third game, beating Jack Pfiester, 8 to 3. Mullin yielded seven hits, but would have had a shutout except for a pair of errors which permitted the Cubs to rack up their runs for a 3 to 1 lead in the fourth inning. The Tigers roared back with five markers in the sixth and two more in the eighth. Cobb connected for four safe hits.

That wound up Detroit's scoring in the Series as Brown and Overall then wrapped up the championship for the Cubs with shutout victories. Brown hurled a four-hitter to win, 3 to 0, and Overall yielded only three safeties in his 2 to 0 triumph in the Series clincher.

Summers was the victim of Brown's whitewashing, going down to his second defeat of the Series, and Donovan again failed to match up against Overall in the second duel between the two aces. The box scores:

Saturday, October 10—At Detroit

Chicago (N.L.)	AB.	R.	H.	O.	A.	E.
Sheckard, lf	6	1	3	1	1	0
Evers, 2b	4	1	2	2	2	1
Schulte, rf	4	2	2	1	0	0
Chance, 1b	4	2	1	12	0	1
Steinfeldt, 3b	3	2	2	0	0	0
Hofman, cf	4	1	1	4	0	0
Tinker, ss	5	1	2	0	4	0
Kling, c	3	0	1	7	1	0
Reulbach, p	3	0	0	0	4	0
Overall, p	1	0	0	0	0	0
Brown, p	0	0	0	0	2	0
Totals	37	10	14	27	14	2

Detroit (A.L.)	AB.	R.	H.	O.	A.	E.
McIntyre, lf	3	1	2	3	0	1
O'Leary, ss	4	0	1	1	3	0
bThomas	1	0	1	0	0	0
cWinter	0	0	0	0	0	0
Crawford, cf	4	1	0	4	0	0
Cobb, rf	4	2	2	0	0	1
Rossman, 1b	4	1	2	12	0	0
Schaefer, 3b	3	0	0	1	2	0
Schmidt, c	4	0	0	4	1	0
Downs, 2b	4	1	1	2	4	1
Killian, p	0	0	0	0	1	0
Summers, p	3	0	1	0	5	0
aJones	1	0	0	0	0	0
Totals	35	6	10	27	16	4

Chicago .... 0 0 4 0 0 0 1 0 5—10
Detroit .... 1 0 0 0 0 0 3 2 0— 6

a Struck out for Summers in ninth. bSingled for O'Leary in ninth. cRan for Thomas in ninth. Two-base hits—Sheckard 2, Downs. Runs batted in—Schulte, Steinfeldt 2, Hofman 2, Tinker 3, Kling, Cobb, Rossman, Downs, Schmidt, Summers. Sacrifice hits—Evers, Schulte, Kling, Brown, Steinfeldt, Cobb, Schaefer. Stolen bases—Chance 2, Hofman, McIntyre. Earned runs—Chicago 8, Detroit 5. Left on bases—Chicago 9, Detroit 7. Struck out—By Reulbach 5, by Brown 1, by Killian 1, by Summers 2. Bases on balls—Off Overall 1, off Brown 1, off Killian 3, off Summers 1. Hit by pitcher—By Overall (McIntyre). Wild pitch—Brown. Hits—Off Reulbach 8 in 6⅔ innings, off Overall 0 in ⅓ inning (pitched to one man in eighth) off Brown 2 in 2 innings, off Killian 5 in 2⅓ innings, off Summers 9 in 6⅔ innings. Winning pitcher—Brown. Losing pitcher—Summers. Umpires—Sheridan (A.L.) and O'Day (N.L.). Time—2:10. Attendance—10,812.

Sunday, October 11—At Chicago

Detroit (A.L.)	AB.	R.	H.	O.	A.	E.
McIntyre, lf	4	0	0	3	0	0
O'Leary, ss	3	0	0	1	1	0
aJones	0	1	0	0	0	0
Crawford, cf	4	0	0	4	0	0
Cobb, rf	4	0	1	1	0	0
Rossman, 1b	4	0	0	8	1	0
Schaefer, 3b	3	0	2	0	1	0
Schmidt, c	3	0	1	7	0	0
Downs, 2b	2	0	0	0	4	0
Donovan, p	2	0	0	0	1	1
Totals	29	1	4	24	8	1

1908 WORLD SERIES

Chicago (N.L.)	AB.	R.	H.	O.	A.	E.
Sheckard, lf	4	1	1	3	0	0
Evers, 2b	4	1	1	0	6	0
Schulte, rf	4	1	1	1	0	0
Chance, 1b	3	0	0	12	0	1
Steinfeldt, 3b	4	0	0	1	1	0
Hofman, cf	3	1	1	0	0	0
Tinker, ss	3	1	1	2	3	0
Kling, c	3	1	1	8	0	0
Overall, p	3	0	1	0	3	0
Totals	31	6	7	27	13	1

Detroit .... 0 0 0   0 0 0   0 0 1—1
Chicago .... 0 0 0   0 0 0   0 6 *—6

aWalked for O'Leary in ninth. Two-base hit—Kling. Three-base hit—Schulte. Home run—Tinker. Runs batted in—Cobb, Sheckard, Evers, Schulte, Tinker 2. Sacrifice hit—Donovan. Stolen bases—Sheckard, Evers, Chance. Double plays—Downs, O'Leary and Rossman; Tinker and Chance. Earned runs—Chicago 6, Detroit 1. Left on bases—Detroit 4, Chicago 2. Struck out—By Overall 5, by Donovan 7. Bases on balls—Off Overall 2, off Donovan 1. Wild pitch—Donovan. Umpires—Klem (N.L.) and Connolly (A.L.). Time—1:30. Attendance—17,760.

Monday, October 12—At Chicago

Detroit (A.L.)	AB.	R.	H.	O.	A.	E.
McIntyre, lf	4	1	1	1	0	0
O'Leary, ss	4	2	0	1	3	1
Crawford, cf	5	1	2	3	0	0
Cobb, rf	5	1	4	0	0	0
Rossman, 1b	4	2	2	9	0	2
Schaefer, 2b	4	0	0	4	4	0
Thomas, c	3	0	1	9	2	0
Coughlin, 3b	3	0	0	0	1	1
Mullin, p	3	1	1	0	2	0
Totals	35	8	11	27	12	4

Chicago (N.L.)	AB.	R.	H.	O.	A.	E.
Sheckard, lf	4	0	0	1	0	0
Evers, 2b	3	1	0	1	6	0
Schulte, rf	4	0	1	1	0	0
Chance, 1b	4	1	2	14	0	1
Steinfeldt, 3b	4	1	1	1	4	1
Hofman, cf	4	0	2	3	1	0
Tinker, ss	3	0	1	3	1	0
Kling, c	3	0	0	3	2	0
Pfiester, p	2	0	0	0	0	0
aHoward	1	0	0	0	0	0
Reulbach, p	0	0	0	0	1	0
Totals	32	3	7	27	15	2

Detroit .... 1 0 0   0 0 5   0 2 0—8
Chicago .... 0 0 0   3 0 0   0 0 0—3

aGrounded out for Pfiester in eighth. Two-base hits—Thomas, Cobb. Three-base hit—Hofman. Runs batted in—Crawford, Cobb 2, Rossman 2, Thomas, Coughlin, Mullin, Chance, Hofman. Sacrifice hits—O'Leary, Coughlin. Stolen bases—Cobb 2, Rossman, Chance 2, Steinfeldt. Double plays—Schaefer and Rossman; Schaefer, O'Leary and Rossman; Evers and Chance; Hofman and Kling. Earned runs—Detroit 7, Chicago 0. Left on bases—Detroit 6, Chicago 3. Struck out—By Mullin 8, by Pfiester 1. Bases on balls—Off Mullin 1, off Pfiester 3, off Reulbach 1. Hits—Off Pfiester 10 in 8 innings, off Reulbach 1 in 1 inning. Losing pitcher—Pfiester. Umpires—O'Day (N.L.) and Sheridan (A.L.). Time—2:10. Attendance—14,543.

Tuesday, October 13—At Detroit

Chicago (N.L.)	AB.	R.	H.	O.	A.	E.
Sheckard, lf	4	0	0	0	0	0
Evers, 2b	5	1	1	0	4	0
Schulte, rf	3	1	2	0	0	0
Chance, 1b	4	1	2	17	0	0
Steinfeldt, 3b	3	0	1	2	3	0
Hofman, cf	4	0	2	1	0	0
Tinker, ss	4	0	0	2	7	0
Kling, c	4	0	2	5	1	0
Brown, p	4	0	0	0	4	0
Totals	35	3	10	27	19	0

Detroit (A.L.)	AB.	R.	H.	O.	A.	E.
McIntyre, lf	4	0	0	1	0	0
O'Leary, ss	4	0	2	2	3	0
Crawford, cf	4	0	2	2	0	0
Cobb, rf	3	0	0	1	0	1
Rossman, 1b	3	0	0	12	1	0
Schaefer, 2b	3	0	0	2	3	0
Schmidt, c	3	0	0	6	2	0
Coughlin, 3b	2	0	0	1	4	0
Summers, p	2	0	0	0	2	0
aJones	1	0	0	0	0	0
Winter, p	0	0	0	0	0	0
Totals	29	0	4	27	15	1

Chicago .... 0 0 2   0 0 0   0 0 1—3
Detroit .... 0 0 0   0 0 0   0 0 0—0

aGrounded out for Summers in eighth. Two-base hit—Crawford. Runs batted in—Chance, Steinfeldt, Hofman. Sacrifice hit—Steinfeldt. Stolen bases—Schulte 2, Evers, Hofman. Double play—Brown Tinker and Chance. Earned runs—Chicago 2, Detroit 0. Left on bases—Chicago 10, Detroit 3. Struck out—By Brown 4, by Summers 5. Bases on balls—Off Summers 3, off Winter 1. Hit by pitcher—By Brown (Coughlin). Hits—Off Summers 9 in 8 innings, off Winter 1 in 1 inning. Losing pitcher—Summers. Passed balls—Kling, Schmidt. Umpires—Connolly (A.L.) and Klem (N.L.). Time—1:35. Attendance—12,907.

Wednesday, October 14—At Detroit

Chicago (N.L.)	AB.	R.	H.	O.	A.	E.
Sheckard, lf	3	0	1	2	0	0
Evers, 2b	4	1	3	2	3	0
Schulte, rf	3	0	1	0	0	0
Chance, 1b	4	0	3	11	0	0
Steinfeldt, 3b	2	0	0	0	3	0
Hofman, cf	4	0	0	2	0	0
Tinker, ss	4	0	1	1	4	0
Kling, c	3	1	0	9	2	0
Overall, p	2	0	1	0	0	0
Totals	29	2	10	27	12	0

Detroit (A.L.)	AB.	R.	H.	O.	A.	E.
McIntyre, lf	3	0	1	2	0	0
O'Leary, ss	4	0	0	2	2	0
Crawford, cf	4	0	1	3	0	0
Cobb, rf	3	0	0	1	0	0
Rossman, 1b	4	0	0	7	3	0
Schaefer, 2b	3	0	0	3	1	0
Schmidt, c	4	0	0	5	4	0
Coughlin, 3b	3	0	1	2	1	0
Donovan, p	2	0	0	1	1	0
Totals	30	0	3	*26	12	0

Chicago .... 1 0 0   0 1 0   0 0 0—2
Detroit .... 0 0 0   0 0 0   0 0 0—0

*Overall out; hit by batted ball. Two-base hits—Evers, McIntyre. Runs batted in—Evers, Chance. Sacrifice hits—Schulte, Steinfeldt, Overall. Stolen base—Donovan. Double plays—Schmidt, Schaefer and Schmidt; O'Leary, Rossman and Coughlin.

Earned runs—Chicago 2, Detroit 0. Left on bases—Detroit 7, Chicago 6. Struck out—By Overall 10, by Donovan 3. Bases on balls—Off Overall 4, off Donovan 3. Wild pitch—Overall. Umpires—Sheridan (A.L.) and O'Day (N.L.). Time—1:25. Attendance—6,210.

COMPOSITE BATTING AVERAGES
Chicago Cubs

Player-Position	G.	AB.	R.	H.	2B.	3B.	HR.	RBI.	BA.
Chance, 1b	5	19	4	8	0	0	0	3	.421
Schulte, rf	5	18	4	7	0	1	0	2	.389
Evers, 2b	5	20	5	7	1	0	0	2	.350
Overall, p	3	6	0	2	0	0	0	0	.333
Hofman, cf	5	19	2	6	0	1	0	4	.316
Tinker, ss	5	19	2	5	0	0	1	5	.263
Steinfeldt, 3b	5	16	3	4	0	0	0	3	.250
Kling, c	5	16	2	4	1	0	0	1	.250
Sheckard, lf	5	21	2	5	2	0	0	1	.238
Reulbach, p	2	3	0	0	0	0	0	0	.000
Brown, p	2	4	0	0	0	0	0	0	.000
Pfiester, p	1	2	0	0	0	0	0	0	.000
Howard, ph	1	1	0	0	0	0	0	0	.000
Totals	5	164	24	48	4	2	1	21	.293

Detroit Tigers

Player-Position	G.	AB.	R.	H.	2B.	3B.	HR.	RBI.	BA.
Thomas, ph-c	2	4	0	2	1	0	0	1	.500
Cobb, rf	5	19	3	7	1	0	0	4	.368
Mullin, p	1	3	1	1	0	0	0	1	.333
Crawford, cf	5	21	2	5	1	0	0	1	.238
McIntyre, lf	5	18	2	4	1	0	0	0	.222
Rossman, 1b	5	19	3	4	0	0	0	3	.211
Summers, p	2	5	0	1	0	0	0	1	.200
Downs, 2b	2	6	1	1	1	0	0	1	.167
O'Leary, ss	5	19	2	3	0	0	0	0	.158
Schaefer, 3b-2b	5	16	2	2	0	0	0	0	.125
Coughlin, 3b	3	8	0	1	0	0	0	1	.125
Schmidt, c	4	14	0	1	0	0	0	1	.071
Killian, p	1	0	0	0	0	0	0	0	.000
Jones, ph	3	2	1	0	0	0	0	0	.000
Donovan, p	2	4	0	0	0	0	0	0	.000
Winter, pr-p	2	0	0	0	0	0	0	0	.000
Totals	5	158	15	32	5	0	0	14	.203

COMPOSITE PITCHING AVERAGES
Chicago Cubs

Pitcher	G.	IP.	H.	R.	E.	SO.	BB.	W.	L.	ERA.
Brown	2	11	6	1	0	5	1	2	0	0.00
Overall	3	18⅓	7	2	2	15	7	2	0	0.98
Reulbach	2	7⅔	9	4	4	5	1	0	0	4.70
Pfiester	1	8	10	8	7	1	3	0	1	7.88
Totals	5	45	32	15	13	26	12	4	1	2.60

Detroit Tigers

Pitcher	G.	IP.	H.	R.	E.	SO.	BB.	W.	L.	ERA.
Mullin	1	9	7	3	0	8	1	1	0	0.00
Winter	1	1	1	0	0	1	0	0	0	0.00
Donovan	2	17	17	8	8	10	4	0	2	4.24
Summers	2	14⅔	18	8	7	7	4	0	2	4.30
Killian	1	2⅓	5	4	3	1	3	0	0	11.57
Totals	5	44	48	24	18	26	13	1	4	3.68

SERIES OF 1909

	W.	L.	Pct.
Pittsburgh N. L.	4	3	.571
Detroit A. L.	3	4	.429

The National League scored its longest run of Series domination to date when the Pirates won over the Tigers in 1909 to make it three straight world championships for the senior circuit.

Hugh Jennings' Detroit team put up a battle, and for the first time in the interleague battling the Series went the limit. Pittsburgh won, four games to three, with the teams alternating all the way, the Pirates capturing the odd-numbered games, one, three, five and seven, and the Tigers the second, fourth and sixth.

Pittsburgh had won its flag with 110 victories, second highest total in National League history, to finish six and one-half games in front of the Cubs, who won 104 games in their bid for four straight pennants. The Tigers won in the American League only after another grim struggle with the Athletics, copping by a margin of three and one-half games.

Jennings' club would have won the Series had it not been for the amazing showing of a Pirate freshman pitcher, Charles (Babe) Adams. In the league race, Adams won 12 games and lost three, and was overshadowed by such other pitchers as Howard Camnitz, Vic Willis and southpaw Al Leifield, who won 25, 22 and 19 decisions, respectively. However, in the Series, the Big Three did not win a game, while the youthful Adams won three and the fourth victory was credited to Nick Maddox, a 13-game winner in the league season.

Adams started the Pirates off well by winning the first game from George Mullin, 4 to 1, giving up six hits. He captured the fifth game, 8 to 4, again yielding six hits, and closed the Series with an 8 to 0 shutout over Bill Donovan and Mullin in the seventh and deciding contest, when, oddly enough, Detroit again made six hits. With the aid of five runs in the first inning, Maddox staggered through to an 8 to 6 Pittsburgh victory in the third contest.

For Detroit, Mullin registered two victories, one a shutout, and Donovan, after pitching in hard luck in 1907 and 1908, finally achieved his only World Series victory in the second game when he checked Pittsburgh on five hits, 7 to 2.

For the first time the batting champions of the two major leagues, Honus Wagner and Ty Cobb, met in the Series. The honors went to the Flying Dutchman, as he avenged his poor showing in 1903 by leading his team at bat with an average of .333. Cobb fell down again, hitting only .231 in what was to be his last World Series.

The most dangerous Tiger on offense was second baseman Jim Delahanty, who led both clubs at bat with a .346 average and had the most hits, nine, including four doubles.

Bill Abstein, Pirate first baseman, struck out 10 times during the Series and was fired by Barney Dreyfuss, Pittsburgh owner, after it was over. Fred Clarke, famous playing manager of the Pirates, hit only .211, but scored seven runs. He was walked four times in the seventh game, when he did not have an official time at bat, and also accounted for both of the home runs made by the Pirates.

The National League champions' merry-go-round on Jennings' catchers continued with the Pirates stealing 18 bases to the Tigers' six, with Wagner getting six of the Pittsburgh pilfers. Cobb stole home in the third inning of the second game.

The box scores:

Friday, October 8—At Pittsburgh

Detroit (A.L.)	AB.	R.	H.	O.	A.	E.
D. Jones, lf	3	0	2	5	0	0
Bush, ss	2	0	0	1	0	1
Cobb, rf	3	1	0	2	0	1
Crawford, cf	4	0	1	1	0	0
Delahanty, 2b	4	0	1	0	4	1
Moriarty, 3b	4	0	0	1	1	0
T. Jones, 1b	3	0	0	10	0	0
aMcIntyre	1	0	0	0	0	0
Schmidt, c	3	0	0	5	1	1
Mullin, p	4	0	1	0	4	0
Totals	31	1	6	24	10	4

Pittsburgh (N.L.)	AB.	R.	H.	O.	A.	E.
Byrne, 3b	3	0	0	2	3	0
Leach, cf	3	0	0	4	0	0
Clarke, lf	4	1	1	2	0	0
Wagner, ss	3	1	1	0	6	0
Miller, 2b	4	0	1	6	0	0
Abstein, 1b	3	1	0	8	1	0
Wilson, rf	3	0	1	0	0	0
Gibson, c	3	1	1	4	0	0
Adams, p	3	0	0	0	2	0
Totals	29	4	5	*26	12	0

| Detroit | 1 0 0 | 0 0 0 | 0 0 0—1 |
| Pittsburgh | 0 0 0 | 1 2 1 | 0 0 *—4 |

*Delahanty out; hit by batted ball in first. aFlied out for T. Jones in ninth. Two-base hits—Wagner, Gibson. Home run—Clarke. Runs batted in—Delahanty, Leach, Clarke, Abstein, Gibson. Sacrifice hit—Cobb. Sacrifice fly—Leach. Stolen bases—Cobb, Miller, Wilson. Earned runs—Pittsburgh 1, Detroit 1. Left on bases—Detroit 8, Pittsburgh 5. Struck out—By Adams 2, by Mullin 4. Bases on balls—Off Adams 4, off Mullin 1. Hit by pitcher—By Mullin (Byrne, Wagner). Passed ball—Schmidt. Umpires—Johnstone (N.L.) and O'Loughlin (A.L.). Time—1:55. Attendance—29,264.

Saturday, October 9—At Pittsburgh

Detroit (A.L.)	AB.	R.	H.	O.	A.	E.
D. Jones, lf	5	1	1	1	0	0
Bush, ss	3	1	1	0	2	0
Cobb, rf	3	1	1	0	0	0
Crawford, cf	4	1	1	3	0	0
Delahanty, 2b	3	1	1	3	1	1
Moriarty, 3b	3	1	1	3	1	0
T. Jones, 1b	3	1	1	8	1	0
Schmidt, c	4	0	2	9	1	1
Donovan, p	4	0	0	0	4	1
Totals	32	7	9	27	10	3

Pittsburgh (N.L.)	AB.	R.	H.	O.	A.	E.
Byrne, 3b	3	1	0	4	3	0
Leach, cf	4	1	2	2	1	0
Clarke, lf	3	0	0	3	0	0
Wagner, ss	4	0	1	1	2	0
Miller, 2b	4	0	1	0	4	0
Abstein, 1b	4	0	1	12	1	1
Wilson, rf	4	0	0	0	0	0
Gibson, c	2	0	0	4	2	0
Camnitz, p	1	0	0	0	1	0
Willis, p	2	0	0	1	2	0
Totals	31	2	5	27	16	1

| Detroit | 0 2 3 | 0 2 0 | 0 0 0—7 |
| Pittsburgh | 2 0 0 | 0 0 0 | 0 0 0—2 |

Two-base hits—Schmidt, Crawford, Leach 2, Miller. Runs batted in—Delahanty 2, Schmidt 4, Leach, Miller. Sacrifice hits—Bush, Clarke. Stolen bases—Cobb, Wagner, Gibson. Double plays—Bush, T. Jones and Moriarty; Miller, Abstein and Byrne. Earned runs—Detroit 6, Pittsburgh 2. Left on bases—Detroit 4, Pittsburgh 5. Struck out—By Donovan 7, by Camnitz 2, by Willis 2. Bases on balls—Off Donovan 2, off Camnitz 1, off Willis 4. Hits—Off Camnitz 6 in 2⅔ innings, off Willis 3 in 6⅓ innings. Losing pitcher—Camnitz. Umpires—Evans (A.L.) and Klem (N.L.). Time—1:45. Attendance—30,915.

Monday, October 11—At Detroit

Pittsburgh (N.L.)	AB.	R.	H.	O.	A.	E.
Byrne, 3b	5	1	2	2	2	1
Leach, cf	4	3	2	1	0	0
Clarke, lf	3	1	0	5	0	0
Wagner, ss	5	1	3	3	4	0
Miller, 2b	4	1	0	3	6	0
Abstein, 1b	4	1	2	8	0	2
Wilson, rf	4	0	1	0	0	0
Gibson, c	4	0	0	5	1	0
Maddox, p	4	0	0	0	1	0
Totals	37	8	10	27	14	3

Detroit (A.L.)	AB.	R.	H.	O.	A.	E.
D. Jones, lf	5	2	1	0	0	0
Bush, ss	5	1	3	4	3	2
Cobb, rf	5	0	2	3	0	0
Crawford, cf	5	0	0	5	0	1
Delahanty, 2b	5	1	3	0	3	0
Moriarty, 3b	3	1	0	0	3	0
T. Jones, 1b	3	1	1	7	0	0
Schmidt, c	4	0	0	4	3	1
Summer, p	0	0	0	0	1	0
Willett, p	2	0	0	1	3	1
aMcIntyre	1	0	0	0	0	0
Works, p	0	0	0	0	1	0
bMullin	1	0	0	0	0	0
Totals	39	6	10	27	14	5

| Pittsburgh | 5 1 0 | 0 0 0 | 0 0 2—8 |
| Detroit | 0 0 0 | 0 0 0 | 4 0 2—6 |

aStruck out for Willett in seventh. bStruck out for Works in ninth. Two-base hits—Abstein, Leach, Delahanty 2, Cobb. Runs batted in—Clarke, Wagner 3, Wilson, Bush 2, Cobb 3, T. Jones. Stolen bases—Wagner 3. Sacrifice fly—Clarke. Earned runs—Pittsburgh 2, Detroit 0. Left on bases—Detroit 8, Pittsburgh 6. Struck out—By Maddox 4, by Works 2. Bases on balls—Off Maddox 2, off Summers 1. Wild pitch—Summers. Hit by pitcher—By Willett (Leach, Clarke). Hits—Off Summers 3 in ⅓ inning, off Willett 3 in 6⅔ innings, off Works 4 in 2 innings. Losing pitcher—Summers. Umpires—O'Loughlin (A.L.), Johnstone (N.L.), Evans (A.L.) and Klem (N.L.). Time—1:56. Attendance—18,277.

Tuesday, October 12—At Detroit

Pittsburgh (N.L.)	AB.	R.	H.	O.	A.	E.
Byrne, 3b	4	0	1	0	2	0
Leach, cf	3	0	0	3	0	0
Clarke, lf	4	0	0	1	0	0
Wagner, ss	3	0	0	2	4	0
Miller, 2b	4	0	1	3	1	2
Abstein, 1b	4	0	1	12	1	2
Wilson, rf	4	0	1	0	0	0
Gibson, c	3	0	1	3	4	0
Leifield, p	1	0	0	0	5	0
aO'Connor	1	0	0	0	0	0
Phillippe, p	1	0	0	0	2	2
Totals	32	0	5	24	19	6

1909 WORLD SERIES

Detroit (A.L.)	AB	R	H	O	A	E
D. Jones, lf	4	1	1	0	0	0
Bush, ss	5	1	1	0	1	0
Cobb, rf	3	0	1	1	0	0
Crawford, cf	4	0	1	2	0	0
Delahanty, 2b	3	0	0	1	3	0
Moriarty, 3b	4	1	2	1	3	0
T. Jones, 1b	3	1	1	13	0	0
Stanage, c	3	0	1	9	1	0
Mullin, p	3	1	0	0	4	0
Totals	32	5	8	27	12	0

Pittsburgh............ 0 0 0 0 0 0 0 0 0—0
Detroit................. 0 2 0 3 0 0 0 0 *—5

aStruck out for Leifield in fifth. Two-base hits—Byrne, Cobb, Bush. Runs batted in—Bush, Cobb 2, Stanage 2. Sacrifice hits—T. Jones, Stanage. Stolen bases—Byrne, Leach. Double play—Wagner and Abstein. Earned runs—Detroit 5, Pittsburgh 0. Left on bases—Detroit 9, Pittsburgh 7. Struck out—By Mullin 10, by Phillippe 1. Bases on balls—Off Mullin 2, off Leifield 1, off Phillippe 1. Hits—Off Leifield 7 in 4 innings, off Phillippe 1 in 4 innings. Hit by pitcher—By Leifield (Cobb, Delahanty). Losing pitcher—Leifield. Umpires Klem (N.L.), Evans (A.L.), Johnstone (N.L.) and O'Loughlin (A.L.). Time—1:57. Attendance—17,036.

Wednesday, Oct. 13—At Pittsburgh

Detroit (A.L.)	AB	R	H	O	A	E
D. Jones, lf	4	1	1	3	0	0
Bush, ss	3	0	0	1	4	0
Cobb, rf	4	1	1	0	0	0
Crawford, cf	4	2	3	1	0	0
Delahanty, 2b	4	0	0	1	1	0
Moriarty, 3b	4	0	0	1	3	0
T. Jones, 1b	4	0	1	11	0	0
Stanage, c	2	0	0	3	0	0
aMcIntyre	1	0	0	0	0	0
Summers, p	3	0	0	0	1	0
Schmidt, c	1	0	0	3	1	1
Willett, p	0	0	0	0	0	0
bMullin	1	0	0	0	0	0
Totals	35	4	6	24	11	1

Pittsburgh (N.L.)	AB	R	H	O	A	E
Byrne, 3b	5	2	2	1	3	0
Leach, cf	4	1	2	3	0	0
Clarke, lf	2	2	2	2	0	0
Wagner, ss	2	1	1	1	2	2
Miller, 2b	4	0	0	1	4	0
Abstein, 1b	3	0	0	11	0	0
Wilson, rf	4	1	1	1	0	0
Gibson, c	4	1	2	8	0	0
Adams, p	3	0	0	0	1	0
Totals	31	8	10	27	7	2

Detroit................. 1 0 0 0 0 2 0 1 0—4
Pittsburgh............ 1 1 1 0 0 0 4 1 *—8

aGrounded out for Stanage in seventh. bFlied out for Willett in ninth. Two-base hits—Crawford, T. Jones, Wilson. Home runs—D. Jones, Crawford, Clarke. Runs batted in—D. Jones, Crawford 2, Clarke 3, Miller, Abstein, Gibson. Sacrifice hits—Clarke, Adams. Stolen bases—Crawford, T. Jones, Wagner 2, Clarke, Gibson. Earned runs—Pittsburgh 7, Detroit 3. Left on bases—Detroit 5, Pittsburgh 5. Struck out—By Summers 4, by Willett 1, by Adams 8. Bases on balls—Off Summers 3, off Adams 1. Hit by pitcher—By Summers (Wagner). Wild pitch—Summers. Hits—Off Summers 10 in 7 innings, off Willett 0 in 1 inning. Losing pitcher—Summers. Umpires—Johnstone (N.L.), O'Loughlin (A.L.), Klem (N.L.) and Evans (A.L.). Time—1:46. Attendance—21,706.

Thursday, October 14—At Detroit

Pittsburgh (N.L.)	AB	R	H	O	A	E
Byrne, 3b	4	1	1	2	4	0
Leach, cf	4	1	0	3	0	0
Clarke, lf	3	1	1	0	0	1
Wagner, ss	4	0	1	3	2	0
Miller, 2b	3	1	2	2	1	1
Abstein, 1b	4	0	1	9	1	0
Wilson, rf	3	0	0	0	1	1
Gibson, c	4	0	1	2	0	0
Willis, p	2	0	0	0	0	0
Camnitz, p	0	0	0	0	1	0
aHyatt	1	0	0	0	0	0
Phillippe, p	0	0	0	1	0	0
bAbbaticchio	1	0	0	0	0	0
Totals	33	4	7	24	10	3

Detroit (A.L.)	AB	R	H	O	A	E
D. Jones, lf-cf	5	1	0	2	0	0
Bush, ss	2	2	1	2	3	1
Cobb, rf	4	0	1	1	0	0
Crawford, cf-1b	3	1	1	1	1	0
Delahanty, 2b	4	0	2	0	4	0
Moriarty, 3b	3	1	1	1	3	0
T. Jones, 1b	4	0	1	13	0	1
McIntyre, lf	0	0	0	0	0	0
Schmidt, c	3	0	1	7	3	1
Mullin, p	4	0	2	0	2	0
Totals	32	5	10	27	16	3

Pittsburgh............ 3 0 0 0 0 0 0 0 1—4
Detroit................. 1 0 0 2 1 1 0 0 *—5

aGrounded out for Camnitz in seventh. bStruck out for Phillippe in ninth. Two-base hits—Wagner, Cobb, Crawford, Delahanty, Mullin. Runs batted in—Clarke, Wagner 2, Cobb, Crawford, Delahanty, Moriarty. Sacrifice hits—Clarke, Wilson. Stolen bases—Miller, D. Jones, Bush. Double plays—Byrne and Abstein; Schmidt and Bush; Schmidt and Moriarty. Earned runs—Detroit 3, Pittsburgh 2. Left on bases—Detroit 9, Pittsburgh 5. Struck out—By Willis 1, by Phillippe 1, by Mullin 5. Bases on balls—Off Willis 4, off Camnitz 1, off Mullin 1. Hit by pitcher—By Willis (Bush). Hits—Off Willis 7 in 5 innings, off Camnitz 2 in 1 inning, off Phillippe 1 in 2 innings. Losing pitcher—Willis. Umpires—Evans (A.L.), Klem (N.L.), O'Loughlin (A.L.) and Johnstone (N.L.). Time—2:00. Attendance—10,535.

Saturday, October 16—At Detroit

Pittsburgh (N.L.)	AB	R	H	O	A	E
Byrne, 3b	0	0	0	0	0	0
Hyatt, cf	3	1	0	0	0	0
Leach, cf-3b	3	2	2	4	2	0
Clarke, lf	0	2	0	5	0	0
Wagner, ss	3	1	1	3	3	0
Miller, 2b	5	0	2	3	0	0
Abstein, 1b	4	1	1	10	0	0
Wilson, rf	4	1	0	0	0	0
Gibson, c	5	0	1	2	1	0
Adams, p	3	0	0	0	4	0
Totals	30	8	7	27	10	0

Detroit (A.L.)	AB	R	H	O	A	E
D. Jones, lf	4	0	1	3	0	1
Bush, ss	3	0	0	2	5	1
Cobb, rf	4	0	0	1	0	0
Crawford, cf	4	0	0	4	0	1
Delahanty, 2b	3	0	2	3	3	0
Moriarty, 3b	1	0	1	1	0	0
O'Leary, 3b	3	0	0	1	1	0
T. Jones, 1b	4	0	1	9	0	0
Schmidt, c	3	0	1	3	2	0
Donovan, p	0	0	0	0	1	0
Mullin, p	3	0	0	0	2	0
Totals	32	0	6	27	14	3

1910 WORLD SERIES

Pittsburgh................ 0 2 0   2 0 3   0 1 0—8
Detroit .... 0 0 0   0 0 0   0 0 0—0

Two-base hits—Leach, Gibson, Abstein, Moriarty, Delahanty, Schmidt. Three-base hit—Wagner. Runs batted in—Hyatt, Clarke, Wagner 2, Miller 2. Sacrifice hits—Leach, Clarke, Wilson, Adams. Sacrifice fly—Hyatt. Stolen bases—Clarke 1, Miller, Abstein. Double play—Bush, Schmidt and Delahanty. Earned runs—Pittsburgh 6, Detroit 0. Left on bases—Pittsburgh 11, Detroit 7. Struck out—By Adams 1, by Mullin 1. Bases on balls—Off Adams 1, off Donovan 6, off Mullin 4. Hit by pitcher—By Adams (Bush), by Donovan (Byrne). Hits—Off Donovan 2 in 3 innings, off Mullin 5 in 6 innings. Losing pitcher—Donovan. Umpires—O'Loughlin (A.L.), Johnstone (N.L.), Evans (A.L.) and Klem (N.L.). Time—2:10. Attendance—17,562.

SERIES OF 1910

	W.	L.	Pct.
Philadelphia A. L.	4	1	.800
Chicago N. L.	1	4	.200

The Cubs won their fourth championship in five years in 1910 and met with a World Series defeat at the hands of the young Athletics, which was almost as unexpected and startling as when Frank Chance's club lost to the White Sox four years earlier. The youthful Mackmen scampered to victory in four games out of five and years later Connie Mack reproached himself for not winning the Series in four straight. His team won the first three games and let the fourth fritter away in the closing innings.

Both clubs won their pennants easily. The Cubs regained the National League championship by a 13-game margin over the second-place Giants, while after a series of close American League races, the Athletics ran away from the second-place Yankees by 14½ games. Both clubs suffered injuries to regular players on the eve of the Series. Second baseman Johnny Evers of the Cubs and center fielder Rube Oldring of the Athletics suffered broken legs. They were replaced by the hard-hitting Heinie Zimmerman and the fleet-footed Amos Strunk, respectively.

The youth of the Athletics was expected to be a handicap, but the Philadelphians hopped all over Chance's array of pitchers. Where the A's hit only .161 while losing to the Giants in 1905, the 1910 Athletics slammed the once-famous Cub chuckers for an average of .316, a mark that stood until 1960 when the Yankees rapped the Pirates for a .338 average. The Cubs hit only .222. The Athletics scored 35 runs, an average of seven a game. Eddie Collins, young Philadelphia second baseman, hit .429 and stole four bases and Frank Baker, third baseman, batted .409. Even Jack Coombs, who pitched three games, hit .385. Danny Murphy, second baseman of the 1905 team, playing right field, poled the only home run.

After Chief Bender, Mack's Indian hurler, held the Cubs to three hits while winning the opening game, 4 to 1, the next three Athletic victories were recorded by Coombs, who pitched 31 league victories that season, 13 of them shutouts. However, in capturing the second, third and fifth games, Coombs was aided by the terrific hitting behind him, winning by scores of 9 to 3, 12 to 5 and 7 to 2. In the second game, Coombs gave up eight hits and walked nine; the Athletics made three double plays and 14 Cubs were left stranded.

Eddie Plank, Mack's third mound ace, had a lame arm, and all of Philadelphia's pitching was done by Coombs and Bender. Bender lost the fourth game, 4 to 3, to King Cole and Miner Brown, Chicago tying in

COMPOSITE BATTING AVERAGES

Pittsburgh Pirates

Player-Position	G.	AB.	R.	H.	2B.	3B.	HR.	RBI.	BA.
Wagner, ss	7	24	4	8	2	1	0	7	.333
Leach, cf-3b	7	25	8	8	4	0	0	2	.320
Byrne, 3b	7	24	5	6	1	0	0	0	.250
Miller, 2b	7	28	2	7	1	0	0	4	.250
Gibson, c	7	25	2	6	2	0	0	0	.240
Abstein, 1b	7	26	3	6	2	0	0	0	.231
Clarke, lf	7	19	7	4	0	0	2	7	.211
Wilson, rf	7	26	2	4	1	0	0	1	.154
Adams, p	3	9	0	0	0	0	0	0	.000
Camnitz, p	2	1	0	0	0	0	0	0	.000
Willis, p	2	4	0	0	0	0	0	0	.000
Maddox, p	1	4	0	0	0	0	0	0	.000
Leifield, p	1	1	0	0	0	0	0	0	.000
O'Connor, ph	1	1	0	0	0	0	0	0	.000
Phillippe, p	2	1	0	0	0	0	0	0	.000
Hyatt, ph-cf	2	4	1	0	0	0	0	1	.000
Abbaticchio, ph	1	1	0	0	0	0	0	0	.000
Totals	7	223	34	49	13	1	2	26	.220

Detroit Tigers

Player-Position	G.	AB.	R.	H.	2B.	3B.	HR.	RBI.	BA.
Delahanty, 2b	7	26	2	9	4	0	0	4	.346
Moriarty, 3b	7	22	4	6	1	0	0	1	.273
Bush, ss	7	23	5	6	1	0	0	3	.261
Crawford, cf-1b	7	28	4	7	3	0	1	3	.250
T. Jones, 1b	7	24	3	6	1	0	0	1	.250
D. Jones, lf-cf	7	30	6	7	0	0	1	1	.233
Cobb, rf	7	26	3	6	3	0	0	6	.231
Schmidt, c	6	18	0	4	2	0	0	4	.222
Stanage, c	2	5	0	1	0	0	0	2	.200
Mullin, p-ph	6	16	1	3	1	0	0	0	.188
McIntyre, ph-lf	4	3	0	0	0	0	0	0	.000
Donovan, p	2	4	0	0	0	0	0	0	.000
Summers, p	2	3	0	0	0	0	0	0	.000
Willett, p	2	2	0	0	0	0	0	0	.000
Works, p	1	0	0	0	0	0	0	0	.000
O'Leary, 3b	1	3	0	0	0	0	0	0	.000
Totals	7	233	28	55	16	0	2	25	.236

COMPOSITE PITCHING AVERAGES

Pittsburgh Pirates

Pitcher	G.	IP.	H.	R.	E.	SO.	BB.	W.	L.	ERA.
Phillippe	2	6	2	0	0	2	1	0	0	0.00
Maddox	1	9	10	6	0	4	2	1	0	0.00
Adams	3	27	18	5	4	11	6	3	0	1.33
Willis	2	11⅔	10	6	4	3	8	0	1	3.08
Leifield	1	4	7	5	5	0	1	0	1	11.25
Camnitz	2	3⅓	8	6	5	2	2	0	1	13.50
Totals	7	61	55	23	18	22	20	4	3	2.66

Detroit Tigers

Pitcher	G.	IP.	H.	R.	E.	SO.	BB.	W.	L.	ERA.
Willett	2	7⅔	3	1	1	0	0	0	0	0.00
Mullin	4	32	22	14	7	20	8	2	1	1.97
Donovan	2	12	7	4	4	7	8	1	1	3.00
Summers	2	7⅓	13	13	7	4	4	0	2	8.59
Works	1	2	4	2	2	2	0	0	0	9.00
Totals	7	61	49	34	20	34	20	3	4	2.95

the ninth and winning in the tenth on Jimmy Archer's double and Jimmy Sheckard's single with two out. Mack always claimed his sentimental side cost him this game, for with his club ahead, 3 to 2, in the eighth, the Athletics had Cole in distress. Mack dismissed a hunch to have Topsy Hartsel bat for Ira Thomas, and the latter ruined a rally by hitting into a double play with the bases full.

With a total attendance of 124,222, the receipts were $173,980. Under a voluntary arrangement made by the club owners, the players shared in the revenue from the fifth game, a Sunday, which compensated for the lowest-attended contest among the first four, and each Athletic drew $2,062.79 and each Cub $1,375.16. The box scores:

Monday, October 17—At Philadelphia

Chicago (N.L.)	AB.	R.	H.	O.	A.	E.
Sheckard, lf	4	0	0	2	0	0
Schulte, rf	2	0	1	0	0	0
Hofman, cf	4	0	0	2	0	0
Chance, 1b	3	0	0	11	2	0
Zimmerman, 2b	3	0	0	2	3	0
Steinfeldt, 3b	3	0	0	0	3	0
Tinker, ss	3	1	1	3	2	0
Kling, c	3	0	1	4	3	0
Overall, p	1	0	0	0	0	0
McIntire, p	1	0	0	0	2	1
aBeaumont	1	0	0	0	0	0
Totals	28	1	3	24	15	1
Phila'phia (A.L.)	AB.	R.	H.	O.	A.	E.
Strunk, cf	3	0	0	1	0	1
Lord, lf	4	1	1	0	0	0
Collins, 2b	2	1	1	2	5	0
Baker, 3b	4	1	3	3	2	0
Davis, 1b	3	0	0	11	0	0
Murphy, rf	3	1	1	1	0	0
Barry, ss	3	0	0	0	4	0
Thomas, c	1	0	0	8	2	1
Bender, p	3	0	1	1	0	0
Totals	26	4	7	27	13	2

Chicago .... 0 0 0   0 0 0   0 0 1—1
Philadelphia ...... 0 2 1   0 0 0   0 1 *—4

aGrounded out for McIntire in ninth. Two-base hits—Baker 2, Lord. Runs batted in—Kling, Baker 2, Murphy, Bender. Sacrifice hits—Davis, Collins. Stolen base—Murphy. Earned runs—Philadelphia 3, Chicago 0. Left on bases—Philadelphia 4, Chicago 2. Struck out—By Bender 8, by Overall 1, by McIntire 2. Bases on balls—Off Bender 2, off Overall 1, off McIntire 3. Hits—Off Overall 6 in 3 innings; off McIntire 1 in 5 innings. Losing pitcher—Overall. Umpires—Connolly (A.L.), O'Day (N.L.), Rigler (N.L.) and Sheridan (A.L.). Time—1:54. Attendance—26,891.

Tuesday, October 18—At Philadelphia

Chicago (N.L.)	AB.	R.	H.	O.	A.	E.
Sheckard, lf	1	1	1	0	1	1
Schulte, rf	3	1	0	0	0	0
Hofman, cf	2	1	1	1	0	0
Chance, 1b	5	0	2	14	0	0
Zimmerman, 2b	3	0	1	1	2	0
Steinfeldt, 3b	5	0	1	0	2	2
Tinker, ss	4	0	2	3	4	0
Kling, c	4	0	0	5	2	0
Brown, p	3	0	0	0	2	0
aBeaumont	1	0	0	0	0	0
Richie, p	0	0	0	0	0	0
Totals	31	3	8	24	13	3
Phila'phia (A.L.)	AB.	R.	H.	O.	A.	E.
Strunk, cf	5	1	2	4	0	0
Lord, lf	5	1	1	1	0	0
Collins, 2b	4	2	3	4	6	0
Baker, 3b	4	1	1	1	1	0
Davis, 1b	5	1	2	7	0	2
Murphy, rf	4	1	1	1	0	0
Barry, ss	3	0	1	3	1	0
Thomas, c	3	2	2	6	1	0
Coombs, p	4	0	1	0	1	2
Totals	37	9	14	27	11	4

Chicago .... 1 0 0   0 0 0   1 0 1—3
Philadelphia ...... 0 0 2   0 1 0   6 0 *—9

aStruck out for Brown in eighth. Two-base hits—Collins 2, Davis, Murphy, Strunk, Tinker, Zimmerman, Sheckard, Steinfeldt. Runs batted in—Chance, Zimmerman 2, Strunk, Collins, Davis 2, Murphy 2, Thomas. Sacrifice hits—Schulte 2, Sheckard, Barry. Sacrifice fly—Zimmerman. Stolen bases—Collins 2. Double plays—Collins and Davis 2; Murphy and Thomas; Tinker and Chance. Earned runs—Philadelphia 7, Chicago 3. Left on bases—Chicago 14, Philadelphia 9. Struck out—By Coombs 5, by Brown 6. Bases on balls—Off Coombs 9, off Brown 4. Hits—Off Brown 13 in 7 innings, off Richie 1 in 1 inning. Losing pitcher—Brown. Umpires—Rigler (N.L.), Sheridan (A.L.), O'Day (N.L.) and Connolly (A.L.). Time—2:25. Attendance—24,597.

Thursday, October 20—At Chicago

Phila'phia (A.L.)	AB.	R.	H.	O.	A.	E.
Strunk, cf	5	1	1	3	0	0
Lord, lf	4	0	1	1	0	0
Collins, 2b	5	1	1	1	1	0
Baker, 3b	5	2	2	2	4	1
Davis, 1b	3	3	3	8	0	0
Murphy, rf	5	2	1	3	1	0
Barry, ss	5	3	3	1	2	0
Thomas, c	4	0	0	8	1	0
Coombs, p	5	0	3	0	0	0
Totals	41	12	15	27	9	1
Chicago (N.L.)	AB.	R.	H.	O.	A.	E.
Sheckard, lf	1	2	0	2	0	0
Schulte, rf	4	0	2	2	0	1
Hofman, cf	3	1	1	2	0	0
Chance, 1b	1	0	0	3	0	0
Archer, 1b	3	0	0	9	0	0
Zimmerman, 2b	4	0	0	4	6	0
Steinfeldt, 3b	4	0	0	0	2	1
Tinker, ss	4	1	3	3	4	2
Kling, c	4	0	0	2	2	0
Reulbach, p	0	0	0	0	1	0
aBeaumont	0	1	0	0	0	0
McIntire, p	0	0	0	0	0	0
Pfiester, p	2	0	0	0	1	0
bNeedham	1	0	0	0	0	0
Totals	31	5	6	27	16	5

Philadelphia ...... 1 2 5   0 0 0   4 0 0—12
Chicago .... 1 2 0   0 0 0   0 2 0— 5

aWalked for Reulbach in second. bFouled out for Pfiester in ninth. Two-base hits—Schulte 2, Tinker, Davis, Coombs, Barry 2. Home run—Murphy. Runs batted in—Baker, Murphy 3, Barry 3, Coombs 3, Schulte 2, Hofman. Sacrifice hit—Lord. Sacrifice fly—Hofman. Stolen base—Tinker. Double plays—Zimmerman, Tinker and Archer; Barry, Collins and Davis; Murphy and Davis. Earned runs—Philadelphia 6, Chicago 5. Left on bases—Philadelphia 7, Chicago 4. Struck out—By Coombs 8, by Pfiester 1. Bases on balls—Off Reulbach 2, off Pfiester 1, off Coombs 4. Hit by pitcher—By McIntire (Davis). Wild pitch—

Coombs. Hits—Off Reulbach 3 in 2 innings, off McIntire 3 in ⅓ inning, off Pfiester 9 in 6⅔ innings. Losing pitcher—McIntire. Umpires—O'Day (N.L.), Sheridan (A.L.), Rigler (N.L.) and Connolly (A.L.). Time—2:07. Attendance—26,210.

Saturday, October 22—At Chicago

Phila'phia (A.L.)	AB.	R.	H.	O.	A.	E.
Strunk, cf	5	0	2	2	0	0
Lord, lf	5	0	0	1	0	0
Collins, 2b	5	1	1	6	1	1
Baker, 3b	4	1	3	3	4	1
Davis, 1b	3	0	1	8	0	1
Murphy, rf	4	0	2	1	0	0
Barry, ss	4	0	0	2	1	0
Thomas, c	4	0	1	5	4	0
Bender, p	3	1	1	0	2	0
Totals	37	3	11	*28	12	3

Chicago (N.L.)	AB.	R.	H.	O.	A.	E.
Sheckard, lf	4	1	1	3	1	0
Schulte, rf	4	2	2	2	0	0
Hofman, cf	3	0	2	1	0	0
Chance, 1b	4	0	2	10	2	0
Zimmerman, 2b	4	0	1	2	2	0
Steinfeldt, 3b	4	0	0	2	4	0
Tinker, ss	3	0	0	1	3	0
Archer, c	4	1	1	8	3	0
Cole, p	2	0	0	1	3	0
aKling	1	0	0	0	0	0
bKane	0	0	0	0	0	0
Brown, p	1	0	0	0	1	1
Totals	34	4	9	30	19	1

Philadelphia .... 0 0 1 2 0 0 0 0 0—3
Chicago .... 1 0 0 1 0 0 0 0 1 1—4

*Chance declared out for Hofman's interference in first; two out when winning run scored. aReached first on Baker's error for Cole in eighth. bRan for Kling in eighth. Two-base hits—Baker, Murphy, Davis, Schulte, Archer. Three-base hits—Strunk, Chance. Runs batted in—Strunk, Baker, Murphy, Sheckard, Hofman, Chance 2. Sacrifice hits—Davis, Murphy, Hofman. Stolen base—Sheckard. Double plays—Bender, Baker and Davis; Cole, Archer and Chance. Earned runs—Chicago 4, Philadelphia 3. Left on bases—Philadelphia 10, Chicago 4. Struck out—By Cole 5, by Brown 1, by Bender 6. Bases on balls—Off Cole 3, off Bender 2. Hit by pitcher—By Cole (Barry). Hits—Off Cole 10 in 8 innings, off Brown 1 in 2 innings. Winning pitcher—Brown. Umpires—Connolly (A.L.), Rigler (N.L.), Sheridan (A.L.) and O'Day (N.L.). Time—2:14. Attendance—19,150.

Sunday, October 23—At Chicago

Phila'phia (A.L.)	AB.	R.	H.	O.	A.	E.
Hartsel, lf	5	2	1	2	0	0
Lord, cf	4	1	1	5	0	0
Collins, 2b	5	0	3	4	4	0
Baker, 3b	5	1	0	0	0	1
Davis, 1b	3	1	0	9	1	0
Murphy, rf	4	2	2	0	0	0
Barry, ss	2	0	0	2	4	0
Lapp, c	4	0	1	4	2	0
Coombs, p	4	0	1	1	3	0
Totals	36	7	9	27	14	1

Chicago (N.L.)	AB.	R.	H.	O.	A.	E.
Sheckard, lf	4	1	2	1	0	0
Schulte, rf	4	0	1	0	0	0
Hofman, cf	3	0	0	1	0	0
Chance, 1b	4	1	2	13	0	0
Zimmerman, 2b	3	0	2	1	5	1
Steinfeldt, 3b	4	0	1	0	1	1
Tinker, ss	4	0	0	1	3	0
Archer, c	4	0	1	10	0	0
Brown, p	3	0	0	0	7	0
aKling	1	0	0	0	0	0
Totals	34	2	9	27	14	2

Philadelphia .... 1 0 0 0 1 0 0 5 0—7
Chicago .... 0 1 0 0 0 0 0 1 0—2

aGrounded out for Brown in ninth. Two-base hits—Chance, Sheckard, Murphy, Collins 2. Runs batted in—Lord, Collins 2, Murphy, Lapp, Chance, Steinfeldt. Sacrifice hits—Zimmerman, Barry. Stolen bases—Hartsel 2, Collins 2, Zimmerman. Earned runs—Philadelphia 4, Chicago 2. Left on bases—Chicago 7, Philadelphia 6. Struck out—By Coombs 4, by Brown 7. Bases on balls—Off Brown 3, off Coombs 1. Wild pitch—Brown. Umpires—O'Day (N.L.), Sheridan (A.L.), Rigler (N.L.) and Connolly (A.L.). Time—2:06. Attendance—27,374.

COMPOSITE BATTING AVERAGES
Philadelphia Athletics

Player-Position	G.	AB.	R.	H.	2B.	3B.	HR.	RBI.	BA.
Collins, 2b	5	21	5	9	4	0	0	3	.429
Baker, 3b	5	22	6	9	3	0	0	4	.409
Coombs, p	3	13	0	5	1	0	0	3	.385
Davis, 1b	5	17	5	6	3	0	0	2	.353
Murphy, rf	5	20	6	7	3	0	1	8	.350
Bender, p	2	6	1	2	0	0	0	1	.333
Strunk, cf	4	18	2	5	1	1	0	2	.278
Thomas, c	4	12	2	3	0	0	0	1	.250
Lapp, c	1	4	0	1	0	0	0	1	.250
Barry, ss	5	17	3	4	2	0	0	3	.235
Hartsel, lf	1	5	2	1	0	0	0	0	.200
Lord, lf-cf	5	22	4	4	2	0	0	1	.182
Totals	5	177	35	56	19	1	1	29	.316

Chicago Cubs

Player-Position	G.	AB.	R.	H.	2B.	3B.	HR.	RBI.	BA.
Chance, 1b	5	17	1	6	1	1	0	4	.353
Schulte, rf	5	17	3	6	3	0	0	2	.353
Tinker, ss	5	18	2	6	2	0	0	0	.333
Sheckard, lf	5	14	5	4	2	0	0	1	.286
Hofman, cf	5	15	2	4	0	0	0	2	.267
Zimmerman, 2b	5	17	0	4	1	0	0	2	.235
Archer, 1b-c	3	11	1	2	1	0	0	0	.182
Steinfeldt, 3b	5	20	0	2	1	0	0	1	.100
Kling, c-ph	5	13	0	1	0	0	0	1	.077
Overall, p	1	1	0	0	0	0	0	0	.000
McIntire, p	2	1	0	0	0	0	0	0	.000
Brown, p	3	7	0	0	0	0	0	0	.000
Richie, p	1	0	0	0	0	0	0	0	.000
Reulbach, p	1	0	0	0	0	0	0	0	.000
Pfiester, p	1	2	0	0	0	0	0	0	.000
Needham, ph	1	1	0	0	0	0	0	0	.000
Cole, p	1	2	0	0	0	0	0	0	.000
Kane, pr	1	0	0	0	0	0	0	0	.000
Beaumont, ph	3	2	1	0	0	0	0	0	.000
Totals	5	158	15	35	11	1	0	13	.222

COMPOSITE PITCHING AVERAGES
Philadelphia Athletics

Pitcher	G.	IP.	H.	R.	E.	SO.	BB.	W.	L.	ERA.
Bender	2	18⅔	12	5	4	14	4	1	1	1.93
Coombs	3	27	23	10	10	17	14	3	0	3.33
Totals	5	45⅔	35	15	14	31	18	4	1	2.76

Chicago Cubs

Pitcher	G.	IP.	H.	R.	E.	SO.	BB.	W.	L.	ERA.
Richie	1	1	1	0	0	0	0	0	0	0.00
Pfiester	1	6⅔	9	5	0	1	1	0	0	0.00
Cole	1	8	10	3	3	5	3	0	0	3.38
Brown	3	18	23	16	11	14	7	1	2	5.50
McIntire	2	5⅓	4	5	4	2	3	0	1	6.80
Overall	1	3	6	3	3	1	1	0	1	9.00
Reulbach	1	2	3	3	2	0	2	0	0	9.00
Totals	5	44	56	35	23	23	17	1	4	4.70

SERIES OF 1911

	W.	L.	Pct.
Philadelphia A. L.	4	2	.667
New York N. L.	2	4	.333

When the clans of Mack and McGraw met in 1911 for the second time as World Series opponents, the A's defeated the Giants, four games to two, in one of the most hotly-contested of all Series. This was the classic in which Frank Baker, Athletics' third baseman, won his nickname, "Home Run" Baker. His sixth-inning, two-run homer in the second game defeated Rube Marquard, 3 to 1, and with Christy Mathewson having a 1 to 0 lead on Jack Coombs in the ninth inning of the third clash, Baker tied the score for Philadelphia with a second homer, banged with one down, the A's eventually winning in the eleventh, 3 to 2. Baker led both teams at bat with a .375 average and was closely followed by Jack Barry, Connie Mack's fair-hitting shortstop, with .368.

The Giants practically pilfered their way to the pennant that season, stealing 347 bases. McGraw tried to follow the same tactics in the World Series, but the Giants got away with only four steals, two by Larry Doyle and two by Buck Herzog, the same as the total of Athletics' larcenies, divided by Eddie Collins and Barry.

The Series did not get under way until October 14 because the National League then ran its schedule to Columbus Day, October 12. Rain later held up the Classic six days between the third and fourth games, and it was not over until October 26.

The first game, played at the Polo Grounds before a crowd of 38,281, the greatest World Series throng up to that time, resulted in a brilliant pitching duel between Mathewson and Chief Bender, New York triumphing, 2 to 1. The hits were six for the Athletics and five for New York, while Bender struck out 11 and Matty five.

Plank finally gained his first Series victory by defeating Marquard in the second game, and fanned Josh Devore, Giant leadoff man, four straight times. Coombs pitched an 11-inning three-hitter to beat Mathewson in the third game. After Baker's homer tied the score in the ninth, the hurling duel continued until Matty's defensive support deserted him in the eleventh, when the A's counted twice with the aid of a pair of errors. In the Giants' half, Herzog rapped a double and scored on an error by Eddie Collins, but Beals Becker, who reached first on the bobble, with two away, then attempted to steal second and was thrown out to end the game.

That's how the Series stood on October 18 as players and fans watched helplessly while rain pelted Philadelphia. When the weather finally dried up, gasoline was burned on the water-soaked field and the teams took the field October 24. Again Bender was superior, defeating Matty, 4 to 2, and giving the A's a three-to-one lead in the Series.

The Mackmen seemed to have the fifth tilt in the bag, going into the ninth with a 3 to 1 lead. Coombs, who pulled a muscle in his side in the sixth, struggled valiantly, but the Giants tied the score with two runs in the ninth, pitcher Otis (Doc) Crandall driving in one with a double and scoring himself. Crandall then received credit for the victory when Doyle scored the winning run for the Giants in the dusk of a late October day on an outfield fly by Fred Merkle in the second half of the tenth with Plank on the hill. Plate umpire Bill Klem later said Doyle did not touch the plate and he would have called him out had the Athletics made a play for Larry as the New York second baseman pranced happily to his club's bench. The great nip-and-tuck Series then collapsed in the sixth game, the Athletics crushing Leon Ames, George Wiltse and Marquard, 13 to 2, as Bender won his fourth World Series game and second of the Series. Despite their brave fight, the Giants were outhit, .244 to .175. The box scores:

Saturday, October 14—At New York

Phila'phia (A.L.)	AB.	R.	H.	O.	A.	E.
Lord, lf	4	0	0	2	0	0
Oldring, cf	4	0	2	1	0	0
Collins, 2b	3	0	0	0	5	1
Baker, 3b	4	1	2	0	1	1
Murphy, rf	3	0	0	1	0	0
Davis, 1b	4	0	1	8	0	0
Barry, ss	3	0	0	0	1	0
Thomas, c	3	0	0	12	2	0
Bender, p	3	0	1	0	1	0
Totals	31	1	6	24	10	2

New York (N.L.)	AB.	R.	H.	O.	A.	E.
Devore, lf	3	0	0	3	0	0
Doyle, 2b	3	0	1	1	0	0
Snodgrass, cf	2	1	0	2	0	0
Murray, rf	3	0	0	1	0	0
Merkle, 1b	4	0	1	11	1	0
Herzog, 3b	3	0	0	0	2	0
Fletcher, ss	4	0	0	2	3	0
Meyers, c	3	1	1	7	1	0
Mathewson, p	3	0	1	0	4	0
Totals	28	2	5	27	11	0

Philadelphia .... 0 1 0 0 0 0 0 0 0—1
New York .... 0 0 0 1 0 0 1 0 *—2

Two-base hits—Oldring 2, Devore, Meyers. Runs batted in—Davis, Devore. Sacrifice hits—Murphy, Murray. Stolen base—Doyle. Earned runs—Philadelphia 1, New York 1. Left on bases—New York 8, Philadelphia 5. Struck out—By Bender 11, by Mathewson 5. Bases on balls—Off Bender 4, off Mathewson 1. Hit by pitcher—Bender (Snodgrass). Passed ball—Meyers. Umpires—Klem (N.L.), Dinneen (A.L.), Brennan (N.L.) and Connolly (A.L.). Time—2:12. Attendance—38,281.

Monday, October 16—At Philadelphia

New York (N.L.)	AB.	R.	H.	O.	A.	E.
Devore, lf	4	0	0	5	0	1
Doyle, 2b	4	0	0	1	2	0
Snodgrass, cf	3	0	2	1	0	0
Murray, rf	4	0	0	0	0	1
Merkle, 1b	3	0	1	7	0	1
Herzog, 3b	3	1	1	1	1	0
Fletcher, ss	3	0	0	1	1	0
Meyers, c	3	0	1	8	1	0
Marquard, p	2	0	0	0	2	0
Crandall, p	1	0	0	0	0	0
Totals	30	1	5	24	7	3

Phila'phia (A.L.)	AB.	R.	H.	O.	A.	E.
Lord, lf	4	1	1	2	1	0
Oldring, cf	3	0	0	1	0	0
Collins, 2b	3	1	2	2	4	0
Baker, 3b	3	1	1	1	1	0
Murphy, rf	3	0	0	0	0	0
Davis, 1b	3	0	0	10	0	0
Barry, ss	3	0	0	2	2	0
Thomas, c	3	0	0	9	0	0
Plank, p	3	0	0	0	2	0
Totals	28	3	4	27	10	0

New York .... 0 1 0 0 0 0 0 0 0—1
Philadelphia .... 1 0 0 0 0 2 0 0 *—3

Two-base hits—Herzog, Collins. Home run—Baker. Runs batted in—Meyers, Baker 2. Sacrifice hit—Oldring. Earned runs—Philadelphia 2, New York 1. Left on bases—New York 3, Philadelphia 2. Struck out—By Marquard 4, by Crandall 2, by Plank 8. Hit by pitcher—Plank (Snodgrass). Wild pitch—Marquard. Hits—Off Marquard 4 in 7 innings, off Crandall 0 in 1 inning. Losing pitcher—Marquard. Umpires—Connolly (A.L.), Brennan (N.L.), Klem (N.L.) and Dinneen (A.L.). Time—1:52. Attendance—26,286.

Tuesday, October 17—At New York

Phila'phia (A.L.)	AB.	R.	H.	O.	A.	E.
Lord, lf	5	0	0	5	0	0
Oldring, cf	5	0	0	0	0	0
Collins, 2b	5	1	2	5	4	2
Baker, 3b	5	2	2	2	1	0
Murphy, rf	5	0	0	2	0	0
Davis, 1b	5	0	2	10	0	0
Barry, ss	3	0	2	1	4	0
Lapp, c	4	0	1	8	6	0
Coombs, p	4	0	0	0	1	0
Totals	41	3	9	33	16	2

New York (N.L.)	AB.	R.	H.	O.	A.	E.
Devore, lf	4	0	0	0	0	0
Doyle, 2b	4	0	0	5	5	0
Snodgrass, cf	3	0	0	3	0	0
Murray, rf	2	0	0	2	1	0
Merkle, 1b	3	0	0	11	1	0
Herzog, 3b	3	1	1	4	3	3
Fletcher, ss	4	0	0	3	4	2
Meyers, c	4	1	1	4	4	0
Mathewson, p	3	0	1	1	4	0
aBecker	1	0	0	0	0	0
Totals	31	2	3	33	22	5

Philadelphia ...... 0 0 0 0 0 0 0 0 1 0 2—3
New York .... 0 0 1 0 0 0 0 0 0 0 1—2

aReached first base on Collins' error for Mathewson in eleventh. Two-base hits—Barry, Herzog. Home run—Baker. Runs batted in—Baker, Murphy, Davis, Devore. Sacrifice hits—Barry, Murray. Stolen bases—Collins, Barry. Double play—Doyle and Fletcher. Earned runs—Philadelphia 1, New York 1. Left on bases—Philadelphia 6, New York 1. Struck out—By Coombs 7, by Mathewson 3. Bases on balls—Off Coombs 4. Umpires—Brennan (N.L.), Connolly (A.L.), Klem (N.L.) and Dinneen (A.L.). Time—2:25. Attendance—37,216.

Tuesday, October 24—At Philadelphia

New York (N.L.)	AB.	R.	H.	O.	A.	E.
Devore, lf	4	1	2	0	0	0
Doyle, 2b	3	1	1	2	0	0
Snodgrass, cf	3	0	0	0	0	0
Murray, rf	4	0	0	1	0	1
Merkle, 1b	4	0	1	12	2	0
Herzog, 3b	4	0	0	1	5	0
Fletcher, ss	4	0	2	0	4	1

	AB.	R.	H.	O.	A.	E.
Meyers, c	4	0	1	7	2	0
Mathewson, p	1	0	0	1	1	1
aBecker	1	0	0	0	0	0
Wiltse, p	0	0	0	0	0	0
Totals	32	2	7	24	14	3

Phila'phia (A.L.)	AB.	R.	H.	O.	A.	E.
Lord, lf	4	0	1	2	0	0
Oldring, cf	3	0	3	0	0	0
Collins, 2b	3	1	2	2	4	0
Baker, 3b	3	1	2	4	3	1
Murphy, rf	4	1	2	0	0	0
Davis, 1b	4	1	1	10	0	0
Barry, ss	4	0	3	1	1	0
Thomas, c	3	0	0	5	2	0
Bender, p	4	0	0	0	1	0
Totals	32	4	11	27	11	1

New York .... 2 0 0 0 0 0 0 0 0—2
Philadelphia ...... 0 0 0 3 1 0 0 0 *—4

aGrounded out for Mathewson in eighth. Two-base hits—Merkle, Meyers, Baker 2, Murphy 2, Davis, Barry 2. Three-base hit—Doyle. Runs batted in—Doyle, Snodgrass, Baker, Murphy, Davis, Thomas. Sacrifice hits—Oldring, Collins. Sacrifice flies—Snodgrass, Thomas. Double play—Baker and Davis. Earned runs—Philadelphia 4, New York 2. Left on bases—Philadelphia 8, New York 6. Struck out—by Mathewson 5, by Wiltse 1, by Bender 4. Bases on balls—Off Mathewson 1, off Bender 2. Hits—Off Mathewson 10 in 7 innings, off Wiltse 1 in 1 inning. Losing pitcher—Mathewson. Umpires—Dinneen (A.L.), Klem (N.L.), Connolly (A.L.) and Brennan (N.L.). Time—1:49. Attendance—24,355.

Wednesday, October 25—At New York

Phila'phia (A.L.)	AB.	R.	H.	O.	A.	E.
Lord, lf	5	0	0	2	0	0
Oldring, cf	5	1	2	0	0	0
Collins, 2b	3	0	0	1	1	1
Baker, 3b	4	0	0	1	2	0
Murphy, rf	4	0	1	4	0	0
Davis, 1b	4	0	0	7	2	0
Barry, ss	4	0	1	3	4	0
Lapp, c	4	1	1	10	2	0
Coombs, p	4	1	2	1	1	0
bStrunk	0	0	0	0	0	0
Plank, p	0	0	0	0	0	0
Totals	37	3	7	c29	12	1

New York (N.L.)	AB.	R.	H.	O.	A.	E.
Devore, lf	5	0	1	3	0	0
Doyle, 2b	5	1	4	3	4	1
Snodgrass, cf	4	0	0	2	0	0
Murray, rf	5	0	0	1	0	0
Merkle, 1b	2	1	0	12	0	0
Herzog, 3b	4	0	1	1	3	0
Fletcher, ss	4	1	1	4	3	1
Meyers, c	3	0	1	5	3	0
Marquard, p	0	0	0	0	0	0
aBecker	1	0	0	0	0	0
Ames, p	1	0	0	0	0	0
Crandall, p	1	1	1	0	2	0
Totals	35	4	9	30	15	2

Philadelphia .... 0 0 3 0 0 0 0 0 0 0—3
New York .... 0 0 0 0 0 0 1 0 2 1—4

aFlied out for Marquard in third. bRan for Coombs in tenth. cTwo out when winning run scored. Two-base hits—Doyle 2, Fletcher, Crandall. Home run—Oldring. Runs batted in—Oldring 3, Devore, Merkle, Meyers, Crandall. Sacrifice hit—Snodgrass. Sacrifice flies—Merkle, Meyers. Stolen bases—Collins, Barry, Doyle, Herzog. Earned runs—New York 3, Philadelphia 0. Left on bases—Philadelphia 5, New York 8. Double plays—Meyers and Doyle; Lapp and Collins. Struck out—By Coombs 9, by Marquard 2, by Ames 2. Bases on balls—Off Coombs 2, off Marquard 1. Hit by pitcher—By Coombs (Merkle). Wild pitch—Crandall. Hits—Off Marquard 3 in 3 innings, off Ames 2 in 4 innings, off Crandall 2 in 3 innings, off Coombs 8 in 9 innings, off Plank 1 in 2/3 inning. Winning pitcher—Crandall. Losing pitcher—Plank. Umpires—Klem (N.L.), Dinneen (A.L.), Connolly (A.L.) and Brennan (N.L.). Time—2:33. Attendance—33,228.

Thursday, Oct. 26—At Philadelphia

New York (N.L.)	AB.	R.	H.	O.	A.	E.
Devore, lf	4	0	0	5	0	0
Doyle, 2b	4	1	1	1	4	0
Snodgrass, cf	4	0	0	1	0	0
Murray, rf	3	0	0	0	0	1
Merkle, 1b	4	0	0	9	0	1
Herzog, 3b	4	1	1	0	0	0
Fletcher, ss	4	0	0	1	2	0
Meyers, c	3	0	1	6	0	0
Wilson, c	1	0	0	1	0	0
Ames, p	1	0	1	0	2	1
aCrandall	0	0	0	0	0	0
Wiltse, p	1	0	0	0	1	0
Marquard, p	0	0	0	0	0	0
Totals	33	2	4	24	10	3

Phila'phia (A.L.)	AB.	R.	H.	O.	A.	E.
Lord, lf	5	1	3	1	0	0
Oldring, cf	5	1	1	3	0	1
Collins, 2b	4	1	0	2	4	0
Baker, 3b	5	2	2	2	2	0
Murphy, rf	4	3	4	1	0	1
Davis, 1b	4	2	1	9	1	0
McInnis, 1b	0	0	0	1	0	0
Barry, ss	2	2	1	2	1	3
Thomas, c	3	1	1	5	1	0
Bender, p	4	0	0	1	4	0
Totals	36	13	13	27	13	5

```
New York ........ 1 0 0   0 0 0   0 0 1— 2
Philadelphia .... 0 0 1   4 0 1   7 0 *—13
```

aWalked for Ames in fifth. Two-base hits—Doyle, Lord 2, Murphy, Barry. Runs batted in—Fletcher, Lord, Collins, Baker, Murphy, Davis 2, Barry 2. Sacrifice hits—Collins, Barry. Sacrifice fly—Barry. Stolen base—Herzog. Earned runs—Philadelphia 10, New York 0. Left on bases—New York 6, Philadelphia 3. Struck out—By Ames 4, by Wiltse 1, by Marquard 2, by Bender 5. Bases on balls—Off Ames 1, off Bender 2. Wild pitches—Marquard, Bender. Hits—Off Ames 4 in 4 innings, off Wiltse 7 in 2⅓ innings, off Marquard 2 in 1⅔ innings. Losing pitcher—Ames. Umpires—Connolly (A.L.), Brennan (N.L.), Klem (N.L.) and Dinneen (A.L.). Time—2:12. Attendance—20,485.

COMPOSITE BATTING AVERAGES
Philadelphia Athletics

Player-Position	G.	AB.	R.	H.	2B.	3B.	HR.	RBI.	BA.
Baker, 3b	6	24	7	9	2	0	2	5	.375
Barry, ss	6	19	2	7	4	0	0	2	.368
Murphy, rf	6	23	4	7	3	0	0	3	.304
Collins, 2b	6	21	4	6	1	0	0	1	.286
Lapp, c	2	8	1	2	0	0	0	0	.250
Coombs, p	2	8	1	2	0	0	0	0	.250
Davis, 1b	6	24	3	5	1	0	0	5	.208
Oldring, cf	6	25	2	5	2	0	1	3	.200
Lord, lf	6	27	2	5	2	0	0	0	.185
Bender, p	3	11	0	1	0	0	0	0	.091
Thomas, c	4	12	1	1	0	0	0	1	.083
Plank, p	2	3	0	0	0	0	0	0	.000
Strunk, ph	1	1	0	0	0	0	0	0	.000
McInnis, 1b	1	0	0	0	0	0	0	0	.000
Totals	6	205	27	50	15	0	3	21	.244

New York Giants

Player-Position	G.	AB.	R.	H.	2B.	3B.	HR.	RBI.	BA.
Ames, p	2	2	0	1	0	0	0	0	.500
Crandall, p-ph	3	2	1	1	1	0	0	1	.500
Doyle, 2b	6	23	3	7	3	1	0	1	.304
Meyers, c	6	20	2	6	2	0	0	2	.300
Mathewson, p	3	7	0	2	0	0	0	0	.286
Herzog, 3b	6	21	3	4	2	0	0	0	.190
Devore, lf	6	24	1	4	1	0	0	3	.167
Merkle, 1b	6	20	1	3	1	0	0	1	.150
Fletcher, ss	6	23	1	3	1	0	0	1	.130
Snodgrass, cf	6	19	1	2	0	0	0	1	.105
Murray, rf	6	21	0	0	0	0	0	0	.000
Marquard, p	3	2	0	0	0	0	0	0	.000
Becker, ph	3	5	0	0	0	0	0	0	.000
Wiltse, p	2	1	0	0	0	0	0	0	.000
Wilson, p	1	1	0	0	0	0	0	0	.000
Totals	6	189	13	33	11	1	0	10	.175

COMPOSITE PITCHING AVERAGES
Philadelphia Athletics

Pitcher	G.	IP.	H.	R.	E.	SO.	BB.	W.	L.	ERA.
Bender	3	26	16	6	3	20	8	2	1	1.04
Coombs	2	20	11	5	3	16	6	1	0	1.35
Plank	2	9⅔	6	2	2	8	0	1	1	1.86
Totals	6	55⅔	33	13	8	44	14	4	2	1.29

New York Giants

Pitcher	G.	IP.	H.	R.	E.	SO.	BB.	W.	L.	ERA.
Crandall	2	4	2	0	0	2	0	1	0	0.00
Marquard	3	11⅔	9	6	2	8	1	0	1	1.54
Mathewson	3	27	25	8	6	13	2	1	2	2.00
Ames	2	8	6	5	2	6	1	0	1	2.25
Wiltse	2	3⅓	8	8	7	2	0	0	0	18.90
Totals	6	54	50	27	17	31	4	2	4	2.83

SERIES OF 1912

	W.	L.	T.	Pct.
Boston A. L.	4	3	1	.571
New York N. L.	3	4	1	.429

Featured by an 11-inning, 6 to 6 tie in the second clash, which stretched the event to eight games, and by a tense final contest, which went 10 innings, the classic between the Red Sox and Giants provided the thriller-diller of all World Series play up to that time. The Series saw John McGraw's men, winner of only one game in the first five, tie up the Series with a heroic uphill fight, have victory within their grasp in the deciding game, and then see it fritter away on school-boy blunders.

Both clubs had brilliant league seasons. The Red Sox, with Joe Wood winning 34 games, ten of them shutouts, while losing only five, broke in on the Athletics' pennant trust, easily capturing the flag with 105 victories, the high in the American up to that time. They beat Washington, the second-place club, by 14 games. With Rube Marquard running off his 19 straight winning streak in the first half of the season, the McGrawites repeated handily in their league, winning 103 games and finishing ten games in front of the runner-up Pirates. A sturdy pitching youngster, Jeff Tesreau, joined Christy Mathewson, Marquard, Leon Ames and George Wiltse on the Giant staff.

Wood topped off his fine season record with three victories and one defeat, while Hugh Bedient won one game for Boston and pitched seven innings of the crucial eighth game. Marquard won two games for the Giants and Tesreau one. Despite his brilliant pitching, Mathewson had to be satisfied with one tie game out of three starting assignments. Buck Herzog, third baseman of the defeated Giants, was the star of the Series, hitting .400 and playing inspired ball at the hot corner. Tris Speaker led the Boston regulars at bat with an even .300 and turned in the only unassisted double play ever made by an outfielder in a World Series. Harry Hooper saved the Series for Boston with a dazzling catch to rob Larry Doyle of a homer in the fifth inning of the eighth game.

After Wood defeated Tesreau in the Polo Grounds opener, 4 to 3, the Giants and Red Sox struggled to an 11-inning, 6 to 6 tie in Boston the next day, Mathewson opposing southpaw Ray Collins, Charley Hall and Bedient. Marquard then put New York back in the Series with a 2 to 1 decision over Bucky O'Brien, but Boston gained that big three-to-one edge by winning the fourth and fifth games, Wood defeating Tesreau again, 3 to 1, and Bedient winning a brilliant 2 to 1 decision over Mathewson.

The Giants then came back gamely and, by knocking out O'Brien and Wood in the first innings of the sixth and seventh games, tied up the Series with impressive 5 to 2 and 11 to 4 victories. The final game, in Boston, saw Mathewson trying to win it for New York, with Bedient again opposing Big Six. The Giants scored an early run in the third, but pinch-hitter Olaf Henriksen, batting for Bedient, tied the score for Boston in the seventh with a pinch double. Wood then went on the firing line for the Red Sox and gave up a Giant run in the first half of the tenth. However, in the second half, center fielder Fred Snodgrass made a two-base muff of pinch-hitter Clyde Engle's easy fly. After Harry Hooper was retired, Steve Yerkes walked. Speaker raised an easy pop foul between first baseman Fred Merkle and catcher Chief Meyers, just outside the first base coach's box. It dropped between the two players; Speaker, his batting life saved, singled in Engle with the tying run, and sent Yerkes to third, from where the Boston second baseman scored the winning run on Larry Gardner's long outfield fly to Josh Devore. The box scores:

Tuesday, October 8—At New York

Boston (A.L.)	AB.	R.	H.	O.	A.	E.
Hooper, rf	3	1	1	1	0	0
Yerkes, 2b	4	0	1	0	1	0
Speaker, cf	3	1	1	0	1	0
Lewis, lf	4	0	0	2	0	0
Gardner, 3b	4	0	0	1	1	0
Stahl, 1b	4	0	0	6	1	0
Wagner, ss	3	1	2	5	3	1
Cady, c	3	0	1	11	1	0
Wood, p	3	1	0	1	1	0
Totals	31	4	6	27	9	1

New York (N.L.)	AB.	R.	H.	O.	A.	E.
Devore, lf	3	1	0	0	0	0
Doyle, 2b	4	1	2	2	7	0
Snodgrass, cf	4	0	1	2	0	0
Murray, rf	3	0	1	1	0	0
Merkle, 1b	4	1	1	12	0	0
Herzog, 3b	4	0	2	1	1	0
Meyers, c	3	0	1	6	1	0
bBecker	0	0	0	0	0	0
Fletcher, ss	4	0	0	3	1	1
Tesreau, p	2	0	0	0	2	0
aMcCormick	1	0	0	0	0	0
Crandall, p	1	0	0	0	1	0
Totals	33	3	8	27	13	1

Boston .... 0 0 0   0 0 1   3 0 0—4
New York .... 0 0 2   0 0 0   0 0 1—3

aFlied out for Tesreau in seventh. bRan for Meyers in ninth. Two-base hits—Hooper, Wagner, Doyle. Three-base hit—Speaker. Runs batted in—Hooper, Yerkes 2, Lewis, Murray 2, Meyers. Sacrifice hits—Hooper, Cady. Double play—Stahl and Wood. Earned runs—Boston 4, New York 3. Left on bases—Boston 6, New York 6. Struck out—By Wood 11, by Tesreau 4, by Crandall 2. Bases on balls—Off Wood 2, off Tesreau 4. Hit by pitcher—By Wood (Meyers). Hits—Off Tesreau 5 in 7 innings, off Crandall 1 in 2 innings. Losing pitcher—Tesreau. Umpires—Klem (N.L.), Evans (A.L.), Rigler (N.L.) and O'Loughlin (A.L.). Time—2:10. Attendance—35,730.

Wednesday, October 9—At Boston

New York (N.L.)	AB.	R.	H.	O.	A.	E.
Snodgrass, lf-rf	4	1	1	0	0	0
Doyle, 2b	5	0	1	2	5	0
Becker, cf	4	1	0	0	1	0
Murray, rf-lf	5	2	3	3	0	0
Merkle, 1b	5	1	0	19	0	1
Herzog, 3b	4	1	3	2	4	0
Meyers, c	4	0	2	5	0	0
aShafer, ss	0	0	0	0	3	0
Fletcher, ss	4	0	0	1	3	3
bMcCormick	0	0	0	0	0	0
Wilson, c	0	0	0	0	1	1
Mathewson, p	5	0	0	1	6	0
Totals	40	6	11	33	23	5

Boston (A.L.)	AB.	R.	H.	O.	A.	E.
Hooper, rf	5	1	3	3	0	0
Yerkes, 2b	5	1	1	3	4	0
Speaker, cf	5	2	2	2	0	0
Lewis, lf	5	2	2	2	0	1
Gardner, 3b	4	0	0	2	0	0
Stahl, 1b	5	0	2	10	0	0
Wagner, ss	5	0	0	5	5	0
Carrigan, c	5	0	0	6	4	0
Collins, p	3	0	0	0	1	0
Hall, p	1	0	0	0	0	0
Bedient, p	1	0	0	0	0	0
Totals	44	6	10	33	14	1

New York .... 0 1 0   1 0 0   0 3 0   1 0—6
Boston .... 3 0 0   0 1 0   0 1 0   1 0—6

Stopped by darkness.

aRan for Meyers in tenth. bHit sacrifice fly for Fletcher in tenth. Two-base hits—Snodgrass, Murray, Herzog, Lewis 2, Hooper. Three-base hits—Murray, Merkle, Herzog, Yerkes, Speaker. Runs batted in—Murray 2, Herzog 2, Meyers, McCormick, Yerkes, Gardner, Stahl 2. Sacrifice hit—Gardner. Sacrifice flies—Herzog, McCormick. Stolen bases—Snodgrass, Herzog, Hooper 2, Stahl. Double play—Fletcher and Herzog. Earned runs—

1912 WORLD SERIES

New York 4, Boston 2. Left on bases—New York 9, Boston 6. Struck out—By Mathewson 4, by Collins 5, by Bedient 1. Bases on balls—Off Hall 4, off Bedient 1. Hit by pitcher—By Bedient (Snodgrass). Hits—Off Collins 9 in 7⅓ innings, off Hall 2 in 2⅔ innings, off Bedient 0 in 1 inning. Umpires—O'Loughlin (A.L.), Rigler (N.L.), Klem (N.L.) and Evans (A.L.). Time—2:38. Attendance—30,148.

Thursday, October 10—At Boston

New York (N.L.)	AB.	R.	H.	O.	A.	E.
Devore, lf	4	0	2	2	0	0
Doyle, 2b	3	0	0	3	1	0
Snodgrass, cf	4	0	1	0	0	0
Murray, rf	4	1	1	5	0	0
Merkle, 1b	3	0	0	5	0	1
Herzog, 3b	2	1	1	1	3	0
Meyers, c	4	0	1	8	1	0
Fletcher, ss	3	0	1	3	2	0
Marquard, p	1	0	0	0	2	0
Totals	28	2	7	27	9	1

Boston (A.L.)	AB.	R.	H.	O.	A.	E.
Hooper, rf	3	0	0	1	0	0
Yerkes, 2b	4	0	1	3	5	0
Speaker, cf	4	0	1	3	1	0
Lewis, lf	4	1	2	4	0	0
Gardner, 3b	3	0	1	0	2	0
Stahl, 1b	4	0	2	11	1	0
cHenriksen	0	0	0	0	0	0
Wagner, ss	4	0	0	1	3	0
Carrigan, c	2	0	0	3	1	0
aEngle	1	0	0	0	0	0
O'Brien, p	2	0	0	1	5	0
bBall	1	0	0	0	0	0
Cady, c	1	0	0	0	1	0
Bedient, p	0	0	0	0	0	0
Totals	33	1	7	27	15	0

New York .... 0 1 0 0 1 0 0 0 0—2
Boston .... 0 0 0 0 0 0 0 0 1—1

aFlied out for Carrigan in eighth. bStruck out for O'Brien in eighth. cRan for Stahl in ninth. Two-base hits—Murray, Herzog, Stahl, Gardner. Runs batted in—Herzog, Fletcher, Gardner. Sacrifice hits—Merkle, Marquard, Gardner. Sacrifice fly—Herzog. Stolen bases—Devore, Fletcher, Wagner. Double play—Speaker and Stahl. Earned runs—New York 2, Boston 1. Left on bases—Boston 7, New York 6. Struck out—By Marquard 6, by O'Brien 3. Bases on balls—Off Marquard 1, off O'Brien 3. Hit by pitcher—By Bedient (Herzog). Hits—Off O'Brien 6 in 8 innings, off Bedient 1 in 1 inning. Losing pitcher—O'Brien. Umpires—Evans (A.L.), Klem (N.L.), O'Loughlin (A.L.) and Rigler (N.L.). Time—2:16. Attendance—34,624.

Friday, October 11—At New York

Boston (A.L.)	AB.	R.	H.	O.	A.	E.
Hooper, rf	4	0	1	1	0	0
Yerkes, 2b	3	0	1	2	5	0
Speaker, cf	4	0	1	2	0	0
Lewis, lf	4	0	0	1	0	0
Gardner, 3b	3	2	2	0	2	0
Stahl, 1b	3	1	0	9	0	0
Wagner, ss	3	0	0	2	3	1
Cady, c	4	0	1	10	0	0
Wood, p	4	0	2	0	2	0
Totals	32	3	8	27	12	1

New York (N.L.)	AB.	R.	H.	O.	A.	E.
Devore, lf	4	0	1	0	0	0
Doyle, 2b	4	0	1	4	1	0
Snodgrass, cf	4	0	0	2	0	0
Murray, rf	4	0	1	3	0	0
Merkle, 1b	4	0	1	8	0	0
Herzog, 3b	4	1	2	2	1	0
Meyers, c	4	0	0	5	1	1
Fletcher, ss	4	0	1	3	6	0
Tesreau, p	2	0	1	0	2	0
aMcCormick	1	0	1	0	0	0
Ames, p	0	0	0	0	1	0
Totals	35	1	9	27	12	1

Boston .... 0 1 0 1 0 0 0 0 1—3
New York .... 0 0 0 0 0 0 1 0 0—1

aSingled for Tesreau in seventh. Two-base hits—Speaker, Fletcher. Three-base hit—Gardner. Runs batted in—Cady, Wood, Fletcher. Sacrifice hits—Yerkes, Stahl. Stolen bases—Stahl, Merkle. Double play—Fletcher and Merkle. Earned runs—Boston 3. New York 1. Left on bases—New York 7, Boston 7. Struck out—By Wood 8, by Tesreau 5. Bases on balls—Off Tesreau 2, off Ames 1. Wild pitch—Tesreau. Hits—Off Tesreau 5 in 7 innings, off Ames 3 in 2 innings. Losing pitcher—Tesreau. Umpires—Rigler (N.L.), O'Loughlin (A.L.), Evans (A.L.) and Klem (N.L.). Time—2:06. Attendance—36,502.

Saturday, October 12—At Boston

New York (N.L.)	AB.	R.	H.	O.	A.	E.
Devore, lf	2	0	0	0	0	0
Doyle, 2b	4	0	0	0	3	1
Snodgrass, cf	4	0	0	2	0	0
Murray, rf	3	0	0	1	0	0
Merkle, 1b	4	1	1	15	0	0
Herzog, 3b	4	0	0	2	3	0
Meyers, c	3	0	1	2	0	0
Fletcher, ss	2	0	0	2	2	0
aMcCromick	1	0	0	0	0	0
bShafer, ss	0	0	0	1	1	0
Mathewson, p	3	0	1	0	3	0
Totals	30	1	3	24	13	1

Boston (A.L.)	AB.	R.	H.	O.	A.	E.
Hooper, rf	4	1	2	4	0	0
Yerkes, 2b	4	1	1	3	3	0
Speaker, cf	3	0	1	3	0	0
Lewis, lf	3	0	0	1	0	0
Gardner, 3b	3	0	0	3	2	1
Stahl, 1b	3	0	0	7	0	0
Wagner, ss	3	0	1	1	1	0
Cady, c	3	0	0	5	0	0
Bedient, p	3	0	0	0	0	0
Totals	29	2	5	27	6	1

New York .... 0 0 0 0 0 0 1 0 0—1
Boston .... 0 0 2 0 0 0 0 0 *—2

aReached first on Gardner's error for Fletcher in seventh. bRan for McCormick in seventh. Two-base hit—Merkle. Three-base hits—Hooper, Yerkes. Runs batted in—Yerkes, Speaker. Double play—Wagner, Yerkes and Stahl. Earned runs—Boston 2, New York 0. Left on bases—New York 5, Boston 3. Struck out—By Mathewson 2, by Bedient 4. Bases on balls—Off Bedient 3. Umpires—O'Loughlin (A.L.), Rigler (N.L.) Klem (N.L.) and Evans (A.L.). Time—1:43. Attendance—34,683.

Monday, October 14—At New York

Boston (A.L.)	AB.	R.	H.	O.	A.	E.
Hooper, rf	4	0	1	2	2	0
Yerkes, 2b	4	0	2	3	1	1
Speaker, cf	3	0	0	5	0	0
Lewis, lf	4	0	0	0	0	0
Gardner, 3b	4	1	0	0	1	0
Stahl, 1b	4	1	2	8	0	0
Wagner, ss	4	0	0	3	0	0

1912 WORLD SERIES

	AB.	R.	H.	O.	A.	E.
Cady, c	3	0	1	3	2	1
O'Brien, p	0	0	0	0	1	0
aEngle	1	0	1	0	0	0
Collins, p	2	0	0	0	2	0
Totals	33	2	7	24	9	2

New York (N.L.)	AB.	R.	H.	O.	A.	E.
Devore, lf	4	0	1	2	0	1
Doyle, 2b	4	1	1	1	1	0
Snodgrass, cf	4	0	1	6	0	0
Murray, rf	3	1	2	7	0	0
Merkle, 1b	3	1	2	4	1	0
Herzog, 3b	3	1	1	1	1	0
Meyers, c	3	1	2	6	0	0
Fletcher, ss	3	0	1	0	2	0
Marquard, p	3	0	0	0	2	1
Totals	30	5	11	27	7	2

Boston .... 0 2 0 0 0 0 0 0 0—2
New York ..... 5 0 0 0 0 0 0 0 *—5

aDoubled for O'Brien in second. Two-base hits—Engle, Merkle, Herzog. Three-base hit—Meyers. Runs batted in—Engle 2, Merkle, Herzog, Fletcher. Stolen bases—Speaker, Doyle, Herzog, Meyers. Double plays—Fletcher, Doyle and Merkle; Hooper and Stahl. Earned runs—New York 3, Boston 0. Left on bases—Boston 5, New York 1. Struck out—By Marquard 3, by O'Brien 1, by Collins 1. Bases on balls—Off Marquard 1. Balk—O'Brien. Hits—Off O'Brien 6 in 1 inning, off Collins 5 in 7 innings. Losing pitcher—O'Brien. Umpires—Klem (N.L.), Evans (A.L.), O'Loughlin (A.L.) and Rigler (N.L.). Time—1:58. Attendance—30,622.

Tuesday, October 15—At Boston

New York (N.L.)	AB.	R.	H.	O.	A.	E.
Devore, rf	4	2	1	3	1	1
Doyle, 2b	4	3	3	2	3	2
Snodgrass, cf	5	1	2	1	0	0
Murray, lf	4	0	0	1	0	0
Merkle, 1b	5	1	2	10	0	1
Herzog, 3b	4	2	1	0	2	0
Meyers, c	4	1	3	6	0	0
Wilson, c	1	0	1	2	0	0
Fletcher, ss	5	1	1	2	4	0
Tesreau, p	4	0	2	0	6	0
Totals	40	11	16	27	16	4

Boston (A.L.)	AB.	R.	H.	O.	A.	E.
Hooper, rf	3	0	1	1	1	0
Yerkes, 2b	4	0	0	1	4	0
Speaker, cf	4	1	1	4	0	1
Lewis, lf	4	1	1	3	0	0
Gardner, 3b	4	1	1	2	0	1
Stahl, 1b	5	0	1	11	0	0
Wagner, ss	5	0	1	4	4	0
Cady, c	4	1	0	1	2	0
Wood, p	0	0	0	0	1	0
Hall, p	3	0	3	0	5	1
Totals	36	4	9	27	18	3

New York ..... 6 1 0 0 0 2 1 0 1—11
Boston .... 0 1 0 0 0 0 2 1 0— 4

Two-base hits—Snodgrass, Hall, Lewis. Home runs—Doyle, Gardner. Runs batted in—Doyle 2, Snodgrass 2, Merkle, Meyers, Tesreau 2, Hooper, Lewis, Gardner. Sacrifice hit—Murray. Sacrifice fly—Hooper. Stolen bases—Devore 2, Doyle. Double plays—Devore and Meyers; Speaker (unassisted). Earned runs—New York 7, Boston 2. Left on bases—Boston 12, New York 8. Struck out—By Tesreau 6, by Hall 1. Bases on balls—Off Tesreau 5, off Hall 5. Hit by pitcher—By Tesreau (Gardner). Wild pitches—Tesreau 2. Hits—Off Wood 7 in 1 inning, off Hall 9 in 8 innings. Losing pitcher—Wood. Umpires—Evans (A.L.), Klem (N.L.), O'Loughlin (A.L.) and Rigler (N.L.). Time—2:21. Attendance—32,694.

Wednesday, October 16—At Boston

New York (N.L.)	AB.	R.	H.	O.	A.	E.
Devore, rf	3	1	1	3	1	0
Doyle, 2b	5	0	0	1	5	0
Snodgrass, cf	4	0	1	4	1	1
Murray, lf	5	1	2	3	0	0
Merkle, 1b	5	0	1	10	0	0
Herzog, 3b	5	0	2	2	1	0
Meyers, c	3	0	0	4	1	0
Fletcher, ss	3	0	1	2	3	0
bMcCormick	1	0	0	0	0	0
Shafer, ss	0	0	0	0	0	0
Mathewson, p	4	0	1	0	3	0
Totals	38	2	9	*29	15	2

Boston (A.L.)	AB.	R.	H.	O.	A.	E.
Hooper, rf	5	0	0	3	0	0
Yerkes, 2b	4	1	1	0	3	0
Speaker, cf	4	0	2	2	0	1
Lewis, lf	4	0	0	1	0	0
Gardner, 3b	3	0	1	1	4	2
Stahl, 1b	4	1	2	15	0	0
Wagner, ss	3	0	1	3	5	1
Cady, c	4	0	0	5	3	0
Bedient, p	2	0	0	0	1	0
aHenriksen	1	0	1	0	0	0
Wood, p	0	0	0	0	2	0
cEngle	1	1	0	0	0	0
Totals	35	3	8	30	18	5

New York ..... 0 0 1 0 0 0 0 0 0 1—2
Boston .... 0 0 0 0 0 0 1 0 0 2—3

aDoubled for Bedient in seventh. bFlied out for Fletcher in ninth. cReached second on Snodgrass' error for Wood in tenth. *Two out when winning run scored. Two-base hits—Murray 2, Herzog, Gardner, Stahl, Henriksen. Runs batted in—Murray, Merkle, Speaker, Gardner, Henriksen. Sacrifice hit—Meyers. Sacrifice fly—Gardner. Stolen base—Devore. Earned runs—Boston 1, New York 2. Left on bases—New York 11, Boston 9. Struck out—By Mathewson 4, by Bedient 2, by Wood 2. Bases on balls—Off Mathewson 5, off Bedient 3, off Wood 1. Hits—Off Bedient 6 in 7 innings, off Wood 3 in 3 innings. Winning pitcher—Wood. Umpires—O'Loughlin (A.L.), Rigler (N.L.), Klem (N.L.) and Evans (A.L.). Time—2:39. Attendance—17,034.

COMPOSITE BATTING AVERAGES
Boston Red Sox

Player-Position	G.	AB.	R.	H.	2B.	3B.	HR.	RBI.	BA.
Henriksen, pr-ph	2	1	0	1	1	0	0	1	1.000
Hall, p	2	4	0	3	1	0	0	0	.750
Engle, ph	3	3	1	1	1	0	0	2	.333
Speaker, cf	8	30	4	9	1	2	0	2	.300
Hooper, rf	8	31	3	9	2	1	0	2	.290
Wood, p	4	7	1	2	0	0	0	1	.286
Stahl, 1b	8	32	3	9	2	0	0	2	.281
Yerkes, 2b	8	32	3	8	0	2	0	4	.250
Gardner, 3b	8	28	4	5	2	1	1	4	.179
Wagner, ss	8	30	1	5	1	0	0	0	.167
Lewis, lf	8	32	4	5	3	0	0	2	.156
Cady, c	7	22	1	3	0	0	0	1	.136
Carrigan, c	2	7	0	0	0	0	0	0	.000
Collins, p	2	5	0	0	0	0	0	0	.000
Bedient, p	4	6	0	0	0	0	0	0	.000
O'Brien, p	2	2	0	0	0	0	0	0	.000
Ball, ph	1	1	0	0	0	0	0	0	.000
Totals	8	273	25	60	14	6	1	21	.220

1913 WORLD SERIES

New York Giants

Player-Position	G.	AB.	R.	H.	2B.	3B.	HR.	RBI.	BA.
Wilson, c	2	1	0	1	0	0	0	0	1.000
Herzog, 3b	8	30	6	12	4	1	0	4	.400
Tesreau, p	3	8	0	3	0	0	0	2	.375
Meyers, c	8	28	2	10	0	1	0	3	.357
Murray, rf-lf	8	31	5	10	4	1	0	5	.323
Merkle, 1b	8	33	5	9	2	1	0	3	.273
McCormick, ph	5	4	0	1	0	0	0	1	.250
Devore, lf	7	24	4	6	0	0	0	0	.250
Doyle, 2b	8	33	5	8	1	0	1	2	.242
Snod'ss, cf-lf-rf	8	33	2	7	2	0	0	2	.212
Fletcher, ss	8	28	1	5	1	0	0	3	.179
Mathewson, p	3	12	0	2	0	0	0	0	.167
Becker, pr-cf	2	4	1	0	0	0	0	0	.000
Crandall, p	1	1	0	0	0	0	0	0	.000
Shafer, pr-ss	3	0	0	0	0	0	0	0	.000
Marquard, p	2	4	0	0	0	0	0	0	.000
Ames, p	1	0	0	0	0	0	0	0	.000
Totals	8	274	31	74	14	4	1	25	.270

COMPOSITE PITCHING AVERAGES
Boston Red Sox

Pitcher	G.	IP.	H.	R.	E.	SO.	BB.	W.	L.	ERA.
Bedient	4	18	10	2	1	7	7	1	0	0.50
Collins	2	14½	14	5	3	6	0	0	0	1.88
Hall	2	10⅔	11	6	4	1	9	0	0	3.38
Wood	4	22	27	11	9	21	3	3	1	3.68
O'Brien	2	9	12	7	5	4	3	0	2	5.00
Totals	8	74	74	31	22	39	22	4	3	2.68

New York Giants

Pitcher	G.	IP.	H.	R.	E.	SO.	BB.	W.	L.	ERA.
Crandall	1	2	1	0	0	2	0	0	0	0.00
Marquard	2	18	14	3	1	9	2	2	0	0.50
Mathewson	3	28⅔	23	11	5	10	5	0	2	1.57
Tesreau	3	23	19	10	8	15	11	1	2	3.13
Ames	1	2	3	1	1	0	1	0	0	4.50
Totals	8	73⅔	60	25	15	36	19	3	4	1.83

SERIES OF 1913

	W.	L.	Pct.
Philadelphia A. L.	4	1	.800
New York N. L.	1	4	.200

The Athletics and Giants met for the third time within a period of nine years, and the 1913 Series resulted in an easy victory for the American League entry, the A's winning four out of five games.

What chance there was for New York was largely ruined by a succession of accidents. Center fielder Fred Snodgrass suffered from a Charley horse and made only two brief appearances in the Series. First baseman Fred Merkle also suffered a leg injury, and while he missed only one game, he limped through the Series. John McGraw's first-string catcher, Chief Meyers, suffered a broken finger in the first game, but Larry McLean, the Indian's fill-in, caught well and was the batting leader of the Series, with a .500 average.

The only game lost by the Mackmen was a ten-inning shutout to Christy Mathewson in the second clash, and they again clearly showed their superiority, with a team batting average of .264 against .201 for the Giants.

For the second successive time, Frank Baker led the Athletics at bat, with an average of .450, and hit his third World Series home run against the Giants. The brilliant Eddie Collins followed Baker with .421 and stole three bases.

Chief Bender won both of his starts for the Athletics, bringing his World Series victory total to six. He scattered 11 hits to win the opener, 6 to 4, and then decisioned the Giants in the fourth game, 6 to 5.

After losing the second game, in which he blanked the Giants for nine innings, Eddie Plank finally vanquished his old college opponent, Matty, in the fifth set-to, winding up the Series with a sizzling two-hitter.

The fourth Philadelphia victory was hurled by Joe Bush, then only 21 years old. He went the distance in the third contest for an easy five-hit, 8 to 2 triumph.

Mack went through the Series with only 12 players, using only two catchers and three pitchers.

While New York won only one game, the play of the Giants in the second game was one of the heroic stands of World Series baseball. McGraw was compelled to play George Wiltse, southpaw pitcher, at first base, infielder Art Shafer in center field and Larry McLean, a second-stringer, behind the bat. With Matty and Plank battling brilliantly and the score, 0 to 0, the A's put runners on third and second with none out in the ninth inning. On successive plays Wiltse shot down the winning run at the plate and the third man was retired at first base.

Following this great stand, the Giants reached Plank for three runs in the tenth. McLean opened the inning with a single. Following a sacrifice, Matty himself slashed a hit to right-center, scoring the first run. An error and hit batsman then filled the bases and Art Fletcher settled the game with a two-run single.

The box scores:

Tuesday, October 7—At New York

Phila'phia (A.L.)	AB.	R.	H.	O.	A.	E.
E. Murphy, rf	4	0	1	2	0	0
Oldring, lf	4	0	1	2	0	0
Collins, 2b	3	3	3	4	6	0
Baker, 3b	4	1	3	1	3	0
McInnis, 1b	3	0	1	10	0	0
Strunk, cf	4	1	0	3	0	0
Barry, ss	4	1	1	1	3	1
Schang, c	4	0	1	4	1	0
Bender, p	4	0	0	0	2	0
Totals	34	6	11	27	15	1

New York (N.L.)	AB.	R.	H.	O.	A.	E.
Shafer, cf	5	0	1	3	0	0
Doyle, 2b	4	1	2	2	2	0
Fletcher, ss	4	0	2	2	2	0
Burns, lf	4	0	1	3	0	0
Herzog, 3b	4	0	0	1	2	0
Murray, rf	4	0	2	1	0	0
Meyers, c	4	0	0	4	2	0
Merkle, 1b	4	2	2	11	0	0
Marquard, p	0	0	0	0	6	0
aMcCormick	1	1	1	0	0	0
Crandall, p	1	0	0	0	0	0
Tesreau, p	0	0	0	0	1	0
bMcLean	1	0	0	0	0	0
Totals	36	4	11	27	15	0

```
Philadelphia .............  0 0 0   3 2 0   0 1 0—6
New York ..................  0 0 1   0 3 0   0 0 0—4
```

aSingled for Marquard in fifth. bPopped out for Tesreau in ninth. Two-base hits—McInnis, Barry, Burns. Three-base hits—Collins, Schang. Home run—Baker. Runs batted in—Baker 3, McInnis, Schang 2, Doyle 2, Fletcher 2. Sacrifice hits—McInnis, Marquard. Stolen base—Collins. Double play—Barry, Collins and McInnis. Left on bases—New York 6, Philadelphia 4. Earned runs—Philadelphia 6, New York 3. Struck out—By Bender 4, by Marquard 1, by Crandall 1, by Tesreau 1. Bases on balls—Off Marquard 1, off Tesreau 1. Hits—Off Marquard 8 in 5 innings, off Crandall 3 in 2 innings (pitched to three batters in eighth), off Tesreau 0 in 2 innings. Losing pitcher—Marquard. Umpires—Klem (N.L.), Egan (A.L.), Rigler (N.L.) and Connolly (A.L.). Time—2:06. Attendance—36,291.

Wednesday, Oct. 8—At Philadelphia

New York (N.L.)	AB.	R.	H.	O.	A.	E.
Herzog, 3b	5	1	0	1	4	0
Doyle, 2b	4	0	0	3	5	2
Fletcher, ss	5	0	2	1	3	0
Burns, lf	4	0	0	4	0	0
Shafer, cf	5	0	0	0	0	0
Murray, rf	4	0	0	0	0	0
McLean, c	4	0	2	5	1	0
aGrant	0	1	0	0	0	0
Wilson, c	0	0	0	1	0	0
Snodgrass, 1b	1	0	1	1	1	0
bWiltse, 1b	2	0	0	13	3	0
Mathewson, p	3	1	2	1	3	0
Totals	37	3	7	30	20	2

Phila'phia (A.L.)	AB.	R.	H.	O.	A.	E.
E. Murphy, rf	5	0	0	5	0	0
Oldring, lf	5	0	1	4	0	0
Collins, 2b	4	0	1	2	2	1
Baker, 3b	5	0	2	0	0	1
McInnis, 1b	4	0	0	5	0	0
Strunk, cf	3	0	1	4	0	0
Barry, ss	4	0	1	2	1	0
Lapp, c	4	0	1	7	1	0
Plank, p	4	0	1	1	2	0
Totals	38	0	8	30	6	2

```
New York ...............  0 0 0   0 0 0   0 0 0   3—3
Philadelphia ...........  0 0 0   0 0 0   0 0 0   0—0
```

aRan for McLean in tenth. bRan for Snodgrass in third; went to first base. Runs batted in—Fletcher 2, Mathewson. Sacrifice hits—Wiltse, Collins. Left on bases—Philadelphia 10, New York 8. Earned runs—New York 2, Philadelphia 0. Struck out—By Mathewson 5, by Plank 6. Bases on balls—Off Mathewson 1, off Plank 2. Hit by pitcher—By Plank (Doyle). Umpires—Connolly (A.L.), Rigler (N.L.), Klem (N.L.) and Egan (A.L.). Time—2:22. Attendance—20,563.

Thursday, October 9—At New York

Phila'phia (A.L.)	AB.	R.	H.	O.	A.	E.
E. Murphy, rf	5	1	2	2	0	0
Oldring, lf	5	3	2	0	0	0
Collins, 2b	5	2	3	5	4	0
Baker, 3b	4	1	2	3	1	0
McInnis, 1b	4	0	0	9	0	0
Strunk, cf	4	0	0	1	0	0
Barry, ss	4	0	1	2	3	0
Schang, c	4	1	1	5	2	1
Bush, p	4	0	1	0	1	0
Totals	39	8	12	27	11	1

New York (N.L.)	AB.	R.	H.	O.	A.	E.
Herzog, 3b	4	0	0	1	0	0
Doyle, 2b	4	0	1	5	1	0
Fletcher, ss	2	0	1	2	2	1
Burns, lf	4	0	0	3	0	0
Shafer, cf	3	1	1	2	0	0
Murray, rf	3	1	1	4	0	0
McLean, c	2	0	1	3	1	0
bCooper	0	0	0	0	0	0
Wilson, c	2	0	0	2	0	0
Merkle, 1b	2	0	0	3	0	0
aWiltse, 1b	0	0	0	2	0	0
Tesreau, p	2	0	0	0	0	0
Crandall, p	1	0	0	0	2	0
Totals	29	2	5	27	6	1

```
Philadelphia ...........  3 2 0   0 0 0   2 1 0—8
New York ................  0 0 0   0 1 0   1 0 0—2
```

aRan for Merkle in seventh. bRan for McLean in sixth. Two-base hit—Shafer. Three-base hit—Collins. Home run—Schang. Runs batted in—Collins 3, Baker 2, Schang, Murray, McLean. Stolen bases—Oldring, Collins, Baker, Fletcher, Murray, Cooper. Double plays—Bush, Barry and McInnis; Schang and Collins; Collins and Barry; Doyle (unassisted). Left on bases—New York 5, Philadelphia 4. Earned runs—Philadelphia 7, New York 1. Struck out—By Bush 3, by Tesreau 3, by Crandall 1. Bases on balls—Off Bush 4. Hit by pitcher—By Bush (Fletcher). Hits—Off Tesreau 11 in 6⅓ innings, off Crandall 1 in 2⅔ innings. Losing pitcher—Tesreau. Umpires—Rigler (N.L.), Connolly (A.L.), Klem (N.L.) and Egan (A.L.). Time—2:11. Attendance—36,896.

Friday, October 10—At Philadelphia

New York (N.L.)	AB.	R.	H.	O.	A.	E.
Snodgrass, cf	2	0	0	2	0	0
Herzog, 3b	2	0	1	2	0	0
Doyle, 2b	4	0	0	2	4	0
Fletcher, ss	4	1	0	1	0	0
Burns, lf	4	2	2	2	0	0
Shafer, 3b-cf	4	0	1	1	0	0
Murray, rf	2	1	1	2	0	0
McLean, c	2	0	2	1	1	0
aCooper	0	0	0	0	0	0
Wilson, c	1	0	0	1	0	0
cCrandall	1	0	0	0	0	0
Merkle, 1b	4	1	1	10	1	2
Demaree, p	1	0	0	0	2	0
bMcCormick	1	0	0	0	0	0
Marquard, p	1	0	0	0	2	0
dGrant	1	0	0	0	0	0
Totals	34	5	8	24	11	2

Phila'phia (A.L.)	AB.	R.	H.	O.	A.	E.
E. Murphy, rf	5	0	0	3	0	0
Oldring, lf	4	0	2	1	0	0
Collins, 2b	4	0	0	3	3	0
Baker, 3b	4	0	0	2	0	0
McInnis, 1b	4	1	1	7	0	0
Strunk, cf	2	2	1	3	0	0
Barry, ss	4	2	3	2	2	0
Schang, c	2	1	2	6	1	0
Bender, p	4	0	0	0	3	0
Totals	33	6	9	27	9	0

```
New York ..............  0 0 0   0 0 0   3 2 0—5
Philadelphia ..........  0 1 0   3 2 0   0 0 *—6
```

aRan for McLean in fifth. bFlied out for Demaree in fifth. cGrounded out for Wilson in ninth. dFouled out for Marquard in ninth. Two-base hits—Burns, Barry 2. Three-base hits—Shafer, Oldring. Home run—Merkle. Runs batted in—Barry 2, Bender, Schang 3, Burns, Shafer, Merkle 3. Sacrifice hit—Strunk. Stolen bases—Burns, Murray,

Collins. Left on bases—Philadelphia 7, New York 4. Earned runs—New York 5, Philadelphia 4. Struck out—By Marquard 2, by Bender 5. Bases on balls—Off Demaree 1, off Marquard 2, off Bender 1. Hit by pitcher—By Bender (Murray). Hits—Off Demaree 7 in 4 innings, off Marquard 2 in 4 innings. Losing pitcher—Demaree. Passed ball—McLean. Umpires—Egan (A.L.), Klem (N.L.), Connolly (A.L.) and Rigler (N.L.). Time —2:09. Attendance—20,568.

Saturday, October 11—At New York

Phila'phia (A.L.)	AB.	R.	H.	O.	A.	E.
E. Murphy, rf	3	1	2	3	0	0
Oldring, lf	4	2	0	3	0	0
Collins, 2b	3	0	1	2	3	0
Baker, 3b	3	0	2	0	2	0
McInnis, 1b	2	0	0	14	0	0
Strunk, cf	4	0	0	2	0	0
Barry, ss	4	0	0	2	7	0
Schang, c	4	0	1	1	0	0
Plank, p	3	0	0	0	1	1
Totals	30	3	6	27	13	1

New York (N.L.)	AB.	R.	H.	O.	A.	E.
Herzog, 3b	4	0	0	1	2	0
Doyle, 2b	4	0	0	1	7	1
Fletcher, ss	3	0	0	2	3	0
Burns, lf	3	0	0	2	0	1
Shafer, cf	2	1	0	2	0	0
Murray, rf	3	0	0	2	0	0
McLean, c	3	0	1	3	1	0
Merkle, 1b	3	0	0	14	0	0
Mathewson, p	2	0	1	0	2	0
aCrandall	1	0	0	0	0	0
Totals	28	1	2	27	15	2

Philadelphia .... 1 0 2   0 0 0   0 0 0—3
New York .... 0 0 0   0 1 0   0 0 0—1

aGrounded out for Mathewson in ninth. Runs batted in—McLean. Baker 2, McInnis. Sacrifice hits—Collins, McInnis. Sacrifice flies—Baker, McInnis. Double plays—Collins, Barry and McInnis; Barry, Collins and McInnis. Left on bases—Philadelphia 5, New York 1. Earned runs—Philadelphia 2, New York 0. Struck out—By Plank 1, by Mathewson 2. Bases on balls—Off Plank 1, off Mathewson 1. Umpires—Klem (N.L.), Egan (A.L.), Rigler (N.L.) and Connolly (A.L.). Time —1:39. Attendance—36,632.

COMPOSITE BATTING AVERAGES
Philadelphia Athletics

Player-Position	G.	AB.	R.	H.	2B.	3B.	HR.	RBI.	BA.
Baker, 3b	5	20	2	9	0	0	1	7	.450
Collins, 2b	5	19	5	8	0	2	0	3	.421
Schang, c	4	14	2	5	0	1	1	6	.357
Barry, ss	5	20	3	6	3	0	0	2	.300
Oldring, lf	5	22	5	6	0	1	0	1	.273
Lapp, c	1	4	0	1	0	0	0	0	.250
Bush, p	1	4	0	1	0	0	0	0	.250
E. Murphy, rf	5	22	2	5	0	0	0	0	.227
Plank, p	2	7	0	1	0	0	0	0	.143
McInnis, 1b	5	17	0	2	1	0	0	2	.118
Strunk, cf	5	17	3	2	0	0	0	1	.118
Bender, p	2	8	0	0	0	0	0	1	.000
Totals	5	174	23	46	4	4	2	23	.264

New York Giants

Player-Position	G.	AB.	R.	H.	2B.	3B.	HR.	RBI.	BA.
Mathewson, p	2	5	1	3	0	0	0	1	.600
McCormick, ph	2	2	1	1	0	0	0	0	.500
McLean, ph-c	5	12	0	6	0	0	0	2	.500
Snodgrass, 1b-cf	2	3	0	1	0	0	0	0	.333
Fletcher, ss	5	18	1	5	0	0	0	4	.278
Murray, rf	5	16	2	4	0	0	0	1	.250
Merkle, 1b	4	13	3	3	0	0	1	3	.231
Shafer, cf-3b	5	19	2	3	1	0	1	1	.158
Burns, lf	5	19	2	3	2	0	0	1	.158
Doyle, 2b	5	20	1	3	0	0	0	2	.150

Player-Position	G.	AB.	R.	H.	2B.	3B.	HR.	RBI.	BA.
Herzog, 3b	5	19	1	1	0	0	0	0	.053
Meyers, c	1	4	0	0	0	0	0	0	.000
Marquard, p	2	1	0	0	0	0	0	0	.000
Crandall, p-ph	4	4	0	0	0	0	0	0	.000
Tesreau, p	2	2	0	0	0	0	0	0	.000
Grant, pr-ph	2	1	1	0	0	0	0	0	.000
Wilson, c	3	3	0	0	0	0	0	0	.000
Wiltse, pr-1b	2	2	0	0	0	0	0	0	.000
Cooper, pr	2	0	0	0	0	0	0	0	.000
Demaree, p	1	1	0	0	0	0	0	0	.000
Totals	5	164	15	33	3	1	1	15	.201

COMPOSITE PITCHING AVERAGES
Philadelphia Athletics

Pitcher	G.	IP.	H.	R.	E.	SO.	BB.	W.	L.	ERA.
Plank	2	19	9	4	2	7	3	1	1	0.95
Bush	1	9	5	2	1	3	4	1	0	1.00
Bender	2	18	19	9	8	9	1	2	0	4.00
Totals	5	46	33	15	11	19	8	4	1	2.15

New York Giants

Pitcher	G.	IP.	H.	R.	E.	SO.	BB.	W.	L.	ERA.
Mathewson	2	19	14	3	2	7	2	1	1	.095
Crandall	2	4⅔	4	2	2	2	0	0	0	3.86
Demaree	1	4	7	4	2	0	1	0	1	4.50
Tesreau	2	8⅓	11	7	6	4	1	0	1	6.48
Marquard	2	9	10	7	7	3	3	0	1	7.00
Totals	5	45	46	23	19	16	7	1	4	3.80

SERIES OF 1914

	W.	L.	Pct.
Boston N. L.	4	0	1.000
Philadelphia A. L.	0	4	.000

Following setbacks in three straight World Series for the Giants and four running for the National League, the senior circuit regained the top in 1914 with the most sensational of all Series victories, a thrilling four-straight clean-up of the great Athletics by George Stallings' "miracle" Boston Braves. Despite the fact that the Braves had won the National League championship in a spectacular climb which took them from the cellar in mid-July, the Athletics were overwhelming favorites, especially when Red Smith, regular third baseman of the Boston club, broke a leg on the eve of the Series. The Athletics, winning their fourth flag in five years and with three world championship triumphs behind them, were expected to put the Boston upstarts in their place. Instead, the Athletics were the first club to be counted out in four games. The Hub end of the Series was played at Fenway Park, home of Boston's Red Sox.

Stallings won the Series with the famous pitching trio which spearheaded his successful pennant campaign, Dick Rudolph, Bill James and George Tyler, the latter a lefthander. Rudolph won the first and fourth games, and James was credited with the second and third contests. After pitching a 1 to 0 two-hit shutout over Eddie Plank in the second game, Big Bill, relieving Tyler, pitched the last two frames of the 12-inning third tiff, yielding no hits and getting credit for the victory. The defeated Athletic pitchers, besides Plank, were Chief Bender, Joe Bush and Bob Shawkey.

Hank Gowdy was the biggest individual

hero for the National Leaguers since Christy Mathewson shut out the A's three times in 1905. Hank was red hot and no Athletic pitcher could cool him off. A .243 hitter in the league season, Gowdy hit .545 in the Series, his six hits including only one single. His collection contained a homer, triple and three doubles. Hank also walked five times. Johnny Evers, an old thorn for the American League with the Cubs, batted .438, while the Trojan and Rabbit Maranville, the youthful Brave shortstop, played brilliant ball around the midway.

The Athletics, who had lost only four games in their previous three Series, were completely submerged, hitting a weak .172 against Boston's .244. Of Mack's players taking part in all four games, Frank Baker again led at bat with an average of only .250, but such old favorites as Eddie Collins, Jack Barry and Rube Oldring hit only .214, .071 and .067, respectively. Part of the poor showing of the A's was attributed by Mack to the fact that the club was torn with dissension over Federal League offers. Bender and Plank pitched in the Series with Federal League contracts in their pockets, and the battling marked their last days in Athletic uniforms, as was the case with Collins, Baker and Jack Coombs, who were sold to other clubs during the winter. Barry, Eddie Murphy and Shawkey followed early in 1915. The box scores:

Friday, October 9—At Philadelphia

Boston (N.L.)	AB.	R.	H.	O.	A.	E.
Moran, rf	5	0	0	0	0	1
Evers, 2b	4	1	1	2	2	1
Connolly, lf	3	1	1	1	1	0
Whitted, cf	3	2	1	1	0	0
Schmidt, 1b	4	1	2	11	1	0
Gowdy, c	3	2	3	9	1	0
Maranville, ss	4	0	2	2	3	0
Deal, 3b	4	0	0	1	2	0
Rudolph, p	4	0	1	0	3	0
Totals	34	7	11	27	13	2
Phil'phia (A.L.)	AB.	R.	H.	O.	A.	E.
Murphy, rf	4	0	1	0	0	0
Oldring, lf	3	0	0	2	0	0
Collins, 2b	3	0	0	2	2	0
Baker, 3b	4	0	1	3	4	0
McInnis, 1b	2	1	0	10	1	0
Strunk, cf	4	0	2	0	0	0
Barry, ss	4	0	0	3	3	0
Schang, c	2	0	0	3	0	0
Lapp, c	1	0	0	2	1	0
Bender, p	2	0	0	1	3	0
Wyckoff, p	1	0	1	1	0	0
Totals	30	1	5	27	14	0

Boston.................. 0 2 0   0 1 3   0 1 0—7
Philadelphia.......... 0 1 0   0 0 0   0 0 0—1

Two-base hits—Gowdy, Baker, Wyckoff. Three-base hits—Gowdy, Whitted. Runs batted in—Whitted 2, Schmidt, Gowdy, Maranville 2. Sacrifice hit—Oldring. Stolen bases—Moran, Schmidt, Gowdy. Double plays—Schmidt and Deal; Barry, Collins and McInnis; Bender and McInnis; Baker and McInnis; Bender, Barry and McInnis. Left on bases—Philadelphia 6, Boston 3. Earned runs—Boston 7, Philadelphia 0. Struck out—By Bender 3, by Wyckoff 2, by Rudolph 8. Bases on balls—Off Bender 2, off Wyckoff 1, off Rudolph 3. Hits—Off Bender 8 in 5⅓ innings, off Wyckoff 3 in 3⅔ innings. Losing pitcher—Bender. Umpires—Dinneen (A.L.), Klem (N.L.), Byron (N.L.) and Hildebrand (A.L.). Time—1:58. Attendance—20,562.

Saturday, October 10—At Philadelphia

Boston (N.L.)	AB.	R.	H.	O.	A.	E.
Mann, rf	5	0	2	0	0	0
Evers, 2b	4	0	2	0	3	0
Cather, lf	5	0	0	2	0	0
Whitted, cf	3	0	0	1	0	0
Schmidt, 1b	4	0	1	12	1	0
Gowdy, c	2	0	1	8	1	0
Maranville, ss	2	0	1	2	4	1
Deal, 3b	4	1	1	2	2	0
James, p	4	0	0	0	3	0
Totals	33	1	7	27	14	1
Phil'phia (A.L.)	AB.	R.	H.	O.	A.	E.
Murphy, rf	3	0	0	2	0	0
Oldring, lf	3	0	0	0	0	0
Collins, 2b	3	0	1	5	2	0
Baker, 3b	3	0	0	2	3	0
McInnis, 1b	3	0	0	7	0	1
Strunk, cf	3	0	0	4	0	0
Barry, ss	2	0	0	2	6	0
Schang, c	3	0	1	5	2	0
Plank, p	2	0	0	0	1	0
aWalsh	0	0	0	0	0	0
Totals	25	0	2	27	14	1

Boston.................. 0 0 0   0 0 0   0 0 1—1
Philadelphia.......... 0 0 0   0 0 0   0 0 0—0

aWalked for Plank in ninth. Two-base hits—Schang, Deal. Run batted in—Whitted. Sacrifice hit—Maranville. Stolen bases—Deal 2, Barry. Double play—Maranville and Schmidt. Left on bases—Boston 11, Philadelphia 1. Earned run—Boston 1. Struck out—By James 8, by Plank 6. Bases on balls—Off James 3, off Plank 4. Hit by pitcher—By Plank (Maranville). Passed ball—Schang. Umpires—Hildebrand (A.L.), Byron (N.L.), Klem (N.L.) and Dinneen (A.L.). Time—1:56. Attendance—20,562.

Monday, October 12—At Boston

Phil'phia (A.L.)	AB.	R.	H.	O.	A.	E.
Murphy, rf	5	2	2	2	0	0
Oldring, lf	5	0	0	1	0	0
Collins, 2b	4	0	1	1	4	0
Baker, 3b	5	0	2	4	4	0
McInnis, 1b	5	1	1	18	0	0
Walsh, cf	4	0	1	1	0	0
Barry, ss	5	0	0	0	7	0
Schang, c	4	1	1	6	1	1
Bush, p	5	0	0	0	5	1
Totals	42	4	8	*33	21	2
Boston (N.L.)	AB.	R.	H.	O.	A.	E.
Moran, rf	4	1	0	2	0	0
Evers, 2b	5	0	3	3	5	0
Connolly, lf	4	0	0	1	0	1
Whitted, cf	5	0	0	2	0	0
Schmidt, 1b	5	1	1	17	1	0
Deal, 3b	5	0	1	2	3	0
Maranville, ss	4	1	1	2	3	0
Gowdy, c	4	1	3	6	0	0
cMann	0	1	0	0	0	0
Tyler, p	3	0	0	1	5	0
aDevore	1	0	0	0	0	0
James, p	0	0	0	0	2	0
bGilbert	0	0	0	0	0	0
Totals	40	5	9	36	19	1

```
Philadelphia ............1 0 0  1 0 0  0 0 0  2 0 0—4
Boston ....................0 1 0  1 0 0  0 0 0  2 0 1—5
```

aFanned for Tyler in tenth. bWalked for James in twelfth. cRan for Gowdy in twelfth. *None out when winning run scored. Two-base hits—Murphy 2, Gowdy 2, McInnis, Deal, Baker. Home run—Gowdy. Runs batted in—Collins, Baker 2, Walsh, Connolly, Maranville, Gowdy 2. Sacrifice hits—Oldring, Moran. Sacrifice flies—Collins, Connolly. Stolen bases—Collins, Evers, Maranville 2. Double play—Evers, Maranville and Schmidt. Left on bases—Philadelphia 10, Boston 8. Earned runs—Boston 4, Philadelphia 4. Struck out—By Bush 4, by Tyler 4, by James 1. Bases on balls—Off Bush 4, off Tyler 3, off James 3. Hits—Off Tyler 8 in 10 innings, off James 0 in 2 innings. Winning pitcher—James. Umpires—Klem (N.L.), Dinneen (A.L.), Byron (N.L.) and Hildebrand (A.L.). Time—3:06. Attendance—35,520.

Tuesday, October 13—At Boston

Phil'phia. (A.L.)	AB.	R.	H.	O.	A.	E.
Murphy, rf	4	0	0	0	0	0
Oldring, lf	4	0	1	3	0	0
Collins, 2b	4	0	1	1	4	0
Baker, 3b	4	0	1	1	4	0
McInnis, 1b	4	0	1	15	1	0
Walsh, cf	2	0	1	1	0	0
Barry, ss	3	1	1	0	5	0
Schang, c	3	0	0	3	0	0
Shawkey, p	2	0	1	0	3	0
Pennock, p	1	0	0	0	1	0
Totals	31	1	7	24	18	0

Boston (N.L.)	AB.	R.	H.	O.	A.	E.
Moran, rf	4	1	1	0	0	0
Evers, 2b	3	1	1	3	6	0
Connolly, lf	2	0	0	0	1	0
aMann, lf	2	0	0	1	0	0
Whitted, cf	3	0	2	1	0	0
Schmidt, 1b	4	0	1	12	0	0
Gowdy, c	2	0	0	8	2	0
Maranville, ss	3	0	0	1	3	0
Deal, 3b	3	0	0	1	4	0
Rudolph, p	2	1	1	0	0	0
Totals	28	3	6	27	16	0

```
Philadelphia ............ 0 0 0   0 1 0   0 0 0—1
Boston .................... 0 0 0   1 2 0   0 0 *—3
```

aLined out for Connolly in sixth. Two-base hits—Walsh, Shawkey, Moran. Runs batted in—Shawkey, Evers 2, Schmidt. Stolen base—Whitted. Double play—Gowdy and Evers. Left on bases—Boston 5, Philadelphia 4. Earned runs—Philadelphia 3, Boston 1. Struck out—By Pennock 3, by Rudolph 7. Bases on balls—Off Shawkey 2, off Pennock 2, off Rudolph 1. Wild pitch—Rudolph. Hits—Off Shawkey 4 in 5 innings, off Pennock 2 in 3 innings. Passed ball—Schang. Losing pitcher—Shawkey. Umpires—Byron (N.L.), Hildebrand (A.L.), Klem (N.L.) and Dinneen (A.L.). Time—1:49. Attendance—34,345.

COMPOSITE BATTING AVERAGES
Boston Braves

Player-Position	G.	AB.	R.	H.	2B.	3B.	HR.	RBI.	BA.
Gowdy, c	4	11	2	6	3	1	3		.545
Evers, 2b	4	16	2	7	0	0	0	2	.438
Rudolph, p	2	6	1	2	0	0	0		.333
Maranville, ss	4	13	1	4	0	0	0	3	.308
Schmidt, 1b	4	17	2	5	0	0	0	2	.294
Mann, rf-pr-ph	3	7	1	2	0	0	0		.286
Whitted, cf	4	14	2	3	0	1	0	3	.214
Deal, 3b	4	16	2	2	2	0	0	0	.125
Connolly, lf	3	9	1	1	0	0	1	1	.111
Moran, rf	3	13	2	1	1	0	0	0	.077
Cather, lf	1	5	0	0	0	0	0	0	.000
James, p	2	4	0	0	0	0	0	0	.000
Tyler, p	1	3	0	0	0	0	0	0	.000
Devore, ph	1	1	0	0	0	0	0	0	.000
Gilbert, ph	1	0	0	0	0	0	0	0	.000
Totals	4	135	16	33	6	2	1	14	.244

Philadelphia Athletics

Player-Position	G.	AB.	R.	H.	2B.	3B.	HR.	RBI.	BA.
Wyckoff, p	1	1	0	1	1	0	0	0	1.000
Shawkey, p	1	2	0	1	1	0	0	1	.500
Walsh, ph-cf	3	6	0	2	1	0	0	1	.333
Strunk, cf	2	7	0	2	0	0	0	0	.286
Baker, 3b	4	16	0	4	2	0	0	2	.250
Collins, 2b	4	14	0	3	0	0	0	1	.214
Murphy, rf	4	16	2	3	2	0	0	0	.188
Schang, c	4	12	1	2	1	0	0	0	.167
McInnis, 1b	4	14	2	2	1	0	0	0	.143
Barry, ss	4	14	1	1	0	0	0	0	.071
Oldring, lf	4	15	0	1	0	0	0	0	.067
Lapp, c	1	1	0	0	0	0	0	0	.000
Bender, p	1	2	0	0	0	0	0	0	.000
Plank, p	1	2	0	0	0	0	0	0	.000
Pennock, p	1	1	0	0	0	0	0	0	.000
Bush, p	1	5	0	0	0	0	0	0	.000
Totals	4	128	6	22	9	0	0	5	.172

COMPOSITE PITCHING AVERAGES
Boston Braves

Pitcher	G.	IP.	H.	R.	E.	SO.	BB.	W.	L.	ERA.
James	2	11	2	0	0	9	6	2	0	0.00
Rudolph	2	18	12	2	1	15	4	2	0	0.50
Tyler	1	10	8	4	4	4	3	0	0	3.60
Totals	4	39	22	6	5	28	13	4	0	1.15

Philadelphia Athletics

Pitcher	G.	IP.	H.	R.	E.	SO.	BB.	W.	L.	ERA.
Pennock	1	3	2	0	0	3	2	0	0	0.00
Plank	1	9	7	1	1	6	4	0	1	1.00
Wyckoff	1	3⅔	3	1	1	2	1	0	0	2.45
Bush	1	11	9	5	4	4	4	0	1	3.27
Shawkey	1	5	4	3	3	2	0	0	1	5.40
Bender	1	5⅓	8	6	6	3	2	0	1	10.13
Totals	4	37	33	16	15	18	15	0	4	3.65

SERIES OF 1915

	W.	L.	Pct.
Boston A. L.	4	1	.800
Philadelphia N. L.	1	4	.200

Following the rout of its representative in the 1914 World Series, the American League came back with vengeance in 1915 when the Red Sox, commanded by Bill Carrigan, defeated the Phillies, managed by Pat Moran, by four games to one.

Philadelphia won the National League pennant with a percentage of .592, the lowest to capture a flag in the parent circuit up to that time. However, Moran had the outstanding pitcher of the year, Grover Alexander, who checked in with 31 victories, 12 of them shutouts, and the home run leader in Gavvy Cravath, who hit 24 round-trippers, the high for this century until Babe Ruth revolutionized the four-ply industry. The Red Sox had captured their American League flag in a furious race with the Tigers, winning 101 games to 100 for Detroit. The Red Sox, playing three fewer games, finished two and one-half lengths in front.

After Alexander, then truly Alex the Great, had defeated Ernie Shore in the first game, 3 to 1, the Red Sox won four straight by one run—three in a row by 2 to 1 and the final, 5 to 4. Whereas the Boston Braves' end of the 1914 Series was played in Fenway Park, the American League field, the Boston games of the 1915 event were played in the newly-constructed National League park, Braves Field, and the third game of the Series, and first played in Boston, set an attendance record of 42,300.

For the first time in the history of the event, the President of the United States came up from Washington to attend a Series game. Woodrow Wilson was present at the second contest, played in Philadelphia, and tossed out the first ball, which was returned to him by umpire Charlie Rigler as a souvenir after one pitch.

The Boston heroes were outfielders Duffy Lewis and Harry Hooper, who hit .444 and .350, respectively, with Hooper poling two home runs in the last game, and the pitching staff, especially George Foster, who not only won his two games but hit .500, getting four hits in eight times at bat. Foster checked the Phillies on three hits in the second game and then scattered nine in capturing the finale.

The other winning Red Sox pitchers were Hubert (Dutch) Leonard and Shore. Leonard hurled a three-hitter to defeat Alexander, 2 to 1, in the great righthander's second appearance in the Series. Eating his heart out on the Boston bench was Babe Ruth, young southpaw hurler of the Red Sox, who was the American League leader in games won and lost that season with 18 victories and six defeats. However, Manager Bill Carrigan used Babe only once as a pinch-hitter in his first of 10 Series.

The Red Sox outhit the Phillies, .264 to .182, with virtually the entire Philadelphia club falling down, with the exception of first baseman Fred Luderus, who hit .438 and bashed one home run.

The box scores:

Friday, October 8—At Philadelphia

Boston (A.L.)	AB.	R.	H.	O.	A.	E.
Hooper, rf	5	0	1	0	0	0
Scott, ss	3	1	1	2	2	0
Speaker, cf	2	1	0	1	0	0
Hoblitzel, 1b	4	0	1	12	0	0
Lewis, lf	4	0	2	2	0	0
Gardner, 3b	3	0	1	0	1	0
Barry, 2b	4	0	1	4	4	0
Cady, c	2	0	0	3	2	0
aHenriksen	1	0	0	0	0	0
Shore, p	3	0	1	0	4	1
bRuth	1	0	0	0	0	0
Totals	32	1	8	24	13	1

Phila'phia (N.L.)	AB.	R.	H.	O.	A.	E.
Stock, 3b	3	1	0	0	2	0
Bancroft, ss	4	1	1	4	1	0
Paskert, cf	3	1	1	1	0	0
Cravath, rf	2	0	0	1	0	0
Luderus, 1b	4	0	1	10	0	1
Whitted, lf	2	0	1	3	0	0
Niehoff, 2b	3	0	0	1	4	0
Burns, c	3	0	0	7	0	0
Alexander, p	3	0	1	0	5	0
Totals	27	3	5	27	12	1

Boston .... 0 0 0 0 0 0 0 1 0—1
Philadelphia ...... 0 0 0 1 0 0 0 2 *—3

aReached first on Luderus' error for Cady in ninth. bGrounded out for Shore in ninth. Runs batted in—Lewis, Cravath, Luderus, Whitted. Sacrifice hits—Scott, Gardner, Cady, Cravath. Stolen bases—Whitted, Hoblitzel. Left on bases—Boston 9, Philadelphia 5. Earned runs—Philadelphia 3, Boston 1. Struck out—By Alexander 6, by Shore 2. Bases on balls—Off Alexander 2, off Shore 4. Umpires—Klem (N.L.), O'Loughlin (A.L.), Evans (A.L.) and Rigler (N.L.). Time—1:58. Attendance—19,343.

Saturday, October 9—At Philadelphia

Boston (A.L.)	AB.	R.	H.	O.	A.	E.
Hooper, rf	3	1	1	2	0	0
Scott, ss	3	0	0	0	3	0
aHenriksen	1	0	0	0	0	0
Cady, c	0	0	0	3	0	0
Speaker, cf	4	0	1	3	0	0
Hoblitzel, 1b	4	0	1	8	3	0
Lewis, lf	4	0	1	1	0	0
Gardner, 3b	4	1	2	0	2	0
Barry, 2b	4	0	1	0	3	0
Thomas, c	3	0	0	6	0	0
Janvrin, ss	1	0	0	1	0	0
Foster, p	4	0	3	3	0	0
Totals	35	2	10	27	11	0

Phila'phia (N.L.)	AB.	R.	H.	O.	A.	E.
Stock, 3b	4	0	0	0	2	0
Bancroft, ss	4	0	1	2	2	0
Paskert, cf	4	0	0	1	0	0
Cravath, rf	3	1	1	1	0	0
Luderus, 1b	3	0	1	9	1	0
Whitted, lf	3	0	0	3	0	0
Niehoff, 2b	3	0	0	4	1	0
Burns, c	3	0	0	6	3	1
Mayer, p	3	0	0	1	3	0
Totals	30	1	3	27	12	1

Boston .... 1 0 0 0 0 0 0 0 1—2
Philadelphia ...... 0 0 0 0 1 0 0 0 0—1

aPopped out for Scott in seventh. Two-base hits—Foster, Cravath, Luderus. Runs batted in—Foster, Luderus. Left on bases—Boston 8, Philadelphia 2. Earned runs—Boston 1, Philadelphia 1. Struck out—By Foster 8, by Mayer 7. Bases on balls—Off Mayer 2. Umpires—Rigler (N.L.), Evans (A.L.), O'Loughlin (A.L.) and Klem (N.L.). Time—2:05. Attendance—20,306.

Monday, October 11—At Boston

Phila'phia (N.L.)	AB.	R.	H.	O.	A.	E.
Stock, 3b	3	0	1	1	0	0
Bancroft, ss	3	0	1	4	1	0
Paskert, cf	4	0	0	7	0	0
Cravath, rf	4	0	0	2	0	0
Luderus, 1b	3	0	0	3	1	0
Whitted, lf	3	0	0	2	0	0
Niehoff, 2b	3	0	0	0	2	0
Burns, c	3	1	1	5	2	0
Alexander, p	2	0	0	2	0	0
Totals	28	1	3	*26	6	0

Boston (A.L.)	AB.	R.	H.	O.	A.	E.
Hooper, rf	4	1	1	2	0	0
Scott, ss	3	0	0	2	1	0
Speaker, cf	3	1	2	2	0	0
Hoblitzel, 1b	3	0	0	9	0	1
Lewis, lf	4	0	3	1	0	0
Gardner, 3b	3	0	0	1	6	0
Barry, 2b	3	0	0	2	1	0
Carrigan, c	2	0	0	8	0	0
Leonard, p	3	0	0	0	2	0
Totals	28	2	6	27	10	1

1915 WORLD SERIES

```
Philadelphia ............... 0 0 1   0 0 0   0 0 0—1
Boston ..................... 0 0 0   1 0 0   0 0 1—2
```

*Two out when winning run scored. Two-base hit—Stock. Three-base hit—Speaker. Runs batted in—Bancroft, Hoblitzel, Lewis. Sacrifice hits—Bancroft, Alexander, Stock, Scott. Sacrifice fly—Hoblitzel. Double play—Burns, Bancroft and Luderus. Left on bases—Boston 4, Philadelphia 3. Earned runs—Boston 2, Philadelphia 1. Struck out—By Leonard 6, by Alexander 4. Bases on balls—Off Alexander 2. Umpires—O'Loughlin (A.L.), Klem (N.L.), Rigler (N.L.) and Evans (A.L.). Time—1:48. Attendance—42,300.

Tuesday, October 12—At Boston

Phila'phia (N.L.)	AB.	R.	H.	O.	A.	E.
Stock, 3b	4	0	1	0	3	0
Bancroft, ss	2	0	0	0	0	0
Paskert, cf	4	0	0	5	0	0
Cravath, rf	4	1	1	0	0	0
Luderus, 1b	4	0	3	5	0	0
aDugey	0	0	0	0	0	0
Becker, lf	0	0	0	0	0	0
Whitted, lf-1b	3	0	0	4	0	0
Niehoff, 2b	3	0	0	3	1	0
Burns, c	3	0	1	7	2	0
Chalmers, p	3	0	1	0	4	0
bByrne	1	0	0	0	0	0
Totals	31	1	7	24	10	0

Boston (A.L.)	AB.	R.	H.	O.	A.	E.
Hooper, rf	4	0	1	2	0	0
Scott, ss	4	0	0	2	4	0
Speaker, cf	3	0	1	1	0	0
Hoblitzel, 1b	4	1	3	5	2	0
Lewis, lf	2	0	1	6	1	0
Gardner, 3b	4	0	0	2	2	0
Barry, 2b	2	1	0	3	1	1
Cady, c	3	0	2	6	1	0
Shore, p	2	0	0	0	1	0
Totals	28	2	8	27	12	1

```
Philadelphia ............... 0 0 0   0 0 0   0 1 0—1
Boston ..................... 0 0 1   0 0 1   0 0 *—2
```

aRan for Luderus in eighth. bFlied out for Chalmers in ninth. Two-base hit—Lewis. Three-base hit—Cravath. Runs batted in—Luderus, Hooper, Lewis. Stolen base—Dugey. Sacrifice hits—Whitted, Shore, Lewis. Left on bases—Philadelphia 8, Boston 7. Earned runs—Boston 2, Philadelphia 1. Double plays—Scott, Barry, Hoblitzel and Barry; Chalmers, Burns and Whitted. Struck out—By Shore 4, by Chalmers 6. Bases on balls—Off Shore 4, off Chalmers 3. Umpires—Evans (A.L.), Rigler (N.L.), O'Loughlin (A.L.) and Klem (N.L.). Time—2:05. Attendance—41,096.

Wednesday, Oct. 13—At Philadelphia

Boston (A.L.)	AB.	R.	H.	O.	A.	E.
Hooper, rf	4	2	3	2	0	1
Scott, ss	5	0	0	2	2	0
Speaker, cf	5	0	1	3	0	0
Hoblitzel, 1b	1	0	0	1	0	0
aGainor, 1b	3	1	1	9	0	0
Lewis, lf	4	1	1	0	0	0
Gardner, 3b	3	1	1	2	3	0
Barry, 2b	4	0	1	1	0	0
Thomas, c	2	0	1	4	3	0
Cady, c	1	0	0	2	1	0
Foster, p	4	0	1	1	3	0
Totals	36	5	10	27	12	1

Phila'phia (N.L.)	AB.	R.	H.	O.	A.	E.
Stock, 3b	3	0	0	1	1	0
Bancroft, ss	4	1	2	3	6	1
Paskert, cf	4	1	2	3	0	0
Cravath, rf	3	0	0	1	0	0
bDugey	0	0	0	0	0	0
Becker, rf	0	0	0	0	0	0
Luderus, 1b	2	1	2	13	2	0
Whitted, lf	4	0	0	2	0	0
Niehoff, 2b	4	1	1	1	2	0
Burns, c	4	0	1	2	2	0
Mayer, p	1	0	0	1	0	0
Rixey, p	2	0	1	0	1	0
cKillefer	1	0	0	0	0	0
Totals	32	4	9	27	14	1

```
Boston ..................... 0 1 1   0 0 0   0 2 1—5
Philadelphia ............... 2 0 0   2 0 0   0 0 0—4
```

aHit into double play for Hoblitzel in third inning. bRan for Cravath in eighth. cGrounded out for Rixey in ninth. Two-base hit—Luderus. Three-base hit—Gardner. Home runs—Hooper 2, Lewis, Luderus. Runs batted in—Luderus 3, Hooper 2, Lewis 2, Barry. Double plays—Foster, Thomas and Hoblitzel; Bancroft and Luderus. Left on bases—Boston 7, Philadelphia 5. Earned runs—Boston 5, Philadelphia 3. Struck out—By Foster 5, by Rixey 2. Bases on balls—Off Foster 2, off Rixey 2. Hit by pitcher—By Foster (Stock, Luderus), by Rixey (Hooper). Hits—Off Mayer 6 in 2⅓ innings, off Rixey 4 in 6⅔ innings. Losing pitcher—Rixey. Umpires—Klem (N.L.), O'Loughlin (A.L.), Evans (A.L.) and Rigler (N.L.). Time—2:15. Attendance—20,306.

COMPOSITE BATTING AVERAGES

Boston Red Sox

Player-Position	G.	AB.	R.	H.	2B.	3B.	HR.	RBI.	BA.
Foster, p	2	8	0	4	1	0	0	1	.500
Lewis, lf	5	18	1	8	1	0	1	5	.444
Hooper, rf	5	20	4	7	0	0	2	3	.350
Cady, c	4	6	0	2	0	0	0	0	.333
Gainor, 1b	1	3	1	1	0	0	0	0	.333
Hoblitzel, 1b	5	16	1	5	0	0	0	1	.313
Speaker, cf	5	17	2	5	0	1	0	0	.294
Gardner, 3b	5	17	2	4	0	1	0	0	.235
Shore, p	2	5	0	1	0	0	0	0	.200
Thomas, c	2	5	0	1	0	0	0	0	.200
Barry, 2b	5	17	1	3	0	0	0	1	.176
Scott, ss	5	18	0	1	0	0	0	0	.056
Janvrin, ss	1	1	0	0	0	0	0	0	.000
Carrigan, c	1	2	0	0	0	0	0	0	.000
Henriksen, ph	2	2	0	0	0	0	0	0	.000
Ruth, ph	1	1	0	0	0	0	0	0	.000
Leonard, p	1	3	0	0	0	0	0	0	.000
Totals	5	159	12	42	2	2	3	11	.264

Philadelphia Phillies

Player-Position	G.	AB.	R.	H.	2B.	3B.	HR.	RBI.	BA.
Rixey, p	1	2	0	1	0	0	0	0	.500
Luderus, 1b	5	16	1	7	2	0	1	6	.438
Chalmers, p	1	3	0	1	0	0	0	0	.333
Bancroft, ss	5	17	2	5	0	0	0	1	.294
Alexander, p	2	5	0	1	0	0	0	0	.200
Burns, c	5	16	1	3	0	0	0	0	.188
Paskert, cf	5	19	2	3	0	0	0	0	.158
Cravath, rf	5	16	2	2	1	1	0	1	.125
Stock, 3b	5	17	1	2	1	0	0	0	.118
Whitted, lf-1b	5	15	0	1	0	0	0	1	.067
Niehoff, 2b	5	16	1	1	0	0	0	0	.063
Mayer, p	2	4	0	0	0	0	0	0	.000
Dugey, pr	2	0	0	0	0	0	0	0	.000
Becker, lf	2	0	0	0	0	0	0	0	.000
Byrne, ph	1	1	0	0	0	0	0	0	.000
Killefer, ph	1	1	0	0	0	0	0	0	.000
Totals	5	148	10	27	4	1	1	9	.182

COMPOSITE PITCHING AVERAGES

Boston Red Sox

Pitcher	G.	IP.	H.	R.	E.	SO.	BB.	W.	L.	ERA.
Leonard	1	9	3	1	1	6	0	1	0	1.00
Foster	2	18	12	5	4	13	2	2	0	2.00
Shore	2	17	12	4	4	6	8	1	1	2.12
Totals	5	44	27	10	9	25	10	4	1	1.84

Philadelphia Phillies

Pitcher	G.	IP.	H.	R.	E.	SO.	BB.	W.	L.	ERA.
Alexander	2	17⅔	14	3	3	10	4	1	1	1.53
Chalmers	1	8	8	2	2	6	3	0	1	2.25
Mayer	2	11½	16	4	3	7	2	0	1	2.38
Rixey	1	6⅔	4	3	2	2	2	0	1	2.70
Totals	5	43⅔	42	12	10	25	11	1	4	2.06

SERIES OF 1916

	W.	L.	Pct.
Boston A. L.	4	1	.800
Brooklyn N. L.	1	4	.200

Bill Carrigan's Red Sox were without Tris Speaker, the team's top performer, in 1916, but the club, with Chick Shorten and Clarence (Tilly) Walker alternating in center field, repeated its American League victory and kept unsullied its World Series record by defeating the Dodgers, led by Wilbert Robinson, by the same margin in which the Phillies were downed the year before, four games to one. Brooklyn had won its first National League flag since 1900 after a hard four-cornered battle with the three other eastern clubs.

It was Uncle Robby's plan to defeat the Red Sox largely with lefthanders, as he started Rube Marquard, winner of two games over the Hub team in 1912, twice and Sherry Smith once. However, his lone victory was pitched by Jack Coombs, who defeated Carl Mays in the third game, played in Brooklyn, 4 to 3. Coombs only lasted until the seventh, big Jeff Pfeffer saving the game.

In many respects, the 1916 Series was history repeating itself. Duffy Lewis and Harry Hooper again led the Boston regulars at bat with averages of .353 and .333, respectively, while the Red Sox pitching staff again performed brilliantly. While George Foster, the 1915 star, made only one relief appearance, Ernie Shore took two games and the Boston lefthanders, Hubert (Dutch) Leonard and Babe Ruth, each won one game.

Making his first World Series appearance as a pitcher, Ruth defeated Smith in 14 innings in the second game, 2 to 1, for the longest World Series game on record. The Babe pitched scoreless ball after Hi Myers, Brooklyn's center fielder, hit him for a first-inning home run. Ruth yielded only six hits and Smith seven. Ruth failed to get a hit in five attempts and fanned twice. Dick Hoblitzel, the Red Sox first baseman, walked four times.

Shore earned a 6 to 5 victory in the opener after Carl Mays came on in the ninth inning to quell a Dodger rally at four runs. In the finale Shore tossed a three-hitter to win handily, 4 to 1.

Leonard's triumph came in the fourth game when he checked the Dodgers on five safeties, 6 to 2.

Casey Stengel was Brooklyn's batting leader with an average of .364 for four games, while a hit for Coombs gave him a World Series lifetime average of .333 for six games. His pitching record was five victories and no defeats.

Only two bases were stolen by the two teams; Harry Hooper for the Red Sox and Zack Wheat for the Dodgers.

For the second successive year, the Red Sox played at Braves Field because of the larger seating capacity, and the fifth and last game, played on Columbus Day, produced a new attendance record—42,620. The attendance and receipts were the largest of any five-game Series played up to that time, as was the players' pool of $162,927.45. The box scores:

Saturday, October 7—At Boston

Brooklyn (N.L.)	AB.	R.	H.	O.	A.	E.
Myers, cf	5	0	2	1	0	0
Daubert, 1b	4	0	0	5	1	0
Stengel, rf	4	2	2	1	0	1
Wheat, lf	4	1	2	3	0	0
Cutshaw, 2b	3	1	0	5	2	1
Mowrey, 3b	3	1	1	1	2	0
Olson, ss	4	0	1	2	1	2
Meyers, c	4	0	1	6	3	0
Marquard, p	2	0	0	0	0	0
aJohnston	1	0	1	0	0	0
Pfeffer, p	0	0	0	0	0	0
bMerkle	0	0	0	0	0	0
Totals	34	5	10	24	9	4

Boston (A.L.)	AB.	R.	H.	O.	A.	E.
Hooper, rf	4	2	1	1	1	0
Janvrin, 2b	4	1	2	2	8	1
Walker, cf	4	1	2	0	0	0
Hoblitzel, 1b	5	2	1	14	0	0
Lewis, lf	3	0	1	0	0	0
Gardner, 3b	4	0	1	1	3	0
Scott, ss	2	0	0	2	4	0
Cady, c	1	0	0	7	0	0
Thomas, c	0	0	0	0	0	0
Shore, p	4	0	0	0	3	0
Mays, p	0	0	0	0	0	0
Totals	31	6	8	27	19	1

Brooklyn............ 0 0 0 1 0 0 0 4—5
Boston............... 0 0 1 0 1 0 3 1 *—6

aSingled for Marquard in eighth. bWalked for Pfeffer in ninth. Two-base hits—Lewis, Hooper, Janvrin, Wheat, Meyers. Runs batted in—Myers, Wheat, Mowrey, Merkle, Walker, Hoblitzel, Lewis, Gardner, Scott. Sacrifice hits—Scott, Janvrin, Lewis. Sacrifice fly—Scott. Double plays—Janvrin, Scott and Hoblitzel; Hooper and Cady; Gardner, Janvrin and Hoblitzel; Shore, Scott, Janvrin and Hoblitzel. Left on bases—Boston 11, Brooklyn 6. Earned runs—Boston 4, Brooklyn 3. Struck out—By Marquard 6, by Shore 5. Bases on balls—Off Marquard 4, off Pfeffer 2, off Shore 3. Hit by pitcher—By Shore (Cutshaw). Passed ball—Meyers. Hits—Off Marquard 7 in 7 innings, off Pfeffer 1 in 1 inning, off Shore 9 in 8⅔ innings, off Mays 1 in ⅓ inning. Winning pitcher—Shore. Losing pitcher—Marquard. Umpires—Connolly (A.L.), O'Day (N.L.), Quigley (N.L.) and Dinneen (A.L.). Time—2:16. Attendance—36,117.

Monday, October 9—At Boston

Brooklyn (N.L.)	AB.	R.	H.	O.	A.	E.
Johnston, rf	5	0	1	1	0	0
Daubert, 1b	5	0	0	18	1	0
Myers, cf	6	1	1	4	1	0

1916 WORLD SERIES

	AB.	R.	H.	O.	A.	E.
Wheat, lf	5	0	0	2	0	0
Cutshaw, 2b	5	0	0	5	6	1
Mowrey, 3b	5	0	1	3	5	0
Olson, ss	2	0	1	2	4	0
Miller, c	5	0	1	4	1	0
Smith, p	5	0	1	1	7	0
Totals	43	1	6	*40	25	2

Boston (A.L.)	AB.	R.	H.	O.	A.	E.
Hooper, rf	6	0	1	2	1	0
Janvrin, 2b	6	0	1	4	5	0
Walker, cf	3	0	0	2	1	0
Walsh, cf	3	0	0	1	0	0
Hoblitzel, 1b	2	0	0	21	1	0
aMcNally	0	1	0	0	0	0
Lewis, lf	3	0	1	1	0	0
Gardner, 3b	5	0	0	3	7	1
bGainor	1	0	1	0	0	0
Scott, ss	4	1	2	1	8	0
Thomas, c	4	0	1	5	4	0
Ruth, p	5	0	0	2	4	0
Totals	42	2	7	42	31	1

Brooklyn........... 1 0 0   0 0 0   0 0 0   0 0—1
Boston .... 0 0 1   0 0 0   0 0 0   0 1—2

aRan for Hoblitzel in fourteenth. bSingled for Gardner in fourteenth. *One out when winning run scored. Two-base hits—Smith, Janvrin. Three-base hits—Scott, Thomas. Home run—Myers. Runs batted in—Gainor, Ruth, Myers. Sacrifice hits—Lewis 2, Thomas, Olson 2. Double plays—Scott, Janvrin and Hoblitzel; Mowrey, Cutshaw and Daubert; Myers and Miller. Left on bases—Boston 9, Brooklyn 5. Earned runs—Boston 2, Brooklyn 1. Struck out—By Smith 2, by Ruth 4. Bases on balls—Off Smith 6, off Ruth 3. Umpires—Dinneen (A.L.), Quigley (N.L.), O'Day (N.L.) and Connolly (A.L.). Time—2:32. Attendance—41,373.

Tuesday, October 10—At Brooklyn

Boston (A.L.)	AB.	R.	H.	O.	A.	E.
Hooper, rf	4	1	2	1	0	0
Janvrin, 2b	4	0	1	0	0	0
Shorten, cf	4	0	3	0	0	0
Hoblitzel, 1b	4	0	1	12	2	0
Lewis, lf	4	0	0	1	1	0
Gardner, 3b	3	1	0	2	0	1
Scott, ss	3	0	0	1	7	0
Thomas, c	3	0	0	5	0	0
Mays, p	1	0	0	0	4	0
aHenriksen	0	1	0	0	0	0
Foster, p	1	0	0	1	2	0
Totals	31	3	7	24	16	1

Brooklyn (N.L.)	AB.	R.	H.	O.	A.	E.
Myers, cf	3	0	0	3	0	0
Daubert, 1b	4	1	3	7	0	0
Stengel, rf	3	0	1	2	1	0
Wheat, lf	2	1	1	4	0	0
Cutshaw, 2b	4	0	1	4	0	0
Mowrey, 3b	3	1	0	2	1	0
Olson, ss	4	1	2	1	2	0
Miller, c	3	0	0	4	2	0
Coombs, p	3	0	1	0	2	0
Pfeffer, p	1	0	1	0	1	0
Totals	30	4	10	27	9	0

Boston .... 0 0 0   0 0 2   1 0 0—3
Brooklyn .... 0 0 1   1 2 0   0 0 *—4

aWalked for Mays in sixth. Three-base hits—Olson, Daubert, Hooper. Home run—Gardner. Runs batted in—Cutshaw, Olson 2, Coombs, Hooper, Shorten, Gardner. Sacrifice hits—Stengel, Miller, Myers. Stolen base—Wheat. Left on bases —Brooklyn 9, Boston 2. Earned runs—Brooklyn 3, Boston 3. Struck out—By Mays 2, by Foster 1, by Coombs 1, by Pfeffer 3. Bases on balls—Off Mays 3, off Coombs 1. Hit by pitcher—By Mays (Myers). Wild pitch—Foster. Hits—Off Mays 7 in 5 innings, off Foster 3 in 3 innings, off Coombs 7 in 6⅓ innings, off Pfeffer 0 in 2⅔ innings. Winning pitcher—Coombs. Losing pitcher—Mays. Umpires—O'Day (N.L.), Connolly (A.L.), Quigley (N.L.) and Dinneen (A.L.). Time—2:01. Attendance—21,087.

Wednesday, October 11—At Brooklyn

Boston (A.L.)	AB.	R.	H.	O.	A.	E.
Hooper, rf	4	1	2	3	0	0
Janvrin, 2b	5	1	0	1	2	1
Walker, cf	4	0	1	2	0	0
Hoblitzel, 1b	3	1	2	8	0	0
Lewis, lf	4	2	2	6	0	0
Gardner, 3b	3	1	1	1	3	0
Scott, ss	4	0	0	3	3	0
Carrigan, c	3	0	2	3	1	0
Leonard, p	3	0	0	0	1	0
Totals	33	6	10	27	10	1

Brooklyn (N.L.)	AB.	R.	H.	O.	A.	E.
Johnston, rf	4	1	1	0	0	1
Myers, cf	4	1	1	1	0	0
Merkle, 1b	3	0	1	9	1	1
Wheat, lf	4	0	1	0	0	1
Cutshaw, 2b	4	0	1	3	2	0
Mowrey, 3b	3	0	0	1	4	0
Olson, ss	3	0	0	2	2	0
Meyers, c	3	0	0	11	3	0
cStengel	0	0	0	0	0	0
Marquard, p	1	0	0	0	2	0
aPfeffer	1	0	0	0	0	0
Cheney, p	0	0	0	0	0	1
bO'Mara	1	0	0	0	0	0
Rucker, p	0	0	0	0	0	0
dGetz	1	0	0	0	0	0
Totals	32	2	5	27	14	4

Boston .... 0 3 0   1 1 0   1 0 0—6
Brooklyn .... 2 0 0   0 0 0   0 0 0—2

aFanned for Marquard in fourth. bStruck out for Cheney in seventh. cRan for Meyers in ninth. dGrounded out for Rucker in ninth. Two-base hits—Lewis, Cutshaw, Hoblitzel. Three-base hit—Johnston. Home run—Gardner. Runs batted in—Myers, Cutshaw, Hoblitzel, Gardner 3, Carrigan. Sacrifice hits—Carrigan, Gardner. Stolen base—Hooper. Left on bases—Brooklyn 7, Boston 5. Earned runs—Boston 5, Brooklyn 1. Struck out—By Leonard 3, by Marquard 3, by Cheney 5, by Rucker 3. Bases on balls—Off Leonard 4, off Marquard 2, off Cheney 1. Wild pitch—Leonard. Passed ball—Meyers. Hits—Off Marquard 5 in 4 innings, off Cheney 4 in 3 innings, off Rucker 1 in 2 innings. Losing pitcher—Marquard. Umpires—Quigley (N.L.), Dinneen (A.L.), O'Day (N.L.) and Connolly (A.L.). Time—2:30. Attendance—21,662.

Thursday, October 12—At Boston

Brooklyn (N.L.)	AB.	R.	H.	O.	A.	E.
Myers, cf	4	0	0	0	0	0
Daubert, 1b	4	0	0	10	1	0
Stengel, rf	4	0	1	0	0	0
Wheat, lf	4	0	0	5	0	0
Cutshaw, 2b	3	1	0	2	3	0
Mowrey, 3b	3	0	1	1	3	1
Olson, ss	3	0	0	2	3	2
Meyers, c	3	0	1	4	2	0
Pfeffer, p	2	0	0	0	1	0
aMerkle	1	0	0	0	0	0
Dell, p	0	0	0	0	0	0
Totals	31	1	3	24	13	3

1917 WORLD SERIES

Boston (A.L.)	AB.	R.	H.	O.	A.	E.
Hooper, rf	3	2	1	1	0	0
Janvrin, 2b	4	0	2	0	1	0
Shorten, cf	3	0	1	3	0	0
Hoblitzel, 1b	3	0	0	14	1	0
Lewis, lf	3	1	2	1	0	0
Gardner, 3b	2	0	0	0	5	0
Scott, ss	3	0	0	2	3	2
Cady, c	3	1	1	4	1	0
Shore, p	3	0	0	2	3	0
Totals	27	4	7	27	14	2

Brooklyn .... 0 1 0   0 0 0   0 0 0—1
Boston .... 0 1 2   0 1 0   0 0 *—4

aFlied out for Pfeffer in eighth. Two-base hit—Janvrin. Three-base hit—Lewis. Runs batted in—Janvrin, Shorten, Gardner. Sacrifice hits—Mowrey, Lewis, Shorten. Sacrifice fly—Gardner. Left on bases—Brooklyn 5, Boston 4. Earned runs—Boston 2, Brooklyn 0. Struck out—By Pfeffer 2, by Shore 4. Bases on balls—Off Pfeffer 2, off Shore 1. Wild pitches—Pfeffer 2. Passed ball—Cady. Hits—Off Pfeffer 6 in 7 innings, off Dell 1 in 1 inning. Losing pitcher—Pfeffer. Umpires—Connolly (A.L.), O'Day (N.L.), Quigley (N.L.) and Dinneen (A.L.). Time—1:43. Attendance—42,620.

COMPOSITE BATTING AVERAGES
Boston Red Sox

Player-Position	G.	AB.	R.	H.	2B.	3B.	HR.	RBI.	BA.
Gainor, ph	1	1	0	1	0	0	0	1	1.000
Carrigan, c	1	3	0	2	0	0	0	1	.667
Shorten, cf	2	7	0	4	0	0	0	2	.571
Lewis, lf	5	17	3	6	2	1	0	1	.353
Hooper, rf	5	21	6	7	1	0	0	1	.333
Walker, cf	3	11	1	3	0	1	0	1	.273
Cady, c	2	4	1	1	0	0	0	0	.250
Hoblitzel, 1b	5	17	3	4	1	0	0	2	.235
Janvrin, 2b	5	23	2	5	3	0	0	1	.217
Gardner, 3b	5	17	2	3	0	0	2	6	.176
Thomas, c	3	7	0	1	0	1	0	0	.143
Scott, ss	5	16	1	2	0	1	0	1	.125
Shore, p	2	7	0	0	0	0	0	0	.000
Mays, p	2	1	0	0	0	0	0	0	.000
Walsh, cf	1	3	0	0	0	0	0	0	.000
McNally, pr	1	0	1	0	0	0	0	0	.000
Ruth, p	1	5	0	0	0	0	0	1	.000
Henriksen, ph	1	0	1	0	0	0	0	0	.000
Foster, p	1	1	0	0	0	0	0	0	.000
Leonard, p	1	3	0	0	0	0	0	0	.000
Totals	5	164	21	39	7	6	2	18	.238

Brooklyn Dodgers

Player-Position	G.	AB.	R.	H.	2B.	3B.	HR.	RBI.	BA.
Stengel, rf-ph	4	11	2	4	0	0	0	0	.364
Coombs, p	1	3	0	1	0	0	0	1	.333
Johnston, ph-rf	3	10	1	3	0	1	0	0	.300
Olson, ss	5	16	1	4	0	1	0	2	.250
Pfeffer, p-ph	4	4	0	1	0	0	0	0	.250
Merkle, ph-1b	3	4	0	1	0	0	0	1	.250
Wheat, lf	5	19	2	4	0	1	0	1	.211
Meyers, c	3	10	0	2	0	1	0	0	.200
Smith, p	1	5	0	1	1	0	0	0	.200
Myers, cf	5	22	2	4	0	0	1	3	.182
Daubert, 1b	4	17	1	3	0	1	0	0	.176
Mowrey, 3b	5	17	2	3	0	0	0	1	.176
Miller, c	2	8	0	1	0	0	0	0	.125
Cutshaw, 2b	5	19	2	2	1	0	0	2	.105
Marquard, p	2	3	0	0	0	0	0	0	.000
O'Mara, ph	1	1	0	0	0	0	0	0	.000
Rucker, p	1	0	0	0	0	0	0	0	.000
Getz, ph	1	1	0	0	0	0	0	0	.000
Cheney, p	1	0	0	0	0	0	0	0	.000
Dell, p	1	0	0	0	0	0	0	0	.000
Totals	5	170	13	34	2	5	1	11	.200

COMPOSITE PITCHING AVERAGES
Boston Red Sox

Pitcher	G.	IP.	H.	R.	E.	SO.	BB.	W.	L.	ERA.
Foster	1	3	3	0	0	1	0	0	0	0.00
Ruth	1	14	6	1	1	4	3	1	0	0.64
Leonard	1	9	5	2	1	3	4	1	0	1.00
Shore	2	17⅔	12	6	2	9	4	2	0	1.53
Mays	2	5⅓	8	4	3	2	3	0	1	5.06
Totals	5	49	34	13	8	19	14	4	1	1.47

Brooklyn Dodgers

Pitcher	G.	IP.	H.	R.	E.	SO.	BB.	W.	L.	ERA.
Rucker	1	2	1	0	0	3	0	0	0	0.00
Dell	1	1	1	0	0	0	0	0	0	0.00
Smith	1	13⅓	7	2	2	2	6	0	1	1.35
Pfeffer	3	10⅔	7	5	2	5	4	0	1	1.69
Cheney	1	3	4	2	1	5	1	0	0	3.00
Coombs	1	6⅓	7	3	3	1	1	1	0	4.26
Marquard	2	11	12	9	8	9	6	0	2	6.55
Totals	5	47⅓	39	21	16	25	18	1	4	3.04

SERIES OF 1917

	W.	L.	Pct.
Chicago A. L.	4	2	.667
New York N. L.	2	4	.333

The 1917 World Series, the first since the entry of the U. S. into World War I, brought together teams representing the two largest cities of the country, the New York Giants and the Chicago White Sox. It resulted in the fourth reverse for John McGraw's team in seven years as the White Sox, led by Clarence (Pants) Rowland, defeated the Polo Grounders, four games to two. After the White Sox won the first two games in Chicago, the Giants evened the Series when Rube Benton and Ferdie Schupp pitched successive shutout victories at the Polo Grounds, New York. The Sox then clinched the decision by winning the fifth and sixth games by scores of 8 to 5 and 4 to 2.

Chicago's fourth inning in the sixth clash, when it scored three runs on only two hits, was almost as tragic a session for McGraw as the tenth inning of the last game of the 1912 Series. Third baseman Heinie Zimmerman made a two-base wild throw on Eddie Collins and right fielder Dave Robertson followed with a schoolboy muff of Joe Jackson's fly. Later, in a run-down play, Zimmerman chased Collins over the plate with a run. Zim was hardly to blame, as catcher Bill Rariden and first baseman Walter Holke had left the home station uncovered.

Urban (Red) Faber, Chicago righthander, became the seventh pitcher in a modern World Series to be credited with three victories. He also was charged with one defeat. Faber tried to steal third in the fifth inning of the second game with Buck Weaver resting serenely on the base. Eddie Cicotte notched the other White Sox victory, a 2 to 1 pitching duel with Harry (Slim) Sallee in the first game. Reb Russell, Chicago lefthander who won 15 games and lost five for Rowland during the regular season, started the fifth contest, but was knocked out in less than an inning, the victory going to Faber, Rowland's fourth hurler, who pitched two hitless shutout frames.

McGraw, with three great lefthanders on his pitching staff, set a Series precedent by starting a southpaw in every game, giving Sallee, Schupp and Benton two assignments apiece. Sallee lost the opener to Cicotte on the margin of a homer by Hap Felsch in the fourth inning.

After Faber won the second contest, with the loss going to Fred Anderson, who had replaced Schupp in the second inning, Benton gained a 2 to 0 triumph over Cicotte and Schupp and then came back to post a 5 to 0 victory over Faber. McGraw's men failed to hold a 5 to 2 lead in the fifth game and then bowed out ingloriously in the finale.

In addition to his historic scoring play in the sixth game, Eddie Collins hit .409 and stole three bases. By playing in his twenty-sixth World Series game, Eddie set a new record, topping the one held by his former associate, Jack Barry, by one game.

Notwithstanding his muff in the sixth game, Robertson starred for the Giants, hitting hard throughout the Series and getting 11 hits in 22 times at bat for an average of .500. Benny Kauff, the former Federal League batting ace, hit only .160 for the Giants, but connected for two home runs in the fourth game, the one won by Schupp from Faber and Dave Danforth, 5 to 0.

Despite the fact the nation had been at war six months when the Series was played, it attracted the usual interest, with total attendance of 186,654 and gate receipts of $425,878. The players' pool totaled $152,888.58. The box scores:

Saturday, October 6—At Chicago

New York (N.L.)	AB.	R.	H.	O.	A.	E.
Burns, lf	3	0	1	2	0	0
Herzog, 2b	4	0	1	3	1	0
Kauff, cf	4	0	0	0	0	0
Zimmerman, 3b	4	0	0	1	3	0
Fletcher, ss	4	0	0	2	3	0
Robertson, rf	4	0	1	0	1	0
Holke, 1b	3	0	2	14	0	0
McCarty, c	3	1	1	2	1	1
Sallee, p	3	0	1	0	6	0
Totals	32	1	7	24	15	1

Chicago (A.L.)	AB.	R.	H.	O.	A.	E.
J. Collins, rf	4	1	3	1	0	0
McMullin, 3b	3	0	1	0	3	0
E. Collins, 2b	3	0	0	2	1	0
Jackson, lf	3	0	0	5	0	0
Felsch, cf	3	1	1	4	0	0
Gandil, 1b	3	0	1	10	1	0
Weaver, ss	3	0	0	2	1	1
Schalk, c	3	0	0	3	0	0
Cicotte, p	3	0	1	0	4	0
Totals	28	2	7	27	10	1

New York...... 0 0 0 0 1 0 0 0 0—1
Chicago........ 0 0 1 1 0 0 0 0 *—2

Runs batted in—Sallee, McMullin, Felsch. Two-base hits—McMullin, Robertson, J. Collins. Three-base hit—McCarty. Home run—Felsch. Sacrifice hit—McMullin. Stolen bases—Burns, Gandil. Double play—Weaver, E. Collins and Gandil. Left on bases—New York 5, Chicago 3. Earned runs—Chicago 2, New York 1. Struck out —By Cicotte 2, by Sallee 2. Bases on balls—Off Cicotte 1. Umpires—O'Loughlin (A.L.), Klem (N.L.), Rigler (N.L.) and Evans (A.L.). Time—1:48. Attendance—32,000.

Sunday, October 7—At Chicago

New York (N.Y.)	AB.	R.	H.	O.	A.	E.
Burns, lf	3	0	1	0	0	0
Herzog, 2b	4	0	0	3	0	0
Kauff, cf	4	0	0	2	0	0
Zimmerman, 3b	4	0	0	4	2	0
Fletcher, ss	4	0	1	2	2	1
Robertson, rf	3	1	2	2	0	0
Holke, 1b	3	1	1	5	0	0
McCarty, c	1	0	1	5	0	0
Rariden, c	2	0	1	1	3	0
Schupp, p	1	0	0	0	1	0
Anderson, p	0	0	0	0	1	0
Perritt, p	1	0	1	0	0	0
bWilhoit	1	0	0	0	0	0
Tesreau, p	0	0	0	0	0	0
Totals	31	2	8	24	9	1

Chicago (A.L.)	AB.	R.	H.	O.	A.	E.
J. Collins, rf	1	0	0	0	1	0
aLeibold, rf	3	1	1	0	0	0
McMullin, 3b	5	1	1	0	3	0
E. Collins, 2b	4	1	2	4	2	0
Jackson, lf	3	1	3	0	1	0
Felsch, cf	4	1	1	2	1	0
Gandil, 1b	4	0	1	12	1	0
Weaver, ss	4	1	3	7	6	0
Schalk, c	4	1	1	1	2	1
Faber, p	3	0	1	1	4	0
Totals	35	7	14	27	21	1

New York...... 0 2 0 0 0 0 0 0 0—2
Chicago........ 0 2 0 5 0 0 0 0 *—7

aStruck out for J. Collins in second. bLined into double play for Perritt in eighth. Runs batted in—McCarty, Jackson 2, E. Collins, McMullin, Leibold, Weaver, Gandil. Stolen bases—E. Collins 2, Jackson. Double plays—Herzog (unassisted); Faber, Weaver and Gandil; Felsch, E. Collins and Weaver; Weaver and Gandil. Left on bases—Chicago 7, New York 3. Earned runs—Chicago 7, New York 2. Struck out—By Schupp 2, by Anderson 3, by Tesreau 1, by Faber 1. Bases on balls—Off Schupp 1, off Perritt 1, off Tesreau 1, off Faber 1. Hits—Off Schupp 4 in 1⅓ innings, off Anderson 5 in 2 innings, off Perritt 5 in 3⅔ innings, off Tesreau 0 in 1 inning. Passed ball—McCarty. Losing pitcher—Anderson. Umpires—Evans (A.L.), Rigler (N.L.), Klem (N.L.) and O'Loughlin (A.L.). Time—2:13. Attendance—32,000.

Wednesday, October 10—At New York

Chicago (A.L.)	AB.	R.	H.	O.	A.	E.
J. Collins, rf	4	0	0	1	0	2
McMullin, 3b	4	0	0	0	1	0
E. Collins, 2b	4	0	2	3	2	0
Jackson, lf	4	0	0	0	0	0
Felsch, cf	3	0	1	5	0	0
Gandil, 1b	3	0	0	6	0	0
Weaver, ss	3	0	2	0	2	0
Schalk, c	3	0	0	9	0	0
Cicotte, p	3	0	0	0	1	1
Totals	31	0	5	24	6	3

New York (N.L.)	AB.	R.	H.	O.	A.	E.
Burns, lf	4	0	1	1	0	0
Herzog, 2b	4	0	1	1	1	0
Kauff, cf	4	0	0	0	0	0
Zimmerman, 3b	4	0	1	0	3	0
Fletcher, ss	4	0	0	1	4	1
Robertson, rf	4	1	3	1	0	0

1917 WORLD SERIES

	AB.	R.	H.	O.	A.	E.
Holke, 1b	4	1	1	15	0	1
Rariden, c	2	0	1	7	4	0
Benton, p	3	0	0	1	2	0
Totals	33	2	8	27	14	2

Chicago .... 0 0 0 0 0 0 0 0 0—0
New York .... 0 0 0 2 0 0 0 0 *—2

Runs batted in—Holke, Burns. Two-base hits—Holke, Weaver. Three-base hit—Robertson. Sacrifice hit—Rariden. Stolen base—Robertson. Double play—Rariden and Herzog. Left on bases—New York 8, Chicago 8. Earned runs—New York 2. Struck out—By Cicotte 8, by Benton 5. Umpires—Klem (N.L.), O'Loughlin (A.L.), Evans (A.L.) and Rigler (N.L.). Time—1:55. Attendance—33,616.

Thursday, October 11—At New York

Chicago (A.L.)	AB.	R.	H.	O.	A.	E.
J. Collins, rf	4	0	2	0	0	0
McMullin, 3b	4	0	1	1	2	0
E. Collins, 2b	3	0	1	0	6	0
Jackson, lf	4	0	0	0	0	0
Felsch, cf	4	0	0	2	1	0
Gandil, 1b	4	0	1	15	0	0
Weaver, ss	3	0	0	0	1	0
Schalk, c	3	0	2	6	3	0
Faber, p	2	0	0	0	4	0
aRisberg	1	0	0	0	0	0
Danforth, p	0	0	0	0	1	0
Totals	32	0	7	24	18	0

New York (N.L.)	AB.	R.	H.	O.	A.	E.
Burns, lf	4	1	1	2	0	0
Herzog, 2b	3	1	1	3	4	1
Kauff, cf	4	2	2	1	0	0
Zimmerman, 3b	4	0	1	2	2	0
Fletcher, ss	4	1	2	1	3	0
Robertson, rf	3	0	1	1	0	0
Holke, 1b	2	0	1	9	0	0
Rariden, c	3	0	0	7	1	0
Schupp, p	3	0	1	1	3	0
Totals	30	5	10	27	13	1

Chicago .... 0 0 0 0 0 0 0 0 0—0
New York .... 0 0 0 1 1 0 1 2 *—5

aFlied out for Faber in eighth. Runs batted in—Kauff 3, Schupp, Rariden. Two-base hit—E. Collins. Three-base hit—Zimmerman. Home runs—Kauff 2. Sacrifice hit—Herzog. Stolen base—E. Collins. Double plays—Herzog, Fletcher and Holke; Faber, Schalk and Gandil. Left on bases—Chicago 6, New York 3. Earned runs—New York 5. Struck out—By Faber 3, by Danforth 2, by Schupp 7. Bases on balls—Off Schupp 1. Hit by pitcher—By Faber (Holke). Wild pitch—Faber. Hits—Off Faber 7 in 7 innings, off Danforth 3 in 1 inning. Losing pitcher—Faber. Umpires—Rigler (N.L.), Evans (A.L.), O'Loughlin (A.L.) and Klem (N.L.). Time—2:09. Attendance—27,746.

Saturday, October 13—At Chicago

New York (N.L.)	AB.	R.	H.	O.	A.	E.
Burns, lf	4	2	1	3	0	0
Herzog, 2b	5	0	1	0	1	1
Kauff, cf	5	0	2	2	0	0
Zimmerman, 3b	5	1	1	1	2	1
Fletcher, ss	5	1	1	2	3	1
Thorpe, rf	0	0	0	0	0	0
Robertson, rf	5	0	3	2	0	0
Holke, 1b	5	0	0	11	0	0
Rariden, c	3	1	3	3	1	0
Sallee, p	3	0	0	0	2	0
Perritt, p	0	0	0	0	0	0
Totals	40	5	12	24	9	3

Chicago (A.L.)	AB.	R.	H.	O.	A.	E.
J. Collins, rf	5	1	1	1	0	1
McMullin, 3b	3	0	0	1	4	0
E. Collins, 2b	4	2	3	1	4	0
Jackson, lf	5	2	3	3	0	0
Felsch, cf	5	1	3	0	0	0
Gandil, 1b	5	1	1	10	2	1
Weaver, ss	4	1	1	2	2	3
Schalk, c	3	0	1	9	0	0
Russell, p	0	0	0	0	0	0
Cicotte, p	1	0	0	0	2	0
aRisberg	1	0	1	0	0	0
Williams, p	0	0	0	0	0	1
bLynn	1	0	0	0	0	0
Faber, p	0	0	0	0	1	0
Totals	37	8	14	27	15	6

New York .... 2 0 0 2 0 0 1 0 0—5
Chicago .... 0 0 1 0 0 1 3 3 *—8

aSingled for Cicotte in sixth. bFanned for Williams in seventh. Runs batted in—Kauff 2, Robertson, Rariden, Burns, Felsch 2, Gandil 2, Risberg, E. Collins. Two-base hits—Kauff, Felsch, Fletcher, Gandil. Sacrifice hits—Sallee, McMullin. Stolen bases—Kauff, Robertson, Schalk. Double plays—McMullin and Gandil; McMullin, E. Collins and Gandil. Left on bases—New York 11, Chicago 10. Earned runs—Chicago 7, New York 4. Struck out—By Cicotte 3, by Williams 3, by Faber 1, by Sallee 2. Bases on balls—Off Russell 1, off Cicotte 1, off Sallee 4. Hits—Off Russell 2 in 0 innings (pitched to three batters in first inning), off Cicotte 8 in 6 innings, off Williams 2 in 1 inning, off Faber 0 in 2 innings, off Sallee 13 in 7⅓ innings, off Perritt 1 in ⅔ inning. Winning pitcher—Faber. Losing pitcher—Sallee. Umpires—O'Loughlin (A.L.), Klem (N.L.), Rigler (N.L.) and Evans (A.L.). Time—2:37. Attendance—27,323.

Monday, October 15—At New York

Chicago (A.L.)	AB.	R.	H.	O.	A.	E.
J. Collins, rf	3	0	0	1	0	0
bLeibold, rf	2	0	1	1	0	0
McMullin, 3b	5	0	0	0	1	0
E. Collins, 2b	4	1	1	1	8	0
Jackson, lf	4	1	1	1	0	0
Felsch, cf	3	1	0	3	0	0
Gandil, 1b	4	0	2	14	0	0
Weaver, ss	4	1	1	2	2	0
Schalk, c	3	0	1	4	1	1
Faber, p	2	0	0	0	0	0
Totals	34	4	7	27	12	1

New York (N.L.)	AB.	R.	H.	O.	A.	E.
Burns, lf	4	1	0	2	0	0
Herzog, 2b	4	0	2	2	5	0
Kauff, cf	4	0	0	2	0	1
Zimmerman, 3b	4	0	0	1	2	1
Fletcher, ss	4	0	1	1	2	0
Robertson, rf	3	0	0	1	1	1
Holke, 1b	4	0	1	12	0	0
Rariden, c	3	1	0	7	1	0
Benton, p	1	0	0	0	0	0
aWilhoit	0	0	0	0	0	0
Perritt, p	1	0	1	0	1	0
cMcCarty	1	0	0	0	0	0
Totals	33	2	6	27	12	3

Chicago .... 0 0 0 3 0 0 0 0 1—4
New York .... 0 0 0 0 2 0 0 0 0—2

aWalked for Benton in fifth. bPopped up for J. Collins in seventh. cGrounded out for Perritt in ninth. Runs batted in—Herzog 2, Gandil 2, Leibold. Two-base hit—Holke. Three-base hit—Herzog. Sacrifice hit—Faber. Left on bases—Chicago 7, New York 7. Earned runs—New York 2, Chicago 1. Struck out—By Faber 4, by Benton 3, by Perritt 3. Bases on balls—Off Faber 2, off Benton 1, off Perritt 2. Hit by pitcher—By Faber (Robertson). Hits—Off Benton 4 in 5 innings, off Perritt 3 in 4 innings. Passed ball—Schalk. Losing pitcher—Benton. Umpires—Klem (N.L.), O'Loughlin (A.L.), Evans (A.L.) and Rigler (N.L.). Time—2:18. Attendance—33,969.

COMPOSITE BATTING AVERAGES
Chicago White Sox

Player-Position	G.	AB.	R.	H.	2B.	3B.	HR.	RBI.	BA.
Risberg, ph	2	2	0	1	0	0	0	1	.500
E. Collins, 2b	6	22	4	9	1	0	0	2	.409
Leibold, ph-rf	2	5	1	2	0	0	0	0	.400
Weaver, ss	6	21	3	7	1	0	0	1	.333
Jackson, lf	6	23	4	7	0	0	0	2	.304
J. Collins, rf	6	21	2	6	1	0	0	0	.286
Felsch, cf	6	22	4	6	1	0	1	3	.273
Schalk, c	6	19	1	5	0	0	0	0	.263
Gandil, 1b	6	23	1	6	1	0	0	5	.261
Cicotte, p	3	7	0	1	0	0	0	0	.143
Faber, p	4	7	0	1	0	0	0	0	.143
McMullin, 3b	6	24	1	3	1	0	0	2	.125
Danforth, p	1	0	0	0	0	0	0	0	.000
Russell, p	1	0	0	0	0	0	0	0	.000
Williams, p	1	0	0	0	0	0	0	0	.000
Lynn, ph	1	1	0	0	0	0	0	0	.000
Totals	6	197	21	54	6	0	1	18	.274

New York Giants

Player-Position	G.	AB.	R.	H.	2B.	3B.	HR.	RBI.	BA.
Perritt, p	3	2	0	2	0	0	0	0	1.000
Robertson, rf	6	22	3	11	1	1	0	1	.500
McCarty, c-ph	3	5	1	2	0	1	0	1	.400
Rariden, c	5	13	2	5	0	0	0	2	.385
Holke, 1b	6	21	2	6	2	0	0	1	.286
Herzog, 2b	6	24	1	6	0	1	0	2	.250
Schupp, p	2	4	0	1	0	0	0	1	.250
Burns, lf	6	22	3	5	0	0	0	2	.227
Fletcher, ss	6	25	2	5	1	0	0	0	.200
Sallee, p	2	6	0	1	0	0	0	1	.167
Kauff, cf	6	25	2	4	1	0	2	5	.160
Zimmerman, 3b	6	25	1	3	0	1	0	0	.120
Anderson, p	1	0	0	0	0	0	0	0	.000
Wilhoit, ph	2	1	0	0	0	0	0	0	.000
Tesreau, p	1	0	0	0	0	0	0	0	.000
Benton, p	2	4	0	0	0	0	0	0	.000
Thorpe, rf	1	0	0	0	0	0	0	0	.000
Totals	6	199	17	51	5	4	2	16	.256

COMPOSITE PITCHING AVERAGES
Chicago White Sox

Pitcher	G.	IP.	H.	R.	E.	SO.	BB.	W.	L.	ERA.
Cicotte	3	23	23	6	5	13	2	1	1	1.96
Faber	4	27	21	7	7	9	3	3	1	2.33
Williams	1	1	2	1	1	3	0	0	0	9.00
Danforth	1	1	3	2	2	2	0	0	0	18.00
Russell	1	0	2	1	1	0	1	0	0	......
Totals	6	52	51	17	16	27	6	4	2	2.77

New York Giants

Pitcher	G.	IP.	H.	R.	E.	SO.	BB.	W.	L.	ERA.
Benton	2	14	9	3	0	8	1	1	1	0.00
Tesreau	1	1	0	0	0	1	1	0	0	0.00
Schupp	2	10⅓	11	2	2	9	2	1	0	1.74
Perritt	3	8⅓	9	2	2	3	3	0	0	2.16
Sallee	2	15⅓	20	10	9	4	4	0	2	5.28
Anderson	1	2	5	4	4	3	0	0	1	18.00
Totals	6	51	54	21	17	28	11	2	4	3.00

SERIES OF 1918

	W.	L.	Pct.
Boston A. L.	4	2	.667
Chicago N. L.	2	4	.333

The major leagues were ordered to suspend their seasons by Labor Day in 1918 by the Work-or-Fight order of General Crowder, the Provost Marshal, but the two championship clubs were given special dispensation to play the World Series after the early September holiday. The American League won by the same margin as in 1917, four games to two, Ed Barrow's Boston Red Sox defeating the Chicago Cubs, managed by Fred Mitchell. It again gave the American League four Series triumphs in succession, and eight in nine years; it also was the Red Sox' fifth World Series victory without a setback.

Unlike the 1917 Series, when war had touched it only lightly, the great struggle in Europe threw a heavy shadow over the 1918 Series. Both of the contending clubs lost heavily in playing personnel to the armed services. The famous Grover Cleveland Alexander, purchased by the Chicago club from the Phillies the winter before, was drafted early in the 1918 season, and the Red Sox lost such former World Series stars as Duffy Lewis, Jack Barry, Dutch Leonard, Dick Hoblitzel, Chick Shorten and others to the armed services.

The World Series admission prices were lowered and though the Cubs transferred their home games to Comiskey Park because of the greater capacity, it scarcely was needed as the best crowd was only 27,054 and receipts for the entire Series came to only $179,619, less than any time since 1910.

Hitting during the Series was very light, and the Red Sox won with the low average of .186 against .210 for the Cubs. The fielding was particularly brilliant and steady, Boston making only one error for the exceptional fielding mark of .996. The Cubs were guilty of only five boots themselves. The Red Sox' hero of the Series was George Whiteman, a war outfield replacement, whose five hits were made at particularly opportune times. He also made several great catches.

Barrow started to experiment with Babe Ruth in the outfield in this season, and the Babe attracted attention by hitting .300 in 95 games and tying Clarence (Tilly) Walker of the Athletics for the home-run lead in the American League with 11.

However, when the World Series started, Ruth was Barrow's hurler and he started Boston off well by defeating Jim Vaughn in a great lefthanded pitching duel, 1 to 0. Ruth also pitched seven and one-third scoreless innings in the fourth game before Chicago counted two runs in the eighth. Including 13⅓ scoreless innings in the 1916 Series, it gave Ruth a total of 29⅔ consecutive scoreless World Series innings—a record that stood until Whitey Ford topped it in 1961. Joe Bush pitched the ninth inning of the fourth game, Ruth going to left field, but Babe received credit for his second victory of the Series. Mitchell's strategy was to keep Ruth out of the Series as much as possible by pitching lefthanders, and Vaughn and George Tyler each started three games. Ruth was held to one long triple in five times at bat in the three games in which he appeared.

In addition to Ruth's two victories, the two other Boston triumphs went to Carl Mays. Bush and Sad Sam Jones each lost a game for the Red Sox. Vaughn and Tyler each won a game for Chicago; Big Jim was charged with two defeats and Tyler with one. The fourth Chicago reverse went to Shufflin' Phil Douglas.

The batting leader for the regulars of both sides was Charley Pick, Cub second baseman, with .389. Catcher Wally Schang batted .444 for the Red Sox, but was at bat only nine times and did not appear in the first game.

For the first time, the second, third and fourth-place clubs shared in the receipts and the players competing in the Series, demanding larger shares, held a sit-down strike before the fifth game at Boston, and delayed its start before capitulating. Each member of the Red Sox received $890 and each of the Cubs $535 under the new plan, after deductions for war charities, the smallest in Series' history, although the original divisions were $1,102.51 and $671.09. The box scores:

Thursday, September 5—At Chicago

Boston (A.L.)	AB.	R.	H.	O.	A.	E.
Hooper, rf	4	0	1	4	0	0
Shean, 2b	2	1	1	0	3	0
Strunk, cf	3	0	0	2	0	0
Whiteman, lf	4	0	2	5	0	0
McInnis, 1b	2	0	1	10	0	0
Scott, ss	4	0	0	0	3	0
Thomas, 3b	3	0	0	1	1	0
Agnew, c	3	0	0	5	0	0
Ruth, p	3	0	0	0	1	0
Totals	28	1	5	27	8	0

Chicago (N.L.)	AB.	R.	H.	O.	A.	E.
Flack, rf	3	0	1	2	0	0
Hollocher, ss	3	0	0	2	1	0
Mann, lf	4	0	1	0	0	0
Paskert, cf	4	0	2	2	0	0
Merkle, 1b	3	0	1	9	2	0
Pick, 2b	3	0	0	1	1	0
aO'Farrell	1	0	0	0	0	0
Deal, 3b	4	0	1	1	3	0
bMcCabe	0	0	0	0	0	0
Killefer, c	4	0	0	7	2	0
Vaughn, p	3	0	0	3	5	0
Totals	32	0	6	27	14	0

Boston .... 0 0 0   1 0 0   0 0 0—1
Chicago .... 0 0 0   0 0 0   0 0 0—0

aPopped out for Pick in ninth. bRan for Deal in ninth. Run batted in—McInnis. Sacrifice hits—Strunk, McInnis, Hollocher. Left on bases—Chicago 8, Boston 5. Earned run—Boston 1. Struck out—By Ruth 4, by Vaughn 6. Bases on balls—Off Ruth 1, off Vaughn 3. Hit by pitcher—By Ruth (Flack). Umpires—O'Day (N.L.), Hildebrand (A.L.), Klem (N.L.) and Owens (A.L.). Time—1:50. Attendance—19,274.

Friday, September 6—At Chicago

Boston (A.L.)	AB.	R.	H.	O.	A.	E.
Hooper, rf	3	0	1	1	0	0
Shean, 2b	4	0	1	5	2	0
Strunk, cf	4	1	1	1	2	0
Whiteman, lf	3	0	1	3	0	1
McInnis, 1b	4	0	1	7	0	0
Scott, ss	3	0	0	3	2	0
Thomas, 3b	2	0	0	1	1	0
bDubuc	1	0	0	0	0	0
Agnew, c	2	0	0	2	4	0
aSchang, c	2	0	1	1	0	0
Bush, p	2	0	0	0	3	0
Totals	30	1	6	24	14	1

Chicago (N.L.)	AB.	R.	H.	O.	A.	E.
Flack, rf	4	0	2	4	1	0
Hollocher, ss	4	0	1	5	4	0
Mann, lf	4	0	0	0	0	0
Paskert, cf	4	0	0	2	0	0
Merkle, 1b	2	1	1	6	1	0
Pick, 2b	2	1	1	4	4	0
Deal, 3b	2	0	0	1	1	1
Killefer, c	2	1	1	4	2	0
Tyler, p	3	0	1	1	2	0
Totals	27	3	7	27	15	1

Boston .... 0 0 0   0 0 0   0 0 1—1
Chicago .... 0 3 0   0 0 0   0 0 *—3

aSingled for Agnew in eighth. bStruck out for Thomas in ninth. Runs batted in—Whiteman, Killefer, Tyler 2. Two-base hit—Killefer. Three base hits—Hollocher, Strunk, Whiteman. Sacrifice hits—Scott, Deal. Double plays—Killefer and Pick; Hollocher, Pick and Merkle. Left on bases—Chicago 4, Boston 7. Earned runs—Boston 1, Chicago 3. Struck out—By Tyler 2. Bases on balls—Off Tyler 4, off Bush 3. Umpires—Hildebrand (A.L.), Klem (N.L.), Owens (A.L.) and O'Day (N.L.). Time—1:58. Attendance—20,040.

Saturday, September 7—At Chicago

Boston (A.L.)	AB.	R.	H.	O.	A.	E.
Hooper, rf	3	0	1	3	0	0
Shean, 2b	4	0	0	1	2	0
Strunk, cf	4	0	1	1	0	0
Whiteman, lf	3	1	1	3	0	0
McInnis, 1b	4	1	1	12	0	0
Schang, c	4	0	2	6	3	0
Scott, ss	4	0	1	1	5	0
Thomas, 3b	3	0	1	0	2	0
Mays, p	3	0	0	0	2	0
Totals	32	2	7	27	14	0

Chicago (N.L.)	AB.	R.	H.	O.	A.	E.
Flack, rf	3	0	0	3	1	0
Hollocher, ss	3	0	0	1	3	1
Mann, lf	4	0	2	1	0	0
Paskert, cf	4	0	1	1	0	0
Merkle, 1b	4	0	0	9	2	0
Pick, 2b	4	1	2	0	0	0
Deal, 3b	3	0	1	1	1	0
aBarber	0	0	0	0	0	0
Killefer, c	3	0	1	8	0	0
Vaughn, p	3	0	0	3	3	0
Totals	31	1	7	27	10	1

Boston .... 0 0 0   2 0 0   0 0 0—2
Chicago .... 0 0 0   0 1 0   0 0 0—1

aAnnounced as batter for Deal in ninth. Runs batted in—Schang, Scott, Killefer. Two-base hits—Mann, Pick. Sacrifice hit—Hollocher. Stolen bases—Whiteman, Schang, Pick. Double plays—Hollocher and Merkle; Vaughn and Merkle. Left on bases—Boston 5, Chicago 5. Earned runs—Boston 2, Chicago 1. Struck out—By Mays 4, by Vaughn 7. Bases on balls—Off Mays 1, off Vaughn 1. Hit by pitcher—By Vaughn (Whiteman). Passed ball—Schang. Umpires—Klem (N.L.),

1918 WORLD SERIES

Owens (A.L.), O'Day (N.L.) and Hildebrand (A.L.). Time—1:57. Attendance—27,054.

Monday, September 9—At Boston

Chicago (N.L.)	AB.	R.	H.	O.	A.	E.
Flack, rf	4	0	1	3	0	0
Hollocher, ss	4	0	0	2	0	0
Mann, lf	4	0	1	2	0	0
Paskert, cf	4	0	0	3	0	0
Merkle, 1b	3	0	1	9	1	0
Pick, 2b	2	0	2	0	2	0
aZeider, 3b	0	0	0	1	2	0
Deal, 3b	2	0	1	1	3	0
bO'Farrell	1	0	0	0	0	0
Wortman, 2b	1	0	0	1	0	0
Killefer, c	2	1	0	1	0	0
eBarber	1	0	0	0	0	0
Tyler, p	0	0	0	1	4	0
cHendrix	1	0	1	0	0	0
dMcCabe	0	1	0	0	0	0
Douglas, p	0	0	0	0	0	1
Totals	29	2	7	24	12	1

Boston (A.L.)	AB.	R.	H.	O.	A.	E.
Hooper, rf	3	0	0	1	0	0
Shean, 2b	3	0	1	4	4	0
Strunk, cf	4	0	0	0	0	0
Whiteman, lf	3	1	0	1	0	0
Bush, p	0	0	0	0	0	0
McInnis, 1b	3	1	1	16	1	0
Ruth, p-lf	2	0	1	0	4	0
Scott, ss	3	0	0	3	8	0
Thomas, 3b	3	0	0	2	3	0
Agnew, c	2	0	0	0	1	0
Schang, c	1	1	1	0	0	0
Totals	27	3	4	27	21	0

Chicago .... 0 0 0 0 0 0 0 2 0—2
Boston .... 0 0 0 2 0 0 0 1 *—3

aWalked for Pick in seventh. bHit into double play for Deal in seventh. cSingled for Tyler in eighth. dRan for Hendrix in eighth. eHit into double play for Killefer in ninth. Runs batted in—Ruth 2, Hollocher, Mann, Shean. Three-base hit—Ruth. Sacrifice hits—Hooper, Ruth. Stolen base—Shean. Double plays—Ruth, Scott and McInnis; Scott, Shean and McInnis 2. Left on bases—Chicago 6, Boston 4. Earned runs—Chicago 2, Boston 2. Struck out—By Tyler 1. Bases on balls—Off Tyler 2, off Ruth 6. Wild pitch—Ruth. Hits—Off Tyler 3 in 7 innings, off Douglas 1 in 1 inning, off Ruth 7 in 8 innings (pitched to two batters in ninth), off Bush 0 in 1 inning. Passed balls—Killefer 2. Winning pitcher—Ruth. Losing pitcher—Douglas. Umpires—Owens (A.L.), O'Day (N.L.), Hildebrand (A.L.) and Klem (N.L.). Time—1:50. Attendance—22,183.

Tuesday, September 10—At Boston

Chicago (N.L.)	AB.	R.	H.	O.	A.	E.
Flack, rf	2	1	0	1	0	0
Hollocher, ss	3	2	3	2	5	0
Mann, lf	3	0	1	2	0	0
Paskert, cf	3	0	0	3	0	0
Merkle, 1b	3	0	1	11	1	0
Pick, 2b	4	0	1	4	3	0
Deal, 3b	4	0	0	0	0	0
Killefer, c	4	0	0	4	0	0
Vaughn, p	4	0	1	0	3	0
Totals	30	3	7	27	12	0

Boston (A.L.)	AB.	R.	H.	O.	A.	E.
Hooper, rf	4	0	1	1	0	0
Shean, 2b	3	0	1	3	2	0
Strunk, cf	4	0	1	4	0	0
Whiteman, lf	3	0	1	2	0	0
McInnis, 1b	3	0	0	9	0	0
Scott, ss	3	0	1	4	0	0
Thomas, 3b	3	0	1	1	1	0
Agnew, c	2	0	0	5	1	0
aSchang, c	1	0	0	1	0	0
Jones, p	1	0	0	1	3	0
bMiller	1	0	0	0	0	0
Totals	28	0	5	27	13	0

Chicago .... 0 0 1 0 0 0 0 2 0—3
Boston .... 0 0 0 0 0 0 0 0 0—0

aStruck out for Agnew in eighth. bFlied out for Jones in ninth. Runs batted in—Mann, Paskert 2. Two-base hits—Mann, Paskert, Strunk. Sacrifice hits—Mann, Shean. Stolen base—Hollocher. Double plays—Merkle and Hollocher; Hollocher, Pick and Merkle 2; Whiteman and Shean. Left on bases—Chicago 6, Boston 3. Earned runs—Chicago 3. Struck out—By Vaughn 4, by Jones 5. Bases on balls—Off Vaughn 1, off Jones 5. Umpires—O'Day (N.L.), Hildebrand (A.L.), Klem (N.L.) and Owens (A.L.). Time—1:42. Attendance—24,694.

Wednesday, September 11—At Boston

Chicago (N.L.)	AB.	R.	H.	O.	A.	E.
Flack, rf	3	1	1	2	0	1
Hollocher, ss	4	0	0	0	4	0
Mann, lf	3	0	0	2	0	0
Paskert, cf	2	0	0	5	0	0
Merkle, 1b	3	0	1	8	2	0
Pick, 2b	3	0	1	3	1	0
Deal, 3b	2	0	0	2	1	0
aBarber	1	0	0	0	0	0
Zeider, 3b	0	0	0	0	0	0
Killefer, c	2	0	0	2	0	0
bO'Farrell, c	1	0	0	0	0	0
Tyler, p	2	0	0	0	3	1
cMcCabe	1	0	0	0	0	0
Hendrix, p	0	0	0	0	0	0
Totals	27	1	3	24	13	2

Boston (A.L.)	AB.	R.	H.	O.	A.	E.
Hooper, rf	3	0	0	1	0	0
Shean, 2b	3	1	0	2	4	0
Strunk, cf	4	0	2	0	0	0
Whiteman, lf	4	0	0	2	0	0
Ruth, lf	0	0	0	1	0	0
McInnis, 1b	4	0	1	16	1	0
Scott, ss	4	0	1	3	3	0
Thomas, 3b	2	0	0	1	2	0
Schang, c	1	0	0	1	2	0
Mays, p	2	1	1	0	6	0
Totals	27	2	5	27	18	0

Chicago .... 0 0 0 1 0 0 0 0 0—1
Boston .... 0 0 2 0 0 0 0 0 *—2

aLined out for Deal in eighth. bPopped out for Killefer in eighth. cFouled out for Tyler in eighth. Run batted in—Merkle. Sacrifice hits—Hooper, Thomas. Stolen base—Flack. Left on bases—Boston 8, Chicago 2. Earned runs—Boston 0, Chicago 1. Struck out—By Tyler 1, by Mays 1. Bases on balls—Off Tyler 5, off Mays 2. Hit by pitcher—By Mays (Mann). Hits—Off Tyler 5 in 7 innings, off Hendrix 0 in 1 inning. Losing pitcher—Tyler. Umpires—Hildebrand (A.L.), Klem (N.L.), Owens (A.L.) and O'Day (N.L.). Time—1:46. Attendance—15,238.

COMPOSITE BATTING AVERAGES
Boston Red Sox

Player-Position	G.	AB.	R.	H.	2B.	3B.	HR.	RBI.	BA.
Schang, ph-c	5	9	1	4	0	0	0	1	.444
Whiteman, lf	6	20	2	5	0	1	0	1	.250
McInnis, 1b	6	20	2	5	0	0	0	1	.250

Player-Position	G.	AB.	R.	H.	2B.	3B.	HR.	RBI.	BA.
Shean, 2b	6	19	2	4	1	0	0	0	.211
Hooper, rf	6	20	0	4	0	0	0	0	.200
Ruth, p-lf	3	5	0	1	0	1	0	2	.200
Mays, p	2	5	1	1	0	0	0	0	.200
Strunk, cf	6	23	1	4	1	1	0	0	.174
Thomas, 3b	6	16	0	2	0	0	0	0	.125
Scott, ss	6	21	0	2	0	0	0	1	.095
Agnew, c	4	9	0	0	0	0	0	0	.000
Dubuc, ph	1	1	0	0	0	0	0	0	.000
Bush, p	2	2	0	0	0	0	0	0	.000
Jones, p	1	1	0	0	0	0	0	0	.000
Miller, ph	1	1	0	0	0	0	0	0	.000
Totals	6	172	9	32	2	3	0	6	.186

Chicago Cubs

Player-Position	G.	AB.	R.	H.	2B.	3B.	HR.	RBI.	BA.
Hendrix, ph	2	1	0	1	0	0	0	0	1.000
Pick, 2b	6	18	2	7	1	0	0	0	.389
Merkle, 1b	6	18	1	5	0	0	0	1	.278
Flack, rf	6	19	2	5	0	0	0	0	.263
Mann, lf	6	22	0	5	2	0	0	2	.227
Tyler, p	3	5	0	1	0	0	0	2	.200
Hollocher, ss	6	21	2	4	0	1	0	1	.190
Paskert, cf	6	21	0	4	1	0	0	2	.190
Deal, 3b	6	17	0	3	0	0	0	0	.176
Killefer, c	6	17	2	2	1	0	0	2	.118
Zeider, ph-3b	2	0	0	0	0	0	0	0	.000
Wortman, 2b	1	1	0	0	0	0	0	0	.000
O'Farrell, ph-c	3	3	0	0	0	0	0	0	.000
McCabe, pr-ph	3	1	1	0	0	0	0	0	.000
Barber, ph	2	2	0	0	0	0	0	0	.000
Vaughn, p	3	10	0	0	0	0	0	0	.000
Douglas, p	1	0	0	0	0	0	0	0	.000
Totals	6	176	10	37	5	1	0	10	.210

COMPOSITE PITCHING AVERAGES
Boston Red Sox

Pitcher	G.	IP.	H.	R.	E.	SO.	BB.	W.	L.	ERA.
Mays	2	18	10	2	2	5	3	2	0	1.00
Ruth	2	17	13	2	2	4	7	2	0	1.06
Jones	1	9	7	3	3	5	5	0	1	3.00
Bush	2	9	7	3	3	0	3	0	1	3.00
Totals	6	53	37	10	10	14	18	4	2	1.70

Chicago Cubs

Pitcher	G.	IP.	H.	R.	E.	SO.	BB.	W.	L.	ERA.
Douglas	1	1	1	1	0	0	0	0	1	0.00
Hendrix	1	1	0	0	0	0	0	0	0	0.00
Vaughn	3	27	17	3	3	17	5	1	2	1.00
Tyler	3	23	14	5	3	4	11	1	1	1.17
Totals	6	52	32	9	6	21	16	2	4	1.04

SERIES OF 1919

	W.	L.	Pct.
Cincinnati N. L.	5	3	.625
Chicago A. L.	3	5	.375

After the close of World War I, baseball made a strong comeback in 1919, even though the two major leagues had cut the usual 154-game schedule to 140 games. The White Sox, world champions of 1917, after dropping to sixth in 1918, easily regained the American League championship under Kid Gleason, the former coach of the team, while the Cincinnati Reds, directed by the former Philadelphia manager, Pat Moran, won their first National League pennant, beating out New York by nine games.

There was intense interest in the World Series, especially in the Midwest, and the old National Commission voted to increase the length of the event, making it five victories out of nine, instead of four out of seven. The players received a cut of the first five games.

Unfortunately, what should have been one of the greatest of all Series developed into the blackest chapter in baseball history. Cincinnati won the Series, five games to three, but it later was charged that eight of the White Sox players, including some of the club's top stars, had conspired with gamblers to throw the games.

Observers noted there were some suspicious circumstances during the Series, but the full scandal did not break until nearly a year afterwards, when in the closing weeks of the 1920 season Ban Johnson, president of the American League, received full details of the alleged conspiracy. As a result, eight Chicago players, five regulars, two first-string pitchers and a utility infielder, were dropped from the ranks of Organized Ball. The eight were Joe Jackson, Oscar (Hap) Felsch, Arnold (Chick) Gandil, George (Buck) Weaver, Charles (Swede) Risberg, Fred McMullin, Eddie Cicotte and Claude Williams.

John A. Heydler, National League president, and Manager Moran of the Cincinnati team always contended that the Reds could have won without any help from the conspirators on the White Sox. They pointed out that the Reds had a magnificent pitching staff in Walter (Dutch) Ruether, Hod Eller, Harry Sallee, Jimmy Ring, Ray Fisher and the Cuban, Adolfo Luque, which enabled them to win the flag with a percentage of .686.

The general impression later was that after the first game, in which Ruether defeated Cicotte, 9 to 1, with the White Sox star being taken out in the fourth inning, the Series was played more or less on its merits. Proof of that was cited in the fact that two of the expelled Chicago stars, Jackson and Weaver, led their team at bat, with .375 and .324, respectively.

Edd Roush, the National League batting king, was held to .214, and Cincinnati's next best hitter during the championship season, Heine Groh, hit .172. The batting leader among the Red regulars was Earle (Greasy) Neale with a .357 average.

The player gaining the most glory from the Series was Dickie Kerr, diminutive Sox lefthander, who won two games, one a three-hit shutout. In winning a 5 to 0 calcimining for the Reds in the fifth game, Eller struck out six Chicago players in order.

After Cincinnati won four of the first five games, the White Sox bounced back for a ten-inning, 5 to 4 victory behind Kerr and a 4 to 1 triumph behind Cicotte. However, the Reds then exploded a 16-hit attack in the eighth and final game to win handily, 10 to 5, as Eller earned his second victory.

The receipts of $722,414 were the greatest up to that time and the attendance of 236,928 was second only to the eight-game Giant-Red Sox Series of 1912. The players' pool hit a new high mark with $260,349.66, as did the winning and losing shares. Each

Red received $5,207.01 and each White Sox player $3,254.36. The division was made and checks sent out long before there were any detailed charges. The box scores:

Wednesday, October 1—At Cincinnati

Chicago (A.L.)	AB.	R.	H.	O.	A.	E.
J. Collins, rf	4	0	1	0	0	0
E. Collins, 2b	4	0	1	3	3	0
Weaver, 3b	4	0	1	0	1	0
Jackson, lf	4	1	0	3	0	0
Felsch, cf	3	0	0	4	0	0
Gandil, 1b	4	0	2	7	0	1
Risberg, ss	2	0	0	5	6	0
Schalk, c	3	0	0	2	2	0
Cicotte, p	1	0	0	0	3	0
Wilkinson, p	1	0	0	0	0	0
aMcMullin	1	0	1	0	0	0
Lowdermilk, p	0	0	0	0	1	0
Totals	31	1	6	24	16	1

Cincinnati (N.L.)	AB.	R.	H.	O.	A.	E.
Rath, 2b	3	2	1	4	2	0
Daubert, 1b	4	1	3	9	0	0
Groh, 3b	3	1	1	0	3	0
Roush, cf	3	0	0	8	0	0
Duncan, lf	4	0	2	1	0	0
Kopf, ss	4	1	0	1	3	1
Neale, rf	4	2	3	3	0	0
Wingo, c	3	1	1	1	2	0
Ruether, p	3	1	3	0	2	0
Totals	31	9	14	27	12	1

Chicago .... 0 1 0 0 0 0 0 0 0—1
Cincinnati .... 1 0 0 5 0 0 2 1 *—9

aSingled for Wilkinson in eighth. Runs batted in—Gandil, Rath, Daubert, Groh 2, Duncan, Wingo, Ruether 3. Two-base hit—Rath. Three-base hits—Ruether 2, Daubert. Sacrifice hits—Felsch, Rath, Roush, Wingo. Sacrifice fly—Groh. Stolen base—Roush. Double plays—Risberg and E. Collins; Risberg, E. Collins and Gandil. Left on bases—Cincinnati 7, Chicago 5. Earned runs—Cincinnati 8, Chicago 0. Struck out—By Cicotte 1, by Wilkinson 1, by Ruether 1. Bases on balls—Off Cicotte 2, off Lowdermilk 1, off Ruether 1. Hit by pitcher—By Cicotte (Rath), by Lowdermilk (Daubert). Hits—Off Cicotte 7 in 3⅔ innings, off Wilkinson 5 in 3⅓ innings, off Lowdermilk 2 in 1 inning. Losing pitcher—Cicotte. Umpires—Rigler (N.L.), Evans (A.L.), Nallin (A.L.) and Quigley (N.L.). Time—1:42. Attendance—30,511.

Thursday, October 2—At Cincinnati

Chicago (A.L.)	AB.	R.	H.	O.	A.	E.
J. Collins, rf	4	0	0	2	0	0
E. Collins, 2b	3	0	0	2	3	0
Weaver, 3b	4	0	2	3	0	0
Jackson, lf	4	0	3	1	0	0
Felsch, cf	2	0	0	5	1	0
Gandil, 1b	4	0	1	7	0	0
Risberg, ss	4	1	1	2	2	1
Schalk, c	4	1	2	2	2	0
Williams, p	3	0	1	0	2	0
aMcMullin	1	0	0	0	0	0
Totals	33	2	10	24	10	1

Cincinnati (N.L.)	AB.	R.	H.	O.	A.	E.
Rath, 2b	3	1	0	1	2	0
Daubert, 1b	3	0	0	12	2	1
Groh, 3b	2	1	0	0	1	0
Roush, cf	2	1	1	5	0	0
Duncan, lf	1	1	0	1	0	0
Kopf, ss	3	0	1	3	6	0
Neale, rf	3	0	1	1	0	1
Rariden, c	3	0	1	3	0	0
Sallee, p	3	0	0	1	3	0
Totals	23	4	4	27	14	2

Chicago .... 0 0 0 0 0 0 2 0 0—2
Cincinnati .... 0 0 0 3 0 1 0 0 *—4

aGrounded out for Williams in ninth. Runs batted in—Roush, Kopf 2, Neale. Two-base hits—Jackson, Weaver. Three base hit—Kopf. Sacrifice hits—Felsch 2, Daubert, Duncan. Stolen base—Gandil. Double plays—Kopf and Daubert; E. Collins and Gandil; Felsch, E. Collins and Gandil; Rath, Kopf and Daubert. Left on bases—Chicago 7, Cincinnati 3. Earned runs—Cincinnati 3, Chicago 0. Struck out—By Williams 1, by Sallee 2. Bases on balls—Off Williams 6, off Sallee 1. Balk—Sallee. Umpires—Evans (A.L.), Quigley (N.L.), Nallin (A.L.) and Rigler (N.L.). Time—1:42. Attendance—29,690.

Friday, October 3—At Chicago

Cincinnati (N.L.)	AB.	R.	H.	O.	A.	E.
Rath, 2b	4	0	0	3	3	0
Daubert, 1b	4	0	0	14	1	0
Groh, 3b	3	0	0	2	5	0
Roush, cf	3	0	0	0	0	0
Duncan, lf	3	0	1	0	0	0
Kopf, ss	3	0	1	1	1	0
Neale, rf	3	0	0	1	0	0
Rariden, c	3	0	0	2	3	0
Fisher, p	2	0	1	0	5	1
aMagee	1	0	0	0	0	0
Luque, p	0	0	0	1	0	0
Totals	29	0	3	24	18	1

Chicago (A.L.)	AB.	R.	H.	O.	A.	E.
Leibold, rf	4	0	0	2	0	0
E. Collins, 2b	4	0	1	1	5	0
Weaver, 3b	4	0	1	0	4	0
Jackson, lf	3	1	2	1	0	0
Felsch, cf	2	1	0	1	0	0
Gandil, 1b	3	0	1	14	1	0
Risberg, ss	2	1	1	4	6	0
Schalk, c	3	0	1	4	0	0
Kerr, p	3	0	0	0	0	0
Totals	28	3	7	27	16	0

Cincinnati .... 0 0 0 0 0 0 0 0 0—0
Chicago .... 0 2 0 1 0 0 0 0 *—3

aFlied out for Fisher in eighth. Runs batted in—Gandil 2, Schalk. Three-base hit—Risberg. Double plays—Groh, Rath and Daubert; Risberg and E. Collins. Left on bases—Cincinnati 3, Chicago 3. Earned runs—Chicago 2. Struck out—by Kerr 4, by Fisher 1, by Luque 1. Bases on balls—Off Fisher 2, off Kerr 1. Hits—Off Fisher 7 in 7 innings, off Luque 0 in 1 inning. Losing pitcher—Fisher. Umpires—Quigley (N.L.), Nallin (A.L.), Rigler (N.L.) and Evans (A.L.). Time—1:30. Attendance—29,126.

Saturday, October 4—At Chicago

Cincinnati (N.L.)	AB.	R.	H.	O.	A.	E.
Rath, 2b	4	0	1	5	1	1
Daubert, 1b	4	0	0	9	1	0
Groh, 3b	4	0	0	2	3	1
Roush, cf	3	0	0	2	0	0
Duncan, lf	3	1	0	1	0	0
Kopf, ss	3	1	1	1	1	0
Neale, rf	3	0	1	2	0	0
Wingo, c	3	0	2	2	0	0
Ring, p	3	0	0	1	2	0
Totals	30	2	5	27	8	2

1919 WORLD SERIES

Chicago (A.L.)	AB.	R.	H.	O.	A.	E.
Leibold, rf	5	0	0	0	0	0
E. Collins, 2b	3	0	0	3	5	0
Weaver, 3b	4	0	0	0	3	0
Jackson, lf	4	0	1	3	0	0
Felsch, cf	3	0	1	0	0	0
Gandil, 1b	4	0	1	14	0	0
Risberg, ss	3	0	0	3	4	0
Schalk, c	1	0	0	4	3	0
Cicotte, p	3	0	0	0	2	2
aMurphy	1	0	0	0	0	0
Totals	31	0	3	27	17	2

Cincinnati............ 0 0 0   0 2 0   0 0 0—2
Chicago............... 0 0 0   0 0 0   0 0 0—0

aFlied out for Cicotte in ninth. Runs batted in—Kopf, Neale. Two-base hits—Jackson, Neale. Sacrifice hit—Felsch. Stolen base—Risberg. Double plays—Cicotte, Risberg and Gandil; E. Collins, Risberg and Gandil. Left on bases—Chicago 10, Cincinnati 1. Earned runs—Cincinnati 0. Struck out—By Cicotte 2, by Ring 2. Bases on balls—Off Ring 3. Hit by pitcher—By Ring (E. Collins, Schalk). Umpires—Nallin (A.L.), Rigler (N.L.), Evans (A.L.) and Quigley (N.L.). Time—1:37. Attendance—34,363.

Monday, October 6—At Chicago

Cincinnati (N.L.)	AB.	R.	H.	O.	A.	E.
Rath, 2b	3	1	1	0	3	0
Daubert, 1b	2	0	0	11	0	0
Groh, 3b	3	1	0	1	2	0
Roush, cf	4	2	1	2	0	0
Duncan, lf	2	0	0	2	0	0
Kopf, ss	3	0	1	0	4	0
Neale, rf	4	0	0	1	0	0
Rariden, c	4	0	0	10	0	0
Eller, p	3	1	1	0	2	0
Totals	28	5	4	27	11	0

Chicago (A.L.)	AB.	R.	H.	O.	A.	E.
Leibold, rf	3	0	0	1	0	0
E. Collins, 2b	4	0	0	1	2	1
Weaver, 3b	4	0	2	1	2	0
Jackson, lf	4	0	0	3	0	0
Felsch, cf	3	0	0	7	0	1
Gandil, 1b	3	0	0	8	1	0
Risberg, ss	3	0	0	1	2	1
Schalk, c	2	0	1	3	2	0
Lynn, c	1	0	0	1	0	0
Williams, p	2	0	0	1	0	0
aMurphy	1	0	0	0	0	0
Mayer, p	0	0	0	0	0	0
Totals	30	0	3	27	9	3

Cincinnati............ 0 0 0   0 0 4   0 0 1—5
Chicago............... 0 0 0   0 0 0   0 0 0—0

aFanned for Williams in eighth. Runs batted in—Rath, Roush 2, Duncan, Neale. Two-base hit—Eller. Three-base hits—Roush, Weaver. Sacrifice hits—Daubert 2, Kopf. Sacrifice fly—Duncan. Stolen base—Roush. Left on bases—Chicago 4, Cincinnati 3. Earned runs—Cincinnati 4. Struck out—By Williams 3, by Eller 9. Bases on balls—Off Williams 2, off Mayer 1, off Eller 1. Passed ball—Schalk. Hits—Off Williams 4 in 8 innings, off Mayer 0 in 1 inning. Losing pitcher—Williams. Umpires—Rigler (N.L.), Evans (A.L.), Quigley (N.L.) and Nallin (A.L.). Time—1:45. Attendance—34,379.

Tuesday, October 7—At Cincinnati

Chicago (A.L.)	AB.	R.	H.	O.	A.	E.
J. Collins, rf	3	0	0	2	0	0
aLeibold, rf	1	0	0	0	0	0
E. Collins, 2b	4	0	0	4	6	0
Weaver, 3b	5	2	3	2	1	0
Jackson, lf	4	1	2	1	1	0
Felsch, cf	5	1	2	2	0	1
Gandil, 1b	4	0	1	11	0	0
Risberg, ss	4	1	0	3	5	2
Schalk, c	2	0	1	4	2	0
Kerr, p	3	0	1	1	4	0
Totals	35	5	10	30	19	3

Cincinnati (N.L.)	AB.	R.	H.	O.	A.	E.
Rath, 2b	5	0	1	4	1	0
Daubert, 1b	4	1	2	8	0	0
Groh, 3b	4	0	1	2	2	0
Roush, cf	4	1	1	7	2	0
Duncan, lf	5	0	1	2	0	0
Kopf, ss	4	0	1	1	5	0
Neale, rf	4	1	3	3	0	0
Rariden, c	4	0	1	3	0	0
Ruether, p	2	1	1	0	0	0
Ring, p	2	0	0	0	1	0
Totals	38	4	11	30	11	0

Chicago.............. 0 0 0   0 1 3   0 0 0   1—5
Cincinnati........... 0 0 2   2 0 0   0 0 0   0—4

aGrounded out for J. Collins in seventh. Runs batted in—E. Collins, Jackson, Felsch, Gandil, Schalk, Duncan 2, Ruether. Two-base hits—Groh, Duncan, Ruether, Weaver 2, Felsch. Three-base hit—Neale. Sacrifice hits—Daubert, Kerr. Sacrifice fly—E. Collins. Stolen bases—Leibold, Schalk, Rath, Daubert. Double plays—Jackson and Schalk; Roush and Groh; Risberg, E. Collins and Gandil, Roush and Rath; Kopf and Rath. Left on bases—Cincinnati 8, Chicago 8. Earned runs—Chicago 5, Cincinnati 3. Struck out—By Ring 2, by Kerr 2. Bases on balls—Off Ruether 3, off Ring 3, off Kerr 2. Hit by pitcher—By Kerr (Roush). Hits—Off Ruether 6 in 5 (pitched to three batters in sixth inning), off Ring 4 in 5 innings. Losing pitcher—Ring. Umpires—Evans (A.L.), Quigley (N.L.), Nallin (A.L.) and Rigler (N.L.). Time—2:06. Attendance—32,006.

Wednesday, October 8—At Cincinnati

Chicago (A.L.)	AB.	R.	H.	O.	A.	E.
J. Collins, cf-rf	5	2	3	1	0	0
E. Collins, 2b	4	1	2	3	6	1
Weaver, 3b	4	1	0	2	2	0
Jackson, lf	4	0	2	3	0	0
Felsch, rf-cf	4	0	2	2	0	0
Gandil, 1b	4	0	0	9	0	0
Risberg, ss	4	0	0	3	2	0
Schalk, c	4	0	1	4	1	0
Cicotte, p	4	0	0	0	2	0
Totals	37	4	10	27	13	1

Cincinnati (N.L.)	AB.	R.	H.	O.	A.	E.
Rath, 2b	5	0	1	3	3	1
Daubert, 1b	4	0	0	10	1	1
Groh, 3b	4	1	1	0	2	1
Roush, cf	4	0	0	3	1	1
Duncan, lf	4	0	1	1	0	0
Kopf, ss	4	0	1	2	5	0
Neale, rf	4	0	1	3	0	0
Wingo, c	1	0	1	5	1	0
Sallee, p	1	0	0	0	1	0
Fisher, p	0	0	0	0	1	0
aRuether	1	0	0	0	0	0
Luque, p	1	0	1	0	0	0
bMagee	1	0	1	0	0	0
cSmith	0	0	0	0	0	0
Totals	34	1	7	27	16	4

Chicago............................ 1 0 1   0 2 0   0 0 0—4
Cincinnati..................... 0 0 0   0 0 1   0 0 0—1

aFouled out for Fisher in fifth. bSingled for Luque in ninth. cRan for Magee in ninth. Runs batted in—Jackson 2, Felsch 2, Duncan. Two-base hits—J. Collins, Groh. Sacrifice hit—E. Collins. Double play—Kopf and Daubert. Left on bases—Cincinnati 9, Chicago 7. Earned runs—Chicago 2, Cincinnati 1. Struck out—By Cicotte 4, by Fisher 1, by Luque 5. Bases on balls—Off Cicotte 3. Hits—Off Sallee 9 in 4⅓ innings, off Fisher 0 in ⅔ inning, off Luque 1 in 4 innings. Losing pitcher—Sallee. Umpires—Quigley (N.L.), Nallin (A.L.), Rigler (N.L.) and Evans (A.L.). Time—1:47. Attendance—13,923.

Thursday, October 9—At Chicago

Cincinnati (N.L.)	AB.	R.	H.	O.	A.	E.
Rath, 2b	4	1	2	2	2	0
Daubert, 1b	4	2	2	8	0	0
Groh, 3b	6	2	2	1	1	0
Roush, cf	5	2	3	3	0	1
Duncan, lf	4	1	2	1	0	0
Kopf, ss	3	1	1	1	3	0
Neale, rf	3	0	1	4	0	0
Rariden, c	5	0	2	7	0	1
Eller, p	4	1	1	0	0	0
Totals	38	10	16	27	6	2

Chicago (A.L.)	AB.	R.	H.	O.	A.	E.
Leibold, cf	5	0	1	2	2	0
E. Collins, 2b	5	1	3	4	1	0
Weaver, 3b	5	1	2	1	5	0
Jackson, lf	5	2	3	2	1	0
Felsch, rf	4	0	0	2	0	0
Gandil, 1b	4	1	1	9	0	0
Risberg, ss	3	0	0	2	3	0
Schalk, c	4	0	1	6	3	1
Williams, p	0	0	0	0	0	0
James, p	2	0	0	0	0	0
Wilkinson, p	1	0	0	0	2	0
aMurphy	0	0	0	0	0	0
Totals	38	5	10	27	16	1

Cincinnati................. 4 1 0   0 1 3   0 1 0—10
Chicago..................... 0 0 1   0 0 0   0 4 0— 5

aHit by pitcher for Wilkinson in ninth. Runs batted in—Roush 4, Duncan 3, Neale, Rariden 2, Jackson 3, Gandil. Two-base hits—Roush 2, E. Collins, Duncan, Weaver, Jackson. Three-base hits—Kopf, Gandil. Home run—Jackson. Sacrifice hits—Duncan, Daubert. Stolen bases—Neale, Rath, Rariden, E. Collins. Left on bases—Cincinnati 12, Chicago 8. Earned runs—Cincinnati 7, Chicago 4. Struck out—By James 2, by Wilkinson 2, by Eller 6. Bases on balls—Off James 3, off Wilkinson 4, off Eller 1. Hit by pitcher—By James (Eller), by Wilkinson (Roush), by Eller (Murphy). Hits—Off Williams 4 in ⅓ inning, off James 8 in 4⅔ innings (pitched to two batters in sixth inning), off Wilkinson 4 in 4 innings. Losing pitcher—Williams. Umpires—Quigley (N.L.), Nallin (A.L.), Rigler (N.L.) and Evans (A.L.). Time—2:27. Attendance—32,930.

COMPOSITE BATTING AVERAGES
Cincinnati Reds

Player-Position	G.	AB.	R.	H.	2B.	3B.	HR.	RBI.	BA.
Ruether, p-ph	3	6	2	4	1	2	0	4	.667
Wingo, c	3	7	1	4	0	0	0	1	.571
Fisher, p	2	2	0	1	0	0	0	0	.500
Magee, ph	2	2	0	1	0	0	0	0	.500
Neale, rf	8	28	3	10	1	1	0	4	.357
Eller, p	2	7	2	2	1	0	0	0	.286
Duncan, lf	8	26	3	7	2	0	0	8	.269
Daubert, 1b	8	29	4	7	0	1	0	1	.241
Rath, 2b	8	31	5	7	1	0	0	2	.226
Kopf, ss	8	27	3	6	0	2	0	3	.222
Roush, cf	8	28	6	6	2	1	0	7	.214
Rariden, c	5	19	0	4	0	0	0	2	.211
Groh, 3b	8	29	6	5	2	0	0	0	.172
Smith, pr	1	0	0	0	0	0	0	0	.000
Sallee, p	2	4	0	0	0	0	0	0	.000
Luque, p	2	1	0	0	0	0	0	0	.000
Ring, p	2	5	0	0	0	0	0	0	.000
Totals	8	251	35	64	10	7	0	34	.255

Chicago White Sox

Player-Position	G.	AB.	R.	H.	2B.	3B.	HR.	RBI.	BA.
McMullin, ph	2	2	0	1	0	0	0	0	.500
Jackson, lf	8	32	5	12	3	0	1	6	.375
Weaver, 3b	8	34	4	11	4	1	0	0	.324
Schalk, c	8	23	1	7	0	0	0	2	.304
J. Collins, rf-cf	4	16	2	4	1	0	0	0	.250
Gandil, 1b	8	30	1	7	0	1	0	5	.233
E. Collins, 2b	8	31	2	7	1	0	0	1	.226
Williams, p	3	5	0	1	0	0	0	0	.200
Felsch, cf-rf	8	26	2	5	1	0	0	3	.192
Kerr, p	2	6	0	1	0	0	0	0	.167
Risberg, ss	8	25	3	2	0	1	0	0	.080
Leibold, rf-ph	5	18	0	1	0	0	0	0	.056
Cicotte, p	3	8	0	0	0	0	0	0	.000
Wilkinson, p	2	2	0	0	0	0	0	0	.000
Lynn, c	1	1	0	0	0	0	0	0	.000
Murphy, ph	3	2	0	0	0	0	0	0	.000
Lowdermilk, p	1	0	0	0	0	0	0	0	.000
Mayer, p	1	0	0	0	0	0	0	0	.000
James, p	1	2	0	0	0	0	0	0	.000
Totals	8	263	20	59	10	3	1	17	.224

COMPOSITE PITCHING AVERAGES
Cincinnati Reds

Pitcher	G.	IP.	H.	R.	E.	SO.	BB.	W.	L.	ERA.
Luque	2	5	1	0	0	6	0	0	0	0.00
Ring	2	14	7	1	1	4	6	1	1	0.64
Sallee	2	13⅓	19	6	2	2	1	1	1	1.35
Eller	2	18	13	5	4	15	2	2	0	2.00
Fisher	2	7⅔	7	3	2	2	2	0	1	2.35
Ruether	2	14	12	5	4	1	4	1	0	2.57
Totals	8	72	59	20	13	30	15	5	3	1.63

Chicago White Sox

Pitcher	G.	IP.	H.	R.	E.	SO.	BB.	W.	L.	ERA.
Mayer	1	1	0	1	0	0	1	0	0	0.00
Kerr	2	19	14	4	3	6	3	2	0	1.42
Wilkinson	2	7⅓	9	4	2	3	4	0	0	2.45
Cicotte	3	21⅔	19	9	7	7	5	1	2	2.91
James	1	4⅔	8	4	3	2	3	0	0	5.79
Williams	3	16⅓	12	12	12	4	8	0	3	6.61
Lowdermilk	1	1	2	1	1	0	1	0	0	9.00
Totals	8	71	64	35	28	22	25	3	5	3.55

SERIES OF 1920

	W.	L.	Pct.
Cleveland A. L.	**5**	**2**	**.714**
Brooklyn N. L.	**2**	**5**	**.286**

The Cleveland Indians, under the inspired leadership of the former Red Sox outfield star, Tris Speaker, won the 1920 American League pennant after a hot three-cornered race with the White Sox and Yankees. Only three games separated the three clubs at the close of the race. The Tribe brilliantly topped off the victory with a 5 to 2 triumph in the World Series over the Brooklyn Dodgers, who won their second pennant in five years under the direction of Wilbert Robinson, the Dodgers fighting off a strong late-season threat by the Giants. Brooklyn got off to a good start in the classic by winning two games out of three at Ebbets Field, but then blew four straight decisions on the field of their opponents.

Stanley Coveleski, husky Polish spitballer from the Pennsylvania mining country, was the pitching star of the Series, with the greatest exhibition since Christy Mathewson, another Pennsylvanian, blanked the Athletics three times in 1905. Coveleski gave up only one more hit than Matty—15—in defeating the Flatbushers three times, but yielded two runs. In each of his three victories, Stan held the Dodgers to five hits. Coveleski walked two men, against only one by Mathewson in 1905.

An important victory for Speaker was turned in by Walter (Duster) Mails, a Dodger castoff. With Cleveland ahead, three games to two, Mails prevented Brooklyn from tying it up by defeating Sherry Smith in a lefthanded pitching duel, 1 to 0. Mails hurled a three-hitter. Cleveland's other victory was chalked up by Jim Bagby, a 31-game winner that season, who lost the second game, 3 to 0, and then gave up 13 hits in winning an 8 to 1 decision in the fifth game. Jim helped win this one with a homer and single, his round-tripper being the first by a World Series pitcher.

As in 1916, Robinson leaned heavily on his lefthanders, Rube Marquard and Smith, both of whom pitched in two games. The Rube was charged with one defeat, while Smith broke even, losing a heart-breaker in his second start to Mails. After opening his World Series career with a shutout, Burleigh Grimes lost his next two starts. Elmer Smith tagged him for the first World Series grand-slam homer. It came in the first inning of the fifth game. Leon Cadore, who pitched the 26-inning tie against the Braves on May 1, 1920, was Brooklyn's losing pitcher in the fourth game.

Bill Wambsganss, Cleveland's second baseman, made the only unassisted triple play of World Series history in the fifth game. With both Pete Kilduff on second and Otto Miller on first on the move, Clarence Mitchell, Brooklyn pitcher, who had succeeded Grimes, hit a sharp line drive to Wambsganss in the fifth inning. Bill, who was running over to cover his bag, stepped on second base, retiring Kilduff, and then wheeled around and tagged Miller, who had run down from first. Mitchell had the unfortunate experience of hitting into five putouts in his last two times at bat, as he later grounded into a double play.

Steve O'Neill and Charley Jamieson led the Indians at bat, with .333, the same average as was chalked up by Zack Wheat, top man for the Dodgers. Joe Wood, who had won three games as a pitcher for the Red Sox in 1912, played right field for Cleveland against Brooklyn's lefthanders and hit .200.

With shortstop Ray Chapman of Cleveland having been killed by being hit on the temple by a pitched ball hurled by Carl Mays late in the season, the National Commission, with the consent of the Brooklyn club, gave Cleveland permission to play Joe Sewell, procured after the September 1 deadline, at shortstop. The young Alabama collegian hit only .174 and was guilty of six errors. After third baseman Jimmy Johnston of the Dodgers was injured, Cleveland, in turn, permitted Manager Robinson to play Jack Sheehan, who also joined the Brooklyn club in September.

The 1920 Series was played only a fortnight after the 1919 Black Sox scandal broke. Nevertheless, there was the usual interest, and though both clubs had small parks they played to capacity crowds. It was the last Series played under the jurisdiction of the National Commission.

Although the Series went seven games, with the attendance 178,737 and receipts $564,800, the National Commission claimed the leagues and clubs lost approximately $100,000. Each Cleveland share was worth $4,168 and each Brooklyn share $2,419.60. The box scores:

Tuesday, October 5—At Brooklyn

Cleveland (A.L.)	AB.	R.	H.	O.	A.	E.
Evans, lf	2	0	0	1	0	0
bJamieson, lf	1	0	0	0	0	0
Wambsganss, 2b	3	0	0	0	2	0
Speaker, cf	4	0	0	4	0	0
Burns, 1b	3	1	1	9	1	0
eE. Smith rf	1	0	0	0	0	0
Gardner, 3b	4	0	0	1	3	0
Wood, rf	2	2	1	4	0	0
fW. Johnston, 1b	1	0	0	0	1	0
Sewell, ss	3	0	1	3	4	0
O'Neill, c	3	0	2	3	0	0
Coveleski, p	3	0	0	2	2	0
Totals	30	3	5	27	13	0

Brooklyn (N.L.)	AB.	R.	H.	O.	A.	E.
Olson, ss	3	0	2	0	3	0
J. Johnston, 3b	3	0	0	1	3	0
Griffith, rf	4	0	1	1	0	0
Wheat, lf	4	1	1	4	0	0
Myers, cf	4	0	0	1	0	0
Konetchy, 1b	4	0	0	12	1	1
Kilduff, 2b	3	0	0	1	3	0
Krueger, c	3	0	0	7	1	0
Marquard, p	1	0	0	0	0	0
aLamar	1	0	0	0	0	0
Mamaux, p	0	0	0	0	1	0
cMitchell	1	0	1	0	0	0
dNeis	0	0	0	0	0	0
Cadore, p	0	0	0	0	1	0
Totals	31	1	5	27	13	1

Cleveland .... 0 2 0   1 0 0   0 0 0—3
Brooklyn .... 0 0 0   0 0 0   1 0 0—1

aPopped out for Marquard in sixth. bGrounded out for Evans in eighth. cSingled for Mamaux in eighth. dRan for Mitchell in eighth. eGrounded out for Burns in ninth. fGrounded out for Wood in ninth. Runs batted in—O'Neill 2, Konetchy. Two base hits—O'Neill 2, Wood, Wheat. Sacrifice hits—Wambsganss, J. Johnston. Double play—Konetchy, Krueger and J. Johnston. Left on bases—Brooklyn 5, Cleveland 3. Earned runs—Brooklyn 1, Cleveland 1. Struck out—By Marquard 4, by Mamaux 3, by Coveleski 3. Bases on balls—Off Marquard 2, off Coveleski 1. Hits—Off Marquard 5 in 6 innings, off Mamaux 0 in 2 innings, off Ca-

1920 WORLD SERIES

dore 0 in 1 inning. Losing pitcher—Marquard. Umpires—Klem (N.L.), Connolly (A.L.), O'Day (N.L.) and Dinneen (A.L.). Time—1:41. Attendance—23,573.

Wednesday, October 6—At Brooklyn

Cleveland (A.L.)	AB.	R.	H.	O.	A.	E.
Jamieson, lf	4	0	1	2	0	0
Wambsganss, 2b	3	0	0	3	0	0
bBurns	0	0	0	0	0	0
Lunte, 2b	0	0	0	0	0	0
Speaker, cf	3	0	2	2	0	0
E. Smith, rf	4	0	0	3	0	0
Gardner, 3b	3	0	2	1	2	0
W. Johnston, 1b	4	0	0	3	3	0
Sewell, ss	4	0	0	1	1	0
O'Neill, c	4	0	1	7	2	0
Bagby, p	2	0	0	2	1	1
aGraney	1	0	0	0	0	0
Uhle, p	0	0	0	0	0	0
cNunamaker	1	0	1	0	0	0
Totals	33	0	7	24	9	1

Brooklyn (N.L.)	AB.	R.	H.	O.	A.	E.
Olson, ss	4	1	1	3	2	0
J. Johnston, 3b	4	1	1	0	1	0
Griffith, rf	4	0	2	3	0	0
Wheat, lf	3	0	1	3	0	0
Myers, cf	3	0	1	2	0	0
Konetchy, 1b	3	0	0	10	1	0
Kilduff, 2b	3	0	0	2	3	0
Miller, c	3	0	0	3	1	0
Grimes, p	3	1	1	1	4	0
Totals	30	3	7	27	12	0

Cleveland .... 0 0 0 0 0 0 0 0 0—0
Brooklyn .... 1 0 1 0 1 0 0 0 *—3

aStruck out for Bagby in seventh. bWalked for Wambsganss in eighth. cSingled for Uhle in ninth. Runs batted in—Griffith 2, Wheat. Two-base hits—Wheat, Gardner, Griffith, Speaker. Stolen base—J. Johnston. Double play—Gardner, O'Neill, W. Johnston and O'Neill. Left on bases—Cleveland 10, Brooklyn 4. Earned runs—Brooklyn 2. Struck out—By Uhle 3, by Grimes 2. Bases on balls—Off Bagby 1, off Grimes 4. Hits—Off Bagby 7 in 6 innings, off Uhle 0 in 2 innings. Losing pitcher—Bagby. Umpires—Connolly (A.L.), O'Day (N.L.), Dinneen (A.L.) and Klem (N.L.). Time—1:55. Attendance—22,559.

Thursday, October 7—At Brooklyn

Cleveland (A.L.)	AB.	R.	H.	O.	A.	E.
Evans, lf	4	0	0	2	0	0
Wambsganss, 2b	3	0	0	2	2	0
Speaker, cf	4	1	1	2	0	0
Burns, 1b	3	0	0	12	0	0
Gardner, 3b	3	0	0	0	0	0
Wood, rf	3	0	0	1	0	0
Sewell, ss	2	0	0	2	3	1
O'Neill, c	3	0	2	2	2	0
bJamieson	0	0	0	0	0	0
Uhle, p	0	0	0	0	1	0
Caldwell, p	0	0	0	0	0	0
Mails, p	2	0	0	1	3	0
cNunamaker, c	1	0	0	0	0	0
Totals	28	1	3	24	11	1

Brooklyn (N.L.)	AB.	R.	H.	O.	A.	E.
Olson, ss	2	1	1	0	6	0
J. Johnston, 3b	3	0	0	0	4	0
Griffith, rf	1	1	0	2	0	0
aNeis, rf	3	0	0	0	0	0
Wheat, lf	4	0	3	1	0	1
Myers, cf	4	0	2	1	0	0
Konetchy, 1b	3	0	0	17	2	0
Kilduff, 2b	1	0	0	2	6	0
Miller, c	1	0	0	2	0	0
S. Smith, p	3	0	0	2	2	0
Totals	25	2	6	27	20	1

Cleveland .... 0 0 0 1 0 0 0 0 0—1
Brooklyn .... 2 0 0 0 0 0 0 0 *—2

aGrounded out for Griffith in third. bRan for O'Neill in eighth. cHit into double play for Mails in eighth. Runs batted in—Wheat, Myers. Two-base hit—Speaker. Sacrifice hits—J. Johnston, Kilduff, Miller. Double plays—Mails and Burns; Olson, Kilduff and Konetchy; Wambsganss, Sewell and Burns; J. Johnston, Kilduff and Konetchy. Left on bases—Brooklyn 7, Cleveland 2. Earned runs—Brooklyn 1, Cleveland 0. Struck out—By Mails 2, by S. Smith 2. Bases on balls—Off Caldwell 1, off Mails 4, off S. Smith 2. Hits—Off Caldwell 2 in ⅓ inning, off Mails 3 in 6⅔ innings, off Uhle 1 in 1 inning. Losing pitcher—Caldwell. Umpires—O'Day (N.L.), Dinneen (A.L.), Klem (N.L.) and Connolly (A.L.). Time—1:47. Attendance—25,088.

Saturday, October 9—At Cleveland

Brooklyn (N.L.)	AB.	R.	H.	O.	A.	E.
Olson, ss	4	0	1	1	3	0
J. Johnston, 3b	4	1	2	1	0	0
fNeis	0	0	0	0	0	0
Griffith, rf	4	0	1	1	0	0
Wheat, lf	4	0	0	0	0	1
Myers, cf	3	0	0	6	1	0
Konetchy, 1b	2	0	0	5	0	0
Kilduff, 2b	3	0	1	2	3	0
Miller, c	3	0	0	7	0	0
Cadore, p	0	0	0	1	0	0
Mamaux, p	1	0	0	0	0	0
Marquard, p	0	0	0	0	1	0
dLamar	1	0	0	0	0	0
Pfeffer, p	1	0	0	0	0	0
Totals	30	1	5	24	8	1

Cleveland (A.L.)	AB.	R.	H.	O.	A.	E.
Jamieson, lf	2	0	0	1	0	0
cEvans, lf	3	0	1	0	0	0
Wambsganss, 2b	4	2	2	4	6	0
Speaker, cf	5	2	2	3	0	0
E. Smith, rf	1	0	1	1	0	0
aBurns, 1b	2	0	1	7	0	1
Gardner, 3b	3	0	1	2	3	0
W. Johnston, 1b	1	0	0	4	0	0
bWood, rf	2	0	0	0	0	0
eGraney, rf	1	0	0	0	0	0
Sewell, ss	4	0	2	1	7	1
O'Neill, c	2	0	1	4	0	0
Coveleski, p	4	1	1	0	2	0
Totals	34	5	12	27	18	2

Brooklyn .... 0 0 0 1 0 0 0 0 0—1
Cleveland .... 2 0 2 0 0 1 0 0 *—5

aSingled for E. Smith in third. bFlied out for W. Johnston in third. cFlied out for Jamieson in fourth. dGrounded out for Marquard in sixth. eForced runner for Wood in seventh. fRan for J. Johnston in ninth. Runs batted in—Griffith, Wambsganss, E. Smith, Burns, Gardner. Two-base hit—Griffith. Sacrifice fly—Gardner. Double plays—Myers, Olson and Kilduff; Sewell, Wambsganss and Burns; Gardner, Wambsganss and Burns. Left on bases—Cleveland 10, Brooklyn 3. Earned runs—Cleveland 4, Brooklyn 1. Struck out—By Cadore 1, by Mamaux 1, by Coveleski 4, Marquard 2, by Pfeffer 1. Bases on balls—Off Cadore 1, off Marquard 1, off Coveleski 1, off Pfeffer 2. Wild pitch—Pfeffer. Hits—Off Cadore 4 in 1 (pitched to two batters in second inning), off Mamaux 2 in 1 (pitched to two batters in third inning), off Marquard 2 in 3 innings, off Pfeffer 4 in 3 innings. Passed ball—Miller. Losing pitcher—Cadore. Umpires—Dinneen (A.L.), Klem (N.L.), Connolly (A.L.) and O'Day (N.L.). Time—1:45. Attendance—25,734.

Sunday, October 10—At Cleveland

Brooklyn (N.L.)	AB.	R.	H.	O.	A.	E.
Olson, ss	4	0	2	3	5	0
Sheehan, 3b	3	0	1	1	1	1
Griffith, rf	4	0	0	0	0	0
Wheat, lf	4	1	2	3	0	0
Myers, cf	4	0	2	0	0	0
Konetchy, 1b	4	0	2	9	2	0
Kilduff, 2b	4	0	1	5	6	0
Miller, c	2	0	2	0	1	0
Krueger, c	2	0	1	2	1	0
Grimes, p	1	0	0	0	1	0
Mitchell, p	2	0	0	1	0	0
Totals	34	1	13	24	17	1

Cleveland (A.L.)	AB.	R.	H.	O.	A.	E.
Jamieson, lf	4	1	2	2	1	0
aGraney, lf	1	0	0	0	0	0
Wambsganss, 2b	5	1	1	7	2	0
Speaker, cf	3	2	1	1	0	0
E. Smith, rf	4	1	3	0	0	0
Gardner, 3b	4	0	1	2	2	1
W. Johnston, 1b	3	1	2	9	0	0
Sewell, ss	3	0	0	2	4	0
O'Neill, c	2	1	0	3	1	1
Thomas, c	0	0	0	1	0	0
Bagby, p	4	1	2	0	2	0
Totals	33	8	12	27	13	2

Brooklyn .... 0 0 0 0 0 0 0 0 1—1
Cleveland .... 4 0 0 3 1 0 0 0 *—8

aStruck out for Jamieson in eighth. Runs batted in—E. Smith 4, Bagby 3, Gardner, Konetchy. Three-base hits—Konetchy, E. Smith. Home Runs—E. Smith, Bagby. Sacrifice hits—Sheehan, W. Johnston. Double plays—Olson, Kilduff and Konetchy; Jamieson and O'Neill; Gardner, Wambsganss and W. Johnston; W. Johnston, Sewell and W. Johnston. Triple play—Wambsganss, unassisted. Left on bases—Brooklyn 7, Cleveland 6. Earned runs—Cleveland 7, Brooklyn 1. Struck out—By Bagby 3, by Mitchell 1. Bases on balls—Off Grimes 1, off Mitchell 3. Wild pitch—Bagby. Hits—Off Grimes 9 in 3⅓ innings, off Mitchell 3 in 4⅔ innings. Passed ball—Miller. Losing pitcher—Grimes. Umpires—Klem (N.L.), Connolly (A.L.), O'Day (N.L.) and Dineen (A.L.). Time—1:49. Attendance—26,884.

Monday, October 11—At Cleveland

Brooklyn (N.L.)	AB.	R.	H.	O.	A.	E.
Olson, ss	4	0	1	4	1	0
Sheehan, 3b	4	0	0	0	3	0
Neis, rf	2	0	0	3	0	0
aKrueger	1	0	0	0	0	0
Griffith, rf	0	0	0	0	0	0
Wheat, lf	4	0	0	2	0	0
Myers, cf	4	0	1	1	0	0
Konetchy, 1b	3	0	1	9	0	0
bMcCabe	0	0	0	0	0	0
Kilduff, 2b	4	0	0	3	2	0
Miller, c	3	0	0	3	3	0
S. Smith, p	3	0	0	0	3	0
Totals	32	0	3	24	12	0

Cleveland (A.L.)	AB.	R.	H.	O.	A.	E.
Evans, lf	4	0	3	4	0	0
Wambsganss, 2b	4	0	0	1	2	0
Speaker, cf	3	1	1	3	0	0
Burns, 1b	2	0	1	10	0	0
Gardner, 3b	3	0	0	2	2	1
Wood, rf	3	0	1	2	0	0
Sewell, ss	3	0	1	2	3	2
O'Neill, c	3	0	0	3	2	0
Mails, p	3	0	0	0	1	0
Totals	28	1	7	27	10	3

Brooklyn .... 0 0 0 0 0 0 0 0 0—0
Cleveland .... 0 0 0 0 0 1 0 0 *—1

aForced runner for Neis in eighth. bRan for Konetchy in ninth. Run batted in—Burns. Two-base hits—Burns, Olson. Left on bases—Brooklyn 7, Cleveland 4. Earned runs—Cleveland 1. Struck out—By Mails 4, by S. Smith 1. Bases on balls—Off Mails 2, off S. Smith 1. Umpires—Connolly (A.L.), O'Day (N.L.), Dinneen (A.L.) and Klem (N.L.). Time—1:34. Attendance—27,194.

Tuesday, October 12—At Cleveland

Brooklyn (N.L.)	AB.	R.	H.	O.	A.	E.
Olson, ss	4	0	0	1	1	0
Sheehan, 3b	4	0	1	2	1	1
Griffith, rf	4	0	3	0	0	0
Wheat, lf	4	0	2	3	0	0
Myers, cf	4	0	0	3	0	0
Konetchy, 1b	4	0	1	8	0	0
Kilduff, 2b	3	0	0	1	4	0
Miller, c	2	0	0	2	1	0
bLamar	1	0	0	0	0	0
Krueger, c	0	0	0	1	0	0
Grimes, p	2	0	1	0	2	1
cSchmandt	1	0	0	0	0	0
Mamaux, p	0	0	0	0	0	0
Totals	33	0	5	24	9	2

Cleveland (A.L.)	AB.	R.	H.	O.	A.	E.
Jamieson, lf	4	1	2	3	0	0
Wambsganss, 2b	4	0	1	4	3	0
Speaker, cf	3	1	1	3	0	0
E. Smith, rf	3	0	0	3	1	0
Gardner, 3b	4	1	1	1	3	0
W. Johnston, 1b	2	0	1	11	1	0
Sewell, ss	4	0	0	6	2	2
O'Neill, c	4	0	1	0	0	0
Coveleski, p	3	1	0	0	1	1
Totals	31	3	7	a26	15	3

Brooklyn .... 0 0 0 0 0 0 0 0 0—0
Cleveland .... 0 0 0 1 1 0 1 0 *—3

aOlson out; hit by batted ball in third. bGrounded out for Miller in seventh. cGrounded out for Grimes in eighth. Runs batted in—Jamieson, Speaker. Two-base hits—O'Neill, Jamieson. Three-base hit—Speaker. Stolen bases—W. Johnston, Jamieson. Left on bases—Cleveland 8, Brooklyn 6. Earned runs—Cleveland 2, Brooklyn 0. Struck out—By Coveleski 1, by Grimes 2, by Mamaux 1. Bases on balls—Off Grimes 4. Hits—Off Grimes 7 in 7 innings, off Mamaux 0 in 1 inning. Losing pitcher—Grimes. Umpires—O'Day (N.L.), Dinneen (A.L.), Klem (N.L.) and Connolly (A.L.). Time—1:55. Attendance—27,525.

COMPOSITE BATTING AVERAGES
Cleveland Indians

Player-Position	G.	AB.	R.	H.	2B.	3B.	HR.	RBI.	BA.
Nunamaker, ph-c	2	2	0	1	0	0	0	0	.500
O'Neill, c	7	21	1	7	3	0	0	2	.333
Bagby, p	2	6	1	2	0	0	1	3	.333
Jamieson, ph-lf	6	15	2	5	1	0	0	1	.333
Speaker, cf	7	25	6	8	2	1	0	1	.320
E. Smith, ph-rf	5	13	1	4	0	1	1	5	.308
Evans, lf-ph	4	13	0	4	0	0	0	0	.308

Player-Position	G.	AB.	R.	H.	2B.	3B.	HR.	RBI.	BA.
Burns, 1b-ph	5	10	1	3	1	0	0	3	.300
W. Jo'ton, ph-1b	5	11	1	3	0	0	0	0	.273
Gardner, 3b	7	24	1	5	1	0	0	2	.208
Wood, rf-ph	4	10	2	2	1	0	0	0	.200
Sewell, ss	7	23	0	4	0	0	0	0	.174
Wambsganss, 2b	7	26	3	4	0	0	0	1	.154
Coveleski, p	3	10	2	1	0	0	0	0	.100
Lunte, 2b	1	0	0	0	0	0	0	0	.000
Graney, ph-rf-lf	3	3	0	0	0	0	0	0	.000
Uhle, p	2	0	0	0	0	0	0	0	.000
Caldwell, p	1	0	0	0	0	0	0	0	.000
Mails, p	2	5	0	0	0	0	0	0	.000
Thomas, c	1	0	0	0	0	0	0	0	.000
Totals	7	217	21	53	9	2	2	18	.244

Brooklyn Dodgers

Player-Position	G.	AB.	R.	H.	2B.	3B.	HR.	RBI.	BA.
Mitchell, ph-p	2	3	0	1	0	0	0	0	.333
Grimes, p	3	6	1	2	0	0	0	0	.333
Wheat, lf	7	27	2	9	2	0	0	2	.333
Olson, ss	7	25	2	8	1	0	0	0	.320
Myers, cf	7	26	0	6	0	0	0	1	.231
J. Johnston, 3b	4	14	2	3	0	0	0	0	.214
Griffith, rf	7	21	1	4	2	0	0	3	.190
Sheehan, 3b	3	11	0	2	0	0	0	0	.182
Konetchy, 1b	7	23	0	4	0	1	0	2	.174
Krueger, c-ph	4	6	1	0	0	0	0	0	.167
Miller, c	6	14	0	2	0	0	0	0	.143
Kilduff, 2b	7	21	0	2	0	0	0	0	.095
Lamar, ph	3	3	0	0	0	0	0	0	.000
Neis, pr-rf	4	5	0	0	0	0	0	0	.000
Marquard, p	2	1	0	0	0	0	0	0	.000
Mamaux, p	3	1	0	0	0	0	0	0	.000
Cadore, p	2	0	0	0	0	0	0	0	.000
S. Smith, p	2	6	0	0	0	0	0	0	.000
Pfeffer, p	1	1	0	0	0	0	0	0	.000
McCabe, pr	1	0	0	0	0	0	0	0	.000
Schmandt, ph	1	1	0	0	0	0	0	0	.000
Totals	7	215	8	44	5	1	0	8	.205

COMPOSITE PITCHING AVERAGES
Cleveland Indians

Pitcher	G.	IP.	H.	R.	E.	SO.	BB.	W.	L.	ERA.
Mails	2	15⅔	6	0	0	6	6	1	0	0.00
Uhle	2	3	1	0	0	3	0	0	0	0.00
Coveleski	3	27	15	2	2	8	2	3	0	0.67
Bagby	2	15	20	4	3	3	1	1	1	1.80
Caldwell	1	⅓	2	1	0	1	0	0	1	27.00
Totals	7	61	44	8	6	20	10	5	2	0.89

Brooklyn Dodgers

Pitcher	G.	IP.	H.	R.	E.	SO.	BB.	W.	L.	ERA.
Mitchell	1	4⅔	3	1	0	1	3	0	0	0.00
S. Smith	2	17	10	2	1	3	3	1	1	0.53
Marquard	2	9	7	3	1	6	3	0	1	1.00
Pfeffer	1	3	4	1	1	1	2	0	0	3.00
Grimes	3	19⅓	23	10	9	4	9	1	2	4.19
Mamaux	3	4	2	2	2	5	0	0	0	4.50
Cadore	2	2	4	2	2	1	1	0	1	9.00
Totals	7	59	53	21	16	21	21	2	5	2.44

SERIES OF 1921

	W.	L.	Pct.
New York N. L.	5	3	.625
New York A. L.	3	5	.375

For the first time, the Series was played under the administration of Commissioner K. M. Landis; for the first time it was an all-New York affair; for the first time the team winning the first two games eventually lost, and for the second time all the games were staged in one city, the Giants defeating the Yankees, five out of eight. All of the games were played at the Polo Grounds, then the home park of both clubs.

The American Leaguers, piloted by Miller Huggins, captured the first two games by identical scores, 3 to 0, and also won the fifth, but John McGraw's Giants then won the last three in succession. The Yanks were handicapped by losing Babe Ruth after the fifth game because of an infected arm and wrenched knee, and in the last two contests they also lost Mike McNally with a disabled throwing arm.

Ruth hit a homer in the fourth game, led the Yankee regulars in batting with .313, although striking out eight times; drew five walks and stole second and third in succession in the second contest.

McNally stole home in the first game and Bob Meusel in the second. An error by Roger Peckinpaugh in the final game let in the winning run. George Kelly struck out ten times. Jess Barnes, after relieving Fred Toney, accounted for seven consecutive outs through strikeouts, three walks intervening, in the sixth game, beating Hod Eller's record, and Frankie Frisch had four hits in four times at bat in the first tilt.

Jess Barnes won two games for the Giants, Phil Douglas captured two and lost one, and Art Nehf won one and lost two, yielding only four hits, for a victory in the payoff game.

Waite Hoyt won two and lost one for the Yankees, pitching a two-hit shutout in the second contest; Waite gave up only two runs, both unearned, and tied Christy Mathewson's 1905 record by pitching 27 innings in one Series without yielding an earned run. Carl Mays won one and lost two, his triumph being a shutout in the first tilt, and Bob Shawkey and Jack Quinn each lost one.

In the first game, not a fly ball was hit to the Giants' outfield off Douglas and Barnes. However, Elmer Miller led off the first inning with a single and, after a sacrifice, Ruth singled to give Mays the only run he really needed to win. McNally stole home in the fifth. Meusel smashed what should have been a triple in the sixth, but was called out for failing to tag first base, but Peckinpaugh scored with the third Yankee run. Hoyt not only held the Giants to two singles in the second game, but also drove in his club's first run with a base hit in the fourth inning. Hoyt also won the fifth game, 3 to 1, but was defeated, 1 to 0, by Nehf in the finale.

The decisive game had a dramatic ending.

With Aaron Ward on first, and one down for the Bombers, Johnny Rawlings made a sensational stop off Frank Baker, throwing the former Mackman out at first, and Kelly cut down Ward at third on a perfect throw to Frisch when he tried to advance two bases on the play.

Attendance and financial records were broken, 269,976 paying $900,233. The split among the second and third-place clubs, resumed in 1919, was continued under the new administration and record-breaking dividends of $5,265 went to each Giant and $3,510 to each Yankee. The box scores:

Wednesday, Oct. 5—At Polo Grounds

New York (A.L.)	AB	R	H	O	A	E
Miller, cf	4	1	1	0	0	0
Peckinpaugh, ss	3	1	1	1	9	0
Ruth, lf	3	0	1	4	0	0
R. Meusel, rf	4	0	0	1	0	0
Pipp, 1b	2	0	0	17	0	0
Ward, 2b	3	0	1	3	5	0
McNally, 3b	4	1	2	0	0	0
Schang, c	2	0	0	1	1	0
Mays, p	3	0	1	0	3	0
Totals	28	3	7	27	18	0

New York (N.L.)	AB	R	H	O	A	E
Burns, cf	4	0	0	0	0	0
Bancroft, ss	4	0	0	1	3	0
Frisch, 3b	4	0	4	1	4	0
Youngs, rf	3	0	0	0	0	0
Kelly, 1b	4	0	0	14	1	0
E. Meusel, lf	3	0	0	0	1	0
Rawlings, 2b	2	0	1	3	5	0
Snyder, c	3	0	0	7	1	0
Douglas, p	2	0	0	0	3	0
bSmith	1	0	0	0	0	0
Barnes, p	0	0	0	0	0	0
Totals	30	0	5	a26	18	0

Yankees .... 1 0 0 0 1 1 0 0 0—3
Giants .... 0 0 0 0 0 0 0 0 0—0

aSchang out; hit by batted ball in seventh. bFlied out for Douglas in eighth. Runs batted in—Ruth, R. Meusel. Two-base hit—McNally. Three-base hit—Frisch. Sacrifice hits—Peckinpaugh, Pipp, Schang, Youngs. Stolen bases—McNally 2, Frisch. Double plays—Frisch, Rawlings and Kelly; Peckinpaugh, Ward and Pipp. Left on bases—Yankees 5, Giants 6. Earned runs—Yankees 3. Struck out—By Mays 1, by Douglas 6, by Barnes 1. Bases on balls—Off Douglas 4. Hit by pitcher—By Mays (Rawlings). Hits—Off Douglas 5 in 8 innings, off Barnes 2 in 1 inning. Passed ball—Snyder. Losing pitcher—Douglas. Umpires—Rigler (N.L.), Moriarty (A.L.), Quigley (N.L.) and Chill (A.L.). Time—1:38. Attendance—30,202.

Thursday, Oct. 6—At Polo Grounds

New York (N.L.)	AB	R	H	O	A	E
Burns, cf	3	0	0	1	0	0
Bancroft, ss	4	0	0	3	3	0
Frisch, 3b	4	0	1	3	2	1
Youngs, rf	2	0	0	2	0	0
Kelly, 1b	4	0	0	12	2	0
E. Meusel, lf	2	0	0	0	0	0
Rawlings, 2b	3	0	1	2	2	0
Smith, c	3	0	0	1	1	1
Nehf, p	2	0	0	0	3	1
Totals	27	0	2	24	13	3

New York (A.L.)	AB	R	H	O	A	E
Miller, cf	3	0	0	1	0	0
Peckinpaugh, ss	3	0	0	3	1	0
Ruth, lf	1	1	0	0	0	0
R. Meusel, rf	4	1	1	1	0	0
Pipp, 1b	3	0	0	14	0	0
Ward, 2b	4	1	1	4	7	0
McNally, 3b	3	0	0	0	3	0
Schang, c	2	0	0	4	2	0
Hoyt, p	3	0	1	0	2	0
Totals	26	3	3	27	15	0

Giants .... 0 0 0 0 0 0 0 0 0—0
Yankees .... 0 0 0 1 0 0 0 2 *—3

Runs batted in—Pipp, Hoyt. Stolen bases—Ruth 2, R. Meusel. Double plays—Frisch and Rawlings; Rawlings, Kelly and Smith; McNally, Ward and Pipp. Left on bases—Yankees 6, Giants 5. Earned runs—Yankees 1. Struck out—By Hoyt 5. Bases on balls—Off Nehf 7, off Hoyt 5. Passed ball—Smith. Umpires—Moriarty (A.L.), Quigley (N.L.), Chill (A.L.) and Rigler (N.L.). Time—1:55. Attendance—34,939.

Friday, October 7—At Polo Grounds

New York (A.L.)	AB	R	H	O	A	E
Miller, cf	5	1	1	2	0	0
Peckinpaugh, ss	3	1	0	4	2	0
Ruth, lf	3	0	1	1	0	0
aFewster, lf	0	1	0	0	0	0
R. Meusel, rf	3	0	2	1	0	0
Pipp, 1b	3	0	0	12	0	0
Ward, 2b	4	0	2	1	5	0
McNally, 3b	3	0	0	0	2	0
Schang, c	2	1	1	2	2	0
Devormer, c	1	0	0	1	0	0
Shawkey, p	1	1	1	0	0	0
Quinn, p	2	0	0	0	1	0
Collins, p	0	0	0	0	0	0
Rogers, p	0	0	0	0	1	0
bBaker	1	0	0	0	0	0
Totals	31	5	8	24	13	0

New York (N.L.)	AB	R	H	O	A	E
Burns, cf	6	1	4	1	0	0
Bancroft, ss	5	1	1	3	2	0
Frisch, 3b	2	3	2	2	1	0
Youngs, rf	3	2	2	0	1	0
Kelly, 1b	3	1	0	7	1	0
E. Meusel, lf	5	2	3	2	0	0
Rawlings, 2b	5	0	2	3	5	0
Snyder, c	5	1	4	8	2	0
Toney, p	0	0	0	0	1	0
Barnes, p	5	2	2	1	1	0
Totals	39	13	20	27	14	0

Yankees .... 0 0 4 0 0 0 0 1 0— 5
Giants .... 0 0 4 0 0 0 8 1 *—13

aRan for Ruth in eighth. bFlied out for Rogers in ninth. Runs batted in—Miller, Ruth 2, Pipp, Ward, Kelly, Bancroft, Youngs 4, E. Meusel 3, Rawlings 3, Snyder. Two-base hits—R. Meusel, Youngs, E. Meusel, Burns. Three-base hits—Burns, Youngs. Sacrifice hits—Pipp, Bancroft. Stolen bases—Burns, Frisch, E. Meusel. Double plays—Ward and Pipp; Quinn, Peckinpaugh and Pipp. Left on bases—Giants 10, Yankees 5. Earned runs—Giants 13, Yankees 5. Struck out—By Toney 1, by Barnes 7, by Quinn 2, by Rogers 1. Bases on balls—Off Shawkey 4, off Toney 2, off Barnes 2, off Quinn 2, off Collins 1. Hit by pitcher—By Barnes (McNally). Wild pitch—Barnes. Hits—Off Toney 4 in 2 (pitched to five batters in third inning), off Barnes 4 in 7 innings, off Shawkey 5 in 2⅓ innings, off Quinn 8 in 3⅔ (pitched to five batters in seventh inning), off Collins 4 in ⅔ inning, off Rogers 3 in 1⅓ innings. Winning pitcher—Barnes. Losing pitcher—Quinn. Umpires—Quigley (N.L.), Chill (A.L.), Rigler (N.L.) and Moriarty (A.L.). Time—2:40. Attendance—36,509.

Sunday, October 9—At Polo Grounds

New York (N.L.)	AB	R	H	O	A	E
Burns, cf	4	0	2	0	0	0
Bancroft, ss	4	0	0	4	1	1
Frisch, 3b	4	0	1	1	3	0
Youngs, rf	4	0	1	1	0	0
Kelly, 1b	4	1	1	9	0	0
E. Meusel, lf	4	1	2	0	0	0
Rawlings, 2b	4	1	2	1	4	0
Snyder, c	4	1	0	10	2	0
Douglas, p	2	0	0	1	2	0
Totals	34	4	9	27	12	1

1921 WORLD SERIES

New York (A.L.)	AB.	R.	H.	O.	A.	E.
Miller, cf	4	0	0	1	0	0
Peckinpaugh, ss	4	0	1	2	6	0
Ruth, lf	4	1	2	2	0	0
R. Meusel, rf	4	0	0	1	0	0
Pipp, 1b	4	0	1	17	0	0
Ward, 2b	2	0	0	1	7	0
McNally, 3b	3	1	1	1	2	1
Schang, c	3	0	2	2	1	0
Mays, p	3	0	0	0	3	0
Totals	31	2	7	27	19	1

Giants................ 0 0 0 0 0 0 0 3 1—4
Yankees............. 0 0 0 0 1 0 0 0 1—2

Runs batted in—Burns 2, E. Meusel, Rawlings, Ruth, Schang. Two-base hits—Burns, Kelly. Three-base hits—Schang, E. Meusel. Home run—Ruth. Sacrifice hits—Douglas, Ward. Double play—Ward, Peckinpaugh and Pipp. Left on bases—Giants 4, Yankees 3. Earned runs—Giants 4, Yankees 2. Struck out—By Douglas 8, by Mays 1. Umpires—Chill (A.L.), Rigler (N.L.), Moriarty (A.L.) and Quigley (N.L.). Time—1:38. Attendance—36,372.

Monday, Oct. 10—At Polo Grounds

New York (A.L.)	AB.	R.	H.	O.	A.	E.
Miller, cf	3	0	1	2	0	0
Peckinpaugh, ss	4	0	1	3	3	0
Ruth, lf	4	1	1	2	0	0
R. Meusel, rf	4	1	2	1	2	0
Pipp, 1b	3	0	0	6	1	0
Ward, 2b	3	0	0	5	3	1
McNally, 3b	2	1	0	1	1	0
Schang, c	3	0	1	7	1	0
Hoyt, p	3	0	0	0	1	0
Totals	29	3	6	27	12	1

New York (N.L.)	AB.	R.	H.	O.	A.	E.
Burns, cf	5	0	1	2	0	0
Bancroft, ss	4	1	1	3	5	0
Frisch, 3b	4	0	2	1	6	1
Youngs, rf	3	0	1	0	0	0
Kelly, 1b	4	0	3	11	1	0
E. Meusel, lf	4	0	1	3	0	0
Rawlings, 2b	4	0	1	0	2	0
Smith, c	3	0	0	6	1	0
Nehf, p	3	0	0	1	1	0
aSnyder	1	0	0	0	0	0
Totals	35	1	10	27	12	1

Yankees............. 0 0 1 2 0 0 0 0 0—3
Giants................ 1 0 0 0 0 0 0 0 0—1

aFanned for Nehf in ninth. Runs batted in—Miller, R. Meusel, Ward, Kelly. Two-base hits—Schang, E. Meusel, R. Meusel, Miller, Rawlings. Sacrifice hits—Miller, Pipp, Ward. Double play—Schang and Ward. Left on bases—Giants 9, Yankees 3. Earned runs—Yankees 3, Giants 0. Struck out—By Hoyt 6, by Nehf 5. Bases on balls—Off Hoyt 2, off Nehf 1. Umpires—Rigler (N.L.), Moriarty (A.L.), Quigley (N.L.) and Chill (A.L.). Time—1:50. Attendance—35,758.

Tuesday, Oct. 11—At Polo Grounds

New York (N.L.)	AB.	R.	H.	O.	A.	E.
Burns, cf	3	1	1	0	0	0
Bancroft, ss	5	0	2	0	2	0
Frisch, 3b	4	2	0	1	2	0
Youngs, rf	5	0	1	2	0	0
Kelly, 1b	4	1	3	7	1	0
E. Meusel, lf	4	1	2	2	0	0
Rawlings, 2b	5	0	0	5	2	0
Snyder, c	4	2	2	10	0	0

	AB.	R.	H.	O.	A.	E.
Toney, p	0	0	0	0	0	0
Barnes, p	4	1	2	0	0	0
Totals	38	8	13	27	7	0

New York (A.L.)	AB.	R.	H.	O.	A.	E.
Fewster, lf	3	2	1	5	0	0
Peckinpaugh, ss	5	0	0	3	1	0
Miller, cf	5	1	1	1	0	0
R. Meusel, rf	3	1	1	2	0	0
Pipp, 1b	4	0	1	2	0	0
Ward, 2b	4	0	1	3	1	1
McNally, 3b	4	0	0	3	0	1
Schang, c	2	0	1	8	3	0
Harper, p	0	0	0	0	0	0
Shawkey, p	3	1	1	0	0	0
aBaker	1	0	0	0	0	0
Piercy, p	0	0	0	0	0	0
Totals	34	5	7	27	5	2

Giants................ 0 3 0 4 0 1 0 0 0—8
Yankees............. 3 2 0 0 0 0 0 0 0—5

aGrounded out for Shawkey in eighth. Runs batted in—Bancroft 2, Frisch, Kelly 2, E. Meusel 2, Snyder, Fewster 2, R. Meusel, Ward 2. Home runs—E. Meusel, Snyder, Fewster. Sacrifice hit—Burns. Stolen bases—Frisch, Pipp. Double plays—Schang and McNally; Schang and Ward. Left on bases—Giants 8, Yankees 7. Earned runs—Giants 6, Yankees 5. Struck out—By Barnes 10, by Harper 1, by Shawkey 5, by Piercy 2. Bases on balls—Off Toney 1, off Barnes 4, off Harper 2, off Shawkey 2. Hits—Off Toney 3 in ⅔ inning, off Barnes 4 in 8⅓ innings, off Harper 3 in 1⅓ innings, off Shawkey 8 in 6⅔ innings, off Piercy 2 in 1 inning. Winning pitcher—Barnes. Losing pitcher—Shawkey. Umpires—Moriarty (A.L.), Quigley (N.L.), Chill (A.L.) and Rigler (N.L.). Time—2:31. Attendance—34,283.

Wednesday, Oct. 12—At Polo Grounds

New York (A.L.)	AB.	R.	H.	O.	A.	E.
Fewster, lf	4	0	1	0	0	0
Peckinpaugh, ss	4	0	2	0	4	0
Miller, cf	3	0	0	2	1	0
R. Meusel, rf	4	0	0	1	0	0
Pipp, 1b	4	1	1	13	0	0
Ward, 2b	3	0	0	0	4	1
McNally, 3b	1	0	1	0	2	0
Baker, 3b	3	0	2	1	0	0
aDevormer	0	0	0	0	0	0
Schang, c	4	0	1	7	0	0
Mays, p	3	0	0	0	2	0
Totals	33	1	8	24	13	1

New York (N.L.)	AB.	R.	H.	O.	A.	E.
Burns, cf	4	0	2	3	0	0
Bancroft, ss	4	0	1	2	2	0
Frisch, 3b	4	0	0	2	3	0
Youngs, rf	3	1	1	2	0	0
Kelly, 1b	3	0	0	13	0	0
E. Meusel, lf	3	0	1	0	1	0
Rawlings, 2b	3	1	0	2	3	0
Snyder, c	3	0	1	3	0	0
Douglas, p	3	0	0	1	5	0
Totals	30	2	6	27	14	0

Yankees............. 0 1 0 0 0 0 0 0 0—1
Giants................ 0 0 0 1 0 0 1 0 *—2

aRan for Baker in ninth. Runs batted in—McNally, E. Meusel, Snyder. Two-base hits—Peckinpaugh, Bancroft, Pipp, Burns 2, Snyder. Sacrifice hit—Ward. Stolen base—Youngs. Left on bases—Yankees 7, Giants 1. Struck out—By Mays 7, by Douglas 3. Bases on balls—Off Douglas 1. Wild pitch—

Douglas. Umpires—Quigley (N.L.), Chill (A.L.), Rigler (N.L.) and Moriarty (A.L.). Time—1:40. Attendance—36,503.

Thursday, Oct. 13—At Polo Grounds

New York (N.L.)	AB.	R.	H.	O.	A.	E.
Burns, cf	4	0	1	3	0	0
Bancroft, ss	3	1	0	0	4	0
Frisch, 3b	4	0	0	2	3	0
Youngs, rf	2	0	1	0	0	0
Kelly, 1b	4	0	0	13	1	0
E. Meusel, lf	4	0	1	1	0	0
Rawlings, 2b	4	0	3	4	4	0
Snyder, c	2	0	0	4	0	0
Nehf, p	4	0	0	0	0	0
Totals	31	1	6	27	12	0

New York (A.L.)	AB.	R.	H.	O.	A.	E.
Fewster, lf	3	0	0	2	0	0
Peckinpaugh, ss	2	0	0	2	2	1
Miller, cf	4	0	1	1	0	0
R. Meusel, rf	4	0	0	2	0	0
Pipp, 1b	3	0	1	11	0	0
aRuth	1	0	0	0	0	0
Ward, 2b	3	0	1	0	2	0
Baker, 3b	3	0	0	1	3	0
Schang, c	3	0	0	8	1	0
Hoyt, p	3	0	1	0	3	0
Totals	29	0	4	27	11	1

Giants .... 1 0 0 0 0 0 0 0 0—1
Yankees .... 0 0 0 0 0 0 0 0 0—0

aGrounded out for Pipp in ninth. Runs batted in—None (run scored on Peckinpaugh's error). Two-base hits—Rawlings 2. Sacrifice hits—Snyder 2. Stolen base—Youngs. Left on bases—Giants 9, Yankees 7. Earned runs—None. Double plays—Bancroft, Rawlings and Kelly; Rawlings, Kelly and Frisch. Struck out—By Nehf 3, by Hoyt 7. Bases on balls—Off Nehf 5, off Hoyt 4. Wild pitch—Nehf. Umpires—Chill (A.L.), Rigler (N.L.), Moriarty (A.L.) and Quigley (N.L.). Time—1:58. Attendance—25,410.

COMPOSITE BATTING AVERAGES

New York Giants

Player-Position	G.	AB.	R.	H.	2B.	3B.	HR.	RBI.	BA.
Barnes, p	3	9	3	4	0	0	0	0	.444
Snyder, c-ph	7	22	4	8	1	0	1	3	.364
E. Meusel, lf	8	29	4	10	2	1	1	7	.345
Rawlings, 2b	8	30	2	10	3	0	0	2	.333
Burns, cf	8	33	2	11	4	1	0	2	.333
Frisch, 3b	8	30	5	9	0	1	0	1	.300
Youngs, rf	8	25	3	7	1	1	0	4	.280
Kelly, 1b	8	30	3	7	1	0	0	4	.233
Bancroft, ss	8	33	3	5	1	0	0	3	.152
Douglas, p	3	7	0	0	0	0	0	0	.000
Smith, ph-c	3	7	0	0	0	0	0	0	.000
Nehf, p	3	9	0	0	0	0	0	0	.000
Toney, p	2	0	0	0	0	0	0	0	.000
Totals	8	264	29	71	13	4	2	28	.269

New York Yankees

Player-Position	G.	AB.	R.	H.	2B.	3B.	HR.	RBI.	BA.
Shawkey, p	2	4	2	2	0	0	0	0	.500
Ruth, lf-ph	6	16	3	5	0	0	1	4	.313
Schang, c	8	21	1	6	1	1	0	1	.286
Baker, ph-3b	4	8	0	2	0	0	0	0	.250
Ward, 2b	8	26	1	6	0	0	0	4	.231
Hoyt, p	3	9	0	2	0	0	0	1	.222
McNally, 3b	7	20	3	4	1	0	0	0	.200
Fewster, pr-lf	4	10	3	2	0	0	1	2	.200
R. Meusel, rf	8	30	3	6	2	0	0	3	.200
Peckinpaugh, ss	8	28	2	5	1	0	0	0	.179
Miller, cf	8	31	3	5	1	0	0	2	.161
Pipp, 1b	8	26	1	4	1	0	0	0	.154
Mays, p	3	9	0	1	0	0	0	0	.111
Devormer, c-pr	2	1	0	0	0	0	0	0	.000
Quinn, p	1	2	0	0	0	0	0	0	.000

Player-Position	G.	AB.	R.	H.	2B.	3B.	HR.	RBI.	BA.
Collins, p	1	0	0	0	0	0	0	0	.000
Rogers, p	1	0	0	0	0	0	0	0	.000
Harper, p	1	0	0	0	0	0	0	0	.000
Piercy, p	1	0	0	0	0	0	0	0	.000
Totals	8	241	22	50	7	1	2	20	.207

COMPOSITE PITCHING AVERAGES

New York Giants

Pitcher	G.	IP.	H.	R.	E.	SO.	BB.	W.	L.	ERA.
Nehf	3	26	13	6	4	8	13	1	2	1.38
Barnes	3	16⅓	10	3	3	18	6	2	0	1.65
Douglas	3	26	20	6	6	17	5	2	1	2.08
Toney	2	2⅔	7	7	7	1	3	0	0	23.63
Totals	8	71	50	22	20	44	27	5	3	2.53

New York Yankees

Pitcher	G.	IP.	H.	R.	E.	SO.	BB.	W.	L.	ERA.
Hoyt	3	27	18	2	0	18	11	2	1	0.00
Piercy	1	1	2	0	0	2	0	0	0	0.00
Mays	3	26	20	6	5	9	0	1	2	1.73
Shawkey	2	9	13	9	7	5	6	0	1	7.00
Rogers	1	1⅓	3	1	1	1	0	0	0	6.75
Quinn	1	3⅔	8	4	4	2	2	0	1	9.82
Harper	1	1⅓	3	3	3	1	2	0	0	20.25
Collins	1	⅔	4	4	4	0	1	0	0	54.00
Totals	8	70	71	29	24	38	22	3	5	3.09

SERIES OF 1922

	W.	L.	T.	Pct.
New York N. L.	4	0	1	1.000
New York A. L.	0	4	1	.000

The two New York clubs again were opponents in the 1922 World Series, the Giants having won the pennant by a seven-game margin over the Cincinnati Reds, while the Yankees nosed out the St. Louis Browns by one game in a race that went down to the wire.

The Giants not only repeated their Series triumph of the previous year, but handed an even more unpleasant dose to the Yankees, who could do no better than gain a 10-inning tie in one game, the second. So disappointed was the Yankee ownership over the rout that Col. T. L. Huston, half owner of the club, called for the dismissal of Manager Miller Huggins after the last game. When Col. Jacob Ruppert, president of the club, refused to accede to his request, it widened the breach between the two partners, which resulted in Huston selling his half-interest to Ruppert the following winter.

At the suggestion of Commissioner K. M. Landis, the Series again was returned to its former length, four games out of seven. The second contest was called at the end of the 10th inning, with the score tied at 3 to 3, by George Hildebrand, the American League umpire behind the plate, because of darkness. Shortly before, Bill Klem, National League umpire, had conferred with Hildebrand and reminded him of the final inning of the 14-inning Red Sox-Brooklyn game in Boston in 1916, which was ended almost in dusk. There was nearly half an hour of daylight after Hildebrand called the game, and indignant fans followed Landis with a chorus of boos as he walked across the field. They were under the impression Landis had advised the umpires to call the game. As a result of the ensuing disorder, the Commissioner ordered the receipts of the game turned over to New York charities. A sum of approximately $120,000 was involved.

The main reason for the Yankee failure was the poor showing of Babe Ruth, slugging star of the American League team, who collected only two hits, a double and a single, in 17 times at bat for a humble average of .118. While the Giants outhit the Yankees, .309 to .203, the American Leaguers further ruined their chances by careless base-running. Repeatedly, shortstop Dave Bancroft of the Giants cut in on outfield throws and trapped unwary Yankees between bases.

The highlights of the Series were the brilliant all-round play of the two Giant infielders, third baseman Heine Groh and second baseman Frankie Frisch, who had a batting circus, garnering averages of .474 and .471, respectively. Aaron Ward, the Yankees' second baseman, matched Frisch's .471 with a meek .154; both of his hits were homers. Only three circuit clouts were hit, the other being made by left fielder Emil Meusel of the Giants.

Art Nehf, John Scott, Hugh McQuillan and Wilfred (Rosy) Ryan were each credited with Giant victories, Ryan getting his win as a relief pitcher for Nehf in the first game. Scott, a mid-season free agent pick-up by Manager John McGraw, shut out the Yanks with four hits in the third clash. Joe Bush lost two games for the American Leaguers, while Carl Mays and Waite Hoyt dropped one each. Bob Shawkey and Jess Barnes pitched the 10-inning tie.

Three turned out to be the key number of the Series, figuring in the score of every game. The Giants won the opener, 3 to 2; the tie game ended, 3 to 3 and McGraw's men then swept the next three contests, 3 to 0, 4 to 3 and 5 to 3.

All the games again were played at the Polo Grounds, and it was McGraw's last world championship. It was the third Series in which an American League club failed to win a game. The box scores:

Wednesday, Oct. 4—At Polo Grounds

New York (A.L.)	AB.	R.	H.	O.	A.	E.
Witt, cf	4	0	1	1	0	0
Dugan, 3b	4	1	1	0	1	0
Ruth, rf	4	0	1	1	0	0
Pipp, 1b	4	0	1	10	0	0
R. Meusel, lf	4	1	2	0	0	0
Schang, c	2	0	1	7	1	0
Ward, 2b	1	0	0	5	4	0
Scott, ss	3	0	0	0	4	0
Bush, p	3	0	0	0	0	0
Hoyt, p	0	0	0	0	0	0
Totals	29	2	7	24	10	0

New York (N.L.)	AB.	R.	H.	O.	A.	E.
Bancroft, ss	4	1	1	3	2	0
Groh, 3b	3	1	3	2	3	0
Frisch, 2b	4	1	2	2	4	0
E. Meusel, lf	4	0	1	0	0	0
Youngs, rf	3	0	0	1	1	2
Kelly, 1b	4	0	2	9	0	0
Stengel, cf	4	0	1	4	0	0
Snyder, c	3	0	1	6	2	0
Nehf, p	2	0	0	0	1	1
aEarl Smith	1	0	0	0	0	0
Ryan, p	0	0	0	0	0	0
Totals	32	3	11	27	13	3

Yankees................ 0 0 0   0 0 1   1 0 0—2
Giants................. 0 0 0   0 0 0   0 3 *—3

aHit into double play for Nehf in seventh. Runs batted in—E. Meusel 2, Youngs, Ruth, Ward. Three-base hits—Groh, Witt. Sacrifice hits—Schang 2, Ward, Youngs. Double plays—Snyder and Bancroft; Youngs and Frisch; Scott, Ward and Pipp; Frisch and Kelly. Left on bases—Giants 7, Yankees 4. Earned runs—Giants 3, Yankees 1. Struck out—By Bush 3, by Hoyt 2, by Nehf 3, by Ryan 2. Bases on balls—Off Bush 1, off Nehf 1. Hits—Off Nehf 6 in 7 innings, off Ryan 1 in 2 innings, off Bush 11 in 7 (pitched to four batters in eighth), off Hoyt 0 in 1 inning. Passed ball—Schang. Winning pitcher—Ryan. Losing pitcher—Bush. Umpires—Klem (N.L.), Hildebrand (A.L.), McCormick (N.L.) and Owens (A.L.). Time—2:08. Attendance—36,514.

Thursday, Oct. 5—At Polo Grounds

New York (N.L.)	AB.	R.	H.	O.	A.	E.
Bancroft, ss	5	0	1	1	0	1
Groh, 3b	4	1	1	1	3	0
Frisch, 2b	4	1	2	1	4	0
E. Meusel, lf	4	1	1	0	0	0
Youngs, rf	3	0	1	1	0	0
Kelly, 1b	4	0	0	15	0	0
Stengel, cf	1	0	1	0	0	0
aCunningham, cf	2	0	0	2	0	0
bEarl Smith	1	0	0	0	0	0
King, cf	0	0	0	0	0	0
Snyder, c	4	0	1	9	1	0
J. Barnes, p	4	0	0	0	4	0
Totals	36	3	8	30	12	1

New York (A.L.)	AB.	R.	H.	O.	A.	E.
Witt, cf	5	0	1	1	1	0
Dugan, 3b	5	1	2	3	0	0
Ruth, rf	4	1	1	5	0	0
Pipp, 1b	5	0	1	11	0	0
R. Meusel, lf	4	0	1	1	0	0
Schang, c	4	0	0	5	0	0
Ward, 2b	4	1	1	3	5	0
Scott, ss	4	0	1	1	3	0
Shawkey, p	4	0	0	2	2	0
Totals	39	3	8	30	11	0

Giants................ 3 0 0   0 0 0   0 0 0—3
Yankees............... 1 0 0   1 0 0   0 1 0—3
Stopped by darkness.

aRan for Stengel in second. bStruck out for Cunningham in ninth. Runs batted in—E. Meusel 3, Ward, R. Meusel, Pipp. Two-base hits—Dugan, Ruth, R. Meusel. Home runs—E. Meusel, Ward. Stolen base—Frisch. Double play—Scott, Ward and Pipp. Left on bases—Yankees 8, Giants 5. Earned runs—Giants 3, Yankees 2. Struck out—By Shawkey 4, by J. Barnes 6. Bases on balls—Off Shawkey 2, off J. Barnes 2. Wild pitches—Shawkey 2. Umpires—Hildebrand (A.L.), McCormick (N.L.), Owens (A.L.) and Klem (N.L.). Time—2:40. Attendance—37,020.

1922 WORLD SERIES

Friday, Oct. 6—At Polo Grounds

New York (A.L.)	AB	R	H	O	A	E
Witt, cf	3	0	0	1	0	0
Dugan, 3b	4	0	0	2	4	0
Ruth, rf	3	0	0	0	0	0
Pipp, 1b	4	0	1	10	1	0
R. Meusel, lf	4	0	1	1	1	0
Schang, c	3	0	1	2	2	0
Ward, 2b	2	0	0	2	4	1
aElmer Smith	1	0	0	0	0	0
McNally, 2b	0	0	0	1	1	0
E. Scott, ss	3	0	0	4	1	0
Hoyt, p	2	0	1	1	2	0
bBaker	1	0	0	0	0	0
Jones, p	0	0	0	0	1	0
Totals	30	0	4	24	17	1

New York (N.L.)	AB	R	H	O	A	E
Bancroft, ss	3	2	0	0	5	0
Groh, 3b	4	1	2	2	2	0
Frisch, 2b	2	0	2	1	5	1
E. Meusel, lf	4	0	1	1	0	0
Youngs, rf	4	0	3	2	0	0
Kelly, 1b	3	0	2	15	1	0
Cunningham, cf	3	0	1	3	0	0
Earl Smith, c	4	0	1	2	1	0
J. Scott, p	4	0	1	1	1	0
Totals	31	3	12	27	15	1

```
Yankees ........ 0 0 0   0 0 0   0 0 0—0
Giants ......... 0 0 2   0 0 0   1 0 *—3
```

aStruck out for Ward in seventh. bGrounded out for Hoyt in eighth. Runs batted in—Frisch 2, E. Meusel. Two-base hit—Schang. Sacrifice hits—Frisch, Kelly. Stolen base—Pipp. Double play—Ward and Pipp. Left on bases—Giants 9, Yankees 5. Earned runs—Giants 1. Struck out—By Hoyt 2, by J. Scott 2. Bases on balls—Off Hoyt 2, off Jones 1, off J. Scott 1. Hit by pitcher—By J. Scott (Ruth). Hits—Off Hoyt 11 in 7 innings, off Jones 1 in 1 inning. Losing pitcher—Hoyt. Umpires—McCormick (N.L.), Owens (A.L.), Klem (N.L.) and Hildebrand (A.L.). Time—1:48. Attendance—37,620.

Saturday, Oct. 7—At Polo Grounds

New York (N.L.)	AB	R	H	O	A	E
Bancroft, ss	3	1	2	3	5	0
Groh, 3b	4	1	1	0	3	0
Frisch, 2b	3	0	0	4	3	0
E. Meusel, lf	4	0	1	1	0	0
Youngs, rf	4	0	2	3	0	0
Kelly, 1b	4	0	0	8	0	0
Cunningham, cf	3	0	0	3	2	0
Snyder, c	4	1	2	5	0	1
McQuillan, p	4	1	1	0	0	0
Totals	33	4	9	27	13	1

New York (A.L.)	AB	R	H	O	A	E
Witt, cf	4	1	2	4	0	0
Dugan, 3b	4	1	1	0	3	0
Ruth, rf	3	0	0	1	0	0
Pipp, 1b	4	0	2	12	3	0
R. Meusel, lf	4	0	1	5	0	0
Schang, c	4	0	1	1	1	0
Ward, 2b	4	1	1	0	2	0
Scott, ss	2	0	0	4	2	0
Mays, p	2	0	0	0	4	0
aElmer Smith	1	0	0	0	0	0
Jones, p	0	0	0	0	0	0
Totals	32	3	8	27	15	0

```
Giants .......... 0 0 0   0 4 0   0 0 0—4
Yankees ......... 2 0 0   0 0 0   1 0 0—3
```

aStruck out for Mays in eighth. Runs batted in—Bancroft 2, E. Meusel, Youngs, Pipp, R. Meusel, Ward. Two-base hits—McQuillan, Witt, Pipp. Home run—Ward. Sacrifice hit—Frisch. Stolen base—R. Meusel. Double plays—Frisch, Bancroft and Kelly; Pipp and Scott. Left on bases—Giants 5, Yankees 4. Earned runs—Giants 4, Yankees 2. Struck out—By Mays 1, by McQuillan 4. Bases on balls—Off Mays 2, off McQuillan 2. Hits—Off Mays 9 in 8 innings, off Jones 0 in 1 inning. Losing pitcher—Mays. Umpires—Owens (A.L.), Klem (N.L.), Hildebrand (A.L.) and McCormick (N.L.). Time—1:41. Attendance—36,242.

Sunday, Oct. 8—At Polo Grounds

New York (A.L.)	AB	R	H	O	A	E
Witt, cf	2	0	0	0	0	0
aMcMillan, cf	2	0	0	1	0	0
Dugan, 3b	3	1	1	0	1	0
Ruth, rf	3	0	0	2	0	0
Pipp, 1b	4	0	1	8	0	0
R. Meusel, lf	4	1	1	0	0	0
Schang, c	3	0	0	4	0	0
Ward, 2b	2	1	0	3	1	0
Scott, ss	2	0	1	5	5	0
Bush, p	3	0	1	1	3	0
Totals	28	3	5	24	10	0

New York (N.L.)	AB	R	H	O	A	E
Bancroft, ss	4	0	0	2	5	0
Groh, 3b	4	0	2	1	3	0
Frisch, 2b	4	1	2	2	4	0
E. Meusel, lf	4	2	1	1	0	0
Youngs, rf	2	0	0	2	1	0
Kelly, 1b	3	0	2	14	0	0
Cunningham, cf	2	0	1	2	0	0
bEarl Smith	1	0	0	0	0	0
King, cf	1	0	1	0	0	0
Snyder, c	4	0	1	3	2	0
Nehf, p	1	0	0	0	2	0
Totals	30	5	10	27	17	0

```
Yankees ........ 1 0 0   0 1 0   1 0 0—3
Giants ......... 0 2 0   0 0 0   0 3 *—5
```

aGrounded out for Witt in fifth. bStruck out for Cunningham in seventh. Runs batted in—Kelly 2, Cunningham 2, King, Pipp, Scott, Bush. Two-base hit—Frisch. Sacrifice hits—Ruth, Scott, Kelly, Schang. Double plays—Bush, Scott and Pipp 2; Ward, Scott and Pipp. Left on bases—Giants 6, Yankees 4. Earned runs—Giants 5, Yankees 3. Struck out—By Bush 3, by Nehf 3. Bases on balls—Off Bush 4, off Nehf 2. Hit by pitcher—By Nehf (Dugan). Wild pitch—Nehf. Umpires—Klem (N.L.), Hildebrand (A.L.), McCormick (N.L.) and Owens (A.L.). Time—2:00. Attendance—38,551.

COMPOSITE BATTING AVERAGES

New York Giants

Player-Position	G	AB	R	H	2B	3B	HR	RBI	BA
King, cf	2	1	0	1	0	0	0	1	1.000
Groh, 3b	5	19	4	9	0	1	0	0	.474
Frisch, 2b	5	17	3	8	1	0	0	2	.471
Stengel, cf	2	5	0	2	0	0	0	0	.400
Youngs, rf	5	16	2	6	0	0	0	2	.375
Snyder, c	4	15	0	5	0	0	0	0	.333
Kelly, 1b	5	18	0	5	0	0	0	2	.278
J. Scott, p	1	4	0	1	0	0	0	0	.250
McQuillan, p	1	4	1	1	0	0	0	0	.250
E. Meusel, lf	5	20	3	5	0	0	1	7	.250
Cunn'ham, pr-cf	4	10	0	2	0	0	0	2	.200
Bancroft, ss	5	19	4	4	0	0	0	2	.211
Ea. Smith, ph-c	4	7	0	1	0	0	0	0	.143
Nehf, p	2	3	1	0	0	0	0	0	.000
Ryan, p	1	0	0	0	0	0	0	0	.000
J. Barnes, p	1	4	0	0	0	0	0	0	.000
Totals	5	162	18	50	2	1	1	18	.309

New York Yankees

Player-Position	G.	AB.	R.	H.	2B.	3B.	HR.	RBI.	BA.
Hoyt, p	2	2	0	1	0	0	0	0	.500
R. Meusel, lf	5	20	2	6	1	0	0	2	.300
Pipp, 1b	5	21	0	6	1	0	0	3	.286
Dugan, 3b	5	20	4	5	1	0	0	0	.250
Witt, cf	5	18	1	4	1	1	0	0	.222
Schang, c	5	16	0	3	1	0	0	0	.188
Bush, p	2	6	0	1	0	0	0	1	.167
Ward, 2b	5	13	3	2	0	0	2	3	.154
eScott, ss	5	14	0	2	0	0	0	1	.143
Ruth, rf	5	17	1	2	1	0	0	1	.118
Shawkey, p	1	4	0	0	0	0	0	0	.000
El. Smith, ph	2	2	0	0	0	0	0	0	.000
McNally, 2b	1	0	0	0	0	0	0	0	.000
Baker, ph	1	1	0	0	0	0	0	0	.000
Jones, p	2	0	0	0	0	0	0	0	.000
Mays, p	1	2	0	0	0	0	0	0	.000
McMillan, ph-cf	1	2	0	0	0	0	0	0	.000
Totals	5	158	11	32	6	1	2	11	.203

COMPOSITE PITCHING AVERAGES

New York Giants

Pitcher	G.	IP.	H.	R.	E.	SO.	BB.	W.	L.	ERA.
J. Scott	1	9	4	0	0	2	1	1	0	0.00
Ryan	1	2	1	0	0	2	0	1	0	0.00
J. Barnes	1	10	8	3	2	6	2	0	0	1.80
McQuillan	1	9	8	3	2	4	2	1	0	2.00
Nehf	2	16	11	5	4	6	3	1	0	2.25
Totals	5	46	32	11	8	20	8	4	0	1.57

New York Yankees

Pitcher	G.	IP.	H.	R.	E.	SO.	BB.	W.	L.	ERA.
Jones	2	2	1	0	0	0	1	0	0	0.00
Hoyt	2	8	11	3	1	4	2	0	1	1.13
Shawkey	1	10	8	3	3	4	2	0	0	2.70
Mays	1	8	9	4	4	1	2	0	1	4.50
Bush	2	15	21	8	8	6	5	0	2	4.80
Totals	5	43	50	18	16	15	12	0	4	3.35

SERIES OF 1923

	W.	L.	Pct.
New York A. L.	4	2	.667
New York N. L.	2	4	.333

After losing two successive Series to the Giants, the Yankees finally rewarded their president, Col. Jacob Ruppert, with his first world championship in 1923 when, meeting the Giants for the third straight time, the Bronx Bombers emerged the victors, four games to two. Yankee Stadium was opened the preceding spring, and for the first time the New York American League club played its home Series games on its own field. However, the new field did not bring the Yankees luck, as they won all three games played at the Polo Grounds, home of the Giants, but lost two of the three games played at the Stadium. Casey Stengel, the Giants' center fielder, was the hero of both Giant victories. Stengel's ninth-inning inside-the-park homer won the first game for the Giants, 5 to 4, and his seventh-inning belt into the right field bleachers in the third game decided a 1 to 0 pitching duel between Art Nehf and Sad Sam Jones in the former's favor. With the fifth game, also played at the Stadium and won by the Yanks, 8 to 1, drawing a new record crowd of 62,817, the Series was the first to hit the million-dollar mark in receipts.

Unlike their tough fight in 1922, the Yankees spreadeagled the field in 1923, winning their third straight pennant by a margin of 16 games over Detroit, while the Giants had a tussle to defeat Cincinnati by four and one-half games. First baseman Wally Pipp of the Yankees sprained his ankle late in the season, and John McGraw, Giant manager, refused to waive the September 1 rule to let the Yankees use a young first baseman recalled from Hartford of the Eastern League—Lou Gehrig. Pipp, taped up for the Series, played good ball and batted .250.

For the first time since Babe Ruth pitched 29 consecutive scoreless innings for the Red Sox, he gained World Series stardom. He hit .368, and crashed through for three homers, two coming in succession in the second game, as well as a triple, a double and three singles. Ruth also walked eight times. The Ruth home-run era began to tell in the Series box scores, as there were ten homers, five for each team. Bob Meusel, while hitting only .269 for the Huggins entry, drove in eight runs. Aaron Ward, Yankee second baseman, hit .417, the same as Stengel, the leading Polo Grounder. Frankie Frisch sparkled afield and batted an even .400.

Southpaw Herb Pennock won two games for the Yankees, and Bob Shawkey and Joe Bush each one. Art Nehf and Wilfred (Rosy) Ryan each chalked up one victory for the Giants, while Nehf, Hugh McQuillan, Jack Bentley and Jack Scott were the McGraw losers.

After Stengel's bat led the Giants to victory in the first and third games, the Yankees' hitters went to work. They pounded out 13 safeties to win the fourth contest, 8 to 4, and then unloaded 14 hits in capturing the fifth game, 8 to 1, as Bush silenced the Giants on three hits—all by Emil Meusel.

However, the Yankees' big offensive inning, which made them world champions, was the eighth of the sixth game. With the Giants trailing, three games to two, McGraw pitched Nehf, always effective against the Bronx Bombers. The crack left-hander pitched great ball for seven innings and went into the eighth leading, 4 to 1, the lone Yank run being a Ruth homer in the first. With one out, Wally Schang and Everett Scott bunched singles and Nehf walked two pinch-hitters, Fred Hofmann and Joe Bush, on eight straight balls, forcing in a run. Ryan relieved Nehf and walked Joe Dugan, forcing in another tally. Ryan next fanned Ruth, but Bob Meusel hit a single, which took an awkward bound over the pitcher's head, and when it was misplayed in center field by Bill Cunningham, all three runners on the bases scored.

Bob Meusel drove in eight runs for a Series record, while George Kelly, Giant first baseman, also established a record with 19 putouts in the sixth game.

All financial and attendance records were broken, and the fifth game also set a new mark, with 62,817 paying $201,459.

The total attendance was 301,430 and receipts $1,063,815. A Yankee share was worth $6,143.49, not topped until 1935, and each Giant's losing share amounted to $4,112.88, high until surpassed in 1928. The box scores:

Wednesday, October 10—At Yankee Stadium

New York (N.L.)	AB.	R.	H.	O.	A.	E.
Bancroft, ss	4	1	1	3	0	0
Groh, 3b	4	1	2	1	3	0
Frisch, 2b	4	0	1	2	2	0
Youngs, rf	3	0	0	1	0	0
E. Meusel, lf	4	0	0	6	0	0
Stengel, cf	3	1	2	2	0	0
Cunningham, cf	0	0	0	1	0	0
Kelly, 1b	4	1	1	5	2	0
Gowdy, c	0	0	0	1	0	0
aMaguire	0	1	0	0	0	0
Snyder, c	2	0	0	4	1	0
Watson, p	0	0	0	0	1	0
bBentley	1	0	1	0	0	0
cGearin	0	0	0	0	0	0
Ryan, p	2	0	0	1	2	0
Totals	31	5	8	27	11	0

New York (A.L.)	AB.	R.	H.	O.	A.	E.
Witt, cf	5	0	1	5	0	0
Dugan, 3b	4	0	1	0	3	0
Ruth, rf	4	1	1	3	0	0
R. Meusel, lf	4	0	1	0	0	0
Pipp, 1b	4	0	2	10	0	0
Ward, 2b	4	1	2	6	3	0
Schang, c	3	1	2	2	2	1
Scott, ss	2	0	0	1	6	0
dHendrick	1	0	0	0	0	0
Johnson, ss	0	0	0	0	1	0
Hoyt, p	1	0	0	0	0	0
Bush, p	3	1	2	0	2	0
Totals	35	4	12	27	17	1

Giants	0 0 4	0 0 0	0 0 1—5
Yankees	1 2 0	0 0 0	1 0 0—4

aRan for Gowdy in third. bSingled for Watson in third. cRan for Bentley in third. dFlied out for Scott in eighth. Runs batted in—Groh 2, Witt 2, Dugan, R. Meusel, Bancroft, Frisch, Stengel. Two-base hits—R. Meusel, Bush, Schang. Three-base hits—Groh, Ruth, Dugan. Home run—Stengel. Sacrifice hit—Scott. Stolen base—Bancroft. Double plays—Ryan, Groh and Frisch; Frisch and Snyder; Scott, Ward and Pipp 2. Left on bases—Yankees 7, Giants 2. Earned runs—Giants 5, Yankees 4. Struck out—By Watson 1, by Ryan 2, by Bush 2. Bases on balls—Off Watson 1, off Ryan 1, off Hoyt 1, off Bush 2. Wild pitch—Ryan. Hits—Off Hoyt 4 in 2⅓ innings, off Bush 4 in 6⅔ innings, off Watson 4 in 2 innings, off Ryan 8 in 7 innings. Winning pitcher—Ryan. Losing pitcher—Bush. Umpires—Evans (A.L.), O'Day (N.L.), Nallin (A.L.) and Hart (N.L.). Time—2:05. Attendance—55,307.

Thursday, Oct. 11—At Polo Grounds

New York (A.L.)	AB.	R.	H.	O.	A.	E.
Witt, cf	5	0	0	1	0	0
Dugan, 3b	4	0	1	2	3	0
Ruth, rf	3	2	2	3	0	0
R. Meusel, lf	4	0	1	4	0	0
Pipp, 1b	3	1	1	13	0	0
Ward, 2b	4	1	2	3	4	0
Schang, c	4	0	1	1	0	0
Scott, ss	4	0	2	0	6	0
Pennock, p	3	0	0	0	1	0
Totals	34	4	10	27	14	0

New York (N.L.)	AB.	R.	H.	O.	A.	E.
Bancroft, ss	4	0	0	0	6	0
Groh, 3b	3	1	1	0	1	0
Frisch, 2b	4	0	2	2	6	0
Youngs, rf	4	0	2	0	0	2
E. Meusel, lf	4	1	2	4	0	0
Cunningham, cf	3	0	0	1	0	0
aGowdy	1	0	0	0	0	0
Stengel, cf	0	0	0	1	0	0
Kelly, 1b	4	0	1	16	1	0
Snyder, c	4	0	0	3	1	0
McQuillan, p	1	0	0	0	0	0
Bentley, p	2	0	1	0	2	0
bJackson	1	0	0	0	0	0
Totals	35	2	9	27	17	2

Yankees	0 1 0	2 1 0	0 0 0—4
Giants	0 1 0	0 0 1	0 0 0—2

aFlied out for Cunningham in eighth. bFlied out for Bentley in ninth. Runs batted in—Ruth 2, Ward, Scott, E. Meusel, Youngs. Two-base hits—Bentley, Dugan. Home runs—Ward, E. Meusel, Ruth 2. Double plays—Bancroft, Frisch and Kelly 2; Scott, Ward and Pipp. Left on bases—Yankees 8, Giants 7. Earned runs—Yankees 4, Giants 2. Struck out—By McQuillan 1, by Pennock 1. Bases on balls—Off McQuillan 2, off Bentley 2, off Pennock 1. Hit by pitcher—By Bentley (Pennock). Hits—Off McQuillan 5 in 3⅔ innings, off Bentley 5 in 5⅓ innings. Losing pitcher—McQuillan. Umpires—O'Day (N.L.), Nallin (A.L.), Hart (N.L.) and Evans (A.L.). Time—2:08. Attendance—40,402.

Friday, Oct. 12—At Yankee Stadium

New York (N.L.)	AB.	R.	H.	O.	A.	E.
Bancroft, ss	3	0	0	3	5	0
Groh, 3b	4	0	0	1	5	0
Frisch, 2b	4	0	2	4	4	0
Youngs, rf	4	0	0	2	0	0
E. Meusel, lf	4	0	0	1	0	0
Stengel, cf	3	1	1	1	0	0
Kelly, 1b	3	0	0	10	0	0
Snyder, c	3	0	0	5	0	0
Nehf, p	3	0	1	0	1	0
Totals	31	1	4	27	15	0

New York (A.L.)	AB.	R.	H.	O.	A.	E.
Witt, cf	4	0	1	3	0	0
Dugan, 3b	4	0	1	1	0	0
Ruth, rf-1b	2	0	1	4	0	0
R. Meusel, lf	4	0	5	5	0	0
Pipp, 1b	2	0	0	8	0	0
Haines, rf	1	0	0	0	0	0
Ward, 2b	4	0	1	0	3	0
Schang, c	4	0	1	3	0	0
Scott, ss	3	0	1	3	4	1
Jones, p	2	0	0	0	2	0
aHofmann	1	0	0	0	0	0
Bush, p	0	0	0	0	0	0
Totals	31	0	6	27	9	1

Giants	0 0 0	0 0 0	1 0 0—1
Yankees	0 0 0	0 0 0	0 0 0—0

aPopped out for Jones in eighth. Run batted in—Stengel. Two-base hit—Dugan. Home run—Stengel. Double plays—Jones, Scott and Pipp; Bancroft, Frisch and Kelly; Frisch, Bancroft and Kelly. Left on bases—Yankees 7, Giants 5. Earned run—Giants 1. Struck out—By Nehf 4, by Jones 3. Bases on balls—Off Nehf, 3, off Jones 2. Hits—Off Jones 4 in 8 innings, off Bush 0 in 1 inning. Losing pitcher—Jones. Umpires—Nallin (A.L.), Hart (N.L.), Evans (A.L.) and O'Day (N.L.). Time—2:05. Attendance—62,430.

1923 WORLD SERIES

Saturday, Oct. 13—At Polo Grounds

New York (A.L.)	AB.	R.	H.	O.	A.	E.
Witt, cf	4	0	3	1	0	0
Dugan, 3b	5	1	0	2	3	0
Ruth, rf	3	2	1	2	0	1
R. Meusel, lf	5	0	1	3	0	0
Pipp, 1b	4	1	2	9	1	0
Ward, 2b	4	2	2	2	5	0
Schang, c	3	1	1	5	0	0
E. Scott, ss	5	1	2	2	1	0
Shawkey, p	3	0	1	1	2	0
Pennock, p	1	0	0	0	0	0
Totals	37	8	13	27	12	1

New York (N.L.)	AB.	R.	H.	O.	A.	E.
Bancroft, ss	5	0	1	2	3	0
Groh, 3b	3	0	0	1	2	0
Frisch, 2b	5	0	2	4	4	0
Youngs, rf	5	2	4	0	0	0
E. Meusel, lf	5	1	1	1	0	0
Stengel, cf	2	1	2	4	0	0
dCunningham	1	0	0	0	0	0
Kelly, 1b	5	0	2	7	0	0
Snyder, c	4	0	0	8	1	0
J. Scott, p	0	0	0	0	0	1
Ryan, p	0	0	0	0	0	0
McQuillan, p	2	0	0	0	1	0
aBentley	1	0	1	0	0	0
bMaguire	0	0	0	0	0	0
Jonnard, p	0	0	0	0	0	0
cO'Connell	0	0	0	0	0	0
Barnes, p	0	0	0	0	0	0
Totals	38	4	13	27	7	1

Yankees ..... 0 6 1 1 0 0 0 0 0—8
Giants ..... 0 0 0 0 0 0 0 3 1—4

aSingled for McQuillan in seventh. bRan for Bentley in seventh. cHit by pitcher for Jonnard in eighth. dStruck out for Stengel in ninth. Runs batted in—Witt 2, R. Meusel 2, E. Scott 2, Ward, Shawkey, Youngs, Stengel, Kelly, Snyder. Two-base hits—Witt 2, Ruth. Three-base hit—R. Meusel. Home run—Youngs. Sacrifice hits—Schang 2, Shawkey, Witt. Double plays—Shawkey, Dugan and Pipp; Dugan and Pipp. Left on bases—Giants 12, Yankees 10. Earned runs—Yankees 5, Giants 4. Struck out—By Shawkey 2, by Pennock 1, by J. Scott 1, by Barnes 2, by McQuillan 2. Bases on balls—Off Shawkey 4, off McQuillan 2, off Jonnard 1, off Ryan 1. Hit by pitcher—By Shawkey (O'Connell). Hits—Off Shawkey 12 in 7⅔ innings, off Pennock 1 in 1⅓ innings, off J. Scott 4 in 1 (pitched to four batters in second inning), off Ryan 2 in ⅔ inning, off McQuillan 6 in 5⅓ innings, off Jonnard 1 in 1 inning, off Barnes 0 in 1 inning. Winning pitcher—Shawkey. Losing pitcher—J. Scott. Umpires—Hart (N.L.), Evans (A.L.), O'Day (N.L.) and Nallin (A.L.). Time—2:32. Attendance—46,302.

Sunday, Oct. 14—At Yankee Stadium

New York (N.L.)	AB.	R.	H.	O.	A.	E.
Bancroft, ss	4	0	0	2	3	0
Groh, 3b	4	0	0	0	2	0
Frisch, 2b	4	0	0	4	1	1
Youngs, rf	3	0	0	2	1	0
E. Meusel, lf	4	1	3	0	0	0
Stengel, cf	3	0	0	3	0	0
Kelly, 1b	2	0	0	6	1	1
Gowdy, c	3	0	0	6	0	0
Bentley, p	0	0	0	0	0	0
J. Scott, p	1	0	0	0	0	0
Barnes, p	1	0	0	1	2	0
aO'Connell	1	0	0	0	0	0
Jonnard, p	0	0	0	0	1	0
Totals	30	1	3	24	11	2

New York (A.L.)	AB.	R.	H.	O.	A.	E.
Witt, cf	4	1	1	5	0	0
Dugan, 3b	5	3	4	0	3	0
Ruth, rf	4	2	1	4	0	0
R. Meusel, lf	5	1	3	1	0	0
Pipp, 1b	3	0	0	11	2	0
Ward, 2b	4	0	2	0	5	0
Schang, c	4	0	1	3	0	0
E. Scott, ss	4	0	1	1	1	0
Bush, p	4	1	1	2	1	0
Totals	37	8	14	27	12	0

Giants ..... 0 1 0 0 0 0 0 0 0—1
Yankees ..... 3 4 0 1 0 0 0 0 *—8

aStruck out for Barnes in eighth. Runs batted in—Dugan 3, R. Meusel 3, Pipp 2, Stengel. Two-base hit—E. Meusel. Three-base hits—E. Meusel, R. Meusel. Home run—Dugan. Sacrifice hit—Pipp. Stolen base—Ward. Left on bases—Yankees 9, Giants 4. Double play—Bancroft and Frisch. Earned runs—Yankees 7, Giants 1. Struck out—By Bush 3, by Bentley 1, by J. Scott 1, by Barnes 2, by Jonnard 1. Bases on balls—Off Bush 2, off Bentley 2, off J. Scott 1. Hits—Off Bentley 5 in 1⅓ innings, off J. Scott 5 in 2 innings, off Barnes 4 in 3⅔ innings, off Jonnard 0 in 1 inning. Losing pitcher—Bentley. Umpires—Evans (A.L.), O'Day (N.L.), Nallin (A.L.) and Hart (N.L.). Time—1:55. Attendance—62,817.

Monday, Oct 15—At Polo Grounds

New York (A.L.)	AB.	R.	H.	O.	A.	E.
Witt, cf	3	0	0	3	1	0
cBush	0	0	0	0	0	0
dJohnson	0	1	0	0	0	0
Jones, p	0	0	0	0	1	0
Dugan, 3b	3	1	0	2	1	0
Ruth, rf	3	1	1	1	0	0
R. Meusel, lf	4	0	1	1	0	0
Pipp, 1b	4	0	0	12	0	0
Ward, 2b	4	0	1	0	7	0
Schang, c	4	1	1	7	0	0
Scott, ss	4	1	1	1	2	0
Pennock, p	2	0	0	0	1	0
aHofmann	0	0	0	0	0	0
bHaines, cf	0	1	0	0	0	0
Totals	31	6	5	27	13	0

New York (N.L.)	AB.	R.	H.	O.	A.	E.
Bancroft, ss	4	0	0	1	7	0
Groh, 3b	4	1	1	1	2	0
Frisch, 2b	4	2	3	1	5	0
Youngs, rf	4	0	2	0	0	0
E. Meusel, lf	4	0	1	1	0	0
Cunningham, cf	3	0	1	0	0	1
eStengel, cf	1	0	0	0	0	0
Kelly, 1b	4	0	0	19	0	0
Snyder, c	4	1	2	4	0	0
Nehf, p	3	0	0	0	5	0
Ryan, p	0	0	0	0	0	0
fBentley	1	0	0	0	0	0
Totals	36	4	10	27	19	1

Yankees ..... 1 0 0 0 0 0 0 5 0—6
Giants ..... 1 0 0 1 1 1 0 0 0—4

aWalked for Pennock in eighth. bRan for Hofmann in eighth. cWalked for Witt in eighth. dRan for Bush in eighth. eFouled out for Cunningham in eighth. fGrounded out for Ryan in ninth. Runs batted in—R. Meusel 2, Ruth, Dugan, Bush, Youngs, E. Meusel, Cunningham, Snyder. Three-base hit—Frisch. Home runs—Ruth, Snyder. Double play—Nehf, Bancroft and Kelly. Left on bases—Giants 5, Yankees 2. Earned runs—Yankees 5, Giants 4. Struck out—By Nehf 3, by Ryan 1, by Pennock 6. Bases on balls—Off Nehf 3, off Ryan 1.

Hits—Off Nehf 4 in 7⅓ innings, off Ryan 1 in 1⅔ innings, off Pennock 9 in 7 innings, off Jones 1 in 2 innings. Winning pitcher—Pennock. Losing pitcher—Nehf. Umpires—O'Day (N.L.), Nallin (A.L.), Hart (N.L.) and Evans (A.L.). Time—2:05. Attendance—34,172.

COMPOSITE BATTING AVERAGES
New York Yankees

Player-Position	G.	AB.	R.	H.	2B.	3B.	HR.	RBI.	BA.
Bush, p-ph	4	7	2	3	1	0	0	1	.429
Ward, 2b	6	24	4	10	0	0	1	2	.417
Ruth, rf-1b	6	19	8	7	1	1	3	3	.368
Shawkey, p	1	3	0	1	0	0	0	1	.333
Schang, c	6	22	3	7	1	0	0	0	.318
Scott, ss	6	22	2	7	0	0	0	3	.318
Dugan, 3b	6	25	5	7	2	1	1	5	.280
R. Meusel, lf	6	26	1	7	1	2	0	8	.269
Pipp, 1b	6	20	2	5	0	0	0	2	.250
Witt, cf	6	25	1	6	2	0	0	4	.240
Johnson, ss-pr	2	0	1	0	0	0	0	0	.000
Pennock, p	3	6	0	0	0	0	0	0	.000
Jones, p	2	2	0	0	0	0	0	0	.000
Haines, rf-cf-pr	2	1	1	0	0	0	0	0	.000
Hofmann, ph	2	1	0	0	0	0	0	0	.000
Hoyt, p	1	1	0	0	0	0	0	0	.000
Hendrick, ph	1	1	0	0	0	0	0	0	.000
Totals	6	205	30	60	8	4	5	29	.293

New York Giants

Player-Position	G.	AB.	R.	H.	2B.	3B.	HR.	RBI.	BA.
Bentley, ph-p	5	5	0	3	1	0	0	0	.600
Stengel, cf-ph	6	12	3	5	0	0	2	4	.417
Frisch, 2b	6	25	2	10	0	1	0	1	.400
Youngs, rf	6	23	2	8	0	0	1	3	.348
E. Meusel, lf	6	25	3	7	1	1	1	2	.280
Groh, 3b	6	22	3	4	0	1	0	2	.182
Kelly, 1b	6	22	1	4	0	0	0	1	.182
Nehf, p	2	6	0	1	0	0	0	0	.167
Cun'ham, cf-ph	4	7	0	1	0	0	0	1	.143
Snyder, c	5	17	1	2	0	0	1	2	.118
Bancroft, ss	6	24	1	2	0	0	0	1	.083
Ryan, p	3	2	0	0	0	0	0	0	.000
Gowdy, c-ph	3	4	0	0	0	0	0	0	.000
Maguire, pr	2	0	1	0	0	0	0	0	.000
McQuillan, p	2	3	0	0	0	0	0	0	.000
J. Scott, p	2	1	0	0	0	0	0	0	.000
Jonnard, p	2	0	0	0	0	0	0	0	.000
O'Connell, ph	2	1	0	0	0	0	0	0	.000
Barnes, p	2	1	0	0	0	0	0	0	.000
Watson, p	1	0	0	0	0	0	0	0	.000
Gearin, pr	1	0	0	0	0	0	0	0	.000
Jackson, ph	1	1	0	0	0	0	0	0	.000
Totals	6	201	17	47	2	3	5	17	.234

COMPOSITE PITCHING AVERAGES
New York Yankees

Pitcher	G.	IP.	H.	R.	E.	SO.	BB.	W.	L.	ERA.
Jones	2	10	5	1	1	3	2	0	1	0.90
Bush	3	16⅔	7	2	2	5	4	1	1	1.08
Shawkey	1	7⅔	12	3	3	2	4	1	0	3.52
Pennock	3	17½	19	7	7	8	1	2	0	3.63
Hoyt	1	2⅓	4	4	4	0	1	0	0	15.43
Totals	6	54	47	17	17	18	12	4	2	2.83

New York Giants

Pitcher	G.	IP.	H.	R.	E.	SO.	BB.	W.	L.	ERA.
Barnes	2	4⅔	4	0	0	4	0	0	0	0.00
Jonnard	2	2	1	0	0	1	1	0	0	0.00
Ryan	3	9⅓	11	5	1	3	3	1	0	0.96
Nehf	2	16½	10	5	5	7	6	1	1	2.76
McQuillan	2	9	11	5	5	3	4	0	1	5.00
Bentley	2	6⅔	10	8	7	1	4	0	1	9.45
J. Scott	2	3	9	4	4	2	1	0	1	12.00
Watson	1	2	4	3	3	1	1	0	0	13.50
Totals	6	53	60	30	25	22	20	2	4	4.25

SERIES OF 1924

	W.	L.	Pct.
Washington A. L.	4	3	.571
New York N. L.	3	4	.429

In the most thrilling and exciting Series played since the Red Sox and Giants battled to eight games in 1912, the Washington Senators, after winning their first major league championship, won the 1924 World Series from the Giants, the ultimate decision hinging on a tricky bounder which hopped over the head of Fred Lindstrom, substitute third baseman, in the twelfth inning of the seventh and final game. President and Mrs. Calvin Coolidge were in attendance at three of the games played in Washington, and the Senators' victory was followed by a frenzy of delight in the Capital, which topped anything in the game's annals to that time.

Washington, after a stubborn season-long contest, blocked the efforts of the Yankees to make it four straight in their league, defeating New York by a scant two-game margin. The Senators were led by their then 27-year-old, first-year boy manager, Stanley (Bucky) Harris. The Giants made it four straight in the National League after a bitter three-cornered fight with Brooklyn and Pittsburgh. It was John McGraw's tenth and last pennant and he finished only a game and one-half ahead of his old Oriole and Giant chum, Wilbert Robinson, manager of the Dodgers.

Much of the interest in the Series was attached to the fact that Walter Johnson, famous hill star of the Senators, was getting his first World Series chance in his eighteenth season with the club. Johnson contributed 23 victories against only seven defeats to Washington's first pennant, but he proved a disappointment in his early games of the Series. The Giants lashed Walter for 14 hits to win the opener for Art Nehf, 4 to 3 in 12 innings, and for 13 more while taking the fifth game, 6 to 2. Entering the pay-off battle in the ninth inning, Ol' Barney then proved one of his team's heroes by holding off the Giants through four gruelling sessions to get credit for the 12-inning deciding game, 4 to 3.

Lady Luck rode with the Senators in this closing game, as they had three kisses from the fickle Goddess of Fortune. With the Giants leading, 3 to 1, in the eighth inning, and the championship in their grasp, Harris hit a grounder to Lindstrom, which jumped over the infielder's head, sending in Washington's two tying runs. In the twelfth inning, Hank Gowdy, behind the bat for the Giants, caught his foot in his mask while trying to catch Muddy Ruel's easy foul fly. His life saved, Ruel doubled for only his second hit of the Series, and he scored the tally that settled the Series when another hopper by Earl McNeely, Washington center fielder, also hit a pebble or hard bit of clay in front of Lindstrom and bounced over Freddy's head.

After the Giants won the first game, the two clubs alternated in winning until the seventh game. Though an injury limited Roger Peckinpaugh, Washington shortstop, to four games, he was his team's batting leader with an average of .417. However, Goose Goslin and Harris were the most potent hitters, each driving in seven runs, with respective averages of .344 and .333. The Goose hit three home runs and Harris two. Bucky also played great ball in the field. Though performing mostly against righthanders, Bill Terry, Giant first baseman, hit .429 for five games, his six hits including a homer and a triple. Clark Griffith had Harris jockey his pitchers in the last game, having righthander Warren (Curly) Ogden pitch to two batters and later shifting to lefthander George Mogridge to put Terry out of action for the day.

Washington's first-string southpaw, Tom Zachary, won two games, and Mogridge and Johnson captured the other two. Johnson struck out 12 men in the first game and 20 in his 24 innings. Fred Marberry lost the third game for Washington. Nehf, Hugh McQuillan and Jack Bentley each was credited with one of New York's victories; Bentley lost two games and Nehf and Virgil Barnes one each.

The box scores:

Saturday, October 4—At Washington

New York (N.L.)	AB.	R.	H.	O.	A.	E.
Lindstrom, 3b	5	0	0	1	3	0
aBentley	0	0	0	0	0	0
bSouthworth, cf	0	1	0	1	1	0
Frisch, 2b-3b	5	0	2	3	3	0
Youngs, rf	6	0	2	2	0	0
Kelly, cf-2b	5	1	1	4	1	0
Terry, 1b	5	1	3	15	0	0
Wilson, lf	6	0	2	4	0	0
Jackson, ss	3	0	0	2	6	1
Gowdy, c	3	0	1	4	1	0
Nehf, p	5	1	3	0	2	0
Totals	43	4	14	36	17	1

Wash'gton (A.L.)	AB.	R.	H.	O.	A.	E.
McNeely, cf	5	1	1	4	0	1
Harris, 2b	6	0	2	3	3	0
Rice, rf	5	0	2	0	1	0
Goslin, lf	6	0	1	2	0	0
Judge, 1b	4	0	1	6	0	0
Bluege, 3b	5	1	1	2	2	0
Peckinpaugh, ss	5	0	2	4	4	0
Ruel, c	3	0	0	15	2	0
Johnson, p	4	0	0	1	0	0
cShirley	1	1	0	0	0	0
Totals	44	3	10	36	13	1

New York..............0 1 0 1 0 0 0 0 0 0 0 2—4
Washington...........0 0 0 0 0 1 0 0 1 0 0 1—3

aWalked for Lindstrom in twelfth. bRan for Bentley in twelfth. cSafe on Jackson's error for Johnson in twelfth. Runs batted in—Kelly 2, Terry, Youngs, Peckinpaugh, Harris, Rice. Two-base hits—Frisch, McNeely, Youngs, Peckinpaugh. Home runs—Kelly, Terry. Sacrifice hits—Kelly, Jackson. Stolen bases—Frisch, Rice, Peckinpaugh. Double plays—Peckinpaugh and Harris; Jackson, Frisch and Terry; Bluege, Harris and Judge. Left on bases—New York 11, Washington 10. Earned runs—New York 3, Washington 2. Struck out—By Johnson 12, by Nehf 3. Bases on balls—Off Johnson 6, off Nehf 5. Passed ball—Ruel. Umpires—Connolly (A.L.), Klem (N.L.), Dinneen (A.L.) and Quigley (N.L.). Time—3:07. Attendance—35,760.

Sunday, October 5—At Washington

New York (N.L.)	AB.	R.	H.	O.	A.	E.
Lindstrom, 3b	3	0	1	0	7	0
Frisch, 2b	3	1	1	2	2	0
Youngs, rf	4	0	1	0	0	0
Kelly, 1b	3	2	1	14	1	0
Meusel, lf	4	0	1	1	0	0
Wilson, cf	4	0	1	0	0	0
Jackson, ss	4	0	0	1	2	0
Gowdy, c	3	0	0	6	2	0
Bentley, p	3	0	0	1	2	0
Totals	31	3	6	a25	16	0

Wash'gton (A.L.)	AB.	R.	H.	O.	A.	E.
McNeely, cf	4	0	0	0	0	0
Harris, 2b	3	1	1	3	5	1
Rice, rf	3	1	2	4	0	0
Goslin, lf	4	1	1	1	0	0
Judge, 1b	2	1	1	15	0	0
Bluege, 3b	3	0	0	0	5	0
Peckinpaugh, ss	4	0	1	2	6	0
Ruel, c	3	0	0	1	0	0
Zachary, p	2	0	0	1	2	0
Marberry, p	0	0	0	0	0	0
Totals	28	4	6	27	18	1

New York...............0 0 0 0 0 0 1 0 2—3
Washington..........2 0 0 0 1 0 0 0 1—4

aOne out when winning run scored. Runs batted in—Goslin 2, Harris, Peckinpaugh, Kelly, Wilson. Two-base hit—Peckinpaugh. Home runs—Goslin, Harris. Sacrifice hits—Rice, Bluege. Stolen base—Rice. Double plays—Bluege, Harris and Judge 2; Harris, Peckinpaugh and Judge. Left on bases—Washington 5, New York 4. Earned runs—Washington 4, New York 3. Struck out—By Bentley 6, by Marberry 1. Bases on balls—Off Bentley 4, off Zachary 3. Hits—Off Zachary 6 in 8⅔ innings, off Marberry 0 in ⅓ inning. Passed ball—Gowdy. Winning pitcher—Zachary. Umpires—Klem (N.L.), Dinneen (A.L.), Quigley (N.L.) and Connolly (A.L.). Time—1:58. Attendance—35,922.

Monday, October 6—At New York

Wash'gton (A.L.)	AB.	R.	H.	O.	A.	E.
Leibold, cf	4	0	0	2	0	0
Harris, 2b	5	1	1	2	4	1
Rice, rf	3	1	1	1	0	0
Goslin, lf	5	0	1	3	1	0
Judge, 1b	5	1	3	5	0	0
Bluege, 3b-ss	3	1	1	2	2	0
Peckinpaugh, ss	1	0	0	0	0	0
Miller, 3b	2	0	1	2	0	1
Ruel, c	3	0	0	7	0	0
Marberry, p	1	0	0	0	1	0
aTate	1	0	0	0	0	0
Russell, p	0	0	0	0	1	0
bMcNeely	1	0	0	0	0	0
Martina, p	0	0	0	0	0	0
cShirley	1	0	1	0	0	0
Speece, p	0	0	0	0	2	0
Totals	34	4	9	24	11	2

New York (N.L.)	AB.	R.	H.	O.	A.	E.
Lindstrom, 3b	4	0	1	3	1	0
Frisch, 3b	4	0	2	4	6	0
Youngs, rf	4	0	1	2	0	0
Kelly, cf	4	1	2	2	0	0
Southworth, cf	0	0	0	0	0	0
Terry, 1b	4	1	2	10	0	0
Wilson, lf	4	0	0	4	0	0
Jackson, ss	4	2	1	0	1	0
Gowdy, c	4	0	2	2	0	0
McQuillan, p	0	1	0	0	2	0
Ryan, p	2	1	1	0	0	0
Jonnard, p	0	0	0	0	0	0
Watson, p	0	0	0	0	0	0
Totals	34	6	12	27	10	0

1924 WORLD SERIES

Washington............ 0 0 0   2 0 0   0 1 1—4
New York............... 0 2 1   1 0 1   0 1 *—6

aWalked for Marberry in fourth. bFlied out for Russell in seventh. cSingled for Martina in eighth. Runs batted in—Gowdy 2, Ryan, Lindstrom, Miller, Shirley. Two-base hits—Judge, Lindstrom. Home run—Ryan. Sacrifice hits—Miller, Ryan. Stolen base—Jackson. Double plays—McQuillan, Frisch and Terry; Marberry, Bluege, Harris and Judge. Left on bases—Washington 13, New York 8. Earned runs—New York 3, Washington 4. Struck out—By Marberry 4, by Martina 1, by Ryan 2. Bases on balls—Off Marberry 2, off Ryan 3, off Jonnard 1, off McQuillan 5. Hit by pitcher—By Marberry (Frisch). Wild pitch—Marberry. Hits—Off Marberry 5 in 3 innings, off Russell 4 in 3 innings, off Martina 0 in 1 inning off Speece 3 in 1 inning, off McQuillan 2 in 3⅔ innings, off Ryan 7 in 4⅔ innings, off Jonnard 0 in 0 (pitched to one batter in ninth), off Watson 0 in ⅔ inning. Winning pitcher—McQuillan. Losing pitcher—Marberry. Umpires—Dinneen (A.L.), Quigley (N.L.), Connolly (A.L.) and Klem (N.L.). Time—2:25. Attendance—47,608.

Tuesday, October 7—At New York

Wash'gton (A.L.)	AB	R	H	O	A	E
McNeely, cf	5	2	3	3	0	0
Harris, 2b	5	2	2	2	8	0
Rice, rf	5	0	0	1	1	1
Goslin, lf	4	2	4	3	0	0
Judge, 1b	4	1	1	11	1	0
Bluege, ss	4	0	3	2	3	1
Ruel, c	3	0	0	5	0	0
Miller, 3b	4	0	0	0	2	1
Mogridge, p	4	0	0	0	0	0
Marberry, p	0	0	0	0	0	0
Totals	38	7	13	27	15	3

New York (N.L.)	AB	R	H	O	A	E
Lindstrom, 3b	4	1	3	1	2	0
Frisch, 2b	4	0	0	3	3	0
Youngs, rf	4	1	0	0	0	0
Kelly, 1b	5	1	1	11	1	0
Meusel, lf	2	0	0	2	0	1
Wilson, cf	4	0	1	3	0	0
Jackson, ss	4	0	0	0	3	0
Gowdy, c	4	1	1	6	1	0
Barnes, p	0	0	0	1	1	0
aTerry	1	0	0	0	0	0
Baldwin, p	0	0	0	0	0	0
bSouthworth	1	0	0	0	0	0
Dean, p	0	0	0	0	0	0
cBentley	1	0	0	0	0	0
Totals	34	4	6	27	11	1

Washington............ 0 0 3   0 2 0   0 2 0—7
New York............... 1 0 0   0 0 1   0 1 1—4

aGrounded out for Barnes in fifth. bReached first on Miller's error for Baldwin in seventh. cStruck out for Dean in ninth. Runs batted in—Goslin 4, Bluege 2, Youngs, Wilson 2, Lindstrom. Two-base hits—Kelly, McNeely, Wilson. Home run—Goslin. Sacrifice hit—Ruel. Left on bases—New York 9, Washington 5. Earned runs—Washington 5, New York 2. Struck out—By Mogridge 2, by Marberry 2, by Barnes 3, by Baldwin 1, by Dean 2. Bases on balls—Off Mogridge 5, off Marberry 1. Wild pitch—Barnes. Hits—Off Mogridge 3 in 7⅓ innings, off Marberry 3 in 1⅔ innings, off Barnes 9 in 5 innings, off Baldwin 1 in 2 innings, off Dean 3 in 2 innings. Winning pitcher—Mogridge. Losing pitcher—Barnes. Umpires—Quigley (N.L.), Connolly (A.L.), Klem (N.L.) and Dinneen (A.L.). Time—2:10. Attendance—49,243.

Wednesday, October 8—At New York

Wash'gton (A.L.)	AB	R	H	O	A	E
McNeely, cf	4	0	1	1	0	0
Harris, 2b	5	0	1	8	2	0
Rice, rf	4	0	0	1	2	0
Goslin, lf	4	1	2	1	0	0
Judge, 1b	4	1	3	3	2	0
Bluege, ss	3	0	0	0	2	0
Ruel, c	2	0	0	6	2	0
Miller, 3b	3	0	1	3	1	0
aLeibold	1	0	0	0	0	0
Johnson, p	3	0	1	1	2	1
bTate	0	0	0	0	0	0
cTaylor	0	0	0	0	0	0
Totals	33	2	9	24	13	1

New York (N.L.)	AB	R	H	O	A	E
Lindstrom, 3b	5	0	4	1	1	0
Frisch, 2b	5	0	1	1	6	0
Youngs, rf	3	0	1	1	1	0
Kelly, cf	4	1	1	2	0	0
Terry, 1b	2	1	1	12	1	0
Wilson, lf	3	0	0	3	1	0
Jackson, ss	3	1	1	1	2	0
Gowdy, c	4	2	1	6	0	0
Bentley, p	3	1	2	0	1	0
McQuillan, p	1	0	1	0	0	0
Totals	33	6	13	27	13	0

Washington............ 0 0 0   1 0 0   0 1 0—2
New York............... 0 0 1   0 2 0   0 3 *—6

aFlied out for Miller in ninth. bWalked for Johnson in ninth. cRan for Tate in ninth. Runs batted in—Lindstrom 2, Bentley 2, Jackson, McQuillan, Miller, Goslin. Two-base hit—Frisch. Three-base hit—Terry. Home runs—Bentley, Goslin. Sacrifice hits—Wilson, Jackson, Bluege. Double plays—Rice, Johnson and Ruel; Bluege, Harris and Judge. Left on bases—Washington 9, New York 8. Earned runs—New York 3, Washington 2. Struck out—By Johnson 3, by Bentley 4, by McQuillan 1. Bases on balls—Off Johnson 2, off Bentley 3, off McQuillan 1. Hit by pitcher—By Johnson (Youngs). Hits—Off Bentley 9 in 7⅓ innings, off McQuillan 0 in 1⅔ innings. Winning pitcher—Bentley. Umpires—Connolly (A.L.), Klem (N.L.), Dinneen (A.L.) and Quigley (N.L.). Time—2:30. Attendance—49,211.

Thursday, October 9—At Washington

New York (N.L.)	AB	R	H	O	A	E
Lindstrom, 3b	4	0	0	1	1	0
Frisch, 2b	4	0	2	1	2	0
Youngs, rf	4	1	0	1	0	0
Kelly, 1b	4	0	2	11	1	1
bSouthworth	0	0	0	0	0	0
Meusel, lf	4	0	0	1	0	0
Wilson, cf	4	0	2	1	0	0
Jackson, ss	3	0	0	3	2	0
Gowdy, c	3	0	1	5	1	0
Nehf, p	2	0	0	0	4	0
aSnyder	1	0	0	0	0	0
Ryan, p	0	0	0	0	1	0
Totals	33	1	7	24	12	1

Wash'gton (A.L.)	AB	R	H	O	A	E
McNeely, cf	2	1	0	1	0	0
Harris, 2b	4	0	1	4	5	0
Rice, rf	4	0	1	4	0	0
Goslin, lf	4	0	0	1	0	0
Judge, 1b	3	0	0	11	0	0
Bluege, 3b-ss	3	0	0	1	3	0
Peckinpaugh, ss	2	1	2	1	4	0
Taylor, 3b	0	0	0	0	0	0
Ruel, c	2	0	0	4	1	0
Zachary, p	3	0	0	0	2	0
Totals	27	2	4	27	15	0

New York .... 1 0 0   0 0 0   0 0 0—1
Washington .... 0 0 0   0 2 0   0 0 *—2

aFlied out for Nehf in eighth. bRan for Kelly in ninth. Runs batted in—Harris 2, Kelly. Two-base hits—Frisch 2. Sacrifice hit—Ruel. Stolen bases—McNeely, Bluege. Double play—Harris, Peckinpaugh and Judge. Left on bases—Washington 7, New York 5. Earned runs—Washington 2, New York 1. Struck out—By Nehf 4, by Ryan 1, by Zachary 3. Bases on balls—Off Nehf 4, off Ryan 1. Hits—Off Nehf 4 in 7 innings, off Ryan 0 in 1 inning. Losing pitcher—Nehf. Umpires—Klem (N.L.), Dinneen (A.L.), Quigley (N.L.) and Connolly (A.L.). Time—1:57. Attendance—34,254.

Friday, October 10—At Washington

New York (N.L.)	AB.	R.	H.	O.	A.	E.
Lindstrom, 3b	5	0	1	0	3	0
Frisch, 2b	5	0	2	3	4	0
Youngs, rf-lf	2	1	0	2	0	0
Kelly, cf-1b	6	1	1	8	1	0
Terry, 1b	2	0	0	6	1	0
aMeusel, lf-rf	3	0	1	1	0	0
Wilson, lf-cf	5	1	1	4	0	0
Jackson, ss	6	0	0	1	4	2
Gowdy, c	6	0	1	8	0	1
Barnes, p	4	0	0	1	2	0
Nehf, p	0	0	0	0	0	0
McQuillan, p	0	0	0	0	0	0
eGroh	1	0	1	0	0	0
fSouthworth	0	0	0	0	0	0
Bentley, p	0	0	0	0	0	0
Totals	45	3	8	g34	15	3

Wash'gton (A.L.)	AB.	R.	H.	O.	A.	E.
McNeely, cf	6	0	1	0	0	0
Harris, 2b	5	1	3	4	1	0
Rice, rf	5	0	0	2	0	0
Goslin, lf	5	0	2	3	0	0
Judge, 1b	4	0	1	11	1	1
Bluege, ss	5	0	0	1	7	2
Taylor, 3b	2	0	0	0	3	1
bLeibold	1	1	1	0	0	0
Miller, 3b	2	0	0	1	1	0
Ruel, c	5	2	2	13	0	0
Ogden, p	0	0	0	0	0	0
Mogridge, p	1	0	0	0	0	0
Marberry, p	1	0	0	1	0	0
cTate	0	0	0	0	0	0
dShirley	0	0	0	0	0	0
Johnson, p	2	0	0	0	1	0
Totals	44	4	10	36	14	4

New York .... 0 0 0   0 0 3   0 0 0   0 0 0—3
Washington .... 0 0 0   1 0 0   0 2 0   0 0 1—4

aFlied out for Terry in sixth. bDoubled for Taylor in eighth. cWalked for Marberry in eighth. dRan for Tate in eighth. eSingled for McQuillan in eleventh. fRan for Groh in eleventh. gOne out when winning run scored. Runs batted in—Harris 3, McNeely, Meusel. Two-base hits—Lindstrom, Leibold, Ruel, Goslin, McNeely. Three-base hit—Frisch. Home run—Harris. Sacrifice hits—Meusel, Lindstrom. Stolen base—Youngs. Double plays—Kelly and Jackson; Jackson, Frisch and Kelly; Johnson, Bluege and Judge. Left on bases—New York 14, Washington 8. Earned runs—Washington 4, New York 1. Struck out—By Ogden 1, by Mogridge 3, by Marberry 3, by Johnson 5, by Barnes 6, by McQuillan 1. Bases on balls—Off Ogden 1, off Mogridge 1, off Marberry 1, off Johnson 2, off Barnes 1, off Bentley 1. Hits—Off Ogden 0 in ⅓ inning, off Mogridge 4 in 4⅔ (pitched to two batters in sixth inning), off Marberry 1 in 3 innings, off Johnson 3 in 4 innings, off Barnes 6 in 7⅔ innings, off Nehf 1 in ⅔ inning, off McQuillan 0 in 1⅓ innings, off Bentley 3 in 1⅓ innings. Winning pitcher—Johnson. Losing pitcher—Bentley. Umpires—Dinneen (A.L.), Quigley (N.L.), Connolly (A.L.), and Klem (N.L.). Time—3:00. Attendance—31,667.

COMPOSITE BATTING AVERAGES
Washington Senators

Player-Position	G.	AB.	R.	H.	2B.	3B.	HR.	RBI.	BA.
Shirley, ph-pr	3	2	1	1	0	0	0	1	.500
Peckinpaugh, ss	4	12	1	5	2	0	0	2	.417
Judge, 1b	7	26	4	10	1	0	0	0	.385
Goslin, lf	7	32	4	11	1	0	3	7	.344
Harris, 2b	7	33	5	11	0	0	2	7	.333
McNeely, cf-ph	7	27	4	6	3	0	0	1	.222
Rice, rf	7	29	2	6	0	0	0	1	.207
Bluege, 3b-ss	7	26	2	5	0	0	0	2	.192
Miller, 3b	4	11	0	2	0	0	0	2	.182
Leibold, cf-ph	3	6	1	1	1	0	0	0	.167
Johnson, p	3	9	0	1	0	0	0	0	.111
Ruel, c	7	21	2	2	1	0	0	0	.095
Marberry, p	4	2	0	0	0	0	0	0	.000
Taylor, pr-3b	3	2	0	0	0	0	0	0	.000
Tate, ph	3	0	0	0	0	0	0	0	.000
Zachary, p	2	5	0	0	0	0	0	0	.000
Mogridge, p	2	5	0	0	0	0	0	0	.000
Russell, p	1	0	0	0	0	0	0	0	.000
Martina, p	1	0	0	0	0	0	0	0	.000
Speece, p	1	0	0	0	0	0	0	0	.000
Ogden, p	1	0	0	0	0	0	0	0	.000
Totals	7	248	26	61	9	0	5	23	.246

New York Giants

Player-Position	G.	AB.	R.	H.	2B.	3B.	HR.	RBI.	BA.
Groh, ph	1	1	0	1	0	0	0	0	1.000
McQuillan, p	3	1	1	1	0	0	0	1	1.000
Ryan, p	2	2	1	1	0	0	1	1	.500
Terry, 1b-ph	5	14	3	6	0	1	1	4	.429
Nehf, p	3	7	1	3	0	0	0	0	.429
Frisch, 2b-3b	7	30	1	10	4	1	0	0	.333
Lindstrom, 3b	7	30	1	10	2	0	0	4	.333
Kelly, cf-2b-1b	7	31	7	9	1	0	1	4	.290
Bentley, ph-p	5	7	1	2	0	0	1	2	.286
Gowdy, c	7	27	3	7	0	0	0	2	.259
Wilson, lf-cf	7	30	1	7	1	0	0	3	.233
Youngs, rf-lf	7	27	3	5	1	0	0	2	.185
Meusel, lf-rf	4	13	0	2	0	0	0	1	.154
Jackson, ss	7	27	3	2	0	0	0	1	.074
So'wo'h, pr-cf-ph	5	1	1	0	0	0	0	0	.000
Barnes, p	2	4	0	0	0	0	0	0	.000
Jonnard, p	1	0	0	0	0	0	0	0	.000
Watson, p	1	0	0	0	0	0	0	0	.000
Baldwin, p	1	0	0	0	0	0	0	0	.000
Dean, p	1	0	0	0	0	0	0	0	.000
Snyder, ph	1	1	0	0	0	0	0	0	.000
Totals	7	253	27	66	9	2	4	22	.261

COMPOSITE PITCHING AVERAGES
Washington Senators

Pitcher	G.	IP.	H.	R.	E.	SO.	BB.	W.	L.	ERA.
Martina	1	1	0	0	0	1	0	0	0	0.00
Ogden	1	⅓	0	0	0	1	1	0	0	0.00
Marberry	4	8	9	6	1	10	4	0	1	1.13
Zachary	2	17⅔	13	4	4	3	3	2	0	2.04
Johnson	3	24	30	10	6	20	11	1	2	2.25
Mogridge	2	12	7	4	3	5	6	1	0	2.25
Russell	1	3	4	2	1	0	0	0	0	3.00
Speece	1	1	3	1	1	0	0	0	0	9.00
Totals	7	67	66	27	16	40	25	4	3	2.15

New York Giants

Pitcher	G.	IP.	H.	R.	E.	SO.	BB.	W.	L.	ERA.
Baldwin	1	2	1	0	0	1	0	0	0	0.00
Dean	1	2	3	2	0	2	0	0	0	0.00
Jonnard	1	0	0	0	0	0	1	0	0	0.00
Watson	1	⅔	0	0	0	0	0	0	0	0.00
Nehf	3	19⅔	15	5	4	7	9	1	1	1.83
McQuillan	3	7	2	2	2	2	6	1	0	2.57
Ryan	2	⅔	2	1	1	0	0	0	0	3.18
Bentley	3	17⅔	18	7	7	10	8	1	2	3.57
Barnes	2	12⅔	15	8	8	9	1	0	1	5.68
Totals	7	67⅓	61	26	23	34	29	3	4	3.07

SERIES OF 1925

	W.	L.	Pct.
Pittsburgh N. L.	4	3	.571
Washington A. L.	3	4	.429

Washington easily repeated in the American League in 1925, defeating the second-place Athletics by eight and one-half games, and in the National League, Pittsburgh, a hot contender in 1924, finally smashed the Giants' four-year pennant domination, Bill McKechnie's first winner defeating New York also by eight and one-half games. The subsequent World Series made history, as the Pirates staged a comeback unparalleled in a seven-game Series, winning out after they were trailing, three games to one. In only one other Series, in 1903, which also involved the Pittsburgh club, had a club overcome such a deficit, the Red Sox doing it in a nine-game Series.

The 1925 Pirates eventually won out on a muddy, rain-soaked field in Pittsburgh, overcoming an early 4 to 0 Washington lead in the deciding game to win, 9 to 7. At no time in the Series were the Buccos ahead until the eighth inning of the last game, when in the wet and gloom of a rainy afternoon Kiki Cuyler, Pittsburgh right fielder, climaxed a great day and Series by doubling off Walter Johnson with the bases full, sending across the winning run.

Johnson pitched much better than in the preceding fall against the Giants, holding the Pirates to one run in winning the first and fourth games. He won the opener from Lee Meadows and Johnny Morrison, 4 to 1, giving up only five hits, and four days later hurled a six-hit, 4 to 0 shutout. However, Johnson could not get his stuff on the soggy, rain-bespattered ball in the closing game, despite the fact that his club gave him seven runs, four in the first inning. The Pirates, proving steady warriors in the wet going, banged Walter for 15 hits in the grand finale. Pittsburgh's pitching hero was Ray Kremer, who, after winning the sixth game, 3 to 2, tying up the Series, also received credit for the seventh game by pitching four innings in a relief role, giving up only one hit, a home run by Roger Peckinpaugh.

Peckinpaugh, chosen the Most Valuable Player of the American League on the eve of the Series, was the goat of the titular battling and largely responsible for Washington blowing its early lead. This usually steady shortstop established a World Series record by committing eight errors on his 40 chances, several of them being made on double-play balls.

The tight Series was reflected in the closeness of the batting, as the Pirates hit .265, compared to .262 for the Senators. A Series record was established with 12 homers, eight going to the American Leaguers. The hitting of the entire Washington outfield was spectacular. Joe (Moon) Harris was especially tough on the Pirate pitchers, getting 11 hits for 22 bases and an average of .440. He poled three homers, as did Goose Goslin. Sam Rice made the most hits for either team, 12, and batted .364. Sam also made a phenomenal catch on Earl Smith, Pirate catcher, robbing him of a home run, as he dived into a temporary bleacher after catching the ball.

Max Carey, the Pirates' captain, was the batting leader of the entire Series, hitting .458. Another Pirate hero was Stuffy McInnis, former Athletic and Red Sox first baseman. After the Pirates trailed, three games to one, McKechnie benched first baseman George Grantham and sent Stuffy to the bag and he helped spark a drive which enabled Pittsburgh to win three straight games.

Kremer and Vic Aldridge were each credited with two of the Pirate victories, while Kremer, Lee Meadows and Emil Yde each lost a game. Johnson won two games for the Senators and lost one; Alex Ferguson took one and dropped one, while Stanley Coveleski, hero of the Cleveland Series five years before, suffered two Senator losses. The box scores:

Wednesday, October 7—At Pittsburgh

Wash'ton (A.L.)	AB.	R.	H.	O.	A.	E.
Rice, cf-rf	4	0	2	3	0	0
S. Harris, 2b	3	0	0	1	0	0
Goslin, lf	4	1	1	0	0	0
Judge, 1b	3	0	0	5	2	0
J. Harris, rf	4	2	2	4	0	0
McNeely, cf	0	0	0	1	0	0
Bluege, 3b	4	1	2	0	2	0
Peckinpaugh, ss	4	0	1	3	2	1
Ruel, c	3	0	0	10	2	0
Johnson, p	3	0	0	0	0	0
Totals	32	4	8	27	8	1

Pittsburgh (N.L.)	AB.	R.	H.	O.	A.	E.
Moore, 2b	4	0	0	1	1	0
Carey, cf	2	0	0	3	0	0
Cuyler, rf	4	0	1	0	0	0
Barnhart, lf	4	0	1	0	0	0
Traynor, 3b	4	1	2	1	3	0
Wright, ss	4	0	0	1	5	0
Grantham, 1b	3	0	0	15	1	0
Smith, c	3	0	1	5	0	0
aBigbee	0	0	0	0	0	0
Gooch, c	0	0	0	1	0	0
Meadows, p	1	0	0	0	2	0
bMcInnis	1	0	0	0	0	0
Morrison, p	0	0	0	0	1	0
Totals	30	1	5	27	13	0

Washington .... 0 1 0   0 2 0   0 0 1—4
Pittsburgh .... 0 0 0   0 1 0   0 0 0—1

aRan for Smith in eighth. bFanned for Meadows in eighth. Runs batted in—J. Harris, Rice 2, Bluege, Traynor. Home runs—J. Harris, Traynor. Sacrifice hit—Judge. Stolen bases—Grantham, Bigbee. Double plays—Peckinpaugh and Judge; Grantham (unassisted). Left on bases—Pittsburgh 5, Washington 3. Earned runs—Washington 4, Pittsburgh 1. Struck out—By Johnson 10, by Meadows 4, by Morrison 1. Bases on balls—Off Johnson 1. Hit by pitcher—By Johnson (Carey 2), by Meadows (S. Harris). Hits—Off Meadows 6 in

1925 WORLD SERIES

8 innings, off Morrison 2 in 1 inning. Losing pitcher—Meadows. Umpires—Rigler (N.L.), Owens (A.L.), McCormick (N.L.) and Moriarty (A.L.). Time—1:57. Attendance—41,723.

Thursday, October 8—At Pittsburgh

Wash'ton (A.L.)	AB.	R.	H.	O.	A.	E.
Rice, cf	5	0	2	2	0	0
S. Harris, 2b	3	0	0	4	4	0
Goslin, lf	4	0	0	0	0	0
Judge, 1b	4	1	1	11	0	0
J. Harris, rf	3	0	2	0	0	0
bMcNeely	0	1	0	0	0	0
Bluege, 3b	2	0	0	0	1	0
aMyer, 3b	1	0	1	1	0	0
Peckinpaugh, ss	3	0	1	1	7	2
Ruel, c	3	0	1	5	0	0
cVeach	0	0	0	0	0	0
Coveleski, p	2	0	0	0	2	0
dRuether	1	0	0	0	0	0
Totals	31	2	8	24	14	2

Pittsburgh (N.L.)	AB.	R.	H.	O.	A.	E.
Moore, 2b	4	1	0	3	1	0
Carey, cf	4	0	2	4	0	0
Cuyler, rf	3	1	1	1	0	0
Barnhart, lf	4	0	1	3	0	0
Traynor, 3b	3	0	0	0	2	0
Wright, ss	4	1	2	1	5	0
Grantham, 1b	4	0	0	9	1	0
Smith, c	3	0	1	6	2	0
Aldridge, p	3	0	0	0	2	0
Totals	32	3	7	27	13	0

Washington .... 0 1 0   0 0 0   0 0 1—2
Pittsburgh .... 0 0 0   1 0 0   0 2 *—3

aRan for Bluege in sixth. bRan for J. Harris in ninth. cSacrificed for Ruel in ninth. dStruck out for Coveleski in ninth. Runs batted in—Cuyler 2, Wright, Veach, Judge. Home runs—Wright, Cuyler. Sacrifice hits—S. Harris, Coveleski, Veach, Cuyler. Left on bases—Washington 8, Pittsburgh 7. Earned runs—Pittsburgh 2, Washington 2. Struck out—By Coveleski 3, by Aldridge 4. Bases on balls—Off Coveleski 1, off Aldridge 2. Hit by pitcher—By Aldridge (Bluege). Balk—Aldridge. Passed ball—Ruel. Umpires—Owens (A.L.), McCormick (N.L.), Moriarty (A.L.) and Rigler (N.L.). Time—2:04. Attendance—43,364.

Saturday, October 10—At Washington

Pittsburgh (N.L.)	AB.	R.	H.	O.	A.	E.
Moore, 2b	3	0	1	2	2	0
Carey, cf	4	0	2	3	0	1
Cuyler, rf	4	1	1	1	0	0
Barnhart, lf	5	0	1	2	0	0
Traynor, 3b	4	1	1	1	3	0
Wright, ss	3	1	0	1	2	1
Grantham, 1b	4	0	0	8	1	0
Smith, c	3	0	1	5	2	1
Kremer, p	3	0	1	0	1	0
dBigbee	1	0	0	0	0	0
Totals	34	3	8	a23	11	3

Wash'ton (A.L.)	AB.	R.	H.	O.	A.	E.
Rice, cf-rf	5	1	2	2	0	0
S. Harris, 2b	3	1	1	4	2	0
Goslin, lf	4	1	2	3	0	0
Judge, 1b	3	0	1	8	0	0
J. Harris, rf	4	0	2	0	0	0
Marberry, p	0	0	0	0	0	0
Myer, 3b	3	0	0	0	1	0
Peckinpaugh, ss	4	0	1	2	3	1
Ruel, c	3	0	1	8	2	0
Ferguson, p	2	1	0	0	0	0
bLeibold	0	0	0	0	0	0
cMcNeely, cf	0	1	0	0	0	0
Totals	31	4	10	27	7	1

Pittsburgh .... 0 1 0   1 0 1   0 0 0—3
Washington .... 0 0 1   0 0 1   2 0 *—4

aMyer out, hit by his own batted ball in seventh. bWalked for Ferguson in seventh. cRan for Leibold in seventh. dBatted for Kremer in ninth. Runs batted in—Judge 2, J. Harris, Goslin, Wright, Barnhart, Kremer. Two-base hits—Judge, Cuyler, Carey. Three-base hit—Traynor. Home run—Goslin. Double plays—Peckinpaugh, S. Harris and Judge; Moore and Grantham. Sacrifice hits—S. Harris, Marberry. Sacrifice flies—Wright, Judge. Left on bases— Pittsburgh 11, Washington 9. Earned runs—Washington 4, Pittsburgh 2. Struck out—By Ferguson 5, by Marberry 2, by Kremer 5. Bases on balls—Off Ferguson 4, off Kremer 3. Hit by pitcher—By Ferguson (Carey), by Marberry (Cuyler). Hits—Off Ferguson 6 in 7 innings, off Marberry 2 in 2 innings. Passed ball—Smith. Winning pitcher—Ferguson. Umpires—McCormick (N.L.), Moriarty (A.L.), Rigler (N.L.) and Owens (A.L.). Time—2:10. Attendance—36,495.

Sunday, October 11—At Washington

Pittsburgh (N.L.)	AB.	R.	H.	O.	A.	E.
Moore, 2b	4	0	1	3	3	0
Carey, cf	3	0	1	0	0	0
Cuyler, rf	4	0	0	0	0	0
Barnhart, lf	3	0	0	2	1	0
Traynor, 3b	4	0	2	0	3	0
Wright, ss	4	0	0	3	4	1
Grantham, 1b	3	0	2	10	3	0
Gooch, c	3	0	0	6	3	0
Yde, p	1	0	0	0	0	0
Morrison, p	1	0	0	2	0	0
aBigbee	1	0	0	0	0	0
Adams, p	0	0	0	0	0	0
Totals	31	0	6	24	19	1

Wash'ton (A.L.)	AB.	R.	H.	O.	A.	E.
Rice, cf	5	1	2	2	0	0
S. Harris, 2b	3	1	1	6	7	0
Goslin, lf	3	1	3	0	0	0
J. Harris, rf	4	1	1	2	0	0
Judge, 1b	3	0	0	9	0	0
Peckinpaugh, ss	4	0	1	0	2	0
Ruel, c	3	0	3	5	0	0
Myer, 3b	4	0	0	2	0	0
Johnson, p	4	0	1	1	1	0
Totals	33	4	12	27	10	0

Pittsburgh .... 0 0 0   0 0 0   0 0 0—0
Washington .... 0 0 4   0 0 0   0 0 *—4

aPopped out for Morrison in eighth. Runs batted in—Goslin 3, J. Harris. Two-base hit—Ruel. Home runs—Goslin, J. Harris. Stolen bases—Carey, Peckinpaugh. Double plays—Traynor, Moore and Grantham; S. Harris and Judge 2. Left on bases—Washington 9, Pittsburgh 6. Earned runs—Washington 3. Struck out—By Johnson 2, by Morrison 4, by Yde 1. Bases on balls—Off Johnson 2, off Morrison 1, off Yde 3. Hits—Off Yde 5 in 2⅓ innings, off Morrison 5 in 4⅔ innings, off Adams 2 in 1 inning. Losing pitcher—Yde. Umpires—Moriarty (A.L.), Rigler (N.L.), Owens (A.L.) and McCormick (N.L.). Time—2:00. Attendance—38,701.

Monday, October 12—At Washington

Pittsburgh (N.L.)	AB.	R.	H.	O.	A.	E.
Moore, 2b	4	1	1	3	2	0
Carey, cf	4	2	2	0	0	0
Cuyler, rf	4	1	2	4	0	0
Barnhart, lf	4	1	2	1	0	0
Traynor, 3b	3	0	1	1	0	0
Wright, ss	5	1	2	1	3	0
McInnis, 1b	5	0	1	12	2	0

	AB.	R.	H.	O.	A.	E.
Smith, c	3	0	2	5	2	0
Aldridge, p	4	0	0	0	2	0
Totals	36	6	13	27	11	0
Wash'ton (A.L.)	AB.	R.	H.	O.	A.	E.
Rice, cf	5	1	2	3	0	0
S. Harris, 2b	3	0	0	2	3	0
Goslin, lf	4	0	1	5	0	0
Judge, 1b	3	0	0	11	0	0
J. Harris, rf	3	1	2	0	0	0
Peckinpaugh, ss	3	0	0	4	3	1
Ruel, c	3	0	1	1	1	0
Bluege, 3b	4	0	1	1	5	0
Coveleski, p	1	0	0	0	2	0
Ballou, p	0	0	0	0	0	0
aLeibold	1	1	1	0	0	0
Zachary, p	0	0	0	0	0	0
Marberry, p	0	0	0	0	0	0
bAdams	1	0	0	0	0	0
Totals	31	3	8	27	14	1

```
Pittsburgh............ 0 0 2  0 0 0  2 1 1—6
Washington........... 1 0 0  1 0 0  1 0 0—3
```

aDoubled for Ballou in seventh. bGrounded out for Marberry in ninth. Runs batted in—Barnhart 2, Traynor, Cuyler, McInnis, Wright, Goslin, J. Harris, Rice. Two-base hits—Goslin, Bluege, Leibold, Wright. Home run—J. Harris. Sacrifice hits—Traynor, E. Smith, S. Harris 2, Peckinpaugh. Stolen bases—Carey, Barnhart. Double plays—Bluege, S. Harris and Judge; Coveleski, Peckinpaugh and Judge; E. Smith and Traynor. Left on bases—Pittsburgh 10, Washington 8. Earned runs—Pittsburgh 6, Washington 3. Struck out—By Aldridge 5, by Ballou 1. Bases on balls—Off Aldridge 4, off Coveleski 4, off Zachary 1. Hits—Off Coveleski 9 in 6⅓ innings, off Ballou 0 in ⅔ inning, off Zachary 3 in 1⅔ innings, off Marberry 1 in ⅓ inning. Losing pitcher—Coveleski. Umpires—Rigler (N.L.), Owens (A.L.), McCormick (N.L.) and Moriarty (A.L.). Time—2:26. Attendance—35,899.

Tuedsay, October 13—At Pittsburgh

Wash'ton (A.L.)	AB.	R.	H.	O.	A.	E.
Rice, cf	4	0	0	2	0	0
S. Harris, 2b	3	0	0	3	0	0
cVeach	1	0	0	0	0	0
Ballou, p	0	0	0	0	0	0
Goslin, lf	3	1	1	2	0	0
J. Harris, rf	4	0	1	2	0	0
Judge, 1b	4	0	1	9	0	0
Bluege, 3b	4	1	1	0	6	0
Peckinpaugh, ss	3	0	1	0	3	1
Severeid, c	3	0	1	6	0	1
aMcNeely	0	0	0	0	0	0
S. Adams, 2b	0	0	0	0	0	0
Ferguson, p	2	0	0	0	1	0
bLeibold	1	0	0	0	0	0
Ruel, c	0	0	0	0	0	0
Totals	32	2	6	24	10	2
Pittsburgh (N.L.)	AB.	R.	H.	O.	A.	E.
Moore, 2b	3	2	2	2	4	0
Carey, cf	2	1	0	0	0	0
Cuyler, rf	3	0	0	2	0	0
Barnhart, lf	3	0	1	2	0	0
Traynor, 3b	4	0	2	1	4	0
Wright, ss	3	0	0	3	2	0
McInnis, 1b	4	0	1	12	1	0
Smith, c	4	0	1	3	1	0
Kremer, p	3	0	0	2	3	1
Totals	29	3	7	27	15	1

```
Washington........... 1 1 0  0 0 0  0 0 0—2
Pittsburgh............ 0 0 2  0 1 0  0 0 *—3
```

aRan for Severeid in eighth. bPopped out for Ferguson in eighth. cGrounded out for S. Harris in eighth. Runs batted in—Moore, Traynor, Goslin, Barnhart, Peckinpaugh. Two-base hits—Peckinpaugh, Barnhart, J. Harris. Home runs—Goslin, Moore. Sacrifice hits—Carey, Cuyler. Stolen bases—Traynor, McNeely. Double play—Judge (unassisted). Left on bases—Pittsburgh 8, Washington 4. Earned runs—Pittsburgh 3, Washington 2. Struck out—By Kremer 3, by Ferguson 6. Bases on balls—Off Kremer 1, off Ferguson 2, off Ballou 1. Hits—Off Ferguson 7 in 7 innings, off Ballou 0 in 1 inning. Losing pitcher—Ferguson. Umpires—Owens (A.L.), McCormick (N.L.), Moriarty (A.L.) and Rigler (N.L.). Time—1:57. Attendance—43,810.

Thursday, October 15—At Pittsburgh

Wash'ton (A.L.)	AB.	R.	H.	O.	A.	E.
Rice, cf	5	2	2	3	0	0
S. Harris, 2b	5	0	0	6	3	0
Goslin, lf	4	2	1	2	0	0
J. Harris, rf	3	1	1	1	1	0
Judge, 1b	3	1	1	6	0	0
Bluege, 3b	4	0	1	0	0	0
aPeckinpaugh, ss	3	1	1	0	2	2
Ruel, c	4	0	0	6	0	0
Johnson, p	4	0	0	0	3	0
Totals	35	7	7	24	9	2
Pittsburgh (N.L.)	AB.	R.	H.	O.	A.	E.
Moore, 2b	4	3	1	2	0	1
Carey, cf	5	3	4	3	0	0
Cuyler, rf	4	0	2	4	0	1
Barnhart, lf	5	0	1	2	0	0
Oldham, p	0	0	0	0	0	0
Traynor, 3b	4	0	1	1	3	0
Wright, ss	4	0	1	1	3	0
McInnis, 1b	4	0	2	7	0	0
Smith, c	4	0	1	4	0	0
cYde	0	1	0	0	0	0
Gooch, c	0	0	0	2	0	0
Aldridge, p	0	0	0	0	0	0
Morrison, p	1	1	0	0	0	0
bGrantham	1	0	0	0	0	0
Kremer, p	1	0	1	0	1	0
dBigbee, lf	1	1	1	0	0	0
Totals	38	9	15	27	7	2

```
Washington........... 4 0 0  2 0 0  0 1 0—7
Pittsburgh............ 0 0 3  0 1 0  2 3 *—9
```

aPeckinpaugh given base in first inning on Smith's interference. bFlied out for Morrison in fourth. cRan for Smith in eighth. dDoubled for Kremer in eighth. Runs batted in—Barnhart, Moore, Carey 2, Traynor, Bluege, Ruel, J. Harris 2, Bigbee, Peckinpaugh 2. Two-base hits—Carey 3, Moore, J. Harris, Cuyler 2, Smith, Bigbee. Three-base hit—Traynor. Home run—Peckinpaugh. Sacrifice hit—Cuyler. Stolen base—Carey. Double play—S. Harris and Judge. Left on bases—Pittsburgh 7, Washington 5. Earned runs—Washington 7, Pittsburgh 5. Struck out—By Morrison 2, by Kremer 1, by Oldham 2, by Johnson 3. Bases on balls—Off Aldridge 3, off Johnson 1. Wild pitches—Aldridge 2. Hits—Off Aldridge 2 in ⅓ inning, off Morrison 4 in 3⅔ innings, off Kremer 1 in 4 innings, off Oldham 0 in 1 inning. Winning pitcher—Kremer. Umpires—McCormick (N.L.), Moriarty (A.L.), Rigler (N.L.) and Owens (A.L.). Time—2:31. Attendance—42,856.

COMPOSITE BATTING AVERAGES
Pittsburgh Pirates

Player-Position	G.	AB.	R.	H.	2B.	3B.	HR.	RBI.	BA.
Morrison, p	3	2	1	1	0	0	0	0	.500
Carey, cf	7	24	6	11	4	0	0	2	.458

1926 WORLD SERIES

Player-Position	G.	AB.	R.	H.	2B.	3B.	HR.	RBI.	BA.
Smith, c	6	20	0	7	1	0	0	0	.350
Traynor, 3b	7	26	2	9	0	2	1	4	.346
Bigbee, pr-ph-lf	4	3	1	1	1	0	0	1	.333
McInnis, ph-1b	4	14	0	4	0	0	0	1	.286
Cuyler, rf	7	26	3	7	3	0	1	6	.269
Barnhart, lf	7	28	1	7	1	0	0	5	.250
Moore, 2b	7	26	7	6	1	0	1	2	.231
Wright, ss	7	27	3	5	1	0	1	3	.185
Kremer, p	3	7	0	1	0	0	0	1	.143
Grantham, 1b-ph	5	15	0	2	0	0	0	0	.133
Aldridge, p	3	7	0	0	0	0	0	0	.000
Gooch, c	3	3	0	0	0	0	0	0	.000
Yde, p-pr	2	1	1	0	0	0	0	0	.000
Meadows, p	1	1	0	0	0	0	0	0	.000
C. Adams, p	1	0	0	0	0	0	0	0	.000
Oldham, p	1	0	0	0	0	0	0	0	.000
Totals	7	230	25	61	12	2	4	25	.265

Washington Senators

Player-Position	G.	AB.	R.	H.	2B.	3B.	HR.	RBI.	BA.
Leibold, ph	3	2	1	1	1	0	0	0	.500
J. Harris, rf	7	25	5	11	2	0	3	6	.440
Rice, cf-rf	7	33	5	12	0	0	0	3	.364
Severeid, c	1	3	0	1	0	0	0	0	.333
Ruel, c	7	19	0	6	1	0	0	1	.316
Goslin, lf	7	26	6	8	1	0	3	6	.308
Bluege, 3b	5	18	2	5	1	0	0	2	.278
Peckinpaugh, ss	7	24	1	6	1	0	1	3	.250
Myer, 3b	3	8	0	2	0	0	0	0	.250
Judge, 1b	7	23	2	4	1	0	1	3	.174
Johnson, p	3	11	0	1	0	0	0	0	.091
S. Harris, 2b	7	23	2	2	0	0	0	0	.087
McNeely, cf-pr	4	0	2	0	0	0	0	0	.000
Ferguson, p	2	4	0	0	0	0	0	0	.000
Veach, ph	2	1	0	0	0	0	0	1	.000
Coveleski, p	2	3	0	0	0	0	0	0	.000
Marberry, p	2	0	0	0	0	0	0	0	.000
Ballou, p	2	0	0	0	0	0	0	0	.000
S. Adams, ph-2b	2	1	0	0	0	0	0	0	.000
Ruether, ph	1	1	0	0	0	0	0	0	.000
Zachary, p	1	0	0	0	0	0	0	0	.000
Totals	7	225	26	59	8	0	8	25	.262

COMPOSITE PITCHING AVERAGES
Pittsburgh Pirates

Pitcher	G.	IP.	H.	R.	E.	SO.	BB.	W.	L.	ERA.
C. Adams	1	1	2	0	0	0	0	0	0	0.00
Oldham	1	1	0	0	0	2	0	0	0	0.00
Morrison	3	9⅓	11	3	3	5	1	0	0	2.89
Kremer	3	21	17	7	7	9	4	2	1	3.00
Meadows	1	8	6	3	3	4	0	0	1	3.38
Aldridge	3	18⅓	18	9	9	9	2	0	2	4.42
Yde	1	2⅓	5	4	3	1	3	0	1	11.70
Totals	7	61	59	26	25	30	17	4	3	3.69

Washington Senators

Pitcher	G.	IP.	H.	R.	E.	SO.	BB.	W.	L.	ERA.
Marberry	2	2⅓	3	0	0	2	0	0	0	0.00
Ballou	2	1⅔	0	0	0	1	1	0	0	0.00
Johnson	3	26	26	10	6	15	4	2	1	2.08
Ferguson	2	14	13	6	5	11	6	1	1	3.21
Coveleski	2	14⅓	16	7	6	3	5	0	2	3.77
Zachary	1	1⅔	3	2	2	0	1	0	0	10.80
Totals	7	60	61	25	19	32	17	3	4	2.85

SERIES OF 1926

	W.	L.	Pct.
St. Louis N. L.	4	3	.571
New York A. L.	3	4	.429

For the third time in three years, the World Series games went to the limit in 1926 when the St. Louis Cardinals, under the management of Rogers Hornsby, who led them to their first National League championship, defeated the Yankees, four games to three, in a dramatic, rip-snorting classic.

The Cardinals won their first pennant largely because the St. Louis management was willing to take on Grover Cleveland Alexander in the middle of the season after Alex had had a battle on the subject of discipline with the Chicago manager, Joe McCarthy. The Cards beat out the Reds in a tight struggle with one of the lowest averages ever to win a National League flag—.578. The Yankees, a seventh-placer in 1925, had made a remarkable comeback and won their flag with a .591 percentage, the lowest by any New York pennant winner.

St. Louis' big Series hero was Alexander, then 39 years old, returning to the World Series wars after 11 years. He won the second and sixth games for Hornsby, and then came back to save the seventh and deciding contest for St. Louis in one of the real nerve-throbbing moments of Series history. With the Cardinals leading, 3 to 2, Alex was called to Jess Haines' relief with the bases full in the seventh inning and Tony Lazzeri up. As freshman slugger of the Yanks, Push 'Em Up Tony ranked second that year only to Babe Ruth in American League runs batted in. Lazzeri hit one vicious foul down the third base line and then fanned. In his two and one-third innings, Alexander did not give up a hit. In winning the second game, 6 to 2, Alexander held the Yankees to four hits. After Earle Combs opened New York's third inning with a single, Alexander retired the next 21 Yankees in order.

Haines blanked the Bronx Bombers with five hits, 4 to 0, in the third game. It was to be 16 years later before another National League pitcher, also a Cardinal—southpaw Ernie White—again would dip the Yanks in the whitewash pail. Haines also received credit for St. Louis' victory in the seventh game. Willie Sherdel, crack St. Louis southpaw, lost two pitching duels to New York's lefthanded ace, Herb Pennock, 2 to 1, in the opener and 3 to 2, in 10 innings, in the fifth game. Herb's first effort was a three-hitter.

Waite Hoyt won his third World Series game, 10 to 5, with the aid of some terrific heavy artillery by Babe Ruth in the fourth contest, played in St. Louis. The Babe knocked out three home runs, the first two being in successive times at bat off Flint Rhem, the Redbirds' starter, and the third, in the sixth inning, off Herman Bell, third of five chuckers used by St. Louis. The Bambino banged a three-and-two pitch on a line far up in the center field bleachers for the longest drive in the history of Sportsman's Park. Ruth also hit a fourth homer off Haines at the Stadium in the seventh game. The Babe hit .300 for the Series, and got only two singles in addition to his four round-trippers, but St. Louis pitchers passed him 11 times. He walked with two out in the ninth inning of the last game and went out stealing for the last out, a much criticized play. Lou Gehrig, in his first Series, hit .348.

The Cardinals' slugging hero was the lowest hitting regular on Hornsby's squad, Tommy Thevenow, .256-hitting shortstop during the championship season. In the Series, he led both clubs, with an average of .417.

Total attendance was 328,051 and receipts were $1,207,864, a mark not excelled until 1936. Each share for the Cardinals was $5,584.51, and the Yankees, $3,417.75, not record-breaking, for the fourth-place clubs were cut in for the first time since 1918 and all first-division teams were included thereafter. The box scores:

Saturday, October 2—At New York

St. Louis (N.L.)	AB.	R.	H.	O.	A.	E.
Douthit, cf	3	1	1	1	0	0
Southworth, rf	3	0	0	1	0	0
Holm, rf	1	0	0	0	0	0
Hornsby, 2b	4	0	0	3	2	0
Bottomley, 1b	4	0	2	10	0	0
L. Bell, 3b	3	0	0	1	1	1
Hafey, lf	4	0	0	5	1	0
O'Farrell, c	2	0	0	1	1	0
Thevenow, ss	2	0	0	1	7	0
Sherdel, p	2	0	0	1	2	0
aFlowers	1	0	0	0	0	0
Haines, p	0	0	0	0	0	0
Totals	29	1	3	24	14	1

New York (A.L.)	AB.	R.	H.	O.	A.	E.
Combs, cf	3	1	1	2	0	0
Koenig, ss	4	0	1	0	4	0
Ruth, rf	3	1	1	1	0	0
Meusel, lf	1	0	0	3	0	0
Gehrig, 1b	4	0	1	14	0	0
Lazzeri, 2b	4	0	1	0	4	0
Dugan, 3b	3	0	1	1	3	0
Severeid, c	3	0	0	6	1	0
Pennock, p	2	0	0	0	3	0
Totals	27	2	6	27	15	0

St. Louis........... 1 0 0 0 0 0 0 0 0—1
New York........ 1 0 0 0 0 1 0 0 *—2

aFlied out for Sherdel in eighth. Runs batted in—Gehrig 2, Bottomley. Two-base hit—Douthit. Sacrifice hits—Pennock, Meusel, Thevenow. Double play—Thevenow, Hornsby and Bottomley. Left on bases—New York 7, St. Louis 5. Earned runs—New York 2, St. Louis 1. Struck out—By Sherdel 1, by Pennock 4. Bases on balls—Off Sherdel 3, off Haines 1, off Pennock 3. Hits—Off Sherdel 6 in 7 innings, off Haines 0 in 1 inning. Losing pitcher—Sherdel. Umpires—Dinneen (A.L.), O'Day (N.L.), Hildebrand (A.L.) and Klem (N.L.). Time—1:48. Attendance—61,658.

Sunday, October 3—At New York

St. Louis (N.L.)	AB.	R.	H.	O.	A.	E.
Douthit, cf	4	1	1	0	0	0
Southworth, rf	5	2	3	0	0	0
Hornsby, 2b	3	0	1	3	5	0
Bottomley, 1b	5	0	2	13	0	0
L. Bell, 3b	4	0	0	0	4	0
Hafey, lf	4	0	0	1	0	0
O'Farrell, c	4	1	2	10	1	0
Thevenow, ss	4	2	3	1	4	0
Alexander, p	4	0	0	0	4	1
Totals	37	6	12	27	18	1

New York (A.L.)	AB.	R.	H.	O.	A.	E.
Combs, cf	3	0	1	1	0	0
Koenig, ss	4	0	0	1	3	0
Ruth, rf	4	0	0	1	0	0
Meusel, lf	4	1	1	3	0	0
Gehrig, 1b	3	0	0	12	0	0
Lazzeri, 2b	3	1	1	2	2	0
Dugan, 3b	3	0	1	1	1	0
Severeid, c	2	0	0	5	1	0
aPaschal	1	0	0	0	0	0
Collins, c	0	0	0	1	0	0
Shocker, p	2	0	0	0	2	0
Shawkey, p	0	0	0	0	0	0
bRuether	1	0	0	0	0	0
Jones, p	0	0	0	0	0	0
Totals	30	2	4	27	9	0

St. Louis........... 0 0 2 0 0 0 3 0 1—6
New York........ 0 2 0 0 0 0 0 0 0—2

aFanned out for Severeid in eighth. bGrounded out for Shawkey in eighth. Runs batted in—Southworth 3, Bottomley 2, Thevenow, Lazzeri. Two-base hits—Hornsby, O'Farrell. Home runs—Southworth, Thevenow. Sacrifice hit—Hornsby. Double play—Alexander, Thevenow and Bottomley. Left on bases—St. Louis 7, New York 2. Earned runs—St. Louis 6, New York 1. Struck out—By Shocker 2, by Shawkey 2, by Jones 1, by Alexander 10. Bases on balls—Off Jones 2, off Alexander 1. Hits—Off Shocker 10 in 7 innings, off Shawkey 0 in 1 inning, off Jones 2 in 1 inning. Losing pitcher—Shocker. Umpires—O'Day (N.L.), Hildebrand (A.L.), Klem (N.L.) and Dinneen (A.L.). Time—1:57. Attendance—63,600.

Tuesday, October 5—At St. Louis

New York (A.L.)	AB.	R.	H.	O.	A.	E.
Combs, cf	3	0	1	4	0	0
Koenig, ss	4	0	0	2	3	1
Ruth, lf	3	0	1	0	0	0
Meusel, rf	4	0	0	1	0	0
Gehrig, 1b	4	0	2	10	0	0
Lazzeri, 2b	4	0	0	4	6	0
Dugan, 3b	3	0	1	0	2	0
Severeid, c	2	0	0	3	0	0
Ruether, p	2	0	0	0	2	0
Shawkey, p	0	0	0	0	0	0
aPaschal	0	0	0	0	0	0
Thomas, p	0	0	0	0	0	0
Totals	29	0	5	24	13	1

St. Louis (N.L.)	AB.	R.	H.	O.	A.	E.
Douthit, cf	3	0	0	1	0	0
Southworth, rf	3	1	2	2	0	0
Hornsby, 2b	4	0	1	1	5	0
Bottomley, 1b	4	0	1	13	0	0
L. Bell, 3b	4	1	1	0	4	0
Hafey, lf	3	0	1	4	0	0
O'Farrell, c	2	0	0	5	0	0
Thevenow, ss	3	1	0	1	2	0
Haines, p	3	1	2	0	2	0
Totals	29	4	8	27	13	0

New York........ 0 0 0 0 0 0 0 0 0—0
St. Louis........... 0 0 0 3 1 0 0 0 *—4

aWalked for Shawkey in eighth. Runs batted in—Haines 2, Bottomley. Two-base hit—Hafey. Home run—Haines. Sacrifice hits—Severeid, Southworth, Hafey. Double plays—Hornsby, Thevenow and Bottomley; Koenig, Lazzeri and Gehrig; Thevenow, Hornsby and Bottomley. Left on bases—New York 6, St. Louis 5. Earned runs—St. Louis 2. Struck out—By Haines 3, by Ruether 1, by Shawkey 1. Bases on balls—Off Haines 3, off Ruether 2. Hits—Off Ruether 7 in 4⅓ innings, off Shawkey 0 in 2⅔ innings, off Thomas 1 in 1 inning. Losing pitcher—Ruether. Umpires—Hildebrand (A.L.), Klem (N.L.), Dinneen (A.L.) and O'Day (N.L.). Time—1:41. Attendance—37,708.

Wednesday, October 6—At St. Louis

New York (A.L.)	AB.	R.	H.	O.	A.	E.
Combs, cf	5	2	2	4	0	0
Koenig, ss	6	1	1	1	3	1
Ruth, lf	3	4	3	1	1	0
Meusel, rf	2	1	1	1	0	0
Gehrig, 1b	3	0	2	8	0	0
Lazzeri, 2b	3	1	1	1	3	0
Dugan, 3b	4	0	1	1	2	0
Severeid, c	4	1	3	10	0	0
Hoyt, p	4	0	0	0	0	0
Totals	34	10	14	27	9	1

St. Louis (N.L.)	AB.	R.	H.	O.	A.	E.
Douthit, cf	5	1	2	2	2	0
Southworth, rf	5	0	3	1	2	0
Hornsby, 2b	5	1	2	3	4	0
Bottomley, 1b	4	0	1	6	1	0
L. Bell, 3b	4	0	1	3	0	0
Hafey, lf	5	1	1	0	0	0
O'Farrell, c	4	1	2	8	1	0
Thevenow, ss	4	1	2	3	2	0
Rhem, p	1	0	0	0	1	0
aToporcer	0	0	0	0	0	0
Reinhart, p	0	0	0	0	0	0
H. Bell, p	0	0	0	0	0	0
bFlowers	1	0	0	0	0	0
Hallahan, p	0	0	0	1	0	0
cHolm	1	0	0	0	0	0
Keen, p	0	0	0	0	1	0
Totals	39	5	14	27	14	0

New York .... 1 0 1 1 4 2 1 0 0—10
St. Louis .... 1 0 0 3 0 0 0 0 1— 5

aHit sacrifice fly for Rhem in fourth. bStruck out for H. Bell in sixth. cStruck out for Hallahan in eighth. Runs batted in—Ruth 4, Dugan 2, Koenig, Lazzeri, Combs, Hornsby, L. Bell, Douthit, Toporcer, Thevenow. Two-base hits—Lazzeri, Dugan, Thevenow, Douthit, Koenig, Gehrig, Combs. Home runs—Ruth 3. Sacrifice hits—Gehrig. Sacrifice flies—L. Bell, Lazzeri, Toporcer. Stolen base—Hornsby. Left on bases—New York 10, St. Louis 2. Earned runs—New York 10, St. Louis 2. Struck out—By Rhem 4, by H. Bell, 1, by Hallahan 1, by Hoyt 8. Bases on balls—Off Rhem 2, off Reinhart 4, off H. Bell 1, off Hallahan 3, off Hoyt 1. Balk—H. Bell. Hits—Off Rhem 7 in 4 innings, off Reinhart 1 in 0 (pitched to five batters in fifth inning), off H. Bell 4 in 2 innings, off Hallahan 2 in 2 innings, off Keen 0 in 1 inning. Losing pitcher—Reinhart. Umpires—Klem (N.L.), Dinneen (A.L.), O'Day (N.L.) and Hildebrand (A.L.). Time—2:38. Attendance—38,825.

Thursday, October 7—At St. Louis

New York (A.L.)	AB.	R.	H.	O.	A.	E.
Combs, cf	4	0	1	2	0	0
Koenig, ss	5	1	2	3	5	1
Ruth, lf	3	0	0	3	0	0
Meusel, rf	3	0	0	0	0	0
Gehrig, 1b	3	1	2	14	0	0
Lazzeri, 2b	4	0	2	3	2	0
Dugan, 3b	3	0	0	0	1	0
aPaschal	1	0	1	0	0	0
Gazella, 3b	0	0	0	1	2	0
Severeid, c	5	0	0	4	1	0
Pennock, p	4	1	1	0	2	0
Totals	35	3	9	30	13	1

St. Louis (N.L.)	AB.	R.	H.	O.	A.	E.
Holm, cf	4	0	0	1	0	0
Southworth, rf	4	0	0	2	0	0
Hornsby, 2b	4	0	0	3	3	0
Bottomley, 1b	4	1	1	12	0	0
L. Bell, 3b	4	1	2	2	3	0
Hafey, lf	4	0	0	6	0	0
O'Farrell, c	4	0	3	2	3	0
Thevenow, ss	4	0	1	1	3	1
Sherdel, p	3	0	0	1	3	0
bFlowers	1	0	0	0	0	0
Totals	36	2	7	30	15	1

New York ...... 0 0 0 0 0 1 0 0 1 1—3
St. Louis ...... 0 0 0 1 0 0 1 0 0 0—2

aSingled for Dugan in ninth. bPopped out for Sherdel in tenth. Runs batted in—Koenig, Paschal, Lazzeri, L. Bell, O'Farrell. Two-base hits—Bottomley, Pennock, L. Bell, Gehrig. Sacrifice hits—Meusel 2. Sacrifice fly—Lazzeri. Stolen base—Southworth. Double plays—Hornsby and Bottomley; Lazzeri, Koenig and Gehrig. Left on bases—New York 11, St. Louis 5. Earned runs—New York 2, St. Louis 2. Struck out—By Pennock 4, by Sherdel 2. Bases on balls—Off Pennock 1, off Sherdel 5. Hit by pitcher—By Sherdel (Gazella). Wild pitch—Sherdel. Passed ball—Severeid. Umpires—Dinneen (A.L.), O'Day (N.L.), Hildebrand (A.L.) and Klem (N.L.). Time—2:28. Attendance—39,552.

Saturday, October 9—At New York

St. Louis (N.L.)	AB.	R.	H.	O.	A.	E.
Holm, cf	5	1	2	4	0	0
Southworth, rf	5	3	2	2	1	0
Hornsby, 2b	4	1	1	0	2	0
Bottomley, 1b	5	2	2	11	0	0
L. Bell, 3b	4	1	3	1	1	1
Hafey, lf	3	0	1	2	0	0
O'Farrell, c	4	0	0	6	0	0
Thevenow, ss	3	1	2	1	5	1
Alexander, p	2	1	0	0	2	0
Totals	35	10	13	27	11	2

New York (A.L.)	AB.	R.	H.	O.	A.	E.
Combs, cf	5	0	2	2	0	0
Koenig, ss	5	0	0	3	2	0
Ruth, rf	3	0	0	0	1	0
Meusel, lf	3	1	2	2	0	0
Gehrig, 1b	4	0	1	9	1	0
Lazzeri, 2b	4	0	0	2	1	1
Dugan, 3b	4	1	2	3	2	0
Severeid, c	3	0	1	6	3	0
aAdams	0	0	0	0	0	0
Collins, c	1	0	0	0	0	0
Shawkey, p	2	0	0	0	1	0
Shocker, p	0	0	0	0	0	0
bPaschal	1	0	0	0	0	0
Thomas, p	0	0	0	0	2	0
cRuether	1	0	0	0	0	0
Totals	36	2	8	27	13	1

St. Louis .... 3 0 0 0 1 0 5 0 1—10
New York .... 0 0 0 1 0 0 1 0 0— 2

aRan for Severeid in seventh. bFanned for Shocker in seventh. cGrounded out for Thomas in ninth. Runs batted in—L. Bell 4, Hornsby 3, Holm, Southworth, Bottomley, Combs, Gehrig. Two-base hits—Bottomley 2, Meusel, Southworth, Hafey, Combs. Three-base hits—Meusel, Southworth. Home run—L. Bell. Sacrifice hits—Hafey, Alexander 2. Stolen base—Ruth. Double plays—Gehrig and Koenig; Southworth and Thevenow. Left on bases—New York 9, St. Louis 4. Earned runs—St. Louis 9, New York 2. Struck out—By Alexander 6, by Shawkey 4, by Shocker 1. Bases on balls—Off Alexander 2, off Shawkey 2. Hit by pitcher—By Thomas (Thevenow). Hits—Off Shawkey 8 in 6⅓ innings, off Shocker 3 in ⅔ inning, off Thomas 2 in 2 innings. Losing pitcher—Shawkey. Umpires—O'Day (N.L.), Hildebrand (A.L.), Klem (N.L.) and Dinneen (A.L.). Time—2:05. Attendance—48,615.

Sunday, October 10—At New York

St. Louis (N.L.)	AB.	R.	H.	O.	A.	E.
Holm, cf	5	0	0	2	0	0
Southworth, rf	4	0	0	0	0	0
Hornsby, 2b	4	0	2	4	1	0
Bottomley, 1b	3	1	1	14	0	0
L. Bell, 3b	4	1	0	0	4	0
Hafey, lf	4	1	2	3	0	0
O'Farrell, c	3	0	0	3	2	0
Thevenow, ss	4	0	2	1	3	0
Haines, p	2	0	1	0	4	0
Alexander, p	1	0	0	0	0	0
Totals	34	3	8	27	14	0

New York (A.L.)	AB.	R.	H.	O.	A.	E.
Combs, cf	5	0	2	2	0	0
Koenig, ss	4	0	0	2	3	1
Ruth, rf	1	1	1	2	0	0
Meusel, lf	4	0	1	3	0	1
Gehrig, 1b	2	0	0	11	0	0
Lazzeri, 2b	4	0	2	2	1	0
Dugan, 3b	4	1	2	2	3	1
Severeid, c	3	0	2	3	1	0
aAdams	0	0	0	0	0	0
Collins, c	1	0	0	0	0	0
Hoyt, p	2	0	0	0	1	0
bPaschal	1	0	0	0	0	0
Pennock, p	1	0	0	0	1	0
Totals	32	2	8	27	10	3

St. Louis	0	0	0	3	0	0	0	0 0—3
New York	0	0	1	0	0	1	0	0 0—2

aRan for Severeid in sixth. bGrounded out for Hoyt in sixth. Runs batted in—O'Farrell, Thevenow 2, Ruth, Severeid. Two-base hit—Severeid. Home run—Ruth. Sacrifice hits—Haines, Koenig, Bottomley. Sacrifice fly—O'Farrell. Struck out—By Haines 2, by Alexander 1, by Hoyt 2. Left on bases—New York 10, St. Louis 7. Earned runs—St. Louis 0, New York 2. Bases on balls—Off Haines 5, off Alexander 1. Hits—Off Hoyt 5 in 6 innings, off Pennock 3 in 3 innings, off Haines 8 in 6⅔ innings, off Alexander 0 in 2⅓ innings. Winning pitcher—Haines. Losing pitcher—Hoyt. Umpires—Hildebrand (A.L.), Klem (N.L.), Dinneen (A.L.) and O'Day (N.L.). Time—2:15. Attendance—38,093.

COMPOSITE BATTING AVERAGES
St. Louis Cardinals

Player-Position	G.	AB.	R.	H.	2B.	3B.	HR.	RBI.	BA.
Haines, p	3	5	1	3	0	0	1	2	.600
Thevenow, ss	7	24	5	10	1	0	1	4	.417
Bottomley, 1b	7	29	4	10	3	0	0	5	.345
Southworth, rf	7	29	6	10	1	1	1	4	.345
O'Farrell, c	7	23	2	7	1	0	0	2	.304
Douthit, cf	4	15	3	4	2	0	0	1	.267
L. Bell, 3b	7	27	4	7	1	0	1	6	.259
Hornsby, 2b	7	28	2	7	1	0	0	4	.250
Hafey, lf	7	27	2	5	2	0	0	0	.185
Holm, rf-ph-cf	5	16	1	2	0	0	0	1	.125
Alexander, p	3	7	1	0	0	0	0	0	.000
Flowers, ph	3	3	0	0	0	0	0	0	.000
Sherdel, p	2	5	0	0	0	0	0	0	.000
Rhem, p	1	1	0	0	0	0	0	0	.000
Toporcer, ph	1	1	0	0	0	0	0	1	.000
Reinhart, p	1	0	0	0	0	0	0	0	.000
H. Bell, p	1	0	0	0	0	0	0	0	.000
Hallahan, p	1	0	0	0	0	0	0	0	.000
Keen, p	1	0	0	0	0	0	0	0	.000
Totals	7	239	31	65	12	1	4	30	.272

New York Yankees

Player-Position	G.	AB.	R.	H.	2B.	3B.	HR.	RBI.	BA.
Combs, cf	7	28	3	10	2	0	0	2	.357
Gehrig, 1b	7	23	1	8	2	0	0	3	.348
Dugan, 3b	7	24	2	8	1	0	0	2	.333
Ruth, rf	7	20	6	6	0	0	4	5	.300
Severeid, c	7	22	1	6	1	0	0	1	.273
Paschal, ph	5	4	0	1	0	0	0	1	.250
Meusel, lf	7	21	3	5	1	1	0	0	.238
Lazzeri, 2b	7	26	2	5	1	0	0	3	.192
Pennock, p	3	7	1	1	1	0	0	1	.143
Koenig, ss	7	32	2	4	1	0	0	2	.125
Ruether, ph-p	3	4	0	0	0	0	0	0	.000
Collins, c	3	2	0	0	0	0	0	0	.000
Shawkey, p	3	2	0	0	0	0	0	0	.000
Hoyt, p	2	6	0	0	0	0	0	0	.000
Shocker, p	2	2	0	0	0	0	0	0	.000
Thomas, p	2	0	0	0	0	0	0	0	.000
Adams, p	2	0	0	0	0	0	0	0	.000
Gazella, 3b	1	0	0	0	0	0	0	0	.000
Jones, p	1	0	0	0	0	0	0	0	.000
Totals	7	223	21	54	10	1	4	19	.242

COMPOSITE PITCHING AVERAGES
St. Louis Cardinals

Pitcher	G.	IP.	H.	R.	E.	SO.	BB.	W.	L.	ERA.
Keen	1	1	0	0	0	0	0	0	0	0.00
Haines	3	16⅔	13	2	2	5	9	2	0	1.08
Alexander	3	20⅓	12	4	3	17	4	2	0	1.33
Sherdel	2	17	15	5	4	3	8	0	2	2.12
Hallahan	1	2	1	1	1	3	0	0	0	4.50
Rhem	1	4	7	3	3	4	2	0	0	6.75
H. Bell	1	2	4	2	2	1	1	0	0	9.00
Reinhart	1	0	1	4	4	0	4	0	1	...
Totals	7	63	54	21	19	31	31	4	3	2.71

New York Yankees

Pitcher	G.	IP.	H.	R.	E.	SO.	BB.	W.	L.	ERA.
Hoyt	2	15	19	8	2	8	1	1	1	1.20
Pennock	3	22	13	3	3	8	4	2	0	1.23
Thomas	2	3	3	1	1	0	0	0	0	3.00
Ruether	1	4⅓	7	4	2	1	2	0	0	4.15
Shawkey	3	10	8	7	6	7	2	0	1	5.40
Shocker	2	7⅔	13	7	7	3	0	0	1	8.22
Jones	1	1	2	1	1	1	2	0	0	9.00
Totals	7	63	65	31	22	28	11	3	4	3.14

SERIES OF 1927

	W.	L.	Pct.
New York A. L.	4	0	1.000
Pittsburgh N. L.	0	4	.000

The Yankees bounced back strongly from their 1926 Series reverse, rolling over the Pittsburgh Pirates in four straight games. It was the first time the American League won the inter-league fall battling without suffering a loss, and started the Yankees on their famous World Series parade.

Many fans considered the 1927 Bombers the greatest of all Yankee teams. The club set an American League record with 110 victories, a winning percentage of .714, and finished 19 games ahead of the second-place Athletics. It was also the year Babe Ruth reached his home run peak of 60 and young Lou Gehrig knocked in 175 runs, then a major league record. On the other hand the Pirates, led by Donie Bush, won their pennant only after a hard four-cornered struggle with St. Louis, New York and Chicago. They eventually nosed out the Cardinals by one and one-half games.

Against the Pirates, Miller Huggins' Yanks won practically as easily as they had done in their league season. Some said the Yankees overawed the Pirates during batting practice at Forbes Field before the first game by the barrage of balls they drove into the stands. However, New York really won on great pitching by Herb Pennock, Waite Hoyt, George Pipgras and Wilcy Moore, rather than on the Yankee slugging. As far as homers went, the Series resembled the pre-Ruthian home run period, as only two circuit clouts were hit, both by Ruth. Gehrig, worried over his mother, who was undergoing an operation in New York, was held to four hits, but all were for extra bases, two triples and two doubles. The Series batting star was Yankee shortstop Mark Koenig, who bagged nine hits in 18 times at bat for an average of .500. Ruth hit .400. The two Waners, then still comparative youngsters, did the most effective hitting for the Pirates, Lloyd batting .400 and Paul .333.

The Buccaneers virtually beat themselves in the opener. Paul Waner missed a shoestring attempt on a short fly by Lou Gehrig in the first inning, the ball going through for a run-producing triple. In the third, errors by George Grantham and Earl Smith enabled the Yanks to pick up three runs as Hoyt won, 5 to 4, with Moore's help.

After Pipgras copped the second contest for New York, 6 to 2, Pennock, easily winning the third game, 8 to 1, pitched the classic of the Series, as he retired 22 Pittsburgh batsmen in a row before Pie Traynor singled in the eighth. The Pirates made one more safety in the ninth to give Herb a three-hitter. It was Pennock's fifth World Series victory against no defeats.

The Pirate pitching was generally unsteady and the big thrill of the Series was saved for the ninth inning of the fourth game, played at Yankee Stadium. With Wilcy Moore, usually used as a relief pitcher, drawing the starting assignment, the Yanks had a lead of 3 to 1 up to the seventh, when the Pirates tied the score. Carmen Hill went out for a pinch-hitter during the rally and John Miljus retired the Yankees in the seventh and eighth. In the ninth, he walked Earle Combs, first man up, and Koenig beat out a bunt. Both moved up on a wild pitch, and Ruth was intentionally passed, filling the bases with none out. With Combs making a fake start for the plate with each pitch, Miljus fanned Gehrig and Bob Meusel. Then, working on Tony Lazzeri, he made his second wild pitch of the inning (Johnny Gooch was the Pirate catcher), and Combs scampered over the plate with the winning run. The box scores:

Wednesday, October 5—At Pittsburgh

New York (A.L.)	AB.	R.	H.	O.	A.	E.
Combs, cf	4	0	0	4	0	0
Koenig, ss	4	2	1	2	2	0
Ruth, rf	4	2	3	5	0	0
Gehrig, 1b	2	1	1	9	0	0
Meusel, lf	3	0	0	2	0	1
Lazzeri, 2b	4	0	1	2	5	0
Dugan, 3b	3	0	0	0	0	0
Collins, c	2	0	0	3	0	0
Hoyt, p	3	0	0	0	0	0
Moore, p	1	0	0	0	2	0
Totals	30	5	6	27	10	1

Pittsburgh (N.L.)	AB.	R.	H.	O.	A.	E.
L. Waner, cf	4	2	1	1	0	0
Barnhart, lf	5	0	1	3	0	0
P. Waner, rf	4	0	3	3	0	0
Wright, ss	2	1	1	1	5	0
Traynor, 3b	4	0	1	1	2	0
Grantham, 2b	3	0	0	5	3	1
Harris, 1b	4	0	1	8	2	0
Smith, c	4	0	0	4	1	1
Kremer, p	2	1	1	0	0	0
Miljus, p	1	0	0	1	2	0
aBrickell	1	0	0	0	0	0
Totals	34	4	9	27	15	2

New York.................. 1 0 3   0 1 0   0 0 0—5
Pittsburgh................ 1 0 1   0 1 0   0 1 0—4

aGrounded out for Miljus in ninth. Runs batted in—Gehrig 2, Meusel, Lazzeri, Barnhart, P. Waner, Wright, Harris. Two-base hits—Koenig, Lazzeri, L. Waner, P. Waner, Kremer. Three-base hit—Gehrig. Sacrifice hits—Gehrig, Dugan, Wright 2. Double plays—Lazzeri and Gehrig; Wright, Grantham and Harris. Left on bases—Pittsburgh 7, New York 4. Earned runs—Pittsburgh 4, New York 2. Struck out—By Hoyt 2, by Kremer 1, by Miljus 3. Bases on balls—Off Hoyt 1, off Kremer 3, off Miljus 1. Hit by pitcher—By Hoyt (L. Waner). Hits—Off Hoyt 8 in 7⅓ innings, off Moore 1 in 1⅔ innings, off Kremer 5 in 5 innings, off Miljus 1 in 4 innings. Winning pitcher—Hoyt. Losing pitcher—Kremer. Umpires—Quigley (N.L.), Nallin (A.L.), Moran (N.L.) and Ormsby (A.L.). Time—2:04. Attendance—41,467.

Thursday, October 6—At Pittsburgh

New York (A.L.)	AB.	R.	H.	O.	A.	E.
Combs, cf	4	1	1	5	0	0
Koenig, ss	5	1	3	3	1	0
Ruth, rf	3	0	0	3	0	0
Gehrig, 1b	3	1	1	6	0	0
Meusel, lf	5	1	2	2	0	0
Lazzeri, 2b	4	0	2	2	2	0
Dugan, 3b	5	1	1	1	0	0
Bengough, c	3	1	0	4	0	0
Pipgras, p	3	0	1	1	2	0
Totals	35	6	11	27	5	0

Pittsburgh (N.L.)	AB.	R.	H.	O.	A.	E.
L. Waner, cf	3	2	1	7	0	1
Barnhart, lf	3	0	2	1	0	0
P. Waner, rf	3	0	1	5	0	0
Wright, ss	4	0	0	0	0	1
Traynor, 3b	4	0	1	3	0	0
Grantham, 2b	4	0	2	1	2	0
Harris, 1b	4	0	0	3	0	0
Gooch, c	3	0	0	7	1	0
Aldridge, p	2	0	0	0	2	0
Cvengros, p	0	0	0	0	0	0
aSmith	1	0	0	0	0	0
Dawson, p	0	0	0	0	0	0
Totals	31	2	7	27	5	2

New York.................. 0 0 3   0 0 0   0 3 0—6
Pittsburgh................ 1 0 0   0 0 0   0 1 0—2

aGrounded out for Cvengros in eighth. Runs batted in—Combs, Ruth, Lazzeri, Koenig. Barnhart, P. Waner. Two-base hits—Gehrig, Traynor,

Grantham. Three-base hit—L. Waner. Sacrifice hits—Gehrig, Lazzeri, Barnhart, P. Waner. Sacrifice fly—Ruth. Stolen base—Meusel. Double play—Lazzeri and Koenig. Left on bases—New York 10, Pittsburgh 2. Earned runs—New York 6, Pittsburgh 2. Struck out—By Aldridge 4, by Pipgras 2. Bases on balls—Off Aldridge 4, off Pipgras 1. Hit by pitcher—By Cvengros (Combs). Wild pitch—Aldridge. Hits—Off Aldridge 10 in 7⅓ innings, off Cvengros 1 in ⅔ inning, off Dawson 0 in 1 inning. Losing pitcher—Aldridge. Umpires—Nallin (A.L.), Moran (N.L.), Ormsby (A.L.) and Quigley (N.L.). Time—2:20. Attendance—41,634.

Friday, October 7—At New York

Pittsburgh (N.L.)	AB.	R.	H.	O.	A.	E.
L. Waner, cf	4	0	1	1	1	0
Rhyne, 2b	4	0	0	0	6	0
P. Waner, rf	4	0	0	0	0	0
Wright, ss	3	0	0	3	2	0
Traynor, 3b	3	1	1	0	3	1
Barnhart, lf	3	0	1	0	1	0
Harris, 1b	3	0	0	11	0	0
Gooch, c	2	0	0	9	0	0
bSpencer, c	1	0	0	0	0	0
Meadows, p	2	0	0	0	1	0
Cvengros, p	0	0	0	0	0	0
cGroh	1	0	0	0	0	0
Totals	30	1	3	24	14	1

New York (A.L.)	AB.	R.	H.	O.	A.	E.
Combs, cf	4	2	2	5	0	0
Koenig, ss	4	2	2	1	2	0
Ruth, rf	4	1	1	1	0	0
Gehrig, 1b	3	0	2	12	0	0
Meusel, lf	4	0	0	2	0	0
Lazzeri, 2b	4	1	1	1	7	0
Dugan, 3b	3	1	1	1	2	0
Grabowski, c	2	0	0	3	0	0
aDurst	1	0	0	0	0	0
Bengough, c	1	0	0	0	0	0
Pennock, p	4	1	0	1	1	0
Totals	34	8	9	27	12	0

Pittsburgh......... 0 0 0 0 0 0 0 1 0—1
New York.......... 2 0 0 0 0 0 6 0 *—8

aGrounded out for Grabowski in seventh. bGrounded out for Gooch in eighth. cPopped out for Cvengros in ninth. Runs batted in—Combs, Koenig, Ruth 3, Gehrig 2, Pennock, Barnhart. Two-base hits—Barnhart, Koenig, Gehrig. Three-base hit—Gehrig. Home run—Ruth. Sacrifice hit—Dugan. Left on bases—New York 4, Pittsburgh 2. Earned runs—New York 8, Pittsburgh 1. Struck out—By Pennock 1, by Meadows 1, by Cvengros 2. Base on balls—Off Meadows 1. Hits—Off Meadows 7 in 6⅓ innings, off Cvengros 2 in 1⅔ innings. Losing pitcher—Meadows. Umpires—Moran (N.L.), Ormsby (A.L.), Quigley (N.L.) and Nallin (A.L.). Time—2:04. Attendance—60,695.

Saturday, October 8—At New York

Pittsburgh (N.L.)	AB.	R.	H.	O.	A.	E.
L. Waner, cf	4	1	3	0	0	1
Barnhart, lf	5	0	1	2	0	0
P. Waner, rf	4	0	1	0	0	0
Wright, ss	4	0	1	6	0	0
Traynor, 3b	4	0	0	1	4	0
Grantham, 2b	4	0	2	0	2	0
Harris, 1b	4	0	2	13	0	0
Smith, c	3	0	0	6	0	0
aYde	0	1	0	0	0	0
Gooch, c	0	0	0	0	0	0

	AB.	R.	H.	O.	A.	E.
Hill, p	1	0	0	0	0	0
bBrickell	1	1	0	0	0	0
Miljus, p	1	0	0	0	0	0
Totals	35	3	10	c26	12	1

New York (A.L.)	AB.	R.	H.	O.	A.	E.
Combs, cf	4	3	2	2	0	0
Koenig, ss	5	0	3	0	3	0
Ruth, rf	4	1	2	1	0	0
Gehrig, 1b	5	0	0	14	2	0
Meusel, lf	5	0	0	2	0	0
Lazzeri, 2b	3	0	0	5	4	1
Dugan, 3b	4	0	1	1	4	0
Collins, c	3	0	3	2	1	0
Moore, p	4	0	1	0	3	1
Totals	37	4	12	27	17	2

Pittsburgh......... 1 0 0 0 0 0 2 0 0—3
New York.......... 1 0 0 0 2 0 0 0 1—4

aRan for Smith in seventh. bReached first on Lazzeri's error for Hill in seventh. cTwo out when winning run scored. Runs batted in—Ruth 3, Wright, Barnhart, P. Waner. Two-base hit—Collins. Home run—Ruth. Sacrifice hits—L. Waner, P. Waner. Stolen base—Ruth. Double plays—Lazzeri and Gehrig; Dugan, Lazzeri and Gehrig; Traynor, Wright and Harris. Left on bases—New York 11, Pittsburgh 9. Earned runs—New York 4, Pittsburgh 1. Struck out—By Hill 6, by Miljus 3, by Moore 2. Bases on balls—Off Hill 1, off Miljus 3, off Moore 2. Wild pitches—Miljus 2. Hits—Off Hill 9 in 6 innings, off Miljus 3 in 2⅔ innings. Losing pitcher—Miljus. Umpires—Ormsby (A.L.), Quigley (N.L.), Nallin (A.L.) and Moran (N.L.). Time—2:15. Attendance—57,909.

COMPOSITE BATTING AVERAGES
New York Yankees

Player-Position	G.	AB.	R.	H.	2B.	3B.	HR.	RBI.	BA.
Collins, c	2	5	0	3	1	0	0	0	.600
Koenig, ss	4	18	5	9	2	0	0	2	.500
Ruth, rf	4	15	4	6	0	0	2	7	.400
Pipgras, p	1	3	0	1	0	0	0	0	.333
Combs, cf	4	16	6	5	0	0	0	0	.313
Gehrig, 1b	4	13	2	4	2	2	0	4	.308
Lazzeri, 2b	4	15	1	4	1	0	0	2	.267
Dugan, 3b	4	15	2	3	0	0	0	0	.200
Moore, p	2	5	0	1	0	0	0	0	.200
Meusel, lf	4	17	1	2	0	0	0	1	.118
Bengough, c	2	4	1	0	0	0	0	0	.000
Pennock, p	1	4	1	0	0	0	0	1	.000
Hoyt, p	1	3	0	0	0	0	0	0	.000
Grabowski, c	1	2	0	0	0	0	0	0	.000
Durst, ph	1	1	0	0	0	0	0	0	.000
Totals	4	136	23	38	6	2	2	19	.279

Pittsburgh Pirates

Player-Position	G.	AB.	R.	H.	2B.	3B.	HR.	RBI.	BA.
Kremer, p	1	2	1	1	1	0	0	0	.500
L. Waner, cf	4	15	5	6	1	1	0	0	.400
Grantham, 2b	3	11	0	4	1	0	0	0	.364
P. Waner, rf	4	15	0	5	1	0	0	3	.333
Barnhart, lf	4	16	0	5	1	0	0	4	.313
Traynor, 3b	4	15	1	3	1	0	0	0	.200
Harris, 1b	4	15	0	3	0	0	0	1	.200
Wright, ss	4	13	1	2	0	0	0	2	.154
Smith, c-ph	3	8	0	0	0	0	0	0	.000
Miljus, p	2	2	0	0	0	0	0	0	.000
Brickell, ph	2	2	1	0	0	0	0	0	.000
Gooch, c	3	5	0	0	0	0	0	0	.000
Aldridge, p	1	2	0	0	0	0	0	0	.000
Cvengros, p	2	0	0	0	0	0	0	0	.000
Dawson, p	1	0	0	0	0	0	0	0	.000
Rhyne, 2b	1	4	0	0	0	0	0	0	.000
Spencer, c	1	1	0	0	0	0	0	0	.000
Meadows, p	1	2	0	0	0	0	0	0	.000
Groh, ph	1	1	0	0	0	0	0	0	.000
Yde, pr	1	0	1	0	0	0	0	0	.000
Hill, p	1	1	0	0	0	0	0	0	.000
Totals	4	130	10	29	6	1	0	10	.223

COMPOSITE PITCHING AVERAGES
New York Yankees

Pitcher	G.	IP.	H.	R.	E.	SO.	BB.	W.	L.	ERA.
Moore	2	10⅔	11	3	1	2	2	1	0	0.84
Pennock	1	9	3	1	1	1	0	1	0	1.00
Pipgras	1	9	7	2	2	2	1	1	0	2.00
Hoyt	1	7⅓	8	4	4	2	1	1	0	4.91
Totals	4	36	29	10	8	7	4	4	0	2.00

Pittsburgh Pirates

Pitcher	G.	IP.	H.	R.	E.	SO.	BB.	W.	L.	ERA.
Dawson	1	1	0	0	0	0	0	0	0	0.00
Miljus	2	6⅔	4	1	1	6	4	0	1	1.35
Kremer	1	5	5	2	1	3	0	0	1	3.60
Cvengros	2	2⅓	3	1	1	2	0	0	0	3.86
Hill	1	6	9	3	3	6	1	0	0	4.50
Aldridge	1	7⅓	10	6	6	4	4	0	1	7.36
Meadows	1	6⅓	7	7	7	6	1	0	1	9.95
Totals	4	34⅔	38	23	20	25	13	0	4	5.19

SERIES OF 1928

	W.	L.	Pct.
New York A. L.	4	0	1.000
St. Louis N. L.	0	4	.000

Continuing where they left off at the end of the 1927 Series, the Yankees vanquished the Cardinals, led by Bill McKechnie, in another four-straight sweep in 1928, giving Miller Huggins' remarkable club a record of eight consecutive victories in two successive Series.

The remarkable part of the 1928 victory was that the Yankees were in poor shape for the title games. Herb Pennock, who had a 17-6 record for the season with a 2.56 ERA, was out with a lame arm, and Earle Combs, the Bombers' brilliant center fielder, had a broken finger and appeared at bat only once, going up as a pinch-hitter in the fourth game. In addition, Tony Lazzeri, the team's second baseman, had a lame arm, and Leo Durocher, a fresh rookie infielder, finished each of the four games at the middle station. Babe Ruth suffered from a lame ankle and limped through the Series.

Unlike the 1927 American League runaway, the Yanks won their 1928 flag only after a nip-and-tuck struggle, as the club blew a 13½-game early-July lead, the Athletics passing them by a half-game in September. However, the champions came through when they had to, took an important late-season series from the Mackmen and defeated them for the pennant by two and one-half games. The Cardinals had their usual stiff battle in the National League, winning the flag from the Giants by two games. So disappointed was Sam Breadon, president of the Cardinals, at his club's crushing Series defeat that he demoted his manager, Bill McKechnie, to Rochester, bringing up Billy Southworth for his first fling at the Cardinal managerial job.

The sensational hitting of Ruth and Lou Gehrig featured the games. In no other Series up to that time did two batsmen so dominate the classic. The Babe hit .625, the highest batting average in World Series history. Unlike 1926, when the Cardinals passed him 11 times, McKechnie permitted his hurlers to pitch to Ruth and he walked only once. He hit three home runs in one game—the second Series in which he had done so, and both times in St. Louis. Willie Sherdel, the little southpaw, and Grover Alexander, then 41, were the victims of this final Ruthian bombardment in the last game.

The younger member of the slugging duo, Gehrig, was almost as tough, with an average of .545. Four of Lou's six hits were homers and one a double, and while Ruth outscored him, nine runs to five, Lou knocked in nine counters to four for the Babe.

Waite Hoyt won two games for New York, bringing his World Series victories to six. With Pennock out of the Series, Tom Zachary, former Washington southpaw, came through with a well-pitched victory for New York in the third contest. George Pipgras won the second game of the Yankees' four straight.

The Cardinals fell down badly at bat, hitting only .206, with but one regular, the veteran shortstop, Walter Maranville, batting .308. The box scores:

Thursday, October 4—At New York

St. Louis (N.L.)	AB.	R.	H.	O.	A.	E.
Douthit, cf	3	0	0	2	0	0
High, 3b	4	0	0	0	1	0
Frisch, 2b	4	0	0	1	6	0
Bottomley, 1b	3	1	2	10	0	0
Hafey, lf	4	0	0	3	0	0
Harper, rf	3	0	1	2	0	0
Wilson, c	3	0	0	3	0	0
Maranville, ss	2	0	0	2	0	1
aOrsatti	0	0	0	0	0	0
Thevenow, ss	0	0	0	1	0	0
Sherdel, p	2	0	0	0	3	0
bHolm	1	0	0	0	0	0
Johnson, p	0	0	0	0	0	0
Totals	29	1	3	24	10	1

New York (A.L.)	AB.	R.	H.	O.	A.	E.
Paschal, cf	4	0	0	4	0	0
Durst, cf	0	0	0	0	0	0
Koenig, ss	4	1	1	2	3	0
Ruth, rf	4	2	3	3	0	0
Gehrig, 1b	4	0	2	6	0	0
Meusel, lf	4	1	1	2	0	0
Lazzeri, 2b	2	0	0	0	2	0
Durocher, 2b	1	0	0	0	0	0
Dugan, 3b	3	0	0	2	0	0
Bengough, c	3	0	0	8	1	0
Hoyt, p	3	0	0	0	1	0
Totals	32	4	7	27	7	0

St. Louis........ 0 0 0 0 0 0 1 0 0—1
New York...... 1 0 0 2 0 0 0 1 *—4

aWalked for Maranville in eighth. bLined out for Sherdel in eighth. Runs batted in—Gehrig 2, Meusel 2, Bottomley. Two-base hits—Ruth 2, Gehrig. Home runs—Meusel, Bottomley. Left on bases—New York 4, St. Louis 4. Earned runs—New York 4, St. Louis 1. Struck out—By Hoyt 6, by Sherdel 2. Bases on balls—Off Hoyt 3. Hits—Off Sherdel 4 in 7 innings, off Johnson 3 in 1 inning. Losing pitcher—Sherdel. Umpires—Owens (A.L.),

1928 WORLD SERIES

Rigler (N.L.), McGowan (A.L.) and Pfirman (N.L.). Time—1:49. Attendance—61,425.

Friday, October 5—At New York

St. Louis (N.L.)	AB.	R.	H.	O.	A.	E.
Douthit, cf	4	0	0	2	1	0
High, 3b	3	0	0	0	1	0
Frisch, 2b	3	0	2	2	3	0
Bottomley, 1b	4	0	0	9	0	0
Hafey, lf	4	0	0	3	0	0
Harper, rf	3	1	0	1	0	0
Wilson, c	4	1	1	5	2	0
Maranville, ss	3	1	1	2	1	0
Alexander, p	1	0	0	0	1	0
Mitchell, p	2	0	0	0	1	1
cOrsatti	1	0	0	0	0	0
Totals	32	3	4	24	10	1

New York (A.L.)	AB.	R.	H.	O.	A.	E.
Durst, cf	2	1	2	0	0	0
aPaschal, cf	2	0	1	1	0	0
Koenig, ss	5	0	0	1	2	1
Ruth, lf	3	2	2	1	0	0
Gehrig, 1b	3	2	1	9	0	0
Meusel, lf	3	2	1	2	0	0
Lazzeri, 2b	3	0	0	1	1	0
Durocher, 2b	0	0	0	0	0	0
Robertson, 3b	2	1	0	2	1	0
bDugan, 3b	0	0	0	1	0	0
Bengough, c	3	1	1	9	0	0
Pipgras, p	2	0	0	0	1	0
Totals	28	9	8	27	5	2

St. Louis .... 0 3 0   0 0 0   0 0 0—3
New York .... 3 1 4   0 0 0   1 0 *—9

aSingled for Durst in third. bHit sacrifice fly for Robertson in seventh. cGrounded out for Mitchell in ninth. Runs batted in—Durst, Paschal, Gehrig 3, Dugan, Meusel, Bengough, Pipgras, Douthit, Wilson, Alexander. Two-base hits—Ruth, Meusel, Wilson. Home run—Gehrig. Sacrifice hits—Lazzeri, Pipgras. Sacrifice fly—Dugan. Stolen bases—Frisch 2, Meusel. Double plays—Koenig, Lazzeri and Gehrig; Frisch, Maranville and Bottomley. Left on bases—St. Louis 6, New York 5. Earned runs—New York 8, St. Louis 3. Struck out—By Pipgras 8, by Alexander 1, by Mitchell 2. Bases on balls—Off Pipgras 4, off Alexander 4, off Mitchell 2. Hit by pitcher—By Mitchell (Pipgras). Hits—Off Alexander 6 in 2⅔ innings, off Mitchell 2 in 5⅓ innings. Losing pitcher—Alexander. Umpires—Rigler (N.L.), McGowan (A.L.), Pfirman (N.L.) and Owens (A.L.). Time—2:04. Attendance—60,714.

Sunday, October 7—At St. Louis

New York (A.L.)	AB.	R.	H.	O.	A.	E.
Durst, cf	5	1	0	3	0	0
Koenig, ss	5	0	1	1	4	0
Ruth, lf	4	2	2	2	1	0
Gehrig, 1b	2	2	2	11	0	0
Meusel, rf	3	1	0	1	0	0
Lazzeri, 2b	3	1	0	0	2	1
Durocher, 2b	0	0	0	1	1	0
Robertson, 3b	4	0	1	0	0	1
Bengough, c	4	0	1	8	0	0
Zachary, p	4	0	0	0	1	0
Totals	34	7	7	27	9	2

St. Louis (N.L.)	AB.	R.	H.	O.	A.	E.
Douthit, cf	4	1	1	2	0	0
High, 3b	5	1	2	2	2	0
Frisch, 2b	2	1	1	2	3	0
Bottomley, 1b	4	0	1	6	1	0
Hafey, lf	4	0	2	1	0	1
Holm, rf	4	0	1	4	0	0
Wilson, c	4	0	0	6	0	2
Maranville, ss	4	0	1	4	1	0
Haines, p	2	0	0	0	1	0
Johnson, p	0	0	0	0	0	0
aBlades	1	0	0	0	0	0
Rhem, p	0	0	0	0	0	0
bOrsatti	1	0	0	0	0	0
Totals	35	3	9	27	8	3

New York .... 0 1 0   2 0 3   1 0 0—7
St. Louis .... 2 0 0   0 1 0   0 0 0—3

aStruck out for Johnson in seventh. bFanned for Rhem in ninth. Runs batted in—Gehrig 3, Robertson, Ruth, Bottomley 2, High. Two-base hit—High. Three-base hit—Bottomley. Home runs—Gehrig 2. Sacrifice hit—Frisch. Stolen bases—Meusel, Lazzeri. Double plays—High, Frisch and Bottomley; Koenig, Durocher and Gehrig. Left on bases—St. Louis 8, New York 4. Earned runs—New York 3, St. Louis 3. Struck out—By Zachary 7, by Haines 3, by Johnson 1, by Rhem 1. Bases on balls—Off Zachary 1, off Haines 3, off Johnson 1. Hit by pitcher—By Zachary (Douthit). Hits—Off Haines 6 in 6 innings, off Johnson 1 in 1 inning, off Rhem 0 in 2 innings. Losing pitcher—Haines. Umpires—McGowan (A.L.), Pfirman (N.L.), Owens (A.L.) and Rigler (N.L.). Time—2:09. Attendance—39,602.

Tuesday, October 9—At St. Louis

New York (A.L.)	AB.	R.	H.	O.	A.	E.
Paschal, cf	4	0	1	3	0	0
Durst, cf	1	1	1	0	0	0
Koenig, ss	5	0	1	4	2	1
Ruth, lf	5	3	3	2	0	0
Gehrig, 1b	2	1	1	7	0	0
Meusel, rf	5	1	1	0	0	0
Lazzeri, 2b	4	1	3	1	2	0
Durocher, 2b	1	0	0	0	0	0
Dugan, 3b	3	0	0	0	0	0
aRobertson, 3b	2	0	0	0	0	0
Bengough, c	3	0	1	8	1	0
bCombs	0	0	0	0	0	0
Collins, c	1	0	1	2	0	0
Hoyt, p	4	0	1	0	2	1
Totals	40	7	15	27	7	2

St. Louis (N.L.)	AB.	R.	H.	O.	A.	E.
Orsatti, cf	5	1	2	4	0	0
High, 3b	5	0	3	0	1	0
Frisch, 2b	4	0	0	3	1	0
Bottomley, 1b	3	0	0	11	1	0
Hafey, lf	3	0	1	1	0	0
Harper, rf	3	0	0	2	0	0
Smith, c	4	0	3	3	1	0
cMartin	0	1	0	0	0	0
Maranville, ss	4	1	2	3	1	0
Sherdel, p	3	0	0	0	0	0
Alexander, p	0	0	0	0	3	0
dHolm	1	0	0	0	0	0
Totals	35	3	11	27	8	0

New York .... 0 0 0   1 0 0   4 2 0—7
St. Louis .... 0 0 1   1 0 0   0 0 1—3

aFielder's choice for Dugan in seventh. bHit sacrifice fly for Bengough in seventh. cRan for Smith in ninth. dGrounded out for Alexander in ninth. Runs batted in—Ruth 3, Durst, Gehrig, Robertson, Combs, Frisch, Holm. Two-base hits—Lazzeri, Collins, Orsatti, High, Maranville. Home runs—Ruth 3, Durst, Gehrig. Sacrifice hit—Hoyt. Sacrifice flies—Frisch, Combs. Stolen bases—Lazzeri, Maranville. Double plays—Bottomley and Maranville; Koenig and Gehrig. Left on bases—New York 11, St. Louis 9. Earned runs—New

York 7, St. Louis 2. Struck out—By Hoyt 8, by Sherdel 1, by Alexander 1. Bases on balls—Off Hoyt 3, off Sherdel 3. Hits—Off Sherdel 11 in 6⅓ innings, off Alexander 4 in 2⅔ innings. Losing pitcher—Sherdel. Umpires—Pfirman (N.L.), Owens (A.L.), Rigler (N.L.) and McGowan (A.L.). Time—2:25. Attendance—37,331.

COMPOSITE BATTING AVERAGES
New York Yankees

Player-Position	G.	AB.	R.	H.	2B.	3B.	HR.	RBI.	BA.
Collins, c	1	1	0	1	1	0	0	0	1.000
Ruth, rf	4	16	9	10	3	0	3	4	.625
Gehrig, 1b	4	11	5	6	1	0	4	9	.545
Durst, cf	4	8	3	3	0	0	1	2	.375
Lazzeri, 2b	4	12	2	3	1	0	0	0	.250
Bengough, c	4	13	1	3	0	0	0	1	.231
Paschal, cf-ph	3	10	0	2	0	0	0	0	.200
Meusel, lf	4	15	5	3	1	0	1	3	.200
Dugan, 3b-ph	3	6	0	1	0	0	0	1	.167
Koenig, ss	4	19	1	3	0	0	0	0	.158
Hoyt, p	2	7	0	1	0	0	0	0	.143
Robertson, 3b-ph	3	8	1	1	0	0	0	2	.125
Durocher, 2b	4	2	0	0	0	0	0	0	.000
Zachary, p	1	4	0	0	0	0	0	0	.000
Pipgras, p	1	2	0	0	0	0	0	1	.000
Combs, ph	1	0	0	0	0	0	0	1	.000
Totals	4	134	27	37	7	0	9	25	.276

St. Louis Cardinals

Player-Position	G.	AB.	R.	H.	2B.	3B.	HR.	RBI.	BA.
Smith, c	1	4	0	3	0	0	0	0	.750
Maranville, ss	4	13	2	4	1	0	0	0	.308
High, 3b	4	17	1	5	2	0	0	1	.294
Orsatti, ph-cf	4	7	1	2	1	0	0	0	.286
Frisch, 2b	4	13	1	3	0	0	0	1	.231
Bottomley, 1b	4	14	1	3	0	1	3	3	.214
Hafey, lf	4	15	0	3	0	0	0	0	.200
Holm, ph-rf	3	6	0	1	0	0	0	1	.167
Harper, rf	3	9	1	1	0	0	0	0	.111
Douthit, cf	3	11	1	1	0	0	0	0	.091
Wilson, c	3	11	1	1	0	0	0	1	.091
Thevenow, ss	1	0	0	0	0	0	0	0	.000
Sherdel, p	2	5	0	0	0	0	0	0	.000
Johnson, p	2	0	0	0	0	0	0	0	.000
Alexander, p	2	1	0	0	0	0	0	1	.000
Mitchell, p	1	2	0	0	0	0	0	0	.000
Haines, p	1	2	0	0	0	0	0	0	.000
Blades, ph	1	1	0	0	0	0	0	0	.000
Rhem, p	1	0	0	0	0	0	0	0	.000
Martin, ph	1	0	1	0	0	0	0	0	.000
Totals	4	131	10	27	5	1	1	9	.206

COMPOSITE PITCHING AVERAGES
New York Yankees

Pitcher	G.	IP.	H.	R.	E.	SO.	BB.	W.	L.	ERA.
Hoyt	2	18	14	4	3	14	6	2	0	1.50
Pipgras	1	9	4	3	3	8	4	1	0	3.00
Zachary	1	9	9	3	3	7	1	1	0	3.00
Totals	4	36	27	10	9	29	11	4	0	2.25

St. Louis Cardinals

Pitcher	G.	IP.	H.	R.	E.	SO.	BB.	W.	L.	ERA.
Rhem	1	2	0	0	0	1	0	0	0	0.00
Mitchell	1	5⅔	2	1	1	2	2	0	0	1.59
Johnson	2	2	4	2	1	1	1	0	0	4.50
Haines	1	6	6	3	3	3	0	0	1	4.50
Sherdel	2	13⅓	15	7	7	3	3	0	2	4.73
Alexander	2	5	10	11	11	2	4	0	1	19.80
Totals	4	34	37	27	23	12	13	0	4	6.09

SERIES OF 1929

	W.	L.	Pct.
Philadelphia A. L.	4	1	.800
Chicago N. L.	1	4	.200

The Philadelphia Athletics and Chicago Cubs met again in 1929, and the verdict was the same as in their 1910 encounter, a victory for the A's in five games. Through a quirk of fate, Joe McCarthy, who was one of a crowd of 5,000 Philadelphia fans to welcome the victorious Athletics back from Chicago in 1910, was in command of the Bruins 19 years later. Connie Mack had made a great comeback; his club followed up its flashy 1928 finish with a surprising 18-game margin over the second-place Yankees. With a club of clouters and aided by some magnificent pitching from Charlie Root, Pat Malone and Guy Bush, the Cubs also won an easy pennant, beating Pittsburgh by ten and one-half games.

The series was a string of bitter disappointments for the Cubs. Mack crossed them in the first game by pitching Howard Ehmke, who had hurled only 55 innings during the entire American League season. However, not only did Ehmke get the A's off to a fine start by defeating Root in the opener, 3 to 1, but he struck out 13 batters, a Series record that stood until Carl Erskine whiffed 14 Yankees in 1953. The following day, George Earnshaw collaborated with Lefty Grove on another 13-strikeout effort for the Mackmen while winning the second game, 9 to 3.

After Chicago, with Bush in the box, won the third game, 3 to 1, the National League club apparently had the Series tied up with a victory in the fourth game, McCarthy's men leading, 8 to 0, after six and one-half innings. Root appeared on his way to a shutout when the Athletics struck with the most terrific inning of all World Series history—15 men went to bat, and the A's scored ten runs, eventually winning, 10 to 8. In vain McCarthy rushed in Art Nehf, Sheriff Blake and Malone. During the big inning, the rampaging White Elephants made ten hits and were helped by a walk and a hit batsman. The most damaging play of the frame was a misjudged fly from Mule Haas' bat by Hack Wilson, the ball going for an inside-the-park homer, scoring three runs. Al Simmons had opened the riotous inning with a home run. Pinch-hitter George Burns, batting for Ed Rommel made two of the A's outs.

The Cubs had almost as bitter a blow two days later when the A's pulled out the last game, played in Philadelphia, 3 to 2, scoring all of their runs after one was out in the ninth. President Herbert Hoover came up from Washington to see the game. With the Cubs leading, 2 to 0, Malone retired pinch-hitter Walter French in the ninth. Max Bishop then singled and Haas tied the score by poling his second home run in two days. Malone retired Mickey Cochrane, but Simmons doubled, Jimmy Foxx was intentionally passed and Bing Miller drove in the winning run with another two-bagger.

Jimmie Dykes led the Athletics at bat with .421, Cochrane following with .400. Miller hit .368 and Foxx .350, the latter delivering two valuable homers, the first helping to defeat Root in the opening clash. While Grove did not start a game, Lefty produced two sensational relief jobs, giving no runs, yielding only three hits and striking out ten in six and one-third innings.

Even though Wilson was the goat of the fatal seventh inning of the fourth game, he batted .471, leading the regulars of both clubs. Rogers Hornsby, the National League's Most Valuable Player of 1929, had a disappointing Series, hitting only .238 and striking out eight times. The box scores:

Tuesday, October 8—At Chicago

Phila'phia (A.L.)	AB.	R.	H.	O.	A.	E.
Bishop, 2b	4	0	0	2	1	0
Haas, cf	3	0	0	1	0	0
Cochrane, c	3	1	1	14	1	0
Simmons, lf	4	1	0	2	0	0
Foxx, 1b	4	1	2	4	0	0
Miller, rf	4	0	1	3	0	0
Dykes, 3b	4	0	1	1	1	1
Boley, ss	4	0	0	0	0	0
Ehmke, p	4	0	1	0	2	0
Totals	34	3	6	27	5	1

Chicago (N.L.)	AB.	R.	H.	O.	A.	E.
McMillan, 3b	4	0	1	1	2	0
English, ss	4	0	2	1	3	2
Hornsby, 2b	4	0	0	1	3	0
Wilson, cf	4	0	0	3	0	0
Cuyler, rf	4	1	1	1	0	0
Stephenson, lf	4	0	2	4	0	0
Grimm, 1b	2	0	2	8	0	0
Taylor, c	2	0	0	6	0	0
aHeathcote	1	0	0	0	0	0
Gonzalez, c	0	0	0	2	0	0
cBlair	1	0	0	0	0	0
Root, p	2	0	0	0	0	0
bHartnett	1	0	0	0	0	0
Bush, p	0	0	0	0	2	0
dTolson	1	0	0	0	0	0
Totals	34	1	8	27	10	2

Philadelphia .... 0 0 0 0 0 0 1 0 2—3
Chicago .... 0 0 0 0 0 0 0 0 1—1

aFlied out for Taylor in seventh. bStruck out for Root in seventh. cForced runner for Gonzalez in ninth. dStruck out for Bush in ninth. Runs batted in—Foxx, Miller 2, Stephenson. Two-base hit—English. Home run—Foxx. Sacrifice hit—Grimm. Double play—English, Hornsby and Grimm. Left on bases—Chicago 8, Philadelphia 6. Earned runs—Philadelphia 1, Chicago 1. Struck out—By Ehmke 13, by Root 5. Bases on balls—Off Ehmke 1, off Root 2. Hits—Off Root 3 in 7 innings, off Bush 3 in 2 innings. Losing pitcher—Root. Umpires—Klem (N.L.), Dinneen (A.L.), Moran (N.L.) and Van Graflan (A.L.). Time—2:03. Attendance—50,740.

Wednesday, October 9—At Chicago

Phila'phia (A.L.)	AB.	R.	H.	O.	A.	E.
Bishop, 2b	4	0	0	0	4	0
Haas, cf	5	1	1	1	0	0
Cochrane, c	2	2	1	14	0	0
Simmons, lf	4	2	2	2	0	0
Foxx, 1b	5	2	3	7	0	0
Miller, rf	4	0	1	0	0	0
Dykes, 3b	4	1	3	1	1	0
Boley, ss	3	0	1	2	2	0
Earnshaw, p	3	1	0	0	0	0
Grove, p	2	0	0	0	1	0
Totals	36	9	12	27	8	0

Chicago (N.L.)	AB.	R.	H.	O.	A.	E.
McMillan, 3b	4	0	0	1	0	0
English, ss	5	0	1	2	3	1
Hornsby, 2b	4	1	1	3	2	0
Wilson, cf	3	1	3	4	0	0
Cuyler, rf	4	0	0	1	0	0
Stephenson, lf	5	1	1	2	0	0
Grimm, 1b	4	0	2	6	1	0
Taylor, c	4	0	2	8	1	0
Malone, p	1	0	0	0	1	0
Blake, p	1	0	1	0	0	0
aHeathcote	0	0	0	0	0	0
bHartnett	1	0	0	0	0	0
Carlson, p	0	0	0	0	1	0
cGonzalez	1	0	0	0	0	0
Nehf, p	0	0	0	0	0	0
Totals	37	3	11	27	9	1

Philadelphia .... 0 0 3 3 0 0 1 2 0—9
Chicago .... 0 0 0 0 3 0 0 0 0—3

aAnnounced for Blake in fifth. bStruck out for Heathcote in fifth. cStruck out for Carlson in eighth. Runs batted in—Haas, Simmons 4, Foxx 3, Dykes, Stephenson, Grimm, Taylor. Two-base hits—Foxx, English. Home runs—Simmons, Foxx. Sacrifice hits—Miller, Boley 2. Double plays—English, Hornsby and Grimm; Bishop, Boley and Foxx. Left on bases—Chicago 12, Philadelphia 9. Earned runs—Philadelphia 6, Chicago 3. Struck out—By Malone 5, by Blake 1, by Carlson 2, by Earnshaw 7, by Grove 6. Bases on balls—Off Malone 5, off Carlson 1, off Earnshaw 4, off Grove 1. Hits—Off Malone 5 in 3⅔ innings, off Blake 2 in 1⅓ innings, off Carlson 5 in 3 innings, off Nehf 0 in 1 inning, off Earnshaw 8 in 4⅔ innings, off Grove 3 in 4⅓ innings. Winning pitcher—Earnshaw. Losing pitcher—Malone. Umpires—Dinneen (A.L.), Moran (N.L.), Van Graflan (A.L.) and Klem (N.L.). Time—2:29. Attendance—49,987.

Friday, October 11—At Philadelphia

Chicago (N.L.)	AB.	R.	H.	O.	A.	E.
McMillan, 3b	4	0	0	1	1	0
English, ss	4	1	0	0	2	1
Hornsby, 2b	4	1	2	2	1	0
Wilson, cf	3	0	2	3	0	0
Cuyler, rf	4	0	1	3	0	0
Stephenson, lf	4	0	1	4	0	0
Grimm, 1b	4	0	0	9	0	0
Taylor, c	4	0	0	5	2	0
Bush, p	3	1	0	0	1	0
Totals	34	3	6	27	7	1

Phila'phia (A.L.)	AB.	R.	H.	O.	A.	E.
Bishop, 2b	4	0	1	3	4	0
Haas, cf	5	0	2	0	0	0
Cochrane, c	3	1	2	12	0	0
Simmons, lf	3	0	0	0	0	0
Foxx, 1b	4	0	0	9	0	0
Miller, rf	4	0	1	2	0	0
Dykes, 3b	4	0	1	1	0	1
Boley, ss	4	0	2	0	2	0
Earnshaw, p	2	0	0	0	2	0
aSumma	1	0	0	0	0	0
Totals	34	1	9	27	8	1

Chicago .... 0 0 0 0 0 3 0 0 0—3
Philadelphia .... 0 0 0 0 1 0 0 0 0—1

aStruck out for Earnshaw in ninth. Runs batted in—Miller, Hornsby, Cuyler 2. Two-base hits—Hornsby, Stephenson. Three-base hit—Wilson. Sacrifice hits—Simmons, Earnshaw. Left on bases—Philadelphia 10, Chicago 6. Earned runs—Chicago 1, Philadelphia 1. Struck out—By Earnshaw 10, by Bush 4. Bases on balls—Off Earnshaw 2, off

1929 WORLD SERIES

Bush 2. Wild pitch—Bush. Umpires—Moran (N.L.), Van Graflan (A.L.), Klem (N.L.) and Dinneen (A.L.). Time—2:09. Attendance—29,921.

Saturday, October 12—At Philadelphia

Chicago (N.L.)	AB.	R.	H.	O.	A.	E.
McMillan, 3b	4	0	0	1	3	0
English, ss	4	0	0	2	1	0
Hornsby, 2b	5	2	2	1	1	0
Wilson, cf	3	1	2	3	0	0
Cuyler, rf	4	2	3	0	0	1
Stephenson, lf	4	1	1	2	1	0
Grimm, 1b	4	2	2	7	0	0
Taylor, c	3	0	0	8	1	0
Root, p	3	0	0	0	0	0
Nehf, p	0	0	0	0	0	0
Blake, p	0	0	0	0	0	0
Malone, p	0	0	0	0	0	0
bHartnett	1	0	0	0	0	0
Carlson, p	0	0	0	0	1	0
Totals	35	8	10	24	8	2

Phila'phia (A.L.)	AB.	R.	H.	O.	A.	E.
Bishop, 2b	5	1	2	2	3	0
Haas, cf	4	1	1	2	0	0
Cochrane, c	4	1	2	9	0	0
Simmons, lf	5	2	2	0	0	0
Foxx, 1b	4	2	2	10	0	0
Miller, rf	3	1	2	3	0	1
Dykes, 3b	4	1	3	0	2	0
Boley, ss	3	1	1	1	5	0
Quinn, p	2	0	0	0	0	0
Walberg, p	0	0	0	0	0	1
Rommel, p	0	0	0	0	0	0
aBurns	2	0	0	0	0	0
Grove, p	0	0	0	0	0	0
Totals	36	10	15	27	10	2

Chicago .... 0 0 0   2 0 5   1 0 0—8
Philadelphia ..... 0 0 0   0 0 0   10 0 *—10

aPopped out and struck out for Rommel in seventh. bStruck out for Malone in eighth. Runs batted in—Cuyler 2, Stephenson, Grimm 2, Taylor, Bishop, Haas 3, Simmons, Foxx, Dykes 3, Boley. Two-base hits—Cochrane, Dykes. Three-base hit—Hornsby. Home runs—Grimm, Haas, Simmons. Sacrifice hits—Taylor, Haas, Boley. Double play—Dykes, Bishop and Foxx. Left on bases—Philadelphia 6, Chicago 4. Earned runs—Philadelphia 10, Chicago 6. Struck out—By Quinn 2, by Walberg 2, by Grove 4, by Root 3, by Malone 2, by Carlson 1. Bases on balls—Off Quinn 2, off Rommel 1, off Nehf 1. Hit by pitcher—By Malone (Miller). Hits—Off Quinn 7 in 5 innings (pitched to four batters in sixth), off Walberg 1 in 1 inning, off Rommel 2 in 1 inning, off Grove 0 in 2 innings, off Root 9 in $6\frac{1}{3}$ innings, off Nehf 1 in 0 inning (pitched to two batters in seventh), off Blake 2 in 0 inning (pitched to two batters in seventh), off Malone 1 in $\frac{2}{3}$ inning, off Carlson 2 in 1 inning. Winning pitcher—Rommel. Losing pitcher—Blake. Umpires—Van Graflan (A.L.), Klem (N.L.), Dinneen (A.L.) and Moran (N.L.). Time—2:12. Attendance—29,921.

Monday, October 14—At Philadelphia

Chicago (N.L.)	AB.	R.	H.	O.	A.	E.
McMillan, 3b	4	0	1	2	3	0
English, ss	4	0	1	3	3	0
Hornsby, 2b	4	0	0	2	4	1
Wilson, cf	4	0	1	1	0	0
Cuyler, rf	4	1	1	3	0	0
Stephenson, lf	2	1	1	1	0	0
Grimm, 1b	4	0	1	10	0	0
Taylor, c	4	0	1	4	0	0
Malone, p	3	0	1	0	0	0
Totals	33	2	8	b26	10	1

Phila'phia (A.L.)	AB.	R.	H.	O.	A.	E.
Bishop, 2b	4	1	1	2	1	0
Haas, cf	4	1	1	1	0	0
Cochrane, c	3	0	0	10	1	0
Simmons, lf	4	1	2	0	0	0
Foxx, 1b	3	0	0	8	1	0
Miller, rf	4	0	2	5	0	0
Dykes, 3b	3	0	0	0	1	0
Boley, ss	3	0	0	1	2	0
Ehmke, p	1	0	0	0	2	0
Walberg, p	1	0	0	0	1	0
aFrench	1	0	0	0	0	0
Totals	31	3	6	27	9	0

Chicago .... 0 0 0   2 0 0   0 0 0—2
Philadelphia ..... 0 0 0   0 0 0   0 0 3—3

aStruck out for Walberg in ninth. bTwo out when winning run scored. Runs batted in—Grimm, Taylor, Haas 2, Miller. Two-base hits—Cuyler, Malone, Simmons, Miller. Home run—Haas. Stolen base—McMillan. Double plays—Hornsby and Grimm; English, Hornsby and Grimm. Left on bases—Chicago 6, Philadelphia 4. Earned runs—Philadelphia 3, Chicago 2. Struck out—By Walberg 6, by Malone 4. Bases on balls—Off Ehmke 2, off Malone 2. Hits—Off Ehmke 6 in $3\frac{2}{3}$ innings, off Walberg 2 in $5\frac{1}{3}$ innings. Winning pitcher—Walberg. Umpires—Klem (N.L.), Dinneen (A.L.), Moran (N.L.) and Van Graflan (A.L.). Time—1:42. Attendance—29,921.

COMPOSITE BATTING AVERAGES
Philadelphia Athletics

Player-Position	G.	AB.	R.	H.	2B.	3B.	HR.	RBI.	BA.
Dykes, 3b	5	19	2	8	1	0	0	4	.421
Cochrane, c	5	15	5	6	1	0	0	0	.400
Miller, rf	5	19	1	7	1	0	0	4	.368
Foxx, 1b	5	20	5	7	1	0	2	5	.350
Simmons, lf	5	20	6	6	1	0	2	5	.300
Haas, cf	5	21	3	5	0	0	2	6	.238
Boley, ss	5	17	1	4	0	0	0	1	.235
Ehmke, p	2	5	0	1	0	0	0	0	.200
Bishop, 2b	5	21	2	4	0	0	0	1	.190
Earnshaw, p	2	5	1	0	0	0	0	0	.000
Grove, p	2	2	0	0	0	0	0	0	.000
Summa, ph	1	1	0	0	0	0	0	0	.000
Quinn, p	1	2	0	0	0	0	0	0	.000
Walberg, p	2	1	0	0	0	0	0	0	.000
Rommel, p	1	0	0	0	0	0	0	0	.000
Burns, ph	1	2	0	0	0	0	0	0	.000
French, ph	1	1	0	0	0	0	0	0	.000
Totals	5	171	26	48	5	0	6	26	.281

Chicago Cubs

Player-Position	G.	AB.	R.	H.	2B.	3B.	HR.	RBI.	BA.
Blake, p	2	1	0	1	0	0	0	0	1.000
Wilson, cf	5	17	2	8	0	1	0	0	.471
Grimm, 1b	5	18	2	7	0	0	1	4	.389
Stephenson, lf	5	19	3	6	1	0	0	3	.316
Cuyler, rf	5	20	4	6	1	0	0	4	.300
Malone, p	3	4	0	1	0	0	0	0	.250
Hornsby, 2b	5	21	4	5	1	1	0	1	.238
English, ss	5	21	1	4	2	0	0	0	.190
Taylor, c	5	17	0	3	0	0	0	3	.176
McMillan, 3b	5	20	0	2	0	0	0	0	.100
Heathcote, ph	1	1	0	0	0	0	0	0	.000
Gonzalez, c-ph	2	1	0	0	0	0	0	0	.000
Blair, ph	1	1	0	0	0	0	0	0	.000
Root, p	2	5	0	0	0	0	0	0	.000
Hartnett, ph	3	3	0	0	0	0	0	0	.000
Bush, p	2	3	1	0	0	0	0	0	.000
Tolson, ph	1	1	0	0	0	0	0	0	.000
Carlson, p	2	1	0	0	0	0	0	0	.000
Nehf, p	2	0	0	0	0	0	0	0	.000
Totals	5	173	17	43	6	2	1	15	.249

COMPOSITE PITCHING AVERAGES
Philadelphia Athletics

Pitcher	G.	IP.	H.	R.	E.	SO.	BB.	W.	L.	ERA.
Grove	2	$6\frac{1}{3}$	3	0	0	10	1	0	0	0.00
Walberg	2	$6\frac{1}{3}$	3	1	0	8	0	1	0	0.00
Ehmke	2	$12\frac{2}{3}$	14	3	3	13	3	1	0	2.13
Earnshaw	2	$13\frac{2}{3}$	14	6	4	17	6	1	1	2.63

Pitcher	G.	IP.	H.	R.	E.	BB.	SO.	W.	L.	ERA.
Quinn	1	5	7	6	5	2	2	0	0	9.00
Rommel	1	1	2	1	1	0	1	1	0	9.00
Totals	5	45	43	17	13	50	13	4	1	2.60

Chicago Cubs

Pitcher	G.	IP.	H.	R.	E.	SO.	BB.	W.	L.	ERA.
Bush	2	11	12	3	1	4	2	1	0	0.82
Malone	3	13	12	9	6	11	7	0	2	4.15
Root	2	13⅓	12	7	7	8	2	0	1	4.73
Carlson	2	4	7	3	3	3	1	0	0	6.75
Blake	2	1⅓	4	2	2	1	0	0	1	13.50
Nehf	2	1	1	2	2	0	1	0	0	18.00
Totals	5	43⅔	48	26	21	27	13	1	4	4.33

SERIES OF 1930

	W.	L.	Pct.
Philadelphia A. L.	4	2	.667
St. Louis N. L.	2	4	.333

The Athletics spreadeagled the American League field in 1930, winning over Washington by eight games, and then followed up their pennant victory by defeating the Cardinals in the World Series, four games to two. Managed by Gabby Street, the Cards were an upstart club, which came from 12 games in arrears in August to snatch the National League pennant from the Cubs, Giants and Dodgers. A September record of 21 victories against only four defeats put them over, two games ahead of their Chicago rivals.

The Series gave Connie Mack his fifth world title, which was the record up to that date. It also was the third time that the American League entrant won four straight sets from its National opponents. After the Athletics won the first two games on their home grounds, the Cards tied it up by winning the next two on their field, one of their victories being a shutout. Then, the American Leaguers grabbed the big end of the purse by winning the fifth and sixth games.

George Earnshaw pitched magnificently for the Mackmen, faring far better than against the Cubs the preceding fall. He gained two victories, in each of which he gave up only one run, and also pitched shutout ball for seven innings of the fifth game, when he gave way to a pinch-hitter. In 25 innings, the big righthander yielded only 13 hits and fanned 19. The fifth game eventually went to Bob Grove, who also won the first tilt for the Athletics.

Bill Hallahan and Jess Haines each won a game for St. Louis, the lefthander pitching a seven-hit shutout in the third game. Burleigh Grimes who had come to St. Louis from Boston early in the 1930 season, suffered two reverses for Street's team and both were tough engagements to lose. Burleigh dropped the opener, 5 to 2, to Grove, a game in which the Cards made nine hits and the Athletics only five. However, all five of the Mackmen's blows were for extra bases. Mickey Cochrane and Al Simmons hit homers, Jimmie Foxx and Mule Haas triples and Jimmie Dykes a double, each Philadelphia hit accounting for a run.

With the Series even at two victories apiece, Grimes squared off with Earnshaw in the fifth game, played in St. Louis. Neither team scored until the ninth, when Cochrane opened by drawing a pass. Grimes retired Simmons, but Foxx awed the crowd by hitting a homer into the left-field bleachers. The A's garnered only five hits in this game and the Cardinals only three off Earnshaw and Grove.

The general excellence of the pitching was told in the club batting averages, the losing Cardinals hitting .200 and the victorious Athletics only .197, a sharp drop from their .281 against the Cubs in 1929. Simmons and Foxx, the two Athletic cleanup sluggers, did most of the club's hitting, racking up averages of .364 and .333, respectively.

Again the spectators were provided some rare batting rallies, although there was nothing like the 10-run outburst in one inning as the Athletics made in the seventh frame of the fourth game in the 1929 Series. The Mackmen pounded five hits in the first game and seven in the sixth, all for extra bases, and each drive was converted into a run.

Shortstop Charley Gelbert led the regular St. Louis players on the offense with an average of .353. Chick Hafey, the Redbirds' left fielder, set a World Series record by hitting five doubles. He made six safeties for a .273 average. The box scores:

Wednesday, Oct. 1—At Philadelphia

St. Louis (N.L.)	AB.	R.	H.	O.	A.	E.
Douthit, cf	4	0	0	0	0	0
Adams, 3b	3	0	1	1	2	0
Frisch, 2b	4	0	2	1	2	0
Bottomley, 1b	4	0	0	12	0	0
Hafey, lf	4	0	1	2	0	0
Blades, rf	3	0	0	2	0	0
Mancuso, c	4	1	1	6	1	0
Gelbert, ss	4	1	2	0	4	0
Grimes, p	3	0	2	0	3	0
aPuccinelli	1	0	0	0	0	0
Totals	34	2	9	24	12	0

Phila'phia (A.L.)	AB.	R.	H.	O.	A.	E.
Bishop, 2b	3	1	0	2	3	0
Dykes, 3b	4	0	1	1	1	0
Cochrane, c	3	1	1	7	0	0
Simmons, lf	3	1	1	2	0	0
Foxx, 1b	3	1	1	8	0	0
Miller, rf	2	0	0	2	0	0
Haas, cf	3	1	1	3	0	0
Boley, ss	2	0	0	2	3	0
Grove, p	3	0	0	0	0	0
Totals	26	5	5	27	7	0

St. Louis .... 0 0 2   0 0 0   0 0 0—2
Philadelphia .... 0 1 0   1 0 1   1 1 *—5

aFouled out for Grimes in ninth. Runs batted in—Miller, Simmons, Dykes, Boley, Cochrane, Douthit, Adams. Two-base hits—Dykes, Frisch, Hafey. Three-base hits—Foxx, Haas. Home runs—Cochrane, Simmons. Sacrifice hits—Miller, Boley, Douthit, Adams. Left on bases—St. Louis 8,

1930 WORLD SERIES

Philadelphia 2. Earned runs—Philadelphia 5, St. Louis 2. Struck out—By Grove 5, by Grimes 6. Bases on balls—Off Grove 1, off Grimes 3. Umpires—Moriarty (A.L.), Rigler (N.L.), Geisel (A.L.) and Reardon (N.L.). Time—1:48. Attendance—32,295.

Thursday, Oct. 2—At Philadelphia

St. Louis (N.L.)	AB.	R.	H.	O.	A.	E.
Douthit, cf	4	0	0	4	0	0
Adams, 3b	4	0	1	0	1	0
Frisch, 2b	4	0	1	1	1	1
Bottomley, 1b	4	0	0	7	0	0
Hafey, lf	4	0	0	2	0	0
Watkins, rf	4	1	1	0	0	0
Mancuso, c	3	0	1	7	0	0
Gelbert, ss	3	0	1	3	1	0
Rhem, p	1	0	0	0	0	1
Lindsey, p	1	0	1	0	0	0
aFisher	1	0	0	0	0	0
Johnson, p	0	0	0	0	0	0
Totals	33	1	6	24	3	2

Phila'phia (A.L.)	AB.	R.	H.	O.	A.	E.
Bishop, 2b	2	1	0	3	0	0
Dykes, 3b	3	0	1	4	2	0
Cochrane, c	3	2	1	9	0	1
Simmons, lf	4	2	2	3	0	0
Foxx, 1b	3	0	1	3	2	0
Miller, rf	4	0	1	1	0	0
Haas, cf	4	0	0	2	0	0
Boley, ss	4	1	1	1	1	1
Earnshaw, p	3	0	0	1	0	0
Totals	30	6	7	27	5	2

St. Louis............ 0 1 0 0 0 0 0 0 0—1
Philadelphia...... 2 0 2 2 0 0 0 0 *—6

aStruck out for Lindsey in seventh. Runs batted in—Watkins, Cochrane, Foxx, Simmons, Miller, Dykes 2. Two base hits—Dykes, Simmons, Foxx, Frisch. Home runs—Cochrane, Watkins. Sacrifice hit—Dykes. Stolen base—Frisch. Double plays—Gelbert, unassisted; Dykes and Foxx. Left on bases—St. Louis 6, Philadelphia 5. Earned runs—Philadelphia 6, St. Louis 1. Struck out—By Earnshaw 8, by Rhem 3, by Lindsey 2, by Johnson 2. Bases on balls—Off Earnshaw 1, off Rhem 2, off Johnson 2. Hits—Off Rhem 7 in 3⅓ innings, off Lindsey 0 in 2⅔ innings, off Johnson 0 on 2 innings. Losing pitcher—Rhem. Umpires—Rigler (N.L.), Geisel (A.L.), Reardon (N.L.) and Moriarty (A.L.). Time—1:47. Attendance—32,295.

Saturday, October 4—At St. Louis

Phila'phia (A.L.)	AB.	R.	H.	O.	A.	E.
Bishop, 2b	4	0	3	0	2	0
Dykes, 3b	4	0	0	1	1	0
Cochrane, c	2	0	0	6	0	0
Simmons, lf	4	0	2	1	1	0
Foxx, 1b	4	0	1	11	1	0
Miller, rf	4	0	0	1	0	0
Haas, cf	3	0	0	1	0	0
aMoore	1	0	1	0	0	0
Boley, ss	4	0	0	3	5	0
Walberg, p	2	0	0	0	0	0
Shores, p	0	0	0	0	0	0
Quinn, p	0	0	0	0	1	0
bMcNair	1	0	0	0	0	0
Totals	33	0	7	24	11	0

St. Louis (N.L.)	AB.	R.	H.	O.	A.	E.
Douthit, cf	4	1	2	3	0	0
Adams, 3b	4	0	0	0	0	0
Frisch, 2b	4	0	2	2	5	0
Bottomley, 1b	4	1	1	14	0	0
Hafey, lf	4	1	2	0	0	0
Blades, rf	2	1	1	1	0	0
Watkins, rf	2	1	1	1	0	0
Wilson, c	4	0	2	6	0	0
Gelbert, ss	3	0	1	0	4	0
Hallahan, p	2	0	0	0	1	0
Totals	33	5	10	27	10	0

Philadelphia...... 0 0 0 0 0 0 0 0 0—0
St. Louis............ 0 0 0 1 1 0 2 1 *—5

aSingled for Haas in ninth. bFlied out for Quinn in ninth. Runs batted in—Douthit, Gelbert, Wilson 2, Hafey. Two-base hits—Bottomley, Hafey, Simmons. Home run—Douthit. Double play—Gelbert, Frisch and Bottomley. Left on bases—Philadelphia 11, St. Louis 5. Earned runs—St. Louis 5. Struck out—By Walberg 3, by Quinn 1, by Hallahan 6. Bases on balls—Off Walberg 1, off Hallahan 5. Hits—Off Walberg 4 in 4⅔ innings, off Shores 3 in 1⅓ innings (pitched to three batters in seventh), off Quinn 3 in 2 innings. Losing pitcher—Walberg. Umpires—Geisel (A.L.), Reardon (N.L.), Moriarty (A.L.) and Rigler (N.L.). Time—1:55. Attendance—36,944.

Sunday, October 5—At St. Louis

Phila'phia (A.L.)	AB.	R.	H.	O.	A.	E.
Bishop, 2b	3	1	1	2	2	0
Dykes, 3b	2	0	0	1	0	1
Cochrane, c	4	0	0	3	0	0
Simmons, lf	3	0	2	0	0	0
Foxx, 1b	4	0	1	6	0	0
Miller, rf	4	0	0	7	0	0
Haas, cf	3	0	0	4	0	0
Boley, ss	4	0	0	1	1	0
Grove, p	3	0	0	0	0	0
Totals	30	1	4	24	3	1

St. Louis (N.L.)	AB.	R.	H.	O.	A.	E.
Douthit, cf	4	0	0	0	0	0
Adams, 3b	4	0	0	2	2	0
Frisch, 2b	4	0	0	3	2	1
Bottomley, 1b	4	0	0	9	0	0
Hafey, lf	3	1	1	3	0	0
Blades, rf	3	1	0	7	0	0
Wilson, c	3	0	1	3	0	0
Gelbert, ss	2	1	2	0	4	0
Haines, p	2	0	1	0	1	0
Totals	29	3	5	27	9	1

Philadelphia...... 1 0 0 0 0 0 0 0 0—1
St. Louis............ 0 0 1 2 0 0 0 0 *—3

Runs batted in—Simmons, Haines, Gelbert. Two-base hit—Hafey. Three-base hit—Gelbert. Sacrifice hits—Dykes, Haines. Double play—Gelbert, Frisch and Bottomley. Left on bases—Philadelphia 7, St. Louis 4. Earned runs—St. Louis 1, Philadelphia 1. Struck out—By Haines 2, by Grove 3. Bases on balls—Off Haines 4, off Grove 1. Wild pitch—Haines. Umpires—Reardon (N.L.), Moriarty (A.L.), Rigler (N.L.) and Geisel (A.L.). Time—1:41. Attendance—39,946.

Monday, October 6—At St. Louis

Phila'phia (A.L.)	AB.	R.	H.	O.	A.	E.
Bishop, 2b	4	0	0	1	0	0
Dykes, 3b	3	0	0	0	1	0
Cochrane, c	3	1	1	7	1	0
Simmons, lf	4	0	3	0	0	0
Foxx, 1b	4	1	2	12	0	0
Miller, rf	4	0	0	0	0	0
Haas, cf	4	0	1	2	0	0
Boley, ss	3	0	1	2	1	0
Earnshaw, p	2	0	0	0	4	0
aMoore	0	0	0	0	0	0
Grove, p	0	0	0	0	1	0
Totals	31	2	5	27	8	0

St. Louis (N.L.)	AB.	R.	H.	O.	A.	E.
Douthit, cf	4	0	0	2	0	0
Adams, 3b	4	0	1	0	1	0
Frisch, 2b	4	0	1	3	3	1
Bottomley, 1b	4	0	0	9	1	0
Hafey, lf	3	0	0	1	0	0
Watkins, rf	3	0	0	1	0	0
bBlades	0	0	0	0	0	0
Wilson, c	4	0	1	9	1	0
Gelbert, ss	2	0	0	2	8	0
Grimes, p	2	0	0	0	0	0
Totals	30	0	3	27	14	1

Philadelphia	0 0 0	0 0 0	0 0 2	—2		
St. Louis	0 0 0	0 0 0	0 0 0	—0		

aWalked for Earnshaw in eighth. bWalked for Watkins in ninth. Runs batted in—Foxx 2. Two-base hit—Wilson. Home run—Foxx. Sacrifice hit—Grimes. Double play—Adams, Frisch and Bottomley. Left on bases—St. Louis 8, Philadelphia 5. Earned runs—Philadelphia 2. Struck out—By Earnshaw 5, by Grove 2, by Grimes 7. Bases on balls—Off Earnshaw 3, off Grove 1, off Grimes 3. Hits—Off Earnshaw 2 in 7 innings, off Grove 1 in 2 innings. Winning pitcher—Grove. Umpires—Moriarty (A.L.), Rigler (N.L.), Geisel (A.L.) and Reardon (N.L.). Time—1:58. Attendance—38,844.

Wednesday, Oct. 8—At Philadelphia

St. Louis (N.L.)	AB.	R.	H.	O.	A.	E.
Douthit, cf	4	0	0	5	0	0
Adams, 3b	2	0	0	1	1	0
cHigh, 3b	2	1	1	0	0	0
Watkins, rf	3	0	0	3	0	1
Frisch, 2b	4	0	1	3	1	0
Hafey, lf	4	0	2	1	0	0
Bottomley, 1b	2	0	0	6	0	0
Wilson, c	4	0	0	5	0	0
Gelbert, ss	3	0	0	0	2	0
Hallahan, p	0	0	0	0	0	0
aFisher	1	0	1	0	0	0
Johnson, p	0	0	0	0	0	0
bBlades	1	0	0	0	0	0
Lindsey, p	0	0	0	0	1	0
dOrsatti	1	0	0	0	0	0
Bell, p	0	0	0	0	1	0
Totals	31	1	5	24	7	1

Phila'phia (A.L.)	AB.	R.	H.	O.	A.	E.
Bishop, 2b	2	2	0	0	2	0
Dykes, 3b	2	2	2	1	1	0
Cochrane, c	3	1	1	8	0	0
Simmons, cf-lf	4	1	1	3	0	0
Foxx, 1b	3	1	1	12	0	0
Miller, rf	3	0	2	1	0	0
Moore, lf	2	0	0	0	0	0
Haas, cf	1	0	0	2	0	0
Boley, ss	4	0	0	0	2	0
Earnshaw, p	4	0	0	0	2	0
Totals	28	7	7	27	7	0

St. Louis	0 0 0	0 0 0	0 0 1	—1	
Philadelphia	2 0 1	2 1 1	0 0 *	—7	

aDoubled for Hallahan in third. bStruck out for Johnson in sixth. cGrounded out for Adams in sixth. dGrounded out for Lindsey in eighth. Runs batted in—Cochrane 2, Miller, Simmons, Dykes 2, Haas, Hafey. Two-base hits—Dykes, Cochrane, Foxx, Miller 2, Hafey 2, Fisher. Home runs—Dykes, Simmons. Sacrifice hits—Cochrane, Miller, Haas. Double play—Foxx, unassisted. Left on bases—St. Louis 6, Philadelphia 6. Earned runs—Philadelphia 7, St. Louis 1. Struck out—By Hallahan 2, by Johnson 2, by Earnshaw 6. Bases on balls—Off Hallahan 3, off Johnson 1, off Lindsey 1, off Earnshaw 3. Hit by pitcher—By Hallahan (Bishop). Passed ball—Wilson. Hits—Off Hallahan 2 in 2 innings, off Johnson 4 in 3 innings, off Lindsey 1 in 2 innings, off Bell 0 in 1 inning. Losing pitcher—Hallahan. Umpires—Rigler (N.L.), Geisel (A.L.), Reardon (N.L.) and Moriarty (A.L.). Time—1:46. Attendance—32,295.

COMPOSITE BATTING AVERAGES
Philadelphia Athletics

Player-Position	G.	AB.	R.	H.	2B.	3B.	HR.	RBI.	BA.
Simmons, lf-cf	6	22	4	8	2	0	2	4	.364
Foxx, 1b	6	21	3	7	2	1	3	.333	
Moore, ph-lf	3	3	0	1	0	0	0	0	.333
Bishop, 2b	6	18	5	4	0	0	0	0	.222
Dykes, 3b	6	18	2	4	3	0	1	5	.222
Cochrane, c	6	18	5	4	1	0	2	4	.222
Miller, rf	6	21	0	3	2	0	0	3	.143
Haas, cf	6	18	1	2	0	1	0	1	.111
Boley, ss	6	21	1	2	0	0	0	1	.095
Grove, p	3	6	0	0	0	0	0	0	.000
Earnshaw, p	3	9	0	0	0	0	0	0	.000
Walberg, p	1	2	0	0	0	0	0	1	.000
Shores, p	1	0	0	0	0	0	0	0	.000
Quinn, p	1	0	0	0	0	0	0	0	.000
McNair, ph	1	1	0	0	0	0	0	0	.000
Totals	6	178	21	35	10	2	6	21	.197

St. Louis Cardinals

Player-Position	G.	AB.	R.	H.	2B.	3B.	HR.	RBI.	BA.
Lindsey, p	2	1	0	1	0	0	0	0	1.000
Haines, p	1	2	0	1	0	0	0	0	.500
High, ph-3b	1	2	1	1	0	0	0	0	.500
Fisher, p	2	2	0	1	0	0	0	0	.500
Grimes, p	2	5	0	2	0	0	0	0	.400
Gelbert, ss	6	17	2	6	0	1	0	2	.353
Mancuso, c	2	7	1	2	0	0	0	0	.286
Hafey, lf	6	22	2	6	5	0	0	0	.273
Wilson, c	4	15	0	4	1	0	0	2	.267
Frisch, 2b	6	24	5	5	2	0	0	0	.208
Watkins, rf	4	12	2	2	0	0	1	1	.167
Adams, 3b	6	21	0	3	0	0	0	1	.143
Blades, rf-ph	5	9	2	1	0	0	0	0	.111
Douthit, cf	6	24	1	2	0	0	1	2	.083
Bottomley, 1b	6	22	1	1	1	0	0	0	.045
Johnson, p	2	0	0	0	0	0	0	0	.000
Hallahan, p	2	2	0	0	0	0	0	0	.000
Puccinelli, ph	1	1	0	0	0	0	0	0	.000
Rhem, p	1	1	0	0	0	0	0	0	.000
Orsatti, ph	1	1	0	0	0	0	0	0	.000
Bell, p	1	0	0	0	0	0	0	0	.000
Totals	6	190	12	38	10	1	2	11	.200

COMPOSITE PITCHING AVERAGES
Philadelphia Athletics

Pitcher	G.	IP.	H.	R.	E.	SO.	BB.	W.	L.	ERA.
Earnshaw	3	25	13	2	2	19	7	2	0	0.72
Grove	3	19	15	5	3	10	3	2	1	1.42
Walberg	1	4⅔	4	2	2	3	1	0	1	3.86
Quinn	1	2	3	1	1	1	0	0	0	4.50
Shores	1	1⅓	3	2	2	0	0	0	0	13.50
Totals	6	52	38	12	10	33	11	4	2	1.73

St. Louis Cardinals

Pitcher	G.	IP.	H.	R.	E.	SO.	BB.	W.	L.	ERA.
Bell	1	1	0	0	0	0	0	0	0	0.00
Haines	1	9	4	1	1	2	4	1	0	1.00
Hallahan	2	11	9	2	2	8	8	1	1	1.63
Lindsey	2	4⅔	1	1	1	2	1	0	0	1.93
Grimes	2	17	10	7	7	13	6	0	2	3.71
Johnson	2	5	4	4	4	3	0	0	0	7.20
Rhem	1	3⅓	7	6	6	3	2	0	1	16.20
Totals	6	51	35	21	21	32	24	2	4	3.71

SERIES OF 1931

	W.	L.	Pct.
St. Louis N. L.	4	3	.571
Philadelphia A. L.	3	4	.429

Connie Mack won his ninth and last pennant in 1931 with 107 victories, the highest victory total of his career, and a percentage of .704, the second best in the American

League. The A's star lefthander, Bob Grove, had one winning streak of 16 straight and finished with 31 victories against only four defeats, and Al Simmons won the league's batting championship with an average of .390.

Yet, with a chance to be the first manager to win three straight world championships, Mack's club lost a thrilling seven-game Series to Gabby Street's Cardinals. The Cardinals had one of their best clubs that year; they won 101 games and romped to the flag easily, edging the second-place Giants by 13 games.

The main reason for the Cardinal victory was the wild ride on which John (Pepper) Martin, the Wild Horse of the Osage, took Mack, Mickey Cochrane, Connie's star catcher, and the Athletic pitching aces, Bob Grove and George Earnshaw, through the Series. Pepper stole five bases and hit an even .500, his 12 blows including four doubles and a homer. He scored five runs and drove in five, batting across four in the fifth game.

Bill Hallahan and Burleigh Grimes, who had pitched well in the 1930 Series, were even better in 1931 and, next to Martin, were the heroes of the Cardinal victory. Hallahan's southpaw magic completely befuddled the American League champions; he pitched two victories, one a shutout, and went to Grimes' rescue when the Athletics threatened to pull out the Series in the ninth inning of the seventh game. Hallahan gave up only one run and 12 hits in 18⅓ innings. In winning the third game, 5 to 2, Grimes pitched a two-hitter, the first Philadelphia safety coming in the eighth inning. Burleigh blanked the A's for eight frames in the seventh game, but was relieved by Hallahan in the ninth with two runs in and the tying tallies on bases. Paul Derringer, an 18-game freshman winner of 1931, suffered two of the Redbird losses; Syl Johnson dropped the other.

Two days consumed in traveling and one rainy day stretched the Series through 10 days and made it possible for Mack to pitch Grove and Earnshaw three times each. Grove won two games and lost one, and Earnshaw reversed this procedure. Mack's other starter was Waite Hoyt, who lost the fifth game to Hallahan, 5 to 1. Though suffering two defeats, Earnshaw really pitched better than Grove. After losing the second game to Hallahan, 2 to 0, big George evened up the Series by winning the fourth game, 3 to 0, giving up only two hits. Picked by Mack to oppose Grimes in the seventh and deciding game, Earnshaw saw the Cards score four early tallies on erratic support and fluke hits, topped by George Watkins' two-run homer in the third. After that, he retired the next 15 men in order before retiring for a pinch-hitter.

Outside of Martin's big splurge, the hitting was light, the Cardinals averaging .236 and the Athletics .220. Next to Martin's .500, the best Cardinal figure was Watkins' .286. Al Simmons and Jimmie Foxx again looked after most of Mack's power with averages of .333 and .348, respectively. Al hit two homers and Jimmie one. Cochrane fell down hard; in addition to failing to stop Martin's steals, Mickey hit only .160, being held to four safeties, all singles, in his 25 plate appearances.

It was the third straight year that President Hoover witnessed a Series since entering the White House. The President went to Philadelphia for the third game and this was the only time he did not see the Mackmen win in the classic. Burleigh Grimes, who was 38 years old the previous August, beat Grove, 5 to 2, on two hits. The box scores:

Thursday, October 1—At St. Louis

Phila'phia (A.L.)	AB.	R.	H.	O.	A.	E.
Bishop, 2b	5	1	1	0	3	0
Haas, cf	5	1	1	2	0	0
Cochrane, c	4	2	2	7	0	0
Simmons, lf	4	1	1	3	0	0
Foxx, 1b	4	0	2	9	0	0
Miller, rf	4	0	0	3	0	0
Dykes, 3b	3	0	2	1	1	0
Williams, ss	4	1	2	2	5	0
Grove, p	4	0	0	0	0	0
Totals	37	6	11	27	9	0

St. Louis (N.L.)	AB.	R.	H.	O.	A.	E.
High, 3b	4	0	1	0	1	0
cMancuso	1	0	0	0	0	0
Roettger, rf	5	1	2	1	0	0
Frisch, 2b	4	1	2	5	1	0
Bottomley, 1b	4	0	0	6	1	0
Hafey, lf	4	0	1	0	0	0
Martin, cf	4	0	3	2	0	0
Wilson, c	4	0	0	12	2	0
Gelbert, ss	4	0	2	1	5	0
Derringer, p	2	0	0	0	0	0
aFlowers	1	0	0	0	0	0
Johnson, p	0	0	0	0	0	0
bBlades	1	0	0	0	0	0
Totals	38	2	12	27	10	0

Philadelphia .... 0 0 4   0 0 0   2 0 0—6
St. Louis .... 2 0 0   0 0 0   0 0 0—2

aGrounded out for Derringer in seventh. bStruck out for Johnson in ninth. cFouled out for High in ninth. Runs batted in—Simmons 3, Foxx 2, Haas, Martin, Bottomley. Two-base hits—Haas, Martin, Gelbert. Home run—Simmons. Stolen bases—Hafey, Martin. Double plays—Bottomley, unassisted; Bishop, Williams and Foxx. Left on bases—St. Louis 9, Philadelphia 7. Earned runs—Philadelphia 6, St. Louis 2. Struck out—By Grove 7, by Derringer 9, by Johnson 2. Bases on balls—Off Derringer 3. Hits—Off Derringer 11 in 7 innings, off Johnson 0 in 2 innings. Losing pitcher—Derringer. Umpires—Klem (N.L.), Nallin (A.L.), Stark (N.L.) and McGowan (A.L.). Time—1:55. Attendance—38,529.

Friday, October 2—At St. Louis

Phila'phia (A.L.)	AB.	R.	H.	O.	A.	E.
Bishop, 2b	5	0	0	1	5	0
Haas, cf	4	0	1	5	0	0
Cochrane, c	2	0	0	5	0	0
Simmons, lf	4	0	0	1	0	0
Foxx, 1b	2	0	1	11	1	0

1931 WORLD SERIES

	AB.	R.	H.	O.	A.	E.
Miller, rf	4	0	1	0	0	0
Dykes, 3b	2	0	0	0	2	0
Williams, ss	2	0	0	1	2	0
Earnshaw, p	3	0	0	0	2	0
aMoore	1	0	0	0	0	0
Totals	29	0	3	24	12	0

St. Louis (N.L.)	AB.	R.	H.	O.	A.	E.
Flowers, 3b	4	0	0	2	1	0
Watkins, rf	4	0	2	1	0	0
Frisch, 2b	4	0	1	4	4	0
Bottomley, 1b	3	0	0	7	0	0
Hafey, lf	4	0	0	4	0	0
Martin, cf	3	2	2	0	0	0
Wilson, c	3	0	0	7	0	1
Gelbert, ss	2	0	1	2	3	0
Hallahan, p	2	0	0	0	0	0
Totals	29	2	6	27	8	1

Philadelphia .... 0 0 0   0 0 0   0 0 0—0
St. Louis .... 0 1 0   0 0 0   1 0 *—2

aStruck out and reached first base on Wilson's error for Earnshaw in ninth. Runs batted in—Wilson, Gelbert. Two-base hits—Watkins, Frisch, Martin. Sacrifice hits—Gelbert, Hallahan, Dykes. Stolen bases—Martin 2. Double play—Frisch, Gelbert and Bottomley. Left on bases—Philadelphia 10, St. Louis 6. Earned runs—St. Louis 2. Struck out—By Hallahan 8, by Earnshaw 5. Bases on balls—Off Hallahan 7, off Earnshaw 1. Wild pitch—Hallahan. Umpires—Nallin (A.L.), Stark (N.L.), McGowan (A.L.) and Klem (N.L.). Time—1:49. Attendance—35,947.

Monday, October 5—At Philadelphia

St. Louis (N.L.)	AB.	R.	H.	O.	A.	E.
Adams, 3b	3	0	0	0	1	0
Flowers, 3b	1	0	0	1	0	0
Roettger, rf	5	0	1	1	0	0
bWatkins, rf	0	1	0	0	0	0
Frisch, 2b	5	0	1	4	3	0
Bottomley, 1b	4	1	1	11	0	0
Hafey, lf	5	1	1	2	0	0
Martin, cf	4	2	2	2	0	0
Wilson, c	4	0	3	5	0	0
Gelbert, ss	4	0	1	1	6	0
Grimes, p	4	0	2	0	2	0
Totals	39	5	12	27	12	0

Phila'phia (A.L.)	AB.	R.	H.	O.	A.	E.
Bishop, 2b	3	0	0	2	3	0
Haas, cf	4	0	0	0	0	0
Cochrane, c	3	0	0	2	0	0
cMcNair	0	1	0	0	0	0
Simmons, lf	4	1	1	3	0	0
Foxx, 1b	2	0	0	16	0	0
Miller, rf	3	0	1	2	0	0
Dykes, 3b	3	0	0	1	4	0
Williams, ss	3	0	0	1	6	0
Grove, p	2	0	0	0	0	0
aCramer	1	0	0	0	0	0
Mahaffey, p	0	0	0	0	1	0
Totals	28	2	2	27	14	0

St. Louis .... 0 2 0   2 0 0   0 1—5
Philadelphia .... 0 0 0   0 0 0   0 0 2—2

aPopped out for Grove in eighth. bRan for Roettger in ninth. cRan for Cochrane in ninth. Runs batted in—Grimes 2, Gelbert, Wilson, Bottomley, Simmons 2. Two-base hits—Roettger, Bottomley, Martin. Home run—Simmons. Double play—Gelbert, Frisch and Bottomley. Left on bases—St. Louis 9, Philadelphia 8. Earned runs—St. Louis 5, Philadelphia 2. Struck out—By Grove 2, by Grimes 5. Bases on balls—Off Grove 1, off Mahaffey 1, off Grimes 4. Hits—Off Grove 11 in 8 innings, off Mahaffey 1 in 1 inning. Losing pitcher—Grove. Umpires—Stark (N.L.), McGowan (A.L.), Klem (N.L.) and Nallin (A.L.). Time—2:10. Attendance—32,295.

Tuesday, October 6—At Philadelphia

St. Louis (N.L.)	AB.	R.	H.	O.	A.	E.
Flowers, 3b	1	0	0	0	1	0
High, 3b	3	0	0	0	1	0
Watkins, rf	4	0	0	2	0	0
Frisch, 2b	3	0	0	1	2	0
Bottomley, 1b	3	0	0	7	0	1
Hafey, lf	3	0	0	0	0	0
Martin, cf	3	0	2	4	0	0
Wilson, c	3	0	0	6	0	0
Gelbert, ss	3	0	0	4	4	0
Johnson, p	2	0	0	0	1	0
Lindsey, p	0	0	0	0	0	0
aCollins	1	0	0	0	0	0
Derringer, p	0	0	0	0	1	0
Totals	29	0	2	24	10	1

Phila'phia (A.L.)	AB.	R.	H.	O.	A.	E.
Bishop, 2b	4	1	2	0	0	0
Haas, cf	3	0	1	1	0	0
Cochrane, c	3	0	0	9	0	0
Simmons, lf	4	0	2	5	0	0
Foxx, 1b	3	1	1	7	0	0
Miller, rf	4	1	1	4	0	0
Dykes, 3b	4	0	2	0	1	0
Williams, ss	4	0	1	0	1	0
Earnshaw, p	3	0	0	1	3	0
Totals	32	3	10	27	5	0

St. Louis .... 0 0 0   0 0 0   0 0 0—0
Philadelphia .... 1 0 0   0 0 2   0 0 *—3

aStruck out for Lindsey in eighth. Runs batted in—Dykes, Foxx, Simmons. Two-base hits—Simmons, Miller, Martin. Home run—Foxx. Sacrifice hit—Haas. Stolen bases—Frisch, Martin. Double play—Frisch, Gelbert and Bottomley. Left on bases—Philadelphia 8, St. Louis 3. Earned runs—Philadelphia 3. Struck out—By Earnshaw 8, by Johnson 2, by Lindsey 2, by Derringer 1. Bases on balls—Off Earnshaw 1, off Johnson 1, off Lindsey 1. Hits—Off Johnson 9 in 5⅔ innings, off Lindsey 1 in 1⅓ innings, off Derringer 0 in 1 inning. Losing pitcher—Johnson. Umpires—McGowan (A.L.), Klem (N.L.), Nallin (A.L.) and Stark (N.L.). Time—1:58. Attendance—32,295.

Wednesday, Oct. 7—At Philadelphia

St. Louis (N.L.)	AB.	R.	H.	O.	A.	E.
Adams, 3b	1	0	1	0	0	0
aHigh, 3b	4	1	0	2	3	0
Watkins, rf	3	1	0	3	0	0
Frisch, 2b	4	1	2	6	1	0
Martin, cf	4	1	3	0	0	0
Hafey, lf	4	0	1	1	0	0
Bottomley, 1b	4	1	2	7	1	0
Wilson, c	4	0	2	7	0	0
Gelbert, ss	4	0	1	1	2	0
Hallahan, p	4	0	0	0	0	0
Totals	36	5	12	27	7	0

Phila'phia (A.L.)	AB.	R.	H.	O.	A.	E.
Bishop, 2b	2	0	0	3	2	0
bMcNair, 2b	2	0	0	1	1	0
Haas, cf	2	0	0	2	0	0
cMoore, lf	2	0	1	1	0	0
Cochrane, c	4	0	0	3	2	0
Simmons, lf-cf	4	1	3	5	0	0
Foxx, 1b	3	0	2	8	1	0
Miller, rf	4	0	0	2	0	0
Dykes, 3b	4	0	1	0	1	0

1931 WORLD SERIES

	AB.	R.	H.	O.	A.	E.
Williams, ss	4	0	1	2	5	0
Hoyt, p	2	0	0	0	0	0
Walberg, p	0	0	0	0	0	0
dHeving	1	0	0	0	0	0
Rommel, p	0	0	0	0	0	0
eBoley	1	0	0	0	0	0
Totals	35	1	9	27	12	0

St. Louis .... 1 0 0   0 0 2   0 1 1—5
Philadelphia .... 0 0 0   0 0 0   1 0 0—1

aRan for Adams in first. bFouled out for Bishop in sixth. cFlied out for Haas in sixth. dFlied out for Walberg in eighth. eStruck out for Rommel in ninth. Runs batted in—Martin 4, Gelbert, Miller. Two-base hits—Frisch, Simmons. Home run—Martin. Stolen base—Watkins. Double plays—Bishop and Foxx; Gelbert, Bottomley and Wilson. Left on bases—Philadelphia 8, St. Louis 5. Earned runs—St. Louis 5, Philadelphia 1. Struck out—By Hallahan 4, by Hoyt 1, by Walberg 2. Bases on balls—Off Hallahan 1, off Walberg 1. Hits—Off Hoyt 7 in 6 innings, off Walberg 2 in 2 innings, off Rommel 3 in 1 inning. Losing pitcher—Hoyt. Umpires—Klem (N.L.), Nallin (A.L.), Stark (N.L.) and McGowan (A.L.). Time—1:56. Attendance—32,295.

Friday, October 9—At St. Louis

Phila'phia (A.L.)	AB.	R.	H.	O.	A.	E.
Bishop, 2b	4	2	1	4	4	0
Haas, cf	2	0	0	5	0	0
Cochrane, c	5	0	1	6	0	1
Simmons, lf	4	1	1	2	0	0
Foxx, 1b	5	2	2	7	0	0
Miller, rf	3	1	1	1	0	0
Dykes, 3b	3	1	0	1	0	0
Williams, ss	4	1	2	1	3	0
Grove, p	4	0	0	0	0	0
Totals	34	8	8	27	7	1

St. Louis (N.L.)	AB.	R.	H.	O.	A.	E.
Flowers, 3b	4	1	1	0	2	1
Roettger, rf	4	0	1	2	0	0
Frisch, 2b	4	0	1	1	4	0
Martin, cf	3	0	0	1	0	0
Hafey, lf	4	0	1	1	0	1
Bottomley, 1b	4	0	0	11	0	0
Wilson, c	3	0	0	6	0	0
Mancuso, c	0	0	0	2	0	0
Gelbert, ss	3	0	1	3	5	0
Derringer, p	0	0	0	0	1	0
Johnson, p	0	0	0	0	0	0
aBlades	1	0	0	0	0	0
Lindsey, p	0	0	0	0	0	0
bCollins	1	0	0	0	0	0
Rhem, p	0	0	0	0	0	0
Totals	31	1	5	27	12	2

Philadelphia .... 0 0 0   0 4 0   4 0 0—8
St. Louis .... 0 0 0   0 0 1   0 0 0—1

aStruck out for Johnson in sixth. bGrounded out for Lindsey in eighth. Runs batted in—Simmons 2, Cochrane, Haas, Dykes, Frisch. Two-base hits—Flowers, Williams. Sacrifice hits—Haas, Miller, Derringer. Double plays—Frisch, Gelbert and Bottomley; Bishop, Williams and Foxx. Left on bases—Philadelphia 8, St. Louis 5. Earned runs—Philadelphia 2, St. Louis 1. Struck out—By Grove 7, by Derringer 4, by Johnson 2, by Rhem 1. Bases on balls—Off Grove 1, off Derringer 4, off Lindsey 2. Hit by pitcher—By Lindsey (Miller). Wild pitch—Derringer. Hits—Off Derringer 4 in 4⅔ innings, off Johnson 1 in 1⅓ innings, off Lindsey 3 in 2 innings, off Rhem 1 in 1 inning. Losing pitcher—Derringer. Umpires—Nallin (A.L.), Stark (N.L.), McGowan (A.L.) and Klem (N.L.). Time—1:57. Attendance—39,401.

Saturday, October 10—At St. Louis

Phila'phia (A.L.)	AB.	R.	H.	O.	A.	E.
Bishop, 2b	4	0	0	2	1	0
Haas, cf	3	0	0	2	0	0
Cochrane, c	4	0	0	8	2	0
Simmons, lf	3	0	1	0	0	0
Foxx, 1b	4	0	0	11	0	1
Miller, rf	4	1	3	0	0	0
Dykes, 3b	3	1	0	1	3	0
Williams, ss	4	0	2	0	2	0
Earnshaw, p	2	0	0	0	2	0
aTodt	0	0	0	0	0	0
Walberg, p	0	0	0	0	0	0
bCramer	1	0	1	0	0	0
Totals	32	2	7	24	10	1

St. Louis (N.L.)	AB.	R.	H.	O.	A.	E.
High, 3b	4	2	3	1	4	0
Watkins, rf	3	2	2	2	0	0
Frisch, 2b	3	0	0	2	4	0
Martin, cf	3	0	0	1	0	0
Orsatti, lf	3	0	0	1	0	0
Bottomley, 1b	3	0	0	12	0	0
Wilson, c	2	0	0	7	1	0
Gelbert, ss	3	0	0	1	4	0
Grimes, p	3	0	0	0	1	0
Hallahan, p	0	0	0	0	0	0
Totals	27	4	5	27	14	0

Philadelphia .... 0 0 0   0 0 0   0 0 2—2
St. Louis .... 2 0 2   0 0 0   0 0 *—4

aWalked for Earnshaw in eighth. bSingled for Walberg in ninth. Runs batted in—Watkins 2, Cramer 2. Home run—Watkins. Sacrifice hit—Frisch. Stolen base—Martin. Double plays—Frisch, Gelbert and Bottomley; Dykes, Bishop and Foxx. Left on bases—Philadelphia 8, St. Louis 3. Earned runs—St. Louis 3, Philadelphia 2. Struck out—By Grimes 6, by Earnshaw 7, by Walberg 2. Bases on balls—Off Grimes 5, off Earnshaw 2, off Walberg 1. Wild pitch—Earnshaw. Hits—Off Grimes 7 in 8⅔ innings, off Hallahan 0 in ⅓ inning, off Earnshaw 4 in 7 innings, off Walberg 1 in 1 inning. Winning pitcher—Grimes. Losing pitcher—Earnshaw. Umpires—Stark (N.L.), McGowan (A.L.), Klem (N.L.) and Nallin (A.L.). Time—1:57. Attendance—20,805.

COMPOSITE BATTING AVERAGES
St. Louis Cardinals

Player-Position	G.	AB.	R.	H.	2B.	3B.	HR.	RBI.	BA.
Martin, cf	7	24	5	12	4	0	1	5	.500
Watkins, rf-pr	5	14	4	4	1	0	1	2	.286
Grimes, p	2	7	0	2	0	0	0	2	.286
Roettger, rf	3	14	1	4	1	0	0	0	.286
High, 3b-pr	4	15	3	4	0	0	0	0	.267
Gelbert, ss	7	23	0	6	1	0	0	3	.261
Frisch, 2b	7	27	2	7	2	0	0	1	.259
Adams, 3b	2	4	0	1	0	0	0	0	.250
Wilson, c	7	23	0	5	0	0	0	2	.217
Hafey, lf	6	24	1	4	0	0	0	0	.167
Bottomley, 1b	7	25	2	4	1	0	0	2	.160
Flowers, ph-3b	5	11	1	1	1	0	0	0	.091
Mancuso, ph-c	2	1	0	0	0	0	0	0	.000
Derringer, p	3	2	0	0	0	0	0	0	.000
Johnson, p	3	2	0	0	0	0	0	0	.000
Blades, ph	2	1	0	0	0	0	0	0	.000
Hallahan, p	3	6	0	0	0	0	0	0	.000
Lindsey, p	2	0	0	0	0	0	0	0	.000
Collins, ph	2	2	0	0	0	0	0	0	.000
Rhem, p	1	0	0	0	0	0	0	0	.000
Orsatti, lf	1	3	0	0	0	0	0	0	.000
Totals	7	229	19	54	11	0	2	17	.236

1932 WORLD SERIES

Philadelphia Athletics

Player-Position	G.	AB.	R.	H.	2B.	3B.	HR.	RBI.	BA.
Cramer, ph	2	2	0	1	0	0	0	2	.500
Foxx, 1b	7	23	3	8	0	0	1	3	.348
Simmons, lf-cf	7	27	4	9	2	0	2	8	.333
Moore, ph-lf	2	3	0	1	0	0	0	0	.333
Williams, ss	7	25	2	8	1	0	0	1	.320
Miller, rf	7	26	3	7	1	0	0	1	.269
Dykes, 3b	7	22	2	5	0	0	0	2	.227
Cochrane, c	7	25	2	4	0	0	0	1	.160
Bishop, 2b	7	27	4	4	0	0	0	0	.148
Haas, cf	7	23	1	3	1	0	0	2	.130
Grove, p	3	10	0	0	0	0	0	0	.000
Earnshaw, p	3	8	0	0	0	0	0	0	.000
McNair, pr-ph-2b	2	2	1	0	0	0	0	0	.000
Walberg, p	2	0	0	0	0	0	0	0	.000
Mahaffey, p	1	0	0	0	0	0	0	0	.000
Hoyt, p	1	2	0	0	0	0	0	0	.000
Heving, ph	1	1	0	0	0	0	0	0	.000
Rommel, p	1	0	0	0	0	0	0	0	.000
Boley, ph	1	1	0	0	0	0	0	0	.000
Todt, ph	1	0	0	0	0	0	0	0	.000
Totals	7	227	22	50	5	0	3	20	.220

COMPOSITE PITCHING AVERAGES
St. Louis Cardinals

Pitcher	G.	IP.	H.	R.	E.	SO.	BB.	W.	L.	ERA.
Rhem	1	1	1	0	0	1	0	0	0	0.00
Hallahan	3	18⅓	12	1	1	12	8	2	0	0.49
Grimes	2	17⅔	9	4	4	11	9	2	0	2.04
Johnson	3	9	10	3	3	6	1	0	1	3.00
Derringer	3	12⅔	14	10	6	14	7	0	2	4.26
Lindsey	2	3⅓	4	4	2	2	3	0	0	5.40
Totals	7	62	50	22	16	46	28	4	3	2.32

Philadelphia Athletics

Pitcher	G.	IP.	H.	R.	E.	SO.	BB.	W.	L.	ERA.
Earnshaw	3	24	12	6	5	20	4	1	2	1.88
Grove	3	26	28	7	7	16	2	2	1	2.42
Walberg	2	3	3	1	1	4	2	0	0	3.00
Hoyt	1	6	7	3	3	1	0	0	1	4.50
Mahaffey	1	1	1	1	1	0	1	0	0	9.00
Rommel	1	1	3	1	1	0	0	0	0	9.00
Totals	7	61	54	19	18	41	9	3	4	2.66

SERIES OF 1932

	W.	L.	Pct.
New York A. L.	4	0	1.000
Chicago N. L.	0	4	.000

Joe McCarthy, released by the late William Wrigley, owner of the Cubs, in the last week of the 1930 National League season because he wanted a manager who could bring him a world championship, had sweet revenge on the Chicagoans in the 1932 Series. As manager of the New York Yankees, he led the A. L. club to a smashing four-straight victory over the Bruins, the Chicago defeat being little less than a debacle. The Yankees hit .313 and buried the Cubs under an avalanche of 37 runs, an average of better than nine a game. It was the third straight Series swept by the Yankees in successive games.

As the Athletics of 1929 had stopped the Yankees' run of three straight pennants, so the Yanks of 1932 halted the A's after three successive championships. McCarthy's club matched the 107 Athletic victories of the year before and beat out the A's by 13 games. The Cubs were a mediocre championship club and won the National League pennant under the inspired leadership of Charlie Grimm, who replaced Rogers Hornsby as manager on August 2. In contrast to the Yankees' .695 percentage, the Cubs' .584 was one of the lowest in all National League history.

The classic saw the greatest one-man show of World Series history by Lou Gehrig, Yankee first baseman, topping that of Hank Gowdy in 1914, Babe Ruth in 1928 and Pepper Martin in 1931. While Gehrig hit .529 against Ruth's .625 in 1928, his run production was much higher. Larrupin' Lou was responsible for 14 markers. In the four games, he connected for nine hits, including three homers and a double, walked twice, fanned only once, scored nine runs, and drove in eight.

Playing in his 10th and last World Series and seventh with a winning club, Ruth drove out two homers. Tony Lazzeri also poled two round-trippers. The Yankees, and especially Ruth, rode the Cubs hard all through the Series because they had voted only a fraction of a share to the former Yankee shortstop, Mark Koenig, who had played great ball for Chicago after joining them in the latter part of the season. While the feud raged hot, Ruth got away with one of the more brazen and defiant gestures of all baseball history.

In the fifth inning of the third game, at Chicago, with Charlie Root pitching, Ruth in pantomime, pointed to the most distant part of Wrigley Field, took two deliberate strikes, and then hit a homer to the bleacher to which he had pointed. Gehrig followed with another four-bagger. Ruth and Gehrig each bagged two homers in this game, and Kiki Cuyler and Gabby Hartnett hit for the circuit for the Cubs. In sharp contrast, pitcher George Pipgras of the Yanks set a Series record by fanning five times in succession.

The Cubs gave Windy City fans a thrill in the fourth clash by banging Johnny Allen for four runs in the first inning. But the joy of Chicago fans folded into gloom as the contest aged, the Bombers shellacking five hurlers and bounding on to a 13 to 6 triumph to sweep the Series in four straight.

Charley Ruffing, Vernon Gomez, Pipgras and Wilcy Moore each won a game for the Yanks, the last-named as a relief hurler. Riggs Stephenson was one Cub who wasn't hypnotized by the Yankees, hitting .444. The box scores:

Wednesday, Sept. 28—At New York

Chicago (N.L.)	AB.	R.	H.	O.	A.	E.
Herman, 2b	5	2	2	1	2	0
English, 3b	4	1	1	2	1	1
Cuyler, rf	5	1	1	2	0	0
Stephenson, lf	5	0	3	2	0	0
Moore, cf	4	0	0	1	0	0
Grimm, 1b	3	0	0	8	1	0
Hartnett, c	5	1	2	4	2	0
Koenig, ss	4	1	1	4	3	0
Bush, p	1	0	0	0	2	0
Grimes, p	1	0	0	0	0	0

1932 WORLD SERIES

	AB.	R.	H.	O.	A.	E.
aGudat	1	0	0	0	0	0
Smith, p	0	0	0	0	0	0
Totals	38	6	10	24	11	1
New York (A.L.)	AB.	R.	H.	O.	A.	E.
Combs, cf	4	2	2	3	0	0
Sewell, 3b	4	1	1	2	1	0
Ruth, rf	3	3	1	1	0	1
Gehrig, 1b	4	3	2	7	1	0
Lazzeri, 2b	4	1	1	1	2	0
Dickey, c	3	0	1	11	0	0
Chapman, lf	4	1	0	1	0	0
Crosetti, ss	2	1	0	0	0	1
Ruffing, p	4	0	0	1	3	0
Totals	32	12	8	27	7	2

Chicago............. 2 0 0   0 0 0   2 2 0— 6
New York.......... 0 0 0   3 0 5   3 1 *—12

aStruck out for Grimes in eighth. Runs batted in—Stephenson 3, Gehrig 2, Dickey 2, Chapman 2, Combs 2, Ruth, Lazzeri, Koenig, Herman, Sewell. Two-base hits—Combs, Hartnett 2. Three-base hit—Koenig. Home run—Gehrig. Sacrifice hit—Crosetti. Stolen base—Cuyler. Double play—Herman, Koenig and Grimm. Left on base—Chicago 11, New York 4. Earned runs—New York 12, Chicago 4. Struck out—By Ruffing 10, by Bush 2, by Smith 1. Bases on balls—Off Ruffing 6, off Bush 5, off Grimes 1. Hit by pitcher—By Grimes (Dickey). Wild pitch—Grimes. Hits—Off Bush 3 in 5⅓ innings, off Grimes 3 in 1⅔ innings, off Smith 2 in 1 inning. Losing pitcher—Bush. Umpires—Dinneen (A.L.), Klem (N.L.), Van Graflan (A.L.) and Magerkurth (N.L.). Time—2:31. Attendance—41,459.

Thursday, Sept. 29—At New York

Chicago (N.L.)	AB.	R.	H.	O.	A.	E.
Herman, 2b	4	1	1	1	6	0
English, 3b	4	0	1	0	0	0
Cuyler, rf	4	0	1	1	0	0
Stephenson, lf	4	1	2	0	0	0
Demaree, cf	4	0	1	1	0	0
Grimm, 1b	4	0	2	8	0	0
Hartnett, c	3	0	1	9	2	0
Jurges, ss	3	0	0	4	3	0
Warneke, p	3	0	0	0	2	0
aHemsley	1	0	0	0	0	0
Totals	34	2	9	24	13	0
New York (A.L.)	AB.	R.	H.	O.	A.	E.
Combs, cf	3	1	1	4	0	0
Sewell, 3b	3	1	1	0	1	0
Ruth, rf	3	1	1	3	0	0
Gehrig, 1b	4	2	3	5	0	0
Lazzeri, 2b	4	0	1	3	1	0
Dickey, c	3	0	2	8	0	0
Chapman, lf	4	0	1	1	1	0
Crosetti, ss	3	0	0	3	3	1
Gomez, p	3	0	0	0	3	0
Totals	30	5	10	27	9	1

Chicago............. 1 0 1   0 0 0   0 0 0—2
New York.......... 2 0 2   0 1 0   0 0 *—5

aFanned for Warneke in ninth. Runs batted in—Dickey 2, Chapman 2, Stephenson, Gehrig, Demaree. Two-base hits—Herman, Stephenson. Three-base hit—Cuyler. Sacrifice hit—Jurges. Double plays—Warneke, Hartnett and Jurges; Hartnett and Herman; Herman, Jurges and Grimm 2. Left on bases—Chicago 7, New York 5. Earned runs—New York 5, Chicago 1. Struck out—By Gomez 8, by Warneke 7. Bases on balls—Off Gomez 1, off Warneke 4. Umpires—Klem (N.L.), Van Graflan (A.L.), Magerkurth (N.L.) and Dinneen (A.L.). Time—1:46. Attendance-50,709.

Saturday, October 1—At Chicago

New York (A.L.)	AB.	R.	H.	O.	A.	E.
Combs, cf	5	1	0	1	0	0
Sewell, 3b	2	1	0	2	2	0
Ruth, lf	4	2	2	2	0	0
Gehrig, 1b	5	2	2	13	1	0
Lazzeri, 2b	4	1	0	3	4	1
Dickey, c	4	0	1	2	1	0
Chapman, rf	4	0	2	0	0	0
Crosetti, ss	4	0	1	4	4	0
Pipgras, p	5	0	0	0	0	0
Pennock, p	0	0	0	0	1	0
Totals	37	7	8	27	13	1
Chicago (N.L.)	AB.	R.	H.	O.	A.	E.
Herman, 2b	4	1	0	1	2	1
English, 3b	4	0	0	3	0	0
Cuyler, rf	4	1	3	1	0	0
Stephenson, lf	4	0	1	1	0	0
Moore, cf	3	1	0	3	0	0
Grimm, 1b	4	0	1	8	0	0
Hartnett, c	4	1	1	10	1	1
Jurges, ss	4	1	3	3	3	2
Root, p	2	0	0	0	0	0
Malone, p	0	0	0	0	0	0
aGudat	1	0	0	0	0	0
May, p	0	0	0	0	0	0
Tinning, p	0	0	0	0	0	0
bKoenig	0	0	0	0	0	0
cHemsley	1	0	0	0	0	0
Totals	35	5	9	27	9	4

New York.......... 3 0 1   0 2 0   0 0 1—7
Chicago............. 1 0 2   1 0 0   0 0 1—5

aPopped out for Malone in seventh. bAnnounced for Tinning in ninth. cStruck out for Koenig in ninth. Runs batted in—Ruth 4, Gehrig 2, Cuyler 2, Grimm, Chapman, Hartnett. Two-base hits—Chapman, Cuyler, Jurges, Grimm. Home runs—Ruth 2, Gehrig 2, Cuyler, Hartnett. Stolen base—Jurges. Double plays—Sewell, Lazzeri and Gehrig; Herman, Jurges and Grimm. Left on bases—New York 11, Chicago 6. Earned runs—New York 5, by Root 4, by Malone 4, by May 1, by Tinning 1, by Pipgras 1, by Pennock 1. Bases on balls—Off Root 3, off Malone 4, off Pipgras 3. Hit by pitcher—By May (Sewell). Hits—Off Root 6 in 4⅓ innings, off Malone 1 in 2⅔ innings, off May 1 in 1⅓ innings, off Tinning 0 in ⅔ inning, off Pipgras 9 in 8 innings (pitched to two batters in ninth), off Pennock 0 in 1 inning. Winning pitcher—Pipgras. Losing pitcher—Root. Umpires—Van Graflan (A.L.), Magerkurth (N.L.), Dinneen (A.L.) and Klem (N.L.). Time—2:11. Attendance—49,986.

Sunday, October 2—At Chicago

New York (A.L.)	AB.	R.	H.	O.	A.	E.
Combs, cf	4	4	3	2	0	0
Sewell, 3b	6	1	3	0	2	1
Ruth, lf	5	0	1	2	0	0
Byrd, lf	0	0	0	0	0	0
Gehrig, 1b	4	2	2	12	0	1
Lazzeri, 2b	5	2	3	1	4	0
Dickey, c	6	2	3	4	0	0
Chapman, rf	5	0	2	4	0	0
Crosetti, ss	6	1	1	2	5	2
Allen, p	0	0	0	0	0	0
W. Moore, p	3	0	1	0	1	0
aRuffing	0	0	0	0	0	0
bHoag	0	1	0	0	0	0
Pennock, p	1	0	0	0	0	0
Totals	45	13	19	27	12	4

1933 WORLD SERIES

Chicago (N.L.)	AB.	R.	H.	O.	A.	E.
Herman, 2b	5	1	1	2	2	0
English, 3b	5	1	1	1	0	0
Cuyler, rf	5	0	1	0	0	0
Stephenson, lf	5	1	2	1	0	0
Demaree, cf	3	1	1	3	0	1
Grimm, 1b	4	2	2	4	2	0
Hartnett, c	4	0	1	8	0	0
cHack	0	0	0	0	0	0
Grimes, p	0	0	0	0	0	0
Jurges, ss	4	0	1	5	2	0
Bush, p	0	0	0	0	0	0
Warneke, p	1	0	0	1	0	0
May, p	2	0	0	1	0	0
Tinning, p	0	0	0	0	1	0
dHemsley, c	1	0	0	0	0	0
Totals	39	6	9	27	7	1

New York	1	0	2	0	0	2	4	0	4—13
Chicago	4	0	0	0	0	1	0	0	1— 6

aWalked for W. Moore in seventh. bRan for Ruffing in seventh. cRan for Hartnett in eighth. dFanned for Tinning in eighth. Runs batted in—Gehrig 3, Demaree 3, Lazzeri 4, Jurges, Combs 2, Sewell 2, Ruth, Chapman, English. Two-base hits—Gehrig, Sewell, Crosetti, Chapman, Grimm. Home runs—Demaree, Lazzeri 2, Combs. Double play—Herman, Jurges and Grimm. Left on bases—New York 13, Chicago 7. Earned runs—New York 13, Chicago 4. Struck out—By Tinning 2, by W. Moore 1, by Pennock 3, by Warneke 1, by May 3. Bases on balls—Off Grimes 1, off Bush 1, off Warneke 1, off May 3, off Pennock 1. Hit by pitcher—By Bush (Ruth), by May (Gehrig). Hits—Off Bush 2 in ⅓ inning, off Warneke 5 in 2⅔ innings, off May 8 in 3⅓ innings, off Tinning 0 in 1⅔ innings, off Grimes 4 in 1 inning, off Allen 5 in ⅔ inning, off W. Moore 2 in 5⅓ innings, off Pennock 2 in 3 innings. Winning pitcher—W. Moore. Losing pitcher—May. Umpires—Magerkurth (N.L.), Dinneen (A.L.), Klem (N.L.) and Van Graflan (A.L.). Time—2:27. Attendance—49,844.

COMPOSITE BATTING AVERAGES
New York Yankees

Player-Position	G.	AB.	R.	H.	2B.	3B.	HR.	RBI.	BA.
Gehrig, 1b	4	17	9	9	1	0	3	8	.529
Dickey, c	4	16	2	7	0	0	0	4	.438
Combs, cf	4	16	8	6	1	0	1	4	.375
Sewell, 3b	4	15	4	5	1	0	0	3	.333
Ruth, rf	4	15	6	5	0	0	2	6	.333
Moore, p	1	3	0	1	0	0	0	0	.333
Lazzeri, 2b	4	17	4	5	0	0	2	5	.294
Chapman, lf	4	17	1	5	2	0	0	6	.294
Crosetti, ss	4	15	2	2	1	0	0	0	.133
Ruffing, p-ph	2	4	0	0	0	0	0	0	.000
Gomez, p	1	3	0	0	0	0	0	0	.000
Pipgras, p	1	5	0	0	0	0	0	0	.000
Pennock, p	2	1	0	0	0	0	0	0	.000
Byrd, lf	1	0	0	0	0	0	0	0	.000
Allen, p	1	0	0	0	0	0	0	0	.000
Hoag, pr	1	0	1	0	0	0	0	0	.000
Totals	4	144	37	45	6	0	8	36	.313

Chicago Cubs

Player-Position	G.	AB.	R.	H.	2B.	3B.	HR.	RBI.	BA.
Stephenson, lf	4	18	2	8	1	0	0	4	.444
Jurges, ss	3	11	1	4	1	0	0	1	.364
Grimm, 1b	4	15	2	5	2	0	0	1	.333
Hartnett, c	4	16	2	5	2	0	1	1	.313
Demaree, cf	2	7	1	2	0	0	1	4	.286
Cuyler, rf	4	18	2	5	1	1	0	2	.278
Koenig, ss-ph	2	4	1	1	0	1	0	1	.250
Herman, 2b	4	18	5	4	0	0	0	1	.222
English, 3b	4	17	2	3	0	0	0	1	.176
Moore, cf	2	7	1	0	0	0	0	0	.000
Bush, p	2	1	0	0	0	0	0	0	.000
Grimes, p	2	1	0	0	0	0	0	0	.000
Gudat, ph	2	2	0	0	0	0	0	0	.000
Smith, p	1	0	0	0	0	0	0	0	.000
Warneke, p	2	4	0	0	0	0	0	0	.000
Hemsley, ph-c	3	3	0	0	0	0	0	0	.000
Root, p	1	2	0	0	0	0	0	0	.000
Malone, p	1	0	0	0	0	0	0	0	.000
May, p	2	2	0	0	0	0	0	0	.000
Tinning, p	2	0	0	0	0	0	0	0	.000
Hack, pr	1	0	0	0	0	0	0	0	.000
Totals	4	146	19	37	8	2	3	16	.253

COMPOSITE PITCHING AVERAGES
New York Yankees

Pitcher	G.	IP.	H.	R.	E.	SO.	BB.	W.	L.	ERA.
W. Moore	1	5⅓	2	1	0	1	0	1	0	0.00
Gomez	1	9	9	2	1	8	1	1	0	1.00
Pennock	2	4	2	1	1	4	1	0	0	2.25
Ruffing	1	9	10	6	4	10	6	1	0	4.00
Pipgras	1	8	9	5	4	1	3	1	0	4.50
Allen	1	⅔	5	4	3	0	0	0	0	40.50
Totals	4	36	37	19	13	24	11	4	0	3.25

Chicago Cubs

Pitcher	G.	IP.	H.	R.	E.	SO.	BB.	W.	L.	ERA.
Malone	1	2⅔	1	0	0	4	4	0	0	0.00
Tinning	2	2⅓	0	0	0	3	0	0	0	0.00
Warneke	2	10⅔	15	7	7	8	5	0	1	5.91
Smith	1	1	2	1	1	1	0	0	0	9.00
Root	1	4⅓	6	6	5	4	3	0	1	10.38
May	2	4⅔	9	7	6	4	3	0	1	11.57
Bush	2	5⅔	5	9	9	2	6	0	1	14.29
Grimes	2	2⅔	7	7	7	0	2	0	0	23.63
Totals	4	34	45	37	35	26	23	0	4	9.26

SERIES OF 1933

	W.	L.	Pct.
New York N. L.	4	1	.800
Washington A. L.	1	4	.200

Following the Cubs' humiliating defeat of 1932, the Giants put the National League back on top with a four-to-one victory over the Washington Senators. It was the first National League victory in five games since 1922, when the Giants also won in that number of clashes, holding the Yankees to one tie.

The two pennant winners of 1933 were distinct dark horses. Finishing the 1932 season tied with the Cardinals for sixth place, the Giants won their first pennant under the leadership of Bill Terry, the club's hard-hitting first baseman. While Terry's team captured only one more game than did the Cubs of 1932, the club had fairly comfortable going and won by a five-game margin over Pittsburgh. Clark Griffith, in Washington, had the same success with his second boy manager, Joe Cronin, as he had with Bucky Harris in 1924. Joe, managing the club from shortstop, won his first of two pennants at the age of 27. His club won 99 games and had a seven-game margin on the Yankees at the finish.

Terry won his first Giant pennant largely on the great work of his pitching staff, Carl Hubbell, Hal Schumacher, Freddy Fitzsimmons and Roy Parmelee, starters, and Adolfo Luque and Herman Bell, relievers. Hubbell won 23 games, ten of them shutouts, and led National League pitchers with an earned-run rating of 1.66. Schumacher bagged 19 decisions and ranked third in the earned-run table—2.15. That kind of pitching, helped by timely batting

1933 WORLD SERIES

by Mel Ott and Terry, subdued the Senators in quick time.

Hubbell won two games and Schumacher and Luque one each. Washington's lone victory was a five-hit, 4 to 0 shutout scored by southpaw Earl Whitehill in the third game. Hubbell held the Senators to five hits while winning the opener, 4 to 2, and then won an 11-inning, 2 to 1 duel from Monte Weaver and Jack Russell in the fourth clash. Schumacher took the second game, 6 to 1, with the aid of a big six-run, sixth-inning explosion against Alvin Crowder, in which the most potent blow was Lefty O'Doul's pinch-hit, which drove across two tallies. In Schumacher's second start, he was knocked out by Fred Schulte's three-run homer in the sixth frame, canceling his 3 to 0 lead. Luque then took hold and held off the Senators until the tenth, when Mel Ott made the Giants world champions with a home run. Crowder, Cronin's 24-game winner during the championship season, was his biggest disappointment, getting knocked from the box in both of his starts.

The Giants, batting .263 in the National League, hit .267 in the Series, while Washington, leading the American League at bat with .287, hit only .214 against Terry's pitching wizards. Ott was New York's batting hero with an average of .389 and two round-trip drives. George Davis, the Giants' lightly regarded .258-hitting center fielder, pressed Mel with .368.

Schulte was Washington's batting leader, with .333; Joe Cronin held up his end with .318. President Franklin Delano Roosevelt attended the third game, played in Washington, and threw out the first ball. The players staged a veritable football scrimmage in going after the pellet. Outfielder Heinie Manush finally retrieved it and presented it to pitcher Whitehill after the game. The box scores:

Tuesday, October 3—At New York

Wash'gton (A.L.)	AB.	R.	H.	O.	A.	E.
Myer, 2b	4	1	1	2	2	3
Goslin, rf	4	0	0	1	0	0
Manush, lf	4	1	0	2	0	0
Cronin, ss	4	0	2	0	2	0
Schulte, cf	4	0	2	4	0	0
Kuhel, 1b	4	0	0	8	1	0
Bluege, 3b	4	0	0	0	2	0
Sewell, c	3	0	0	6	1	0
Stewart, p	1	0	0	0	0	0
Russell, p	1	0	0	1	3	0
aHarris	0	0	0	0	0	0
Thomas, p	0	0	0	0	0	0
Totals	33	2	5	24	11	3

New York (N.L.)	AB.	R.	H.	O.	A.	E.
Moore, lf	4	1	0	1	0	0
Critz, 2b	4	1	1	2	2	1
Terry, 1b	4	1	1	9	0	0
Ott, rf	4	1	4	0	0	0
Davis, cf	4	0	2	0	0	0
Jackson, 3b	4	0	0	0	4	0
Mancuso, c	4	0	0	12	1	0
Ryan, ss	4	0	1	3	3	1
Hubbell, p	3	0	1	0	1	0
Totals	35	4	10	27	11	2

Washington...... 0 0 0   1 0 0   0 0 1—2
New York........ 2 0 2   0 0 0   0 0 *—4

aWalked for Russell in eighth. Runs batted in—Ott 3, Jackson, Cronin, Kuhel. Home run—Ott. Double play—Mancuso and Ryan. Left on bases—New York 7, Washington 6. Earned runs—New York 2, Washington 0. Struck out—By Hubbell 10, by Russell 3, by Thomas 2. Bases on balls—Off Hubbell 2. Hits—Off Stewart 6 in 2 innings (pitched to three batters in third), off Russell 4 in 5 innings, off Thomas 0 in 1 inning. Losing pitcher—Stewart. Umpires—Moran (N.L.), Moriarty (A.L.), Pfirman (N.L.) and Ormsby (A.L.). Time—2:07. Attendance—46,672.

Wednesday, October 4—At New York

Wash'gton (A.L.)	AB.	R.	H.	O.	A.	E.
Myer, 2b	3	0	0	1	3	0
Goslin, rf	4	1	2	0	0	0
Manush, lf	3	0	1	1	0	0
Cronin, ss	4	0	0	3	4	0
Schulte, cf	4	0	0	1	0	0
Kuhel, 1b	3	0	0	15	1	0
Bluege, 3b	2	0	0	0	3	0
cHarris	1	0	0	0	0	0
Sewell, c	3	0	0	3	0	0
dBolton	1	0	0	0	0	0
Crowder, p	2	0	1	0	1	0
Thomas, p	0	0	0	0	0	0
bRice	1	0	1	0	0	0
McColl, p	0	0	0	0	1	0
Totals	31	1	5	24	13	0

New York (N.L.)	AB.	R.	H.	O.	A.	E.
Moore, lf	4	0	2	4	0	0
Critz, 2b	3	1	1	1	3	0
Terry, 1b	4	1	1	10	0	0
Ott, rf	2	1	0	4	0	0
Davis, cf	2	0	1	1	0	0
aO'Doul	1	1	1	0	0	0
Peel, cf	1	0	0	0	0	0
Jackson, 3b	3	1	1	1	5	0
Mancuso, c	4	1	1	4	1	0
Ryan, ss	4	0	1	2	3	0
Schumacher, p	4	0	1	0	2	0
Totals	32	6	10	27	14	0

Washington...... 0 0 1   0 0 0   0 0 0—1
New York........ 0 0 0   0 0 6   0 0 *—6

aSingled for Davis in sixth. bSingled for Thomas in seventh. cGrounded out for Bluege in ninth. dGrounded out for Sewell in ninth. Runs batted in—Goslin, O'Doul 2, Jackson, Mancuso, Schumacher, Moore. Two-base hit—Terry. Home run—Goslin. Sacrifice hit—Jackson. Double plays—Cronin, Myer and Kuhel; Jackson, Critz and Terry. Left on bases—Washington 7, New York 6. Earned runs—New York 6, Washington 1. Struck out—By Schumacher 2, by Crowder 3. Bases on balls—Off Schumacher 4, off Crowder 3. Wild pitch—Schumacher. Hits—Off Crowder 9 in 5⅔ innings, off Thomas 1 in ⅓ inning, off McColl 0 in 2 innings. Losing pitcher—Crowder. Umpires—Moriarty (A.L.), Pfirman (N.L.), Ormsby (A.L.) and Moran (N.L.). Time—2:09. Attendance—35,461.

Thursday, October 5—At Washington

New York (N.L.)	AB.	R.	H.	O.	A.	E.
Moore, lf	4	0	0	2	1	0
Critz, 2b	4	0	1	2	4	0

1933 WORLD SERIES

	AB.	R.	H.	O.	A.	E.
Terry, 1b	4	0	0	9	0	0
Ott, rf	3	0	0	1	0	0
Davis, cf	4	0	1	3	0	0
Jackson, 3b	3	0	1	0	2	0
Mancuso, c	4	0	0	4	1	0
Ryan, ss	3	0	0	3	3	0
Fitzsimmons, p	2	0	1	0	1	0
aPeel	1	0	1	0	0	0
Bell, p	0	0	0	0	0	0
Totals	32	0	5	24	12	0

Wash'gton (A.L.)	AB.	R.	H.	O.	A.	E.
Myer, 2b	4	1	3	3	3	0
Goslin, rf	4	1	1	2	0	0
Manush, lf	4	0	3	3	0	0
Cronin, ss	4	0	1	0	2	1
Schulte, cf	4	0	2	1	0	0
Kuhel, 1b	3	0	0	15	0	0
Bluege, 3b	3	1	1	0	6	0
Sewell, c	3	1	1	3	0	0
Whitehill, p	3	0	0	0	4	0
Totals	32	4	9	27	15	1

```
New York ......... 0 0 0   0 0 0   0 0 0—0
Washington ....... 2 1 0   0 0 0   1 0 *—4
```

aSingled for Fitzsimmons in eighth. Runs batted in—Cronin, Schulte, Myer 2. Two-base hits—Goslin, Bluege, Schulte, Myer, Jackson. Stolen base—Sewell. Double plays—Cronin, Myer and Kuhel; Moore and Mancuso. Left on bases—New York 7, Washington 4. Earned runs—Washington 4. Struck out—By Whitehill 2, by Fitzsimmons 2. Bases on balls—Off Whitehill 2. Wild pitch—Whitehill. Hits—Off Fitzsimmons 9 in 7 innings, off Bell 0 in 1 inning. Losing pitcher—Fitzsimmons. Umpires—Pfirman (N.L.), Ormsby (A.L.), Moran (N.L.) and Moriarty (A.L.). Time—1:55. Attendance—25,727.

Friday, October 6—At Washington

New York (N.L.)	AB.	R.	H.	O.	A.	E.
Moore, lf	5	0	2	3	0	0
Critz, 2b	6	0	0	9	5	0
Terry, 1b	5	1	2	9	0	0
Ott, rf	4	0	2	4	0	0
Davis, cf	4	0	1	1	0	0
Jackson, 3b	5	1	1	0	2	0
Mancuso, c	2	0	0	5	0	0
Ryan, ss	5	0	2	1	5	0
Hubbell, p	4	0	1	1	3	1
Totals	40	2	11	33	15	1

Wash'gton (A.L.)	AB.	R.	H.	O.	A.	E.
Myer, 2b	4	0	2	6	4	0
Goslin, rf-lf	4	0	1	1	0	0
Manush, lf	2	0	0	1	0	0
Harris, rf	1	0	0	2	0	0
Cronin, ss	5	0	1	1	4	0
Schulte, cf	5	0	1	2	0	0
Kuhel, 1b	5	1	1	14	1	0
Bluege, 3b	3	0	0	2	1	0
Sewell, c	4	0	2	4	1	0
Weaver, p	4	0	0	0	6	0
Russell, p	0	0	0	0	0	0
aBolton	1	0	0	0	0	0
Totals	38	1	8	33	17	0

```
New York ......... 0 0 0   1 0 0   0 0 0   0 1—2
Washington ....... 0 0 0   0 0 0   1 0 0   0 0—1
```

aHit into double play for Russell in eleventh. Runs batted in—Terry, Ryan, Sewell. Two-base hit—Moore. Home run—Terry. Sacrifice hits—Goslin, Bluege 2, Davis, Hubbell, Mancuso. Double plays—Myer and Kuhel; Ryan, Critz and Terry. Left on bases—New York 12, Washington 11. Earned runs—New York 2, Washington 0. Struck out—By Weaver 3, by Russell 1, by Hubbell 5. Bases on balls—Off Weaver 4, off Hubbell 4. Hits—Off Weaver 11 in 10⅓ innings, off Russell 0 in ⅔ inning. Losing pitcher—Weaver. Umpires—Ormsby (A.L.), Moran (N.L.), Moriarty (A.L.) and Pfirman (N.L.). Time—2:59. Attendance—26,762.

Saturday, October 7—At Washington

New York (N.L.)	AB.	R.	H.	O.	A.	E.
Moore, lf	5	0	1	3	0	0
Critz, 2b	5	0	0	2	4	0
Terry, 1b	5	0	2	13	1	0
Ott, rf	5	1	1	1	0	0
Davis, cf	5	1	2	1	0	0
Jackson, 3b	3	1	1	2	4	1
Mancuso, c	3	1	1	7	1	0
Ryan, ss	2	0	1	0	5	0
Schumacher, p	3	0	1	0	0	0
Luque, p	1	0	1	1	0	0
Totals	37	4	11	30	15	1

Wash'gton (A.L.)	AB.	R.	H.	O.	A.	E.
Myer, 2b	5	0	0	3	1	0
Goslin, rf	4	0	1	4	1	0
Manush, lf	5	1	1	3	0	0
Cronin, ss	5	1	3	3	3	0
Schulte, cf	4	1	2	1	0	0
aKerr	0	0	0	0	0	0
Kuhel, 1b	5	0	2	7	0	0
Bluege, 3b	4	0	1	1	1	0
Sewell, c	4	0	0	7	0	0
Crowder, p	2	0	0	0	2	0
Russell, p	1	0	0	1	1	0
Totals	39	3	10	30	9	0

```
New York ......... 0 2 0   0 0 1   0 0 0   1—4
Washington ....... 0 0 0   0 0 3   0 0 0   0—3
```

aRan for Schulte in tenth. Runs batted in—Schumacher 2, Mancuso, Ott, Schulte 3. Two-base hits—Davis, Mancuso. Home runs—Schulte, Ott. Sacrifice hits—Ryan, Jackson. Double plays—Jackson and Terry; Cronin and Kuhel. Left on bases—Washington 9, New York 7. Earned runs—New York 4, Washington 3. Struck out—By Crowder 4, by Russell 3, by Schumacher 1, by Luque 3. Bases on balls—Off Crowder 2, off Schumacher 1, off Luque 2. Wild pitches—Crowder, Schumacher. Hits—Off Crowder 7 in 5⅓ innings, off Russell 4 in 4⅔ innings, off Schumacher 8 in 5 ⅔ innings, off Luque 2 in 4⅓ innings. Winning pitcher—Luque. Losing pitcher—Russell. Umpires—Moran (N.L.), Moriarty (A.L.), Pfirman (N.L.) and Ormsby (A.L.). Time—2:38. Attendance—28,454.

COMPOSITE BATTING AVERAGES
New York Giants

Player-Position	G.	AB.	R.	H.	2B.	3B.	HR.	RBI.	BA.
O'Doul, ph	1	1	1	1	0	0	0	2	1.000
Luque, p	1	1	0	1	0	0	0	0	1.000
Fitzsimmons, p	1	2	0	1	0	0	0	0	.500
Peel, cf-ph	2	2	0	1	0	0	0	0	.500
Ott, rf	5	18	3	7	0	0	2	4	.389
Davis, cf	5	19	1	7	1	0	0	0	.368
Hubbell, p	2	7	0	2	0	0	0	0	.286
Schumacher, p	2	7	0	2	0	0	0	3	.286
Ryan, ss	5	18	0	5	0	0	0	1	.278
Terry, 1b	5	22	3	6	1	0	1	1	.273
Moore, lf	5	22	1	5	1	0	0	1	.227
Jackson, 3b	5	18	3	4	1	0	0	2	.222
Critz, 2b	5	22	2	3	0	0	0	0	.136
Mancuso, c	5	17	2	2	1	0	0	2	.118
Bell, p	1	0	0	0	0	0	0	0	.000
Totals	5	176	16	47	5	0	3	16	.267

Washington Senators

Player-Position	G.	AB.	R.	H.	2B.	3B.	HR.	RBI.	BA.
Rice, ph	1	1	0	1	0	0	0	0	1.000
Schulte, cf	5	21	1	7	1	0	1	4	.333
Cronin, ss	5	22	1	7	0	0	0	2	.318
Myer, 2b	5	20	2	6	1	0	0	2	.300
Crowder, p	2	4	0	1	0	0	0	0	.250
Goslin, rf	5	20	2	5	1	0	1	1	.250
Sewell, c	5	17	1	3	0	0	0	1	.176
Kuhel, 1b	5	20	1	3	0	0	0	1	.150
Bluege, 3b	5	16	1	2	1	0	0	0	.125
Manush, lf	5	18	2	2	0	0	0	0	.111
Stewart, p	1	1	0	0	0	0	0	0	.000
Russell, p	3	2	0	0	0	0	0	0	.000
Harris, ph-rf	3	2	0	0	0	0	0	0	.000
Thomas, p	2	0	0	0	0	0	0	0	.000
Bolton, ph	2	2	0	0	0	0	0	0	.000
McColl, p	1	0	0	0	0	0	0	0	.000
Whitehill, p	1	3	0	0	0	0	0	0	.000
Weaver, p	1	4	0	0	0	0	0	0	.000
Kerr, pr	1	0	0	0	0	0	0	0	.000
Totals	5	173	11	37	4	0	2	11	.214

COMPOSITE PITCHING AVERAGES

New York Giants

Pitcher	G.	IP.	H.	R.	E.	SO.	BB.	W.	L.	ERA.
Hubbell	2	20	13	3	0	15	6	2	0	0.00
Luque	1	4⅓	2	0	0	5	2	1	0	0.00
Bell	1	1	0	0	0	0	0	0	0	0.00
Schumacher	2	14⅔	13	4	4	3	5	1	0	2.45
Fitzsimmons	1	7	9	4	4	2	0	0	1	5.14
Totals	5	47	37	11	8	25	13	4	1	1.53

Washington Senators

Pitcher	G.	IP.	H.	R.	E.	SO.	BB.	W.	L.	ERA.
Whitehill	1	9	5	0	0	2	2	1	0	0.00
McColl	1	2	0	0	0	0	0	0	0	0.00
Thomas	2	1⅓	1	0	0	2	0	0	0	0.00
Russell	3	10⅓	8	1	1	7	0	0	1	0.87
Weaver	1	10⅓	11	2	2	3	4	0	1	1.74
Crowder	2	11	16	9	9	7	5	0	1	7.36
Stewart	1	2	6	4	2	0	0	0	1	9.00
Totals	5	46	47	16	14	21	11	1	4	2.74

SERIES OF 1934

	W.	L.	Pct.
St. Louis N. L.	4	3	.571
Detroit A. L.	3	4	.429

Bouncing back strongly after second-division finishes in 1932 and '33, the Cardinals regained the World Series heights in 1934, defeating the Detroit Tigers, winners of their first American League flag in 25 years under the aggressive management of Mickey Cochrane, four games to three. It was the third time the Redbirds won a Series which went the limit, and they repeated the procedure of 1926, coming from behind to tie the Series by taking the sixth game, and then winding it up with an 11 to 0 rout to clinch the event. Detroit's debacle in the last game, after a close Series, was the worst since the Athletics wound up their 1911 Series with the Giants with a 13 to 2 shellacking.

To qualify for the World Series, the Cardinals, managed this time by Frankie Frisch, the star second baseman, had to beat out the Giants, 1933 world champions, on the last day of the season. The St. Louis club was helped by the collapse of Bill Terry's New Yorkers in the last fortnight of the campaign. The Giants lost six of their last seven contests to the Braves, Phillies and the sixth-place Dodgers, giving the Cards the pennant by two games. Under Cochrane's inspiration, the Tigers won their first pennant since 1909.

The two Dean brothers, Dizzy and Paul, made pitching history for the Cards. Dizzy, by winning 30 games, became the first National League pitcher since Grover Alexander in 1917 to reach the 30-victory class. His younger brother, Paul, won 19, including a late September no-hitter against Brooklyn. The famous brothers won a pair of games each in the Series. Dizzy also lost a game and made a fourth appearance in the Series, in the fourth game, as a pinch-runner for Virgil Davis, when he was hit on the head by Billy Rogell, Tiger shortstop, and had to be carried off the field.

Lynwood (Schoolboy) Rowe pitched brilliantly for Detroit in winning a 12-inning, 3 to 2 decision over Bill Hallahan and Bill Walker in the second game. After two early runs were scored by the Redbirds, Rowe pitched a no-hitter for seven innings and gave up only one hit in his last nine. With the Series three to two in Detroit's favor, Rowe missed a chance to clinch the set when he lost the sixth game to Paul Dean, 4 to 3. Elden Auker won an easy 10 to 4 victory for Detroit in the fourth game, but was the victim of St. Louis' final outburst in the one-sided deciding contest, played in Detroit. After holding off Dizzy Dean for two innings, Auker went out during a seven-run fusilade. Tommy Bridges won the fifth game for Detroit, 3 to 1.

The final game was marked by an unfortunate spectacle, in which Commissioner K. M. Landis had the umpires order Joe Medwick, Cardinal left fielder, from the game. In the sixth inning, Medwick collided forcibly with third baseman Marv Owen of Detroit, and when he returned to his position in the last half of the inning, Detroit fans bombarded him with over-ripe fruit, vegetables, lunch boxes and newspapers. Landis removed Medwick to stop the disturbance.

Ducky Wucky had a great Series, hitting .379, his 11 safeties including a homer and the disturbance-provoking triple. Pepper Martin, moved in to third base, again rode high, posting a .355 average. He stole two more bases on Cochrane. Charley Gehringer, Tiger second sacker, was Detroit's all-round star, with a batting average of .379, and fielding brilliantly. Hank Greenberg hit .321, but four of his nine hits came in Auker's 10 to 4 victory; Hank fanned nine times, most of his whiffs coming in the clutch.

The entry of Henry Ford as a $100,000 sponsor for the broadcasts of the games, to continue for four years, and the sixth million-dollar gate, boosted the receipts to $1,128,995, after the 1933 low. The box scores:

1934 WORLD SERIES

Wednesday, October 3—At Detroit

St. Louis (N.L.)	AB	R	H	O	A	E
Martin, 3b	5	1	1	1	1	0
Rothrock, rf	4	0	2	0	0	0
Frisch, 2b	4	0	0	2	4	0
Medwick, lf	5	2	4	2	0	0
Collins, 1b	4	2	1	13	1	0
DeLancey, c	5	0	1	7	1	0
Orsatti, cf	4	1	2	1	0	2
Fullis, cf	1	0	1	0	0	0
Durocher, ss	5	0	0	0	4	0
J. Dean, p	5	2	1	1	2	0
Totals	42	8	13	27	13	2

Detroit (A.L.)	AB	R	H	O	A	E
White, cf	2	1	0	6	0	0
Cochrane, c	4	0	1	2	0	0
Gehringer, 2b	4	0	2	2	3	1
Greenberg, 1b	4	2	2	8	1	1
Goslin, lf	4	0	2	3	0	0
Rogell, ss	4	0	1	1	4	1
Owen, 3b	4	0	0	2	1	2
Fox, rf	4	0	0	3	0	0
Crowder, p	1	0	0	0	0	0
aDoljack	1	0	0	0	0	0
Marberry, p	0	0	0	0	1	0
Hogsett, p	1	0	0	0	1	0
bG. Walker	1	0	0	0	0	0
Totals	34	3	8	27	11	5

St. Louis .... 0 2 1 0 1 4 0 0 0—8
Detroit .... 0 0 1 0 0 1 0 1 0—3

aFlied out for Crowder in fifth. bStruck out for Hogsett in ninth. Runs batted in—Martin, Rothrock 2, Medwick 2, DeLancey 2, Gehringer, Greenberg, Goslin. Two-base hits—DeLancey, J. Dean. Home runs—Medwick, Greenberg. Sacrifice hits—Rothrock, Frisch. Double play—DeLancey and Frisch. Left on bases—St. Louis 10, Detroit 6. Earned runs—St. Louis 5, Detroit 3. Struck out—By J. Dean 6, by Crowder 1, by Hogsett 1. Bases on balls—Off J. Dean 2, off Crowder 1. Hits—Off Crowder 6 in 5 innings, off Marberry 4 in ⅔ inning, off Hogsett 3 in 3⅓ innings. Losing pitcher—Crowder. Umpires—Owens (A.L.), Klem (N.L.), Geisel (A.L.) and Reardon (N.L.). Time—2:13. Attendance—42,505.

Thursday, October 4—At Detroit

St. Louis (N.L.)	AB	R	H	O	A	E
Martin, 3b	5	1	2	1	1	1
Rothrock, rf	4	0	0	4	0	0
Frisch, 2b	5	0	1	3	6	1
Medwick, lf	5	0	1	0	0	0
Collins, 1b	5	0	1	12	2	0
DeLancey, c	5	1	1	10	0	0
Orsatti, cf	4	0	1	2	0	0
Durocher, ss	4	0	0	1	3	0
Hallahan, p	3	0	0	1	3	1
W. Walker, p	1	0	0	0	1	0
Totals	41	2	7	b34	16	3

Detroit (A.L.)	AB	R	H	O	A	E
White, cf	4	0	0	4	0	0
aG. Walker	1	0	1	0	0	0
Doljack, rf	1	0	0	1	0	0
Cochrane, c	4	0	0	8	0	0
Gehringer, 2b	4	1	1	3	6	0
Greenberg, 1b	4	0	0	13	0	0
Goslin, lf	6	0	2	3	1	0
Rogell, ss	4	1	1	1	2	0
Owen, 3b	5	0	0	0	1	0
Fox, rf	5	1	2	2	0	0
Rowe, p	4	0	0	1	0	0
Totals	42	3	7	36	12	0

St. Louis .... 0 1 1 0 0 0 0 0 0 0 0 0—2
Detroit .... 0 0 0 1 0 0 0 0 1 0 0 1—3

aSingled for White in ninth. bOne out when winning run scored. Runs batted in—Goslin, Fox, G. Walker, Medwick, Orsatti. Two-base hits—Rogell, Fox, Martin. Three-base hit—Orsatti. Sacrifice hits—Rowe, Rothrock. Stolen base—Gehringer. Left on bases—Detroit 13, St. Louis 4. Earned runs—Detroit 3, St. Louis 2. Struck out—By Rowe 7, by Hallahan 6, by W. Walker 2. Bases on balls—Off Hallahan 4, off W. Walker 3. Hits—Off Hallahan 6 in 8⅓ innings, off W. Walker 1 in 3 innings. Losing pitcher—W. Walker. Umpires—Klem (N.L.), Geisel (A.L.), Reardon (N.L.) and Owens (A.L.). Time—2:49. Attendance—43,451.

Friday, October 5—At St. Louis

Detroit (A.L.)	AB	R	H	O	A	E
White, cf	5	1	2	4	0	0
Cochrane, c	3	0	0	6	3	0
Gehringer, 2b	5	0	2	3	3	0
Greenberg, 1b	4	0	1	6	0	0
Goslin, lf	4	0	1	2	0	0
Rogell, ss	4	0	1	1	2	2
Owen, 3b	3	0	0	1	0	0
Fox, rf	4	0	1	1	0	0
Bridges, p	1	0	0	0	0	0
Hogsett, p	2	0	0	0	1	0
Totals	35	1	8	24	9	2

St. Louis (N.L.)	AB	R	H	O	A	E
Martin, 3b	3	2	2	2	1	0
Rothrock, rf	4	1	1	5	0	1
Frisch, 2b	4	0	2	2	1	0
Medwick, lf	4	0	1	3	0	0
Collins, 1b	4	1	2	3	0	0
DeLancey, c	4	0	1	9	0	0
Orsatti, cf	2	0	0	1	0	0
Durocher, ss	3	0	0	2	1	0
P. Dean, p	3	0	0	0	0	0
Totals	31	4	9	27	3	1

Detroit .... 0 0 0 0 0 0 0 0 1—1
St. Louis .... 1 1 0 0 2 0 0 0 *—4

Runs batted in—Rothrock 2, Frisch, P. Dean, Greenberg. Two-base hits—Martin, DeLancey, Gehringer. Three-base hits—Martin, Rothrock, Greenberg. Double plays—Cochrane and Gehringer; Rogell, Gehringer and Greenberg. Left on bases—Detroit 13, St. Louis 6. Earned runs—St. Louis 4, Detroit 1. Struck out—By P. Dean 7, by Bridges 3, by Hogsett 2. Bases on balls—Off P. Dean 5, off Bridges 1, off Hogsett 1. Hit by pitcher—By P. Dean (Owen), by Bridges (Orsatti). Hits—Off Bridges 8 in 4 innings (pitched to three batters in fifth), off Hogsett 1 in 4 innings. Losing pitcher—Bridges. Umpires—Geisel (A.L.), Reardon (N.L.), Owens (A.L.) and Klem (N.L.). Time—2:07. Attendance—34,073.

Saturday, October 6—At St. Louis

Detroit (A.L.)	AB	R	H	O	A	E
White, cf	4	2	1	2	0	0
Cochrane, c	5	2	1	1	0	0
Gehringer, 2b	4	2	2	4	4	1
Goslin, lf	3	2	0	3	0	0
Rogell, ss	5	1	2	4	3	0
Greenberg, 1b	5	1	4	10	2	0
Owen, 3b	5	0	2	1	2	0
Fox, rf	4	0	1	2	0	0
Auker, p	4	0	0	0	2	0
Totals	39	10	13	27	13	1

1934 WORLD SERIES

St. Louis (N.L.)	AB.	R.	H.	O.	A.	E.
Martin, 3b	4	0	1	1	2	3
Rothrock, rf	5	0	0	3	0	0
Frisch, 2b	5	1	1	2	4	0
Medwick, lf	3	1	2	0	0	0
Collins, 1b	4	0	2	9	1	0
DeLancey, c	2	0	0	8	1	1
Orsatti, cf	4	1	2	2	1	0
Durocher, ss	4	1	1	2	1	0
Carleton, p	1	0	0	0	0	0
Vance, p	0	0	0	0	0	0
aV. Davis	1	0	1	0	0	0
bJ. Dean	0	0	0	0	0	0
W. Walker, p	1	0	0	0	0	1
Haines, p	0	0	0	0	0	0
cCrawford	1	0	0	0	0	0
Mooney, p	0	0	0	0	1	0
Totals	35	4	10	27	11	5

Detroit .... 0 0 3 1 0 0 1 5 0—10
St. Louis .... 0 1 1 2 0 0 0 0 0— 4

aSingled for Vance in fourth. bRan for V. Davis in fourth. cGrounded out for Haines in eighth. Runs batted in—Rogell 4, Greenberg 3, Owen, Collins 2, Orsatti, V. Davis. Two-base hits—Cochrane, Greenberg 2, Fox, Collins. Sacrifice hits—Cochrane, Gehringer, Goslin, Auker. Stolen bases—White, Greenberg, Owen. Double plays—Auker, Rogell and Greenberg; Greenberg and Rogell; Rogell and Greenberg. Left on bases—Detroit 12, St. Louis 8. Earned runs—Detroit 7, St. Louis 3. Struck out—By Auker 1, by Carleton 2, by Vance 3, by Haines 2. Bases on balls—Off Auker 4, off Carleton 2, off Vance 1, off W. Walker 3. Wild pitch—Vance. Hits—Off Carleton 4 in 2⅔ innings, off Vance 2 in 1⅓ innings, off W. Walker 5 in 3⅓ innings, off Haines 1 in ⅔ inning, off Mooney 1 in 1 inning. Losing pitcher—W. Walker. Umpires—Reardon (N.L.), Owens (A.L.), Klem (N.L.) and Geisel (A.L.). Time—2:43. Attendance—37,492.

Sunday, October 7—At St. Louis

Detroit (A.L.)	AB.	R.	H.	O.	A.	E.
White, cf	2	0	0	2	0	0
Cochrane, c	4	0	1	10	0	0
Gehringer, 2b	4	1	1	4	1	0
Goslin, lf	4	0	1	1	0	0
Rogell, ss	4	1	2	0	2	0
Greenberg, 1b	3	1	0	6	0	0
Owen, 3b	4	0	0	1	0	0
Fox, rf	4	0	1	3	0	0
Bridges, p	4	0	1	0	2	0
Totals	33	3	7	27	5	0

St. Louis (N.L.)	AB.	R.	H.	O.	A.	E.
Martin, 3b	4	0	2	0	1	0
Rothrock, rf	4	0	0	2	0	0
Frisch, 2b	4	0	1	2	3	0
Medwick, lf	4	0	0	3	0	0
Collins, 1b	4	0	1	5	1	0
DeLancey, c	4	1	1	6	0	0
Fullis, cf	3	0	0	5	0	1
dOrsatti	1	0	0	0	0	0
Durocher, ss	2	0	1	3	2	0
aV. Davis	1	0	1	0	0	0
bWhitehead, ss	0	0	0	1	0	0
J. Dean, p	2	0	0	0	0	0
cCrawford	1	0	0	0	0	0
Carleton, p	0	0	0	0	0	0
Totals	34	1	7	27	7	1

Detroit .... 0 1 0 0 0 2 0 0 0—3
St. Louis .... 0 0 0 0 0 0 1 0 0—1

aSingled for Durocher in eighth. bRan for V. Davis in eighth. cFlied out for J. Dean in eighth. dForced runner for Fullis in ninth. Runs batted in—Gehringer, Greenberg, Fox, DeLancey. Two-base hits—Goslin, Fox, Martin. Home runs—Gehringer, DeLancey. Double play—Collins, Durocher and Collins. Left on bases—Detroit 7, St. Louis 6. Earned Runs—Detroit 2, St. Louis 1. Struck out—By Bridges 7, by J. Dean 6. Bases on balls—Off J. Dean 3. Hit by pitcher—By J. Dean (White). Wild pitch—Bridges. Hits—Off J. Dean 6 in 8 innings, off Carleton 1 in 1 inning. Losing pitcher—J. Dean. Umpires—Owens (A.L.), Klem (N.L.), Geisel (A.L.) and Reardon (N.L.). Time—1:58. Attendance—38,536.

Monday, October 8—At Detroit

St. Louis (N.L.)	AB.	R.	H.	O.	A.	E.
Martin, 3b	5	1	1	1	2	0
Rothrock, rf	4	1	2	1	0	0
Frisch, 2b	4	0	0	2	3	1
Medwick, lf	4	0	2	0	0	0
Collins, 1b	4	0	0	8	0	0
DeLancey, c	4	0	0	6	4	0
Orsatti, cf	4	0	1	7	0	0
Durocher, ss	4	2	3	2	2	0
P. Dean, p	3	0	1	0	0	1
Totals	36	4	10	27	11	2

Detroit (A.L.)	AB.	R.	H.	O.	A.	E.
White, cf	2	2	0	0	0	0
Cochrane, c	4	0	3	7	0	0
Gehringer, 2b	4	1	1	0	4	0
Goslin, lf	4	0	1	4	0	1
Rogell, ss	4	0	0	1	2	0
Greenberg, 1b	4	0	1	10	0	0
Owen, 3b	4	0	0	3	3	0
Fox, rf	4	0	1	2	0	0
Rowe, p	3	0	0	0	0	0
Totals	33	3	7	27	9	1

St. Louis .... 1 0 0 0 2 0 1 0 0—4
Detroit .... 0 0 1 0 0 2 0 0 0—3

Runs batted in—Martin, Rothrock, Medwick, P. Dean, Cochrane, Greenberg. Two-base hits—Rothrock, Durocher, Fox. Sacrifice hits—P. Dean, Rowe. Left on bases—Detroit 6, St. Louis 6. Earned runs—St. Louis 3, Detroit 1. Struck out—By P. Dean 4, by Rowe 5. Bases on balls—Off P. Dean 2. Umpires—Klem (N.L.), Geisel (A.L.), Reardon (N.L.) and Owens (A.L.). Time—1:58. Attendance—44,551.

Tuesday, October 9—At Detroit

St. Louis (N.L.)	AB.	R.	H.	O.	A.	E.
Martin, 3b	5	3	2	0	1	0
Rothrock, rf	5	1	2	4	0	0
Frisch, 2b	5	1	1	3	5	0
Medwick, lf	4	1	1	1	0	0
Fullis, lf	1	0	1	1	0	0
Collins, 1b	5	1	4	7	2	1
DeLancey, c	5	1	1	5	0	0
Orsatti, cf	3	1	1	2	0	0
Durocher, ss	5	1	2	3	4	0
J. Dean, p	5	1	2	1	0	0
Totals	43	11	17	27	12	1

Detroit (A.L.)	AB.	R.	H.	O.	A.	E.
White, cf	4	0	0	3	0	1
Cochrane, c	4	0	0	2	2	0
Hayworth, c	0	0	0	1	0	0
Gehringer, 2b	4	0	2	3	5	1
Goslin, lf	4	0	0	4	0	1
Rogell, ss	4	0	1	3	2	0
Greenberg, 1b	4	0	1	7	0	0
Owen, 3b	4	0	0	1	2	0
Fox, rf	3	0	2	3	0	0
Auker, p	0	0	0	0	0	0
Rowe, p	0	0	0	0	0	0

1935 WORLD SERIES

	AB.	R.	H.	O.	A.	E.
Hogsett, p	0	0	0	0	0	0
Bridges, p	2	0	0	0	0	0
Marberry, p	0	0	0	0	0	0
aG. Walker	1	0	0	0	0	0
Crowder, p	0	0	0	0	0	0
Totals	34	0	6	27	11	3

St. Louis	0 0 7	0 0 2	2 0 0—11
Detroit	0 0 0	0 0 0	0 0 0— 0

aFlied out for Marberry in eighth. Runs batted in—Martin, Rothrock, Frisch 3, Medwick, Collins 2, DeLancey, J. Dean. Two-base hits—Rothrock 2, Frisch, DeLancey, J. Dean, Fox 2. Three-base hits—Medwick, Durocher. Stolen bases—Martin 2. Double play—Owen, Gehringer and Greenberg. Left on bases—St. Louis 9, Detroit 7. Earned runs—St. Louis 9. Struck out—By J. Dean 5, by Auker 1, by Bridges 2, by Crowder 1. Bases on balls—Off Auker 1, off Hogsett 2, off Marberry 1. Hits—Off Auker 6 in 2⅓ innings, off Rowe 2 in ⅓ inning, off Hogsett 2 in 0 (pitched to four batters in third inning), off Bridges 6 in 4⅓ innings, off Marberry 1 in 1 inning, off Crowder 0 in 1 inning. Losing pitcher—Auker. Umpires—Geisel (A.L.), Reardon (N.L.), Owens (A.L.) and Klem (N.L.). Time—2:19. Attendance—40,902.

COMPOSITE BATTING AVERAGES
St. Louis Cardinals

Player-Position	G.	AB.	R.	H.	2B.	3B.	HR.	RBI.	BA.
V. Davis, ph	2	2	0	2	0	0	0	1	1.000
Fullis, p	3	5	0	2	0	0	0	0	.400
Medwick, lf	7	29	4	11	0	1	1	5	.379
Collins, 1b	7	30	4	11	1	0	0	4	.367
Martin, 3b	7	31	8	11	3	1	0	3	.355
Orsatti, cf	7	22	3	7	0	1	0	2	.318
Durocher, ss	7	27	4	7	1	1	0	0	.259
J. Dean, p-pr	4	12	3	3	2	0	0	1	.250
Rothrock, rf	7	30	3	7	3	1	0	6	.233
Frisch, 2b	7	31	2	6	1	0	0	4	.194
DeLancey, c	7	29	3	5	3	0	1	4	.172
P. Dean, p	2	6	0	1	0	0	0	2	.167
Hallahan, p	1	1	0	0	0	0	0	0	.000
W. Walker, p	2	2	0	0	0	0	0	0	.000
Carleton, p	2	1	0	0	0	0	0	0	.000
Vance, p	1	0	0	0	0	0	0	0	.000
Whitehead, pr-ss	1	0	0	0	0	0	0	0	.000
Haines, p	1	0	0	0	0	0	0	0	.000
Crawford, ph	2	2	0	0	0	0	0	0	.000
Mooney, p	1	0	0	0	0	0	0	0	.000
Totals	7	262	34	73	14	5	2	32	.279

Detroit Tigers

Player-Position	G.	AB.	R.	H.	2B.	3B.	HR.	RBI.	BA.
Gehringer, 2b	7	29	5	11	1	0	1	2	.379
G. Walker, ph	3	3	0	1	0	0	0	1	.333
Greenberg, 1b	2	7	1	2	0	0	1	2	.286
Fox, rf	7	28	1	8	6	0	0	2	.286
Rogell, ss	7	29	3	8	1	0	0	4	.276
Goslin, lf	7	29	2	7	1	0	0	2	.241
Cochrane, c	7	28	2	6	1	0	0	1	.214
Bridges, p	3	7	0	1	0	0	0	0	.143
White, cf	7	23	6	3	0	0	0	0	.130
Owen, 3b	7	29	0	2	0	0	0	1	.069
Auker, p	2	4	0	0	0	0	0	0	.000
Doljack, ph-cf	2	2	0	0	0	0	0	0	.000
Crowder, p	2	1	0	0	0	0	0	0	.000
Marberry, p	2	0	0	0	0	0	0	0	.000
Rowe, p	3	7	0	0	0	0	0	0	.000
Hogsett, p	3	3	0	0	0	0	0	0	.000
Hayworth, c	1	0	0	0	0	0	0	0	.000
Totals	7	250	23	56	12	1	2	20	.224

COMPOSITE PITCHING AVERAGES
St. Louis Cardinals

Pitcher	G.	IP.	H.	R.	E.	SO.	BB.	W.	L.	ERA.
Haines	1	⅔	1	0	0	2	0	0	0	0.00
Mooney	1	1	1	0	0	0	0	0	0	0.00
Vance	1	1⅓	2	1	0	3	1	0	0	0.00
P. Dean	2	18	15	4	2	11	7	2	0	1.00
J. Dean	3	26	20	6	5	17	5	2	1	1.73
Hallahan	1	8⅓	6	2	2	6	4	0	0	2.16

Pitcher	G.	IP.	H.	R.	E.	SO.	BB.	W.	L.	ERA.
W. Walker	2	6⅓	6	7	5	2	6	0	0	7.11
Carleton	2	3⅔	5	3	3	2	2	0	0	7.36
Totals	7	65⅓	56	23	17	43	25	4	3	2.34

Detroit Tigers

Pitcher	G.	IP.	H.	R.	E.	SO.	BB.	W.	L.	ERA.
Hogsett	3	7⅓	6	1	1	3	3	0	0	1.23
Crowder	2	6	6	4	1	2	1	0	1	1.50
Rowe	3	21⅓	19	8	7	12	0	1	1	2.95
Bridges	3	17⅓	21	9	7	12	1	1	1	3.63
Auker	2	11⅓	16	8	7	2	5	1	1	5.56
Marberry	2	1⅔	5	4	4	0	1	0	0	21.60
Totals	7	65	73	34	27	31	11	3	4	3.74

SERIES OF 1935

	W.	L.	Pct.
Detroit A. L.	4	2	.667
Chicago N. L.	2	4	.333

Two early World Series rivals of the first decade of the century—the Detroit Tigers and Chicago Cubs—clashed again in 1935 after an interval of 26 years. Both clubs had established reputations as World Series punching bags. The Tigers won the Series, four games to two, their first triumph after four reverses, while the Cubs' defeat made it five straight setbacks for the team which was almost invincible under Frank Chance in the Series of 1907 and 1908.

Mickey Cochrane's Bengals had repeated in the American League, after a close struggle with the Yankees. Detroit's winning margin was three games. The Cubs again were commanded by Charlie Grimm, the 1932 chief, and their pennant victory was made possible by a sensational 21-game September winning streak, which continued almost to the last day of the season. The momentum of that drive carried the National Leaguers to a 3 to 0 victory in the first game, which Lon Warneke won in Detroit from Schoolboy Rowe, but the Tigers took four of the next five games.

Detroit was victorious in the Series despite the loss of Hank Greenberg, the American League's Most Valuable Player of 1935, with a broken wrist in the second game. It was a heavy loss, as Greenberg had banged in 170 runs for Detroit that season. Cochrane was forced to switch third baseman Marvin Owen to first and play Herman (Flea) Clifton at third base. The pair proved a heavy load for the Tiger team to carry, getting only one hit between them in 36 times at bat, but timely wallops by Charley Gehringer, Pete Fox, Goose Goslin and Cochrane eventually turned the battling in Detroit's favor. Gehringer hit almost exactly what he did the year before—.375, four points below his 1934 average.

The Series was marked by repeated arguments between the Cubs and umpire George Moriarty and, after the classic was over, Commissioner Landis slapped $200 fines on the arbiter and on Manager Grimm, Woody English, Billy Herman and Bill Jurges of the Chicago club for use of improper language.

1935 WORLD SERIES

Tommy Bridges won two games for the Tigers; in his second World Series in as many years, Alvin Crowder finally managed to hang up a victory, while Rowe captured one game in a relief role and suffered both of the Detroit defeats. Warneke gained Chicago's two victories; Larry French lost two games, and other Cub reverses went to Charlie Root and Tex Carleton. Light hitting hurt the Bruin pitchers, as there was a lack of any cleanup punch in the Chicago lineup. Billy Herman, batting second, led the Cubs at bat with .333 and knocked in six runs. No other Chicago player drove in more than two counters. The Cubs batted .238 against .258 for the Tigers.

Warneke hurled a four-hitter in his opening-game triumph and then was credited with a 3 to 1 victory in the fifth game, although a muscle injury forced the Arkansas Hummingbird to leave the mound in the sixth inning. Bill Lee finished to protect Lon's decision.

Much of the excitement was saved for the ninth inning of the sixth and final game, in which Bridges faced French. Chicago needed the game to tie, and both pitchers were hit fairly hard, each club getting 12 safeties. Stan Hack stunned Detroit fandom by opening the ninth with a triple, but the crowd went wild when Bridges fanned Bill Jurges, tossed French out at first and retired Augie Galan on an outfield fly.

The crowd enthusiasm turned to pandemonium a few minutes later when Cochrane singled with one out, took second on Gehringer's out, and scored the winning run on Goslin's clean single to right. Detroit became a madhouse, with the bedlam unabated until daylight the following morning. The box scores:

Wednesday, October 2—At Detroit

Chicago (N.L.)	AB.	R.	H.	O.	A.	E.
Galan, lf	4	1	1	2	0	0
Herman, 2b	3	1	0	0	3	0
Lindstrom, cf	3	0	1	2	0	0
Hartnett, c	4	0	2	1	0	0
Demaree, rf	4	1	2	1	0	0
Cavarretta, 1b	3	0	0	17	0	0
Hack, 3b	4	0	0	1	3	0
Jurges, ss	4	0	1	2	2	0
Warneke, p	3	0	0	1	8	0
Totals	32	3	7	27	16	0

Detroit (A.L.)	AB.	R.	H.	O.	A.	E.
White, cf	4	0	1	2	0	0
Cochrane, c	4	0	0	8	1	0
Gehringer, 2b	3	0	0	3	4	0
Greenberg, 1b	3	0	0	9	0	1
Goslin, lf	3	0	0	1	0	1
Fox, rf	4	0	2	1	0	0
Rogell, ss	4	0	0	3	0	0
Owen, 3b	3	0	0	0	0	0
Rowe, p	3	0	1	0	4	1
Totals	31	0	4	27	9	3

Chicago............ 2 0 0 0 0 0 0 0 1—3
Detroit............. 0 0 0 0 0 0 0 0 0—0

Runs batted in—Hartnett, Demaree. Two-base hits—Galan, Fox, Rowe. Home run—Demaree. Sacrifice hits—Herman, Lindstrom, Cavarretta. Double play—Cochrane and Gehringer. Left on bases—Detroit 8, Chicago 5. Earned runs—Chicago 2. Struck out—By Rowe 8, by Warneke 1. Bases on balls—Off Warneke 4. Passes ball—Cochrane. Umpires—Moriarty (A.L.), Quigley (N.L.), McGowan (A.L.) and Stark (N.L.). Time—1:51. Attendance—47,391.

Thursday, October 3—At Detroit

Chicago (N.L.)	AB.	R.	H.	O.	A.	E.
Galan, lf	4	0	0	3	1	0
Herman, 2b	4	0	1	2	6	0
Lindstrom, cf	3	0	0	1	0	0
Hartnett, c	4	0	1	4	2	0
Demaree, rf	4	0	1	0	1	0
Cavarretta, 1b	4	1	0	9	0	0
Hack, 3b	3	0	1	2	1	0
Jurges, ss	3	1	1	3	1	0
Root, p	0	0	0	0	0	0
Henshaw, p	1	0	0	0	1	0
Kowalik, p	2	1	1	0	2	1
aKlein	1	0	0	0	0	0
Totals	33	3	6	24	15	1

Detroit (A.L.)	AB.	R.	H.	O.	A.	E.
White, cf	3	2	1	3	0	0
Cochrane, c	2	1	1	2	0	0
Gehringer, 2b	3	2	2	2	5	0
Greenberg, 1b	3	1	1	8	2	2
Goslin, lf	3	0	0	2	0	0
Fox, rf	4	0	1	4	0	0
Rogell, ss	4	0	2	3	2	0
Owen, 3b	2	1	0	2	0	0
Bridges, p	4	1	1	1	2	0
Totals	28	8	9	27	11	2

Chicago............ 0 0 0 0 1 0 2 0 0—3
Detroit............. 4 0 0 3 0 0 1 0 *—8

aFlied out for Kowalik in ninth. Runs batted in—Cochrane, Gehringer 3, Fox, Greenberg 2, Jurges, Herman 2. Two-base hits—Cochrane, Rogell, Demaree. Home run—Greenberg. Sacrifice hit—Owen. Double plays—Bridges, Rogell and Greenberg; Rogell, Gehringer and Greenberg; Herman and Cavarretta; Jurges, Herman and Cavarretta. Left on bases—Chicago 7, Detroit 5. Earned runs—Detroit 8, Chicago 2. Struck out—By Henshaw 2, by Kowalik 1, by Bridges 2. Bases on balls—Off Henshaw 5, off Kowalik 1, off Bridges 4. Hit by pitcher—By Henshaw (Owen), by Kowalik (Greenberg). Wild pitch—Henshaw. Hits—Off Root 4 in 0 (pitched to four batters in first inning), off Henshaw 2 in 3⅔ innings, off Kowalik 3 in 4⅓ innings. Losing pitcher—Root. Umpires—Quigley (N.L.), McGowan (A.L.), Stark (N.L.) and Moriarty (A.L.). Time—1:59. Attendance—46,742.

Friday, October 4—At Chicago

Detroit (A.L.)	AB.	R.	H.	O.	A.	E.
White, cf	5	1	2	5	0	0
Cochrane, c	5	0	0	4	2	1
Gehringer, 2b	5	1	2	4	7	0
Goslin, lf	5	2	3	2	0	0
Fox, rf	5	1	2	0	0	0
Rogell, ss	5	0	3	2	4	0
Owen, 1b	5	1	0	15	0	0
Clifton, 3b	4	0	0	0	5	1
Auker, p	2	0	0	0	2	0
aWalker	1	0	0	0	0	0
Hogsett, p	0	0	0	1	0	0
Rowe, p	2	0	0	0	0	0
Totals	44	6	12	33	20	2

1935 WORLD SERIES

Chicago (N.L.)	AB.	R.	H.	O.	A.	E.
Galan, lf	4	0	2	1	0	0
Herman, 2b	5	0	1	3	2	1
Lindstrom, cf-3b	5	2	2	2	1	1
Hartnett, c	4	0	0	8	3	0
Demaree, rf-cf	4	1	1	2	0	0
Cavarretta, 1b	5	0	0	10	1	1
Hack, 3b-ss	5	2	2	3	2	0
Jurges, ss	1	1	0	3	4	0
bKlein, rf	2	1	1	1	0	0
Lee, p	1	0	0	0	1	0
Warneke, p	0	0	0	0	0	0
cO'Dea	1	0	1	0	0	0
French, p	0	0	0	0	0	0
dStephenson	1	0	0	0	0	0
Totals	38	5	10	33	14	3

Detroit .... 0 0 0   0 0 1   0 4 0   0 1—6
Chicago .... 0 2 0   0 1 0   0 0 2   0 0—5

aHit into double play for Auker in seventh. bSingled for Jurges in ninth. cSingled for Warneke in ninth. dStruck out for French in eleventh. Runs batted in—Demaree, Lee, Galan 2, O'Dea, Fox, Goslin 2, Rogell, White. Two base hits—Lindstrom, Gehringer, Goslin. Three-base hit—Fox. Home run—Demaree. Sacrifice hits—Lee 2, Hartnett. Stolen base—Hack. Double plays—Rogell, Gehringer and Owen; Gehringer, Rogell and Owen; Jurges, Herman and Cavarretta. Left on bases—Detroit 8, Chicago 7. Earned runs—Detroit 5, Chicago 4. Struck out—By Auker 1, by Rowe 3, by Lee 3, by Warneke 2, by French 1. Bases on balls—Off Auker 2, off Hogsett 1, off Lee 3. Hit by pitcher—By Hogsett (Jurges). Hits—Off Auker 6 in 6 innings, off Hogsett 0 in 1 inning, off Rowe 4 in 4 innings, off Lee 7 in 7⅓ innings, off Warneke 2 in 1⅔ innings, off French 3 in 2 innings. Winning pitcher—Rowe. Losing pitcher—French. Umpires—McGowan (A.L.), Stark (N.L.), Moriarty (A.L.) and Quigley (N.L.). Time—2:27. Attendance—45,532.

Saturday, October 5—At Chicago

Detroit (A.L.)	AB.	R.	H.	O.	A.	E.
White, cf	3	0	1	0	0	0
Cochrane, c	4	0	1	6	0	0
Gehringer, 2b	4	0	2	3	3	0
Goslin, lf	3	0	1	1	0	0
Fox, rf	5	0	1	0	0	0
Rogell, ss	3	0	0	2	2	0
Owen, 1b	4	0	0	13	1	0
Clifton, 3b	4	1	0	0	4	0
Crowder, p	3	1	1	2	2	0
Totals	33	2	7	27	12	0

Chicago (N.L.)	AB.	R.	H.	O.	A.	E.
Galan, lf	4	0	0	2	0	1
Herman, 2b	4	0	1	4	1	0
Lindstrom, cf	4	0	0	3	0	0
Hartnett, c	4	1	1	7	0	0
Demaree, rf	4	0	1	4	0	0
Cavarretta, 1b	4	0	2	3	1	0
Hack, 3b	4	0	0	0	0	0
Jurges, ss	1	0	0	4	2	1
Carleton, p	1	0	0	0	2	0
aKlein	1	0	0	0	0	0
Root, p	0	0	0	0	1	0
Totals	31	1	5	27	7	2

Detroit .... 0 0 1   0 0 1   0 0 0—2
Chicago .... 0 1 0   0 0 0   0 0 0—1

aGrounded out for Carleton in seventh. Runs batted in—Hartnett, Gehringer. Two-base hits—Fox, Gehringer, Herman. Home run—Hartnett. Sacrifice hit—Gehringer. Stolen base—Gehringer. Double plays—Jurges and Herman; Rogell, Gehringer and Owen. Left on bases—Detroit 13, Chicago 6. Earned runs—Chicago 1, Detroit 1. Struck out—By Crowder 5, by Carleton 4, by Root 2. Bases on balls—Off Crowder 3, off Carleton 7, off Root 1. Balk—Carleton. Hits—Off Carleton 6 in 7 innings, off Root 1 in 2 innings. Losing pitcher—Carleton. Umpires—Stark (N.L.), Moriarty (A.L.), Quigley (N.L.) and McGowan (A.L.). Time—2:28. Attendance—49,350.

Sunday, October 6—At Chicago

Detroit (A.L.)	AB.	R.	H.	O.	A.	E.
White, cf	4	0	0	4	0	0
Cochrane, c	4	0	2	5	0	0
Gehringer, 2b	4	1	1	2	2	0
Goslin, lf	3	0	1	4	0	0
Fox, rf	4	0	2	0	1	0
Rogell, ss	4	0	0	1	1	0
Owen, 1b	3	0	0	5	4	1
aWalker	1	0	0	0	0	0
Clifton, 3b	3	0	0	0	0	0
Rowe, p	3	0	1	3	1	0
Totals	33	1	7	24	9	1

Chicago (N.L.)	AB.	R.	H.	O.	A.	E.
Galan, lf	4	1	0	2	0	0
Herman, 2b	4	1	2	3	3	0
Klein, rf	4	1	2	3	0	0
Hartnett, c	4	0	1	4	0	0
Demaree, cf	4	0	1	1	0	0
Cavarretta, 1b	4	0	0	11	1	0
Hack, 3b	2	0	0	0	0	0
Jurges, ss	3	0	1	1	4	0
Warneke, p	2	0	1	1	1	0
Lee, p	0	0	0	1	0	0
Totals	31	3	8	27	9	0

Detroit .... 0 0 0   0 0 0   0 0 1—1
Chicago .... 0 0 2   0 0 0   1 0 *—3

aGrounded out for Owen in ninth. Runs batted in—Klein 2, Herman, Fox. Two-base hit—Herman. Three-base hit—Herman. Home run—Klein. Sacrifice hit—Lee. Double play—Jurges and Cavarretta. Left on bases—Detroit 7, Chicago 6. Earned runs—Chicago 2, Detroit 1. Struck out—By Rowe 3, by Warneke 2, by Lee 2. Bases on balls—Off Rowe 1, off Lee 2. Hits—Off Warneke 6 in 6 innings, off Lee 4 in 3 innings. Winning pitcher—Warneke. Umpires—Moriarty (A.L.), Quigley (N.L.), McGowan (A.L.) and Stark (N.L.). Time—1:49. Attendance—49,237.

Monday, October 7—At Detroit

Chicago (N.L.)	AB.	R.	H.	O.	A.	E.
Galan, lf	5	0	1	2	0	0
Herman, 2b	4	1	3	3	4	0
Klein, rf	4	0	1	0	0	0
Hartnett, c	4	0	2	9	1	0
Demaree, cf	4	0	0	0	0	0
Cavarretta, 1b	4	0	1	8	0	0
Hack, 3b	4	0	2	0	4	0
Jurges, ss	4	1	1	3	2	0
French, p	4	1	1	1	2	0
Totals	37	3	12	*26	13	0

Detroit (A.L.)	AB.	R.	H.	O.	A.	E.
Clifton, 3b	5	0	0	2	0	0
Cochrane, c	5	2	3	7	0	0
Gehringer, 2b	5	0	2	0	4	0
Goslin, lf	5	0	1	2	0	0
Fox, rf	4	0	0	3	1	1
Walker, cf	2	1	1	0	0	0
Rogell, ss	4	1	2	2	3	0
Owen, 1b	3	0	1	11	0	0
Bridges, p	4	0	0	0	3	0
Totals	37	4	12	27	11	1

```
Chicago.................... 0 0 1   0 2 0   0 0 0—3
Detroit..................... 1 0 0   1 0 1   0 0 1—4
```

*Two out when winning run scored. Runs batted in—Herman 3, Fox, Bridges, Owen, Goslin. Two-base hits—Fox, Gehringer, Rogell, Hack. Three-base hit—Hack. Home run—Herman. Sacrifice hit—Walker. Double play—Gehringer, Rogell and Owen. Left on bases—Detroit 10, Chicago 7. Earned runs—Detroit 4, Chicago 3. Struck out—By French 7, by Bridges 7. Bases on balls—Off French 2. Umpires—Quigley (N.L.), McGowan (A.L.), Stark (N.L.) and Moriarty (A.L.). Time—1:57. Attendance—48,420.

COMPOSITE BATTING AVERAGES
Detroit Tigers

Player-Position	G.	AB.	R.	H.	2B.	3B.	HR.	RBI.	BA.
Fox, rf	6	26	1	10	3	1	0	4	.385
Gehringer, 2b	6	24	4	9	3	0	0	4	.375
Crowder, p	1	3	1	1	0	0	0	0	.333
Cochrane, c	6	24	3	7	1	0	0	1	.292
Rogell, ss	6	24	1	7	2	0	0	1	.292
Goslin, lf	6	22	2	6	1	0	0	3	.273
White, cf	5	19	3	5	0	0	0	1	.263
Rowe, p	3	8	0	2	1	0	0	0	.250
Walker, ph-cf	3	4	1	1	0	0	0	0	.250
Greenberg, 1b	2	6	1	1	0	0	1	2	.167
Bridges, p	2	8	1	1	0	0	0	1	.125
Owen, 3b-1b	6	20	2	1	0	0	0	1	.050
Clifton, 3b	4	16	1	0	0	0	0	0	.000
Auker, p	1	2	0	0	0	0	0	0	.000
Hogsett, p	1	0	0	0	0	0	0	0	.000
Totals	6	206	21	51	11	1	1	18	.248

Chicago Cubs

Player-Position	G.	AB.	R.	H.	2B.	3B.	HR.	RBI.	BA.
O'Dea, ph	1	1	0	1	0	0	0	1	1.000
Kowalik, p	1	2	1	1	0	0	0	0	.500
Herman, 2b	6	24	3	8	2	1	1	6	.333
Klein, ph-rf	5	12	2	4	0	0	1	2	.333
Hartnett, c	6	24	1	7	0	0	1	2	.292
Demaree, rf-cf	6	24	2	6	1	0	2	2	.250
French, p	2	4	1	1	0	0	0	0	.250
Jurges, ss	6	16	3	4	0	0	0	1	.250
Hack, 3b-ss	6	22	2	5	1	1	0	0	.227
Lindstrom, cf-3b	4	15	0	3	1	0	0	0	.200
Warneke, p	3	5	0	1	0	0	0	0	.200
Galan, lf	6	25	2	4	1	0	0	2	.160
Cavarretta, 1b	6	24	1	3	0	0	0	0	.125
Root, p	2	0	0	0	0	0	0	0	.000
Henshaw, p	1	1	0	0	0	0	0	0	.000
Lee, p	2	1	0	0	0	0	0	1	.000
Stephenson, ph	1	1	0	0	0	0	0	0	.000
Carleton, p	1	1	0	0	0	0	0	0	.000
Totals	6	202	18	48	6	2	5	17	.238

COMPOSITE PITCHING AVERAGES
Detroit Tigers

Pitcher	G.	IP.	H.	R.	E.	SO.	BB.	W.	L.	ERA.
Hogsett	1	1	0	0	0	0	1	0	0	0.00
Crowder	1	9	5	1	1	5	3	1	0	1.00
Bridges	2	18	18	6	5	9	4	2	0	2.50
Rowe	3	21	19	8	6	14	1	1	2	2.57
Auker	1	6	6	3	2	1	2	0	0	3.00
Totals	6	55	48	18	14	29	11	4	2	2.29

Chicago Cubs

Pitcher	G.	IP.	H.	R.	E.	SO.	BB.	W.	L.	ERA.
Warneke	3	16⅔	9	1	1	5	4	2	0	0.54
Carleton	1	7	6	2	1	4	7	0	1	1.29
Kowalik	1	4⅓	3	1	1	1	0	0	0	2.08
French	2	10⅔	15	5	4	8	2	0	2	3.38
Lee	2	10⅓	11	5	4	5	0	0	0	3.48
Henshaw	1	3⅔	2	3	3	2	5	0	0	7.36
Root	2	2	5	4	4	2	1	0	1	18.00
Totals	6	54⅔	51	21	18	27	25	2	4	2.96

SERIES OF 1936

	W.	L.	Pct.
New York A. L.	4	2	.667
New York N. L.	2	4	.333

Meeting again in the 1936 World Series, after an interval of 13 years, the two New York clubs, the Yankees and Giants, clashed in their fourth so-called Subway Series, with victory perching on the American League banner, four games to two. Despite two bitter setbacks by such overwhelming scores of 18 to 4 and 13 to 5, the Giants made the Series closer than the final result indicated. The Yankees had seven-run innings in each of their big games, the second batch coming in the ninth frame of the payoff contest.

Joe DiMaggio, the famous rookie from the Far West, joined the Yankees in 1936, and his acquisition helped to put the Bronx Bombers, runners-up for three consecutive years, over the top that season. They won the pennant in a breeze, with a 19½-game lead over the Tigers. After playing listless ball in the early part of the season, the Giants put on a strong campaign in August and September, beating out the Cubs and Cardinals by five games.

The Polo Grounders were again built around their ace pitcher, Carl Hubbell, the National League's Most Valuable Player, who had his best season, with 26 victories against only six defeats. Hubbell closed the 1936 National League season with a winning streak of 16 straight. He made it 17 in a row when he defeated Charley Ruffing on a wet field in the World Series opener, 6 to 1, to end a Yankee streak of 12 straight Series victories. Carl held the Yanks to seven hits and the only run against him came on a homer by George Selkirk in the third inning. Dick Bartell tied the score with a circuit clout in the fifth and the Giants then went ahead in the sixth on Mel Ott's double and a single by Gus Mancuso. A four-run outburst in the eighth clinched the verdict.

In his next start, King Carl lost to Monte Pearson, 5 to 2, in the fourth game, Lou Gehrig hitting Hub for a two-run homer in the third inning. Lou also clouted a round-tripper off Freddy Fitzsimmons, but closed the Series with an average of .292, his first under .300.

The heavy hitting of the Yankees in two games gave them a team batting average of .302 against .246 for the Giants. Alvin (Jake) Powell, the Yankees' left fielder, procured that year in a trade for Ben Chapman, led both clubs with .455. Tony Lazzeri became the second player to hit a homer with the bases full in the classic, turning the trick in the second game.

Aggressive Dick Bartell carried off batting honors for the Giants with .381. Bill Terry, Giant manager, ended his playing career with the Series and hit .240.

Lefty Gomez won a pair of games, and he was lucky enough to be the pitcher in the two big Yankee scoring contests. Pearson and Bump Hadley each brought in the other well-pitched games for Joe McCarthy's men. Ruffing did not have much luck in this Series, as he lost the first game, and Pat Malone, who relieved Red in the fifth struggle, was charged with the ten-inning, 5 to 4 Yankee defeat. Selkirk hit his second homer of the Series in the contest. The Giants settled the overtime battle when Jo-Jo Moore doubled, Bartell sacrificed and Manager Terry flied out to DiMaggio in the tenth inning.

In addition to Hubbell's results, Hal Schumacher also won one and dropped one for the Giants, while Fitzsimmons lost two. Freddy's 2 to 1 defeat in the third game was a tough one, as he yielded only four hits against 11 off Hadley and Malone. With the score tied, 1 to 1, in the eighth, Powell on third and two out, Frank Crosetti banged a single off Fitz' glove, driving in what proved to be the winning run. The box scores:

Wednesday, Sept. 30—Polo Grounds

Yankees (A.L.)	AB.	R.	H.	O.	A.	E.
Crosetti, ss	4	0	1	1	3	1
Rolfe, 3b	3	0	1	2	1	0
DiMaggio, cf	4	0	1	3	0	0
Gehrig, 1b	3	0	0	7	0	0
Dickey, c	4	0	0	8	0	1
Powell, lf	4	0	3	2	0	0
Lazzeri, 2b	3	0	0	1	2	0
Selkirk, rf	4	1	1	0	0	0
Ruffing, p	3	0	0	0	1	0
Totals	32	1	7	24	7	2

Giants (N.L.)	AB.	R.	H.	O.	A.	E.
Moore, lf	5	0	0	0	0	0
Bartell, ss	4	1	2	1	2	0
Terry, 1b	4	1	2	12	2	0
Ott, rf	2	2	2	0	0	0
Ripple, cf	2	0	0	0	0	0
Mancuso, c	3	1	1	9	1	0
Whitehead, 2b	3	1	0	3	4	0
Jackson, 3b	4	0	0	1	1	0
Hubbell, p	4	0	2	1	2	1
Totals	31	6	9	27	12	1

Yankees............ 0 0 1 0 0 0 0 0 0—1
Giants............. 0 0 0 0 1 1 0 4 *—6

Runs batted in—Bartell, Mancuso, Whitehead, Jackson, Hubbell, Selkirk. Two-base hits—Ott, Crosetti, Powell. Home runs—Bartell, Selkirk. Sacrifice hits—Ripple 2, Rolfe. Double play—Whitehead and Terry. Left on bases—Giants 7, Yankees 7. Earned runs—Giants 4, Yankees 1. Struck out—By Ruffing 5, by Hubbell 8. Bases on balls—Off Ruffing 4, off Hubbell 1. Hit by pitcher—By Hubbell (Gehrig). Umpires—Pfirman (N.L.), Geisel (A.L.), Magerkurth (N.L.) and Summers (A.L.). Time—2:40. Attendance—39,419.

Friday, October 2—At Polo Grounds

Yankees (A.L.)	AB.	R.	H.	O.	A.	E.
Crosetti, ss	5	4	3	0	1	0
Rolfe, 3b	4	3	2	2	0	0
DiMaggio, cf	5	2	3	6	0	0
Gehrig, 1b	5	1	2	6	0	0
Dickey, c	5	3	1	8	0	0
Selkirk, rf	5	1	1	2	0	0
Powell, lf	3	2	2	2	0	0
Lazzeri, 2b	4	1	1	1	3	0
Gomez, p	5	1	1	0	0	0
Totals	41	18	17	27	4	0

Giants (N.L.)	AB.	R.	H.	O.	A.	E.
Moore, lf	5	0	0	2	0	0
Bartell, ss	3	0	1	2	2	0
Terry, 1b	5	0	2	6	1	0
Leiber, cf	4	0	0	7	1	0
Ott, rf	4	0	0	4	0	0
Mancuso, c	2	2	1	3	2	0
Whitehead, 2b	4	0	0	2	1	0
Jackson, 3b	4	1	1	0	2	1
Schumacher, p	0	0	0	0	0	0
Smith, p	0	0	0	0	0	0
Coffman, p	0	0	0	0	1	0
aDavis	1	1	1	0	0	0
Gabler, p	0	0	0	1	0	0
bDanning	1	0	0	0	0	0
Gumbert, p	0	0	0	0	0	0
Totals	33	4	6	27	10	1

Yankees............ 2 0 7 0 0 1 2 0 6—18
Giants............. 0 1 0 3 0 0 0 0 0— 4

aSingled for Coffman in fourth. bStruck out for Gabler in eighth. Runs batted in—Lazzeri 5, Dickey 5, Gehrig 3, DiMaggio 2, Gomez 2, Terry 2, Bartell, Rolfe. Two-base hits—Bartell, Mancuso, DiMaggio. Home runs—Dickey, Lazzeri. Sacrifice hit—DiMaggio. Stolen base—Powell. Double play—Leiber, Jackson and Bartell. Left on bases—Giants 9, Yankees 6. Earned runs—Yankees 17, Giants 4. Struck out—By Schumacher 1, by Coffman 1, by Gumbert 1, by Gomez 8. Bases on balls—Off Schumacher 4, off Smith 1, off Gabler 3, off Gumbert 1, off Gomez 7. Wild pitches—Schumacher, Gomez. Hits—Off Schumacher 3 in 2 innings (pitched to three batters in third), off Smith 2 in ⅓ inning, off Coffman 2 in 1⅔ innings, off Gabler 5 in 4 innings, off Gumbert 5 in 1 inning. Losing pitcher—Schumacher. Umpires—Geisel (A.L.), Magerkurth (N.L.), Summers (A.L.) and Pfirman (N.L.). Time—2:49. Attendance—43,543.

Saturday, Oct. 3—At Yankee Stadium

Giants (N.L.)	AB.	R.	H.	O.	A.	E.
Moore, lf	5	0	1	2	0	0
Bartell, ss	3	0	1	0	1	0
Terry, 1b	4	0	1	5	1	0
Ott, rf	4	0	2	4	0	0
Ripple, cf	4	1	1	2	0	0
Mancuso, c	4	0	1	7	0	0
Whitehead, 2b	4	0	0	3	4	0
Jackson, 3b	2	0	1	0	1	0
cKoenig	1	0	0	0	0	0
Fitzsimmons, p	3	0	2	1	1	0
dLeslie	1	0	1	0	0	0
eDavis	0	0	0	0	0	0
Totals	35	1	11	24	8	0

Yankees (A.L.)	AB.	R.	H.	O.	A.	E.
Crosetti, ss	4	0	1	4	5	0
Rolfe, 3b	4	0	0	3	1	0
DiMaggio, cf	3	0	1	2	0	0
Gehrig, 1b	3	1	1	10	1	0
Dickey, c	2	0	0	3	2	0
Selkirk, rf	3	0	1	2	0	0
Powell, lf	2	1	0	1	0	0
Lazzeri, 2b	2	0	0	2	2	0
Hadley, p	2	0	0	0	3	0
aRuffing	1	0	0	0	0	0
bJohnson	0	0	0	0	0	0
Malone, p	0	0	0	0	0	0
Totals	26	2	4	27	14	0

Giants............. 0 0 0 0 1 0 0 0 0—1
Yankees............ 0 1 0 0 0 0 0 1 *—2

aForced runner for Hadley in eighth. bRan for Ruffing in eighth. cGrounded out for Jackson in ninth. dSingled for Fitzsimmons in ninth. eRan for Leslie in ninth. Runs batted in—Crosetti, Gehrig, Ripple. Two-base hit—DiMaggio. Home

1936 WORLD SERIES

runs—Gehrig, Ripple. Sacrifice hits—Lazzeri, Bartell. Double plays—Crosetti and Gehrig; Bartell, Whitehead and Terry. Left on bases—Giants 9, Yankees 3. Earned runs—Yankees 2, Giants 1. Struck out—By Fitzsimmons 5, by Hadley 2, by Malone 1. Bases on balls—Off Fitzsimmons 2, off Hadley 1. Hits—Off Hadley 10 in 8 innings, off Malone 1 in 1 inning. Winning pitcher—Hadley. Umpires—Magerkurth (N.L.), Summers (A.L.), Pfirman (N.L.) and Geisel (A.L.). Time—2:01. Attendance—64,842.

Sunday, Oct. 4—At Yankee Stadium

Giants (N.L.)	AB.	R.	H.	O.	A.	E.
Moore, lf	3	0	1	2	0	0
Bartell, ss	4	1	1	3	4	0
Terry, 1b	3	0	0	10	1	0
Ott, rf	4	0	0	0	0	0
Ripple, cf	4	0	2	3	0	0
Mancuso, c	4	0	0	3	0	0
Whitehead, 2b	3	0	0	2	5	0
cKoenig	1	0	1	0	0	0
Jackson, 3b	4	0	1	0	3	1
Hubbell, p	2	0	0	1	0	0
aLeslie	1	0	1	0	0	0
bDavis	0	1	0	0	0	0
Gabler, p	0	0	0	0	0	0
Totals	33	2	7	24	13	1

Yankees (A.L.)	AB.	R.	H.	O.	A.	E.
Crosetti, ss	4	1	2	4	1	0
Rolfe, 3b	3	1	2	1	2	0
DiMaggio, cf	4	0	0	1	0	0
Gehrig, 1b	4	2	2	7	0	0
Dickey, c	4	0	0	8	0	0
Powell, lf	4	1	1	2	0	0
Lazzeri, 2b	4	0	0	3	4	0
Selkirk, rf	3	0	1	0	0	1
Pearson, p	4	0	2	1	2	0
Totals	34	5	10	27	11	1

Giants............ 0 0 0   1 0 0   0 1 0—2
Yankees......... 0 1 3   0 0 0   0 1 *—5

aSingled for Hubbell in eighth. bRan for Leslie in eighth. cSingled for Whitehead in ninth. Runs batted in—Gehrig 2, Rolfe, Powell, Selkirk, Terry, Ripple. Two-base hits—Crosetti, Gehrig, Pearson. Home run—Gehrig. Double play—Bartell, Whitehead and Terry. Left on bases—Yankees 7, Giants 6. Earned runs—Yankees 4, Giants 2. Struck out—By Pearson 7, by Hubbell 2. Bases on balls—Off Pearson 2, off Hubbell 1, off Gabler 1. Wild pitch—Hubbell. Hits—Off Hubbell 8 in 7 innings, off Gabler 2 in 1 inning. Losing pitcher—Hubbell. Umpires—Summers (A.L.), Pfirman (N.L.), Geisel (A.L.) and Magerkurth (N.L.). Time—2:12. Attendance—66,669.

Monday, Oct. 5—At Yankee Stadium

Giants (N.L.)	AB.	R.	H.	O.	A.	E.
Moore, lf	5	2	2	1	0	0
Bartell, ss	4	1	1	2	2	1
Terry, 1b	5	0	0	6	2	0
Ott, rf	5	1	1	1	0	1
Ripple, cf	2	1	1	2	0	0
Mancuso, c	3	0	2	14	2	0
Whitehead, 2b	4	0	1	3	4	0
Jackson, 3b	4	0	0	1	1	1
Schumacher, p	4	0	0	0	2	0
Totals	36	5	8	30	13	3

Yankees (A.L.)	AB.	R.	H.	O.	A.	E.
Crosetti, ss	5	0	0	2	3	1
Rolfe, 3b	5	0	2	3	1	0
DiMaggio, cf	4	0	1	4	0	0
Gehrig, 1b	4	0	1	5	1	0
Dickey, c	5	0	1	8	0	0
bSeeds	0	0	0	0	0	0
Selkirk, rf	4	2	2	2	0	0
Powell, lf	4	1	1	2	0	0
Lazzeri, 2b	3	1	1	3	1	0
Ruffing, p	1	0	0	1	2	0
aJohnson	1	0	0	0	0	0
Malone, p	1	0	1	0	2	0
Totals	37	4	10	30	10	1

Giants............ 3 0 0   0 0 1   0 0 0   1—5
Yankees......... 0 1 1   0 0 2   0 0 0   0—4

aStruck out for Ruffing in sixth. bRan for Dickey in tenth. Runs batted in—Bartell, Terry, Ripple, Whitehead, Crosetti, Selkirk, Lazzeri. Two-base hits—Moore 2, Bartell, Mancuso, DiMaggio. Home run—Selkirk. Sacrifice hits—Bartell, Mancuso. Double plays—Schumacher, Terry and Mancuso; Bartell, Whitehead and Terry; Mancuso and Whitehead; Crosetti, Lazzeri and Gehrig. Left on bases—Yankees 9, Giants 5. Earned runs—Giants 4, Yankees 3. Struck out—By Schumacher 10, by Ruffing 7, by Malone 1. Bases on balls—Off Schumacher 6, off Ruffing 1, off Malone 1. Wild pitch—Schumacher. Hits—Off Ruffing 7 in 6 innings, off Malone 1 in 4 innings. Losing pitcher—Malone. Umpires—Pfirman (N.L.), Geisel (A.L.), Magerkurth (N.L.) and Summers (A.L.). Time—2:45. Attendance—50,024.

Tuesday, October 6—At Polo Grounds

Yankees (A.L.)	AB.	R.	H.	O.	A.	E.
Crosetti, ss	4	0	0	0	1	0
Rolfe, 3b	6	1	3	3	2	1
DiMaggio, cf	6	1	3	2	0	1
Gehrig, 1b	5	1	1	10	0	0
Dickey, c	5	2	0	3	0	0
Selkirk, rf	5	2	2	3	0	0
Powell, lf	5	3	3	3	0	0
Lazzeri, 2b	4	2	3	3	5	0
Gomez, p	3	0	1	0	3	0
Murphy, p	2	1	1	0	0	0
Totals	45	13	17	27	11	2

Giants (N.L.)	AB.	R.	H.	O.	A.	E.
Moore, lf	5	2	2	2	0	0
Bartell, ss	3	2	2	0	2	0
Terry, 1b	4	0	1	6	0	0
Leiber, cf	2	0	0	6	0	0
Mayo, 3b	1	0	0	0	0	0
Ott, rf	4	1	2	3	0	0
Mancuso, c	3	0	0	4	0	0
aLeslie	1	0	0	0	0	0
Danning, c	1	0	0	3	0	1
Whitehead, 2b	3	0	0	1	2	0
bRipple, cf	0	0	0	1	0	0
Jackson, 3b	3	0	1	0	0	0
cKoenig, 2b	1	0	0	1	0	0
Fitzsimmons, p	1	0	0	0	1	0
Castleman, p	2	0	1	0	0	0
dDavis	1	0	0	0	0	0
Coffman, p	0	0	0	0	0	0
Gumbert, p	0	0	0	0	0	0
Totals	35	5	9	27	5	1

Yankees......... 0 2 1   2 0 0   0 1 7—13
Giants............ 2 0 0   0 1 0   1 1 0— 5

aFouled out for Mancuso in seventh. bWalked for Whitehead in seventh. cFanned for Jackson in seventh. dFlied out for Castleman in eighth. Runs batted in—Powell 4, Rolfe 2, Crosetti, DiMaggio, Gehrig, Lazzeri, Gomez, Murphy, Ott 3, Moore, Terry. Two-base hits—Bartell, Ott. Three-base hit—Selkirk. Home runs—Moore, Ott, Powell. Sacrifice hits—Terry, Leiber. Left on bases—Yankees

11, Giants 10. Earned runs—Yankees 13, Giants 5. Struck out—By Gomez 1, by Murphy 1, by Fitzsimmons 1, by Castleman 5, by Gumbert 1. Bases on balls—Off Gomez 4, off Murphy 1, off Castleman 2, off Gumbert 3, off Coffman 1. Hits—Off Gomez 8 in 6⅓ innings, off Murphy 1 in 2⅔ innings, off Fitzsimmons 9 in 3⅔ innings, off Castleman 3 in 4⅓ innings, off Coffman 3 in 0 inning (pitched to five batters in ninth), off Gumbert 2 in 1 inning. Winning pitcher—Gomez. Losing pitcher—Fitzsimmons. Umpires—Geisel (A.L.), Magerkurth (N.L.), Summers (A.L.) and Pfirman (N.L.). Time—2:50. Attendance—38,427.

SERIES OF 1937

	W.	L.	Pct.
New York A. L.	4	1	.800
New York N. L.	1	4	.200

Despite the fact that the Giants won one game from the Yankees in 1937, when the two New York clubs met for the fifth time and the second successive year, the victory of Joe McCarthy's troupe was the easiest ever gained by the American League, with the possible exception of 1932, when the Yanks buried the Cubs four straight under an avalanche of hits and runs. After winning three successive games by scores of 8 to 1, 8 to 1 and 5 to 1, the Yankees dropped a game to the Giant ace, Carl Hubbell, 7 to 3, and then wound up the Series with a 4 to 2 victory. While the Yankees hit only .249 against .237 for the Giants, the American Leaguers made their 42 hits good for 68 bases, getting six doubles, four triples and four homers in the five games.

By scoring the one-sided victory, the Yankees became the first club to win six world championships, breaking a tie with the Athletics. It also gave them a run of 20 victories out of 23 games since they started their great World Series drive in 1927.

The Yankees again won the pennant in one of the American League's typical one-sided races, defeating Detroit by 13 games. The Giants, with Johnny McCarthy replacing the veteran leader, Bill Terry, at first base, again had to come from behind in September to win, beating out the Cubs by three games.

Hubbell again had a splendid season for the Giants, winning 22 games and losing eight. The big disappointment came for Giant fans when the great Carl was knocked out during a seven-run broadside by the Yankees in the sixth inning of the first game. A freak of the session was that the winning Yankee pitcher, the weak-hitting Vernon Gomez, walked twice in the big frame. In the second game, the Yankees ganged up on Cliff Melton, a 20-game winner in his freshman year. In the third game, Monte Pearson, who was relieved by Johnny Murphy with two out in the ninth, won an impressive five-hit decision over Hal Schumacher.

Hubbell captured the fourth game for the Polo Grounders when the Giants cuffed Bump Hadley for six runs in the second inning. The Yanks then wound it up with Gomez defeating Melton, Al Smith and Don Brennan. The Giants outhit the Yanks, 10 to 8, in the final clash, but McCarthy's great team cashed in heavily on home runs by Joe DiMaggio and Myril Hoag. Gomez' second victory enabled him to tie the World Series record of the earlier famous Yankee southpaw, Herb Pennock, five victories against no defeats.

Tony Lazzeri, playing his sixth and last

COMPOSITE BATTING AVERAGES
New York Yankees

Player-Position	G.	AB.	R.	H.	2B.	3B.	HR.	RBI.	BA.
Malone, p	2	1	0	1	0	0	0	0	1.000
Pearson, p	1	4	0	2	1	0	0	0	.500
Murphy, p	1	2	1	1	0	0	0	1	.500
Powell, lf	6	22	8	10	1	0	1	5	.455
Rolfe, 3b	6	25	5	10	0	0	0	4	.400
DiMaggio, cf	6	26	3	9	3	0	0	3	.346
Selkirk, rf	6	24	6	8	0	1	2	3	.333
Gehrig, 1b	6	24	5	7	1	0	2	7	.292
Crosetti, ss	6	26	5	7	2	0	0	3	.269
Lazzeri, 2b	6	20	4	5	0	0	1	7	.250
Gomez, p	2	8	1	2	0	0	0	3	.250
Dickey, c	6	25	5	3	0	0	1	5	.120
Ruffing, p-ph	3	5	0	0	0	0	0	0	.000
Johnson, pr-ph	2	1	0	0	0	0	0	0	.000
Hadley, p	1	2	0	0	0	0	0	0	.000
Seeds, pr	1	0	0	0	0	0	0	0	.000
Totals	6	215	43	65	8	1	7	41	.302

New York Giants

Player-Position	G.	AB.	R.	H.	2B.	3B.	HR.	RBI.	BA.
Leslie, ph	3	3	0	2	0	0	0	0	.667
Castleman, p	1	2	0	1	0	0	0	0	.500
Fitzsimmons, p	2	4	0	2	0	0	0	0	.500
Davis, ph-pr	4	2	2	1	0	0	0	0	.500
Bartell, ss	6	21	5	8	3	0	1	3	.381
Hubbell, p	2	6	0	2	0	0	0	1	.333
Koenig, ph-2b	3	3	0	1	0	0	0	0	.333
Ripple, cf-ph	5	12	2	4	0	0	1	3	.333
Ott, rf	6	23	4	7	2	0	1	3	.304
Mancuso, c	6	19	3	5	2	0	0	1	.263
Terry, 1b	6	25	1	6	0	0	0	5	.240
Moore, lf	6	28	4	6	2	0	0	1	.214
Jackson, 3b	6	21	1	4	0	0	0	1	.190
Whitehead, 2b	6	21	1	1	0	0	0	2	.048
Leiber, cf	2	6	0	0	0	0	0	0	.000
Schumacher, p	2	4	0	0	0	0	0	0	.000
Smith, p	1	0	0	0	0	0	0	0	.000
Coffman, p	2	0	0	0	0	0	0	0	.000
Gabler, p	2	0	0	0	0	0	0	0	.000
Danning, ph-c	2	2	0	0	0	0	0	0	.000
Gumbert, p	2	0	0	0	0	0	0	0	.000
Mayo, 3b	1	1	0	0	0	0	0	0	.000
Totals	6	203	23	50	9	0	4	20	.246

COMPOSITE PITCHING AVERAGES
New York Yankees

Pitcher	G.	IP.	H.	R.	E.	SO.	BB.	W.	L.	ERA.
Hadley	1	8	10	1	1	2	1	1	0	1.12
Malone	2	5	2	1	1	2	1	0	1	1.80
Pearson	1	9	7	2	2	7	2	1	0	2.00
Murphy	1	2⅔	1	1	1	1	0	0	0	3.38
Ruffing	2	14	16	10	7	12	5	0	1	4.50
Gomez	2	15⅓	14	8	8	9	11	2	0	4.70
Totals	6	54	50	23	20	33	21	4	2	3.33

New York Giants

Pitcher	G.	IP.	H.	R.	E.	SO.	BB.	W.	L.	ERA.
Castleman	1	4⅓	3	1	1	5	2	0	0	2.08
Hubbell	2	16	15	5	4	10	2	1	1	2.25
Schum'er	2	12	13	9	7	11	10	1	1	5.25
Fitzsimmons	2	11⅔	13	7	7	6	2	0	2	5.40
Gabler	2	5	7	4	4	0	4	0	0	7.20
Coffman	2	1⅓	5	6	6	1	1	0	0	32.40
Gumbert	2	2	7	8	8	2	4	0	0	36.00
Smith	1	⅓	2	3	3	0	1	0	0	81.00
Totals	6	53	65	43	40	35	26	2	4	6.79

1937 WORLD SERIES

World Series with the Yanks, made it a good one, leading both teams at bat with an average of .400, his six hits including a homer and a triple. Hoag, substituting for Tommy Henrich, injured earlier in the season, had a fine Series. Lou Gehrig, handicapped by a bad case of lumbago, hit .294, his five hits including a double, triple and homer. The round-tripper, made off Hubbell in the Giants' lone victory, was Lou's tenth and last in World Series play. Joe Moore, the Giants' left fielder and leadoff man, did the best work for the Terry troupe, getting nine hits and batting .391.

Wed., Oct. 6—At Yankee Stadium

Giants (N.L.)	AB.	R.	H.	O.	A.	E.
Moore, lf	4	0	2	4	0	0
Bartell, ss	4	0	1	1	2	1
Ott, 3b	4	0	0	1	2	0
Leiber, cf	4	0	0	3	0	0
Ripple, rf	3	1	1	2	0	0
McCarthy, 1b	4	0	1	8	0	0
Mancuso, c	3	0	0	4	1	0
Whitehead, 2b	3	0	1	1	4	1
Hubbell, p	2	0	0	0	1	0
Gumbert, p	0	0	0	0	0	0
Coffman, p	0	0	0	0	0	0
aBerger	1	0	0	0	0	0
Smith, p	0	0	0	0	0	0
Totals	32	1	6	24	10	2

Yankees (A.L.)	AB.	R.	H.	O.	A.	E.
Crosetti, ss	4	1	1	0	2	0
Rolfe, 3b	4	1	1	0	0	0
DiMaggio, cf	4	0	2	4	0	0
Gehrig, 1b	2	1	0	9	0	0
Dickey, c	3	1	1	3	0	0
Hoag, lf	4	1	0	5	0	0
Selkirk, rf	4	1	1	3	0	0
Lazzeri, 2b	4	1	1	3	2	0
Gomez, p	2	1	0	0	2	0
Totals	31	8	7	27	6	0

Giants.................. 0 0 0   0 1 0   0 0 0—1
Yankees................. 0 0 0   0 0 7   0 1 *—8

aFlied out for Coffman in eighth. Runs batted in—Rolfe, DiMaggio 2, Dickey, Selkirk 2, Lazzeri, Mancuso. Two-base hit—Whitehead. Home run—Lazzeri. Double plays—Crosetti, Lazzeri and Gehrig; Ott, Whitehead and McCarthy. Left on bases—Yankees 6, Giants 5. Earned runs—Yankees 5, Giants 1. Struck out—By Gomez 2, by Hubbell 3. Bases on balls—Off Gomez 1, off Hubbell 3, off Coffman 4. Hits—Off Hubbell 6 in 5⅓ innings, off Gumbert 0 in 0 inning (pitched to one batter in sixth), off Coffman 0 in 1⅔ innings, off Smith 0 in 1 inning. Losing pitcher—Hubbell. Umpires—Ormsby (A.L.), Barr (N.L.), Basil (A.L.) and Stewart (N.L.). Time—2:20. Attendance—60,573.

Thursday, Oct. 7—At Yankee Stadium

Giants (N.L.)	AB.	R.	H.	O.	A.	E.
Moore, lf	5	0	2	2	0	0
Bartell, ss	4	1	2	3	5	0
Ott, 3b	4	0	1	2	1	0
Ripple, rf	4	0	0	0	0	0
McCarthy, 1b	4	0	0	8	1	0
Chiozza, cf	4	0	1	3	0	0
Mancuso, c	4	0	0	4	0	0
Whitehead, 2b	3	0	1	2	3	0
Melton, p	1	0	0	0	0	0
Gumbert, p	0	0	0	0	0	0
Coffman, p	1	0	0	0	1	0
aLeslie	0	0	0	0	0	0
Totals	34	1	7	24	11	0

Yankees (A.L.)	AB.	R.	H.	O.	A.	E.
Crosetti, ss	5	0	0	1	4	0
Rolfe, 3b	5	0	0	0	3	0
DiMaggio, cf	4	1	2	4	0	0
Gehrig, 1b	2	1	0	11	0	0
Dickey, c	4	1	2	8	0	0
Hoag, lf	4	2	1	2	0	0
Selkirk, rf	4	2	2	1	0	0
Lazzeri, 2b	3	1	2	0	2	0
Ruffing, p	4	0	2	0	2	0
Totals	35	8	12	27	11	0

Giants.................. 1 0 0   0 0 0   0 0 0—1
Yankees................. 0 0 0   0 2 4   2 0 *—8

aWalked for Coffman in ninth. Runs batted in—Dickey, Hoag, Selkirk 3, Ruffing 3, Ott. Two-base hits—Hoag, Selkirk, Ruffing, Moore, Bartell. Double play—Bartell, Whitehead and McCarthy. Left on bases—Giants 9, Yankees 6. Earned runs—Yankees 8, Giants 1. Struck out—By Ruffing 8, by Melton 2, by Gumbert 1, by Coffman 1. Bases on balls—Off Ruffing 3, off Melton 1, off Gumbert 1, off Coffman 1. Hits—Off Melton 6 in 4 innings, off Gumbert 4 in 1⅓ innings, off Coffman 2 in 2⅔ innings. Losing pitcher—Melton. Umpires—Barr (N.L.), Basil (A.L.), Stewart (N.L.) and Ormsby (A.L.). Time—2:11. Attendance—57,675.

Friday, October 8—At Polo Grounds

Yankees (A.L.)	AB.	R.	H.	O.	A.	E.
Crosetti, ss	4	0	0	1	7	0
Rolfe, 3b	4	1	2	1	1	0
DiMaggio, cf	5	0	1	5	0	0
Gehrig, 1b	5	1	1	12	0	0
Dickey, c	5	1	1	5	0	0
Selkirk, rf	4	2	1	0	0	0
Hoag, lf	4	0	2	0	0	0
Lazzeri, 2b	2	0	1	3	3	0
Pearson, p	3	0	0	0	0	0
Murphy, p	0	0	0	0	0	0
Totals	36	5	9	27	11	0

Giants (N.L.)	AB.	R.	H.	O.	A.	E.
Moore, lf	4	0	1	2	0	0
Bartell, ss	4	0	0	3	2	0
Ott, 3b	4	0	1	1	3	0
Ripple, rf	4	1	1	5	0	0
McCarthy, 1b	3	0	1	7	0	2
Chiozza, cf	3	0	1	3	0	1
Danning, c	4	0	0	5	0	0
Whitehead, 2b	3	0	0	1	4	0
Schumacher, p	1	0	0	0	1	0
aBerger	1	0	0	0	0	0
Melton, p	0	0	0	0	0	1
bLeslie	1	0	0	0	0	0
Brennan, p	0	0	0	0	0	0
Totals	32	1	5	27	10	4

Yankees................. 0 1 2   1 1 0   0 0 0—5
Giants.................. 0 0 0   0 0 0   1 0 0—1

aStruck out for Schumacher in sixth. bFouled out for Melton in eighth. Runs batted in—Gehrig, Dickey, Selkirk, Lazzeri, McCarthy. Two-base hits—Rolfe 2, McCarthy. Three-base hit—Dickey. Sacrifice hit—Hoag. Double play—Whitehead, Bartell and McCarthy. Left on bases—Yankees 11, Giants 6. Earned runs—Yankees 4, Giants 1. Struck out—By Pearson 4, by Schumacher 3. Bases on balls—Off Pearson 2, off Schumacher 4, off Melton 2. Wild pitch—Schumacher. Hits—Off Pearson 5 in 8⅔ innings, off Murphy 0 in ⅓ inning, off Schumacher 9 in 6 innings, off Melton 0 in 2 innings, off Brennan 0 in 1 inning. Winning pitcher—Pearson. Losing pitcher—Schumacher. Umpires—Basil (A.L.), Stewart (N.L.), Ormsby (A.L.) and Barr (N.L.). Time—2:07. Attendance—37,385.

Saturday, Oct. 9—At Polo Grounds

Yankees (A.L.)	AB.	R.	H.	O.	A.	E.
Crosetti, ss	4	1	0	2	3	0
Rolfe, 3b	4	1	2	0	2	0
DiMaggio, cf	4	0	0	2	0	0
Gehrig, 1b	4	1	1	10	0	0
Dickey, c	4	0	0	3	1	0
Hoag, lf	4	0	2	3	0	0
Selkirk, rf	3	0	0	0	0	0
Lazzeri, 2b	3	0	1	4	4	0
Hadley, p	0	0	0	0	0	0
Andrews, p	2	0	0	0	1	0
aPowell	1	0	0	0	0	0
Wicker, p	0	0	0	0	0	0
Totals	33	3	6	24	11	0

Giants (N.L.)	AB.	R.	H.	O.	A.	E.
Moore, lf	5	1	1	1	0	0
Bartell, ss	5	1	1	3	2	2
Ott, 3b	5	0	1	1	0	1
Ripple, rf	2	0	1	3	0	0
Leiber, cf	3	2	2	3	0	0
McCarthy, 1b	4	1	2	9	0	0
Danning, c	4	0	3	4	0	0
Whitehead, 2b	3	1	1	3	5	0
Hubbell, p	4	1	0	0	2	0
Totals	35	7	12	27	9	3

Yankees .... 1 0 1 0 0 0 0 0 1—3
Giants .... 0 6 0 0 0 0 1 0 *—7

aFanned for Andrews in eighth. Runs batted in—Moore, Bartell, Leiber 2, Danning 2, Hubbell, DiMaggio, Gehrig. Two-base hit—Danning. Three-base hit—Rolfe. Home run—Gehrig. Stolen base—Whitehead. Double plays—Whitehead and Bartell; Hubbell, Whitehead and McCarthy. Left on bases—Giants 8, Yankees 4. Earned runs—Giants 7, Yankees 2. Struck out—By Hubbell 4, by Andrews 1. Bases on balls—Off Hubbell 1, off Andrews 4. Hits—Off Hadley 6 in 1½ innings, off Andrews 6 in 5⅔ innings, off Wicker 0 in 1 inning. Losing pitcher—Hadley. Umpires—Stewart (N.L.), Ormsby (A.L.), Barr (N.L.) and Basil (A.L.). Time—1:57. Attendance—44,293.

Sunday, Oct. 10—At Polo Grounds

Yankees (A.L.)	AB.	R.	H.	O.	A.	E.
Crosetti, ss	4	0	0	2	1	0
Rolfe, 3b	3	0	1	1	0	0
DiMaggio, cf	5	1	1	3	0	0
Gehrig, 1b	4	0	2	8	1	0
Dickey, c	3	0	0	7	0	0
Hoag, lf	4	1	1	1	0	0
Selkirk, rf	4	0	1	3	0	0
Lazzeri, 2b	3	1	1	1	5	0
Gomez, p	4	1	1	1	0	0
Totals	34	4	8	27	8	0

Giants (N.L.)	AB.	R.	H.	O.	A.	E.
Moore, lf	5	0	3	4	0	0
Bartell, ss	4	1	1	3	3	0
Ott, 3b	3	0	1	1	0	3
Ripple, rf	4	0	2	1	0	0
Leiber, cf	4	0	2	1	0	0
McCarthy, 1b	4	0	0	6	0	0
Danning, c	4	0	0	11	1	0
Whitehead, 2b	4	0	1	1	1	0
Melton, p	2	0	0	0	0	0
aRyan	1	0	0	0	0	0
Smith, p	0	0	0	0	1	0
bMancuso	1	0	0	0	0	0
Brennan, p	0	0	0	0	0	0
cBerger	1	0	0	0	0	0
Totals	36	2	10	27	6	0

Yankees .... 0 1 1 0 2 0 0 0 0—4
Giants .... 0 0 2 0 0 0 0 0 0—2

aStruck out for Melton in fifth. bFlied out for Smith in seventh. cGrounded out for Brennan in ninth. Runs batted in—DiMaggio, Hoag, Ott 2, Gomez, Gehrig. Two-base hits—Whitehead, Gehrig. Three-base hits—Gehrig, Lazzeri. Home runs—DiMaggio, Hoag, Ott. Sacrifice hit—Rolfe. Double play—Gehrig, unassisted. Left on bases—Yankees 9, Giants 8. Earned runs—Yankees 4, Giants 2. Struck out—By Gomez 6, by Melton 5, by Smith 1, by Brennan 1. Bases on balls—Off Gomez 1, off Melton 3, off Brennan 1. Hit by pitcher—By Smith (Lazzeri). Wild pitch—Melton. Hits—Off Melton 6 in 5 innings, off Smith 1 in 2 innings, off Brennan 1 in 2 innings. Losing pitcher—Melton. Umpires—Ormsby (A.L.), Barr (N.L.), Basil (A.L.) and Stewart (N.L.). Time—2:06. Attendance—38,216.

COMPOSITE BATTING AVERAGES
New York Yankees

Player-Position	G.	AB.	R.	H.	2B.	3B.	HR.	RBI.	BA.
Ruffing, p	1	4	0	2	1	0	0	3	.500
Lazzeri, 2b	5	15	3	6	0	1	1	2	.400
Hoag, lf	5	20	4	6	1	0	1	2	.300
Rolfe, 3b	5	20	3	6	2	1	0	1	.300
Gehrig, 1b	5	17	4	5	1	1	1	3	.294
DiMaggio, cf	5	22	2	6	0	0	1	4	.273
Selkirk, rf	5	19	5	5	1	0	0	6	.263
Dickey, c	5	19	3	4	0	1	0	3	.211
Gomez, p	2	6	2	1	0	0	0	1	.167
Crosetti, ss	5	21	2	1	0	0	0	0	.048
Pearson, p	1	3	0	0	0	0	0	0	.000
Murphy, p	1	0	0	0	0	0	0	0	.000
Hadley, p	1	0	0	0	0	0	0	0	.000
Andrews, p	1	2	0	0	0	0	0	0	.000
Powell, ph	1	1	0	0	0	0	0	0	.000
Wicker, p	1	0	0	0	0	0	0	0	.000
Totals	5	169	28	42	6	4	4	25	.249

New York Giants

Player-Position	G.	AB.	R.	H.	2B.	3B.	HR.	RBI.	BA.
Moore, lf	5	23	1	9	1	0	0	1	.391
Leiber, cf	3	11	2	4	0	0	0	2	.364
Ripple, rf	5	17	2	5	0	0	0	0	.294
Chiozza, cf	2	7	0	2	0	0	0	0	.286
Whitehead, 2b	5	16	1	4	2	0	0	0	.250
Danning, c	3	12	0	3	1	0	0	2	.250
Bartell, ss	5	21	3	5	1	0	0	1	.238
McCarthy, 1b	5	19	1	4	1	0	0	1	.211
Ott, 3b	5	20	1	4	0	0	1	3	.200
Mancuso, c-ph	3	8	0	0	0	0	0	1	.000
Hubbell, p	2	6	1	0	0	0	0	1	.000
Gumbert, p	2	0	0	0	0	0	0	0	.000
Coffman, p	2	0	0	0	0	0	0	0	.000
Berger, ph	3	0	0	0	0	0	0	0	.000
Smith, p	2	0	0	0	0	0	0	0	.000
Melton, p	3	2	0	0	0	0	0	0	.000
Leslie, ph	2	1	0	0	0	0	0	0	.000
Schumacher, p	1	1	0	0	0	0	0	0	.000
Brennan, p	2	1	0	0	0	0	0	0	.000
Ryan, ph	1	1	0	0	0	0	0	0	.000
Totals	5	169	12	40	6	0	1	12	.237

COMPOSITE PITCHING AVERAGES
New York Yankees

Pitcher	G.	IP.	H.	R.	E.	SO.	BB.	W.	L.	ERA.
Murphy	1	⅓	0	0	0	0	0	0	0	0.00
Wicker	1	1	0	0	0	0	0	0	0	0.00
Ruffing	1	9	7	1	1	8	3	1	0	1.00
Pearson	1	8⅔	5	1	1	4	2	1	0	1.04
Gomez	2	18	16	3	3	8	2	2	0	1.50
Andrews	1	5⅔	6	2	2	1	4	0	0	3.18
Hadley	1	1⅓	6	5	5	0	0	0	1	33.75
Totals	5	44	40	12	12	21	11	4	1	2.45

1938 WORLD SERIES

Pitcher	G.	IP.	H.	R.	E.	SO.	BB.	W.	L.	ERA.
New York Giants										
Brennan	2	3	1	0	0	1	1	0	0	0.00
Smith	2	3	2	1	1	1	0	0	0	3.00
Hubbell	2	14½	12	10	6	7	4	1	1	3.77
Coffman	2	4⅓	2	2	2	1	5	0	0	4.15
Melton	3	11	12	6	6	7	6	0	2	4.91
Schum'er	1	6	9	5	4	3	4	0	1	6.00
Gumbert	2	1⅓	4	4	4	1	1	0	0	27.00
Totals	5	43	42	28	23	21	21	1	4	4.81

SERIES OF 1938

	W.	L.	Pct.
New York A. L.	4	0	1.000
Chicago N. L.	0	4	.000

Joe McCarthy, Yankee pilot, winning his fourth American League and third straight championship in 1938, took a double revenge on his former National League club, the Cubs, in the World Series, poking the snouts of the Bruins into the dirt for the second time in four straight games. It gave McCarthy the distinction of being the first manager to win three successive world championships and gave him eight straight World Series victories against Chicago, his former team, led in 1938 by Gabby Hartnett.

An ill omen of the tragedy that awaited Lou Gehrig, great first baseman and captain of the Yankees, was that the victory was achieved with little aid from his once lethal bat. In the four games he did not get an extra-base hit or drive in a run, his four singles standing out in sharp contrast to nine hits for 19 bases and eight runs batted in in the four-game Series with the Cubs only six years before. However, Lou closed his World Series career with the fine average of .361 for 34 games in seven sets of battles.

The Yankees of 1938 were one of McCarthy's best clubs, winning 99 games. The club had a nine and one-half game edge on the Red Sox and loafed all through September. The Cubs, on the other hand, won their race with a great September drive, and, aided by a Pirate collapse, managed to win the National League flag with 89 victories and the low percentage of .586.

While the Yankees did not overwhelm the Cubs at bat as completely as in 1932, hitting .274 against .243 for Chicago, the American Leaguers outscored the Cubs, 22 runs to nine. Bill Dickey, Yankee catcher who hit .438 against the Cubs in 1932, his first World Series, came back in '38 with a .400 average. Joe Gordon, in his freshman year with the Bombers, also hit .400 and drove in six runs.

The Yankee pitching was so good that McCarthy had to make only one mound change and that was occasioned by the use of a pinch-hitter for Vernon Gomez in the second game. Red Ruffing won two well-pitched games, taking the opener from Bill Lee in Chicago, 3 to 1, and the closing game at Yankee Stadium from the General and a succession of relief men, 8 to 3.

Gomez was credited with the Yanks' 6 to 3 victory in the second game, enabling him to tie Chief Bender and Waite Hoyt with six triumphs apiece in classic competition. However, El Goofo was rapped for nine hits in his seven innings on the mound and was behind, 3 to 2, when George Selkirk opened the eighth with a single. After Myril Hoag batted for Gomez and forced Selkirk, Crosetti came through with his circuit clout to give Lefty his triumph. DiMaggio's homer iced it in the ninth.

Monte Pearson hurled the third game for the Yankees, and turned in a five-hit, 5 to 2 performance.

Lee, whose 22 victories helped the Cubs win the National League pennant, was Hartnett's biggest disappointment, losing both of his starts. The other Chicago defeats went to Dizzy Dean and Clay Bryant. His speed gone, Dizzy got by with his nothing ball for seven innings in the second game, and seemed on the point of a spectacular victory when Frank Crosetti and Joe DiMaggio sank him with a pair of two-run homers in the eighth and ninth. Most of the Cub hitting was done by three players, Stan Hack, Joe Marty and Phil Cavarretta. The first-named batted .471; Marty hit an even .500 for three games, and Cavarretta, .462. It was the sixth straight World Series setback for the Cubs. The box scores:

Wednesday, October 5—At Chicago

New York (A.L.)	AB.	R.	H.	O.	A.	E.
Crosetti, ss	4	0	1	4	6	0
Rolfe, 3b	5	0	1	0	1	0
Henrich, rf	4	1	2	0	0	1
DiMaggio, cf	4	0	0	2	0	0
Gehrig, 1b	3	1	1	10	0	0
Dickey, c	4	1	4	6	3	0
Selkirk, lf	4	0	1	1	0	0
Gordon, 2b	4	0	2	4	2	0
Ruffing, p	3	0	0	0	1	0
Totals	35	3	12	27	13	1

Chicago (N.L.)	AB.	R.	H.	O.	A.	E.
Hack, 3b	4	0	3	1	1	0
Herman, 2b	4	0	1	2	5	1
Demaree, lf	4	0	0	2	0	0
Cavarretta, rf	4	0	2	1	1	0
Reynolds, cf	4	0	0	3	0	0
Hartnett, c	3	0	1	6	2	0
Collins, 1b	3	1	2	10	1	0
Jurges, ss	3	0	1	1	3	0
Lee, p	2	0	0	1	0	0
aO'Dea	1	0	0	0	0	0
Russell, p	0	0	0	0	0	0
Totals	32	1	9	27	13	1

New York .... 0 2 0   0 0 0   1 0 0—3
Chicago .... 0 0 1   0 0 0   0 0 0—1

aForced runner for Lee in eighth. Runs batted in—Dickey, Selkirk, Gordon, Hack. Two-base hits—Crosetti, Henrich, Gordon. Three-base hit—Hartnett. Sacrifice hit—Ruffing. Stolen base—Dickey. Double plays—Crosetti and Gehrig; Gordon, Crosetti and Gehrig; Jurges, Herman and Collins; Collins, unassisted. Left on bases—New

York 8, Chicago 4. Earned runs—New York 3, Chicago 1. Struck out—By Ruffing 5, by Lee 6. Base on balls—Off Lee 1. Hit by pitcher—By Lee (Crosetti). Hits—Off Lee 11 in 8 innings, off Russell 1 in 1 inning. Losing pitcher—Lee. Umpires—Moran (N.L.), Kolls (A.L.), Sears (N.L.) and Hubbard (A.L.). Time—1:53. Attendance—43,642.

Thursday, October 6—At Chicago

New York (A.L.)	AB.	R.	H.	O.	A.	E.
Crosetti, ss	4	1	1	5	3	0
Rolfe, 3b	4	0	0	0	2	2
Henrich, rf	4	1	1	2	0	0
DiMaggio, cf	4	2	2	4	0	0
Gehrig, 1b	3	1	1	6	0	0
Dickey, c	4	0	0	6	2	0
Selkirk, lf	3	0	1	0	0	0
Powell, lf	0	0	0	0	0	0
Gordon, 2b	4	0	1	4	3	0
Gomez, p	2	0	0	0	1	0
aHoag	1	1	0	0	0	0
Murphy, p	0	0	0	0	0	0
Totals	33	6	7	27	11	2

Chicago (N.L.)	AB.	R.	H.	O.	A.	E.
Hack, 3b	5	2	2	0	3	0
Herman, 2b	4	1	1	5	5	0
Demaree, rf	3	0	1	1	0	0
Marty, cf	4	0	3	2	0	0
Reynolds, lf	3	0	0	4	0	0
Hartnett, c	4	0	0	5	0	0
Collins, 1b	4	0	1	10	0	0
Jurges, ss	3	0	0	4	1	0
Dean, p	3	0	2	0	2	0
French, p	0	0	0	1	0	0
bCavarretta	1	0	1	0	0	0
Totals	34	3	11	27	11	0

New York........ 0 2 0   0 0 0   0 2 2—6
Chicago......... 1 0 2   0 0 0   0 0 0—3

aForced runner for Gomez in eighth. bSingled for French in ninth. Runs batted in—Marty 3, Crosetti 2, DiMaggio 2, Gordon 2. Two-base hits—Marty, Gordon. Home runs—Crosetti, DiMaggio. Sacrifice hit—Demaree. Double plays—Crosetti, Gordon and Gehrig; Gordon, Crosetti and Gehrig; Herman, Jurges and Collins. Left on bases—Chicago 7, New York 2. Earned runs—New York 6, Chicago 3. Struck out—By Gomez 5, by Murphy 1, by Dean 2, by French 2. Bases on balls—Off Gomez 1, off Murphy 1, off Dean 1, off French 1. Hits—Off Gomez 9 in 7 innings, off Murphy 2 in 2 innings, off Dean 7 in 8 innings (pitched to two batters in ninth), off French 0 in 1 inning. Winning pitcher—Gomez. Losing pitcher—Dean. Umpires—Kolls (A.L.), Sears (N.L.), Hubbard (A.L.) and Moran (N.L.). Time—1:53. Attendance—42,108.

Saturday, October 8—At New York

Chicago (N.L.)	AB.	R.	H.	O.	A.	E.
Hack, 3b	3	1	1	2	0	0
Herman, 2b	3	0	0	1	1	1
Cavarretta, rf	4	0	1	2	0	0
Marty, cf	4	1	3	3	0	0
Reynolds, lf	4	0	0	0	0	0
Hartnett, c	4	0	0	3	1	0
Collins, 1b	4	0	0	8	0	0
Jurges, ss	3	0	0	5	3	0
bLazzeri	1	0	0	0	0	0
Bryant, p	2	0	0	0	0	0
Russell, p	0	0	0	0	0	0
aGalan	1	0	0	0	0	0
French, p	0	0	0	0	2	0
cO'Dea	1	0	0	0	0	0
Totals	34	2	5	24	7	1

New York (A.L.)	AB.	R.	H.	O.	A.	E.
Crosetti, ss	3	0	0	1	0	1
Rolfe, 3b	4	0	1	0	1	0
Henrich, rf	4	0	0	3	0	0
DiMaggio, cf	3	1	1	1	0	0
Gehrig, 1b	4	1	1	4	1	0
Dickey, c	3	1	1	12	0	0
Selkirk, lf	3	0	0	2	0	0
Gordon, 2b	4	1	2	2	3	1
Pearson, p	3	1	1	2	0	0
Totals	31	5	7	27	5	2

Chicago......... 0 0 0   0 1 0   0 1 0—2
New York........ 0 0 0   0 2 2   0 1 *—5

aPopped out for Russell in seventh. bGrounded out for Jurges in ninth. cFlied out for French in ninth. Runs batted in—Gordon 3, Marty 2, Rolfe, Dickey. Two-base hit—Hack. Home runs—Dickey, Gordon, Marty. Left on bases—New York 8, Chicago 7. Earned runs—New York 5, Chicago 1. Struck out—By Pearson 9, by Bryant 3. Bases on balls—Off Pearson 2, off Bryant 5, off Russell 1. Hits—Off Bryant 6 in 5⅓ innings, off Russell 0 in ⅔ inning, off French 1 in 2 innings. Losing pitcher—Bryant. Umpires—Sears (N.L.), Hubbard (A.L.), Moran (N.L.) and Kolls (A.L.). Time—1:57. Attendance—55,236.

Sunday, October 9—At New York

Chicago (N.L.)	AB.	R.	H.	O.	A.	E.
Hack, 3b	5	0	2	1	0	0
Herman, 2b	5	0	1	1	3	0
Cavarretta, rf	4	1	2	1	0	0
Marty, cf	4	0	0	2	0	0
Demaree, lf	3	1	0	3	0	0
O'Dea, c	3	1	1	5	0	0
Collins, 1b	4	0	0	10	0	0
Jurges, ss	4	0	2	1	0	1
Lee, p	1	0	0	0	0	0
aGalan	1	0	0	0	0	0
Root, p	0	0	0	0	0	0
bLazzeri	1	0	0	0	0	0
Page, p	0	0	0	0	1	0
French, p	0	0	0	0	0	0
Carleton, p	0	0	0	0	0	0
Dean, p	0	0	0	0	0	0
cReynolds	1	0	0	0	0	0
Totals	36	3	8	24	4	1

New York (A.L.)	AB.	R.	H.	O.	A.	E.
Crosetti, ss	5	0	2	6	1	0
Rolfe, 3b	5	0	1	0	0	0
Henrich, rf	4	1	1	1	0	0
DiMaggio, cf	4	1	1	3	0	0
Gehrig, 1b	4	1	1	5	2	0
Dickey, c	4	0	1	7	0	0
Hoag, lf	4	2	2	1	0	0
Gordon, 2b	3	2	1	2	4	1
Ruffing, p	3	1	1	2	3	0
Totals	36	8	11	27	10	1

Chicago......... 0 0 0   1 0 0   0 2 0—3
New York........ 0 3 0   0 0 1   0 4 *—8

aFanned for Lee in fourth. bFanned for Root in seventh. cFlied out for Dean in ninth. Runs batted in—Crosetti 4, O'Dea 2, Henrich, Hoag, Ruffing. Two-base hits—Crosetti, Hoag, Cavarretta, Jurges. Three-base hit—Crosetti. Home runs—Henrich, O'Dea. Stolen bases—Rolfe, Gordon. Left on bases—Chicago 8, New York 6. Earned runs—New York 5, Chicago 2. Struck out—By Ruffing 6, by Lee 2, by Root 1. Bases on balls—Off Ruffing 2, off Carleton 2. Wild pitches—Carleton 2. Hits—Off Lee 4 in 3 innings, off Root 3 in 3 innings, off Page 2 in 1⅓ innings, off French 0 in ⅓ inning, off Carleton 1 in 0 inning (pitched to three batters in eighth), off Dean 1 in ⅓ inning. Losing pitcher—Lee. Umpires—Hubbard (A.L.), Moran (N.L.), Kolls (A.L.) and Sears (N.L.). Time—2:11. Attendance—59,847.

COMPOSITE BATTING AVERAGES
New York Yankees

Player-Position	G.	AB.	R.	H.	2B.	3B.	HR.	RBI.	BA.
Dickey, c	4	15	2	6	0	0	1	2	.400
Gordon, 2b	4	15	3	6	2	0	1	6	.400
Hoag, ph-lf	2	5	3	2	1	0	0	1	.400
Pearson, p	1	3	1	1	0	0	0	0	.333
Gehrig, 1b	4	14	4	4	0	0	0	0	.286
DiMaggio, cf	4	15	4	4	0	0	1	2	.267
Crosetti, ss	4	16	1	4	2	1	1	6	.250
Henrich, rf	4	16	3	4	1	0	1	1	.250
Selkirk, lf	3	10	0	2	0	0	0	1	.200
Rolfe, 3b	4	18	0	3	0	0	0	1	.167
Ruffing, p	2	6	1	1	0	0	0	1	.167
Powell, lf	1	0	0	0	0	0	0	0	.000
Gomez, p	1	2	0	0	0	0	0	0	.000
Murphy, p	1	0	0	0	0	0	0	0	.000
Totals	4	135	22	37	6	1	5	21	.274

Chicago Cubs

Player-Position	G.	AB.	R.	H.	2B.	3B.	HR.	RBI.	BA.
Dean, p	2	3	0	2	0	0	0	0	.666
Marty, cf	3	12	1	6	1	0	1	5	.500
Hack, 3b	4	17	3	8	1	0	0	1	.471
Cavarretta, rf-ph	4	13	1	6	1	0	0	0	.462
Jurges, ss	4	13	0	3	1	0	0	0	.231
O'Dea, ph-c	3	5	1	1	0	0	1	2	.200
Herman, 2b	4	16	1	3	0	0	0	0	.188
Collins, 1b	4	15	1	2	0	0	0	0	.133
Demaree, lf	3	10	1	1	0	0	0	0	.100
Hartnett, c	3	11	0	1	0	1	0	0	.091
Reynolds, cf-lf-ph	4	12	0	0	0	0	0	0	.000
Lee, p	2	3	0	0	0	0	0	0	.000
Russell, p	2	0	0	0	0	0	0	0	.000
French, p	3	0	0	0	0	0	0	0	.000
Lazzeri, ph	2	2	0	0	0	0	0	0	.000
Bryant, p	1	2	0	0	0	0	0	0	.000
Galan, ph	2	2	0	0	0	0	0	0	.000
Root, p	1	0	0	0	0	0	0	0	.000
Page, p	1	0	0	0	0	0	0	0	.000
Carleton, p	1	0	0	0	0	0	0	0	.000
Totals	4	136	9	33	4	1	2	8	.243

COMPOSITE PITCHING AVERAGES
New York Yankees

Pitcher	G.	IP.	H.	R.	E.	SO.	BB.	W.	L.	ERA.
Murphy	1	2	2	0	0	1	1	0	0	0.00
Pearson	1	9	5	2	1	9	2	1	0	1.00
Ruffing	2	18	17	4	3	11	2	2	0	1.50
Gomez	1	7	9	3	3	5	1	1	0	3.86
Totals	4	36	33	9	7	26	6	4	0	1.75

Chicago Cubs

Pitcher	G.	IP.	H.	R.	E.	SO.	BB.	W.	L.	ERA.
Russell	2	1⅔	1	0	0	0	1	0	0	0.00
Lee	2	11	15	6	3	8	1	0	2	2.45
French	3	3⅓	1	1	1	2	1	0	0	2.70
Root	1	3	3	1	1	1	0	0	0	3.00
Dean	2	8⅓	8	6	6	2	1	0	1	6.48
Bryant	1	5⅓	6	4	4	3	5	0	1	6.75
Page	1	1⅓	2	2	2	0	0	0	0	13.50
Carleton	1	0	1	2	2	0	2	0	0	.....
Totals	4	34	37	22	19	16	11	0	4	5.03

SERIES OF 1939

	W.	L.	Pct.
New York A. L.	4	0	1.000
Cincinnati N. L.	0	4	.000

The Yankees made it four straight in the American League in 1939, and despite the fact that Lou Gehrig had bowed out of the New Yorkers' lineup early in the season, the Bronx Steam Roller continued flattening National League opponents as Bill McKechnie's Cincinnati Reds became the fourth straight victim of the Bombers in the World Series. The first club to win four consecutive world championships in modern competition—in fact, no other club had been able to cop more than two in succession—the Yankees gained the eighth title in their history and their fifth in four straight games over a 12-year span.

It was the old story in the American League this year. Gehrig performed in only the first eight championship games and finished the season in his sad role of non-playing captain. Babe Dahlgren succeeded Gehrig at first base, while a new young slugger from Maryland, Charlie Keller, helped replace Larrupin' Lou's old punch. The Yankee percentage mounted to .702 and the victory total to 106—17 laps ahead of the second-place Red Sox. Cincinnati repelled a late-season threat by the Cardinals and topped the Redbirds by four and one-half games.

The breaks in the Series went to the Yankees, and they took advantage of every opportunity, scoring runs on daring chances. The Series, however, was much closer than any of the other "four straight" events taken by the Yankees. Cincinnati played good ball up to near the end; after playing errorless ball to the ninth inning of the fourth game, they were guilty of four miscues in the last two frames. The team batting averages were low, .206 for the Yanks against .203 for the Reds. However, the terrific dynamite in the New York hits enabled the Bombers to score 20 runs against eight for Cincinnati. Each club banged out 27 hits, but the Yankees had seven home runs and the Reds none.

Keller, the Yankees' freshman slugger, was the Series sensation, with a real Gehrig touch. He batted .438, drove in six runs and his seven hits included three homers, a triple and a double. Frank McCormick, Red first baseman and cleanup hitter, was the only Red to live up to his promise, batting .400.

Red Ruffing entered the five-victory class by winning the opener, 2 to 1, from Derringer, Charley giving up four hits against six off Paul. The second game was a two-hit shutout by Monte Pearson, the classic of his four World Series victories. Monte duplicated the 1927 game of Herb Pennock against Pittsburgh, pitching no-hit ball until one was out in the eighth when Ernie Lombardi bashed Cincinnati's first safety. Vernon Gomez started the third game for the Yankees, but retired because of a sore arm after pitching one inning. Bump Hadley, taking over in the second, received credit for his second World Series victory in a freak 7 to 3 decision. Cincinnati outhit the Yankees, ten to five, but four of the five New York hits were homers. Johnny Murphy, the third New York pitcher, received credit for the ten-inning last game.

The Reds won their 1939 pennant largely on the pitching of Bucky Walters, the league's Most Valuable Player, and Derringer, the pair winning 27 and 25 games, respectively. However, in the Series, Walters was charged with two defeats and Derringer and Gene Thompson one each.

The final game, pitched by Derringer and Walters, left an ugly taste in the mouths of Red rooters. With Cincinnati leading, 4 to 2, New York tied it in the ninth when shortstop Billy Myers messed up a double-play ball. In the tenth, errors by Myers, Ival Goodman and Lombardi helped the rampaging Yanks score three runs, DiMaggio tallying the third as the stunned Lombardi lay prostrate a few feet from the plate. The box scores:

Wednesday, October 4—At New York

Cincinnati (N.L.)	AB.	R.	H.	O.	A.	E.
Werber, 3b	4	0	0	0	1	0
Frey, 2b	4	0	0	2	2	0
Goodman, rf	2	1	0	4	0	0
McCormick, 1b	3	0	2	9	1	0
Lombardi, c	3	0	0	7	0	0
Craft, cf	3	0	1	2	0	0
Berger, lf	3	0	0	1	0	0
Myers, ss	3	0	1	0	1	0
Derringer, p	3	0	0	1	0	0
Totals	28	1	4	*25	5	0

New York (A.L.)	AB.	R.	H.	O.	A.	E.
Crosetti, ss	4	0	0	1	7	0
Rolfe, 3b	4	0	0	1	2	0
Keller, rf	4	1	1	2	0	0
DiMaggio, cf	3	0	1	2	0	0
Dickey, c	4	0	1	4	0	0
Selkirk, lf	3	0	0	2	0	0
Gordon, 2b	3	1	1	2	4	0
Dahlgren, 1b	3	0	1	13	0	0
Ruffing, p	3	0	1	0	3	0
Totals	31	2	6	27	16	0

Cincinnati.................. 0 0 0   1 0 0   0 0 0—1
New York.................. 0 0 0   0 1 0   0 0 1—2

*One out when winning run scored. Runs batted in—Dickey, Dahlgren, McCormick. Two-base hit—Dahlgren. Tree-base hit—Keller. Stolen base—Goodman. Double plays—Rolfe, Gordon and Dahlgren; Ruffing, Crosetti, Gordon and Dahlgren; Gordon, Crosetti and Dahlgren. Left on bases—New York 5, Cincinnati 1. Earned runs—New York 2, Cincinnati 1. Struck out—By Ruffing 4, by Derringer 7. Bases on balls—Off Ruffing 1, off Derringer 1. Umpires—McGowan (A.L.), Reardon (N.L.), Summers (A.L.) and Pinelli (N.L.). Time—1:33. Attendance—58,541.

Thursday, October 5—At New York

Cincinnati (N.L.)	AB.	R.	H.	O.	A.	E.
Werber, 3b	3	0	1	0	1	0
Frey, 2b	4	0	0	2	2	0
Goodman, rf	3	0	0	1	0	0
McCormick, 1b	3	0	0	7	0	0
Lombardi, c	3	0	1	5	1	0
aBordagaray	0	0	0	0	0	0
Hershberger, c	0	0	0	0	0	0
Craft, cf	3	0	0	3	1	0
Berger, lf	3	0	0	1	0	0
Myers, ss	3	0	0	5	3	0
Walters, p	2	0	0	0	4	0
bGamble	1	0	0	0	0	0
Totals	28	0	2	24	11	0

New York (A.L.)	AB.	R.	H.	O.	A.	E.
Crosetti, ss	4	0	1	1	2	0
Rolfe, 3b	4	1	1	1	1	0
Keller, rf	4	1	2	0	0	0
DiMaggio, cf	4	0	1	4	0	0
Dickey, c	3	0	1	8	1	0
Selkirk, lf	3	0	1	3	0	0
Gordon, 2b	3	0	0	2	0	0
Dahlgren, 1b	3	2	2	8	0	0
Pearson, p	2	0	0	0	5	0
Totals	30	4	9	27	9	0

Cincinnati.................. 0 0 0   0 0 0   0 0 0—0
New York.................. 0 0 3   1 0 0   0 0 *—4

aRan for Lombardi in eighth. bFanned for Walters in ninth. Runs batted in—Crosetti, Keller, Dickey, Dahlgren. Two-base hits—Keller, Dahlgren. Home run—Dahlgren. Sacrifice hit—Pearson. Double plays—Dickey and Crosetti; Walters, Myers and McCormick. Left on bases—New York 3, Cincinnati 2. Earned runs—New York 4. Struck out—By Pearson 8, by Walters 5. Base on balls—Off Pearson 1. Umpires—Reardon (N.L.), Summers (A.L.), Pinelli (N.L.) and McGowan (A.L.). Time—1:27. Attendance—59,791.

Saturday, October 7—At Cincinnati

New York (A.L.)	AB.	R.	H.	O.	A.	E.
Crosetti, ss	4	1	0	2	2	0
Rolfe, 3b	4	1	1	0	2	0
Keller, rf	3	3	2	2	0	0
DiMaggio, cf	4	1	2	2	0	0
Dickey, c	3	1	1	5	1	0
Selkirk, lf	2	0	0	3	0	0
Gordon, 2b	4	0	0	3	5	0
Dahlgren, 1b	4	0	0	9	2	0
Gomez, p	1	0	0	0	0	0
Hadley, p	3	0	0	1	1	1
Totals	32	7	5	27	13	1

Cincinnati (N.L.)	AB.	R.	H.	O.	A.	E.
Werber, 3b	4	1	1	3	2	0
Frey, 2b	4	0	0	2	2	0
Goodman, rf	5	1	3	2	0	0
McCormick, 1b	5	0	2	9	0	0
Lombardi, c	3	0	1	5	0	0
bBordagaray	0	0	0	0	0	0
Hershberger, c	1	0	0	1	0	0
Craft, cf	4	0	0	2	0	0
Berger, lf	4	0	0	0	0	0
Myers, ss	3	1	2	1	4	0
Thompson, p	1	0	1	0	0	0
Grissom, p	0	0	0	0	0	0
aBongiovanni	1	0	0	0	0	0
Moore, p	1	0	0	0	2	0
Totals	36	3	10	27	10	0

New York.................. 2 0 2   0 3 0   0 0 0—7
Cincinnati.................. 1 2 0   0 0 0   0 0 0—3

aGrounded out for Grissom in sixth. bRan for Lombardi in seventh. Runs batted in—Keller 4, DiMaggio 2, Dickey, Werber, Goodman, Lombardi. Home runs—Keller 2, DiMaggio, Dickey. Sacrifice hit—Thompson. Double play—Rolfe, Gordon and Dahlgren. Left on bases—Cincinnati 11, New York 3. Earned runs—New York 7, Cincinnati 3. Struck out—By Gomez 1, by Hadley 2, by Thompson 3, by Moore 2. Bases on balls—Off Hadley 3, off Thompson 4, off Grissom 1. Hit by pitcher—By Hadley (Lombardi). Wild pitch—Thompson. Hits—Off Gomez 3 in 1 inning, off Hadley 7 in 8 innings, off Thompson 5 in 4⅔ innings, off Grissom 0 in 1⅓ innings, off Moore 0 in 3 innings. Winning pitcher—Hadley. Losing pitcher—Thompson. Umpires—Summers (A.L.), Pinelli (N.L.), McGowan (A.L.) and Reardon (N.L.). Time—2:01. Attendance—32,723.

1940 WORLD SERIES

Sunday, October 8—At Cincinnati

New York (A.L.)	AB.	R.	H.	O.	A.	E.
Crosetti, ss	4	1	0	2	3	0
Rolfe, 3b	4	0	0	1	3	1
Keller, rf	5	3	2	2	0	0
DiMaggio, cf	5	2	2	3	0	0
Dickey, c	5	1	1	10	0	0
Selkirk, lf	4	0	1	1	0	0
Gordon, 2b	4	0	1	0	3	0
Dahlgren, 1b	4	0	0	11	0	0
Hildebrand, p	1	0	0	0	0	0
Sundra, p	0	0	0	0	0	0
Murphy, p	2	0	0	0	3	0
Totals	38	7	7	30	12	1

Cincinnati (N.L.)	AB.	R.	H.	O.	A.	E.
Werber, 3b	5	0	2	0	1	0
Frey, 2b	5	0	0	3	4	0
Goodman, rf	5	1	2	3	1	1
McCormick, 1b	4	1	2	7	1	0
Lombardi, c	5	0	1	4	0	1
Craft, cf	1	0	0	0	0	0
Simmons, lf	4	1	1	3	0	0
Berger, lf-cf	5	0	0	4	0	0
Myers, ss	3	1	1	5	1	2
Derringer, p	2	0	1	1	0	0
aHershberger	1	0	1	0	0	0
Walters, p	1	0	0	0	0	0
Totals	41	4	11	30	8	4

New York .... 0 0 0 0 0 0 2 0 2 3—7
Cincinnati .... 0 0 0 0 0 0 3 1 0 0—4

aSingled for Derringer in seventh. Runs batted in—Keller, DiMaggio, Dickey 2, Gordon, Werber, Lombardi, Berger, Hershberger. Two-base hits—Selkirk, Goodman, McCormick, Simmons. Three-base hit—Myers. Home runs—Keller, Dickey. Sacrifice hits—Rolfe, McCormick. Left on bases—Cincinnati 9, New York 5. Earned runs—New York 4, Cincinnati 4. Struck out—By Hildebrand 3, by Sundra 2, by Murphy 2, by Derringer 2, by Walters 1. Bases on balls—Off Sundra 1, off Derringer 2, off Walters 1. Hits—Off Hildebrand 2 in 4 innings, off Sundra 4 in 2⅔ innings, off Murphy 5 in 3⅓ innings, off Derringer 3 in 7 innings, off Walters 4 in 3 innings. Winning pitcher—Murphy. Losing pitcher—Walters. Umpires—Pinelli (N.L.), McGowan (A.L.), Reardon (N.L.) and Summers (A.L.). Time—2:04. Attendance—32,794.

COMPOSITE BATTING AVERAGES
New York Yankees

Player-Position	G.	AB.	R.	H.	2B.	3B.	HR.	RBI.	BA.
Keller, rf	4	16	8	7	1	1	3	6	.438
Ruffing, p	1	3	0	1	0	0	0	0	.333
DiMaggio, cf	4	16	3	5	0	0	1	3	.313
Dickey, c	4	15	2	4	0	0	2	5	.267
Dahlgren, 1b	4	14	2	3	2	0	1	2	.214
Selkirk, lf	4	12	0	2	1	0	0	0	.167
Gordon, 2b	4	14	1	2	0	0	0	1	.143
Rolfe, 3b	4	16	2	2	0	0	0	0	.125
Crosetti, ss	4	16	2	1	0	0	0	1	.063
Pearson, p	1	2	0	0	0	0	0	0	.000
Gomez, p	1	1	0	0	0	0	0	0	.000
Hadley, p	1	3	0	0	0	0	0	0	.000
Hildebrand, p	1	1	0	0	0	0	0	0	.000
Sundra, p	1	0	0	0	0	0	0	0	.000
Murphy, p	1	2	0	0	0	0	0	0	.000
Totals	4	131	20	27	4	1	7	18	.206

Cincinnati Reds

Player-Position	G.	AB.	R.	H.	2B.	3B.	HR.	RBI.	BA.
Thompson, p	1	1	0	1	0	0	0	0	1.000
Hershberger, c-ph	3	2	0	1	0	0	0	1	.500
McCormick, 1b	4	15	1	6	1	0	0	1	.400
Goodman, rf	4	15	3	5	1	0	0	1	.333
Myers, ss	4	12	2	4	0	1	0	0	.333
Werber, 3b	4	16	1	4	0	0	2	0	.250
Simmons, lf	1	4	1	1	1	0	0	0	.250
Lombardi, c	4	14	0	3	0	0	0	2	.214
Derringer, p	2	5	0	1	0	0	0	0	.200
Craft, cf	4	11	0	1	0	0	0	0	.091
Frey, 2b	4	17	0	0	0	0	0	0	.000
Berger, lf-cf	4	15	0	0	0	0	0	1	.000
Bordagaray, pr	2	0	0	0	0	0	0	0	.000
Walters, p	2	3	0	0	0	0	0	0	.000
Gamble, ph	1	1	0	0	0	0	0	0	.000
Grissom, p	1	0	0	0	0	0	0	0	.000
Bongiovanni, ph	1	1	0	0	0	0	0	0	.000
Moore, p	1	1	0	0	0	0	0	0	.000
Totals	4	133	8	27	3	1	0	8	.203

COMPOSITE PITCHING AVERAGES
New York Yankees

Pitcher	G.	IP.	H.	R.	E.	SO.	BB.	W.	L.	ERA.
Pearson	1	9	2	0	0	8	1	1	0	0.00
Hildebrand	1	4	2	0	0	3	0	0	0	0.00
Sundra	1	2⅔	4	3	0	2	1	0	0	0.00
Ruffing	1	9	4	1	1	4	1	1	0	1.00
Hadley	1	8	7	2	2	3	1	0	0	2.25
Murphy	1	3⅓	5	1	1	2	0	1	0	2.70
Gomez	1	1	3	1	1	1	0	0	0	9.00
Totals	4	37	27	8	5	22	6	4	0	1.22

Cincinnati Reds

Pitcher	G.	IP.	H.	R.	E.	SO.	BB.	W.	L.	ERA.
Moore	1	3	0	0	0	2	0	0	0	0.00
Grissom	1	1⅓	0	0	0	0	1	0	0	0.00
Derringer	2	15⅓	9	4	4	9	3	0	1	2.35
Walters	2	11	13	9	6	6	1	0	2	4.91
Thompson	1	4⅔	5	7	7	3	4	0	1	13.50
Totals	4	35⅓	27	20	17	20	9	0	4	4.33

SERIES OF 1940

	W.	L.	Pct.
Cincinnati N. L.	4	3	.571
Detroit A. L.	3	4	.429

The Cincinnati Reds rebounded from their four straight losses to the Yankees in 1939 by defeating Detroit, led by Del Baker, in four out of seven games, giving the National League its first World Series triumph since 1934, when the Tigers lost to the St. Louis Cardinals, also in seven games. In 1940, there was a break in the usual major league procedure. The Reds won the National League flag by a comfortable 12-game margin over Brooklyn, while the Tigers, smashing the Yankee pennant trust, clinched their sixth American League flag on the next-to-last day of the season, beating Cleveland by one game and New York by two. The Tigers' average of .584 was the lowest percentage figure for a flag winner in American League history up to that time.

Three pitchers dominated the 1940 Series—Paul Derringer and Bucky Walters of the Reds and Buck Newsom of the Tigers, each winning two games.

Tommy Bridges of Detroit gained the other victory while Derringer and Newsom each lost one game. Schoolboy Rowe, who had won 16 games while losing only three during the regular season, failed in both of his starts, being knocked out in the fourth inning of the second game and in the first frame of the sixth contest.

The lead see-sawed back and forth until the final game, no team being more than one victory ahead. The Tigers got off in front in the first game, knocking out Derringer in the second inning when they scored five runs on five hits, a walk, two errors and a sacrifice, Newsom going on to a 7 to 2 win. Newsom's father, who saw the triumph, died early the next morning in the Netherland Plaza Hotel, Cincinnati's World Series headquarters.

Walters squared the Series for the Reds in the second game, yielding only three hits for a 5 to 3 verdict. Bucky got off to a shaky start, walking the first two men he faced and both scored, but the Reds rapped Rowe for a tying pair in the second inning and then went ahead in the third, when Jimmy Ripple homered with a man on base.

Walters' triumph broke a string of ten straight American League victories in World Series competition since Carl Hubbell of the Giants defeated the Yankees in 1937.

Home runs by Rudy York and Pinky Higgins in the seventh inning of the third contest broke up a pitching duel between Jim Turner and Bridges, and Detroit went on to win, 7 to 4. Turner had battled Bridges on even terms until the Tigers' four-run explosion in the seventh snapped a 1-all tie.

Derringer, who was knocked out in the opening tilt, came back in the fourth contest to set the Tigers down with five safeties, 5 to 2, and even the Series for the second time. The victory broke the jinx which had haunted Derringer's World Series efforts. With St. Louis in 1931, he had been beaten twice by the Athletics and, with the Reds, he lost the opening game of the 1939 classic as well as the '40 lidlifter.

In the best pitching performance of the Series, Newsom limited the Reds to three singles in the fifth contest for an 8 to 0 shutout to put the Tigers back in the lead. Hank Greenberg led the 13-hit Detroit attack with a homer and two singles to drive in four runs.

Walters, however, duplicated the shutout feat in the sixth game, scattering five hits to win, 4 to 0, and even the Series again. Rowe was kayoed during a two-run Red uprising in the first inning.

Newsom, returning to the mound after only one day's rest, hurled a superb game in the final contest, limiting the Reds to seven hits, in a duel with Derringer.

Derringer allowed the same number of safeties, but doubles by Frank McCormick and Jimmy Ripple and Billy Myers' long fly brought in two Cincinnati runs in the seventh frame, enough to win, 2 to 1, and give the Reds the Series.

Billy Werber, the Reds' third sacker, led his team at bat with an average of .370. With Ernie Lombardi limping with an ankle injury and catching only one game, Coach Jimmie Wilson became one of Cincinnati's outstanding heroes. He jumped into the breach behind the bat, caught six games, hit .353 and stole the only base of the Series. Bruce Campbell, Greenberg and Higgins were the Tiger batting stalwarts, with .360, .357 and .333, respectively, while each hit a home run. The box scores:

Wednesday, October 2—At Cincinnati

Detroit (A.L.)	AB.	R.	H.	O.	A.	E.
Bartell, ss	4	0	2	2	0	1
McCosky, cf	5	0	2	2	0	0
Gehringer, 2b	4	0	0	4	3	0
Greenberg, lf	5	1	1	4	0	0
York, 1b	4	2	2	6	1	0
Campbell, rf	3	1	2	3	0	0
Higgins, 3b	4	1	1	0	5	0
Sullivan, c	3	1	0	5	2	0
Newsom, p	4	1	0	1	0	0
Totals	36	7	10	27	11	1

Cincinnati (N.L.)	AB.	R.	H.	O.	A.	E.
Werber, 3b	4	1	1	1	2	1
M. McCormick, cf	4	0	1	2	0	0
Goodman, rf	4	1	2	1	0	0
F. McCormick, 1b	3	0	0	7	1	0
Ripple, lf	4	0	1	2	0	0
Wilson, c	2	0	0	9	1	0
aRiggs	1	0	0	0	0	0
Baker, c	1	0	1	3	0	1
Joost, 2b	4	0	2	2	1	0
Myers, ss	4	0	0	0	1	1
Derringer, p	0	0	0	0	1	0
Moore, p	2	0	0	0	1	0
bCraft	1	0	0	0	0	0
Riddle, p	0	0	0	0	0	0
Totals	34	2	8	27	8	3

Detroit .... 0 5 0   0 2 0   0 0 0—7
Cincinnati ..... 0 0 0   1 0 0   0 1 0—2

aStruck out for Wilson in seventh. bFlied out for Moore in eighth. Runs batted in—Bartell 2, McCosky, Campbell 2, Higgins 2, Goodman, Ripple. Two-base hits—Werber, M. McCormick, Goodman. Three-base hit—York. Home run—Campbell. Sacrifice hit—Campbell. Double plays—Higgins, Gehringer and York; Wilson and Joost. Left on bases—Detroit 8, Cincinnati 6. Earned runs—Detroit 6, Cincinnati 2. Struck out—By Newsom 4, by Derringer 1, by Moore 7, by Riddle 2. Bases on balls—Off Newsom 1, off Derringer 1, off Moore 4. Hits—Off Derringer 5 in 1⅓ innings, off Moore 5 in 6⅔ innings, off Riddle 0 in 1 inning. Losing pitcher—Derringer. Umpires—Klem (N.L.), Ormsby (A.L.), Ballanfant (N.L.) and Basil (A.L.). Time—2:09. Attendance—31,793.

Thursday, October 3—At Cincinnati

Detroit (A.L.)	AB.	R.	H.	O.	A.	E.
Bartell, ss	3	1	0	3	2	0
McCosky, cf	2	1	0	4	0	0
Gehringer, 2b	4	1	1	0	3	0
Greenberg, lf	3	0	1	1	0	0
York, 1b	4	0	0	10	0	0
Campbell, rf	4	0	0	3	0	0
Higgins, 3b	3	0	1	1	4	0
Tebbetts, c	3	0	0	2	0	1
Rowe, p	1	0	0	0	0	0
Gorsica, p	2	0	0	0	1	0
Totals	29	3	3	24	10	1

Cincinnati (N.L.)	AB.	R.	H.	O.	A.	E.
Werber, 3b	3	0	1	2	4	0
M. McCormick, cf	4	0	0	3	0	0
Goodman, rf	4	1	1	0	0	0
F. McCormick, 1b	4	1	1	9	0	0

1940 WORLD SERIES

	AB.	R.	H.	O.	A.	E.
Ripple, lf	4	1	1	3	0	0
Wilson, c	4	1	2	4	0	0
Joost, 2b	4	0	1	2	2	0
Myers, ss	3	0	1	3	3	0
Walters, p	3	1	1	0	2	0
Totals	33	5	9	27	11	0

Detroit .... 2 0 0   0 0 1   0 0 0—3
Cincinnati .... 0 2 2   1 0 0   0 0 *—5

Runs batted in—Werber, Ripple 2, Joost, Myers, Gehringer, Greenberg. Two-base hits—Werber, Walters, Greenberg, Higgins. Home run—Ripple. Double play—Werber, Joost and F. McCormick. Left on bases—Cincinnati 5, Detroit 3. Earned runs—Cincinnati 5, Detroit 3. Struck out—By Walters 4, by Rowe 1, by Gorsica 1. Bases on balls—Off Walters 4, off Rowe 1. Hits—Off Rowe 8 in 3⅓ innings, off Gorsica 1 in 4⅔ innings. Losing pitcher—Rowe. Umpires—Ormsby (A.L.), Ballanfant (N.L.), Basil (A.L.) and Klem (N.L.). Time—1:54. Attendance—30,640.

Friday, October 4—At Detroit

Cincinnati (N.L.)	AB.	R.	H.	O.	A.	E.
Werber, 3b	4	1	3	2	3	0
M. McCormick, cf	5	0	2	3	0	1
Goodman, rf	4	0	1	1	0	0
F. McCormick, 1b	4	0	0	9	1	0
Ripple, lf	4	1	1	2	0	0
Lombardi, c	3	0	1	4	0	0
Baker, c	1	1	0	2	0	0
Joost, 2b	4	0	1	1	2	0
Myers, ss	4	0	1	0	3	0
Turner, p	2	0	0	0	1	0
Moore, p	0	0	0	0	0	0
aRiggs	1	1	0	0	0	0
Beggs, p	0	0	0	0	0	0
bFrey	1	0	0	0	0	0
Totals	37	4	10	24	10	1

Detroit (A.L.)	AB.	R.	H.	O.	A.	E.
Bartell, ss	4	0	1	3	3	0
McCosky, cf	4	1	2	4	0	0
Gehringer, 2b	4	0	1	2	4	0
Greenberg, lf	4	2	2	1	0	0
York, 1b	4	1	2	8	0	0
Campbell, rf	4	2	3	4	0	0
Higgins, 3b	4	1	2	0	3	1
Tebbetts, c	4	0	0	5	1	0
Bridges, p	3	0	0	0	1	0
Totals	35	7	13	27	12	1

Cincinnati .... 1 0 0   0 0 0   0 1 2—4
Detroit .... 0 0 0   1 0 0   4 2 *—7

aForced runner for Moore in eighth. bFlied out for Beggs in ninth. Runs batted in—York 2, Campbell, Higgins, Werber, M. McCormick, Goodman, Joost. Two-base hits—McCosky, Campbell, Higgins, Werber, Lombardi. Three-base hit—Greenberg. Home runs—York, Higgins. Double plays—Werber, Joost and F. McCormick; Myers, F. McCormick and Baker. Left on bases—Cincinnati 7, Detroit 4. Earned runs—Detroit 6, Cincinnati 3. Struck out—By Bridges 5, by Turner 4, by Beggs 1. Base on balls—Off Bridges 1. Hits—Off Turner 8 in 6 innings (pitched to four batters in seventh), off Moore 2 in 1 inning, off Beggs 3 in 1 inning. Losing pitcher—Turner. Umpires—Ballanfant (N.L.), Basil (A.L.), Klem (N.L.) and Ormsby (A.L.). Time—2:08. Attendance—52,877.

Saturday, October 5—At Detroit

Cincinnati (N.L.)	AB.	R.	H.	O.	A.	E.
Werber, 3b	3	2	2	2	1	0
M. McCormick, cf	5	1	2	3	0	0
Goodman, rf	5	2	2	1	0	0
F. McCormick, 1b	5	0	2	13	0	1
Ripple, lf	2	0	1	0	0	0
bArnovich, lf	1	0	0	2	0	0
Wilson, c	5	0	1	4	0	0
Joost, 2b	5	0	1	0	1	0
Myers, ss	3	0	0	2	6	0
Derringer, p	4	0	0	0	3	0
Totals	38	5	11	27	11	1

Detroit (A.L.)	AB.	R.	H.	O.	A.	E.
Bartell, ss	4	0	1	0	0	0
dFox	1	0	0	0	0	0
McCosky, cf	2	1	1	2	0	0
Gehringer, 2b	4	0	0	5	3	0
Greenberg, lf	4	0	1	2	0	0
York, 1b	2	0	0	13	1	0
Campbell, rf	4	1	1	1	0	0
Higgins, 3b	4	0	2	1	9	0
Sullivan, c	2	0	0	2	0	0
Trout, p	1	0	0	0	1	0
Smith, p	1	0	0	0	1	0
aAverill	1	0	0	0	0	0
McKain, p	0	0	0	0	1	0
cTebbetts	1	0	0	0	0	0
Totals	31	2	5	27	16	1

Cincinnati .... 2 0 1   1 0 0   0 1 0—5
Detroit .... 0 0 1   0 0 1   0 0 0—2

aFlied out for Smith in sixth. bFlied out for Ripple in seventh. cGrounded out for McKain in ninth. dFlied out for Bartell in ninth. Runs batted in—M. McCormick, Goodman 2, Ripple, Greenberg, Higgins. Two-base hits—M. McCormick, Goodman, Ripple, Greenberg. Three-base hit—Higgins. Sacrifice hit—Arnovich. Double plays—Joost, Myers and F. McCormick; Derringer, Myers and F. McCormick. Left on bases—Cincinnati 11, Detroit 8. Earned runs—Cincinnati 4, Detroit 2. Struck out—By Derringer 4, by Trout 1, by Smith 1. Bases on balls—Off Derringer 6, off Trout 1, off Smith 3. Wild pitch—McKain. Hits—Off Trout 6 in 2 innings (pitched to 3 men in third), off Smith 1 in 4 innings, off McKain 4 in 3 innings. Losing pitcher—Trout. Umpires—Basil (A.L.), Klem (N.L.), Ormsby (A.L.) and Ballanfant (N.L.). Time—2:06. Attendance—54,093.

Sunday, October 6—At Detroit

Cincinnati (N.L.)	AB.	R.	H.	O.	A.	E.
Werber, 3b	4	0	1	0	0	0
M. McCormick, cf	4	0	1	5	1	0
Goodman, rf	4	0	0	1	0	0
F. McCormick, 1b	4	0	1	5	0	0
Ripple, lf	2	0	0	4	0	0
Wilson, c	1	0	0	3	1	0
aBaker, c	2	0	0	2	0	0
Joost, 2b	3	0	0	2	1	0
Myers, ss	2	0	0	2	0	0
Thompson, p	1	0	0	0	1	0
Moore, p	0	0	0	0	0	0
bFrey	1	0	0	0	0	0
Vander Meer, p	0	0	0	0	0	0
cRiggs	1	0	0	0	0	0
Hutchings, p	0	0	0	0	1	0
Totals	29	0	3	24	5	0

Detroit (A.L.)	AB.	R.	H.	O.	A.	E.
Bartell, ss	4	1	2	0	1	0
McCosky, cf	3	2	2	3	0	0
Gehringer, 2b	4	2	2	2	4	0
Greenberg, lf	5	2	3	1	0	0

1940 WORLD SERIES

	AB.	R.	H.	O.	A.	E.
York, 1b	4	0	0	7	0	0
Campbell, rf	4	0	3	2	0	0
Higgins, 3b	2	0	0	1	3	0
Sullivan, c	4	1	1	11	0	0
Newsom, p	4	0	0	0	0	0
Totals	34	8	13	27	8	0

Cincinnati .... 0 0 0 0 0 0 0 0 0—0
Detroit .... 0 0 3 4 0 0 0 1 *—8

aStruck out for Wilson in fifth. bGrounded out for Moore in fifth. cStruck out for Vander Meer in eighth. Runs batted in—Bartell, Greenberg 4, Campbell 2. Two-base hit—Bartell. Home run—Greenberg. Sacrifice hit—Newsom. Double play—Bartell, Gehringer and York. Left on bases—Cincinnati 4, Detroit 13. Earned runs—Detroit 8. Struck out—By Newsom 7, by Thompson 2, by Vander Meer 2. Bases on balls—Off Newsom 2, off Thompson 4, off Moore 2, off Vander Meer 3, off Hutchings 1. Wild pitch—Hutchings. Passed ball—Wilson. Hits—Off Thompson 8 in 3⅓ innings, off Moore in 1 in ⅔ inning, off Vander Meer 2 in 3 innings, off Hutchings 2 in 1 inning. Losing pitcher—Thompson. Umpires—Klem (N.L.), Ormsby (A.L.), Ballanfant (N.L.) and Basil (A.L.). Time—2:26. Attendance—55,189.

Monday, October 7—At Cincinnati

Detroit (A.L.)	AB.	R.	H.	O.	A.	E.
Bartell, ss	3	0	2	0	4	0
bSullivan	1	0	0	0	0	0
Croucher, ss	0	0	0	0	0	0
McCosky, cf	4	0	0	1	0	0
Gehringer, 2b	4	0	0	2	1	0
Greenberg, lf	3	0	0	2	0	0
York, 1b	4	0	2	10	0	0
Campbell, rf	3	0	0	2	0	0
Higgins, 3b	3	0	1	1	2	0
Tebbetts, c	3	0	0	6	2	0
Rowe, p	0	0	0	0	1	0
Gorsica, p	2	0	0	0	5	0
aAverill	1	0	0	0	0	0
Hutchinson, p	0	0	0	0	0	0
Totals	31	0	5	24	15	0

Cincinnati (N.L.)	AB.	R.	H.	O.	A.	E.
Werber, 3b	5	1	2	1	3	0
M. McCormick, cf	3	0	1	4	0	0
Goodman, rf	4	1	2	2	0	0
F. McCormick, 1b	4	0	1	10	1	1
Ripple, lf	2	0	2	2	0	0
Wilson, c	3	1	1	4	0	0
Joost, 2b	3	0	0	2	4	0
Myers, ss	4	0	2	2	4	1
Walters, p	4	1	1	0	2	0
Totals	32	4	10	27	14	2

Detroit .... 0 0 0 0 0 0 0 0 0—0
Cincinnati .... 2 0 0 0 0 1 0 1 *—4

aReached first on F. McCormick's error for Gorsica in eighth. bFlied out for Bartell in eighth. Runs batted in—Goodman, Ripple, Walters 2. Two-base hits—Werber, Bartell. Home run—Walters. Sacrifice hits—M. McCormick, Goodman. Double plays—Joost, Myers and F. McCormick; Werber, Joost and F. McCormick; F. McCormick, Myers and F. McCormick; Gorsica, Tebbetts and York. Left on bases—Cincinnati 11, Detroit 6. Earned runs—Cincinnati 4. Struck out—By Walters 2, by Gorsica 3, by Hutchinson 1. Bases on balls—Off Walters 2, off Gorsica 4, off Hutchinson 5. Hits—Off Rowe 4 in ⅓ inning, off Gorsica 5 in 6⅔ innings, off Hutchinson 1 in 1 inning. Losing pitcher—Rowe. Umpires—Ormsby (A.L.), Ballanfant (N.L.), Basil (A.L.) and Klem (N.L.). Time—2:01. Attendance—30,481.

Tuesday, October 8—At Cincinnati

Detroit (A.L.)	AB.	R.	H.	O.	A.	E.
Bartell, ss	4	0	0	3	2	0
McCosky, cf	3	0	0	3	0	0
Gehringer, 2b	4	0	2	3	2	0
Greenberg, lf	4	0	2	1	0	0
York, 1b	4	0	0	5	0	0
Campbell, rf	3	0	0	2	0	0
Higgins, 3b	4	0	1	0	4	0
Sullivan, c	3	1	1	6	0	0
Newsom, p	2	0	1	1	0	0
cAverill	1	0	0	0	0	0
Totals	32	1	7	24	8	0

Cincinnati (N.L.)	AB.	R.	H.	O.	A.	E.
Werber, 3b	4	0	0	1	3	1
M. McCormick, cf	4	0	2	4	0	0
Goodman, rf	4	0	0	3	0	0
F. McCormick, 1b	4	1	1	6	1	0
Ripple, lf	3	1	1	1	0	0
Wilson, c	2	0	2	2	0	0
Joost, 2b	2	0	0	5	1	0
aLombardi	0	0	0	0	0	0
bFrey, 2b	0	0	0	0	1	0
Myers, ss	3	0	1	5	1	0
Derringer, p	3	0	0	0	1	0
Totals	29	2	7	27	8	1

Detroit .... 0 0 1 0 0 0 0 0 0—1
Cincinnati .... 0 0 0 0 0 0 2 0 *—2

aWalked for Joost in seventh. bRan for Lombardi in seventh. cGrounded out for Newsom in ninth. Runs batted in—Ripple, Myers. Two-base hits—M. McCormick, F. McCormick, Ripple, Higgins. Sacrifice hits—Wilson, Newsom. Stolen base—Wilson. Double play—Gehringer, Bartell and York. Left on bases—Detroit 8, Cincinnati 5. Earned runs—Cincinnati 2, Detroit 0. Struck out—By Derringer 1, by Newsom 6. Bases on balls—Off Derringer 3, off Newsom 1. Umpires—Ballanfant (N.L.), Basil (A.L.), Klem (N.L.) and Ormsby (A.L.). Time—1:47. Attendance—26,854.

COMPOSITE BATTING AVERAGES
Cincinnati Reds

Player-Position	G.	AB.	R.	H.	2B.	3B.	HR.	RBI.	BA.
Werber, 3b	7	27	5	10	4	0	0	2	.370
Wilson, c	6	17	2	6	0	0	0	0	.353
Ripple, lf	7	21	3	7	2	0	1	6	.333
Lombardi, c-ph	2	3	0	1	1	0	0	0	.333
M. McCormick, cf	7	29	1	9	3	0	0	2	.310
Walters, p	2	7	2	2	1	0	1	2	.286
Goodman, rf	7	29	5	8	2	0	0	5	.276
Baker, c	3	4	1	1	0	0	0	0	.250
F. McCormick, 1b	7	28	2	6	1	0	0	0	.214
Joost, 2b	7	25	0	5	0	0	0	2	.200
Myers, ss	7	23	0	3	0	0	0	2	.130
Aronvich, ph-lf	1	1	0	0	0	0	0	0	.000
Riggs, ph	3	3	1	0	0	0	0	0	.000
Derringer, p	3	7	0	0	0	0	0	0	.000
Moore, p	3	2	0	0	0	0	0	0	.000
Riddle, p	1	0	0	0	0	0	0	0	.000
Turner, p	1	2	0	0	0	0	0	0	.000
Beggs, p	1	0	0	0	0	0	0	0	.000
Thompson, p	1	1	0	0	0	0	0	0	.000
Vander Meer, p	1	0	0	0	0	0	0	0	.000
Hutchings, p	1	0	0	0	0	0	0	0	.000
Frey, ph-pr-2b	3	2	0	0	0	0	0	0	.000
Craft, ph	1	1	0	0	0	0	0	0	.000
Totals	7	232	22	58	14	0	2	21	.250

Detroit Tigers

Player-Position	G.	AB.	R.	H.	2B.	3B.	HR.	RBI.	BA.
Campbell, rf	7	25	4	9	1	0	1	5	.360
Greenberg, lf	7	28	5	10	2	1	1	6	.357
Higgins, 3b	7	24	2	8	3	1	1	6	.333
McCosky, cf	7	23	5	7	1	0	0	1	.304
Bartell, ss	7	26	2	7	2	0	0	3	.269
York, 1b	7	26	3	6	0	1	1	2	.231
Gehringer, 2b	7	28	3	6	0	0	0	1	.214
Sullivan, c-ph	5	13	3	2	0	0	0	0	.154

Player-Position	G.	AB.	R.	H.	2B.	3B.	HR.	RBI.	BA.
Newsom, p	3	10	1	1	0	0	0	0	.100
Croucher, ss	1	0	0	0	0	0	0	0	.000
Tebbetts, c-ph	4	11	0	0	0	0	0	0	.000
Rowe, p	2	1	0	0	0	0	0	0	.000
Gorsica, p	2	4	0	0	0	0	0	0	.000
Bridges, p	1	3	0	0	0	0	0	0	.000
Trout, p	1	1	0	0	0	0	0	0	.000
Smith, p	1	1	0	0	0	0	0	0	.000
McKain, p	1	0	0	0	0	0	0	0	.000
Hutchinson, p	1	0	0	0	0	0	0	0	.000
Averill, ph	3	3	0	0	0	0	0	0	.000
Fox, ph	1	1	0	0	0	0	0	0	.000
Totals	7	228	28	56	9	3	4	24	.246

COMPOSITE PITCHING AVERAGES
Cincinnati Reds

Pitcher	G.	IP.	H.	R.	E.	SO.	BB.	W.	L.	ERA.
Vander Meer	1	3	2	0	0	2	3	0	0	0.00
Riddle	1	1	0	0	0	2	0	0	0	0.00
Walters	2	18	8	3	3	6	6	2	0	1.50
Derringer	3	19⅓	17	8	6	6	10	2	1	2.79
Moore	3	8⅓	8	3	3	7	6	0	0	3.24
Turner	1	6	8	5	5	4	0	0	1	7.50
Hutchings	1	1	2	1	1	0	1	0	0	9.00
Beggs	1	1	3	2	1	1	0	0	0	9.00
Thompson	1	3⅓	8	6	6	2	4	0	1	16.20
Totals	7	61	56	28	25	30	30	4	3	3.69

Detroit Tigers

Pitcher	G.	IP.	H.	R.	E.	SO.	BB.	W.	L.	ERA.
Gorsica	2	11⅓	6	1	1	4	4	0	0	0.79
Newsom	3	26	18	4	4	17	4	2	1	1.38
Smith	1	4	1	1	1	1	3	0	0	2.25
McKain	1	3	4	1	1	0	0	0	0	3.00
Bridges	1	9	10	4	3	5	1	1	0	3.00
Hutchinson	1	1	1	1	1	1	1	0	0	9.00
Trout	1	2	6	3	2	1	1	0	1	9.00
Rowe	2	3⅔	12	7	7	1	1	0	2	17.18
Totals	7	60	58	22	20	30	15	3	4	3.00

SERIES OF 1941

	W.	L.	Pct.
New York A. L.	4	1	.800
Brooklyn N. L.	1	4	.200

Returning as American League pennant winners for the twelfth time, the Yankees added their ninth Series triumph and eighth in succession in tripping the Dodgers, the first Brooklyn team to win a National League flag since 1920, in four games out of five. The loss of the second contest to the Dodgers broke a Yankee string of ten straight victories in the fall classic. The 1941 triumph was the sixth for Manager Joe McCarthy.

The Yankees, regaining the American League pennant, won in their usual runaway. Brooklyn, winning its first flag in 21 years under Leo Durocher, had a ding-dong finish with St. Louis, beating the Cards by two and one-half games.

Two unusual incidents marked the Series. Freddy Fitzsimmons, after holding the Yankees scoreless for seven innings in the third game, was hit on the knee by a liner in the last play of that frame and forced to retire. The American League team then scored two runs in the eighth off Hugh Casey to win. In the fourth contest, with two out in the ninth inning, the Dodgers ahead, 4 to 3, and Tommy Henrich swinging for the third strike that would have retired the side, catcher Mickey Owen missed the ball and the Yankees went on to stage a four-run rally to win, 7 to 4.

Red Ruffing, Johnny Murphy (in relief), Marius Russo and Ernie Bonham were credited with the Yankee victories and Whit Wyatt pitched the lone win for the Dodgers, also being charged with a loss, as was Curt Davis, while Casey lost two in relief roles. Spurgeon Chandler suffered the Yankee defeat.

Ruffing joined Chief Bender, Waite Hoyt and Vernon Gomez in the six-victory class by besting Davis in the opener, 3 to 2. Joe Gordon homered for the first Yank tally in the second inning, a pass and Bill Dickey's two-bagger plated another marker in the fourth frame and then, in the sixth, what proved to be the deciding run counted on another walk and singles by Dickey and Gordon.

In their only win, the Dodgers reversed the 3 to 2 score in the second tilt, crowding four of their six hits into two innings to give Wyatt a victory over Chandler. Russo turned in a four-hitter in the third game against Fitzsimmons' seven-inning scoreless pitching, until Freddy was forced out, and won, 2 to 1, as the Yankees bunched singles by Red Rolfe, Henrich, Joe DiMaggio and Charlie Keller off Casey in the eighth frame for two runs. The Dodgers scored on a double by Dixie Walker and a single by Pee Wee Reese.

Scoring four runs in the ninth inning of the fourth game—after Henrich had apparently struck out for the final out—on a single by DiMaggio, a double by Keller, a walk and a double by Gordon, the Yankees mopped up, 7 to 4.

Four-hit pitching by Bonham gave the Yankees a 3 to 1 win over Wyatt in the final game, the Dodgers scoring only in the third inning on a double by Wyatt, a single by Lew Riggs and Pete Reiser's long fly to Henrich. The Yankees scored all they needed in the second inning on a pass, single by Dickey, wild pitch and another one-bagger by Gordon. Henrich iced the cake with a homer in the fifth.

Even though the breaks were with the Yankees, they outhit Brooklyn, .247 to .182. Gordon and Keller were the batting kings of the Bombers with averages of .500 and .389, respectively, each driving in five runs. Joe Medwick led the Dodgers who played in all five games with the low average of .235. The box scores:

Wednesday, October 1—At New York

Brooklyn (N.L.)	AB.	R.	H.	O.	A.	E.
Walker, rf	3	0	0	3	0	0
Herman, 2b	3	0	0	0	6	0
Reiser, cf	3	0	0	4	0	0
Camilli, 1b	4	0	0	7	2	0
Medwick, lf	4	0	1	4	0	0
Lavagetto, 3b	4	1	0	0	0	0
Reese, ss	4	1	3	4	2	0
Owen, c	2	0	1	1	0	0

1941 WORLD SERIES

	AB.	R.	H.	O.	A.	E.
aRiggs	1	0	1	0	0	0
Franks, c	1	0	0	0	1	0
Davis, p	2	0	0	1	0	0
Casey, p	0	0	0	0	0	0
bWasdell	1	0	0	0	0	0
Allen, p	0	0	0	0	0	0
Totals	32	2	6	24	11	0

New York (A.L.)	AB.	R.	H.	O.	A.	E.
Sturm, 1b	3	0	1	7	0	0
Rolfe, 3b	3	0	1	2	2	0
Henrich, rf	4	0	0	0	0	0
DiMaggio, cf	4	0	0	5	0	0
Keller, lf	2	2	0	4	0	0
Dickey, c	4	0	2	6	0	0
Gordon, 2b	2	1	2	0	2	0
Rizzuto, ss	4	0	0	3	5	1
Ruffing, p	3	0	0	0	0	0
Totals	29	3	6	27	9	1

Brooklyn.......... 0 0 0   0 1 0   1 0 0—2
New York........ 0 1 0   1 0 1   0 0 *—3

aSingled for Owen in seventh. bFouled out for Casey in seventh. Runs batted in—Gordon 2, Dickey, Owen, Riggs. Two-base hit—Dickey. Three-base hit—Owen. Home run—Gordon. Double plays—Rolfe and Rizzuto; Gordon, Rizzuto and Sturm. Left on bases—New York 8, Brooklyn 6. Earned runs—New York 3, Brooklyn 1. Struck out—By Ruffing 5, by Davis 1. Bases on balls—Off Ruffing 3, off Davis 3, off Allen 2. Hit by pitcher—By Allen (Sturm). Hits—Off Davis 6 in 5⅓ innings, off Casey 0 in ⅔ innings, off Allen 0 in 2 innings. Losing pitcher—Davis. Umpires—McGowan (A.L.), Pinelli (N.L.), Grieve (A.L.) and Goetz (N.L.). Time—2:08. Attendance—68,540.

Thursday, October 2—At New York

Brooklyn (N.L.)	AB.	R.	H.	O.	A.	E.
Walker, rf	4	1	0	4	0	0
Herman, 2b	4	0	1	4	4	0
Reiser, cf	4	0	0	2	1	0
Camilli, 1b	3	1	1	8	1	0
Medwick, lf	4	1	2	0	0	0
Lavagetto, 3b	3	0	1	1	1	0
Reese, ss	4	0	0	2	4	2
Owen, c	2	0	1	6	1	0
Wyatt, p	3	0	0	0	1	0
Totals	31	3	6	27	13	2

New York (A.L.)	AB.	R.	H.	O.	A.	E.
Sturm, 1b	5	0	1	11	0	0
Rolfe, 3b	5	0	1	1	2	0
Henrich, rf	4	1	1	0	0	0
DiMaggio, cf	3	0	0	4	0	0
Keller, lf	4	1	2	1	0	0
Dickey, c	4	0	0	5	1	0
aBordagaray	0	0	0	0	0	0
Rosar, c	0	0	0	0	0	0
Gordon, 2b	1	0	1	2	7	1
Rizzuto, ss	4	0	1	3	5	0
Chandler, p	2	0	1	0	0	0
Murphy, p	1	0	0	0	0	0
bSelkirk	1	0	1	0	0	0
Totals	34	2	9	27	15	1

Brooklyn.......... 0 0 0   0 2 1   0 0 0—3
New York........ 0 1 1   0 0 0   0 0 0—2

aRan for Dickey in eighth. bSingled for Murphy in ninth. Runs batted in—Chandler, Keller, Reese, Owen, Camilli. Two-base hits—Henrich, Medwick. Double plays—Reese, Herman and Camilli; Gordon, Rizzuto and Sturm 2; Dickey and Gordon. Left on bases—New York 10, Brooklyn 4. Earned runs—Brooklyn 2, New York 2. Struck out—By Wyatt 5, by Chandler 2, by Murphy 2. Bases on balls—Off Wyatt 5, off Chandler 2, off Murphy 1. Hits—Off Chandler 4 in 5 innings (pitched to two batters in sixth), off Murphy 2 in 4 innings. Losing pitcher—Chandler. Umpires—Pinelli (N.L.), Grieve (A.L.), Goetz (N.L.) and McGowan (A.L.). Time—2:31. Attendance—66,248.

Saturday, October 4—At Brooklyn

New York (A.L.)	AB.	R.	H.	O.	A.	E.
Sturm, 1b	4	0	1	12	0	0
Rolfe, 3b	4	1	2	1	2	0
Henrich, rf	3	1	1	2	0	0
DiMaggio, cf	4	0	2	2	0	0
Keller, lf	4	0	1	2	0	0
Dickey, c	4	0	0	4	1	0
Gordon, 2b	3	0	1	2	4	0
Rizzuto, ss	3	0	0	2	3	0
Russo, p	4	0	0	0	4	0
Totals	33	2	8	27	14	0

Brooklyn (N.L.)	AB.	R.	H.	O.	A.	E.
Reese, ss	4	0	1	3	1	0
Herman, 2b	1	0	0	0	1	0
Coscarart, 2b	2	0	0	0	3	0
Reiser, cf	4	0	1	5	0	0
Medwick, lf	4	0	1	3	0	0
Lavagetto, 3b	3	0	0	1	0	0
Camilli, 1b	3	0	0	11	0	0
Walker, rf	3	1	1	2	0	0
Owen, c	3	0	0	2	1	0
Fitzsimmons, p	2	0	0	0	2	0
Casey, p	0	0	0	0	0	0
French, p	0	0	0	0	0	0
aGalan	1	0	0	0	0	0
Allen, p	0	0	0	0	0	0
Totals	30	1	4	27	8	0

New York........ 0 0 0   0 0 0   0 2 0—2
Brooklyn.......... 0 0 0   0 0 0   0 1 0—1

aFanned for French in eighth. Runs batted in—DiMaggio, Keller, Reese. Two-base hits—Reiser, Walker. Three-base hit—Gordon. Stolen bases—Rizzuto, Sturm. Double plays—Rizzuto and Sturm; Reese and Camilli. Left on bases—New York 7, Brooklyn 4. Earned runs—New York 2, Brooklyn 1. Struck out—By Russo 5, by Fitzsimmons 1. Bases on balls—Off Russo 2, off Fitzsimmons 3. Hits—Off Fitzsimmons 4 in 7 innings, off Casey 4 in ⅓ inning, off French 0 in ⅔ inning, off Allen 0 in 1 inning. Losing pitcher—Casey. Umpires—Grieve (A.L.), Goetz (N.L.), McGowan (A.L.) and Pinelli (N.L.). Time—2:22. Attendance—33,100.

Sunday, October 5—At Brooklyn

New York (A.L.)	AB.	R.	H.	O.	A.	E.
Sturm, 1b	5	0	2	9	1	0
Rolfe, 3b	5	1	2	0	2	0
Henrich, rf	4	1	0	3	0	0
DiMaggio, cf	4	1	2	2	0	0
Keller, lf	5	1	4	1	0	0
Dickey, c	2	2	0	7	0	0
Gordon, 2b	5	1	2	2	3	0
Rizzuto, ss	4	0	0	2	3	0
Donald, p	2	0	0	0	1	0
Breuer, p	1	0	0	0	1	0
bSelkirk	1	0	0	0	0	0
Murphy, p	1	0	0	1	0	0
Totals	39	7	12	27	11	0

Brooklyn (N.L.)	AB.	R.	H.	O.	A.	E.
Reese, ss	5	0	0	2	4	0
Walker, rf	5	1	2	5	0	0
Reiser, cf	5	1	2	1	0	0
Camilli, 1b	4	0	2	10	1	0

1942 WORLD SERIES

	AB.	R.	H.	O.	A.	E.
Riggs, 3b	3	0	0	0	2	0
Medwick, lf	2	0	0	1	0	0
Allen, p	0	0	0	0	0	0
Casey, p	2	0	1	0	3	0
Owen, c	2	1	0	2	1	1
Coscarart, 2b	3	1	0	4	2	0
Higbe, p	1	0	1	0	1	0
French, p	0	0	0	0	0	0
aWasdell, lf	3	0	1	2	0	0
Totals	35	4	9	27	14	1

New York............ 1 0 0   2 0 0   0 0 4—7
Brooklyn............ 0 0 0   2 2 0   0 0 0—4

aDoubled for French in fourth. bGrounded out for Breuer in eighth. Runs batted in—Keller 3, Sturm 2, Gordon 2, Wasdell 2, Reiser 2. Two-base hits—Keller 2, Walker, Camilli, Wasdell, Gordon. Home run—Reiser. Double play—Gordon, Rizzuto and Sturm. Left on bases—New York 11, Brooklyn 8. Earned runs—Brooklyn 4, New York 3. Struck out—By Donald 2, by Breuer 2, by Murphy 1, by Higbe 1, by Casey 1. Bases on balls—Off Donald 3, off Breuer 1, off Higbe 2, off Casey 2, off Allen 1. Hit by pitcher—By Allen (Henrich). Hits —Off Donald 6 in 4 innings (pitched to two batters in fifth), off Breuer 3 in 3 innings, off Murphy 0 in 2 innings, off Higbe 6 in 3⅔ innings, off French 0 in ⅓ inning, off Allen 1 in ⅔ inning, off Casey 5 in 4⅓ innings. Winning pitcher—Murphy. Losing pitcher—Casey. Umpires—Goetz (N.L.), McGowan (A.L.), Pinelli (N.L.) and Grieve (A.L.). Time—2:54. Attendance—33,813.

Monday, October 6—At Brooklyn

New York (A.L.)	AB.	R.	H.	O.	A.	E.
Sturm, 1b	4	0	1	9	0	0
Rolfe, 3b	3	0	0	3	0	0
Henrich, rf	3	1	1	1	0	0
DiMaggio, cf	4	0	1	6	0	0
Keller, lf	3	1	0	4	0	0
Dickey, c	4	1	1	2	0	0
Gordon, 2b	3	0	1	0	3	0
Rizzuto, ss	3	0	1	2	2	0
Bonham, p	4	0	0	0	1	0
Totals	31	3	6	27	6	0

Brooklyn (N.L.)	AB.	R.	H.	O.	A.	E.
Walker, rf	3	0	1	0	0	0
Riggs, 3b	4	0	1	1	3	0
Reiser, cf	4	0	1	2	0	0
Camilli, 1b	4	0	0	9	1	0
Medwick, lf	3	0	0	0	0	0
Reese, ss	3	0	0	2	3	1
bWasdell	1	0	0	0	0	0
Owen, c	3	0	0	9	1	0
Coscarart, 2b	2	0	0	3	3	0
aGalan	1	0	0	0	0	0
Herman, 2b	0	0	0	0	2	0
Wyatt, p	3	1	1	1	1	0
Totals	31	1	4	27	14	1

New York............ 0 2 0   0 1 0   0 0 0—3
Brooklyn............ 0 0 1   0 0 0   0 0 0—1

aFouled out for Coscarart in seventh. bFlied out for Reese in ninth. Runs batted in—Gordon, Reiser, Henrich. Two-base hit—Wyatt. Three-base hit—Reiser. Home run—Henrich. Left on bases—New York 6, Brooklyn 5. Earned runs—New York 3, Brooklyn 1. Double plays—Owen and Riggs; Reese, Coscarart and Camilli; Herman, Reese and Camilli. Struck out—By Bonham 2, by Wyatt 9. Bases on balls—Off Bonham 2, off Wyatt 5. Wild pitch—Wyatt. Umpires—McGowan (A.L.), Pinelli (N.L.), Grieve (A.L.) and Goetz (N.L.). Time—2:13. Attendance—34,072.

COMPOSITE BATTING AVERAGES
New York Yankees

Player-Position	G.	AB.	R.	H.	2B.	3B.	HR.	RBI.	BA.
Gordon, 2b	5	14	2	7	1	1	1	5	.500
Chandler, p	1	2	0	1	0	0	0	1	.500
Selkirk, ph	2	2	0	1	0	0	0	0	.500
Keller, lf	5	18	5	7	2	0	0	5	.389
Rolfe, 3b	5	20	2	6	0	0	0	0	.300
Sturm, 1b	5	21	0	6	0	0	0	2	.286
DiMaggio, cf	5	19	1	5	0	0	0	1	.263
Henrich, rf	5	18	4	3	1	0	1	1	.167
Dickey, c	5	18	3	3	1	0	0	1	.167
Rizzuto, ss	5	18	0	2	0	0	0	0	.111
Rosar, c	1	0	0	0	0	0	0	0	.000
Ruffing, p	1	3	0	0	0	0	0	0	.000
Murphy, p	2	2	0	0	0	0	0	0	.000
Russo, p	1	4	0	0	0	0	0	0	.000
Donald, p	1	2	0	0	0	0	0	0	.000
Breuer, p	1	1	0	0	0	0	0	0	.000
Bonham, p	1	4	0	0	0	0	0	0	.000
Bordagaray, pr	1	0	0	0	0	0	0	0	.000
Totals	5	166	17	41	5	1	2	16	.247

Brooklyn Dodgers

Player-Position	G.	AB.	R.	H.	2B.	3B.	HR.	RBI.	BA.
Higbe, p	1	1	0	1	0	0	0	1	1.000
Casey, p	3	2	0	1	0	0	0	0	.500
Riggs, ph-3b	3	8	0	2	0	0	0	1	.250
Medwick, lf	5	17	1	4	1	0	0	0	.235
Walker, rf	5	18	3	4	2	0	0	0	.222
Reiser, cf	5	20	1	4	1	1	1	3	.200
Reese, ss	5	20	1	4	0	0	0	0	.200
Wasdell, ph-lf	3	5	0	1	1	0	0	2	.200
Camilli, 1b	5	18	1	3	1	0	0	1	.167
Owen, c	5	12	1	2	0	1	0	2	.167
Wyatt, p	2	6	1	1	1	0	0	0	.167
Herman, 2b	4	8	0	1	0	0	0	0	.125
Lavagetto, 3b	3	10	1	1	0	0	0	0	.100
Coscarart, 2b	3	7	1	0	0	0	0	0	.000
Franks, c	1	1	0	0	0	0	0	0	.000
Davis, p	1	2	0	0	0	0	0	0	.000
Allen, p	3	0	0	0	0	0	0	0	.000
Fitzsimmons, p	1	2	0	0	0	0	0	0	.000
French, p	2	0	0	0	0	0	0	0	.000
Galan, ph	2	2	0	0	0	0	0	0	.000
Totals	5	159	11	29	7	2	1	11	.182

COMPOSITE PITCHING AVERAGES
New York Yankees

Pitcher	G.	IP.	H.	R.	E.	SO.	BB.	W.	L.	ERA.
Murphy	2	6	2	0	0	3	1	1	0	0.00
Breuer	1	3	3	0	0	2	1	0	0	0.00
Ruffing	1	9	6	2	1	5	3	1	0	1.00
Bonham	1	9	4	1	1	2	2	1	0	1.00
Russo	1	9	4	1	1	5	2	1	0	1.00
Chandler	1	5	4	3	2	2	2	0	1	3.60
Donald	1	4	6	4	4	2	3	0	0	9.00
Totals	5	45	29	11	9	21	14	4	1	1.80

Brooklyn Dodgers

Pitcher	G.	IP.	H.	R.	E.	SO.	BB.	W.	L.	ERA.
Fitzsimmons	1	7	4	0	0	1	3	0	0	0.00
Allen	3	3⅔	0	0	0	3	0	0	0	0.00
French	2	1	0	0	0	0	0	0	0	0.00
Wyatt	2	18	15	5	5	14	10	1	1	2.50
Casey	3	5⅓	9	6	2	1	2	0	2	3.38
Davis	1	5⅓	4	3	3	3	0	1	0	5.06
Higbe	1	3⅔	6	3	3	1	2	0	0	7.36
Totals	5	44	41	17	13	18	23	1	4	2.66

SERIES OF 1942

	W.	L.	Pct.
St. Louis N. L.	4	1	.800
New York A. L.	1	4	.200

In one of the biggest upsets since the "miracle" Braves scalped the famous Athletics four straight in the 1914 World Series, the Cardinals, winners of a sensational National League race, dethroned the supposedly invincible Yankees, chronic persecutors of National League champions, four games to one, in the 1942 classic. The startling upset was not so much that St. Louis won, for any club posting 106 league victories was bound to claim respect, but that after losing the first game, the Cardinals should set back the Bronx Bombers four straight. In those four games, the Yankees lost as many World Series decisions as they did in the eight Series in which they engaged from 1927 to 1941, inclusive. It also was the first time since 1915 that a club dropped four in a row after opening with a victory.

Under the brilliant leadership of Billy Southworth, the Cardinals, trailing the Dodgers by ten and one-half games as late as mid-August, piled up 106 victories, the best National League pennant performance since Pittsburgh in 1909, and finally nosed out Brooklyn. The second-place Dodgers won 104 games. The Yankees captured 103 games in winning their sixth flag in seven years.

The Series proved a jinx to the two men selected the Most Valuable Players of 1942, Mort Cooper, ace pitcher of the Cardinals, and Joe Gordon, second sacker of the Yankees, though the awards were not announced until after the Series. With 22 victories against seven defeats, Cooper was the spearhead of St. Louis' pennant drive, but in the Series he twice was knocked out of the box and charged with the lone Cardinal defeat. Gordon was the goat of the Series, getting only two hits for an average of .095, and he threw away the last game when he let Walker Cooper pick him off second base in the ninth inning, spiking New York's final threat.

Southworth's heroes were a pair of freshmen—pitchers Johnny Beazley and third baseman Whitey Kurowski—and southpaw Ernie White. Beazley, who had a 21-6 record during the regular season, won two games, besting Ernie Bonham in the second game, 4 to 3, and Red Ruffing in the fifth contest, 4 to 2. Kurowski hit a game-winning triple in the second tilt and then won the finale with a two-run homer in the ninth inning. White pitched a 2 to 0 shutout in the third game, marking the first time the Yanks had been blanked in Series competition since Jess Haines turned the trick in 1926. The fourth St. Louis victory was credited to Max Lanier, who did a neat relief job in annexing the fourth game, 9 to 6.

The lone Yankee victory was pitched by Ruffing, who established a new record by scoring his seventh World Series victory in the first game, 7 to 4. Ruffing had a no-hit game until two were out in the eighth, when Terry Moore singled. That was one putout longer than Herb Pennock went against the Pirates in 1927 and Monte Pearson against the Reds in 1939 in their bids for World Series no-hitters. Ruffing then was within one putout of a two-hit shutout in the ninth when the Cardinals drove him out with a succession of hits and walks. Before Spud Chandler could retire the side, the Redbirds scored four runs and had the potential tying runs on bases. There is no doubt the Cards found themselves in that inning, for prior to that they were a jittery bunch of kids and were guilty of four errors.

Chandler suffered the toughest of the four Yankee reverses, for in eight innings of the third game only four Cards reached base on him and he yielded only one clean hit. The "crabbing" of the Yanks on a sacrifice bunt by Marty Marion, forcing the shortstop to bat over again, when he beat out an infield hit in the third inning, was responsible for the lone run off Chandler.

The Yankees outhit the Cards, .247 to .239; outfielded them .973 to .947; had three homers to the Cardinals' two, and three steals to none for St. Louis, but they could not come through in the pinches. Their best work was done by their first two hitters, Phil Rizzuto and Red Rolfe, who batted .381 and .353, respectively. The only Cardinal to bat .300 was Jimmy Brown, who just made that mark. The box scores:

Wednesday, Sept. 30—At St. Louis

New York (A.L.)	AB.	R.	H.	O.	A.	E.
Rizzuto, ss	4	0	0	2	2	0
Rolfe, 3b	5	2	2	0	1	0
Cullenbine, rf	3	1	1	1	0	0
DiMaggio, cf	5	2	3	3	0	0
Keller, lf	4	0	0	4	0	0
Gordon, 2b	5	0	0	2	1	0
Dickey, c	4	1	2	9	0	0
Hassett, 1b	4	1	2	5	1	0
Ruffing, p	4	0	1	0	0	0
Chandler, p	0	0	0	1	0	0
Totals	38	7	11	27	5	0

St. Louis (N.L.)	AB.	R.	H.	O.	A.	E.
Brown, 2b	4	0	1	1	2	1
T. Moore, cf	4	0	2	2	0	0
Slaughter, rf	3	0	1	1	0	1
Musial, lf	4	0	0	1	0	0
W. Cooper, c	4	1	1	8	1	0
Hopp, 1b	4	0	0	11	1	0
Kurowski, 3b	3	0	0	1	0	0
bSanders	0	1	0	0	0	0
Marion, ss	4	1	1	3	2	0
M. Cooper, p	2	0	0	0	1	0
Gumbert, p	0	0	0	0	0	0
aWalker	1	0	0	0	0	0
Lanier, p	0	0	0	0	1	2
cO'Dea	1	0	1	0	0	0
dCrespi	0	1	0	0	0	0
Totals	34	4	7	27	8	4

New York .... 0 0 0 1 1 0 0 3 2—7
St. Louis .... 0 0 0 0 0 0 0 0 4—4

aStruck out for Gumbert in eighth. bWalked for Kurowski in ninth. cSingled for Lanier in ninth. dRan for O'Dea in ninth. Runs batted in—Hassett 2, DiMaggio, Marion 2, O'Dea, T. Moore. Two-base hits—Hassett, Cullenbine. Three-base hit—Marion. Sacrifice hit—Cullenbine. Left on bases—New York 9, St. Louis 9. Earned runs—St. Louis 4, New York 3. Struck out—By Ruffing 8, by M.

1942 WORLD SERIES

Cooper 7, by Lanier 1. Bases on balls—Off Ruffing 6, off M. Cooper 3, off Lanier 1. Hits—Off Ruffing 5 in 8⅔ innings, off Chandler 2 in ⅓ inning, off M. Cooper 10 in 7⅔ innings, off Gumbert 0 in ⅓ inning, off Lanier 1 in 1 inning. Winning pitcher—Ruffing. Losing pitcher—M. Cooper. Umpires—Magerkurth (N.L.), Summers (A.L.), Barr (N.L.) and Hubbard (A.L.). Time—2:35. Attendance—34,769.

Thursday, October 1—At St. Louis

New York (A.L.)	AB.	R.	H.	O.	A.	E.
Rizzuto, ss	4	0	1	0	3	1
Rolfe, 3b	4	0	1	0	2	0
Cullenbine, rf	4	1	1	2	0	0
DiMaggio, cf	4	1	1	7	0	0
Keller, lf	4	1	2	1	0	0
Gordon, 2b	4	0	1	0	3	0
Dickey, c	4	0	2	5	0	0
aStainback	0	0	0	0	0	0
Hassett, 1b	4	0	1	9	0	1
Bonham, p	2	0	0	0	0	0
bRuffing	1	0	0	0	0	0
Totals	35	3	10	24	8	2

St. Louis (N.L.)	AB.	R.	H.	O.	A.	E.
Brown, 2b	3	1	0	0	3	0
Moore, cf	3	1	0	2	0	0
Slaughter, rf	4	1	1	2	1	0
Musial, lf	4	0	1	5	0	0
W. Cooper, c	4	0	1	4	0	0
Hopp, 1b	3	1	2	11	0	0
Kurowski, 3b	3	0	1	2	1	0
Marion, ss	3	0	0	1	4	0
Beazley, p	3	0	0	0	0	0
Totals	30	4	6	27	9	0

New York .... 0 0 0   0 0 0   0 3 0—3
St. Louis .... 2 0 0   0 0 0   1 1 *—4

aRan for Dickey in ninth. bFlied out for Bonham in ninth. Runs batted in—W. Cooper 2, Keller 2, DiMaggio, Musial, Kurowski. Two-base hits—Slaughter, W. Cooper, Rolfe, Gordon. Three-base hit—Kurowski. Home run—Keller. Sacrifice hit—T. Moore. Stolen bases—Rizzuto, Cullenbine. Double play—Brown, Marion and Hopp. Left on bases—New York 7, St. Louis 4. Earned runs—St. Louis 4, New York 3. Struck out—By Bonham 3, by Beazley 4. Bases on balls—Off Bonham 1, off Beazley 2. Umpires—Summers (A.L.), Barr (N.L.), Hubbard (A.L.) and Magerkurth (N.L.). Time—1:57. Attendance—34,255.

Saturday, October 3—At New York

St. Louis (N.L.)	AB.	R.	H.	O.	A.	E.
Brown, 2b	4	1	1	1	2	0
T. Moore, cf	4	0	0	3	0	0
Slaughter, rf	4	0	1	3	0	0
Musial, lf	3	0	1	2	0	0
W. Cooper, c	4	0	0	8	0	1
Hopp, 1b	4	0	0	8	0	0
Kurowski, 3b	2	1	1	2	2	0
Marion, ss	3	0	1	0	1	0
White, p	2	0	0	0	0	0
Totals	30	2	5	27	5	1

New York (A.L.)	AB.	R.	H.	O.	A.	E.
Rizzuto, ss	4	0	2	2	6	0
Hassett, 1b	1	0	0	1	0	0
Crosetti, 3b	3	0	0	1	1	0
Cullenbine, rf	4	0	1	0	0	0
DiMaggio, cf	4	0	2	2	0	0
Gordon, 2b	4	0	0	3	3	0
Keller, lf	4	0	0	2	1	0
Dickey, c	3	0	1	5	0	0
Priddy, 3b-1b	3	0	0	10	1	0

	AB.	R.	H.	O.	A.	E.
Chandler, p	2	0	0	1	2	0
aRuffing	1	0	0	0	0	0
Breuer, p	0	0	0	0	0	1
Turner, p	0	0	0	0	0	0
Totals	33	0	6	27	15	1

St. Louis .... 0 0 1   0 0 0   0 0 1—2
New York .... 0 0 0   0 0 0   0 0 0—0

aFanned for Chandler in eighth. Runs batted in—Brown, Slaughter. Sacrifice hit—White. Stolen base—Rizzuto. Double play—Keller and Dickey. Left on bases—New York 6, St. Louis 4. Earned runs—St. Louis 1. Struck out—By White 6, by Chandler 3. Bases on balls—Off Chandler 1, off Turner 1. Hits—Off Chandler 3 in 8 innings, off Breuer 2 in 0 inning (pitched to three batters in ninth), off Turner 0 in 1 inning. Losing pitcher—Chandler. Umpires—Barr (N.L.), Hubbard (A.L.), Magerkurth (N.L.) and Summers (A.L.). Time—2:30. Attendance—69,123.

Sunday, October 4—At New York

St. Louis (N.L.)	AB.	R.	H.	O.	A.	E.
Brown, 2b	6	0	2	1	5	0
T. Moore, cf	3	0	2	6	0	0
Slaughter, rf	4	1	0	1	0	0
Musial, lf	3	2	2	3	0	0
W. Cooper, c	5	1	2	2	0	0
Hopp, 1b	3	2	1	7	0	0
Kurowski, 3b	3	1	1	1	0	1
Marion, ss	4	1	0	6	4	0
M. Cooper, p	3	1	1	0	0	0
Gumbert, p	0	0	0	0	0	0
Pollet, p	0	0	0	0	0	0
aSanders	1	0	0	0	0	0
Lanier, p	1	0	1	0	0	0
Totals	36	9	12	27	9	1

New York (A.L.)	AB.	R.	H.	O.	A.	E.
Rizzuto, ss	5	1	3	4	2	0
Rolfe, 3b	4	2	2	2	2	0
Cullenbine, rf	4	1	2	0	0	0
DiMaggio, cf	4	0	0	5	0	0
Keller, lf	4	1	1	4	0	0
Gordon, 2b	4	1	0	3	2	0
Dickey, c	4	0	0	2	0	1
Priddy, 1b	4	0	1	7	2	0
Borowy, p	1	0	0	0	1	0
Donald, p	2	0	0	0	0	0
Bonham, p	0	0	0	0	2	0
bRosar	1	0	1	0	0	0
Totals	37	6	10	27	11	1

St. Louis .... 0 0 0   6 0 0   2 0 1—9
New York .... 1 0 0   0 0 5   0 0 0—6

aPopped out for Pollet in seventh. bSingled for Bonham in ninth. Runs batted in—Cullenbine 2, Kurowski 2, M. Cooper 2, T. Moore, Musial, Keller 3, Priddy, W. Cooper, Marion, Lanier. Two-base hits—T. Moore, Musial, Rolfe, Priddy. Home run—Keller. Sacrifice hits—Hopp, T. Moore, Kurowski. Double play—Marion and Brown. Left on bases—St. Louis 10, New York 5. Earned runs—St. Louis 9, New York 5. Struck out—By M. Cooper 2, by Borowy 1, by Donald 1. Bases on balls—Off M. Cooper 1, off Borowy 3, off Donald 2, off Bonham 2. Hits—Off M. Cooper 7 in 5⅓ innings, off Gumbert 1 in ⅓ inning, off Pollet 0 in ⅓ inning, off Lanier 2 in 3 innings, off Borowy 6 in 3 innings (pitched to six batters in fourth), off Donald 3 in 3 innings (pitched to three batters in seventh), off Bonham 3 in 3 innings. Winning pitcher—Lanier. Losing pitcher—Donald. Umpires—Hubbard (A.L.), Magerkurth (N.L.), Summers (A.L.) and Barr (N.L.). Time—2:28. Attendance—69,902.

1943 WORLD SERIES

Monday, October 5—At New York

St. Louis (N.L.)	AB.	R.	H.	O.	A.	E.
Brown, 2b	3	0	2	3	4	2
T. Moore, cf	3	1	1	3	0	0
Slaughter, rf	4	1	2	2	0	0
Musial, lf	4	0	0	2	0	0
W. Cooper, c	4	1	2	2	1	0
Hopp, 1b	3	0	0	9	2	1
Kurowski, 3b	4	1	1	1	1	0
Marion, ss	4	0	0	3	5	0
Beazley, p	4	0	1	2	0	1
Totals	33	4	9	27	13	4

New York (A.L.)	AB.	R.	H.	O.	A.	E.
Rizzuto, ss	4	1	2	7	1	0
Rolfe, 3b	4	1	1	1	0	0
Cullenbine, rf	4	0	0	3	0	0
DiMaggio, cf	4	0	1	3	0	0
Keller, lf	4	0	1	1	0	0
Gordon, 2b	4	0	1	3	3	0
Dickey, c	4	0	0	4	0	0
aStainback	0	0	0	0	0	0
Priddy, 1b	3	0	0	5	1	1
Ruffing, p	3	0	1	0	1	0
bSelkirk	1	0	0	0	0	0
Totals	35	2	7	27	6	1

St. Louis........ 0 0 0   1 0 1   0 0 2—4
New York...... 1 0 0   1 0 0   0 0 0—2

aRan for Dickey in ninth. bGrounded out for Ruffing in ninth. Runs batted in—Rizzuto, Slaughter, DiMaggio, W. Cooper, Kurowski 2. Home runs—Rizzuto, Slaughter, Kurowski. Sacrifice hits—T. Moore, Hopp. Double plays—Gordon, Rizzuto and Priddy; Hopp, Marion and Brown. Left on bases—New York 7, St. Louis 5. Earned runs—St. Louis 4, New York 2. Struck out—By Beazley 2, by Ruffing 3. Bases on balls—Off Beazley 1, off Ruffing 1. Umpires—Magerkurth (N.L.), Summers (A.L.), Barr (N.L.) and Hubbard (A.L.). Time—1:58. Attendance—69,052.

COMPOSITE BATTING AVERAGES
St. Louis Cardinals

Player-Position	G.	AB.	R.	H.	2B.	3B.	HR.	RBI.	BA.
Lanier, p	2	1	0	1	0	0	0	1	1.000
O'Dea, ph	1	1	0	1	0	0	0	1	1.000
Brown, 2b	5	20	2	6	0	0	0	1	.300
T. Moore, cf	5	17	2	5	1	0	0	2	.294
W. Cooper, c	5	21	3	6	1	0	0	4	.286
Kurowski, 3b	5	15	3	4	0	1	1	5	.267
Slaughter, rf	5	19	3	5	1	0	1	2	.263
Musial, lf	5	18	2	4	1	0	0	2	.222
M. Cooper, p	2	5	1	1	0	0	0	2	.200
Hopp, 1b	5	17	3	3	0	0	0	0	.176
Beazley, p	2	7	0	1	0	0	0	0	.143
Marion, ss	5	18	2	2	0	1	0	3	.111
Gumbert, p	2	0	0	0	0	0	0	0	.000
White, p	1	2	0	0	0	0	0	0	.000
Pollet, p	1	0	0	0	0	0	0	0	.000
Crespi, pr	1	0	1	0	0	0	0	0	.000
Sanders, ph	2	1	0	0	0	0	0	0	.000
Walker, ph	1	1	0	0	0	0	0	0	.000
Totals	5	163	23	39	4	2	2	23	.239

New York Yankees

Player-Position	G.	AB.	R.	H.	2B.	3B.	HR.	RBI.	BA.
Rosar, ph	1	1	0	1	0	0	0	0	1.000
Rizzuto, ss	5	21	2	8	0	0	1	1	.381
Rolfe, 3b	4	17	5	6	2	0	0	0	.353
DiMaggio, cf	5	21	3	7	0	0	0	3	.333
Hassett, 1b	3	9	1	3	1	0	0	2	.333
Cullenbine, rf	5	19	3	5	1	0	0	2	.263
Dickey, c	5	19	1	5	0	0	0	0	.263
Ruffing, p-ph	4	9	0	2	0	0	0	0	.222
Keller, lf	5	20	2	4	0	0	2	5	.200
Priddy, 3b1-1b	3	10	0	1	1	0	0	1	.100
Gordon, 2b	5	21	1	2	1	0	0	0	.095
Crosetti, 3b	1	3	0	0	0	0	0	0	.000
Chandler, p	2	2	0	0	0	0	0	0	.000
Bonham, p	2	2	0	0	0	0	0	0	.000
Breuer, p	1	0	0	0	0	0	0	0	.000
Turner, p	1	0	0	0	0	0	0	0	.000
Borowy, p	1	1	0	0	0	0	0	0	.000
Donald, p	1	2	0	0	0	0	0	0	.000
Selkirk, ph	1	1	0	0	0	0	0	0	.000
Stainback, pr	2	0	0	0	0	0	0	0	.000
Totals	5	178	18	44	6	0	3	14	.247

COMPOSITE PITCHING AVERAGES
St. Louis Cardinals

Pitcher	G.	IP.	H.	R.	E.	SO.	BB.	W.	L.	ERA.
White	1	9	6	0	0	6	0	1	0	0.00
Lanier	2	4	3	2	0	1	1	1	0	0.00
Gumbert	2	⅔	1	1	0	0	0	0	0	0.00
Pollet	1	⅓	0	0	0	0	0	0	0	0.00
Beazley	2	18	17	5	5	6	3	2	0	2.50
M. Cooper	2	13	17	10	8	9	4	0	1	5.54
Totals	5	45	44	18	13	22	8	4	1	2.60

New York Yankees

Pitcher	G.	IP.	H.	R.	E.	SO.	BB.	W.	L.	ERA.
Turner	1	1	0	0	0	1	0	0	0	0.00
Breuer	1	0	2	1	0	0	0	0	0	0.00
Chandler	2	8⅓	5	1	3	1	1	1	0	1.08
Ruffing	2	17⅔	14	8	11	7	1	1	1	4.08
Bonham	2	11	9	5	5	3	3	0	1	4.09
Donald	1	3	3	2	2	1	2	0	1	6.00
Borowy	1	3	6	6	6	1	3	0	0	18.00
Totals	5	44	39	23	22	19	17	1	4	4.50

SERIES OF 1943

	W.	L.	Pct.
New York A. L.	4	1	.800
St. Louis N. L.	1	4	.200

The Yankees, who had bowed to the Cardinals in the 1942 Series, gained quick revenge on their St. Louis rivals, winning in the same manner in which they had been defeated the year before—four games to one. After the Bronx Bombers won the opener, the Cooper brothers, Morton and Walker, playing despite the death of their father the morning of the second game, formed the Cardinals' battery for a victory that raised the hopes of Redbird fans for a duplication of 1942, when Billy Southworth's club lost the opener and then copped four straight. But this time history did not repeat itself as the New Yorkers swept the next three contests, with one play—Johnny Lindell's crashing slide into third baseman Whitey Kurowski—providing the turning point of the Series.

As a result, the Yankees gained their tenth world championship and seventh under the management of Joe McCarthy, but it was to be the last for Marse Joe, who was unable to win another pennant before leaving the New York helm in 1946.

Both the Cardinals and the Yankees breezed to their league titles. The Redbirds, who had a real battle with the Dodgers in 1942, although winning 106 games during the season, achieved their '43 flag with one less triumph, but were able to finish 18 games ahead of the second-place Cincinnati Reds. The Yankees raised their pennant with 98 victories and a lead of 13½ games over the Washington Senators.

Starting off as they did the previous year, the Yankees opened the Series on the win-

1943 WORLD SERIES

ning side, copping the first game, 4 to 2, behind Spud Chandler. The New Yorkers took advantage of an error and wild pitch by Max Lanier to score two of their runs. Joe Gordon homered for another tally. Mort Cooper's 4 to 3 decision over Ernie Bonham in the second game was achieved with the aid of homers by Marty Marion, the Cardinals' leading hitter in the Series with a mark of .357, and Ray Sanders.

The key play of the classic occurred in the eighth inning of the third game when the Cards blew up after holding a 2 to 1 lead in a duel between Al Brazle and Hank Borowy. Lindell opened the inning with a single and advanced to second on Harry Walker's fumble of the hit in the outfield. George Stirnweiss, batting for Borowy, bunted to Sanders, whose throw had Lindell nailed at third, but Johnny barged into Kurowski, knocking the ball from his hand, and both runners were safe. Tuck Stainback then flied out, Lindell holding third, but Stirnweiss moved to second after the catch.

The Cardinals handed an intentional pass to Frankie Crosetti, filling the bases, but Billy Johnson, who paced the Bombers at bat with an even .300 in the Series, knocked the strategy topsy-turvy with a triple that cleared the sacks. A walk and three more hits added a pair of runs before the Yankees were retired.

The Redbirds scored only one run in the final two games, picking up a tainted marker off Marius Russo, who beat them, 2 to 1, and then being blanked by Chandler, who gained his 2 to 0 triumph when Bill Dickey smashed a homer off Cooper with Charlie Keller on base in the sixth inning. Cooper fanned the first five batters to face him, but received no hitting support from his teammates, who stranded 11 men on base. The box scores:

Tuesday, October 5—At New York

St. Louis (N.L.)	AB.	R.	H.	O.	A.	E.
Klein, 2b	4	0	1	0	2	1
Walker, cf	4	0	0	2	0	0
Musial, rf	4	0	1	1	0	0
W. Cooper, c	4	1	1	7	1	0
Kurowski, 3b	3	0	0	1	1	0
Sanders, 1b	4	1	2	8	0	0
Litwhiler, lf	3	0	0	3	0	0
Marion, ss	3	0	1	2	3	0
Lanier, p	2	0	1	0	1	1
aGarms	1	0	0	0	0	0
Brecheen, p	0	0	0	0	1	0
Totals	32	2	7	24	9	2

New York (A.L.)	AB.	R.	H.	O.	A.	E.
Stainback, rf	4	0	1	2	1	0
Crosetti, ss	4	2	1	3	3	1
Johnson, 3b	4	1	2	0	3	0
Keller, lf	4	0	1	0	0	0
Gordon, 2b	3	1	1	4	8	0
Dickey, c	4	0	1	4	0	0
Etten, 1b	4	0	0	11	0	1
Lindell, cf	3	0	0	3	0	0
Chandler, p	3	0	1	0	2	0
Totals	33	4	8	27	17	2

St. Louis............ 0 1 0 0 1 0 0 0 0—2
New York........... 0 0 0 2 0 2 0 0 *—4

aFanned for Lanier in eighth. Two-base hit—Marion. Home run—Gordon. Sacrifice hit—Kurowski. Runs batted in—Marion, Lanier, Gordon, Dickey. Stolen base—Crosetti. Double plays—Klein, Marion and Sanders; Gordon, Crosetti and Etten. Bases on balls—Off Chandler 1, off Brecheen 1. Struck out—By Lanier 7, by Chandler 3, by Brecheen 1. Pitching record—Lanier 7 hits, 4 runs in 7 innings; Brecheen 1 hit, 0 runs in 1 inning. Wild pitch—Lanier. Earned runs—New York 2, St. Louis 1. Left on bases—New York 6, St. Louis 5. Losing pitcher—Lanier. Umpires—Rommel (A.L.), Reardon (N.L.), Rue (A.L.) and Stewart (N.L.). Time—2:07. Attendance—68,676.

Wednesday, October 6—At New York

St. Louis (N.L.)	AB.	R.	H.	O.	A.	E.
Klein, 2b	4	0	1	4	4	0
Walker, cf	5	0	1	5	0	1
Musial, rf	4	1	1	2	0	0
W. Cooper, c	3	0	1	5	0	1
Kurowski, 3b	4	1	1	0	1	0
Sanders, 1b	3	1	1	8	0	0
Litwhiler, lf	3	0	0	3	0	0
Marion, ss	3	1	1	0	3	0
M. Cooper, p	3	0	0	0	0	0
Totals	32	4	7	27	8	2

New York (A.L.)	AB.	R.	H.	O.	A.	E.
Crosetti, ss	4	1	2	2	2	0
aMetheny, rf	3	0	0	2	0	0
Johnson, 3b	4	1	2	0	1	0
Keller, lf	4	1	1	3	0	0
Dickey, c	3	0	0	9	2	0
Etten, 1b	4	0	0	4	0	0
Gordon, 2b	4	0	1	4	0	0
Stainback, cf	3	0	0	3	0	0
Bonham, p	2	0	0	0	0	0
bWeatherly	1	0	0	0	0	0
Murphy, p	0	0	0	0	1	0
Totals	32	3	6	27	6	0

St. Louis............ 0 0 1 3 0 0 0 0 0—4
New York........... 0 0 0 1 0 0 0 2 3—3

aAwarded first base in sixth on W. Cooper's interference. bFouled out for Bonham in eighth. Two-base hit—Johnson. Three-base hit—Keller. Home runs—Marion, Sanders. Sacrifice hits—W. Cooper, M. Cooper. Runs batted in—Kurowski, Sanders 2, Marion, Keller 2, Etten. Stolen base—Marion. Double play—Marion, Klein and Sanders. Bases on balls—Off Bonham 3, off Murphy 1, off M. Cooper 1. Struck out—By Bonham 9, by M. Cooper 4. Pitching record—Bonham 6 hits, 4 runs in 8 innings, Murphy 1 hit, 0 runs in 1 inning. Earned runs—St. Louis 4, New York 3. Left on bases—St. Louis 7, New York 4. Losing pitcher—Bonham. Umpires—Reardon (N.L.), Rue (A.L.), Stewart (N.L.) and Rommel (A.L.). Time—2:08. Attendance—68,578.

Thursday, October 7—At New York

St. Louis (N.L.)	AB.	R.	H.	O.	A.	E.
Klein, 2b	4	0	0	2	2	0
Walker, cf	4	0	1	1	0	1
Musial, rf	3	1	1	1	1	0
W. Cooper, c	4	0	1	3	2	0
Kurowski, 3b	3	1	1	2	2	2
bO'Dea	1	0	0	0	0	0
Sanders, 1b	3	0	0	9	2	0
Litwhiler, lf	4	0	2	3	0	0
Marion, ss	2	0	0	2	4	1
Brazle, p	3	0	0	1	2	0
Krist, p	0	0	0	0	0	0
Brecheen, p	0	0	0	0	0	0
Totals	31	2	6	24	15	4

1943 WORLD SERIES

New York (A.L.)	AB.	R.	H.	O.	A.	E.
Stainback, cf	4	0	1	1	0	0
Crosetti, ss	2	1	0	2	4	0
Johnson, 3b	4	1	1	0	1	0
Keller, lf	3	1	0	2	0	0
Gordon, 2b	4	0	1	3	2	0
Dickey, c	4	0	2	6	1	0
Etten, 1b	4	0	1	9	1	0
Lindell, rf	3	1	1	2	0	0
Borowy, p	2	1	1	2	0	0
aStirnweiss	1	1	0	0	0	0
Murphy, p	0	0	0	0	0	0
Totals	31	6	8	27	9	0

```
St. Louis .......... 0 0 0   2 0 0   0 0 0—2
New York .......... 0 0 0   0 0 1   0 5 *—6
```

aReached first on Kurowski's error on fielder's choice at third base for Borowy in eighth. bPopped out for Kurowski in ninth. Two-base hits—Walker, Kurowski, Borowy. Three-base hit—Johnson. Sacrifice hit—Crosetti. Runs batted in—Johnson 3, Gordon, Etten, Litwhiler 2. Double plays—Crosetti, Gordon and Etten; Marion, Klein and Sanders. Bases on balls—Off Borowy 3, off Brazle 2. Struck out—By Brazle 4, by Borowy 4, by Murphy 1. Pitching record—Borowy 6 hits, 2 runs in 8 innings; Murphy, 0 hits, 0 runs in 1 inning; Brazle 5 hits, 6 runs in 7⅓ innings; Krist 1 hit, 0 runs in 0 inning (pitched to one batter); Brecheen 2 hits, 0 runs in ⅔ inning. Earned runs—New York 3, St. Louis 2. Left on bases—St. Louis 5, New York 4. Winning pitcher—Borowy. Losing pitcher—Brazle. Umpires—Rue (A.L.), Stewart (N.L.), Rommell (A.L.) and Reardon (N.L.). Time—2:10. Attendance—69,990.

Sunday, October 10—At St. Louis

New York (A.L.)	AB.	R.	H.	O.	A.	E.
Stainback, cf	3	0	0	1	0	0
Crosetti, ss	4	0	1	2	2	1
Johnson, 3b	4	0	0	1	2	0
Keller, lf	4	0	1	4	0	0
Gordon, 2b	4	1	1	3	7	0
Dickey, c	3	0	1	2	0	0
Etten, 1b	4	0	1	11	0	0
Lindell, rf	3	0	0	3	0	0
Russo, p	3	1	2	0	2	0
Totals	32	2	6	27	13	2

St. Louis (N.L.)	AB.	R.	H.	O.	A.	E.
Klein, 2b	5	0	0	1	4	1
Walker, cf	4	0	0	2	0	0
Musial, rf	4	0	2	2	1	0
W. Cooper, c	4	0	1	7	0	0
Kurowski, 3b	4	0	0	2	1	0
Sanders, 1b	4	1	1	9	1	0
Litwhiler, lf	4	0	1	2	0	0
Marion, ss	3	0	2	2	1	0
Lanier, p	2	0	0	0	1	0
aDemaree	1	0	0	0	0	0
bWhite	0	0	0	0	0	0
Brecheen, p	0	0	0	0	1	0
cNarron	1	0	0	0	0	0
Totals	36	1	7	27	10	1

```
New York .......... 0 0 0   1 0 0   0 1 0—2
St. Louis .......... 0 0 0   0 0 0   1 0 0—1
```

aReached first on Johnson's error for Lanier in seventh. bRan for Demaree in seventh. cGrounded out for Brecheen in ninth. Two-base hits—Russo 2, Litwhiler, Marion, Gordon. Sacrifice hit—Stainback. Runs batted in—Crosetti, Dickey. Stolen base—Keller. Bases on balls—Off Lanier 1, off Brecheen 2, off Russo 1. Struck out—By Lanier 5, by Brecheen 2, by Russo 2. Pitching record—Lanier 4 hits, 1 run in 7 innings; Brecheen 2 hits, 1 run in 2 innings. Earned runs—New York 2, St. Louis 0. Left on bases—New York 7, St. Louis 9. Losing pitcher—Brecheen. Umpires—Stewart (N.L.), Rommel (A.L.), Reardon (N.L.) and Rue (A.L.). Time—2:06. Attendance—36,196.

Monday, October 11—At St. Louis

New York (A.L.)	AB.	R.	H.	O.	A.	E.
Crosetti, ss	4	0	1	0	5	1
Metheny, rf	5	0	1	1	0	0
Lindell, rf	0	0	0	0	0	0
Johnson, 3b	4	0	1	1	2	0
Keller, lf	3	1	1	1	1	0
Dickey, c	4	1	1	7	0	0
Etten, 1b	3	0	1	11	1	0
Gordon, 2b	2	0	0	6	6	0
Stainback, cf	3	0	1	0	0	0
Chandler, p	3	0	0	0	2	0
Totals	31	2	7	27	17	1

St. Louis (N.L.)	AB.	R.	H.	O.	A.	E.
Klein, 2b	5	0	0	3	1	0
Garms, lf	4	0	0	1	0	0
Musial, rf	3	0	0	1	0	0
W. Cooper, c	2	0	1	6	0	1
O'Dea, c	2	0	2	2	0	0
Kurowski, 3b	4	0	2	3	3	0
Sanders, 1b	3	0	1	7	2	0
Hopp, cf	4	0	0	1	0	0
Marion, ss	3	0	1	2	3	0
M. Cooper, p	2	0	0	0	1	0
aWalker	1	0	1	0	0	0
Lanier, p	0	0	0	0	1	0
Dickson, p	0	0	0	1	0	0
bLitwhiler	1	0	1	0	0	0
Totals	34	0	10	27	11	1

```
New York .......... 0 0 0   0 0 2   0 0 0—2
St. Louis .......... 0 0 0   0 0 0   0 0 0—0
```

aSingled for M. Cooper in seventh. bSingled for Dickson in ninth. Home run—Dickey. Sacrifice hits—Marion, Garms, Stainback, Chandler. Runs batted in—Dickey 2. Double plays—Crosetti, Gordon and Etten; Klein, Marion and Sanders. Bases on balls—Off Chandler 2, off M. Cooper 2, off Lanier 2, off Dickson 1. Struck out—By M. Cooper 6, by Lanier 1, by Chandler 7. Pitching record—M. Cooper 5 hits, 2 runs in 7 innings; Lanier 2 hits, 0 runs in 1⅓ innings; Dickson 0 hits, 0 runs in ⅔ inning. Wild pitch—M. Cooper. Earned runs—New York 2. Left on bases—St. Louis 11, New York 9. Losing pitcher—M. Cooper. Umpires—Rommel (A.L.), Reardon (N.L.), Rue (A.L.) and Stewart (N.L.). Time—2:24. Attendance—33,872.

COMPOSITE BATTING AVERAGES
New York Yankees

Player-Position	G.	AB.	R.	H.	2B.	3B.	HR.	RBI.	BA.
Russo, p	1	3	1	2	2	0	0	0	.667
Borowy, p	1	2	1	1	1	0	0	0	.500
Johnson, 3b	5	20	3	6	1	1	0	3	.300
Dickey, c	5	18	1	5	0	0	1	4	.278
Crosetti, ss	5	18	4	5	0	0	0	1	.278
Gordon, 2b	5	17	2	4	1	0	1	2	.235
Keller, lf	5	18	3	4	0	1	0	2	.222
Stainback, rf	5	17	0	3	0	0	0	0	.176
Chandler, p	2	6	0	1	0	0	0	0	.167
Metheny, rf	2	8	0	1	0	0	0	0	.125
Lindell, cf	4	9	1	1	0	0	0	0	.111
Etten, 1b	5	19	0	2	0	0	0	2	.105
Bonham, p	1	2	0	0	0	0	0	0	.000
Murphy, p	2	0	0	0	0	0	0	0	.000
Stirnweiss, ph	1	1	1	0	0	0	0	0	.000
Weatherly, ph	1	1	0	0	0	0	0	0	.000
Totals	5	159	17	35	5	2	2	14	.220

St. Louis Cardinals

Player-Position	G.	AB.	R.	H.	2B.	3B.	HR.	RBI.	BA.
O'Dea, ph-c	2	3	0	2	0	0	0	0	.667
Marion, ss	5	14	1	5	2	0	1	2	.357
W. Cooper, c	5	17	1	5	0	0	0	0	.294
Sanders, 1b	5	17	3	5	0	0	1	2	.294
Musial, rf	5	18	2	5	0	0	0	0	.278
Litwhiler, lf-ph	5	15	0	4	1	0	0	2	.267
Lanier, p	3	4	0	1	0	0	0	1	.250
Kurowski, 3b	5	18	2	4	1	0	0	1	.222
Walker, cf-ph	5	18	0	3	1	0	0	0	.167
Klein, 2b	5	22	0	3	0	0	0	0	.136
Garms, ph-lf	2	5	0	0	0	0	0	0	.000
Hopp, cf	1	4	0	0	0	0	0	0	.000
Brecheen, p	3	0	0	0	0	0	0	0	.000
M. Cooper, p	2	5	0	0	0	0	0	0	.000
Brazle, p	1	3	0	0	0	0	0	0	.000
Krist, p	1	0	0	0	0	0	0	0	.000
Dickson, p	1	0	0	0	0	0	0	0	.000
Demaree, ph	1	1	0	0	0	0	0	0	.000
Narron, ph	1	1	0	0	0	0	0	0	.000
White, pr	1	0	0	0	0	0	0	0	.000
Totals	5	165	9	37	5	0	2	8	.224

COMPOSITE PITCHING AVERAGES
New York Yankees

Pitcher	G.	IP.	H.	R.	E.	SO.	BB.	W.	L.	ERA.
Russo	1	9	7	1	0	2	1	1	0	0.00
Murphy	2	2	1	0	0	1	1	0	0	0.00
Chandler	2	18	17	2	1	10	3	2	0	0.50
Borowy	1	8	6	2	2	4	3	1	0	2.25
Bonham	1	8	6	4	4	9	3	0	1	4.50
Totals	5	45	37	9	7	26	11	4	1	1.40

St. Louis Cardinals

Pitcher	G.	IP.	H.	R.	E.	SO.	BB.	W.	L.	ERA.
Krist	1	0	1	0	0	0	0	0	0	0.00
Dickson	1	⅔	0	0	0	0	1	0	0	0.00
Lanier	3	15⅓	13	5	3	13	3	0	1	1.76
Brecheen	3	3⅔	5	1	1	3	3	0	1	2.45
M. Cooper	2	16	11	5	5	10	3	1	1	2.81
Brazle	1	7⅓	5	6	3	4	2	0	1	3.68
Totals	5	43	35	17	12	30	12	1	4	2.51

SERIES OF 1944

	W.	L.	Pct.
St. Louis N. L.	4	2	.667
St. Louis A. L.	2	4	.333

Although the Cubs and the White Sox had met in 1906 and the Yankees had opposed the Giants five times (1921-22-23-36-37) and the Dodgers once, in 1941, no city other than Chicago or New York had witnessed a World Series between two home clubs until the Cardinals and the Browns engaged in the "Trolley Series" of 1944. The Browns, who had won the American League pennant for the first time in their history, failed to measure up to their more experienced rivals and went down to defeat, four games to two.

Managed by Billy Southworth, who became the first National League pilot to win three consecutive flags since John McGraw led the Giants to four pennants from 1921 to '24, the Cardinals also became the first senior circuit club to cop over 100 games in each of three straight seasons. The Birds won 106 in 1942, 105 in '43 and 105 again in '44.

Meanwhile, the Browns engaged in a knock-down, drag-out fight with the Tigers before clinching the American League honors by the margin of one game. The Browns swept their final four-game series with the Yankees, winning the last game on the final day of the season, 5 to 2, with the aid of a pair of two-run homers by Chet Laabs. In Detroit, Dutch Leonard, named to pitch the windup for the Senators against the Tigers, received a telephone call offering him a bribe if he would not bear down. The pitcher hung up on his mysterious caller, then went out and beat the Bengals, 4 to 1.

The fall classic between the two St. Louis rivals was marked by superb pitching for both clubs and inept fielding by the Browns, who committed 10 errors, seven of them coming during innings in which the Cardinals scored. The Birds had only one bobble and none by their infield, which handled 123 chances without slipping. The pitchers struck out a record total of 92 batters, 49 of them by Cardinal moundsmen and 43 by the Browns' hurlers.

The opening game proved a heartbreaker for Morton Cooper, the Birds' ace, who yielded only two hits in a duel with Denny Galehouse, but was defeated, 2 to 1, when Gene Moore singled and George McQuinn homered in the fourth inning. The second game developed into an extra-inning battle, with the Cardinals winning in the eleventh, 3 to 2, on a single by Ray Sanders, a sacrifice and a single by pinch-hitter Ken O'Dea. The Browns forged ahead again in the third game, routing Ted Wilks with four runs in the third inning to give Jack Kramer a 6 to 2 decision, but the Cardinals then swept the next three contests to close out the Series.

After Harry Brecheen vanquished Sig Jakucki, 5 to 1, with the aid of a two-run homer by Stan Musial, Cooper turned the tables on Galehouse with a shutout, 2 to 0, winning on circuit clouts by Sanders and Danny Litwhiler. A wild throw by Vern Stephens helped the Cardinals score three runs in the fourth inning of the sixth game and enabled Max Lanier to post the clinching 3 to 1 triumph with relief assistance from Wilks, who disposed of the last 11 Browns in succession.

McQuinn topped the Series hitters with .438, while Emil Verban's .412 was high for the Cardinal batsmen. The box scores:

Wednesday, October 4—At St. Louis

Browns (A.L.)	AB.	R.	H.	O.	A.	E.
Gutteridge, 2b	4	0	0	1	2	0
Kreevich, cf	4	0	0	6	0	0
Laabs, lf	4	0	0	2	0	0
Stephens, ss	3	0	0	1	3	0
Moore, rf	3	1	1	1	0	0
McQuinn, 1b	3	1	1	10	0	0
Christman, 3b	3	0	0	1	1	0
Hayworth, c	3	0	0	5	0	0
Galehouse, p	2	0	0	0	2	0
Totals	29	2	2	27	8	0

1944 WORLD SERIES

Cardinals (N.L.)	AB.	R.	H.	O.	A.	E.
Hopp, cf	5	0	1	1	0	0
Sanders, 1b	3	0	1	12	0	0
Musial, rf	3	0	1	2	0	0
W. Cooper, c	3	0	0	8	0	0
Kurowski, 3b	4	0	1	0	3	0
Litwhiler, lf	2	0	0	1	0	0
Fallon, 2b	1	0	0	0	0	0
Marion, ss	4	1	2	1	4	0
Verban, 2b	2	0	1	1	1	0
aBergamo, lf	1	0	1	0	0	0
M. Cooper, p	2	0	0	0	3	0
bGarms	1	0	0	0	0	0
Donnelly, p	0	0	0	0	1	0
cO'Dea	1	0	0	0	0	0
Totals	32	1	7	27	12	0

```
Browns........... 0 0 0   2 0 0   0 0 0—2
Cardinals........ 0 0 0   0 0 0   0 0 1—1
```

aWalked for Verban in seventh. bGrounded out for M. Cooper in seventh. cFlied out for Donnelly in ninth, scoring Marion. Two-base hits—Marion 2. Home run—McQuinn. Sacrifice hit—Musial. Runs batted in—McQuinn 2, O'Dea. Double play—Gutteridge, Stephens and McQuinn. Bases on balls—Off M. Cooper 3, off Galehouse 4. Struck out—By M. Cooper 4, by Donnelly 2, by Galehouse 5. Pitching record—M. Cooper 2 hits, 2 runs in 7 innings; Donnelly 0 hits, 0 runs in 2 innings. Earned runs—Browns 2, Cardinals 1. Left on bases—Browns 3, Cardinals 9. Losing pitcher—M. Cooper. Umpires—Sears (N.L.), McGowan (A.L.), Dunn (N.L.) and Pipgras (A.L.). Time—2:05. Attendance—33,242.

Thursday, October 5—At St. Louis

Browns (A.L.)	AB.	R.	H.	O.	A.	E.
Gutteridge, 2b	4	0	0	5	4	1
Kreevich, cf	5	0	2	1	0	0
Laabs, lf	4	0	0	1	0	0
cZarilla, lf	1	0	0	0	0	0
Stephens, ss	5	0	0	2	5	0
McQuinn, 1b	2	0	1	13	1	0
Christman, 3b	5	0	0	0	5	1
Moore, rf	5	1	2	1	0	0
Hayworth, c	5	1	1	7	1	0
Potter, p	2	0	0	1	1	2
aMancuso	1	0	1	0	0	0
bShirley	0	0	0	0	0	0
Muncrief, p	1	0	0	0	0	0
Totals	40	2	7	x31	17	4

Cardinals (N.L.)	AB.	R.	H.	O.	A.	E.
Bergamo, lf	5	0	0	0	0	0
Hopp, cf	5	0	0	2	0	0
Musial, rf	5	0	1	2	0	0
W. Cooper, c	4	0	0	15	0	0
Sanders, 1b	3	2	1	8	1	0
Kurowski, 3b	4	0	2	1	4	0
Marion, ss	3	0	0	2	6	0
Verban, 2b	3	1	1	3	0	0
dO'Dea	1	0	1	0	0	0
Lanier, p	2	0	0	0	0	0
Donnelly, p	1	0	0	0	1	0
Totals	36	3	7	33	12	0

```
Browns........... 0 0 0   0 0 0   2 0 0   0 0—2
Cardinals........ 0 0 1   1 0 0   0 0 0   0 1—3
```

aSingled for Potter in seventh. bRan for Mancuso in seventh. cForced Kreevich for Laabs in tenth. dSingled for Verban in eleventh, scoring Sanders. xOne out when winning run scored. Two-base hits—W. Cooper, Kurowski, Hayworth, Kreevich, McQuinn. Sacrifice hits—Lanier, W. Cooper, Kurowski. Runs batted in—Bergamo, Verban, Hayworth, Mancuso. O'Dea. Double plays—Stephens and Gutteridge; Stephens, Gutteridge and McQuinn. Bases on balls—Off Lanier 3, off Donnelly 1, off Potter 2, off Muncrief 3. Struck out—By Lanier 6, by Donnelly 7, by Potter 3, by Muncrief 4. Pitching record—Potter 4 hits, 2 runs in 6 innings; Muncrief 3 hits, 1 run in 4⅓ innings; Lanier 5 hits, 2 runs in 7 innings (none out in eighth); Donnelly 2 hits, 0 runs in 4 innings. Earned runs—Browns 2, Cardinals 1. Left on bases—Browns 9, Cardinals 10. Winning pitcher—Donnelly. Losing pitcher—Muncrief. Umpires—McGowan (A.L.), Dunn (N.L.), Pipgras (A.L.) and Sears (N.L.). Time—2:32. Attendance—35,076.

Friday, October 6—At St. Louis

Cardinals (N.L.)	AB.	R.	H.	O.	A.	E.
Litwhiler, lf	5	0	0	0	0	0
Hopp, cf	4	1	1	1	0	0
Musial, rf	4	0	1	2	0	0
W. Cooper, c	4	0	2	5	0	0
Sanders, 1b	3	0	1	11	0	0
Kurowski, 3b	4	1	0	0	4	0
Marion, ss	4	0	2	2	5	0
Verban, 2b	2	0	0	3	1	0
aGarms	1	0	0	0	0	0
Fallon, 2b	1	0	0	0	0	0
Wilks, p	1	0	0	0	0	0
Schmidt, p	1	0	0	0	0	0
bBergamo	0	0	0	0	0	0
Jurisich, p	0	0	0	0	0	0
Byerly, p	0	0	0	0	0	0
cO'Dea	1	0	0	0	0	0
Totals	35	2	7	24	10	0

Browns (A.L.)	AB.	R.	H.	O.	A.	E.
Gutteridge, 2b	4	1	1	2	1	1
Kreevich, cf	4	0	0	1	0	0
Moore, rf	4	1	1	3	0	0
Stephens, ss	2	2	1	1	1	1
McQuinn, 1b	3	1	3	6	0	0
Zarilla, lf	4	1	1	2	0	0
Christman, 3b	4	0	1	1	0	0
Hayworth, c	2	0	0	11	0	0
Kramer, p	4	0	0	0	2	0
Totals	31	6	8	27	4	2

```
Cardinals........ 1 0 0   0 0 0   1 0 0—2
Browns........... 0 0 4   0 0 0   2 0 *—6
```

aFlied out for Verban in seventh. bWalked for Schmidt in seventh. cGrounded out for Byerly in ninth. Two-base hits—Gutteridge, McQuinn, W. Cooper. Runs batted in—McQuinn 2, Zarilla, Christman, W. Cooper, Marion. Double play—Marion and Sanders. Bases on balls—Off Kramer 2, off Wilks 3, off Schmidt 1, off Jurisich 1. Struck out—By Kramer 10, by Wilks 3, by Schmidt 1, by Byerly 1. Pitching record—Wilks 5 hits, 4 runs in 2⅔ innings; Schmidt 1 hit, 0 runs in 3⅓ innings; Jurisich 2 hits, 2 runs in ⅔ inning; Byerly 0 hits, 0 runs in 1⅓ innings. Wild pitch—Schmidt. Passed ball—W. Cooper. Earned runs—Browns 6, Cardinals 0. Left on bases—Cardinals 8, Browns 6. Losing pitcher—Wilks. Umpires—Dunn (N.L.), Pipgras (A.L.), Sears (N.L.) and McGowan (A.L.). Time—2:19. Attendance—34,737.

Saturday, October 7—At St. Louis

Cardinals (N.L.)	AB.	R.	H.	O.	A.	E.
Litwhiler, lf	4	1	2	2	0	0
Hopp, cf	5	2	2	4	0	0
Musial, rf	4	2	3	2	0	0
W. Cooper, c	4	0	2	4	0	0
Sanders, 1b	5	1	1	9	0	0
Kurowski, 3b	4	0	0	0	3	0
Marion, ss	4	0	1	1	3	0

	AB.	R.	H.	O.	A.	E.
Verban, 2b	4	0	1	4	3	0
Brecheen, p	4	0	0	1	3	0
Totals	38	5	12	27	12	0
Browns (A.L.)	AB.	R.	H.	O.	A.	E.
Gutteridge, 2b	4	0	2	3	2	1
Kreevich, cf	5	0	1	4	2	0
Moore, rf	3	1	0	1	0	0
Stephens, ss	4	0	1	1	6	0
Laabs, lf	4	0	2	1	0	0
McQuinn, 1b	3	0	1	9	0	0
Christman, 3b	4	0	1	0	1	0
Hayworth, c	2	0	0	5	0	0
Mancuso, c	2	0	1	3	0	0
Jakucki, p	0	0	0	0	1	0
aClary	1	0	0	0	0	0
Hollingsworth, p	1	0	0	0	1	0
bByrnes	0	0	0	0	0	0
Shirley, p	0	0	0	0	1	0
cTurner	1	0	0	0	0	0
Totals	34	1	9	27	14	1

Cardinals............ 2 0 2 0 0 1 0 0 0—5
Browns.............. 0 0 0 0 0 0 0 1 0—1

aFlied out for Jakucki in third. bWalked for Hollingsworth in seventh. cFlied out for Shirley in ninth. Two-base hits—Marion, Laabs, Musial. Three-base hit—W. Cooper. Home run—Musial. Runs batted in—Musial 2, W. Cooper, Marion. Double plays—Kurowski, Verban and Sanders; Marion, Verban and Sanders. Bases on balls—Off Hollingsworth 2, off Shirley 1, off Brecheen 4. Struck out—By Jakucki 4, by Hollingsworth 1, by Shirley 1, by Brecheen 4. Pitching record—Jakucki 5 hits, 4 runs in 3 innings; Hollingsworth 5 hits, 1 run in 4 innings; Shirley 2 hits, 0 runs in 2 innings. Earned runs—Cardinals 4, Browns 1. Left on bases—Cardinals 9, Browns 10. Losing pitcher—Jakucki. Umpires—Pipgras (A.L.), Sears (N.L.), McGowan (A.L.) and Dunn (N.L.). Time—2:22. Attendance—35,455.

Sunday, October 8—At St. Louis

Cardinals (N.L.)	AB.	R.	H.	O.	A.	E.
Litwhiler, lf	4	1	2	0	0	0
Hopp, cf	4	0	0	3	0	0
Musial, rf	3	0	1	1	0	1
W. Cooper, c	4	0	0	13	0	0
Sanders, 1b	4	1	1	4	0	0
Kurowski, 3b	4	0	1	3	0	0
Marion, ss	4	0	0	1	2	0
Verban, 2b	3	0	1	2	0	0
M. Cooper, p	2	0	0	0	3	0
Totals	32	2	6	27	5	1
Browns (A.L.)	AB.	R.	H.	O.	A.	E.
Gutteridge, 2b	2	0	0	1	0	0
aBaker, 2b	1	0	0	0	0	0
Kreevich, cf	4	0	2	5	0	0
Moore, rf	4	0	0	2	0	0
Stephens, ss	4	0	3	1	1	1
McQuinn, 1b	3	0	0	6	0	0
Zarilla, lf	4	0	0	0	0	0
Christman, 3b	3	0	0	0	1	0
bByrnes	1	0	0	0	0	0
Hayworth, c	3	0	1	12	1	0
cLaabs	1	0	0	0	0	0
Galehouse, p	3	0	1	0	3	0
dChartak	1	0	0	0	0	0
Totals	34	0	7	27	6	1

Cardinals............ 0 0 0 0 0 1 0 1 0—2
Browns.............. 0 0 0 0 0 0 0 0 0—0

aFanned for Gutteridge in seventh. bFanned for Christman in ninth. cFanned for Hayworth in ninth. dFanned for Galehouse in ninth. Two-base hits—Litwhiler, Musial, Kreevich, Stephens. Home runs—Sanders, Litwhiler. Sacrifice hit—M. Cooper. Runs batted in—Sanders, Litwhiler. Double play—Stephens and McQuinn. Bases on balls—Off Galehouse 1, off M. Cooper 2. Struck out—By Galehouse 10, by M. Cooper 12. Earned runs—Cardinals 2. Left on bases—Cardinals 5, Browns 9. Umpires—Sears (N.L.), Pipgras (A.L.), Dunn (N.L.) and McGowan (A.L.). Time—2:04. Attendance—36,568.

Monday, October 9—At St. Louis

Browns (A.L.)	AB.	R.	H.	O.	A.	E.
Gutteridge, 2b	3	0	0	3	2	0
bBaker, 2b	1	0	0	1	0	0
Kreevich, cf	4	0	1	3	0	0
Moore, rf	3	0	0	0	0	0
Stephens, ss	4	0	0	3	3	1
Laabs, lf	2	1	1	1	1	0
McQuinn, 1b	2	0	1	6	1	0
Christman, 3b	3	0	0	1	1	0
cByrnes	1	0	0	0	0	0
Hayworth, c	2	0	0	5	0	1
dChartak	1	0	0	0	0	0
Potter, p	2	0	0	1	1	0
Muncrief, p	0	0	0	0	0	0
aZarilla	1	0	0	0	0	0
Kramer, p	0	0	0	0	1	0
Totals	29	1	3	24	11	2
Cardinals (N.L.)	AB.	R.	H.	O.	A.	E.
Litwhiler, lf	5	0	0	2	0	0
Hopp, cf	4	0	1	3	0	0
Musial, rf	4	0	0	2	0	0
W. Cooper, c	3	1	2	10	0	0
Sanders, 1b	3	1	1	7	1	0
Kurowski, 3b	3	1	1	0	1	0
Marion, ss	3	0	0	0	2	0
Verban, 2b	3	0	3	2	2	0
Lanier, p	2	0	2	1	1	0
Wilks, p	1	0	0	0	1	0
Totals	31	3	10	27	8	0

Browns............... 0 1 0 0 0 0 0 0 0—1
Cardinals............ 0 0 0 3 0 0 0 0 *—3

aFanned for Muncrief in seventh. bFanned for Gutteridge in seventh. cFanned for Christman in ninth. dFanned for Hayworth in ninth. Two-base hit—Kreevich. Three-base hit—Laabs. Sacrifice hits—McQuinn, Wilks, Marion. Runs batted in—McQuinn, Kurowski, Verban, Lanier. Bases on balls—Off Lanier 5, off Potter 1, off Muncrief 1, off Kramer 2. Struck out—By Lanier 5, by Wilks 4, by Potter 3, by Kramer 2. Pitching record—Potter 6 hits, 3 runs in 3⅔ innings; Muncrief 2 hits, 0 runs in 2⅓ innings; Kramer 2 hits, 0 runs in 2 innings; Lanier 3 hits, 1 run in 5⅓ innings; Wilks 0 hits, 0 runs in 3⅔ innings. Wild pitch—Lanier. Winning pitcher—Lanier. Losing pitcher—Potter. Earned runs—Browns 1, Cardinals 1. Left on bases—Browns 7, Cardinals 10. Umpires—McGowan (A.L.), Dunn (N.L.), Pipgras (A.L.) and Sears (N.L.). Time—2:06. Attendance—31,630.

COMPOSITE BATTING AVERAGES
St. Louis Cardinals

Player-Position	G.	AB.	R.	H.	2B.	3B.	HR.	RBI.	BA.
Lanier, p	2	4	0	2	0	0	0	1	.500
Verban, 2b	6	17	1	7	0	0	0	2	.412
O'Dea, ph	3	3	0	1	0	0	0	2	.333
W. Cooper, c	6	22	1	7	2	1	0	2	.318
Musial, rf	6	23	2	7	2	0	1	2	.304
Sanders, 1b	6	21	5	6	0	0	1	1	.286
Marion, ss	6	22	1	5	3	0	0	2	.227
Kurowski, 3b	6	23	2	5	1	0	0	1	.217
Litwhiler, lf	5	20	2	4	1	0	1	1	.200

Player-Position	G.	AB.	R.	H.	2B.	3B.	HR.	RBI.	BA.
Hopp, cf	6	27	2	5	0	0	0	0	.185
Fallon, 2b	2	2	0	0	0	0	0	0	.000
Bergamo, ph-lf	3	6	0	0	0	0	0	1	.000
M. Cooper, p	2	4	0	0	0	0	0	0	.000
Donnelly, p	2	1	0	0	0	0	0	0	.000
Wilks, p	2	2	0	0	0	0	0	0	.000
Schmidt, p	1	1	0	0	0	0	0	0	.000
Jurisich, p	1	0	0	0	0	0	0	0	.000
Byerly, p	1	0	0	0	0	0	0	0	.000
Brecheen, p	1	4	0	0	0	0	0	0	.000
Garms, ph	2	2	0	0	0	0	0	0	.000
Totals	6	204	16	49	9	1	3	15	.240

St. Louis Browns

Player-Position	G.	AB.	R.	H.	2B.	3B.	HR.	RBI.	BA.
Mancuso, ph-c	2	3	0	2	0	0	0	1	.667
McQuinn, 1b	6	16	2	7	2	0	1	5	.438
Kreevich, cf	6	26	0	6	3	0	0	0	.231
Stephens, ss	6	22	2	5	1	0	0	0	.227
Laabs, lf-ph	5	15	1	3	1	1	0	0	.200
Galehouse, p	2	5	0	1	0	0	0	0	.200
Moore, rf	6	22	4	4	0	0	0	0	.182
Gutteridge, 2b	6	21	1	3	1	0	0	0	.143
Hayworth, c	6	17	2	2	1	0	0	1	.118
Zarilla, ph-lf	4	10	1	1	0	0	0	1	.100
Christman, 3b	6	22	0	2	0	0	0	1	.091
Baker, ph-2b	2	2	0	0	0	0	0	0	.000
Potter, p	2	4	0	0	0	0	0	0	.000
Muncrief, p	2	1	0	0	0	0	0	0	.000
Kramer, p	2	4	0	0	0	0	0	0	.000
Jakucki, p	1	0	0	0	0	0	0	0	.000
Clary, ph	1	1	0	0	0	0	0	0	.000
Hollingsworth, p	1	1	0	0	0	0	0	0	.000
Shirley, pr-p	2	0	0	0	0	0	0	0	.000
Byrnes, ph	3	2	0	0	0	0	0	0	.000
Turner, ph	1	1	0	0	0	0	0	0	.000
Chartak, ph	2	2	0	0	0	0	0	0	.000
Totals	6	197	12	36	9	1	1	9	.183

COMPOSITE PITCHING AVERAGES
St. Louis Cardinals

Pitcher	G.	IP.	H.	R.	E.	SO.	BB.	W.	L.	ERA.
Donnelly	2	6	2	0	0	9	1	1	0	0.00
Schmidt	1	3⅓	1	0	0	1	1	0	0	0.00
Byerly	1	1⅓	0	0	0	1	0	0	0	0.00
Brecheen	1	9	9	1	1	4	4	1	0	1.00
M. Cooper	2	16	9	2	2	16	5	1	1	1.13
Lanier	2	12⅓	8	3	3	11	8	1	0	2.19
Wilks	2	6⅓	5	4	4	7	3	0	1	5.68
Jurisich	1	⅔	2	2	2	0	1	0	0	27.00
Totals	6	55	36	12	12	49	23	4	2	1.96

St. Louis Browns

Pitcher	G.	IP.	H.	R.	E.	SO.	BB.	W.	L.	ERA.
Kramer	2	11	9	2	0	12	4	1	0	0.00
Shirley	1	2	2	0	0	1	1	0	0	0.00
Potter	2	9⅔	10	5	1	6	3	0	1	0.93
Muncrief	2	6⅔	5	1	1	4	4	0	1	1.35
Galehouse	2	18	13	3	3	15	5	1	1	1.50
H'lingsworth	1	4	5	1	1	1	2	0	0	2.25
Jakucki	1	3	5	4	3	4	0	0	1	9.00
Totals	6	54⅓	49	16	9	43	19	2	4	1.49

SERIES OF 1945

	W.	L.	Pct.
Detroit A. L.	4	3	.571
Chicago N. L.	3	4	.429

The World Series jinx, which had persistently dogged the Cubs throughout their history, continued its hex hold on Chicago's National League representatives, who suffered their seventh straight Series setback and eighth in 10 appearances when they lost to the Tigers, four games to three. The Bengals' only previous world championship also had been gained at the expense of the Cubs, in 1935, and oddly enough, the Tigers were the victims on the two occasions that the Bruins won the title, in 1907 and '08.

Breaking the Cardinals' three-year pennant monopoly, the Cubs, led by Charlie Grimm, won honors in the senior league on the next to the last day of the season after a stubbornly-contested battle with the second-place St. Louisans. The addition of Hank Borowy in a $100,000 "waiver deal" with the Yankees, July 27, paid pennant dividends for the Cubs, as the Jersey righthander won 11 and lost only two after switching circuits. The Tigers also had tough opposition from the Senators, but wrapped up the flag on the last day of the campaign when Hank Greenberg, back from service in the Army Air Force, hit a grand-slam homer to defeat the Browns.

The Cubs unfurled the two pitching masterpieces of the Series when Borowy posted a shutout over Hal Newhouser in the first game and Claude Passeau pitched a one-hitter in the third, yielding a lone single to Rudy York in the second inning. However, the Bruins, who had Borowy to thank for winning the pennant, were forced to call on him in all of the last three games of the Classic and he was unequal to the task, winning one and losing two.

Phil Cavarretta of the Cubs topped the hitters with a mark of .432 and Roger Cramer paced the Tigers with .379, but Greenberg was the batting hero of the Series. Of his seven hits, five were for extra bases, including three doubles and two homers. His first round-tripper with two men on base won the second game and his second homer tied up the sixth game, although the Cubs finally won it in the twelfth.

After Newhouser was defeated by Borowy in the opener, 9 to 0, Virgil Trucks, who had exchanged his Army uniform for baseball flannels less than a week before, put the Tigers back on an even keel with a 4-1 triumph in the second contest. Passeau followed with his great performance, blanking the Bengals, 3 to 0. His one-hitter surpassed the similar feat of Ed Reulbach of the Cubs against the White Sox in 1906, since Passeau walked only one man, who was erased in a twin-killing, while Big Ed passed six, hit a batter and was handicapped by two errors behind him. Chicago's backing of Passeau was perfect.

That was the end of fine pitching for the Cubs in the Series, but the Tigers came back with a five-hitter by Dizzy Trout and two superb efforts by Newhouser, who wound up with a total of 22 strikeouts to his credit, setting a record for a seven-game classic. Trout mastered the Cubs, 4 to 1, in the fourth game and Newhouser posted an 8 to 4 triumph in a return meeting with Borowy in the fifth contest.

The sixth game proved a box score nightmare with 38 players, 19 for each team. The Cubs were the victims of a bad break in the sixth inning when Jimmy Outlaw's hard smash to the box ripped the nail off the middle finger of Passeau's right hand, forcing the hurler to leave the game in the next frame. The Tigers then bombarded Hank Wyse and Ray Prim for four runs in the eighth to tie the score.

Borowy, who had been routed in the sixth inning the previous day, took over in the ninth and hurled four frames of shutout relief to cop the 12-inning slugfest, 8 to 7. The Cubs' winning run was propelled home on a freakish hit by Stan Hack, scoring Bill Schuster from first. Hack's drive looked like an ordinary one-base blow to left, but the ball hopped queerly over Greenberg's shoulder and rolled to the wall. The scorers voted it a single for Hack, an error for Greenberg and no run batted in, but the decision brought a torrent of protest. Five hours after the game, the scorers changed their ruling, awarding a double and RBI to Hack and taking away Greenberg's error.

After a day of rest, Borowy returned to the mound again in the seventh and final game, but the Cubs' weary righthander failed to retire a single batter, being rapped for a quick run on successive singles by Skeeter Webb, Eddie Mayo and Roger Cramer. With Paul Derringer on the hill in relief, a sacrifice by Greenberg, an intentional pass to Roy Cullenbine, a not-intended walk to Outlaw which forced in a run, and Paul Richards' base-cleaning double gave Steve O'Neill's Tigers a total of five tallies and eased the way for Newhouser's clinching 9 to 3 victory. The box scores:

Wednesday, October 3—At Detroit

Chicago, (N.L.)	AB.	R.	H.	O.	A.	E.
Hack, 3b	5	0	1	3	0	0
Johnson, 2b	5	2	2	3	4	0
Lowrey, lf	4	0	0	1	0	0
Cavarretta, 1b	4	3	3	8	1	0
Pafko, cf	4	3	3	4	1	0
Nicholson, rf	4	1	2	0	0	0
Livingston, c	4	0	2	5	0	0
Hughes, ss	3	0	0	2	4	0
Borowy, p	3	0	0	1	1	0
Totals	36	9	13	27	11	0
Detroit (A.L.)	AB.	R.	H.	O.	A.	E.
Webb, ss	4	0	1	1	2	0
dMcHale	1	0	0	0	0	0
Mayo, 2b	4	0	2	4	1	0
Cramer, cf	3	0	0	6	0	0
Greenberg, lf	2	0	1	0	0	0
Cullenbine, rf	3	0	0	0	0	0
York, 1b	3	0	1	8	0	0
Outlaw, 3b	4	0	1	1	4	0
Richards, c	2	0	0	7	2	0
bHostetler	1	0	0	0	0	0
Newhouser, p	1	0	0	0	1	0
Benton, p	0	0	0	0	0	0
aEaton	1	0	0	0	0	0
Tobin, p	1	0	0	0	1	0
Mueller, p	0	0	0	0	0	0
cBorom	1	0	0	0	0	0
Totals	31	0	6	27	11	0

Chicago.......... 4 0 3 0 0 0 2 0 0—9
Detroit............ 0 0 0 0 0 0 0 0 0—0

aFanned for Benton in fourth. bGrounded out for Richards in ninth. cGrounded out for Mueller in ninth. dFlied out for Webb in ninth. Two-base hits—Johnson, Pafko. Three-base hit—Nicholson. Home run—Cavarretta. Sacrifice hits—Lowrey, Borowy. Runs batted in—Nicholson 3, Livingston 2, Pafko, Cavarretta 2. Stolen bases—Johnson, Pafko. Double plays—Hughes, Johnson and Cavarretta; Johnson, Hughes and Cavarretta. Bases on balls—Off Newhouser 1, off Borowy 5, off Tobin 1, off Mueller 1. Struck out—By Newhouser 3, by Borowy 4, by Benton 1, by Mueller 1. Pitching record—Off Newhouser 8 hits, 7 runs in 2⅔ innings; off Benton 1 hit, 0 runs in 1⅓ innings; off Tobin 4 hits, 2 runs in 3 innings; off Mueller 0 hits, 0 runs in 2 innings. Hit by pitcher—By Borowy 1 (Greenberg). Passed balls—Richards 2. Earned runs—Chicago 9. Left on bases—Detroit 10, Chicago 5. Losing pitcher—Newhouser. Umpires—Summers (A.L.), Jorda (N.L.), Passarella (A.L.) and Conlan (N.L.). Time—2:10. Attendance—54,637.

Thursday, October 4—At Detroit

Chicago (N.L.)	AB.	R.	H.	O.	A.	E.
Hack, 3b	3	0	3	0	2	0
Johnson, 2b	3	0	0	2	4	0
Lowrey, lf	4	0	2	3	0	0
Cavarretta, 1b	4	1	1	8	0	0
Pafko, cf	4	0	0	4	0	0
Nicholson, rf	3	0	1	2	0	0
Gillespie, c	4	0	0	3	0	0
Hughes, ss	3	0	0	2	2	0
Wyse, p	2	0	0	0	0	0
aSecory	1	0	0	0	0	0
Erickson, p	0	0	0	0	0	0
bBecker	1	0	0	0	0	0
Totals	32	1	7	24	8	0
Detroit (A.L.)	AB.	R.	H.	O.	A.	E.
Webb, ss	4	1	2	0	4	0
Mayo, 2b	3	1	0	3	3	0
Cramer, cf	4	1	3	2	0	0
Greenberg, lf	3	1	1	2	1	0
Cullenbine, rf	2	0	0	2	0	0
York, 1b	4	0	0	11	1	0
Outlaw, 3b	4	0	1	1	0	0
Richards, c	4	0	0	5	0	0
Trucks, p	3	0	0	1	1	0
Totals	31	4	7	27	10	0

Chicago.......... 0 0 0 1 0 0 0 0 0—1
Detroit............ 0 0 0 0 4 0 0 0 *—4

aFlied out for Wyse in seventh. bFanned for Erickson in ninth. Two-base hits—Cavarretta, Hack. Home run—Greenberg. Sacrifice hit—Johnson. Runs batted in—Nicholson, Cramer, Greenberg 3. Bases on balls—Off Wyse 3, off Erickson 1, off Trucks 3. Struck out—By Wyse 1, by Erickson 1, by Trucks 4. Pitching record—Off Wyse 5 hits, 4 runs in 6 innings; off Erickson 2 hits, 0 runs in 2 innings. Earned runs—Detroit 4, Chicago 1. Left on bases—Chicago 8, Detroit 7. Losing pitcher—Wyse. Umpires—Jorda (N.L.), Passarella (A.L.), Conlan (N.L.) and Summers (A.L.). Time—1:48. Attendance—53,636.

Friday, October 5—At Detroit

Chicago (N.L.)	AB.	R.	H.	O.	A.	E.
Hack, 3b	5	0	2	1	1	0
Johnson, 2b	5	0	0	1	1	0
Lowrey, lf	4	1	2	4	0	0
Cavarretta, 1b	2	0	1	10	1	0
Pafko, cf	2	1	0	3	0	0

1945 WORLD SERIES

	AB.	R.	H.	O.	A.	E.
Nicholson, rf	4	0	1	3	0	0
Livingston, c	4	1	1	3	0	0
Hughes, ss	3	0	1	1	4	0
Passeau, p	4	0	0	1	2	0
Totals	33	3	8	27	9	0

Detroit (A.L.)	AB.	R.	H.	O.	A.	E.
Webb, ss	3	0	0	2	3	1
dMcHale	1	0	0	0	0	0
Mayo, 2b	3	0	0	2	1	1
Cramer, cf	3	0	0	4	0	0
Greenberg, lf	3	0	0	1	0	0
Cullenbine, rf	3	0	0	1	0	0
York, 1b	3	0	1	12	0	0
Outlaw, 3b	3	0	0	0	3	0
Swift, c	1	0	0	2	0	0
aBorom	0	0	0	0	0	0
Richards, c	1	0	0	3	1	0
Overmire, p	1	0	0	0	1	0
bWalker	1	0	0	0	0	0
Benton, p	0	0	0	0	3	0
cHostetler	1	0	0	0	0	0
Totals	27	0	1	27	12	2

Chicago	0 0 0	2 0 0	1 0 0—3
Detroit	0 0 0	0 0 0	0 0 0—0

aRan for Swift in sixth; doubled up with Walker. bGrounded into double play for Overmire in sixth. cGrounded out for Benton in ninth. dFouled out for Webb in ninth. Two-base hits—Lowrey, Livingston, Hack. Sacrifice hits—Cavarretta, Hughes, Pafko. Runs batted in—Nicholson, Hughes, Passeau. Double play—Johnson and Cavarretta. Bases on balls—Off Overmire 2, off Passeau 1. Struck out—By Overmire 2, by Benton 3, by Passeau 1. Pitching record—Off Overmire 4 hits, 2 runs in 6 innings; off Benton, 4 hits, 1 run in 3 innings. Earned runs—Chicago 3. Left on bases—Chicago 8, Detroit 1. Losing pitcher—Overmire. Umpires—Passarella (A.L.), Conlan (N.L.), Summers (A.L.) and Jorda (N.L.). Time—1:55. Attendance—55,500.

Saturday, October 6—At Chicago

Detroit (A.L.)	AB.	R.	H.	O.	A.	E.
Webb, ss	5	0	0	1	3	0
Mayo, 2b	3	1	0	1	1	0
Cramer, cf	4	1	2	4	0	0
Greenberg, lf	3	1	1	1	0	0
Cullenbine, rf	3	1	1	1	0	0
York, 1b	3	0	0	10	0	1
Outlaw, 3b	4	0	1	0	3	0
Richards, c	4	0	1	7	0	0
Trout, p	4	0	1	2	2	0
Totals	33	4	7	27	12	1

Chicago (N.L.)	AB.	R.	H.	O.	A.	E.
Hack, 3b	4	0	0	2	2	0
Johnson, 2b	4	1	2	1	3	0
Lowrey, lf	4	0	1	3	0	0
Cavarretta, 1b	4	0	0	10	1	0
Pafko, cf	4	0	0	1	0	0
Nicholson, rf	4	0	0	1	0	1
Livingston, c	3	0	1	4	1	0
Hughes, ss	1	0	0	3	3	0
bBecker	1	0	1	0	0	0
cMerullo, ss	0	0	0	1	0	0
Prim, p	0	0	0	0	1	0
Derringer, p	0	0	0	0	0	0
aSecory	1	0	0	0	0	0
Vandenberg, p	0	0	0	1	0	0
dGillespie	1	0	0	0	0	0
Erickson, p	0	0	0	0	0	0
Totals	31	1	5	27	11	1

Detroit	0 0 0	4 0 0	0 0 0—4
Chicago	0 0 0	0 0 1	0 0 0—1

aFanned for Derringer in fifth. bSingled for Hughes in seventh. cRan for Becker in seventh, failing to advance. dGrounded out for Vandenberg in seventh. Two-base hit—Cullenbine. Three-base hit—Johnson. Sacrifice hit—Prim. Runs batted in—Greenberg, Cullenbine, Outlaw, Richards. Bases on balls—Off Prim 1, off Derringer 2, off Erickson 1, off Trout 1. Struck out—By Prim 1, by Derringer 1, by Erickson 2, by Trout 6. Pitching record—Off Prim 3 hits, 4 runs in 3⅓ innings; off Derringer 2 hits, 0 runs in 1⅔ innings; off Vandenberg 0 hits, 0 runs in 2 innings; off Erickson 2 hits, 0 runs in 2 innings. Passed ball—Livingston. Earned runs—Detroit 4, Chicago 0. Left on bases—Detroit 6, Chicago 5. Losing pitcher—Prim. Umpires—Conlan (N.L.), Summers (A.L.), Jorda (N.L.) and Passarella (A.L.). Time—2:00. Attendance—42,923.

Sunday, October 7—At Chicago

Detroit (A.L.)	AB.	R.	H.	O.	A.	E.
Webb, ss	4	1	1	2	4	0
Mayo, 2b	4	0	2	2	1	0
Cramer, cf	4	2	1	1	0	0
Greenberg, lf	5	3	3	0	0	0
Cullenbine, rf	4	1	2	1	0	0
York, 1b	5	1	1	9	2	0
Outlaw, 3b	4	0	0	0	3	0
Richards, c	4	0	1	11	1	0
Newhouser, p	3	0	0	1	3	0
Totals	37	8	11	27	14	0

Chicago (N.L.)	AB.	R.	H.	O.	A.	E.
Hack, 3b	3	0	1	2	2	1
Johnson, 2b	3	0	0	1	3	0
Lowrey, lf	4	1	1	1	0	0
Cavarretta, 1b	3	1	1	10	0	0
Pafko, cf	4	1	0	5	0	1
Nicholson, rf	4	0	1	1	0	0
Livingston, c	4	0	1	4	0	0
Merullo, ss	2	0	0	2	1	0
bWilliams	1	0	0	0	0	0
Schuster, ss	1	0	0	1	2	0
Borowy, p	1	1	1	0	1	0
Vandenberg, p	0	0	0	0	1	0
Chipman, p	0	0	0	0	0	0
aSauer	1	0	0	0	0	0
Derringer, p	0	0	0	0	0	0
cSecory	1	0	1	0	0	0
Erickson, p	0	0	0	0	1	0
Totals	32	4	7	27	11	2

Detroit	0 0 1	0 0 4	1 0 2—8
Chicago	0 0 1	0 0 0	2 0 1—4

aFanned for Chipman in sixth. bCalled out on strikes for Merullo in seventh. cSingled for Derringer in eighth. Two-base hits—Borowy, Greenberg 3, Livingston, Cullenbine, Cavarretta. Sacrifice hits—Outlaw, Cullenbine, Johnson. Runs batted in—Cramer, Hack, Greenberg, York, Newhouser, Webb, Outlaw, Nicholson 2, Livingston, Cullenbine 2. Double plays—Mayo, York, Webb and Mayo; Johnson, Merullo and Cavarretta. Bases on balls—Off Borowy 1; off Vandenberg 1; off Chipman 1; off Newhouser 2. Struck out—By Borowy 4, by Newhouser 9. Pitching record—Off Borowy 8 hits, 5 runs in 5 innings (pitched to four in sixth); off Vandenberg 0 hits, 0 runs in ⅔ inning; off Chipman 0 hits, 0 runs in ⅓ inning; off Derringer 1 hit, 1 run in 2 innings; off Erickson 2 hits, 2 runs in 1 inning. Hit by pitcher—Erickson 1 (Cramer). Earned runs—Detroit 8, Chicago 4. Left on bases—Detroit 9, Chicago 4. Losing pitch-

1945 WORLD SERIES

er—Borowy. Umpires—Summers (A.L.), Jorda (N.L.), Passarella (A.L.) and Conlan (N.L.). Time—2:18. Attendance—43,463.

Monday, October 8—At Chicago

Detroit (A.L.)	AB.	R.	H.	O.	A.	E.
Webb, ss	3	0	0	3	3	0
cHostetler	1	0	0	0	0	0
Hoover, ss	3	1	1	1	1	0
Mayo, 2b	6	0	1	4	5	0
Cramer, cf	6	1	2	2	0	0
Greenberg, lf	5	2	1	4	0	0
Cullenbine, rf	5	1	2	1	0	0
York, 1b	6	0	2	9	1	0
Outlaw, 3b	5	0	1	2	0	0
Richards, c	0	0	0	4	1	1
aMaier	1	0	1	0	0	0
Swift, c	2	1	1	5	1	0
Trucks, p	1	0	0	0	0	0
Caster, p	0	0	0	0	0	0
bMcHale	1	0	0	0	0	0
Bridges, p	0	0	0	0	0	0
Benton, p	0	0	0	0	0	0
dWalker	1	1	1	0	0	0
Trout, p	2	0	0	0	3	0
Totals	48	7	13	j35	15	1

Chicago (N.L.)	AB.	R.	H.	O.	A.	E.
Hack, 3b	5	1	4	3	3	2
Johnson, 2b	4	0	0	2	6	1
Lowrey, lf	5	1	1	6	1	0
Cavarretta, 1b	5	1	2	15	0	0
Pafko, cf	6	0	2	1	1	0
Nicholson, rf	5	0	0	1	0	0
Livingston, c	3	2	2	2	2	0
eGillespie	1	0	0	0	0	0
Williams, c	1	0	0	1	1	0
Hughes, ss	4	1	3	4	3	0
fBecker	0	0	0	0	0	0
gBlock	0	0	0	0	0	0
Merullo, ss	0	0	0	1	1	0
hSecory	1	0	1	0	0	0
iSchuster	0	1	0	0	0	0
Passeau, p	3	1	0	0	1	0
Wyse, p	1	0	0	0	0	0
Prim, p	0	0	0	0	0	0
Borowy, p	2	0	0	0	0	0
Totals	46	8	15	36	19	3

Detroit............ 0 1 0 0 0 0 2 4 0 0 0 0—7
Chicago........... 0 0 0 0 4 1 2 0 0 0 0 1—8

aSingled for Richards in sixth. bCalled out on strikes for Caster in sixth. cReached first base on error for Webb in seventh. dDoubled for Benton in eighth. eGrounded out for Livingston in ninth. fWalked for Hughes in ninth. gFailed to advance running for Becker in ninth. hSingled for Merullo in twelfth. iScored for Secory, pinch-running in twelfth. jTwo out when winning run was scored. Two-base hits—York, Livingston, Hughes, Walker, Pafko, Hack. Home run—Greenberg. Sacrifice hits—Johnson 2. Runs batted in—Richards, Hack 3, Cavarretta 2, Hughes 2, York, Livingston, Cullenbine, Hoover, Greenberg, Mayo, Cramer. Stolen base—Cullenbine. Double plays—Mayo, Webb, Richards and Webb; Merullo, Johnson and Cavarretta; Mayo, Hoover and York. Bases on balls—Off Trucks 2; off Bridges 3; off Wyse 1; off Trout 2; off Passeau 6. Struck out—By Trucks 3; by Passeau 2; by Caster 1; by Bridges 1; by Benton 1; by Trout 3. Pitching record—Off Trucks 7 hits, 4 runs in 4⅓ innings; off Caster 0 hits, 0 runs in ⅔ inning; off Bridges 3 hits, 3 runs in 1⅔ innings; off Benton 1 hit, 0 runs in ⅓ inning; off Trout 4 hits, 1 run in 4⅔ innings; off Passeau 5 hits, 3 runs in 6⅔ innings; off Wyse 3 hits, 3 runs in ⅔ inning; off Prim 1 hit, 1 run in ⅔ inning; off Borowy 4 hits, 0 runs in 4 innings. Earned runs—Chicago 8, Detroit 5. Left on bases—Detroit 12, Chicago 12. Winning pitcher—Borowy. Losing pitcher—Trout. Umpires—Jorda (N.L.), Passarella (A.L.), Conlan (N.L.) and Summers (A.L.). Time—3:28. Attendance—41,708.

Wednesday, October 10—At Chicago

Detroit (A.L.)	AB.	R.	H.	O.	A.	E.
Webb, ss	4	2	1	0	5	0
Mayo, 2b	5	2	2	2	1	0
Cramer, cf	5	2	3	2	0	0
Greenberg, lf	2	0	0	0	0	0
Mierkowicz, lf	0	0	0	0	0	0
Cullenbine, rf	2	2	0	2	0	0
York, 1b	4	0	0	8	1	0
Outlaw, 3b	4	1	1	1	2	0
Richards, c	4	0	2	9	0	0
Swift, c	1	0	0	2	0	0
Newhouser, p	4	0	0	1	2	1
Totals	35	9	9	27	11	1

Chicago (N.L.)	AB.	R.	H.	O.	A.	E.
Hack, 3b	5	0	0	1	3	0
Johnson, 2b	5	1	1	3	3	0
Lowrey, lf	4	1	2	3	0	0
Cavarretta, 1b	4	1	3	10	0	0
Pafko, cf	4	0	1	6	0	0
Nicholson, rf	4	0	1	1	0	0
Livingston, c	4	0	1	4	1	0
Hughes, ss	3	0	1	1	1	0
Borowy, p	0	0	0	0	0	0
Derringer, p	0	0	0	0	0	0
Vandenberg, p	1	0	0	0	1	0
aSauer	1	0	0	0	0	0
Erickson, p	0	0	0	0	0	0
bSecory	1	0	0	0	0	0
Passeau, p	0	0	0	0	0	0
Wyse, p	0	0	0	0	0	0
cMcCullough	1	0	0	0	0	0
Totals	37	3	10	27	9	0

Detroit............ 5 1 0 0 0 0 1 2 0—9
Chicago........... 1 0 0 1 0 0 0 1 0—3

aFanned for Vandenberg in fifth. bCalled out on strikes for Erickson in seventh. cFanned for Wyse in ninth. Two-base hits—Richards 2, Mayo, Nicholson, Johnson. Three-base hit—Pafko. Sacrifice hit—Greenberg. Runs batted in—Cramer, Outlaw, Richards 4, Cavarretta, York, Pafko, Mayo, Greenberg, Nicholson. Stolen bases—Outlaw, Cramer. Double play—Webb, Mayo and York. Bases on balls—Off Newhouser 1; off Vandenberg 1; off Derringer 5; off Erickson 1; off Passeau 1. Struck out—By Newhouser 10; by Vandenberg 3; by Erickson 2. Pitching record—Off Borowy 3 hits, 3 runs in 0 inning (pitched to three batters); off Derringer 2 hits, 3 runs in 1⅔ innings; off Vandenberg 1 hit, 0 runs in 3⅓ innings; off Erickson 2 hits, 1 run in 2 innings; off Passeau 1 hit, 2 runs in 1 inning; off Wyse 0 hits, 0 runs in 1 inning. Wild pitch—Newhouser. Earned runs—Detroit 9, Chicago 3. Left on bases—Detroit 8, Chicago 8. Losing pitcher—Borowy. Umpires—Passarella (A.L.), Conlan (N.L.), Summers (A.L.) and Jorda (N.L.). Time—2:31. Attendance—41,590.

COMPOSITE BATTING AVERAGES
Detroit Tigers

Player-Position	G.	AB.	R.	H.	2B.	3B.	HR.	RBI.	BA.
Maier, ph	1	1	0	1	0	0	0	0	1.000
Walker, ph	2	2	1	1	1	0	0	0	.500
Cramer, cf	7	29	7	11	0	0	0	4	.379
Hoover, ss	1	3	1	1	0	0	0	1	.333
Greenberg, lf	7	23	7	7	3	0	2	7	.304

1946 WORLD SERIES

Player-Position	G.	AB.	R.	H.	2B.	3B.	HR.	RBI.	BA.
Mayo, 2b	7	28	4	7	1	0	0	2	.250
Swift, c	3	4	1	1	0	0	0	0	.250
Cullenbine, rf	7	22	5	5	2	0	0	4	.227
Richards, c	7	19	0	4	2	0	0	6	.211
Webb, ss	7	27	4	5	0	0	0	1	.185
York, 1b	7	28	1	5	1	0	0	3	.179
Outlaw, 3b	7	28	1	5	0	0	0	3	.179
Trout, p	2	6	0	1	0	0	0	0	.167
Mierkowicz, lf	1	0	0	0	0	0	0	0	.000
Newhouser, p	3	8	0	0	0	0	0	1	.000
Benton, p	3	0	0	0	0	0	0	0	.000
Tobin, p	1	1	0	0	0	0	0	0	.000
Mueller, p	1	0	0	0	0	0	0	0	.000
Trucks, p	2	4	0	0	0	0	0	0	.000
Overmire, p	1	1	0	0	0	0	0	0	.000
Caster, p	1	0	0	0	0	0	0	0	.000
Bridges, p	1	0	0	0	0	0	0	0	.000
McHale, ph	3	3	0	0	0	0	0	0	.000
Borom, ph-pr	2	1	0	0	0	0	0	0	.000
Eaton, ph	1	1	0	0	0	0	0	0	.000
Hostetler, ph	3	3	0	0	0	0	0	0	.000
Totals	7	242	32	54	10	0	2	32	.223

Chicago Cubs

Player-Position	G.	AB.	R.	H.	2B.	3B.	HR.	RBI.	BA.
Becker, ph	3	2	0	1	0	0	0	0	.500
Cavarretta, 1b	7	26	7	11	2	0	1	5	.423
Secory, ph	5	5	0	2	0	0	0	0	.400
Hack, 3b	7	30	1	11	3	0	0	4	.367
Livingston, c	6	22	3	8	3	0	0	4	.364
Lowrey, lf	7	29	4	9	1	0	0	0	.310
Hughes, ss	6	17	1	5	1	0	0	3	.294
Pafko, cf	7	28	5	6	2	1	0	2	.214
Nicholson, rf	7	28	1	6	1	0	0	8	.214
Johnson, 2b	7	29	4	5	2	1	0	0	.172
Borowy, p	4	6	1	1	1	0	0	0	.167
Gillespie, c-ph	3	6	0	0	0	0	0	0	.000
Merullo, pr-ss	3	2	0	0	0	0	0	0	.000
Schuster, ss-pr	2	1	1	0	0	0	0	0	.000
Williams, ph-c	2	2	0	0	0	0	0	0	.000
Wyse, p	3	3	0	0	0	0	0	0	.000
Erickson, p	4	0	0	0	0	0	0	0	.000
Passeau, p	3	7	1	0	0	0	0	1	.000
Prim, p	2	0	0	0	0	0	0	0	.000
Vandenberg, p	3	1	0	0	0	0	0	0	.000
Chipman, p	1	0	0	0	0	0	0	0	.000
Derringer, p	2	0	0	0	0	0	0	0	.000
Block, pr	1	0	0	0	0	0	0	0	.000
McCullough, ph	1	1	0	0	0	0	0	0	.000
Sauer, ph	2	2	0	0	0	0	0	0	.000
Totals	7	247	29	65	16	3	1	27	.263

COMPOSITE PITCHING AVERAGES

Detroit Tigers

Pitcher	G.	IP.	H.	R.	E.	SO.	BB.	W.	L.	ERA.
Mueller	1	2	0	0	0	1	1	0	0	0.00
Caster	1	⅔	0	0	0	1	0	0	0	0.00
Trout	2	13⅔	9	2	1	9	3	1	1	0.66
Benton	3	4⅔	6	1	1	5	0	0	0	1.93
Overmire	1	6	4	2	2	2	2	0	1	3.00
Trucks	2	13½	14	5	5	7	5	1	0	3.38
Tobin	1	3	4	2	2	0	1	0	0	6.00
Newhouser	3	20⅔	25	14	14	22	4	2	1	6.10
Bridges	1	1⅔	3	3	3	1	3	0	0	16.20
Totals	7	65⅔	65	29	28	48	19	4	3	3.84

Chicago Cubs

Pitcher	G.	IP.	H.	R.	E.	SO.	BB.	W.	L.	ERA.
Vandenberg	3	6	1	0	0	3	3	0	0	0.00
Chipman	1	⅓	0	0	0	0	1	0	0	0.00
Passeau	3	16⅔	7	5	5	3	8	1	0	2.70
Erickson	4	7	8	3	3	5	3	0	0	3.86
Borowy	4	18	21	8	8	8	6	2	2	4.00
Derringer	3	5½	5	4	4	1	7	0	0	6.75
Wyse	3	7⅔	8	7	6	1	4	0	1	7.04
Prim	2	4	4	5	4	1	1	0	1	9.00
Totals	7	65	54	32	30	22	33	3	4	4.15

SERIES OF 1946

	W.	L.	Pct.
St. Louis N. L.	4	3	.571
Boston A. L.	3	4	.429

Never beaten in a World Series that went the limit, the Cardinals maintained their record by defeating the Red Sox, marking the fourth time that they had gained the world championship in a seven-game battle. The Redbirds previously performed the feat against the Yankees in 1926, the Athletics in '31 and the Tigers in '34, in addition to winning in two shorter classics and losing in three.

Under Eddie Dyer, in his freshman year as pilot, the St. Louisans ended the National League season in a tie with Brooklyn and then qualified for the Series by winning two straight games from the Dodgers in the first pennant playoff in major league history. The Red Sox romped to the A.L. flag, finishing 12 games ahead of the second-place Detroit Tigers. The title climaxed years of effort by Owner Tom Yawkey to develop a champion, but the pride of Boston was humbled when the Red Sox became the first Hub representative ever to bow in blue-ribbon competition. The Sox had won the World Series in all five of their previous appearances in 1903, '12, '15, '16, and '18.

The failure of Ted Williams, who batted .200 with just five hits, all singles, was a big factor in the Red Sox' loss. However, Bobby Doerr, who missed one game and part of another because of migraine headaches, hit .409, and Rudy York walloped two homers, a triple and a double for the Bosox. Harry Walker was the hitting pace-setter for the Cardinals, with .412.

Opening the Series, the Cardinals lost the first game, for the eighth time in the nine fall events in which they had participated. The Birds appeared to have the jinx whipped when they held a 2 to 1 lead going into the ninth inning, but a freak hop on a grounder by Pinky Higgins enabled the Sox to tie the score and they beat Howard Pollet in the tenth, 3 to 2, on a homer by York.

Harry Brecheen blanked the Red Sox, 3 to 0, on four singles in the second game, but the Cardinals were slapped with the whitewash brush in the next encounter, losing 4 to 0 to Dave (Boo) Ferriss. George Munger, aided by a 20-hit attack, was an easy 12 to 3 victor for the Cardinals in the fourth game. The Hubites went ahead in the Series for the third time when Joe Dobson chalked up a four-hit, 6 to 3 triumph in the fifth game.

With their backs to the wall, the Cardinals called on Brecheen and the crafty southpaw, who again drew Mickey Harris as his opponent, beat the Red Sox for the second time, 4 to 1.

Murry Dickson opposed Ferriss at the start of the payoff game, but the Redbirds kayoed the Red Sox righthander and held a 3 to 1 lead going into the eighth inning. Bosox Manager Joe Cronin then called on two pinch-hitters and both delivered, Glen Russell rapping a single to center and stopping at third on a double by George Metko-

1946 WORLD SERIES

vich. Brecheen replaced Dickson and almost emerged unscathed when Wally Moses fanned and Johnny Pesky lined to Slaughter, whose throw kept the runners from advancing. However, Dom DiMaggio came through with a double, driving in two runs to tie the score.

In the home half of the eighth, Enos Slaughter singled off Bob Klinger, but both Kurowski and Del Rice were retired. Walker then hit safely to left-center and Slaughter made his famous three-base sprint to the plate, much to the surprise and chagrin of shortstop Pesky, whose split-second delay in relaying the ball home enabled the fleet-footed Cardinal to count with the clinching run. The box scores:

Sunday, October 6—At St. Louis

Boston (A.L.)	AB.	R.	H.	O.	A.	E.
McBride, rf	5	0	1	1	0	1
Moses, rf	0	0	0	1	0	0
Pesky, ss	5	0	0	0	3	1
DiMaggio, cf	5	0	2	1	1	0
Williams, lf	3	0	1	4	0	0
York, 1b	4	2	1	10	0	0
Doerr, 2b	4	0	1	4	4	0
Higgins, 3b	4	0	2	2	0	0
aGutteridge	0	1	0	0	0	0
Johnson, p	1	0	0	0	2	0
H. Wagner, c	3	0	0	6	1	0
bRussell, 3b	1	0	1	0	0	0
Hughson, p	2	0	0	0	1	0
cPartee, c	1	0	0	1	0	0
Totals	38	3	9	30	12	2

St. Louis (N.L.)	AB.	R.	H.	O.	A.	E.
Schoendienst, 2b	5	1	2	2	5	0
Moore, cf	4	0	0	3	1	0
Musial, 1b	5	0	1	13	0	0
Slaughter, rf	4	0	1	3	0	0
Kurowski, 3b	3	1	1	1	4	0
Garagiola, c	4	0	1	4	0	0
Walker, lf	2	0	1	3	0	0
dDusak, lf	1	0	0	0	0	0
Marion, ss	3	0	0	1	3	0
Pollet, p	4	0	0	0	0	0
Totals	35	2	7	30	13	0

Boston............ 0 1 0 0 0 0 0 0 1 1—3
St. Louis......... 0 0 0 0 0 1 0 1 0 0—2

aRan for Higgins in ninth and scored. bSingled for H. Wagner in ninth. cFanned for Hughson in ninth. dFlied out for Walker in ninth. Two-base hits—Musial, Garagiola. Three-base hit—Slaughter. Home run—York. Sacrifice hits—Marion, Moore. Runs batted in—Higgins, McBride, York, Musial, Garagiola. Stolen base—Schoendienst. Bases on balls—Off Pollet 4; off Hughson 2. Struck out—By Pollet 3; by Hughson 5; by Johnson 1. Hit by pitcher—By Pollet (York); by Hughson (Kurowski). Pitching record—Off Hughson, 7 hits, 2 runs in 8 innings; off Johnson, 0 hits, 0 runs in 2 innings. Earned runs—Boston 3, St. Louis 2. Left on bases—Boston 10, St. Louis 8. Winning pitcher—Johnson. Umpires—Ballanfant (N.L.), Hubbard (A.L.), Barlick (N.L.), Berry (A.L.). Time—2:39. Attendance—36,218.

Monday, October 7—At St. Louis

Boston (A.L.)	AB.	R.	H.	O.	A.	E.
McBride, rf	4	0	1	3	0	0
Pesky, ss	4	0	0	3	2	0
DiMaggio, cf	4	0	1	3	0	0
Williams, lf	4	0	0	1	0	0
York, 1b	2	0	0	6	2	0
Doerr, 2b	4	0	1	4	5	0
Higgins, 3b	2	0	0	0	2	1
Partee, c	2	0	0	1	0	0
H. Wagner, c	1	0	0	2	0	0
Harris, p	2	0	1	1	0	0
aCulberson	1	0	0	0	0	0
Dobson, p	0	0	0	0	0	0
Totals	30	0	4	24	11	1

St. Louis (N.L.)	AB.	R.	H.	O.	A.	E.
Schoendienst, 2b	3	0	0	2	3	0
Moore, cf	3	0	1	3	0	0
Musial, 1b	4	0	0	11	0	0
Kurowski, 3b	4	0	1	1	1	0
Slaughter, rf	4	0	0	2	0	0
Dusak, lf	2	0	1	1	0	0
bSisler	1	0	0	0	0	0
Walker, lf	0	0	0	1	0	0
Marion, ss	4	0	0	2	6	0
Rice, c	2	2	2	4	0	0
Brecheen, p	3	1	1	0	0	0
Totals	30	3	6	27	10	0

Boston............ 0 0 0 0 0 0 0 0 0—0
St. Louis......... 0 0 1 0 2 0 0 0 *—3

aFlied out for Harris in eighth. bGrounded out for Dusak in eighth. Two-base hits—Rice, Dusak. Sacrifice hit—Schoendienst. Runs batted in—Brecheen, Moore, Musial. Double play—Marion and Musial. Bases on balls—Off Harris 3; off Brecheen 3. Struck out—By Harris 3; by Brecheen 4. Pitching record—Off Harris, 6 hits, 3 runs in 7 innings; off Dobson, 0 hits, 0 runs in 1 inning. Earned runs—St. Louis 2. Left on bases Boston 6, St. Louis 7. Losing pitcher—Harris. Umpires—Hubbard (A.L.), Barlick (N.L.), Berry (A.L.), Ballanfant (N.L.). Time—1:56. Attendance—35,815.

Wednesday, October 9—At Boston

St. Louis (N.L.)	AB.	R.	H.	O.	A.	E.
Schoendienst, 2b	4	0	0	3	2	1
Moore, cf	4	0	0	1	0	0
Musial, 1b	3	0	1	8	1	0
Slaughter, rf	4	0	1	4	0	0
Kurowski, 3b	3	0	0	1	0	0
Garagiola, c	3	0	1	3	1	0
Walker, lf	3	0	1	2	0	0
Marion, ss	3	0	1	2	3	0
Dickson, p	2	0	1	0	2	0
aSisler	1	0	0	0	0	0
Wilks, p	0	0	0	0	1	0
Totals	30	0	6	24	10	1

Boston (A.L.)	AB.	R.	H.	O.	A.	E.
Moses, rf	3	0	0	2	0	0
Pesky, ss	4	1	2	1	3	0
DiMaggio, cf	4	0	1	4	1	0
Williams, lf	3	1	1	2	0	0
York, 1b	4	2	2	12	0	0
Doerr, 2b	4	0	2	2	8	0
Higgins, 3b	3	0	0	1	0	0
H. Wagner, c	3	0	0	3	0	0
Ferriss, p	4	0	0	0	3	0
Totals	32	4	8	27	15	0

St. Louis......... 0 0 0 0 0 0 0 0 0—0
Boston............ 3 0 0 0 0 0 0 1 *—4

aForced Walker while batting for Dickson in eighth. Two-base hits—DiMaggio, Dickson, Doerr. Three-base hit—Musial. Home run—York. Sacrifice hit—H. Wagner. Runs batted in—York 3. Stolen base—Musial. Double plays—DiMaggio and Pesky; Pesky, Doerr and York. Bases on balls —Off Ferriss 1; off Dickson 3. Struck out—By Dickson 4; by Ferriss 2. Pitching record—Off Dickson, 6 hits, 3 runs in 7 innings; off Wilks, 2 hits, 1 run in one inning. Passed ball—Garagiola. Earned runs—Boston 3. Left on bases—St. Louis 4, Boston 8. Losing pitcher—Dickson. Umpires—Barlick (N.L.), Berry (A.L.), Ballanfant (N.L.), Hubbard (A.L.). Time—1:54. Attendance—34,500.

Thursday, October 10—At Boston

St. Louis (N.L.)	AB.	R.	H.	O.	A.	E.
Schoendienst, 2b	6	1	1	1	4	0
Moore, cf	4	1	1	3	0	0
Musial, 1b	5	1	1	6	1	0
Slaughter, rf	6	4	4	5	1	0
Kurowski, 3b	5	2	4	2	0	0
Garagiola, c	5	1	4	4	0	0
Walker, lf	2	1	1	3	0	0
Marion, ss	4	1	3	2	1	1
Munger, p	4	0	1	1	0	0
Totals	41	12	20	27	7	1

Boston (A.L.)	AB.	R.	H.	O.	A.	E.
Moses, rf	5	0	4	1	0	0
Pesky, ss	5	0	0	3	2	1
DiMaggio, cf	4	1	0	3	1	0
Williams, lf	3	1	1	0	1	0
York, 1b	3	0	1	9	0	0
Doerr, 2b	3	1	2	4	6	0
Gutteridge, 2b	0	0	0	0	0	0
Higgins, 3b	4	0	1	2	1	1
H. Wagner, c	4	0	0	5	1	0
Hughson, p	0	0	0	0	0	1
Bagby, p	1	0	0	0	1	0
aMetkovich	1	0	0	0	0	0
Zuber, p	0	0	0	0	0	0
bMcBride	1	0	0	0	0	0
Brown, p	0	0	0	0	0	0
Ryba, p	0	0	0	0	0	1
Dreisewerd, p	0	0	0	0	0	0
cCulberson	1	0	0	0	0	0
Totals	35	3	9	27	14	4

St. Louis............ 0 3 3 0 1 0 1 0 4—12
Boston.............. 0 0 0 1 0 0 0 2 0— 3

aFlied out for Bagby in fifth. bBounced out for Zuber in seventh. cLined out for Dreisewerd in ninth. Two-base hits—Kurowski 2, Musial, York, Slaughter, Garagiola, Marion. Home runs—Slaughter, Doerr. Sacrifice hits—Marion, Moore, Munger, Walker. Runs batted in—Slaughter, Walker, Marion 3, Musial 2, Garagiola 3, York, Kurowski, Doerr 2. Double plays—Slaughter and Garagiola; Doerr, Pesky and York; Schoendienst and Musial; Pesky and Doerr. Bases on balls—Off Munger 3; off Bagby 1; off Zuber 1; off Brown 1; off Ryba 1. Struck out—By Hughson 1; by Bagby 1; by Zuber 1; by Munger 2. Pitching record—Off Hughson, 5 hits, 6 runs in 2 innings (pitched to three batters in third); off Bagby, 6 hits, 1 run in 3 innings; off Zuber, 3 hits, 1 run in 2 innings; off Brown, 4 hits, 3 runs in 1 inning (pitched to three batters in ninth); off Ryba 2 hits, 1 run in ⅔ inning; off Dreisewerd, 0 hits, 0 runs in ⅓ inning. Earned runs—St. Louis 8, Boston 1. Left on bases—St. Louis 10, Boston 8. Losing pitcher—Hughson. Umpires—Berry (A.L.), Ballanfant (N.L.), Hubbard (A.L.) and Barlick (N.L.). Time—2:31. Attendance—35,645.

Friday, October 11—At Boston

St. Louis (N.L.)	AB.	R.	H.	O.	A.	E.
Schoendienst, 2b	4	0	1	3	1	0
Moore, cf	4	0	0	2	0	0
Musial, 1b	3	1	1	7	0	0
Slaughter, rf	2	0	0	0	0	0
Dusak, lf	1	0	0	0	0	0
Kurowski, 3b	4	1	0	3	1	0
Garagiola, c	4	1	0	7	1	0
Walker, lf-rf	4	0	2	1	0	0
Marion, ss	4	0	0	1	7	1
Pollet, p	0	0	0	0	0	0
Brazle, p	2	0	0	0	1	0
aJones	1	0	0	0	0	0
Beazley, p	0	0	0	0	1	0
Totals	33	3	4	24	12	1

Boston (A.L.)	AB.	R.	H.	O.	A.	E.
Gutteridge, 2b	5	0	2	0	2	0
Pesky, ss	5	1	3	2	2	2
DiMaggio, cf	3	1	1	3	0	0
Williams, lf	5	0	1	4	0	0
York, 1b	2	1	0	8	0	1
Higgins, 3b	4	1	1	0	1	0
Culberson, rf	3	1	2	2	0	0
Partee, c	3	1	1	8	1	0
Dobson, p	3	0	0	0	1	0
Totals	33	6	11	27	7	3

St. Louis............ 0 1 0 0 0 0 0 0 2— 3
Boston.............. 1 1 0 0 0 1 3 0 *— 6

aFanned for Brazle in eighth. Two-base hits—Walker, Musial, DiMaggio, Higgins. Home run—Culberson. Sacrifice hits—Dobson, DiMaggio. Runs batted in—Walker 3, Williams, Gutteridge, Culberson, Higgins, Partee. Stolen bases—Slaughter, Culberson, Pesky. Double plays—Partee and Pesky; Marion, Schoendienst and Musial. Bases on balls—Off Brazle 6; off Dobson 1. Struck out—By Brazle 4; by Beazley 1; by Dobson 8. Hit by pitcher—By Dobson (Slaughter). Pitching record —Off Pollet, 3 hits, 1 run in ⅓ inning; off Brazle, 7 hits, 5 runs in 6⅔ innings; off Beazley, 1 hit, 0 runs in 1 inning. Earned runs—Boston 5, St. Louis 0. Left on bases—St. Louis 5, Boston 11. Wild pitch—Beazley. Losing pitcher—Brazle. Umpires—Ballanfant (N.L.), Hubbard (A.L.), Barlick (N.L.) and Berry (A.L.). Time—2:23. Attendance—35,982.

Sunday, October 13—At St. Louis

Boston (A.L.)	AB.	R.	H.	O.	A.	E.
Culberson, rf	4	0	0	5	0	0
Pesky, ss	3	0	1	2	3	0
DiMaggio, cf	4	0	1	5	0	0
Williams, lf	3	0	0	2	0	0
York, 1b	4	1	1	4	0	0
Doerr, 2b	3	0	1	1	1	0
Higgins, 3b	3	0	1	1	1	0
Partee, c	3	0	0	4	0	0
Harris, p	1	0	0	0	0	0
Hughson, p	1	0	0	0	0	0
aMcBride	1	0	0	0	0	0
Johnson, p	0	0	0	0	0	0
Totals	30	1	7	24	5	0

St. Louis (N.L.)	AB.	R.	H.	O.	A.	E.
Schoendienst, 2b	4	1	1	4	3	0
Moore, cf	4	0	1	2	0	0
Musial, 1b	4	1	1	9	0	0
Kurowski, 3b	4	0	1	2	2	0
Slaughter, rf	2	0	0	2	0	0
Dusak, lf	0	0	0	0	1	0
bWalker, lf	3	1	0	1	0	0
Marion, ss	4	1	2	2	1	0
Rice, c	3	0	1	5	1	0
Brecheen, p	4	1	0	0	2	0
Totals	32	4	8	27	10	0

Boston............................ 0 0 0   0 0 0   1 0 0—1
St. Louis........................ 0 0 3   0 0 0   0 1 *—4

aFouled out for Hughson in eighth. bLined out for Dusak in third and then played left field. Two-base hits—Schoendienst, Marion. Three-base hit—York. Runs batted in—Moore, Kurowski, Slaughter, Doerr, Marion. Double plays—Kurowski, Schoendienst and Musial 2; Brecheen, Schoendienst, Marion and Musial. Bases on balls—Off Brecheen 2; off Harris 1; off Hughson 1; off Johnson 2. Struck out—By Brecheen 6; by Harris 2; by Hughson 2. Pitching record—Off Harris, 5 hits, 3 runs in 2⅔ innings; off Hughson, 2 hits, 0 runs in 4⅓ innings; off Johnson, 1 hit, 1 run in 1 inning. Earned runs—Boston 1, St. Louis 4. Left on bases—Boston 4, St. Louis 8. Losing pitcher—Harris. Umpires—Hubbard (A.L.), Barlick (N.L.), Berry (A.L.) and Ballanfant (N.L). Time—1:56. Attendance—35,768.

Tuesday, October 15—At St. Louis

Boston (A.L.)	AB.	R.	H.	O.	A.	E.
Moses, rf................	4	1	1	1	0	0
Pesky, ss................	4	0	1	2	1	0
DiMaggio, cf.........	3	0	1	0	0	0
cCulberson, cf......	0	0	0	0	0	0
Williams, lf...........	4	0	0	3	1	0
York, 1b................	4	0	1	10	1	0
dCampbell.............	0	0	0	0	0	0
Doerr, 2b...............	4	0	2	3	7	0
Higgins, 3b............	4	0	0	0	1	0
H. Wagner, c.........	2	0	0	4	0	0
aRussell.................	1	1	1	0	0	0
Partee, c................	1	0	0	0	0	0
Ferriss, p...............	2	0	0	0	0	0
Dobson, p..............	0	0	0	0	1	0
bMetkovich...........	1	1	1	0	0	0
Klinger, p...............	0	0	0	1	0	0
Johnson, p.............	0	0	0	0	0	0
eMcBride...............	1	0	0	0	0	0
Totals	35	3	8	24	12	0

St. Louis (N.L.)	AB.	R.	H.	O.	A.	E.
Schoendienst, 2b ...	4	0	2	2	3	0
Moore, cf	4	0	1	3	0	0
Musial, 1b	3	0	1	6	0	0
Slaughter, rf	3	1	1	4	0	0
Kurowski, 3b	4	1	1	3	1	1
Garagiola, c	3	0	0	4	0	0
Rice, c	1	0	0	0	0	0
Walker, lf	3	1	2	3	0	0
Marion, ss	2	0	0	2	1	0
Dickson, p	3	1	1	0	1	0
Brecheen, p	1	0	0	0	0	0
Totals	31	4	9	27	6	1

Boston............................ 1 0 0   0 0 0   0 2 0—3
St. Louis........................ 0 1 0   0 2 0   0 1 *—4

aSingled for H. Wagner in eighth. bDoubled for Dobson in eighth. cRan for DiMaggio in eighth. dRan for York in ninth. eRolled out for Johnson in ninth. Two-base hits—Musial, Kurowski, Dickson, DiMaggio, Metkovich, Walker. Sacrifice hit—Marion. Runs batted in—DiMaggio 3, Walker 2, Dickson, Schoendienst. Bases on balls—Off Ferriss 1; off Dobson 2; off Klinger 1; off Dickson 1. Struck out—By Ferriss 1; by Dobson 2; by Dickson 3; by Brecheen 1. Pitching record—Off Ferriss, 7 hits, 3 runs in 4⅓ innings; off Dobson, 0 hits, 0 runs in 2⅔ innings; off Klinger, 2 hits, 1 run in ⅔ inning; off Johnson, 0 hits, 0 runs in ⅓ inning; off Dickson, 5 hits, 3 runs in 7 innings (pitched to two batters in eighth); off Brecheen, 3 hits, 0 runs in 2 innings. Earned runs—Boston 3, St. Louis 4. Left on bases

—Boston 6, St. Louis 8. Winning pitcher—Brecheen. Losing pitcher—Klinger. Umpires—Barlick (N.L.), Berry (A.L.), Ballanfant (N.L.) and Hubbard (A.L.). Time—2:17. Attendance—36,143.

COMPOSITE BATTING AVERAGES
St. Louis Cardinals

Player-Position	G.	AB.	R.	H.	2B.	3B.	HR.	RBI.	BA.
Rice, c......................	3	6	2	3	1	0	0	0	.500
Walker, lf-rf-ph........	7	17	3	7	2	0	0	6	.412
Dickson, p................	2	5	1	2	2	0	0	1	.400
Slaughter, rf.............	7	25	5	8	1	1	1	2	.320
Garagiola, c.............	5	19	2	6	2	0	0	4	.316
Kurowski, 3b............	7	27	5	8	3	0	0	2	.296
Dusak, ph-lf	4	4	0	1	1	0	0	0	.250
Marion, ss	7	24	1	6	2	0	0	4	.250
Munger, p................	1	4	0	1	0	0	0	0	.250
Schoendienst, 2b.....	7	30	3	7	1	0	0	1	.233
Musial, 1b................	7	27	3	6	4	1	0	4	.222
Moore, cf.................	7	27	1	4	0	0	0	2	.148
Brecheen, p.............	3	8	2	1	0	0	0	1	.125
Pollet, p...................	2	4	0	0	0	0	0	0	.000
Wilks, p...................	1	0	0	0	0	0	0	0	.000
Brazle, p..................	1	2	0	0	0	0	0	0	.000
Beazley, p................	1	0	0	0	0	0	0	0	.000
Jones, ph.................	1	1	0	0	0	0	0	0	.000
Sisler, ph	2	2	0	0	0	0	0	0	.000
Totals	7	232	28	60	19	2	1	27	.259

Boston Red Sox

Player-Position	G.	AB.	R.	H.	2B.	3B.	HR.	RBI.	BA.
Russell, ph-3b	2	2	1	2	0	0	0	0	1.000
Metkovich, ph	2	2	1	1	1	0	0	0	.500
Moses, rf..................	4	12	1	5	0	0	0	0	.417
Doerr, 2b..................	6	22	1	9	1	0	1	3	.409
Gutteridge, pr-2b	3	5	1	2	0	0	0	1	.400
Harris, p...................	3	3	0	1	0	0	0	0	.333
Hughson, p..............	3	3	0	1	0	0	0	0	.333
York, 1b...................	7	23	6	6	1	1	2	5	.261
DiMaggio, cf............	7	27	2	7	3	0	0	3	.259
Pesky, ss..................	7	30	2	7	0	0	0	0	.233
C'son, ph-rf-cf-pr ...	5	9	1	2	0	0	1	1	.222
Higgins, 3b...............	7	24	1	5	1	0	0	2	.208
Williams, lf	7	25	2	5	0	0	0	1	.200
McBride, rf-ph.........	5	12	0	2	0	0	0	1	.167
Partee, ph-c.............	5	10	1	1	0	0	0	1	.100
H. Wagner, c...........	5	13	0	0	0	0	0	0	.000
Johnson, p...............	3	1	0	0	0	0	0	0	.000
Dobson, p................	3	3	0	0	0	0	0	0	.000
Ferriss, p..................	2	6	0	0	0	0	0	0	.000
Bagby, p...................	1	0	0	0	0	0	0	0	.000
Zuber, p...................	1	0	0	0	0	0	0	0	.000
Brown, p..................	1	0	0	0	0	0	0	0	.000
Ryba, p....................	1	0	0	0	0	0	0	0	.000
Dreiseword, p..........	1	0	0	0	0	0	0	0	.000
Klinger, p.................	1	0	0	0	0	0	0	0	.000
Campbell, pr............	1	0	0	0	0	0	0	0	.000
Totals	7	233	20	56	7	1	4	18	.240

COMPOSITE PITCHING AVERAGES
St. Louis Cardinals

Pitcher	G.	IP.	H.	R.	E.	SO.	BB.	W.	L.	ERA.
Wilks	1	1	2	1	0	0	0	0	0	0.00
Beazley	1	1	1	0	0	1	0	0	0	0.00
Brecheen	3	20	14	5	1	11	5	3	0	0.45
Munger	1	9	9	3	1	2	3	1	0	1.00
Pollet	2	10⅓	12	4	4	3	4	0	1	3.48
Dickson	2	14	11	6	6	7	4	0	1	3.86
Brazle	1	6⅔	7	5	4	4	6	0	1	5.40
Totals	7	62	56	20	16	28	22	4	3	2.32

Boston Red Sox

Pitcher	G.	IP.	H.	R.	E.	SO.	BB.	W.	L.	ERA.
Dobson	3	12⅔	4	3	0	10	3	1	0	0.00
Ryba	1	⅔	2	1	0	0	1	0	0	0.00
Dreiseword	1	⅓	0	0	0	0	0	0	0	0.00
Ferriss	2	13⅓	13	3	3	4	2	1	0	2.03
Johnson	3	3⅓	1	1	1	2	1	0	0	2.75
Bagby	1	3	6	1	1	1	0	0	0	3.00
Hughson	3	14⅓	14	8	5	8	3	0	0	3.14
Zuber	1	2	3	1	1	1	1	0	0	4.50
Harris	2	9⅔	11	6	5	5	4	0	2	4.66
Klinger	1	⅔	2	1	1	0	1	0	1	13.50
Brown	1	1	4	3	3	0	1	0	0	27.00
Totals	7	61	60	28	20	30	19	3	4	2.95

SERIES OF 1947

	W.	L.	Pct.
New York A. L.	4	3	.571
Brooklyn N. L.	3	4	.429

In a dramatic Series, which was made notable by the closest bid for a no-hit game in World Series play up to that time, the Yankees defeated the Dodgers to capture their eleventh championship over a period of 25 years. The big drama of the classic occurred in the fourth game when Floyd Bevens held the Dodgers hitless until two were out in the ninth inning, only to have a pinch-double by Cookie Lavagetto wreck the righthander's effort and beat the Yankees, 3 to 2.

Bevens, who had won only seven games while losing 13 during the regular season, was wild in his performance against the Dodgers, issuing a total of 10 walks. Two of them, plus a sacrifice and an infield out, produced a run for Brooklyn in the fifth inning. In the final frame, with one away, Carl Furillo walked and Johnny Jorgensen fouled out. Al Gionfriddo then ran for Furillo and stole second in a maneuver that paved the way for the Dodger victory. With Pete Reiser at the plate for Hugh Casey, Manager Bucky Harris of the Yankees made a move which will always be the subject of debate. Although Reiser had been kept out of the starting lineup by a leg injury, the Yankee manager ordered Bevens to walk the pinch-hitter, who represented the potential winning run. Eddie Miksis ran for Reiser and Lavagetto batted for Eddie Stanky. On Bevens' second pitch, Cookie crashed a double off the right field wall to break Bevens' spell and drive in two runs to beat the Yanks.

The Dodgers, under the leadership of Burt Shotton, who took over as manager following the suspension of Leo Durocher for the season, entered the Series after a close battle for the pennant with the Cardinals. Harris who had won the American League flag as a freshman pilot with the Senators in 1924, duplicated the feat in his first year at the helm of the Yankees. The Bombers who racked up 19 straight victories in July, breezed home with a 12-length lead over the Tigers.

For a team which failed to produce a single route-going pitcher in the seven games of the classic, the Dodgers put up a remarkable fight. Their hurling hero was Casey, who relieved in six of the games and chalked up two victories without defeat. Tommy Henrich of the Yankees, with .323, and Pee Wee Reese, with .304, paced the batters who participated in every contest.

The Series accounted for two "firsts," being the first to be televised and the first to produce total receipts of over $2,000,000. With $175,000 from radio rights and $65,000 for TV, the gross reached $2,021,348.92.

Opening the competition, the first 12 Yankees were retired in succession by Ralph Branca before the Bombers broke loose with five runs in the fifth inning to gain a 5 to 3 victory. Allie Reynolds spaced nine hits and fanned six to register a 10 to 3 triumph for the Yankees in the second game, but the Dodgers kayoed Bobo Newsom, their former teammate, to win, 9 to 8, in the next meeting.

After the Dodgers wrecked Bevens' no-hit aspirations, Shea, making his second start of the Series, hurled a four-hitter to put the Yankees back in the lead, gaining a 2 to 1 decision when Joe DiMaggio belted a homer off Rex Barney in the fifth inning. The desperate Dodgers then came back to tie the classic for the second time, winning, 8 to 6. Thirty-eight players broke into the lineup, and it remained for a substitute performer, Gionfriddo, to star again with a sensational catch that saved the game for the Dodgers. Gionfriddo went into the game as a defensive measure in the sixth inning, with the Dodgers leading, 8 to 5. His opportunity came in that frame, with two Yankees on base and two out, when he raced to the left field bullpen and pulled down a 415-foot drive by DiMaggio that looked like a score-tying home run.

Shea, two-time freshman winner, started for the Yanks in the seventh and final game, but was kayoed in the second inning when the Dodgers scored twice. The Yankees picked up a tally off Hal Gregg in their half and drove him from the box in the fourth inning. Bobby Brown, batting for Bevens, who had replaced Shea, doubled to drive in the tying run and Henrich then singled off Hank Behrman to score the payoff tally for the third time in the Series. Joe Page, the ace Yankee fireman, hurled the last five innings and allowed only one hit—a single by Miksis in the ninth—to receive credit for the decisive victory. The box scores:

Tuesday, Sept. 30—At New York

Brooklyn (N.L.)	AB.	R.	H.	O.	A.	E.
Stanky, 2b	4	0	1	0	4	0
Robinson, 1b	2	1	0	8	1	0
Reiser, cf-lf	4	1	1	3	0	0
Walker, rf	4	0	2	1	0	0
Hermanski, lf	2	0	0	2	0	0
bFurillo, cf	1	0	1	2	0	0
Edwards, c	4	0	0	8	0	0
Jorgensen, 3b	2	0	0	0	1	0
cLavagetto, 3b	2	0	0	0	0	0
Reese, ss	4	1	1	0	2	0
Branca, p	2	0	0	0	0	0
Behrman, p	0	0	0	0	1	0
dMiksis	1	0	0	0	0	0
Casey, p	0	0	0	0	0	0
Totals	32	3	6	24	9	0

New York (A.L.)	AB.	R.	H.	O.	A.	E.
Stirnweiss, 2b	4	0	0	3	1	0
Henrich, rf	4	0	1	3	0	0
Berra, c	4	0	0	5	0	0

1947 WORLD SERIES

	AB.	R.	H.	O.	A.	E.
DiMaggio, cf	4	1	1	2	0	0
McQuinn, 1b	3	1	0	7	2	0
Johnson, 3b	2	1	0	1	2	0
Lindell, lf	3	0	1	3	0	0
Rizzuto, ss	2	1	1	1	3	0
Shea, p	1	0	0	1	2	0
aBrown	0	1	0	0	0	0
Page, p	1	0	0	1	2	0
Totals	28	5	4	27	12	0

Brooklyn........... 1 0 0 0 0 1 1 0 0—3
New York.......... 0 0 0 0 5 0 0 0 *—5

aWalked for Shea in fifth. bSingled for Hermanski in sixth. cPopped out for Jorgensen in seventh. dStruck out for Behrman in seventh. Two-base hit—Lindell. Runs batted in—Walker, Lindell 2, Brown, Henrich 2, Furillo. Stolen bases—Robinson, Reese. Double play—Johnson and McQuinn. Bases on balls—Off Shea 2; off Branca 3; off Page 1. Struck out—By Shea 3; by Branca 5; by Page 2; by Casey 1. Hit by pitcher—By Branca 1 (Johnson). Pitching record—Off Shea 2 hits, 1 run in 5 innings; off Page 4 hits, 2 runs in 4 innings; off Branca 2 hits, 5 runs in 4 innings (pitched to six batters in fifth); off Behrman 1 hit, no runs in 2 innings; off Casey 1 hit, no runs in 2 innings. Earned runs—New York 5, Brooklyn 3. Left on bases—Brooklyn 5, New York 3. Wild pitch—Page. Balk—Shea. Winning pitcher—Shea. Losing pitcher—Branca. Umpires—McGowan (A.L.), Pinelli (N.L.), Rommel (A.L.), Goetz (N.L.), Magerkurth (N.L.) and Boyer (A.L.). Time—2:36. Attendance—73,365.

Wednesday, October 1—At New York

Brooklyn (N.L.)	AB.	R.	H.	O.	A.	E.
Stanky, 2b	4	0	1	3	2	1
Robinson, 1b	4	0	2	5	0	1
Reiser, cf	4	0	1	4	0	1
Walker, rf	4	1	1	1	0	0
Hermanski, lf	3	1	0	3	0	0
Edwards, c	4	0	1	5	1	0
Reese, ss	3	1	2	0	0	0
Jorgensen, 3b	4	0	1	3	5	0
Lombardi, p	2	0	0	0	0	0
Gregg, p	0	0	0	0	2	0
aVaughan	1	0	0	0	0	0
Behrman, p	0	0	0	0	0	0
Barney, p	0	0	0	0	0	0
bGionfriddo	1	0	0	0	0	0
Totals	34	3	9	24	10	2

New York (A.L.)	AB.	R.	H.	O.	A.	E.
Stirnweiss, 2b	4	2	3	1	2	0
Henrich, rf	4	1	2	3	0	0
Lindell, lf	4	1	2	1	0	0
DiMaggio, cf	4	0	1	4	0	0
McQuinn, 1b	5	1	2	6	1	0
Johnson, 3b	5	2	2	1	2	0
Rizzuto, ss	5	0	1	3	4	0
Berra, c	3	1	0	6	1	1
Reynolds, p	4	2	2	1	0	0
Totals	38	10	15	27	10	1

Brooklyn........... 0 0 1 1 0 0 0 0 1—3
New York.......... 1 0 1 1 2 1 4 0 *—10

aFlied out for Gregg in seventh. bForced Jorgensen while batting for Barney in ninth. Two-base hits—Rizzuto, Lindell, Robinson. Three-base hits—Stirnweiss, Lindell, Johnson. Home runs—Walker, Henrich. Sacrifice hit—Henrich. Runs batted in—Robinson, Lindell 2, Walker, Rizzuto, Henrich, McQuinn, Reynolds, Johnson, Stirnweiss, Jorgensen. Stolen base—Reese. Double plays—Jorgensen, Stanky and Robinson; Stirnweiss, Rizzuto and McQuinn. Bases on balls—Off Lombardi 1; off Gregg 1; off Behrman 1; off Barney 1; off Reynolds 2. Struck out—By Reynolds 6; by Lombardi 3; by Gregg 2. Pitching record—Off Lombardi 9 hits, 5 runs in 4 innings (pitched to two batters in fifth); off Gregg 2 hits, 1 run in 2 innings; off Behrman 3 hits, 4 runs in ⅓ inning; off Barney 1 hit, no runs in 1⅔ innings. Wild pitches—Behrman, Barney. Earned runs—New York 10, Brooklyn 3. Left on bases—New York 9, Brooklyn 6. Losing pitcher—Lombardi. Umpires—Pinelli (N.L.), Rommel (A.L.), Goetz (N.L.), McGowan (A.L.), Boyer (A.L.) and Magerkurth (N.L.). Time—2:36. Attendance—69,865.

Thursday, October 2—At Brooklyn

New York (A.L.)	AB.	R.	H.	O.	A.	E.
Stirnweiss, 2b	5	0	2	2	3	0
Henrich, rf	4	0	1	0	0	0
Lindell, lf	4	1	2	0	0	0
DiMaggio, cf	4	1	2	3	0	0
McQuinn, 1b	4	0	0	8	1	0
Johnson, 3b	4	1	1	2	1	0
Rizzuto, ss	5	0	1	5	2	0
Lollar, c	3	2	2	2	1	0
eBerra, c	2	1	1	2	0	0
Newsom, p	0	0	0	0	1	0
Raschi, p	0	0	0	0	0	0
bClark	0	1	0	0	0	0
Drews, p	0	0	0	0	2	0
cPhillips	1	0	0	0	0	0
Chandler, p	0	0	0	0	0	0
dBrown	1	1	1	0	0	0
Page, p	1	0	0	0	0	0
Totals	38	8	13	24	11	0

Brooklyn (N.L.)	AB.	R.	H.	O.	A.	E.
Stanky, 2b	4	2	1	4	5	0
Robinson, 1b	4	1	2	10	1	0
Reiser, cf	0	0	0	0	0	0
aFurillo, cf	3	1	2	0	0	1
Walker, rf	5	0	2	1	0	0
Hermanski, lf	3	2	1	4	0	0
Edwards, c	4	1	1	5	0	0
Reese, ss	3	1	1	1	3	0
Jorgensen, 3b	4	0	2	1	3	0
Hatten, p	2	1	1	0	0	0
Branca, p	1	0	0	0	0	0
Casey, p	1	0	0	1	1	0
Totals	34	9	13	27	13	1

New York........... 0 0 2 2 2 1 1 0 0—8
Brooklyn........... 0 6 1 2 0 0 0 0 *—9

aDoubled for Reiser in second. bWalked for Raschi in third. cFlied out for Drews in fourth. dDoubled for Chandler in sixth. eHomered for Lollar in seventh. Two-base hits—Edwards, Stanky, Furillo, Lollar, Brown, Henrich, Jorgensen. Home runs—DiMaggio, Berra. Sacrifice hit—Robinson. Runs batted in—Edwards, Reese, Stanky, Furillo 2, Lindell, DiMaggio 3, Jorgensen, Lollar, Stirnweiss, Walker, Hermanski, Henrich, Berra. Stolen bases—Robinson, Walker. Double plays—Reese, Stanky and Robinson; Stanky and Robinson. Bases on balls—Off Newsom 2; off Hatten 3; off Chandler 3; off Branca 2; off Page 1; off Casey 1. Struck out—By Hatten 3; by Branca 1; by Chandler 1; by Page 3; by Casey 1. Hit by pitcher—Drews (Hermanski). Pitching record—Off Newsom 5 hits, 5 runs in 1⅔ innings; off Raschi 2 hits, 1 run in ⅓ inning; off Drews 1 hit, 1 run in 1 inning; off Chandler 2 hits, 2 runs in 2 innings; off Page 3 hits, no runs in 3 innings; off Hatten 8 hits, 6 runs in 4⅓ innings; off Branca 4 hits, 2 runs in 2 innings; off Casey 1 hit, no runs in 2⅔ innings. Wild pitches—Drews, Page. Passed

1947 WORLD SERIES

ball—Lollar. Earned runs—Brooklyn 9, New York 8. Left on bases—Brooklyn 9, New York 9. Winning pitcher—Casey. Losing pitcher—Newsom. Umpires—Rommel (A.L.), Goetz (N.L.), McGowan (A.L.), Pinelli (N.L.), Magerkurth (N.L.) and Boyer (A.L.). Time—3:05. Attendance—33,098.

Friday, October 3—At Brooklyn

New York (A.L.)	AB.	R.	H.	O.	A.	E.
Stirnweiss, 2b	4	1	2	2	1	0
Henrich, rf	5	0	1	2	0	0
Berra, c	4	0	0	6	1	1
DiMaggio, cf	2	0	0	2	0	0
McQuinn, 1b	4	0	1	7	0	0
Johnson, 3b	4	1	1	3	2	0
Lindell, lf	3	0	2	3	0	0
Rizzuto, ss	4	0	1	1	2	0
Bevens, p	3	0	0	0	1	0
Totals	33	2	8	f26	7	1

Brooklyn (N.L.)	AB.	R.	H.	O.	A.	E.
Stanky, 2b	1	0	0	2	3	0
eLavagetto	1	0	1	0	0	0
Reese, ss	4	0	0	3	5	1
Robinson, 1b	4	0	0	11	1	0
Walker, rf	2	0	0	0	1	0
Hermanski, lf	4	0	0	2	0	0
Edwards, c	4	0	0	7	1	1
Furillo, cf	3	0	0	2	0	0
bGionfriddo	0	1	0	0	0	0
Jorgensen, 3b	2	1	0	0	1	0
Taylor, p	0	0	0	0	0	0
Gregg, p	1	0	0	0	1	0
aVaughan	0	0	0	0	0	0
Behrman, p	0	0	0	0	1	0
Casey, p	0	0	0	0	0	0
cReiser	0	0	0	0	0	0
dMiksis	0	1	0	0	0	0
Totals	26	3	1	27	15	3

New York......... 1 0 0   1 0 0   0 0 0—2
Brooklyn........... 0 0 0   0 1 0   0 0 2—3

aWalked for Gregg in seventh. bRan for Furillo in ninth. cWalked for Casey in ninth. dRan for Reiser in ninth. eDoubled for Stanky in ninth. fTwo out when winning run was scored. Two-base hits—Lindell, Lavagetto. Three-base hit—Johnson. Sacrifice hits—Stanky, Bevens. Runs batted in—DiMaggio, Lindell, Reese, Lavagetto 2. Stolen bases—Rizzuto, Reese, Gionfriddo. Double plays—Reese, Stanky and Robinson; Gregg, Reese and Robinson; Casey, Edwards and Robinson. Bases on balls—Off Taylor 1; off Gregg 3; off Bevens 10. Struck out—By Gregg 5; by Bevens 5. Pitching record—Off Taylor 2 hits, 1 run in 0 inning (pitched to four batters); off Gregg 4 hits, 1 run in 7 innings; off Behrman 2 hits, 0 runs in 1⅓ innings; off Casey 0 hits, 0 runs in ⅔ inning. Wild pitch—Bevens. Earned runs—Brooklyn 3, New York 1. Left on bases—New York 9, Brooklyn 8. Winning pitcher—Casey. Umpires—Goetz (N.L.), McGowan (A.L.), Pinelli (N.L.), Rommel (A.L.), Boyer (A.L.) and Magerkurth (N.L.). Time—2:20. Attendance—33,443.

Saturday, October 4—At Brooklyn

New York (A.L.)	AB.	R.	H.	O.	A.	E.
Stirnweiss, 2b	3	0	0	3	4	0
Henrich, rf	4	0	2	1	0	0
Lindell, lf	2	0	0	3	0	0
DiMaggio, cf	4	1	1	3	0	0
McQuinn, 1b	4	0	0	7	0	0
Johnson, 3b	3	0	0	2	1	0
A. Robinson, c	3	1	0	7	0	0
Rizzuto, ss	2	0	0	1	1	0
Shea, p	4	0	2	0	1	0
Totals	29	2	5	27	7	0

Brooklyn (N.L.)	AB.	R.	H.	O.	A.	E.
Stanky, 2b	3	0	0	2	2	0
cReiser	0	0	0	0	0	0
dMiksis, 2b	0	0	0	1	1	1
Reese, ss	2	0	0	2	3	0
J. Robinson, 1b	4	0	1	5	0	0
Walker, rf	4	0	0	0	0	0
Hermanski, lf	4	0	1	2	0	0
Edwards, c	3	0	1	9	2	0
eLombardi	0	0	0	0	0	0
Furillo, cf	3	0	0	2	0	0
Jorgensen, 3b	4	0	0	3	0	0
Barney, p	1	0	0	0	1	0
Hatten, p	0	0	0	0	0	0
aGionfriddo	0	1	0	0	0	0
Behrman, p	0	0	0	0	0	0
bVaughan	1	0	1	0	0	0
Casey, p	0	0	0	1	0	0
fLavagetto	1	0	0	0	0	0
Totals	30	1	4	27	10	1

New York......... 0 0 0   1 1 0   0 0 0—2
Brooklyn........... 0 0 0   0 0 1   0 0 0—1

aWalked for Hatten in sixth. bDoubled for Behrman in seventh. cWalked for Stanky in seventh. dRan for Reiser in seventh. eRan for Edwards in ninth. fFanned for Casey in ninth. Two-base hits—Henrich, Vaughan, Shea. Home run—DiMaggio. Sacrifice hit—Furillo. Runs batted in—Shea, DiMaggio, J. Robinson. Double plays—Reese, Stanky and J. Robinson; Reese, Miksis and J. Robinson. Bases on balls—Off Barney 9; off Shea 5; off Behrman 1. Struck out—By Barney 3; by Shea 7; by Hatten 1; by Behrman 2; by Casey 1. Hit by pitcher—By Casey (Lindell). Pitching record—Off Barney 3 hits, 2 runs in 4⅔ innings; off Hatten 0 hits, 0 runs in 1⅓ innings; off Behrman 1 hit, 0 runs in 1 inning; off Casey 1 hit, 0 runs in 2 innings. Wild pitch—Barney. Passed balls—Edwards 2. Earned runs—New York 2, Brooklyn 1. Left on bases—New York 11, Brooklyn 8. Losing pitcher—Barney. Umpires—McGowan (A.L.), Pinelli (N.L.), Rommel (A.L.), Goetz (N.L.), Magerkurth (N.L.) and Boyer (A.L.). Time—2:46. Attendance—34,379.

Sunday, October 5—At New York

Brooklyn (N.L.)	AB.	R.	H.	O.	A.	E.
Stanky, 2b	5	2	2	4	2	0
Reese, ss	4	2	3	2	1	0
J. Robinson, 1b	5	1	2	7	1	0
Walker, rf	5	0	1	3	0	0
Hermanski, lf	1	0	0	0	0	0
bMiksis, lf	1	0	0	0	0	0
Gionfriddo, lf	2	0	0	1	0	0
Edwards, c	4	1	1	5	0	0
Furillo, cf	4	1	2	4	1	0
Jorgensen, 3b	2	0	0	1	1	1
cLavagetto, 3b	2	0	0	0	1	0
Lombardi, p	1	0	0	0	0	0
Branca, p	1	0	0	0	1	0
dBragan	1	0	1	0	0	0
eBankhead	0	1	0	0	0	0
Hatten, p	1	0	0	0	0	0
Casey, p	0	0	0	0	1	0
Totals	39	8	12	27	9	1

New York (A.L.)	AB.	R.	H.	O.	A.	E.
Stirnweiss, 2b	5	0	0	1	6	0
Henrich, rf-lf	5	1	2	1	0	0
Lindell, lf	2	1	2	0	0	0
Berra, rf	3	0	0	0	0	0

1947 WORLD SERIES

	AB.	R.	H.	O.	A.	E.
DiMaggio, cf	5	1	1	5	0	0
Johnson, 3b	5	1	2	1	5	0
Phillips, 1b	1	0	0	4	0	0
aBrown	1	0	1	0	0	0
McQuinn, 1b	1	0	0	6	0	0
Rizzuto, ss	4	0	1	6	1	0
Lollar, c	1	1	1	0	0	0
A. Robinson, c	4	1	2	2	0	1
Reynolds, p	0	0	0	0	0	0
Drews, p	2	0	0	0	1	0
Page, p	0	0	0	0	0	0
Newsom, p	0	0	0	0	0	0
fClark	1	0	0	0	0	0
Raschi, p	0	0	0	0	0	0
gHouk	1	0	1	0	0	0
Wensloff, p	0	0	0	0	1	0
hFrey	1	0	0	0	0	0
Totals	42	6	15	27	14	2

Brooklyn........ 2 0 2 0 0 4 0 0 0—8
New York........ 0 0 4 1 0 0 0 0 1—6

aSingled for Phillips in third. bPopped out for Hermanski in fifth. cFlied out for Jorgensen in sixth. dDoubled for Branca in sixth. eRan for Bragan in sixth. fLined out for Newsom in sixth. gSingled for Raschi in seventh. hForced A. Robinson for Wensloff in ninth. Two-base hits—Reese, J. Robinson, Walker, Lollar, Furillo, Bragan. Runs batted in—J. Robinson, Walker, Stirnweiss, Lindell, Johnson, Brown, Berra, Lavagetto, Reese 2, Frey, Bragan. Double play—Rizzuto and Phillips. Bases on balls—Off Reynolds 1; off Drews 1; off Hatten 4. Struck out—By Lombardi 2; by Branca 2; by Page 1; by Raschi 1. Pitching record—Off Reynolds 6 hits, 4 runs in 2⅓ innings; off Drews 1 hit, 0 runs in 2 innings; off Page 4 hits, 4 runs in 1 inning; off Newsom 1 hit, 0 runs in ⅔ inning; off Raschi 0 hits, 0 runs in 1 inning; off Wensloff 0 hits, 0 runs in 2 innings; off Lombardi 5 hits, 4 runs in 2⅔ innings; off Branca 6 hits, 1 run in 2⅓ innings; off Hatten 3 hits, 1 run in 3 innings (pitched to two batters in ninth); off Casey 1 hit, 0 runs in 1 inning. Wild pitch—Lombardi. Passed ball—Lollar. Earned runs—Brooklyn 7, New York 6. Left on bases—New York 13, Brooklyn 6. Winning pitcher—Branca. Losing pitcher—Page. Umpires—Pinelli (N.L.), Rommel (A.L.), Goetz (N.L.), McGowan (A.L.), Boyer (A.L.) and Magerkurth (N.L.). Time—3:19. Attendance—74,065.

Monday, October 6—At New York

Brooklyn (N.L.)	AB.	R.	H.	O.	A.	E.
Stanky, 2b	4	0	1	3	1	0
Reese, ss	3	0	0	0	1	0
J. Robinson, 1b	4	0	0	3	2	0
Walker, rf	3	0	0	3	0	0
Hermanski, lf	2	1	1	2	0	0
bMiksis, lf	2	0	1	2	0	0
Edwards, c	4	1	2	5	0	0
Furillo, cf	3	0	1	4	0	0
Jorgensen, 3b	2	0	1	0	1	0
dLavagetto, 3b	1	0	0	0	0	0
Gregg, p	2	0	0	1	0	0
Behrman, p	0	0	0	1	0	0
Hatten, p	0	0	0	0	0	0
Barney, p	0	0	0	0	0	0
eHodges	1	0	0	0	0	0
Casey, p	0	0	0	0	0	0
Totals	31	2	7	24	5	0

New York (A.L.)	AB.	R.	H.	O.	A.	E.
Stirnweiss, 2b	2	0	0	5	4	0
Henrich, lf	5	0	1	2	0	0
Berra, rf	3	0	0	1	0	0
cClark, rf	1	0	1	2	0	0
DiMaggio, cf	3	0	0	3	0	0
McQuinn, 1b	2	1	0	7	0	0
Johnson, 3b	3	2	1	1	1	0
A. Robinson, c	3	0	0	4	2	0
Rizzuto, ss	4	2	3	2	2	0
Shea, p	0	0	0	0	0	0
Bevens, p	1	0	0	0	0	0
aBrown	1	0	1	0	0	0
Page, p	2	0	0	0	0	0
Totals	30	5	7	27	9	0

Brooklyn........ 0 2 0 0 0 0 0 0 0—2
New York........ 0 1 0 2 0 1 1 0 *—5

aDoubled for Bevens in fourth. bGrounded out for Hermanski in sixth. cSingled for Berra in sixth. dPopped out for Jorgensen in seventh. eStruck out for Barney in seventh. Two-base hits—Jorgensen, Brown. Three-base hits—Hermanski, Johnson. Sacrifice hit—McQuinn. Runs batted in—Edwards, Jorgensen, Rizzuto, Brown, Henrich, Clark, A. Robinson. Stolen base—Rizzuto. Double play—Rizzuto, Stirnweiss and McQuinn. Bases on balls—Off Shea 1; off Bevens 1; off Gregg 4; off Behrman 3. Struck out—By Gregg 3; by Bevens 2; by Behrman 1; by Page 1; by Hatten 1. Pitching record—Off Gregg 3 hits, 3 runs in 3⅔ innings; off Behrman 2 hits, 1 run in 1⅔ innings; off Hatten 1 hit, 0 runs in ⅓ inning; off Casey 1 hit, 1 run in 2 innings; off Shea 4 hits, 2 runs in 1⅓ innings; off Bevens 2 hits, 0 runs in 2⅔ innings; off Page 1 hit, 0 runs in 5 innings. Earned runs—New York 5, Brooklyn 2. Left on bases—New York 9, Brooklyn 4. Winning pitcher—Page. Losing pitcher—Gregg. Umpires—Rommel (A.L.), Goetz (N.L.), McGowan (A.L.), Pinelli (N.L.) Magerkurth (N.L.) and Boyer (A.L.). Time—2:19. Attendance—71,548.

COMPOSITE BATTING AVERAGES
New York Yankees

Player-Position	G.	AB.	R.	H.	2B.	3B.	HR.	RBI.	BA.
Brown, ph	4	3	2	3	2	0	0	3	1.000
Houk, ph	1	1	0	1	0	0	0	0	1.000
Lollar, c	2	4	3	3	2	0	0	1	.750
Reynolds, p	2	4	2	2	0	0	0	1	.500
Lindell, lf	6	18	3	9	3	1	0	7	.500
Clark, ph-rf	3	2	1	1	0	0	0	1	.500
Shea, p	3	5	0	2	1	0	0	1	.400
Henrich, rf-lf	7	31	2	10	2	0	1	5	.323
Rizzuto, ss	7	26	3	8	1	0	0	2	.308
Johnson, 3b	7	26	8	7	0	3	0	2	.269
Stirnweiss, 2b	7	27	3	7	0	1	0	3	.259
DiMaggio, cf	7	26	4	6	0	0	2	5	.231
A. Robinson, c	3	10	2	2	0	0	0	1	.200
Berra, c-ph-rf	6	19	2	3	0	0	1	2	.158
McQuinn, 1b	7	23	3	3	0	0	0	1	.130
Page, p	4	4	0	0	0	0	0	0	.000
Newsom, p	2	0	0	0	0	0	0	0	.000
Raschi, p	2	0	0	0	0	0	0	0	.000
Drews, p	2	2	0	0	0	0	0	0	.000
Phillips, ph-1b	2	2	0	0	0	0	0	0	.000
Chandler, p	1	0	0	0	0	0	0	0	.000
Bevens, p	2	4	0	0	0	0	0	0	.000
Wensloff, p	1	0	0	0	0	0	0	0	.000
Frey, ph	1	1	0	0	0	0	0	1	.000
Totals	7	238	38	67	11	5	4	36	.282

Brooklyn Dodgers

Player-Position	G.	AB.	R.	H.	2B.	3B.	HR.	RBI.	BA.
Bragan, ph	1	1	0	1	1	0	0	1	1.000
Vaughan, ph	3	2	0	1	1	0	0	0	.500
Furillo, ph-cf	6	17	2	6	2	0	0	3	.353
Hatten, p	4	3	1	1	0	0	0	0	.333
Reese, ss	7	23	5	7	1	0	0	4	.304
Robinson, 1b	7	27	3	7	2	0	0	3	.259
Miksis, ph-2b-lf	5	4	1	1	0	0	0	0	.255

Player-Position	G.	AB.	R.	H.	2B.	3B.	HR.	RBI.	BA.
Reiser, cf-lf-ph	5	8	1	2	0	0	0	0	.250
Stanky, 2b	7	25	4	6	1	0	0	2	.240
Walker, rf	7	27	1	6	1	0	1	4	.222
Edwards, c	7	27	3	6	1	0	0	2	.222
Jorgensen, 3b	7	20	1	4	2	0	0	3	.200
Hermanski, lf	7	19	4	3	0	1	0	1	.158
Lavagetto, ph-3b	5	7	0	1	1	0	0	3	.143
G'friddo, ph-pr-lf	4	3	2	0	0	0	0	0	.000
Branca, p	3	4	0	0	0	0	0	0	.000
Casey, p	6	1	0	0	0	0	0	0	.000
Gregg, p	3	3	0	0	0	0	0	0	.000
Barney, p	3	1	0	0	0	0	0	0	.000
Taylor, p	1	0	0	0	0	0	0	0	.000
Lombardi, p-pr	3	3	0	0	0	0	0	0	.000
Bankhead, pr	1	0	1	0	0	0	0	0	.000
Hodges, ph	1	1	0	0	0	0	0	0	.000
Totals	7	226	29	52	13	1	1	26	.230

COMPOSITE PITCHING AVERAGES
New York Yankees

Pitcher	G.	IP.	H.	R.	E.	BB.	SO.	W.	L.	ERA.
Wensloff	1	2	0	0	0	0	0	0	0	0.00
Shea	3	15⅓	10	4	4	10	8	2	0	2.35
Bevens	2	11⅓	3	3	3	7	11	0	1	2.38
Drews	2	3	2	1	1	0	1	0	0	3.00
Page	4	13	12	6	6	7	2	1	1	4.15
Reynolds	2	11⅓	15	7	6	6	3	1	0	4.76
Raschi	2	1⅓	2	1	1	1	0	0	0	6.75
Chandler	1	2	2	2	2	1	3	0	0	9.00
Newsom	2	2⅓	6	5	5	0	2	0	1	19.29
Totals	7	61⅔	52	29	28	32	30	4	3	4.09

Brooklyn Dodgers

Pitcher	G.	IP.	H.	R.	E.	BB.	SO.	W.	L.	ERA.
Taylor	1	0	2	1	0	0	1	0	0	0.00
Casey	6	10⅓	5	1	1	3	1	2	0	0.87
Barney	3	6⅔	4	2	2	3	10	0	1	2.70
Gregg	3	12⅔	9	5	5	10	8	0	1	3.55
Hatten	4	9	12	7	7	5	7	0	0	7.00
Behrman	5	6⅓	9	5	5	3	5	0	0	7.11
Branca	3	8⅓	12	8	8	8	5	1	1	8.64
Lombardi	2	6⅔	14	9	9	5	1	0	1	12.15
Totals	7	60	67	38	37	37	38	3	4	5.55

SERIES OF 1948			
	W.	L.	Pct.
Cleveland A. L.	4	2	.667
Boston N. L.	2	4	.333

With a Navy veteran of World War II, southpaw Gene Bearden, in a hero's role, the Indians won the American League pennant in a one-game playoff with the Red Sox and then also defeated Boston's National League Braves to add the world championship to their laurels. Bearden pitched the Indians to their flag victory in the playoff with the Red Sox, shut out the Braves in his only Series start and then, hurling with cool, calm courage, worked out of a tough inning to save the Tribe's decision as a relief hurler in the Classic clincher.

Lou Boudreau's Indians, who were in third place, four and one-half games behind after Labor Day, made a stretch drive to the top, but blew their chance to win over the regulation distance when they lost to the Tigers on the last day of the season while the Red Sox beat the Yankees. In the playoff the next day in Boston, Boudreau smashed two homers and Bearden posted a five-hitter to defeat the Red Sox, 8 to 3, for his twentieth victory of the season. Meanwhile, in the National League, the Braves won handily for Billy Southworth to give the Hub its first senior circuit championship in 34 years and its second in modern history. The Indians also were making only their second appearance in a Series, the previous one being in 1920.

A veteran member of the Tribe, Bob Feller, who had waited ten years for his Series chance, suffered a heart-breaking defeat in the opening game when he lost to Johnny Sain, 1 to 0, although allowing only two hits. The lone run counted in the eighth inning after a hotly-disputed decision by umpire Bill Stewart on a pickoff attempt by the Indians. Bill Salkeld walked to open the stanza and Phil Masi ran for him. Mike McCormick sacrificed and Eddie Stanky drew an intentional pass. Feller and Boudreau then attempted the pick-off on Masi at second, Feller whirling and throwing to his manager, who cut in behind the runner. Masi slid back and was called safe, although Boudreau argued vehemently that he had made the tag before the runner reached the bag. Sain then flied out, but Tommy Holmes came through with a single, driving in the run that meant the game.

The Indians overcame their disappointment and clicked off three straight victories as the Series proceeded, with Bob Lemon beating Warren Spahn, 4 to 1; Bearden posting a 2 to 0 decision on five hits, and Steve Gromek sending Sain down to defeat, 2 to 1, with the aid of a 410-foot home run by Larry Doby. Another Boudreau-Stewart rhubarb occurred in the first inning of this game when the Cleveland pilot was called out on a close play trying to stretch a double.

What had been a pitchers' Series turned into a donnybrook of slugging in the next game as the Braves routed three pitchers, including Feller, with a six-run rally in the seventh inning to win, 11 to 5. Bob Elliott smashed two homers off Feller in successive times at bat in the first and third innings.

In the sixth and final contest, Lemon coasted along to a 4 to 1 lead, when the Braves suddenly came to life, loading the bases with only one out in the eighth inning. Bearden stepped into the breach and retired Clint Conatser on an outfield fly, but one run scored. Another clattered across the plate when pinch-hitter Masi doubled, cutting the Indians' lead to 4 to 3, but Bearden grabbed Mike McCormick's hot smash and the danger was over.

Earl Torgeson of the Braves led the hitters with an average of .389, while Doby topped Cleveland with .318. The box scores:

Wednesday, October 6—At Boston

Cleveland (A.L.)	AB.	R.	H.	O.	A.	E.
Mitchell, lf	4	0	0	2	0	0
Doby, cf	4	0	1	3	0	0
Boudreau, ss	4	0	0	2	1	0

1948 WORLD SERIES

	AB.	R.	H.	O.	A.	E.
Gordon, 2b	4	0	1	1	1	0
Keltner, 3b	4	0	1	1	1	0
Judnich, rf	4	0	0	2	0	0
Robinson, 1b	3	0	0	10	1	0
Hegan, c	3	0	1	2	1	0
Feller, p	2	0	0	1	4	0
Totals	32	0	4	24	9	0

Boston (N.L.)	AB.	R.	H.	O.	A.	E.
Holmes, rf	4	0	1	5	0	0
Dark, ss	4	0	0	1	1	0
Torgeson, 1b	2	0	0	4	0	0
Elliott, 3b	3	0	0	1	0	2
Rickert, lf	3	0	1	5	0	0
Salkeld, c	1	0	0	5	1	0
aMasi, c	0	1	0	1	0	0
M. McCormick, cf	2	0	0	5	0	0
Stanky, 2b	2	0	0	0	1	0
bSisti, 2b	0	0	0	0	0	0
Sain, p	3	0	0	0	0	0
Totals	24	1	2	27	3	2

Cleveland .... 0 0 0 0 0 0 0 0 0—0
Boston .... 0 0 0 0 0 0 0 1 *—1

aRan for Salkeld in eighth. bRan for Stanky in eighth. Run batted in—Holmes. Sacrifice hits—Feller, Salkeld, M. McCormick. Stolen bases—Hegan, Gordon, Torgeson. Bases on balls—Off Feller 3. Struck out—By Feller 2, by Sain 6. Left on bases—Cleveland 6, Boston 4. Earned run—Boston 1. Umpires—Barr (N.L.), Summers (A.L.), Stewart (N.L.), Grieve (A.L.), Paparella (A.L.) and Pinelli (N.L.). Time—1:42. Attendance—40,135.

Thursday, October 7—At Boston

Cleveland (A.L.)	AB.	R.	H.	O.	A.	E.
Mitchell, lf	5	1	1	1	0	0
Clark, rf	3	0	0	2	0	0
Kennedy, rf	1	0	1	0	0	0
Boudreau, ss	5	1	2	4	2	0
Gordon, 2b	4	1	1	2	3	1
Keltner, 3b	4	0	0	0	0	0
Doby, cf	4	0	2	0	0	0
Robinson, 1b	3	0	1	8	3	0
Hegan, c	3	1	0	7	0	0
Lemon, p	4	0	0	3	6	0
Totals	36	4	8	27	14	1

Boston (N.L.)	AB.	R.	H.	O.	A.	E.
Holmes, rf	4	0	0	2	1	0
Dark, ss	4	1	1	0	2	2
Torgeson, 1b	4	0	2	14	0	0
Elliott, 3b	4	0	1	1	5	1
Rickert, lf	4	0	1	5	0	0
Salkeld, c	1	0	1	2	0	0
aMasi, c	1	0	0	1	0	0
M. McCormick, cf	4	0	2	1	0	0
Stanky, 2b	2	0	1	1	3	0
Spahn, p	2	0	0	0	1	0
Barrett, p	0	0	0	0	0	0
bF. McCormick	1	0	0	0	0	0
Potter, p	0	0	0	0	0	0
cSanders	1	0	0	0	0	0
Totals	32	1	8	27	13	3

Cleveland .... 0 0 0 2 1 0 0 0 1—4
Boston .... 1 0 0 0 0 0 0 0 0—1

aRan for Salkeld in sixth. bStruck out for Barrett in seventh. cGrounded out to Lemon for Potter in ninth. Two-base hits—Boudreau, Doby, Stanky. Runs batted in—Elliott, Gordon, Doby, Boudreau, Kennedy. Sacrifice hits—Stanky, Clark. Double plays—Holmes and Torgeson; Boudreau, Gordon and Robinson; Gordon, Boudreau and Robinson. Bases on balls—Off Lemon 3, off Spahn 2. Struck out—By Lemon 5, by Spahn 1, by Barrett 1, by Potter 1. Pitching record—Off Spahn 6 hits, 3 runs in 4⅓ innings; off Barrett 1 hit, 0 runs in 2⅔ innings; off Potter 1 hit, 1 run in 2 innings. Earned runs—Cleveland 3, Boston 0. Left on bases—Cleveland 8, Boston 8. Losing pitcher—Spahn. Umpires—Summers (A.L.), Stewart (N.L.), Grieve (A.L.), Barr, Pinelli (N.L.) and Paparella (A.L.). Time—2:14. Attendance—39,633.

Friday, October 8—At Cleveland

Boston (N.L.)	AB.	R.	H.	O.	A.	E.
Holmes, rf	4	0	0	2	0	0
Dark, ss	4	0	1	3	2	1
M. McCormick, lf	4	0	1	6	0	0
Elliott, 3b	3	0	1	2	1	0
F. McCormick, 1b	3	0	1	5	1	0
Conatser, cf	3	0	0	1	0	0
Masi, c	3	0	0	2	0	0
Stanky, 2b	3	0	1	2	3	0
Bickford, p	0	0	0	0	0	0
Voiselle, p	1	0	0	1	0	0
aRyan	1	0	0	0	0	0
Barrett, p	0	0	0	0	0	0
Totals	29	0	5	24	7	1

Cleveland (A.L.)	AB.	R.	H.	O.	A.	E.
Mitchell, lf	3	0	0	2	0	0
Doby, cf	3	0	1	1	0	0
Boudreau, ss	3	0	0	1	2	0
Gordon, 2b	4	0	0	3	4	0
Keltner, 3b	3	1	0	0	4	0
Judnich, rf	3	0	0	1	0	0
Robinson, 1b	3	0	1	14	0	0
Hegan, c	3	0	1	5	0	0
Bearden, p	3	1	2	0	6	0
Totals	28	2	5	27	16	0

Boston .... 0 0 0 0 0 0 0 0 0—0
Cleveland .... 0 0 1 1 0 0 0 0 *—2

aStruck out for Voiselle in eighth. Two-base hits—Bearden, Dark. Run batted in—Hegan. Sacrifice hit—Bickford. Double plays—Dark, Stanky and F. McCormick; Bearden, Gordon and Robinson; Keltner, Gordon and Robinson. Bases on balls—Off Bickford 5. Struck out—By Bearden 4, by Bickford 1. Pitching record—Off Bickford 4 hits, 2 runs in 3⅓ innings; off Voiselle 1 hit, 0 runs in 3⅔ innings; off Barrett 0 hits, 0 runs in 1 inning. Left on bases—Cleveland 7, Boston 3. Earned runs—Cleveland 1. Losing pitcher—Bickford. Umpires—Stewart (N.L.), Grieve (A.L.), Barr (N.L.), Summers (A.L.), Paparella (A.L.) and Pinelli (N.L.). Time—1:36. Attendance—70,306.

Saturday, October 9—At Cleveland

Boston (N.L.)	AB.	R.	H.	O.	A.	E.
Holmes, rf	4	0	0	0	1	0
Dark, ss	4	0	0	2	5	0
Torgeson, 1b	3	0	2	11	2	0
Elliott, 3b	4	0	0	2	2	0
Rickert, lf	4	1	2	2	0	0
M. McCormick, cf	4	0	1	1	0	0
Masi, c	3	0	0	3	1	0
aSalkeld	1	0	0	0	0	0
Stanky, 2b	3	0	1	1	1	0
Sain, p	2	0	1	2	2	0
Totals	32	1	7	24	14	0

Cleveland (A.L.)	AB.	R.	H.	O.	A.	E.
Mitchell, lf	4	1	1	2	0	0
Doby, cf	3	1	1	2	0	0
Boudreau, ss	3	0	1	2	4	0
Gordon, 2b	3	0	0	4	1	0

1948 WORLD SERIES

	AB.	R.	H.	O.	A.	E.
Keltner, 3b	3	0	0	1	2	0
Judnich, rf	3	0	0	1	0	0
Kennedy, rf	0	0	0	1	0	0
Robinson, 1b	3	0	2	8	1	0
Hegan, c	2	0	0	5	1	0
Gromek, p	3	0	0	1	1	0
Totals	27	2	5	27	10	0

```
Boston ........................ 0 0 0  0 0 0  1 0 0—1
Cleveland ................... 1 0 1  0 0 0  0 0 *—2
```

aFlied out for Masi in ninth. Two-base hits—Torgeson 2, Boudreau. Home runs—Doby, Rickert. Runs batted in—Boudreau, Doby, Rickert. Sacrifice hits—Sain, Hegan. Double play—Boudreau, Boston 1. Bases on balls—Off Gromek 1. Struck out—By Sain 3, by Gromek 2. Left on bases—Boston 6, Cleveland 2. Earned runs—Cleveland 2, Boston 1. Umpires—Grieve (A.L.), Barr (N.L.), Summers (A.L.), Stewart (N.L.), Pinelli (N.L.) and Paparella (A.L.). Time—1:31. Attendance—81,897.

Sunday, October 10—At Cleveland

Boston (N.L.)	AB.	R.	H.	O.	A.	E.
Holmes, rf	5	2	2	0	0	0
Dark, ss	4	1	1	1	1	0
Torgeson, 1b	5	1	2	10	1	0
Elliott, 3b	4	3	2	1	3	0
Rickert, lf	5	1	1	3	0	0
Salkeld, c	4	2	1	8	0	0
M. McCormick, cf	5	1	1	2	0	0
Stanky, 2b	3	0	1	1	2	0
Potter, p	2	0	1	1	0	0
Spahn, p	2	0	0	0	1	0
Totals	39	11	12	27	8	0

Cleveland (A.L.)	AB.	R.	H.	O.	A.	E.
Mitchell, lf	3	1	1	3	0	0
Doby, cf	4	0	0	4	0	1
Boudreau, ss	4	0	2	0	3	0
Gordon, 2b	3	1	1	2	1	0
Keltner, 3b	3	1	0	1	1	1
Judnich, rf	3	1	1	3	0	0
bBoone	1	0	0	0	0	0
Peck, rf	0	0	0	0	0	0
Robinson, 1b	4	0	0	8	2	0
Hegan, c	4	1	1	4	1	0
Feller, p	2	0	0	1	0	0
Klieman, p	0	0	0	0	0	0
Christopher, p	0	0	0	0	0	0
Paige, p	0	0	0	0	0	0
aRosen	1	0	0	0	0	0
Muncrief, p	0	0	0	1	0	0
cTipton	1	0	0	0	0	0
Totals	33	5	6	27	8	2

```
Boston ..................... 3 0 1  0 0 1  6 0 0—11
Cleveland ................ 1 0 0  4 0 0  0 0 0— 5
```

aPopped out for Paige in seventh. bStruck out for Judnich in eighth. cStruck out for Muncrief in ninth. Two-base hit—Boudreau. Home runs—Elliott 2, Mitchell, Hegan, Salkeld. Runs batted in—Elliott 4, Mitchell, Judnich, Hegan 3, Salkeld, Torgeson, Rickert, M. McCormick, Stanky, Spahn. Sacrifice hit—Dark. Bases on balls—Off Potter 2, off Spahn 1, off Feller 2, off Klieman 2. Struck out—By Feller 5, by Spahn 7. Pitching record—Off Potter 5 hits, 5 runs in 3⅓ innings; off Spahn 1 hit, 0 runs in 5⅔ innings; off Feller 8 hits, 7 runs in 6⅓ innings; off Klieman 1 hit, 3 runs in 0 innings (pitched to three batters in seventh); off Christopher 2 hits, 1 run in 0 inning (pitched to two batters in seventh); off Paige 0 hits, 0 runs in ⅔ inning; off Muncrief 1 hit, 0 runs in 2 innings.

Balk—Paige. Earned runs—Boston 11, Cleveland 5. Left on bases—Boston 6, Cleveland 4. Winning pitcher—Spahn. Losing pitcher—Feller. Umpires—Barr (N.L.), Summers (A.L.), Stewart (N.L.), Grieve (A.L.), Paparella (A.L.) and Pinelli (N.L.). Time—2:39. Attendance—86,288.

Monday, October 11—At Boston

Cleveland (A.L.)	AB.	R.	H.	O.	A.	E.
Mitchell, lf	4	1	1	3	0	0
Kennedy, lf	1	0	0	1	0	0
Doby, rf	4	0	2	1	0	0
Boudreau, ss	3	0	1	2	2	0
Gordon, 2b	4	1	1	3	3	0
Keltner, 3b	4	1	1	0	3	0
Tucker, cf	3	1	1	3	1	0
Robinson, 1b	4	0	2	12	0	0
Hegan, c	4	0	1	2	2	0
Lemon, p	3	0	0	0	3	0
Bearden, p	1	0	0	0	1	0
Totals	35	4	10	27	15	0

Boston (N.L.)	AB.	R.	H.	O.	A.	E.
Holmes, rf	5	1	2	1	0	0
Dark, ss	4	0	1	0	1	0
Torgeson, 1b	4	1	1	5	1	0
Elliott, 3b	3	1	3	4	3	0
Rickert, lf	3	0	0	5	0	0
bConatser, cf	1	0	0	0	0	0
Salkeld, c	2	0	0	4	1	0
cMasi, c	1	0	1	3	0	0
M. McCor'k, cf-lf	4	0	1	2	0	0
Stanky, 2b	1	0	0	3	2	0
dRyan	1	0	0	0	0	0
Voiselle, p	1	0	0	0	0	0
aF. McCormick	1	0	0	0	0	0
Spahn, p	0	0	0	0	1	0
eSisti	1	0	0	0	0	0
Totals	31	3	9	27	9	0

```
Cleveland ............... 0 0 1  0 0 2  0 1 0—4
Boston ..................... 0 0 0  1 0 0  0 2 0—3
```

aGrounded out for Voiselle in seventh. bFlied out for Rickert in eighth, scoring Holmes. cDoubled for Salkeld in eighth. dRan for Stanky in ninth. eBunted into double play for Spahn in ninth. Two-base hits—Mitchell, Boudreau, Torgeson, Masi. Home run—Gordon. Runs batted in—Boudreau, M. McCormick, Gordon, Hegan, Robinson, Conatser, Masi. Sacrifice hit—Voiselle. Double plays—Tucker and Robinson; Lemon, Boudreau and Robinson; Gordon, Boudreau and Robinson; Elliott, Stanky and Torgeson; Hegan and Gordon. Bases on balls—Off Lemon 4, off Bearden 1, off Voiselle 2. Struck out—By Voiselle 2, by Spahn 4, by Lemon 1. Pitching record—Off Voiselle 7 hits, 3 runs in 7 innings; off Spahn 3 hits, 1 run in 2 innings; off Lemon 8 hits, 3 runs in 7⅓ innings; off Bearden 1 hit, 0 runs in 1⅔ innings. Hit by pitcher—By Voiselle (Boudreau). Balk—Lemon. Left on bases—Cleveland 7, Boston 7. Earned runs—Cleveland 4, Boston 3. Winning pitcher—Lemon. Losing pitcher—Voiselle. Umpires—Summers (A.L.), Stewart (N.L.), Grieve (A.L.), Barr (N.L.), Pinelli (N.L.) and Paparella (A.L.). Time—2:17. Attendance—40,103.

COMPOSITE BATTING AVERAGES
Cleveland Indians

Player-Position	G.	AB.	R.	H.	2B.	3B.	HR.	RBI.	BA.
Bearden, p	2	4	1	2	1	0	0	0	.500
Kennedy, rf	3	2	0	1	0	0	0	1	.500
Tucker, cf	1	3	1	1	0	0	0	0	.333
Doby, cf	6	22	1	7	1	0	1	2	.318
Robinson, 1b	6	20	0	6	0	0	0	1	.300
Boudreau, ss	6	22	1	6	4	0	0	3	.273

1949 WORLD SERIES

Player-Position	G.	AB.	R.	H.	2B.	3B.	HR.	RBI.	BA.
Hegan, c	6	19	2	4	0	0	1	5	.211
Gordon, 2b	6	22	3	4	0	0	1	2	.182
Mitchell, lf	6	23	4	4	1	0	1	1	.174
Keltner, 3b	6	21	3	2	0	0	0	0	.095
Judnich, rf	4	13	1	1	0	0	0	1	.077
Clark, rf	1	3	0	0	0	0	0	0	.000
Peck, rf	1	0	0	0	0	0	0	0	.000
Feller, p	2	4	0	0	0	0	0	0	.000
Lemon, p	2	7	0	0	0	0	0	0	.000
Gromek, p	1	3	0	0	0	0	0	0	.000
Boone, ph	1	1	0	0	0	0	0	0	.000
Klieman, p	1	0	0	0	0	0	0	0	.000
Christopher, p	1	0	0	0	0	0	0	0	.000
Paige, p	1	0	0	0	0	0	0	0	.000
Muncrief, p	1	0	0	0	0	0	0	0	.000
Tipton, ph	1	1	0	0	0	0	0	0	.000
Rosen, ph	1	1	0	0	0	0	0	0	.000
Totals	6	191	17	38	7	0	4	16	.199

Boston Braves

Player-Position	G.	AB.	R.	H.	2B.	3B.	HR.	RBI.	BA.
Potter, p	2	2	0	1	0	0	0	0	.500
Torgeson, 1b	5	18	2	7	3	0	0	1	.389
Elliott, 3b	6	21	4	7	0	0	2	5	.333
Stanky, 2b	6	14	0	4	1	0	0	1	.286
M. McCor'k, cf-lf	6	23	1	6	0	0	0	2	.261
Salkeld, c-ph	5	9	2	2	0	0	1	1	.222
Rickert, lf	5	19	2	4	0	0	1	2	.211
F. McCo'k, ph-1b	3	5	0	1	0	0	0	0	.200
Sain, p	2	5	0	1	0	0	0	0	.200
Holmes, rf	6	26	3	5	0	0	0	1	.192
Dark, ss	6	24	2	4	1	0	0	0	.167
Masi, pr-c	5	8	1	1	0	0	0	1	.125
Conatser, cf-ph	2	4	0	0	0	0	0	1	.000
Sisti, pr-2b	2	1	0	0	0	0	0	0	.000
Spahn, p	3	4	0	0	0	0	0	1	.000
Barrett, p	2	0	0	0	0	0	0	0	.000
Bickford, p	1	0	0	0	0	0	0	0	.000
Voiselle, p	2	2	0	0	0	0	0	0	.000
Ryan, ph-pr	2	1	0	0	0	0	0	0	.000
Sanders, ph	1	1	0	0	0	0	0	0	.000
Totals	6	187	17	43	6	0	4	16	.230

COMPOSITE PITCHING AVERAGES
Cleveland Indians

Pitcher	G.	IP.	H.	R.	E.	SO.	BB.	W.	L.	ERA.
Bearden	2	10⅔	6	0	0	4	1	1	0	0.00
Muncrief	1	2	1	0	0	0	0	0	0	0.00
Paige	1	⅔	0	0	0	0	0	0	0	0.00
Gromek	1	9	7	1	1	2	1	1	0	1.00
Lemon	2	16⅓	16	4	3	6	7	2	0	1.65
Feller	2	14⅓	10	8	8	7	5	0	2	5.02
Klieman	1	0	1	3	3	0	2	0	0	......
Christopher	1	0	2	1	1	0	0	0	0	......
Totals	6	53	43	17	16	19	16	4	2	2.72

Boston Braves

Pitcher	G.	IP.	H.	R.	E.	SO.	BB.	W.	L.	ERA.
Barrett	2	3⅔	1	0	0	1	0	0	0	0.00
Sain	2	17	9	2	2	9	0	1	1	1.06
Voiselle	2	10⅔	8	3	3	2	2	0	1	2.53
Bickford	1	3⅓	4	2	1	1	5	0	1	2.70
Spahn	3	12	10	4	4	12	3	1	1	3.00
Potter	2	5⅓	6	6	5	1	2	0	0	8.44
Totals	6	52	38	17	15	26	12	2	4	2.60

SERIES OF 1949

	W.	L.	Pct.
New York A. L.	4	1	.800
Brooklyn N. L.	1	4	.200

Although the long history of the World Series is replete with pitching masterpieces, including 1905, when all five games between the Giants and the Athletics ended in shutouts, no previous classic ever began with the rivals swapping 1 to 0 thrillers until the Yankees and the Dodgers exchanged minimum score verdicts in 1949. However, after winning the first game behind Allie Reynolds and losing the second to Preacher Roe, the Yankees clicked off three straight victories for their twelfth World Series triumph and the Dodgers' fifth successive failure.

The 1949 Series also marked the first time that the lights were used in a world championship contest. When the Yankees came to bat at ten minutes before 5 o'clock in the ninth inning of the final tilt, the game was halted while Ebbets Field's mazdas were switched on at Commissioner A. B. Chandler's request.

Neither of the pennant races was decided until the last day of the season. The Yankees, one length behind going into their final two-game set with the Red Sox, beat the Boston club 5 to 4, October 1, to tie for the lead and then copped the flag with a 5 to 3 triumph on the last day. The Dodgers, with a precarious one-game lead on the final day of the campaign, were forced into extra innings by the Phillies, but won in the tenth, 9 to 7, to stave off a tie with the Cardinals. The champions finished with the same season record—97-57.

The first game of the Series produced a scintillating twirling battle between Reynolds and Don Newcombe. Allie blanked the Dodgers on two hits, while Newcombe permitted only four until the ninth inning, when Tommy Henrich rapped a home run to win for the Yanks. Roe reversed the tables in the second game in another magnificent hurling duel with Vic Raschi. The Dodgers scored the lone tally in the second stanza when Jackie Robinson doubled and counted on Gil Hodges' single.

For eight innings of the third game, fans were treated to another tense battle, this time between Tommy Byrne and Ralph Branca. The Yankees took a 1 to 0 lead in the third inning on a pass, single by Byrne and Phil Rizzuto's fly, but Brooklyn tied the score in the fourth on a home run by Pee Wee Reese. With Joe Page replacing Byrne, the two clubs then squared off on even terms until the ninth, when the Yankees drove Branca from the mound, scoring three runs before Jack Banta halted the outburst.

With one out, Yogi Berra walked, Joe DiMaggio fouled out, Bobby Brown singled and Gene Woodling walked to load the bases. Johnny Mize then batted for Cliff Mapes and singled, sending Berra and Brown across the plate. After Banta replaced Branca, Coleman's single drove in the third run. This proved to be the big marker because, in the home half of the ninth, both Luis Olmo and Roy Campanella smashed homers before Page fanned Bruce Edwards to bring the inning to a close.

Newcombe, returning to the mound after two days rest, and Ed Lopat were the rival hurlers in the fourth game, but the Dodgers' righthander fell apart in the fourth inning and was hammered for three runs on a pass and doubles by Brown, Cliff Mapes and Lopat. In the next inning, the Bombers added three more off Joe Hatten when Brown tripled with the bases loaded. Lopat, leading by 6 to 0, suddenly folded in the sixth inning and the Dodgers drove him from the box with four runs before Reynolds came in to retire the last ten batters in succession. In their big inning, the Dodgers clipped off seven singles to tie a Series record, but a double play after the first two hits held down their run production.

Needing only one more victory for the title, the Yankees went to work in a hurry in the fifth game, piling up a lead of 10 to 2 in the first six innings, with a homer by DiMaggio accounting for one of the tallies. The Dodgers, with their backs to the wall, made their final bid in the seventh, when they kayoed Raschi with four runs, three of them on a circuit clout by Gil Hodges. Page relieved Vic after this blow and blanked the Brooks the rest of the way to bring the Series to an end.

The Yankees batted only .226 as a team in the classic and the Dodgers hit an even more feeble .210. Reese was the plate leader with a mark of .316 among the players who took part in all five games. Henrich's .263 was high for the champions' regulars. The box scores:

Wednesday, October 5—At New York

Brooklyn (N.L.)	AB.	R.	H.	O.	A.	E.
Reese, ss	4	0	1	2	2	0
Jorgensen, 3b	3	0	1	0	2	0
Snider, cf	4	0	0	3	0	0
Robinson, 2b	4	0	0	4	0	0
Hermanski, lf	3	0	0	0	0	0
Furillo, rf	3	0	0	0	0	0
Hodges, 1b	2	0	0	4	0	0
Campanella, c	2	0	0	11	0	0
Newcombe, p	3	0	0	0	0	0
Totals	28	0	2	*24	4	0

New York (A.L.)	AB.	R.	H.	O.	A.	E.
Rizzuto, ss	4	0	0	1	2	0
Henrich, 1b	4	1	1	9	0	0
Berra, c	3	0	0	9	0	0
DiMaggio, cf	3	0	0	1	0	0
Lindell, lf	3	0	1	0	0	0
Johnson, 3b	3	0	0	2	3	0
Mapes, rf	3	0	0	4	0	0
Coleman, 2b	3	0	1	1	2	1
Reynolds, p	3	0	2	0	1	0
Totals	29	1	5	27	8	1

Brooklyn.................. 0 0 0 0 0 0 0 0 0—0
New York................ 0 0 0 0 0 0 0 0 1—1

*None out when winning run scored. Two-base hits—Jorgensen, Reynolds, Coleman. Home run—Henrich. Run batted in—Henrich. Stolen base—Reese. Sacrifice hit—Hodges. Double play—Reynolds, Coleman and Henrich. Bases on balls—Off Reynolds 4. Struck out—By Reynolds 9, by Newcombe 11. Earned run—New York 1. Left on bases—Brooklyn 6, New York 4. Winning pitcher—Reynolds. Losing pitcher—Newcombe. Umpires—Hubbard (A.L.), Reardon (N.L.), Passarella (A.L.), Jorda (N.L.), Hurley (A.L.), Barr (N.L.). Time—2:24. Attendance—66,230.

Thursday, October 6—At New York

Brooklyn (N.L.)	AB.	R.	H.	O.	A.	E.
Reese, ss	4	0	0	1	3	1
Jorgensen, 3b	4	0	1	1	4	0
Snider, cf	4	0	1	3	1	0
Robinson, 2b	3	1	1	3	1	0
Hermanski, rf	3	0	1	2	0	0
dFurillo	1	0	0	0	0	0
McCormick, rf	0	0	0	1	0	0
Rackley, lf	2	0	0	0	0	0
Olmo, lf	2	0	1	2	0	0
Hodges, 1b	3	0	1	9	1	0
Campanella, c	2	0	1	4	0	0
Roe, p	3	0	0	1	1	1
Totals	31	1	7	27	11	2

New York (A.L.)	AB.	R.	H.	O.	A.	E.
Rizzuto, ss	3	0	1	0	6	0
Henrich, 1b	4	0	0	11	1	0
Bauer, rf	4	0	1	1	0	0
DiMaggio, cf	4	0	1	1	0	0
Lindell, lf	4	0	0	2	1	1
Johnson, 3b	4	0	1	0	2	0
Coleman, 2b	4	0	1	6	3	0
Silvera, c	2	0	0	6	0	0
aMize	1	0	1	0	0	0
bStirnweiss	0	0	0	0	0	0
Niarhos, c	0	0	0	0	0	0
Raschi, p	2	0	0	0	0	0
cBrown	1	0	0	0	0	0
Page, p	0	0	0	0	0	0
Totals	33	0	6	27	13	1

Brooklyn.................. 0 1 0 0 0 0 0 0 0—1
New York................ 0 0 0 0 0 0 0 0 0—0

aSingled for Silvera in eighth. bRan for Mize in eighth. cStruck out for Raschi in eighth. dPopped out for Hermanski in ninth. Two-base hits—Robinson, Coleman, Jorgensen. Three-base hit—Hermanski. Run batted in—Hodges. Sacrifice hits—Rizzuto, Robinson. Stolen bases—Rizzuto, Johnson. Double play—Rizzuto, Coleman and Henrich. Base on balls—Off Raschi 1. Struck out—By Raschi 4, by Roe 3. Pitching record—Off Raschi 6 hits, 1 run in 8 innings; off Page 1 hit, no runs in 1 inning. Earned run—Brooklyn 1. Left on bases—Brooklyn 5, New York 7. Winning pitcher—Roe. Losing pitcher—Raschi. Umpires—Reardon (N.L.), Passarella (A.L.), Jorda (N.L.), Hubbard (A.L.), Hurley (A.L.), Barr (N.L.). Time—2:30. Attendance—70,053.

Friday, October 7—At Brooklyn

New York (A.L.)	AB.	R.	H.	O.	A.	E.
Rizzuto, ss	4	0	0	0	0	0
Henrich, 1b	3	0	0	10	0	0
Berra, c	3	1	0	7	2	0
DiMaggio, cf	4	0	0	4	0	0
Brown, 3b	4	1	1	0	2	0
Woodling, lf	3	1	1	2	0	0
Mapes, rf	2	1	0	2	0	0
aMize	1	0	1	0	0	0
bBauer, rf	0	0	0	0	0	0
Coleman, 2b	4	0	1	2	4	0
Byrne, p	1	0	1	0	0	0
Page, p	3	0	0	0	1	0
Totals	32	4	5	27	9	0

Brooklyn (N.L.)	AB.	R.	H.	O.	A.	E.
Reese, ss	2	1	1	1	2	0
Miksis, 3b	4	0	1	3	1	0
Furillo, rf	4	0	1	2	0	0
Robinson, 2b	2	0	0	2	3	0
Hodges, 1b	3	0	0	8	0	0
Olmo, lf	4	1	1	0	0	0
Snider, cf	4	0	0	3	0	0

1949 WORLD SERIES

	AB	R	H	O	A	E
Campanella, c	4	1	1	7	0	0
Branca, p	3	0	0	1	0	0
Banta, p	0	0	0	0	0	0
cEdwards	1	0	0	0	0	0
Totals	31	3	5	27	6	0

New York............ 0 0 1 0 0 0 0 0 3—4
Brooklyn............ 0 0 0 1 0 0 0 0 2—3

aSingled for Mapes in ninth. bRan for Mize in ninth. cStruck out for Banta in ninth. Two-base hit—Woodling. Home runs—Reese, Olmo, Campanella. Runs batted in—Rizzuto, Reese, Mize 2, Coleman, Olmo, Campanella. Double play—Berra and Coleman. Bases on balls—Off Branca 4, off Byrne 2, off Page 2. Struck out—By Branca 6, by Byrne 1, by Page 4, by Banta 1. Pitching record—Off Byrne 2 hits, 1 run in 3⅓ innings; off Page 3 hits, 2 runs in 5⅔ innings; off Branca 4 hits, 4 runs in 8⅔ innings; off Banta 1 hit, 0 runs in ⅓ inning. Hit by pitcher—By Byrne 1 (Reese). Earned runs—New York 4, Brooklyn 3. Left on bases—New York 5, Brooklyn 6. Winning pitcher—Page. Losing pitcher—Branca. Umpires—Passarella (A.L.), Jorda (N.L.), Hubbard (A.L.), Reardon (N.L.), Barr (N.L.), Hurley (A.L.). Time—2:30. Attendance—32,788.

Saturday, October 8—At Brooklyn

New York (A.L.)	AB	R	H	O	A	E
Rizzuto, ss	4	0	2	1	4	0
Henrich, 1b	4	1	3	10	0	0
Berra, c	5	1	1	10	1	0
DiMaggio, cf	3	1	0	1	0	0
R. Brown, 3b	3	1	2	0	3	0
Woodling, lf	3	1	0	2	0	0
Mapes, rf	2	1	1	1	0	0
aBauer, rf	2	0	0	2	0	0
Coleman, 2b	4	0	0	0	0	0
Lopat, p	3	0	1	0	1	0
Reynolds, p	1	0	0	0	0	0
Totals	34	6	10	27	9	0

Brooklyn (N.L.)	AB	R	H	O	A	E
Reese, ss	4	1	2	0	2	0
Miksis, 3b	2	0	0	0	2	1
cCox, 3b	2	0	1	0	0	0
Snider, cf	4	0	0	4	0	0
Robinson, 2b	3	1	1	2	3	0
Hodges, 1b	4	1	1	8	1	0
Olmo, lf	4	1	1	2	1	0
Campanella, c	4	0	1	5	2	0
Hermanski, rf	4	0	2	4	0	0
Newcombe, p	1	0	0	1	1	0
Hatten, p	0	0	0	0	0	0
bT. Brown	1	0	0	0	0	0
Erskine, p	0	0	0	0	0	0
dJorgensen	1	0	0	0	0	0
Banta, p	0	0	0	0	0	0
eWhitman	1	0	0	0	0	0
Totals	35	4	9	27	12	1

New York............ 0 0 0 3 3 0 0 0 0—6
Brooklyn............ 0 0 0 0 0 4 0 0 0—4

aFlied out for Mapes in fifth. bFlied out for Hatten in fifth. cSingled for Miksis in sixth. dStruck out for Erskine in sixth. eStruck out for Banta in ninth. Two-base hits—Reese, R. Brown, Mapes, Lopat. Three-base hit—R. Brown. Runs batted in—Mapes 2, Lopat, R. Brown 3, Robinson, Olmo, Campanella, Hermanski. Double plays—Miksis, Campanella and Robinson; Rizzuto and Henrich. Bases on balls—Off Newcombe 3, off Lopat 1, off Hatten 2, off Banta 1. Struck out—By Lopat 4, by Reynolds 5, by Banta 2. Pitching record—Off Newcombe 5 hits, 3 runs in 3⅔ innings; off Hatten 3 hits, 3 runs in 1⅓ innings; off Erskine 1 hit, 0 runs in 1 inning; off Banta 1 hit, 0 runs in 3 innings; off Lopat 9 hits, 4 runs in 5⅔ innings; off Reynolds 0 hits, 0 runs in 3⅓ innings. Earned runs—New York 6, Brooklyn 4. Left on bases—New York 7, Brooklyn 5. Winning pitcher—Lopat. Losing pitcher—Newcombe. Umpires—Jorda (N.L.), Hubbard (A.L.), Reardon (N.L.), Passarella (A.L.), Hurley (A.L.) and Barr (N.L.). Time—2:42. Attendance—33,934.

Sunday, October 9—At Brooklyn

New York (N.L.)	AB	R	H	O	A	E
Rizzuto, ss	3	2	0	3	3	0
Henrich, 1b	4	2	1	8	0	0
Berra, c	5	0	0	11	0	0
DiMaggio, cf	4	1	1	0	0	0
R. Brown, 3b	4	2	3	0	1	0
Woodling, lf	4	2	3	3	0	0
Mapes, rf	3	1	0	1	0	1
Coleman, 2b	5	0	2	1	0	0
Raschi, p	3	0	1	0	0	0
Page, p	1	0	0	0	1	0
Totals	36	10	11	27	5	1

Brooklyn (N.L.)	AB	R	H	O	A	E
Reese, ss	5	0	2	1	0	0
Jorgensen, 3b	3	1	0	0	0	0
eMiksis	1	0	1	0	0	0
Snider, cf	5	2	2	5	0	0
Robinson, 2b	4	0	1	1	2	1
Hermanski, rf	3	1	1	1	0	0
Hodges, 1b	5	1	2	9	1	0
Rackley, lf	3	0	0	2	0	0
cOlmo, lf	1	0	0	2	0	0
Campanella, c	3	1	1	5	0	0
Barney, p	0	0	0	1	1	1
Banta, p	0	0	0	0	1	0
aT. Brown	1	0	0	0	0	0
Erskine, p	0	0	0	0	0	0
Hatten, p	0	0	0	0	0	0
bCox	1	0	0	0	0	0
Palica, p	0	0	0	0	1	0
dEdwards	1	0	1	0	0	0
Minner, p	0	0	0	0	1	0
Totals	37	6	11	27	7	2

New York............ 2 0 3 1 1 3 0 0 0—10
Brooklyn............ 0 0 1 0 0 1 4 0 0— 6

aStruck out for Banta in fifth. bStruck out for Hatten in sixth. cStruck out for Rackley in seventh. dSingled for Palica in eighth. eDoubled for Jorgensen in ninth. Two-base hits—Campanella, Woodling 2, Snider, Coleman, Miksis. Three-base hit—R. Brown. Home runs—DiMaggio, Hodges. Runs batted in—DiMaggio 2, R. Brown 2, Coleman 3, Raschi, Berra, Reese, Hermanski, Robinson, Hodges 3. Sacrifice hits—Rizzuto, Mapes. Double play—Page, Rizzuto and Henrich. Bases on balls—Off Barney 6, off Erskine 1, off Palica 1, off Raschi 4, off Page 1. Struck out—By Barney 2, by Banta 2, by Palica 1, by Raschi 7, by Page 4. Pitching record—off Barney 3 hits, 5 runs in 2⅔ innings; off Banta 3 hits, 2 runs in 2⅓ innings; off Erskine 2 hits, 3 runs in ⅔ inning; off Hatten 1 hit, 0 runs in ⅓ inning; off Palica 1 hit, 0 runs in 2 innings; off Minner 1 hit, 0 runs in 1 inning; off Raschi 9 hits, 6 runs in 6⅔ innings; off Page 2 hits, 0 runs in 2⅓ innings. Earned runs—New York 10, Brooklyn 6. Left on bases—New York 9, Brooklyn 9. Winning pitcher—Raschi. Losing pitcher—Barney. Umpires—Hubbard (A.L.), Reardon (N.L.), Passarella (A.L.), Jorda (N.L.), Barr (N.L.) and Hurley (A.L.). Time—3:04. Attendance—33,711.

COMPOSITE BATTING AVERAGES
New York Yankees

Player-Position	G.	AB.	R.	H.	2B.	3B.	HR.	RBI.	BA.
Byrne, p	1	1	1	0	1	0	0	0	1.000
Mize, ph	2	2	0	2	0	0	0	2	1.000
R. Brown, ph-3b	4	12	4	6	1	2	0	5	.500
Reynolds, p	2	4	0	2	1	0	0	0	.500
Woodling, lf	3	10	4	4	3	0	0	0	.400
Lopat, p	1	3	0	1	1	0	0	1	.333
Henrich, 1b	5	19	4	5	0	0	1	1	.263
Coleman, 2b	5	20	0	5	3	0	0	4	.250
Raschi, p	2	5	0	1	0	0	0	1	.200
Rizzuto, ss	5	18	2	3	0	0	0	1	.167
Bauer, rf-pr-ph	3	6	0	1	0	0	0	0	.167
Lindell, lf	2	7	0	1	0	0	0	0	.143
Johnson, 3b	2	7	0	1	0	0	0	0	.143
DiMaggio, cf	5	18	2	2	0	0	1	2	.111
Mapes, rf	4	10	3	1	1	0	0	2	.100
Berra, c	4	16	2	1	0	0	0	1	.063
Niarhos, c	1	0	0	0	0	0	0	0	.000
Silvera, c	1	2	0	0	0	0	0	0	.000
Page, p	3	4	0	0	0	0	0	0	.000
Stirnweiss, pr	1	0	0	0	0	0	0	0	.000
Totals	5	164	21	37	10	2	2	20	.226

Brooklyn Dodgers

Player-Position	G.	AB.	R.	H.	2B.	3B.	HR.	RBI.	BA.
Edwards, ph	2	2	0	1	0	0	0	0	.500
Cox, ph-3b	2	3	0	1	0	0	0	0	.333
Reese, ss	5	19	2	6	1	0	1	2	.316
Hermanski, lf-rf	4	13	1	4	0	1	0	2	.308
Miksis, 3b-ph	3	7	0	2	1	0	0	0	.286
Olmo, lf	4	11	2	3	0	0	1	2	.273
Campanella, c	5	15	2	4	1	0	1	2	.267
Hodges, 1b	5	17	2	4	0	0	1	4	.235
Robinson, 2b	5	16	2	3	1	0	0	2	.188
Jorgensen, 3b-ph	4	11	1	2	2	0	0	0	.182
Snider, cf	5	21	2	3	1	0	0	1	.143
Furillo, rf-ph	3	8	0	1	0	0	0	0	.125
Newcombe, p	2	4	0	0	0	0	0	0	.000
McCormick, rf	1	0	0	0	0	0	0	0	.000
Rackley, lf	2	5	0	0	0	0	0	0	.000
Roe, p	1	3	0	0	0	0	0	0	.000
Branca, p	1	3	0	0	0	0	0	0	.000
Banta, p	3	1	0	0	0	0	0	0	.000
Hatten, p	2	0	0	0	0	0	0	0	.000
Erskine, p	2	0	0	0	0	0	0	0	.000
Barney, p	1	0	0	0	0	0	0	0	.000
Palica, p	1	1	0	0	0	0	0	0	.000
Minner, p	1	0	0	0	0	0	0	0	.000
Whitman, ph	1	1	0	0	0	0	0	0	.000
T. Brown, ph	2	2	0	0	0	0	0	0	.000
Totals	5	162	14	34	7	1	4	14	.210

COMPOSITE PITCHING AVERAGES
New York Yankees

Pitcher	G.	IP.	H.	R.	E.	SO.	BB.	W.	L.	ERA.
Reynolds	2	12⅓	2	0	0	14	4	1	0	0.00
Page	3	9	6	2	2	8	3	1	0	2.00
Byrne	1	3⅓	2	1	1	1	2	0	0	2.70
Raschi	2	14⅔	15	7	7	11	5	1	1	4.30
Lopat	1	5⅔	9	4	4	4	1	1	0	6.35
Totals	5	45	34	14	14	38	15	4	1	2.80

Brooklyn Dodgers

Pitcher	G.	IP.	H.	R.	E.	SO.	BB.	W.	L.	ERA.
Roe	1	9	6	0	0	3	0	1	0	0.00
Palica	1	2	1	0	0	1	1	0	0	0.00
Minner	1	1	1	0	0	0	0	0	0	0.00
Newcombe	2	11⅔	10	4	4	11	3	0	2	3.09
Banta	3	5⅔	5	2	2	4	1	0	0	3.18
Branca	1	8⅔	4	4	4	6	4	0	1	4.15
Hatten	2	1⅔	4	3	3	0	2	0	0	16.20
Erskine	2	1⅔	3	3	3	1	1	0	0	16.20
Barney	1	2⅔	3	5	5	2	6	0	1	16.88
Totals	5	44	37	21	21	27	18	1	4	4.29

SERIES OF 1950

	W.	L.	Pct.
New York A. L.	4	0	1.000
Philadelphia N. L.	0	4	.000

The Yankees, who had registered the last previous World Series sweep, rolling over the Cincinnati Reds in 1939, accomplished the feat for the sixth time while gaining their thirteenth world championship with four straight victories over the Phillies. Superb pitching and fielding—rather than vaunted Yankee hitting—carried Casey Stengel's Bombers to their second straight title as they held Eddie Sawyer's Whiz Kids to just five runs, only three of them earned, in the swiftly-completed Series.

The National Leaguers ran out of gas after a terrific battle with the Dodgers for the right to oppose the Yankees. Reversing the outcome of the 1949 finale, the Phillies squeezed out a ten-inning, 4 to 1 victory on a homer by Dick Sisler to grab the flag on the last day of the season. A triumph for Brooklyn would have thrown the race into a tie.

The American League race was a four-team dogfight for most of the season, but the addition of rookie Ed (Whitey) Ford, who won nine straight games after being called up from Kansas City on June 29, enabled the New Yorkers to finish in front by three lengths over the Detroit Tigers.

With Robin Roberts, the Phillies' ace, suffering from overwork after pitching in three games in the final five days of the campaign, Manager Sawyer of the Phils pulled a surprise when he selected Jim Konstanty to open the Series. The bespectacled righthander had made 74 league relief appearances—then a major league record—during the season, but had not started a single game. Given his big chance, he almost made good, but a double by Bobby Brown and two outfield flies in the fourth inning resulted in his defeat in a brilliant mound duel with Vic Raschi, marking the third straight year that the Series had started with a 1 to 0 battle. It also was the Yankees' ninth consecutive opening-day triumph since Carl Hubbell beat them in 1936.

Roberts drew Allie Reynolds as his opponent in the second game and the two star righthanders matched pitches on fairly even terms until the tenth inning, when Joe DiMaggio smashed a homer to give the Yankees a 2 to 1 victory.

Gran Hamner, who topped the Phillies in batting with an average of .429, proved the goat in the third game when his error in the eighth inning enabled the Yankees to tie the score at 2 to 2 and paved the way for their ninth-inning victory. The Phillies held a 2 to 1 lead with two out in the eighth when Ken Heintzelman suddenly lost control and filled the bases with three straight passes. Konstanty relieved and induced Brown to ground to Hamner, but the shortstop bobbled the ball as the tying run tallied.

In the ninth inning, with Russ Meyer on the mound for the Phillies, Jimmy Bloodworth figured in two successive plays that resulted in infield hits for the Yankees. The veteran second baseman first fumbled a tricky grounder by Gene Woodling and then stopped, but couldn't hold, a line drive by Phil Rizzuto. Jerry Coleman followed with a single into left-center, scoring Woodling for a 3 to 2 victory.

Needing only one more decision, the Yankees kayoed rookie Bob Miller with two runs in the initial frame of the fourth game and added three more off Konstanty in the sixth, one tally coming on a homer by Yogi Berra. Ford, the rookie southpaw on the mound for the Bombers, had a shutout within his grasp until the ninth inning, when Woodling's muff of a fly by Andy Seminick with two out enabled the Phils to score two tallies. Woodling, who matched Hamner's batting mark of .429, thus joined the Phils' shortstop in the goat class, although his error was of less importance.

The Phils opened the ninth with a single by Willie Jones. Del Ennis was hit by a pitched ball and, after a forceout by Sisler, Hamner fanned. Seminick followed with his deep fly to Woodling, who dropped the ball as Jones and pinch-runner Ken Johnson crossed the plate. When Mike Goliat kept the Phillies going with a single, Stengel called on Reynolds and the Big Chief fanned pinch-hitter Stan Lopata to end the Series. The box scores:

Wednesday, Oct. 4—At Philadelphia

New York (A.L.)	AB.	R.	H.	O.	A.	E.
Woodling, lf	3	0	1	1	0	0
Rizzuto, ss	3	0	1	0	2	0
Berra, c	4	0	0	7	0	0
DiMaggio, cf	2	0	0	3	0	0
Mize, 1b	4	0	0	7	0	0
Hopp, 1b	0	0	0	3	0	0
Brown, 3b	4	1	1	0	0	0
Johnson, 3b	0	0	0	0	0	0
Bauer, rf	4	0	1	5	0	0
Coleman, 2b	4	0	0	1	2	0
Raschi, p	3	0	1	0	3	0
Totals	31	1	5	27	7	0
Phila'phia (N.L.)	AB.	R.	H.	O.	A.	E.
Waitkus, 1b	3	0	0	9	2	0
Ashburn, cf	4	0	0	2	0	0
Sisler, lf	4	0	0	3	0	0
Ennis, rf	3	0	0	4	0	0
Jones, 3b	3	0	1	4	3	1
Hamner, ss	3	0	0	0	1	0
Seminick, c	3	0	1	1	1	0
Goliat, 2b	3	0	0	3	2	0
Konstanty, p	2	0	0	1	0	0
aWhitman	1	0	0	0	0	0
Meyer, p	0	0	0	0	1	0
Totals	29	0	2	27	10	1

New York............ 0 0 0   1 0 0   0 0 0—1
Philadelphia........ 0 0 0   0 0 0   0 0 0—0

aFlied out for Konstanty in eighth. Two-base hit—Brown. Run batted in—Coleman. Sacrifice hits—Rizzuto, Raschi. Bases on balls—Off Konstanty 4, off Raschi 1. Struck out—By Raschi 5. Pitching record—Konstanty 4 hits, 1 run in 8 innings; Meyer 1 hit, 0 runs in 1 inning. Earned runs—New York 1. Left on bases—New York 9, Philadelphia 3. Winning pitcher—Raschi. Losing pitcher—Konstanty. Umpires—Conlan (N.L.), McGowan (A.L.), Boggess (N.L.), Berry (A.L.), Barlick (N.L.) and McKinley (A.L.). Time—2:17. Attendance—30,746.

Thursday, October 5—At Philadelphia

New York (A.L.)	AB.	R.	H.	O.	A.	E.
Woodling, lf	5	0	2	2	0	0
Rizzuto, ss	4	0	0	2	1	0
Berra, c	5	0	1	7	0	0
DiMaggio, cf	5	1	1	3	0	0
Mize, 1b	4	0	1	6	0	0
Johnson, 3b	1	0	0	0	2	0
Brown, 3b	4	0	2	0	0	0
bHopp, 1b	1	0	0	3	0	0
Bauer, rf	5	0	1	1	0	0
Coleman, 2b	3	1	1	5	6	0
Reynolds, p	3	0	1	1	2	0
Totals	40	2	10	30	11	0
Phila'phia (N.L.)	AB.	R.	H.	O.	A.	E.
Waitkus, 1b	4	0	2	8	0	0
Ashburn, cf	5	0	2	4	0	0
Sisler, lf	5	0	0	3	0	0
Ennis, rf	4	0	0	1	0	0
Jones, 3b	4	0	0	3	0	0
Hamner, ss	3	0	2	2	2	0
Seminick, c	2	0	0	5	0	0
aCaballero	0	0	0	0	0	0
Silvestri, c	0	0	0	1	0	0
cWhitman	0	0	0	0	0	0
Lopata, c	0	0	0	1	0	0
Goliat, 2b	4	1	1	2	2	0
Roberts, p	2	0	0	0	0	0
dMayo	0	0	0	0	0	0
Totals	33	1	7	30	4	0

New York............ 0 1 0   0 0 0   0 0 0   1—2
Philadelphia........ 0 0 0   0 1 0   0 0 0   0—1

aRan for Seminick in seventh. bRan for Brown in eighth. cIntentionally walked for Silvestri in ninth. dWalked for Roberts in tenth. Two-base hits—Ashburn, Waitkus, Coleman, Hamner. Three-base hit—Hamner. Home run—DiMaggio. Runs batted in—Woodling, Ashburn, DiMaggio. Sacrifice hits—Roberts, Waitkus. Stolen base—Hamner. Double plays—Johnson, Coleman and Hopp; Rizzuto, Coleman and Hopp. Bases on balls—Off Roberts 3, off Reynolds 4. Struck out—By Reynolds 6, by Roberts 5. Earned runs—New York 2, Philadelphia 1. Left on bases—New York 11, Philadelphia 8. Winning pitcher—Reynolds. Losing pitcher—Roberts. Umpires—McGowan (A.L.), Boggess (N.L.), Berry (A.L.), Conlan (N.L.), McKinley (A.L.) and Barlick (N.L.). Time—3:06. Attendance—32,660.

Friday, October 6—At New York

Phila'phia (N.L.)	AB.	R.	H.	O.	A.	E.
Waitkus, 1b	5	0	1	8	0	0
Ashburn, cf	4	0	1	0	0	0
Jones, 3b	3	0	1	1	2	0
Ennis, rf	4	1	1	3	0	0
Sisler, lf	4	0	1	2	1	0
Mayo, lf	0	0	0	1	0	0
Hamner, ss	4	1	3	2	2	1
Seminick, c	2	0	1	5	0	1
Goliat, 2b	3	0	1	4	1	0
dCaballero	0	0	0	0	0	0
Bloodworth, 2b	0	0	0	0	0	0
Heintzelman, p	2	0	0	0	2	0
Konstanty, p	0	0	0	0	0	0
eWhitman	1	0	0	0	0	0
Meyer, p	0	0	0	0	0	0
Totals	32	2	10	f26	8	2

New York (A.L.)	AB.	R.	H.	O.	A.	E.
Rizzuto, ss	3	1	1	1	1	0
Coleman, 2b	4	1	3	3	1	0
Berra, c	2	0	0	6	1	0
DiMaggio, cf	3	0	1	1	0	0
Bauer, lf	3	0	0	1	0	0
bBrown	1	0	0	0	0	0
cJensen	0	0	0	0	0	0
Ferrick, p	0	0	0	0	0	0
Mize, 1b	4	0	0	9	2	0
Collins, 1b	0	0	0	1	1	0
Johnson, 3b	4	0	0	1	3	0
Mapes, rf	4	0	0	3	0	0
Lopat, p	2	0	1	1	4	0
aWoodling, lf	2	1	1	0	0	0
Totals	32	3	7	27	13	0

Philadelphia	0 0 0	0 0 1	1 0 0—2
New York	0 0 1	0 0 0	0 1 1—3

aPopped out for Lopat in eighth. bSafe on error for Bauer in eighth. cRan for Brown in eighth. dRan for Goliat in ninth. eBatted for Konstanty in ninth and was safe on fielder's choice. fTwo out when winning run scored. Two-base hits—Ennis, Hamner. Runs batted in—Coleman 2, Sisler, Goliat. Stolen base—Rizzuto. Sacrifice hits—Seminick 2, Heintzelman, Jones. Double play—Hamner and Waitkus. Bases on balls—Off Heintzelman 6, off Ferrick 1. Struck out—By Heintzelman 3, by Meyer 1, by Lopat 5. Pitching record—Lopat 9 hits, 2 runs in 8 innings; Ferrick 1 hit, 0 runs in 1 inning; Heintzelman 4 hits, 2 runs in 7⅔ innings; Konstanty 0 hits, 0 runs in ⅓ inning; Meyer 3 hits, 1 run in ⅔ inning. Left on bases—Philadelphia 8, New York 9. Earned runs—Philadelphia 2, New York 2. Winning pitcher—Ferrick. Losing pitcher—Meyer. Umpires—Boggess (N.L.), Berry (A.L.), Conlan (N.L.), McGowan (A.L.), Barlick (N.L.) and McKinley (A.L.). Time—2:35. Attendance—64,505.

Saturday, October 7—At New York

Phila'phia (N.L.)	AB.	R.	H.	O.	A.	E.
Waitkus, 1b	3	0	1	9	1	0
Ashburn, cf	4	0	0	3	0	0
Jones, 3b	4	1	2	0	4	0
Ennis, rf	3	0	1	1	0	0
Sisler, lf	4	0	0	2	0	0
bK. Johnson	0	1	0	0	0	0
Hamner, ss	4	0	1	2	2	0
Seminick, c	4	0	0	3	1	0
cMayo	0	0	0	0	0	0
Goliat, 2b	4	0	1	4	4	1
Miller, p	0	0	0	0	0	0
Konstanty, p	2	0	1	0	1	0
aCaballero	1	0	0	0	0	0
Roberts, p	0	0	0	0	0	0
dLopata	1	0	0	0	0	0
Totals	34	2	7	24	13	1

New York (A.L.)	AB.	R.	H.	O.	A.	E.
Woodling, lf	4	1	2	4	0	1
Rizzuto, ss	4	0	0	2	4	0
Berra, c	4	2	2	10	0	0
DiMaggio, cf	3	1	2	1	0	0
Mize, 1b	3	0	1	5	1	0
Hopp, 1b	1	0	0	1	1	0
Brown, 3b	3	1	1	0	1	1
W. Johnson, 3b	1	0	0	0	0	0
Bauer, rf	3	0	0	1	0	0
Coleman, 2b	3	0	0	2	3	0
Ford, p	3	0	0	1	0	0
Reynolds, p	0	0	0	0	0	0
Totals	32	5	8	27	10	2

Philadelphia	0 0 0	0 0 0	0 0 2—2
New York	2 0 0	0 0 3	0 0 *—5

aStruck out for Konstanty in eighth. bRan for Sisler in ninth. cRan for Seminick in ninth. dStruck out for Roberts in ninth. Two-base hits—Jones, DiMaggio. Three-base hit—Brown. Home run—Berra. Runs batted in—Berra 2, DiMaggio, Brown, Bauer. Double plays—Mize and Berra; Coleman, Rizzuto and Mize. Bases on balls—Off Ford 1. Struck out—By Ford 7, by Konstanty 3, by Reynolds 1. Pitching record—Miller 2 hits, 2 runs in ⅓ inning; Konstanty 5 hits, 3 runs in 6⅔ innings; Roberts 1 hit, 0 runs in 1 inning; Ford 7 hits, 2 runs in 8⅔ innings; Reynolds 0 hits, 0 runs in ⅓ inning. Hit by pitcher—By Konstanty (DiMaggio), by Ford (Ennis). Wild pitch—Miller. Left on bases—Philadelphia 7, New York 4. Earned runs—Philadelphia 0, New York 4. Winning pitcher—Ford. Losing pitcher—Miller. Umpires—Berry (A.L.), Conlan (N.L.), McGowan (A.L.), Boggess (N.L.), McKinley (A.L.) and Barlick (N.L.). Time—2:05. Attendance—68,098.

COMPOSITE BATTING AVERAGES

New York Yankees

Player-Position	G.	AB.	R.	H.	2B.	3B.	HR.	RBI.	BA.
Lopat, p	1	2	0	1	0	0	0	0	.500
Woodling, lf-ph	4	14	2	6	0	0	0	1	.429
Brown, 3b-ph	4	12	2	4	1	1	0	1	.333
Raschi, p	1	3	0	1	0	0	0	0	.333
Reynolds, p	2	3	0	1	0	0	0	0	.333
DiMaggio, cf	4	13	2	4	1	0	1	2	.308
Coleman, 2b	4	14	2	4	1	0	0	3	.286
Berra, c	4	15	2	3	0	0	1	2	.200
Rizzuto, ss	4	14	1	2	0	0	0	0	.143
Mize, 1b	4	15	0	2	0	0	0	0	.133
Bauer, rf-lf	4	15	0	2	0	0	0	1	.133
Collins, 1b	1	0	0	0	0	0	0	0	.000
Mapes, rf	1	4	0	0	0	0	0	0	.000
Hopp, 1b-pr	3	2	0	0	0	0	0	0	.000
W. Johnson, 3b	4	6	0	0	0	0	0	0	.000
Ferrick, p	1	0	0	0	0	0	0	0	.000
Ford, p	1	3	0	0	0	0	0	0	.000
Jensen, pr	1	0	0	0	0	0	0	0	.000
Totals	4	135	11	30	3	1	2	10	.222

Philadelphia Phillies

Player-Position	G.	AB.	R.	H.	2B.	3B.	HR.	RBI.	BA.
Hamner, ss	4	14	1	6	2	1	0	0	.429
Jones, 3b	4	14	1	4	1	0	0	0	.286
Waitkus, 1b	4	15	0	4	1	0	0	0	.267
Konstanty, p	3	4	0	1	0	0	0	0	.250
Goliat, 2b	4	14	1	3	0	0	0	1	.214
Seminick, c	4	11	0	2	0	0	0	0	.182
Ashburn, cf	4	17	0	3	1	0	0	1	.176
Ennis, rf	4	14	1	2	1	0	0	0	.143
Sisler, lf	4	17	0	1	0	0	0	1	.059
Silvestri, c	1	0	0	0	0	0	0	0	.000
Lopata, c-ph	2	1	0	0	0	0	0	0	.000
Bloodworth, 2b	1	0	0	0	0	0	0	0	.000
Mayo, ph-lf-pr	3	0	0	0	0	0	0	0	.000
Meyer, p	2	0	0	0	0	0	0	0	.000
Roberts, p	2	2	0	0	0	0	0	0	.000
Heintzelman, p	1	2	0	0	0	0	0	0	.000
Miller, p	1	0	0	0	0	0	0	0	.000
Whitman, ph	3	2	0	0	0	0	0	0	.000
K. Johnson, pr	1	0	1	0	0	0	0	0	.000
Caballero, pr-ph	3	1	0	0	0	0	0	0	.000
Totals	4	128	5	26	6	1	0	3	.203

COMPOSITE PITCHING AVERAGES

New York Yankees

Pitcher	G.	IP.	H.	R.	E.	SO.	BB.	W.	L.	ERA.
Raschi	1	9	2	0	0	5	1	1	0	0.00
Ford	1	8⅔	7	2	0	7	1	1	0	0.00
Ferrick	1	1	1	0	0	0	1	1	0	0.00
Reynolds	2	10⅓	7	1	1	7	4	1	0	0.87
Lopat	1	8	9	2	2	5	0	0	0	2.25
Totals	4	37	26	5	3	24	7	4	0	0.73

Philadelphia Phillies

Pitcher	G.	IP.	H.	R.	E.	SO.	BB.	W.	L.	ERA.
Heintzelman	1	7⅔	4	2	1	3	6	0	0	1.17
Roberts	2	11	11	2	2	5	3	0	1	1.64
Konstanty	3	15	9	4	4	3	4	0	1	2.40
Meyer	2	1⅔	4	1	1	1	0	0	1	5.40
Miller	1	⅓	2	2	1	0	0	0	1	27.00
Totals	4	35⅔	30	11	9	12	13	0	4	2.27

SERIES OF 1951

	W.	L.	Pct.
New York A. L.	4	2	.667
New York N. L.	2	4	.333

After winning the National League pennant on Bobby Thomson's historic home run in the third playoff game with the Brooklyn Dodgers, the Giants of Leo Durocher were unable to continue their "miracle" drive against Casey Stengel's Yankees, who captured the Series in six games for their third straight world championship for the Old Professor and the fourteenth for the Bombers in 18 classics.

A day of rain, after the Giants had captured two of the first three games, was tabbed by many observers as the turning point of the Series. Stengel's pitching staff was in bad shape but, as a result of the postponement, Allie Reynolds was able to return to the mound in the fourth contest—and from there on, it was a breeze for the Yankees.

The Giants on the other hand, were hurt by the fact that their two 23-game winners, Sal Maglie and Larry Jansen, apparently were pitched out as a result of their labors during the regular season. Neither won a game in the Series.

Jansen was defeated twice and Maglie once. Also, George Spencer, who had been the Giants' relief mainstay, appearing in 57 games and winning 10 while losing four, was ineffective in two appearances. In a total of only three and one-third innings, the Yanks hammered him for seven runs.

The Polo Grounders captured the senior circuit pennant with one of the greatest stretch drives in major league history, climaxed by a dramatic finish right out of the story books. Trailing Brooklyn by 13½ games at one point in August, the Giants copped 37 of their last 44 contests during the regular race to wind up in a first-place tie with the Dodgers. The Giants won the first game of the playoffs, 3 to 1, and the Dodgers romped off with the second, 10 to 0. Then, in the ninth inning of the final game, with Brooklyn leading, 4 to 2, one out and two Giants on base, Thomson teed off against Ralph Branca for the homer that pulled the game out of the fire, 5 to 4, and gave Durocher's Cinderella club the flag.

The race in the American League also was hotly contested, but the Yankees beat off the threat of the Indians and went on to win by five lengths over the Cleveland club. The high spot of the Bombers' dash to the wire occurred on September 28 when Reynolds pitched his second no-hitter of the season to beat the Boston Red Sox, 8 to 0, in the first game of a doubleheader and Vic Raschi followed with an 11 to 3 decision in the nightcap to post the two victories the Yankees needed to clinch the league championship.

Like Eddie Sawyer in 1950, Durocher made a surprise pitching selection for the opener of the Series, naming southpaw Dave Koslo, who had a modest 10-9 record during the regular season. However, the veteran lefthander came through in great shape to defeat Reynolds, 5 to 1. Monty Irvin collected four hits for the Giants and his theft of home in the first inning was the first in the Series since 1928. Al Dark smashed a homer with two men on base in the sixth to clinch the victory.

Eddie Lopat's five-hit hurling stopped the Giants in the second game, 3 to 1, but Jim Hearn put the National Leaguers in front again in the third contest, winning, 6 to 2, in a game that was featured by Eddie Stanky's famous "drop-kick." The Polo Grounders were ahead, 1 to 0, with one out in the fifth inning when Stanky coaxed a pass from Raschi. The Giants put on the hit-and-run with Dark at the plate, but catcher Yogi Berra called for a pitchout and pegged straight to Phil Rizzuto, who had the ball waiting as Stanky slid into second. Stanky, however, kicked the ball out of Phil's hand, scrambled to his feet and high-tailed for third. Dark singled Stanky home and the Giants proceeded to count four more times before the side was retired.

Rain then interrupted the Series for a day and Reynolds, with an additional 24 hours of rest, vanquished the Giants, 6 to 2. The fifth game was strictly "no contest" after the third inning, when Gil McDougald, the Yankees' rookie third baseman, smashed a grand-slam homer, entering his name in the record books along with Elmer Smith (1920) and Tony Lazzeri (1936) as the only players to accomplish the batting feat in World Series play. Lopat, who hurled another five-hitter, had easy sailing to a 13 to 1 decision.

The sixth and final game was a battle to the wire, with Hank Bauer in the hero's role as the Yankees nosed out the Giants, 4 to 3. With the score tied, 1 to 1, Bauer tripled off Koslo with the bases loaded in the sixth inning to provide the hit that ultimately won the game, but the big right fielder had to come up with a sensational catch in the ninth inning to save the victory.

Opening the final frame, Stanky singled, Dark bunted safely and Whitey Lockman singled to short center to load the bases. Bob Kuzava replaced Johnny Sain on the mound for the Yankees and one run tallied on Monty Irvin's fly to Gene Woodling for the first out. The other runners advanced and another counter crossed the plate after Thomson also flied to Woodling, leaving the Yankees only one run ahead, with the potential tying tally on base. Sal Yvars then batted for Henry Thompson and sliced a low line drive to right field. Bauer, racing in, made a spectacular sitting catch of the

1951 WORLD SERIES

ball, only six inches off the ground, to climax the Series.

Irvin led the hitters with .458 and tied Dave Robertson's 1917 mark for most hits in a six-game classic—11. Rizzuto was the top batter among the Yankee regulars, with .320. The box scores:

Thursday, Oct. 4—At Yankee Stadium

Giants (N.L.)	AB.	R.	H.	O.	A.	E.
Stanky, 2b	4	1	0	4	2	0
Dark, ss	5	1	2	1	2	0
Thompson, rf	3	1	0	3	0	1
Irvin, lf	5	1	4	4	0	0
Lockman, 1b	4	0	1	4	1	0
Thomson, 3b	3	0	1	2	2	0
Mays, cf	5	0	0	2	0	0
Westrum, c	3	1	2	5	0	0
Koslo, p	3	0	0	2	0	0
Totals	35	5	10	27	7	1

Yankees (A.L.)	AB.	R.	H.	O.	A.	E.
Mantle, rf	3	0	0	4	0	0
Rizzuto, ss	4	0	2	1	2	0
Bauer, lf	4	0	0	0	0	0
DiMaggio, cf	4	0	0	3	0	0
Berra, c	4	0	1	5	1	0
McDougald, 3b	4	1	1	0	2	0
Coleman, 2b	3	0	1	3	3	0
Collins, 1b	3	0	1	11	0	0
bMize	1	0	0	0	0	0
Reynolds, p	2	0	1	0	3	0
Hogue, p	0	0	0	0	1	0
aBrown	1	0	0	0	0	0
Morgan, p	0	0	0	0	1	0
cWoodling	1	0	0	0	0	0
Totals	34	1	7	27	13	1

Giants .... 2 0 0 0 0 3 0 0 0—5
Yankees .... 0 1 0 0 0 0 0 0 0—1

aStruck out for Hogue in eighth. bPopped out for Collins in ninth. cStruck out for Morgan in ninth. Runs batted in—Lockman, Dark 3. Two-base hits—Lockman, McDougald. Three-base hit—Irvin. Home run—Dark. Stolen base—Irvin. Sacrifices—Koslo 2. Double play—McDougald, Coleman and Collins. Left on bases—Giants 13, Yankees 9. Earned runs—Giants 5, Yankees 1. Bases on balls—Off Reynolds 7, off Morgan 1, off Koslo 3. Struck out—By Reynolds 1, by Morgan 3, by Koslo 3. Pitching record—Off Reynolds 8 hits, 5 runs in 6 innings; off Hogue 0 hits, 0 runs in 1 inning; off Morgan 2 hits, 0 runs in 2 innings. Winning pitcher—Koslo. Losing pitcher—Reynolds. Umpires—Summers (A.L.), Ballanfant (N.L.), Paparella (A.L.), Barlick (N.L.), Stevens (A.L.) and Gore (N.L.). Time—2:58. Attendance—65,673.

Friday, Oct. 5—At Yankee Stadium

Giants (N.L.)	AB.	R.	H.	O.	A.	E.
Stanky, 2b	3	0	0	1	4	0
Dark, ss	4	0	1	0	4	0
Thomson, 3b	4	0	0	2	3	0
Irvin, lf	4	1	3	3	0	0
Lockman, 1b	4	0	1	11	0	1
Mays, cf	4	0	0	2	0	0
Westrum, c	2	0	0	5	0	0
bSchenz	0	0	0	0	0	0
Hartung, rf	1	0	0	0	0	0
Thompson, rf	2	0	0	0	0	0
aRigney	1	0	0	0	0	0
Spencer, p	0	0	0	0	0	0
Jansen, p	2	0	0	0	0	0
cNoble, c	1	0	0	0	0	0
Totals	32	1	5	24	11	1

Yankees (A.L.)	AB.	R.	H.	O.	A.	E.
Mantle, rf	2	1	1	0	0	0
Bauer, rf	2	0	0	1	0	0
Rizzuto, ss	4	0	1	2	2	0
McDougald, 2b-3b	3	0	1	2	3	0
DiMaggio, cf	3	0	0	4	0	0
Berra, c	3	0	0	2	0	0
Woodling, lf	3	0	0	4	0	0
Brown, 3b	3	0	1	0	4	0
dMartin	0	1	0	0	0	0
Coleman, 2b	0	0	0	1	0	0
Collins, 1b	3	1	1	9	2	0
Lopat, p	3	0	1	2	2	0
Totals	29	3	6	27	13	0

Giants .... 0 0 0 0 0 0 1 0 0—1
Yankees .... 1 1 0 0 0 0 0 1 *—3

aFlied out for Thompson in seventh. bRan for Westrum in seventh. cFouled out for Jansen in seventh. dRan for Brown in eighth. Runs batted in—McDougald, Collins, Rigney, Lopat. Home run—Collins. Stolen base—Irvin. Double play—Dark, Stanky and Lockman. Left on bases—Giants 6, Yankees 2. Earned runs—Yankees 3, Giants 1. Bases on balls—Off Lopat 2. Struck out—By Jansen 5, by Lopat 1. Pitching record—Off Jansen 4 hits, 2 runs in 6 innings; off Spencer 2 hits, 1 run in 2 innings. Winning pitcher—Lopat. Losing pitcher—Jansen. Umpires—Ballanfant (N.L.), Paparella (A.L.), Barlick (N.L.), Summers (A.L.), Gore (N.L.) and Stevens (A.L.). Time—2:05. Attendance—66,018.

Saturday, Oct. 6—At Polo Grounds

Yankees (A.L.)	AB.	R.	H.	O.	A.	E.
Woodling, lf	4	1	1	3	0	0
Rizzuto, ss	4	1	1	2	4	1
McDougald, 2b	3	0	2	2	2	0
DiMaggio, cf	4	0	0	4	0	0
Berra, c	3	0	1	5	1	1
Brown, 3b	3	0	0	0	1	0
Collins, 1b	3	0	0	6	0	0
Bauer, rf	4	0	0	2	0	0
Raschi, p	1	0	0	0	0	0
Hogue, p	0	0	0	0	0	0
aHopp	0	0	0	0	0	0
Ostrowski, p	0	0	0	0	0	0
bMize	1	0	0	0	0	0
Totals	30	2	5	24	8	2

Giants (N.L.)	AB.	R.	H.	O.	A.	E.
Stanky, 2b	2	1	1	2	2	0
Dark, ss	4	1	1	4	4	0
Thompson, rf	3	1	1	1	0	0
Irvin, lf	3	1	0	2	0	0
Lockman, 1b	4	1	1	10	1	1
Thomson, 3b	4	1	1	3	4	0
Mays, cf	4	0	2	3	0	0
Westrum, c	4	0	0	2	1	1
Hearn, p	3	0	0	0	2	0
Jones, p	0	0	0	0	1	0
Totals	31	6	7	27	15	2

Yankees .... 0 0 0 0 0 0 0 1 1—2
Giants .... 0 1 0 0 5 0 0 0 *—6

aWalked for Hogue in seventh. bFlied out for Ostrowski in ninth. Runs batted in—Mays, Dark, Lockman 3, Collins, Woodling. Two-base hit—Thomson. Home runs—Lockman, Dark. Double plays—Stanky, Dark and Lockman; Hearn, Dark, Lockman and Dark; Rizzuto, McDougald and Collins. Left on bases—Yankees 10, Giants 5. Earned runs—Yankees 2, Giants 1. Bases on balls—Off Raschi 3, off Hearn 8. Struck out—By Raschi 3, by Ostrowski 1, by Hearn 1. Pitching record—Off Raschi 5 hits, 6 runs in 4⅓ innings; off Hogue

1 hit, 0 runs in 1⅔ innings; off Ostrowski 1 hit, 0 runs in 2 innings; off Hearn 4 hits, 1 run in 7⅔ innings; off Jones 1 hit, 1 run in 1⅓ innings. Hit by pitcher—By Raschi 1 (Stanky), by Hearn 1 (Rizzuto). Winning pitcher—Hearn. Losing pitcher—Raschi. Umpires—Paparella (A.L.), Barlick (N.L.), Summers (A.L.), Ballanfant (N.L.), Stevens (A.L.) and Gore (N.L.). Time—2:42. Attendance—52,035.

Monday, Oct. 8—At Polo Grounds

Yankees (A.L.)	AB.	R.	H.	O.	A.	E.
Bauer, rf	4	0	2	0	0	0
Rizzuto, ss	5	1	1	5	5	0
Berra, c	5	1	1	8	1	0
DiMaggio, cf	5	1	2	2	0	0
Woodling, lf	4	2	1	1	0	0
McDougald, 2b-3b	4	0	1	3	2	0
Brown, 3b	4	1	2	0	0	0
Coleman, 2b	0	0	0	1	1	0
Collins, 1b	3	0	1	7	0	0
Reynolds, p	4	0	1	0	2	0
Totals	38	6	12	27	11	0

Giants (N.L.)	AB.	R.	H.	O.	A.	E.
Stanky, 2b	4	0	1	3	0	1
Dark, ss	4	1	3	2	1	0
Thompson, rf	3	1	0	1	0	0
Irvin, lf	4	0	2	3	0	0
Lockman, 1b	4	0	0	4	0	0
Thomson, 3b	2	0	2	2	3	1
Mays, cf	4	0	0	5	1	0
Westrum, c	2	0	0	7	1	0
Maglie, p	1	0	0	0	0	0
aLohrke	1	0	0	0	0	0
Jones, p	0	0	0	0	0	0
bRigney	1	0	0	0	0	0
Kennedy, p	0	0	0	0	0	0
Totals	30	2	8	27	6	2

Yankees .... 0 1 0   1 2 0   2 0 0—6
Giants .... 1 0 0   0 0 0   0 0 1—2

aPopped out for Maglie in fifth. bStruck out for Jones in eighth. Runs batted in—Irvin, Collins, Reynolds, DiMaggio 2, McDougald, Thomson. Two-base hits—Dark 3, Woodling, Brown. Home run—DiMaggio. Double plays—Rizzuto, McDougald and Collins; Reynolds, Rizzuto and Collins 2; Rizzuto, Coleman and Collins. Left on bases—Yankees 8, Giants 5. Earned runs—Yankees 4, Giants 2. Bases on balls—Off Maglie 2, off Jones 1, off Reynolds 4. Struck out—By Maglie 3, by Jones 2, by Kennedy 2, by Reynolds 7. Pitching record—Off Maglie 8 hits, 4 runs in 5 innings; off Jones 4 hits, 2 runs in 3 innings; off Kennedy 0 hits, 0 runs in 1 inning. Winning pitcher—Reynolds. Losing pitcher—Maglie. Umpires—Barlick (N.L.), Summers (A.L.), Ballanfant (N.L.), Paparella (A.L.), Gore (N.L.) and Stevens (A.L.). Time—2:57. Attendance—49,010.

Tuesday, Oct. 9—At Polo Grounds

Yankees (A.L.)	AB.	R.	H.	O.	A.	E.
Woodling, lf	3	3	1	5	0	1
Rizzuto, ss	4	3	2	0	6	0
Berra, c	4	2	1	3	0	0
DiMaggio, cf	5	0	3	3	0	0
Mize, 1b	3	1	1	6	0	0
Bauer, rf	1	0	0	0	0	0
McDougald, 2b-3b	5	1	1	2	2	0
Brown, 3b	3	0	2	1	3	0
cColeman, 2b	1	1	0	0	1	0
Collins, rf-1b	5	1	1	7	0	0
Lopat, p	5	0	0	0	2	0
Totals	39	13	12	27	14	1

Giants (N.L.)	AB.	R.	H.	O.	A.	E.
Stanky, 2b	4	0	0	1	4	0
Dark, ss	4	1	2	2	3	0
Thomson, 3b	4	0	0	1	3	0
Irvin, lf	4	0	2	2	0	1
Lockman, 1b	4	0	0	9	3	0
Mays, cf	2	0	0	2	0	0
Hartung, rf	3	0	0	1	1	1
Westrum, c	3	0	1	7	0	0
Jansen, p	0	0	0	1	1	0
aLohrke	1	0	0	0	0	0
Kennedy, p	0	0	0	0	1	0
bRigney	1	0	0	0	0	0
Spencer, p	0	0	0	0	1	0
Corwin, p	0	0	0	1	0	0
dWilliams	1	0	0	0	0	0
Konikowski, p	0	0	0	0	0	0
Totals	31	1	5	27	17	3

Yankees .... 0 0 5   2 0 2   4 0 0—13
Giants .... 1 0 0   0 0 0   0 0 0— 1

aStruck out for Jansen in third. bFlied out for Kennedy in fifth. cRan for Brown in seventh. dGrounded out for Corwin in eighth. Runs batted in—DiMaggio 3, McDougald 4, Rizzuto 3, Mize. Two-base hits—Westrum, Mize, DiMaggio. Three-base hit—Woodling. Home runs—McDougald, Rizzuto, Mize. Double plays—Lopat, McDougald and Mize, Left on bases—Yankees 7, Giants 4. Earned runs—Yankees 13, Giants 0. Bases on balls—Off Jansen 4, off Kennedy 1, off Spencer 3, off Lopat 1. Struck out—By Jansen 1, by Kennedy 2, by Corwin 1, by Lopat 3. Pitching record—Off Jansen 3 hits, 5 runs in 3 innings; off Kennedy 3 hits, 2 runs in 2 innings; off Spencer 4 hits, 6 runs in 1⅓ innings; off Corwin 1 hit, 0 runs in 1⅔ innings; off Konikowski 1 hit, 0 runs in 1 inning. Wild pitch—Corwin. Winning pitcher—Lopat. Losing pitcher—Jansen. Umpires—Summers (A.L.), Ballanfant (N.L.), Paparella (A.L.), Barlick (N.L.), Stevens (A.L.) and Gore (N.L.). Time—2:31. Attendance—47,530.

Wed., Oct. 10—At Yankee Stadium

Giants (N.L.)	AB.	R.	H.	O.	A.	E.
Stanky, 2b	5	1	1	3	4	0
Dark, ss	3	1	1	1	2	0
Lockman, 1b	5	0	3	10	0	0
Irvin, lf	4	0	0	3	0	0
Thomson, 3b	4	0	1	2	0	0
Thompson, rf	3	0	1	0	0	1
dYvars	1	0	0	0	0	0
Westrum, c	3	0	1	3	0	0
bWilliams	0	0	0	0	0	0
Jansen, p	0	0	0	0	1	0
Mays, cf	3	1	2	2	0	0
Koslo, p	2	0	0	0	1	0
aRigney	1	0	1	0	0	0
Hearn, p	0	0	0	0	0	0
cNoble, c	1	0	0	0	1	0
Totals	35	3	11	24	9	1

Yankees (A.L.)	AB.	R.	H.	O.	A.	E.
Rizzuto, ss	4	0	1	4	4	0
Coleman, 2b	4	1	1	2	1	0
Berra, c	4	1	2	4	0	0
DiMaggio, cf	2	1	1	1	0	0
McDougald, 3b	4	0	0	1	3	0
Mize, 1b	2	1	1	6	0	0
Collins, 1b	1	0	0	0	0	0
Bauer, rf	3	0	1	4	0	0
Woodling, lf	3	0	0	5	0	0
Raschi, p	1	0	0	0	0	0
Sain, p	1	0	0	0	0	0
Kuzava, p	0	0	0	0	0	0
Totals	29	4	7	27	8	0

1952 WORLD SERIES

```
Giants .................... 0 0 0  0 1 0  0 0 2—3
Yankees .................. 1 0 0  0 0 3  0 0 *—4
```

aSingled for Koslo in seventh. bRan for Westrum in eighth. cCalled out on strikes for Hearn in eighth. dLined out for Thompson in ninth. Runs batted in—McDougald, Stanky, Bauer 3, Irvin, Thomson. Two-base hits—Lockman, Berra, DiMaggio. Three-base hit—Bauer. Double plays—Rizzuto and Mize 2; Rizzuto, Coleman and Mize; Dark, Stanky and Lockman. Left on bases—Giants 12, Yankees 5. Earned runs—Yankees 4, Giants 2. Bases on balls—Off Raschi 5, off Sain 2, off Koslo 4. Struck out—By Raschi 1, by Sain 2, by Koslo 3. Pitching records—Off Koslo 5 hits, 4 runs in 6 innings; off Hearn 1 hit, 0 runs in 1 inning; off Jansen 1 hit, 0 runs in 1 inning; off Raschi 7 hits, 1 run in 6 innings (pitched to two batters in seventh); off Sain 4 hits, 2 runs in 2 innings (pitched to three batters in ninth); off Kuzava 0 hits, 0 runs in 1 inning. Wild pitch—Koslo. Passed ball—Berra. Winning pitcher—Raschi. Losing pitcher—Koslo. Umpires—Ballanfant (N.L.), Paparella (A.L.), Barlick (N.L.), Summers (A.L.), Gore (N.L.) and Stevens (A.L.). Time—2:59. Attendance—61,711.

COMPOSITE PITCHING AVERAGES
New York Yankees

Pitcher	G.	IP.	H.	R.	E.	SO.	BB.	W.	L.	ERA.
Hogue	2	2⅔	1	0	0	0	0	0	0	0.00
Morgan	1	2	2	0	0	3	1	0	0	0.00
Ostrowski	1	2	1	0	0	1	0	0	0	0.00
Kuzava	1	1	0	0	0	0	0	0	0	0.00
Lopat	2	18	10	2	1	4	3	2	0	0.50
Raschi	2	10⅓	12	7	1	4	8	1	1	0.87
Reynolds	2	15	16	7	7	8	11	1	1	4.20
Sain	1	2	4	2	2	2	2	0	0	9.00
Totals	6	53	46	18	11	22	25	4	2	1.87

New York Giants

Pitcher	G.	IP.	H.	R.	E.	SO.	BB.	W.	L.	ERA.
Corwin	1	1⅔	1	0	0	1	0	0	0	0.00
Konikowski	1	1	1	0	0	0	0	0	0	0.00
Hearn	2	8⅔	5	1	1	1	8	1	0	1.04
Jones	2	4⅓	5	3	1	2	1	0	0	2.08
Koslo	2	15	12	5	5	6	7	1	1	3.00
Kennedy	2	3	3	2	2	4	1	0	0	6.00
Jansen	3	10	8	7	7	6	4	0	2	6.30
Maglie	1	5	8	4	4	3	2	0	1	7.20
Spencer	2	3⅓	6	7	7	0	3	0	0	18.90
Totals	6	52	49	29	27	23	26	2	4	4.67

SERIES OF 1952

	W.	L.	Pct.
New York A. L.	4	3	.571
Brooklyn N. L.	3	4	.429

COMPOSITE BATTING AVERAGES
New York Yankees

Player-Position	G.	AB.	R.	H.	2B.	3B.	HR.	RBI.	BA.
Brown, ph-3b	5	14	5	5	1	0	0	0	.357
Reynolds, p	2	6	0	2	0	0	0	1	.333
Rizzuto, ss	6	25	5	8	0	0	1	3	.320
Mize, ph-1b	4	7	2	2	1	0	0	1	.286
DiMaggio, cf	6	23	3	6	2	0	0	5	.261
Berra, c	6	23	4	6	1	0	0	0	.261
McDougald, 3b-2b	6	23	2	6	1	0	1	7	.261
Coleman, 2b-pr	5	8	2	2	0	0	0	0	.250
Collins, 1b-rf	6	18	5	4	0	0	1	3	.222
Mantle, rf	2	5	1	1	0	0	0	0	.200
Bauer, lf-rf	6	18	0	3	0	1	0	3	.167
Woodling, ph-lf	6	18	6	3	1	1	1	1	.167
Lopat, p	2	8	0	1	0	0	0	1	.125
Hogue, p	2	0	0	0	0	0	0	0	.000
Morgan, p	1	0	0	0	0	0	0	0	.000
Raschi, p	2	2	0	0	0	0	0	0	.000
Ostrowski, p	1	0	0	0	0	0	0	0	.000
Sain, p	1	1	0	0	0	0	0	0	.000
Kuzava, p	1	0	0	0	0	0	0	0	.000
Hopp, ph	1	0	1	0	0	0	0	0	.000
Martin, pr	1	0	1	0	0	0	0	0	.000
Totals	6	199	29	49	7	2	5	25	.246

New York Giants

Player-Position	G.	AB.	R.	H.	2B.	3B.	HR.	RBI.	BA.
Irvin, lf	6	24	3	11	0	1	0	2	.458
Dark, ss	6	24	5	10	3	0	1	4	.417
Rigney, ph	4	4	0	1	0	0	0	1	.250
Lockman, 1b	6	25	1	6	2	0	1	4	.240
Thomson, 3b	6	21	1	5	1	0	0	2	.238
Westrum, c	6	17	1	4	1	0	0	0	.235
Mays, cf	6	22	1	4	0	0	0	1	.182
Thompson, rf	5	14	3	2	0	0	0	0	.143
Stanky, 2b	6	22	3	3	0	0	0	1	.136
Noble, ph-c	2	2	0	0	0	0	0	0	.000
Hartung, rf	2	4	0	0	0	0	0	0	.000
Koslo, p	2	5	0	0	0	0	0	0	.000
Spencer, p	2	0	0	0	0	0	0	0	.000
Jansen, p	3	2	0	0	0	0	0	0	.000
Hearn, p	2	3	0	0	0	0	0	0	.000
Jones, p	2	0	0	0	0	0	0	0	.000
Maglie, p	1	1	0	0	0	0	0	0	.000
Kennedy, p	2	0	0	0	0	0	0	0	.000
Corwin, p	1	0	0	0	0	0	0	0	.000
Konikowski, p	1	0	0	0	0	0	0	0	.000
Yvars, ph	1	1	0	0	0	0	0	0	.000
Lohrke, ph	2	2	0	0	0	0	0	0	.000
Williams, ph-pr	2	1	0	0	0	0	0	0	.000
Schenz, pr	1	0	0	0	0	0	0	0	.000
Totals	6	194	18	46	7	1	2	15	.237

Winning their fourth straight world championship in a hard-fought Series with the Dodgers, the Yankees, under Manager Casey Stengel, tied the record set by the Bronx Bombers of 1936, '37, '38 and '39, who captured the game's highest honors for four consecutive years under Manager Joe McCarthy. But while Marse Joe's Manglers for his fourth straight title included Frankie Crosetti, Red Rolfe, Tommy Henrich, Joe DiMaggio, Bill Dickey, George Selkirk, Charlie Keller and Joe Gordon among his regulars, Stengel achieved his triumph with stars of lesser note, who were nevertheless true to the Yankee tradition when the chips were down.

The Dodgers put up their most gallant Series fight, but went down to defeat for the sixth time in as many appearances in the fall classic. Manager Chuck Dressen's Flatbushers jumped off in front by winning the first game. From then on, the two clubs alternated in winning until the Yankees swept the final two tilts, with Billy Martin's last-moment catch of a pop fly by Jackie Robinson with the bases loaded and two men out in the seventh inning of the payoff game sealing the Dodgers' doom.

To many experts, the 1952 American League pennant represented Stengel's top achievement as the Yankee skipper. Despite the retirement of DiMaggio, the loss of three players to military service and a shoulder injury that sidelined Ed Lopat for a good part of the season, Ol' Case was able to deliver his fourth flag, a feat achieved previously by only two managers—McCarthy with the Yankees of 1936 to '39 and John J. McGraw with the New York Giants of 1921 to '24. The rise of Mickey

Mantle to stardom, the spectacular pitching of Allie Reynolds and Stengel's judicious juggling of his available talent enabled the Yankees to edge out Cleveland by two games.

The Dodgers, who had been bested in photo finishes in 1950 and '51, came through for Dressen, but only after the Giants had almost succeeded in another of their stretch drives. Chuck's crew feasted on the last three clubs in the standings, winning 17 from Cincinnati, 18 from Boston and 19 from Pittsburgh. Joe Black, the 28-year-old righthander who was not even on the club's roster at the start of spring training, proved the Dodgers' life-saver. Although used strictly in relief until the final eight days of the campaign, when he started twice, Black led the Brooks with 15 victories against four losses. He worked in 56 games.

Dressen started his best bet, Black, in the Series and the big righthander responded with a 4 to 2 victory over Reynolds. Robinson and Duke Snider walloped homers off Allie's deliveries and Pee Wee Reese clouted one against reliever Ray Scarborough. Gil McDougald homered for the Yanks. Vic Raschi evened the Series for the Yankees with a 7 to 1 triumph in the second game, but Preacher Roe regained Brooklyn's advantage in the third contest, winning 5 to 3, despite boundary belts by Yogi Berra and Johnny Mize. Berra, however, wore the goat's horns. In the ninth inning, with the Dodgers ahead only 3 to 2, the backstop let one of relief pitcher Tom Gorman's serves get away from him and two runners scored, nullifying the homer socked by pinch-hitter Mize in the home half of the frame.

Reynolds, who bowed to Black in the opener, gained revenge on his mound opponent with a 2 to 0 shutout, another homer by Mize producing the Yankees' first run. Carl Erskine of the Dodgers, although rapped for five runs in the fifth frame of the next game, including the third circuit clout of the Series for Mize, settled down and retired the last 19 men in succession to win a 6 to 5 verdict in 11 innings. Snider, who rapped a two-run homer for the Brooks in the fifth and then tied the score at 5-all with a single in the seventh, drove in the winning counter with a double off relief pitcher Johnny Sain.

Snider, the Duke of Flatbush, walloped two more homers for the Dodgers in the sixth game—his string of four tying a Series record—but there was a standoff in the slugging department when Berra and Mickey Mantle also hit four-baggers for the Yanks. A single by Gene Woodling, a balk by Billy Loes and Raschi's single off the young hurler's knee in the sixth inning proved the difference as the Bombers won, 3 to 2, to tie the classic for the third time.

The seventh and deciding game was a tight, tense battle, with Stengel exercising all of his managerial wiles in the manipulation of his pitchers. Lopat started against Black, but after the Yankees tallied in the fourth inning, the Dodgers chased the Bombers' southpaw, filling the bases with none out. Reynolds choked off the threat, with only one run scoring on an outfield fly. A homer by Woodling in the fifth put the Yanks in front again, but the Dodgers once more knotted the count in their half. Mantle then homered in the sixth and drove in another tally with a single in the seventh to make the score 4 to 2.

The drama of the game came in the Dodgers' half of the seventh. Reynolds, arm-weary, had gone out for a pinch-hitter and Raschi had replaced him. Carl Furillo walked and, after Rocky Nelson popped up, Billy Cox singled and Pee Wee Reese drew a pass to load the bases. It was evident that Raschi didn't have it and Stengel summoned Bob Kuzava, his southpaw stopper in the final game of the '51 Series, to face the dangerous Snider. The count went to a full three-and-two, but on the next pitch, Duke reached for a high pitch and popped out.

Kuzava next faced the righthanded-hitting Robinson and again the count went to three-and-two. With all three Dodger runners on the move, Jackie swung at a high curve and lifted it into the air near the mound. It was first baseman Joe Collins' ball, but he appeared to lose sight of it. As Kuzava stood transfixed, Martin made a desperate dash from his second-base position and, running at full speed, grabbed the ball in his gloved hand about knee high. Two Dodgers had already crossed the plate and another was rounding third when Martin's catch snuffed out the rally. Kuzava then blanked the Flatbushers with ease in the eighth and ninth to preserve the 4 to 2 victory and give the title to the Bombers.

The conquest was the Yankees' fifteenth success in 19 appearances in the fall classic, the sixth straight year the American League entrant had won and the circuit's thirty-second triumph in 49 blue-ribbon battles. The last time a National League club won the championship was when the St. Louis Cardinals defeated the Boston Red Sox in 1946.

The closeness of the Series was reflected in the race for batting honors, which almost ended in a four-way tie. However, Woodling led the way among the players in all seven games, hitting .348, three points more than Mantle, Reese and Snider, who deadlocked with averages of .345. The box scores:

Wednesday, October 1—At Brooklyn

New York (A.L.)	AB.	R.	H.	O.	A.	E.
Bauer, rf	4	0	0	2	0	0
Rizzuto, ss	4	0	1	2	1	0

1952 WORLD SERIES

	AB.	R.	H.	O.	A.	E.
Mantle, cf	4	0	2	2	0	0
Berra, c	4	0	0	7	2	0
Collins, 1b	4	0	0	8	0	0
Noren, lf	3	0	0	1	0	0
McDougald, 3b	2	1	1	0	4	1
Martin, 2b	3	0	1	2	1	0
Reynolds, p	2	0	0	0	1	1
aWoodling	1	1	1	0	0	0
Scarborough, p	0	0	0	0	1	0
Totals	31	2	6	24	10	2

Brooklyn (N.L.)	AB.	R.	H.	O.	A.	E.
Cox, 3b	3	0	0	1	2	0
Reese, ss	4	2	2	4	1	0
Snider, cf	4	1	2	2	0	0
Robinson, 2b	2	1	1	1	4	0
Campanella, c	3	0	1	6	0	0
Pafko, lf	3	0	0	3	1	0
Hodges, 1b	3	0	0	6	3	0
Furillo, rf	3	0	0	3	0	0
Black, p	3	0	0	1	0	0
Totals	28	4	6	27	11	0

New York	0	0	1	0	0	0	0	1	0—2
Brooklyn	0	1	0	0	0	2	0	1	*—4

aTripled for Reynolds in eighth. Runs batted in—Robinson, McDougald, Snider 2, Bauer, Reese. Two-base hit—Snider. Three-base hit—Woodling. Home runs—Robinson, McDougald, Snider, Reese. Double plays—Martin and Collins; Cox, Robinson and Hodges. Left on bases—New York 4, Brooklyn 2. Earned runs—New York 2, Brooklyn 4. Bases on balls—Off Reynolds 2, off Black 2. Struck out—By Reynolds 4, by Scarborough 1, by Black 6. Pitching records—Off Reynolds 5 hits, 3 runs in 7 innings; off Scarborough 1 hit, 1 run in 1 inning. Wild pitch—Reynolds. Winning pitcher—Black. Losing pitcher—Reynolds. Umpires—Pinelli (N.L.), Passarella (A.L.), Goetz (N.L.), McKinley (A.L.), Boggess (N.L.) and Honochick (A.L.). Time—2:21. Attendance—34,861.

Thursday, October 2—At Brooklyn

New York (A.L.)	AB.	R.	H.	O.	A.	E.
Bauer, rf	4	0	1	3	0	0
Rizzuto, ss	4	0	0	2	2	0
Mantle, cf	5	2	3	2	0	0
Woodling, lf	4	1	1	2	0	0
Berra, c	3	0	2	10	2	0
Collins, 1b	3	1	0	8	1	0
McDougald, 3b	3	2	1	0	1	0
Martin, 2b	4	1	2	0	1	0
Raschi, p	3	0	0	0	0	0
Totals	33	7	10	27	7	0

Brooklyn (N.L.)	AB.	R.	H.	O.	A.	E.
Cox, 3b	4	0	0	1	0	0
Reese, ss	3	1	1	2	5	0
Snider, cf	4	0	1	1	0	0
Robinson, 2b	3	0	0	3	3	0
Campanella, c	4	0	1	7	3	0
Pafko, lf	4	0	0	2	0	0
Hodges, 1b	3	0	0	9	0	1
Furillo, rf	3	0	0	0	0	0
Erskine, p	2	0	0	0	1	0
Loes, p	0	0	0	0	0	0
aNelson	0	0	0	0	0	0
Lehman, p	0	0	0	0	1	0
Totals	30	1	3	27	13	1

New York	0	0	0	1	1	5	0	0	0—7
Brooklyn	0	0	1	0	0	0	0	0	0—1

aWalked for Loes in seventh inning. Runs batted in—Campanella, Berra, Martin 4, McDougald. Two-base hit—Mantle. Home run—Martin. Stolen base—McDougald. Double play—Reese, Robinson and Hodges. Left on bases—New York 6, Brooklyn 7. Earned runs—New York 6, Brooklyn 1. Bases on balls—Off Raschi 5, off Erskine 6, off Lehman 1. Struck out—By Raschi 9, by Erskine 4, by Loes 2. Pitching records—Off Erskine 6 hits, 4 runs in 5 innings (none out in sixth); off Loes 2 hits, 3 runs in 2 innings; off Lehman 2 hits, 0 runs in 2 innings. Wild pitch—Erskine. Winning pitcher—Raschi. Losing pitcher—Erskine. Umpires—Passarella (A.L.), Goetz (N.L.), McKinley (A.L.), Pinelli (N.L.), Honochick (A.L.) and Boggess (N.L.). Time—2:47. Attendance—33,792.

Friday, October 3—At New York

Brooklyn (N.L.)	AB.	R.	H.	O.	A.	E.
Furillo, rf	5	1	1	0	0	0
Reese, ss	5	1	3	1	4	0
Robinson, 2b	4	2	2	2	3	0
Campanella, c	5	0	1	9	1	0
Pafko, lf	5	0	2	2	0	0
Snider, cf	5	0	1	3	0	0
Hodges, 1b	3	0	0	9	2	0
Cox, 3b	2	1	1	0	2	0
Roe, p	2	0	0	1	0	0
Totals	36	5	11	27	12	0

New York (A.L.)	AB.	R.	H.	O.	A.	E.
Rizzuto, ss	4	0	0	4	4	0
Collins, 1b	4	0	0	7	0	0
bSain	1	0	0	0	0	0
Mantle, cf	4	0	0	6	0	0
Woodling, lf	4	0	1	2	0	0
Berra, c	4	1	3	1	1	1
Bauer, rf	2	1	0	3	0	0
McDougald, 3b	4	0	0	1	2	1
Martin, 2b	1	0	0	3	3	0
Lopat, p	2	0	1	0	0	0
Gorman, p	0	0	0	0	0	0
aMize	1	1	1	0	0	0
Totals	31	3	6	27	10	2

Brooklyn	0	0	1	0	1	0	0	1	2—5
New York	0	1	0	0	0	0	0	1	1—3

aHomered for Gorman in ninth. bFlied out for Collins in ninth. Runs batted in—Lopat, Robinson, Reese, Pafko, Berra, Mize. Two-base hits—Furillo, Berra. Home runs—Berra, Mize. Sacrifice hits—Bauer, Roe 2. Stolen bases—Snider, Reese, Robinson. Double plays—Rizzuto and Martin; McDougald and Collins. Left on bases—Brooklyn 10, New York 8. Earned runs—Brooklyn 5, New York 3. Bases on balls—Off Roe 5, off Lopat 4. Struck out—By Roe 5. Pitching records—Off Lopat 10 hits, 5 runs in 8⅓ innings; off Gorman 1 hit, 0 runs in ⅔ inning. Hit by pitched ball—By Roe 1 (Martin). Passed ball—Berra. Winning pitcher—Roe. Losing pitcher—Lopat. Umpires—Goetz (N.L.), McKinley (A.L.), Pinelli (N.L.), Passarella (A.L.), Boggess (N.L.) and Honochick (A.L.). Time—2:56. Attendance—66,698.

Saturday, October 4—At New York

Brooklyn (N.L.)	AB.	R.	H.	O.	A.	E.
Cox, 3b	3	0	0	2	2	0
bNelson	1	0	0	0	0	0
Morgan, 3b	0	0	0	0	1	0
Reese, ss	4	0	2	3	3	1
Snider, cf	4	0	0	5	0	0
Robinson, 2b	4	0	0	0	2	0
Campanella, c	3	0	0	4	0	0
Pafko, lf	3	0	1	2	0	0
Hodges, 1b	2	0	0	10	0	0
Furillo, rf	2	0	1	1	0	0
Black, p	1	0	0	0	2	0
aShuba	1	0	0	0	0	0
Rutherford, p	0	0	0	0	0	0
Totals	28	0	4	24	10	1

1952 WORLD SERIES

New York (A.L.)	AB.	R.	H.	O.	A.	E.
McDougald, 3b	3	0	0	0	1	0
Rizzuto, ss	2	0	0	1	3	0
Mantle, cf	3	1	1	4	0	0
Mize, 1b	3	1	2	4	2	0
cCollins, 1b	0	0	0	1	0	0
Berra, c	4	0	0	12	1	0
Wooding, lf	3	0	1	1	0	0
Bauer, rf	4	0	0	1	0	0
Martin, 2b	3	0	0	2	1	1
Reynolds, p	3	0	0	1	0	0
Totals	28	2	4	27	8	1

```
Brooklyn....... 0 0 0  0 0 0  0 0 0—0
New York....... 0 0 0  1 0 0  0 1 *—2
```

aFlied out for Black in eighth. bStruck out for Cox in eighth. cRan for Mize in eighth. Run batted in—Mize. Two-base hits—Woodling, Mize. Three-base hit—Mantle. Home run—Mize. Sacrifice—Furillo. Double play—Rizzuto, Martin and Mize. Left on bases—Brooklyn 5, New York 8. Earned runs—New York 2. Bases on balls—Off Black 5, off Rutherford 1, off Reynolds 3. Struck out—By Reynolds 10, by Black 2, by Rutherford 1. Pitching records—Off Black 3 hits, 1 run in 7 innings; off Rutherford 1 hit, 1 run in 1 inning. Winning pitcher—Reynolds. Losing pitcher—Black. Umpires—McKinley (A.L.), Pinelli (N.L.), Passarella (A.L.), Goetz (N.L.), Honochick (A.L.), Boggess (N.L.). Time—2:33. Attendance—71,787.

Sunday, October 5—At New York

Brooklyn (N.L.)	AB.	R.	H.	O.	A.	E.
Cox, 3b	5	2	3	2	2	0
Reese, ss	5	0	1	1	1	0
Snider, cf	5	1	3	4	0	0
Robinson, 2b	2	1	0	2	1	0
Shuba, lf	2	0	1	4	0	0
Furillo, rf	4	0	1	3	0	0
Campanella, c	5	0	0	6	1	0
Pafko, rf-lf	4	0	1	3	0	0
Holmes, lf	1	0	0	2	0	0
Hodges, 1b	3	0	0	6	0	0
Erskine, p	4	1	0	0	1	0
Totals	40	6	10	33	6	0

New York (A.L.)	AB.	R.	H.	O.	A.	E.
McDougald, 3b	4	1	0	0	2	0
Rizzuto, ss	5	1	1	1	4	1
Mantle, cf	5	0	1	1	0	0
Mize, 1b	5	1	1	9	1	0
Berra, c	4	0	0	10	1	0
Woodling, lf	4	0	0	5	0	0
Bauer, rf	3	1	0	1	0	0
Martin, 2b	4	1	1	6	3	0
Blackwell, p	1	0	0	0	1	0
aNoren	1	0	1	0	0	0
Sain, p	2	0	0	0	2	0
Totals	38	5	5	33	14	1

```
Brooklyn....... 0 1 0  0 3 0  1 0 0  0 1—6
New York....... 0 0 0  0 5 0  0 0 0  0 0—5
```

aSingled for Blackwell in fifth. Runs batted in—Pafko, Reese, Snider 4, Noren, McDougald, Mize 3. Two-base hits—Furillo, Snider. Home runs—Snider, Mize. Stolen base—Robinson. Sacrifices—Erskine, Cox, Reese. Double plays—Martin, Rizzuto and Mize; McDougald, Berra and Mize. Left on bases—Brooklyn 11, New York 3. Earned runs—Brooklyn 6, New York 5. Bases on balls—Off Erskine 3, off Blackwell 3, off Sain 3. Struck out—By Erskine 6, by Blackwell 4, by Sain 3. Pitching records—Off Blackwell 4 hits, 4 runs in 5 innings; off Sain 6 hits, 2 runs in 6 innings. Hit by pitched ball—By Sain 1 (Snider). Winning pitcher—Erskine. Losing pitcher—Sain. Umpires—Pinelli (N.L.), Passarella (A.L.), Goetz (N.L.), McKinley (A.L.), Boggess (N.L.), Honochick (A.L.). Time—3:00. Attendance—70,536.

Monday, October 6—At Brooklyn

New York (A.L.)	AB.	R.	H.	O.	A.	E.
McDougald, 3b	4	0	1	1	2	0
Rizzuto, ss	4	0	1	2	2	0
Mantle, cf	3	1	1	0	0	0
Mize, 1b	3	0	0	7	0	0
Collins, 1b	1	0	0	2	0	0
Berra, c	5	1	1	12	0	0
Woodling, lf	3	1	2	3	0	0
Noren, rf	4	0	2	0	0	0
Bauer, rf	0	0	0	0	0	0
Martin, 2b	4	0	0	0	3	0
Raschi, p	3	0	1	0	1	0
Reynolds, p	1	0	0	0	0	0
Totals	35	3	9	27	8	0

Brooklyn (N.L.)	AB.	R.	H.	O.	A.	E.
Cox, 3b	5	0	2	1	3	0
Reese, ss	4	0	0	5	2	1
Snider, cf	3	2	2	4	0	0
Robinson, 2b	4	0	0	2	2	0
Shuba, lf	4	0	1	2	0	0
aAmoros	0	0	0	0	0	0
Holmes, lf	0	0	0	0	0	0
Campanella, c	4	0	1	5	0	0
Hodges, 1b	3	0	0	7	1	0
bNelson	1	0	0	0	0	0
Furillo, rf	3	0	1	1	0	0
Loes, p	3	0	1	0	2	0
Roe, p	0	0	0	0	0	0
cPafko	1	0	0	0	0	0
Totals	35	2	8	27	10	1

```
New York....... 0 0 0  0 0 0  2 1 0—3
Brooklyn....... 0 0 0  0 0 1  0 1 0—2
```

aRan for Shuba in eighth. bStruck out for Hodges in ninth. cPopped out for Roe in ninth. Runs batted in—Snider 2, Berra, Raschi, Mantle. Two-base hits—Cox, Shuba. Home runs—Snider 2, Berra, Mantle. Stolen base—Loes. Double play—Hodges, Reese and Robinson. Left on bases—New York 11, Brooklyn 8. Earned runs—New York 3, Brooklyn 2. Bases on balls—Off Raschi 1, off Reynolds 1, off Loes 5, off Roe 1. Struck out—By Raschi 9, by Reynolds 2, by Loes 3, by Roe 1. Pitching records—Off Raschi 8 hits, 2 runs in 7⅔ innings; off Reynolds 0 hits, 0 runs in 1⅓ innings; off Loes 9 hits, 3 runs in 8⅓ innings; 0 runs in ⅔ inning. Balk—Loes. Winning pitcher—Raschi. Losing pitcher—Loes. Umpires—Passarella (A.L.), Goetz (N.L.), McKinley (A.L.), Pinelli (N.L.), Honochick (A.L.), Boggess (N.L.). Time—2:56. Attendance—30,037.

Tuesday, October 7—At Brooklyn

New York (A.L.)	AB.	R.	H.	O.	A.	E.
McDougald, 3b	5	1	2	2	3	2
Rizzuto, ss	4	1	1	1	1	0
Mantle, cf	5	1	2	1	0	0
Mize, 1b	3	0	2	6	0	0
Collins, 1b	0	0	0	1	0	0
Berra, c	4	0	0	7	0	0
Woodling, lf	4	1	2	5	0	1
Noren, rf	2	0	1	0	0	0
aBauer, rf	1	0	0	0	0	0
Martin, 2b	4	0	1	2	4	0
Lopat, p	1	0	0	0	1	0
Reynolds, p	1	0	0	0	0	1
bHouk	1	0	0	0	0	0
Raschi, p	0	0	0	0	0	0
Kuzava, p	1	0	0	0	0	0
Totals	36	4	10	27	9	4

1953 WORLD SERIES

Brooklyn (N.L.)	AB	R	H	O	A	E
Cox, 3b	5	1	2	2	3	1
Reese, ss	4	0	1	2	2	0
Snider, cf	4	1	1	4	0	0
Robinson, 2b	4	0	1	0	4	0
Campanella, c	4	0	2	2	0	0
Hodges, 1b	4	0	0	13	0	0
Shuba, lf	3	0	1	1	0	0
dPafko	1	0	0	0	0	0
Holmes, lf	0	0	0	0	0	0
Furillo, lf	3	0	0	3	0	0
Black, p	2	0	0	0	0	0
Roe, p	0	0	0	0	0	0
cNelson	1	0	0	0	0	0
Erskine, p	0	0	0	0	0	0
eMorgan	1	0	0	0	0	0
Totals	36	2	8	27	9	1

New York .... 0 0 0 1 1 1 1 0 0—4
Brooklyn .... 0 0 0 1 1 0 0 0 0—2

aSafe on error for Noren in sixth. bGrounded out for Reynolds in seventh. cPopped out for Roe in seventh. dStruck out for Shuba in eighth. eFlied out for Erskine in ninth. Runs batted in—Mize, Hodges, Woodling, Reese, Mantle 2. Two-base hits—Rizzuto, Cox. Home runs—Woodling, Mantle. Sacrifice—Rizzuto. Double plays—Robinson, Reese and Hodges; Rizzuto, Martin and Mize. Left on bases—New York 8, Brooklyn 9. Earned runs—New York 4, Brooklyn 2. Bases on balls—Off Raschi 2, off Black 1, off Erskine 1. Struck out—By Lopat 3, by Reynolds 2, by Kuzava 2, by Black 1, by Roe 1. Pitching records—Off Lopat 4 hits, 1 run in 3 innings (pitched to three batters in fourth); off Reynolds 3 hits, 1 run in 3 innings; off Raschi 1 hit, 0 runs in ⅓ inning; off Kuzava 0 hits, 0 runs in 2⅔ innings; off Black 6 hits, 3 runs in 5⅓ innings; off Roe 3 hits, 1 run in 1⅔ innings; off Erskine 1 hit, 0 runs in 2 innings. Winning pitcher—Reynolds. Losing pitcher—Black. Umpires—Goetz (N.L.), McKinley (A.L.), Pinelli (N.L.), Passarella (A.L.), Boggess (N.L.), Honochick (A.L.). Time—2:54. Attendance—33,195.

COMPOSITE BATTING AVERAGES
New York Yankees

Player-Position	G	AB	R	H	2B	3B	HR	RBI	BA
Mize, ph-1b	5	15	3	6	1	0	3	6	.400
Woodling, ph-lf	7	23	4	8	1	1	1	3	.348
Mantle, cf	7	29	5	10	1	1	2	3	.345
Lopat, p	2	3	0	1	0	0	0	1	.333
Noren, lf-ph-rf	4	10	0	3	0	0	0	1	.300
Martin, 2b	7	23	2	5	0	0	1	4	.217
Berra, c	7	28	2	6	1	0	2	3	.214
McDougald, 3b	7	25	5	5	0	0	1	3	.200
Raschi, p	3	6	0	1	0	0	0	1	.167
Rizzuto, ss	7	27	2	4	1	0	0	0	.148
Bauer, rf-ph	7	18	2	1	0	0	0	1	.056
Collins, 1b-pr	6	12	1	0	0	0	0	0	.000
Reynolds, p	4	7	0	0	0	0	0	0	.000
Scarborough, p	1	0	0	0	0	0	0	0	.000
Gorman, p	1	0	0	0	0	0	0	0	.000
Blackwell, p	1	1	0	0	0	0	0	0	.000
Kuzava, p	1	1	0	0	0	0	0	0	.000
Sain, ph-p	2	3	0	0	0	0	0	0	.000
Houk, ph	1	1	0	0	0	0	0	0	.000
Totals	7	232	26	50	5	2	10	24	.216

Brooklyn Dodgers

Player-Position	G	AB	R	H	2B	3B	HR	RBI	BA
Snider, cf	7	29	5	10	2	0	4	8	.345
Reese, ss	7	29	4	10	0	0	1	4	.345
Loes, p	2	3	0	1	0	0	0	0	.333
Shuba, ph-lf	4	10	0	3	1	0	0	0	.300
Cox, 3b	7	27	4	8	0	0	0	0	.296
Campanella, c	7	28	0	6	0	0	0	1	.214
Pafko, lf-rf-ph	7	21	0	4	0	0	0	0	.190
Robinson, 2b	7	23	4	4	0	0	1	2	.174
Furillo, rf	7	23	1	4	2	0	0	0	.174
Holmes, lf	3	1	0	0	0	0	0	0	.000
Morgan, 3b-ph	2	1	0	0	0	0	0	0	.000
Hodges, 1b	7	21	1	0	0	0	0	1	.000
Black, p	3	6	0	0	0	0	0	0	.000
Erskine, p	3	6	1	0	0	0	0	0	.000
Lehman, p	1	0	0	0	0	0	0	0	.000
Roe, p	3	2	0	0	0	0	0	0	.000
Rutherford, p	1	0	0	0	0	0	0	0	.000
Amoros, pr	1	0	0	0	0	0	0	0	.000
Nelson, ph	4	3	0	0	0	0	0	0	.000
Totals	7	233	20	50	7	0	6	18	.215

COMPOSITE PITCHING AVERAGES
New York Yankees

Pitcher	G	IP	H	R	E	SO	BB	W	L	ERA
Kuzava	1	2⅔	0	0	0	2	0	0	0	0.00
Gorman	1	⅔	1	0	0	0	0	0	0	0.00
Raschi	3	17	12	3	3	18	8	2	0	1.59
Reynolds	4	20⅓	12	4	4	18	6	2	1	1.77
Sain	1	6	6	2	2	3	3	0	1	3.00
Lopat	2	11⅓	14	6	6	3	4	0	1	4.76
Blackwell	1	5	4	4	4	4	3	0	0	7.20
Scarborough	1	1	1	1	1	1	0	0	0	9.00
Totals	7	64	50	20	20	49	24	4	3	2.81

Brooklyn Dodgers

Pitcher	G	IP	H	R	E	SO	BB	W	L	ERA
Lehman	1	2	2	0	0	1	0	0	0	0.00
Black	3	21⅓	15	6	6	9	8	1	2	2.53
Roe	3	11⅓	9	4	4	7	6	1	0	3.18
Loes	2	10⅓	11	6	5	5	5	0	1	4.35
Erskine	3	18	12	9	9	16	10	1	1	4.50
Rutherford	1	1	1	1	1	1	1	0	0	9.00
Totals	7	64	50	26	25	32	31	3	4	3.52

SERIES OF 1953

	W.	L.	Pct.
New York A. L.	4	2	.667
Brooklyn N. L.	2	4	.333

Cagey Casey Stengel and his incredible New York Yankees won their fifth straight world championship, a feat never before accomplished by any team or manager, when they defeated the Brooklyn Dodgers, four games to two, in the Golden Jubilee World Series of 1953. As befitted the history-making event, surviving members of the first World Series of 1903 attended the games as special guests of honor.

The triumph over the Dodgers, who became the real patsies of Series competition, with seven straight setbacks, gave the Yankees the amazing record of 15 world titles in their last 16 appearances and 16 in 20 tries. It also was the seventh straight victory for the American League and the thirty-third against 17 defeats since the inter-loop rivalry started.

The Dodgers, who clubbed their way to an easy pennant victory, setting numerous slugging marks along the way, continued their strong hitting in the series, with a team average of .300. But the Dodgers' defense cracked, with seven errors, and their pitching faltered, although Carl Erskine emerged with the outstanding mound performance when he fanned 14 Yankees in the third game to break the record of 13 strikeouts set by Howard Ehmke of the Athletics against the Cubs in 1929.

The star of the classic for the Yankees was Billy Martin, their scrappy second baseman. Only a .257 batter during the regular campaign, Billy the Kid broke loose in a fantastic .500 streak, with 12 hits to set a new high for a six-game Series. He rapped two homers, two triples, one double and seven singles for 23 total bases and drove in eight runs, including the winning marker in the ninth inning of the final game.

Mickey Mantle was both goat and hero for the Yankees, striking out eight times, including five times in succession, but coming through with a two-run homer to win the second game and a grand-slam for the winning edge in the fifth.

Allie Reynolds, the Big Chief, who switched from starting assignments to the bullpen to become the Yanks' relief ace during their pennant drive, drew the opening nod against Erskine in the Series lid-lifter and was staked to a 4 to 0 lead in the first inning.

Junior Gilliam homered for the Dodgers in the fifth frame and Yogi Berra connected for the Yanks in their half off Jim Hughes, Erskine's successor. The Brooks then routed Reynolds with three runs in the sixth on a round-tripper by Gil Hodges, a single by Billy Cox and a pinch-hit homer by George Shuba. Johnny Sain relieving Reynolds, gave up the tying tally in the seventh, but Collins immediately snapped the deadlock with a homer off Clem Labine and the Yanks added another trio off Ben Wade in the eighth to clinch their 9 to 5 victory.

Two southpaw "junkmen"—Preacher Roe and Eddie Lopat—opposed each other in the second contest, but the Dodgers' vet went down to a 4 to 2 defeat, although yielding only five hits while the crafty Yankee gave up nine. Despite using eight righthanded batters against Lopat, the Dodgers stranded ten runners, with Duke Snider, lone lefty in the Brooklyn lineup, leaving five aboard in five tries. Martin hit a homer off Roe in the seventh inning to tie the score, and in the eighth Hank Bauer singled and Mantle followed with his winning drive.

Two games down, Manager Chuck Dressen had no alternative but to call on Erskine again and Carl, with only one day of rest, responded with his 14-strikeout masterpiece. The righthander racked up 11 of his whiffs against lefthanded batters, fanning Mantle and Collins four times apiece. However, Erskine had to battle Vic Raschi every inch of the way before gaining a 3 to 2 triumph. Martin's single to open the Yankee fifth set up the game's first run, but Jackie Robinson's double, a balk and a squeeze by Cox enabled the Dodgers to tie the score in their half of the inning. Robinson singled in another Brooklyn run in the sixth, but New York knotted the game in the eighth on Woodling's ace. Roy Campanella homered in the Dodger eighth for the winning run.

The Dodgers squared the Series with a 7 to 3 victory in the fourth game after pounding Whitey Ford for three runs in the first inning. Duke Snider hit a homer and two doubles for four RBIs to pace the Brooks' 12-hit attack. Meanwhile, except for Gil McDougald's two-run homer in the fifth, the Yankees were held in check by Billy Loes until the ninth, when the first three Bombers reached base. Labine relieved and retired both Phil Rizzuto and Johnny Mize, but Mantle singled to score Gene Woodling. However, the rally was abruptly snuffed when Martin attempted to tally from second on the hit and was nailed at the plate on left fielder Don Thompson's strong throw to Campanella.

That was the last Dodger victory as the Yankees exploded with Mantle's grand-slam and other round-trippers by Martin, Woodling and McDougald to win an 11 to 7 slugfest in the fifth game. Mantle delivered his jackpot wallop on the first pitch by Russ Meyer, who had just relieved Johnny Podres, in the third inning.

The payoff sixth game saw Erskine make another effort to save the Dodgers, but he was unequal to the strain and gave up three runs in the first two innings. Ford, who lasted only one inning in the fourth game, came back to hold the Brooks to six hits and one run for seven stanzas with the Dodger marker being made possible by Jackie Robinson's theft of third while Ford held the ball in the sixth inning. At the start of the eighth inning Stengel sent Reynolds to the mound to protect the lead, but Furillo, N. L. batting champion, smashed a two-run homer in the ninth.

However, in the last of the ninth, Bauer worked Labine for a pass. Berra lined out, but Mantle beat out an infield hit. Martin then cracked a single to center and the Series was over.

A boost in ticket prices resulted in several new Series records for receipts. Box seats were hiked from $8 to $10, grandstand reserved seats from $6 to $7 and bleachers from $1 to $2. Only standing room tickets remained the same at $4.

Box scores of the games follow:

Wednesday, Sept. 30—At New York

Brooklyn (N.L.)	AB.	R.	H.	O.	A.	E.
Gilliam, 2b	5	1	2	3	3	0
Reese, ss	3	0	0	3	3	0
Snider, cf	5	0	2	3	0	0
Robinson, lf	4	0	0	0	0	0
Campanella, c	4	1	1	6	3	0
Hodges, 1b	5	1	3	7	0	0
Furillo, rf	4	0	1	2	0	1
Cox, 3b	5	1	2	0	1	0
Erskine, p	0	0	0	0	0	0
aBelardi	1	0	0	0	0	0
Hughes, p	1	0	0	0	0	1
bShuba	1	1	1	0	0	0
Labine, p	1	0	0	0	1	0
Wade, p	0	0	0	0	0	0
Totals	39	5	12	24	11	2

1953 WORLD SERIES

New York (A.L.)	AB.	R.	H.	O.	A.	E.
McDougald, 3b	5	0	0	3	2	0
Collins, 1b	4	2	2	6	0	0
Bauer, rf	5	1	2	4	0	0
Berra, c	4	1	2	8	2	0
Mantle, cf	3	1	1	0	0	0
Woodling, lf	3	1	1	4	0	0
Martin, 2b	4	1	3	1	2	0
Rizzuto, ss	3	1	0	1	1	0
Reynolds, p	1	0	0	0	0	0
Sain, p	2	1	1	0	0	0
Totals	34	9	12	27	7	0

Brooklyn........... 0 0 0 0 1 3 1 0 0—5
New York.......... 4 0 0 0 1 0 1 3 *—9

aStruck out for Erskine in second. bHomered for Hughes in sixth. Runs batted in—Bauer, Martin 3, Gilliam, Berra, Hodges, Shuba, Furillo, Collins 2, Sain 2. Two-base hits—Cox, Snider, Sain. Three-base hits—Bauer, Martin. Home runs—Gilliam, Berra, Hodges, Shuba, Collins. Stolen base—Martin. Left on bases—Brooklyn 12, New York 6. Earned runs—Brooklyn 5, New York 9. Bases on balls—Off Reynolds 3, off Sain 1, off Erskine 3, off Hughes 1, off Wade 1. Struck out—By Reynolds 6, by Erskine 1, by Hughes 3, by Labine 1, by Wade 2. Pitching records—Off Erskine 2 hits, 4 runs in 1 inning; off Hughes 3 hits, 1 run in 4 innings; off Labine 4 hits, 1 run in 1⅔ innings; off Wade 3 hits, 3 runs in 1⅓ innings; off Reynolds 7 hits, 4 runs in 5⅓ innings; off Sain 5 hits, 1 run in 3⅔ innings. Hit by pitcher—By Reynolds 1 (Campanella). Winning pitcher—Sain. Losing pitcher—Labine. Umpires—Grieve (A.L.), Stewart (N.L.), Hurley (A.L.), Gore (N.L.), Soar (A.L.) and Dascoli (N.L.). Time—3:10. Attendance—69,374.

Thursday, October 1—At New York

Brooklyn (N.L.)	AB.	R.	H.	O.	A.	E.
Gilliam, 2b	5	0	0	1	2	0
Reese, ss	3	0	2	0	1	0
Snider, cf	5	0	0	2	0	0
Robinson, lf	4	0	1	3	0	0
Campanella, c	4	0	0	5	1	0
Hodges, 1b	3	1	2	9	1	0
Furillo, rf	4	1	2	3	0	1
Cox, 3b	3	0	1	0	2	0
Roe, p	3	0	0	1	1	0
aWilliams	1	0	1	0	0	0
Totals	35	2	9	24	10	1

New York (A.L.)	AB.	R.	H.	O.	A.	E.
Woodling, lf	3	1	0	1	0	0
Collins, 1b	3	0	0	15	0	0
Bauer, rf	4	1	1	1	0	0
Berra, c	3	0	0	4	0	0
Mantle, cf	3	1	1	4	0	0
McDougald, 3b	3	0	0	0	3	0
Martin, 2b	3	1	2	1	5	0
Rizzuto, ss	2	0	1	1	5	0
Lopat, p	3	0	0	0	2	0
Totals	27	4	5	27	15	0

Brooklyn........... 0 0 0 2 0 0 0 0 0—2
New York.......... 1 0 0 0 0 0 1 2 *—4

aSingled for Roe in ninth. Runs batted in—Berra, Cox 2, Martin, Mantle 2. Two-base hits—Rizzuto, Cox, Furillo. Three-base hit—Reese. Home runs—Martin, Mantle. Sacrifice hit—Rizzuto. Stolen base—Hodges. Double play—Martin, Rizzuto and Collins. Left on bases—Brooklyn 10, New York 5. Earned runs—Brooklyn 2, New York 4. Bases on balls—Off Lopat 4, off Roe 4. Struck out—By Lopat 3, by Roe 4. Hit by pitcher—By Roe 1 (McDougald). Winning pitcher—Lopat. Losing pitcher—Roe. Umpires—Stewart (N.L.), Hurley (A.L.), Gore (N.L.), Grieve (A.L.), Dascoli (N.L.) and Soar (A.L.). Time—2:42. Attendance—66,786.

Friday, October 2—At Brooklyn

New York (A.L.)	AB.	R.	H.	O.	A.	E.
McDougald, 3b	4	0	1	2	3	0
cNoren	0	0	0	0	0	0
Collins, 1b	5	0	0	8	0	0
Bauer, rf	4	1	1	1	0	0
Berra, c	1	0	1	4	1	0
Mantle, cf	4	0	0	2	0	0
Woodling, lf	4	0	1	0	0	0
Martin, 2b	3	1	1	3	4	0
Rizzuto, ss	3	0	1	3	3	0
aBollweg	1	0	0	0	0	0
Raschi, p	2	0	0	1	1	0
bMize	1	0	0	0	0	0
Totals	32	2	6	24	12	0

Brooklyn (N.L.)	AB.	R.	H.	O.	A.	E.
Gilliam, 2b	4	0	1	1	2	0
Reese, ss	4	0	1	1	4	0
Snider, cf	3	1	1	0	0	0
Hodges, 1b	2	0	1	8	1	0
Campanella, c	4	1	1	14	0	0
Furillo, rf	4	0	0	1	0	0
Robinson, lf	4	1	3	1	0	0
Thompson, lf	0	0	0	0	0	0
Cox, 3b	3	0	0	0	1	0
Erskine, p	3	0	1	1	2	0
Totals	31	3	9	27	10	0

New York........... 0 0 0 0 1 0 0 1 0—2
Brooklyn........... 0 0 0 0 1 1 0 1 *—3

aStruck out for Rizzuto in ninth. bStruck out for Raschi in ninth. cWalked for McDougald in ninth. Runs batted in—McDougald, Cox, Robinson, Woodling, Campanella. Two-base hit—Robinson. Home run—Campanella. Sacrifice hits—Raschi, Cox. Double play—Rizzuto, Martin and Collins. Left on bases—New York 9, Brooklyn 8. Earned runs—New York 2, Brooklyn 3. Bases on balls—Off Erskine 3, off Raschi 3. Struck out—By Erskine 14, by Raschi 4. Hit by pitcher—By Erskine (Berra 2). Wild pitch—Erskine. Balk—Raschi. Winning pitcher—Erskine. Losing pitcher—Raschi. Umpires—Hurley (A.L.), Gore (N.L.), Grieve (A.L.), Stewart (N.L.), Soar (A.L.) and Dascoli (N.L.). Time—3:00. Attendance—35,270.

Saturday, October 3—At Brooklyn

New York (A.L.)	AB.	R.	H.	O.	A.	E.
Mantle, cf	5	0	1	1	0	0
Collins, 1b	4	0	0	9	1	0
Bauer, rf	4	0	1	4	0	0
Berra, c	4	0	2	4	0	0
Woodling, lf	3	1	1	1	0	0
Martin, 2b	4	1	2	4	2	0
McDougald, 3b	3	1	1	0	5	0
Rizzuto, ss	4	0	1	0	2	0
Ford, p	0	0	0	0	0	0
Gorman, p	1	0	0	0	1	0
aBollweg	1	0	0	0	0	0
Sain, p	0	0	0	0	0	0
bNoren	1	0	0	0	0	0
Schallock, p	0	0	0	0	1	0
cMize	1	0	0	0	0	0
Totals	35	3	9	24	11	0

Brooklyn (N.L.)	AB.	R.	H.	O.	A.	E.
Gilliam, 2b	5	1	3	2	2	0
Reese, ss	5	0	0	2	1	0
Robinson, lf	4	0	1	1	0	0

1953 WORLD SERIES

	AB.	R.	H.	O.	A.	E.
Thompson, lf	0	0	0	0	1	0
Hodges, 1b	4	1	0	5	1	0
Campanella, c	2	2	0	10	0	0
Snider, cf	4	1	3	5	0	0
Furillo, rf	4	1	1	2	0	0
Cox, 3b	4	1	2	0	1	0
Loes, p	3	0	2	0	0	0
Labine, p	0	0	0	0	0	0
Totals	35	7	12	27	6	0

New York........... 0 0 0   0 2 0   0 0 1—3
Brooklyn............ 3 0 0   1 0 2   1 0 *—7

aStruck out for Gorman in fifth. bPopped out for Sain in seventh. cFlied out for Schallock in ninth. Runs batted in—Robinson, Snider 4, Gilliam 2, McDougald 2, Mantle. Two-base hits—Gilliam 3, Snider 2, Cox. Three-base hit—Martin. Home runs—McDougald, Snider. Sacrifice hit—Loes. Left on bases—New York 7, Brooklyn 7. Earned runs—New York 3, Brooklyn 7. Bases on balls—Off Loes 2, off Ford 1, off Schallock 1. Struck out—By Loes 8, by Gorman 1, by Sain 1, by Schallock 1, by Labine 1. Pitching records—Off Ford 3 hits, 3 runs in 1 inning; off Gorman 4 hits, 1 run in 3 innings; off Sain 3 hits, 2 runs in 2 innings; off Schallock 2 hits, 1 run in 2 innings; off Loes 8 hits, 3 runs in 8 innings (pitched to three batters in ninth); off Labine 1 hit, 0 runs in 1 inning. Wild pitch—Ford. Winning pitcher—Loes. Losing pitcher—Ford. Umpires—Gore (N.L.), Grieve (A.L.), Stewart (N.L.), Hurley (A.L.), Dascoli (N.L.) and Soar (A.L.). Time—2:46. Attendance—36,775.

Sunday, October 4—At Brooklyn

New York (A.L.)	AB.	R.	H.	O.	A.	E.
Woodling, lf	3	1	1	2	1	0
Collins, 1b	5	2	1	6	2	0
Bauer, rf	3	1	0	1	0	0
Berra, c	4	2	2	6	0	0
Mantle, cf	5	1	1	2	0	0
Martin, 2b	5	1	2	3	2	0
McDougald, 3b	5	1	2	0	1	0
Rizzuto, ss	3	2	1	4	6	1
McDonald, p	2	0	1	3	0	0
Kuzava, p	1	0	0	0	0	0
Reynolds, p	0	0	0	0	0	0
Totals	36	11	11	27	12	1

Brooklyn (N.L.)	AB.	R.	H.	O.	A.	E.
Gilliam, 2b	4	2	2	4	3	0
Reese, ss	5	0	1	0	1	0
Snider, cf	5	0	2	3	0	0
Robinson, lf	5	1	1	0	0	0
Campanella, c	4	2	3	8	3	0
Hodges, 1b	4	0	2	11	1	1
Furillo, rf	4	1	1	0	0	0
Cox, 3b	4	1	1	1	4	0
Podres, p	1	0	1	0	1	0
Meyer, p	1	0	0	0	1	0
aBelardi	1	0	0	0	0	0
Wade, p	0	0	0	0	0	0
bShuba	0	0	0	0	0	0
cWilliams	1	0	0	0	0	0
Black, p	0	0	0	0	0	0
Totals	39	7	14	27	14	1

New York........... 1 0 5   0 0 0   3 1 1—11
Brooklyn............ 0 1 0   0 1 0   0 4 1— 7

aGrounded out for Meyer in seventh. bAnnounced for Wade in eighth. cStruck out for Shuba in eighth. Runs batted in—Woodling, Mantle 4, Snider, Martin 2, McDonald, Berra, Furillo, Cox 3, McDougald, Gilliam. Two-base hits—McDonald, Collins. Three-base hit—McDougald. Home runs—Woodling, Mantle, Martin, Cox, McDougald, Gilliam. Sacrifice hits—McDonald, Bauer. Stolen base—Rizzuto. Double plays—Woodling and Berra; Rizzuto and Collins; Martin, Rizzuto and Collins. Left on bases—New York 7, Brooklyn 6. Earned runs—New York 6, Brooklyn 6. Bases on balls—Off Podres 2, off Meyer 4. Struck out—By Meyer 5, by Black 2, by McDonald 3, by Kuzava 1. Pitching records—Off Podres 1 hit, 5 runs in 2⅔ innings; off Meyer 8 hits, 4 runs in 4⅓ innings; off Wade 1 hit, 1 run in 1 inning; off Black 1 hit, 1 run in 1 inning; off McDonald 12 hits, 6 runs in 7⅔ innings; off Kuzava 2 hits, 1 run in ⅔ inning; off Reynolds 0 hits, 0 runs in ⅔ inning. Hit by pitcher—By Podres (Bauer), by McDonald (Gilliam). Winning pitcher—McDonald. Losing pitcher—Podres. Umpires—Grieve (A.L.), Stewart (N.L.), Hurley (A.L.), Gore (N.L.), Soar (A.L.) and Dascoli (N.L.). Time—3:02. Attendance—36,775.

Monday, October 5—At New York

Brooklyn (N.L.)	AB.	R.	H.	O.	A.	E.
Gilliam, 2b	4	0	0	4	4	1
Reese, ss	4	0	1	1	4	0
Robinson, lf	4	1	2	3	0	0
Campanella, c	4	0	1	4	0	0
Hodges, 1b	4	0	0	7	0	0
Snider, cf	3	1	0	4	1	0
Furillo, rf	4	1	3	2	0	0
Cox, 3b	4	0	1	0	1	1
Erskine, p	1	0	0	0	0	1
aWilliams	0	0	0	0	0	0
Milliken, p	0	0	0	0	0	0
bMorgan	1	0	0	0	0	0
Labine, p	1	0	0	0	1	0
Totals	34	3	8	i25	11	3

New York (A.L.)	AB.	R.	H.	O.	A.	E.
Woodling, lf	4	1	2	1	0	0
Collins, 1b	3	0	1	5	1	0
cMize	1	0	0	0	0	0
Bollweg, 1b	0	0	0	0	0	0
Bauer, rf	3	2	1	3	0	0
Berra, c	5	0	2	10	0	0
Mantle, cf	4	0	1	5	0	0
Martin, 2b	5	0	2	1	0	0
McDougald, 3b	4	0	0	0	0	0
Rizzuto, ss	4	1	2	2	2	0
Ford, p	3	0	1	0	1	0
Reynolds, p	1	0	1	0	0	0
Totals	37	4	13	27	4	0

Brooklyn........... 0 0 0   0 0 1   0 0 2—3
New York........... 2 1 0   0 0 0   0 0 1—4

aWalked for Erskine in fifth. bLined out for Milliken in seventh. cGrounded out for Collins in eighth. One out when winning run scored. Runs batted in—Berra, Martin 2, Woodling, Campanella, Furillo 2. Two-base hits—Berra, Furillo, Martin, Robinson. Home run—Furillo. Stolen base—Robinson. Double plays—Cox, Gilliam and Hodges; Snider, Gilliam and Campanella; Labine, Gilliam and Hodges. Left on bases—Brooklyn 6, New York 13. Earned runs—Brooklyn 3, New York 4. Bases on balls—Off Erskine 3, off Milliken 1, off Labine 1, off Ford 1, off Reynolds 1. Struck out—By Ford 7, by Reynolds 3, by Erskine 1, by Labine 1. Pitching records—Off Erskine 6 hits, 3 runs in 4 innings; off Milliken 2 hits, 0 runs in 2 innings; off Labine 5 hits, 1 run in 2⅓ innings; off Ford 6 hits, 1 run in 7 innings; off Reynolds 2 hits, 2 runs in 2 innings. Winning pitcher—Reynolds. Losing pitcher—Labine. Umpires—Stewart (N.L.), Hurley (A.L.), Gore (N.L.), Grieve (A.L.), Dascoli (N.L.) and Soar (A.L.). Time—2:55. Attendance—62,370.

COMPOSITE BATTING AVERAGES
New York Yankees

Player-Position	G.	AB.	R.	H.	2B.	3B.	HR.	RBI.	BA.
Martin, 2b	6	24	5	12	1	2	2	8	.500
McDonald, p	1	2	0	1	1	0	0	1	.500
Reynolds, p	3	2	0	1	0	0	0	0	.500
Sain, p	2	2	1	1	1	0	0	2	.500
Berra, c	6	21	3	9	1	0	1	4	.429
Ford, p	2	3	0	1	0	0	0	0	.333
Rizzuto, ss	6	19	4	6	1	0	0	0	.316
Woodling, lf	6	20	5	6	0	0	1	3	.300
Bauer, rf	6	23	6	6	0	1	0	1	.261
Mantle, cf	6	24	3	5	0	0	2	7	.208
McDougald, 3b	6	24	2	4	0	1	2	4	.167
Collins, 1b	6	24	4	4	1	0	1	2	.167
Bollweg, ph-1b	3	2	0	0	0	0	0	0	.000
Lopat, p	1	3	0	0	0	0	0	0	.000
Raschi, p	1	2	0	0	0	0	0	0	.000
Gorman, p	1	1	0	0	0	0	0	0	.000
Schallock, p	1	0	0	0	0	0	0	0	.000
Kuzava, p	1	1	0	0	0	0	0	0	.000
Mize, ph	3	3	0	0	0	0	0	0	.000
Noren, ph	2	1	0	0	0	0	0	0	.000
Totals	6	201	33	56	6	4	9	32	.279

Brooklyn Dodgers

Player-Position	G.	AB.	R.	H.	2B.	3B.	HR.	RBI.	BA.
Shuba, ph	2	1	1	1	0	0	1	2	1.000
Podres, p	1	1	0	1	0	0	0	0	1.000
Loes, p	1	3	0	2	0	0	0	0	.667
Williams, ph	3	2	0	1	0	0	0	0	.500
Hodges, 1b	6	22	3	8	0	0	1	1	.364
Furillo, rf	6	24	4	8	2	0	1	4	.333
Snider, cf	6	25	3	8	3	0	1	5	.320
Robinson, lf	6	25	3	8	2	0	0	2	.320
Cox, 3b	6	23	3	7	3	0	1	6	.304
Gilliam, 2b	6	27	4	8	3	0	2	4	.296
Campanella, c	6	22	6	6	0	0	1	2	.273
Erskine, p	3	4	0	1	0	0	0	0	.250
Reese, ss	6	24	0	5	0	1	0	0	.208
Thompson, lf	2	0	0	0	0	0	0	0	.000
Hughes, p	1	1	0	0	0	0	0	0	.000
Labine, p	3	2	0	0	0	0	0	0	.000
Wade, p	2	0	0	0	0	0	0	0	.000
Roe, p	1	3	0	0	0	0	0	0	.000
Meyer, p	1	1	0	0	0	0	0	0	.000
Black, p	1	0	0	0	0	0	0	0	.000
Milliken, p	1	0	0	0	0	0	0	0	.000
Belardi, ph	2	2	0	0	0	0	0	0	.000
Morgan, ph	1	1	0	0	0	0	0	0	.000
Totals	6	213	27	64	13	1	8	26	.300

COMPOSITE PITCHING AVERAGES
New York Yankees

Pitcher	G.	IP.	H.	R.	E.	SO.	BB.	W.	L.	ERA.
Lopat	1	9	9	2	2	3	4	1	0	2.00
Gorman	1	3	4	1	1	1	0	0	0	3.00
Raschi	1	8	9	3	3	4	3	0	1	3.38
Ford	2	8	9	4	4	7	2	0	1	4.50
Schallock	1	2	2	1	1	1	1	0	0	4.50
Sain	2	5⅔	8	3	3	1	1	1	0	4.76
McDonald	1	7⅔	12	6	5	3	0	1	0	5.87
Reynolds	3	8	9	6	6	9	4	1	0	6.75
Kuzava	1	⅔	2	1	1	1	0	0	0	13.50
Totals	6	52	64	27	26	30	15	4	2	4.50

Brooklyn Dodgers

Pitcher	G.	IP.	H.	R.	E.	SO.	BB.	W.	L.	ERA.
Milliken	1	2	2	0	0	1	0	0	0	0.00
Hughes	1	4	3	1	1	3	1	0	0	2.25
Loes	1	8	8	3	3	8	2	1	0	3.38
Podres	1	2⅔	1	5	1	0	2	0	1	3.38
Labine	3	5	10	2	2	3	1	0	2	3.60
Roe	1	8	5	4	4	4	4	0	1	4.50
Erskine	3	14	14	9	9	16	9	1	0	5.79
Meyer	1	4⅓	8	4	3	5	4	0	0	6.23
Black	1	1	1	1	1	2	0	0	0	9.00
Wade	2	2⅔	4	4	4	2	1	0	0	15.43
Totals	6	51⅓	56	33	28	43	25	2	4	4.91

SERIES OF 1954

	W.	L.	Pct.
New York N. L.	4	0	1.000
Cleveland A. L.	0	4	.000

After losing seven straight World Series, the National League smashed the American League's domination when the New York Giants, under Manager Leo Durocher, crushed the Cleveland Indians in four games. The Indians had broken the supremacy of the New York Yankees, world champions for five consecutive years, and had set a league record of 111 victories, making their collapse in the Classic one of the most astonishing reversals of form in Series history.

The Giants, fifth in 1953, had been transformed into a pennant-winning club by the return of Willie Mays from the Army and the acquisition of southpaw Johnny Antonelli from the Braves in a winter deal for outfielder Bobby Thomson. Antonelli posted 21 victories and Mays copped the batting title with a mark of .345.

In the Series, Mays made a sensational catch to save the first game. Antonelli won the second contest and stopped the Indians in relief in the clincher. But principal honors went to a man from the bench—Dusty Rhodes, the pinch-hitting hero of the Giants' sweep. The husky clutch-clouter hit a pinch-homer to win the first game and delivered vital pinch singles in the second and third encounters. He also hit a homer in the second game after going into the lineup.

Sal Maglie, starting the lidlifter for the Giants against Bob Lemon, fell behind, 2 to 0, in the first inning when Al Smith was nicked by a pitched ball, Bobby Avila singled and Vic Wertz tripled. The Giants tied the score in the third on singles by Whitey Lockman and Alvin Dark, Don Mueller's forceout, a pass to Mays and a single by Hank Thompson. Mays' great catch came in the eighth inning, with two on base, when he raced to the wall in front of the center field bleachers and, with his back to the plate, snared a 460-foot drive by Wertz.

The smash came off Don Liddle, who had just replaced Maglie. Marv Grissom, the American League castoff, then took the mound and went on to gain the 5 to 2 victory in 10 innings. With one out in the tenth, Mays walked for the second time and promptly stole second. Thompson drew an intentional pass and Rhodes, batting for Monte Irvin, hit Lemon's first pitch for a 260-foot Chinese homer into the right field stands.

Antonelli, taking the mound against Early Wynn in the second game, threw a gopher to Smith on his first delivery. He yielded seven more safeties and walked six, but stopped every Indian threat. Wynn walked Mays in the fifth inning and Thompson singled. Rhodes stepped to the plate again for Irvin and dropped a Texas League single into short center, scoring Mays with the tying run. After Davey Williams fanned for the first out, Wes Westrum walked. Antonelli then grounded to Avila, forcing Westrum at second, but Thompson scored with the Giants' second marker. Rhodes went to left field and iced the 3 to 1 victory with a powerful homer in the seventh.

Shifting to Cleveland the Giants won again, 6 to 2, behind the four-hit hurling of Ruben Gomez and Hoyt Wilhelm. The National Leaguers scored a run off Mike Garcia in the first inning on two singles, around an error, and routed the Big Bear with a three-run attack in the third. After two singles and an intentional walk loaded the bases. Rhodes rapped another pinch-single on the first pitch to drive in two runs. Williams' squeeze bunt plated the other tally.

The Giants mopped up in the fourth game, 7 to 4, to become only the second National League club to sweep a Series in four games (without a tie), the other being the Miracle Boston Braves of 1914. Durocher started lefty Don Liddle, while Lopez called on Lemon. Bob, pitching with two days of rest, was routed in the fifth inning and Hal Newhouser failed in relief as the Giants took a 7 to 0 lead.

With Hank Majeski hitting a pinch-homer, the Indians rallied to rout both Liddle and Wilhelm, but Antonelli wrapped up the verdict with a hitless relief performance in the final one and two-thirds innings.

The Series was the most lucrative in history for the players, who shared in a record pool of $881,763.72. A full slice for the Giants amounted to $11,147.90 and for the Indians $6,712.50, both new highs for Classic money. The attendance of 251,507 also set a new record for a four-game Series. The box scores follow:

Wednesday, Sept. 29—At New York

Cleveland (A.L.)	AB.	R.	H.	O.	A.	E.
Smith, lf	4	1	1	1	0	0
Avila, 2b	5	1	1	2	3	0
Doby, cf	3	0	1	3	0	0
Rosen, 3b	5	0	1	1	3	0
Wertz, 1b	5	0	4	11	1	0
dRegalado	0	0	0	0	0	0
Grasso, c	0	0	0	1	0	0
Philley, rf	3	0	0	0	0	0
aMajeski	0	0	0	0	0	0
bMitchell	0	0	0	0	0	0
Dente, ss	0	0	0	0	0	0
Strickland, ss	3	0	0	2	3	0
cPope, rf	1	0	0	0	0	0
Hegan, c	4	0	0	6	1	0
eGlynn, 1b	1	0	0	0	0	0
Lemon, p	4	0	0	1	1	0
Totals	38	2	8	¡28	12	0

New York (N.L.)	AB.	R.	H.	O.	A.	E.
Lockman, 1b	5	1	1	9	0	0
Dark, ss	4	0	2	3	2	0
Mueller, rf	5	0	2	2	0	2
Mays, cf	3	1	0	2	0	0
Thompson, 3b	3	1	1	3	3	0
Irvin, lf	3	0	0	5	0	1
fRhodes	1	1	1	0	0	0
Williams, 2b	4	0	0	1	1	0
Westrum, c	4	0	2	5	0	0
Maglie, p	3	0	0	0	2	0
Liddle, p	0	0	0	0	0	0
Grissom, p	1	0	0	0	0	0
Totals	36	5	9	30	8	3

Cleveland .... 2 0 0   0 0 0   0 0 0—2
New York .... 0 0 2   0 0 0   0 0 0 3—5

aAnnounced as batter for Philley in eighth. bWalked for Majeski in eighth. cCalled out on strikes for Strickland in eighth. dRan for Wertz in tenth. eStruck out for Hegan in tenth. fHit home run for Irvin in tenth. iOne out when winning run scored. Runs batted in—Wertz 2, Mueller, Thompson, Rhodes 3. Two-base hit—Wertz. Three-base hit—Wertz. Home run—Rhodes. Stolen base—Mays. Sacrifice hits—Irvin, Dente. Left on bases—Cleveland 13, New York 9. Earned runs—New York 5, Cleveland 2. Bases on balls—Off Lemon 5, off Maglie 2, off Grissom 3. Struck out—By Maglie 2, by Grissom 2, by Lemon 6. Pitching records—Off Maglie 7 hits, 2 runs in 7 innings (pitched to two batters in eighth); off Liddle 0 hits, 0 runs in ⅓ inning; off Grissom 1 hit 0 runs in 2⅔ innings. Hit by pitcher—By Maglie (Smith). Wild pitch—Lemon. Winning pitcher—Grissom. Losing pitcher—Lemon. Umpires—Barlick (N.L.), Berry (A.L.), Conlan (N.L.), Stevens (A.L.), Warneke (N.L.), Napp (A.L.). Time—3:11. Attendance—52,751.

Thursday, Sept. 30—At New York

Cleveland (A.L.)	AB.	R.	H.	O.	A.	E.
Smith, lf	4	1	2	3	0	0
Avila, 2b	4	0	1	2	2	0
Doby, cf	5	0	0	2	0	0
Rosen, 3b	3	0	1	0	0	0
bRegalado, 3b	1	0	0	0	0	0
Wertz, 1b	3	0	1	5	1	0
Westlake, rf	3	0	1	3	0	0
Strickland, ss	3	0	0	1	1	0
cPhilley	1	0	0	0	0	0
Dente, ss	0	0	0	0	0	0
Hegan, c	4	0	1	7	0	0
Wynn, p	2	0	1	1	1	0
dMajeski	1	0	0	0	0	0
Mossi, p	0	0	0	0	1	0
Totals	34	1	8	24	6	0

New York (N.L.)	AB.	R.	H.	O.	A.	E.
Lockman, 1b	4	0	0	8	0	0
Dark, ss	4	0	1	0	6	0
Mueller, rf	4	0	0	1	0	0
Mays, cf	2	1	0	1	0	0
Thompson, 3b	3	1	1	1	3	0
Irvin, lf	1	0	0	2	0	0
aRhodes, lf	2	1	2	1	0	0
Williams, 2b	3	0	0	4	0	0
Westrum, c	2	0	0	9	0	0
Antonelli, p	3	0	0	0	1	0
Totals	28	3	4	27	10	0

Cleveland .... 1 0 0   0 0 0   0 0 0—1
New York .... 0 0 0   0 2 0   1 0 *—3

aSingled for Irvin in fifth. bRan for Rosen in seventh. cStruck out for Strickland in eighth. dGrounded out for Wynn in eighth. Runs batted in—Smith, Rhodes 2, Antonelli. Two-base hits—Hegan, Wynn. Home runs—Smith, Rhodes. Sacrifice fly—Wynn. Left on bases—Cleveland 13, New York 3. Earned runs—New York 3, Cleveland 1. Bases on balls—Off Antonelli 6, off Wynn 2. Struck out—By Antonelli 9, by Wynn 5. Pitching records—Off Wynn 4 hits, 3 runs in 7 innings; off Mossi 0 hits, 0 runs in 1 inning. Wild pitch—Wynn. Winning pitcher—Antonelli. Losing pitcher—Wynn. Umpires—Berry (A.L.), Conlan (N.L.), Stevens (A.L.), Barlick (N.L.), Warneke (N.L.), Napp (A.L.). Time—2:50. Attendance—49,099.

1954 WORLD SERIES

Friday, October 1—At Cleveland

New York (N.L.)	AB.	R.	H.	O.	A.	E.
Lockman, 1b	4	1	1	13	0	0
Dark, ss	4	0	1	2	2	1
Mueller, rf	5	2	2	0	0	0
Mays, cf	5	1	3	2	0	0
Thompson, 3b	3	2	1	0	3	0
Irvin, lf	1	0	0	0	0	0
aRhodes, lf	3	0	1	3	0	0
Williams, 2b	2	0	0	2	5	0
Westrum, c	4	0	1	4	0	0
Gomez, p	4	0	0	1	2	0
Wilhelm, p	0	0	0	0	0	0
Totals	35	6	10	27	12	1

Cleveland (A.L.)	AB.	R.	H.	O.	A.	E.
Smith, lf	3	0	0	0	0	0
Avila, 2b	2	0	0	4	1	0
Doby, cf	4	0	1	2	0	0
Wertz, 1b	4	1	1	6	1	0
Majeski, 3b	4	0	2	2	1	0
Philley, rf	3	0	1	1	0	0
Strickland, ss	3	0	0	3	4	1
fPope	1	0	0	0	0	0
Hegan, c	2	0	0	8	1	0
dGlynn	1	1	1	0	0	0
Naragon, c	0	0	0	1	0	0
Garcia, p	0	0	0	0	1	1
bLemon	1	0	0	0	0	0
Houtteman, p	0	0	0	0	0	0
cRegalado	1	0	0	0	0	0
Narleski, p	0	0	0	0	1	0
eMitchell	1	0	0	0	0	0
Mossi, p	0	0	0	0	0	0
Totals	30	2	4	27	10	2

New York .... 1 0 3 0 1 1 0 0 0—6
Cleveland .... 0 0 0 0 0 0 1 1 0—2

aSingled for Irvin in third. bStruck out for Garcia in third. cGrounded out for Houtteman in fifth. dDoubled for Hegan in eighth. eGrounded out for Narleski in eighth. fGrounded out for Strickland in ninth. Runs batted in—Mays 2, Rhodes, Williams, Westrum, Wertz, Smith. Two-base hits—Thompson, Glynn. Home run—Wertz. Sacrifice hits—Avila, Williams, Dark. Double plays—Dark, Williams and Lockman; Strickland and Wertz. Left on bases—New York 9, Cleveland 5. Earned runs—New York 5, Cleveland 2. Bases on balls—Off Garcia 3, off Houtteman 1, off Narleski 1, off Gomez 3. Struck out—By Garcia 3, by Houtteman 1, by Narleski 2, by Mossi 1, by Gomez 2, by Wilhelm 2. Pitching records—Off Garcia 5 hits, 4 runs in 3 innings; off Houtteman 2 hits, 1 run in 2 innings; off Narleski 1 hit, 1 run in 3 innings; off Mossi 2 hits, 0 runs in 1 inning; off Gomez 4 hits, 2 runs in 7⅓ innings; off Wilhelm 0 hits, 0 runs in 1⅔ innings. Wild pitch—Garcia. Winning pitcher—Gomez. Losing pitcher—Garcia. Umpires—Conlan (N.L.), Stevens (A.L.), Barlick (N.L.), Berry (A.L.), Napp (A.L.), Warneke (N.L.). Time—2:28. Attendance—71,555.

Saturday, October 2—At Cleveland

New York (N.L.)	AB.	R.	H.	O.	A.	E.
Lockman, 1b	5	0	0	10	1	0
Dark, ss	5	2	3	2	2	0
Mueller, rf	4	1	3	0	0	0
Mays, cf	4	1	1	5	0	0
Thompson, 3b	2	2	1	1	2	0
Irvin, lf	4	1	2	1	0	0
Williams, 2b	2	0	0	3	3	1
Westrum, c	1	0	0	5	0	0
Liddle, p	3	0	0	0	1	1
Wilhelm, p	1	0	0	0	1	1
Antonelli, p	0	0	0	0	0	0
Totals	31	7	10	27	10	3

Cleveland (A.L.)	AB.	R.	H.	O.	A.	E.
Smith, lf	3	0	0	0	0	0
cPope, lf	1	0	0	0	0	0
eMitchell	1	0	0	0	0	0
Avila, 2b	4	0	0	4	4	0
Doby, cf	4	0	0	0	0	0
Rosen, 3b	4	0	1	1	0	0
Wertz, 1b	4	1	2	11	3	1
Westlake, rf	4	0	0	3	0	1
Dente, ss	3	1	0	1	1	0
Hegan, c	3	1	1	6	1	0
Lemon, p	1	0	0	1	1	0
Newhouser, p	0	0	0	0	0	0
Narleski, p	0	0	0	0	0	0
aMajeski	1	1	1	0	0	0
Mossi, p	0	0	0	0	1	0
bRegalado	1	0	1	0	0	0
Garcia, p	0	0	0	0	1	0
dPhilley	1	0	0	0	0	0
Totals	35	4	6	27	12	2

New York .... 0 2 1 0 4 0 0 0 0—7
Cleveland .... 0 0 0 0 3 0 1 0 0—4

aHit home run for Narleski in fifth. bSingled for Mossi in seventh. cGrounded out for Smith in seventh. dStruck out for Garcia in ninth. eFouled out for Pope in ninth. Runs batted in—Westrum 2, Mays, Thompson, Irvin 2, Majeski 3, Regalado. Two-base hits—Irvin, Wertz, Mays. Home run—Majeski. Sacrifice hits—Williams, Westrum, Mueller. Sacrifice flies—Westrum 2. Double plays—Thompson, Williams and Lockman; Dente, Avila and Wertz. Left on bases—New York 7, Cleveland 6. Earned runs—New York 6, Cleveland 1. Bases on balls—Off Lemon 3, off Newhouser 1, off Liddle 1, off Garcia 1, off Antonelli 1. Struck out—By Lemon 5, by Garcia 1, by Liddle 2, by Wilhelm 1, by Antonelli 3. Pitching records—Off Lemon 7 hits, 6 runs in 4 innings (pitched to three batters in fifth); off Newhouser 1 hit, 1 run in 0 inning (pitched to two batters in fifth); off Narleski 0 hits, 0 runs in 1 inning; off Mossi 1 hit, 0 runs in 2 innings; off Garcia 1 hit, 0 runs in 2 innings; off Liddle 5 hits, 4 runs in 6⅔ innings; off Wilhelm 1 hit, 0 runs in ⅔ inning; off Antonelli 0 hits, 0 runs in 1⅔ innings. Wild pitch—Liddle. Winning pitcher—Liddle. Losing pitcher—Lemon. Umpires—Stevens (A.L.), Barlick (N.L.), Berry (A.L.), Conlan (N.L.), Warneke (N.L.), Napp (A.L.). Time—2:52. Attendance—78,102.

COMPOSITE BATTING AVERAGES

New York Giants

Player-Position	G.	AB.	R.	H.	2B.	3B.	HR.	RBI.	BA.
Rhodes, ph-lf	3	6	2	4	0	0	2	7	.667
Dark, ss	4	17	2	7	0	0	0	1	.412
Mueller, rf	4	18	4	7	0	0	0	1	.389
Thompson, 3b	4	11	6	4	1	0	0	2	.364
Mays, cf	4	14	4	4	1	0	0	3	.286
Westrum, c	4	11	0	3	0	0	0	3	.273
Irvin, lf	4	9	1	2	1	0	0	2	.222
Lockman, 1b	4	18	2	2	0	0	0	0	.111
Williams, 2b	4	11	0	0	0	0	0	1	.000
Maglie, p	1	3	0	0	0	0	0	0	.000
Liddle, p	2	3	0	0	0	0	0	0	.000
Grissom, p	1	1	0	0	0	0	0	0	.000
Antonelli, p	2	3	0	0	0	0	0	1	.000
Gomez, p	1	4	0	0	0	0	0	0	.000
Wilhelm, p	2	1	0	0	0	0	0	0	.000
Totals	4	130	21	33	3	0	2	20	.254

Cleveland Indians

Player-Position	G.	AB.	R.	H.	2B.	3B.	HR.	RBI.	BA.
Wynn, p	1	2	0	1	1	0	0	0	.500
Wertz, 1b	4	16	2	8	2	1	1	3	.500
Glynn, ph-1b	2	2	1	1	1	0	0	0	.500
Rega'do, pr-3b-ph	4	3	0	1	0	0	0	1	.333
Rosen, 3b	3	12	0	3	0	0	0	0	.250
Smith, lf	4	14	2	3	0	0	1	2	.214
Majeski, ph-3b	4	6	1	1	0	0	1	3	.167

1955 WORLD SERIES

Player-Position	G.	AB.	R.	H.	2B.	3B.	HR.	RBI.	BA.
Hegan, c	4	13	1	2	1	0	0	0	.154
Westlake, rf	2	7	0	1	0	0	0	0	.143
Avila, 2b	4	15	0	2	0	0	0	0	.133
Doby, cf	4	16	0	2	0	0	0	0	.125
Philley, rf-ph	4	8	0	1	0	0	0	0	.125
Naragon, c	1	0	0	0	0	0	0	0	.000
Grasso, c	1	0	0	0	0	0	0	0	.000
Dente, ss	3	3	1	0	0	0	0	0	.000
Strickland, ss	3	9	0	0	0	0	0	0	.000
Pope, ph-rf	3	3	0	0	0	0	0	0	.000
Mossi, p	3	0	0	0	0	0	0	0	.000
Garcia, p	2	0	0	0	0	0	0	0	.000
Houtteman, p	1	0	0	0	0	0	0	0	.000
Narleski, p	2	0	0	0	0	0	0	0	.000
Newhouser, p	1	0	0	0	0	0	0	0	.000
Lemon, p-ph	3	6	0	0	0	0	0	0	.000
Totals	4	137	9	26	5	1	3	9	.190

COMPOSITE PITCHING AVERAGES

New York Giants

Pitcher	G.	IP.	H.	R.	E.	SO.	BB.	W.	L.	ERA.
Grissom	1	2⅔	1	0	0	2	3	1	0	0.00
Wilhelm	2	2⅓	1	0	0	3	0	0	0	0.00
Antonelli	2	10⅔	8	1	1	12	7	1	0	0.84
Liddle	2	7	5	4	1	2	1	1	0	1.29
Gomez	1	7⅓	4	2	2	2	3	1	0	2.35
Maglie	1	7	7	2	2	2	2	0	0	2.57
Totals	4	37	26	9	6	23	16	4	0	1.46

Cleveland Indians

Pitcher	G.	IP.	H.	R.	E.	SO.	BB.	W.	L.	ERA.
Mossi	3	4	3	0	0	1	0	0	0	0.00
Narleski	2	4	1	1	1	2	1	0	0	2.25
Wynn	1	7	4	3	3	5	2	0	1	3.86
Houtteman	1	2	2	1	1	1	1	0	0	4.50
Garcia	2	5	6	4	3	4	4	0	1	5.40
Lemon	2	13⅓	16	11	10	11	8	0	2	6.75
Newhouser	1	0	1	1	1	0	1	0	0	......
Totals	4	35⅓	33	21	19	24	17	0	4	4.84

SERIES OF 1955

	W.	L.	Pct.
Brooklyn N. L.	4	3	.571
New York A. L.	3	4	.429

The Brooklyn Dodgers, always a bridesmaid but never a bride in seven previous World Series appearances, reached the altar of success for the first time when Manager Walt Alston's National League champions defeated the New York Yankees of Casey Stengel and set a new record as the first club to battle from behind after losing the first two games in a seven-game Series.

The dramatic comeback of the Flatbush Flock reached its climax in the final contest when Johnny Podres, 23-year-old southpaw, baffled the Bronx Bombers and posted his second victory of the Classic, 2 to 0. A fortuitous switch in the Brooklyn lineup, sending Sandy Amoros into left field, proved the decisive move. The fleet-footed Cuban made a one-handed catch of a drive by Yogi Berra and started a game-saving double play in the sixth inning.

The Brooks may have had it too easy during the regular campaign. They romped to the flag by a 13½-game margin over Milwaukee.

The Yankees, meanwhile, regained the A.L. championship from the Cleveland Indians by three lengths. The title was the sixth for Stengel in his seven seasons at the helm. The defeat in the Series was the first for Ol' Casey, but injuries played an important part in the outcome. Mickey Mantle, crippled with a bad leg, appeared in only three games, one of them as a pinch-hitter, and Hank Bauer saw limited action because of a pulled muscle.

Coming from their pennant picnic, the Dodgers faltered under the pressure of the Series and lost the opening game in Yankee Stadium, 6 to 5. Big Don Newcombe, 20-game winner for the Brooks, was kayoed in the sixth inning and Manager Alston, exhibiting a lack of confidence, failed to use him during the rest of the Classic.

First baseman Joe Collins, only a .234 hitter during the season but a typical Yankee "money" player, slammed two homers as the hero of the victory. Collins delivered a solo swat in the fourth inning and hammered another drive with Berra on base in the sixth. Elston Howard, also homered, connecting with Collins on base in the second inning.

Carl Furillo and Duke Snider rapped boundary belts for the Brooks. The cannonading set a pattern for the Series, which produced a seven-game homer record for both clubs—17.

Tommy Byrne, the reclaimed southpaw who returned from the minors to win 16 games for the Yankees, provided the dramatics in the second contest with a five-hit performance for a 4 to 2 victory. The lefthander, noted for his potent bat at the plate, also supplied a sharp single to cap the Bombers' four-run outburst against Billy Loes in the fourth inning.

Moving to Ebbets Field for the third game, the Dodgers snapped back with an 8 to 3 victory behind Podres, who posted his twenty-third birthday. The lefthander, only a mediocre moundsman during the season with a 9-10 record, doled out seven hits, including a homer by Mantle, who played despite his limp.

The N.L. champs uncorked their siege guns and pounded out an 8 to 5 victory in the next encounter to knot the Series at two-all. The determined Brooks slammed an assortment of five pitchers for 14 hits, featuring homers by Roy Campanella, Gil Hodges and Snider.

Snider whacked two more homers, increasing his all-time Series total to nine, to lead the Dodgers to a 5 to 3 victory in the fifth game, enabling the Brooks to go ahead for the first time in the Classic. Amoros also hit for the circuit, connecting off Bob Grim after a single by Hodges in the second inning.

Manager Alston gambled with rookie Roger Craig as a starter and he lasted until the seventh inning. After Bob Cerv homered and Howard walked, Clem Labine made his fourth appearance in five games and successfully protected young Craig's decision.

The Yanks, who won the second game by scoring all their runs in one inning, pulled the trick again in the sixth game, piling up five markers in the opening stanza for a 5 to 1 victory to force the Series to a seventh and final contest. Having succeeded with Craig, Alston tried his luck with another young pitcher, Karl Spooner, but the southpaw was kayoed after retiring only one batter. Moose Skowron capped the first-inning outburst with a three-run homer into the right field seats.

Ford won his second game of the Series, stopping the Dodgers on four hits.

In the finale, Podres came through with his brilliant shutout. Although nicked for eight hits, the courageous lefthander was equal to every emergency. Cool and calm, he relied on a high, hard fast ball and a deceptive changeup to humble the Yankees.

Byrne, Bob Grim and Bob Turley pitched for the Yanks and yielded a total of only five hits. However, in the fourth inning, Campanella doubled and scored on a single by Hodges. Reese singled in the sixth and Snider, bunting for a sacrifice, was safe when he brushed the ball out of Skowron's glove while running down the line. Campanella moved the runners along and, after Furillo walked, Hodges tagged reliever Grim for a sacrifice fly.

With Zimmer out of the game, Junior Gilliam shifted from left field to second base and Amoros went to left in the move that paid off handsomely for the Dodgers in the Yankees' half of the inning.

Martin walked to open the threat and Gil McDougald bunted safely. With Berra at bat, Amoros played toward center for the lefthanded slugger and appeared to have little chance to make a catch when Yogi sliced a fly ball just inside the left field foul line. Racing at top speed, Sandy made a glove-handed grab of the ball for the most spectacular catch of the Series. A sharp relay from Amoros to Reese to Hodges doubled McDougald off first. Both McDougald and Martin had sprung into motion with the crack of the bat. Had the ball fallen safely, the Yankees not only would have tied the score, but Berra would have reached second or third, putting the potential winning run on base with none out. The box scores:

Wednesday, Sept. 28—At New York

Brooklyn (N.L.)	AB.	R.	H.	O.	A.	E.
Gilliam, lf	3	0	0	2	0	0
Reese, ss	5	0	1	2	5	0
Snider, cf	5	1	2	1	0	0
Campanella, c	5	0	0	5	1	0
Furillo, rf	4	2	3	1	0	0
Hodges, 1b	4	0	1	12	1	0
J. Robinson, 3b	4	2	1	0	2	0
Zimmer, 2b	2	0	1	1	3	0
Newcombe, p	3	0	0	0	1	0
Bessent, p	0	0	0	0	1	0
bKellert	1	0	1	0	0	0
cHoak	0	0	0	0	0	0
Labine, p	0	0	0	0	0	0
Totals	36	5	10	24	14	0

New York (A.L.)	AB.	R.	H.	O.	A.	E.
Bauer, rf	4	0	2	3	0	0
McDougald, 3b	4	0	1	2	1	1
Noren, cf	4	0	0	4	0	0
Berra, c	3	1	1	5	0	0
Collins, 1b	3	3	2	6	1	0
Howard, lf	3	1	1	1	0	0
Martin, 2b	3	0	2	2	3	0
Rizzuto, ss	2	0	0	3	2	0
aE. Robinson	0	0	0	0	0	0
J. Coleman, ss	1	0	0	0	0	0
Ford, p	2	1	0	1	3	0
Grim, p	0	0	0	0	0	0
Totals	29	6	9	27	10	1

Brooklyn......... 0 2 1   0 0 0   0 2 0—5
New York......... 0 2 1   1 0 2   0 0 *—6

aBatted for Rizzuto in sixth when Martin was out attempting to steal home. bSingled for Bessent in eighth. cRan for Kellert in eighth. Runs batted in—Furillo, Zimmer 2, Howard 2, Snider, Noren, Collins 3. Three-base hits—J. Robinson, Martin. Home runs—Furillo, Howard, Snider, Collins 2. Stolen base—J. Robinson. Sacrifice fly—Zimmer. Double plays—Zimmer and Hodges; Martin, Rizzuto and Collins; Hodges, Reese and Hodges. Left on bases—Brooklyn 9, New York 2. Earned runs—Brooklyn 3, New York 6. Bases on balls—Off Ford 4, off Newcombe 2, off Labine 1. Struck out—By Ford 2, by Newcombe 4, by Grim 2. Pitching records—Off Newcombe 8 hits, 6 runs in 5⅔ innings; off Bessent 0 hits, 0 runs in 1⅓ innings; off Ford 9 hits, 5 runs in 8 innings; off Labine 1 hit, 0 runs in 1 inning, off Grim 1 hit, 0 runs in 1 inning. Winning pitcher—Ford. Losing pitcher—Newcombe. Umpires—Summers (A.L.), Ballanfant (N.L.), Honochick (A.L.), Dascoli (N.L.), Flaherty (A.L.) and Donatelli (N.L.). Time—2:31. Attendance—63,869

Thursday, Sept. 29—At New York

Brooklyn (N.L.)	AB.	R.	H.	O.	A.	E.
Gilliam, lf	4	0	1	0	1	0
Reese, ss	4	1	2	2	3	0
Snider, cf	4	0	1	2	0	0
Campanella, c	3	0	0	11	2	0
Furillo, rf	3	0	0	0	0	0
Hodges, 1b	3	0	0	6	1	0
J. Robinson, 3b	2	1	0	1	1	0
Zimmer, 2b	3	0	1	2	2	2
Loes, p	1	0	0	0	0	0
Bessent, p	0	0	0	0	0	0
cKellert	1	0	0	0	0	0
Spooner, p	0	0	0	0	1	0
dHoak	0	0	0	0	0	0
Labine, p	0	0	0	0	0	0
Totals	28	2	5	24	11	2

New York (A.L.)	AB.	R.	H.	O.	A.	E.
Bauer, rf	1	0	1	3	0	0
Cerv, cf	3	0	0	0	0	0
McDougald, 3b	4	0	1	1	0	0
Noren, cf-lf	3	0	0	4	0	0
Berra, c	3	1	2	6	1	0
Collins, 1b	3	1	0	5	0	0
Howard, lf-rf	4	1	1	2	1	0
Martin, 2b	3	1	1	2	3	0
Rizzuto, ss	1	0	1	2	1	0
aE. Robinson	0	0	0	0	0	0

	AB.	R.	H.	O.	A.	E.
bJ. Coleman, ss	1	0	0	2	2	0
Byrne, p	3	0	1	0	0	0
Totals	29	4	8	27	8	0

Brooklyn.............. 0 0 0   1 1 0   0 0 0—2
New York.............. 0 0 0   4 0 0   0 0 *—4

aHit by pitch for Rizzuto in fourth. bRan for E. Robinson in fourth. cHit into double play for Bessent in fifth. dWalked for Spooner in eighth. Runs batted in—Snider, Howard, Martin, Byrne 2, Gilliam. Two-base hit—Reese. Double plays—Campanella and Zimmer; Zimmer, Reese and Hodges; Hodges and Reese; J. Coleman, Martin and Collins; Berra and Martin; Martin, J. Coleman and Collins. Left on bases—Brooklyn 4, New York 5. Earned runs—New York 4, Brooklyn 2. Bases on balls—Off Byrne 5, off Loes, 1, off Spooner 1. Struck out—By Byrne 6, by Loes 5, by Spooner 5, by Labine 1. Pitching records—Off Loes 7 hits, 4 runs in 3⅔ innings; off Bessent 0 hits, 0 runs in ⅓ inning; off Spooner 1 hit, 0 runs in 3 innings; off Labine 0 hits, 0 runs in 1 inning. Hit by pitcher—By Loes (Berra, E. Robinson). Winning pitcher—Byrne. Losing pitcher—Loes. Umpires—Ballanfant (N.L.), Honochick (A.L.), Dascoli (N.L.), Summers (A.L.), Flaherty (A.L.) and Donatelli (N.L.). Time—2:28. Attendance—64,707.

Friday, September 30—At Brooklyn

New York (A.L.)	AB.	R.	H.	O.	A.	E.
Cerv, lf-cf	4	0	0	3	0	0
McDougald, 3b	4	0	1	0	3	0
Berra, c	4	0	1	4	0	0
Mantle, cf-rf	4	1	1	2	0	0
Skowron, 1b	4	1	2	5	2	0
Howard, rf-lf	4	0	0	5	0	0
Martin, 2b	4	0	0	3	0	0
Rizzuto, ss	2	1	1	2	1	0
Turley, p	1	0	0	0	0	0
Morgan, p	0	0	0	0	0	0
aBauer	1	0	0	0	0	0
Kucks, p	0	0	0	0	0	0
bCarey	1	0	1	0	0	0
Sturdivant, p	0	0	0	0	1	0
Totals	33	3	7	24	7	0

Brooklyn (N.L.)	AB.	R.	H.	O.	A.	E.
Gilliam, 2b	3	1	1	2	3	0
Reese, ss	3	1	1	1	2	0
Snider, cf	4	1	1	1	0	0
Campanella, c	5	1	3	6	0	1
Furillo, rf	5	0	1	1	0	0
Hodges, 1b	5	0	0	14	0	0
Robinson, 3b	5	2	2	0	7	0
Amoros, lf	1	1	1	2	1	0
Podres, p	3	1	1	0	1	0
Totals	34	8	11	27	14	1

New York.............. 0 2 0   0 0 0   1 0 0—3
Brooklyn.............. 2 2 0   2 0 0   2 0 *—8

aFlied out for Morgan in fifth. bTripled for Kucks in seventh. Runs batted in—Campanella 3, Mantle, Gilliam, Reese 2, Furillo, Carey, Amoros. Two-base hits—Skowron, Furillo, Robinson, Campanella. Three-base hit—Carey. Home runs—Campanella, Mantle. Sacrifice hit—Podres. Double play—Reese, Gilliam and Hodges. Left on bases—Brooklyn 11, New York 5. Earned runs—Brooklyn 8, New York 2. Bases on balls—Off Podres 2, off Turley 2, off Morgan 3, off Kucks 1, off Sturdivant 1. Struck out—By Podres 6, by Turley 1, by Morgan 1. Pitching records—Off Turley 3 hits, 4 runs in 1⅓ innings; off Morgan 3 hits, 2 runs in 2⅔ innings; off Kucks 1 hit, 0 runs in 2 innings; off Sturdivant 4 hits, 2 runs in 2 innings. Hit by pitcher—By Turley (Amoros). Winning pitcher—Podres. Losing pitcher—Turley. Umpires—Honochick (A.L.), Dascoli (N.L.), Summers (A.L.), Ballanfant (N.L.), Donatelli (N.L.) and Flaherty (A.L.). Time—2:20. Attendance—34,209.

Saturday, October 1—At Brooklyn

New York (A.L.)	AB.	R.	H.	O.	A.	E.
Noren, cf	5	0	1	3	0	0
McDougald, 3b	5	1	1	1	1	0
Mantle, rf	5	0	1	2	0	0
Berra, c	3	0	1	4	1	0
Collins, 1b	2	2	0	11	1	0
Howard, lf	3	1	1	0	0	0
Martin, 2b	4	1	2	3	3	0
Rizzuto, ss	3	0	1	2	2	0
Larsen, p	2	0	0	0	1	0
Kucks, p	0	0	0	0	1	0
aE. Robinson	1	0	1	0	0	0
bCarroll	0	0	0	0	0	0
R. Coleman, p	0	0	0	0	0	0
Morgan, p	0	0	0	0	0	0
cSkowron	1	0	0	0	0	0
Sturdivant, p	0	0	0	0	0	0
Totals	34	5	9	24	10	0

Brooklyn (N.L.)	AB.	R.	H.	O.	A.	E.
Gilliam, 2b	4	1	2	1	4	0
Reese, ss	4	1	2	1	2	0
Snider, cf	4	1	1	6	0	0
Campanella, c	5	2	3	4	0	0
Furillo, rf	5	1	2	1	0	0
Hodges, 1b	4	1	3	11	0	0
J. Robinson, 3b	4	0	0	1	2	0
Amoros, lf	3	1	1	2	0	0
Erskine, p	1	0	0	0	1	0
Bessent, p	1	0	0	0	1	0
Labine, p	2	0	0	0	2	0
Totals	37	8	14	27	12	0

New York.............. 1 1 0   1 0 2   0 0 0—5
Brooklyn.............. 0 0 1   3 3 0   1 0 *—8

aSingled for Kucks in sixth. bRan for E. Robinson in sixth. cFlied out for Morgan in eighth. Runs batted in—McDougald, Gilliam, Martin 2, Campanella, Hodges 3, Snider 3, E. Robinson. Two-base hits—Gilliam, Campanella, Martin. Home runs—McDougald, Campanella, Hodges, Snider. Stolen bases—Rizzuto, Collins, Gilliam. Sacrifice hits—Howard, Reese. Double play—J. Robinson, Gilliam and Hodges. Left on bases—Brooklyn 9, New York 7. Earned runs—Brooklyn 8, New York 5. Bases on balls—Off Erskine 2, off Bessent 1, off Labine 1, off Larsen 2, off Sturdivant 1. Struck out—By Erskine 3, by Larsen 2, by Kucks 1, by R. Coleman 1. Pitching records—Off Erskine 3 hits, 3 runs in 3 innings (pitched to two batters in fourth); off Bessent 3 hits, 0 runs in 1⅔ innings; off Larsen 5 hits, 5 runs in 4 innings (pitched to one batter in fifth); off Kucks 3 hits, 2 runs in 1 inning; off R. Coleman 5 hits, 1 run in 1 inning (pitched to three batters in seventh); off Morgan 0 hits, 0 runs in 1 inning; off Sturdivant 1 hit, 0 runs in 1 inning; off Labine 3 hits, 2 runs in 4⅓ innings. Winning pitcher—Labine. Losing pitcher—Larsen. Umpires—Dascoli (N.L.), Summers (A.L.), Ballanfant (N.L.), Honochick (A.L.), Donatelli (N.L.) and Flaherty (A.L.). Time—2:57. Attendance—36,242.

Sunday, October 2—At Brooklyn

New York (A.L.)	AB.	R.	H.	O.	A.	E.
Howard, lf	4	0	1	0	0	0
Noren, cf	4	0	0	2	0	0
McDougald, 3b	3	0	0	1	2	0

1955 WORLD SERIES

	AB.	R.	H.	O.	A.	E.
Berra, c	4	2	2	9	1	0
Collins, rf-1b	3	0	0	0	0	0
E. Robinson, 1b	2	0	1	6	0	0
cCarroll	0	0	0	0	0	0
Bauer, rf	0	0	0	0	0	0
Martin, 2b	4	0	1	4	3	0
Rizzuto, ss	1	0	0	2	0	0
aSkowron	1	0	0	0	0	0
J. Coleman, ss	1	0	0	0	1	0
dCarey	1	0	0	0	0	0
Grim, p	2	0	0	0	1	0
bCerv	1	1	1	0	0	0
Turley, p	0	0	0	0	1	0
eByrne	1	0	0	0	0	0
Totals	32	3	6	24	9	0
Brooklyn (N.L.)	AB.	R.	H.	O.	A.	E.
Gilliam, 2b	3	0	1	1	5	0
Reese, ss	3	0	0	4	3	1
Snider, cf	4	2	3	0	0	0
Campanella, c	3	0	0	6	0	0
Furillo, rf	4	1	1	1	0	0
Hodges, 1b	3	1	2	14	1	0
J. Robinson, 3b	3	0	1	0	3	1
Amoros, lf	4	1	1	1	0	0
Craig, p	0	0	0	0	1	0
Labine, p	2	0	0	0	1	0
Totals	29	5	9	27	14	2

New York ...... 0 0 0 1 0 0 1 1 0—3
Brooklyn ...... 0 2 1 0 1 0 0 1 *—5

aFouled out for Rizzuto in fourth. bHomered for Grim in seventh. cRan for E. Robinson in eighth. dGrounded out for J. Coleman in ninth. eGrounded out for Turley in ninth. Runs batted in—Amoros 2, Snider 2, Martin, Cerv, Berra, J. Robinson. Two-base hit—Snider. Home runs—Amoros, Snider 2, Cerv, Berra. Sacrifice hits—Craig, Hodges. Double plays—Gilliam, Reese and Hodges; Martin and E. Robinson; J. Coleman, Martin and E. Robinson; Hodges, Reese and Hodges; J. Robinson, Gilliam and Hodges. Left on bases—New York 7, Brooklyn 7. Earned runs—New York 5, Brooklyn 1. Bases on balls—Off Craig 5, off Grim 4, off Turley 1. Struck out—By Craig 4, by Labine 1, by Grim 5, by Turley 5. Pitching records—Off Craig 4 hits, 2 runs in 6 innings (pitched to two batters in seventh), off Grim 6 hits, 4 runs in 6 innings, off Turley 3 hits, 1 run in 2 innings, off Labine 2 hits, 1 run in 3 innings. Winning pitcher—Craig. Losing pitcher—Grim. Umpires—Summers (A.L.), Ballanfant (N.L.), Honochick (A.L.), Dascoli (N.L.), Donatelli (N.L.) and Flaherty (A.L.). Time—2:40. Attendance—36,796.

Monday, October 3—At New York

Brooklyn (N.L.)	AB.	R.	H.	O.	A.	E.
Gilliam, 2b-lf	3	0	1	0	0	0
Reese, ss	4	1	1	3	2	0
Snider, cf	1	0	0	1	0	0
aZimmer, 2b	2	0	0	1	1	0
Campanella, c	3	0	0	5	0	0
Furillo, rf	3	0	1	1	0	0
Hodges, 1b	3	0	0	7	1	0
J. Robinson, 3b	4	0	1	2	3	1
Amoros, lf-cf	4	0	1	2	0	0
Spooner, p	0	0	0	0	0	0
Meyer, p	2	0	0	0	1	0
cKellert	1	0	0	0	0	0
Roebuck, p	0	0	0	2	0	0
Totals	30	1	4	24	8	1
New York (A.L.)	AB.	R.	H.	O.	A.	E.
Rizzuto, ss	3	1	0	1	5	0
Martin, 2b	4	0	1	4	2	0
McDougald, 3b	3	1	0	0	5	0
Berra, c	3	1	2	8	0	0
Bauer, rf	4	1	3	0	0	0
Skowron, 1b	2	1	1	6	0	0
bCollins, 1b	1	0	0	5	1	0
Cerv, cf	4	0	1	2	0	0
Howard, lf	4	0	0	1	0	0
Noren, lf	0	0	0	0	0	0
Ford, p	4	0	0	0	1	0
Totals	32	5	8	27	14	0

Brooklyn ...... 0 0 0 1 0 0 0 0 0—1
New York ...... 5 0 0 0 0 0 0 0 *—5

aStruck out for Snider in fourth. bWalked for Skowron in fifth. cPopped out for Meyer in seventh. Runs batted in—Berra, Bauer, Skowron 3, Furillo. Home run—Skowron. Stolen base—Rizzuto. Double plays—McDougald, Martin and Skowron; J. Robinson and Hodges. Left on bases—Brooklyn 7, New York 7. Bases on balls—Off Ford 4, off Spooner 2, off Meyer 2. Struck out—By Ford 8, by Spooner 1, by Meyer 4. Pitching records—Off Spooner 3 hits, 5 runs in ⅓ inning; off Meyer 4 hits, 0 runs in 5⅔ innings, off Roebuck 1 hit, 0 runs in 2 innings. Earned runs—Brooklyn 1, New York 5. Hit by pitcher—By Ford (Furillo). Wild pitch—Ford. Winning pitcher—Ford. Losing pitcher—Spooner. Umpires—Ballanfant (N.L.), Honochick (A.L.), Dascoli (N.L.), Summers (A.L.), Flaherty (A.L.) and Donatelli (N.L.). Time—2:34. Attendance—64,022.

Tuesday, October 4—At New York

Brooklyn (N.L.)	AB.	R.	H.	O.	A.	E.
Gilliam, lf-2b	4	0	1	2	0	0
Reese, ss	4	1	1	2	6	0
Snider, cf	3	0	0	2	0	0
Campanella, c	3	1	1	5	0	0
Furillo, rf	3	0	0	3	0	0
Hodges, 1b	2	0	1	10	0	0
Hoak, 3b	3	0	1	1	1	0
Zimmer, 2b	2	0	0	0	2	0
aShuba	1	0	0	0	0	0
Amoros, lf	0	0	0	2	1	0
Podres, p	4	0	0	0	1	0
Totals	29	2	5	27	11	0
New York (A.L.)	AB.	R.	H.	O.	A.	E.
Rizzuto, ss	3	0	1	1	3	0
Martin, 2b	3	0	1	1	6	0
McDougald, 3b	4	0	3	1	1	0
Berra, c	4	0	1	4	1	0
Bauer, rf	4	0	0	1	0	0
Skowron, 1b	4	0	1	11	1	1
Cerv, cf	4	0	0	5	0	0
Howard, lf	4	0	1	2	0	0
Byrne, p	2	0	0	0	2	0
Grim, p	0	0	0	1	0	0
bMantle	1	0	0	0	0	0
Turley, p	0	0	0	0	0	0
Totals	33	0	8	27	14	1

Brooklyn ...... 0 0 0 1 0 1 0 0 0—2
New York ...... 0 0 0 0 0 0 0 0 0—0

aGrounded out for Zimmer in sixth. bPopped out for Grim in seventh. Runs batted in—Hodges 2. Two-base hits—Skowron, Campanella, Berra. Sacrifice hits—Snider, Campanella. Sacrifice fly—Hodges. Double play—Amoros, Reese and Hodges. Left on bases—Brooklyn 8, New York 8. Earned runs—Brooklyn 1, New York 0. Bases on balls—Off Byrne 3, off Grim 1, off Turley 1, off Podres 2. Struck out—By Byrne 2, by Grim 1, by Turley 1, by Podres 4. Pitching records—Off Byrne 3 hits, 2 runs in 5⅓ innings; off Grim 1 hit, 0 runs in 1⅔ innings; off Turley 1 hit, 0 runs in 2 innings. Wild pitch—Grim. Winning pitcher—Podres. Losing pitcher—Byrne. Umpires—Honochick (A.L.), Dascoli (N.L.), Summers (A.L.), Ballanfant (N.L.), Flaherty (A.L.) and Donatelli (N.L.). Time—2:44. Attendance—62,465.

Pitcher	G.	IP.	H.	R.	E.	BB.	SO.	W.	L.	ERA.
R. Coleman	1	1	5	1	1	0	0	0	0	9.00
Larsen	1	4	5	5	5	2	2	0	1	11.25
Totals	7	60	58	31	28	38	33	3	4	4.20

SERIES OF 1956

	W.	L.	Pct.
New York A. L.	4	3	.571
Brooklyn N. L.	3	4	.429

COMPOSITE BATTING AVERAGES
Brooklyn Dodgers

Player-Position	G.	AB.	R.	H.	2B.	3B.	HR.	RBI.	BA.
Amoros, lf-cf	5	12	3	4	0	0	1	3	.333
Kellert, ph	3	3	0	1	0	0	0	0	.333
Hoak, pr-ph-3b	3	3	0	1	0	0	0	0	.333
Snider, cf	7	25	5	8	1	0	4	7	.320
Reese, ss	7	27	5	8	1	0	0	2	.296
Furillo, rf	7	27	4	8	1	0	1	3	.296
Gilliam, lf-2b	7	24	2	7	1	0	0	3	.292
Hodges, 1b	7	24	2	7	0	0	1	5	.292
Campanella, c	7	27	4	7	3	0	2	4	.259
Zimmer, 2b-ph	4	9	0	2	0	0	0	2	.222
J. Robinson, 3b	6	22	5	4	1	1	0	1	.182
Podres, p	2	7	1	1	0	0	0	0	.143
Newcombe, p	1	3	0	0	0	0	0	0	.000
Bessent, p	3	1	0	0	0	0	0	0	.000
Labine, p	4	4	0	0	0	0	0	0	.000
Loes, p	1	1	0	0	0	0	0	0	.000
Spooner, p	2	0	0	0	0	0	0	0	.000
Erskine, p	1	1	0	0	0	0	0	0	.000
Craig, p	1	0	0	0	0	0	0	0	.000
Meyer, p	1	2	0	0	0	0	0	0	.000
Roebuck, p	1	0	0	0	0	0	0	0	.000
Shuba, ph	1	1	0	0	0	0	0	0	.000
Totals	7	223	31	58	8	1	9	30	.260

New York Yankees

Player-Position	G.	AB.	R.	H.	2B.	3B.	HR.	RBI.	BA.
E. Rob'son, ph-1b	4	3	0	2	0	0	0	1	.667
Carey, ph	2	2	0	1	0	1	0	1	.500
Bauer, rf-ph	6	14	1	6	0	0	0	1	.429
Berra, c	7	24	5	10	1	0	1	2	.417
Skowron, 1b-ph	5	12	2	4	2	0	1	3	.333
Martin, 2b	7	25	2	8	1	0	0	4	.320
Rizzuto, ss	7	15	2	4	0	0	0	1	.267
McDougald, 3b	7	27	2	7	0	0	1	1	.259
Mantle, cf-rf-ph	3	10	1	2	0	0	1	1	.200
Howard, lf-rf	7	26	3	5	0	0	1	3	.192
Collins, 1b-rf-ph	5	12	6	2	0	0	2	3	.167
Byrne, p-ph	3	6	0	1	0	0	0	2	.167
Cerv, cf-lf-ph	5	16	1	2	0	0	1	1	.125
Noren, cf-lf	5	16	0	1	0	0	0	1	.063
J. Coleman, ss-pr	3	3	0	0	0	0	0	0	.000
Ford, p	2	6	1	0	0	0	0	0	.000
Grim, p	3	2	0	0	0	0	0	0	.000
Turley, p	3	1	0	0	0	0	0	0	.000
Morgan, p	2	0	0	0	0	0	0	0	.000
Kucks, p	2	0	0	0	0	0	0	0	.000
Sturdivant, p	2	0	0	0	0	0	0	0	.000
Larsen, p	1	2	0	0	0	0	0	0	.000
R. Coleman, p	1	0	0	0	0	0	0	0	.000
Carroll, pr	2	0	0	0	0	0	0	0	.000
Totals	7	222	26	55	4	2	8	25	.248

COMPOSITE PITCHING AVERAGES
Brooklyn Dodgers

Pitcher	G.	IP.	H.	R.	E.	SO.	BB.	W.	L.	ERA.
Meyer	1	5⅔	4	0	0	4	2	0	0	0.00
Bessent	3	3⅓	3	0	0	1	1	0	0	0.00
Roebuck	1	2	1	0	0	0	0	0	0	0.00
Podres	2	18	15	3	2	10	4	2	0	1.00
Labine	4	9⅓	6	3	3	2	2	1	0	2.89
Craig	1	6	4	2	2	4	5	1	0	3.00
Erskine	1	3	3	3	3	3	2	0	0	9.00
Newcombe	1	5⅔	8	6	6	4	2	0	1	9.53
Loes	1	3⅔	7	4	4	5	1	0	1	9.82
Spooner	2	3⅓	4	5	5	6	3	0	1	13.50
Totals	7	60	55	26	25	39	22	4	3	3.75

New York Yankees

Pitcher	G.	IP.	H.	R.	E.	SO.	BB.	W.	L.	ERA.
Byrne	2	14⅓	8	4	3	8	8	1	1	1.88
Ford	2	17	13	6	4	10	8	2	0	2.12
Grim	3	8⅔	8	4	4	8	5	0	1	4.15
Morgan	2	3⅔	3	2	2	1	3	0	0	4.91
Kucks	2	3	4	2	2	1	1	0	0	6.00
Sturdivant	2	3	5	2	2	0	2	0	0	6.00
Turley	3	5⅓	7	5	5	7	4	0	1	8.44

The first perfect game, as well as the first no-hit, no-run performance, in World Series history—a feat that wrote the name of Don Larsen indelibly in the all-time annals of Organized Ball—featured the remarkable comeback of the New York Yankees, who won their seventeenth world championship and their sixth in seven Classic appearances under Manager Casey Stengel by defeating the Brooklyn Dodgers in a dramatic seven-game battle.

There were other heroes in the Series—and at least one goat. Yogi Berra, the Yankees' great catcher, and his teammate Bill Skowron, each homered with the bases loaded, marking the first time that two grand-slams had been hit in one Series. Enos Slaughter, 40-year-old outfielder, won one game for the Bombers with a three-run homer, and five Yankee pitchers —Whitey Ford, Tom Sturdivant, Larsen, Bob Turley and Johnny Kucks—reeled off consecutive complete games.

Sal Maglie and Clem Labine hurled brilliantly for the Dodgers, but the National League champions had the goat in big Don Newcombe, their 27-game winner during the regular season. The powerful right-hander failed ignobly. Kayoed in the second game, although the Dodgers came back to win it, Newk started the final contest and, with the chips down, once more was pounded from the mound.

The Yankees won the American League pennant easily, moving into first place to stay on May 16 and finishing the year with a margin of nine games over the Cleveland Indians. The Dodgers, wrapped in a three-club tussle with the Milwaukee Braves and Cincinnati Reds, did not emerge with the flag until the last day of the season.

In 1955, the Dodgers had romped to the pennant and then proceeded to lose the first two games of the Series before coming back to win the world championship. This year, the situation and results were the exact reverse. The Yankees had trouble getting back in gear, after their breeze during the regular campaign, and the Dodgers swept to victory in the first two games.

With President Eisenhower in the crowd at the Ebbets Field inaugural, the Brooks pounded out a 6 to 3 triumph behind the crafty hurling of Maglie, the 39-year-old righthander, who won honors as the "Comeback Player of the Year" in the National League. The Barber made a shaky start, giving up two runs in the first inning on a single by Slaughter and a homer by Mickey Mantle, but he yielded only seven more hits the remainder of the way and struck out ten Yankees.

Manager Stengel nominated Ford for the opener, defying Ebbets Field's reputation as a jinx park for lefthanders. The Dodgers made the hex stand up. In the second inning, Jackie Robinson homered, Gil Hodges singled and Carl Furillo doubled to tie the score and in the third, singles by Pee Wee Reese and Duke Snider and a homer by Hodges clinched the verdict for the Brooks.

The second game produced one of the most amazing scoring comebacks in Series history when the Dodgers fell behind, 6 to 0, after one and one-half innings, but smashed ahead to gain a 13 to 8 victory. Newcombe gave up one run in the first inning and then was routed in the second during a five-run outburst that included Berra's grand-slam homer.

While the crowd of 36,217 watched with incredulity, the Dodgers rallied with six runs off Larsen, Kucks and Tommy Byrne in their half of the second. Oddly enough, all six runs were unearned as the result of an error by first baseman Joe Collins, the first bobble in Series play for the Yankee veteran.

While Don Bessent, in a seven-inning relief performance, held the Yankees to six hits and two runs, the Dodgers proceeded to hammer Sturdivant, Tom Morgan and Mickey McDermott for their remaining tallies. Stengel used seven pitchers in the three-hour, 26-minute game, longest by time in Series history.

The foldup might have shattered the morale of many clubs, but not the Bombers. Moving to Yankee Stadium, the American League champions shook off the two defeats and won three straight games in their home park.

Ford, defeated in the opener, returned to the mound and beat the Dodgers, 5 to 3, in the third game when Slaughter came through with his homer off Roger Craig in the sixth inning after singles by Hank Bauer and Berra. Slaughter's homer wiped out a 2 to 1 Dodger lead.

Sturdivant followed with a 6 to 2 victory on a six-hit effort. After taking an early 3 to 1 lead against Carl Erskine, the Yankees clinched their verdict when Mantle hit for the circuit off Ed Roebuck in the sixth inning and Bauer delivered a round-tripper with a man on base off Don Drysdale in the seventh. The homer was the first for Bauer in 36 Series games in which he had appeared.

Larsen then turned in his perfect performance in the fifth game, cutting down 27 consecutive batters to win, 2 to 0, in a game that mounted in tension as 64,519 watched from the stands and millions more heard the play-by-play over radio or saw the masterpiece unfold over television. The flawless gem was the first in the major leagues since April 30, 1922, and the first no-hitter achieved in 307 Series games since the start of the Classic in 1903.

The righthander pitched without a windup, using a style he adopted late in the season. He threw three balls to only one batter —Reese in the first inning—and fanned seven, including pinch-hitter Dale Mitchell, called out on strikes to end the game. Mantle came up with one of the outstanding defensive plays, racing to deep left-center for a back-handed grab of a line drive by Hodges in the fifth inning.

Maglie, on the mound for the Dodgers, was superb in defeat. The veteran yielded just five hits, but one was a homer by Mantle in the fourth. The other Yankee run scored in the sixth on a single by Andy Carey, a sacrifice by Larsen and a single by Bauer.

With their backs to the wall the Dodgers called on Labine in the sixth game, as the Series returned to Ebbets Field, and the righthander, making his first Classic start, after eight previous relief appearances, came through with a 1 to 0 victory over Turley in ten innings.

Turley, who copied Larsen in discarding the windup, fanned 11 and yielded only three hits going into the Dodgers' tenth. After Labine flied out to open the frame, Jim Gilliam walked and Reese sacrificed. The Yanks handed an intentional pass to Snider, the eighth walk issued by Turley, to bring up Robinson, who had left five runners stranded in three earlier turns at bat. But this time Jackie lined Turley's second pitch to left field, Slaughter charged in and then, too late, realized his mistake as the ball soared over his head to the wall for a hit, scoring Gilliam with the winning run.

In the final game, the Yankees demonstrated their complete mastery of the Dodgers, smashing four homers behind the three-hit pitching of Kucks to wrap up the title with a 9 to 0 victory. Berra, feasting on Newcombe's offerings, belted two homers off the Dodger ace, each with a man on base. Elston Howard kayoed Newk with another homer in the fourth inning and Skowron delivered the crowning blow with his grand-slam off Craig in the seventh.

The box scores:

Wednesday, October 3—At Brooklyn

New York (A.L.)	AB.	R.	H.	O.	A.	E.
Bauer, rf	5	0	2	3	0	0
Slaughter, lf	5	1	3	3	0	0
Mantle, cf	3	1	1	4	1	0
Berra, c	3	0	0	4	0	0
Skowron, 1b	4	0	0	5	3	1
McDougald, ss	4	0	0	2	6	0
Martin, 2b-3b	3	1	1	2	1	0
Carey, 3b	3	0	1	0	1	0
cCollins	1	0	0	0	0	0
Turley, p	0	0	0	0	0	0

1956 WORLD SERIES

	AB.	R.	H.	O.	A.	E.
Ford, p	1	0	0	1	0	0
aWilson	1	0	0	0	0	0
Kucks, p	0	0	0	0	0	0
bCerv	1	0	1	0	0	0
Morgan, p	0	0	0	0	0	0
dByrne	1	0	0	0	0	0
G. Coleman, 2b	0	0	0	0	0	0
Totals	35	3	9	24	12	1

Brooklyn (N.L.)	AB.	R.	H.	O.	A.	E.
Gilliam, 2b	3	0	0	3	1	0
Reese, ss	4	1	2	1	1	0
Snider, cf	3	1	1	1	0	0
Robinson, 3b	4	1	1	2	2	0
Hodges, 1b	4	2	2	4	0	0
Furillo, rf	4	0	1	2	0	0
Campanella, c	4	1	1	11	1	0
Amoros, lf	3	0	1	3	0	0
Maglie, p	3	0	0	0	0	0
Totals	32	6	9	27	5	0

New York............ 2 0 0 1 0 0 0 0 0—3
Brooklyn............ 0 2 3 1 0 0 0 0 *—6

aStruck out for Ford in fourth. bSingled for Kucks in sixth. cStruck out for Carey in eighth. dFouled out for Morgan in eighth. Runs batted in—Mantle 2, Robinson, Furillo, Hodges 3, Martin, Amoros. Two-base hits—Furillo, Campanella. Home runs—Mantle, Robinson, Hodges, Martin. Stolen base—Gilliam. Double plays—Skowron, McDougald and Martin; Gilliam, Reese and Hodges. Left on bases—New York 9, Brooklyn 4. Earned runs—Brooklyn 6, New York 3. Bases on balls—Off Maglie 4, off Morgan 2. Struck out—By Maglie 10. by Ford 1, by Kucks 1, by Turley 2. Pitching records—Off Ford 6 hits, 5 runs in 3 innings; off Kucks 2 hits, 1 run in 2 innings; off Morgan 1 hit, 0 runs in 2 innings; off Turley 0 runs, 0 hits in 1 inning. Winning pitcher—Maglie. Losing pitcher—Ford. Umpires—Pinelli (N.L.), Soar (A.L.), Boggess (N.L.), Napp (A.L.), Gorman (N.L.) and Runge (A.L.). Time—2:32. Attendance—34,479.

Friday, October 5—At Brooklyn

New York (A.L.)	AB.	R.	H.	O.	A.	E.
McDougald, ss	3	0	1	1	0	0
Slaughter, lf	4	3	2	1	0	0
Mantle, cf	4	1	1	2	0	0
Berra, c	4	1	2	10	0	0
Collins, 1b	4	0	1	3	0	1
Bauer, rf	5	0	1	2	0	1
Martin, 3b-2b	4	1	1	3	2	0
G. Coleman, 2b	2	0	0	2	2	0
dSkowron	1	0	0	0	0	0
Carey, 3b	0	0	0	0	1	0
Larsen, p	1	1	1	0	0	0
Kucks, p	0	0	0	0	0	0
Byrne, p	0	0	0	0	0	0
Sturdivant, p	0	0	0	0	0	0
Morgan, p	1	1	1	0	0	0
Turley, p	0	0	0	0	0	0
bSiebern	1	0	0	0	0	0
McDermott, p	1	0	1	0	0	0
Totals	35	8	12	24	5	2

Brooklyn (N.L.)	AB.	R.	H.	O.	A.	E.
Gilliam, 2b	3	1	1	5	3	0
Reese, ss	6	1	1	2	5	0
Snider, cf	4	3	2	6	0	0
Robinson, 3b	4	2	2	0	2	0
Hodges, 1b	3	2	3	6	0	0
Amoros, lf	4	1	0	0	0	0
cJackson	1	0	0	0	0	0
Cimoli, lf	0	0	0	1	0	0

	AB.	R.	H.	O.	A.	E.
Furillo, rf	4	2	2	2	0	0
Campanella, c	3	1	0	5	0	0
Newcombe, p	0	0	0	0	0	0
Roebuck, p	0	0	0	0	1	0
aMitchell	1	0	0	0	0	0
Bessent, p	2	0	1	0	0	0
Totals	35	13	12	27	11	0

New York............ 1 5 0 1 0 0 0 0 1— 8
Brooklyn............ 0 6 1 2 2 0 0 2 *—13

aFouled out for Roebuck in second. bFlied out for Turley in sixth. cStruck out for Amoros in seventh. dStruck out for G. Coleman in eighth. Runs batted in—Collins 2, Larsen, Berra 4, Campanella, Reese 2, Snider 3, Bessent, Slaughter, Hodges 4, Gilliam 2. Two-base hits—Hodges 2. Home runs—Berra, Snider. Sacrifice hits—G. Coleman, McDougald, Bessent. Sacrifice flies—Campanella, Slaughter. Double plays—Martin and Collins; Reese, Gilliam and Hodges. Left on bases—Brooklyn 11, New York 7. Earned runs—New York 8, Brooklyn 6. Bases on balls—Off Newcombe 2, off Bessent 2, off Larsen 4, off Sturdivant 2, off Morgan 2, off McDermott 3. Struck out—By Bessent 4, by Byrne 1, by Sturdivant 2, by Morgan 3, by Turley 1, by McDermott 3. Pitching records—Off Newcombe 6 hits, 6 runs in 1⅔ innings; off Roebuck 0 hits, 0 runs in ⅓ inning; off Bessent 6 hits, 2 runs in 7 innings; off Larsen 1 hit, 4 runs in 1⅔ innings; off Kucks 1 hit, 1 run in 0 inning (pitched to one batter in second); off Byrne 1 hit, 1 run in ⅓ inning; off Sturdivant 2 hits, 1 run in ⅔ inning; off Morgan 5 hits, 4 runs in 2 innings; off Turley 0 hits, 0 runs in ⅓ inning; off McDermott 2 hits, 2 runs in 3 innings. Wild pitch—Bessent. Winning pitcher—Bessent. Losing pitcher—Morgan. Umpires—Soar (A.L.), Boggess (N.L.), Napp (A.L.), Pinelli (N.L.), Runge (A.L.) and Gorman (N.L.). Time—3:26. Attendance—36,217.

Saturday, October 6—At New York

Brooklyn (N.L.)	AB.	R.	H.	O.	A.	E.
Gilliam, lf	4	0	0	2	0	0
Reese, ss	4	1	2	2	3	0
Snider, cf	3	0	0	4	0	0
Robinson, 3b	3	1	1	0	0	0
Hodges, 1b	3	1	1	5	1	0
Furillo, rf	4	0	2	1	0	0
Campanella, c	3	0	1	7	0	0
Neal, 2b	4	0	0	2	2	1
Craig, p	2	0	1	1	1	0
aJackson	1	0	0	0	0	0
Labine, p	0	0	0	0	0	0
Totals	31	3	8	24	7	1

New York (A.L.)	AB.	R.	H.	O.	A.	E.
Bauer, rf	4	1	2	2	1	0
Collins, 1b	4	1	0	8	0	0
Mantle, cf	4	0	1	2	0	0
Berra, c	4	1	2	8	1	0
Slaughter, lf	3	1	2	1	0	0
Martin, 2b	4	1	1	1	3	0
McDougald, ss	2	0	1	4	2	0
Carey, 3b	3	0	0	1	5	1
Ford, p	3	0	0	0	0	0
Totals	31	5	8	27	12	1

Brooklyn............ 0 1 0 0 0 1 1 0 0—3
New York............ 0 1 0 0 0 3 0 1 *—5

aFlied out for Craig in seventh. Runs batted in—Campanella, Martin, Snider, Slaughter 3, Berra. Two-base hits—Berra, Furillo. Three-base hit—Reese. Home runs—Martin, Slaughter. Sacrifice flies—Campanella, Snider. Double plays—Martin, McDougald and Collins; Craig, Reese and Hodges;

Neal, Reese and Hodges. Left on bases—Brooklyn 5, New York 4. Earned runs—New York 4, Brooklyn 2. Bases on balls—Off Ford 2, off Craig 1, off Labine 1. Struck out—By Ford 7, by Craig 4, by Labine 2. Pitching records—Off Craig 7 hits, 4 runs in 6 innings; off Labine 1 hit, 1 run in 2 innings. Winning pitcher—Ford. Losing pitcher—Craig. Umpires—Boggess (N.L.), Napp (A.L.), Pinelli (N.L.), Soar (A.L.), Gorman (N.L.), Runge (A.L.). Time—2:17. Attendance—73,977.

Sunday, October 7—At New York

Brooklyn (N.L.)	AB.	R.	H.	O.	A.	E.
Gilliam, 2b	4	0	0	1	4	0
Reese, ss	4	0	1	1	2	0
Snider, cf	4	1	1	3	0	0
Robinson, 3b	3	1	1	0	2	0
Hodges, 1b	4	0	1	10	1	0
Amoros, lf	3	0	0	2	0	0
Furillo, rf	3	0	0	0	0	0
Campanella, c	2	0	2	6	0	0
Erskine, p	1	0	0	1	2	0
aWalker	1	0	0	0	0	0
Roebuck, p	0	0	0	0	0	0
bMitchell	1	0	0	0	0	0
Drysdale, p	0	0	0	0	0	0
cJackson	1	0	0	0	0	0
Totals	31	2	6	24	11	0

New York (A.L.)	AB.	R.	H.	O.	A.	E.
Bauer, rf	4	1	1	1	0	0
Collins, 1b	3	1	1	8	2	1
Mantle, cf	3	2	1	4	0	0
Berra, c	4	0	1	8	1	0
Slaughter, lf	3	1	0	1	0	0
Martin, 2b	4	0	1	3	3	0
McDougald, ss	2	0	0	3	3	0
Carey, 3b	3	1	1	0	0	1
Sturdivant, p	3	0	1	2	0	0
Totals	29	6	7	27	9	2

Brooklyn............ 0 0 0 1 0 0 0 0 1—2
New York........... 1 0 0 2 0 1 2 0 *—6

aHit into double play for Erskine in fifth. bFlied out for Roebuck in seventh. cCalled out on strikes for Drysdale in ninth. Runs batted in—Berra, Hodges, Martin, McDougald, Mantle Bauer 2, Campanella. Two-base hits—Collins, Snider, Robinson. Home runs—Mantle, Bauer. Stolen base—Mantle. Sacrifice fly—McDougald. Double plays—Gilliam, Reese and Hodges; Collins (unassisted); Martin, McDougald and Collins. Left on bases—Brooklyn 8, New York 3. Earned runs—New York 6, Brooklyn 2. Bases on balls—Off Sturdivant 6, off Erskine 2, off Drysdale 1. Struck out—By Sturdivant 7, by Erskine 2, by Roebuck 2, by Drysdale 1. Pitching records—Off Erskine 4 hits, 3 runs in 4 innings; off Roebuck 1 hit, 1 run in 2 innings; off Drysdale 2 hits, 2 runs in 2 innings. Winning pitcher—Sturdivant. Losing pitcher—Erskine. Umpires—Napp (A.L.), Pinelli (N.L.), Soar (A.L.), Boggess (N.L.), Runge (A.L.), Gorman (N.L.). Time—2:43. Attendance—69,705.

Monday, October 8—At New York

Brooklyn (N.L.)	AB.	R.	H.	O.	A.	E.
Gilliam, 2b	3	0	0	2	0	0
Reese, ss	3	0	0	4	2	0
Snider, cf	3	0	0	1	0	0
Robinson, 3b	3	0	0	2	4	0
Hodges, 1b	3	0	0	5	1	0
Amoros, lf	3	0	0	3	0	0
Furillo, rf	3	0	0	0	0	0
Campanella, c	3	0	0	7	2	0
Maglie, p	2	0	0	0	1	0
aMitchell	1	0	0	0	0	0
Totals	27	0	0	24	10	0

New York (A.L.)	AB.	R.	H.	O.	A.	E.
Bauer, rf	4	0	1	4	0	0
Collins, 1b	4	0	1	7	0	0
Mantle, cf	3	1	1	4	0	0
Berra, c	3	0	0	7	0	0
Slaughter, lf	2	0	0	1	0	0
Martin, 2b	3	0	1	3	4	0
McDougald, ss	2	0	0	0	2	0
Carey, 3b	3	1	1	1	1	0
Larsen, p	2	0	0	0	1	0
Totals	26	2	5	27	8	0

Brooklyn............ 0 0 0 0 0 0 0 0 0—0
New York........... 0 0 0 1 0 1 0 0 *—2

aCalled out on strikes for Maglie in ninth. Runs batted in—Mantle, Bauer. Home run—Mantle. Sacrifice hit—Larsen. Double plays—Reese and Hodges; Hodges, Campanella, Robinson, Campanella and Robinson. Left on bases—Brooklyn 0, New York 3. Earned runs—New York 2, Brooklyn 0. Bases on balls—Off Maglie 2. Struck out—By Larsen 7, by Maglie 5. Umpires—Pinelli (N.L.), Soar (A.L.), Boggess (N.L.), Napp (A.L.), Gorman (N.L.), Runge (A.L.). Time—2:06. Attendance—64,519.

Tuesday, October 9—At Brooklyn

New York (A.L.)	AB.	R.	H.	O.	A.	E.
Bauer, rf	5	0	2	2	0	0
Collins, 1b	5	0	2	4	1	0
Mantle, cf	3	0	0	2	0	0
Berra, c	4	0	2	12	0	0
Slaughter, lf	3	0	0	1	1	0
Martin, 2b	4	0	1	3	1	0
McDougald, ss	4	0	0	3	0	0
Carey, 3b	4	0	0	2	0	0
Turley, p	4	0	0	0	2	0
Totals	36	0	7	a29	5	0

Brooklyn (N.L.)	AB.	R.	H.	O.	A.	E.
Gilliam, 2b	3	1	1	0	7	0
Reese, ss	4	0	0	2	3	0
Snider, cf	2	0	1	4	0	0
Robinson, 3b	4	0	1	1	1	0
Hodges, 1b	3	0	0	14	0	0
Amoros, lf	3	0	0	2	0	0
Furillo, rf	4	0	0	2	0	0
Campanella, c	4	0	0	5	0	0
Labine, p	4	0	1	0	3	0
Totals	31	1	4	30	14	0

New York........... 0 0 0 0 0 0 0 0 0 0—0
Brooklyn............ 0 0 0 0 0 0 0 0 0 1—1

aTwo out when winning run scored. Run batted in—Robinson. Two-base hits—Berra, Collins, Labine. Sacrifice hit—Reese. Double play—Gilliam, Reese and Hodges. Left on bases—Brooklyn 10, New York 8. Earned runs—Brooklyn 1, New York 0. Bases on balls—Off Labine 2, off Turley 8. Struck out—By Labine 5, by Turley 11. Winning pitcher—Labine. Losing pitcher—Turley. Umpires—Soar (A.L.), Boggess (N.L.), Napp (A.L.), Pinelli (N.L.), Runge (A.L.), Gorman (N.L.). Time—2:37. Attendance—33,224.

Wednesday, October 10—At Brooklyn

New York (A.L.)	AB.	R.	H.	O.	A.	E.
Bauer, rf	5	1	1	0	0	0
Martin, 2b	5	2	2	2	6	0
Mantle, cf	4	1	1	0	0	0
Berra, c	3	3	2	1	1	0
Skowron, 1b	5	1	1	16	1	0
Howard, lf	5	1	2	2	0	0
McDougald, ss	4	0	1	3	3	0
Carey, 3b	3	0	0	2	2	0
Kucks, p	3	0	0	1	2	0
Totals	37	9	10	27	15	0

1957 WORLD SERIES

Brooklyn (N.L.)	AB.	R.	H.	O.	A.	E.
Gilliam, 2b	4	0	0	6	2	0
Reese, ss	2	0	0	2	5	1
Snider, cf	4	0	2	1	0	0
Robinson, 3b	3	0	0	0	1	0
Hodges, 1b	3	0	0	10	2	0
Amoros, lf	3	0	0	0	0	0
Furillo, rf	3	0	1	0	0	0
Campanella, c	3	0	0	8	0	0
Newcombe, p	1	0	0	0	1	0
Bessent, p	0	0	0	0	0	0
aMitchell	1	0	0	0	0	0
Craig, p	0	0	0	0	0	0
Roebuck, p	0	0	0	0	0	0
bWalker	1	0	0	0	0	0
Erskine, p	0	0	0	0	0	0
Totals	28	0	3	27	11	1

New York......... 2 0 2 1 0 0 4 0 0—9
Brooklyn.......... 0 0 0 0 0 0 0 0 0—0

aGrounded out for Bessent in sixth. bGrounded out for Roebuck in eighth. Runs batted in—Berra 4, Howard, Skowron 4. Two-base hits—Mantle, Howard. Home runs—Berra 2, Howard, Skowron. Stolen base—Bauer. Sacrifice hit—Kucks. Double plays—Kucks, Martin and Skowron; McDougal and Skowron. Left on bases—New York 6, Brooklyn 4. Earned runs—New York 9, Brooklyn 0. Bases on balls—Off Newcombe 1, off Bessent 1, off Craig 2, off Kucks 3. Struck out—By Newcombe 4, by Bessent 1, by Roebuck 3, by Kucks 1. Pitching records—Off Newcombe 5 hits, 5 runs in 3 innings (pitched to one batter in fourth); off Bessent 2 hits, 0 runs in 3 innings; off Craig 3 hits, 4 runs in 0 innings (pitched to 5 batters in seventh); off Roebuck 0 hits, 0 runs in 2 innings; off Erskine 0 hits, 0 runs in 1 inning. Wild pitch—Craig. Winning pitcher—Kucks. Losing pitcher—Newcombe. Umpires—Boggess (N.L.), Napp (A.L.), Pinelli (N.L.), Soar (A.L.), Gorman (N.L.), Runge (A.L.). Time—2:19. Attendance—33,782.

COMPOSITE BATTING AVERAGES
New York Yankees

Player-Position	G.	AB.	R.	H.	2B.	3B.	HR.	RBI.	BA.
McDermott, p	1	1	0	1	0	0	0	0	1.000
Cerv, ph	1	1	0	1	0	0	0	0	1.000
Morgan, p	2	1	1	1	0	0	0	0	1.000
Howard, lf	1	5	1	2	1	0	1	1	.400
Berra, c	7	25	5	9	2	0	3	10	.360
Slaughter, lf	6	20	6	7	0	0	1	4	.350
Larsen, p	2	3	1	1	0	0	0	1	.333
Sturdivant, p	2	3	0	1	0	0	0	0	.333
Martin, 2b-3b	7	27	5	8	0	0	2	3	.296
Bauer, rf	7	32	3	9	0	0	1	3	.281
Mantle, cf	7	24	6	6	1	0	3	4	.250
Collins, ph-1b	6	21	2	5	2	0	0	0	.238
Carey, 3b	7	19	2	3	0	0	0	0	.158
McDougald, ss	7	21	0	3	0	0	1	0	.143
Skowron, 1b-ph	3	10	1	1	0	0	1	4	.100
G. Coleman, 2b	2	2	0	0	0	0	0	0	.000
Turley, p	3	4	0	0	0	0	0	0	.000
Ford, p	2	4	0	0	0	0	0	0	.000
Kucks, p	3	3	0	0	0	0	0	0	.000
Byrne, ph-p	2	1	0	0	0	0	0	0	.000
Siebern, ph	1	1	0	0	0	0	0	0	.000
Wilson, ph	1	1	0	0	0	0	0	0	.000
Totals	7	229	33	58	6	0	12	33	.253

Brooklyn Dodgers

Player-Position	G.	AB.	R.	H.	2B.	3B.	HR.	RBI.	BA.
Bessent, p	2	2	0	1	0	0	0	1	.500
Craig, p	2	2	0	1	0	0	0	0	.500
Snider, cf	7	23	5	7	1	0	1	4	.304
Hodges, 1b	7	23	5	7	2	0	1	8	.304
Robinson, 3b	7	24	5	6	1	0	1	2	.250
Labine, p	2	4	0	1	1	0	0	0	.250
Furillo, rf	7	25	2	6	2	0	0	1	.240
Reese, ss	7	27	3	6	0	1	0	2	.222
Campanella, c	7	22	2	4	1	0	0	3	.182
Gilliam, 2b-lf	7	24	2	2	0	0	2	2	.083

Player-Position	G.	AB.	R.	H.	2B.	3B.	HR.	RBI.	BA.
Amoros, lf	6	19	1	1	0	0	0	1	.053
Cimoli, lf	1	0	0	0	0	0	0	0	.000
Maglie, p	2	5	0	0	0	0	0	0	.000
Newcombe, p	2	1	0	0	0	0	0	0	.000
Roebuck, p	3	0	0	0	0	0	0	0	.000
Neal, 2b	1	4	0	0	0	0	0	0	.000
Erskine, p	2	1	0	0	0	0	0	0	.000
Drysdale, p	1	0	0	0	0	0	0	0	.000
Walker, ph	2	2	0	0	0	0	0	0	.000
Mitchell, ph	4	4	0	0	0	0	0	0	.000
Jackson, ph	3	3	0	0	0	0	0	0	.000
Totals	7	215	25	42	8	1	3	24	.195

COMPOSITE PITCHING AVERAGES
New York Yankees

Pitcher	G.	IP.	H.	R.	E.	SO.	BB.	W.	L.	ERA.
Larsen	2	10⅔	1	4	0	7	4	1	0	0.00
Byrne	1	⅓	1	1	0	1	0	0	0	0.00
Turley	3	11	4	1	1	14	8	0	1	0.82
Kucks	3	11	6	2	1	2	3	1	0	0.82
Sturdivant	2	9⅔	8	3	3	9	8	1	0	2.79
McDermott	1	3	2	2	1	3	2	0	0	3.00
Ford	2	12	14	8	7	8	2	1	1	5.25
Morgan	2	4	6	4	4	3	4	0	1	9.00
Totals	7	61⅔	42	25	17	47	32	4	3	2.48

Brooklyn Dodgers

Pitcher	G.	IP.	H.	R.	E.	SO.	BB.	W.	L.	ERA.
Labine	2	12	8	1	0	7	3	1	0	0.00
Bessent	2	10	8	2	2	5	3	1	0	1.80
Roebuck	3	4⅓	1	1	1	5	0	0	0	2.08
Maglie	2	17	16	5	5	15	6	1	1	2.65
Erskine	2	5	4	3	3	2	2	0	1	5.40
Drysdale	1	2	2	2	2	1	1	0	0	9.00
Craig	2	6	10	8	8	4	3	0	1	12.00
Newcombe	2	4⅔	11	11	11	4	3	0	1	21.21
Totals	7	61	58	33	32	43	21	3	4	4.72

SERIES OF 1957

	W.	L.	Pct.
Milwaukee N. L.	4	3	.571
New York A. L.	3	4	.429

The sensational pitching of Lew Burdette, who posted three victories and hurled 24 consecutive scoreless innings to join the select ranks of World Series work horses, enabled the Braves to bring Milwaukee its first championship in a brilliantly contested Classic with the New York Yankees. Although batting only .209, lowest average for a winning team in seven-game Series history, the Braves made efficient use of their hits and were superb on defense to upset the Yanks, four games to three.

Veteran Warren Spahn won the Braves' other game, but it took a courageous comeback by his teammates to gain the decision. Burdette, on the other hand was superlative. In this era of power, the righthander, once a Yankee, racked up 4 to 2, 1 to 0 and 5 to 0 victories to become the first Series pitcher to turn in three complete-game triumphs since Stan Coveleski of the Indians turned the trick against the Dodgers in 1920.

The Yankees, qualifying for their eighth Series appearance in nine seasons under Manager Casey Stengel, shook off the challenge of the White Sox to win the American League pennant by eight games. Manager Fred Haney's Braves, after showing signs of weakening under the pressure of a drive by the Cardinals, finished strong to capture the National League flag by a similar margin of eight lengths.

Opening the Series at Yankee Stadium, Whitey Ford sent the Bombers in front with a 3 to 1 victory over Spahn. The Braves avoided a shutout in the seventh when Wes Covington doubled and Red Schoendienst singled.

Burdette, who was traded to the Braves in a deal for Johnny Sain in 1951, appeared against the Yankees in the second game and started his amazing Series work with his 4 to 2 victory. After the success with Ford, Manager Stengel nominated another lefthander, Bobby Shantz, who had made a successful comeback during the season after being obtained from the Athletics, but the little southpaw failed to match Whitey's performance.

The Braves scored their winning runs in the fourth, breaking a 2-all deadlock. Joe Adcock and Andy Pafko singled. Covington, after fouling off two attempted bunts, looped a single into left-center. Adcock scored and when Tony Kubek failed to flag Enos Slaughter's throw to third, Pafko also crossed the plate with an insurance run.

After a day off for traveling, the Series opponents resumed their action in Milwaukee, where Kubek, the Yankees' 21-year-old versatile rookie, made a smashing debut in his home town. Tony hit two homers, one in the first inning and the other in the seventh, to pace the Bombers to a 12 to 3 victory. A Series record was set and two were tied in the game. The Braves left 14 men on base to match one mark and equalled another when their six pitchers issued 11 passes. Bob Turley and Don Larsen, who hurled for the Yankees, walked eight and the combined total of 19 for the two clubs set a Series record.

Bob Buhl, who started for the Braves, was routed in the opening frame after Kubek's first homer, two walks, a sacrifice fly and a single by Harry Simpson produced three runs.

The fourth game demonstrated the Braves' spirit. After the Yanks scored in the first inning, the Braves exploded for four runs in the fourth inning off Tom Sturdivant on homers by Hank Aaron and Frank Torre. Spahn carried his 4 to 1 lead into the ninth inning and had two out, two men on base and a count of three balls and two strikes on first baseman Elston Howard when disaster struck the vet southpaw. Howard drove the next pitch over the left field wall for a homer to tie the score.

Haney stuck with Spahn, even in the tenth, when Kubek beat out an infield hit and Bauer tripled to send the Yankees in front. However, in the home half, a bit of shoe polish helped make Series history. Nippy Jones, batting for Spahn, was hit on the foot by a pitch thrown by Tommy Byrne, the Yankees' fourth pitcher in the game, but Umpire Augie Donatelli's view had been obstructed. Jones retrieved the ball and showed the ump a tell-tale smudge of black from the polish on his shoe.

Jones was waved to first as a hit batsman and Felix Mantilla came in to run for him. Bob Grim relieved Byrne. Johnny Logan greeted the change with a double, scoring Mantilla with the tying run. Mathews then hit a homer to win the game.

It was Burdette's turn to pitch again in the fifth game and the righthander gained his 1 to 0 victory in a magnificent duel with Ford. The lone run scored after two were out in the sixth inning. Mathews beat out a two-hopper to Jerry Coleman. Aaron popped a single to short right field and Adcock lined a sharp single to right for the only run that Burdette needed.

Once more there was an open date for travel and when the Series resumed in New York, Turley tossed a four-hitter to give the Yankees a 3 to 2 victory. All the runs in the game scored on homers. Yogi Berra connected off Buhl with Slaughter on base in the third inning, but round-trippers by Torre in the fifth and Aaron in the seventh knotted the count at 2 to 2. In the Yanks' half, with Ernie Johnson on the mound in relief for the Braves, Bauer belted the game-winning drive.

In normal rotation, the Braves would have started Spahn in the payoff contest, but the lefthander had been felled by the flu. Manager Haney had no choice but to call on Burdette, with only two days of rest, and the righthander rose to the occasion with his 5 to 0 triumph. The Braves routed Larsen while scoring four runs in the fourth inning. Crandall wrapped up the day's scoring and the Series with a homer off Byrne, fifth Yankee pitcher, in the eighth inning. The box scores:

Wednesday, October 2—At New York

Milwaukee (N.L.)	AB.	R.	H.	O.	A.	E.
Schoendienst, 2b	4	0	1	1	2	0
Logan, ss	3	0	0	2	3	0
Mathews, 3b	2	0	0	0	1	0
Aaron, cf	4	0	1	2	0	0
Adcock, 1b	4	0	0	7	0	0
Torre, 1b	0	0	0	1	0	0
Pafko, rf	4	0	0	3	0	0
Covington, lf	4	1	2	4	0	0
Crandall, c	4	0	1	4	1	0
Spahn, p	1	0	0	0	1	0
Johnson, p	0	0	0	0	1	0
aJones	1	0	0	0	0	0
McMahon, p	0	0	0	0	0	0
Totals	31	1	5	24	9	0

New York (A.L.)	AB.	R.	H.	O.	A.	E.
Bauer, rf	4	0	1	1	0	0
McDougald, ss	4	0	1	2	6	0
Mantle, cf	4	0	2	2	0	0
Skowron, 1b	1	0	0	2	0	0
Howard, 1b	2	1	1	3	1	1
Collins, 1b	1	0	0	5	0	0
Berra, c	3	1	1	5	0	0

1957 WORLD SERIES

	AB.	R.	H.	O.	A.	E.
Carey, 3b	3	0	1	2	2	0
Coleman, 2b	3	1	2	3	4	0
Kubek, lf	3	0	0	1	0	0
Ford, p	3	0	0	1	1	0
Totals	31	3	9	27	14	1

Milwaukee	0	0 0	0 0 0	1 0 0—1
New York	0	0 0	0 1 2	0 0 *—3

aGrounded out for Johnson in seventh. Runs batted in—Bauer, Carey, Coleman, Schoendienst. Two-base hits—Coleman, Bauer, Covington. Sacrifice hit—Coleman. Double plays—McDougald, Coleman and Howard; Crandall and Logan. Left on bases—Milwaukee 7, New York 7. Earned runs—Milwaukee 3, New York 1. Bases on balls—Off Ford 4, off Spahn 1, off McMahon 1. Struck out—By Ford 5, by Johnson 1, by McMahon 3. Pitching records—Off Spahn 7 hits, 3 runs in 5⅓ innings; off Johnson 0 hits, 0 runs in ⅔ inning; off McMahon 2 hits, 0 runs in 2 innings. Winner—Ford. Loser—Spahn. Umpires—Paparella (A.L.), Conlan (N.L.), McKinley (A.L.), Donatelli (N.L.), Secory (N.L.), Chylak (A.L.). Time—2:10. Attendance—69,476.

Thursday, October 3—At New York

Milwaukee (N.L.)	AB.	R.	H.	O.	A.	E.
Schoendienst, 2b	4	0	0	1	3	0
Logan, ss	3	1	1	3	3	0
Mathews, 3b	4	0	0	1	2	0
Aaron, cf	4	1	1	2	0	0
Adcock, 1b	4	1	2	8	1	0
Torre, 1b	0	0	0	2	0	0
Pafko, rf	4	1	1	2	0	0
Covington, lf	4	0	2	3	0	0
Crandall, c	3	0	1	5	0	0
Burdette, p	3	0	0	0	4	0
Totals	33	4	8	27	13	0

New York (A.L.)	AB.	R.	H.	O.	A.	E.
Bauer, rf	5	1	1	3	0	0
McDougald, ss	4	0	0	2	3	0
Mantle, cf	3	0	0	2	0	1
Berra, c	4	0	0	6	0	0
Slaughter, lf	3	1	1	2	0	0
Simpson, 1b	4	0	0	10	1	0
Kubek, 3b	4	0	2	1	1	1
Coleman, 2b	2	0	1	1	1	0
bCollins	1	0	0	0	0	0
Shantz, p	1	0	0	0	1	0
Ditmar, p	1	0	0	0	0	0
aLumpe	1	0	1	0	0	0
Grim, p	0	0	0	0	0	0
cHoward	1	0	1	0	0	0
dRichardson	0	0	0	0	0	0
Totals	34	2	7	27	7	2

Milwaukee	0 1 1	2 0 0	0 0 0—4
New York	0 1 1	0 0 0	0 0 0—2

aSingled for Ditmar in seventh. bPopped out for Coleman in ninth. cSingled for Grim in ninth. dRan for Howard in ninth. Runs batted in—Adcock, Coleman, Logan, Bauer, Covington. (Pafko scored on Kubek's error in fourth). Two-base hit—Slaughter. Three-base hit—Aaron. Home runs—Logan, Bauer. Sacrifice hit—Burdette. Double play—McDougald and Simpson. Left on bases—New York 8, Milwaukee 5. Earned runs—Milwaukee 3, New York 2. Bases on balls—Off Shantz 1, off Burdette 3. Struck out—By Shantz 3, by Ditmar 1, by Grim 2, by Burdette 5. Pitching records—Off Shantz 6 hits, 4 runs in 3 innings (pitched to three batters in fourth); off Ditmar 1 hit, 0 runs in 4 innings; off Grim 1 hit, 0 runs in 2 innings. Hit by pitcher—By Ditmar (Logan). Winner—Burdette. Loser—Shantz. Umpires—Conlan (N.L.), McKinley (A.L.), Donatelli (N.L.), Paparella (A.L.), Secory (N.L.), Chylak (A.L.). Time—2:26. Attendance—65,202.

Saturday, October 5—At Milwaukee

New York (A.L.)	AB.	R.	H.	O.	A.	E.
Bauer, rf	5	1	1	3	0	0
Kubek, lf	5	3	3	4	0	0
Mantle, cf	3	2	2	1	0	0
Berra, c	4	2	1	7	0	0
McDougald, ss	1	2	0	3	3	0
Simpson, 1b	1	0	1	0	0	0
aHoward, 1b	2	0	0	6	0	0
Collins, 1b	1	0	0	1	0	0
Lumpe, 3b	5	0	1	2	3	0
Coleman, 2b	4	1	0	0	1	0
Turley, p	1	0	0	0	0	0
Larsen, p	2	1	0	0	0	0
Totals	34	12	9	27	7	0

Milwaukee (N.L.)	AB.	R.	H.	O.	A.	E.
Schoendienst, 2b	5	0	3	0	2	0
Logan, ss	4	1	2	0	1	0
Mathews, 3b	2	0	0	3	6	0
Aaron, cf	5	1	2	2	0	0
Covington, lf	3	0	0	2	0	0
Adcock, 1b	3	0	0	9	1	0
Trowbridge, p	0	0	0	0	0	0
dJones	1	0	0	0	0	0
McMahon, p	0	0	0	0	1	0
fPafko	0	0	0	0	0	0
Hazle, rf	4	1	0	0	0	0
Rice, c	3	0	1	5	1	0
eDeMerit	0	0	0	0	0	0
Crandall, c	1	0	0	0	0	0
Buhl, p	0	0	0	0	1	1
Pizarro, p	1	0	0	0	0	0
Conley, p	0	0	0	1	0	0
bSawatski	1	0	0	0	0	0
Johnson, p	0	0	0	0	1	0
cTorre, 1b	2	0	0	3	0	0
Totals	35	3	8	27	14	1

New York	3 0 2	2 0 0	5 0 0—12
Milwaukee	0 1 0	0 2 0	0 0 0— 3

aWalked for Simpson in third. bFanned for Conley in fourth. cGrounded out for Johnson in sixth. dGrounded out for Trowbridge in seventh. eRan for Rice in eighth. fHit by pitched ball for McMahon in ninth. Runs batted in—Kubek 4, McDougald, Simpson, Schoendienst, Lumpe 2, Mantle 2, Aaron 2, Bauer 2. Home runs—Kubek 2, Mantle, Aaron. Stolen base—McDougald. Sacrifice fly—McDougald. Double play—Schoendienst and Torre. Left on bases—Milwaukee 14, New York 7. Earned runs—New York 11, Milwaukee 3. Bases on balls—Off Buhl 2, off Pizarro 2, off Conley 1, off E. Johnson 1, off Trowbridge 3, off McMahon 2, off Turley 4, off Larsen 4. Struck out—By Pizarro 1, by E. Johnson 2, by Trowbridge 1, by McMahon 2, by Turley 2, by Larsen 4. Pitching records—Off Buhl 2 hits, 3 runs in ⅔ inning; off Turley 3 hits, 1 run in 1⅓ innings; off Pizarro 3 hits, 2 runs in 1⅔ innings; off Conley 2 hits, 2 runs in 1⅔ innings; off E. Johnson 0 hits, 0 runs in 2 innings; off Trowbridge 2 hits, 5 runs in 1 inning; off McMahon 0 hits, 0 runs in 2 innings; off Larsen 5 hits, 2 runs in 7⅓ innings. Hit by pitcher—By Larsen (Pafko). Wild pitch—Turley. Passed ball—Rice. Winner—Larsen. Loser—Buhl. Umpires—McKinley (A.L.), Donatelli (N.L.), Paparella (A.L.). Conlan (N.L.), Chylak (A.L.), Secory (N.L.). Time—3:18. Attendance—45,804.

Sunday, October 6—At Milwaukee

New York (A.L.)	AB	R	H	O	A	E
Kubek, lf-cf	5	1	2	1	0	0
Bauer, rf	5	0	1	0	0	0
Mantle, cf	5	1	0	1	0	0
Slaughter, lf	0	0	0	0	0	0
Berra, c	3	1	2	8	0	0
McDougald, ss	4	1	2	1	2	0
Howard, 1b	4	1	1	13	0	0
Collins, 1b	0	0	0	0	1	0
Carey, 3b	4	0	1	1	4	0
Coleman, 2b	4	0	1	3	4	0
Sturdivant, p	1	0	0	0	1	0
aSimpson	1	0	0	0	0	0
Shantz, p	0	0	0	0	0	0
bLumpe	1	0	1	0	0	0
Kucks, p	0	0	0	0	0	0
Byrne, p	1	0	0	0	0	0
Grim, p	0	0	0	0	0	0
Totals	38	5	11	f28	12	0

Milwaukee (N.L.)	AB	R	H	O	A	E
Schoendienst, 2b	4	0	1	3	3	0
Logan, ss	4	2	1	1	10	0
Mathews, 3b	4	2	2	1	4	0
Aaron, cf	3	1	2	1	0	0
Covington, lf	4	0	0	0	0	0
Torre, 1b	3	1	1	15	1	0
cAdcock, 1b	1	0	0	1	0	0
Hazle, rf	2	0	0	2	0	0
Pafko, rf	2	0	0	3	0	0
Crandall, c	4	0	0	2	0	0
Spahn, p	3	0	0	1	2	0
dJones	0	0	0	0	0	0
eMantilla	0	1	0	0	0	0
Totals	34	7	7	30	20	0

```
New York .........  1 0 0   0 0 0   0 0 3   1—5
Milwaukee ........  0 0 0   4 0 0   0 0 0   3—7
```

aHit into double play for Sturdivant in fifth. bSingled for Shantz in eighth. cGrounded out for Torre in ninth. dHit by pitch for Spahn in tenth. eRan for Jones in tenth. fOne out when winning run scored. Runs batted in—McDougald, Aaron 3, Torre, Howard 3, Bauer, Logan, Mathews 2. Two base hits—Mathews, Carey, Schoendienst, Logan. Three-base hit—Bauer. Home runs—Aaron, Torre, Howard, Mathews. Stolen base—Covington. Sacrifice hit—Schoendienst. Double plays—Schoendienst and Torre; Logan, Schoendienst and Torre 2. Left on bases—New York 4, Milwaukee 4. Earned runs—Milwaukee 7, New York 5. Bases on balls—Off Spahn 1, off Sturdivant 1, off Shantz 1, off Kucks 1. Struck out—By Spahn 2, by Sturdivant 1, by Shantz 4, by Kucks 1, by Byrne 1. Pitching records—Off Sturdivant 4 hits, 4 runs in 4 innings; off Shantz 0 hits, 0 runs in 3 innings; off Kucks 1 hit, 0 runs in ⅔ inning; off Byrne 0 hit, 1 run in 1⅓ innings (pitched to one batter in tenth); off Grim 2 hits, 2 runs in ⅓ inning. Hit by pitcher —By Byrne (Jones). Winner—Spahn. Loser—Grim. Umpires—Donatelli (N.L.), Paparella (A.L.), Conlan (N.L.), McKinley (A.L.), Chylak (A.L.), Secory (N.L.). Time—2:31. Attendance—45,804.

Monday, October 7—At Milwaukee

New York (A.L.)	AB	R	H	O	A	E
Bauer, rf	4	0	2	0	0	0
Kubek, cf	3	0	0	4	0	0
McDougald, ss	4	0	1	1	7	0
Berra, c	4	0	1	4	1	0
Slaughter, lf	3	0	2	3	0	0
Simpson, 1b	3	0	0	8	0	0
Lumpe, 3b	3	0	0	0	2	0
Coleman, 2b	3	0	1	4	2	0

	AB	R	H	O	A	E
aMantle	0	0	0	0	0	0
Turley, p	0	0	0	0	0	0
Ford, p	2	0	0	0	0	0
bHoward	1	0	0	0	0	0
Richardson, 2b	0	0	0	0	0	0
Totals	30	0	7	24	11	0

Milwaukee (N.L.)	AB	R	H	O	A	E
Schoendienst, 2b	1	0	0	0	0	0
Mantilla, 2b	3	0	0	2	7	0
Logan, ss	4	0	0	3	3	0
Mathews, 3b	3	1	1	1	2	0
Aaron, cf	3	0	2	0	0	0
Adcock, 1b	3	0	1	13	0	1
Torre, 1b	0	0	0	1	0	0
Pafko, rf	3	0	2	1	0	0
Covington, lf	2	0	0	1	0	0
Crandall, c	3	0	0	5	3	0
Burdette, p	3	0	0	0	2	0
Totals	28	1	6	27	17	1

```
New York .........  0 0 0   0 0 0   0 0 0—0
Milwaukee ........  0 0 0   0 0 1   0 0 *—1
```

aRan for Coleman in eighth. bStruck out for Ford in eighth. Run batted in—Adcock. Sacrifice hits—Kubek, Covington. Double plays—Crandall and Logan; Mathews, Mantilla and Adcock; McDougald, Coleman and Simpson; Logan and Adcock. Left on bases—Milwaukee 5, New York 4. Earned runs—Milwaukee 1, New York 0. Bases on balls—Off Ford 1. Struck out—By Burdette 5, by Ford 2, by Turley 2. Pitching records—Off Ford 6 hits, 1 run in 7 innings; off Turley 0 hits, 0 runs in 1 inning. Winner—Burdette. Loser—Ford. Umpires—Paparella (A.L.), Conlan (N.L.), McKinley (A.L.), Donatelli (N.L.), Chylak (A.L.), Secory (N.L.). Time—2:00. Attendance—45,811.

Wednesday, October 9—At New York

Milwaukee (N.L.)	AB	R	H	O	A	E
Mantilla, 2b	3	0	0	2	1	0
Logan, ss	4	0	0	2	1	0
Mathews, 3b	3	0	1	0	0	0
Aaron, cf	4	1	1	1	0	0
Covington, lf	4	0	0	1	1	0
Torre, 1b	3	1	2	7	1	0
Hazle, rf	3	0	0	0	0	0
Rice, c	3	0	0	10	1	0
Buhl, p	1	0	0	0	1	0
E. Johnson, p	1	0	0	1	2	0
aSawatski	1	0	0	0	0	0
McMahon, p	0	0	0	0	1	0
Totals	30	2	4	24	9	0

New York (A.L.)	AB	R	H	O	A	E
Bauer, rf	4	1	1	1	0	0
Kubek, cf	4	0	0	3	0	0
Slaughter, lf	2	1	0	0	0	0
Berra, c	4	1	3	10	0	0
McDougald, ss	3	0	1	2	2	0
Lumpe, 3b	3	0	1	1	1	0
Simpson, 1b	3	0	0	6	0	0
Collins, 1b	0	0	0	1	1	0
Coleman, 2b	2	0	1	1	3	0
Turley, p	3	0	0	2	2	0
Totals	28	3	7	27	9	0

```
Milwaukee ........  0 0 0   0 1 0   1 0 0—2
New York .........  0 0 2   0 0 0   1 0 *—3
```

aStruck out for E. Johnson in eighth. Runs batted in—Berra 2, Torre, Aaron, Bauer. Two-base hits—Mathews, Coleman, Berra. Home runs—Berra, Torre, Aaron, Bauer. Sacrifice hit—McDougald. Double plays—Rice and Logan; Covington and Rice; Turley, McDougald and Collins.

Left on bases—New York 6, Milwaukee 3. Earned runs—New York 3, Milwaukee 2. Bases on balls—Off Turley 2, off Buhl 4. Struck out—By Turley 8, by Buhl 4, by E. Johnson 5. Pitching records—Off Buhl 4 hits, 2 runs in 2⅔ innings; off E. Johnson 2 hits, 1 run in 4⅓ innings; off McMahon 1 hit, 0 run in 1 inning. Wild pitch—Buhl. Winner—Turley. Loser—E. Johnson. Umpires—Conlan (N.L.), McKinley (A.L.), Donatelli (N.L.), Paparella (A.L.), Secory (N.L.), Chylak (A.L.). Time—2:09. Attendance—61,408.

Thursday, October 10—At New York

Milwaukee (N.L.)	AB.	R.	H.	O.	A.	E.
Hazle, rf	4	1	2	3	0	0
dPafko, rf	1	0	0	0	0	0
Logan, ss	5	1	1	2	4	0
Mathews, 3b	4	1	1	3	4	1
Aaron, cf	5	1	2	3	0	0
Covington, lf	3	0	1	2	0	0
Torre, 1b	2	0	0	8	0	0
Mantilla, 2b	4	0	0	2	0	0
Crandall, c	4	1	2	4	0	0
Burdette, p	2	0	0	0	3	0
Totals	34	5	9	27	11	1

New York (A.L.)	AB.	R.	H.	O.	A.	E.
Bauer, rf	4	0	1	2	0	0
Slaughter, lf	4	0	0	2	0	0
Mantle, cf	4	0	1	2	0	0
Berra, c	3	0	0	4	1	1
McDougald, ss	4	0	1	2	1	1
Kubek, 3b	4	0	1	3	4	1
Coleman, 2b	4	0	2	4	3	0
Collins, 1b	2	0	0	5	0	0
Sturdivant, p	0	0	0	0	0	0
cHoward	1	0	0	0	0	0
Byrne, p	1	0	1	0	0	0
Larsen, p	0	0	0	0	1	0
Shantz, p	0	0	0	0	0	0
aLumpe	1	0	0	0	0	0
Ditmar, p	0	0	0	0	0	0
bSkowron, 1b	3	0	0	3	2	0
Totals	35	0	7	27	12	3

Milwaukee	0	0	4	0	0	0	0	1	0—5
New York	0	0	0	0	0	0	0	0	0—0

aStruck out for Shantz in third. bHit into forceout for Ditmar in fifth. cStruck out for Sturdivant in seventh. dFouled out for Hazle in eighth. Runs batted in—Mathews 2, Aaron, Torre, Crandall. Two-base hits—Bauer, Mathews. Home run—Crandall. Sacrifice hits—Burdette, Mathews, Covington. Double play—McDougald, Coleman and Skowron. Left on bases—New York 9, Milwaukee 8. Earned runs—Milwaukee 3, New York 0. Bases on balls—Off Burdette 1, off Larsen 1, off Byrne 2. Struck out—By Burdette 3, by Larsen 2, by Ditmar 1, by Sturdivant 1. Pitching records—Off Larsen 3 hits, 3 runs in 2⅓ innings; off Shantz 2 hits, 1 run in ⅔ inning; off Ditmar 1 hit, 0 runs in 2 innings; off Sturdivant 2 hits, 0 runs in 2 innings; off Byrne 1 hit, 1 run in 2 innings. Winner—Burdette. Loser—Larsen. Umpires—McKinley (A.L.), Donatelli (N.L.), Paparella (A.L.), Conlan (N.L.), Chylak (A.L.), Secory (N.L.). Time—2:34. Attendance—61,207.

COMPOSITE BATTING AVERAGES
Milwaukee Braves

Player-Position	G.	AB.	R.	H.	2B.	3B.	HR.	RBI.	BA.
Aaron, cf	7	28	5	11	0	1	3	7	.393
Torre, 1b-ph	7	10	2	3	0	0	2	3	.300
Schoendienst, 2b	5	18	0	5	1	0	0	2	.278
Mathews, 3b	7	22	4	5	0	0	1	4	.227
Pafko, rf-ph	6	14	1	3	0	0	0	0	.214
Crandall, c	6	19	1	4	0	0	1	1	.211
Covington, lf	7	24	1	5	1	0	0	1	.208
Adcock, 1b-ph	5	15	1	3	0	0	0	2	.200
Logan, ss	7	27	5	5	1	0	1	2	.185
Rice, c	2	6	0	1	0	0	0	0	.167
Hazle, rf	4	13	2	2	0	0	0	0	.154
Mantilla, pr-2b	4	10	1	0	0	0	0	0	.000
Spahn, p	2	4	0	0	0	0	0	0	.000
Johnson, p	3	1	0	0	0	0	0	0	.000
McMahon, p	3	0	0	0	0	0	0	0	.000
Trowbridge, p	1	0	0	0	0	0	0	0	.000
Buhl, p	2	1	0	0	0	0	0	0	.000
Pizarro, p	1	1	0	0	0	0	0	0	.000
Conley, p	1	0	0	0	0	0	0	0	.000
Burdette, p	3	8	0	0	0	0	0	0	.000
Jones, ph	3	2	0	0	0	0	0	0	.000
DeMerit, pr	1	0	0	0	0	0	0	0	.000
Sawatski, ph	2	2	0	0	0	0	0	0	.000
Totals	7	225	23	47	6	1	8	22	.209

New York Yankees

Player-Position	G.	AB.	R.	H.	2B.	3B.	HR.	RBI.	BA.
Byrne, p	2	2	0	1	0	0	0	0	.500
Coleman, 2b	7	22	2	8	2	0	0	2	.364
Berra, c	7	25	5	8	1	0	1	2	.320
Carey, 3b	2	7	0	2	1	0	0	1	.286
Kubek, lf-3b-cf	7	28	4	8	0	0	2	4	.286
Lumpe, ph-3b	6	14	0	4	0	0	0	2	.286
Howard, 1b-ph	6	11	2	3	0	0	1	3	.273
Mantle, cf-pr	6	19	3	5	0	0	1	2	.263
Bauer, rf	7	31	3	8	2	1	2	6	.258
McDougald, ss	7	24	3	6	0	0	0	2	.250
Slaughter, lf	5	12	2	3	1	0	0	0	.250
Simpson, 1b-ph	5	12	0	1	0	0	0	1	.083
Richardson, pr-2b	2	0	0	0	0	0	0	0	.000
Skowron, 1b-ph	2	4	0	0	0	0	0	0	.000
Collins, 1b-ph	6	5	0	0	0	0	0	0	.000
Ford, p	2	5	0	0	0	0	0	0	.000
Shantz, p	3	1	0	0	0	0	0	0	.000
Ditmar, p	2	1	0	0	0	0	0	0	.000
Grim, p	2	0	0	0	0	0	0	0	.000
Turley, p	3	4	0	0	0	0	0	0	.000
Larsen, p	2	2	1	0	0	0	0	0	.000
Sturdivant, p	2	1	0	0	0	0	0	0	.000
Kucks, p	1	0	0	0	0	0	0	0	.000
Totals	7	230	25	57	7	1	7	25	.248

COMPOSITE PITCHING AVERAGES
Milwaukee Braves

Pitcher	G.	IP.	H.	R.	E.	SO.	BB.	W.	L.	ERA.
McMahon	3	5	3	0	0	5	3	0	0	0.00
Burdette	3	27	21	2	2	13	4	3	0	0.67
Johnson	3	7	2	1	1	8	1	0	1	1.29
Spahn	2	15⅓	18	8	8	2	2	1	1	4.70
Buhl	2	3⅓	6	5	4	4	6	0	1	10.80
Pizarro	1	1⅔	3	2	2	1	2	0	0	10.80
Conley	1	1⅔	2	2	2	0	1	0	0	10.80
Trowbridge	1	1	2	5	5	1	3	0	0	45.00
Totals	7	62	57	25	24	34	22	4	3	3.48

New York Yankees

Pitcher	G.	IP.	H.	R.	E.	SO.	BB.	W.	L.	ERA.
Ditmar	2	6	2	0	0	2	0	0	0	0.00
Kucks	1	⅔	1	0	0	1	1	0	0	0.00
Ford	2	16	11	2	2	7	5	1	1	1.13
Turley	3	11⅔	7	3	3	12	6	1	0	2.31
Larsen	2	9⅔	8	5	4	6	5	1	1	3.72
Shantz	2	6⅔	8	5	3	7	2	0	1	4.05
Byrne	2	3⅓	1	2	2	1	2	0	0	5.40
Sturdivant	2	6	6	4	4	2	1	0	0	6.00
Grim	2	2½	3	2	2	2	0	0	1	7.71
Totals	7	62⅓	47	23	20	40	22	3	4	2.89

SERIES OF 1958

	W.	L.	Pct.
New York A. L.	4	3	.571
Milwaukee N. L.	3	4	.429

Picking themselves off the floor, the New York Yankees, perennial American League champions, made a courageous comeback to defeat the Braves, four games to three, gaining dramatic revenge for their loss of the title to the Milwaukee National League champions in 1957.

The Yankees' triumph must rate as the greatest in the remarkable history of the club. Manager Casey Stengel's crew lost three of the first four games and appeared doomed to defeat, but the Yankees' pride and indomitable spirit drove them to their upset of the Braves. Only once before in the World Series had any club, trailing by three games to one, overcome such a deficit in a seven-game Classic. The Pittsburgh Pirates achieved the feat against the Washington Senators in 1925.

For Manager Stengel, the world championship was his seventh, putting him in a tie with Joe McCarthy, who also copped his seven with the Yankees. By defeating the Braves, the New Yorkers completed the cycle of beating every National League club in at least one Series.

The Yankees had two big heroes, with No. 1 honors going to Hank Bauer, the fighting Marine of World War II, who collected 10 hits, four of them homers, and drove in eight runs, the most for any player on either club. In the third game of the Series, the only one won by the Bombers in the first four, Bauer banged out three of his team's four hits and drove in all four of its runs. Led by Hammering Hank, the Yankees pounded a total of 10 homers in the Series to only three for the Braves.

Ranking next to Bauer among the Yankee laureates was Bob Turley. Shelled quickly in his first start, the fast-balling righthander came back to win the fifth game, save the sixth and win the seventh. In the clincher, he replaced Don Larsen and held the Braves to two hits and one run in the last six and two-thirds innings.

Lew Burdette, who wrote his name in the history books with his three complete-game victories for Milwaukee in 1957, beat the Yankees again in his first start, but then was unable to continue his mastery, losing his next two efforts. On the other hand, Warren Spahn, shaky winner of one game in '57, was the standout in defeat for the Braves. The veteran lefthander won two games before being handed a heartbreaking loss in his third start.

Spahn drew first blood in the Series opener at Milwaukee, beating the Yankees in 10 innings, 4 to 3. The Bombers belted two homers, the first by Bill Skowron in the fourth inning and the other by Bauer after a pass to Whitey Ford in the fifth.

Trailing, 3 to 2, the Braves knotted the count in the eighth after Eddie Mathews walked and stopped at third on a double by Hank Aaron. Ryne Duren, bespectacled relief ace of the Yankees, came in to replace Ford and fanned Joe Adcock, but Wes Covington drove a sacrifice fly, Mathews scoring with the tying run. In the tenth, Adcock and Del Crandall singled. Billy Bruton, who missed the 1957 Series, undergoing an operation for an injured knee, then came through in the clutch with two out, rapping a long single to drive in the winning run.

Burdette, starting the second game, was on the ropes in the first inning, but the Braves exploded in their half for seven runs, the most ever made in the opening frame of a Series game, to enable the right-hander to rack up a 13 to 5 verdict. The Yanks, after loading the bases, scored only one run in the first on a forceout before Yogi Berra grounded into a double play. However, the run ruined Burdette's hopes of breaking Babe Ruth's 1916-18 record of pitching $29\frac{2}{3}$ consecutive scoreless innings. Lew's streak was stopped at 24 innings.

The Braves opened their outburst against Turley with a homer by Bruton, and Burdette himself supplied the coup de grace with a three-run homer off reliever Duke Maas. Burdette was only the sixth pitcher in World Series history to hit for the circuit.

Burdette was tagged for two homers by Mickey Mantle and one by Bauer. He had a three-hitter going into the ninth when Bauer homered, Gil McDougald singled and Mantle walloped his second round-tripper of the game.

After an open date for travel, the Series was resumed at Yankee Stadium, where Bauer staged his one-man batting show to help the Bombers to a 4 to 0 victory behind the hurling of Larsen and Duren. Larsen, who had not pitched a complete game since July 18, because of an elbow ailment, was withdrawn after seven innings when he showed signs of tiring and Duren finished. They held the Braves to six hits.

Bob Rush, formerly of the Cubs, limited the Yankees to only three safeties. However, in the fifth inning, after Norm Siebern walked, Jerry Lumpe popped up and Skowron grounded out, Siebern taking second. Manager Fred Haney ordered an intentional pass for McDougald, but the strategy backfired when Rush also walked Larsen and Bauer followed with a pop-fly single to right field, Siebern and Skowron scoring. In the seventh, with Don McMahon on the mound for the Braves, Enos Slaughter drew a pass, batting for Larsen, and Bauer clinched the victory with a home run.

Spahn returned to the mound for his second start the next day and turned in one of the finer performances of Series history, hurling a two-hitter to shut out the Yankees, 3 to 0. In achieving the victory, the crafty southpaw stopped Bauer's streak of hitting safely in 17 straight Series games.

Young Siebern, playing left, the difficult sun field at Yankee Stadium, was the goat of the Bombers' loss. In the sixth inning, Siebern lost track of a fly by Red Schoendienst, letting the ball drop for a triple. With the infield drawn in for a possible play at the plate, shortstop Tony Kubek missed connections with Johnny Logan's grounder for an error, the run scoring. The Braves nicked Ford for another marker in the seventh. Siebern again was blinded by the rays of the sun on a fly by Logan in the eighth, the ball bouncing into the stands for an automatic double. Mathews then whacked a legitimate double to score Logan.

As events turned out, that was the Braves' last victory. The Yankees started their comeback behind Turley, who beat the Braves the next day, 7 to 0, for the third shutout in as many consecutive games at Yankee Stadium. Turley pitched a five-hitter.

The Yankees scored their initial run on a homer by McDougald in the third inning. In the sixth, Elston Howard, playing left field in place of Siebern, made a catch that could well be called the turning point of the Series. Bruton led off the frame with a single. Schoendienst followed with a sliced looper to left. Howard, racing in, dived and made a sliding, one-handed grab of the ball. Bruton, already past second, was the easy victim of a double play. Mathews then singled for a hit that would have produced two runs and perhaps turned the tide in the Braves' favor, except for Howard's fielding feat.

The catch sparked the Yankees, who caught fire in their half to kayo Burdette, their former nemesis, during a six-run outburst.

Returning to Milwaukee, the rivals squared off again after an open date. Spahn, winner over the Yankees in two 10-inning games, one in 1957 and the other in his first start in the '58 Series, was forced to battle into overtime once more, but this time luck turned sour for the veteran lefty, who was defeated in 10 innings, 4 to 3.

Bauer, who was stopped cold by Spahn in their previous meeting in the fourth game, regained the upper hand with a homer for the Yankees in the first inning. However, Ford, pitching like Spahn with only two days of rest, proved unequal to the assignment. The Braves rapped him for the tying run in their half of the opening frame. In the second, Covington, Andy Pafko and Spahn singled to send the Braves ahead, 2 to 1. It was the third straight game in which Spahn had come through with an RBI. When Schoendienst walked, Art Ditmar relieved Ford and emerged from the jam with the aid of questionable base-running by the Braves. Johnny Logan lifted a shallow fly to Howard in left and Pafko, running after the catch on the command of Coach Billy Herman, was easily doubled at the plate. The Yanks tied the score in the sixth.

McDougald shattered the deadlock with a homer in the tenth. Then, with two away, Howard and Berra rapped singles. Manager Fred Haney removed Spahn and brought in Don McMahon, who was clipped for another single by Skowron, driving in what proved to be the winning run. The Braves rallied in their half, scoring once on a walk to Logan and singles by Aaron and Adcock. However, with two away, Turley replaced Duren and retired pinch-hitter Frank Torre on a soft liner to McDougald at second.

Having used Turley in the game-saving role, Manager Stengel switched to Larsen to start the climactic seventh contest, while the Braves brought back Burdette for his third appearance. Larsen was not in form, but the Braves failed to take full advantage of their opportunity after loading the bases in the first inning, scoring only one run.

The Yankees were presented with two gift runs in the second inning. Berra walked to open the stanza and Torre then was charged with two successive throwing errors, one on a bunt by Howard and the other on a grounder by Lumpe, loading the bases. Berra scored when Skowron forced Lumpe and Howard tallied on a sacrifice fly by Kubek.

In the third inning, when Bruton and Aaron singled with one out, Manager Stengel called on Turley to take the mound for the Yankees. Bullet Bob quickly erased the Braves' threat. The Braves had a short-lived period of contention when Crandall homered in the sixth, but the Yankees were not to be denied with the big Series money at stake. In the eighth inning, with two out, Berra doubled and Howard singled to break the 2-2 tie. Carey also singled and Skowron then tomahawked the Braves with a three-run homer to wrap up the deciding 6 to 2 victory.

The box scores:

Wednesday, October 1—At Milwaukee

New York (A.L.)	AB.	R.	H.	O.	A.	E.
Bauer, rf	5	1	2	0	0	0
McDougald, 2b	4	0	2	1	2	0
Mantle, cf	3	0	0	3	0	0
Howard, lf	5	0	0	4	0	0
Berra, c	4	0	2	13	2	0
Skowron, 1b	4	1	2	7	0	0
Carey, 3b	4	0	0	0	2	0
Kubek, ss	4	0	0	1	1	1
Ford, p	2	1	0	0	0	0
Duren, p	1	0	0	0	0	0
Totals	36	3	8	†29	7	1

Milwaukee (N.L.)	AB.	R.	H.	O.	A.	E.
Schoendienst, 2b	4	0	0	2	2	0
Logan, ss	4	0	1	2	3	0
bTorre	1	0	0	0	0	0
Mantilla, ss	0	0	0	0	0	0
Mathews, 3b	3	1	0	1	3	0
Aaron, rf	4	1	1	3	0	0
Adcock, 1b	5	1	2	8	2	0
Covington, lf	4	0	0	2	1	0

1958 WORLD SERIES

	AB.	R.	H.	O.	A.	E.
Crandall, c	5	1	2	7	0	0
Pafko, cf	3	0	1	4	0	0
aBruton, cf	2	0	1	0	0	0
Spahn, p	4	0	2	1	2	0
Totals	39	4	10	30	13	0

New York......... 0 0 0   1 2 0   0 0 0   0–3
Milwaukee........ 0 0 0   2 0 0   0 1 0   1–4

aStruck out for Pafko in ninth. bPopped out for Logan in ninth. iTwo out when winning run scored. Runs batted in—Bauer 2, Skowron, Covington, Crandall, Spahn, Bruton. Two-base hits—Logan, Berra, Aaron. Home runs—Skowron, Bauer. Sacrifice fly—Covington. Left on bases—New York 7, Milwaukee 11. Earned runs—Milwaukee 4, New York 3. Bases on balls—Off Spahn 4, off Ford 3, off Duren 1. Struck out—By Spahn 6, by Ford 8, by Duren 5. Pitching records—Off Ford 6 hits, 3 runs in 7 innings (pitched to two batters in eighth); off Duren 4 hits, 1 run in 2⅔ innings. Wild pitches—Spahn, Ford. Passed ball—Berra. Winner—Spahn. Loser—Duren. Umpires—Barlick (N.L.), Berry (A.L.), Gorman (N.L.), Flaherty (A.L.), Jackowski (N.L.), Umont (A.L.). Time—3:09. Attendance—46,367.

Thursday, October 2—At Milwaukee

New York (A.L.)	AB.	R.	H.	O.	A.	E.
Bauer, rf	4	2	2	1	0	0
McDougald, 2b	4	1	1	0	6	0
Mantle, cf	3	2	2	3	0	0
Howard, lf	1	0	0	1	0	0
Siebern, lf	3	0	1	2	0	0
Berra, c	4	0	0	3	0	0
Skowron, 1b	4	0	0	11	0	0
Carey, 3b	2	0	0	1	2	0
cSlaughter	1	0	0	0	0	0
Richardson, 3b	1	0	0	0	0	0
Kubek, ss	3	0	0	2	2	0
Turley, p	0	0	0	0	0	0
Maas, p	0	0	0	0	0	0
Kucks, p	1	0	1	0	0	0
aLumpe	1	0	0	0	0	0
Dickson, p	0	0	0	0	0	0
dThroneberry	1	0	0	0	0	0
Monroe, p	0	0	0	0	0	0
Totals	33	5	7	24	10	0

New York......... 1 0 0   1 0 0   0 0 3– 5
Milwaukee........ 7 1 0   0 0 0   2 3 *–13

Milwaukee (N.L.)	AB.	R.	H.	O.	A.	E.
Bruton, cf	4	2	3	3	0	0
Schoendienst, 2b	5	2	2	2	6	0
Mathews, 3b	5	2	2	0	0	1
Aaron, rf	4	2	2	1	0	0
Covington, lf	4	1	3	1	0	0
bMantilla	0	1	0	0	0	0
Pafko, lf	0	0	0	1	0	0
Torre, 1b	5	0	1	10	1	0
Crandall, c	2	1	0	5	1	0
Logan, ss	4	1	1	3	5	0
Burdette, p	4	1	1	1	0	0
Totals	37	13	15	27	13	1

aFlied out for Kucks in fifth. bRan for Covington in seventh. cGrounded out for Carey in eighth. dStruck out for Dickson in eighth. Runs batted in—Bauer, Mantle 3, Howard, Bruton, Mathews 2, Covington 2, Pafko, Torre, Crandall, Logan 2, Burdette 3. Two-base hits—Schoendienst 2, Mathews. Home runs—Bruton, Burdette, Mantle 2, Bauer. Sacrifice flies—Crandall, Pafko. Stolen base—Mathews. Double plays—Schoendienst, Logan and Torre; Logan, Schoendienst and Torre. Left on bases—New York 2, Milwaukee 5. Earned runs—Milwaukee 13, New York 4. Bases on balls—Off Burdette 1, off Turley 1, off Maas 1, off Monroe 1. Struck out—By Burdette 5, by Turley 1, by Dickson 1, by Monroe 1. Pitching records—Off Turley 3 hits, 4 runs in ⅓ inning; off Maas 2 hits, 3 runs in ⅓ inning; off Kucks 3 hits, 1 run in 3⅓ innings; off Dickson 4 hits, 2 runs in 3 innings; off Monroe 3 hits, 3 runs in 1 inning. Winning pitcher—Burdette. Losing pitcher—Turley. Umpires—Berry (A.L.), Gorman (N.L.), Flaherty (A.L.), Barlick (N.L.), Umont (A.L.) and Jackowski (N.L.). Time—2:43. Attendance—46,367.

Saturday, October 4—At New York

Milwaukee (N.L.)	AB.	R.	H.	O.	A.	E.
Bruton, cf	3	0	0	2	0	0
Schoendienst, 2b	4	0	2	1	3	0
Mathews, 3b	3	0	0	0	1	0
Aaron, rf	3	0	0	1	0	0
Covington, lf	3	0	1	4	0	0
Torre, 1b	4	0	2	9	0	0
Crandall, c	4	0	1	4	1	0
Logan, ss	3	0	0	2	0	0
Rush, p	2	0	0	0	3	0
aHanebrink	1	0	0	0	0	0
McMahon, p	0	0	0	1	0	0
cWise	1	0	0	0	0	0
Totals	31	0	6	24	8	0

New York (A.L.)	AB.	R.	H.	O.	A.	E.
Bauer, rf	4	1	3	2	0	0
Kubek, ss	4	0	0	2	2	0
Mantle, cf	2	0	0	4	0	0
Berra, c	4	0	0	9	2	0
Siebern, lf	2	1	0	2	0	0
Lumpe, 3b	3	0	1	2	1	0
Richardson, 3b	1	0	0	0	0	0
Skowron, 1b	4	0	0	4	1	0
McDougald, 2b	2	1	0	1	0	0
Larsen, p	1	0	0	1	0	0
bSlaughter	0	1	0	0	0	0
Duren, p	0	0	0	0	1	0
Totals	27	4	4	27	7	0

Milwaukee........ 0 0 0   0 0 0   0 0 0–0
New York......... 0 0 0   0 2 0   2 0 *–4

aPopped out for Rush in seventh. bWalked for Larsen in seventh. cStruck out for McMahon in ninth. Runs batted in—Bauer 4. Home run—Bauer. Double plays—Crandall and Torre; Duren, Kubek and Skowron. Left on bases—Milwaukee 10, New York 4. Earned runs—New York 4, Milwaukee 0. Bases on balls—Off Larsen 3, off Duren 3, off Rush 5, off McMahon 2. Struck out—By Larsen 8, by Duren 1, by Rush 2, by McMahon 2. Pitching records—Off Larsen 6 hits, 0 runs in 7 innings; off Duren 0 hits, 0 runs in 2 innings; off Rush 3 hits, 2 runs in 6 innings; off McMahon 1 hit, 2 runs in 2 innings. Wild pitch—Duren. Winning pitcher—Larsen. Losing pitcher—Rush. Umpires—Gorman (N.L.), Flaherty (A.L.), Barlick (N.L.), Berry (A.L.), Jackowski (N.L.) and Umont (A.L.). Time—2:42. Attendance—71,599.

Sunday, October 5—At New York

Milwaukee (N.L.)	AB.	R.	H.	O.	A.	E.
Schoendienst, 2b	5	1	1	2	2	0
Logan, ss	5	1	1	1	5	0
Mathews, 3b	4	0	1	1	1	0
Aaron, cf-rf	4	0	2	2	0	0
Adcock, 1b	3	0	0	9	0	0
bTorre, 1b	1	0	0	2	0	0
Crandall, c	3	0	2	8	0	0
Covington, lf	3	0	0	1	0	0

1958 WORLD SERIES

	AB.	R.	H.	O.	A.	E.
cBruton, cf	0	0	0	1	0	0
Pafko, rf-lf	4	0	1	0	0	0
Spahn, p	4	0	1	0	2	0
Totals	36	3	9	27	10	0

New York (A.L.)	AB.	R.	H.	O.	A.	E.
Siebern, lf	3	0	0	1	0	0
McDougald, 2b	4	0	0	4	4	0
Bauer, rf	4	0	0	0	0	0
Mantle, cf	4	0	1	2	0	0
Skowron, 1b	3	0	1	10	0	0
Berra, c	3	0	0	7	0	0
Richardson, 3b	2	0	0	0	0	0
aHoward	1	0	0	0	0	0
Carey, 3b	0	0	0	0	1	0
Kubek, ss	2	0	0	2	6	1
dSlaughter	1	0	0	0	0	0
Dickson, p	0	0	0	0	0	0
Ford, p	1	0	0	1	1	0
Kucks, p	0	0	0	0	0	0
eLumpe, ss	1	0	0	0	0	0
Totals	29	0	2	27	12	1

Milwaukee .... 0 0 0 0 0 1 1 1 0—3
New York .... 0 0 0 0 0 0 0 0 0—0

aCalled out on strikes for Richardson in seventh. bPopped out for Adcock in eighth. cRan for Covington in eighth. dCalled out on strikes for Kubek in eighth. ePopped out for Kucks in eighth. Runs batted in—Mathews, Spahn. Two-base hits—Aaron, Pafko, Logan, Mathews. Three-base hits—Mantle, Schoendienst. Double play—McDougald, Kubek and Skowron. Left on bases—Milwaukee 8, New York 4. Earned runs—Milwaukee 2, New York 0. Bases on balls—Off Ford 1, off Kucks 1, off Spahn 2. Struck out—By Ford 6, by Spahn 7. Pitching records—Off Ford 8 hits, 3 runs in 7 innings (pitched to two batters in eighth); off Kucks 1 hit, 0 runs in 1 inning; off Dickson 0 hits, 0 runs in 1 inning. Wild pitch—Ford. Winning pitcher—Spahn. Losing pitcher—Ford. Umpires—Flaherty (A.L.), Barlick (N.L.), Berry (A.L.), Gorman (N.L.), Umont (A.L.) and Jackowski (N.L.). Time—2:17. Attendance—71,563.

Monday, October 6—At New York

Milwaukee (N.L.)	AB.	R.	H.	O.	A.	E.
Bruton, cf	3	0	2	2	0	0
Schoendienst, 2b	3	0	1	0	1	0
Mathews, 3b	4	0	1	1	3	0
Aaron, rf	4	0	0	1	0	0
Covington, lf	4	0	1	2	0	0
bWise	0	0	0	0	0	0
Torre, 1b	3	0	0	9	1	0
Crandall, c	3	0	0	8	1	0
Logan, ss	3	0	0	0	3	0
Burdette, p	2	0	0	1	0	0
Pizarro, p	0	0	0	0	1	0
aHanebrink	1	0	0	0	0	0
Willey, p	0	0	0	0	0	0
Totals	30	0	5	24	10	0

New York (A.L.)	AB.	R.	H.	O.	A.	E.
Bauer, rf	4	1	1	2	0	0
Lumpe, 3b	3	0	1	0	1	0
Richardson, 3b	1	0	0	0	1	0
Mantle, cf	3	1	2	2	0	0
Berra, c	4	1	1	11	0	0
Howard, lf	3	1	0	3	1	0
Skowron, 1b	4	1	1	5	1	0
McDougald, 2b	4	2	2	3	1	0
Kubek, ss	4	0	1	1	1	0
Turley, p	3	0	1	0	0	0
Totals	33	7	10	27	6	0

Milwaukee .... 0 0 0 0 0 0 0 0 0—0
New York .... 0 0 1 0 0 6 0 0 *—7

aFouled out for Pizarro in eighth. bRan for Covington in ninth. Runs batted in—Berra, Skowron, McDougald 3, Turley 2. Two-base hits—Berra, McDougald. Home run—McDougald. Sacrifice hit—Schoendienst. Double plays—Mathews and Torre; Howard, McDougald and Skowron. Left on bases—Milwaukee 7, New York 4. Earned runs—New York 7, Milwaukee 0. Bases on balls—Off Turley 3, off Burdette 1, off Pizarro 1. Struck out—By Turley 10, by Burdette 4, by Pizarro 3, by Willey 2. Pitching records—Off Burdette 8 hits, 6 runs in 5⅓ innings; off Pizarro 2 hits, 1 run in 1⅔ innings; off Willey 0 hits, 0 runs in 1 inning. Wild pitch—Pizarro. Winning pitcher—Turley. Losing pitcher—Burdette. Umpires—Barlick (N.L.), Berry (A.L.), Gorman (N.L.), Flaherty (A.L.), Jackowski (N.L.) and Umont (A.L.). Time—2:19. Attendance—65,279.

Wednesday, October 8—At Milwaukee

New York (A.L.)	AB.	R.	H.	O.	A.	E.
Carey, 3b	5	0	0	0	1	0
McDougald, 2b	5	1	2	6	4	0
Bauer, rf	5	1	2	0	0	0
Mantle, cf	5	1	1	0	0	0
Howard, lf	5	1	2	3	1	0
Berra, c	4	0	2	14	1	0
Skowron, 1b	4	0	1	6	2	0
Kubek, ss	2	0	0	0	1	0
aSlaughter	1	0	0	0	0	0
Duren, p	2	0	0	0	0	0
Turley, p	0	0	0	0	0	0
Ford, p	1	0	0	0	0	0
Ditmar, p	1	0	0	1	0	1
bLumpe, ss	1	0	0	0	1	0
Totals	41	4	10	30	11	1

Milwaukee (N.L.)	AB.	R.	H.	O.	A.	E.
Schoendienst, 2b	4	1	2	6	2	1
Logan, ss	2	1	0	1	3	2
Mathews, 3b	5	0	0	1	3	0
Aaron, rf	5	0	3	2	0	0
Adcock, 1b	4	0	1	6	0	0
cMantilla	0	0	0	0	0	0
Crandall, c	4	0	0	7	1	0
dTorre	1	0	0	0	0	0
Covington, lf	4	1	2	3	0	0
Pafko, cf	2	0	1	3	0	0
Bruton, cf	2	0	0	3	0	1
Spahn, p	4	0	1	1	2	0
McMahon, p	0	0	0	0	0	0
Totals	37	3	10	30	11	4

New York .... 1 0 0 0 0 1 0 0 0 2—4
Milwaukee .... 1 1 0 0 0 0 0 0 0 1—3

aGrounded out for Kubek in sixth. bStruck out for Ditmar in sixth. cRan for Adcock in tenth. dPopped out for Crandall in tenth. Runs batted in—McDougald, Bauer, Berra, Skowron, Aaron 2, Spahn. Two-base hit—Schoendienst. Home runs—Bauer, McDougald. Sacrifice hits—Logan 2. Sacrifice fly—Berra. Double plays—Howard and Berra; Crandall and Schoendienst. Left on bases—New York 10, Milwaukee 9. Earned runs—New York 4, Milwaukee 3. Bases on balls—Off Spahn 2, off Ford 1, off Duren 2. Struck out—By Spahn 5, by McMahon 1, by Ford 2, by Ditmar 2, by Duren 8. Pitching records—Off Spahn 9 hits, 4 runs in 9⅔ innings; off McMahon 1 hit, 0 runs in ⅓ inning; off Ford 5 hits, 2 runs in 1⅓ innings; off Ditmar 2 hits, 0 runs in 3⅔ innings; off Duren 3 hits, 1 run in 4⅔ innings; off Turley 0 hits, 0 runs in ⅓ inning. Winning pitcher—Duren. Losing pitcher—Spahn. Umpires—Berry (A.L.), Gorman (N.L.), Flaherty

(A.L.), Barlick (N.L.), Umont (A.L.) and Jackowski (N.L.). Time—3:07. Attendance—46,367.

Thursday, October 9—At Milwaukee

New York (A.L.)	AB.	R.	H.	O.	A.	E.
Bauer, rf	5	0	0	2	0	0
McDougald, 2b	5	0	2	3	6	0
Mantle, cf	4	0	0	2	0	0
Berra, c	4	2	1	3	1	0
Howard, lf	3	2	2	3	0	0
Lumpe, 3b	3	0	0	0	2	0
Carey, 3b	1	1	1	1	0	0
Skowron, 1b	4	1	2	12	0	0
Kubek, ss	2	0	0	1	2	0
Larsen, p	1	0	0	0	0	0
Turley, p	2	0	0	0	1	0
Totals	34	6	8	27	12	0

Milwaukee (N.L.)	AB.	R.	H.	O.	A.	E.
Schoendienst, 2b	5	1	1	5	3	0
Bruton, cf	3	0	1	1	0	0
Torre, 1b	2	0	0	10	0	2
Aaron, rf	3	0	1	4	0	0
Covington, lf	4	0	0	1	0	0
Mathews, 3b	1	0	0	1	2	0
Crandall, c	4	1	1	4	1	0
Logan, ss	4	0	0	1	5	0
Burdette, p	3	0	0	0	2	0
McMahon, p	0	0	0	0	0	0
aAdcock	1	0	1	0	0	0
bMantilla	0	0	0	0	0	0
Totals	30	2	5	27	13	2

```
New York ............. 0 2 0   0 0 0   0 4 0—6
Milwaukee ........... 1 0 0   0 0 1   0 0 0—2
```

aSingled for McMahon in ninth. bRan for Adcock in ninth. Runs batted in—Skowron 4, Kubek, Howard, Covington, Crandall. Two-base hits—McDougald, Berra. Home runs—Crandall, Skowron. Sacrifice hits—Torre, Howard, Turley. Sacrifice fly—Kubek. Stolen base—Howard. Double play—McDougald and Skowron. Left on bases—New York 7, Milwaukee 8. Earned runs—New York 4, Milwaukee 2. Bases on balls—Off Larsen 3, off Turley 3, off Burdette 2, off McMahon 1. Struck out—By Larsen 1, by Turley 2, by Burdette 3, by McMahon 2. Pitching records—Off Larsen 3 hits, 1 run in 2⅓ innings; off Turley 2 hits, 1 run in 6⅔ innings; off Burdette 7 hits, 6 runs in 8 innings; off McMahon 1 hit, 0 runs in 1 inning. Winning pitcher—Turley. Losing pitcher—Burdette. Umpires—Gorman (N.L.), Flaherty (A.L.), Barlick (N.L.), Berry (A.L.), Jackowski (N.L.) and Umont (A.L.). Time—2:31. Attendance—46,367.

COMPOSITE BATTING AVERAGES
New York Yankees

Player-Position	G.	AB.	R.	H.	2B.	3B.	HR.	RBI.	BA.
Kucks, p	2	1	0	1	0	0	0	0	1.000
Bauer, rf	7	31	6	10	1	0	4	8	.323
McDougald, 2b	7	28	5	9	2	0	2	4	.321
Skowron, 1b	7	27	3	7	0	0	2	7	.259
Mantle, cf	7	24	4	6	0	1	2	3	.250
Howard, lf-ph	6	18	4	4	0	0	0	2	.222
Berra, c	7	27	3	6	3	0	0	2	.222
Turley, p	4	5	0	1	0	0	0	2	.200
Lumpe, ph-3b-ss	6	12	0	2	0	0	0	0	.167
Siebern, lf	3	8	1	1	0	0	0	0	.125
Carey, 3b	5	12	1	1	0	0	0	0	.083
Kubek, ss	7	21	0	1	0	0	0	1	.048
Richardson, 3b	4	5	0	0	0	0	0	0	.000
Ford, p	3	4	1	0	0	0	0	0	.000
Duren, p	3	3	0	0	0	0	0	0	.000
Maas, p	1	0	0	0	0	0	0	0	.000
Dickson, p	2	0	0	0	0	0	0	0	.000
Monroe, p	1	0	0	0	0	0	0	0	.000
Larsen, p	2	2	0	0	0	0	0	0	.000
Ditmar, p	1	1	0	0	0	0	0	0	.000
Slaughter, ph	4	3	1	0	0	0	0	0	.000
Throneberry, ph	1	1	0	0	0	0	0	0	.000
Totals	7	233	29	49	5	1	10	29	.210

Milwaukee Braves

Player-Position	G.	AB.	R.	H.	2B.	3B.	HR.	RBI.	BA.
Bruton, ph-cf-pr	7	17	2	7	0	0	1	2	.412
Spahn, p	3	12	0	4	0	0	0	3	.333
Pafko, cf-lf-rf	4	9	0	3	0	0	0	0	.333
Aaron, rf-cf	7	27	3	9	2	0	0	2	.333
Adcock, 1b-ph	4	13	1	4	0	0	0	0	.308
Schoendienst, 2b	7	30	5	9	3	1	0	0	.300
Covington, lf	7	26	2	7	0	0	0	4	.269
Crandall, c	7	25	4	6	0	0	1	3	.240
Torre, ph-1b	7	17	0	3	0	0	0	1	.176
Mathews, 3b	7	25	3	4	2	0	0	1	.160
Logan, ss	7	25	3	3	2	0	0	2	.120
Burdette, p	3	9	1	1	0	0	1	3	.111
Mantilla, ss-pr	4	0	1	0	0	0	0	0	.000
Rush, p	1	2	0	0	0	0	0	0	.000
McMahon, p	3	0	0	0	0	0	0	0	.000
Willey, p	1	0	0	0	0	0	0	0	.000
Pizarro, p	1	0	0	0	0	0	0	0	.000
Wise, ph-pr	2	1	0	0	0	0	0	0	.000
Hanebrink, ph	2	2	0	0	0	0	0	0	.000
Totals	7	240	25	60	10	1	3	24	.250

COMPOSITE PITCHING AVERAGES
New York Yankees

Pitcher	G.	IP.	H.	R.	E.	SO.	BB.	W.	L.	ERA.
Ditmar	1	3⅔	2	0	0	2	0	0	0	0.00
Larsen	2	9⅓	9	1	1	9	6	1	0	0.96
Duren	3	9⅓	7	2	2	14	6	1	1	1.93
Kucks	2	4⅓	4	1	1	0	1	0	0	2.08
Turley	4	16⅓	10	5	5	13	7	2	1	2.76
Ford	3	15⅓	19	8	7	16	5	0	1	4.11
Dickson	2	4	4	2	2	1	0	0	0	4.50
Monroe	1	1	3	3	3	1	1	0	0	27.00
Maas	1	⅓	2	3	3	0	1	0	0	81.00
Totals	7	63⅔	60	25	24	56	27	4	3	3.39

Milwaukee Braves

Pitcher	G.	IP.	H.	R.	E.	SO.	BB.	W.	L.	ERA.
Willey	1	1	0	0	0	2	0	0	0	0.00
Spahn	3	28⅔	19	7	7	18	8	2	1	2.20
Rush	1	6	3	2	2	2	5	0	1	3.00
McMahon	3	3⅓	2	2	2	5	3	0	0	5.40
Pizarro	1	1⅔	2	1	1	3	1	0	0	5.40
Burdette	3	22⅓	22	17	14	12	4	1	2	5.64
Totals	7	63	49	29	26	42	21	3	4	3.71

SERIES OF 1959

	W.	L.	Pct.
Los Angeles N. L.	4	2	.667
Chicago A. L.	2	4	.333

The California Gold Rush had its diamond version in the richest Series in history, and one of the most dramatic from the standpoint of the clubs involved, when the Dodgers brought the world championship to Los Angeles by defeating the White Sox, four games to two.

Three of the contests were played in Los Angeles Memorial Coliseum, the huge football stadium converted into a baseball field for use by the Dodgers. Each game set an attendance record, drawing successive crowds of 92,394, 92,650 and 92,706 for a total of 277,750. With the addition of 143,034 for the three games at Comiskey Park in Chicago, the attendance total of 420,784 broke all Series gate records and the net receipts of $5,628,809.44, including $3,000,000 for the TV-radio rights, surpassed all previous money marks.

The Dodgers tried for 65 years before winning a world crown for Brooklyn, but it took them only two years to accomplish the same feat after moving to the West Coast. They were the first club ever to rise from seventh place one year—their finish in 1958—to the throne the next season. But, before doing so, Manager Walt Alston's crew had to win out in a red-hot pennant race, climaxed by the third playoff in the annals of the National League.

Tied with the Milwaukee Braves at the end of the regular schedule, the Dodgers proceeded to sweep two successive games from the defending champions, 3 to 2 and 6 to 5, to capture the flag.

The White Sox won their first pennant in the American League since 1919, when the infamous "Black Sox" played the Cincinnati Reds. Bill Veeck and his associates hit the jackpot in their first year of ownership of the club after acquiring the majority stock interest of Mrs. Dorothy Comiskey Rigney. Featuring tight defense, speed on the bases and strong pitching, Al Lopez' "Go-Go" Sox finished five games in front of runner-up Cleveland.

A National League castoff, Ted Kluszewski, was the hero in a losing cause for the White Sox. The veteran first baseman, formerly with the Cincinnati Reds and Pittsburgh Pirates, drove in 10 runs to set a record for RBIs in a six-game Series and tie the mark for most RBIs in a Classic of any length.

The Dodgers had heroes aplenty. Catcher Johnny Roseboro earned his share of the laurels for his work in throwing the brakes on the running of the White Sox. Charley Neal won one game with a pair of homers, Gil Hodges decided another with a mammoth round-tripper, Carl Furillo came through with a winning pinch-single and Chuck Essegian set a Series record as the first pinch-hitter ever to deliver two home runs.

However, one player stood out above all others. Larry Sherry, 24-year-old right-hander, relieved in all four games that the Dodgers won, picking up two victories and saving two. For the first time, no complete game was pitched in the Classic by the staff of either club. Sherry's remarkable work proved the big difference. In a total of 12⅔ innings, he allowed only eight hits and one run.

Opening the Series in Chicago, the White Sox, who often had been compared to Charles A. (The Old Roman) Comiskey's Hitless Wonders of 1906, came up with a surprising display of power to overwhelm the Dodgers, 11 to 0. The Pale Hose tied the Series record for the most one-sided shutout, matching the St. Louis Cardinals' victory over the Detroit Tigers in the final game of 1934.

After starting with two runs in the first inning, the Windy City crew exploded for seven in the third, with the aid of three errors, two by Duke Snider and one by Neal. Kluszewski featured the outburst with a homer and then homered again, after a single by Jim Landis, to wrap up the run production in the fourth inning. Early Wynn, breezing behind his big lead, left the mound in the eighth, when his elbow stiffened, and Gerry Staley completed the shutout.

A club with less spirit and desire might have been discouraged by the walloping, but the Dodgers came back to win the second game, 4 to 3.

The White Sox again jumped off to a 2 to 0 lead in the first inning off Johnny Podres. The Dodgers broke their drouth when Neal homered off Bob Shaw in the fifth inning.

In the seventh, with two out, Essegian batted for Podres and came through with a round-tripper to tie the score at 2 to 2. Jim Gilliam walked and Neal then belted his second homer of the game to send the Dodgers ahead.

Sherry, making his first relief appearance of the Series, was on the ropes in the eighth when Kluszewski and Sherm Lollar singled. Torgeson ran for Kluszewski. Al Smith then slammed a double to deep left-center, scoring Torgeson, but Lollar was nailed at the plate on Wally Moon's throw to Maury Wills and the shortstop's relay to Roseboro.

After an open date for travel, the Dodgers opened the California phase of the Classic with a 3 to 1 victory for Don Drysdale, who had Sherry's help in gaining the decision. Dick Donovan, pitching for the White Sox, yielded only one single and did not issue a pass in the first six innings, but his teammates wasted several scoring chances.

In the seventh, after Neal singled, Donovan's control deserted him. With two out, both Norm Larker and Hodges drew passes to load the bases. Staley then replaced Donovan. The Dodgers countered with Furillo, who batted for Don Demeter and rapped a ground single into center field scoring two runs.

The White Sox, fighting back, kayoed Drysdale in the eighth, but Sherry pitched out of the jam at the expense of only one run.

Sherry once more was the "toast of Los Angeles" when the Dodgers won the fourth game of the Series, 4 to 3, on a homer by Hodges in the eighth inning.

Roger Craig and Wynn, mound opponents in the opener, faced each other again. The Dodgers chased Wynn in the third inning, scoring four runs after two were out. Although in frequent trouble, Craig staved off the White Sox until the seventh. With one run in, two on and two out, Lollar proceeded to tie the score with a homer.

Sherry took the mound for the Dodgers in the eighth and was the winner when

Hodges blasted his homer off Staley to the right of the screen in left-center field.

On the verge of elimination, the White Sox came back courageously to gain a 1 to 0 victory in a game that was highlighted by the maneuvering of Managers Lopez and Alston. The only run was scored off Sandy Koufax in the fourth inning when Fox singled, took third on another single by Landis and came home when Lollar grounded into a double play.

For the first time in Series history, three pitchers—Shaw, Billy Pierce and Donovan—combined in a shutout. Pierce's role was relatively minor, except that his appearance figured in the strategic moves of the managers in the eighth inning.

The victory of the White Sox forced the clubs to return to Chicago. After another open date for traveling, the Dodgers brought the Classic to a conclusion by blasting their way to a 9 to 3 triumph.

Wynn, making his third start of the Series, was belted for two runs in the third inning when Moon walked and Snider homered. The Dodgers then kayoed the veteran righthander during a six-run explosion in the fourth.

Podres, with an 8 to 0 lead, appeared all set for an easy victory, but the lefthander hit Landis with a pitch in the home half of the fourth, walked Lollar and was tagged for a homer by Kluszewski. When Smith drew a walk, that was all for Podres. Sherry relieved, and that was all for the White Sox. The hard-firing youngster blanked the A.L. champs over the remainder of the route.

In the ninth, Essegian batted for Snider and homered off Ray Moore to write a record finish to the Series.

The box scores:

Thursday, October 1—At Chicago

Los Ang. (N.L.)	AB.	R.	H.	O.	A.	E.
Gilliam, 3b	4	0	1	0	1	0
Neal, 2b	4	0	2	0	3	1
Moon, lf	4	0	1	2	0	0
Snider, cf	2	0	0	2	0	2
Demeter, cf	1	0	0	0	0	0
Larker, rf	4	0	1	4	0	0
Hodges, 1b	4	0	2	10	0	0
Roseboro, c	4	0	0	5	0	0
Wills, ss	3	0	1	1	2	0
cFurillo	1	0	0	0	0	0
Craig, p	1	0	0	0	1	0
Churn, p	0	0	0	0	1	0
Labine, p	0	0	0	0	0	0
aEssegian	1	0	0	0	0	0
Koufax, p	0	0	0	0	0	0
bFairly	1	0	0	0	0	0
Klippstein, p	0	0	0	0	1	0
Totals	34	0	8	24	9	3

Chicago (A.L.)	AB.	R.	H.	O.	A.	E.
Aparicio, ss	5	0	0	3	3	0
Fox, 2b	4	2	1	2	2	0
Landis, cf	4	3	3	1	0	0
Kluszewski, 1b	4	2	3	8	2	0
Lollar, c	3	1	0	7	0	0
Goodman, 3b	2	1	1	0	0	0
Esposito, 3b	2	0	0	1	0	0
Smith, lf	4	1	2	2	0	0
Rivera, rf	4	1	0	2	0	0
Wynn, p	3	0	1	1	1	0
Staley, p	1	0	0	0	1	0
Totals	36	11	11	27	9	0

Los Angeles .... 0 0 0   0 0 0   0 0 0— 0
Chicago .... 2 0 7   2 0 0   0 0 *—11

aStruck out for Labine in fifth. bGrounded out for Koufax in seventh. cFlied out for Wills in ninth. Runs batted in—Landis, Kluszewski 5, Lollar, Goodman, Wynn. Two-base hits—Fox, Smith 2, Wynn. Home runs—Kluszewski 2. Stolen base—Neal. Sacrifice fly—Lollar. Double play—Aparicio, Fox and Kluszewski. Left on bases—Los Angeles 8, Chicago 3. Earned runs—Chicago 7, Los Angeles 0. Bases on balls—Off Wynn 1, off Craig 1. Struck out—By Wynn 6, by Staley 1, by Craig 1, by Labine 1, by Koufax 1, by Klippstein 2. Pitching records—Off Wynn 6 hits, 0 runs in 7 innings (pitched to one batter in eighth); off Staley 2 hits, 0 runs in 2 innings; off Craig 5 hits, 5 runs in 2⅓ innings; off Churn 5 hits, 6 runs in ⅔ inning (pitched to two batters in fourth); off Labine 0 hits, 0 runs in 1 inning; off Koufax 0 hits, 0 runs in 2 innings; off Klippstein 1 hit, 0 runs in 2 innings. Winner—Wynn. Loser—Craig. Umpires—Summers (A.L.), Dascoli (N.L.), Hurley (A.L.), Secory (N.L.), Rice (A.L.), Dixon (N.L.). Time—2:35. Attendance—48,013.

Friday, October 2—At Chicago

Los Ang. (N.L.)	AB.	R.	H.	O.	A.	E.
Gilliam, 3b	4	1	1	1	1	0
Neal, 2b	5	2	2	2	4	0
Moon, lf	3	0	1	1	1	0
Snider, cf	4	0	1	1	0	0
Demeter, cf	0	0	0	0	0	0
Larker, rf	3	0	0	4	0	0
Sherry, p	1	0	0	1	1	0
Hodges, 1b	4	0	0	10	1	0
Roseboro, c	4	0	1	6	0	0
Wills, ss	4	0	1	1	6	1
Podres, p	2	0	1	0	0	0
aEssegian	1	1	1	0	0	0
Fairly, rf	1	0	0	0	0	0
Totals	36	4	9	27	14	1

Chicago (A.L.)	AB.	R.	H.	O.	A.	E.
Aparicio, ss	5	1	2	3	1	0
Fox, 2b	4	0	0	0	5	0
Landis, cf	3	1	0	2	0	0
Kluszewski, 1b	4	0	1	9	0	0
bTorgeson, 1b	0	1	0	0	0	0
Lollar, c	4	0	2	4	0	0
Smith, lf	3	0	1	2	0	0
Phillips, 3b	3	0	1	2	0	0
cGoodman, 3b	1	0	0	0	0	0
McAnany, rf	3	0	0	3	0	0
Rivera, rf	1	0	0	2	0	0
Shaw, p	3	0	1	0	1	0
Lown, p	0	0	0	0	0	0
dCash	1	0	0	0	0	0
Totals	35	3	8	27	7	0

Los Angeles .... 0 0 0   0 1 0   3 0 0—4
Chicago .... 2 0 0   0 0 0   0 1 0—3

aHit home run for Podres in seventh. bRan for Kluszewski in eighth. cStruck out for Phillips in eighth. dGrounded out for Lown in ninth. Runs batted in—Neal 3, Essegian, Kluszewski, Lollar, Smith. Two-base hits—Aparicio, Phillips, Smith. Home runs—Neal 2, Essegian. Stolen bases—Moon, Gilliam. Left on bases—Chicago 8, Los Angeles 7. Earned runs—Los Angeles 4, Chicago 3. Bases on balls—Off Podres 3, off Shaw 1, off Lown 1. Struck out—By Podres 3, by Sherry 1, by Shaw 1, by Lown 3. Pitching records—Off Podres 5 hits, 2 runs in 6 innings; off Sherry 3 hits, 1 run in 3 innings; off Shaw 8 hits, 4 runs in 6⅔ innings; off Lown 1 hit, 0 runs in 2⅓ innings. Winner—Podres. Loser—Shaw. Umpires—Dascoli (N.L.), Hurley (A.L.), Secory (N.L.), Summers (A.L.), Rice (A.L.) and Dixon (N.L.). Time—2:21. Attendance—47,368.

Sunday, October 4—At Los Angeles

Chicago (A.L.)	AB	R	H	O	A	E
Aparicio, ss	4	0	2	0	3	0
Fox, 2b	4	0	3	3	6	0
Landis, cf	5	0	1	2	0	0
Kluszewski, 1b	3	1	1	11	1	0
Lollar, c	4	0	2	5	1	0
Goodman, 3b	3	0	2	1	1	0
cEsposito, 3b	0	0	0	0	0	0
Smith, lf	4	0	0	0	0	0
Rivera, rf	3	0	0	1	0	0
Donovan, p	3	0	1	1	1	0
Staley, p	0	0	0	0	0	0
dCash	1	0	0	0	0	0
Totals	34	1	12	24	13	0

Los Ang. (N.L.)	AB	R	H	O	A	E
Gilliam, 3b	4	0	0	3	2	0
Neal, 2b	4	1	2	3	2	0
Moon, rf	4	0	0	1	0	0
Larker, lf	2	1	0	1	0	0
Hodges, 1b	2	0	1	6	1	0
Demeter, cf	2	0	0	0	0	0
aFurillo	1	0	1	0	0	0
bFairly, cf	0	0	0	0	0	0
Roseboro, c	3	0	0	9	3	0
Wills, ss	3	1	1	3	2	0
Drysdale, p	2	0	0	1	1	0
Sherry, p	0	0	0	0	0	0
Totals	27	3	5	27	11	0

Chicago .... 0 0 0 0 0 0 0 1 0—1
Los Angeles .... 0 0 0 0 0 0 2 1 *—3

aSingled for Demeter in seventh. bRan for Furillo in seventh. cRan for Goodman in eighth. dStruck out for Staley in ninth. Runs batted in—Furillo 2, Neal. Two-base hit—Neal. Stolen base—Landis. Sacrifice hit—Sherry. Double plays—Aparicio, Fox and Kluszewski; Roseboro and Neal; Gilliam, Neal and Hodges; Wills, Neal and Hodges. Left on bases—Chicago 11, Los Angeles 3. Earned runs—Chicago 1, Los Angeles 3. Bases on balls—Off Drysdale 4, off Donovan 2. Struck out—By Drysdale 5, by Sherry 3, by Donovan 5. Pitching records—Off Drysdale 11 hits, 1 run in 7 innings (pitched to two batters in eighth); off Sherry 1 hit, 0 runs in 2 innings; off Donovan 2 hits, 2 runs in 6⅔ innings; off Staley 3 hits 1 run in 1⅓ innings. Hit by pitcher—By Sherry (Goodman). Winner—Drysdale. Loser—Donovan. Umpires—Hurley (A.L.), Secory (N.L.), Summers (A.L.), Dascoli (N.L.), Dixon (N.L.) and Rice (A.L.). Time—2:33. Attendance—92,394.

Monday, October 5—At Los Angeles

Chicago (A.L.)	AB	R	H	O	A	E
Landis, cf	5	1	1	0	0	1
Aparicio, ss	3	0	1	0	2	1
Fox, 2b	5	1	3	3	4	0
Kluszewski, 1b	4	1	2	9	0	0
Lollar, c	4	1	1	6	2	0
Goodman, 3b	4	0	0	0	0	0
Smith, lf	3	0	2	3	0	0
Rivera, rf	3	0	0	3	1	0

	AB	R	H	O	A	E
Wynn, p	1	0	0	0	1	0
Lown, p	0	0	0	0	0	0
aCash	1	0	0	0	0	0
Pierce, p	0	0	0	0	0	1
cTorgeson	1	0	0	0	0	0
Staley, p	0	0	0	0	0	0
Totals	34	4	10	24	10	3

Los Ang. (N.L.)	AB	R	H	O	A	E
Gilliam, 3b	4	0	0	0	1	0
Neal, 2b	4	0	0	4	4	0
Moon, rf-lf	4	1	2	3	0	0
Larker, lf	2	1	1	0	0	0
bFurillo, rf	1	0	0	0	0	0
Fairly, rf	1	0	0	0	0	0
Hodges, 1b	4	2	2	10	0	0
Demeter, cf	3	1	2	1	0	0
Roseboro, c	3	0	1	7	0	0
Wills, ss	4	0	1	2	6	0
Craig, p	2	0	0	0	1	0
Sherry, p	0	0	0	0	0	0
Totals	32	5	9	27	12	0

Chicago .... 0 0 0 0 0 0 4 0 0—4
Los Angeles .... 0 0 4 0 0 0 0 1 *—5

aStruck out for Lown in fourth. bStruck out for Larker in fifth. cGrounded out for Pierce in seventh. Runs batted in—Kluszewski, Lollar 3, Hodges 2, Roseboro. Two-base hit—Fox. Home runs—Lollar, Hodges. Stolen bases—Aparicio, Wills. Sacrifice hits—Roseboro, Craig, Aparicio. Double plays—Wills, Neal and Hodges; Neal, Wills and Hodges. Left on bases—Chicago 9, Los Angeles 6. Earned runs—Los Angeles 4, Chicago 4. Bases on balls—Off Craig 4, off Sherry 1, off Pierce 1. Struck out—By Craig 7, by Wynn 2, by Pierce 2, by Staley 2. Pitching records—Off Craig 10 hits, 4 runs in 7 innings; off Sherry 0 hits, 0 runs in 2 innings; off Wynn 8 hits, 4 runs in 2⅔ innings; off Lown 0 hits, 0 runs in ⅓ inning; off Pierce 0 hits, 0 runs in 3 innings; off Staley 1 hit, 1 run in 2 innings. Passed ball—Lollar. Winner—Sherry. Loser—Staley. Umpires—Secory (N.L.), Summers (A.L.), Dascoli (N.L.), Hurley (A.L.), Dixon (N.L.) and Rice (A.L.). Time—2:30. Attendance—92,650.

Tuesday, October 6—At Los Angeles

Chicago (A.L.)	AB	R	H	O	A	E
Aparicio, ss	4	0	2	3	5	0
Fox, 2b	3	1	1	4	4	0
Landis, cf	4	0	1	2	0	0
Lollar, c	4	0	0	1	0	0
Kluszewski, 1b	4	0	0	12	0	0
Smith, rf-lf	4	0	0	1	0	0
Phillips, 3b	3	0	1	1	2	0
McAnany, lf	1	0	0	1	0	0
Rivera, rf	0	0	0	2	0	0
Shaw, p	1	0	0	0	3	0
Pierce, p	0	0	0	0	0	0
Donovan, p	0	0	0	0	0	0
Totals	28	1	5	27	14	0

Los Ang. (N.L.)	AB	R	H	O	A	E
Gilliam, 3b	5	0	4	0	3	0
Neal, 2b	5	0	1	5	2	0
Moon, rf-cf	4	0	1	0	0	0
Larker, lf	4	0	0	3	1	0
Hodges, 1b	4	0	3	7	1	0
Demeter, cf	3	0	0	4	0	0
eFairly	0	0	0	0	0	0
fRepulski, rf	0	0	0	0	0	0
Roseboro, c	3	0	0	6	1	0
gFurillo	1	0	0	0	0	0
Pignatano, c	0	0	0	1	0	0
Wills, ss	2	0	0	1	2	0

1959 WORLD SERIES

	AB.	R.	H.	O.	A.	E.
aEssegian	0	0	0	0	0	0
bZimmer, ss	1	0	0	0	1	0
Koufax, p	2	0	0	0	0	0
cSnider	1	0	0	0	0	0
dPodres	0	0	0	0	0	0
Williams, p	0	0	0	0	0	0
hSherry	1	0	0	0	0	0
Totals	36	0	9	27	11	0

Chicago.............. 0 0 0 1 0 0 0 0 0—1
Los Angeles....... 0 0 0 0 0 0 0 0 0—0

aWalked for Wills in seventh. bRan for Essegian in seventh. cHit into force play for Koufax in seventh. dRan for Snider in seventh. eAnnounced as batter for Demeter in eighth. fWalked intentionally for Fairly in eighth. gPopped out for Roseboro in eighth. hGrounded out for Williams in ninth. Runs batted in—None (run scored on Lollar's double play). Three-base hit—Hodges. Stolen base—Gilliam. Sacrifice hits—Shaw 2. Double play—Neal and Hodges. Left on bases—Chicago 5, Los Angeles 11. Earned runs—Chicago 1, Los Angeles 0. Bases on balls—Off Koufax 1, off Williams 2, off Shaw 1. Struck out—By Koufax 6, by Williams 1, by Shaw 1. Pitching records—Off Koufax 5 hits, 1 run in 7 innings; off Williams 0 hits, 0 runs in 2 innings; off Shaw 9 hits, 0 runs in 7⅓ innings; off Pierce 0 hits, 0 runs in 0 innings (pitched to one batter in eighth); off Donovan 0 hits, 0 runs in 1⅔ innings. Wild pitch—Shaw. Winner—Shaw. Loser—Koufax. Umpires—Summers (A.L.), Dascoli (N.L.), Hurley (A.L.), Secory (N.L.), Dixon (N.L.) and Rice (A.L.). Time—2:28. Attendance—92,706.

Thursday, October 8—At Chicago

Los Ang. (N.L.)	AB.	R.	H.	O.	A.	E.
Gilliam, 3b	4	1	0	0	2	0
Neal, 2b	5	1	3	4	4	0
Moon, lf	4	2	1	3	0	0
Snider, cf-rf	3	1	1	2	0	0
eEssegian	1	1	1	0	0	0
Fairly, rf	0	0	0	0	0	0
Hodges, 1b	5	0	1	10	0	0
Larker, rf	1	0	1	0	0	0
aDemeter, cf	3	1	1	4	0	0
Roseboro, c	4	0	0	2	0	0
Wills, ss	4	1	1	2	3	0
Podres, p	2	1	1	0	1	0
Sherry, p	2	0	2	0	2	0
Totals	38	9	13	27	12	0

Chicago (A.L.)	AB.	R.	H.	O.	A.	E.
Aparicio, ss	5	0	1	1	2	1
Fox, 2b	4	0	1	2	2	0
Landis, cf	3	1	1	2	0	0
Lollar, c	3	1	0	5	2	0
Kluszewski, 1b	4	1	2	10	0	0
Smith, lf	2	0	0	2	0	0
Phillips, 3b-rf	4	0	1	3	1	0
McAnany, rf	1	0	0	1	0	0
bGoodman, 3b	3	0	0	0	1	0
Wynn, p	1	0	0	0	1	0
Donovan, p	0	0	0	0	0	0
Lown, p	0	0	0	0	0	0
cTorgeson	0	0	0	0	0	0
Staley, p	0	0	0	0	1	0
dRomano	1	0	0	0	0	0
Pierce, p	0	0	0	0	0	0
Moore, p	0	0	0	0	0	0
fCash	1	0	0	0	0	0
Totals	32	3	6	27	9	1

Los Angeles....... 0 0 2 6 0 0 0 0 1—9
Chicago.............. 0 0 0 3 0 0 0 0 0—3

aRan for Larker in fourth. bStruck out for McAnany in fourth. cWalked for Lown in fourth. dGrounded out for Staley in seventh. eHomered for Snider in ninth. fFlied out for Moore in ninth. Runs batted in—Neal 2, Moon 2, Snider 2, Essegian, Wills, Podres, Kluszewski 3. Two-base hits—Podres, Neal, Fox, Kluszewski. Home runs—Snider, Moon, Kluszewski, Essegian. Sacrifice hit—Roseboro. Double play—Podres, Neal and Hodges. Left on bases—Los Angeles 7, Chicago 7. Earned runs—Los Angeles 9, Chicago 3. Bases on balls—Off Wynn 3, off Donovan 1, off Podres 3, off Sherry 1. Struck out—By Wynn 2, by Pierce 1, by Moore 1, by Podres 1, by Sherry 1. Pitching records—Off Wynn 5 hits, 5 runs in 3⅓ innings; off Donovan 2 hits, 3 runs in 0 innings (pitched to three batters in fourth); off Lown 1 hit, 0 runs in ⅔ innings; off Staley 2 hits, 0 runs in 3 innings; off Pierce 2 hits, 0 runs in 1 inning; off Moore 1 hit, 1 run in 1 inning; off Podres 2 hits, 3 runs in 3⅓ innings; off Sherry 4 hits, 0 runs in 5⅔ innings. Hit by pitcher—By Podres (Landis). Winner—Sherry. Loser—Wynn. Umpires—Dascoli (N.L.), Hurley (A.L.), Secory (N.L.), Summers (A.L.), Rice (A.L.) and Dixon (N.L.). Time—2:33. Attendance—47,653.

COMPOSITE BATTING AVERAGES
Los Angeles Dodgers

Player-Position	G.	AB.	R.	H.	2B.	3B.	HR.	RBI.	BA.
Essegian, ph	4	3	2	2	0	0	2	2	.667
Sherry, p-ph	5	4	0	2	0	0	0	0	.500
Podres, p-pr	3	4	1	2	1	0	0	1	.500
Hodges, 1b	6	23	2	9	0	1	1	2	.391
Neal, 2b	6	27	4	10	2	0	2	6	.370
Moon, lf-rf-cf	6	23	3	6	0	0	1	2	.261
Demeter, cf-pr	6	12	2	3	0	0	0	0	.250
Wills, ss	6	20	2	5	0	0	0	1	.250
Furillo, ph-rf	4	4	0	1	0	0	0	2	.250
Gilliam, 3b	6	25	2	6	0	0	0	0	.240
Snider, cf-rf-ph	4	10	1	2	0	0	1	2	.200
Larker, rf-lf	6	16	2	3	0	0	0	0	.188
Roseboro, c	6	21	0	2	0	0	0	1	.095
Zimmer, pr-ss	1	1	0	0	0	0	0	0	.000
Pignatano, c	1	1	0	0	0	0	0	0	.000
Fairly, ph-rf-cf-pr	6	3	0	0	0	0	0	0	.000
Craig, p	2	3	0	0	0	0	0	0	.000
Churn, p	1	0	0	0	0	0	0	0	.000
Labine, p	1	0	0	0	0	0	0	0	.000
Koufax, p	2	2	0	0	0	0	0	0	.000
Klippstein, p	1	0	0	0	0	0	0	0	.000
Drysdale, p	1	2	0	0	0	0	0	0	.000
Williams, p	1	0	0	0	0	0	0	0	.000
Repulski, ph-rf	1	0	0	0	0	0	0	0	.000
Totals	6	203	21	53	3	1	7	19	.261

Chicago White Sox

Player-Position	G.	AB.	R.	H.	2B.	3B.	HR.	RBI.	BA.
Kluszewski, 1b	6	23	5	9	1	0	3	10	.391
Fox, 2b	6	24	4	9	3	0	0	0	.375
Donovan, p	3	3	0	1	0	0	0	0	.333
Aparicio, ss	6	26	1	8	1	0	0	0	.308
Phillips, 3b-rf	3	10	0	3	1	0	0	0	.300
Landis, cf	6	24	6	7	0	0	0	1	.292
Smith, lf-rf	6	20	1	5	3	0	0	1	.250
Shaw, p	2	4	0	1	0	0	0	0	.250
Goodman, 3b-ph	5	13	1	3	0	0	0	1	.231
Lollar, c	6	22	3	5	0	0	1	5	.227
Wynn, p	3	5	0	1	1	0	0	1	.200
Esposito, 3b-pr	2	2	0	0	0	0	0	0	.000
Rivera, rf	5	11	1	0	0	0	0	0	.000
Tor'son, pr-1b-ph	3	1	1	0	0	0	0	0	.000
McAnany, lf-rf	3	5	0	0	0	0	0	0	.000
Staley, p	4	0	0	0	0	0	0	0	.000
Lown, p	2	0	0	0	0	0	0	0	.000
Pierce, p	3	0	0	0	0	0	0	0	.000
Moore, p	1	0	0	0	0	0	0	0	.000
Cash, ph	4	4	0	0	0	0	0	0	.000
Romano, ph	2	1	0	0	0	0	0	0	.000
Totals	6	199	23	52	10	0	4	19	.261

COMPOSITE PITCHING AVERAGES

Los Angeles Dodgers

Pitcher	G.	IP.	H.	R.	E.	SO.	BB.	W.	L.	ERA.
Williams	1	2	0	0	0	1	2	0	0	0.00
Klippstein	1	2	1	0	0	2	0	0	0	0.00
Labine	1	1	0	0	0	1	0	0	0	0.00
Sherry	4	12⅔	8	1	1	5	2	2	0	0.71
Koufax	2	9	5	1	1	7	1	0	1	1.00
Drysdale	1	7	11	1	1	5	4	1	0	1.29
Podres	2	9⅓	7	5	5	4	6	1	0	4.82
Craig	2	9⅓	15	9	9	8	5	0	1	8.68
Churn	1	⅔	5	6	2	0	0	0	0	27.00
Totals	6	53	52	23	19	33	20	4	2	3.23

Chicago White Sox

Pitcher	G.	IP.	H.	R.	E.	SO.	BB.	W.	L.	ERA.
Lown	3	3⅓	2	0	0	3	1	0	0	0.00
Pierce	3	4	2	0	0	3	2	0	0	0.00
Staley	4	8⅓	8	2	2	3	0	0	1	2.16
Shaw	2	14	17	4	4	2	2	1	1	2.57
Donovan	3	8⅓	4	5	5	5	3	0	1	5.40
Wynn	3	13	19	9	8	10	4	1	1	5.54
Moore	1	1	1	1	1	1	0	0	0	9.00
Totals	6	52	53	21	20	27	12	2	4	3.46

SERIES OF 1960

	W.	L.	Pct.
Pittsburgh N. L.	4	3	.571
New York A. L.	3	4	.429

Every World Series takes its memorable place in the annals of the National Pastime, but the 1960 meeting of the Pittsburgh Pirates and the New York Yankees must go down in history as the weirdest and whackiest of all blue-ribbon classics. The Yankees shattered records by the dozen and overwhelmed the Pirates in three games by the fantastic scores of 16 to 3, 10 to 0 and 12 to 0, yet when it was all over, the Pirates were the world champions.

Winners in the first game, then slaughtered in the next two, the Bucs refused to quit, coming back with two successive victories. Yankee power asserted itself again in the sixth game, but the Pirates then seized the Bombers' own weapon—the homer—for a Series triumph that was supreme for excitement and thrills.

The Yankees batted .338 as a club, scored 55 runs, collected 91 hits and had 27 extra-base blows, all new Series marks. Ten of their hits were homers. Bobby Richardson, perhaps the lightest hitter of the Bombers over the regular season, turned slugger to set records for most RBIs in a game, six, and most in a Series, 12. The young second baseman also wrote his name into the books as the seventh player to hit a grand-slam homer in Series competition.

The Pirates had a team batting average of .256, with only four homers, and they scored just 27 runs, but Manager Danny Murtaugh's men truly proved themselves a "team of destiny" in a courageous battle that brought stellar honors to virtually every member of the club.

Vern Law won two games for the Pirates and made a bid for a third victory, but an injured right ankle was a factor in preventing the righthander from completing any of his three starts. Harvey Haddix also won two games, receiving credit in relief for the clincher. Roy Face was sensational in three relief appearances before weariness caught up with the little fireman in a fourth attempt. Bill Virdon saved two games with circus catches in center field and Bill Mazeroski was the muscle man with a homer that provided the biggest margin in the first game and the biggest homer of 'em all—the blow that dramatically decided the title.

The Pirates, playing steady and at times inspired ball, won the National League pennant by seven games over the Milwaukee Braves. The Yankees had a tussle for American League honors before breaking away with 15 straight victories at the end of the season to finish eight lengths ahead of the Baltimore Orioles. The flag was the Yankees' twenty-fifth and their tenth in 12 years under Manager Casey Stengel, who brought the club back to the top after a third-place finish in 1959. The Pirates' pennant was their first since 1927.

Law, who hurt his ankle five days before the Series, shook off the injury and pitched the opener in Pittsburgh, but needed Face's help to register a 6 to 4 victory.

The Yankees ignited their Series-long bombardment of the fences with a homer by Roger Maris in the first inning, only to have the Pirates leg their way to three runs off Art Ditmar in the home half of the stanza.

A single by Maris and a pass to Mickey Mantle had Law in trouble in the fourth, but Virdon made a sensational catch of a long smash by Yogi Berra against the right-center field wall. The fielding gem blunted what could have been a big inning for the Yankees, who went on to score only one run on a single by Bill Skowron.

In the Pirates' half, with Jim Coates on the mound for the Yankees, Don Hoak walked and Mazeroski hit a homer, the only round-tripper, it was to develop, that the Pirates collected in the first six games. Another Pittsburgh run scored in the sixth.

Law faltered in the eighth, giving up successive singles to Hector Lopez and Maris, but Face relieved and cut down the heart of the Yankee batting order, retiring Mantle, Berra and Skowron. In the ninth, the little righthander survived a two-run pinch-homer by Elston Howard to wrap up the decision for Law.

The second game would have been a credit to the Yankees' famed "Murderers' Row" of old. The Bombers tore Forbes Field apart with a 19-hit attack that included two tape-measure homers by Mantle, one of them a 478-foot drive over the wall to the right of center field.

Bob Friend started for the Bucs, but trailed, 3 to 1, when he was lifted for a pinch-hitter in the fourth inning. The Yankees then turned the game into a rout, going on to post a 16 to 3 victory.

The Pirates nicked Bob Turley for 13 hits—the 32-hit total for both clubs set a Series record. Despite his overwhelming lead, Turley was unable to last the route. After the Pirates counted twice in the ninth, Bobby Shantz relieved.

After an open date in the schedule, the Series resumed at Yankee Stadium, where Richardson staged his record-breaking performance with the bat in a 10 to 0 victory. Whitey Ford hurled the shutout on a four-hitter.

The Yankees, spoiling the forty-third birthday of Manager Murtaugh of the Pirates, exploded for six runs in the first inning. Bob Cerv, Mantle and Skowron started the fireworks with singles for the first run off Wilmer (Vinegar Bend) Mizell. The lefthander departed after passing Gil McDougald to load the bases.

With Clem Labine on the mound in relief, Howard beat out an infield hit, scoring the second run and leaving the bases loaded for Richardson. Bobby first tried a squeeze bunt, but fouled off the pitch. Then, with a 3-2 count, the Yankee kid clouted his grand-slam homer.

In the fourth, with Fred Green pitching for the Pirates, Ford singled and Mantle smashed a towering homer into the upper deck in left-center field. Successive singles by Skowron, McDougald and Howard filled the bases. Richardson again took advantage of the opportunity, but less dramatically, rapping a two-run single to bring his RBIs for the game to the record-breaking total of six.

Refusing to be buried, the Bucs came back with Law in the fourth game and eked out a 3 to 2 victory, thanks to another superb relief performance by Face.

Skowron tagged Law for a homer in the fourth inning before the Pirates took advantage of a questionable attempted force play by Skowron to score all their runs off Ralph Terry in the fifth.

Terry retired the next two batters, but Law, only a .181 batter during the regular season, ripped off a double, Gino Cimoli scoring the tying run. Terry then had two strikes on Virdon before Bill connected for a looping single to center, scoring Smokey Burgess and Law.

The Yankees rallied in the seventh, scoring on a double by Skowron, single by McDougald and forceout by Richardson. When Johnny Blanchard followed with a pinch-single, Face relieved Law. Cerv greeted Roy with a tremendous drive to right-center, but Virdon pulled down the ball at the 407-foot marker, banging into the wall as he made the catch. Face then proceeded to mow down the Yankees over the remainder of the game.

With the Series tied at two victories each, the Pirates started Haddix in the fifth game, while the Yankees called on Ditmar, who had been kayoed in the first inning of the opener. Ditmar failed again, but an error by McDougald figured in his downfall.

In the second inning, Dick Stuart singled and was forced. Burgess doubled, Cimoli stopping at third. Don Hoak tapped to Kubek, Cimoli scoring. Burgess unwisely tried to take third and would have been out, but McDougald dropped Kubek's throw. Mazeroski took advantage of the break and chopped a double to left field, scoring Burgess and Hoak.

With the Pirates leading, 4 to 2, Haddix lost his stuff in the seventh. Without hesitation, Murtaugh called on Face again and the little relief star turned in his most superb performance of the Series, holding the Yankees hitless for the remainder of the game to lock up a 5 to 2 victory.

Again, there was an open date in the Series while the clubs shifted back to Pittsburgh. With the Yankees' backs to the wall, Manager Stengel called on his southpaw ace, Ford. Whitey breezed to a 12 to 0 victory for his second shutout and the most decisive whitewashing in Classic history. The triumph was his seventh in Series competiton, but his first away from Yankee Stadium.

The Yankees kayoed Friend for the second time and continued their 17-hit attack on four successors.

Squaring off for the seventh and deciding game, the Pirates turned for the third time to Law, while the Yankees started Turley. Bob Skinner, who had been idle since jamming his left thumb in the opener, returned to the Bucs' lineup in left field and Rocky Nelson replaced Stuart at first.

The changes paid off in the first inning when Skinner walked and Nelson smashed a homer. In the second Virdon lined a single to center for two runs to boost the Pirates to a 4 to 0 lead.

The Yankees broke into the scoring column in the fifth when Skowron homered. In the sixth, Richardson singled and Tony Kubek walked as Law began to show the effects of his ankle injury. Murtaugh turned again to Face, who made his fourth appearance of the Series, but the little fellow's overworked arm was not equal to the challenge. Mantle greeted Roy with a single, scoring Richardson, and Berra followed with a three-run homer to send the Yankees ahead, 5 to 4.

Face yielded two more runs in the eighth on a pass to Berra, singles by Skowron and Blanchard and a double by Cletis Boyer, presenting the Pirates with what appeared to be the almost impossible task of overcoming a 7 to 4 deficit. But the Bucs did it!

Opening the home half of the eighth, Cimoli batted for Face and singled off Shantz. Then came the big break of the Series. Virdon rapped a grounder that took a bad hop and struck Kubek in the throat for a hit. Kubek was forced to retire. Dick Groat followed with a single, scoring Cimoli and bringing Coates to the mound for the Yankees. Skinner sacrificed the base runners along, but they were forced to hold up on Nelson's fly to Maris. Roberto Clemente beat out an infield hit, scoring Virdon, but the Pirates were still one run behind. Hal Smith was the batter on the spot and the reserve catcher delivered sensationally with a homer that turned Forbes Field into a bedlam as three runs crossed the plate to give the Bucs a 9 to 7 lead.

But the Yankees weren't through. Friend took the mound in the ninth in an effort to preserve the Pirates' lead and failed dismally when Richardson and pinch-hitter Dale Long both singled. Haddix, coming to the rescue, retired Maris, but Mantle singled to center, scoring Richardson. Then came a crucial play.

Berra shot a sharp two-hop smash that Nelson backhanded just beyond first base. The force of the ball spun him around with his back to the plate. Unable to pick out catcher Smith against the background of the fans, Rocky couldn't make a play on pinch-runner McDougald, racing home with the tying run. Instead, Rocky stepped on first to retire Berra, then looked up toward second only to discover that Mantle was diving back to first. Nelson swiped at Mantle but missed, and the score was knotted.

The victory thus escaped the Pirates for the moment, but the "team of destiny" could not be denied. Stepping to the plate against Terry to open the bottom of the ninth, Mazeroski took one pitch for a ball and then swung at the next for the homer that made the Pirates champions of the world.

The box scores:

Wednesday, October 5—At Pittsburgh

New York (A.L.)	AB.	R.	H.	O.	A.	E.
Kubek, ss	5	0	3	2	4	1
Lopez, lf	5	0	1	0	1	0
Maris, rf	4	2	3	3	0	0
Mantle, cf	3	0	0	3	0	0
Berra, c	4	0	1	4	1	0
Skowron, 1b	4	0	2	9	0	0
Boyer, 3b	0	0	0	0	0	0
aLong	1	0	0	0	0	0
McDougald, 3b	3	0	1	1	1	0
Richardson, 2b	4	1	0	2	2	1
Ditmar, p	0	0	0	0	0	0
Coates, p	1	0	0	0	0	0
bBlanchard	1	0	0	0	0	0
Maas, p	0	0	0	0	0	0
cCerv	1	0	1	0	0	0
Duren, p	0	0	0	0	1	0
dHoward	1	1	1	0	0	0
Totals	37	4	13	24	10	2

Pittsburgh (N.L.)	AB.	R.	H.	O.	A.	E.
Virdon, cf	3	1	1	3	0	0
Groat, ss	4	1	2	2	3	0
Skinner, lf	3	1	1	3	1	0
Cimoli, lf	0	0	0	0	0	0
Stuart, 1b	4	0	1	9	0	0
Clemente, rf	4	0	1	2	0	0
Burgess, c	4	0	0	5	0	0
Hoak, 3b	2	1	0	1	0	0
Mazeroski, 2b	4	2	2	2	3	0
Law, p	1	0	0	0	2	0
Face, p	1	0	0	0	0	0
Totals	30	6	8	27	9	0

New York........ 1 0 0 1 0 0 0 0 2—4
Pittsburgh....... 3 0 0 2 0 1 0 0 *—6

aFlied out for Boyer in second. bGrounded out for Coates in fifth. cSingled for Maas in seventh. dHomered for Duren in ninth. Runs batted in—Maris, Skowron, Howard 2, Virdon, Groat, Skinner, Clemente, Mazeroski 2. Two-base hits—Groat, Virdon. Home runs—Maris, Mazeroski, Howard. Stolen bases—Virdon, Skinner. Sacrifice hit—Law. Double plays—Mazeroski and Stuart; Skinner and Mazeroski; Mazeroski, Groat and Stuart. Left on bases—New York 7, Pittsburgh 6. Earned runs—New York 4, Pittsburgh 6. Bases on balls—Off Ditmar 1, off Coates 1, off Duren 1, off Law 1. Struck out—By Coates 2, by Maas 1, by Duren 1, by Law 3, by Face 1. Pitching records—Off Ditmar 3 hits and 3 runs in ⅓ inning; off Coates 3 hits and 2 runs in 3⅔ innings; off Maas 2 hits and 1 run in 2 innings; off Duren 0 hits and 0 runs in 2 innings; off Law 10 hits and 2 runs in 7 innings (pitched to two batters in eighth); off Face 3 hits and 2 runs in 2 innings. Hit by pitcher—By Coates 1 (Law), by Duren 1 (Skinner). Wild pitch—Law. Winning pitcher—Law. Losing pitcher—Ditmar. Umpires—Boggess (N.L.), Stevens (A.L.), Jackowski (N.L.), Chylak (A.L.), Landes (N.L.), Honochick (A.L.). Time—2:29. Attendance—36,676.

Thursday, October 6—At Pittsburgh

New York (A.L.)	AB.	R.	H.	O.	A.	E.
Kubek, ss-lf	6	3	3	2	3	0
McDougald, 3b	3	1	2	1	0	0
DeMaestri, ss	2	1	1	0	0	0
Maris, rf	5	2	1	3	0	0
Mantle, cf	4	3	2	4	0	0
Berra, lf	4	1	1	1	0	0
Boyer, 3b	2	0	1	0	0	0
Skowron, 1b	6	1	2	11	0	0
Howard, c	5	1	2	1	0	0
Richardson, 2b	4	3	3	4	6	1
Turley, p	4	0	1	0	2	0
Shantz, p	0	0	0	0	1	0
Totals	45	16	19	27	12	1

Pittsburgh (N.L.)	AB.	R.	H.	O.	A.	E.
Virdon, cf	5	0	0	2	0	0
Groat, ss	4	0	1	1	0	1
Gibbon, p	0	0	0	1	0	0
Cheney, p	0	0	0	0	1	0
cChristopher	0	1	0	0	0	0
Clemente, rf	5	0	2	1	0	0
Nelson, 1b	5	1	2	4	3	0
Cimoli, lf	4	1	2	2	0	0
Burgess, c	4	0	2	11	1	0
Hoak, 3b	5	0	2	0	0	0
Mazeroski, 2b	4	0	1	2	2	0
Friend, p	1	0	0	1	1	0
aBaker	1	0	0	0	0	0
Green, p	0	0	0	0	0	0
Labine, p	0	0	0	0	1	0
Witt, p	0	0	0	0	0	0
bSchofield, ss	1	0	1	2	0	0
Totals	39	3	13	27	9	1

New York........ 0 0 2 1 2 7 3 0 1—16
Pittsburgh....... 0 0 0 1 0 0 0 0 2— 3

aPopped out for Friend in fourth. bSingled for Witt in sixth. cHit by pitch for Cheney in ninth. Runs batted in—Kubek, McDougald 2, Mantle 5, Berra 2, Skowron, Howard, Richardson 2, Turley, Cimoli, Hoak. Two-base hits—Mazeroski, McDougald, Hoak 2, Richardson, Boyer. Three-base hit—Howard. Home runs—Mantle 2. Sacrifice hit—Turley. Double play—Shantz, Richardson and Skowron. Left on bases—New York 8, Pittsburgh 13. Earned runs—New York 10, Pittsburgh 2. Bases on balls—Off Turley 3, off Friend 2, off Green 1, off Labine 1, off Cheney 1. Struck out—By Friend 6, by Labine 1, by Gibbon 2, by Cheney 2. Pitching records—Off Turley 13 hits and 3 runs in 8⅓ innings; off Shantz 0 hits and 0 runs in ⅔ inning; off Friend 6 hits and 3 runs in 4 innings; off Green 3 hits and 4 runs in 1 inning (pitched to two batters in sixth); off Labine 3 hits and 5 runs in ⅔ inning, off Witt 2 hits and 0 runs in ⅓ inning; off Gibbon 4 hits and 3 runs in 2 innings; off Cheney 1 hit and 1 run in 1 inning. Hit by pitcher—By Turley (Christopher). Wild pitch—Cheney. Passed balls—Burgess 2. Winning pitcher—Turley. Losing pitcher—Friend. Umpires—Stevens (A.L.), Jackowski (N.L.), Chylak (A.L.), Boggess (N.L.), Landes (N.L.), Honochick (A.L.). Time—3:14. Attendance—37,308.

Saturday, October 8—At New York

Pittsburgh (N.L.)	AB.	R.	H.	O.	A.	E.
Virdon, cf	4	0	1	3	0	0
Groat, ss	4	0	0	1	1	0
Clemente, rf	4	0	1	1	0	0
Stuart, 1b	4	0	1	6	0	0
Cimoli, lf	3	0	0	2	0	0
Smith, c	3	0	0	9	1	0
Hoak, 3b	3	0	0	1	3	0
Mazeroski, 2b	3	0	1	1	3	0
Mizell, p	0	0	0	0	0	0
Labine, p	0	0	0	0	1	0
Green, p	1	0	0	0	0	0
Witt, p	0	0	0	0	0	0
aBaker	1	0	0	0	0	0
Cheney, p	0	0	0	0	0	0
bSchofield	1	0	0	0	0	0
Gibbon, p	0	0	0	0	0	0
Totals	31	0	4	24	9	0

New York (A.L.)	AB.	R.	H.	O.	A.	E.
Cerv, lf	5	1	2	3	0	0
Maris, rf	3	0	0	1	0	0
Berra, rf	1	0	1	1	0	0
Mantle, cf	5	2	2	4	0	0
Skowron, 1b	5	2	2	11	3	0
McDougald, 3b	4	2	1	0	3	0
Howard, c	4	1	2	3	0	0
Richardson, 2b	5	1	2	1	4	0
Kubek, ss	3	0	1	2	1	1
Ford, p	4	1	1	3	4	0
Totals	39	10	16	27	15	1

Pittsburgh............ 0 0 0   0 0 0   0 0 0— 0
New York............. 6 0 0   4 0 0   0 0 *—10

aGrounded out for Witt in sixth. bLined out for Cheney in eighth. Runs batted in—Mantle 2, Skowron, Howard, Richardson 6. Two-base hits—Virdon, Mantle. Home runs—Richardson, Mantle. Double play—Ford, Richardson and Skowron. Left on bases—Pittsburgh 5, New York 9. Earned runs—New York 10, Pittsburgh 0. Bases on balls—Off Mizell 1, off Witt 2, off Gibbon 1, off Ford 1. Struck out—By Green 3, by Witt 1, by Cheney 3, by Ford 3. Pitching records—Off Mizell 3 hits and 4 runs in ⅓ inning; off Labine 1 hit and 2 runs in ⅓ inning; off Green 5 hits and 4 runs in 3 innings; off Witt 3 hits and 0 runs in 1⅓ innings; off Cheney 1 hit and 0 runs in 2 innings; off Gibbon 0 hits and 0 runs in 1 inning. Wild pitches—Green, Witt. Winning pitcher—Ford. Losing pitcher—Mizell. Umpires—Jackowski (N.L.), Chylak (A.L.), Boggess (N.L.), Stevens (A.L.), Honochick (A.L.), Landes (N.L.). Time—2:41. Attendance—70,001.

Sunday, October 9—At New York

Pittsburgh (N.L.)	AB.	R.	H.	O.	A.	E.
Virdon, cf	4	0	1	2	0	0
Groat, ss	4	0	0	1	1	0
Clemente, rf	4	0	1	4	0	0
Stuart, 1b	4	0	0	12	0	0
Cimoli, lf	4	1	1	0	0	0
Burgess, c	3	1	0	5	1	0
Oldis, c	0	0	0	0	0	0
Hoak, 3b	4	0	1	1	3	0
Mazeroski, 2b	3	0	1	2	3	0
Law, p	3	1	2	0	3	0
Face, p	1	0	0	0	1	0
Totals	34	3	7	27	12	0

New York (A.L.)	AB.	R.	H.	O.	A.	E.
Cerv, lf	4	0	1	1	0	0
Kubek, ss	4	0	1	0	2	0
Maris, rf	4	0	0	0	0	0
Mantle, cf	3	0	0	3	0	0
Berra, c	4	0	0	7	0	0
Skowron, 1b	4	2	2	8	1	0
McDougald, 3b	4	0	1	1	1	0
Richardson, 2b	3	0	2	6	3	0
cLong	1	0	0	0	0	0
Terry, p	2	0	0	0	3	0
Shantz, p	0	0	0	0	0	0
aBlanchard	1	0	1	0	0	0
bDeMaestri	0	0	0	0	0	0
Coates, p	0	0	0	1	1	0
Totals	34	2	8	27	11	0

Pittsburgh............ 0 0 0   0 3 0   0 0 0—3
New York............. 0 0 0   1 0 0   1 0 0—2

aSingled for Shantz in seventh. bRan for Blanchard in seventh. cFlied out for Richardson in ninth. Runs batted in—Virdon 2, Law, Skowron, Richardson. Two-base hits—Kubek, Richardson, Skowron, Law. Home run—Skowron. Sacrifice hit—Mazeroski. Double play—Hoak and Stuart. Left on bases—Pittsburgh 6, New York 6. Earned runs—Pittsburgh 3, New York 2. Bases on balls—Off Law 1, off Terry 1. Struck out—By Law 5, by Face 1, by Terry 5, by Shantz 1, by Coates 1. Pitching records—Off Law 8 hits and 2 runs in 6⅓ innings; off Face 0 hits and 0 runs in 2⅔ innings; off Terry 6 hits and 3 runs in 6⅓ innings; of Shantz 0 hits and 0 runs in ⅔ inning; off Coates 1 hit and 0 runs in 2 innings. Winning pitcher—Law. Losing pitcher—Terry. Umpires—Chylak (A.L.), Boggess (N.L.), Stevens (A.L.), Jackowski (N.L.), Landes (N.L.), Honochick (A.L.). Time—2:29. Attendance—67,812.

Monday, October 10—At New York

Pittsburgh (N.L.)	AB.	R.	H.	O.	A.	E.
Virdon, cf	5	0	1	1	0	0
Groat, ss	4	1	1	3	4	1
Clemente, rf	4	0	0	3	0	0
Stuart, 1b	4	0	1	8	0	0
Nelson, 1b	0	0	0	2	0	0
Cimoli, lf	4	1	0	0	0	0
Burgess, c	4	1	2	6	0	0
cChristopher	0	1	0	0	0	0
Oldis, c	0	0	0	0	0	0
Hoak, 3b	4	1	2	1	1	1
Mazeroski, 2b	4	0	1	2	5	0

1960 WORLD SERIES

	AB.	R.	H.	O.	A.	E.
Haddix, p	3	0	1	1	1	0
Face, p	1	0	0	0	0	0
Totals	37	5	10	27	11	2
New York (A.L.)	AB.	R.	H.	O.	A.	E.
McDougald, 3b	4	0	0	2	2	1
Maris, rf	4	1	1	1	0	0
Cerv, lf	4	0	1	4	0	1
Mantle, cf	1	0	0	1	0	0
Skowron, 1b	4	0	0	8	0	0
Howard, c	3	1	1	6	0	0
bBerra, c	1	0	0	2	0	0
Richardson, 2b	4	0	0	2	2	0
Kubek, ss	4	0	1	1	5	0
Ditmar, p	0	0	0	0	0	0
Arroyo, p	1	0	0	0	0	0
Stafford, p	1	0	0	0	1	0
aLopez	1	0	1	0	0	0
Duren, p	0	0	0	0	1	0
dBlanchard	1	0	0	0	0	0
Totals	33	2	5	27	11	2

Pittsburgh .... 0 3 1 0 0 0 0 0 1—5
New York .... 0 1 1 0 0 0 0 0 0—2

aSingled for Stafford in seventh. bGrounded out for Howard in eighth. cRan for Burgess in ninth. dFlied out for Duren in ninth. Runs batted in—Clemente, Hoak 2, Mazeroski 2, Maris, Kubek. Two-base hits—Burgess, Mazeroski, Howard, Groat, Virdon. Home run—Maris. Double plays—Stafford, Kubek and Skowron; Mazeroski and Stuart. Left on bases—Pittsburgh 5, New York 7. Earned runs—Pittsburgh 3, New York 2. Bases on balls—Off Haddix 2, off Face 1. Struck out—By Haddix 6, by Face 1, by Arroyo 1, by Stafford 2, by Duren 4. Pitching records—Off Haddix 5 hits and 2 runs in 6⅓ innings; off Face 0 hits and 0 runs in 2⅔ innings; off Ditmar 3 hits and 3 runs in 1⅓ innings; off Arroyo 2 hits and 1 run in ⅔ inning (pitched to two batters in third); off Stafford 3 hits and 0 runs in 5 innings; off Duren 2 hits and 1 run in 2 innings. Wild pitch—Duren. Passed ball—Burgess. Winning pitcher—Haddix. Losing pitcher—Ditmar. Umpires—Boggess (N.L.), Stevens (A.L.), Jackowski (N.L.), Chylak (A.L.), Landes (N.L.), Honochick (A.L.). Time—2:32. Attendance—62,753.

Wednesday, Oct. 12—At Pittsburgh

New York (A.L.)	AB.	R.	H.	O.	A.	E.
Boyer, 3b	6	1	1	0	5	0
Kubek, ss-lf	5	2	1	2	4	1
Maris, rf	5	1	3	1	0	0
Mantle, cf	4	2	1	2	0	0
Berra, lf	4	3	3	0	0	0
DeMaestri, ss	0	0	0	0	2	0
Skowron, 1b	4	0	2	13	0	0
Howard, c	0	0	0	1	0	0
aGrba	0	0	0	0	0	0
Blanchard, c	4	2	3	4	1	0
Richardson, 2b	5	1	2	4	6	0
Ford, p	4	0	1	0	1	0
Totals	41	12	17	27	19	1
Pittsburgh (N.L.)	AB.	R.	H.	O.	A.	E.
Virdon, cf	4	0	1	4	0	1
Groat, ss	4	0	1	1	1	0
Witt, p	0	0	0	0	0	0
Clemente, rf	4	0	2	4	0	0
Stuart, 1b	4	0	0	10	0	0
Cimoli, lf	4	0	1	1	0	0
Smith, c	4	0	2	4	0	0
Hoak, 3b	2	0	0	1	1	0
Mazeroski, 2b	3	0	0	2	7	0

	AB.	R.	H.	O.	A.	E.
Friend, p	0	0	0	0	2	0
Cheney, p	0	0	0	0	0	0
bBaker	1	0	0	0	0	0
Mizell, p	0	0	0	0	0	0
cNelson	1	0	0	0	0	0
Green, p	0	0	0	0	0	0
Labine, p	0	0	0	0	0	0
dSchofield, ss	1	0	0	0	0	0
Totals	32	0	7	27	11	1

New York .... 0 1 5 0 0 2 2 2 0—12
Pittsburgh .... 0 0 0 0 0 0 0 0 0— 0

aRan for Howard in second. bStruck out for Cheney in third. cStruck out for Mizell in fifth. dGrounded out for Labine in eighth. Runs batted in—Kubek, Mantle 2, Berra 2, Skowron, Blanchard, Richardson 3, Ford 2. Two-base hits—Maris, Skowron, Blanchard 2. Three-base hits—Richardson 2, Boyer. Sacrifice hit—Ford. Sacrifice fly—Skowron. Double plays—Richardson, Kubek and Skowron; Boyer, Richardson and Skowron 2; Groat, Mazeroski and Stuart; Hoak, Mazeroski and Stuart. Left on bases—New York 8, Pittsburgh 6. Earned runs—New York 12, Pittsburgh 0. Bases on balls—Off Ford 1, off Friend 1, off Mizell 1. Struck out—By Ford 5, by Friend 1, by Cheney 1, by Mizell 1, by Labine 1. Pitching records—Off Friend 5 hits and 5 runs in 2 innings (pitched to four batters in third); off Cheney 2 hits and 1 run in 1 inning; off Mizell 1 hit and 0 runs in 2 innings; off Green 3 hits and 2 runs in 0 innings (pitched to three batters in fifth); off Labine 6 hits and 4 runs in 3 innings; off Witt 0 hits and 0 runs in 1 inning. Hit by pitcher—By Friend (Howard, Kubek). Wild pitch—Labine. Winning pitcher—Ford. Losing pitcher—Friend. Umpires—Stevens (A.L.), Jackowski (N.L.), Chylak (A.L.), Boggess (N.L.), Landes (N.L.), Honochick (A.L.). Time—2:38. Attendance—38,580.

Thursday, October 13—At Pittsburgh

New York (A.L.)	AB.	R.	H.	O.	A.	E.
Richardson, 2b	5	2	2	2	5	0
Kubek, ss	3	1	0	3	2	0
DeMaestri, ss	0	0	0	0	0	0
dLong	1	0	1	0	0	0
eMcDougald, 3b	0	1	0	0	0	0
Maris, rf	5	0	0	2	0	1
Mantle, cf	5	1	3	0	0	0
Berra, lf	4	2	1	3	0	0
Skowron, 1b	5	2	2	10	2	0
Blanchard, c	4	0	1	1	1	0
Boyer, 3b-ss	4	0	1	0	3	0
Turley, p	0	0	0	0	0	0
Stafford, p	0	0	0	0	1	0
aLopez	1	0	1	0	0	0
Shantz, p	3	0	1	3	1	0
Coates, p	0	0	0	0	0	0
Terry, p	0	0	0	0	0	0
Totals	40	9	13	f24	15	1
Pittsburgh (N.L.)	AB.	R.	H.	O.	A.	E.
Virdon, cf	4	1	2	3	0	0
Groat, ss	4	1	1	3	2	0
Skinner, lf	2	1	0	1	0	0
Nelson, 1b	3	1	1	7	0	0
Clemente, rf	4	1	1	4	0	0
Burgess, c	3	0	2	0	0	0
bChristopher	0	0	0	0	0	0
Smith, c	1	1	1	1	0	0
Hoak, 3b	3	1	0	3	2	0
Mazeroski, 2b	4	2	2	5	2	0
Law, p	2	0	0	0	1	0
Face, p	0	0	0	0	1	0

	AB.	R.	H.	O.	A.	E.
cCimoli	1	1	1	0	0	0
Friend, p	0	0	0	0	0	0
Haddix, p	0	0	0	0	0	0
Totals	31	10	11	27	6	0

New York............ 0 0 0   0 1 4   0 2 2—9
Pittsburgh........... 2 2 0   0 0 0   0 5 1—10

aSingled for Stafford in third. bRan for Burgess in seventh. cSingled for Face in eighth. dSingled for DeMaestri in ninth. eRan for Long in ninth. fNone out when winning run scored. Runs batted in—Mantle 2, Berra 4, Skowron, Blanchard, Boyer, Virdon 2, Groat, Nelson 2, Clemente, Smith 3, Mazeroski. Two-base hit—Boyer. Home runs—Nelson, Skowron, Berra, Smith, Mazeroski. Sacrifice hit—Skinner. Double plays—Stafford, Blanchard and Skowron; Richardson, Kubek and Skowron; Kubek, Richardson and Skowron. Left on bases—New York 6, Pittsburgh 1. Earned runs—New York 9, Pittsburgh 10. Bases on balls—Off Turley 1, off Stafford 1, off Shantz 1, off Law 1, off Face 1. Struck out—None. Pitching records—Off Turley 2 hits and 3 runs in 1 inning (pitched to one batter in second); off Stafford 2 hits and 1 run in 1 inning; off Shantz 4 hits and 3 runs in 5 innings (pitched to three batters in eighth); off Coates 2 hits and 2 runs in ⅔ inning; off Terry 1 hit and 1 run in ⅓ inning; off Law 4 hits and 3 runs in 5 innings (pitched to two batters in sixth); off Face 6 hits and 4 runs in 3 innings; off Friend 2 hits and 2 runs in 0 inning (pitched to two batters in ninth); off Haddix 1 hit and 0 runs in 1 inning. Winning pitcher—Haddix. Losing pitcher—Terry. Umpires—Jackowski (N.L.), Chylak (A.L.), Boggess (N.L.), Stevens (A.L.), Landes (N.L.), Honochick (A.L.). Time—2:36. Attendance—36,683.

COMPOSITE BATTING AVERAGES
Pittsburgh Pirates

Player-Position	G.	AB.	R.	H.	2B.	3B.	HR.	RBI.	BA.
Smith, c	3	8	1	3	0	0	1	3	.375
Schofield, ph-ss	3	3	0	1	0	0	0	0	.333
Nelson, 1b-ph	4	9	2	3	0	0	1	2	.333
Law, p	3	6	1	2	1	0	0	1	.333
Haddix, p	2	3	0	1	0	0	0	0	.333
Burgess, c	5	18	2	6	1	0	0	0	.333
Mazeroski, 2b	7	25	4	8	2	0	2	5	.320
Clemente, rf	7	29	1	9	0	0	0	3	.310
Cimoli, lf-ph	7	20	4	5	0	0	0	1	.250
Virdon, cf	7	29	2	7	3	0	0	5	.241
Hoak, 3b	7	23	3	5	2	0	0	3	.217
Groat, ss	7	28	3	6	2	0	0	2	.214
Skinner, lf	2	5	2	1	0	0	0	1	.200
Stuart, 1b	5	20	0	3	0	0	0	0	.150
Oldis, c	2	0	0	0	0	0	0	0	.000
Face, p	4	3	0	0	0	0	0	0	.000
Gibbon, p	2	0	0	0	0	0	0	0	.000
Cheney, p	3	0	0	0	0	0	0	0	.000
Friend, p	3	1	0	0	0	0	0	0	.000
Green, p	3	1	0	0	0	0	0	0	.000
Labine, p	3	0	0	0	0	0	0	0	.000
Witt, p	3	0	0	0	0	0	0	0	.000
Mizell, p	2	0	0	0	0	0	0	0	.000
Chris'pher, ph-pr	3	0	2	0	0	0	0	0	.000
Baker, ph	3	3	0	0	0	0	0	0	.000
Totals	7	234	27	60	11	0	4	26	.256

New York Yankees

Player-Position	G.	AB.	R.	H.	2B.	3B.	HR.	RBI.	BA.
DeMaestri, pr-ss	4	2	1	1	0	0	0	0	.500
Howard, ph-c	5	13	4	6	1	1	1	4	.462
Blanchard, ph-c	5	11	2	5	2	0	0	2	.455
Lopez, lf-ph	3	7	0	3	0	0	0	0	.429
Mantle, cf	7	25	8	10	1	0	3	11	.400
Skowron, 1b	7	32	5	12	2	0	2	6	.375
Richardson, 2b	7	30	8	11	2	2	1	12	.367
Cerv, ph-lf	4	14	1	5	0	0	0	0	.357
Shantz, p	3	3	0	1	0	0	0	0	.333
Long, ph	3	3	0	1	0	0	0	0	.333
Kubek, ss-lf	7	30	6	10	1	0	0	3	.333

Player-Position	G.	AB.	R.	H.	2B.	3B.	HR.	RBI.	BA.
Berra, c-lf-rf-ph	7	22	6	7	0	0	1	8	.318
McDougald, 3b-pr	6	18	4	5	1	0	0	2	.278
Maris, rf	7	30	6	8	1	0	2	2	.267
Turley, p	2	4	0	1	0	0	0	1	.250
Ford, p	2	8	1	2	0	0	0	2	.250
Boyer, 3b-ss	4	12	1	3	2	1	0	1	.250
Ditmar, p	2	0	0	0	0	0	0	0	.000
Coates, p	3	1	0	0	0	0	0	0	.000
Maas, p	1	0	0	0	0	0	0	0	.000
Duren, p	2	0	0	0	0	0	0	0	.000
Terry, p	2	2	0	0	0	0	0	0	.000
Arroyo, p	1	1	0	0	0	0	0	0	.000
Stafford, p	2	1	0	0	0	0	0	0	.000
Grba, pr	1	0	0	0	0	0	0	0	.000
Totals	7	269	55	91	13	4	10	54	.338

COMPOSITE PITCHING AVERAGES
Pittsburgh Pirates

Pitcher	G.	IP.	H.	R.	E.	SO.	BB.	W.	L.	ERA.
Witt	3	2⅔	5	0	0	1	2	0	0	0.00
Haddix	2	7⅓	6	2	2	6	2	2	0	2.45
Law	3	18⅓	22	7	7	8	3	2	0	3.44
Cheney	3	4	4	2	2	6	1	0	0	4.50
Face	4	10⅓	9	6	6	4	2	0	0	5.23
Gibbon	2	3	4	3	3	2	1	0	0	9.00
Labine	3	4	13	11	6	2	1	0	0	13.50
Friend	3	6	13	10	9	7	3	0	2	13.50
Mizell	2	2⅓	4	4	4	1	2	0	1	15.43
Green	3	4	11	10	10	3	1	0	0	22.50
Totals	7	62	91	55	49	40	18	4	3	7.11

New York Yankees

Pitcher	G.	IP.	H.	R.	E.	SO.	BB.	W.	L.	ERA.
Ford	2	18	11	0	0	8	2	2	0	0.00
Stafford	2	6	5	1	1	2	1	0	0	1.50
Duren	2	4	2	1	1	5	1	0	0	2.25
Shantz	3	6⅓	4	3	3	1	1	0	0	4.26
Maas	1	2	2	1	1	1	0	0	0	4.50
Turley	2	9⅓	15	6	5	0	4	1	0	4.82
Terry	2	6⅔	7	4	4	5	1	0	2	5.40
Coates	3	6⅓	6	4	4	3	1	0	0	5.68
Arroyo	1	⅔	2	1	1	1	0	0	0	13.50
Ditmar	2	1⅔	6	6	4	0	1	0	2	21.60
Totals	7	61	60	27	24	26	12	3	4	3.54

SERIES OF 1961

	W.	L.	Pct.
New York A. L.	4	1	.800
Cincinnati N. L.	1	4	.200

On the spot as the successor to Casey Stengel, Ralph Houk not only led the New York Yankees to the American League pennant, but piloted the Bombers to triumph in the World Series, defeating the Cincinnati Reds, four games to one. As a result, the Major became only the third manager to win the world championship in his freshman season at the helm, joining Bucky Harris of the 1924 Washington Senators and Eddie Dyer of the 1946 St. Louis Cardinals.

The Yankees achieved their near-sweep with virtually no help from Mickey Mantle. Injured shortly before the regular season ended, Mantle appeared in only two Series games and contributed just one single in six trips. Roger Maris, who hit 61 homers during the campaign, whacked only one round-tripper against the Reds, but it was a winning wallop in the third game. Manager Fred Hutchinson of the Cincy crew called the homer "the most damaging blow of the Series. After that, we couldn't seem to bounce back."

Among many Yankee heroes, the standout was Whitey Ford. With two shutouts over the Pittsburgh Pirates in 1960 already to his credit, the superb southpaw proceeded to set a record of 32 consecutive innings of scoreless pitching in Series competition, breaking Babe Ruth's cherished mark of 29⅔ innings.

Ford started the Yankees on the way with a two-hit, 2 to 0 victory in the opening game at Yankee Stadium. The Bombers used their favorite weapon—the homer—to beat Jim O'Toole. Elston Howard hit for the circuit in the fourth inning and Bill Skowron in the sixth.

Joey Jay, who blossomed out in Cincinnati uniform as a 21-game winner after being cast off by the Milwaukee Braves, posted the Reds' lone victory in the second encounter, hurling a four-hitter to turn back the Yankees, 6 to 2.

After Gordon Coleman of the Reds and Yogi Berra of the Yankees each homered with a man on base in the fourth inning, the Reds went ahead on the daring base-running of Elio Chacon in the fifth. With two away Chacon singled and raced to third on another single by Eddie Kasko. A pitch by Ralph Terry then squirted off Howard's glove and rolled about a dozen feet behind the catcher. Without hesitation, Chacon broke for the plate and slid across safely to snap the 2 to 2 tie.

Johnny Edwards, only a .185 hitter during the season, helped the Reds ice the decision. The Yankees twice passed Gene Freese intentionally to get at Edwards and each time the rookie catcher delivered an RBI hit, rapping a single in the sixth inning and a double in the eighth.

After an open date, the Series moved to Cincinnati, where Bob Purkey suffered a heart-breaking, 3 to 2 loss to the Yankees. The righthander yielded only six hits. However, after the Reds took a 2 to 1 lead against Bill Stafford, Johnny Blanchard delivered a pinch-homer in the eighth inning to tie the score. Then Maris, hitless up to that point in the Series, smashed a drive deep into the right field stands in the ninth inning to decide the outcome. Luis Arroyo was the winner in relief.

Ford returned to the mound in the fourth game and broke Ruth's shutout record before a foot injury forced the lefthander to leave the mound in the sixth inning. Jim Coates relieved and wrapped up the Yankees' 7 to 0 victory. The slump-shackled Reds collected only five hits, while the Yankees pounded 11 off O'Toole and Jim Brosnan.

Berra came up with a stiff shoulder and joined Mantle on the bench for the fifth game. Blanchard and Hector Lopez stepped into their posts in the outfield and led the way to a smashing 13 to 5 victory. Lopez drove in five runs with a triple, homer and squeeze bunt, while Blanchard batted three across with a homer, double and single.

The Yankees kayoed Jay in the first inning, piling up five runs. With an apparent easy victory in reach, Terry again succumbed to his World Series jinx and was removed in the third inning after Frank Robinson hit a three-run homer for the Reds. Bud Daley relieved and held the Reds in check the remainder of the way while the Yankees went on to fatten their lead with another five-run blast at Bill Henry's expense in the fourth inning.

Wally Post homered with a man on base for the Reds in the fifth, but the Yankees scored two more runs in the sixth to tie a blue ribbon to their nineteenth title in 26 fall appearances. The Reds used eight pitchers in the final game, setting a Series record.

Once more, Bobby Richardson was the leading batter. The Yankee second baseman tied the record for most hits in a five-game Series, with nine, while producing a .391 average. The most disappointing performer was Vada Pinson of the Reds, who hit .343 during the regular season and only .091 in the Series.

The box scores:

Wednesday, October 4—At New York

Cincinnati (N.L.)	AB.	R.	H.	O.	A.	E.
Blasingame, 2b	3	0	0	3	2	0
dLynch	1	0	0	0	0	0
Kasko, ss	4	0	1	3	3	0
Pinson, cf	4	0	0	4	0	0
Robinson, lf	2	0	0	0	0	0
Post, rf	3	0	1	2	0	0
Freese, 3b	3	0	0	1	0	0
Coleman, 1b	3	0	0	7	0	0
D. Johnson, c	2	0	0	3	1	0
aCardenas	1	0	0	0	0	0
Zimmerman, c	0	0	0	1	0	0
O'Toole, p	2	0	0	0	0	0
bGernert	1	0	0	0	0	0
Brosnan, p	0	0	0	0	0	0
Totals	29	0	2	24	6	0

New York (A.L.)	AB.	R.	H.	O.	A.	E.
Richardson, 2b	4	0	3	1	4	0
Kubek, ss	3	0	0	2	3	0
Maris, cf-rf	4	0	0	2	0	0
Howard, c	4	1	1	6	0	0
Skowron, 1b	3	1	1	13	0	0
Berra, lf	2	0	0	1	0	0
Lopez, rf	2	0	0	0	0	0
cBlanchard	1	0	0	0	0	0
Reed, cf	0	0	0	0	0	0
Boyer, 3b	3	0	1	2	5	0
Ford, p	3	0	0	0	1	0
Totals	29	2	6	27	13	0

Cincinnati............... 0 0 0   0 0 0   0 0 0—0
New York................ 0 0 0   1 0 1   0 0 *—2

aStruck out for D. Johnson in eighth. bGrounded out for O'Toole in eighth. cPopped out for Lopez in eighth. dPopped out for Blasingame in ninth. Home runs—Howard, Skowron. Runs batted in—Howard, Skowron. Double play—D. Johnson, Kasko and Coleman. Left on bases—Cincinnati 3, New York 8. Earned runs—New York 2.

1961 WORLD SERIES

Bases on balls—Off Ford 1, off O'Toole 4, off Brosnan 1. Struck out—By Ford 6, by O'Toole 2, by Brosnan 1. Pitching records—Off O'Toole 6 hits and 2 runs in 7 innings, off Brosnan 0 hits and 0 runs in 1 inning. Winning pitcher—Ford. Losing pitcher—O'Toole. Umpires—Runge (A.L.), Conlan (N.L.), Umont (A.L.), Donatelli (N.L.), Crawford (N.L.), Stewart (A.L.). Time—2:11. Attendance—62,397.

Thursday, October 5—At New York

Cincinnati (N.L.)	AB.	R.	H.	O.	A.	E.
Chacon, 2b	4	1	1	6	4	0
Kasko, ss	5	0	1	6	4	0
Pinson, cf	5	0	1	2	0	0
Robinson, lf	4	2	0	0	0	0
Coleman, 1b	5	1	2	5	1	0
Post, rf	4	2	2	0	0	0
Freese, 3b	2	0	0	1	1	0
Edwards, c	4	0	2	6	1	0
Jay, p	4	0	0	1	0	0
Totals	37	6	9	27	11	0

New York (A.L.)	AB.	R.	H.	O.	A.	E.
Richardson, 2b	4	0	1	2	3	0
Kubek, ss	4	0	1	1	2	0
Maris, cf	3	1	0	1	0	0
Berra, lf	4	1	2	4	0	1
Blanchard, rf	4	0	0	0	1	0
Howard, c	3	0	0	8	0	0
Skowron, 1b	3	0	0	8	1	0
Boyer, 3b	2	0	0	2	1	1
Terry, p	2	0	0	0	1	0
aLopez	0	0	0	0	0	0
Arroyo, p	0	0	0	1	0	1
bGardner	1	0	0	0	0	0
Totals	30	2	4	27	9	3

Cincinnati .... 0 0 0 2 1 1 0 2 0—6
New York .... 0 0 0 2 0 0 0 0 0—2

aWalked for Terry in seventh. bLined out for Arroyo in ninth. Two-base hits—Post, Edwards, Pinson. Home runs—Coleman, Berra. Runs batted in—Coleman 2, Edwards 2, Berra 2. Double plays—Chacon, Kasko and Coleman 2. Left on bases—Cincinnati 8, New York 7. Earned runs—Cincinnati 3, New York 2. Bases on balls—Off Terry 2, off Arroyo 2, off Jay 6. Struck out—By Terry 7, by Arroyo 1, by Jay 6. Pitching records—Off Terry 6 hits and 4 runs in 7 innings; off Arroyo 3 hits and 2 runs in 2 innings. Passed ball—Howard. Winning pitcher—Jay. Losing pitcher—Terry. Umpires—Conlan (N.L.), Umont (A.L.), Donatelli (N.L.), Runge (A.L.), Crawford (N.L.), Stewart (A.L.). Time—2:43. Attendance—63,083.

Saturday, October 7—At Cincinnati

New York (A.L.)	AB.	R.	H.	O.	A.	E.
Richardson, 2b	4	0	1	2	2	0
Kubek, ss	4	1	1	0	1	0
Maris, rf	4	1	1	2	0	0
Mantle, cf	4	0	0	1	0	0
Reed, cf	0	0	0	0	0	0
Berra, lf	3	0	1	2	0	0
Howard, c	4	0	1	10	0	0
Skowron, 1b	3	0	0	9	1	0
Boyer, 3b	3	0	0	0	3	0
Stafford, p	2	0	0	1	0	1
Daley, p	0	0	0	0	0	0
cBlanchard	1	1	1	0	0	0
Arroyo, p	0	0	0	0	1	0
Totals	32	3	6	27	8	1

Cincinnati (N.L.)	AB.	R.	H.	O.	A.	E.
Chacon, 2b	3	1	1	2	1	0
aLynch	0	0	0	0	0	0
bBlasingame, 2b	0	0	0	0	0	0
fBell	1	0	0	0	0	0
Kasko, ss	4	0	2	3	1	0
Pinson, cf	4	0	0	4	0	0
Robinson, rf	4	0	1	1	0	0
Coleman, 1b	4	0	2	6	3	0
Post, lf	4	0	0	2	0	0
Freese, 3b	3	0	0	2	0	0
Edwards, c	3	1	1	3	0	0
dCardenas	1	0	1	0	0	0
Purkey, p	3	0	0	4	2	0
eGernert	1	0	0	0	0	0
Totals	35	2	8	27	7	0

New York .... 0 0 0 0 0 0 1 1 1—3
Cincinnati .... 0 0 1 0 0 0 1 0 0—2

aIntentionally walked for Chacon in seventh. bRan for Lynch in seventh. cHomered for Daley in eighth. dDoubled for Edwards in ninth. eGrounded out for Purkey in ninth. fGrounded out for Blasingame in ninth. Two-base hits—Robinson, Howard, Edwards, Cardenas. Home runs—Blanchard, Maris. Runs batted in—Berra, Blanchard, Maris, Kasko, Robinson. Stolen base—Richardson. Double play—Kasko (unassisted). Left on bases—New York 3, Cincinnati 8. Earned runs—New York 2, Cincinnati 2. Bases on balls—Off Purkey 1, off Stafford 2. Struck out—By Purkey 3, by Stafford 5, by Arroyo 2. Pitching records—Off Stafford 7 hits and 2 runs in 6⅔ innings; off Daley 0 hits and 0 runs in ⅓ inning; off Arroyo 1 hit and 0 runs in 2 innings. Passed ball—Edwards. Winning pitcher—Arroyo. Losing pitcher—Purkey. Umpires—Umont (A.L.), Donatelli (N.L.), Runge (A.L.), Conlan (N.L.), Stewart (A.L.). Time—2:15. Attendance—32,589.

Sunday, October 8—At Cincinnati

New York (A.L.)	AB.	R.	H.	O.	A.	E.
Richardson, 2b	5	1	3	4	4	0
Kubek, ss	5	0	1	0	4	0
Maris, rf-cf	3	2	0	3	0	0
Mantle, cf	2	0	1	1	0	0
aLopez, rf	3	1	1	3	0	0
Howard, c	4	1	1	3	0	0
Berra, lf	2	1	0	4	0	0
Skowron, 1b	3	0	3	9	0	0
Boyer, 3b	4	0	1	0	2	0
Ford, p	2	1	0	0	0	0
Coates, p	1	0	0	0	0	0
Totals	34	7	11	27	10	0

Cincinnati (N.L.)	AB.	R.	H.	O.	A.	E.
Chacon, 2b	4	0	1	4	4	0
Kasko, ss	4	0	1	1	2	0
Pinson, cf	4	0	0	4	1	1
Robinson, rf	1	0	0	2	0	0
Post, lf	4	0	1	1	0	0
Freese, 3b	4	0	0	1	2	0
Coleman, 1b	4	0	0	5	0	0
D. Johnson, c	2	0	2	5	0	0
cBell	1	0	0	0	0	0
Zimmerman, c	0	0	0	3	0	0
O'Toole, p	1	0	0	1	0	0
bGernert	1	0	0	0	0	0
Brosnan, p	0	0	0	0	0	0
dLynch	1	0	0	0	0	0
Henry, p	0	0	0	0	0	0
Totals	31	0	5	27	9	1

New York .... 0 0 0 1 1 2 3 0 0—7
Cincinnati .... 0 0 0 0 0 0 0 0 0—0

aRan for Mantle in fourth. bHit into force play for O'Toole in fifth. cGrounded out for D. Johnson in seventh. dStruck out for Brosnan in eighth.

1961 WORLD SERIES

Two-base hits—Richardson, Howard, Boyer. Runs batted in—Kubek, Lopez 2, Skowron, Boyer 2. Double plays—Kasko, Chacon and Coleman; Kubek, Richardson and Skowron; Freese, Chacon and Coleman; Coleman (unassisted). Left on bases—New York 6, Cincinnati 7. Earned runs—New York 7. Bases on balls—Off O'Toole 3, off Brosnan 3, off Coates 1. Struck out—By O'Toole 2, by Brosnan 3, by Henry 2, by Ford 1, by Coates 2. Pitching records—Off O'Toole 5 hits and 2 runs in 5 innings; off Brosnan 6 hits and 5 runs in 3 innings; off Henry 0 hits and 0 runs in 1 inning; off Ford 4 hits and 0 runs in 5 innings (pitched to one batter in sixth); off Coates 1 hit and 0 runs in 4 innings. Hit by pitcher—By Ford (Robinson), by Coates (Robinson). Wild pitch—Brosnan. Winning pitcher—Ford. Losing pitcher—O'Toole. Umpires—Donatelli (N.L.), Runge (A.L.), Conlan (N.L.), Umont (A.L.), Crawford (N.L.), Stewart (A.L.). Time—2:27. Attendance—32,589.

Monday, October 9—At Cincinnati

New York (A.L.)	AB.	R.	H.	O.	A.	E.
Richardson, 2b	6	1	1	1	3	0
Kubek, ss	6	2	2	2	1	0
Maris, cf-rf	5	0	1	3	1	0
Blanchard, rf	4	3	3	2	0	0
Reed, cf	0	0	0	0	0	0
Howard, c	5	3	2	4	0	0
Skowron, 1b	5	2	2	7	3	0
Lopez, lf	4	2	2	5	0	0
Boyer, 3b	3	0	2	2	1	0
Terry, p	1	0	0	1	1	0
Daley, p	1	0	0	0	0	1
Totals	40	13	15	27	10	1

Cincinnati (N.L.)	AB.	R.	H.	O.	A.	E.
Blasingame, 2b	4	1	1	2	2	0
eChacon	1	0	0	0	0	0
Kasko, ss	5	1	2	0	3	1
Pinson, cf	5	0	1	4	0	0
Robinson, rf	4	1	2	2	0	0
Coleman, 1b	4	1	1	7	0	1
Post, lf	3	1	2	3	0	0
Freese, 3b	4	0	1	1	1	0
Edwards, c	4	0	1	8	0	0
Jay, p	0	0	0	0	0	0
Maloney, p	0	0	0	0	0	0
K. Johnson, p	0	0	0	0	0	0
aBell	1	0	0	0	0	0
Henry, p	0	0	0	0	1	0
Jones, p	0	0	0	0	0	0
bGernert	1	0	0	0	0	0
Purkey, p	0	0	0	0	1	1
cCardenas	1	0	0	0	0	0
Brosnan, p	0	0	0	0	0	0
dLynch	1	0	0	0	0	0
Hunt, p	0	0	0	0	1	0
Totals	38	5	11	27	9	3

New York	5 1 0	5 0 2	0 0 0	—13
Cincinnati	0 0 3	0 2 0	0 0 0	— 5

aFouled out for K. Johnson in second. bCalled out on strikes for Jones in fourth. cFlied out for Purkey in sixth. dGrounded out for Brosnan in eighth. eGrounded out for Blasingame in ninth. Two-base hits—Howard, Boyer, Maris, Freese, Blanchard, Robinson. Three-base hit—Lopez. Home runs—Blanchard, Robinson, Lopez, Post. Runs batted in—Maris, Blanchard 2, Skowron 3, Lopez 5, Boyer, Daley, Robinson 3, Post 2. Sacrifice hits—Terry, Lopez, Daley. Sacrifice fly—Daley. Left on bases—New York 10, Cincinnati 7. Earned runs—New York 11, Cincinnati 3. Bases on balls—Off Maloney 1, off Henry 2, off Purkey 2, off Hunt 1. Struck out—By Maloney 1, by Henry 1, by Purkey 2, by Brosnan 1, by Hunt 1, by Daley 3. Pitching records—Off Jay 4 hits and 4 runs in ⅔ inning; off Maloney 4 hits and 2 runs in ⅔ inning; off K. Johnson 0 hits and 0 runs in ⅔ inning; off Henry 4 hits and 5 runs in 1⅓ innings; off Jones 0 hits and 0 runs in ⅔ inning; off Purkey 0 hits and 2 runs in 2 innings; off Brosnan 3 hits and 0 runs in 2 innings; off Hunt 0 hits and 0 runs in 1 inning; off Terry 6 hits and 3 runs in 2⅓ innings; off Daley 5 hits and 2 runs in 6⅔ innings. Hit by pitcher—By Daley (Post). Wild pitch—Brosnan. Winning pitcher—Daley. Losing pitcher—Jay. Umpires—Runge (A.L.), Conlan (N.L.), Umont (A.L.), Donatelli (N.L.), Crawford (N.L.), Stewart (A.L.). Time—3:05. Attendance—32,589.

COMPOSITE BATTING AVERAGES
New York Yankees

Player-Position	G.	AB.	R.	H.	2B.	3B.	HR.	RBI.	BA.
Blanchard, ph-rf	4	10	4	4	1	0	2	3	.400
Richardson, 2b	5	23	2	9	1	0	0	0	.391
Skowron, 1b	5	17	3	6	0	0	1	5	.353
Lopez, rf-ph-pr-lf	4	9	3	3	0	1	1	7	.333
Berra, lf	4	11	2	3	0	0	1	3	.273
Boyer, 3b	5	15	0	4	2	0	0	3	.267
Howard, c	5	20	5	5	3	0	1	1	.250
Kubek, ss	5	22	3	5	0	0	0	1	.227
Mantle, cf	2	6	0	1	0	0	0	0	.167
Maris, cf-rf	5	19	4	2	1	0	1	2	.105
Reed, cf	3	0	0	0	0	0	0	0	.000
Ford, p	2	5	1	0	0	0	0	0	.000
Terry, p	2	3	0	0	0	0	0	0	.000
Arroyo, p	2	0	0	0	0	0	0	0	.000
Stafford, p	1	2	0	0	0	0	0	0	.000
Daley, p	2	1	0	0	0	0	0	1	.000
Coates, p	1	1	0	0	0	0	0	0	.000
Gardner, ph	1	1	0	0	0	0	0	0	.000
Totals	5	165	27	42	8	1	7	26	.255

Cincinnati Reds

Player-Position	G.	AB.	R.	H.	2B.	3B.	HR.	RBI.	BA.
D. Johnson, ph	2	4	0	2	0	0	0	0	.500
Edwards, c	3	11	1	4	2	0	0	2	.364
Cardenas, ph	3	3	0	1	1	0	0	0	.333
Post, rf-lf	5	18	3	6	1	0	1	2	.333
Kasko, ss	5	22	1	7	0	0	0	1	.318
Chacon, 2b-ph	4	12	2	3	0	0	0	0	.250
Coleman, 1b	5	20	2	5	0	0	1	2	.250
Robinson, lf-rf	5	15	3	3	2	0	1	4	.200
Blasingame, 2b-pr	3	7	1	1	0	0	0	0	.143
Pinson, cf	5	22	0	2	1	0	0	0	.091
Freese, 3b	5	16	0	1	1	0	0	0	.063
Zimmerman, c	2	0	0	0	0	0	0	0	.000
O'Toole, p	2	3	0	0	0	0	0	0	.000
Brosnan, p	3	0	0	0	0	0	0	0	.000
Jay, p	2	4	0	0	0	0	0	0	.000
Purkey, p	2	3	0	0	0	0	0	0	.000
Henry, p	2	0	0	0	0	0	0	0	.000
Maloney, p	1	0	0	0	0	0	0	0	.000
K. Johnson, p	1	0	0	0	0	0	0	0	.000
Jones, p	1	0	0	0	0	0	0	0	.000
Hunt, p	1	0	0	0	0	0	0	0	.000
Lynch, ph	4	3	0	0	0	0	0	0	.000
Gernert, ph	4	4	0	0	0	0	0	0	.000
Bell, ph	3	3	0	0	0	0	0	0	.000
Totals	5	170	13	35	8	0	3	11	.206

COMPOSITE PITCHING AVERAGES
New York Yankees

Pitcher	G.	IP.	H.	R.	E.	SO.	BB.	W.	L.	ERA.
Ford	2	14	6	0	0	7	1	2	0	0.00
Daley	2	7	5	2	0	3	2	1	0	0.00
Coates	1	4	1	0	0	2	1	0	0	0.00
Arroyo	2	4	4	2	1	3	2	1	0	2.25
Stafford	1	6⅔	7	2	2	5	2	0	0	2.70
Terry	2	9⅓	12	7	5	7	2	0	1	4.82
Totals	5	45	35	13	8	27	8	4	1	1.60

Cincinnati Reds

Pitcher	G.	IP.	H.	R.	E.	SO.	BB.	W.	L.	ERA.
Hunt	1	1	0	0	0	1	1	0	0	0.00
K. Johnson	1	⅔	0	0	0	0	0	0	0	0.00
Jones	1	⅔	0	0	0	0	0	0	0	0.00
Purkey	2	11	6	5	2	5	3	0	1	1.64
O'Toole	2	12	11	4	4	7	0	0	2	3.00

Pitcher	G.	IP.	H.	R.	E.	BB.	SO.	W.	L.	ERA.
Jay	2	9⅔	8	6	6	6	6	1	1	5.59
Brosnan	3	6	9	5	5	5	4	0	0	7.50
Henry	2	2⅓	4	5	5	3	2	0	0	19.29
Maloney	1	⅔	4	2	2	1	1	0	0	27.00
Totals	5	44	42	27	24	25	24	1	4	4.91

SERIES OF 1962

	W.	L.	Pct.
New York A. L.	4	3	.571
San Francisco N. L.	3	4	.429

Going down to the final dramatic pitch, the New York Yankees won their second successive world championship and twentieth in 27 post-season appearances by defeating the San Francisco Giants, four games to three, in a Series that proved excitingly competitive despite the harassment of rain.

There was one postponement in New York and three consecutive days of idleness in San Francisco. With open dates along the way for coast-to-coast travel, the Series stretched out over a total of 13 days, making it the longest Classic by the calendar since the rain-wracked meeting of the New York Giants and Philadelphia Athletics in 1911. That also covered 13 days.

As often happens, the big offensive guns were muffled in the Series and batting honors were captured by lesser lights. Mickey Mantle and Roger Maris, the slugging "M-Men" of the Yankees, batted only .120 and .174, respectively. Willie Mays hit .250 and Orlando Cepeda just .158 for the Giants. In the place of the "big names," Tom Tresh, the Yankees' rookie left fielder, and Jose Pagan, the Giants' shortstop, were the batting leaders. Tresh hit .321 and Pagan .368.

With the pitchers dominating the Classic, the Yankees compiled the lowest batting average in their 27 appearances in the Series, hitting .199 as a club. The Giants had a far more respectable mark of .226 and outscored the Yankees 21-20, but winning when the chips are down is a Yankee trademark.

Lefthander Whitey Ford started the Bombers off on the right foot in the opening game at San Francisco, posting a 6 to 2 victory. After the Yankees scored two runs off Billy O'Dell in the first inning on singles by Bobby Richardson and Tresh and a double by Maris, the Giants had the satisfaction of ending Ford's Series record for scoreless pitching. In the second inning, Mays singled and, with one out, took third on a single by Jim Davenport. When Pagan bunted safely, Mays crossed the plate to snap Ford's string at 33⅔ shutout innings.

The Giants tied the score in the third when Charlie Hiller doubled and Felipe Alou singled, but the Yankees broke away in the seventh on a homer by Cletis Boyer and iced the victory with two more runs in the eighth and one in the ninth.

When the Giants came back to win the second game, 2 to 0, behind Jack Sanford, the victory set a pattern for the see-saw Series. Neither club was able to dominate sufficiently to win twice in succession over the seven-game stretch. Sanford was staked to a lead in the first inning in his duel with Ralph Terry. Hiller smashed Terry's first pitch to right field, where Maris almost made an incredible shoe-top catch, but the ball dropped out of his glove for a double. Felipe Alou sacrificed and when his brother, Matty, grounded out, Hiller scored. Willie McCovey smashed a tremendous homer over the right field wall for an insurance run in the seventh inning.

Shifting to New York, the Series resumed after a day off for travel with the Yankees going ahead when Bill Stafford defeated Billy Pierce, 3 to 2. The Yankees scored all their runs in the seventh inning. Tresh led off with a single and raced to third on another single by Mantle. When Felipe Alou was unable to come up with the ball cleanly on a tough hop in left-center field, Mantle advanced to second. Alou was charged with an error. Maris then singled to drive in two runs and took second when his hit bounced away from McCovey.

Don Larsen, who pitched the only World Series perfect game while with the Yankees in 1956, replaced Pierce. When Elston Howard flied to center, Maris alertly tagged up and sped to third after the catch. That move set up what proved to be the winning run. After Bill Skowron was hit by a pitch. Boyer grounded to Pagan, who attempted to start a double play. Skowron was forced at second, but Boyer beat Hiller's throw to first, Maris scoring on the play. As a result, the Yankees had the run they needed to nip the Giants, who scored in the ninth on a double by Mays and a homer by Ed Bailey.

A grand-slam homer by Hiller, the first ever hit by an N. L. player in Series competition, gave the Giants a 7 to 3 victory in the fourth game. The Giants picked up their first two runs on a homer by Tom Haller off Ford in the second inning. Juan Marichal, San Francisco's ace, fouled a pitch off his index finger, attempting to bunt in the fifth, and was forced to leave the game. Bob Bolin, who replaced him, gave up two runs to the Yankees in the sixth when Mantle and Maris walked and Skowron and Boyer singled. Larsen relieved Bolin and passed Yogi Berra, who batted for Ford, but Tony Kubek went out to retire the side.

Jim Coates took the mound for the Yankees in the seventh and walked Davenport. Haller struck out, but Matty Alou, batting for Pagan, doubled. When Bailey was sent up to swing for Larsen, Marshall Bridges, a southpaw, replaced Coates. Bob Nieman took Bailey's place at the plate and drew an intentional pass to load the bases. Harvey Kuenn popped up and the Yankees seemed out of trouble. Hiller proved otherwise, coming through with his historic home run on a line drive into the right field stands. Larsen was the winner on the exact sixth anniversary of his perfect game in the same park.

Rain delayed the fifth game for one day and when the Series resumed, the Yankees moved in front again with a 5 to 3 victory on a three-run homer by Tresh in the eighth inning. Pagan singled off Terry in the third inning, leading to the Giants' first run, and accounted for their second run with a homer in the fifth. A wild pitch by Sanford and a passed ball by Haller resulted in a matching pair for the Yankees. In the eighth, Kubek and Richardson singled ahead of Tresh's winning wallop. The Giants rallied in the ninth, but had to settle for one run on a single by McCovey and a double by Haller.

Traveling back to San Francisco, the clubs were greeted by torrential rains and three days were spent in idleness before the Classic was able to continue. Billy Pierce then pitched the Giants to a 5 to 2 victory on a brilliant three-hitter, deadlocking the Series at three games apiece. Ford, making his third start for the Yankees, yielded a single to Felipe Alou in the fourth inning and walked Mays. With Cepeda at bat, Ford attempted to pick Alou off second, but threw wild into right-center field, Felipe scoring and Mays reaching third. Cepeda then doubled, counting Mays, and scored himself on a single by Davenport. Maris homered for the Yankees in the fifth, but the Giants came back with two runs on singles by Kuenn, Hiller, Felipe Alou and Cepeda. A double by Boyer and a single by Kubek gave the Yankees a run in the eighth, but Pierce bore down to complete his first Series victory.

With all the chips down, the Yankees won the seventh and final game, 1 to 0, on the four-hit hurling of Terry. The only run off Sanford came in the fifth inning. Skowron and Boyer singled, putting men on first and third. Sanford lost his control, walking Terry on four pitches. Kubek grounded into a double play, Pagan to Hiller to Cepeda, Skowron scoring the all-important run for the Yankees.

The entire dramatics of the Series were climaxed in the Giants' ninth inning. In 1960, Terry threw the home-run ball that Bill Mazeroski hit to win the Series for the Pittsburgh Pirates. This time, the Yankee righthander faced another clutch situation. Matty Alou led off with a safe bunt. Felipe Alou and Hiller struck out, but Mays doubled to right. Maris turned in one of the prize fielding plays of the Series, grabbing the ball on the run and firing to the cut-off man, Richardson, forcing Matty Alou to stop at third.

With McCovey at the plate, Manager Houk came out to talk with Terry. First base was open and the Yankees could have walked the Giants' lefthanded hitter, but Terry decided to pitch to the slugger. McCovey smashed a long foul on the first delivery, took a ball on the next pitch and then shot a vicious line drive toward right, but Richardson threw up his glove at second base—and the Series was over with another world championship for the Yankees. The box scores:

Thursday, Oct. 4—At San Francisco

New York (A.L.)	AB.	R.	H.	O.	A.	E.
Kubek, ss	5	0	2	3	4	0
Richardson, 2b	5	1	1	4	2	0
Tresh, lf	5	2	2	0	0	0
Mantle, cf	4	0	0	1	0	0
Maris, rf	4	1	2	2	0	0
Howard, c	3	1	2	6	0	0
Skowron, 1b	2	0	0	7	0	0
Long, 1b	2	0	1	3	0	0
Boyer, 3b	3	1	1	1	2	0
Ford, p	3	0	0	0	4	0
Totals	36	6	11	27	12	0

San Fran. (N.L.)	AB.	R.	H.	O.	A.	E.
Kuenn, lf	5	0	0	6	0	0
Hiller, 2b	4	1	1	4	4	0
F. Alou, rf	4	0	1	1	0	0
Mays, cf	4	1	3	1	0	0
Cepeda, 1b	4	0	0	6	0	0
Davenport, 3b	2	0	1	0	2	0
Bailey, c	4	0	0	8	0	0
Miller, p	0	0	0	0	1	0
Pagan, ss	4	0	3	1	2	0
O'Dell, p	3	0	1	0	0	0
Larsen, p	0	0	0	0	0	0
Orsino, c	1	0	0	0	0	0
Totals	35	2	10	27	9	0

New York............ 2 0 0 0 0 0 1 2 1—6
San Francisco...... 0 1 1 0 0 0 0 0 0—2

Runs batted in—Maris 2, Howard, Long, Boyer 2, Mays, Pagan. Two-base hits—Maris, Hiller. Home run—Boyer. Stolen bases—Mantle, Tresh. Sacrifice fly—Boyer. Double plays—Richardson, Kubek and Skowron; Boyer, Richardson and Long; Davenport, Hiller and Cepeda. Left on bases—New York 10, San Francisco 8. Earned runs—New York 6, San Francisco 2. Bases on Balls—Off Ford 2, off O'Dell 3, off Larsen 1, off Miller 1. Struck out—By Ford 6, by O'Dell 8. Pitching records—Off O'Dell 9 hits and 5 runs in 7⅓ innings; off Larsen 1 hit and 1 run in 1 inning; off Miller 1 hit and 0 runs in ⅔ inning. Hit by pitcher—By O'Dell (Howard). Winning pitcher—Ford. Losing pitcher—O'Dell. Umpires—Barlick (N.L.), Berry (A.L.), Landes (N.L.), Honochick (A.L.), Burkhart (N.L.) and Soar (A.L.). Time—2:43. Attendance—43,852.

Friday, October 5—At San Francisco

New York (A.L.)	AB.	R.	H.	O.	A.	E.
Kubek, ss	4	0	0	1	1	1
Richardson, 2b	4	0	0	3	3	0
Tresh, lf	3	0	1	0	0	0
Mantle, cf	4	0	1	3	0	0
Maris, rf	3	0	0	0	1	0
Berra, c	2	0	0	6	1	0
Long, 1b	3	0	0	6	3	0
Boyer, 3b	3	0	1	3	2	0
Terry, p	2	0	0	2	0	0

	AB	R	H	O	A	E
aBlanchard	1	0	0	0	0	0
Daley, p	0	0	0	0	0	0
Totals	29	0	3	24	11	1

San Fran. (N.L.)	AB	R	H	O	A	E
Hiller, 2b	3	1	1	0	6	0
F. Alou, rf	2	0	1	0	0	0
M. Alou, lf	4	0	1	1	0	0
Mays, cf	4	0	0	3	0	0
McCovey, 1b	4	1	1	11	1	0
Haller, c	3	0	1	8	1	0
Davenport, 3b	3	0	0	1	0	0
Pagan, ss	1	0	0	2	4	0
Sanford, p	3	0	1	1	1	0
Totals	27	2	6	27	13	0

New York .... 0 0 0 0 0 0 0 0 0—0
San Francisco .... 1 0 0 0 0 0 1 0 *—2

aStruck out for Terry in eighth. Runs batted in—M. Alou, McCovey. Two-base hits—Hiller, Mantle. Home run—McCovey. Stolen base—Tresh. Sacrifice hits—F. Alou, Pagan. Double play—Hiller, Pagan and McCovey. Left on bases—New York 5, San Francisco 6. Earned runs—New York 0, San Francisco 2. Bases on balls—Off Terry 1, off Daley 1, off Sanford 3. Struck out—By Terry 5, Sanford 6. Pitching records—Off Terry 5 hits and 2 runs in 7 innings; off Daley 1 hit and 0 runs in 1 inning. Hit by pitcher—By Terry (Pagan). Winning pitcher—Sanford. Losing pitcher—Terry. Umpires—Berry (A.L.), Landes (N.L.), Honochick (A.L.), Barlick (N.L.), Burkhart (N.L.) and Soar (A.L.). Time—2:11. Attendance—43,910.

Sunday, October 7—At New York

San Fran. (N.L.)	AB	R	H	O	A	E
F. Alou, lf	4	0	0	3	0	1
Hiller, 2b	3	0	0	3	0	0
Mays, cf	4	1	1	6	0	0
McCovey, rf	3	0	0	2	0	1
Cepeda, 1b	4	0	0	4	0	0
Bailey, c	4	1	1	4	0	0
Davenport, 3b	4	0	1	1	1	1
Pagan, ss	3	0	1	1	2	0
Pierce, p	2	0	0	0	0	0
Larsen, p	0	0	0	0	0	0
aM. Alou	1	0	0	0	0	0
Bolin, p	0	0	0	0	0	0
Totals	32	2	4	24	3	3

New York (A.L.)	AB	R	H	O	A	E
Kubek, ss	4	0	1	1	2	0
Richardson, 2b	4	0	0	2	4	0
Tresh, lf	4	1	1	4	0	0
Mantle, cf	3	1	1	2	0	0
Maris, rf	3	1	1	3	0	0
Howard, c	3	0	1	7	0	0
Skowron, 1b	2	0	0	7	0	0
Boyer, 3b	3	0	0	1	2	1
Stafford, p	3	0	0	0	1	0
Totals	29	3	5	27	9	1

San Francisco .... 0 0 0 0 0 0 0 0 2—2
New York .... 0 0 0 0 0 0 3 0 *—3

aHit into force play for Larsen in eighth. Runs batted in—Bailey 2, Maris 2, Boyer. Two-base hits—Davenport, Kubek, Howard, Mays. Home run—Bailey. Double play—Davenport and Hiller. Left on bases—San Francisco 5, New York 3. Earned runs—San Francisco 2, New York 2. Bases on balls—Off Stafford 2. Struck out—By Pierce 3, by Bolin 1, by Stafford 5. Pitching records—Off Pierce 5 hits and 3 runs in 6 innings (pitched to 3 batters in seventh); off Larsen 0 hits and 0 runs in 1 inning; off Bolin 0 hits and 0 runs in 1 inning. Hit by pitcher—By Larsen (Skowron). Winning pitcher—Stafford. Losing pitcher—Pierce. Umpires—Landes (N.L.), Honochick (A.L.), Barlick (N.L.), Berry (A.L.), Soar (A.L.) and Burkhart (N.L.). Time—2:06. Attendance—71,434.

Monday, October 8—At New York

San Fran. (N.L.)	AB	R	H	O	A	E
Kuenn, rf	3	0	0	3	0	0
O'Dell, p	0	0	0	0	0	0
Hiller, 2b	5	1	2	3	2	0
Mays, cf	5	0	1	2	0	0
F. Alou, lf	4	1	1	1	0	0
Cepeda, 1b	4	0	0	8	3	0
Davenport, 3b	2	1	0	1	1	1
Haller, c	4	1	2	6	1	0
Pagan, ss	2	0	1	0	1	0
bM. Alou, rf	2	2	2	1	0	0
Marichal, p	2	0	0	1	0	0
Bolin, p	0	0	0	0	0	0
Larsen, p	0	0	0	1	0	0
cBailey	0	0	0	0	0	0
dNieman	0	0	0	0	0	0
eBowman, ss	1	1	0	0	4	0
Totals	34	7	9	27	12	1

New York (A.L.)	AB	R	H	O	A	E
Kubek, ss	4	1	1	1	4	0
Richardson, 2b	4	0	1	2	3	1
Tresh, lf	5	0	2	1	0	0
Mantle, cf	4	1	0	0	0	0
Maris, rf	3	1	0	3	0	0
Howard, c	4	0	0	7	0	0
Skowron, 1b	4	0	3	12	0	0
Boyer, 3b	4	0	2	1	4	0
Ford, p	2	0	0	0	0	0
aBerra	0	0	0	0	0	0
Coates, p	0	0	0	0	0	0
Bridges, p	0	0	0	0	1	0
fLopez	1	0	0	0	0	0
Totals	35	3	9	27	12	1

San Francisco .... 0 2 0 0 0 0 4 0 1—7
New York .... 0 0 0 0 0 2 0 0 1—3

aWalked for Ford in sixth. bDoubled for Pagan in seventh. cAnnounced for Larsen in seventh. dWalked intentionally for Bailey in seventh. eRan for Nieman in seventh. fGrounded out for Bridges in ninth. Runs batted in—Hiller 4, Haller 2, Tresh, Skowron, Boyer. Two-base hits—F. Alou, M. Alou. Three-base hit—Skowron. Home runs—Haller, Hiller. Sacrifice hit—O'Dell. Double plays—Haller, Hiller, Cepeda and Marichal; Boyer, Richardson and Skowron; Hiller and Cepeda. Left on bases—San Francisco 5, New York 10. Earned runs—San Francisco 6, New York 3. Bases on balls—Off Marichal 2, off Bolin 2, off Larsen 1, off Coates 1, off Bridges 2, off Ford 1. Struck out—By Marichal 4, by Bolin 1, by Ford 3, by Coates 1, by Bridges 3. Pitching record—Off Marichal 2 hits and 0 runs in 4 innings; off Bolin 4 hits and 2 runs in 1⅔ innings; off Larsen 0 hits and 0 runs in ⅓ inning; off O'Dell 3 hits and 1 run in 3 innings; off Ford 5 hits and 2 runs in 6 innings; off Coates 1 hit and 2 runs in ⅓ inning; off Bridges 3 hits and 3 runs in 2⅔ innings. Winning pitcher—Larsen. Losing pitcher—Coates. Umpires—Honochick (A.L.), Barlick (N.L.), Berry (A.L.), Landes (N.L.), Soar (A.L.) and Burkhart (N.L.). Time—2:55. Attendance—66,607.

Wednesday, Oct 10—At New York

San Fran. (N.L.)	AB	R	H	O	A	E
Hiller, 2b	3	0	1	1	3	1
Davenport, 3b	4	0	0	3	0	0
M. Alou, rf	4	0	0	0	0	0

1962 WORLD SERIES

	AB.	R.	H.	O.	A.	E.
Mays, cf	4	0	0	1	0	0
McCovey, 1b	4	1	1	7	3	1
F. Alou, lf	4	0	2	1	0	0
Haller, c	4	0	1	10	0	0
Pagan, ss	4	2	2	2	2	0
Sanford, p	2	0	1	2	1	0
Miller, p	0	0	0	0	0	0
aBailey	1	0	0	0	0	0
Totals	34	3	8	24	9	2

New York (A.L.)	AB.	R.	H.	O.	A.	E.
Kubek, ss	4	1	2	1	2	0
Richardson, 2b	4	2	2	2	2	0
Tresh, lf	3	2	2	2	0	0
Mantle, cf	3	0	0	2	0	0
Maris, rf	3	0	0	3	0	0
Howard, c	4	0	0	7	0	0
Skowron, 1b	3	0	0	9	1	0
Boyer, 3b	3	0	0	1	2	0
Terry, p	3	0	0	0	1	0
Totals	30	5	6	27	8	0

San Francisco	0 0 1	0 1 0	0 0 1—3
New York	0 0 0	1 0 1	0 3 *—5

a Flied out for Miller in ninth. Runs batted in—Hiller, Haller, Pagan, Tresh 3. Two-base hits—Hiller, Tresh, Haller. Three-base hit—F. Alou. Home runs—Pagan, Tresh. Stolen base—Mantle. Sacrifice hits—Sanford, Tresh. Double play—Sanford and McCovey. Left on bases—San Francisco 6, New York 4. Earned runs—San Francisco 3, New York 4. Bases on balls—Off Sanford 1, off Miller 1, off Terry 1. Struck out—By Sanford 10, by Terry 7. Pitching records—Off Sanford 6 hits and 5 runs in 7⅓ innings; off Miller 0 hits and 0 runs in ⅔ inning. Wild pitch—Sanford. Passed ball—Haller. Winning pitcher—Terry. Losing pitcher—Sanford. Umpires—Barlick (N.L.), Berry (A.L.), Landes (N.L.), Honochick (A.L.), Soar (A.L.) and Burkhart (N.L.). Time—2:42. Attendance—63,165.

Monday, Oct. 15—At San Francisco

New York (A.L.)	AB.	R.	H.	O.	A.	E.
Kubek, ss	4	0	1	4	4	0
Richardson, 2b	4	0	0	3	5	0
Tresh, lf	4	0	0	1	0	0
Mantle, cf	4	0	0	0	0	0
Maris, rf	3	1	1	0	0	0
Howard, c	3	0	0	5	1	0
Skowron, 1b	3	0	0	11	0	0
Boyer, 3b	2	1	1	0	2	1
Ford, p	2	0	0	0	0	1
Coates, p	0	0	0	0	0	0
aLopez	1	0	0	0	0	0
Bridges, p	0	0	0	0	0	0
Totals	30	2	3	24	12	2

San Fran. (N.L.)	AB.	R.	H.	O.	A.	E.
Kuenn, lf	4	1	1	2	0	0
M. Alou, lf	0	0	0	1	0	0
Hiller, 2b	4	1	2	4	4	0
F. Alou, rf	4	1	2	1	0	0
Mays, cf	3	1	1	5	0	0
Cepeda, 1b	4	1	3	9	1	0
Davenport, 3b	4	0	1	0	4	1
Bailey, c	4	0	0	3	0	0
Pagan, ss	3	0	0	1	1	0
Pierce, p	3	0	0	1	0	0
Totals	33	5	10	27	10	1

New York	0 0 0	0 1 0	0 1 0—2
San Francisco	0 0 0	3 2 0	0 0 *—5

aFlied out for Coates in eighth. Runs batted in—Kubek, Maris, F. Alou, Cepeda 2, Davenport. Two-base hits—Cepeda, Boyer. Home run—Maris. Stolen base—Mays. Double plays—Kubek, Richardson and Skowron; Howard and Kubek; Davenport, Hiller and Cepeda. Left on bases—New York 3, San Francisco 5. Earned runs—New York 2, San Francisco 5. Bases on balls—Off Ford 7, off Pierce 2. Struck out—By Ford 3, by Coates 2, by Pierce 2. Pitching records—Off Ford 9 hits and 5 runs in 4⅔ innings; off Coates 0 hits and 0 runs in 2⅓ innings; off Bridges 1 hit and 0 runs in 1 inning. Winning pitcher—Pierce. Losing pitcher—Ford. Umpires—Berry (A.L.), Landes (N.L.), Honochick (A.L.), Barlick (N.L.), Burkhart (A.L.) and Soar (A.L.). Time—2:00. Attendance—43,948.

Tuesday, Oct. 16—At San Francisco

New York (A.L.)	AB.	R.	H.	O.	A.	E.
Kubek, ss	4	0	1	1	0	0
Richardson, 2b	2	0	0	3	0	0
Tresh, lf	4	0	1	6	0	0
Mantle, cf	3	0	1	3	0	0
Maris, rf	4	0	0	0	0	0
Howard, c	4	0	0	5	0	0
Skowron, 1b	4	1	1	6	0	0
Boyer, 3b	4	0	2	2	2	0
Terry, p	3	0	1	1	1	0
Totals	32	1	7	27	3	0

San Fran. (N.L.)	AB.	R.	H.	O.	A.	E.
F. Alou, rf	4	0	0	1	0	0
Hiller, 2b	4	0	0	1	3	0
Mays, cf	4	0	1	1	0	0
McCovey, lf	4	0	1	3	0	0
Cepeda, 1b	3	0	0	12	0	0
Haller, c	3	0	0	5	0	0
Davenport, 3b	3	0	0	3	4	0
Pagan, ss	2	0	0	1	2	1
aBailey	1	0	0	0	0	0
Bowman, ss	0	0	0	0	1	0
Sanford, p	2	0	1	0	1	0
O'Dell, p	0	0	0	0	0	0
bM. Alou	1	0	1	0	0	0
Totals	31	0	4	27	11	1

New York	0 0 0	0 1 0	0 0 0—1
San Francisco	0 0 0	0 0 0	0 0 0—0

aFouled out for Pagan in eighth. bBunted safely for O'Dell in ninth. Runs batted in—None (run scored as Kubek hit into double play). Two-base hit—Mays. Three-base hit—McCovey. Double plays—Pagan, Hiller and Cepeda; Davenport and Cepeda. Left on bases—New York 8, San Francisco 4. Earned runs—New York 1, San Francisco 0. Bases on balls—Off Sanford 4. Struck out—By Terry 4, by Sanford 3, by O'Dell 1. Pitching records—Off Sanford 7 hits and 1 run in 7 innings (pitched to 3 batters in eighth); off O'Dell 0 hits and 0 runs in 2 innings. Winning pitcher—Terry. Losing pitcher—Sanford. Umpires—Landes (N.L.), Honochick (A.L.), Barlick (N.L.), Berry (A.L.), Burkhart (N.L.), and Soar (A.L.). Time—2:29. Attendance—43,948.

COMPOSITE BATTING AVERAGES

New York Yankees

Player-Position	G.	AB.	R.	H.	2B.	3B.	HR.	RBI.	BA.
Tresh, lf	7	28	5	9	1	0	1	4	.321
Boyer, 3b	7	22	2	7	1	0	1	4	.318
Kubek, ss	7	29	2	8	1	0	0	1	.276
Skowron, 1b	6	18	1	4	0	1	0	1	.222
Long, 1b	2	5	0	1	0	0	0	1	.200
Maris, rf	7	23	4	4	1	0	1	5	.174
Richardson, 2b	7	27	3	4	0	0	0	0	.148
Howard, c	6	21	1	3	1	0	0	1	.143
Terry, p	3	8	0	1	0	0	0	0	.125
Mantle, cf	7	25	2	3	1	0	0	0	.120
Berra, c-ph	2	2	0	0	0	0	0	0	.000
Ford, p	3	7	0	0	0	0	0	0	.000

Player-Position	G.	AB.	R.	H.	2B.	3B.	HR.	RBI.	BA.
Daley, p	1	0	0	0	0	0	0	0	.000
Stafford, p	1	3	0	0	0	0	0	0	.000
Coates, p	2	0	0	0	0	0	0	0	.000
Bridges, p	2	0	0	0	0	0	0	0	.000
Lopez, ph	2	2	0	0	0	0	0	0	.000
Blanchard, ph	1	1	0	0	0	0	0	0	.000
Totals	7	221	20	44	6	1	3	17	.199

San Francisco Giants

Player-Position	G.	AB.	R.	H.	2B.	3B.	HR.	RBI.	BA.
Sanford, p	3	7	0	3	0	0	0	0	.429
Pagan, ss	7	19	2	7	0	0	1	2	.368
O'Dell, p	3	3	0	1	0	0	0	0	.333
M. Alou, lf-ph-rf	6	12	2	4	1	0	0	1	.333
Haller, c	4	14	1	4	1	0	1	3	.286
Hiller, 2b	7	26	4	7	3	0	1	5	.269
F. Alou, rf-lf	7	26	2	7	1	1	0	1	.269
Mays, cf	7	28	3	7	2	0	0	1	.250
McCovey, 1b-rf-lf	4	15	2	3	0	1	1	1	.200
Cepeda, 1b	5	19	1	3	1	0	0	2	.158
Davenport, 3b	7	22	1	3	1	0	0	1	.136
Kuenn, lf-rf	3	12	1	1	0	0	0	0	.083
Bailey, c-ph	6	14	1	1	0	0	1	2	.071
Orsino, c	1	1	0	0	0	0	0	0	.000
Bowman, pr-ss	2	1	1	0	0	0	0	0	.000
Miller, p	2	0	0	0	0	0	0	0	.000
Larsen, p	3	0	0	0	0	0	0	0	.000
Pierce, p	2	5	0	0	0	0	0	0	.000
Bolin, p	2	0	0	0	0	0	0	0	.000
Marichal, p	1	2	0	0	0	0	0	0	.000
Nieman, ph	1	0	0	0	0	0	0	0	.000
Totals	7	226	21	51	10	2	5	19	.226

COMPOSITE PITCHING AVERAGES
New York Yankees

Pitcher	G.	IP.	H.	R.	E.	SO.	BB.	W.	L.	ERA.
Daley	1	1	1	0	0	0	1	0	0	0.00
Terry	3	25	17	5	5	16	2	2	1	1.80
Stafford	1	9	4	2	2	5	2	0	1	2.00
Ford	3	19⅔	24	9	9	12	4	1	1	4.12
Bridges	2	3⅔	4	3	2	3	2	0	0	4.91
Coates	2	2⅔	1	2	2	3	1	0	1	6.75
Totals	7	61	51	21	20	39	12	4	3	2.95

San Francisco Giants

Pitcher	G.	IP.	H.	R.	E.	SO.	BB.	W.	L.	ERA.
Marichal	1	4	2	0	0	4	2	0	0	0.00
Miller	2	1⅓	1	0	0	0	0	0	0	0.00
Sanford	3	23⅓	16	6	5	19	8	1	2	1.93
Pierce	2	15	8	5	4	5	2	1	1	2.40
Larsen	2	2⅓	1	1	1	0	2	1	0	3.86
O'Dell	2	12⅓	12	6	6	9	3	0	1	4.38
Bolin	2	2⅔	4	2	2	2	2	0	0	6.75
Totals	7	61	44	20	18	39	21	3	4	2.66

SERIES OF 1963

	W.	L.	Pct.
Los Angeles N. L.	4	0	1.000
New York A. L.	0	4	.000

The New York Yankees, winners of 20 world championships, six of them achieved in four-game sweeps, were given a dose of their own medicine for the first time in their long history when the Los Angeles Dodgers bowled over the Bronx Bombers in four straight games.

For the Dodgers, the unprecedented triumph represented redemption for their sins of 1962 when the club collapsed in the last week of the season and lost the National League pennant to the San Francisco Giants in a playoff.

The Yankees, on the other hand, probably were the victims of their own success. Manager Ralph Houk's crew, although beset by injuries that sidelined one regular or another at almost every stage of the campaign, breezed to the club's twenty-eighth American League title with such ease that the players' competitive edge may have been blunted.

Meanwhile, the Dodgers were forced to battle almost down to the wire before clinching the N.L. flag. Manager Walt Alston's men, clinging to a precarious one-length lead, went into St. Louis and knocked off the red-hot Cardinals in three straight games, September 16-18, to settle the issue.

With both Mickey Mantle and Roger Maris back in the lineup, the Yankees were favored in the Series on the assumption that the Bombers' batting would prevail in what shaped up as a pitchers' battle. The Yankees had their canny veteran, Whitey Ford, and two outstanding youngsters, Jim Bouton and Al Downing, to match against Dodger starters Sandy Koufax, Johnny Podres and Don Drysdale, backed by reliever Ron Perranoski.

As it turned out, Maris batted only five times without a hit before suffering an injury in the second game. Mantle came out of the Series with two hits, including a last-gasp homer, in 15 trips and the Yankees, as a club, set a record for lowest batting average in a four-game set—.171.

The Dodgers were scarcely more masterful at the plate, hitting .214, but they capitalized on virtually every break and every Yankee mistake. John Roseboro, who had not hit a homer against a left-hander all season, decided the first game with a "cheapie" off Ford. A fouled-up pickoff play and a tumble by Maris were the big factors in the second game. The Dodgers won the third game on a grounder that skipped off Bobby Richardson's shin and the final contest was decided by the only Yankee error of the Series.

New York clubs of the past had been able to surmount any handicaps but this one was almost helpless against the Dodgers' magnificent pitching. Koufax was sensational in his two starts, Drysdale hurled a tremendous three-hitter and Podres, hero of the Dodgers' first world championship in 1955, worked a stout-hearted game before being relieved by Perranoski with one out in the ninth inning.

The Dodgers used a total of only 13 players. Their heroes included a couple of unexpected stars—Bill Skowron and Dick Tracewski. Skowron, obtained from the Yankees, was pretty much a minor member of the L.A. crew during the season, but Manager Alston started him at first base in the opener of the Series and the sight of Yankee Stadium brought muscles back to the Moose. As a result, he was in the lineup for every game. Tracewski got his chance because of an injury to Ken McMullen and rose to the opportunity with defensive brilliance.

The clubs led with their best—Koufax

against Ford—in the lidlifter and it was all "K" for Koufax. Sensational Sandy broke Carl Erskine's Series record for most strikeouts in a game, whiffing 15, while the Dodgers climbed on Ford for four runs in the second inning to defeat the Yankees, 5-2.

Koufax struck out the first five batters in starting his fanning bee. He added at least one victim in every inning except the sixth. When Richardson went down swinging in the eighth, Sandy tied Erskine's mark. He still needed one more with two out in the ninth when Harry Bright came up as a pinch-hitter for the Yankees. Koufax got his man and, afterwards, Bright said, "I guess I'm the only guy in baseball to have 60,000 people cheering for me to strike out."

Titanic Frank Howard, who proved a nemesis for Ford, belted a tremendous double to the center field wall with one out in the second inning. Skowron brought Howard home with a single and Tracewski followed with another base-hit. Roseboro then came to the plate and lofted his Chinese home run to the lower right field seats, fair by only a few feet.

Singles by Jim Gilliam, Tommy Davis and Skowron produced a run in the third as frosting on the victory cake. Koufax, who gave up six safeties, struggled a bit in the late innings and was deprived of a shutout when Tony Kubek beat out an infield hit in the eighth and Tom Tresh lined a homer into the left field seats.

In 1955, when the former Brooklyn Dodgers beat the Yankees, four games to three, Podres, then 23 years old, was the star with two victories. The southpaw pitched in his youthful form and, with two-out help in the ninth from Perranoski, defeated the Yankees in the second game, 4-1.

Maury Wills opened the first inning with a single to center off Downing. A cross-up in pickoff signals then enabled the Dodger speedster to steal second. When Downing uncorked his throw to first, Joe Pepitone was off the bag, preparing to coming in for a possible bunt by Gilliam, the next batter. Wills streaked to second and beat Pepitone's peg with a headlong slide.

Gilliam singled to right and Wills was forced to stop at third on Maris' throw, but Gilliam alertly took second on the play. Willie Davis followed with a curving line drive to right. Maris had a chance at a catch, but slipped and the ball went over his head for a double, scoring Wills and Gilliam.

Skowron homered in the fourth inning and the Dodgers added a run in the eighth off Ralph Terry, pitching in relief for the Yankees, when Willie Davis doubled and Tommy Davis hit his second triple of the game.

In the Yankees' ninth, Podres got past Mantle, who flied deep to left, but Hector Lopez bounced a ground-rule double into the left field seats. Manager Alston wasted no time in bringing Perranoski to the mound. The ace reliever gave up a run-scoring single to Elston Howard, but quickly disposed of the next two batters to send the Dodgers west with their second victory.

After a day off for travel, the Series resumed at Dodger Stadium and, this time, it was Drysdale's turn to scintillate. The big righthander, handed a tainted run to work with in the first inning, made the tally stand up for a dramatic 1-0 victory in a low-hit duel with Bouton.

After Wills was retired on a bunt to open the Dodgers' first turn at bat, Gilliam walked and Willie Davis lined out. Then came a big break on a wild pitch by Bouton that allowed Gilliam to take second. With a runner in scoring position, the Dodgers quickly capitalized on the situation. Tommy Davis lashed a hard grounder that glanced off the mound and bounced off Richardson's shins into short right-center field for a single that scored Gilliam with the vital run.

The Dodgers had a fearful moment with two out in the ninth inning when Pepitone smashed a drive deep to right, but Ron Fairly backed up and nabbed the ball five feet in front of the fence.

Moving in for the kill, the Dodgers started Koufax in the fourth game and the Yankees countered with Ford. Whitey pitched a superb game, allowing only two hits. One of them was a tape-measure homer by Howard, who also blooped a single to center for the other L.A. safety. Koufax gave up six hits.

Howard's colossal homer in the fifth inning traveled 420 feet into the eighth row of the second tier of the grandstand. It was the first fair ball to be hit into the second deck of Dodger Stadium. Koufax turned back the Yankees until the seventh when Mantle, in his only Series flash of power, belted a long homer to tie the score.

In the Dodgers' half, Gilliam chopped a high-bouncing ball to third. Clete Boyer, timing his leap, speared the ball and fired to first, but Pepitone, blinded by the white shirts of the box seat fans, lost the throw for an error as Gilliam scampered to third. On Ford's next pitch, Willie Davis hit a sacrifice fly to Mantle, who had no chance to throw out Gilliam.

The Yankees made their dying threat in the ninth. Richardson led off with a single, but Koufax cleverly threw change-up curves past Tresh and Mantle for called third strikes.

Howard then grounded to Wills in deep short. Maury made a hurried throw to Tracewski, covering second, and as umpire Tom Gorman's hand went up to signal the Series-ending putout, the ball trickled from Tracewski's glove. The Yankees still were alive—but for only one more pitch by Koufax. Sandy jammed Lopez, the pitch flicked off the Yankee's bat and dribbled toward short. Wills grabbed the ball and threw out the runner to end the Series and start a Dodger celebration.

It was a celebration with a golden glint because the players' pool was the richest in Series history—$1,017,546.43. A full share for the triumphant Dodgers amounted to a record $12,794, while the deflated Yankees gained some balm in the form of a record losing cut of $7,874.32. The box scores:

Wednesday, October 2—At New York

Los Ang. (N.L.)	AB.	R.	H.	O.	A.	E.
Wills, ss	5	0	0	2	0	0
Gilliam, 3b	4	0	1	1	1	0
W. Davis, cf	3	1	0	1	0	0
T. Davis, lf	4	0	3	0	0	0
F. Howard, rf	4	1	1	0	0	0
Fairly, rf	0	0	0	0	0	0
Skowron, 1b	3	1	2	3	0	0
Tracewski, 2b	4	1	1	2	2	0
Roseboro, c	4	1	1	18	0	0
Koufax, p	4	0	0	0	1	0
Totals	35	5	9	27	4	0

New York (A.L.)	AB.	R.	H.	O.	A.	E.
Kubek, ss	4	1	1	1	5	0
Richardson, 2b	3	0	0	2	2	0
Tresh, lf	3	1	1	0	0	0
Mantle, cf	3	0	0	1	0	0
Maris, rf	4	0	0	2	0	0
E. Howard, c	4	0	1	11	0	0
Pepitone, 1b	4	0	2	8	0	0
Boyer, 3b	4	0	1	1	2	0
Ford, p	1	0	0	1	2	0
aLopez	1	0	0	0	0	0
Williams, p	0	0	0	0	0	0
bLinz	1	0	0	0	0	0
Hamilton, p	0	0	0	0	0	0
cBright	1	0	0	0	0	0
Totals	33	2	6	27	11	0

Los Angeles .... 0 4 1 0 0 0 0 0 0—5
New York .... 0 0 0 0 0 0 0 2 0—2

aStruck out for Ford in fifth. bStruck out for Williams in eighth. cStruck out for Hamilton in ninth. Runs batted in—Skowron 2, Roseboro 3, Tresh 2. Two-base hit—F. Howard. Home runs—Roseboro, Tresh. Stolen base—T. Davis. Sacrifice hit—W. Davis. Left on bases—Los Angeles 6, New York 7. Earned runs—Los Angeles 5, New York 2. Bases on balls—Off Koufax 3, off Ford 2. Struck out—By Koufax 15, by Ford 4, by Williams 5, by Hamilton 1. Pitching records—Off Ford 8 hits, 5 runs in 5 innings; off Williams 1 hit, 0 runs in 3 innings; off Hamilton 0 hits, 0 runs in 1 inning. Losing pitcher—Ford. Umpires—Paparella (A.L.), Gorman (N.L.), Napp (A.L.), Crawford (N.L.), Venzon (N.L.) and Rice (A.L.). Time—2:09. Attendance—69,000.

Thursday, October 3—At New York

Los Ang. (N.L.)	AB.	R.	H.	O.	A.	E.
Wills, ss	4	1	2	2	3	0
Gilliam, 3b	4	1	1	1	1	0
W. Davis, cf	4	1	2	3	0	0
T. Davis, lf	4	0	2	6	0	0
F. Howard, rf	3	0	0	2	0	0
bFairly, rf	0	0	0	0	0	0
Skowron, 1b	4	1	2	8	1	0
Tracewski, 2b	3	0	0	0	1	0
Roseboro, c	4	0	0	5	0	0
Podres, p	4	0	1	0	2	1
Perranoski, p	0	0	0	0	0	0
Totals	34	4	10	27	8	1

New York (A.L.)	AB.	R.	H.	O.	A.	E.
Kubek, ss	4	0	0	2	4	0
Richardson, 2b	4	0	1	3	5	0
Tresh, lf	4	0	2	0	0	0
Mantle, cf	4	0	0	0	0	0
Maris, rf	1	0	0	1	0	0
Lopez, rf	3	1	2	1	0	0
E. Howard, c	4	0	2	6	0	0
Pepitone, 1b	3	0	0	13	1	0
Boyer, 3b	4	0	0	0	3	0
Downing, p	1	0	0	0	1	0
aBright	1	0	0	0	0	0
Terry, p	0	0	0	1	1	0
cLinz	1	0	0	0	0	0
Reniff, p	0	0	0	0	0	0
Totals	34	1	7	27	15	0

Los Angeles .... 2 0 0 1 0 0 0 1 0—4
New York .... 0 0 0 0 0 0 0 0 1—1

aCalled out on strikes for Downing in fifth. bWalked intentionally for F. Howard in eighth. cLined out for Terry in eighth. Runs batted in—W. Davis 2, T. Davis, Skowron, E. Howard. Two-base hits—W. Davis 2, Lopez 2. Three-base hits—T. Davis 2. Home run—Skowron. Stolen base—Wills. Double plays—Richardson, Kubek and Pepitone; Kubek, Richardson and Pepitone; Terry, Richardson and Pepitone. Left on bases—Los Angeles 5, New York 7. Earned runs—Los Angeles 4, New York 1. Bases on balls—Off Podres 1, off Downing 1, off Terry 1. Struck out—By Podres 4, by Perranoski 1, by Downing 6. Pitching records—Off Podres 6 hits, 1 run in 8⅓ innings; off Perranoski 1 hit, 0 runs in ⅔ inning; off Downing 7 hits, 3 runs in 5 innings; off Terry 3 hits, 1 run in 3 innings; off Reniff 0 hits, 0 runs in 1 inning. Winning pitcher—Podres. Losing pitcher—Downing. Umpires—Gorman (N.L.), Napp (A.L.), Crawford (N.L.), Paparella (A.L.), Venzon (N.L.) and Rice (A.L.). Time—2:13. Attendance—66,455.

Saturday, October 5—At Los Angeles

New York (A.L.)	AB.	R.	H.	O.	A.	E.
Kubek, ss	4	0	2	2	2	0
Richardson, 2b	3	0	0	1	3	0
Tresh, lf	4	0	0	2	0	0
Mantle, cf	4	0	1	1	0	0
Pepitone, 1b	3	0	0	8	2	0
E. Howard, c	3	0	0	7	1	0
Blanchard, rf	3	0	0	1	0	0
Boyer, 3b	2	0	0	1	1	0
Bouton, p	2	0	0	1	2	0
aBerra	1	0	0	0	0	0
Reniff, p	0	0	0	0	0	0
Totals	29	0	3	24	11	0

Los Ang. (N.L.)	AB.	R.	H.	O.	A.	E.
Wills, ss	4	0	0	1	2	1
Gilliam, 3b	2	1	0	0	0	0
W. Davis, cf	3	0	0	0	0	0
T. Davis, lf	4	0	1	0	0	0
Fairly, rf	1	0	0	3	0	0
Skowron, 1b	3	0	1	10	2	0
Roseboro, c	3	0	1	9	0	0
Tracewski, 2b	3	0	1	3	3	0
Drysdale, p	1	0	0	1	3	0
Totals	24	1	4	27	10	1

New York .... 0 0 0 0 0 0 0 0 0—0
Los Angeles .... 1 0 0 0 0 0 0 0 *—1

1964 WORLD SERIES

aLined out for Bouton in eighth. Run batted in—T. Davis. Sacrifice hits—Richardson, W. Davis. Double plays—Pepitone, Kubek and Pepitone; Richardson, Pepitone and Kubek. Left on bases—New York 5, Los Angeles 6. Earned run—Los Angeles 1. Bases on balls—Off Bouton 5, off Reniff 1, off Drysdale 1. Struck out—By Bouton 4, by Reniff 1, by Drysdale 9. Hit by pitcher—By Drysdale (Pepitone). Wild pitches—Bouton 2. Pitching record—Off Bouton 4 hits and 1 run in 7 innings; off Reniff 0 hits and 0 runs in 1 inning. Losing pitcher—Bouton. Umpires—Napp (A.L.), Crawford (N.L.), Paparella (A.L.), Gorman (N.L.), Rice (A.L.), Venzon (N.L.). Time—2:05. Attendance—55,912.

Sunday, October 6—At Los Angeles

New York (A.L.)	AB.	R.	H.	O.	A.	E.
Kubek, ss	4	0	0	0	2	0
Richardson, 2b	4	0	2	1	4	0
Tresh, lf	4	0	0	1	0	0
Mantle, cf	4	1	1	4	0	0
E. Howard, c	4	0	2	6	1	0
Lopez, rf	4	0	0	1	0	0
Pepitone, 1b	3	0	0	8	3	1
Boyer, 3b	3	0	0	2	0	0
Ford, p	2	0	0	2	0	0
aLinz	1	0	1	0	0	0
Reniff, p	0	0	0	1	0	0
Totals	33	1	6	24	12	1

Los Ang. (N.L.)	AB.	R.	H.	O.	A.	E.
Wills, ss	2	0	0	0	5	0
Gilliam, 3b	3	1	0	0	0	0
W. Davis, cf	2	0	0	2	0	0
T. Davis, lf	3	0	0	0	0	0
F. Howard, rf	3	1	2	2	0	0
Fairly, rf	0	0	0	0	0	0
Skowron, 1b	3	0	0	9	1	0
Roseboro, c	3	0	0	11	0	0
Tracewski, 2b	3	0	0	2	1	1
Koufax, p	2	0	0	1	2	0
Totals	24	2	2	27	9	1

New York .... 0 0 0   0 0 0   1 0 0—1
Los Angeles ...... 0 0 0   0 1 0   1 0 *—2

aSingled for Ford in eighth. Runs batted in—Mantle, W. Davis, F. Howard. Two-base hit—Richardson. Home run—F. Howard, Mantle. Sacrifice fly—W. Davis. Double plays—E. Howard and Pepitone; Kubek, Richardson and Pepitone; Tracewski and Skowron. Left on bases—New York 5, Los Angeles 6. Earned runs—New York 1, Los Angeles 1. Bases on balls—Off Ford 1. Struck out—By Ford 4, by Koufax 8. Pitching record—Off Ford 2 hits and 2 runs in 7 innings; off Reniff 0 hits and 0 runs in 1 inning. Losing pitcher—Ford. Umpires—Crawford (N.L.), Paparella (A.L.), Gorman (N.L.), Napp (A.L.), Rice (A.L.), Venzon (N.L.). Time—1:50. Attendance—55,912.

COMPOSITE BATTING AVERAGES
Los Angeles Dodgers

Player-Position	G.	AB.	R.	H.	2B.	3B.	HR.	RBI.	BA.
T. Davis, lf	4	15	0	6	0	2	0	2	.400
Skowron, 1b	4	13	2	5	0	0	1	3	.385
F. Howard, rf	3	10	2	3	1	0	1	1	.300
Podres, p	1	4	0	1	0	0	0	0	.250
W. Davis, cf	4	12	2	2	2	0	0	3	.167
Gilliam, 3b	4	13	3	2	0	0	0	0	.154
Tracewski, 2b	4	13	1	2	0	0	0	0	.154
Roseboro, c	4	14	2	2	0	0	1	3	.143
Wills, ss	4	15	1	2	0	0	0	0	.133
Koufax, p	2	6	0	0	0	0	0	0	.000
Perranoski, p	1	0	0	0	0	0	0	0	.000
Drysdale, p	1	2	0	0	0	0	0	0	.000
Fairly, rf-pr	4	1	0	0	0	0	0	0	.000
Totals	4	117	12	25	3	2	3	12	.214

New York Yankees

Player-Position	G.	AB.	R.	H.	2B.	3B.	HR.	RBI.	BA.
Linz, ph	3	3	0	1	0	0	0	0	.333
E. Howard, c	4	15	0	5	0	0	0	1	.333
Lopez, ph-rf	3	8	1	2	2	0	0	0	.250
Richardson, 2b	4	14	0	3	1	0	0	0	.214
Tresh, lf	4	15	1	3	0	0	1	2	.200
Kubek, ss	4	16	1	3	0	0	0	0	.188
Pepitone, 1b	4	13	0	2	0	0	0	0	.154
Mantle, cf	4	15	1	2	0	0	1	1	.133
Boyer, 3b	4	13	0	1	0	0	0	0	.077
Maris, rf	2	5	0	0	0	0	0	0	.000
Ford, p	2	3	0	0	0	0	0	0	.000
Williams, p	1	0	0	0	0	0	0	0	.000
Hamilton, p	1	0	0	0	0	0	0	0	.000
Bright, ph	2	2	0	0	0	0	0	0	.000
Downing, p	1	1	0	0	0	0	0	0	.000
Terry, p	1	0	0	0	0	0	0	0	.000
Reniff, p	3	0	0	0	0	0	0	0	.000
Blanchard, rf	1	3	0	0	0	0	0	0	.000
Bouton, p	1	2	0	0	0	0	0	0	.000
Berra, ph	1	1	0	0	0	0	0	0	.000
Totals	4	129	4	22	3	0	2	4	.171

COMPOSITE PITCHING AVERAGES
Los Angeles Dodgers

Pitcher	G.	IP.	H.	R.	E.	SO.	BB.	W.	L.	ERA.
Perranoski	1	⅔	1	0	0	1	0	0	0	0.00
Drysdale	1	9	3	0	0	9	1	1	0	0.00
Podres	1	8½	6	1	1	4	1	1	0	1.08
Koufax	2	18	12	3	3	23	3	2	0	1.50
Totals	4	36	22	4	4	37	5	4	0	1.00

New York Yankees

Pitcher	G.	IP.	H.	R.	E.	SO.	BB.	W.	L.	ERA.
Williams	1	3	1	0	0	5	0	0	0	0.00
Reniff	3	3	0	0	0	1	1	0	0	0.00
Hamilton	1	1	0	0	0	1	0	0	0	0.00
Bouton	1	7	4	1	1	4	5	0	1	1.29
Terry	1	3	3	1	1	0	1	0	0	3.00
Ford	2	12	10	7	6	8	3	0	2	4.50
Downing	1	5	7	3	3	6	1	0	1	5.40
Totals	4	34	25	12	11	25	11	0	4	2.91

SERIES OF 1964

	W.	L.	Pct.
St. Louis N. L.	4	3	.571
New York A. L.	3	4	.429

Pennant-winners and world champions for the first time since 1946, the St. Louis Cardinals defeated the New York Yankees, four games to three, in a Series that was not only dramatic in the field, but historic in its surprising developments.

The day after the classic ended, Johnny Keane resigned as manager of the Cardinals and Yogi Berra was fired as manager of the Yankees. Four days later, October 20, Keane was appointed manager of the Yankees to succeed Berra, who was retained as a special field consultant. However, Berra quit on November 17 and signed as a coach of the New York Mets.

The decision to oust Berra was reached long before he brought the American League pennant to the Yankees in his only season as manager of the club. The Bronx Bombers finished one game ahead of the Chicago White Sox and two in front of the Baltimore Orioles.

The Cardinals won the National League flag on the last day of the season after an almost incredible collapse by the Philadelphia Phillies. Holding a lead of six and one-half lengths with only 12 games to play, the Phillies lost ten in a row before recovering to beat the Cincinnati Reds twice. The Cardinals, after losing a pair to the lowly Mets, exploded for an 11-5 victory to triumph by one game as the Reds and Phillies finished in a tie for second place.

Ironically, President August A. Busch, Jr., of the Cardinals had fired General Manager Bing Devine and Business Manager Art Routzong in August because of his dissatisfaction with the club's pennant progress. Reports at the time that Busch also intended to replace Keane after the season were a factor in the manager's decision to resign, regardless of the outcome of the race.

Keane left them cheering as his Cardinals vanquished the Yankees in the Series. Mickey Mantle, although hobbled by leg trouble that interfered with his defensive work, won one game for the Yankees with a home run. Joe Pepitone iced another with a grand-slam and rookie Mel Stottlemyre was a New York pitching standout. However, the Cardinals had stars up and down their lineup, with chief honors going to Bob Gibson, Tim McCarver and Ken Boyer.

The Yankees, who had gone into the Series without shortstop Tony Kubek, suffered a damaging blow in the first game when Whitey Ford not only lost, 9-5, but went on the shelf with arm trouble for the balance of the classic. It was the fifth consecutive defeat in Series competition for the Bombers. They had dropped four straight to the Dodgers in 1963.

The ace lefthander nursed a 4-2 lead going into the bottom of the sixth inning when the Cardinals exploded. Boyer singled and Mike Shannon smashed a 450-foot homer to tie the score. McCarver doubled to rout Ford. Al Downing relieved, but before the little lefthander could end the outburst, the Cardinals scored twice more on a pinch-single by Carl Warwick and a triple by Curt Flood.

Barney Schultz, veteran knuckleball righthander, pitched the last three innings for the Redbirds allowing one run and preserving the victory for Ray Sadecki.

The Yankees called on Stottlemyre in the second game and the young righthander was superb in an 8-3 victory. Gibson started for the Cardinals and struck out six batters in the first three innings, but the hard-throwing righthander began wavering and went down to defeat after a controversial call in the sixth inning.

Mantle drew a walk to open the stanza. After Elston Howard went out, Pepitone appeared to have pulled away from an inside pitch, but plate umpire Bill McKinley ruled that he had been nicked by the ball. The Cardinals argued violently, but to no avail. Pepitone was waved to first, Mantle moved to second and Tom Tresh promptly singled, scoring Mantle, to break a 1-1 tie.

The Yankees added two runs in the seventh and salted their decision with four more in the ninth.

Schultz, whose relief exploits helped the Cardinals win the pennant, was the hard-luck victim—on only one pitch—when the Yankees won the third game, 2 to 1. Curt Simmons, who started for the Redbirds, gave up the Yanks' initial run in the second inning, but singled off Jim Bouton to drive the tying tally across the plate in the fifth.

The Cardinals removed Simmons for a pinch-hitter in the ninth and then brought Schultz in from the bullpen to face the Yankees. Mantle was the first batter. Schultz threw a knuckleball, but it floated instead of breaking, and Mantle tore into the pitch for a winning home run. With the blow, Mantle broke a tie with Babe Ruth for the most Series homers. The smash was his sixteenth.

The Yanks opened the fourth game by scoring three runs off Sadecki in the first inning, but they were blanked thereafter on two hits by the terrific relief pitching of Roger Craig and Ron Taylor. Craig in his four and two-thirds innings of relief, fanned eight Bomber batters. Downing, meanwhile, downed the Cardinals until the sixth inning when he went down, 4-3, on one swing of Boyer's bat. The blow was a grand-slam homer that followed a pinch-single by Warwick, another single by Curt Flood and an error by Bobby Richardson on Groat's ground ball, which appeared a certain double play that would have retired the Cards.

Two base-running blunders by Mickey Mantle in the first and third innings, broke up scoring chances for the Yankees.

A tremendous defensive play saved Gibson from disaster in the fifth game and the Cardinal righthander went on the defeat the Yankees, 5-2, on a round-tripper by McCarver in the tenth.

With the Cardinals leading, 2-0, Mantle was safe on an error by Dick Groat to open the Yankees' ninth. Pepitone then lashed a line drive that struck the half-turned Gibson and bounced toward third. Bounding of the mound, Gibson grabbed the ball, fired off balance and nipped Pepitone by inches. If Gibson had not made the play, he would have been beaten because Tresh followed with a drive into the right field stands, scoring behind Mantle, to send the game into overtime.

In the tenth, Bill White drew a pass from reliever Pete Mikkelsen and Boyer, intending to sacrifice, bunted safely to the right of the mound. Groat forced Boyer, but McCarver clubbed a fast ball to the right field stands for the winning homer.

The power in the Yankee lineup asserted itself in the sixth game. Roger Maris and Mantle connected against Simmons on consecutive pitches in the sixth inning and Pepitone delivered his grand-slam in the eighth to sew up an 8-3 victory. The blow came off Gordon Richardson, who relieved Schultz with the bases loaded.

With all the money riding on the seventh and final game, the Cardinals once more called on Gibson and the Yankees turned to Stottlemyre, each pitching with two days of rest. The Cardinals, running like the old Gashouse Gang, scored three runs in the fourth inning. Downing relieved in the fifth and failed to retire a batter, throwing four pitches and giving up a homer by Lou Brock, a single by White and a double by Boyer. After Roland Sheldon relieved, White scored on an infield out and Boyer on a sacrifice fly to give the Cardinals a 6-0 lead.

Mantle cut the Yankees' deficit in half in the sixth, smashing a homer with two men on base, but Boyer got one run back for the Cardinals with a drive over the fence against Steve Hamilton in the seventh. Laboring in the ninth, Gibson was tagged for homers by Cletis Boyer, brother of the Cardinals' captain, and Phil Linz. With two out, the batter was Richardson, who had set a Series record by collecting 13 hits. On deck was Maris, the Yankees' home-run threat.

In the clutch situation, Gibson called on all his reserve and retired Richardson on a pop fly to Dal Maxvill as the Cardinals exploded in championship exultation. Maxvill, incidentally, was a standout substitute for Julian Javier, the Cardinals' regular second baseman, who was injured and appeared only briefly.

Gibson set a Series record for strikeouts with 31 in 27 innings. The box scores:

Wednesday, October 7—At St. Louis

New York (A.L.)	AB.	R.	H.	O.	A.	E.
Linz, ss	4	0	0	1	1	0
Richardson, 2b	5	0	2	2	3	0
Maris, cf	4	0	1	0	0	0
Mantle, rf	5	1	2	1	0	1
Howard, c	4	1	2	5	0	0
Tresh, lf	4	1	2	1	0	0
Pepitone, 1b	5	0	0	11	0	0
C. Boyer, 3b	4	1	1	2	4	1
Ford, p	1	0	1	0	1	0
Downing, p	0	0	0	0	0	0
dBlanchard	1	0	1	0	0	0
eHegan	0	1	0	0	0	0
Sheldon, p	0	0	0	1	1	0
Mikkelsen, p	0	0	0	0	0	0
Totals	37	5	12	24	10	2

St. Louis (N.L.)	AB.	R.	H.	O.	A.	E.
Flood, cf	5	1	2	5	0	0
Brock, lf	5	1	2	1	1	0
Groat, ss	4	0	1	1	4	0
K. Boyer, 3b	3	1	1	1	4	0
White, 1b	4	0	0	11	0	0
Shannon, rf	4	3	2	2	0	0
McCarver, c	3	1	2	4	0	0
Maxvill, 2b	2	0	0	2	2	0
aJames	1	0	0	0	0	0
Schultz, p	1	0	0	0	0	0
Sadecki, p	2	0	1	0	1	0
bWarwick	1	0	1	0	0	0
cJavier, 2b	0	1	0	0	1	0
fSkinner	0	0	0	0	0	0
gBuchek, 2b	0	1	0	0	0	0
Totals	35	9	12	27	13	0

New York...... 0 3 0 0 1 0 0 1 0—5
St. Louis...... 1 1 0 0 0 4 0 3 *—9

aPopped out for Maxvill in sixth. bSingled for Sadecki in sixth. cRan for Warwick in sixth. dDoubled for Downing in eighth. eRan for Blanchard in eighth. fWalked intentionally for Javier in eighth. gRan for Skinner in eighth. Runs batted in—Richardson, Tresh 3, Ford, Flood 2, Brock 2, K. Boyer, Shannon 2, Sadecki, Warwick. Two-base hits—Tresh, McCarver, Blanchard, Brock. Three-base hits—McCarver, Flood. Home runs—Tresh, Shannon. Stolen base—C. Boyer. Sacrifice fly—K. Boyer. Double plays—Groat, Maxvill and White; Sheldon and Pepitone. Left on bases—New York 11, St. Louis 7. Earned runs—New York 5, St. Louis 6. Bases on balls—Off Ford 1, off Sheldon 2, off Mikkelsen 1, off Sadecki 5, off Schultz 1. Struck out—By Ford 4, by Downing 1, by Sadecki 2, by Schultz 1. Pitching records—Off Ford 8 hits, 5 runs in 5⅓ innings; off Downing 2 hits, 1 run in 1⅔ innings; off Sheldon 0 hits, 2 runs in ⅔ inning; off Mikkelsen 2 hits, 1 run in ⅓ inning off Sadecki 8 hits, 4 runs in 6 innings; off Schultz 4 hits, 1 run in 3 innings. Passed balls—Howard 2. Winning pitcher—Sadecki. Losing pitcher—Ford. Umpires—Secory (N.L.), McKinley (A.L.), Burkhart (N.L.), Soar (A.L.), V. Smith (N.L.) and A. Smith (A.L.). Time—2:42. Attendance—30,805.

Thursday, October 8—At St. Louis

New York (A.L.)	AB.	R.	H.	O.	A.	E.
Linz, ss	4	2	3	1	8	0
B. Richardson, 2b	5	1	2	4	2	0
Maris, cf	5	1	2	2	0	0
Mantle, rf	4	2	1	0	0	0
Lopez, rf	0	0	0	0	0	0
Howard, c	4	2	1	4	1	0
Pepitone, 1b	4	0	2	14	1	0
Tresh, lf	3	0	1	1	0	0
C. Boyer, 3b	3	0	0	0	3	0
Stottlemyre, p	5	0	0	1	3	0
Totals	37	8	12	27	18	0

St. Louis (N.L.)	AB.	R.	H.	O.	A.	E.
Flood, cf	4	0	0	2	0	0
Brock, lf	4	0	0	1	0	0
White, 1b	3	0	0	7	0	0
K. Boyer, 3b	4	0	0	2	1	0
Groat, ss	3	1	1	2	3	0
McCarver, c	4	0	1	10	0	0
Shannon, rf	4	1	1	2	0	0
Maxvill, 2b	2	0	1	1	3	0
aWarwick	1	1	1	0	0	0
Schultz, p	0	0	0	0	0	0
G. Richardson, p	0	0	0	0	0	0
Craig, p	0	0	0	0	0	0
dJames	1	0	0	0	0	0
Gibson, p	1	0	1	0	0	0
bSkinner	1	0	1	0	0	0
cBuchek, 2b	0	0	0	0	0	0
Totals	32	3	7	27	7	0

New York...... 0 0 0 1 0 1 2 0 4—8
St. Louis...... 0 0 1 0 0 0 0 1 1—3

aSingled for Maxvill in eighth. bDoubled for Gibson in eighth. cRan for Skinner in eighth. dStruck out for Craig in ninth. Runs batted in—Linz, B. Richardson, Mantle 2, Pepitone, Tresh 2, C. Boyer, Flood, Brock, McCarver. Two-base hits—B. Richardson, Howard, Pepitone, Skinner,

Mantle. Three-base hit—Groat. Home run—Linz. Sacrifice hit—Gibson. Sacrifice flies—C. Boyer, Tresh. Double play—Linz, B. Richardson and Pepitone. Left on bases—New York 10, St. Louis 5. Earned runs—New York 8, St. Louis 3. Bases on balls—Off Stottlemyre 2, off Gibson 3, off G. Richardson 2. Struck out—By Stottlemyre 4, by Gibson 9, by Craig 1. Pitching record—Off Gibson 8 hits, 4 runs in 8 innings; off Schultz 2 hits, 2 runs in ⅓ inning; off G. Richardson 2 hits, 2 runs in ⅓ inning; off Craig 0 hits, 0 runs in ⅓ inning. Hit by pitcher—By Gibson (Pepitone). Wild pitch—Gibson. Passed pass—Howard. Winning pitcher—Stottlemyre. Losing pitcher—Gibson. Umpires—McKinley (A.L.), Burkhart (N.L.), Soar (A.L.), V. Smith (N.L.), A. Smith (A.L.) and Secory (A.L.). Time—2:29. Attendance—30,805.

Saturday, October 10—At New York

St. Louis (N.L.)	AB.	R.	H.	O.	A.	E.
Flood, cf	5	0	0	1	0	0
Brock, lf	4	0	0	2	0	0
White, 1b	4	0	1	12	2	0
K. Boyer, 3b	4	0	0	1	3	0
Groat, ss	4	0	1	1	4	0
McCarver, c	2	1	1	3	0	0
Shannon, rf	3	0	1	1	0	0
Maxvill, 2b	3	0	1	1	2	0
aWarwick	0	0	0	0	0	0
Buchek, 2b	0	0	0	0	0	0
Simmons, p	2	0	1	2	1	0
bSkinner	1	0	0	0	0	0
Schultz, p	0	0	0	0	0	0
Totals	32	1	6	i24	12	0

New York (A.L.)	AB.	R.	H.	O.	A.	E.
Linz, ss	4	0	0	0	3	1
Richardson, 2b	4	0	1	4	3	0
Maris, cf	4	0	0	4	0	0
Mantle, rf	3	1	2	3	0	1
Howard, c	2	1	1	2	0	0
Tresh, lf	3	0	0	4	0	0
Pepitone, 1b	2	0	0	8	0	0
C. Boyer, 3b	3	0	1	1	3	0
Bouton, p	3	0	0	1	0	0
Totals	28	2	5	27	9	2

St. Louis............ 0 0 0 0 1 0 0 0 0—1
New York........... 0 1 0 0 0 0 0 0 1—2

aWalked for Maxvill in ninth. bFlied out for Simmons in ninth. iNone out when winning run scored. Runs batted in—Simmons, Mantle, C. Boyer. Two-base hits—C. Boyer, Groat, Mantle, Maxvill. Home run—Mantle. Sacrifice hits—Simmons, Shannon. Double play—Maxvill, Groat and White. Left on bases—St. Louis 9, New York 5. Earned runs—St. Louis 0, New York 2. Bases on balls—Off Simmons 3, off Bouton 3. Struck out—By Simmons 2, by Bouton 2. Pitching record—Off Simmons 4 hits, 1 run in 8 innings; off Schultz 1 hit, 1 run in 0 inning (pitched to one batter in ninth). Winning pitcher—Bouton. Losing pitcher—Schultz. Umpires—Burkhart (N.L.), Soar (A.L.), V. Smith (N.L.), A. Smith (A.L.), Secory (N.L.) and McKinley (A.L.). Time—2:16. Attendance—67,101.

Sunday, October 11—At New York

St. Louis (N.L.)	AB.	R.	H.	O.	A.	E.
Flood, cf	4	1	2	1	0	0
Brock, lf	4	0	0	1	0	0
Groat, ss	4	1	1	1	2	0
K. Boyer, 3b	4	1	1	1	2	1
White, 1b	4	0	0	11	0	0
Shannon, rf	4	0	0	1	0	0
McCarver, c	3	0	1	10	1	0
Maxvill, 2b	3	0	0	1	1	0
Sadecki, p	0	0	0	0	0	0
Craig, p	1	0	0	0	2	0
aWarwick	1	1	1	0	0	0
Taylor, p	1	0	0	0	2	0
Totals	33	4	6	27	11	1

New York (A.L.)	AB.	R.	H.	O.	A.	E.
Linz, ss	4	1	1	0	3	0
Richardson, 2b	4	1	1	1	2	1
Maris, cf	4	1	1	6	0	0
Mantle, rf	2	0	1	2	0	0
Howard, c	3	0	1	9	0	0
Tresh, lf	4	0	0	1	0	0
Pepitone, 1b	3	0	0	8	0	0
C. Boyer, 3b	4	0	1	0	3	0
Downing, p	2	0	0	0	1	0
Mikkelsen, p	0	0	0	0	0	0
bBlanchard	1	0	0	0	0	0
Terry, p	0	0	0	0	0	0
Totals	31	3	6	27	9	1

St. Louis............ 0 0 0 0 0 4 0 0 0—4
New York........... 3 0 0 0 0 0 0 0 0—3

aSingled for Craig in sixth. bFlied out for Mikkelsen in seventh. Runs batted in—K. Boyer 4, Richardson, Mantle, Howard. Two-base hits—Linz, Richardson. Home run—K. Boyer. Double play—Linz, Richardson and Pepitone. Left on bases—St. Louis 4, New York 5. Earned runs—St. Louis 3, New York 2. Bases on balls—Off Craig 3, off Taylor 1, off Downing 2. Struck out—By Craig 8, by Taylor 2, by Downing 4, by Mikkelsen 1, by Terry 3. Pitching record—Off Sadecki 4 hits, 3 runs in ⅓ inning; off Craig 2 hits, 0 runs in 4⅔ innings; off Taylor 0 hits, 0 runs in 4 innings; off Downing 4 hits, 4 runs in 6 innings (pitched to one batter in seventh); off Mikkelsen 0 hits, 0 runs in 1 inning; off Terry 2 hits, 0 runs in 2 innings. Winning pitcher—Craig. Losing pitcher—Downing. Umpires—Soar (A.L.), V. Smith (N.L.), A. Smith (A.L.), Secory (N.L.), McKinley (A.L.) and Burkhart (N.L.). Time—2:18. Attendance—66,312.

Monday, October 12—At New York

St. Louis (N.L.)	AB.	R.	H.	O.	A.	E.
Flood, cf	4	1	1	1	0	0
Brock, lf	5	1	2	1	0	0
White, 1b	4	1	0	7	0	0
aK. Boyer, 3b	4	0	1	3	1	0
Groat, ss	4	1	1	2	2	1
McCarver, c	5	1	3	13	0	0
Shannon, rf	5	0	1	0	0	0
Maxvill, 2b	5	0	1	1	1	0
Gibson, p	4	1	1	1	1	0
Totals	40	5	10	30	5	1

New York (A.L.)	AB.	R.	H.	O.	A.	E.
Linz, ss	5	0	0	1	3	0
Richardson, 2b	5	0	3	5	3	1
Maris, cf	5	0	0	3	0	0
Mantle, rf	3	1	0	1	0	0
Howard, c	3	0	0	9	0	1
Pepitone, 1b	4	0	1	8	1	0
Tresh, lf	3	1	1	1	0	0
C. Boyer, 3b	2	0	0	0	3	0
bBlanchard	1	0	0	0	0	0
Gonzalez, 3b	1	0	0	1	3	0
Stottlemyre, p	2	0	1	0	1	0
cLopez	1	0	0	0	0	0
Reniff, p	0	0	0	0	0	0
Mikkelsen, p	0	0	0	1	0	0
dHegan	1	0	0	0	0	0
Totals	36	2	6	30	14	2

St. Louis............ 0 0 0 0 2 0 0 0 0 3—5
New York.......... 0 0 0 0 0 0 0 0 2 0—2

aReached first on catcher's interference. bPopped out for C. Boyer in seventh. cStruck out for Stottlemyre in tenth. dStruck out for Mikkelsen in tenth. Runs batted in—Brock, White, McCarver 3, Tresh 2. Home runs—Tresh, McCarver. Stolen base—White. Double plays—Maxvill, Groat and White; Linz, Richardson and Pepitone. Left on bases—St. Louis 9, New York 7. Earned runs—St. Louis 4, New York 0. Bases on balls—Off Gibson 2, off Stottlemyre 2, off Mikkelsen 1. Struck out—By Gibson 13, by Stottlemyre 6, by Mikkelsen 3. Pitching record—Off Stottlemyre 6 hits, 2 runs in 7 innings; off Reniff 2 hits, 0 runs in ⅓ inning; off Mikkelsen 2 hits, 3 runs in 2⅔ innings. Hit by pitched ball—By Gibson (Howard). Winning pitcher—Gibson. Losing pitcher—Mikkelsen. Umpires—V. Smith (N.L.), A. Smith (A.L.), Secory (N.L.), McKinley (A.L.), Burkhart (N.L.) and Soar (A.L.). Time—2:37. Attendance—65,633.

Wednesday, October 14—At St. Louis

New York (A.L.)	AB.	R.	H.	O.	A.	E.
Linz, ss................	5	1	1	2	3	0
B. Richardson, 2b....	4	0	2	2	3	0
Maris, cf.............	4	1	1	4	0	0
Mantle, rf............	3	2	1	3	0	0
Howard, c............	4	1	1	5	0	0
Tresh, lf.............	3	2	1	1	0	0
Pepitone, 1b.........	4	1	1	6	2	0
C. Boyer, 3b.........	4	0	1	1	1	0
Bouton, p............	4	0	1	3	0	0
Hamilton, p..........	0	0	0	0	0	0
Totals	35	8	10	27	9	0

St. Louis (N.L.)	AB.	R.	H.	O.	A.	E.
Flood, cf.............	3	2	1	1	0	0
Brock, lf.............	4	0	3	5	0	1
White, 1b............	4	0	0	8	1	0
K. Boyer, 3b.........	4	0	0	0	3	0
Groat, ss.............	4	0	0	3	0	0
McCarver, c..........	4	0	2	8	0	0
Shannon, rf..........	4	1	1	3	0	0
Maxvill, 2b..........	2	0	0	2	3	0
aWarwick	1	0	0	0	0	0
Buchek, 2b..........	1	0	1	0	1	0
Simmons, p..........	2	0	1	0	0	0
Taylor, p	0	0	0	0	0	0
bJames..............	1	0	0	0	0	0
Schultz, p	0	0	0	0	0	0
G. Richardson, p......	0	0	0	0	0	0
Humphreys, p........	0	0	0	0	0	0
cSkinner............	1	0	1	0	0	0
Totals	35	3	10	27	8	1

New York.......... 0 0 0 0 1 2 0 5 0—8
St. Louis............ 1 0 0 0 0 0 0 1 1—3

aFouled out for Maxvill in seventh. bGrounded out for Taylor in seventh. cSingled for Humphreys in ninth. Runs batted in—Maris, Mantle, Howard, Bouton, Pepitone 4, White, Skinner. Two-base hits—Tresh, Brock. Home runs—Maris, Mantle, Pepitone. Stolen base—B. Richardson. Sacrifice hit—B. Richardson. Double plays—B. Richardson, Linz and Pepitone; Maxvill and Groat; Linz, B. Richardson and Pepitone. Left on bases—New York 3, St. Louis 7. Earned runs—New York 8, St. Louis 3. Bases on balls—Off Bouton 2, off Schultz 2. Struck out—By Bouton 5, by Simmons 6, by Humphreys 1. Pitching record—Off Bouton 9 hits, 3 runs in 8⅓ innings; off Hamilton 1 hit, 0 runs in ⅔ inning; off Simmons 7 hits, 3 runs in 6⅓ innings; off Taylor 0 hits, 0 runs in ⅔ inning; off Schultz 2 hits, 4 runs in ⅔ inning; off G. Richardson 1 hit, 1 run in ⅓ inning; off Humphreys 0 hits, 0 runs in 1 inning. Winning pitcher—Bouton. Losing pitcher—Simmons. Umpires—A. Smith (A.L.), Secory (N.L.), McKinley (A.L.), Burkhart (N.L.), Soar (A.L.) and V. Smith (N.L.). Time—2:37. Attendance—30,805.

Thursday, October 15—At St. Louis

New York (A.L.)	AB.	R.	H.	O.	A.	E.
Linz, ss...............	5	1	2	2	0	1
B. Richardson, 2b....	5	1	2	1	3	0
Maris, cf.............	4	1	1	1	0	0
Mantle, rf............	4	1	1	2	0	0
Howard, c	4	0	1	6	1	0
Pepitone, 1b.........	4	0	0	8	2	0
Tresh, lf.............	2	0	1	2	0	0
C. Boyer, 3b..........	4	1	1	1	5	1
Stottlemyre, p........	1	0	0	1	1	0
aHegan	0	0	0	0	0	0
Downing, p..........	0	0	0	0	0	0
Sheldon, p...........	0	0	0	0	0	0
bLopez...............	1	0	0	0	0	0
Hamilton, p	0	0	0	0	0	0
Mikkelsen, p..........	0	0	0	0	1	0
cBlanchard..........	1	0	0	0	0	0
Totals	35	5	9	24	13	2

St. Louis (N.L.)	AB.	R.	H.	O.	A.	E.
Flood, cf.............	5	0	0	2	0	0
Brock, lf.............	4	1	2	0	0	0
White, 1b............	4	1	2	6	0	0
K. Boyer, 3b.........	4	3	3	1	2	0
Groat, ss.............	3	0	0	1	1	1
McCarver, c..........	2	1	1	9	0	0
Shannon, rf..........	4	1	1	3	1	0
Maxvill, 2b..........	3	0	1	5	3	0
Gibson, p............	4	0	0	0	1	0
Totals	33	7	10	27	8	1

New York.......... 0 0 0 0 0 3 0 0 2—5
St. Louis............ 0 0 0 3 3 0 1 0 *—7

aWalked for Stottlemyre in fifth. bStruck out for Sheldon in seventh. cStruck out for Mikkelsen in ninth. Runs batted in—Maxvill, Brock, Groat, McCarver, Mantle 3, K. Boyer, C. Boyer, Linz. Two-base hits—White, K. Boyer. Home runs—Brock, Mantle, K. Boyer, C. Boyer, Linz. Stolen bases—McCarver, Shannon. Sacrifice hit—Maxvill. Sacrifice fly—McCarver. Double play—Groat, Maxvill and White, Shannon and Groat. Left on bases—New York 6, St. Louis 6. Earned runs—New York 5, St. Louis 7. Bases on balls—Off Stottlemyre 2, off Gibson 3. Struck out—By Stottlemyre 2, by Sheldon 2, by Hamilton 2, by Gibson 9. Pitching record—Off Stottlemyre 5 hits, 3 runs in 4 innings; off Downing 3 hits, 3 runs in 0 inning (pitched to three batters in fifth); off Sheldon 0 hits, 0 runs in 2 innings; off Hamilton 2 hits, 1 run in 1⅓ innings; off Mikkelsen 0 hits, 0 runs in ⅔ inning. Winning pitcher—Gibson. Losing pitcher—Stottlemyre. Umpires—Secory (N.L.), McKinley (A.L.), Burkhart (N.L.), Soar (A.L.), V. Smith (N.L.) and A. Smith (A.L.). Time—2:40. Attendance—30,346.

COMPOSITE BATTING AVERAGES
St. Louis Cardinals

Player-Position	G.	AB.	R.	H.	2B.	3B.	HR.	RBI.	BA.
Buchek, pr-2b..........	4	1	1	1	0	0	0	0	1.000
Warwick, ph..........	5	4	2	3	0	0	0	1	.750
Skinner, ph	4	3	0	2	1	0	0	1	.667
Sadecki, p............	2	2	0	1	0	0	0	1	.500
Simmons, p..........	2	4	0	2	0	0	0	1	.500
McCarver, c..........	7	23	4	11	1	1	1	5	.478
Brock, lf	7	30	2	9	2	0	1	5	.300
Gibson, p............	3	9	1	2	0	0	0	0	.222
K. Boyer, 3b.........	7	27	5	6	1	0	2	6	.222
Shannon, rf..........	7	28	6	6	0	0	1	2	.214

1965 WORLD SERIES

Player-Position	G.	AB.	R.	H.	2B.	3B.	HR.	RBI.	BA.
Flood, cf	7	30	5	6	0	1	0	3	.200
Maxvill, 2b	7	20	0	4	1	0	0	1	.200
Groat, ss	7	26	3	5	1	1	0	1	.192
White, 1b	7	27	2	3	1	0	0	2	.111
Javier, pr-2b	1	0	1	0	0	0	0	0	.000
Schultz, p	4	1	0	0	0	0	0	0	.000
G. Richardson, p	2	0	0	0	0	0	0	0	.000
Craig, p	2	1	0	0	0	0	0	0	.000
Taylor, p	2	1	0	0	0	0	0	0	.000
Humphreys, p	1	0	0	0	0	0	0	0	.000
James, ph	3	3	0	0	0	0	0	0	.000
Totals	7	240	32	61	8	3	5	29	.254

New York Yankees

Player-Position	G.	AB.	R.	H.	2B.	3B.	HR.	RBI.	BA.
Ford, p	1	1	0	1	0	0	0	1	1.000
B. Richardson, 2b	7	32	3	13	2	0	0	3	.406
Mantle, rf	7	24	8	8	2	0	3	8	.333
Howard, c	7	24	5	7	1	0	0	2	.292
Tresh, lf	7	22	4	6	2	0	2	7	.273
Blanchard, ph	4	4	0	1	1	0	0	0	.250
Linz, ss	7	31	5	7	1	0	2	2	.226
C. Boyer, 3b	7	24	2	5	1	0	1	3	.208
Maris, cf	7	30	4	6	0	0	1	1	.200
Pepitone, 1b	7	26	1	4	1	0	1	5	.154
Bouton, p	2	7	0	1	0	0	0	1	.143
Stottlemyre, p	3	8	0	1	0	0	0	0	.125
Gonzalez, 3b	1	1	0	0	0	0	0	0	.000
Lopez, rf-ph	3	2	0	0	0	0	0	0	.000
Downing, p	3	2	0	0	0	0	0	0	.000
Sheldon, p	2	0	0	0	0	0	0	0	.000
Mikkelsen, p	4	0	0	0	0	0	0	0	.000
Terry, p	1	0	0	0	0	0	0	0	.000
Reniff, p	1	0	0	0	0	0	0	0	.000
Hamilton, p	2	0	0	0	0	0	0	0	.000
Hegan, pr-ph	3	1	1	0	0	0	0	0	.000
Totals	7	239	33	60	11	0	10	33	.251

COMPOSITE PITCHING AVERAGES
St. Louis Cardinals

Pitcher	G.	IP.	H.	R.	E.	SO.	BB.	W.	L.	ERA.
Craig	2	5	2	0	0	9	3	1	0	0.00
Taylor	2	4⅔	0	0	0	2	1	0	0	0.00
Humphreys	1	1	0	0	0	1	0	0	0	0.00
Simmons	2	14½	11	4	4	8	3	0	1	2.51
Gibson	3	27	23	11	9	31	8	2	1	3.00
Sadecki	2	6⅓	12	7	6	2	5	1	0	8.53
Schultz	4	4	9	8	8	1	3	0	1	18.00
G. Richardson	2	⅔	3	3	3	0	2	0	0	40.50
Totals	7	63	60	33	30	54	25	4	3	4.29

New York Yankees

Pitcher	G.	IP.	H.	R.	E.	SO.	BB.	W.	L.	ERA.
Sheldon	2	2⅔	0	2	0	2	2	0	0	0.00
Terry	1	2	2	0	0	3	0	0	0	0.00
Reniff	1	⅓	2	0	0	0	0	0	0	0.00
Bouton	2	17½	15	4	3	7	5	2	0	1.56
Stottlemyre	3	20	18	8	7	12	6	1	1	3.15
Hamilton	2	2	3	1	1	2	0	0	0	4.50
Mikkelsen	4	4⅔	4	4	3	4	2	0	1	5.79
Downing	3	7⅔	9	8	7	5	2	0	1	8.22
Ford	1	5⅓	8	5	5	4	1	0	1	8.44
Totals	7	62	61	32	26	39	18	3	4	3.77

SERIES OF 1965

	W.	L.	Pct.
Los Angeles N. L.	4	3	.571
Minnesota A. L.	3	4	.429

For the first time since 1907-09, the National League made it three world championships in a row when the amazing Los Angeles Dodgers rallied to defeat the Minnesota Twins, four games to three.

Walter Alston's masterful handling of his club made him the first N.L. manager to win four classics. His other world titles came in 1955, '59 and '63.

The powder-puff Dodgers, who hit just 78 home runs in the regular season, won the pennant with terrific pitching—and pitching proved the difference in the Series against Manager Sam Mele's power-packed Twins, who had clubbed 150 homers.

The American League sluggers appeared on the way to a quick kayo of the Dodgers when they beat Alston's aces, Don Drysdale and Sandy Koufax, in the first two games. But the Twins learned, as N.L. clubs already knew, that it was possible to gain successive victories over Drysdale and Koufax once, but almost impossible to do it twice. The third member of L.A.'s "Big Three," Claude Osteen, also pitched a key decision as the Dodgers gained three of their triumphs by shutouts. The Twins had been blanked only three times in the entire 1965 campaign.

Rising to the Series challenge, the Dodgers reversed batting roles with the Twins, hitting .274 against the A.L. club's .195. Right fielder Ron Fairly, who had been hitless in ten games in previous Series play, broke out with a .379 average to lead all regular performers. His teammate, shortstop Maury Wills, batted .367.

Although Koufax normally would have been the starting pitcher for the Dodgers, the Series opened on a Jewish religious holiday and Drysdale got the assignment for the lidlifter at Metropolitan Stadium against Jim Grant.

After Fairly homered for the Dodgers in the second inning and Don Mincher duplicated the blow in the Twins' half, Minnesota exploded for six runs in the third and Grant had easy sailing to an 8-2 victory. The big blow of the uprising was a three-run homer by Zoilo Versalles. Frank Quilici, the Twins' rookie second baseman, led off with a double and singled on a second trip, tying the Series record for most hits in one inning.

If the Twins surprised everybody by kayoing Drysdale, they shocked the baseball world by coming back to beat Koufax while winning the second game, 5-1. An error by Jim Gilliam on Versalles' sharp grounder, a double by Tony Oliva and a single by Harmon Killebrew gave the Twins two runs off Koufax in the sixth inning and they padded their advantage in the seventh and eighth against Ron Perranoski's relief pitching.

The Twins got steady hurling in Game Two from Jim Kaat, but it took a sensational catch by left fielder Bob Allison to bail the southpaw out of trouble in the fifth inning. After Fairly singled, Jim Lefebvre stroked a curving line drive to left. Allison, who had to go a long way to catch up with the ball, reached for it with one final lunge, grabbed it just as it was about to hit the ground and then slid almost 15 feet on the wet turf. The catch was hailed as one of the greatest in Series history.

After a day off for travel, the clubs resumed competition at Los Angeles and, in a different park, the story was different as Osteen, Drysdale and Koufax racked up consecutive victories. Osteen calcimined the Twins, 4-0, beating Camilo Pascual; Drysdale followed with a 7-2 decision over Grant, and Koufax applied the whitewash, 7-0, in a return duel with Kaat.

When the clubs traveled back to Minnesota, the pressure was on the Twins, who had no choice but to call on Grant. Although having only two days of rest, the big righthander was equal to the challenge, pitching a six-hitter to defeat Osteen, 5-1. After Allison put the Twins in front with a two-run homer in the fourth inning, Grant iced his victory by hitting for the circuit with two men on base in the sixth. He became only the seventh pitcher to smash a homer in Series competition.

Manager Alston of the Dodgers tussled with the problem of whether to use Drysdale or Koufax in the climactic seventh game. He finally passed over the more rested Drysdale and picked Koufax, who had been suffering all year from an arthritic elbow. Manager Mele of the Twins selected Kaat. This was the third meeting of the Series for the two lefthanders and both pitched with only two days between assignments.

Koufax was not at his best, if that can be said about a pitcher who yielded only three hits. From the start of the game, the southpaw had trouble with his curve, but he made his blazing fast ball do the job in a 2-0 victory. He struck out 10.

Lou Johnson, 32-year-old outfielder who came out of the minors to fill in capably after Tommy Davis suffered a fractured leg on May 1, hit a homer off Kaat in the fourth inning to give Koufax the only run he needed. However, the Dodgers went on to add an insurance counter later in the inning on a double by Fairly and a single by Wes Parker.

Gilliam pulled Koufax out of his only tough spot. In the fifth inning, Quilici doubled and Rich Rollins, batting for Kaat, walked. Versalles then smashed a hot grounder down the third base line, but Gilliam dived to his right and made a backhanded grab of the ball. The old pro calmly regained his feet and trotted to third for a forceout of Quilici, taking the steam out of the Twins' threat.

In the ninth, Killebrew singled with one away, but Koufax fired three successive strikes past Earl Battey and then whiffed Allison to wrap up the Series. The box scores:

Wednesday, October 6—At Minnesota

Los Ang. (N.L.)	AB.	R.	H.	O.	A.	E.
Wills, ss	5	0	2	3	2	0
Gilliam, 3b	5	0	1	0	1	0
W. Davis, cf	4	0	1	2	0	0
Fairly, rf	4	1	1	2	0	0
Johnson, lf	4	0	1	4	0	0
Lefebvre, 2b	4	1	1	0	4	1
Parker, 1b	3	0	1	7	0	0
Roseboro, c	4	0	1	6	0	0
Drysdale, p	1	0	0	0	1	0
Reed, p	0	0	0	0	0	0
aCrawford	1	0	1	0	0	0
Brewer, p	0	0	0	0	0	0
bMoon	1	0	0	0	0	0
Perranoski, p	0	0	0	0	1	0
cLeJohn	1	0	0	0	0	0
Totals	37	2	10	24	9	1

Minnesota (A.L.)	AB.	R.	H.	O.	A.	E.
Versalles, ss	5	1	2	3	2	0
Valdespino, lf	4	1	1	4	0	0
Oliva, rf	4	0	0	7	0	0
Killebrew, 3b	3	1	1	3	0	0
Hall, cf	3	0	1	1	0	0
Mincher, 1b	3	2	1	3	0	0
Battey, c	4	0	1	5	0	0
Quilici, 2b	4	1	2	1	1	0
Grant, p	3	2	1	0	0	0
Totals	33	8	10	27	3	0

Los Angeles......... 0 1 0 0 0 0 0 0 1—2
Minnesota............ 0 1 6 0 0 1 0 0 *—8

aSingled for Reed in fifth. bFouled out for Brewer in seventh. cStruck out for Perranoski in ninth. Runs batted in—Wills, Fairly, Versalles 4, Mincher, Battey 2, Quilici. Two-base hits—Quilici, Valdespino, Grant. Home runs—Fairly, Mincher, Versalles. Stolen base—Versalles. Sacrifice hit—Grant. Double play—Perranoski, Wills and Parker. Left on bases—Los Angeles 9, Minnesota 5. Earned runs—Los Angeles 2, Minnesota 4. Bases on balls—Off Drysdale 1, off Perranoski 2, off Grant 1. Struck out—By Drysdale 4, by Reed 1, by Brewer 1, by Grant 5. Pitching records—Off Drysdale 7 hits, 7 runs in 2⅔ innings; off Reed 0 hits, 0 runs in 1⅓ innings; off Brewer 3 hits, 1 run in 2 innings; off Perranoski 0 hits, 0 runs in 2 innings. Wild pitch—Brewer. Losing pitcher—Drysdale. Umpires—Hurley (A.L.), Venzon (N.L.), Flaherty (A.L.), Sudol (N.L.), Stewart (A.L.) and Vargo (N.L.). Time—2:29. Attendance—47,797.

Thursday, October 7—At Minnesota

Los Ang. (N.L.)	AB.	R.	H.	O.	A.	E.
Wills, ss	4	0	1	1	2	0
Gilliam, 3b	4	0	0	0	0	2
W. Davis, cf	4	0	1	1	0	0
Johnson, lf	4	0	0	3	0	1
Fairly, rf	4	1	2	1	0	0
Lefebvre, 2b	4	0	2	2	0	0
Parker, 1b	1	0	1	3	1	0
Roseboro, c	4	0	0	12	1	0
Koufax, p	2	0	0	1	2	0
aDrysdale	1	0	0	0	0	0
Perranoski, p	0	0	0	0	0	0
Miller, p	0	0	0	0	0	0
bTracewski	1	0	0	0	0	0
Totals	33	1	7	24	6	3

Minnesota (A.L.)	AB.	R.	H.	O.	A.	E.
Versalles, ss	5	2	1	0	0	0
Nossek, cf	3	0	1	4	0	0
Oliva, rf	4	1	1	3	0	0
Killebrew, 3b	3	0	2	2	1	0
Battey, c	4	0	1	3	1	0
Allison, lf	4	1	1	2	0	0
Mincher, 1b	4	1	1	7	4	0
Quilici, 2b	2	0	0	1	3	0
Kaat, p	4	0	1	5	0	0
Totals	33	5	9	27	9	0

1965 WORLD SERIES

```
Los Angeles ..................  0 0 0   0 0 0   1 0 0—1
Minnesota ....................  0 0 0   0 0 2   1 2 *—5
```

aStruck out for Koufax in seventh. bLined out for Miller in ninth. Runs batted in—Roseboro, Oliva, Killebrew, Kaat 2. Two-base hits—Oliva, Allison. Three-base hit—Versalles. Sacrifice hits—Parker, Nossek. Left on bases—Los Angeles 8, Minnesota 8. Earned runs—Los Angeles 1, Minnesota 4. Bases on balls—Off Koufax 1, off Perranoski 2, off Kaat 1. Struck out—By Koufax 9, by Perranoski 1, by Kaat 3. Pitching records—Off Koufax 6 hits, 2 runs in 6 innings; off Perranoski 3 hits, 3 runs in 1⅔ innings; off Miller 0 hits, 0 runs in ⅓ inning. Hit by pitcher—By Kaat (Parker). Wild pitch—Perranoski. Balk—Perranoski. Losing pitcher—Koufax. Umpires—Venzon (N.L.), Flaherty (A.L.), Sudol (N.L.), Stewart (A.L.), Vargo (N.L.) and Hurley (A.L.). Time—2:13. Attendance—48,700.

Saturday, October 9—At Los Angeles

Minnesota (A.L.)	AB.	R.	H.	O.	A.	E.
Versalles, ss	3	0	2	3	3	0
Nossek, cf	4	0	1	3	0	0
Oliva, rf	4	0	1	2	0	0
Killebrew, 3b	3	0	0	1	1	0
Battey, c	3	0	0	0	0	0
Zimmerman, c	1	0	0	1	1	0
Allison, lf	3	0	0	3	0	0
Mincher, 1b	3	0	1	7	0	0
Quilici, 2b	3	0	0	4	2	0
Pascual, p	1	0	0	0	1	0
aRollins	1	0	0	0	0	0
Merritt, p	0	0	0	0	2	0
bValdespino	1	0	0	0	0	0
Klippstein, p	0	0	0	0	0	0
Totals	30	0	5	24	10	0

Los Ang. (N.L.)	AB.	R.	H.	O.	A.	E.
Wills, ss	4	0	1	2	5	0
Gilliam, 3b	4	0	1	1	1	0
Kennedy, 3b	0	0	0	0	0	1
W. Davis, cf	4	1	1	2	0	0
Fairly, rf	4	1	1	1	0	0
Johnson, lf	2	0	2	0	0	0
Lefebvre, 2b	2	1	1	1	3	0
Tracewski, 2b	2	0	0	2	3	0
Parker, 1b	3	0	1	14	2	0
Roseboro, c	3	0	1	2	2	0
Osteen, p	2	0	1	2	2	0
Totals	30	4	10	27	18	1

```
Minnesota ....................  0 0 0   0 0 0   0 0 0—0
Los Angeles ..................  0 0 0   2 1 1   0 0 *—4
```

aGrounded out for Pascual in sixth. bPopped out for Merritt in eighth. Runs batted in—Wills, Johnson, Roseboro 2. Two-base hits—Versalles, Gilliam, Johnson 2, Fairly, Wills. Stolen bases—Wills, Parker, Roseboro. Sacrifice hits—Johnson, Osteen. Double plays—Tracewski and Parker; Zimmerman and Versalles; Wills and Parker. Left on bases—Minnesota 5, Los Angeles 6. Earned runs—Minnesota 0, Los Angeles 4. Bases on balls—Off Pascual 1, off Klippstein 1, off Osteen 2. Struck out—By Klippstein 1, by Osteen 2. Pitching records—Off Pascual 8 hits, 3 runs in 5 innings; off Merritt 2 hits, 1 run in 2 innings; off Klippstein 0 hits, 0 runs in 1 inning. Losing pitcher—Pascual. Umpires—Flaherty (A.L.), Sudol (N.L.), Stewart (A.L.), Vargo (N.L.), Hurley (A.L.) and Venzon (N.L.). Time—2:06. Attendance—55,934.

Sunday, October 10—At Los Angeles

Minnesota (A.L.)	AB.	R.	H.	O.	A.	E.
Versalles, ss	4	0	1	3	2	0
Valdespino, lf	4	0	1	2	0	0
Oliva, rf	4	1	1	2	0	0
Killebrew, 3b	2	1	1	1	0	0
Hall, cf	4	0	0	1	0	0
Mincher, 1b	4	0	0	8	0	0
Battey, c	3	0	0	3	2	0
Zimmerman, c	0	0	0	1	0	0
Quilici, 2b	3	0	0	3	3	1
Grant, p	2	0	0	0	0	0
Worthington, p	0	0	0	0	0	1
bNossek	1	0	1	0	0	0
Pleis, p	0	0	0	0	1	0
Totals	31	2	5	24	8	2

Los Ang. (N.L.)	AB.	R.	H.	O.	A.	E.
Wills, ss	4	1	2	1	2	0
Gilliam, 3b	2	1	0	1	1	0
aKennedy, 3b	0	0	0	0	1	0
W. Davis, cf	4	1	2	3	0	0
Fairly, rf	4	1	1	0	0	0
Johnson, lf	4	1	2	1	1	0
Parker, 1b	4	2	2	8	0	0
Roseboro, c	3	0	1	10	1	0
Tracewski, 2b	4	0	0	2	3	0
Drysdale, p	3	0	0	1	0	0
Totals	32	7	10	27	10	0

```
Minnesota ....................  0 0 0   1 0 1   0 0 0—2
Los Angeles ..................  1 1 0   1 0 3   0 1 *—7
```

aRan for Gilliam in seventh. bSingled for Worthington in eighth. Runs batted in—Oliva, Killebrew, Fairly 3, Johnson, Parker. Home runs—Killebrew, Parker, Oliva, Johnson. Stolen bases—Wills, Parker. Double play—Battey and Versalles. Left on bases—Minnesota 4, Los Angeles 4. Earned runs—Minnesota 2, Los Angeles 5. Bases on balls—Off Grant 1, off Worthington 1, off Drysdale 2. Struck out—By Grant 2, by Worthington 2, by Drysdale 11. Pitching records—Off Grant 6 hits and 5 runs in 5 innings (pitched to two batters in sixth); off Worthington 2 hits and 1 run in 2 innings; off Pleis 2 hits and 1 run in 1 inning. Hit by pitcher—By Worthington (Gilliam). Wild pitch—Grant. Losing pitcher—Grant. Umpires—Sudol (N.L.), Stewart (A.L.), Vargo (N.L.), Hurley (A.L.), Venzon (N.L.) and Flaherty (A.L.). Time—2:15. Attendance—55,920.

Monday, October 11—At Los Angeles

Minnesota (A.L.)	AB.	R.	H.	O.	A.	E.
Versalles, ss	4	0	0	2	0	0
Nossek, cf	4	0	1	2	0	0
Oliva, rf	3	0	0	2	0	0
Killebrew, 3b	3	0	1	1	2	0
Battey, c	3	0	0	7	1	0
Allison, lf	2	0	0	3	0	0
Mincher, 1b	3	0	0	5	0	0
Quilici, 2b	3	0	1	2	3	1
Kaat, p	1	0	0	0	1	0
Boswell, p	0	0	0	0	0	0
aRollins	1	0	0	0	0	0
Perry, p	0	0	0	0	1	0
bValdespino	1	0	1	0	0	0
Totals	28	0	4	24	8	1

Los Ang. (N.L.)	AB.	R.	H.	O.	A.	E.
Wills, ss	5	2	4	1	7	0
Gilliam, 3b	4	1	2	0	0	0
Kennedy, 3b	1	0	0	0	0	0
W. Davis, cf	4	1	2	1	0	0
Johnson, lf	5	1	1	2	0	0
Fairly, rf	5	1	3	2	0	0
Parker, 1b	4	0	0	7	0	0

1965 WORLD SERIES

	AB.	R.	H.	O.	A.	E.
Tracewski, 2b	3	0	1	4	2	0
Roseboro, c	2	1	0	10	0	0
Koufax, p	4	0	1	0	1	0
Totals	37	7	14	27	10	0

Minnesota........ 0 0 0   0 0 0   0 0 0—0
Los Angeles..... 2 0 2   1 0 0   2 0 *—7

aFlied out for Boswell in sixth. bSingled for Perry in ninth. Runs batted in—Wills, Gilliam 2, Johnson, Fairly, Koufax. Two-base hits—Wills 2, Fairly. Stolen bases—W. Davis 3, Wills. Sacrifice hits—W. Davis, Parker. Double plays—Wills, Tracewski and Parker 2; Wills and Tracewski. Left on bases—Minnesota 2, Los Angeles 11. Earned runs—Minnesota 0, Los Angeles 6. Bases on balls—Off Boswell 2, off Perry 1, off Koufax 1. Struck out—By Kaat 1, by Boswell 3, by Perry 3, by Koufax 10. Pitching records—Off Kaat 6 hits and 4 runs in 2⅓ innings; off Boswell 3 hits and 1 run in 2⅔ innings; off Perry 5 hits and 2 runs in 3 innings. Losing pitcher—Kaat. Umpires—Stewart (A.L.), Vargo (N.L.), Hurley (A.L.), Venzon (N.L.), Flaherty (A.L.) and Sudol (N.L.). Time—2:34. Attendance—55,801.

Wednesday, October 13—At Minnesota

Los Ang. (N.L.)	AB.	R.	H.	O.	A.	E.
Wills, ss	4	0	1	4	4	0
Gilliam, 3b	4	0	0	0	3	0
W. Davis, cf	4	0	0	1	0	0
Fairly, rf	4	1	2	1	0	0
Johnson, lf	4	0	1	0	0	0
Parker, 1b	4	0	0	10	1	0
Roseboro, c	3	0	1	5	0	0
Tracewski, 2b	3	0	1	2	3	1
Osteen, p	1	0	0	0	1	0
aCrawford	1	0	0	0	0	0
Reed, p	0	0	0	1	0	0
bMoon	1	0	0	0	0	0
Miller, p	0	0	0	0	0	0
Totals	33	1	6	24	12	1

Minnesota (A.L.)	AB.	R.	H.	O.	A.	E.
Versalles, ss	3	0	1	2	3	0
Nossek, cf	4	0	2	4	0	0
Oliva, rf	4	0	2	0	0	0
Killebrew, 3b	4	0	0	1	1	1
Battey, c	4	1	1	5	1	0
Allison, lf	3	2	1	2	0	0
Mincher, 1b	3	0	0	11	0	0
Quilici, 2b	2	1	0	2	4	0
Grant, p	3	1	1	0	1	0
Totals	30	5	6	27	10	1

Los Angeles..... 0 0 0   0 0 0   1 0 0—1
Minnesota........ 0 0 0   2 0 3   0 0 *—5

aStruck out for Osteen in sixth. bGrounded out for Reed in eighth. Runs batted in—Fairly, Allison 2, Grant 3. Three-base hit—Battey. Home runs—Fairly, Allison, Grant. Stolen base—Allison. Double plays—Osteen, Wills and Parker; Battey and Versalles. Left on bases—Los Angeles 5, Minnesota 6. Earned runs—Los Angeles 1, Minnesota 4. Bases on balls—Off Osteen 3, off Reed 2. Struck out—By Osteen 2, by Reed 3, by Grant 5. Pitching records—Off Osteen 4 hits and 2 runs in 5 innings; off Reed 2 hits and 3 runs in 2 innings; off Miller 0 hits and 0 runs in 1 inning. Losing pitcher—Osteen. Umpires—Vargo (N.L.), Hurley (A.L.), Venzon (N.L.), Flaherty (A.L.), Sudol (N.L.) and Stewart (A.L.). Time—2:16. Attendance—49,578.

Thursday, October 14—At Minnesota

Los Ang. (N.L.)	AB.	R.	H.	O.	A.	E.
Wills, ss	4	0	0	2	4	0
Gilliam, 3b	5	0	2	2	1	0
Kennedy, 3b	0	0	0	0	1	0
W. Davis, cf	2	0	0	1	0	0
Johnson, lf	4	1	1	3	0	0
Fairly, rf	4	1	1	0	0	0
Parker, 1b	4	0	2	6	0	0
Tracewski, 2b	4	0	0	1	0	0
Roseboro, c	2	0	1	12	0	0
Koufax, p	3	0	0	0	1	0
Totals	32	2	7	27	7	0

Minnesota (A.L.)	AB.	R.	H.	O.	A.	E.
Versalles, ss	4	0	1	0	2	0
Nossek, cf	4	0	0	0	0	0
Oliva, rf	3	0	0	4	0	1
Killebrew, 3b	3	0	1	2	2	0
Battey, c	4	0	0	8	1	0
Allison, lf	4	0	0	1	0	0
Mincher, 1b	3	0	0	10	0	0
Quilici, 2b	3	0	1	1	3	0
Kaat, p	1	0	0	0	1	0
Worthington, p	0	0	0	1	1	0
aRollins	0	0	0	0	0	0
Klippstein, p	0	0	0	0	0	0
Merritt, p	0	0	0	0	0	0
bValdespino	1	0	0	0	0	0
Perry, p	0	0	0	0	0	0
Totals	30	0	3	27	10	1

Los Angeles..... 0 0 0   2 0 0   0 0 0—2
Minnesota........ 0 0 0   0 0 0   0 0 0—0

aWalked for Worthington in fifth. bFlied out for Merritt in eighth. Runs batted in—Johnson, Parker. Two-base hits—Roseboro, Fairly, Quilici. Three-base hit—Parker. Home run—Johnson. Sacrifice hit—W. Davis. Left on bases—Los Angeles 9, Minnesota 6. Earned runs—Los Angeles 2, Minnesota 0. Bases on balls—Off Koufax 3, off Kaat 1, off Worthington 1, off Klippstein 1, off Perry 1. Struck out—By Koufax 10, by Kaat 2, by Klippstein 2, by Merritt 1, by Perry 1. Pitching records—Off Kaat 5 hits and 2 runs in 3 innings (pitched to three batters in fourth); off Worthington 0 hits and 0 runs in 2 innings; off Klippstein 2 hits and 0 runs in 1⅔ innings; off Merritt 0 hits and 0 runs in 1⅓ innings; off Perry 0 hits and 0 runs in 1 inning. Hit by pitcher—By Klippstein (W. Davis). Losing pitcher—Kaat. Umpires—Hurley (A.L.), Venzon (N.L.), Flaherty (A.L.), Sudol (N.L.), Stewart (A.L.) and Vargo (N.L.). Time—2:27. Attendance—50,596.

COMPOSITE BATTING AVERAGES
Los Angeles Dodgers

Player-Position	G.	AB.	R.	H.	2B.	3B.	HR.	RBI.	BA.
Crawford, ph	2	2	0	1	0	0	0	0	.500
Lefebvre, 2b	3	10	2	4	0	0	0	0	.400
Fairly, rf	7	29	7	11	3	0	2	6	.379
Wills, ss	7	30	3	11	3	0	0	3	.367
Osteen, p	3	3	0	1	0	0	0	0	.333
Parker, 1b	7	23	3	7	0	1	1	2	.304
Johnson, lf	7	27	3	8	2	0	2	4	.296
Roseboro, c	7	21	1	6	1	0	0	3	.286
W. Davis, cf	7	26	3	6	0	0	0	0	.231
Gilliam, 3b	7	28	2	6	1	0	0	0	.214
Tracewski, ph-2b	6	17	0	2	0	0	0	0	.118
Koufax, p	3	9	0	1	0	0	0	1	.111
Kennedy, 3b-pr	4	1	0	0	0	0	0	0	.000
Reed, p	2	0	0	0	0	0	0	0	.000
Brewer, p	1	0	0	0	0	0	0	0	.000
Perranoski, p	2	0	0	0	0	0	0	0	.000
Miller, p	2	0	0	0	0	0	0	0	.000
Drysdale, p-ph	3	5	0	0	0	0	0	0	.000
Moon, ph	2	2	0	0	0	0	0	0	.000
LeJohn, ph	1	1	0	0	0	0	0	0	.000
Totals	7	234	24	64	10	1	5	21	.274

Minnesota Twins

Player-Position	G.	AB.	R.	H.	2B.	3B.	HR.	RBI.	BA.
Killebrew, 3b	7	21	2	6	0	0	1	2	.286
Versalles, ss	7	28	3	8	1	1	1	4	.286
Valdespino, lf-ph	5	11	1	3	1	0	0	0	.273
Grant, p	3	8	3	2	1	0	1	3	.250
Nossek, cf-ph	6	20	0	4	0	0	0	0	.200
Quilici, 2b	7	20	2	4	2	0	0	1	.200
Oliva, rf	7	26	2	5	1	0	1	2	.192
Kaat, p	3	6	0	1	0	0	0	2	.167
Hall, cf	2	7	0	1	0	0	0	0	.143
Mincher, 1b	7	23	3	3	0	0	1	1	.130
Allison, lf	5	16	3	2	1	0	1	2	.125
Battey, c	7	25	1	3	0	1	0	2	.120
Zimmerman, c	2	1	0	0	0	0	0	0	.000
Pascual, p	1	1	0	0	0	0	0	0	.000
Merritt, p	2	0	0	0	0	0	0	0	.000
Klippstein, p	2	0	0	0	0	0	0	0	.000
Worthington, p	2	0	0	0	0	0	0	0	.000
Pleis, p	1	0	0	0	0	0	0	0	.000
Boswell, p	1	0	0	0	0	0	0	0	.000
Perry, p	2	0	0	0	0	0	0	0	.000
Rollins, ph	3	2	0	0	0	0	0	0	.000
Totals	7	215	20	42	7	2	6	19	.195

COMPOSITE PITCHING AVERAGES

Los Angeles Dodgers

Pitcher	G.	IP.	H.	R.	E.	SO.	BB.	W.	L.	ERA.
Miller	2	1⅓	0	0	0	0	0	0	0	0.00
Koufax	3	24	13	2	1	29	5	2	1	0.38
Osteen	2	14	9	2	1	4	5	1	1	0.64
Drysdale	2	11⅔	12	9	5	15	3	1	1	3.86
Brewer	1	2	3	1	1	1	0	0	0	4.50
Perranoski	2	3⅔	3	3	3	1	4	0	0	7.36
Reed	2	3⅓	2	3	3	4	2	0	0	8.10
Totals	7	60	42	20	14	54	19	4	3	2.10

Minnesota Twins

Pitcher	G.	IP.	H.	R.	E.	SO.	BB.	W.	L.	ERA.
Worthington	2	4	2	1	0	2	2	0	0	0.00
Klippstein	2	2⅔	2	0	0	3	2	0	0	0.00
Merritt	2	3⅓	2	1	1	1	0	0	0	2.70
Grant	3	23	22	8	7	12	2	2	1	2.74
Boswell	1	2⅔	3	1	1	3	2	0	0	3.38
Kaat	3	14⅓	18	7	6	6	2	1	2	3.77
Perry	2	4	5	2	2	4	2	0	0	4.50
Pascual	1	5	8	3	3	0	1	0	1	5.40
Pleis	1	1	2	1	1	0	0	0	0	9.00
Totals	7	60	64	24	21	31	13	3	4	3.15

SERIES OF 1966

	W.	L.	Pct.
Baltimore A. L.	4	0	1.000
Los Angeles N. L.	0	4	.000

One of the most astounding of all World Series saw the Baltimore Orioles sweep over the Los Angeles Dodgers in four straight games, restoring some prestige to the American League, which had seen its standard-bearers fall to the National League in three previous fall classics.

The Dodgers, who were forced down to the last day of the regular season to win the N. L. pennant, were admittedly not a power-hitting club, but Manager Walt Alston's forces made use of tremendous pitching, excellent speed and good defense. The Orioles, on the other hand, hit 175 home runs and also were outstanding defensively, but Manager Hank Bauer had to struggle all through the season with his pitching staff, which compiled only 23 complete games. The Dodgers had 52, including 27 route-going performances by Sandy Koufax, their 27-game winner. The Orioles' top pitcher, Jim Palmer, won only 15 games.

With the chips down in the Series, the Dodger staff lived up to its reputation, holding the Orioles to a club batting average of .200, lowest in history for a four-straight winner. But the Orioles staff proved phenomenal, setting a new Series record by holding the Dodgers scoreless for the last 33 innings. In their futility at the plate, the Dodgers also set new marks for fewest runs scored (2), fewest hits (17), fewest total bases (23) and lowest club batting average for a Series of any length (.142).

If there was any consolation for the Dodgers, or the National League, it might have come from the fact that two former N.L. players—Frank Robinson and Moe Drabowsky—were the determining factors in the Orioles' sweep. Robinson, a slugging outfielder obtained in a deal with the Cincinnati Reds, started and finished the Series scoring with homers. Drabowsky, an N.L. castoff, was the lone reliever used by the Orioles and his contribution was of such importance that Manager Bauer said, "The turning point in this Series was when Drabowsky came in to shut the door on the Dodgers in the opener."

The Dodgers, who were forced to use Koufax in the last game of the season to clinch their flag, gave the starting assignment in the opener to Don Drysdale, their big righthander. By the time the first four Orioles had completed their turns at the plate, Drysdale's fate was sealed. After Luis Aparicio, the leadoff man, was retired, Russ Snyder drew a walk and Frank Robinson hammered a homer into the left field seats at Dodger Stadium. Brooks Robinson followed with a drive into the same area, only deeper, and, to all intents and purposes, the Series was over.

In the second inning, the Orioles added a run on a pass to Andy Etchebarren, a sacrifice by Dave McNally and a single by Snyder. The Dodgers picked up one in their half on a homer by Jim Lefebvre and then threatened to break the game wide open in the third before Drabowsky appeared.

McNally, a fireball lefthander, had trouble with his control and, with one out in the third, walked Lou Johnson, Tommy Davis and Lefebvre in succession to load the bases. Taking over in relief, Drabowsky struck out Wes Parker, walked Jim Gilliam to force in a run and then retired Johnny Roseboro.

Going on to complete six and two-thirds innings of sensational work, Drabowsky held the Dodgers to one hit while achieving one of the greatest strikeout performances in Series history. The Polish-born righthander fanned a total of 11, a Series record for a relief pitcher, and in the fourth and fifth innings whiffed six straight batters to tie another classic mark. The victims of his string were Jim Barbieri, Maury Wills, Willie Davis, Johnson, Tommy Davis and

Lefebvre before Parker broke the spell with a fly.

The Orioles tacked on the last run of their 5-2 victory against Joe Moeller in the fourth inning. Dave Johnson doubled and took third on an infield out. After Drabowsky walked, Johnson scored while Aparicio was forcing Drabowsky.

The defeat of Drysdale was damaging to the Dodgers, but all odds favored Los Angeles in the second game when Koufax took the mound with his 27-9 record against Palmer's 15-10. Refusing to be awed, Palmer hurled a four-hitter and beat the Dodgers, 6-0, to become the youngest pitcher to rack up a Series shutout. The righthander was nine days shy of his twenty-first birthday.

While Palmer was the hero, center fielder Willie Davis of the Dodgers was the goat in a defensive collapse by the N.L. champions, who made six errors of commission and several of omission.

After four scoreless innings, Boog Powell led off the fifth with a single for the Orioles. Dave Johnson popped up, trying to bunt, and Paul Blair followed with a fly to deep center. Willie Davis lost the ball in the sun and it dropped at his feet for an error, Powell reaching third and Blair second.

The Dodgers decided to pitch to Etchebarren and the strategy appeared successful when the Orioles' catcher lofted a soft fly to short center. Willie Davis got a bead on the ball, then lost it in the sun and it glanced off his glove for an error. To compound his felonies, the Dodger outfielder grabbed the ball and threw wildly to third base for his third miscue, making him the first player in Series history to commit three errors in one inning.

Powell and Blair both scored, with Etchebarren winding up at third. Aparicio doubled to drive in Etchebarren with the Orioles' third run.

In the sixth inning, Willie Davis and right fielder Ron Fairly both had a chance to snare a long drive by Frank Robinson, but they bluffed each other away and the ball landed untouched for a triple. When Powell followed with a single, the tally, although tainted, constituted the only earned run scored off Koufax in his six innings on the mound. The Orioles iced their victory with two markers off Ron Perranoski in the eighth inning.

The Dodgers lost the first two games to the Minnesota Twins in 1965, but came back to win the Series. History refused to repeat, however, when two pitchers gave the Orioles successive 1-0 victories as they completed the sweep before their hometown fans in Baltimore.

Claude Osteen drew the Dodgers' starting assignment in the third game and allowed only three hits, while the Dodgers collected six off Wally Bunker, but the pitch that made the difference came in the fifth inning. Facing Blair, Osteen threw a fast ball, low and away, but the Orioles' center fielder leaned into it and powered a 430-foot homer into the left field bleachers for a 1-0 victory.

McNally came back to start the fourth game for the Orioles and this time the lefthander had superb control in matching four-hitters with Drysdale. The one pitch that decided their duel was served up by Drysdale to Frank Robinson in the fourth inning. Swinging at a fast ball, Robinson pounded it into the left field seats, 410 feet away, and the Orioles nailed down their second straight 1-0 victory to gain acclaim as world champions. The box scores:

Wednesday, Oct. 5—At Los Angeles

Baltimore (A.L.)	AB.	R.	H.	O.	A.	E.
Aparicio, ss	5	0	0	4	1	0
Snyder, cf-lf	3	1	1	2	0	0
F. Robinson, rf	5	1	2	1	0	0
B. Robinson, 3b	5	1	1	2	1	0
Powell, 1b	5	0	1	3	0	0
Blefary, lf	3	0	1	2	0	0
Blair, cf	0	0	0	0	0	0
D. Johnson, 2b	4	1	2	0	2	0
Etchebarren, c	3	1	1	13	0	0
McNally, p	0	0	0	0	0	0
Drabowsky, p	2	0	0	0	0	0
Totals	35	5	9	27	4	0
Los Ang. (N.L.)	AB.	R.	H.	O.	A.	E.
Wills, ss	3	0	0	6	5	0
W. Davis, cf	4	0	1	1	0	0
L. Johnson, rf	3	1	0	3	0	0
T. Davis, lf	3	0	0	1	0	0
Lefebvre, 2b	3	1	1	3	5	0
Parker, 1b	4	0	1	9	0	0
Gilliam, 3b	2	0	0	1	1	0
Roseboro, c	4	0	0	3	0	0
Drysdale, p	0	0	0	0	1	0
aStuart	1	0	0	0	0	0
Moeller, p	0	0	0	0	0	0
bBarbieri	1	0	0	0	0	0
R. Miller, p	0	0	0	0	1	0
cCovington	1	0	0	0	0	0
Perranoski, p	0	0	0	0	1	0
dFairly	1	0	0	0	0	0
Totals	30	2	3	27	14	0

Baltimore .... 3 1 0 1 0 0 0 0 0—5
Los Angeles .... 0 1 1 0 0 0 0 0 0—2

aFlied out for Drysdale in second. bStruck out for Moeller in fourth. cStruck out for R. Miller in seventh. dStruck out for Perranoski in ninth. Runs batted in—Aparicio, Snyder, F. Robinson 2, B. Robinson, Lefebvre. Gilliam. Two-base hits—Parker, D. Johnson, Powell. Home runs—F. Robinson, B. Robinson. Lefebvre. Stolen base—Wills. Sacrifice hit—McNally. Left on bases—Baltimore 9. Los Angeles 8. Earned runs—Baltimore 5. Los Angeles 2. Bases on balls—Off McNally 5. off Drabowsky 2, off Drysdale 2, off Moeller 1, off R. Miller 2. Struck out—By McNally 1. by Drabowsky 11, by Drysdale 1, by R. Miller 1, by Perranoski 1. Pitching records—Off McNally 2 hits and 2 runs in 2⅓ innings; off Drabowsky 1 hit and 0 runs in 6⅔ innings; off Drysdale 4 hits and 4 runs in 2 innings; off Moeller 1 hit and 1 run in 2 innings; off R. Miller 2 hits and 0 runs in 3 innings; off Perranoski 2 hits and 0 runs in 2 innings. Winning pitcher—Drabowsky. Losing pitcher—Drysdale. Umpires—Jackowski (N.L.), Chylak (A.L.), Pelekoudas (N.L.), Rice (A.L.), Steiner (N.L.) and Drummond (A.L.). Time—2:56. Attendance—55,941.

1966 WORLD SERIES

Thursday, October 6—At Los Angeles

Baltimore (A.L.)	AB	R	H	O	A	E
Aparicio, ss	5	0	2	4	1	0
Blefary, lf	5	0	0	1	0	0
F. Robinson, rf	3	2	1	1	0	0
B. Robinson, 3b	4	1	1	1	1	0
Powell, 1b	3	1	2	8	0	0
D. Johnson, 2b	4	0	2	2	4	0
Blair, cf	3	1	0	4	0	0
Etchebarren, c	3	1	0	6	0	0
Palmer, p	4	0	0	0	2	0
Totals	34	6	8	27	8	0

Los Ang. (N.L.)	AB	R	H	O	A	E
Wills, ss	4	0	0	3	1	0
Gilliam, 3b	4	0	0	2	3	1
W. Davis, cf	4	0	0	2	0	3
Fairly, rf	3	0	0	3	0	1
Lefebvre, 2b	3	0	0	3	0	0
L. Johnson, lf	4	0	1	1	0	0
Roseboro, c	4	0	1	8	1	0
Parker, 1b	2	0	1	5	1	0
Koufax, p	2	0	0	0	1	0
Perranoski, p	0	0	0	0	1	1
Regan, p	0	0	0	0	0	0
aT. Davis	1	0	1	0	0	0
Brewer, p	0	0	0	0	0	0
Totals	31	0	4	27	8	6

Baltimore .... 0 0 0 0 3 1 0 2 0—6
Los Angeles .... 0 0 0 0 0 0 0 0 0—0

aSingled for Regan for eighth. Runs batted in—Aparicio, Powell, D. Johnson. Two-base hits—L. Johnson, Aparicio. Three-base hit—F. Robinson. Sacrifice hit—Powell. Double play—Gilliam, Roseboro and Parker. Left on bases—Baltimore 6, Los Angeles 7. Earned runs—Baltimore 3. Bases on balls—Off Palmer 3, off Koufax 2, off Perranoski 1, off Regan 1. Struck out—By Palmer 6, by Koufax 2, by Perranoski 1, by Regan 1, by Brewer 1. Pitching records—Off Koufax 6 hits and 4 runs in 6 innings; off Perranoski 2 hits and 2 runs in 1⅓ innings; off Regan 0 hits and 0 runs in ⅔ inning; off Brewer 0 hits and 0 runs in 1 inning. Wild pitches—Regan, Palmer. Winning pitcher—Palmer. Losing pitcher—Koufax. Umpires—Chylak (A.L.), Pelekoudas (N.L.), Rice (A.L.), Steiner (N.L.), Drummond (A.L.) and Jackowski (N.L.). Time—2:26. Attendance—55,947.

Saturday, October 8—At Baltimore

Los Ang. (N.L.)	AB	R	H	O	A	E
Wills, ss	3	0	1	1	6	0
Parker, 1b	4	0	1	10	1	0
Regan, p	0	0	0	0	1	0
W. Davis, cf	4	0	0	2	0	0
Fairly, rf-1b	3	0	0	2	0	0
Lefebvre, 2b	4	0	0	3	4	0
L. Johnson, lf-rf	4	0	2	1	0	0
Roseboro, c	3	0	0	4	0	0
Kennedy, 3b	3	0	0	0	2	0
Osteen, p	2	0	0	1	0	0
aT. Davis, lf	1	0	1	0	0	0
Totals	31	0	6	24	14	0

Baltimore (A.L.)	AB	R	H	O	A	E
Aparicio, ss	3	0	1	1	3	0
Blefary, lf	3	0	0	3	0	0
Snyder, lf	0	0	0	0	0	0
F. Robinson, rf	3	0	0	1	0	0
B. Robinson, 3b	2	0	0	1	1	0
Powell, 1b	3	0	1	9	1	0
D. Johnson, 2b	3	0	0	3	3	0
Blair, cf	3	1	1	3	0	0
Etchebarren, c	3	0	0	6	0	0
Bunker, p	2	0	0	0	3	0
Totals	25	1	3	27	11	0

Los Angeles .... 0 0 0 0 0 0 0 0 0—0
Baltimore .... 0 0 0 0 1 0 0 0 *—1

aSingled for Osteen in eighth. Run batted in—Blair. Two-base hit—Parker. Home run—Blair. Sacrifice hit—Wills. Double plays—Aparicio, D. Johnson and Powell; Wills, Lefebvre and Parker; Lefebvre, Wills and Parker. Left on bases—Los Angeles 6, Baltimore 1. Earned run—Baltimore 1. Bases on balls—Off Osteen 1, off Bunker 1. Struck out—By Osteen 3, by Regan 1, by Bunker 6. Pitching records—Off Osteen 3 hits and 1 run in 7 innings; off Regan 0 hits and 0 runs in 1 inning. Winning pitcher—Bunker. Losing pitcher—Osteen. Umpires—Pelekoudas (N.L.), Rice (A.L.), Steiner (N.L.), Drummond (A.L.), Jackowski (N.L.) and Chylak (A.L.). Time—1:55. Attendance—54,445.

Sunday, October 9—At Baltimore

Los Ang. (N.L.)	AB	R	H	O	A	E
Wills, ss	3	0	0	2	3	0
W. Davis, cf	4	0	0	1	0	0
L. Johnson, rf	4	0	1	4	0	0
T. Davis, lf	3	0	0	2	0	0
Lefebvre, 2b	2	0	1	1	1	0
Parker, 1b	3	0	0	7	0	0
Roseboro, c	3	0	0	7	1	0
Kennedy, 3b	2	0	1	0	1	0
aStuart	1	0	0	0	0	0
Drysdale, p	2	0	0	0	2	0
bFerrara	1	0	1	0	0	0
cOliver	0	0	0	0	0	0
Totals	28	0	4	24	8	0

Baltimore (A.L.)	AB	R	H	O	A	E
Aparicio, ss	3	0	1	0	3	0
Snyder, cf-lf	3	0	0	0	0	0
F. Robinson, rf	3	1	1	3	0	0
B. Robinson, 3b	3	0	1	0	3	0
Powell, 1b	3	0	1	7	0	0
Blefary, lf	2	0	0	1	0	0
Blair, cf	0	0	0	2	0	0
D. Johnson, 2b	3	0	0	7	3	0
Etchebarren, c	3	0	0	7	1	0
McNally, p	3	0	0	0	0	0
Totals	26	1	4	27	10	0

Los Angeles .... 0 0 0 0 0 0 0 0 0—0
Baltimore .... 0 0 0 1 0 0 0 0 *—1

aStruck out for Kennedy in ninth. bSingled for Drysdale in ninth. cRan for Ferrara in ninth. Run batted in—F. Robinson. Home run—F. Robinson. Double plays—Lefebvre, Wills and Parker; Aparicio, D. Johnson and Powell; B. Robinson, D. Johnson and Powell; Etchebarren and D. Johnson. Left on bases—Los Angeles 3, Baltimore 2. Earned run—Baltimore 1. Bases on balls—Off Drysdale 1, off McNally 2. Struck out—By Drysdale 5, by McNally 4. Winning pitcher—McNally. Losing pitcher—Drysdale. Umpires—Rice (A.L.), Steiner (N.L.), Drummond (A.L.), Jackowski (N.L.), Chylak (A.L.) and Pelekoudas (N.L.). Time—1:45. Attendance—54,458.

COMPOSITE BATTING AVERAGES

Baltimore Orioles

Player-Position	G.	AB.	R.	H.	2B.	3B.	HR.	RBI.	BA.
Powell, 1b	4	14	1	5	1	0	0	1	.357
F. Robinson, rf	4	14	4	4	0	1	2	3	.286
D. Johnson, 2b	4	14	1	4	0	0	0	0	.286
Aparicio, ss	4	16	0	4	1	0	0	2	.250
B. Robinson, 3b	4	14	2	3	0	0	1	1	.214
Snyder, cf-lf	3	6	1	1	0	0	0	0	.167
Blair, cf	4	6	2	1	0	0	1	1	.167
Etchebarren, c	4	12	0	1	0	0	0	0	.083
Blefary, lf	4	13	0	1	0	0	0	0	.077
McNally, p	2	3	0	0	0	0	0	0	.000

Player-Position	G.	AB.	R.	H.	2B.	3B.	HR.	RBI.	BA.
Drabowsky, p.	1	2	0	0	0	0	0	0	.000
Palmer, p.	1	4	0	0	0	0	0	0	.000
Bunker, p.	1	2	0	0	0	0	0	0	.000
Totals	4	120	13	24	3	1	4	10	.200

Los Angeles Dodgers

Player-Position	G.	AB.	R.	H.	2B.	3B.	HR.	RBI.	BA.
Ferrara, ph.	1	1	0	1	0	0	0	0	1.000
L. Johnson, rf-lf	4	15	1	4	1	0	0	0	.267
T. Davis, lf-ph	4	8	0	2	0	0	0	0	.250
Parker, 1b	4	13	0	3	2	0	0	0	.231
Kennedy, 3b	2	5	0	1	0	0	0	0	.200
Lefebvre, 2b	4	12	1	2	0	0	0	1	.167
Fairly, ph-rf-1b	3	7	0	1	0	0	0	0	.143
Wills, ss	4	13	0	1	0	0	0	0	.077
Roseboro, c	4	14	0	1	0	0	0	0	.071
W. Davis, cf	4	16	0	1	0	0	0	0	.063
Gilliam, 3b	2	6	0	0	0	0	0	1	.000
Drysdale, p	2	2	0	0	0	0	0	0	.000
Moeller, p	1	0	0	0	0	0	0	0	.000
R. Miller, p	1	0	0	0	0	0	0	0	.000
Perranoski, p	2	0	0	0	0	0	0	0	.000
Koufax, p	1	2	0	0	0	0	0	0	.000
Regan, p	2	0	0	0	0	0	0	0	.000
Brewer, p	1	0	0	0	0	0	0	0	.000
Osteen, p	1	2	0	0	0	0	0	0	.000
Covington, ph	1	1	0	0	0	0	0	0	.000
Barbieri, ph	1	1	0	0	0	0	0	0	.000
Stuart, ph	2	2	0	0	0	0	0	0	.000
Oliver, pr	1	0	0	0	0	0	0	0	.000
Totals	4	120	2	17	3	0	1	2	.142

COMPOSITE PITCHING AVERAGES

Baltimore Orioles

Pitcher	G.	IP.	H.	R.	E.	SO.	BB.	W.	L.	ERA.
Palmer	1	9	4	0	0	6	3	1	0	0.00
Bunker	1	9	6	0	0	6	1	1	0	0.00
Drabowsky	1	6⅔	1	0	0	11	2	1	0	0.00
McNally	2	11⅓	6	2	2	5	7	1	0	1.59
Totals	4	36	17	2	2	28	13	4	0	0.50

Los Angeles Dodgers

Pitcher	G.	IP.	H.	R.	E.	SO.	BB.	W.	L.	ERA.
R. Miller	1	3	2	0	0	1	2	0	0	0.00
Regan	2	1⅔	0	0	0	2	1	0	0	0.00
Brewer	1	1	0	0	0	1	0	0	0	0.00
Osteen	1	7	3	1	1	3	1	0	1	1.29
Koufax	1	6	6	4	1	2	2	0	1	1.50
Drysdale	2	10	8	5	5	6	3	0	2	4.50
Moeller	1	2	1	1	1	0	1	0	0	4.50
Perranoski	2	3⅓	4	2	2	2	1	0	0	5.40
Totals	4	34	24	13	10	17	11	0	4	2.65

SERIES OF 1967

	W.	L.	Pct.
St. Louis N. L.	4	3	.571
Boston A. L.	3	4	.429

An "impossible dream" for the Boston Red Sox came within one victory of realization, but finally vanished in cold reality when the American League pennant winners lost the World Series to the National League champion St. Louis Cardinals, four games to three.

The triumph was the Cards' eighth in 11 appearances in the fall classic. It climaxed Stan Musial's first year as general manager of the club as the new working partner of Manager Red Schoendienst, his former teammate. The Redbirds breezed to the N.L. pennant, although their ace righthander, Bob Gibson, suffered a broken bone in his right leg and was out of action from July 15 until September 7. Gibson worked himself back into condition and, in fact, posted the flag-clinching victory on September 18. He was fully rested before the World Series started.

The Red Sox had finished in ninth place in 1966 and nobody figured on them being a pennant contender. But, under Dick Williams, their new manager, the Red Sox came to life in mid-July and engaged in a tense race with the Minnesota Twins, Detroit Tigers and Chicago White Sox. Going into the final week of the season, each of the four clubs had a chance. The White Sox were knocked out on September 29, but the three other clubs did not settle the issue until the last day when the Red Sox, calling on Jim Lonborg, their star pitcher, beat the Twins, 5-3, as the Tigers for the second straight day split a doubleheader with the California Angels.

Unable to use Lonborg in the first game of the World Series, the Red Sox turned to Jose Santiago, who pitched effectively and even hit a homer in his own behalf. However, Santiago was no match for Gibson, who hurled the Cardinals to a 2-1 victory in the game at Boston, allowing only six hits. The Cardinals scored once in the third inning when Lou Brock singled, Curt Flood doubled and Roger Maris grounded out. After Santiago's homer in Boston's half of the frame, the tie held up until the seventh when Brock singled again, stole second and scored on successive infield outs by Flood and Maris.

Lonborg took the mound in the second game and the righthander pitched a one-hitter, the fourth in Series history, to beat the Cardinals, 5-0. Julian Javier doubled, with two out in the eighth inning, for the lone St. Louis safety. Carl Yastrzemski, the Triple-Crown winner of the Red Sox, started his club on the way to victory with a homer off Dick Hughes in the fourth inning. Two walks and an error loaded the bases in the sixth and, after Ron Willis replaced Hughes, Rico Petrocelli hit a sacrifice fly.

In the seventh, Jose Tartabull walked and Dalton Jones beat out an infield hit. The Cardinals summoned southpaw Joe Hoerner to face Yastrzemski, but the left-handed-swinging slugger wrecked the move by smashing his second homer of the game.

The Series shifted to St. Louis and the Cardinals regained the upper hand by winning the third game, 5-2, behind the seven-hit flinging of Nelson Briles. Brock tripled and Flood singled off Gary Bell for a quick Cardinal run in the first inning and two more went on the scoreboard in the second when Tim McCarver singled and Mike Shannon followed with a homer. Brock beat out a bunt in the sixth, raced to third on a wild pick-off throw by reliever Lee Stange and crossed the plate on a single by

Maris. The last St. Louis marker of the game counted off Dan Osinski in the eighth on a single by Maris and a double by Orlando Cepeda.

The Red Sox notched their first run in the sixth on singles by pinch-hitter Mike Andrews and Dalton Jones, around a bunt by Tartabull, who was trying for a hit rather than a sacrifice. Reggie Smith accounted for the other run with a homer in the seventh.

Gibson was back on the mound for the Cardinals in the fourth game and the righthander proved even better than in his first start, yielding only five hits in a 6-0 victory. Santiago, again on the firing line for Boston, was kayoed in the first inning when the Redbirds exploded for four runs. Brock and Flood led off with singles and both scored on a double by Maris. After advancing to third on Cepeda's fly to right field, Maris came home on a single by McCarver. Shannon popped up, but an infield hit by Javier and a single by Dal Maxvill added the fourth run before Bell relieved Santiago and retired Gibson. The Cardinals wound up their scoring in the third inning against Jerry Stephenson on a double by Cepeda, wild pitch, sacrifice fly by McCarver, walk to Shannon and double by Javier.

Needing a victory to prolong the Series, the Red Sox got it from Lonborg, who pitched a three-hitter and beat the Cardinals, 3-1. Southpaw Steve Carlton started for the Cardinals and was tagged with the defeat on an unearned run in the third inning on a single by Joe Foy, Shannon's boot of a bunt by Mike Andrews and a single by Ken Harrelson.

Ron Willis was on the mound for the Cardinals in the ninth inning when the Red Sox added two runs, accounting for their winning margin. George Scott walked and Smith doubled, Scott stopping at third. After an intentional pass to Petrocelli loaded the bases, Jack Lamabe came in from the bullpen to face Elston Howard, who looped a single to right field, scoring Scott and, when Maris' throw to the plate was high, Smith also scored. Thus, a homer by Maris in the Cardinals' half served no purpose, other than to deprive Lonborg of a second shutout.

Returning to Boston, the Red Sox exploded with a record-breaking homer attack to defeat the Cardinals, 8-4, squaring the Series at three victories for each club. Petrocelli, taking aim at the friendly left-field wall in Fenway Park, lofted a homer in the second inning to start the Red Sox scoring. The Cardinals came back with two runs in the third off rookie Gary Waslewski. Javier doubled and scored on a single by Brock, who then stole second and counted on a single by Flood.

In the fourth, Yastrzemski cleared the left-field fence, Smith slashed a line drive into the right field stands and Petrocelli poked a fly over the left-field wall for his second homer of the game and a record for the Red Sox of three in one inning.

The Cardinals rallied once more and tied the score against John Wyatt in the seventh when pinch-hitter Bobby Tolan drew a walk and Brock belted a 450-foot drive into the stands.

Manager Schoendienst, who had used Willis and Briles as relievers for Hughes, brought Lamabe out to face the Red Sox in their half of the seventh. Before the inning was over, Schoendienst had to go to the bullpen three more times, calling on Hoerner, Larry Jaster and Ray Washburn.

Pinch-hitter Jones opened the Red Sox action with a single and Foy followed with a double, scoring Jones. Hoerner faced two batters—Andrews, who singled to score Foy, and Yastrzemski, who also singled, sending Andrews to third. Pinch-hitter Jerry Adair delivered a sacrifice fly against Jaster, sending Andrews home. Singles by Scott and Smith then plated Yastrzemski with the fourth run of the inning before Washburn finally stopped the Red Sox outburst.

When Hal Woodeshick took the mound in the ninth, he became the eighth pitcher used by the Cardinals, tying a Series record. The Red Sox, who finished with Bell, called on three pitchers in the game and the two-club total of 11 set a classic record.

With the entire season wrapped up in one final game, the Red Sox had to turn to Lonborg, although he had had only two days of rest. Gibson, with three days to recuperate, made his third start of the Series. The climactic duel of the two ace righthanders proved onesided as Gibson not only pitched a three-hitter, but also belted a homer, to bring the world championship to the Cardinals with a convincing 7-2 victory.

The Cardinals started their attack on Lonborg with two runs in the third inning on a triple by Maxvill, singles by Flood and Maris and a wild pitch. Two more runs followed in the fifth, the first on Gibson's homer. Brock then singled, stole second and third and scored on a sacrifice fly by Maris. The killing blow followed in the sixth when McCarver doubled, Shannon was safe on an error by Foy and Javier, disdaining the bunt with nobody out, lofted a homer into the net above the left-field fence.

Gibson gave up a Red Sox run in the fifth on a triple by Scott and a wild throw by Javier, handling the relay from Flood. Gibson showed signs of weakening in the eighth, but pitched out of trouble at the expense of only one run. It scored on a double by Petrocelli, a wild pitch, a walk to pinch-hitter Jones and a forceout by another pinch-hitter, Norm Siebern. The box scores:

1967 WORLD SERIES

Wednesday, October 4—At Boston

St. Louis (N.L.)	AB	R	H	O	A	E
Brock, lf	4	2	4	2	0	0
Flood, cf	5	0	1	2	0	0
Maris, rf	4	0	1	3	0	0
Cepeda, 1b	4	0	0	6	0	0
McCarver, c	3	0	0	11	2	0
Shannon, 3b	4	0	2	0	1	0
Javier, 2b	4	0	2	1	1	0
Maxvill, ss	2	0	0	2	2	0
Ro. Gibson, p	4	0	0	0	0	0
Totals	34	2	10	27	6	0

Boston (A.L.)	AB	R	H	O	A	E
Adair, 2b	4	0	0	2	3	0
Jones, 3b	4	0	1	2	2	0
Yastrzemski, lf	4	0	0	4	1	0
Harrelson, rf	3	0	0	0	0	0
Wyatt, p	0	0	0	0	0	0
cFoy	1	0	0	0	0	0
Scott, 1b	3	0	2	8	0	0
Petrocelli, ss	3	0	0	0	0	0
dAndrews	1	0	0	0	0	0
Smith, cf	3	0	1	1	0	0
Ru. Gibson, c	2	0	0	8	0	0
aSiebern, rf	1	0	1	0	0	0
bTartabull, rf	0	0	0	1	0	0
Santiago, p	2	1	1	0	0	0
Howard, c	0	0	0	1	0	0
Totals	31	1	6	27	6	0

St. Louis .... 0 0 1 0 0 0 1 0 0—2
Boston .... 0 0 1 0 0 0 0 0 0—1

aAt bat for Ru. Gibson when side was retired in seventh. bRan for Siebern in eighth. cGrounded out for Wyatt in ninth. dFlied out for Petrocelli in ninth. Runs batted in—Maris 2, Santiago. Two-base hits—Flood, Scott. Home run—Santiago. Stolen bases—Brock 2. Sacrifice hit—Howard. Double plays—Jones and Scott; Jones, Adair and Scott. Left on bases—St. Louis 10, Boston 5. Earned runs—St. Louis 2, Boston 1. Bases on balls—Off Ro. Gibson 1, off Santiago 3, off Wyatt 2. Struck out—By Ro. Gibson 10, by Santiago 5, by Wyatt 1. Pitching records—Off Santiago 10 hits and 2 runs in 7 innings; off Wyatt 0 hits and 0 runs in 2 innings. Balk—Wyatt. Passed ball—Ru. Gibson. Winning pitcher—Ro. Gibson. Losing pitcher—Santiago. Umpires—Stevens (A.L.), Barlick (N.L.), Umont (A.L.), Donatelli (N.L.), Runge (A.L.) and Pryor (N.L.). Time—2:22. Attendance—34,796.

Thursday, October 5—At Boston

St. Louis (N.L.)	AB	R	H	O	A	E
Brock, lf	4	0	0	4	0	0
Flood, cf	3	0	0	3	0	0
Maris, rf	3	0	0	4	0	0
Cepeda, 1b	3	0	0	1	1	0
McCarver, c	3	0	0	9	0	0
Shannon, 3b	3	0	0	1	1	1
Javier, 2b	3	0	1	0	1	0
Maxvill, ss	2	0	0	1	0	0
aTolan	1	0	0	0	0	0
Bressoud, ss	0	0	0	0	0	0
Hughes, p	2	0	0	1	0	0
Willis, p	0	0	0	0	0	0
Hoerner, p	0	0	0	0	0	0
Lamabe, p	0	0	0	0	0	0
bRicketts	1	0	0	0	0	0
Totals	28	0	1	24	3	1

Boston (A.L.)	AB	R	H	O	A	E
Tartabull, rf	4	1	0	2	0	0
Jones, 3b	5	1	2	0	3	0
Yastrzemski, lf	4	2	3	3	0	0
Scott, 1b	4	1	1	12	1	0
Smith, cf	3	0	0	1	0	0
Adair, 2b	4	0	2	1	4	0
Petrocelli, ss	2	0	1	3	5	0
Howard, c	3	0	0	4	0	0
Lonborg, p	4	0	0	1	0	0
Totals	33	5	9	27	13	0

St. Louis .... 0 0 0 0 0 0 0 0 0—0
Boston .... 0 0 0 1 0 1 3 0 *—5

aGrounded out for Maxvill in eighth. bPopped out for Lamabe in ninth. Runs batted in—Yastrzemski 4, Petrocelli. Two-base hit—Javier. Home runs—Yastrzemski 2. Stolen base—Adair. Sacrifice fly—Petrocelli. Left on bases—St. Louis 2, Boston 11. Earned runs—Boston 4. Bases on balls—Off Hughes 3, off Willis 2, off Hoerner 1, off Lonborg 1. Struck out—By Hughes 5, by Willis 1, by Lamabe 2, By Lonborg 4. Pitching records—Off Hughes 4 hits and 2 runs in 5⅓ innings; off Willis 1 hit and 2 runs in ⅔ inning (pitched to two batters in seventh); off Hoerner 2 hits and 1 run in ⅔ inning; off Lamabe 2 hits and 0 runs in 1⅓ innings. Winning pitcher—Lonborg. Losing pitcher—Hughes. Umpires—Barlick (N.L.), Umont (A.L.), Donatelli (N.L.), Runge (A.L.), Pryor (N.L.) and Stevens (A.L.). Time—2:24. Attendance—35,188.

Saturday, October 7—At St. Louis

Boston (A.L.)	AB	R	H	O	A	E
Tartabull, rf	4	0	0	3	0	0
Jones, 3b	4	0	3	2	1	0
Yastrzemski, lf	3	0	0	0	1	0
Scott, 1b	4	0	0	8	1	0
Smith, cf	4	1	2	2	0	0
Adair, 2b	4	0	0	2	2	0
Petrocelli, ss	3	0	0	1	5	0
Howard, c	3	0	1	5	0	0
Bell, p	0	0	0	0	1	0
aThomas	1	0	0	0	0	0
Waslewski, p	0	0	0	1	0	0
bAndrews	1	1	1	0	0	0
Stange, p	0	0	0	0	0	1
cFoy	1	0	0	0	0	0
Osinski, p	0	0	0	0	0	0
Totals	32	2	7	24	11	1

St. Louis (N.L.)	AB	R	H	O	A	E
Brock, lf	4	2	2	2	0	0
Flood, cf	4	0	1	3	0	0
Maris, rf	4	1	2	0	0	0
Cepeda, 1b	4	0	1	13	0	0
McCarver, c	4	1	1	5	1	0
Shannon, 3b	3	1	2	2	2	0
Javier, 2b	3	0	1	0	6	0
Maxvill, ss	3	0	0	2	4	0
Briles, p	3	0	0	0	2	0
Totals	32	5	10	27	15	0

Boston .... 0 0 0 0 0 1 1 0 0—2
St. Louis .... 1 2 0 0 0 1 0 1 *—5

aStruck out for Bell in third. bSingled for Waslewski in sixth. cGrounded out for Stange in eighth. Runs batted in—Jones, Smith, Flood, Maris, Cepeda, Shannon 2. Two-base hit—Cepeda. Three-base hit—Brock. Home runs—Shannon, Smith. Double plays—Bell, Petrocelli and Scott; Javier, Maxvill and Cepeda. Left on bases—Boston 4, St. Louis 3. Earned runs—Boston 2, St. Louis 4. Bases on balls—None. Struck out—By Bell 1, by Waslewski 3, by Briles 4. Pitching record—Off Bell 5 hits and 3 runs in 2 innings; off Waslewski 0 hits and 0 runs in 3 innings; off Stange 3 hits and 1 run in 2 innings; off Osinski 2 hits and 1 run in 1 inning. Hit by pitcher—By Briles (Yastrzemski). Winning pitcher—Briles. Losing pitcher—Bell. Umpires—Umont (A.L.), Donatelli (N.L.), Runge (A.L.), Pryor (N.L.), Stevens (A.L.), Barlick (N.L.). Time—2:15. Attendance—54,575.

Sunday, October 8—At St. Louis

Boston (A.L.)	AB	R	H	O	A	E
Tartabull, rf	4	0	2	1	0	0
Jones, 3b	4	0	0	0	2	0
Yastrzemski, lf	4	0	2	3	0	0
Scott, 1b	4	0	1	9	0	0
Smith, cf	3	0	0	3	0	0
Adair, 2b	4	0	0	2	2	0
Petrocelli, ss	3	0	0	2	4	0
Howard, c	2	0	0	0	0	0
Morehead, p	0	0	0	0	0	0
bSiebern	1	0	0	0	0	0
Brett, p	0	0	0	0	0	0
Santiago, p	0	0	0	0	0	0
Bell, p	0	0	0	0	0	0
aFoy	1	0	0	0	0	0
Stephenson, p	0	0	0	0	0	0
Ryan, c	2	0	0	4	0	0
Totals	32	0	5	24	8	0

St. Louis (N.L.)	AB	R	H	O	A	E
Brock, lf	4	1	2	2	0	0
Flood, cf	4	1	1	3	0	0
Maris, rf	4	1	1	2	0	0
Cepeda, 1b	4	1	1	11	1	0
McCarver, c	3	1	1	7	0	0
Shannon, 3b	3	1	0	0	2	0
Javier, 2b	4	0	2	0	2	0
Maxvill, ss	3	0	1	0	2	0
Gibson, p	3	0	0	2	2	0
Totals	32	6	9	27	9	0

Boston .... 0 0 0   0 0 0   0 0 0—0
St. Louis .... 4 0 2   0 0 0   0 0 *—6

aStruck out for Bell in third. bFlied out for Morehead in eighth. Runs batted in—Maris 2, McCarver 2, Javier, Maxvill. Two-base hits—Maris, Cepeda, Brock, Javier, Yastrzemski. Stolen base—Brock. Sacrifice fly—McCarver. Left on bases—Boston 6, St. Louis 6. Earned runs—St. Louis 6. Bases on balls—Off Stephenson 1, off Morehead 1, off Brett 1, off Gibson 1. Struck out—By Morehead 2, by Brett 1, by Gibson 6. Pitching record—Off Santiago 6 hits and 4 runs in ⅔ inning, off Bell 0 hits and 0 runs in 1⅓ innings, off Stephenson 3 hits and 2 runs in 2 innings, off Morehead 0 hits and 0 runs in 3 innings, off Brett 0 hits and 0 runs in 1 inning. Wild pitch—Stephenson. Winning pitcher—Gibson. Losing pitcher—Santiago. Umpires—Donatelli (N.L.), Runge (A.L.), Pryor (N.L.), Stevens (A.L.), Barlick (N.L.), Umont (A.L.). Time—2:05. Attendance—54,575.

Monday, October 9—At St. Louis

Boston (A.L.)	AB	R	H	O	A	E
Foy, 3b	5	1	1	2	4	0
Andrews, 2b	3	0	1	1	2	0
Yastrzemski, lf	3	0	1	2	0	0
Harrelson, rf	3	0	1	1	0	0
Tartabull, rf	0	0	0	0	0	0
Scott, 1b	3	1	0	14	0	0
Smith, cf	4	1	1	1	0	0
Petrocelli, ss	3	0	0	1	2	1
Howard, c	4	0	1	5	0	0
Lonborg, p	4	0	0	0	2	0
Totals	32	3	6	27	10	1

St. Louis (N.L.)	AB	R	H	O	A	E
Brock, lf	4	0	0	0	0	0
Flood, cf	4	0	0	2	0	0
Maris, rf	4	1	2	3	0	1
Cepeda, 1b	4	0	0	5	0	0
McCarver, c	3	0	0	9	1	0
Shannon, 3b	3	0	0	1	3	1
Javier, 2b	3	0	0	4	3	0
Maxvill, ss	2	0	1	3	4	0
bRicketts	1	0	0	0	0	0
Willis, p	0	0	0	0	0	0
Lamabe, p	0	0	0	0	1	0
Carlton, p	1	0	0	0	0	0
aTolan	1	0	0	0	0	0
Washburn, p	0	0	0	0	1	0
cGagliano	1	0	0	0	0	0
Bressoud, ss	0	0	0	0	0	0
Totals	31	1	3	27	13	2

Boston .... 0 0 1   0 0 0   0 0 2—3
St. Louis .... 0 0 0   0 0 0   0 0 1—1

aStruck out for Carlton in sixth. bGrounded out for Maxvill in eighth. cPopped out for Washburn in eighth. Runs batted in—Harrelson, Howard, Maris. Two-base hits—Yastrzemski, Smith. Home run—Maris. Sacrifice hit—Andrews. Double plays—Javier, Maxvill and Cepeda; McCarver, Javier, McCarver, Shannon, Lamabe and McCarver. Left on bases—Boston 7, St. Louis 3. Earned runs—Boston 1, St. Louis 1. Bases on balls—Off Carlton 2, off Willis 2. Struck out—By Lonborg 4, by Carlton 5, by Washburn 2, by Lamabe 2. Pitching record—Off Carlton 3 hits and 1 run in 6 innings, off Washburn 1 hit and 0 runs in 2 innings, off Willis 1 hit and 2 runs in 0 inning (pitched to three batters in ninth), off Lamabe 1 hit and 0 runs in 1 inning. Wild pitch—Carlton. Winning pitcher—Lonborg. Losing pitcher—Carlton. Umpires—Runge (A.L.), Pryor (N.L.), Stevens (A.L.), Barlick (N.L.), Umont (A.L.), Donatelli (N.L.). Time—2:20. Attendance—54,575.

Wednesday, October 11—At Boston

St. Louis (N.L.)	AB	R	H	O	A	E
Brock, lf	5	2	2	2	0	0
Flood, cf	5	0	1	2	0	0
Maris, rf	4	0	2	2	0	0
Cepeda, 1b	5	0	1	10	0	0
McCarver, c	3	0	0	2	0	0
Shannon, 3b	4	0	1	1	4	0
Javier, 2b	4	1	1	3	3	0
Maxvill, ss	3	0	0	2	2	0
Hughes, p	1	0	0	0	0	0
Willis, p	0	0	0	0	0	0
aSpiezio	1	0	0	0	0	0
Briles, p	0	0	0	0	2	0
bTolan	0	1	0	0	0	0
Lamabe, p	0	0	0	0	0	0
Hoerner, p	0	0	0	0	0	0
Jaster, p	0	0	0	0	0	0
Washburn, p	0	0	0	0	0	0
eRicketts	1	0	0	0	0	0
Woodeshick, p	0	0	0	0	1	0
Totals	36	4	8	24	12	0

Boston (A.L.)	AB	R	H	O	A	E
Foy, 3b	4	1	1	3	3	0
Andrews, 2b	5	1	2	0	2	0
Yastrzemski, lf	4	2	3	2	0	0
Harrelson, rf	3	0	0	1	0	0
Tartabull, rf	0	0	0	0	0	0
dAdair	0	0	0	0	0	0
Bell, p	0	0	0	0	1	0
Scott, 1b	4	0	1	10	1	0
Smith, cf	4	1	2	4	0	0
Petrocelli, ss	3	2	2	1	3	1

1967 WORLD SERIES

	AB.	R.	H.	O.	A.	E.
Howard, c	4	0	0	4	0	0
Waslewski, p	1	0	0	1	0	0
Wyatt, p	0	0	0	0	0	0
cJones	1	1	1	0	0	0
Thomas, rf	1	0	0	1	0	0
Totals	34	8	12	27	10	1

St. Louis .... 0 0 2 0 0 0 2 0 0—4
Boston .... 0 1 0 3 0 0 4 0 *—8

aGrounded out for Willis in fifth. bWalked for Briles in seventh. cSingled for Wyatt in seventh. dHit sacrifice fly for Tartabull in seventh. eFlied out for Washburn in eighth. Runs batted in—Brock 3, Flood, Foy, Andrews, Yastrzemski, Adair, Smith 2, Petrocelli 2. Two-base hits—Javier, Foy, Shannon. Home runs—Petrocelli 2, Yastrzemski, Smith, Brock. Stolen base—Brock. Sacrifice hit—Foy. Sacrifice fly—Adair. Left on bases—St. Louis 9, Boston 7. Earned runs—St. Louis 4, Boston 8. Bases on balls—Off Briles 1, off Washburn 1, off Waslewski 2, off Wyatt 1, off Bell 1. Struck out—By Hughes 2, by Waslewski 4. Pitching record—Off Hughes 5 hits and 4 runs in 3⅔ innings, off Willis 0 hits and 0 runs in ⅓ inning, off Briles 0 hits and 0 runs in 2 innings, off Lamabe 2 hits and 2 runs in ⅓ inning, off Hoerner 2 hits and 2 runs in 0 inning (pitched to two batters in seventh), off Jaster 2 hits and 0 runs in ⅓ inning, off Washburn 0 hits and 0 runs in ⅓ inning, off Woodeshick 1 hit and 0 runs in 1 inning, off Waslewski 4 hits and 2 runs in 5⅓ innings, off Wyatt 1 hit and 0 runs in 1⅔ innings, off Bell 3 hits and 0 runs in 2 innings. Hit by pitcher—By Briles (Waslewski). Winning pitcher—Wyatt. Losing pitcher—Lamabe. Umpires—Pryor (N.L.), Stevens (A.L.), Barlick (N.L.), Umont (A.L.), Donatelli (N.L.), Runge (A.L.). Time—2:48. Attendance—35,188.

Thursday, October 12—At Boston

St. Louis (N.L.)	AB.	R.	H.	O.	A.	E.
Brock, lf	4	1	2	1	0	0
Flood, cf	3	1	1	0	0	0
Maris, rf	3	0	2	1	0	0
Cepeda, 1b	5	0	0	6	2	0
McCarver, c	5	1	1	12	0	0
Shannon, 3b	4	1	0	0	0	0
Javier, 2b	4	1	2	4	4	1
Maxvill, ss	4	1	1	3	3	0
Ro. Gibson, p	4	1	1	0	1	0
Totals	36	7	10	27	10	1

Boston (A.L.)	AB.	R.	H.	O.	A.	E.
Foy, 3b	3	0	0	2	3	1
Morehead, p	0	0	0	0	0	0
Osinski, p	0	0	0	0	0	0
Brett, p	0	0	0	0	0	0
Andrews, 2b	3	0	0	1	2	0
Yastrzemski, lf	3	0	1	2	0	0
Harrelson, rf	4	0	0	3	0	0
Scott, 1b	4	1	1	9	0	0
Smith, cf	3	0	0	2	0	0
Petrocelli, ss	3	1	1	3	2	0
Howard, c	2	0	0	4	1	0
bJones, 3b	0	0	0	0	0	0
Lonborg, p	1	0	0	0	0	0
aTartabull	1	0	0	0	0	0
Santiago, p	0	0	0	0	0	0
cSiebern	1	0	0	0	0	0
Ru. Gibson, c	0	0	0	1	0	0
Totals	28	2	3	27	8	1

St. Louis .... 0 0 2 0 2 3 0 0 0—7
Boston .... 0 0 0 0 1 0 0 1 0—2

aStruck out for Lonborg in sixth. bWalked for Howard in eighth. cHit into force play for Santiago in eighth. Runs batted in—Flood, Maris, Javier 3, Ro. Gibson, Siebern. Two-base hits—McCarver, Brock, Petrocelli. Three-base hits—Maxvill, Scott. Home runs—Ro. Gibson, Javier. Stolen bases—Brock 3. Sacrifice hit—Andrews. Sacrifice fly—Maris. Double play—Maxvill, Javier and Cepeda. Left on bases—St. Louis 7, Boston 3. Earned runs—St. Louis 6, Boston 2. Bases on balls—Off Ro. Gibson 3, off Lonborg 1, off Morehead 3. Struck out—By Ro. Gibson 10, by Lonborg 3, by Santiago 1, by Morehead 1. Pitching record—Off Lonborg 10 hits and 7 runs in 6 innings, off Santiago 0 hits and 0 runs in 2 innings, off Morehead 0 hits and 0 runs in ⅓ inning, off Osinski 0 hits and 0 runs in ⅓ inning, off Brett 0 hits and 0 runs in ⅓ inning. Wild pitches—Lonborg, Ro. Gibson. Winning pitcher—Ro. Gibson. Losing pitcher—Lonborg. Umpires—Stevens (A.L.), Barlick (N.L.), Umont (A.L.), Donatelli (N.L.), Runge (A.L.), Pryor (N.L.). Time—2:23. Attendance—35,188.

COMPOSITE BATTING AVERAGES
St. Louis Cardinals

Player-Position	G.	AB.	R.	H.	2B.	3B.	HR.	RBI.	BA.
Brock, lf	7	29	8	12	2	1	1	3	.414
Maris, rf	7	26	3	10	1	0	1	7	.385
Javier, 2b	7	25	2	9	3	0	1	4	.360
Shannon, 3b	7	24	3	5	1	0	1	2	.208
Flood, cf	7	28	2	5	1	0	0	3	.179
Maxvill, ss	7	19	1	3	0	1	0	1	.158
McCarver, c	7	24	3	3	1	0	0	2	.125
Cepeda, 1b	7	29	1	3	2	0	0	1	.103
Ro. Gibson, p	3	11	1	1	0	0	1	1	.091
Jaster, p	1	0	0	0	0	0	0	0	.000
Woodeshick, p	1	0	0	0	0	0	0	0	.000
Bressoud, ss	2	0	0	0	0	0	0	0	.000
Hoerner, p	2	0	0	0	0	0	0	0	.000
Washburn, p	2	0	0	0	0	0	0	0	.000
Lamabe, p	3	0	0	0	0	0	0	0	.000
Willis, p	1	0	0	0	0	0	0	0	.000
Carlton, p	1	1	0	0	0	0	0	0	.000
Gagliano, ph	1	1	0	0	0	0	0	0	.000
Spiezio, ph	1	1	0	0	0	0	0	0	.000
Tolan, ph	3	2	1	0	0	0	0	0	.000
Briles, p	2	3	0	0	0	0	0	0	.000
Hughes, p	2	3	0	0	0	0	0	0	.000
Ricketts, ph	3	3	0	0	0	0	0	0	.000
Totals	7	229	25	51	11	2	5	24	.223

Boston Red Sox

Player-Position	G.	AB.	R.	H.	2B.	3B.	HR.	RBI.	BA.
Santiago, p	3	2	1	1	0	0	1	1	.500
Yastrzemski, lf	7	25	4	10	2	0	3	5	.400
Jones, 3b-ph	6	18	2	7	0	0	0	0	.389
Siebern, ph-rf	3	3	0	1	0	0	0	1	.333
Andrews, ph-2b	5	13	2	4	0	0	0	1	.308
Smith, cf	7	24	3	6	1	0	2	3	.250
Scott, 1b	7	26	3	6	1	1	0	0	.231
Petrocelli, ss	7	20	3	4	1	0	2	3	.200
Tartab'l, pr-rf-ph	7	13	1	2	0	0	0	0	.154
Foy, ph-3b	6	15	2	2	1	0	0	1	.133
Adair, 2b-ph	5	16	0	2	0	0	0	1	.125
Howard, c	7	18	0	2	0	0	0	1	.111
Harrelson, rf	4	13	0	1	0	0	0	1	.077
Stange, p	1	0	0	0	0	0	0	0	.000
Stephenson, p	1	0	0	0	0	0	0	0	.000
Brett, p	2	0	0	0	0	0	0	0	.000
Morehead, p	2	0	0	0	0	0	0	0	.000
Wyatt, p	2	0	0	0	0	0	0	0	.000
Bell, p	3	0	0	0	0	0	0	0	.000
Osinski, p	2	0	0	0	0	0	0	0	.000
Ryan, c	1	0	0	0	0	0	0	0	.000
Thomas, ph-rf	2	2	0	0	0	0	0	0	.000
Waslewski, p	2	1	0	0	0	0	0	0	.000
Ru. Gibson, c	2	0	0	0	0	0	0	0	.000
Lonborg, p	3	9	0	0	0	0	0	0	.000
Totals	7	222	21	48	6	1	8	19	.216

COMPOSITE PITCHING AVERAGES
St. Louis Cardinals

Pitcher	G.	IP.	H.	R.	E.	SO.	BB.	W.	L.	ERA.
Carlton	1	6	3	1	0	5	2	0	1	0.00

Pitcher	G.	IP.	H.	R.	E.	BB.	SO.	W.	L.	ERA.
Washburn	2	2⅓	1	0	0	2	1	0	0	0.00
Woodeshick	1	1	1	0	0	0	0	0	0	0.00
Jaster	1	⅓	2	0	0	0	0	0	0	0.00
Ro. Gibson	3	27	14	3	3	26	5	3	0	1.00
Briles	2	11	7	2	2	4	1	1	0	1.64
Hughes	2	9	9	6	5	7	3	0	1	5.00
Lamabe	3	2⅔	5	2	2	4	0	0	1	6.75
Willis	3	1	2	4	3	1	4	0	0	27.00
Hoerner	2	⅔	4	3	3	0	1	0	0	40.50
Totals	7	61	48	21	18	49	17	4	3	2.66

Boston Red Sox

Pitcher	G.	IP.	H.	R.	E.	BB.	SO.	W.	L.	ERA.
Morehead	2	3⅓	0	0	0	3	4	0	0	0.00
Stange	1	2	3	1	0	0	0	0	0	0.00
Brett	2	1⅓	0	0	0	1	1	0	0	0.00
Waslewski	2	8⅓	4	2	2	7	2	0	0	2.16
Lonborg	3	24	14	8	7	11	2	2	1	2.63
Wyatt	2	3⅔	1	2	2	1	3	1	0	4.91
Bell	3	5⅓	8	3	3	1	1	0	1	5.06
Santiago	3	9⅔	16	6	6	6	3	0	2	5.59
Osinski	2	1⅓	2	1	1	0	0	0	0	6.75
Stephenson	1	2	3	2	2	0	1	0	0	9.00
Totals	7	61	51	25	23	30	17	3	4	3.39

SERIES OF 1968

	W.	L.	Pct.
Detroit A. L.	4	3	.571
St. Louis N. L.	3	4	.429

Winners of the American League pennant for the first time since 1945, the Detroit Tigers capped a sensational success story by coming from behind to triumph over the National League champion St. Louis Cardinals in the World Series, four games to three.

Denny McLain, who had won 31 games for the Tigers during the regular season, was expected to be the Detroit pitching star, but instead the hero's mantle was donned by southpaw Mickey Lolich, who beat the Cardinals three times, climaxing his work with a victory over Bob Gibson, the St. Louis ace, in the deciding contest.

Of all the Detroit players, the World Series meant the most to Al Kaline, who finally was a member of a pennant-winning team in his 16th season with the Tigers. The veteran outfielder got a chance to appear in the starting lineup only because of a gamble taken by Manager Mayo Smith. Breaking up his regular outfield, Smith moved center fielder Mickey Stanley to shortstop, shifted right fielder Jim Northrup to center and put Kaline in right field.

Although having only limited experience at shortstop, Stanley did nothing to make Smith regret the move. He handled 31 of 33 chances and neither of his errors hurt the Detroit cause. Kaline, meanwhile, became one of the Tigers' stars, batting .379. One of his hits, a two-run single in the fifth game, helped revive the Tigers when they were on the verge of being swept out of the Series.

Before the classic opened, there was a national debate on what would happen when McLain met Gibson, the Cardinals' 22-game winner in the pennant season. The great confrontation proved almost no contest. Gibson not only beat the Tigers, 4-0, but the righthander set a Series record for most strikeouts with 17. That bettered the high of 15 by Sandy Koufax of the Los Angeles Dodgers against the New York Yankees in 1963.

McLain evaded trouble until the fourth inning when walks to Roger Maris and Tim McCarver paved the way for a three-run outburst by the Cardinals. Mike Shannon singled, scoring Maris, and when Willie Horton booted the ball in left field, McCarver advanced to third and Shannon reached second on the error. Julian Javier followed with a ground single to right field, sending both runners across the plate. Lou Brock accounted for the Cardinals' other run, hitting a homer off reliever Pat Dobson in the seventh.

Lolich, who had a 17-9 record in the regular season, drew Nelson Briles (19-11) as his mound opponent in the second game in St. Louis. The Cardinals had feasted on lefthanders during their romp to the N.L. pennant, but they found Lolich something else again. The Tigers' southpaw gave up only six hits and evened the Series with an 8-1 victory.

Briles was tagged for three homers, the first by Horton producing the initial run of the game in the second inning. The blow that was the most embarrassing to Briles came in the third when Lolich, apparently set up as a strikeout victim, tomahawked a high pitch and knocked the ball into the left field corner of the grandstand. The homer was the first of his entire pro career.

The Tigers' third homer of the game was hit by Norm Cash to open the sixth. When Horton followed with an infield hit, Briles was removed. Steve Carlton, in relief, gave up a single to Northrup and a pass to Don Wert, loading the bases. Dick McAuliffe, coming up with two out, lashed a sinking line drive to center field. Running at top speed, Curt Flood barely got the fingertips of his glove on the ball and it bounced off for a single, scoring Horton and Northrup.

In the seventh, singles by Kaline and Cash brought Ron Willis to the mound for the Cardinals. Kaline, who had taken third base on Cash's hit, scored the Tigers' sixth run when Northrup grounded into a double play. The Tigers' final two tallies in the ninth were gifts. With Joe Hoerner pitching, Kaline started the inning with a single and when Cash bunted, both runners were safe on Shannon's wide throw to second. After Ray Oyler sacrificed, Northrup struck out. The Cardinals passed Bill Freehan intentionally to load the bases. Hoerner then failed to relocate the plate, not only walking Wert to force in one run, but passing Lolich to hand the Tigers their final marker of the game.

When the Series shifted to Detroit for the third meeting, the Cardinals exploded for 13 hits, including two homers, and defeated the Tigers, 7-3.

Kaline homered off Ray Washburn, after a single by McAuliffe in the third inning, to give the Tigers a 2-0 lead before the Cardinals took command with four runs in the fifth. Brock singled, stole second and scored on a double by Flood. Earl Wilson, on the mound for the Tigers, pulled a right hamstring muscle pitching to Flood, but he did not leave the game until he walked Maris. Dobson, relieving, retired Orlando Cepeda on a pop fly, but McCarver smashed a three-run homer to put the Cardinals ahead, 4-2.

McAuliffe golfed one of Washburn's pitches into the seats in the home half of the fifth. When Washburn encountered control difficulties in the sixth, walking both Cash and Horton with one out, Manager Red Schoendienst yanked his starter and called on Hoerner for the second time in the Series. This time, the lefthanded fireman was superb, yielding only one hit in the last three and two-thirds innings. Hoerner not only squelched any hopes that the Tigers might have had, but Cepeda helped kill them off by hitting a three-run homer in the seventh. The blow off Don McMahon came after a single by Flood and double by Maris.

Gibson returned to the mound for the Cardinals in the fourth game and had more trouble from the weather than he did with the Tigers. Rain delayed the start of play for 35 minutes and interrupted action for 74 minutes in the third inning, but Gibson did not cool off. The ace righthander pitched a five-hitter and beat the Tigers, 10-1, for his seventh straight complete-game victory in Series competition, a record.

Brock, leading off, started the Cardinals' scoring with a homer off McLain. Maris was safe on an error and scored another run in the first inning on singles by McCarver and Shannon. A single by Flood, a triple by McCarver and a double by Shannon added two runs in the third before the rain halted play. When the clubs resumed the field after their long wait, McLain bowed out and Joe Sparma went in to pitch for the Tigers.

Gibson opened the fourth inning with a homer, becoming the first pitcher with two World Series homers to his credit. Gibson hit his first against the Red Sox in 1967. Brock tripled following Gibson's homer and scored when Maris grounded out after Daryl Patterson came in to pitch for the Tigers. Northrup saved Detroit from a shutout by hitting for the circuit in the home half of the fourth. The Cardinals then piled it on with four runs in the seventh.

Game No. 5, with Lolich again pitching against Briles, produced a play that helped beat the Cardinals, 5-3, and unquestionably turned the Series around in the Tigers' favor.

The Cardinals greeted Lolich with a three-run blast in the first inning on a double by Brock, a single by Flood and a homer by Cepeda. The Tigers pulled close with a pair in the fourth on a triple by Stanley, a sacrifice fly by Cash, another triple by Horton and a single by Northrup.

The key play occurred in the fifth after Brock doubled with one away. When Javier rapped a one-bounce single to Horton in left, Brock raced for home. However, instead of sliding into the plate, the Cardinal speedster came in standing up and was called out on Horton's tremendous throw to Freehan.

As a result, the Cardinals' lead still was only 3-2 when it was Lolich's turn to bat with one out in the seventh inning. Second-guessers figured that if the Cardinals had been ahead by 4-2, Manager Smith would have sent in a pinch-hitter for Lolich. Instead, trailing by only one run, Smith let Lolich bat and the pitcher came through with a single that lit the fires of a Tiger rally. The hit resulted in the removal of Briles. Hoerner relieved for the third time in the Series and failed to retire any of four batters. McAuliffe singled and Stanley walked to load the bases. Kaline singled, driving in two runs, to send the Tigers ahead and Cash followed with another single to plate an insurance marker.

When the clubs returned to St. Louis for the sixth game, Manager Smith decided to call on McLain again, making another of his successful decisions in the Series. McLain, who submitted to a shot of cortisone to ease the miseries of his aching right shoulder, proceeded to stick the needle into the Cardinals and breezed to a 13-1 victory. The defeat was the worst in the Cards' Series history.

After counting twice in the second inning, the Tigers exploded for ten runs in the third to tie a Series record set when the Philadelphia Athletics scored ten times in the seventh to overcome the Chicago Cubs, 10-8, October 12, 1929.

After McAuliffe walked and Stanley and Kaline singled for the Tigers' first run in their big inning, Larry Jaster replaced Washburn on the mound for the Cardinals. Cash singled, scoring Stanley, and Horton walked to load the bases. Northrup then hit a grand-slam homer, the 11th in Series annals. The Tigers were by no means through. After Willis relieved, two walks, one of them intentional, and a hit batsman loaded the bases. Kaline singled for his second hit of the stanza, driving in two runs. Dick Hughes became the Cardinals' fourth pitcher of the inning and two more runs scored on singles by Cash and Horton before the Tigers subsided. Kaline, however, went on to add to his batting laurels with a homer off Carlton in the fifth inning. The Cardinals averted what would have been the worst shutout in Series history when singles by Maris, Cepeda and Javier produced a run off McLain in the ninth.

With everything at stake, Gibson and Lolich faced each other in the seventh game.

The Cardinals ran high, wide and handsome in the Series, stealing a total of 11 bases—seven by Brock, three by Flood and one by Javier—but their tactics backfired in the sixth inning and killed off a scoring opportunity. Brock singled for his 13th hit of the Series. Caught off first base on Lolich's pickoff throw, Brock attempted to race into second but was out on Cash's throw to Stanley. Flood beat out an infield hit with two away and also was caught off first by Lolich and was retired in a rundown. Safety-first baseball by the Cardinals might have made it a different inning.

There were two out in the Tigers' seventh when disaster struck for the Cardinals. Cash looped a single to right and Horton grounded a single through the hole into left field. Northrup then smashed a drive to center field. Flood, momentarily losing sight of the ball against the crowd background in the grandstand, took about three steps in before slipping as he changed directions and headed back toward the wall. The ball sailed over his head for a triple, Cash and Horton scoring. Freehan, who had made only one hit in 22 times at bat up to that point, doubled, scoring Northrup with the Tigers' third run.

The Tigers reached Gibson for their final run in the ninth on singles by Horton, Northrup and Wert, with Dick Tracewski scoring as a pinch-runner for Horton. The Cardinals' last gasp before surrendering their world championship crown came in the last half of the ninth when Shannon hit a homer.

The box scores follow:

Wednesday, October 2—At St. Louis

Detroit (A.L.)	AB.	R.	H.	O.	A.	E.
McAuliffe, 2b	4	0	1	4	0	0
Stanley, ss	4	0	2	3	2	0
Kaline, rf	4	0	1	2	0	0
Cash, 1b	4	0	0	6	1	1
Horton, lf	4	0	1	2	0	1
Northrup, cf	3	0	0	2	0	0
Freehan, c	2	0	0	4	1	1
Wert, 3b	2	0	1	0	1	0
bMathews	1	0	0	0	0	0
Tracewski, 3b	0	0	0	0	0	0
McLain, p	1	0	0	2	0	0
aMatchick	1	0	0	0	0	0
Dobson, p	0	0	0	0	0	0
cBrown	1	0	0	0	0	0
McMahon, p	0	0	0	1	0	0
Totals	31	0	5	24	7	3

St. Louis (N.L.)	AB.	R.	H.	O.	A.	E.
Brock, lf	4	1	1	2	0	0
Flood, cf	4	0	1	1	0	0
Maris, rf	3	1	1	3	0	0
Cepeda, 1b	4	0	0	1	1	0
McCarver, c	3	1	2	17	1	0
Shannon, 3b	4	1	2	0	0	0
Javier, 2b	3	0	1	2	0	0
Maxvill, ss	2	0	0	2	0	0
Gibson, p	2	0	0	1	0	0
Totals	29	4	6	27	2	0

Detroit............... 0 0 0 0 0 0 0 0 0—0
St. Louis........... 0 0 0 3 0 0 1 0 *—4

aGrounded out for McLain in sixth. bStruck out for Wert in eighth. cFlied out for Dobson in eighth. Runs batted in—Brock, Shannon, Javier 2. Two-base hit—Kaline. Three-base hit—McCarver. Home run—Brock. Stolen bases—Brock, Javier, Flood. Sacrifice hit—Gibson. Left on bases—Detroit 5, St. Louis 6. Earned runs—Detroit 0, St. Louis 3. Bases on balls—Off McLain 3, off Dobson 1, off Gibson 1. Struck out—By McLain 3, by Gibson 17. Pitching records—Off McLain, 3 hits, 3 runs in 5 innings; off Dobson 2 hits, 1 run in 2 innings; off McMahon 1 hit, 0 runs in 1 inning. Losing pitcher—McLain. Umpires—Gorman (N.L.), Honochick (A.L.), Landes (N.L.), Kinnamon (A.L.), Harvey (N.L.) and Haller (A.L.). Time—2:29. Attendance—54,692.

Thursday, October 3—At St. Louis

Detroit (A.L.)	AB.	R.	H.	O.	A.	E.
McAuliffe, 2b	5	0	2	1	5	0
Stanley, ss-cf	5	0	1	0	3	1
Kaline, rf	5	2	2	2	0	0
Cash, 1b	5	2	3	11	0	0
Horton, lf	3	2	2	0	0	0
Oyler, ss	0	0	0	0	0	0
Northrup, cf-lf	5	1	1	4	0	0
Freehan, c	4	0	0	9	1	0
Wert, 3b	2	0	0	0	2	0
Lolich, p	4	1	2	0	0	0
Totals	38	8	13	27	11	1

St. Louis (N.L.)	AB.	R.	H.	O.	A.	E.
Brock, lf	3	1	1	0	0	0
Javier, 2b	4	0	2	3	2	0
Flood, cf	3	0	1	2	0	0
Cepeda, 1b	4	0	2	6	0	0
Shannon, 3b	4	0	0	1	3	1
McCarver, c	4	0	0	7	0	0
Davis, rf	4	0	0	4	0	0
Maxvill, ss	3	0	0	4	3	0
Briles, p	2	0	0	0	0	0
Carlton, p	0	0	0	0	0	0
Willis, p	0	0	0	0	0	0
aGagliano	1	0	0	0	0	0
Hoerner, p	0	0	0	0	0	0
Totals	32	1	6	27	8	1

Detroit............... 0 1 1 0 0 3 1 0 2—8
St. Louis........... 0 0 0 0 0 1 0 0 0—1

aGrounded out for Willis in eighth. Runs batted in—McAuliffe 2, Cash, Horton, Wert, Lolich 2, Cepeda. Home runs—Horton, Lolich, Cash. Stolen bases—Brock 2. Sacrifice hit—Oyler. Double plays—Stanley, McAuliffe and Cash; Maxvill and Cepeda; Javier, Maxvill and Cepeda. Left on bases—Detroit 11, St. Louis 6. Earned runs—Detroit 6, St. Louis 1. Bases on balls—Off Lolich 2, off Briles 1, off Carlton 1, off Willis 2, off Hoerner 3. Struck out—By Lolich 9, by Briles 2, by Carlton 1, by Willis 2, by Hoerner 1. Pitching records—Off Briles 7 hits, 4 runs in 5 innings (pitched to two batters in sixth); off Carlton 4 hits, 2 runs in 1 inning (pitched to two batters in seventh); off Willis 1 hit, 0 runs in 2 innings; off Hoerner 1 hit, 2 runs in 1 inning. Losing pitcher—Briles. Umpires—Honochick (A.L.), Landes (N.L.), Kinnamon (A.L.), Harvey (N.L.), Haller (A.L.) and Gorman (N.L.). Time—2:41. Attendance—54,692.

1968 WORLD SERIES

Saturday, October 5—At Detroit

St. Louis (N.L.)	AB.	R.	H.	O.	A.	E.
Brock, lf	4	1	3	5	0	0
Flood, cf	4	2	2	1	0	0
Maris, rf	3	2	1	2	0	0
Cepeda, 1b	5	1	1	10	0	0
McCarver, c	5	1	2	5	0	0
Shannon, 3b	4	0	2	0	1	0
Javier, 2b	4	0	1	2	5	0
Maxvill, ss	4	0	0	2	2	0
Washburn, p	3	0	0	0	1	0
Hoerner, p	2	0	1	0	0	0
Totals	38	7	13	27	9	0

Detroit (A.L.)	AB.	R.	H.	O.	A.	E.
McAuliffe, 2b	4	2	2	0	1	0
Stanley, ss	3	0	0	0	2	0
Kaline, rf	4	1	1	1	0	0
Cash, 1b	3	0	0	8	1	0
Horton, lf	2	0	0	1	0	0
Northrup, cf	4	0	0	7	0	0
Freehan, c	3	0	0	6	2	0
Wert, 3b	4	0	0	3	2	0
Wilson, p	1	0	0	0	2	0
Dobson, p	0	0	0	0	0	0
aMatchick	1	0	0	0	0	0
McMahon, p	0	0	0	0	0	0
Patterson, p	0	0	0	0	0	0
bComer	1	0	1	0	0	0
Hiller, p	0	0	0	1	0	0
cPrice	1	0	0	0	0	0
Totals	31	3	4	27	10	0

St. Louis .... 0 0 0 0 4 0 3 0 0—7
Detroit .... 0 0 2 0 1 0 0 0 0—3

aStruck out for Dobson in fifth. bSingled for Patterson in seventh. cFlied out for Hiller in ninth. Runs batted in—Flood, Cepeda 2, McCarver 3, McAuliffe, Kaline 2. Two-base hits—Flood, Maris. Home runs—Kaline, McCarver, McAuliffe, Cepeda. Stolen bases—Brock 3. Double play—Freehan and Wert. Left on bases—St. Louis 11, Detroit 6. Earned runs—St. Louis 7, Detroit 3. Bases on balls—Off Washburn 4, off Hoerner 1, off Wilson 6, off Hiller 1. Struck out—By Washburn 3, by Hoerner 2, by Wilson 3, by McMahon 1, by Hiller 1. Pitching records—Off Washburn 3 hits and 3 runs in 5⅓ innings; off Hoerner 1 hit and 0 runs in 3⅔ innings; off Wilson 4 hits and 3 runs in 4⅓ innings; off Dobson 2 hits and 1 run in ⅔ inning; off McMahon 3 hits and 3 runs in 1 inning (pitched to three batters in seventh); off Patterson 0 hits and 0 runs in 1 inning; off Hiller 4 hits and 0 runs in 2 innings. Winning pitcher—Washburn. Losing pitcher—Wilson. Umpires—Landes (N.L.), Kinnamon (A.L.), Harvey (N.L.), Haller (A.L.), Gorman (N.L.), Honochick (A.L.). Time—3:17. Attendance—53,634.

Sunday, October 6—At Detroit

St. Louis (N.L.)	AB.	R.	H.	O.	A.	E.
Brock, lf	5	2	3	2	0	0
Flood, cf	5	1	1	3	0	0
Maris, rf	5	1	0	0	0	0
Cepeda, 1b	4	0	1	9	1	0
McCarver, c	5	1	3	10	0	0
Shannon, 3b	5	1	2	1	0	0
Javier, 2b	4	1	2	0	2	0
Maxvill, ss	4	1	0	2	1	0
Gibson, p	3	2	1	0	0	0
Totals	40	10	13	27	4	0

Detroit (A.L.)	AB.	R.	H.	O.	A.	E.
McAuliffe, 2b	4	0	0	2	4	0
Stanley, ss	4	0	0	3	3	0
Kaline, rf	4	0	2	1	0	0
Cash, 1b	4	0	1	10	2	0
Horton, lf	3	0	0	1	0	0
Northrup, cf	4	1	1	5	0	1
Mathews, 3b	2	0	1	0	1	1
Freehan, c	3	0	0	4	1	1
McLain, p	1	0	0	0	0	1
Sparma, p	0	0	0	0	0	0
Patterson, p	0	0	0	0	1	0
aPrice	1	0	0	0	0	0
Lasher, p	0	0	0	1	0	0
bMatchick	1	0	0	0	0	0
Hiller, p	0	0	0	0	0	0
Dobson, p	0	0	0	1	0	0
Totals	31	1	5	27	13	4

St. Louis .... 2 0 2 2 0 0 0 4 0—10
Detroit .... 0 0 0 1 0 0 0 0 0— 1

aStruck out for Patterson in fifth. bFlied out for Lasher in seventh. Runs batted in—Brock 4, Maris, McCarver, Shannon 2, Gibson 2, Northrup. Two-base hits—Kaline, Shannon, Javier, Brock. Three-base hits—McCarver, Brock. Home runs—Brock, Gibson, Northrup. Stolen base—Brock. Double play—Cepeda and Maxvill. Left on bases—St. Louis 7, Detroit 5. Earned runs—St. Louis 7, Detroit 1. Bases on balls—Off Gibson 2, off McLain 1, off Patterson 1, off Hiller 2. Struck out—By Gibson 10, by McLain 3, by Lasher 1. Pitching records—Off McLain 6 hits and 4 runs in 2⅔ innings; off Sparma 2 hits and 2 runs in ⅓ inning (pitched to two batters in fourth); off Patterson 1 hit and 0 runs in 2 innings; off Lasher 0 runs in 2 innings; off Hiller 2 hits and 4 runs in 0 inning (pitched to five batters in eighth); off Dobson 1 hit and 0 runs in 2 innings. Losing pitcher—McLain. Umpires—Kinnamon (A.L.), Harvey (N.L.), Haller (A.L.), Gorman (N.L.), Honochick (A.L.), Landes (N.L.). Time—2:34. Attendance—53,634.

Monday, October 7—At Detroit

St. Louis (N.L.)	AB.	R.	H.	O.	A.	E.
Brock, lf	5	1	3	2	0	0
Javier, 2b	4	0	2	2	1	0
Flood, cf	4	1	1	3	0	0
Cepeda, 1b	4	1	1	7	0	0
Shannon, 3b	4	0	0	1	0	0
McCarver, c	3	0	1	6	0	0
Davis, rf	3	0	0	1	0	0
aGagliano	1	0	0	0	0	0
Maxvill, ss	3	0	0	1	2	0
bSpiezio	1	0	1	0	0	0
cSchofield	0	0	0	0	0	0
Briles, p	2	0	0	0	2	0
Hoerner, p	0	0	0	0	0	0
Willis, p	0	0	0	1	0	0
dMaris	1	0	0	0	0	0
Totals	35	3	9	24	7	0

Detroit (A.L.)	AB.	R.	H.	O.	A.	E.
McAuliffe, 2b	4	1	1	1	2	0
Stanley, ss-cf	3	2	1	2	3	0
Kaline, rf	4	0	2	3	0	0
Cash, 1b	2	0	2	7	1	1
Horton, lf	4	1	1	1	0	0
Oyler, ss	0	0	0	0	1	0
Northrup, cf-lf	3	0	1	2	0	0
Freehan, c	4	0	0	9	1	0
Wert, 3b	3	0	0	0	1	0
Lolich, p	4	1	1	1	2	0
Totals	31	5	9	27	11	1

St. Louis .... 3 0 0 0 0 0 0 0 0—3
Detroit .... 0 0 0 2 0 0 3 0 *—5

aFlied out for Davis in ninth. bSingled for Maxvill in ninth. cRan for Spiezio in ninth. dStruck out for Willis in ninth. Runs batted in—Flood, Cepeda 2, Kaline 2, Cash 2, Northrup. Two-base hits—Brock 2. Three-base hits—Stanley, Horton. Home run—Cepeda. Stolen base—Flood. Sacrifice fly—Cash. Double play—Shannon, Javier and Cepeda. Left on bases—St. Louis 7, Detroit 7. Earned runs—St. Louis 3, Detroit 5. Bases on balls—Off Briles 3, off Hoerner 1, off Lolich 1. Struck out—By Briles 5, by Willis 1, by Lolich 8. Pitching records—Off Briles 6 hits and 3 runs in 6⅓ innings; off Hoerner 3 hits and 2 runs in 0 innings (pitched to four batters in seventh); off Willis 0 hits and 0 runs in 1⅔ innings. Hit by pitcher—By Lolich (Briles). Losing pitcher—Hoerner. Umpires—Harvey (N.L.), Haller (A.L.), Gorman (N.L.), Honochick (A.L.), Landes (N.L.), Kinnamon (A.L.). Time—2:43. Attendance—53,634.

Wednesday, October 9—At St. Louis

Detroit (A.L.)	AB.	R.	H.	O.	A.	E.
McAuliffe, 2b	2	2	0	3	1	0
Stanley, ss-cf	5	2	1	2	1	1
Kaline, rf	4	3	3	7	0	0
Cash, 1b	4	2	3	5	0	0
Horton, lf	3	2	2	0	0	0
Oyler, ss	0	0	0	0	0	0
Northrup, cf-lf	5	1	2	1	0	0
Freehan, c	4	0	1	7	0	0
Wert, 3b	3	1	0	2	2	0
McLain, p	4	0	0	0	1	0
Totals	34	13	12	27	5	1

St. Louis (N.L.)	AB.	R.	H.	O.	A.	E.
Brock, lf	4	0	1	1	0	1
Flood, cf	4	0	0	0	0	0
Maris, rf	4	1	2	2	0	0
Cepeda, 1b	4	0	2	7	2	0
McCarver, c	4	0	1	8	0	0
Shannon, 3b	4	0	1	1	1	0
Javier, 2b	4	0	1	3	2	0
Maxvill, ss	4	0	0	4	6	0
Washburn, p	0	0	0	0	0	0
Jaster, p	0	0	0	0	0	0
Willis, p	0	0	0	0	0	0
Hughes, p	0	0	0	0	0	0
aRicketts	1	0	1	0	0	0
Carlton, p	0	0	0	1	1	0
bTolan	1	0	0	0	0	0
Granger, p	0	0	0	0	1	0
cEdwards	1	0	0	0	0	0
Nelson, p	0	0	0	0	0	0
Totals	35	1	9	27	13	1

Detroit .... 0 2 10   0 1 0   0 0 0—13
St. Louis .... 0 0 0   0 0 0   0 0 1— 1

aSingled for Hughes in third. bStruck out for Carlton in sixth. cStruck out for Granger in eighth. Runs batted in—Kaline 4, Cash 2, Horton 2, Northrup 4, Freehan, Javier. Two-base hit—Horton. Home runs—Northrup, Kaline. Sacrifice hit—McLain. Double plays—Maxvill, Javier and Cepeda 2; Stanley, McAuliffe and Cash; Granger, Maxvill and Cepeda. Left on bases—Detroit 5, St. Louis 7. Earned runs—Detroit 13, St. Louis 1. Bases on balls—Off Washburn 3, off Jaster 1, off Willis 1, off Granger 1. Struck out—By McLain 7, by Washburn 3, by Carlton 2, by Granger 1, by Nelson 1. Pitching records—Off Washburn 4 hits and 5 runs in 2 innings (pitched to three batters in third); off Jaster 2 hits and 3 runs in 0 innings (pitched to three batters in third); off Willis 1 hit and 4 runs in ⅔ inning; off Hughes 2 hits and 0 runs in ⅓ inning; off Carlton 3 hits and 1 run in 3 innings; off Granger 0 hits and 0 runs in 2 innings;

off Nelson 0 hits and 0 runs in 1 inning. Hit by pitcher—By Willis (Wert), by Granger (Kaline, Horton). Losing pitcher—Washburn. Umpires—Haller (A.L.), Gorman (N.L.), Honochick (A.L.), Landes (N.L.), Kinnamon (A.L.), Harvey (N.L.). Time—2:26. Attendance—54,692.

Thursday, October 10—At St. Louis

Detroit (A.L.)	AB.	R.	H.	O.	A.	E.
McAuliffe, 2b	4	0	0	1	3	0
Stanley, ss-cf	4	0	1	5	2	0
Kaline, rf	4	0	0	2	0	0
Cash, 1b	4	1	1	11	2	0
Horton, lf	4	1	2	0	0	0
bTracewski	0	1	0	0	0	0
Oyler, ss	0	0	0	1	0	0
Northrup, cf-lf	4	1	2	1	0	1
Freehan, c	4	0	1	6	0	0
Wert, 3b	3	0	1	0	6	0
Lolich, p	4	0	0	0	2	0
Totals	35	4	8	27	15	1

St. Louis (N.L.)	AB.	R.	H.	O.	A.	E.
Brock, lf	3	0	1	1	0	0
Javier, 2b	4	0	0	3	2	0
Flood, cf	4	0	2	3	0	0
Cepeda, 1b	3	0	0	7	0	0
Shannon, 3b	4	1	1	1	2	0
McCarver, c	3	0	1	8	0	0
Maris, rf	3	0	0	3	0	0
Maxvill, ss	2	0	0	0	1	0
aGagliano	1	0	0	0	0	0
Schofield, ss	0	0	0	0	0	0
Gibson, p	3	0	0	1	0	0
Totals	30	1	5	27	5	0

Detroit .... 0 0 0   0 0 0   3 0 1—4
St. Louis .... 0 0 0   0 0 0   0 0 1—1

aGrounded out for Maxvill in eighth. bRan for Horton in ninth. Runs batted in—Northrup 2, Freehan, Wert, Shannon. Two-base hit—Freehan. Three-base hit—Northrup. Home run—Shannon. Stolen base—Flood. Double play—Stanley and Cash. Left on bases—Detroit 5, St. Louis 5. Earned runs—Detroit 4, St. Louis 1. Bases on balls—Off Lolich 3, off Gibson 1. Struck out—By Lolich 4, by Gibson 8. Umpires—Gorman (N.L.), Honochick (A.L.), Landes (N.L.), Kinnamon (A.L.), Harvey (N.L.), Haller (A.L.). Time—2:07. Attendance—54,692.

COMPOSITE BATTING AVERAGES
Detroit Tigers

Player-Position	G.	AB.	R.	H.	2B.	3B.	HR.	RBI.	BA.
Comer, ph	1	1	0	1	0	0	0	0	1.000
Cash, 1b	7	26	5	10	0	0	1	5	.385
Kaline, rf	7	29	6	11	2	0	2	8	.379
Mathews, ph-3b	2	3	0	1	0	0	0	0	.333
Horton, lf	7	23	6	7	1	1	1	3	.304
Northrup, cf-lf	7	28	4	7	0	1	2	8	.250
Lolich, p	3	12	2	3	0	0	1	2	.250
McAuliffe, 2b	7	27	5	6	0	0	1	3	.222
Stanley, ss-cf	7	28	4	6	0	1	0	0	.214
Wert, 3b	6	17	1	2	0	0	0	2	.118
Freehan, c	7	24	0	2	1	0	0	2	.083
Brown, ph	1	1	0	0	0	0	0	0	.000
Wilson, p	1	1	0	0	0	0	0	0	.000
Price, ph	2	2	0	0	0	0	0	0	.000
Matchick, ph	3	3	0	0	0	0	0	0	.000
McLain, p	3	6	0	0	0	0	0	0	.000
Oyler, ss	4	0	0	0	0	0	0	0	.000
Dobson, p	3	0	0	0	0	0	0	0	.000
Hiller, p	2	0	0	0	0	0	0	0	.000
McMahon, p	2	0	0	0	0	0	0	0	.000
Patterson, p	2	0	0	0	0	0	0	0	.000
Tracewski, 3b-pr	2	0	1	0	0	0	0	0	.000
Lasher, p	1	0	0	0	0	0	0	0	.000
Sparma, p	1	0	0	0	0	0	0	0	.000
Totals	7	231	34	56	4	3	8	33	.242

St. Louis Cardinals

Player-Position	G.	AB.	R.	H.	2B.	3B.	HR.	RBI.	BA.
Ricketts, ph	1	1	0	1	0	0	0	0	1.000
Spiezio, ph	1	1	0	1	0	0	0	0	1.000
Hoerner, p	3	2	0	1	0	0	0	0	.500
Brock, lf	7	28	6	13	3	1	2	5	.464
McCarver, c	7	27	3	9	0	2	1	4	.333
Javier, 2b	7	27	1	9	1	0	0	3	.333
Flood, cf	7	28	4	8	1	0	0	2	.286
Shannon, 3b	7	29	3	8	1	0	1	4	.276
Cepeda, 1b	7	28	2	7	0	0	2	6	.250
Maris, rf-ph	6	19	5	3	1	0	0	1	.158
Gibson, p	3	8	2	1	0	0	1	2	.125
Edwards, ph	1	1	0	0	0	0	0	0	.000
Tolan, ph	1	1	0	0	0	0	0	0	.000
Gagliano, ph	3	3	0	0	0	0	0	0	.000
Washburn, p	2	3	0	0	0	0	0	0	.000
Briles, p	2	4	0	0	0	0	0	0	.000
Davis, rf	2	7	0	0	0	0	0	0	.000
Maxvill, ss	7	22	1	0	0	0	0	0	.000
Willis, p	3	0	0	0	0	0	0	0	.000
Carlton, p	2	0	0	0	0	0	0	0	.000
Schofield, pr-ss	2	0	0	0	0	0	0	0	.000
Granger, p	1	0	0	0	0	0	0	0	.000
Hughes, p	1	0	0	0	0	0	0	0	.000
Jaster, p	1	0	0	0	0	0	0	0	.000
Nelson, p	1	0*	0	0	0	0	0	0	.000
Totals	7	239	27	61	7	3	7	27	.255

COMPOSITE PITCHING AVERAGES

Detroit Tigers

Pitcher	G.	IP.	H.	R.	E.	SO.	BB.	W.	L.	ERA.
Patterson	2	3	1	0	0	0	1	0	0	0.00
Lasher	1	2	1	0	0	1	0	0	0	0.00
Lolich	3	27	20	5	5	21	6	3	0	1.67
McLain	3	16⅔	18	8	6	13	4	1	2	3.24
Dobson	3	4⅔	5	2	2	0	1	0	0	3.86
Wilson	1	4⅓	4	3	3	3	6	0	1	6.23
Hiller	2	2	6	4	3	1	3	0	0	13.50
McMahon	2	2	4	3	3	1	0	0	0	13.50
Sparma	1	⅓	2	2	1	0	0	0	0	27.00
Totals	7	62	61	27	23	40	21	4	3	3.34

St. Louis Cardinals

Pitcher	G.	IP.	H.	R.	E.	SO.	BB.	W.	L.	ERA.
Granger	1	2	0	0	0	1	1	0	0	0.00
Nelson	1	1	0	0	0	1	0	0	0	0.00
Hughes	1	⅓	2	0	0	0	0	0	0	0.00
Gibson	3	27	18	5	5	35	4	2	1	1.67
Hoerner	3	4⅔	4	2	2	3	5	0	1	3.86
Briles	2	11⅓	13	7	7	7	4	0	1	5.56
Carlton	2	4	7	3	3	3	1	0	0	6.75
Willis	3	4⅓	2	4	4	3	4	0	0	8.31
Washburn	2	7⅓	7	8	8	6	7	1	1	9.82
Jaster	1	0*	2	3	3	0	1	0	0	....
Totals	7	62	56	34	32	59	27	3	4	4.65

*Pitched to three batters in third inning of sixth game.

SERIES OF 1969

	W.	L.	Pct.
New York N. L.	4	1	.800
Baltimore A. L.	1	4	.200

The 1969 World Series produced one of the more startling upsets in the history of the classic as the New York Mets defeated the Baltimore Orioles, capturing four straight games after losing the opener.

Never higher than ninth since being awarded an expansion franchise in 1962, the Mets surprised everybody by winning the National League's Eastern Division in handy fashion and then sweeping by the league's Western Division winner, the Atlanta Braves, in three straight games.

The Orioles made shambles of the American League's Eastern Division and then wiped out the Western Division champs, the Minnesota Twins, in three games.

The 1969 Series was the first to open on a Saturday since 1926—October 11, at Memorial Stadium, Baltimore. The opposing pitchers were Mets' ace righthander Tom Seaver and Oriole lefty Mike Cuellar. Leadoff man Don Buford laced Seaver's second pitch of the game off the right field wall for a home run. In the fourth, Elrod Hendricks singled, Dave Johnson walked and Mark Belanger singled for another run. Cuellar then hit a single and Buford doubled to make the score 4-0. The Mets scored a run in the seventh on Al Weis' sacrifice fly, but Baltimore third baseman Brooks Robinson made a great pick-up and throw of pinch-hitter Rod Gaspar's slowly hit grounder to retire the side. The Mets threatened again in the ninth, but Cuellar induced pinch-hitter Art Shamsky to roll out with two runners on base.

In the second game the Mets' Jerry Koosman revived memories of Don Larsen's no-hitter for the Yankees in the 1956 Series as he tossed six hitless frames and nursed a 1-0 lead into the seventh, the result of Donn Clendenon's fourth inning homer. But Paul Blair singled cleanly to left to open the frame and, after two were out, stole second and scored on Brooks Robinson's single up the middle. Oriole hurler Dave McNally retired the first two Mets in the ninth, but Ed Charles, Jerry Grote and Al Weis stroked successive singles to left and the Mets went ahead 2-1. Koosman walked Frank Robinson and Boog Powell with two out in the bottom of the inning and Manager Gil Hodges replaced him with Ron Taylor. Brooks Robinson then grounded a 3-1 pitch to Charles. After some hesitation as to whether or not to try for an unassisted force, Charles finally threw to first for the game's final out.

After a day off for travel, the teams resumed Tuesday at New York's Shea Stadium where the Mets won a 5-0 decision, largely on the strength of center fielder Tommie Agee staging a one-man show that must rank with the greatest ever seen in World Series play.

Agee began his heroics in the first inning when he blasted a home run off Oriole starter Jim Palmer. In the fourth, with men on first and third, he raced to the 396-foot sign in left center to make a backhanded finger-tip catch of Elrod Hendricks' bid for a triple. In the seventh, with two out and the bases loaded, he made a head-long diving grab of Paul Blair's line shot that was going up the alley in right center for extra bases. Either play stands comparison with those of Al Gionfriddo in the 1947 Series and Willie Mays in 1954. By himself, Agee was the difference of six runs in the game.

Besides Agee's homer, the Mets scored two runs in the second off Palmer on pitcher Gary Gentry's double and another in the sixth as a result of Jerry Grote's double. They added one more on Ed Kranepool's home run in the eighth off reliever Dave Leonhard.

Gentry pitched until the seventh when he loaded the bases on walks and was replaced by Nolan Ryan. It was off Ryan that Blair hit his line drive that Agee caught.

The Mets, behind Tom Seaver, won the fourth game, 2-1, in ten innings. Donn Clendenon hit a home run off Mike Cuellar in the second and the run stood up until the ninth when Frank Robinson and Boog Powell singled. Right fielder Ron Swoboda made a diving grab of Brooks Robinson's line drive, a run scoring after the catch. But Swoboda's play was one of the fielding gems of the Series and prevented a second run which surely would have come in had not the catch been made. In the tenth, with Dick Hall on the mound, Don Buford misplayed Jerry Grote's fly and it fell for a two-base hit in short left field. After Al Weis was intentionally walked, lefty Pete Richert replaced Hall. Pinch-hitter J. C. Martin bunted, and when Richert's throw to first hit Martin on the wrist, the ball caromed away enabling pinch-runner Rod Gaspar to score. The Orioles later claimed Martin was out of the base path and should have been called out for "interference." Newspaper pictures proved inconclusive and the play, of course, was allowed to stand. The game was notable in that Earl Weaver became the third manager in Series history to be ejected by an umpire, Shag Crawford doing the honors in the third inning when the Oriole skipper objected too vociferously on ball-and-strike calls.

In the fifth game, the Orioles jumped on Jerry Koosman for three runs in the third when Mark Belanger singled and Dave McNally and Frank Robinson homered. In the sixth inning, Cleon Jones was awarded first base when it was proved by examining the shoe polish on the ball that he had been hit by a pitch. Umpire Lou DiMuro had originally called the pitch a ball. Donn Clendenon immediately followed with his third home run of the Series. Al Weis' homer tied it in the seventh and the Mets clinched the game in the eighth on doubles by Cleon Jones and Ron Swoboda and errors by Boog Powell and Eddie Watt. The final score was 5-3 and the Mets were World Champions.

The old adage that "good pitching will always stop good hitting" was never proved more correct than in this Series. The heavy hitting Orioles had a combined average of but .146. Boog Powell had no extra base hits and Brooks Robinson managed only one single in 19 official at bats for a miserable .053 mark. Dave Johnson wasn't much better at .063. Frank Robinson batted just .188. Much was said about the "miracle" of the Mets. But there was nothing really miraculous. It was simply a combination of the classic ingredients of winning baseball: good pitching, timely hitting and solid fielding.

The box scores:

Saturday, October 11—At Baltimore

New York (N.L.)	AB.	R.	H.	O.	A.	E.
Agee, cf	4	0	0	4	0	0
Harrelson, ss	3	0	1	0	1	0
Jones, lf	4	0	1	1	0	0
Clendenon, 1b	4	1	2	9	1	0
Swoboda, rf	3	0	1	0	0	0
Charles, 3b	4	0	0	1	4	0
Grote, c	4	0	1	6	0	0
Weis, 2b	1	0	0	3	1	1
Seaver, p	1	0	0	0	0	0
aDyer	1	0	0	0	0	0
Cardwell, p	0	0	0	0	0	0
bGaspar	1	0	0	0	0	0
Taylor, p	0	0	0	0	1	0
cShamsky	1	0	0	0	0	0
Totals	31	1	6	24	8	1
Baltimore (A.L.)	AB.	R.	H.	O.	A.	E.
Buford, lf	4	1	2	2	0	0
Blair, cf	3	0	0	2	0	0
F. Robinson, rf	4	0	0	2	0	0
Powell, 1b	4	0	1	11	0	0
B. Robinson, 3b	4	0	0	0	6	0
Hendricks, c	3	1	1	8	0	0
Johnson, 2b	2	1	0	1	3	0
Belanger, ss	3	1	1	1	3	0
Cuellar, p	3	0	1	0	0	0
Totals	30	4	6	27	12	0

```
New York.......... 0 0 0   0 0 0   1 0 0—1
Baltimore......... 1 0 0   3 0 0   0 0 *—4
```

aGrounded out for Seaver in sixth. bGrounded out for Cardwell in seventh. cGrounded out for Taylor in ninth. Runs batted in—Buford 2, Belanger, Cuellar, Weis. Two-base hits—Clendenon, Buford. Home run—Buford. Sacrifice fly—Weis. Double play—Belanger, Johnson and Powell. Left on bases—New York 8, Baltimore 4. Earned runs—New York 1, Baltimore 4. Bases on balls—Off Seaver 1, off Taylor 1, off Cuellar 4. Struck out—By Seaver 3, by Taylor 3, by Cuellar 8. Pitching records—Off Seaver 6 hits and 4 runs in 5 innings; off Cardwell 0 hits and 0 runs in 1 inning; off Taylor 0 hits and 0 runs in 2 innings. Losing pitcher—Seaver. Umpires—Soar (A.L.), Secory (N.L.), Napp (A.L.), Crawford (N.L.), DiMuro (A.L.), Weyer (N.L.). Time—2:13. Attendance—50,429.

Sunday, October 12—At Baltimore

New York (N.L.)	AB.	R.	H.	O.	A.	E.
Agee, cf	4	0	0	3	0	0
Harrelson, ss	3	0	0	3	3	0
Jones, lf	4	0	0	2	0	0
Clendenon, 1b	3	1	1	7	0	0
Swoboda, rf	4	0	0	5	0	0
Charles, 3b	4	1	2	0	3	0
Grote, c	4	0	1	4	0	0
Weis, 2b	3	0	2	3	1	0
Koosman, p	4	0	0	0	1	0
Taylor, p	0	0	0	0	0	0
Totals	33	2	6	27	8	0
Baltimore (A.L.)	AB.	R.	H.	O.	A.	E.
Buford, lf	4	0	0	1	0	0
Blair, cf	4	1	1	2	0	0
F. Robinson, rf	3	0	0	2	0	0
aRettenmund	0	0	0	0	0	0
Powell, 1b	3	0	0	10	1	0
B. Robinson, 3b	4	0	1	0	2	0

1969 WORLD SERIES

	AB.	R.	H.	O.	A.	E.
Johnson, 2b	2	0	0	1	3	0
Etchebarren, c	3	0	0	8	0	0
Belanger, ss	3	0	0	2	4	0
McNally, p	3	0	0	1	1	0
Totals	29	1	2	27	11	0

New York	0 0 0	1 0 0	0 0 1—2
Baltimore	0 0 0	0 0 0	1 0 0—1

aRan for F. Robinson in ninth. Runs batted in—Clendenon, Weis, B. Robinson. Two-base hit—Charles. Home run—Clendenon. Stolen base—Blair. Left on bases—New York 7, Baltimore 4. Earned runs—New York 2, Baltimore 1. Bases on balls—Off Koosman 3, off McNally 3. Struck out—By Koosman 4, by McNally 7. Pitching records—Off Koosman 2 hits and 1 run in 8⅔ innings; off Taylor 0 hits and 0 runs in ⅓ inning. Wild pitch—McNally. Winning pitcher—Koosman. Save—Taylor. Umpires—Secory (N.L.), Napp (A.L.), Crawford (N.L.), DiMuro (A.L.), Weyer (N.L.), Soar (A.L.). Time—2:20. Attendance—50,850.

Tuesday, October 14—At New York

Baltimore (A.L.)	AB.	R.	H.	O.	A.	E.
Buford, lf	3	0	0	2	0	0
Blair, cf	5	0	0	0	0	0
F. Robinson, rf	2	0	1	7	0	0
Powell, 1b	4	0	2	5	1	0
B. Robinson, 3b	4	0	0	0	1	0
Hendricks, c	4	0	0	6	0	0
Johnson, 2b	4	0	0	1	3	0
Belanger, ss	2	0	0	2	0	0
Palmer, p	2	0	0	1	0	1
aMay	0	0	0	0	0	0
Leonhard, p	0	0	0	0	1	0
bDalrymple	1	0	1	0	0	0
cSalmon	0	0	0	0	0	0
Totals	31	0	4	24	6	1

New York (N.L.)	AB.	R.	H.	O.	A.	E.
Agee, cf	3	1	1	6	0	0
Garrett, 3b	1	0	0	1	0	0
Jones, lf	4	0	0	0	0	0
Shamsky, rf	4	0	0	1	0	0
Weis, 2b	0	0	0	0	0	0
Boswell, 2b	3	1	1	0	1	0
Gaspar, rf	1	0	0	2	0	0
Kranepool, 1b	4	1	1	7	0	0
Grote, c	3	1	1	7	0	0
Harrelson, ss	3	1	1	3	5	0
Gentry, p	3	0	1	0	0	0
Ryan, p	0	0	0	0	0	0
Totals	29	5	6	27	6	0

Baltimore	0 0 0	0 0 0	0 0 0—0
New York	1 2 0	0 0 1	0 1 *—5

aWalked for Palmer in seventh. bSingled for Leonhard in ninth. cRan for Dalrymple in ninth. Runs batted in—Agee, Kranepool, Grote, Gentry 2. Two-base hits—Gentry, Grote. Home runs—Agee, Kranepool. Sacrifice hit—Garrett. Left on bases—Baltimore 11, New York 6. Earned runs—Baltimore 0, New York 5. Bases on balls—Off Palmer 4, off Leonhard 1, off Gentry 5, off Ryan 2. Struck out—By Palmer 5, by Leonhard 1, by Gentry 4, by Ryan 3. Pitching records—Off Palmer 5 hits and 4 runs in 6 innings; off Leonhard 1 hit and 1 run in 2 innings; off Gentry 3 hits and 0 runs in 6⅔ innings; off Ryan 1 hit and 0 runs in 2⅓ innings. Winning pitcher—Gentry. Losing pitcher—Palmer. Save—Ryan. Umpires—Napp (A.L.), Crawford (N.L.), DiMuro (A.L.), Weyer (N.L.), Soar (A.L.), Secory (N.L.). Time—2:23. Attendance—56,335.

Wednesday, October 15—At New York

Baltimore (A.L.)	AB.	R.	H.	O.	A.	E.
Buford, lf	5	0	0	2	0	0
Blair, cf	4	0	1	0	0	0
F. Robinson, rf	4	1	1	0	0	0
Powell, 1b	4	0	1	14	0	0
B. Robinson, 3b	3	0	0	0	3	0
Hendricks, c	3	0	0	7	1	0
Johnson, 2b	4	0	0	4	6	0
Belanger, ss	4	0	1	0	6	0
Cuellar, p	2	0	1	0	1	0
aMay	1	0	0	0	0	0
Watt, p	0	0	0	0	0	0
cDalrymple	1	0	1	0	0	0
Hall, p	0	0	0	0	0	0
Richert, p	0	0	0	0	0	1
Totals	35	1	6	27	17	1

New York (N.L.)	AB.	R.	H.	O.	A.	E.
Agee, cf	4	0	1	2	0	0
Harrelson, ss	4	0	1	5	2	0
Jones, lf	4	0	1	1	0	0
Clendenon, 1b	4	1	1	6	3	0
Swoboda, rf	4	0	3	4	0	0
Charles, 3b	3	0	0	2	1	0
bShamsky	1	0	0	0	0	0
Garrett, 3b	0	0	0	0	0	1
Grote, c	4	0	1	7	2	0
dGaspar	0	1	0	0	0	0
Weis, 2b	3	0	2	1	1	0
Seaver, p	3	0	0	2	1	0
eMartin	0	0	0	0	0	0
Totals	34	2	10	30	10	1

Baltimore	0 0 0	0 0 0	0 0 1	0—1
New York	0 1 0	0 0 0	0 0 0	1—2

None out when winning run scored.

aStruck out for Cuellar in eighth. bGrounded out for Charles in ninth. cSingled for Watt in tenth. dRan for Grote in tenth. eSacrificed and was safe on error for Seaver in tenth. Runs batted in—Clendenon, B. Robinson. Two-base hit—Grote. Home run—Clendenon. Sacrifice hit—Martin. Sacrifice fly—B. Robinson. Double plays—Belanger, Johnson and Powell 2; Hendricks and Johnson. Left on bases—Baltimore 7, New York 7. Earned runs—Baltimore 1, New York 1. Bases on balls—Off Hall 1, off Seaver 2. Struck out—By Cuellar 5, by Watt 2, by Seaver 6. Pitching records—Off Cuellar 7 hits and 1 run in 7 innings; off Watt 2 hits and 0 runs in 2 innings; off Hall 1 hit and 1 run in 0 innings (pitched to two batters in tenth); off Richert 0 hits and 0 runs in 0 innings (pitched to one batter in tenth). Losing pitcher—Hall. Umpires—Crawford (N.L.), DiMuro (A.L.), Weyer (N.L.), Soar (A.L.), Secory (N.L.), Napp (A.L.). Time—2:33. Attendance—57,367.

Thursday, October 16—At New York

Baltimore (A.L.)	AB.	R.	H.	O.	A.	E.
Buford, lf	4	0	0	1	0	0
Blair, cf	4	0	0	3	0	0
F. Robinson, rf	3	1	1	2	0	0
Powell, 1b	4	0	1	6	0	1
bSalmon	0	0	0	0	0	0
B. Robinson, 3b	4	0	1	1	4	0
Johnson, 2b	4	0	1	1	0	0
Etchebarren, c	3	0	0	8	0	0
Belanger, ss	3	1	1	2	1	0
McNally, p	2	1	0	0	0	0
aMotton	1	0	0	0	0	0
Watt, p	0	0	0	0	0	1
Totals	32	3	5	24	5	2

1970 WORLD SERIES

New York (N.L.)	AB.	R.	H.	O.	A.	E.
Agee, cf	3	0	1	4	0	0
Harrelson, ss	4	0	0	1	6	0
Jones, lf	3	2	1	3	0	0
Clendenon, 1b	3	1	1	8	0	0
Swoboda, rf	4	1	2	5	0	0
Charles, 3b	4	0	0	0	1	0
Grote, c	4	0	0	5	0	0
Weis, 2b	4	1	1	1	2	0
Koosman, p	3	0	1	0	1	0
Totals	32	5	7	27	10	0

```
Baltimore .............  0 0 3   0 0 0   0 0 0—3
New York ..............  0 0 0   0 0 2   1 2 *—5
```

aGrounded out for McNally in eighth. bRan for Powell in ninth. Runs batted in—McNally 2, F. Robinson, Clendenon 2, Weis, Swoboda. Two-base hits—Koosman, Jones, Swoboda. Home runs—McNally, F. Robinson, Clendenon, Weis. Stolen base—Agee. Left on bases—Baltimore 3, New York 6. Earned runs—Baltimore 3, New York 4. Bases on balls—Off McNally 2, off Koosman 1. Struck out—By McNally 6, by Watt 1, by Koosman 5. Pitching records—Off McNally 5 hits and 3 runs in 7 innings; off Watt 2 hits and 2 runs in 1 inning. Hit by pitcher—By McNally (Jones). Losing pitcher—Watt. Umpires—DiMuro (A.L.), Weyer (N.L.), Soar (A.L.), Secory (N.L.), Napp (A.L.), Crawford (N.L.). Time—2:14. Attendance—57,397.

COMPOSITE BATTING AVERAGES
New York Mets

Player-Position	G.	AB.	R.	H.	2B.	3B.	HR.	RBI.	BA.
Weis, 2b	5	11	1	5	0	0	1	3	.455
Swoboda, rf	4	15	1	6	1	0	0	1	.400
Clendenon, 1b	4	14	4	5	1	0	3	4	.357
Boswell, 2b	1	3	1	1	0	0	0	0	.333
Gentry, p	1	3	0	1	1	0	0	2	.333
Kranepool, 1b	1	4	1	1	0	0	1	1	.250
Grote, c	5	19	1	4	2	0	0	1	.211
Harrelson, ss	5	17	3	3	0	0	0	0	.176
Agee, cf	5	18	1	3	0	0	1	1	.167
Jones, lf	5	19	2	3	1	0	0	0	.158
Koosman, p	2	7	0	1	0	0	0	0	.143
Charles, 3b	4	15	1	2	1	0	0	0	.133
Shamsky, ph-rf	3	6	0	0	0	0	0	0	.000
Seaver, p	2	4	0	0	0	0	0	0	.000
Gaspar, ph-rf-pr	3	2	1	0	0	0	0	0	.000
Garrett, 3b	2	1	0	0	0	0	0	0	.000
Dyer, ph	1	1	0	0	0	0	0	0	.000
Taylor, p	2	0	0	0	0	0	0	0	.000
Cardwell, p	1	0	0	0	0	0	0	0	.000
Martin, ph	1	0	0	0	0	0	0	0	.000
Ryan, p	1	0	0	0	0	0	0	0	.000
Totals	5	159	15	35	8	0	6	13	.220

Baltimore Orioles

Player-Position	G.	AB.	R.	H.	2B.	3B.	HR.	RBI.	BA.
Dalrymple, ph	2	2	0	2	0	0	0	0	1.000
Cuellar, p	2	5	0	2	0	0	0	1	.400
Powell, 1b	5	19	5	5	0	0	0	0	.263
Belanger, ss	5	15	2	3	0	0	0	1	.200
McNally, p	2	5	1	1	0	0	1	2	.200
F. Robinson, rf	5	16	2	3	0	0	1	1	.188
Blair, cf	5	20	1	2	0	0	0	0	.100
Buford, lf	5	20	1	2	1	0	1	2	.100
Hendricks, c	3	10	1	1	0	0	0	0	.100
Johnson, 2b	5	16	1	1	0	0	0	0	.063
B. Robinson, 3b	5	19	0	1	0	0	0	2	.053
Etchebarren, c	2	6	0	0	0	0	0	0	.000
Palmer, p	1	2	0	0	0	0	0	0	.000
May, ph	2	1	0	0	0	0	0	0	.000
Motton, ph	1	1	0	0	0	0	0	0	.000
Salmon, pr	2	0	0	0	0	0	0	0	.000
Watt, p	2	0	0	0	0	0	0	0	.000
Hall, p	1	0	0	0	0	0	0	0	.000
Leonhard, p	1	0	0	0	0	0	0	0	.000
Rettenmund, pr	2	0	0	0	0	0	0	0	.000
Richert, p	1	0	0	0	0	0	0	0	.000
Totals	5	157	9	23	1	0	3	9	.146

COMPOSITE PITCHING AVERAGES
New York Mets

Pitcher	G.	IP.	H.	R.	E.R.	SO.	BB.	W.	L.	ERA.
Gentry	1	6⅔	3	0	0	4	5	1	0	0.00
Taylor	2	2⅓	0	0	0	3	1	0	0	0.00
Ryan	1	2⅓	1	0	0	3	2	0	0	0.00
Cardwell	1	1	0	0	0	0	0	0	0	0.00
Koosman	2	17⅔	7	4	4	9	4	2	0	2.04
Seaver	2	15	12	5	5	9	3	1	1	3.00
Totals	5	45	23	9	9	28	15	4	1	1.80

Saves—Taylor, Ryan.

Baltimore Orioles

Pitcher	G.	IP.	H.	R.	E.R.	SO.	BB.	W.	L.	ERA.
Cuellar	2	16	13	2	2	13	4	1	0	1.13
McNally	2	16	11	5	5	13	5	0	1	2.81
Watt	2	3	4	2	1	3	0	0	1	3.00
Leonhard	1	2	1	1	1	1	1	0	0	4.50
Palmer	1	6	5	4	4	5	4	0	1	6.00
Hall	1	0*	1	1	0	0	1	0	0	0.00
Richert	1	0†	0	0	0	0	0	0	0	0.00
Totals	5	43	35	15	13	35	15	1	4	2.72

*Pitched to two batters in tenth inning of fourth game.
†Pitched to one batter in tenth inning of fourth game.

SERIES OF 1970	W.	L.	Pct.
Baltimore A. L.	4	1	.800
Cincinnati N. L.	1	4	.200

The Baltimore Orioles, victims of an astonishing upset at the hands of the New York Mets the previous year, made amends for that setback by climbing to the top of the baseball world in the 1970 World Series, downing the Cincinnati Reds, four games to one.

Baltimore ran away with the American League's Eastern Division race for the second successive season and, as in 1969, polished off the Western Division winner, again the Minnesota Twins, in three consecutive games.

Cincinnati's Big Red Machine bolted into a wide lead early in the chase for the National League's Western Division crown and then coasted home. The Reds captured the pennant by winning three straight games from the Pittsburgh Pirates, who had survived a three-team dogfight in the Eastern Division.

The 1970 World Series was one in which the hitters distinguished themselves more than the pitchers and in which Brooks Robinson, the Orioles' third baseman, was the outstanding player for his feats both at bat and in the field.

Cincinnati went into the Series with a crippled pitching staff. Wayne Simpson, rookie righthander who had won 14 games during the regular season, was out with a sore shoulder, and 20-game winner, lefty Jim Merritt, nursing a sore elbow, was able to make but one, brief, ineffective appearance.

The Series opened at Cincinnati's Riverfront Stadium on Saturday, October 10. Two historic firsts were recorded: the first World Series game to be played in that particular ball park and the first to be played on artificial turf. The opposing pitchers were a pair of hard-throwing righthanders,

Gary Nolan for Cincinnati and Jim Palmer for Baltimore.

The Reds went right to work on Palmer, scoring a run in their first turn at bat on a double by Bobby Tolan and a single by Johnny Bench. They added two more in the third inning when Tolan walked and Lee May homered over the left field wall.

Nolan pitched hitless ball for three frames but in the fourth Paul Blair beat out a hopper toward third base and Boog Powell followed with an opposite-field homer to left.

Elrod Hendricks knotted the score with a leadoff round-tripper in the fifth and Brooks Robinson put the Orioles ahead in the seventh by smashing a change-up pitch over the left field barrier. This last blow proved to be the winning margin.

But it was in the Cincinnati half of the sixth inning that the crucial action took place. It centered around an incident likely to be rehashed a long time afterward. With one out and Bernie Carbo on third base and Tommy Helms on first, pinch hitter Ty Cline bounced a high chopper in front of the plate. Umpire Ken Burkhart straddled the third base foul line and signaled a fair ball. Hendricks was going to throw to first base but his batterymate, Palmer, yelled for him to tag Carbo, who was coming down the line trying to score. Whirling, Hendricks plowed into Burkhart and lunged for Carbo. From the tangle of bodies, Burkhart jerked his clenched fist skyward to signal "out." Reds' Manager Sparky Anderson and Carbo protested the call.

Burkhart said that he saw Hendricks tag out Carbo. Hendricks, of course, said he had tagged Carbo while falling over Burkhart. Carbo said that he wasn't tagged at all and had scored. Instant replays and sequence photos cast a different light on the episode. Hendricks tagged Carbo with his glove, while holding the ball in his right hand. Carbo slid wide of the plate and tagged it only accidentally when he returned to protest the "out" call. Despite his protest at the time, Anderson remarked after the game, "The umpires didn't beat us. Baltimore did."

Although his home run was the game-winner, Brooks Robinson will be best remembered for an "impossible" play on May's hard smash in the sixth inning. May rifled the ball between Brooks and third base. Robinson took a few quick steps, backhanded the ball when it was past him and while still moving toward foul territory, turned and threw in the same motion, getting the ball to Powell on the bounce, beating May by less than a stride. In view of the fact that Carbo walked as the next hitter and Helms singled him to third to set up the controversial play at the plate, Robinson's play was as vital as his next-inning homer.

In the second game the Reds once again built up a quick early lead. Oriole shortstop Mark Belanger's error opened the gates for three unearned runs in the first inning, the key hits being a double by Lee May and a bunt single by Hal McRae. The Cincinnati club increased its margin to 4-0 in the third inning on Bobby Tolan's home run and chased Oriole starter Mike Cuellar.

But the Orioles roared back. Boog Powell hit a home run in the fourth, and in the next stanza singles by pinch-hitter Chico Salmon, Don Buford and Paul Blair sent Red starter Jim McGlothlin to the showers. Milt Wilcox came on in relief and yielded singles to Powell and Brooks Robinson and a double to Elrod Hendricks. When the side was finally retired by Clay Carroll, the Orioles had plated five tallies and held a 6-4 lead. This was reduced to 6-5 in the sixth inning when Johnny Bench crashed a home run.

The Reds threatened again in the seventh, getting runners on first and second, but Baltimore Manager Earl Weaver called on 40-year-old relief specialist Dick Hall, who slammed the door on Cincinnati by hurling perfect ball the remainder of the game.

The Series scene shifted to Baltimore's Memorial Stadium for the third game and once again Brooks Robinson stood out as the star of stars in a game in which the Orioles took command at the outset.

The opposing pitchers were lefty Dave McNally for Baltimore and veteran right-hander Tony Cloninger for Cincinnati.

In the first inning it appeared the Reds would jump into the lead for the third consecutive game. Hits by Pete Rose and Bobby Tolan resulted in runners at first and second. But B. Robby made a leaping grab of Tony Perez' hopper, stepped on third and fired to first for a double play. An inning later, he raced in for Helms' slow roller and nipped him with a hard throw. In the sixth inning he made a diving stab of Johnny Bench's savage liner to save another hit.

But his fielding wizardry was not the least of Robinson's contributions to the Baltimore cause. He drove in the Orioles' first two runs in the first inning with a bases loaded double.

Singles by Hal McRae and Dave Concepcion, wrapped around an infield out, netted the Reds a run in the second inning. Frank Robinson's home run in the third and Don Buford's home run in the fifth boosted the Orioles' lead to 4-1.

When Paul Blair singled with one out in the sixth, Sparky Anderson decided to remove Cloninger and replace him with Wayne Granger. Granger was promptly greeted by Brooks Robinson's second double of the afternoon. Dave Johnson was given an intentional walk and Andy Etchebarren struck out, leaving it all up to McNally.

The Baltimore pitcher, who bats righthanded although he throws lefthanded, was a strikeout victim in his first two at-bats. A homer hitter in the 1969 Series against the Mets, he worked the count to two-and-two and then drove the next pitch into the left field bleachers, 380 feet away, thus becoming the first pitcher and 12th player to hit a grand slam home run in World Series competition.

With an 8-1 lead, McNally permitted two runs in the seventh inning, Concepcion driving in Lee May with a sacrifice fly and Rose scoring Helms with a single.

The final Oriole run, also in the seventh, resulted from a walk to Boog Powell, a single by Frank Robinson and Blair's double, all off reliever Don Gullett.

For seven innings of the fourth game it appeared that the Orioles were on their way to a four-game sweep, matching their 1966 feat against the Los Angeles Dodgers. They held a 5-3 lead and Jim Palmer, the first-game winner, had held the Reds to five hits.

But Tony Perez walked to lead off the eighth inning and Johnny Bench singled him to third base. Eddie Watt relieved Palmer at this point with Lee May at bat. May drove Watt's first pitch far into the left-field bleachers and that provided a 6-5 Cincinnati victory.

The lead had changed hands twice during the early going. In the second inning, after May walked and Dave Concepcion tripled for the first Cincinnati run, Brooks Robinson homered off Gary Nolan. The Reds, however, regained the lead in the third on Bobby Tolan's walk and singles by Pete Rose and May, but the Orioles again rebounded, this time into a 4-2 lead.

Palmer ignited the outburst with a single. After two were out, Boog Powell walked and Frank Robinson singled for one run. Brooks Robinson's single scored Powell and, when Tolan bobbled the ball the Robinsons moved up to third and second, respectively.

Hendricks' single scored Frank, but Brooks was nipped at the plate on Rose's throw to Bench.

Rose brought the Reds to within one run of a tie in the fifth with a home run, but then gave the run back to the Birds in the sixth.

Brooks Robinson and Hendricks singled. Rose attempted to head off Brooks at third, but the ball skipped past Perez, permitting Robinson to score.

Cincinnati relief pitcher Clay Carroll, who blanked the Orioles for 2⅓ innings in each of the first two games, entered the contest with Hendricks on third base and one out. He struck out Dave Johnson and got Mark Belanger on a fly ball to left field and permitted but one harmless single the rest of the way to notch the victory.

For the fifth game, Cincinnati Manager Sparky Anderson called upon Jim Merritt, who had only pitched nine innings since September 8, when he contracted tendinitis of the elbow. Earl Weaver countered with Mike Cuellar, who had been knocked out of the box in the third inning of the first game.

At the outset it appeared that Cuellar was in for another rough afternoon. Pete Rose's double, a single by Johnny Bench, and doubles by Lee May and Hal McRae sent Cincinnati off to a 3-0 lead before Merritt took the mound. But those three runs were all that the Reds were to get.

Paul Blair's single and Frank Robinson's home run started the Orioles on the road back in their first turn. Merritt exited in the second inning as the Orioles took a 4-3 lead on Dave Johnson's walk and singles by Andy Etchebarren, Mark Belanger and Blair.

The Orioles scored two more runs in the third inning on a double by Boog Powell and singles by Merv Rettenmund and Dave Johnson sandwiched between an infield out. Rettenmund's home run made the score 7-3 in the fifth and the Orioles closed out the scoring with two more tallies in the eighth, Blair scoring from second on Powell's infield out and Frank Robinson crossing the plate on Johnson's single.

Paul Blair led the Series in batting with a .474 mark, although Brooks Robinson hit .429 and led his club in runs batted in. For Cincinnati, Hal McRae batted .455 in three games, while Lee May hit .389 and batted in eight runs. The Orioles as a team batted .292, the Reds only .213, the biggest disappointment being Tony Perez, who could manage just one hit in 18 at bats for an .056 mark.

The box scores follow:

Saturday, October 10—At Cincinnati

Baltimore (A.L.)	AB.	R.	H.	O.	A.	E.
Buford, lf	4	0	1	1	0	0
Blair, cf	4	1	1	7	0	0
Powell, 1b	3	1	1	6	0	0
F. Robinson, rf	4	0	0	2	0	0
B. Robinson, 3b	4	1	1	3	3	1
Hendricks, c	4	1	1	4	1	1
Johnson, 2b	3	0	1	2	0	0
Belanger, ss	3	0	1	2	3	0
Palmer, p	4	0	0	0	0	0
Richert, p	0	0	0	0	0	0
Totals	33	4	7	27	7	2

Cincinnati (N.L.)	AB.	R.	H.	O.	A.	E.
xRose, rf	3	0	0	3	0	0
Tolan, cf	4	2	1	0	0	0
Perez, 3b	3	0	0	0	3	0
Bench, c	4	0	1	12	0	0
May, 1b	4	1	2	7	1	0
Carbo, lf	2	0	0	2	0	0
Helms, 2b	4	0	1	1	1	0
Woodward, ss	2	0	0	2	1	0
aCline	1	0	0	0	0	0
Chaney, ss	0	0	0	0	0	0
bStewart	1	0	0	0	0	0
Nolan, p	2	0	0	0	0	0
Carroll, p	0	0	0	0	0	0
cBravo	1	0	0	0	0	0
Totals	31	3	5	27	6	0

1970 WORLD SERIES

```
Baltimore ..................  0 0 0   2 1 0   1 0 0—4
Cincinnati ..................  1 0 2   0 0 0   0 0 0—3
```

xAwarded first base on catcher's interference. aGrounded into fielder's choice for Woodward in sixth. bStruck out for Chaney in ninth. cStruck out for Carroll in ninth. Runs batted in—Powell 2, B. Robinson, Hendricks, Bench, May 2. Two-base hits—Tolan, Johnson. Home runs—May, Powell, Hendricks, B. Robinson. Stolen base—Tolan. Caught stealing—Carbo. Sacrifice hit—Nolan. Wild pitch—Palmer. Double play—May, Woodward and May. Left on bases—Baltimore 5, Cincinnati 8. Earned runs—Baltimore 4, Cincinnati 3. Bases on balls—Off Nolan 1, off Carroll 2, off Palmer 5. Struck out—By Nolan 7, by Carroll 4, by Palmer 2. Pitching records—Off Nolan 5 hits and 4 runs in 6⅔ innings; off Carroll 0 runs and 2 hits in 2⅓ innings; off Palmer 5 hits and 3 runs in 8⅔ innings; off Richert 0 runs and 0 hits in ⅓ inning. Winning pitcher—Palmer. Losing pitcher—Nolan. Save—Richert. Umpires—Burkhart (N.L.), Flaherty (A.L.), Venzon (N.L.), Stewart (A.L.), Williams (N.L.), Ashford (A.L.). Time—2:24. Attendance—51,531.

Sunday, October 11—At Cincinnati

Baltimore (A.L.)	AB.	R.	H.	O.	A.	E.
Buford, lf	4	1	2	1	1	0
Blair, cf	5	1	2	6	0	1
Powell, 1b	3	2	2	9	2	0
F. Robinson, rf	5	0	0	1	0	0
B. Robinson, 3b	4	1	1	1	6	0
Hendricks, c	3	0	1	3	0	0
Johnson, 2b	3	0	1	5	3	0
Belanger, ss	4	0	0	0	3	1
Cuellar, p	1	0	0	1	0	0
Phoebus, p	0	0	0	0	0	0
aSalmon	1	1	1	0	0	0
Drabowsky, p	1	0	0	1	0	0
Lopez, p	0	0	0	0	0	0
Hall, p	1	0	0	0	0	0
Totals	35	6	10	27	15	2

Cincinnati (N.L.)	AB.	R.	H.	O.	A.	E.
Rose, rf	3	0	0	3	0	0
Tolan, cf	4	2	2	0	0	0
Perez, 3b	4	1	1	0	3	0
Bench, c	3	1	1	5	0	0
May, 1b	4	1	1	13	1	0
McRae, lf	4	0	2	0	0	0
Helms, 2b	4	0	0	4	4	0
Woodward, ss	2	0	0	2	4	0
bCline	1	0	1	0	0	0
Chaney, ss	0	0	0	0	1	0
dCarbo	1	0	0	0	0	0
McGlothlin, p	2	0	0	0	0	0
Wilcox, p	0	0	0	0	0	0
Carroll, p	0	0	0	0	0	0
cBravo	0	0	0	0	0	0
Gullett, p	0	0	0	0	0	0
eStewart	1	0	0	0	0	0
Totals	33	5	7	27	13	0

```
Baltimore ..................  0 0 0   1 5 0   0 0 0—6
Cincinnati ..................  3 0 1   0 0 1   0 0 0—5
```

aSingled for Phoebus in fifth. bSingled for Woodward in seventh. cSacrificed for Carroll in seventh. dGrounded out for Chaney in ninth. eFlied out for Gullett in ninth. Runs batted in—Blair, Powell 2, B. Robinson, Hendricks 2, Tolan, Bench, May 2, McRae. Two-base hits—May, McRae, Hendricks. Home runs—Tolan, Powell, Bench. Sacrifice hit—Bravo. Double plays—Woodward, Helms and May; B. Robinson, Johnson and Powell; May, Woodward and May. Left on bases—Baltimore 7, Cincinnati 4. Earned runs—Baltimore 6, Cincinnati 2. Bases on balls—Off McGlothlin 2, off Gullett 3, off Cuellar 1, off Drabowsky 1. Struck out—By McGlothlin 2, by Carroll 1, by Gullett 2, by Cuellar 1, by Drabowsky 1. Pitching records—Off McGlothlin 6 hits, 4 runs in 4⅓ innings; off Wilcox 3 hits, 0 runs in ⅓ inning; off Carroll 1 hit, 0 runs in 2⅓ innings; off Gullett 0 hits, 0 runs in 2 innings; off Cuellar 4 hits, 4 runs in 2⅓ innings; off Phoebus 1 hit, 0 runs in 1⅔ innings; off Drabowksy 2 hits, 1 run in 2⅓ innings; off Lopez 0 hits, 0 runs in ⅓ inning; off Hall 0 hits, 0 runs in 2⅓ innings. Winning pitcher—Phoebus. Losing pitcher—Wilcox. Save—Hall. Umpires—Flaherty (A.L.), Venzon (N.L.), Stewart (A.L.), Williams (N.L.), Ashford (A.L.) and Burkhart (N.L.). Time—2:26. Attendance—51,531.

Tuesday, October 13—At Baltimore

Cincinnati (N.L.)	AB.	R.	H.	O.	A.	E.
Rose, rf	5	0	2	4	0	0
Tolan, cf	4	0	1	2	0	0
Perez, 3b	3	0	0	0	2	0
Bench, c	4	0	0	5	2	0
May, 1b	3	1	1	9	0	0
McRae, lf	4	1	2	1	1	0
Helms, 2b	4	1	1	3	1	0
Concepcion, ss	3	0	1	0	2	0
Cloninger, p	2	0	0	0	0	0
Granger, p	0	0	0	0	1	0
aWoodward	1	0	1	0	0	0
Gullett, p	0	0	0	0	0	0
bCline	1	0	0	0	0	0
Totals	34	3	9	24	9	0

Baltimore (A.L.)	AB.	R.	H.	O.	A.	E.
Buford, lf	3	2	1	3	0	0
Belanger, ss	4	0	2	3	0	0
Powell, 1b	3	1	0	8	0	0
F. Robinson, rf	4	2	3	2	0	0
Blair, cf	3	1	3	3	0	0
B. Robinson, 3b	4	1	2	3	3	0
Johnson, 2b	2	1	0	4	2	0
Etchebarren, c	4	0	0	5	0	1
McNally, p	4	1	1	0	1	0
Totals	31	9	10	27	9	1

```
Cincinnati ..................  0 1 0   0 0 0   2 0 0—3
Baltimore ..................  2 0 1   0 1 4   1 0 *—9
```

aSingled for Granger in seventh. bGrounded into force play for Gullett in ninth. Runs batted in—Rose, Concepcion 2, Buford, F. Robinson, Blair 2, B. Robinson 2, McNally 4. Two-base hits—B. Robinson 2, Blair. Home runs—F. Robinson, Buford, McNally. Sacrifice fly—Concepcion. Caught stealing—Blair, Johnson. Double plays—B. Robinson and Powell; Bench and Helms. Left on bases—Cincinnati 7, Baltimore 3. Earned runs—Baltimore 9, Cincinnati 3. Bases on balls—Off McNally 2, off Cloninger 3, off Granger 1, off Gullett 1. Struck out—By McNally 5, by Cloninger 3, by Granger 1. Pitching records—Off McNally 9 hits, 3 runs in 9 innings; off Cloninger 6 hits, 5 runs in 5⅓ innings; off Granger 2 hits, 3 runs in ⅔ inning; off Gullett 2 hits, 1 run in 2 innings. Losing pitcher—Cloninger. Umpires—Venzon (N.L.), Stewart (A.L.), Williams (N.L.), Ashford (A.L.), Burkhart (N.L.) and Flaherty (A.L.). Time—2:09. Attendance—51,773.

Wednesday, October 14—At Baltimore

Cincinnati (N.L.)	AB.	R.	H.	O.	A.	E.
Tolan, cf	3	1	1	1	0	1
Rose, rf	5	1	2	1	1	1
Perez, 3b	4	1	0	0	3	1
Bench, c	4	1	1	8	1	0
May, 1b	3	2	2	13	0	0

1970 WORLD SERIES

	AB.	R.	H.	O.	A.	E.
Carbo, lf	4	0	0	2	0	0
Helms, 2b	3	0	1	1	3	0
Concepcion, ss	3	0	1	0	0	0
Carroll, p	1	0	0	0	0	0
Nolan, p	1	0	0	0	1	0
Gullett, p	1	0	0	0	0	0
Woodward, ss	0	0	0	0	0	0
aBravo	1	0	0	0	0	0
Chaney, ss	1	0	0	1	1	0
Totals	34	6	8	27	10	3

Baltimore (A.L.)	AB.	R.	H.	O.	A.	E.
Buford, lf	4	0	0	1	0	0
Blair, cf	3	0	0	3	0	0
Powell, 1b	3	1	0	6	0	0
F. Robinson, rf	4	1	1	1	0	0
B. Robinson, 3b	4	2	4	1	0	0
Hendricks, c	4	0	2	10	1	0
Johnson, 2b	4	0	0	2	3	0
Belanger, ss	3	0	0	3	1	0
bCrowley	1	0	0	0	0	0
Palmer, p	3	1	1	0	0	0
Watt, p	0	0	0	0	0	0
Drabowsky, p	0	0	0	0	0	0
cRettenmund	1	0	0	0	0	0
Totals	34	5	8	27	5	0

Cincinnati............ 0 1 1 0 1 0 0 3 0—6
Baltimore............ 0 1 3 0 0 1 0 0 0—5

aPopped out for Woodward in seventh. bGrounded out for Belanger in ninth. cReached first on Perez' throwing error for Drabowsky in ninth. Runs batted in—Rose, May 4, Concepcion, F. Robinson 2, Hendricks. Three-base hit—Concepcion. Home runs—B. Robinson, Rose, May. Sacrifice hit—Blair. Caught stealing—Tolan. Left on bases—Cincinnati 6, Baltimore 5. Earned runs—Cincinnati 6, Baltimore 4. Bases on balls—Off Palmer 4, off Watt 1, off Nolan 2. Struck out—By Palmer 7, by Watt 3, by Nolan 2, by Gullett 2, by Carroll 4. Pitching records—Off Palmer 7 hits, 5 runs in 7 innings (pitched to two batters in eighth); off Watt 2 hits, 1 run in 1 inning (pitched to one batter in ninth); off Drabowsky 0 hits, 0 runs in 1 inning; off Nolan 4 hits, 4 runs in 2⅔ innings; off Gullett 3 hits, 1 run in 2⅔ innings; off Carroll 1 hit, 0 runs in 3⅔ innings. Winning pitcher—Carroll. Losing pitcher—Watt. Umpires—Stewart (A.L.), Williams (N.L.), Ashford, Burkhart (N.L.), Flaherty (A.L.) and Venzon (N.L.). Time—2:26. Attendance—53,007.

Thursday, October 15—At Baltimore

Cincinnati (N.L.)	AB.	R.	H.	O.	A.	E.
Tolan, cf	4	0	0	1	0	0
Rose, rf	4	1	1	3	0	0
Perez, 3b	4	0	0	3	2	0
Bench, c	4	1	1	6	0	0
May, 1b	4	1	1	6	1	0
McRae, lf	3	0	1	1	0	0
cCorrales	1	0	0	0	0	0
Helms, 2b	3	0	1	1	4	0
Concepcion, ss	3	0	1	2	0	0
Merritt, p	1	0	0	0	0	0
Granger, p	0	0	0	0	0	0
Wilcox, p	0	0	0	0	1	0
aBravo	0	0	0	0	0	0
Cloninger, p	0	0	0	0	1	0
bCarbo	1	0	0	0	0	0
Washburn, p	0	0	0	1	3	0
Carroll, p	0	0	0	0	0	0
Totals	32	3	6	24	12	0

Baltimore (A.L.)	AB.	R.	H.	O.	A.	E.
Belanger, ss	5	0	1	4	4	0
Blair, cf	4	2	3	2	0	0
F. Robinson, rf	5	2	2	1	0	0
Powell, 1b	5	1	2	9	0	0
Rettenmund, lf	4	2	2	3	0	0
B. Robinson, 3b	5	0	1	1	2	0
Johnson, 2b	4	1	3	2	1	0
Etchebarren, c	3	1	1	5	0	0
Cuellar, p	3	0	0	0	1	0
Totals	38	9	15	27	8	0

Cincinnati............ 3 0 0 0 0 0 0 0 0—3
Baltimore............ 2 2 2 0 1 0 0 2 *—9

aWalked for Wilcox in fifth. bGrounded into double play for Cloninger in seventh. cGrounded out for McRae in ninth. Runs batted in—Bench, McRae 2, Belanger, Blair, F. Robinson 2, Powell, Rettenmund 2, Johnson 2. Two-base hits—Rose, May, McRae, Powell, Johnson. Home runs—F. Robinson, Rettenmund. Sacrifice hit—Cuellar. Double play—Cuellar, Belanger and Powell. Left on bases—Cincinnati 3, Baltimore 11. Earned runs—Baltimore 9, Cincinnati 3. Bases on balls—Off Cuellar 1, off Merritt 1, off Cloninger 2, off Washburn 2. Struck out—By Cuellar 4, by Wilcox 2, by Cloninger 1, by Carroll 2. Pitching records—Off Cuellar 6 hits, 3 runs in 9 innings; off Merritt 3 hits, 4 runs in 1⅔ innings; off Granger 5 hits, 2 runs in ⅔ inning; off Wilcox 0 runs, 0 hits in 1⅔ innings; off Cloninger 4 hits, 1 run in 2 innings; off Washburn 2 hits, 2 runs in 1⅓ innings; off Carroll 1 hit, 0 runs in ⅔ inning. Losing pitcher—Merritt. Umpires—Williams (N.L.), Ashford (A.L.), Burkhart (N.L.), Flaherty (A.L.), Venzon (N.L.) and Stewart (A.L.). Time—2:35. Attendance—45,341.

COMPOSITE BATTING AVERAGES
Baltimore Orioles

Player-Position	G.	AB.	R.	H.	2B.	3B.	HR.	RBI.	BA.
Salmon, ph	1	1	1	1	0	0	0	0	1.000
Blair, cf	5	19	5	9	1	0	0	3	.474
B. Robinson, 3b	5	21	5	9	2	0	2	6	.429
R'tenmund, ph-lf	2	5	2	2	0	0	1	2	.400
Hendricks, c	3	11	1	4	1	0	1	4	.364
Johnson, 2b	5	16	2	5	2	0	0	2	.313
Powell, 1b	5	17	6	5	1	0	2	5	.294
F. Robinson, rf	5	22	5	6	0	0	2	4	.273
Buford, lf	4	15	3	4	0	0	1	1	.267
McNally, p	1	4	1	1	0	0	1	4	.250
Etchebarren, c	2	7	1	1	0	0	0	0	.143
Palmer, p	2	7	1	1	0	0	0	0	.143
Belanger, ss	5	19	0	2	0	0	0	1	.105
Drabowsky, p	2	1	0	0	0	0	0	0	.000
Crowley, ph	1	1	0	0	0	0	0	0	.000
Hall, p	1	1	0	0	0	0	0	0	.000
Cuellar, p	2	4	0	0	0	0	0	0	.000
Lopez, p	1	0	0	0	0	0	0	0	.000
Phoebus, p	1	0	0	0	0	0	0	0	.000
Richert, p	1	0	0	0	0	0	0	0	.000
Watt, p	1	0	0	0	0	0	0	0	.000
Totals	5	171	33	50	7	0	10	32	.292

Cincinnati Reds

Player-Position	G.	AB.	R.	H.	2B.	3B.	HR.	RBI.	BA.
McRae, lf	3	11	1	5	2	0	0	3	.455
May, 1b	5	18	6	7	2	0	2	8	.389
Concepcion, ss	3	9	0	3	0	1	0	3	.333
Cline, ph	3	3	0	1	0	0	0	0	.333
Rose, rf	5	20	2	5	1	0	1	2	.250
Helms, 2b	5	18	1	4	0	0	0	0	.222
Bench, c	5	19	3	4	0	0	1	3	.211
Tolan, cf	5	19	5	4	1	0	1	1	.211
Woodward, ss-ph	4	5	0	1	0	0	0	0	.200
Perez, 3b	5	18	2	1	0	0	0	0	.056
Carroll, p	4	1	0	0	0	0	0	0	.000
Chaney, ss	3	1	0	0	0	0	0	0	.000
Gullett, p	3	1	0	0	0	0	0	0	.000
Corrales, ph	1	1	0	0	0	0	0	0	.000
Merritt, p	1	1	0	0	0	0	0	0	.000
Bravo, ph	4	2	0	0	0	0	0	0	.000

Player-Position	G.	AB.	R.	H.	2B.	3B.	HR.	RBI.	BA.
Cloninger, p	2	2	0	0	0	0	0	0	.000
Stewart, ph	2	2	0	0	0	0	0	0	.000
McGlothlin, p	1	2	0	0	0	0	0	0	.000
Nolan, p	2	3	0	0	0	0	0	0	.000
Carbo, lf-ph	4	8	0	0	0	0	0	0	.000
Granger, p	2	0	0	0	0	0	0	0	.000
Wilcox, p	2	0	0	0	0	0	0	0	.000
Washburn, p	1	0	0	0	0	0	0	0	.000
Totals	5	164	20	35	6	1	5	20	.213

COMPOSITE PITCHING AVERAGES
Baltimore Orioles

Pitcher	G.	IP.	H.	R.	E.	SO.	BB.	W.	L.	ERA.
Hall	1	2⅓	0	0	0	0	0	0	0	0.00
Phoebus	1	1⅔	1	0	0	0	1	0	0	0.00
Lopez	1	⅓	0	0	0	0	0	0	0	0.00
Richert	1	⅓	0	0	0	0	0	0	0	0.00
Drabowsky	2	3⅓	2	1	1	1	1	0	0	2.70
McNally	1	9	9	3	3	5	2	1	0	3.00
Cuellar	2	11⅓	10	7	4	5	2	1	0	3.18
Palmer	2	15⅔	11	8	8	9	9	1	0	4.60
Watt	1	1	2	1	1	3	1	0	1	9.00
Totals	5	45	35	20	17	23	15	4	1	3.40

Saves—Richert 1, Hall 1.

Cincinnati Reds

Pitcher	G.	IP.	H.	R.	E.	SO.	BB.	W.	L.	ERA.
Carroll	4	9	5	0	0	11	2	1	0	0.00
Gullett	3	6⅔	5	2	1	4	4	0	1	1.35
Cloninger	2	7⅓	10	6	6	4	5	0	1	7.36
Nolan	2	9⅓	9	8	8	9	3	0	1	7.71
McGlothlin	1	4⅓	6	4	4	2	2	0	0	8.31
Wilcox	2	2	3	2	2	2	0	0	1	9.00
Washburn	1	1⅓	2	2	2	0	2	0	0	13.50
Merritt	1	1⅔	3	4	4	0	1	0	1	21.60
Granger	2	1⅓	7	5	5	1	1	0	0	33.75
Totals	5	43	50	33	32	33	20	1	4	6.70

SERIES OF 1971

	W.	L.	Pct.
Pittsburgh N. L.	4	3	.571
Baltimore A. L.	3	4	.429

Sparked by Roberto Clemente and Steve Blass, the Pittsburgh Pirates came back after losing the first two games of the 1971 World Series to take four of the next five from the Baltimore Orioles, returning baseball's highest prize to the National League after a hiatus of one year and giving the Steel City its first World Championship since 1960.

Besides the batting of Clemente, who hit safely in every game and posted a .414 average for the classic, and the pitching of Blass, who hurled two complete one-run games, one a three-hitter and the other a four-hitter, the Series was notable for the fact that the fourth game, played in Pittsburgh, was the first World Series night game and was witnessed on television by an estimated 61 million people.

The Pirates had reached the Series by breezing to their second straight East Division title in the National League and then beating the San Francisco Giants, surprise winners in the West Division, three consecutive games after losing the first.

The Orioles towroped the American League East for the third successive time and then topped the West Division titlists, the Oakland Athletics, in three straight games.

The Series opened at Baltimore on Saturday, October 9, with the opposing pitchers Dock Ellis, a voluble righthander who had won 19 games for Pittsburgh during the regular season, and southpaw Dave McNally, who had posted his fourth successive 20-game season for the Orioles.

The National Leaguers got on the board when their first sacker, Bob Robertson, opened the second inning with a walk, advanced to second on a wild pitch and scored when shortstop Mark Belanger, after fielding Manny Sanguillen's grounder, uncorked a throw to third which hit Robertson on the helmet and bounced into the Orioles' dugout. Sanguillen moved to third as McNally threw out Jose Pagan and scored on Jackie Hernandez' squeeze bunt. The ball got away from Baltimore catcher Elrod Hendricks and Hernandez took second from where he scored one out later on Dave Cash's single.

The Orioles started their resurgence in their second-inning turn when Frank Robinson tagged Ellis for a leadoff homer.

In the third inning, Baltimore wiped out the Pirate lead and sent Ellis to the showers in the process. Belanger singled, Don Buford followed suit and Merv Rettenmund blasted his second World Series homer to give the Birds a 4-3 lead. When Boog Powell walked, Ellis was removed in favor of righthander Bob Moose.

The scoring for the day was concluded in the fifth inning when Buford hit a homer off of Moose.

The second game of the Series, originally scheduled for Sunday, was rained out and play resumed on Monday.

The 53,239 fans at the game, including Mrs. Richard M. Nixon, saw Brooks Robinson put on a sensational show. The Oriole third baseman rapped three singles, drew two walks and executed one of his patented, miracle plays in leading the Orioles to an 11-3 victory.

In contrast to the first game when three homers drove in all of their runs, the Orioles went to the other extreme in their second triumph. Fourteen singles against six Pirate pitchers bounced off Baltimore bats.

Jim Palmer gained credit for his third Series win in four decisions, although he was lifted by Manager Earl Weaver after eight innings with an eight-run lead.

Bob Johnson, a 9-10 hurler during the regular season, was the Pirate starter. He had pitched a great game during the Championship Series, beating the Giants 2-1, to earn the World Series assignment.

After retiring the Orioles in order in the first inning, Johnson yielded one run in the second when Frank Robinson singled, Elrod Hendricks walked and Brooks Robinson singled for his 10th World Series RBI.

Johnson survived the third, but was shelled in the fourth when, with one out, Frank Robinson singled, Hendricks was hit on the ankle by a pitch, Brooks walked and

Dave Johnson singled for two runs.

Bruce Kison, who distinguished himself in the deciding game of the N.L. Championship Series, replaced Johnson with unhappy results.

Kison, just six days away from his wedding day, exhibited a bridegroom's nervousness by walking Mark Belanger and Palmer for one more run before Don Buford flied out to end the inning.

With Bob Moose on the Pirate hill, the Orioles padded their lead to 10-0 in the fifth.

Merv Rettenmund, hero of the opener, ignited the fuse with a single and, before the Bucs restored order, five more singles, two walks and an error had contributed to six Oriole runs.

Singles by the two Robinsons, around another by Hendricks, produced the final Oriole run in the sixth.

A walk, a single and a homer by Richie Hebner accounted for the Pirates' first three runs in the eighth.

Pittsburgh's Three Rivers Stadium was the scene of the third contest on Tuesday and the tide of battle shifted to the hometown Bucs, who won 3-1.

The righthanded Steve Blass, a 15-game winner during the regular season, tossed a masterful three-hitter at the defending World Champions, who were able to muster their only tally on the strength of a homer by Frank Robinson in the seventh inning.

The Pirates, meanwhile, had scored in the first off veteran lefty Mike Cuellar when Dave Cash doubled, moved to third when first baseman Boog Powell mishandled Al Oliver's grounder and scored as Roberto Clemente grounded into a forceout.

They added another run in the sixth on Manny Sanguillen's double and Jose Pagan's run-producing single.

The bottom of the seventh saw the Pirates, then leading by but one run, put the game on ice because of a missed signal. Clemente reached first when Cuellar's throw to Powell pulled the big first baseman off the bag. Willie Stargell then walked. With Bob Robertson at the plate and the Oriole infield playing deep, Manager Danny Murtaugh decided to play for one or two runs and ordered Robertson to sacrifice. The slugger, who hadn't bunted once all season, missed the sign and smacked a 1-and-1 pitch over the 385-foot mark in right-center field.

The Wednesday night game provided tremendous drama for the vast television audience and the record Pittsburgh baseball crowd of 51,378.

The Orioles struck quickly, knocking out starter Luke Walker in the first inning. Singles by Paul Blair, Mark Belanger and Merv Rettenmund loaded the bases. Blair scored on a passed ball. Frank Robinson walked to reload the bases and Brooks Robinson and Boog Powell stroked sacrifice flies to give the Orioles a 3-0 lead. Walker departed the premises at this juncture and was replaced by Bruce Kison, tall 21-year-old righthander.

The Orioles' attack died when the youngster took the mound. Blair's double with two out in the second inning was their only hit the rest of the evening.

Meanwhile, the Pirates went to work on Pat Dobson, one of Baltimore's four 20-game winners in the 1971 campaign. A walk to Dave Cash, Willie Stargell's double and Al Oliver's single produced two runs in the first. Singles by Richie Hebner, Roberto Clemente and Oliver tied the score in the third inning.

The Pirates scored the decisive run off reliever Eddie Watt in the seventh. With one out, Bob Robertson and Sanguillen singled. When pinch-hitter Vic Davalillo flied to left-center field, Paul Blair dropped the ball, but recovered in time to nail Sanguillen diving back into second base.

Here Murtaugh went to his bench, calling on 21-year-old Milt May, whose dad, Merrill (Pinky) May, was a teammate of Murtaugh on the 1941 Phillies.

Batting for Kison, May lined a single to right to score Robertson.

Now it was up to Dave Giusti and the 31-year-old righthander, who saved 30 Pirate victories in regular season play, spun two perfect innings to preserve the 4-3 victory.

The fifth game of the Series, played at Pittsburgh on Thursday afternoon, was practically no contest.

The Pirates gave the starting assignment to Nelson Briles, a veteran of two previous World Series with the St. Louis Cardinals, and the righthander was in complete control all the way, setting the Baltimore club down on two hits and was never in trouble at any time.

Against such overwhelming opposition, the Birds' Dave McNally, winner of the Series opener, was no match.

Bob Robertson started McNally's downfall with a 410-foot homer to center field on the first pitch of the second inning.

After Manny Sanguillen followed with a single, McNally fanned Jose Pagan and Jackie Hernandez and slipped two strikes past Briles.

Briles worked the count to 3-and-2, then singled to center, scoring Sanguillen, who had stolen second base.

The Bucs scored their third run without benefit of a hit in the third inning. Gene Clines walked and went to second as Roberto Clemente grounded out.

When Brooks Robinson booted Robertson's grounder for the Birds' ninth error of the Series, Clines took third. He scored on a wild pitch.

The Pirates kayoed McNally in the fifth. Clines opened with a triple over Paul Blair's head in center field and Clemente, hitting safely in his twelfth consecutive Series game, singled up the middle.

After a day off, the teams resumed play in Baltimore on Saturday.

Danny Murtaugh nominated Bob Moose to start for the Pirates.

Moose held the Orioles to two hits in the first five innings.

Meanwhile, the Pirates had gained a 2-0 lead, scoring once in the second inning when Al Oliver doubled off Jim Palmer and Bob Robertson singled, and once in the third when Roberto Clemente homered to right field.

Leading off the Orioles' sixth, Don Buford tagged Moose for a home run to right field.

When Hebner booted Dave Johnson's high hopper and Boog Powell singled, Murtaugh went to his bullpen, bringing in Bob Johnson.

With runners on first and third and none out, there appeared to be no way the Orioles could fail to score. But Johnson disappointed most of the 44,174 spectators by retiring Frank Robinson on a pop to shortstop, slipping a third strike past Rettenmund and getting Brooks Robinson to ground to Hebner, who forced Powell at second.

The Pirates were only seven outs away from the world championship when the Orioles scored their second run.

Mark Belanger, who had a perfect day at bat with three walks and a single, ignited the tying spurt with a one-out hit to right field.

After Palmer struck out, Belanger stole second base. Again Murtaugh sent a call to the bullpen, this time for Dave Giusti. The premier reliever walked Buford. Dave Johnson worked the count to 2-and-2 and Giusti threw his favorite palm ball.

On a one-handed, golf-type swing, Johnson arched the ball to short left field for a single as Belanger raced home to tie the score.

Bob Miller took the mound for Pittsburgh in the tenth and Vic Davalillo, who had pinch-hit in the top of the inning, went to center field. With one out, Frank Robinson drew a walk. Merv Rettenmund then dribbled a single up the middle and Robinson moved to third, barely beating Davalillo's good throw.

Brooks Robinson ran the count to one ball and two strikes and then lifted a fly to medium center field. Frank Robinson tagged up and took off. Davalillo's throw to catcher Manny Sanguillen was about ten feet up the third base line. On the second bounce, the ball hopped high. Manny jumped and grabbed the ball, but as he did, Robinson slid between his legs and got the "safe" call from umpire John Kibler, for a 3-2 triumph.

The Orioles had come back from the brink of oblivion and the Series was to reach its climax the next day, a Sunday.

For the final game the starting pitchers were again Steve Blass and Mike Cuellar, the pair who had hooked up in the third contest.

Blass' only misadventure on the cool and cloudy day occurred in the eighth inning. Until that time, the Orioles had managed only two hits, a third-inning single by Don Buford, who was picked off base, and a fifth-inning double by Elrod Hendricks.

Hendricks led off the eighth by grounding a single through the shortstop's normal position which had been vacated by Jackie Hernandez in the Pirate shift.

When Mark Belanger looped a soft single to center field, the Birds had two aboard with none out.

Cuellar was lifted for pinch-hitter Tom Shopay whose sacrifice moved the runners along.

When Buford grounded to Bob Robertson at first base, Hendricks scored and Belanger took third. But Dave Johnson, who tied game No. 6 with a single, wasn't quite up to it this time. The Baltimore second baseman grounded into the hole on the left side.

Hernandez glided to his right, made a sparkling pickup and nailed Johnson with a strong throw.

Roberto Clemente had staked Blass to a 1-0 lead in the fourth inning after Cuellar breezed through the first 11 batters, permitting only two balls to be hit to the outfield.

Roberto drove a high curve ball over the center field wall. It was his second Series homer to go with a triple, two doubles and seven singles.

Through seven innings, Cuellar permitted only one other hit, a single by Manny Sanguillen in the fifth.

The run which won the Series for Pittsburgh was scored in the eighth. Willie Stargell bounced a single to left. On a hit-and-run play, Jose Pagan doubled to deep center and Stargell raced home with the all-important tally.

After his rocky eighth inning, Blass was untouchable in the ninth, setting the Orioles down in order to lock up the championship for the Pirates.

The box scores:

Saturday, October 9—At Baltimore

Pittsburgh (N.L.)	AB.	R.	H.	O.	A.	E.
Cash, 2b	4	0	1	1	3	0
Clines, cf	4	0	0	1	0	0
Clemente, rf	4	0	2	2	0	0
Stargell, lf	3	0	0	2	0	0
Robertson, 1b	3	1	0	8	1	0
Sanguillen, c	4	1	0	6	0	0
Pagan, 3b	4	0	0	2	0	0
Hernandez, ss	2	1	0	0	4	0
bOliver	1	0	0	0	0	0
Ellis, p	1	0	0	1	0	0
Moose, p	1	0	0	0	1	0
aMazeroski	1	0	0	0	0	0
Miller, p	0	0	0	1	1	0
Totals	32	3	3	24	10	0

1971 WORLD SERIES

Baltimore (A.L.)	AB.	R.	H.	O.	A.	E.
Buford, lf	4	2	2	4	0	0
Blair, cf	0	0	0	0	0	0
Rettenmund, cf-lf	4	1	1	4	0	0
Powell, 1b	3	0	0	6	0	0
F. Robinson, 1b	4	1	2	3	0	0
Hendricks, c	4	0	1	9	0	1
B. Robinson, 3b	4	0	1	0	3	0
Johnson, 2b	4	0	1	1	1	0
Belanger, ss	4	1	2	0	2	2
McNally, p	3	0	0	0	1	0
Totals	34	5	10	27	7	3

```
Pittsburgh ............... 0 3 0   0 0 0   0 0 0—3
Baltimore ................ 0 1 3   0 1 0   0 0 *—5
```

aFlied out for Moose in seventh. bStruck out for Hernandez in ninth. Runs batted in—Hernandez, Cash, F. Robinson, Rettenmund 3, Buford. Two-base hit—Clemente. Three-base hit—Belanger. Home runs—F. Robinson, Rettenmund, Buford. Sacrifice hit—Hernandez. Left on bases—Pittsburgh 5, Baltimore 6. Earned runs—Pittsburgh 0, Baltimore 5. Bases on balls—Off McNally 2, off Ellis 1. Struck out—By McNally 9, by Ellis 1, by Moose 4, by Miller 1. Pitching record—Off McNally 3 runs and 3 hits in 9 innings; off Ellis 4 runs and 4 hits in 2⅓ innings; off Moose 1 run and 3 hits in 3⅔ innings; off Miller 0 runs and 3 hits in 2 innings. Wild pitches—McNally, Moose. Losing pitcher—Ellis. Umpires—Chylak (A.L.), Sudol (N.L.), Rice (A.L.), Vargo (N.L.), Odom (A.L.) and Kibler (N.L.). Time—2:06. Attendance—53,229.

Monday, October 11—At Baltimore

Pittsburgh (N.L.)	AB.	R.	H.	O.	A.	E.
Cash, 2b	5	0	0	2	6	0
Hebner, 3b	3	1	1	0	0	0
Clemente, rf	5	0	2	2	0	0
Stargell, lf	3	0	1	2	1	0
Giusti, p	0	0	0	0	0	0
Oliver, cf	5	0	0	1	0	1
Robertson, 1b	3	0	0	8	1	0
Sanguillen, c	5	0	1	4	0	0
Hernandez, ss	2	1	1	2	1	0
dMay	1	0	0	0	0	0
R. Johnson, p	2	0	0	2	0	0
Kison, p	0	0	0	0	0	0
Moose, p	0	0	0	0	0	0
Veale, p	0	0	0	0	1	0
aSands	1	0	0	0	0	0
Miller, p	0	0	0	0	0	0
cDavalillo, lf	1	1	1	1	0	0
Totals	36	3	8	24	10	1

Baltimore (A.L.)	AB.	R.	H.	O.	A.	E.
Buford, lf	5	0	0	2	0	0
Rettenmund, cf-rf	5	1	2	3	0	0
Powell, 1b	5	1	1	4	3	0
F. Robinson, rf	4	2	3	1	0	0
bBlair, pr-cf	1	1	1	1	0	0
Hendricks, c	3	2	1	10	0	0
B. Robinson, 3b	3	2	3	0	1	0
D. Johnson, 2b	5	1	2	1	3	0
Belanger, ss	3	1	0	2	1	1
Palmer, p	2	0	0	2	0	0
Hall, p	0	0	0	1	0	0
Totals	36	11	14	27	8	1

```
Pittsburgh ............... 0 0 0   0 0 0   0 3 0— 3
Baltimore ................ 0 1 0   3 6 1   0 0 *—11
```

aStruck out for Veale in sixth. bRan and scored for F. Robinson in sixth. cSingled and scored for Miller in eighth. dGrounded out for Hernandez in ninth. Runs batted in—B. Robinson 3, D. Johnson 2, Palmer 2, Hendricks, Buford, Rettenmund, Hebner 3. Two-base hit—Clemente. Home run—Hebner. Double plays—Cash and Hernandez; Stargell and Sanguillen. Left on bases—Pittsburgh 14, Baltimore 9. Earned runs—Baltimore 11, Pittsburgh 3. Bases on balls—Off Palmer 8, off R. Johnson 2, off Kison 2, off Veale 2, off Giusti 1. Struck out—By Palmer 10, by R. Johnson 1, by Miller 1. Pitching record—Off Palmer 3 runs and 7 hits in 8 innings; off Hall 0 runs and 1 hit in 1 inning; off R. Johnson 4 runs and 4 hits in 3⅓ innings; off Kison 0 runs and 0 hits in 0 innings (pitched to two batters in fourth); off Moose 5 runs and 5 hits in 1 inning; off Veale 1 run and 1 hit in ⅔ inning; off Miller 1 run and 3 hits in 1 inning; off Giusti 0 runs and 1 hit in 1 inning. Hit by pitcher—By R. Johnson (Hendricks). Winning pitcher—Palmer. Losing pitcher—R. Johnson. Save—Hall. Umpires—Sudol (N.L.), Rice (A.L.), Vargo (N.L.), Odom (A.L.), Kibler (N.L.) and Chylak (A.L.). Time—2:55. Attendance—53,239.

Tuesday, October 12—At Pittsburgh

Baltimore (A.L.)	AB.	R.	H.	O.	A.	E.
Buford, lf	4	0	0	3	0	0
Rettenmund, cf	4	0	0	3	0	0
Powell, 1b	4	0	0	7	0	1
F. Robinson, rf	4	1	2	2	0	0
Hendricks, c	3	0	0	4	1	0
B. Robinson, 3b	3	0	1	1	5	1
Johnson, 2b	3	0	0	3	2	0
Belanger, ss	3	0	0	1	2	0
Cuellar, p	1	0	0	0	0	1
Dukes, p	0	0	0	0	0	0
aShopay	1	0	0	0	0	0
Watt, p	0	0	0	0	0	0
Totals	30	1	3	24	10	3

Pittsburgh (N.L.)	AB.	R.	H.	O.	A.	E.
Cash, 2b	4	1	1	2	2	0
Oliver, cf	4	0	0	2	0	0
Clemente, rf	4	1	1	3	0	0
Stargell, lf	1	1	0	2	0	0
Robertson, 1b	4	1	1	8	1	0
Sanguillen, c	4	1	2	8	0	0
Pagan, 3b	4	2	2	0	0	0
Alley, ss	2	0	0	1	2	0
Hernandez, ss	1	0	0	0	1	0
Blass, p	4	0	0	1	2	0
Totals	32	5	7	27	8	0

```
Baltimore ............... 0 0 0   0 0 0   1 0 0—1
Pittsburgh .............. 1 0 0   0 0 1   3 0 *—5
```

aGrounded out for Dukes in eighth. Runs batted in—Clemente, Pagan, Robertson 3, F. Robinson. Two-base hits—Cash, Pagan, Sanguillen. Home runs—F. Robinson, Robertson. Double play—B. Robinson and Johnson. Left on bases—Baltimore 4, Pittsburgh 9. Earned runs—Baltimore 1, Pittsburgh 4. Bases on balls—Off Cuellar 6, off Blass 2. Struck out—By Cuellar 4, by Watt 1, by Blass 8. Pitching records—Off Cuellar 5 runs and 7 hits in 6 innings (pitched to three batters in seventh); off Dukes 0 runs and 0 hits in 1 inning; off Watt 0 runs and 0 hits in 1 inning; off Blass 1 run and 3 hits in 9 innings. Losing pitcher—Cuellar. Umpires—Rice (A.L.), Vargo (N.L.), Odom (A.L.), Kibler (N.L.), Chylak (A.L.) and Sudol (N.L.). Time—2:20. Attendance—50,403.

Wed., October 13—At Pittsburgh

Baltimore (A.L.)	AB.	R.	H.	O.	A.	E.
Blair, cf	4	1	2	2	1	1
Belanger, ss	4	1	1	3	4	0
Rettenmund, lf	4	1	1	1	0	0
F. Robinson, rf	2	0	0	2	0	0
B. Robinson, 3b	3	0	0	1	1	0

1971 WORLD SERIES

	AB.	R.	H.	O.	A.	E.
Powell, 1b	3	0	0	6	0	0
Johnson, 2b	3	0	0	3	2	0
Etchebarren, c	2	0	0	6	0	0
Dobson, p	2	0	0	0	3	0
Jackson, p	0	0	0	0	0	0
aShopay	1	0	0	0	0	0
Watt, p	0	0	0	0	0	0
Richert, p	0	0	0	0	0	0
Totals	28	3	4	24	11	1

Pittsburgh (N.L.)	AB.	R.	H.	O.	A.	E.
Cash, 2b	4	1	1	3	3	0
Hebner, 3b	5	1	1	1	1	0
Clemente, rf	4	0	3	0	0	0
Stargell, lf	5	1	2	1	0	0
Oliver, cf	4	0	2	6	0	0
Robertson, 1b	4	1	1	11	0	0
Sanguillen, c	4	0	2	4	0	0
Hernandez, ss	3	0	1	1	2	0
bDavalillo	1	0	0	0	0	0
Giusti, p	0	0	0	0	0	0
Walker, p	0	0	0	0	0	0
Kison, p	2	0	0	0	1	0
cMay	1	0	1	0	0	0
dAlley, ss	0	0	0	0	2	0
Totals	37	4	14	27	9	0

Baltimore	3 0 0	0 0 0	0 0 0—3
Pittsburgh	2 0 1	0 0 0	1 0 *—4

aGrounded into fielder's choice for Jackson in seventh. bReached first on Blair's error for Hernandez in seventh. cSingled for Kison in seventh. dRan for May in seventh. Runs batted in—B. Robinson, Powell, Stargell, Oliver 2, May. Two-base hits—Stargell, Oliver, Blair. Stolen bases—Sanguillen, Hernandez. Sacrifice flies—B. Robinson. Powell. Double plays—Hernandez, Cash and Robertson; Belanger, Johnson and Powell. Left on bases—Baltimore 4, Pittsburgh 13. Earned runs—Baltimore 3, Pittsburgh 4. Bases on balls—Off Dobson 3, off Jackson 1, off Walker 1. Struck out—By Dobson 4, by Watt 1, by Richert 1, by Kison 3, by Giusti 1. Pitching records—Off Dobson 3 runs and 3 hits in 5⅓ innings; off Jackson 0 runs and 0 hits in ⅔ inning; off Watt 1 run and 4 hits in 1⅓ innings; off Richert 0 runs and 0 hits in ⅔ inning; off Walker 3 runs and 3 hits in ⅔ inning; off Kison 0 runs and 1 hit in 6⅓ innings; off Giusti 0 runs and 0 hits in 2 innings. Passed ball—Sanguillen. Hit by pitcher—By Kison 3 (Johnson, F. Robinson, Etchebarren). Winning pitcher—Kison. Losing pitcher—Watt. Save—Giusti. Umpires—Vargo (N.L.), Odom (A.L.), Kibler (N.L.), Chylak (A.L.), Sudol (N.L.) and Rice (A.L.). Time—2:48. Attendance—51,378.

Thurs., October 14—At Pittsburgh

Baltimore (A.L.)	AB.	R.	H.	O.	A.	E.
Buford, lf	3	0	0	1	0	0
Blair, cf	4	0	0	3	1	0
Powell, 1b	3	0	1	8	0	0
F. Robinson, rf	3	0	0	1	0	0
Hendricks, c	2	0	0	4	3	0
B. Robinson, 3b	3	0	1	2	2	1
Johnson, 2b	3	0	0	3	1	0
Belanger, ss	3	0	0	2	3	0
McNally, p	1	0	0	0	1	0
Leonhard, p	0	0	0	0	0	0
aShopay	1	0	0	0	0	0
Dukes, p	0	0	0	0	0	0
bRettenmund	1	0	0	0	0	0
Totals	27	0	2	24	11	1

Pittsburgh (N.L.)	AB.	R.	H.	O.	A.	E.
Cash, 2b	4	0	0	5	2	0
Clines, cf	3	2	1	3	0	0
Clemente, rf	4	0	1	4	0	0
Stargell, lf	4	0	1	2	0	0
Robertson, 1b	3	1	1	9	0	0
Sanguillen, c	4	1	1	2	0	0
Pagan, 3b	4	0	1	0	6	0
Hernandez, ss	3	0	2	2	1	0
Briles, p	2	0	1	0	1	0
Totals	31	4	9	27	10	0

Baltimore	0 0 0	0 0 0	0 0 0—0
Pittsburgh	0 2 1	0 1 0	0 0 *—4

aFlied out for Leonhard in sixth. bGrounded out for Dukes in ninth. Runs batted in—Robertson, Briles, Clemente. Three-base hit—Clines. Home run—Robertson. Sacrifice hits—Briles 2. Stolen bases—Clines, Sanguillen. Double plays—Hernandez, Cash and Robertson; Pagan, Cash and Robertson. Left on bases—Baltimore 2, Pittsburgh 9. Earned runs—Pittsburgh 3. Bases on balls—Off McNally 2, off Leonhard 1, off Briles 2. Struck out—By McNally 3, by Dukes 1, by Briles 2. Pitching records—Off McNally 4 runs, 7 hits in 4 innings (pitched to two batters in fifth); off Leonhard 0 runs, 0 hits in 1 inning; off Dukes 0 runs, 2 hits in 3 innings. Wild pitch—McNally. Hit by pitcher—By Dukes (Hernandez). Losing pitcher—McNally. Umpires—Odom (A.L.), Kibler (N.L.), Chylak (A.L.), Sudol (N.L.), Rice (A.L.) and Vargo (N.L.). Time—2:16. Attendance—51,377.

Sat., October 16—At Baltimore

Pittsburgh (N.L.)	AB.	R.	H.	O.	A.	E.
Cash, 2b	5	0	1	3	4	0
Hebner, 3b	4	0	0	0	2	1
Clemente, rf	4	1	2	2	0	0
Stargell, lf	4	0	0	2	0	0
Oliver, cf	5	1	1	2	0	0
Miller, p	0	0	0	0	0	0
Robertson, 1b	4	0	2	9	0	0
Sanguillen, c	4	0	3	8	0	0
Hernandez, ss	4	0	0	2	2	0
Moose, p	1	0	0	0	2	0
R. Johnson, p	1	0	0	0	0	0
Giusti, p	0	0	0	0	0	0
bDavalillo, cf	1	0	0	1	0	0
Totals	37	2	9	c29	10	1

Baltimore (A.L.)	AB.	R.	H.	O.	A.	E.
Buford, lf	4	1	3	3	1	0
D. Johnson, 2b	5	0	1	5	1	0
Powell, 1b	5	0	1	9	1	0
F. Robinson, rf	4	1	0	0	0	0
Rettenmund, cf	5	0	1	4	0	0
B. Robinson, 3b	4	0	1	1	0	0
Hendricks, c	4	0	0	6	0	0
Belanger, ss	1	1	1	2	5	0
Palmer, p	2	0	0	0	1	0
aShopay	1	0	0	0	0	0
Dobson, p	0	0	0	0	0	0
McNally, p	0	0	0	0	0	0
Totals	35	3	8	30	9	0

Pittsburgh	0 1 1	0 0 0	0 0 0—2
Baltimore	0 0 0	0 0 1	1 0 0 1—3

aFlied out for Palmer in ninth. bLined out for Giusti in tenth. cTwo out when winning run scored. Runs batted in—Robertson, Clemente, Buford, D. Johnson, B. Robinson. Two-base hits—Oliver, Buford. Three-base hit—Clemente. Home runs—Clemente, Buford. Sacrifice hits—Moose, Palmer. Sacrifice fly—B. Robinson. Stolen bases—Belanger, Cash. Double play—Hebner, Cash and Robertson. Left on bases—Pittsburgh 9, Baltimore 10. Earned runs—Pittsburgh 2, Baltimore 3. Bases on balls—Off Moose 2, off R. Johnson 1, off Giusti 1, off Miller 1, off Palmer 1, off Dobson 1, off McNally 1. Struck out—By Moose 3, by R. Johnson 2, by Giusti 3, by Palmer 5, by Dobson 1. Pitching records—Off Moose 1 run, 4 hits in 5 innings (pitched to three batters in sixth); off R. Johnson 1 run, 1 hit in 1⅔ innings; off Giusti 0 runs, 2 hits in 2⅓ innings; off Miller 1 run, 1 hit in ⅔ inning; off Palmer 2 runs, 8 hits in 9 innings; off Dobson 0 runs, 1 hit in ⅔ inning; off McNally 0 runs, 0 hits in ⅓ inning. Winning pitcher—McNally. Losing pitcher—Miller. Umpires—Kibler (N.L.), Chylak (A.L.), Sudol (N.L.), Rice (A.L.), Vargo (N.L.) and Odom (A.L.). Time—2:59. Attendance—44,174.

Sunday, October 17—At Baltimore

Pittsburgh (N.L.)	AB.	R.	H.	O.	A.	E.
Cash, 2b	4	0	0	4	3	0
Clines, cf	4	0	0	2	0	0
Clemente, rf	4	1	1	2	0	0
Robertson, 1b	4	0	1	11	1	1
Sanguillen, c	4	0	2	5	0	0
Stargell, lf	4	1	1	0	0	0
Pagan, 3b	3	0	1	0	2	0
Hernandez, ss	3	0	0	2	5	0
Blass, p	3	0	0	1	2	0
Totals	33	2	6	27	13	1

Baltimore (A.L.)	AB.	R.	H.	O.	A.	E.
Buford, lf	3	0	1	0	0	0
Johnson, 2b	4	0	0	2	0	0
Powell, 1b	4	0	0	12	0	0
F. Robinson, rf	4	0	0	3	0	0
Rettenmund, cf	4	0	0	0	0	0
B. Robinson, 3b	2	0	0	1	5	0
Hendricks, c	3	1	2	7	0	0
Belanger, ss	3	0	1	0	3	0
Cuellar, p	2	0	0	0	3	0
aShopay	0	0	0	0	0	0
Dobson, p	0	0	0	0	0	0
McNally, p	0	0	0	0	0	0
Totals	29	1	4	27	13	0

Pittsburgh......... 0 0 0   1 0 0   0 1 0—2
Baltimore.......... 0 0 0   0 0 0   0 1 0—1

aSacrificed for Cuellar in eighth. Runs batted in—Clemente, Pagan, Buford. Two-base hits—Hendricks, Pagan. Home run—Clemente. Sacrifice hit—Shopay. Caught stealing—Buford. Double play—Cash and Robertson. Left on bases—Pittsburgh 4, Baltimore 4. Earned runs—Pittsburgh 2, Baltimore 1. Bases on balls—Off Blass 2. Struck out—By Blass 5, by Cuellar 6, by Dobson 1. Pitching records—Off Blass 1 run and 4 hits in 9 innings; off Cuellar 2 runs and 4 hits in 8 innings; off Dobson 0 runs and 2 hits in ⅔ inning; off McNally 0 runs and 0 hits in ⅓ inning. Losing pitcher—Cuellar. Umpires—Chylak (A.L.), Sudol (N.L.), Rice (A.L.), Vargo (N.L.), Odom (A.L.) and Kibler (N.L.). Time—2:10. Attendance—47,291.

COMPOSITE BATTING AVERAGES
Pittsburgh Pirates

Player-Position	G.	AB.	R.	H.	2B.	3B.	HR.	RBI.	BA.
May, ph	2	2	0	1	0	0	0	1	.500
Briles, p	1	2	0	1	0	0	0	1	.500
Clemente, rf	7	29	3	12	2	1	2	4	.414
Sanguillen, c	7	29	3	11	1	0	0	0	.379
Dav'illo, ph-lf-cf	3	3	1	1	0	0	0	0	.333
Pagan, 3b	4	15	0	4	2	0	0	2	.267
Robertson, 1b	7	25	4	6	0	0	2	5	.240
Hernandez, ss	7	18	2	4	0	0	0	1	.222
Oliver, ph-cf	5	19	1	4	2	0	0	1	.211
Stargell, lf	7	24	3	5	1	0	0	1	.208
Hebner, 3b	3	12	2	2	0	0	1	3	.167
Cash, 2b	7	30	2	4	1	0	0	1	.133
Clines, cf	3	11	2	1	0	1	0	0	.091
Ellis, p	1	1	0	0	0	0	0	0	.000
Mazeroski, ph	1	1	0	0	0	0	0	0	.000
Sands, ph	1	1	0	0	0	0	0	0	.000
Alley, ss-pr	2	2	0	0	0	0	0	0	.000
Kison, p	2	2	0	0	0	0	0	0	.000
Moose, p	3	2	0	0	0	0	0	0	.000
R. Johnson, p	2	3	0	0	0	0	0	0	.000
Blass, p	2	7	0	0	0	0	0	0	.000
Giusti, p	3	0	0	0	0	0	0	0	.000
Miller, p	3	0	0	0	0	0	0	0	.000
Veale, p	1	0	0	0	0	0	0	0	.000
Walker, p	1	0	0	0	0	0	0	0	.000
Totals	7	238	23	56	9	2	5	21	.235

Baltimore Orioles

Player-Position	G.	AB.	R.	H.	2B.	3B.	HR.	RBI.	BA.
Blair, cf-pr	4	9	2	3	1	0	0	0	.333
B. Robinson, 3b	7	22	2	7	0	0	0	5	.318
F. Robinson, rf	7	25	5	7	0	0	2	2	.280
Hendricks, c	6	19	3	5	1	0	0	1	.263
Buford, lf	6	23	3	6	1	0	2	4	.261
Belanger, ss	7	21	4	5	0	1	0	0	.238
Ret'nd, cf-rf-lf-ph	7	27	3	5	0	0	1	4	.185
D. Johnson, 2b	7	27	1	4	0	0	0	3	.148
Powell, 1b	7	27	1	3	0	0	0	1	.111
Dobson, p	3	2	0	0	0	0	0	0	.000
Etchebarren, c	1	2	0	0	0	0	0	0	.000
Cuellar, p	2	3	0	0	0	0	0	0	.000
McNally, p	4	4	0	0	0	0	0	0	.000
Palmer, p	2	4	0	0	0	0	0	2	.000
Shopay, ph	5	4	0	0	0	0	0	0	.000
Dukes, p	2	0	0	0	0	0	0	0	.000
Watt, p	2	0	0	0	0	0	0	0	.000
Hall, p	1	0	0	0	0	0	0	0	.000
Jackson, p	1	0	0	0	0	0	0	0	.000
Leonhard, p	1	0	0	0	0	0	0	0	.000
Richert, p	1	0	0	0	0	0	0	0	.000
Totals	7	219	24	45	3	1	5	22	.205

COMPOSITE PITCHING AVERAGES
Pittsburgh Pirates

Pitcher	G.	IP.	H.	R.	E.	SO.	BB.	W.	L.	ERA.
Briles	1	9	2	0	0	2	2	1	0	0.00
Kison	2	6⅓	1	0	0	3	2	1	0	0.00
Giusti	3	5⅓	3	0	0	4	2	0	0	0.00
Blass	2	18	7	2	2	13	4	2	0	1.00
Miller	3	4⅔	7	2	2	2	1	0	1	3.86
Moose	3	9⅔	12	7	7	7	2	0	0	6.52
R. Johnson	2	5	5	5	5	3	3	0	1	9.00
Veale	1	⅔	1	1	1	0	2	0	0	13.50
Ellis	1	2⅓	4	4	4	1	1	0	1	15.43
Walker	1	⅔	3	3	3	0	1	0	0	40.50
Totals	7	61⅔	45	24	24	35	20	4	3	3.50

Shutout—Briles. Save—Giusti.

Baltimore Orioles

Pitcher	G.	IP.	H.	R.	E.	SO.	BB.	W.	L.	ERA.
Dukes	2	4	2	0	0	1	0	0	0	0.00
Hall	1	1	1	0	0	0	0	0	0	0.00
Leonhard	1	1	0	0	0	0	1	0	0	0.00
Jackson	1	⅔	0	0	0	1	0	0	0	0.00
Richert	1	⅔	0	0	0	0	1	0	0	0.00
McNally	4	13⅔	10	5	3	12	5	2	1	1.98
Palmer	2	17	15	5	5	15	9	1	0	2.65
Cuellar	2	14	11	7	6	10	6	0	2	3.86
Watt	2	2⅓	4	1	1	2	0	0	1	3.86
Dobson	3	6⅔	13	3	3	6	4	0	0	4.05
Totals	7	61	56	23	18	47	26	3	4	2.66

Save—Hall.

SERIES OF 1972

	W.	L.	Pct.
Oakland A. L.	4	3	.571
Cincinnati N. L.	3	4	.429

The Oakland Athletics climbed to the top of the baseball pole in 1972, giving the franchise its first World Series title since 1930, when the club was stationed in Philadelphia. In a World Series in which no less than six of the seven games were decided by one run and in which no starting pitcher managed to go a full nine innings, Oakland defeated the National League champions, the Cincinnati Reds, as Gene Tenace, a relatively obscure catcher, led the way with four home runs and nine runs batted in.

Oakland, after shaking off the Chicago White Sox in the last month of the season to capture the junior circuit's West Division title, won the league crown in a five-game playoff from the Detroit Tigers, winners in the East. The Tigers were the survivors of a four-club dogfight with Boston, Baltimore and New York.

The Cincinnati Reds were an easy winner in the National League West Division and knocked off the defending World Champion Pittsburgh Pirates in an exciting playoff that wasn't decided until the last inning of the fifth game of the Championship Series.

The Athletics, minus the services of their top slugger, Reggie Jackson, sidelined by a pulled hamstring, were in need of somebody to furnish the sock laid dormant by Jackson's injury. In his first two at-bats, Tenace, four days past his 26th birthday, propelled Gary Nolan pitches over the left-field wall at Cincinnati's Riverfront Stadium to give the A's all the runs they needed to win the opening game, 3-2.

The Reds threatened frequently to break the game open and Oakland's starting pitcher, lefty Ken Holtzman, was in hot water throughout. But the National Leaguers left eight men on base and finally were stifled by the relief pitching of Rollie Fingers and Vida Blue.

In the second game, the A's combined stout pitching with a sparkling defense to defeat the Reds, 2-1.

The A's scored their runs on four singles in the second inning and a home run by left fielder Joe Rudi in the third frame, all off Ross Grimsley, the Reds' starter.

Jim (Catfish) Hunter, the righthander who had won 21 games in 28 decisions for the Athletics during the regular season, put on a brilliant display before he tired and was relieved with two outs in the ninth.

Rudi, who had supplied the big blow of a nine-hit attack, furnished the key defensive play when the Reds threatened to pull out the decision in the ninth inning. He raced toward the barrier, looked over his head, turned to his right and leaped a good four feet to spear a line drive off the bat of Denis Menke. The sensational catch came with a runner on first and nobody out. Had the catch not been made, the Reds would have been back in the game as, one out later, pinch-hitter Hal McRae stroked a single to left. Hunter was then removed and Fingers came on to retire pinch-hitter Julian Javier for the final out.

Faced with imminent disaster, the Reds needed brilliant work to keep in contention when the Series resumed following a day off for travel and another day off because of rain, on Wednesday night in Oakland. They got that brilliant work from right-hander Jack Billingham, who allowed just three hits in eight full innings before Clay Carroll relieved and retired the side to give Cincinnati a 1-0 victory.

The only run of the game was scored by the Reds against John (Blue Moon) Odom in the seventh inning. A single by Tony Perez, Menke's sacrifice and a single by Cesar Geronimo constituted the evening's entire output of scoring.

The following night, the Reds apparently had the Series tied up but a furious last-minute rally by Oakland gave the A's a 3-2 verdict and a 3-1 lead in games.

The Reds had a 2-1 lead going into the bottom of the ninth and, with ace reliever Carroll on the mound, seemed home free. But successive singles by pinch-hitter Gonzalo Marquez, Tenace—whose fifth-inning home run had scored the A's only previous tally in the game—pinch-hitter Don Mincher and pinch-hitter Angel Mangual left the Reds staring in mute disbelief and triggered a wild demonstration by the A's bench.

Cincinnati had scored its two runs in the eighth inning on a single by Dave Concepcion, a sacrifice, a base on balls and a double by Bobby Tolan, the last blow off of Vida Blue, who had relieved starter Holtzman.

The fifth game, played on Friday afternoon, was a wild affair that saw the Reds take a first-pitch lead on a home run by Pete Rose, fall behind by two runs, and then come back to give Grimsley, fifth of six Cincinnati pitchers, the 5-4 decision over Fingers, the second of three Oakland moundsmen.

The advantage given Reds' starter Jim McGlothlin was protected for just one inning as a walk to Mike Epstein, a single by George Hendrick and a home run by Tenace gave the A's a 3-1 margin at the end of two frames.

The Reds got one back in the fourth when Menke reached the left-field seats for a home run, only his second hit of the Series. But the A's retaliated in their half of the inning, scoring once on a walk, a sacrifice and a pinch single by Marquez.

Daring base running put Cincinnati within one run of the A's in the fifth inning. Joe Morgan, on first after being walked, came all the way home on a hit-and-run play, the hit being a single by Tolan.

Morgan was again a factor in the eighth inning when the Reds tied the game. He walked, stole second and scored on another single by Tolan.

The winning run for the visitors came across in the ninth when Geronimo singled and reached second on a sacrifice bunt by Grimsley. After third baseman Sal Bando miscued on Concepcion's grounder, Rose lashed a single to center to score Geronimo.

The game ended on a thrilling note when, with one out and pinch-runner Odom at third and pinch-hitter Dave Duncan on first via a single, Campy Campaneris lifted a foul pop behind third base. Morgan made the catch and Odom broke for the plate. Morgan stumbled briefly, regained his balance and fired on target to Johnny Bench. The Reds' catcher stood his ground, took the throw and made the tag. Odom complained on the call to umpire Bob Engel but, as usual, the decision stood.

The Series resumed on Saturday afternoon in Cincinnati and the Reds evened the Series at 3-3 by pounding starter Vida Blue and three relievers for ten hits, including doubles by Morgan and McRae, a triple by Concepcion and a home run by Bench to gain an 8-1 triumph. Grimsley, the second of four Red pitchers, gained credit for the win.

Odom and Billingham were the opposing pitchers in the climactic game of the 1972 baseball season. The latter was the victim of bad luck in the first inning when center fielder Tolan misjudged Mangual's liner, failed to make the catch and Mangual reached third from where he scored on Tenace's bad-hop single.

The Reds got even in the bottom of the fifth on a double by Tony Perez, walks to Geronimo and Concepcion and a sacrifice fly by McRae, pinch-hitting for Billingham.

With Pedro Borbon on the mound for Cincinnati in the sixth, the A's put together a rally that was to win the Series. Campaneris singled up the middle to open the inning but, with two out, was no farther along than third base. Tenace then doubled into the left-field corner for the go-ahead run. Bando sent a long drive to center field. Tolan ran to catch the ball but suddenly his left leg crumpled. He dropped to the ground and was unable to make a play as Bando reached second and pinch-runner Allan Lewis scored. It developed that Tolan had pulled a hamstring muscle and had to be removed from the game.

The Reds made their last gesture in the eighth. Rose singled and Morgan doubled to open the inning. But pinch-hitter Joe Hague popped out. A's Manager Dick Williams ordered Bench intentionally walked, thereby violating one of baseball's cardinal principles, "Never put the winning run on base." But the strategy paid off as a sacrifice fly by Perez produced one tally and Denis Menke flied to left, leaving the home team still a run short.

The Reds got a runner on first with two out in the bottom of the ninth, but Fingers retired Rose on a fly ball for the final out.

The box scores:

Saturday, October 14—At Cincinnati

Oakland (A.L.)	AB.	R.	H.	O.	A.	E.
Campaneris, ss	3	0	2	2	3	0
Rudi, lf	4	0	0	3	0	0
Alou, rf	3	0	0	1	0	0
Epstein, 1b	3	0	0	6	1	0
cLewis	0	0	0	0	0	0
Hegan, 1b	0	0	0	2	0	0
Bando, 3b	4	0	0	0	3	0
Hendrick, cf	2	1	0	2	0	0
Tenace, c	3	2	2	7	2	0
Green, 2b	2	0	0	3	1	0
bMarquez	1	0	0	0	0	0
Kubiak, 2b	0	0	0	1	2	0
Holtzman, p	2	0	0	0	1	0
Fingers, p	0	0	0	0	0	0
Blue, p	0	0	0	0	0	0
Totals	27	3	4	27	13	0
Cincinnati (N.L.)	AB.	R.	H.	O.	A.	E.
Rose, lf	4	0	0	3	0	0
Morgan, 2b	3	0	0	5	5	0
Tolan, cf	4	0	1	2	0	0
Bench, c	3	2	2	1	2	0
Perez, 1b	4	0	2	10	0	0
Menke, 3b	3	0	0	2	2	0
Geronimo, rf	3	0	0	3	0	0
dMcRae	1	0	1	0	0	0
eFoster	0	0	0	0	0	0
Concepcion, ss	2	0	1	1	1	0
Nolan, p	2	0	0	0	1	0
Borbon, p	0	0	0	0	0	0
aUhlaender	1	0	0	0	0	0
Carroll, p	0	0	0	0	1	0
fJavier	1	0	0	0	0	0
Totals	31	2	7	27	13	0

Oakland .... 0 2 0 0 1 0 0 0 0—3
Cincinnati .... 0 1 0 1 0 0 0 0 0—2

aStruck out for Borbon in seventh. bPopped out for Green in eighth. cRan for Epstein in ninth. dSingled for Geronimo in ninth. eRan for McRae in ninth. fGrounded out for Carroll in ninth. Runs batted in—Tenace 3, Concepcion, Menke. Two-base hit—Bench. Home runs—Tenace 2. Sacrifice hits—Campaneris, Concepcion. Left on bases—Oakland 2, Cincinnati 8. Earned runs—Oakland 3, Cincinnati 2. Bases on balls—Off Holtzman 3, off Fingers 1, off Blue 1, off Nolan 2, off Carroll 2. Strikeouts—By Holtzman 3, by Fingers 3, by Blue 1, by Carroll 1. Caught stealing—Campaneris, Tolan, Concepcion, Lewis. Double play—Morgan and Perez. Wild pitch—Blue. Pitching records—Off Holtzman 5 hits, 2 runs in 5 innings (pitched to one batter in sixth); off Fingers 1 hit, 0 runs in 1⅓ innings; off Blue 1 hit, 0 runs in 2⅔ innings; off Nolan 4 hits, 3 runs in 6 innings; off Borbon 0 hits, 0 runs in 1 inning; off Carroll 0 hits and 0 runs in 2 innings. Winning pitcher—Holtzman. Save—Blue. Losing pitcher—Nolan. Umpires—Pelekoudas (N.L.), Honochick (A.L.), Steiner (N.L.), Umont (A.L.), Engel (N.L.), Haller (A.L.). Time—2:18. Attendance—52,918.

Sunday, October 15—At Cincinnati

Oakland (A.L.)	AB.	R.	H.	O.	A.	E.
Campaneris, ss	5	0	1	2	1	0
Alou, rf	4	0	1	4	0	0
Rudi, lf	3	1	2	4	0	0
Epstein, 1b	2	0	0	2	0	1
bLewis	0	0	0	0	0	0
Hegan, 1b	1	0	0	3	0	0
Bando, 3b	4	0	1	0	1	0
Hendrick, cf	4	1	1	3	0	0
Tenace, c	4	0	0	7	0	0
Green, 2b	4	0	2	2	1	0

1972 WORLD SERIES

	AB.	R.	H.	O.	A.	E.
Hunter, p	3	0	1	0	1	1
Fingers, p	0	0	0	0	0	0
Totals	34	2	9	27	4	2
Cincinnati (N.L.)	AB.	R.	H.	O.	A.	E.
Rose, lf	4	0	1	2	1	0
Morgan, 2b	4	0	0	0	3	0
Tolan, cf	4	0	0	1	0	0
Bench, c	3	0	1	8	1	0
Perez, 1b	3	1	2	11	0	0
Menke, 3b	4	0	0	0	2	0
Geronimo, rf	4	0	0	3	0	0
Chaney, ss	2	0	0	2	4	0
dMcRae	1	0	1	0	0	0
eConcepcion	0	0	0	0	0	0
Grimsley, p	1	0	0	0	2	0
aUhlaender	1	0	1	0	0	0
Borbon, p	0	0	0	0	0	0
cHague	1	0	0	0	0	0
Hall, p	0	0	0	0	0	0
fJavier	1	0	0	0	0	0
Totals	33	1	6	27	13	0

```
Oakland .............. 0 1 1   0 0 0   0 0 0—2
Cincinnati .......... 0 0 0   0 0 0   0 0 1—1
```

aDoubled for Grimsley in fifth. bRan for Epstein in sixth. cFlied out for Borbon in seventh. dSingled for Chaney in ninth. eRan for McRae in ninth. fFouled out for Hall in ninth. Runs batted in—Hunter, Rudi, McRae. Two-base hit—Uhlaender. Home run—Rudi. Stolen bases—Morgan, Alou. Caught stealing—Lewis. Double plays—Campaneris, Green and Epstein; Bench and Chaney. Left on bases—Oakland 8, Cincinnati 8. Earned runs—Oakland 2, Cincinnati 1. Bases on balls—Off Hunter 3, off Borbon 1, off Hall 2. Strikeouts—By Hunter 6, by Grimsley 1, by Borbon 4, by Hall 2. Pitching records—Off Hunter 1 run, 6 hits in 8⅔ innings; off Fingers 0 runs, 0 hits in ⅓ inning; off Grimsley 2 runs, 6 hits in 5 innings; off Borbon 0 runs, 0 hits in 2 innings; off Hall 0 runs, 3 hits in 2 innings. Winning pitcher—Hunter. Save—Fingers. Losing pitcher—Grimsley. Umpires—Honochick (A.L.), Steiner (N.L.), Umont (A.L.), Engel (N.L.), Haller (A.L.), Pelekoudas (N.L). Time—2:26. Attendance—53,224.

Wednesday, October 18—At Oakland

Cincinnati (N.L.)	AB.	R.	H.	O.	A.	E.
Rose, lf	3	0	0	0	0	0
Morgan, 2b	3	0	0	3	3	1
Tolan, cf	4	0	1	3	0	0
Bench, c	4	0	0	7	1	1
Perez, 1b	3	1	1	11	0	0
Menke, 3b	2	0	1	0	3	0
Geronimo, rf	4	0	1	0	0	0
Chaney, ss	4	0	0	3	6	0
Billingham, p	4	0	0	0	1	0
Carroll, p	0	0	0	0	1	0
Totals	31	1	4	27	15	2
Oakland (A.L.)	AB.	R.	H.	O.	A.	E.
Campaneris, ss	3	0	0	0	0	0
Alou, rf	3	0	0	0	0	0
Rudi, lf	4	0	0	1	0	0
Epstein, 1b	2	0	0	8	0	1
Bando, 3b	4	0	0	1	1	0
Hendrick, cf	4	0	0	1	0	0
Tenace, c	3	0	0	14	0	1
Green, 2b	2	0	1	0	3	0
aMarquez	1	0	1	0	0	0
bLewis	0	0	0	0	0	0
Kubiak, 2b	0	0	0	2	0	0
Odom, p	2	0	0	0	3	0
cHegan	1	0	0	0	0	0
Blue, p	0	0	0	0	0	0
Fingers, p	0	0	0	0	0	0
Totals	29	0	3	27	7	2

```
Cincinnati .......... 0 0 0   0 0 0   1 0 0—1
Oakland .............. 0 0 0   0 0 0   0 0 0—0
```

aSingled for Green in seventh. bRan for Marquez in seventh. cLined out for Odom in seventh. Run batted in—Geronimo. Stolen bases—Rose, Geronimo, Tolan. Sacrifice hits—Alou, Menke. Double play—Morgan, Chaney and Perez. Left on bases—Cincinnati 8, Oakland 6. Earned run—Cincinnati 1. Bases on balls—Off Billingham 3, off Odom 2, off Blue 1, off Fingers 1. Strikeouts—By Billingham 7, by Odom 11, by Fingers 3. Pitching records—Off Billingham 0 runs, 3 hits in 8 innings (replaced with three balls and no strikes on first batter in ninth); off Carroll 0 runs, 0 hits in 1 inning; off Odom 1 run, 3 hits in 7 innings; off Blue 0 runs, 1 hit in ⅓ inning; off Fingers 0 runs, 0 hits in 1⅔ innings. Winning pitcher—Billingham. Save—Carroll. Losing pitcher—Odom. Umpires—Steiner (N.L.), Umont (A.L.), Engel (N.L.), Haller (A.L.), Pelekoudas (N.L.), Honochick (A.L.). Time—2:24. Attendance—49,410.

Thursday, October 19—At Oakland

Cincinnati (N.L.)	AB.	R.	H.	O.	A.	E.
Rose, lf	4	0	0	3	0	0
Morgan, 2b	3	1	0	2	1	0
Tolan, cf	4	0	1	0	0	0
Bench, c	4	0	2	4	0	0
Perez, 1b	4	0	2	11	0	1
McRae, rf	4	0	1	2	0	0
Geronimo, rf	0	0	0	0	0	0
Menke, 3b	4	0	0	1	4	0
Concepcion, ss	3	1	1	2	5	0
Gullett, p	2	0	0	0	1	0
aJavier	1	0	0	0	0	0
Borbon, p	0	0	0	0	0	0
Carroll, p	0	0	0	0	0	0
Totals	32	2	7	g25	11	1
Oakland (A.L.)	AB.	R.	H.	O.	A.	E.
Campaneris, ss	4	0	0	3	3	0
Alou, rf	3	0	0	2	0	0
Rudi, lf	4	0	2	2	0	0
Bando, 3b	3	0	2	1	4	0
Epstein, 1b	3	0	0	7	0	0
Hegan, 1b	1	0	0	3	1	0
Hendrick, cf	3	0	0	3	0	0
bMarquez	1	0	1	0	0	0
cLewis	0	1	0	0	0	0
Tenace, c	4	2	2	2	1	0
Green, 2b	3	0	1	4	6	0
dMincher	1	0	1	0	0	0
eOdom	0	0	0	0	0	0
Holtzman, p	3	0	0	0	2	1
Blue, p	0	0	0	0	0	0
Fingers, p	0	0	0	0	1	0
fMangual	1	0	1	0	0	0
Totals	34	3	10	27	18	1

```
Cincinnati .......... 0 0 0   0 0 0   0 2 0—2
Oakland .............. 0 0 0   0 1 0   0 0 2—3
```

gOne out when winning run scored.

aSacrificed for Gullett in eighth. bSingled for Hendrick in ninth. cRan for Marquez in ninth. dSingled for Green in ninth. eRan for Mincher in ninth. fSingled for Fingers in ninth. Runs batted in—Tenace, Tolan 2, Mincher, Mangual. Two-base hits—Green, Tolan. Home run—Tenace. Stolen base—Bench. Caught stealing—Perez. Sacrifice hit—Javier. Double plays—Concepcion and

Perez; Holtzman, Green and Hegan. Left on bases—Cincinnati 5, Oakland 8. Earned runs—Oakland 3, Cincinnati 2. Bases on balls—Off Gullett 2, off Blue 1. Strikeouts—By Gullett 4, by Holtzman 1, by Fingers 1. Pitching records—Off Gullett 1 run, 5 hits in 7 innings; off Borbon 1 run, 2 hits in 1⅓ innings; off Carroll 1 run, 3 hits in 0 innings (pitched to three batters in ninth); off Holtzman 1 run, 5 hits in 7⅔ innings; off Blue 1 run, 2 hits in ⅓ inning (pitched to one batter in ninth); off Fingers 0 runs, 0 hits in 1 inning. Winning pitcher—Fingers. Losing pitcher—Carroll. Umpires—Umont (A.L.), Engel (N.L.), Haller (A.L.), Pelekoudas (N.L.), Honochick (A.L.), Steiner (N.L.). Time—2:06. Attendance—49,410.

McGlothlin 2, off Borbon 1, off Grimsley 1, off Hunter 2, off Fingers 1. Strikeouts—By McGlothlin 3, by Hall 1 by Carroll 1, by Hunter 2, by Fingers 4. Pitching records—Off McGlothlin 4 runs, 2 hits in 3 innings (pitched to two batters in fourth); off Borbon 0 runs, 1 hit in 1 inning, off Hall 0 runs, 0 hits in 2 innings; off Carroll 0 runs, 3 hits in 1⅔ innings; off Grimsley 0 runs, 0 hits in ⅔ inning; off Billingham 0 runs, 1 hit in ⅔ inning; off Hunter 3 runs, 5 hits in 4⅔ innings; off Fingers 2 runs, 3 hits in 3⅔ innings; off Hamilton 0 runs, 0 hits in ⅔ inning. Winning pitcher—Grimsley. Save—Billingham. Losing pitcher—Fingers. Umpires—Engel (N.L.), Haller (A.L.), Pelekoudas (N.L.), Honochick (A.L.), Steiner (N.L.), Umont (A.L.). Time—2:26. Attendance—49,410.

Friday, October 20—At Oakland

Cincinnati (N.L.)	AB.	R.	H.	O.	A.	E.
Rose, lf	5	1	3	2	0	0
Morgan, 2b	3	2	0	3	2	0
Tolan, cf	4	0	2	2	0	0
Bench, c	4	0	0	6	2	0
Perez, 1b	4	0	1	10	2	0
Menke, 3b	3	1	1	2	3	0
Geronimo, rf	4	1	1	1	0	0
Chaney, ss	1	0	0	0	1	0
dHague	1	0	0	0	0	0
Carroll, p	0	0	0	1	0	0
Grimsley, p	0	0	0	0	0	0
Billingham, p	0	0	0	0	0	0
McGlothlin, p	1	0	0	0	1	0
Borbon, p	0	0	0	0	1	0
cUhlaender	1	0	0	0	0	0
Hall, p	0	0	0	0	1	0
eConcepcion, ss	2	0	0	0	0	0
Totals	33	5	8	27	13	0

Oakland (A.L.)	AB.	R.	H.	O.	A.	E.
Campaneris, ss	5	0	0	2	3	0
Alou, rf	4	0	0	1	1	1
Rudi, lf	3	0	0	4	0	0
Epstein, 1b	2	1	0	6	0	0
Hegan, 1b	1	0	1	2	0	0
Bando, 3b	3	1	1	0	1	1
Hendrick, cf	2	1	1	3	0	0
fMincher	0	0	0	0	0	0
gMangual, cf	1	0	0	0	0	0
Tenace, c	2	1	1	7	0	0
iOdom	0	0	0	0	0	0
Green, 2b	1	0	0	1	0	0
aMarquez	1	0	1	0	0	0
bLewis	0	0	0	0	0	0
Kubiak, 2b	2	0	1	1	1	0
Hunter, p	2	0	0	0	2	0
Fingers, p	0	0	0	0	1	0
Hamilton, p	0	0	0	0	0	0
hDuncan	1	0	1	0	0	0
Totals	30	4	7	27	9	2

Cincinnati	1 0 0	1 1 0	0 1 1—5
Oakland	0 3 0	1 0 0	0 0 0—4

aSingled for Green in fourth. bRan for Marquez in fourth. cGrounded out for Borbon in fifth. dGrounded out for Chaney in seventh. eFlied out for Hall in seventh. fAnnounced to bat for Hendrick in eighth. gGrounded out for Mincher in eighth. hSingled for Hamilton in ninth. iRan for Tenace in ninth. Runs batted in—Rose 2, Tenace 3, Menke, Marquez, Tolan 2. Two-base hit—Perez. Home runs—Rose, Tenace, Menke. Stolen bases—Tolan 2, Morgan. Sacrifice hits—Menke, Hendrick, Fingers, Grimsley. Double plays—Morgan and Bench; Alou and Tenace. Wild pitch—Fingers. Hit by pitch—By McGlothlin (Rudi). Left on bases—Cincinnati 6, Oakland 6. Earned runs—Cincinnati 5, Oakland 4. Bases on balls—Off

Saturday, October 21—At Cincinnati

Oakland (A.L.)	AB.	R.	H.	O.	A.	E.
Campaneris, ss	4	0	0	2	4	0
Alou, rf	4	0	0	1	0	0
Rudi, lf	4	0	1	1	0	0
Epstein, 1b	4	0	0	6	1	0
Bando, 3b	4	1	2	0	1	0
Mangual, cf	4	0	2	3	0	1
Tenace, c	4	0	1	8	1	0
Green, 2b	2	0	1	2	1	0
aMarquez	1	0	0	0	0	0
Kubiak, 2b	1	0	0	0	0	0
Blue, p	1	0	0	0	1	0
Locker, p	0	0	0	0	0	0
bMincher	0	0	0	0	0	0
cDuncan	1	0	0	0	0	0
Hamilton, p	0	0	0	0	0	0
Horlen, p	0	0	0	1	0	0
Totals	34	1	7	24	9	1

Cincinnati (N.L.)	AB.	R.	H.	O.	A.	E.
Rose, lf	3	1	0	3	0	0
Morgan, 2b	5	1	2	2	1	0
Tolan, cf	4	2	2	3	0	0
Bench, c	2	2	1	5	0	0
Perez, 1b	3	0	1	10	1	0
McRae, rf	3	1	1	2	0	0
Geronimo, rf	1	0	1	0	0	0
Menke, 3b	4	0	0	1	2	0
Concepcion, ss	3	1	2	1	3	0
Nolan, p	1	0	0	0	1	0
Grimsley, p	1	0	0	0	0	0
Borbon, p	0	0	0	0	0	0
Hall, p	2	0	0	0	0	0
Totals	32	8	10	27	8	0

Oakland	0 0 0	0 1 0	0 0 0—1
Cincinnati	0 0 0	1 1 1	5 0 *—8

aGrounded into forceout for Green in seventh. bAnnounced to bat for Locker in seventh. cStruck out for Mincher in seventh. Runs batted in—Bench, Green, Concepcion, Perez, Morgan, Tolan 2, Geronimo 2. Two-base hits—Morgan, Green, McRae. Three-base hit—Concepcion. Home run—Bench. Stolen bases—Tolan 2, Concepcion. Caught stealing—Rose. Sacrifice fly—Concepcion. Wild pitch—Horlen. Left on bases—Oakland 7, Cincinnati 6. Earned runs—Cincinnati 8, Oakland 1. Bases on balls—Off Blue 2, off Hamilton 1, off Horlen 2, off Grimsley 1. Strikeouts—By Blue 4, by Hamilton 1, by Horlen 1, by Nolan 3, by Hall 1. Pitching records—Off Blue 3 runs, 4 hits in 5⅔ innings; off Locker 0 runs, 1 hit in ⅓ inning; off Hamilton 4 runs, 3 hits in ⅔ inning; off Horlen 1 run, 2 hits in 1⅓ innings; off Nolan 1 run, 3 hits in 4⅔ innings; off Grimsley 0 runs, 1 hit in 1 inning; off Borbon 0 runs, 1 hit in 1 inning, off Hall 0 runs, 2 hits in 2⅓ innings. Winning pitcher—Grimsley. Save—Hall. Losing pitcher—Blue. Umpires—

Haller (A.L.), Pelekoudas (N.L.), Honochick (A.L.), Steiner (N.L.), Umont (A.L.), Engel (N.L.). Time—2:21. Attendance—52,737.

lekoudas (N.L.), Honochick (A.L.), Steiner (N.L.), Umont (A.L.), Engel (N.L.), Haller (A.L.). Time—2:50. Attendance—56,040.

Sunday, October 22—At Cincinnati

Oakland (A.L.)	AB.	R.	H.	O.	A.	E.
Campaneris, ss	4	1	2	6	1	1
Mangual, cf	4	1	0	3	0	0
Rudi, lf	3	0	0	5	0	0
Tenace, 1b	3	0	2	3	1	0
bLewis	0	1	0	0	0	0
Hegan, 1b	1	0	0	1	0	0
Bando, 3b	4	0	1	1	1	0
Alou, rf	3	0	0	2	0	0
Duncan, c	3	0	0	5	1	0
Green, 2b	4	0	1	0	1	0
Odom, p	2	0	0	1	0	0
Hunter, p	0	0	0	0	0	0
Holtzman, p	0	0	0	0	0	0
Fingers, p	1	0	0	0	0	0
Totals	32	3	6	27	5	1

Cincinnati (N.L.)	AB.	R.	H.	O.	A.	E.
Rose, lf	5	1	2	1	0	0
Morgan, 2b	3	0	1	3	3	0
Tolan, cf	2	0	0	0	0	1
Foster, rf	0	0	0	0	0	0
dJavier	0	0	0	0	0	0
eHague, rf	1	0	0	0	0	0
Bench, c	3	0	0	10	1	0
Perez, 1b	2	1	1	10	1	0
Menke, 3b	4	0	0	0	7	0
Geronimo, rf-cf	3	0	0	2	0	0
Concepcion, ss	3	0	0	0	2	1
Billingham, p	1	0	0	1	0	0
aMcRae	0	0	0	0	0	0
Borbon, p	0	0	0	0	0	0
Carroll, p	0	0	0	0	1	0
Grimsley, p	0	0	0	0	0	0
cUhlaender	1	0	0	0	0	0
Hall, p	0	0	0	0	1	0
fChaney	0	0	0	0	0	0
Totals	28	2	4	27	16	2

Oakland	1 0 0	0 0 2	0 0 0	—3
Cincinnati	0 0 0	0 1 0	0 1 0	—2

aHit sacrifice fly for Billingham in fifth. bRan for Tenace in sixth. cFlied out for Grimsley in seventh. dAnnounced to bat for Foster in eighth. ePopped out for Javier in eighth. fHit by pitch for Hall in ninth. Runs batted in—Tenace 2, McRae, Bando, Perez. Two-base hits—Perez, Tenace, Bando, Morgan. Stolen base—Bench. Caught stealing—Duncan, Morgan. Sacrifice hits—Mangual, Campaneris. Sacrifice flies—McRae, Perez. Double play—Campaneris and Tenace. Wild pitch—Hunter. Hit by pitch—By Fingers (Chaney). Left on bases—Cincinnati 8, Oakland 8. Earned runs—Oakland 2, Cincinnati 2. Bases on balls—Off Odom 4, off Hunter 1, off Fingers 1, off Billingham 1, off Carroll 2, off Grimsley 1. Strikeouts—By Odom 2, by Hunter 3, by Billingham 4, by Carroll 1, by Grimsley 1, by Hall 3. Pitching records—Off Odom 1 run, 2 hits in 4⅓ innings; off Hunter 1 run, 1 hit in 2⅔ innings (pitched to one batter in eighth); off Holtzman 0 runs, 1 hit in 0 innings (pitched to one batter in eighth); off Fingers 0 runs, 0 hits in 2 innings; off Billingham 1 run, 2 hits in 5 innings; off Borbon 2 runs, 3 hits in ⅔ inning; off Carroll 0 runs, 0 hits in 1 inning; off Grimsley 0 runs, 0 hits in ⅓ inning; off Hall 0 runs, 1 hit in 2 innings. Winning pitcher—Hunter. Save—Fingers. Losing pitcher—Borbon. Umpires—Pe-

COMPOSITE BATTING AVERAGES
Oakland Athletics

Player-Position	G.	AB.	R.	H.	2B.	3B.	HR.	RBI.	BA.
Mincher, ph	3	1	0	1	0	0	0	1	1.000
Marquez, ph	5	5	0	3	0	0	0	1	.600
Tenace, c-1b	7	23	5	8	1	0	4	9	.348
Green, 2b	7	18	0	6	2	0	0	1	.333
Kubiak, 2b	4	3	0	1	0	0	0	0	.333
Mangual, ph-cf	4	10	1	3	0	0	0	1	.300
Bando, 3b	7	26	2	7	1	0	0	1	.269
Rudi, lf	7	25	1	6	0	0	1	1	.240
Hegan, 1b-ph	6	5	0	1	0	0	0	0	.200
Duncan, ph-c	3	5	0	1	0	0	0	0	.200
Hunter, p	3	5	0	1	0	0	0	1	.200
Campaneris, ss	7	28	1	5	0	0	0	0	.179
Hendrick, cf	5	15	3	2	0	0	0	0	.133
Alou, rf	7	24	0	1	0	0	0	0	.042
Fingers, p	6	1	0	0	0	0	0	0	.000
Blue, p	4	1	0	0	0	0	0	0	.000
Odom, p-pr	4	4	0	0	0	0	0	0	.000
Holtzman, p	3	5	0	0	0	0	0	0	.000
Epstein, 1b	6	16	1	0	0	0	0	0	.000
Lewis, pr	6	0	2	0	0	0	0	0	.000
Hamilton, p	2	0	0	0	0	0	0	0	.000
Horlen, p	1	0	0	0	0	0	0	0	.000
Locker, p	1	0	0	0	0	0	0	0	.000
Totals	7	220	16	46	4	0	5	16	.209

Cincinnati Reds

Player-Position	G.	AB.	R.	H.	2B.	3B.	HR.	RBI.	BA.
McRae, ph-rf	5	9	1	4	1	0	0	2	.444
Perez, 1b	7	23	3	10	2	0	0	2	.435
Co'pcion, ss-pr-ph	6	13	2	4	0	1	0	2	.308
Tolan, cf	7	26	2	7	1	0	0	6	.269
Bench, c	7	23	4	6	1	0	1	1	.261
Uhlaender, ph	4	4	0	1	1	0	0	0	.250
Rose, lf	7	28	3	6	0	0	1	2	.214
Geronimo, rf-cf	7	19	1	3	0	0	0	3	.158
Morgan, 2b	7	24	4	3	2	0	0	1	.125
Menke, 3b	7	24	1	2	0	0	1	2	.083
McGlothlin, p	1	1	0	0	0	0	0	0	.000
Gullett, p	1	2	0	0	0	0	0	0	.000
Grimsley, p	4	2	0	0	0	0	0	0	.000
Hall, p	4	2	0	0	0	0	0	0	.000
Javier, ph	4	2	0	0	0	0	0	0	.000
Nolan, p	2	3	0	0	0	0	0	0	.000
Hague, ph-rf	3	3	0	0	0	0	0	0	.000
Billingham, p	3	5	0	0	0	0	0	0	.000
Chaney, ss-ph	4	7	0	0	0	0	0	0	.000
Foster, pr-rf	2	0	0	0	0	0	0	0	.000
Carroll, p	5	0	0	0	0	0	0	0	.000
Borbon, p	6	0	0	0	0	0	0	0	.000
Totals	7	220	21	46	8	1	3	21	.209

COMPOSITE PITCHING AVERAGES
Oakland Athletics

Pitcher	G.	IP.	H.	R.	E.	SO.	BB.	W.	L.	ERA.
Locker	1	⅓	1	0	0	0	0	0	0	0.00
Odom	2	11⅓	5	2	2	13	6	0	1	1.59
Fingers	6	10⅓	4	2	2	11	4	1	1	1.74
Holtzman	3	12⅔	11	3	3	4	3	1	0	2.13
Hunter	3	16	12	5	5	11	6	2	0	2.81
Blue	4	8⅔	8	4	4	5	5	0	1	4.15
Horlen	1	1⅓	2	1	1	1	2	0	0	6.75
Hamilton	2	1⅓	3	4	4	1	1	0	0	27.00
Totals	7	62	46	21	21	46	27	4	3	3.05

Saves—Fingers 2, Blue.

Cincinnati Reds

Pitcher	G.	IP.	H.	R.	E.	SO.	BB.	W.	L.	ERA.
Billingham	3	13⅔	6	1	0	11	4	1	0	0.00
Hall	4	8⅓	6	0	0	7	2	0	0	0.00
Gullett	1	7	5	1	1	4	2	0	1	1.29
Carroll	5	5⅔	6	1	1	3	4	0	1	1.59
Grimsley	4	7	7	2	2	2	3	2	1	2.57
Nolan	2	10⅔	7	4	4	3	2	0	1	3.38
Borbon	6	7	7	3	3	4	2	0	1	3.86
McGlothlin	1	3	2	4	4	3	2	0	0	12.00
Totals	7	62⅓	46	16	15	37	21	3	4	2.17

Saves—Carroll, Billingham, Hall.

SERIES OF 1973

	W.	L.	Pct.
Oakland A. L.	4	3	.571
New York N. L.	3	4	.429

The Oakland Athletics, despite being beset by turmoil and strife, became the first team since the New York Yankees of 1961 and 1962 to win two successive World Series when they defeated the New York Mets, surprise winners of the National League pennant, in a seven-game set.

The A's were favored to win the American League West and they did it in handy fashion. They then went on to down the East Division winners, the Baltimore Orioles, in five games.

The Mets, at one time 12 games off the pace in the National League East and, as late as August 5 in last place, 11½ games out of first, won 20 of their final 28 games to capture their division crown on the day following the last day of the regular season schedule. They then upset the West Division winners, the Cincinnati Reds, the finale of the five-game playoff series being marked by riotous scenes at Shea Stadium.

The Mets had won their divisional laurels with a record of 82-79 and their won-lost percentage of .509 was the lowest ever taken by any team into a World Series.

Two lefties, Jon Matlack and Ken Holtzman, were the opposing pitchers in the first game, played at the Oakland-Alameda County Coliseum. Matlack was in peak form and the A's got only three hits off him. Unfortunately for the New York hurler, all three hits came in the same inning and, sandwiched around an error, proved his undoing. With two out and nobody on base in the third inning, Holtzman doubled down the left-field foul line. Bert Campaneris then grounded to second baseman Felix Millan who let the ball go through his legs, enabling Holtzman to score. Campaneris then stole second and scored on Joe Rudi's single. Sal Bando added a harmless single but the damage was done. The two runs were all the A's needed.

The Mets spent the afternoon hitting line drives all over the park, but their only score came in the fourth inning on a double by Cleon Jones and a single by John Milner. Rollie Fingers relieved Holtzman at the start of the sixth inning and, with ninth-inning help from Darold Knowles, managed to prevent any further scoring. The Series, incidentally, was the second successive one in which no starting pitcher was able to negotiate a complete game.

The second game saw a Series record tied when no less than 11 pitchers trudged to the mound and the game resembled one between the single men and the married men at a company picnic, rather than a contest for baseball's highest prize. The game also marked the last decisive appearances of the great Willie Mays as a playing factor in a major league game.

Lefthander Jerry Koosman started for the Mets but wasn't around very long, departing in the third inning after being racked for two doubles and two triples and permitting three runs.

Koosman's opponent, another lefty, Vida Blue, wasn't much better. After yielding homers in the early innings to Jones and Wayne Garrett, he went to the showers in the sixth. The highlight play of the inning came with the bases loaded, one out, the score 4-3 in favor of the Mets. Knowles was pitching and pinch-hitter Jim Beauchamp was at the plate. Beauchamp bounced an easy grounder back to the mound for what was apparently a double play. However, Knowles threw the ball wildly past catcher Ray Fosse and two runs scored.

The A's picked up a run in the seventh inning, the result of a double by Reggie Jackson following a hit batsman and a walk, but going into the bottom of the ninth they still trailed the Mets by two runs.

Mays had entered the game in the top of the ninth as a pinch-runner for Rusty Staub. When the Mets took the field, Don Hahn moved from center field to right and Mays went to center field, as he had been doing since he first started in the major leagues in 1951.

Pinch-hitter Deron Johnson led off with a line shot to center field. It was the kind of a ball that ten years earlier Mays would have caught without any trouble. But this time the 42-year-old super star was unequal to the task and he fell on his face going for it and the ball fell for a double. Pitcher Tug McGraw retired the next two batters but then walked Bando and Jackson singled to right. Tenace lined a single to left and the score was tied and the game went into extra innings.

The game's action reached its climax in the 12th inning. Bud Harrelson led off the frame with a double to right-center off reliever Fingers. McGraw attempted a sacrifice and popped a bunt over the charging third baseman Bando's head for a single, Harrelson going to third. When Garrett struck out and Millan popped out, it appeared that Fingers would get out of the inning without any damage. But the next hitter was Mays and the aging veteran, who earlier in the game had appeared to be a tragic figure both in the field and on the base paths, still had one hit left in his bat. It came on the second pitch and was a single up the middle, cracking the tie and opening the door for some low comedy which was to quickly follow.

After Jones lined a single to left, loading the bases, Paul Lindblad replaced Fingers. Milner hit a routine grounder to second baseman Mike Andrews which Andrews let go through his legs and two more runs crossed the plate. Jerry Grote, the next batter, also hit a grounder to Andrews and this play resulted in another run when the second sacker's throw pulled Tenace off the bag at first. The inning mercifully ended when Hahn grounded out to Bando.

The A's scored a run in the bottom of the inning, drove McGraw to cover and had the bases loaded with two out when George Stone finally induced Campaneris to ground out to shortstop and end the game. The game lasted four hours and 13 minutes and its conclusion brought a sigh of relief to all concerned.

The next day, a Monday, was supposed to be a day of rest but it brought little rest to the Athletics. Their owner, the ebullient Charles O. Finley, "fired" Andrews for his two errors and had him sent home. This drew the wrath of the other A's players and also the attention of Commissioner Bowie Kuhn who directed Finley to reinstate Andrews and issued a stern rebuke to the embattled magnate.

The scene shifted to New York's Shea Stadium for the third game, played under the arcs, and the opposing pitchers were the aces of their respective clubs, Tom Seaver of the Mets and Jim Hunter of the A's. They had pitched the fifth game of their league playoffs and so were rested until this point.

The Mets got on the board early when Garrett hit Hunter's second pitch of the game into the right-field stands for a home run. Millan followed with a single, went to third when Staub singled on a hit and run play and scored on a wild pitch. But that was the end of the Mets' scoring for the evening.

Seaver pitched powerfully until the sixth frame when the visitors finally broke his service, one run scoring on doubles by Bando and Tenace. Oakland tied the game in the eighth when Campaneris singled, stole second and scored on Joe Rudi's single.

In the bottom of the eighth, Seaver left the game for a pinch-hitter. He had complained to Manager Yogi Berra that he felt "tired." His place on the hill was taken by veteran lefty Ray Sadecki. Sadecki ran into trouble immediately and was replaced by McGraw who shut off a budding Oakland rally.

The Mets left two men on base in the ninth and the A's did likewise in the top of the tenth.

But Oakland scored the winning run in the eleventh. A walk to Ted Kubiak, a passed ball on a strikeout and Campaneris' single produced the decisive tally. The Mets got a man as far as second with one out in the bottom of the inning. Fingers relieved Lindblad and slammed the door to give the A's a 2-1 lead in Series games.

The fourth game marked the celebration of Rusty Staub Night at Shea Stadium. The Mets' right fielder had four hits, including a home run, and a walk in five visits to the plate and drove in five of his team's six runs as the National Leaguers evened up the Series at 2-2 with a 6-1 triumph.

Staub's home run came in the bottom of the first and followed a single by Garrett and a safe bunt by Millan. After an out, a base on balls and another single, Oakland starter Holtzman found himself under the showers and replaced by John Odom.

Oakland was able to muster only a run in the fourth inning, that being produced by an error, a single by Jackson and a ground out.

But the Mets added three more runs in their half of the frame on a single by Hahn, a single by Harrelson, a hit batsman, an error and Staub's second hit of the game. The latter blow drove in the final two tallies.

Matlack, on the mound for the home team, pitched eight strong innings and Sadecki mopped up in the final frame.

The Mets assumed a 3-2 Series lead in the fifth game through the medium of brilliant pitching by Koosman and McGraw and a couple of timely hits. The score was 2-0.

The first Met run came in the bottom of the second when Jones lined a double to left and immediately scored on Milner's ground single to right. The other run came in the sixth when Grote singled to left and Hahn tripled to left-center.

Koosman held the A's to only two hits going into the seventh inning but walked Tenace and gave up a double to Fosse after one out. He was replaced by McGraw, who walked pinch-hitter Johnson to load the bases and then pitched out of the trouble by getting pinch-hitter Mangual to pop out to Harrelson at shortstop and striking out Campaneris. The A's were held hitless in the final two innings and the Mets seemed on their way to baseball's pinnacle.

But, after a day of travel and a return to the West Coast, the A's seemed a different club. The bat of Reggie Jackson, dormant except for an outburst in the second game, came to life and propelled the American Leaguers to a 3-1 victory and set up a seventh game with the crown squarely on the line.

The victim of Jackson's hitting was Met ace Seaver. In the first inning with Joe Rudi on first as the result of a single, and two out, Jackson lined a double to left-center to score Rudi. In the third inning, Jackson lined a double to right-center to score Bando who had reached base on a two-out single.

The two runs were all the A's could muster off Seaver, but they were enough. Hunter pitched a strong game for Oakland until the eighth when he was taken out after giving up a one-out single to pinch-hitter Boswell. His place was taken by Knowles, who promptly gave up singles to

Garrett and Millan for one run. But the lefthander struck out Staub on three pitches. Fingers then took over the pitching chores and the Mets' scoring was over for the afternoon.

The Athletics added an insurance run in the bottom of the inning on Jackson's third hit, a single on which he reached third base as Hahn misplayed the ball, and pinch-hitter Jesus Alou's sacrifice fly.

The seventh game saw the eruption of Oakland's power. Going into the final contest, the American Leaguers had been unable to hit a single homer. But they did in the most important game of all and it sealed the doom of the Mets.

The opposing pitchers were Matlack and Holtzman and a pitchers' duel seemed likely until a sudden explosion took place in the bottom of the third. With one out, Holtzman doubled down the left-field foul line. The next batter, Campaneris homered over the right-field fence. Rudi then lined a single to center. The attack was temporarily halted when Bando popped out. But Jackson then blasted a long home run into the right-center stands to make the score 4-0 as Matlack exited and Harry Parker come on to pitch for the New Yorkers.

Holtzman pitched steadily until the sixth inning when successive doubles by Millan and Staub gave the Mets their first tally of the game and brought on Fingers from the bullpen.

After leaving two runners stranded in the seventh, the Mets made their final gesture in the ninth. Milner led off with a walk. After Grote flied out, Hahn singled. Harrelson tried to beat out a bunt, but was thrown out, leaving runners on second and third. Pinch-hitter Ed Kranepool reached first when Tenace bobbled his grounder, Milner scoring on the play. The Mets now had the tying run at the plate in the person of third baseman Garrett. Knowles replaced Fingers on the mound for Oakland and got Garrett to pop out to Campaneris and close out the 1973 baseball season.

The box scores follow:

Saturday, October 13—At Oakland

New York (N.L.)	AB.	R.	H.	O.	A.	E.
Garrett, 3b	5	0	0	0	0	0
Millan, 2b	4	0	1	1	2	1
Mays, cf	4	0	1	0	0	1
Jones, lf	4	1	2	3	0	0
Milner, 1b	4	0	2	11	0	0
Grote, c	4	0	0	5	2	0
Hahn, rf	2	0	0	0	0	0
cKranepool	1	0	0	0	0	0
Harrelson, ss	2	0	0	4	6	0
dHodges	0	0	0	0	0	0
eMartinez	0	0	0	0	0	0
Matlack, p	0	0	0	0	0	0
bBoswell	1	0	1	0	0	0
McGraw, p	0	0	0	0	0	0
fStaub	0	0	0	0	0	0
gBeauchamp	1	0	0	0	0	0
Totals	32	1	7	24	10	2

Oakland (A.L.)	AB.	R.	H.	O.	A.	E.
Campaneris, ss	4	1	1	3	1	0
Rudi, lf	3	0	1	0	0	0
Bando, 3b	3	0	1	1	3	0
Jackson, cf-rf	3	0	0	4	0	0
Tenace, 1b	3	0	0	11	0	0
Alou, rf	3	0	0	1	0	0
Davalillo, cf	0	0	0	0	0	0
Fosse, c	3	0	0	4	1	0
Green, 2b	2	0	0	2	3	0
Holtzman, p	1	1	1	1	3	0
aMangual	1	0	0	0	0	0
Fingers, p	1	0	0	0	0	0
Knowles, p	0	0	0	0	0	0
Totals	27	2	4	27	11	0

New York........ 0 0 0   1 0 0   0 0 0—1
Oakland.......... 0 0 2   0 0 0   0 0 *—2

aLined out for Holtzman in fifth. bSingled for Matlack in seventh. cLined out for Hahn in ninth. dWalked for Harrelson in ninth. eRan for Hodges in ninth. fAnnounced to bat for McGraw in ninth. gPopped out for Staub in ninth. Runs batted in—Rudi, Milner. Two-base hits—Holtzman, Jones. Three-base hit—Millan. Stolen base—Campaneris. Caught stealing—Green. Sacrifice hits—Matlack, Rudi. Double plays—Holtzman and Tenace; Green, Campaneris and Tenace. Passed ball—Fosse. Left on bases—New York 9, Oakland 5. Earned run—New York 1. Bases on balls—Off Matlack 2, off McGraw 1, off Holtzman 3, off Fingers 1. Struck out—By Matlack 3, by McGraw 1, by Holtzman 2, by Fingers 3. Pitching records—Off Matlack 2 runs and 3 hits in 6 innings; off McGraw 0 runs and 1 hit in 2 innings; off Holtzman 1 run and 4 hits in 5 innings; off Fingers 0 runs and 3 hits in 3⅓ innings; off Knowles 0 runs and 0 hits in ⅔ inning. Winning pitcher—Holtzman. Losing pitcher—Matlack. Save—Knowles. Umpires—Springstead (A.L.), Donatelli (N.L.), Neudecker (A.L.), Pryor (N.L.), Goetz (A.L.), Wendelstedt (N.L.). Time—2:26. Attendance—46,021.

Sunday October 14—At Oakland

New York (N.L.)	AB.	R.	H.	O.	A.	E.
Garrett, 3b	6	1	1	1	5	0
Millan, 2b	6	0	0	4	5	0
Staub, rf	5	0	1	0	0	0
gMays, cf	2	1	1	1	0	0
Jones, lf	5	3	3	0	0	0
Milner, 1b	6	1	2	15	0	0
Grote, c	6	1	2	15	2	0
Hahn, cf-rf	7	1	1	0	0	0
Harrelson, ss	6	1	3	0	4	0
Koosman, p	1	0	0	0	0	1
Sadecki, p	0	0	0	0	1	0
aTheodore	1	0	0	0	0	0
Parker, p	0	0	0	0	0	0
bKranepool	0	0	0	0	0	0
cBeauchamp	1	0	0	0	0	0
McGraw, p	2	1	1	0	2	0
Stone, p	0	0	0	0	0	0
Totals	54	10	15	36	19	1

Oakland (A.L.)	AB.	R.	H.	O.	A.	E.
Campaneris, ss	6	2	1	0	6	0
Rudi, lf	5	1	2	3	1	0
Bando, 3b	5	2	1	1	4	1
Jackson, cf	6	1	4	3	0	0
Tenace, 1b	3	0	1	13	0	1
Alou, rf	6	0	3	2	0	0
Fosse, c	5	0	0	11	0	0
Green, 2b	2	0	0	2	1	0
dMangual	1	0	0	0	0	0
Kubiak, 2b	0	0	0	0	0	0

1973 WORLD SERIES

	AB.	R.	H.	O.	A.	E.
fAndrews, 2b	2	0	0	1	0	2
Blue, p	2	0	0	0	0	0
Pina, p	0	0	0	0	0	0
Knowles, p	0	0	0	0	0	1
eConigliaro	1	0	0	0	0	0
Odom, p	0	0	0	0	0	0
hJohnson	1	0	1	0	0	0
iLewis	0	1	0	0	0	0
Fingers, p	1	0	0	0	1	0
Lindblad, p	0	0	0	0	0	0
jDavalillo	1	0	0	0	0	0
Totals	47	7	13	36	13	5

New York............0 1 1   0 0 4   0 0 0   0 0 4—10
Oakland...............2 1 0   0 0 0   1 0 2   0 0 1— 7

aGrounded out for Sadecki in fifth. bAnnounced to bat for Parker in sixth. cSafe on error for Kranepool in sixth. dStruck out for Green in sixth. eGrounded out for Knowles in seventh. fGrounded out for Kubiak in eighth. gRan for Staub in ninth. hDoubled for Odom in ninth. iRan for Johnson in ninth. jPopped out for Lindblad in twelfth. Runs batted in—Bando, Alou 2, Rudi, Jackson 2, Tenace, Jones, Garrett, Hahn, Harrelson, Mays. Two-base hits—Rudi, Alou, Jackson, Johnson, Harrelson. Three-base hits—McGraw. Home runs—Jones, Garrett. Stolen base—Campaneris. Caught stealing—Rudi, Tenace. Sacrifice hit—McGraw. Double plays—Garrett, Millan and Milner; Rudi and Fosse. Left on bases—New York 15, Oakland 12. Earned runs—New York 5, Oakland 7. Bases on balls—Off Koosman 3, off McGraw 3, off Stone 1, off Blue 2, off Knowles 2. Struck out—By Koosman 4, by Sadecki 3, by McGraw 8, by Blue 4, by Knowles 2, by Odom 2, by Fingers 2. Pitching records—Off Koosman 3 runs and 6 hits in 2⅓ innings; off Sadecki 0 runs and 0 hits in 1⅔ innings; off Parker 0 runs and 1 hit in 1 inning; off McGraw 4 runs and 5 hits in 6 innings (pitched to two batters in twelfth); off Blue 4 runs and 4 hits in 5⅓ innings; off Pina 2 runs and 2 hits in 0 innings (pitched to three batters in sixth); off Knowles 0 runs and 1 hit in 1⅔ innings; off Odom 0 runs and 2 hits in 2 innings; off Fingers 4 runs and 6 hits in 2⅔ innings; off Lindblad 0 runs and 0 hits in ⅓ inning. Hit by pitcher—By Pina (Grote), by McGraw (Campaneris), by Fingers (Jones). Winning pitcher—McGraw. Losing pitcher—Fingers. Save—Stone. Umpires—Donatelli (N.L.), Neudecker (A.L.), Pryor (N.L.), Goetz (A.L.), Wendelstedt (N.L.), Springstead (A.L.). Time—4:13. Attendance—49,151.

Tuesday, October 16—At New York

Oakland (A.L.)	AB.	R.	H.	O.	A.	E.
Campaneris, ss	6	1	3	2	7	0
Rudi, lf	5	0	2	7	0	0
Bando, 3b	4	1	2	0	1	0
Jackson, rf	5	0	0	2	0	0
Tenace, 1b-c	3	0	1	4	0	0
Davalillo, cf-1b	5	0	1	7	0	0
Fosse, c	2	0	0	5	0	0
aBourque, 1b	2	0	1	2	0	0
eLewis	0	0	0	0	0	0
Lindblad, p	1	0	0	0	0	0
Fingers, p	0	0	0	0	0	0
Green, 2b	2	0	0	0	1	0
bAlou	1	0	0	0	0	0
Kubiak, 2b	1	1	0	2	2	0
Hunter, p	2	0	0	0	2	1
cJohnson	1	0	0	0	0	0
Knowles, p	0	0	0	0	0	0
fMangual, cf	2	0	0	1	0	0
Totals	42	3	10	33	12	1

New York (N.L.)	AB.	R.	H.	O.	A.	E.
Garrett, 3b	4	1	2	1	2	0
Millan, 2b	5	1	2	3	2	2
Staub, rf	6	0	2	2	0	0
Jones, lf	5	0	0	2	1	0
Milner, 1b	3	0	1	5	1	0
Grote, c	5	0	0	15	0	0
Hahn, cf	5	0	1	4	1	0
Harrelson, ss	5	0	2	1	3	0
Seaver, p	3	0	0	0	0	0
dBeauchamp	1	0	0	0	0	0
Sadecki, p	0	0	0	0	0	0
McGraw, p	0	0	0	0	1	0
gMays	1	0	0	0	0	0
Parker, p	0	0	0	0	0	0
Totals	43	2	10	33	11	2

Oakland............... 0 0 0   0 0 1   0 1 0   0 1—3
New York............ 2 0 0   0 0 0   0 0 0   0 0—2

aFlied out for Fosse in seventh. bGrounded out for Green in seventh. cStruck out for Hunter in seventh. dFlied out for Seaver in eighth. eRan for Bourque in ninth. fStruck out for Knowles in ninth. gGrounded into force out for McGraw in tenth. Runs batted in—Garrett, Tenace, Rudi, Campaneris. Two-base hits—Rudi, Hahn, Bando, Tenace, Staub. Home run—Garrett. Stolen base—Campaneris. Sacrifice hits—Bando, Millan. Passed ball—Grote. Left on bases—Oakland 10, New York 14. Earned runs—Oakland 2, New York 2. Bases on balls—Off Hunter 3, off Knowles 1, off Lindblad 1, off Seaver 1, off McGraw 1, off Parker 1. Strikeouts—By Hunter 5, by Seaver 12, by McGraw 1, by Parker 1. Pitching records—Off Hunter 2 runs and 7 hits in 6 innings; off Knowles 0 runs and 0 hits in 2 innings; off Lindblad 0 runs and 3 hits in 2 innings (pitched to one batter in eleventh); off Fingers 0 runs and 0 hits in 1 inning; off Seaver 2 runs and 7 hits in 8 innings; off Sadecki 0 runs and 1 hit in 0 innings (pitched to two batters in ninth); off McGraw 0 runs and 1 hit in 2 innings; off Parker 1 run and 1 hit in 1 inning. Wild pitch—Hunter. Winning pitcher—Lindblad. Losing pitcher—Parker. Save—Fingers. Umpires—Neudecker (A.L.), Pryor (N.L.), Goetz (A.L.), Wendelstedt (N.L.), Springstead (A.L.), Donatelli (N.L.). Time—3:15. Attendance—54,817.

Wednesday, October 17—At New York

Oakland (A.L.)	AB.	R.	H.	O.	A.	E.
Campaneris, ss	4	0	0	1	2	0
Rudi, lf	4	0	1	1	1	0
Bando, 3b	3	1	0	3	4	0
Jackson, cf	4	0	1	0	0	0
Tenace, 1b	3	0	1	12	0	0
Alou, rf	4	0	0	1	0	0
Fosse, c	4	0	1	4	2	0
Green, 2b	1	0	0	1	3	1
aMangual	1	0	0	0	0	0
Kubiak, 2b	1	0	0	1	3	0
dJohnson	1	0	1	0	0	0
Holtzman, p	0	0	0	0	0	0
Odom, p	1	0	0	0	1	0
Knowles, p	0	0	0	0	1	0
bConigliaro	1	0	0	0	0	0
Pina, p	0	0	0	0	0	0
cAndrews	1	0	0	0	0	0
Lindblad, p	0	0	0	0	0	0
eDavalillo	0	0	0	0	0	0
Totals	33	1	5	24	17	1

New York (N.L.)	AB.	R.	H.	O.	A.	E.
Garrett, 3b	4	2	1	0	4	1
Millan, 2b	5	1	1	4	1	0
Staub, rf	4	1	4	1	0	0
Jones, lf	3	0	1	2	0	0
Theodore, lf	1	0	0	1	0	0

	AB.	R.	H.	O.	A.	E.
Milner, 1b	3	0	0	9	0	0
Grote, c	4	0	3	7	0	0
Hahn, cf	4	1	1	2	0	0
Harrelson, ss	2	1	1	1	3	0
Matlack, p	3	0	1	0	1	0
Sadecki, p	0	0	0	0	0	0
Totals	33	6	13	27	9	1

Oakland	0 0 0	1 0 0	0 0 0—1
New York	3 0 0	3 0 0	0 0 *—6

aPopped out for Green in fifth. bFlied out for Knowles in fifth. cGrounded out for Pina in eighth. dSingled for Kubiak in ninth. eWalked for Lindblad in ninth. Runs batted in—Staub 5, Tenace. Home run—Staub. Double plays—Bando, Green and Tenace; Knowles, Fosse and Tenace; Kubiak and Tenace. Left on bases—Oakland 9, New York 10. Earned runs—Oakland 1, New York 5. Bases on balls—Off Holtzman 1, off Odom 2, off Knowles 1, off Pina 2, off Matlack 2, off Sadecki 1. Strikeouts—By Knowles 1, by Lindblad 1, by Matlack 5, by Sadecki 2. Pitching records—Off Holtzman 3 runs and 4 hits in ⅓ inning; off Odom 2 runs and 3 hits in 2⅔ innings (pitched to two batters in fourth); off Knowles 1 run and 1 hit in 1 inning; off Pina 0 runs and 4 hits in 3 innings; off Lindblad 0 runs and 1 hit in 1 inning; off Matlack 1 run and 3 hits in 8 innings; off Sadecki 0 runs and 2 hits in 1 inning. Wild pitch—Odom. Hit by pitcher—By Knowles (Garrett), by Matlack (Campaneris). Winning pitcher—Matlack. Losing pitcher—Holtzman. Save—Sadecki. Umpires—Pryor (N.L.), Goetz (A.L.), Wendelstedt (N.L.), Springstead (A.L.), Donatelli (N.L.), Neudecker (A.L.). Time—2:41. Attendance—54,817.

Thursday, October 18—At New York

Oakland (A.L.)	AB.	R.	H.	O.	A.	E.
Campaneris, ss	3	0	1	0	4	1
Rudi, lf	4	0	0	3	0	0
Bando, 3b	3	0	1	1	1	0
Jackson, cf	3	0	0	1	0	0
Tenace, 1b	1	0	0	7	2	0
dOdom	0	0	0	0	0	0
Bourque, 1b	0	0	0	1	1	0
Alou, rf	4	0	0	0	0	0
Fosse, c	4	0	1	6	0	0
Green, 2b	2	0	0	1	0	0
aJohnson	0	0	0	0	0	0
bLewis	0	0	0	0	0	0
Kubiak, 2b	1	0	0	2	2	0
Blue, p	2	0	0	2	1	0
Knowles, p	0	0	0	0	0	0
cMangual	1	0	0	0	0	0
Fingers, p	0	0	0	0	0	0
eConigliaro	1	0	0	0	0	0
Totals	29	0	3	24	11	1

New York (N.L.)	AB.	R.	H.	O.	A.	E.
Garrett, 3b	3	0	0	1	2	1
Millan, 2b	4	0	0	2	1	0
Staub, rf	3	0	1	0	0	0
Jones, lf	4	1	2	2	0	0
Milner, 1b	4	0	2	7	0	0
Grote, c	3	1	1	10	0	0
Hahn, cf	4	0	1	2	0	0
Harrelson, ss	2	0	0	3	4	0
Koosman, p	3	0	0	0	1	0
McGraw, p	1	0	0	0	0	0
Totals	31	2	7	27	8	1

Oakland	0 0 0	0 0 0	0 0 0—0
New York	0 1 0	0 0 1	0 0 *—2

aWalked for Green in seventh. bRan for Johnson in seventh. cPopped out for Knowles in seventh. dRan for Tenace in eighth. eStruck out for Fingers in ninth. Runs batted in—Milner, Hahn. Two-base hits—Jones, Fosse. Three-base hit—Hahn. Sacrifice hit—Grote. Double play—Millan, Harrelson and Milner. Left on bases—Oakland 9, New York 10. Earned runs—New York 2. Bases on balls—Off Blue 1, off Knowles 1, off Fingers 2, off Koosman 4, off McGraw 3. Strikeouts—By Blue 4, by Knowles 1, by Fingers 1, by Koosman 4, by McGraw 4. Pitching records—Off Blue 2 runs and 6 hits in 5⅔ innings; off Knowles 0 runs and 0 hits in ⅔ inning; off Fingers 0 runs and 1 hit in 2 innings; off Koosman 0 runs and 3 hits in 6⅓ innings; off McGraw 0 runs and 0 hits in 2⅔ innings. Wild pitch—Blue. Winning pitcher—Koosman. Losing pitcher—Blue. Save—McGraw. Umpires—Goetz (A.L.), Wendelstedt (N.L.), Springstead (A.L.), Donatelli (N.L.), Neudecker (A.L.), Pryor (N.L.). Time—2:39. Attendance—54,817.

Saturday, October 20—At Oakland

New York (N.L.)	AB.	R.	H.	O.	A.	E.
Garrett, 3b	3	0	1	0	2	1
Millan, 2b	4	0	1	2	1	0
Staub, rf	4	0	1	0	0	0
Jones, lf	4	0	0	1	0	0
Milner, 1b	4	0	1	10	0	0
Grote, c	4	0	1	7	1	0
Hahn, cf	3	0	0	4	0	1
cKranepool	1	0	0	0	0	0
Harrelson, ss	3	0	0	0	2	0
Seaver, p	2	0	0	0	2	0
aBoswell	1	1	1	0	0	0
McGraw, p	0	0	0	0	0	0
Totals	33	1	6	24	8	2

Oakland (A.L.)	AB.	R.	H.	O.	A.	E.
Campaneris, ss	4	0	0	2	4	0
Rudi, lf	3	1	1	3	0	0
Bando, 3b	4	1	1	0	0	0
Jackson, rf-cf	4	1	3	2	0	0
Tenace, c-1b	3	0	0	3	0	0
Davalillo, cf	2	0	0	6	0	0
bAlou, rf	0	0	0	1	0	0
Johnson, 1b	4	0	1	5	1	0
Fosse, c	0	0	0	0	0	0
Green, 2b	3	0	1	4	2	0
Hunter, p	3	0	0	1	0	0
Knowles, p	0	0	0	0	0	0
Fingers, p	0	0	0	0	0	0
Totals	30	3	7	27	7	0

New York	0 0 0	0 0 0	0 1 0—1
Oakland	1 0 1	0 0 0	0 1 *—3

aSingled for Seaver in eighth. bHit sacrifice fly for Davalillo in eighth. cPopped out for Hahn in ninth. Runs batted in—Jackson 2, Alou, Millan. Two-base hits—Jackson 2. Caught stealing—Tenace. Sacrifice fly—Alou. Double play—Grote and Millan. Left on bases—New York 6, Oakland 7. Earned runs—New York 1, Oakland 2. Bases on balls—Off Seaver 2, off McGraw 1, off Hunter 1. Struck out—By Seaver 6, by McGraw 1, by Hunter 1, by Knowles 1. Pitching records—Off Seaver 2 runs and 6 hits in 7 innings; off McGraw 1 run and 1 hit in 1 inning; off Hunter 1 run and 4 hits in 7⅓ innings; off Knowles 0 runs and 2 hits in ⅔ inning; off Fingers 0 runs and 0 hits in 1⅓ innings. Wild pitch—Seaver. Winning pitcher—Hunter. Losing pitcher—Seaver. Save—Fingers. Umpires—Wendelstedt (N.L.), Springstead (A.L.), Donatelli (N.L.), Neudecker (A.L.), Pryor (N.L.), Goetz (A.L.). Time—2:07. Attendance—49,333.

1974 WORLD SERIES

Sunday, October 21—At Oakland

New York (N.L.)	AB.	R.	H.	O.	A.	E.
Garrett, 3b	5	0	0	1	4	0
Millan, 2b	4	1	1	0	1	0
Staub, rf	4	0	2	2	0	0
Jones, lf	3	0	0	1	0	1
Milner, 1b	3	1	0	9	0	0
Grote, c	4	0	1	8	0	0
Hahn, cf	4	0	3	1	0	0
Harrelson, ss	4	0	0	2	2	0
Matlack, p	1	0	0	0	0	0
Parker, p	0	0	0	0	0	0
bBeauchamp	1	0	0	0	0	0
Sadecki, p	0	0	0	0	0	0
cBoswell	1	0	1	0	0	0
Stone, p	0	0	0	0	0	0
dKranepool	1	0	0	0	0	0
eMartinez	0	0	0	0	0	0
Totals	35	2	8	24	7	1

Oakland (A.L.)	AB.	R.	H.	O.	A.	E.
Campaneris, ss	4	2	3	2	4	0
Rudi, lf	3	1	2	3	0	0
Bando, 3b	4	0	0	0	1	0
Jackson, cf-rf	4	1	1	5	0	0
Tenace, c-1b	3	0	0	7	0	1
Alou, rf	1	0	0	0	0	0
aDavalillo, cf	3	0	0	2	0	0
Johnson, 1b	3	0	0	3	0	0
Fosse, c	1	0	1	2	0	0
Green, 2b	4	0	0	3	2	0
Holtzman, p	2	1	1	0	0	0
Fingers, p	1	0	1	0	1	0
Knowles, p	0	0	0	0	0	0
Totals	33	5	9	27	8	1

```
New York .............. 0 0 0   0 0 1   0 0 1—2
Oakland ................ 0 0 4   0 1 0   0 0 *—5
```

aFlied out for Alou in third. bStruck out for Parker in fifth. cSingled for Sadecki in seventh. dSafe on error for Stone in ninth. eRan for Kranepool in ninth. Runs batted in—Campaneris 2, Jackson 2, Rudi, Staub. Two-base hits—Holtzman, Millan, Staub. Home runs—Campaneris, Jackson. Double play—Bando, Campaneris and Green. Left on bases—New York 8, Oakland 6. Earned runs—New York 1, Oakland 5. Bases on balls—Off Matlack 1, off Parker 1, off Holtzman 1, off Fingers 1. Struck out—By Matlack 3, by Parker 1, by Sadecki 1, by Stone 3, by Holtzman 4, by Fingers 2. Pitching records—Off Matlack 4 runs and 4 hits in 2⅔ innings; off Parker 0 runs and 0 hits in 1⅓ innings; off Sadecki 1 run and 2 hits in 2 innings; off Stone 0 runs and 3 hits in 2 innings; off Holtzman 1 run and 5 hits in 5⅓ innings; off Fingers 1 run and 3 hits in 3⅓ innings; off Knowles 0 runs and 0 hits in ⅓ inning. Winning pitcher—Holtzman. Losing pitcher—Matlack. Umpires—Springstead (A.L.), Donatelli (N.L.), Neudecker (A.L.), Pryor (N.L.), Goetz (A.L.), Wendelstedt (N.L.). Time—2:37. Attendance—49,333.

COMPOSITE BATTING AVERAGES
Oakland Athletics

Player-Position	G.	AB.	R.	H.	2B.	3B.	HR.	RBI.	BA.
Holtzman, p	3	3	2	2	2	0	0	0	.667
Bourque, ph-1b	2	2	0	1	0	0	0	0	.500
Rudi, lf	7	27	3	9	2	0	0	4	.333
Fingers, p	6	3	0	1	0	0	0	0	.333
Jackson, cf-rf	7	29	3	9	3	1	1	6	.310
Johnson, ph-1b	6	10	0	3	1	0	0	0	.300
Campaneris, ss	7	31	6	9	0	1	1	3	.290
Bando, 3b	7	26	5	6	3	0	1	1	.231
Alou, rf-ph	7	19	0	3	1	0	0	3	.158
Fosse, c	7	19	0	3	1	0	0	0	.158
Tenace, 1b-c	7	19	0	3	1	0	0	3	.158
Da'lillo, cf-ph-1b	6	11	0	1	0	0	0	0	.091
Green, 2b	7	16	0	1	0	0	0	0	.063
Knowles, p	7	0	0	0	0	0	0	0	.000
Lewis, pr	3	0	1	0	0	0	0	0	.000
Pina, p	2	0	0	0	0	0	0	0	.000
Lindblad, p	3	1	0	0	0	0	0	0	.000
Odom, p-pr	3	1	0	0	0	0	0	0	.000
Conigliaro, ph	3	3	0	0	0	0	0	0	.000
Andrews, ph-2b	2	3	0	0	0	0	0	0	.000
Kubiak, 2b	4	3	1	0	0	0	0	0	.000
Blue, p	2	4	0	0	0	0	0	0	.000
Hunter, p	2	5	0	0	0	0	0	0	.000
Mangual, ph-cf	5	6	0	0	0	0	0	0	.000
Totals	7	241	21	51	12	3	2	20	.212

New York Mets

Player-Position	G.	AB.	R.	H.	2B.	3B.	HR.	RBI.	BA.
Boswell, ph	3	3	1	3	0	0	0	0	1.000
Staub, ph-rf	7	26	1	11	2	0	1	6	.423
McGraw, p	5	3	1	1	0	0	0	0	.333
Milner, 1b	7	27	2	8	0	0	0	2	.296
Jones, lf	7	28	5	8	2	0	1	1	.286
Mays, cf-pr-ph	3	7	1	2	0	0	0	1	.286
Grote, c	7	30	2	8	0	0	0	0	.267
Harrelson, ss	7	24	2	6	1	0	0	1	.250
Matlack, p	3	4	0	1	0	0	0	0	.250
Hahn, rf-cf	7	29	2	7	1	1	0	2	.241
Millan, 2b	7	32	3	6	1	1	0	1	.188
Garrett, 3b	7	30	4	5	0	0	2	2	.167
Martinez, pr	2	0	0	0	0	0	0	0	.000
Hodges, ph	1	0	0	0	0	0	0	0	.000
Stone, p	2	0	0	0	0	0	0	0	.000
Parker, p	3	0	0	0	0	0	0	0	.000
Sadecki, p	4	0	0	0	0	0	0	0	.000
Theodore, ph-lf	2	2	0	0	0	0	0	0	.000
Kranepool, ph	4	3	0	0	0	0	0	0	.000
Beauchamp, ph	4	4	0	0	0	0	0	0	.000
Koosman, p	2	4	0	0	0	0	0	0	.000
Seaver, p	2	5	0	0	0	0	0	0	.000
Totals	7	261	24	66	7	2	4	16	.253

COMPOSITE PITCHING AVERAGES
Oakland Athletics

Pitcher	G.	IP.	H.	R.	E.	SO.	BB.	W.	L.	ERA.
Knowles	7	6⅓	4	1	0	5	5	0	0	0.00
Lindblad	3	3⅓	4	0	0	1	1	1	0	0.00
Pina	2	3	6	2	0	0	2	0	0	0.00
Fingers	6	13⅔	13	5	1	8	4	0	1	0.66
Hunter	2	13⅓	11	3	3	6	4	1	0	2.03
Odom	2	4⅔	5	2	2	2	2	0	0	3.86
Holtzman	3	10⅔	13	5	5	6	5	2	1	4.22
Blue	2	11	10	6	6	8	3	0	1	4.91
Totals	7	66	66	24	17	36	26	4	3	2.32

Saves—Fingers 2, Knowles 2.

New York Mets

Pitcher	G.	IP.	H.	R.	E.	SO.	BB.	W.	L.	ERA.
Parker	3	3⅓	2	1	0	2	2	0	1	0.00
Stone	2	3	4	0	0	3	1	0	0	0.00
Sadecki	4	4⅔	5	1	1	6	1	0	0	1.93
Matlack	3	16⅔	10	7	4	11	5	1	2	2.16
Seaver	2	15	13	4	4	18	3	0	1	2.40
McGraw	5	13⅔	8	5	4	14	9	1	0	2.63
Koosman	2	8⅔	9	3	3	8	7	1	0	3.12
Totals	7	65	51	21	16	62	28	3	4	2.22

Saves—Stone, Sadecki, McGraw.

SERIES OF 1974

	W.	L.	Pct.
Oakland A. L.	4	1	.800
Los Angeles N. L.	1	4	.200

The Oakland Athletics won their third World Series in a row when they defeated the Los Angeles Dodgers, four games to one. Not since the New York Yankees of 1951, en route to winning five straight Series, had a team won three consecutive Classics. All of this was accomplished amidst a background of fist fights, lawsuits, threats of lawsuits, A's Owner

Charles O. Finley's egocentric actions and general disharmony.

Alvin Dark, resurrected from baseball's burial ground by Finley, was the A's manager in 1974, replacing Dick Williams, who left the A's after the conclusion of the 1973 Series. In leading his team to the flag, Dark thus joined Joe McCarthy and Yogi Berra as the only managers to win pennants in both major leagues.

The A's, never really seriously threatened, were winners in the American League's West Division by five games over the surprising Texas Rangers. In the Championship Series, Oakland polished off the Baltimore Orioles in four games. The Orioles had survived an intense dogfight in the A.L. East, narrowly prevailing over the New York Yankees.

The Dodgers raced away to a large early lead in the National League's West Division and managed to stave off a closing bid by the Cincinnati Reds. The L.A. club won the Championship Series in four games over the East Division winners, the Pittsburgh Pirates. Pittsburgh had clinched its divisional laurels the last game of the season, edging out the St. Louis Cardinals.

It was generally felt that the two best teams in baseball were facing each other and the Series was eagerly anticipated by fans throughout the country.

But before there was action on the playing field, there was action off the field. Jim Hunter, the A's ace pitcher, announced that Owner Finley owed him back salary and, unless it was paid immediately, Hunter would declare himself a free agent upon the end of the Series. Former Oakland infielder Mike Andrews, "fired" by Finley during the 1973 Series, filed a two-million dollar libel and slander suit against Finley. Two A's pitchers, Rollie Fingers and John Odom, engaged in fisticuffs in the clubhouse during a workout the day before the first game.

Nevertheless, the main action was on the field. The opposing pitchers for the opening game were A's lefty Ken Holtzman and righthander Andy Messersmith. Oakland got on the board first when Reggie Jackson, leading off the second inning, hit the ball into the left-center pavilion for a home run. The lead was increased in the top of the fifth when Holtzman doubled, moved to third on a wild pitch and scored on Bert Campaneris' squeeze bunt. Holtzman's two-base hit was noteworthy in that he hadn't batted all season because of the American League's use of the designated hitter. It recalled to mind that Holtzman had bashed a double in the first game of the 1973 Series to start the A's off to a win in that one.

A couple of Oakland errors gave the Dodgers a run in their half of the fifth. Dave Lopes was safe when Campaneris fumbled his grounder and he scored all the way from first when Jackson fumbled Bill Buckner's bouncing single to right. When Jimmy Wynn drew a base on balls following Buckner's hit, Fingers replaced Holtzman on the mound for Oakland.

The A's got an insurance run in the eighth and only a sensational play prevented further scoring. Campaneris singled and moved to second on a sacrifice. He scored when Ron Cey threw Sal Bando's grounder into right field, Bando reaching third on the play. Jackson then lifted a fly to right-center. Wynn appeared set to make the catch, but Joe Ferguson cut in front of him and threw a no-bounce strike to home plate to double Bando trying to score.

Los Angeles made its final gesture of the game in the ninth when, with two out and nobody on, Wynn hit a home run. When Steve Garvey followed with a single, Dark brought in his big ace, Hunter, to replace Fingers. Hunter then proceeded to strike out Ferguson and end the game.

Another lefty, Vida Blue, was on the mound for the A's in the second game. His mound rival was the Dodgers' most effective hurler over the last half of the season, righthander Don Sutton. The Dodgers got a run in the second inning on a walk to Cey, a bloop single by Bill Russell and another single by Steve Yeager. They added two more in the sixth when Garvey beat out an infield hit and Ferguson followed with a home run over the center-field fence.

Sutton had the A's shut out going into the ninth. Then he opened the frame by hitting Bando with a pitch. Jackson got a double on a checked swing when the ball went just inside the left-field foul line. Mike Marshall took the mound for Los Angeles and Joe Rudi delivered a single to center to score two runs. Gene Tenace struck out and then the A's made use of their "designated runner," Herb Washington, the track star. Marshall promptly picked Washington off first base and then closed out the game by striking out pinch-hitter Angel Mangual.

After a day off, the Series resumed at Oakland with a Tuesday night game. The Dodgers were forced to make a pitching gamble. With Doug Rau ineffective the last weeks of the regular season, Manager Walter Alston decided to go with the veteran lefty, Al Downing, who had won but five games during the year. Hunter was his opponent.

Downing was kayoed in the fourth inning but his support was something less than adequate. In the third inning, with one out, Bill North singled for the A's and moved to third as Cey was throwing out Campaneris after making a diving stop. Bando walked and Jackson hit a high bounder in front of the plate. It should have been fielded for the third out but Ferguson, catching with Yeager benched to make room for left-handed-hitting Willie Crawford, fumbled the ball and North scored. Rudi then hit a grounder up the middle that Lopes failed to come up with. It was scored as a hit and the second run of the inning came across.

Downing exited in the next stanza when Campaneris singled to score Green who had walked and advanced to second on a sacrifice.

The Dodgers finally broke through in the eighth inning on Buckner's bases empty home run. Dark wasted no time making a pitching change. He immediately brought in Fingers. Even though Fingers yielded a solo homer to Crawford in the ninth, he pitched around an error by Campaneris and the game ended with Russell grounding into a double play.

Messersmith and Holtzman, the starting pitchers in the opening game of the Series, again opposed each other in the fourth contest. And again Holtzman made a mockery of the American League's designated hitter rule by starting the Oakland scoring, this time with a solo home run over the left-field fence in the third inning.

The Dodgers went ahead in the fourth inning when Russell lined a two-out triple to right-center, scoring Garvey, who had singled, and Ferguson, who had walked. It proved to be the only scoring the Dodgers would do that night.

The A's wrapped up the contest with a four-run outburst in the sixth. North opened the inning with a walk and advanced to second when Messersmith threw wildly on an attempted pick-off. Bando plated North with a bloop single to right and Jackson walked. Rudi moved the runners up with a sacrifice and the bases were loaded when Claudell Washington was issued an intentional walk. Jim Holt batted for Ray Fosse and singled to right, scoring two runs. The final tally of the inning came across when Dick Green bounced into a force-out. Fingers replaced Holtzman when the Dodgers threatened in the eighth and prevented further scoring.

The fifth and final game of the Series proved to be the most interesting. The A's began with a rush, scoring in their first turn at bat. Campaneris lined a single to left and was forced at second by North. But North stole second and went on to third when Yeager's throw sailed into center field. Bando's fly ball to left scored North.

Fosse hit a home run into the left-field stands in the second inning and, with Blue apparently breezing along, the A's seemed safely on their way to closing out the Series.

But the Dodgers weren't through. In the sixth inning, Tom Paciorek batted for starting pitcher Sutton and lined a double to left-center. Lopes walked and Buckner sacrificed, putting runners on second and third. Wynn's sacrifice fly got the first run home and Garvey's single tied the game.

The Dodgers brought in their iron fireman, Marshall, to keep their championship hopes alive. Marshall got through the sixth inning without incident but the seventh was another story. The bottom half of the inning was held up six minutes because of unruly spectators throwing debris on the field. When order was restored and the game resumed, Rudi hit Marshall's first pitch for a line drive homer into the left-field stands. That run was to prove decisive but not before further excitement.

Buckner opened the Dodger eighth with a line single to center off A's reliever Rollie Fingers, who had just entered the game. The bounding ball got past North and Buckner, who had second base easily because of the misplay, took off for third. Jackson picked up the ball and threw to Green who, in turn, made a perfect throw to Bando and Buckner was out. It was the most exciting play of the Series and it broke the backs of the Dodgers. They expired peacefully the rest of the game.

The general feeling after the Series was that the A's prevailed over the younger Dodgers because of experience. There were a number of records set during the Series which was the first ever played entirely on the West Coast. For the third consecutive year, no starting pitcher was able to go nine innings.

The box scores follow:

Saturday, October 12—At Los Angeles

Oakland (A.L.)	AB.	R.	H.	O.	A.	E.
Campaneris, ss	2	1	1	0	5	1
North, cf	2	0	0	4	0	0
Bando, 3b	4	0	0	1	1	0
Jackson, rf	3	1	1	0	0	1
C. Washington, rf	0	0	0	0	0	0
Rudi, lf	4	0	2	6	0	0
Tenace, 1b	3	0	1	6	1	0
Fosse, c	3	0	0	7	0	0
Green, 2b	3	0	0	3	2	0
cHolt	1	0	0	0	0	0
Maxvill, 2b	0	0	0	0	0	0
Holtzman, p	1	1	1	0	1	0
Fingers, p	2	0	0	0	0	0
Hunter, p	0	0	0	0	0	0
Totals	28	3	6	27	10	2

Los Ang. (N.L.)	AB.	R.	H.	O.	A.	E.
Lopes, 2b	5	1	0	5	0	0
Buckner, lf	5	0	2	2	0	0
Wynn, cf	4	1	1	1	0	0
Garvey, 1b	5	0	2	6	1	0
dPaciorek	0	0	0	0	0	0
Ferguson, rf-c	3	0	0	2	1	0
Cey, 3b	3	0	1	0	5	1
Russell, ss	4	0	1	2	0	0
Yeager, c	3	0	1	9	1	0
aCrawford, rf	1	0	1	0	0	0
Messersmith, p	3	0	2	0	4	0
bJoshua	1	0	0	0	0	0
Marshall, p	0	0	0	0	0	0
Totals	37	2	11	27	12	1

Oakland............ 0 1 0   0 1 0   0 1 0—3
Los Angeles...... 0 0 0   0 1 0   0 0 1—2

Oakland	IP.	H.	R.	ER.	BB.	SO.
Holtzman	4⅓	7	1	0	2	3
Fingers (W)	4⅓	4	1	1	1	3
Hunter (S)	⅓	0	0	0	0	1

Los Angeles	IP.	H.	R.	ER.	BB.	SO.
Me'ersmith (L)	8	5	3	2	3	8
Marshall	1	1	0	0	1	1

Bases on balls—Off Holtzman 2 (Ferguson, Wynn), off Fingers 1 (Cey), off Messersmith 3 (Holtzman, Jackson, North), off Marshall 1 (Fosse).

Strikeouts—By Holtzman 3 (Lopes, Ferguson, Messersmith), by Fingers 3 (Garvey, Yeager, Russell), by Hunter 1 (Ferguson), by Messersmith 8 (Tenace, Green, North, Bando 2, Rudi, Fosse 2), by Marshall 1 (Fingers).

aSingled for Yeager in eighth. bGrounded out for Messersmith in eighth. cPopped out for Green in ninth. dRan for Garvey in ninth. Runs batted in—Jackson, Campaneris, Wynn. Two-base hit—Holtzman. Home runs—Jackson, Wynn. Sacrifice hits—Campaneris 2, North, Tenace. Caught stealing—Buckner, North. Double plays—Campaneris, Green and Tenace; Ferguson and Yeager. Wild pitch—Messersmith. Hit by pitcher—By Fingers (Ferguson). Left on bases—Oakland 6, Los Angeles 12. Umpires—Gorman (N.L.), Kunkel (A.L.), Harvey (N.L.), Denkinger (N.L.), Luciano (A.L.), Olsen (N.L.). Time—2:43. Attendance—55,974.

Sunday, October 13—At Los Angeles

Oakland (A.L.)	AB.	R.	H.	O.	A.	E.
Campaneris, ss	4	0	1	0	1	0
North, cf	4	0	0	3	0	0
Haney, c	0	0	0	2	0	0
Bando, 3b	3	1	0	0	1	0
Jackson, rf	3	1	2	2	0	0
Rudi, lf	4	0	1	3	0	0
fH. Washington	0	0	0	0	0	0
Tenace, 1b	3	0	0	8	0	0
Fosse, c	2	0	0	5	0	0
aAlou	1	0	0	0	0	0
Odom, p	0	0	0	0	0	0
eMangual	1	0	0	0	0	0
Green, 2b	2	0	0	1	2	0
bHolt	1	0	1	0	0	0
cMaxvill, 2b	0	0	0	0	0	0
Blue, p	2	0	0	0	1	0
dC. Washington, cf	1	0	1	0	0	0
Totals	31	2	6	24	5	0

Los Ang. (N.L.)	AB.	R.	H.	O.	A.	E.
Lopes, 2b	4	0	0	3	2	0
Buckner, lf	4	0	0	3	0	0
Wynn, cf	3	0	0	0	0	0
Garvey, 1b	4	1	2	7	0	0
Ferguson, rf	3	1	1	0	0	0
Cey, 3b	3	1	0	2	1	0
Russell, ss	3	0	1	2	3	1
Yeager, c	3	0	2	10	1	0
Sutton, p	2	0	0	0	1	0
Marshall, p	0	0	0	0	1	0
Totals	29	3	6	27	9	1

Oakland .... 0 0 0   0 0 0   0 2—2
Los Angeles .... 0 1 0   0 0 2   0 0 *—3

Oakland	IP.	H.	R.	ER.	BB.	SO.
Blue (L)	7	6	3	3	2	5
Odom	1	0	0	0	1	2

Los Angeles	IP.	H.	R.	ER.	BB.	SO.
Sutton (W)	8*	5	2	2	2	9
Marshall (S)	1	1	0	0	0	2

*Pitched to two batters in ninth.

Bases on balls—Off Blue 2 (Wynn, Cey), off Odom 1 (Ferguson), off Sutton 2 (Tenace, Jackson).

Strikeouts—By Blue 5 (Buckner, Sutton, Lopes, Wynn 2), by Odom 2 (Wynn, Garvey), by Sutton 9 (Campaneris 2, North, Rudi, Fosse, Blue 2, Green, Alou), by Marshall 2 (Tenace, Mangual).

aStruck out for Fosse in eighth. bSingled for Green in eighth. cRan for Holt in eighth. dSingled for Blue in eighth. eStruck out for Odom in ninth. fRan for Rudi in ninth. Runs batted in—Yeager, Ferguson 2, Rudi 2. Two-base hits—Campaneris, Jackson. Home run—Ferguson. Stolen base—Ferguson. Sacrifice hit—Sutton. Double plays—Sutton, Lopes and Garvey; Russell and Garvey. Wild pitch—Sutton. Hit by pitcher—By Sutton (Bando). Left on bases—Oakland 5, Los Angeles 6. Umpires—Kunkel (A.L.), Harvey (N.L.), Denkinger (A.L.), Olsen (N.L.), Luciano (A.L.), Gorman (N.L.). Time—2:40. Attendance—55,989.

Tuesday, October 15—At Oakland

Los Ang. (N.L.)	AB.	R.	H.	O.	A.	E.
Lopes, 2b	3	0	2	1	0	0
Buckner, lf	4	1	1	2	0	0
Wynn, cf	4	0	1	0	0	0
Garvey, 1b	4	0	1	10	0	0
Crawford, rf	4	1	1	1	0	0
Ferguson, c	3	0	0	9	0	2
dAuerbach	0	0	0	0	0	0
Cey, 3b	4	0	0	1	3	0
Russell, ss	4	0	1	0	3	0
Downing, p	1	0	0	0	3	0
Brewer, p	0	0	0	0	0	0
aLacy	1	0	0	0	0	0
Hough, p	0	0	0	0	0	0
bJoshua	1	0	0	0	0	0
Marshall, p	0	0	0	0	1	0
Totals	33	2	7	24	10	2

Oakland (A.L.)	AB.	R.	H.	O.	A.	E.
North, cf	4	1	1	5	0	0
Campaneris, ss	4	0	2	3	2	1
Bando, 3b	3	1	0	0	1	0
Jackson, rf	3	0	0	2	0	0
C. Washington, rf	0	0	0	0	0	0
Rudi, lf	4	0	1	2	0	0
Tenace, 1b	2	0	1	4	0	0
cH. Washington	0	0	0	0	0	0
Holt, 1b	0	0	0	1	0	0
Fosse, c	4	0	0	5	0	0
Green, 2b	3	1	0	4	4	1
Hunter, p	2	0	0	1	1	0
Fingers, p	0	0	0	0	0	0
Totals	29	3	5	27	8	2

Los Angeles .... 0 0 0   0 0 0   0 1 1—2
Oakland .... 0 0 2   1 0 0   0 0 *—3

Los Angeles	IP.	H.	R.	ER.	BB.	SO.
Downing (L)	3⅔	4	3	1	4	3
Brewer	⅓	0	0	0	0	1
Hough	2	0	0	0	1	4
Marshall	2	1	0	0	0	1

Oakland	IP.	H.	R.	ER.	BB.	SO.
Hunter (W)	7⅓	5	1	1	2	4
Fingers	1⅔	2	1	1	0	1

Bases on balls—Off Downing 4 (Tenace 2, Bando, Green), off Hough 1 (Jackson), off Hunter 1 (Lopes, Ferguson).

Strikeouts—By Downing 3 (North, Green, Hunter), by Brewer 1 (Bando), by Hough 4 (Rudi, Tenace, Hunter, North), by Marshall 1 (Jackson), by Hunter 4 (Ferguson 2, Cey, Lacy), by Fingers 1 (Cey).

aStruck out for Brewer in fifth. bFlied out for Hough in seventh. cRan for Tenace in eighth. dRan for Ferguson in ninth. Runs batted in—Rudi, Campaneris, Buckner, Crawford. Two-base hit—Campaneris. Home runs—Buckner, Craw-

1974 WORLD SERIES

ford. Stolen bases—Lopes 2, Jackson. Sacrifice hit—Hunter. Double plays—Green and Campaneris; Green and Tenace; Green, Campaneris and Holt. Wild pitch—Hough. Left on bases—Los Angeles 6, Oakland 8. Umpires—Harvey (N.L.), Denkinger (A.L.), Olsen (N.L.), Luciano (A.L.), Gorman (N.L.), Kunkel (A.L.). Time—2:35. Attendance—49,347.

Wednesday, October 16—At Oakland

Los Ang. (N.L.)	AB.	R.	H.	O.	A.	E.
Lopes, 2b	4	0	0	8	5	0
Buckner, lf	4	0	1	1	0	0
Wynn, cf	3	0	1	1	0	0
Garvey, 1b	4	1	2	7	2	0
Ferguson, rf	3	1	0	0	0	0
Cey, 3b	4	0	1	0	0	0
Russell, ss	4	0	1	0	4	0
Yeager, c	3	0	1	6	1	0
dJoshua	1	0	0	0	0	0
Messersmith, p	1	0	0	1	0	1
cPaciorek	1	0	0	0	0	0
Marshall, p	0	0	0	0	1	0
Totals	32	2	7	24	13	1

Oakland (A.L.)	AB.	R.	H.	O.	A.	E.
Campaneris, ss	3	0	0	1	4	0
North, cf	3	1	0	3	0	0
Bando, 3b	3	1	1	0	4	0
Jackson, rf	3	1	1	0	0	0
Rudi, 1b-lf	3	0	0	10	0	0
C. Washington, lf	3	1	2	0	0	0
Tenace, 1b	0	0	0	1	0	0
Fosse, c	2	0	1	6	0	0
aHolt	1	0	1	0	0	0
bH. Washington	0	0	0	0	0	0
Haney, c	0	0	0	4	0	0
Green, 2b	2	0	0	2	4	0
Holtzman, p	3	1	1	0	2	0
Fingers, p	0	0	0	0	0	0
Totals	26	5	7	27	14	0

Los Angeles.................. 0 0 0   2 0 0   0 0 0—2
Oakland....................... 0 0 1   0 0 4   0 0 *—5

Los Angeles	IP.	H.	R.	ER.	BB.	SO.
Me'rsmith (L)	6	6	5	5	4	4
Marshall	2	1	0	0	0	2

Oakland	IP.	H.	R.	ER.	BB.	SO.
Holtzman (W)	7⅔	6	2	2	2	7
Fingers (S)	1⅓	1	0	0	0	2

Bases on balls—Off Messersmith 4 (Bando, North, Jackson, C. Washington), off Holtzman 2 (Ferguson, Wynn).

Strikeouts—By Messersmith 4 (Bando, Fosse, Jackson, Holtzman), by Marshall 2 (North, C. Washington), by Holtzman 7 (Wynn, Garvey, Lopes 2, Cey, Messersmith, Yeager), by Fingers 2 (Ferguson, Russell).

aSingled for Fosse in sixth. bRan for Holt in sixth. cGrounded out for Messersmith in seventh. dGrounded into double play for Yeager in ninth. Runs batted in—Holtzman, Russell 2, Bando, Holt 2, Green. Two-base hits—Buckner, Yeager, Wynn. Three-base hit—Russell. Home run—Holtzman. Caught stealing—Campaneris. Sacrifice hits—Messersmith, Green, Rudi. Double plays—Lopes and Garvey; Russell, Lopes and Garvey; Green, Campaneris and Tenace. Wild pitch—Holtzman. Hit by pitcher—By Messersmith (Campaneris). Left on bases—Los Angeles 6, Oakland 4. Umpires—Denkinger (A.L.), Olsen (N.L.), Luciano (A.L.), Gorman (N.L.), Kunkel (A.L.), Harvey (N.L.). Time—2:17. Attendance—49,347.

Thursday, October 17—At Oakland

Los Ang. (N.L.)	AB.	R.	H.	O.	A.	E.
Lopes, 2b	2	1	0	2	2	0
Buckner, lf	3	0	1	3	0	0
Wynn, cf	2	0	0	3	0	0
Garvey, 1b	4	0	1	4	0	0
Ferguson, rf	4	0	1	3	0	0
Cey, 3b	3	0	1	2	0	0
Russell, ss	3	0	0	0	1	0
bCrawford	1	0	0	0	0	0
Yeager, c	2	0	0	7	1	1
cJoshua	1	0	0	0	0	0
Sutton, p	1	0	0	0	1	0
aPaciorek	1	1	1	0	0	0
Marshall, p	0	0	0	0	1	0
Totals	27	2	5	24	6	1

Oakland (A.L.)	AB.	R.	H.	O.	A.	E.
Campaneris, ss	4	0	2	2	4	0
North, cf	4	1	0	2	0	1
Bando, 3b	3	0	0	1	3	0
Jackson, rf	2	0	0	2	1	0
Rudi, 1b-lf	3	1	2	7	0	0
C. Washington, lf	3	0	1	3	0	0
Fingers, p	0	0	0	0	1	0
Fosse, c	3	1	1	4	1	0
Green, 2b	3	0	0	5	2	0
Blue, p	2	0	0	0	2	0
Odom, p	0	0	0	0	0	0
Tenace, 1b	1	0	0	1	0	0
Totals	28	3	6	27	14	1

Los Angeles.................. 0 0 0   0 0 2   0 0 0—2
Oakland....................... 1 1 0   0 0 0   1 0 *—3

Los Angeles	IP.	H.	R.	ER.	BB.	SO.
Sutton	5	4	2	2	1	3
Marshall (L)	3	2	1	1	0	4

Oakland	IP.	H.	R.	ER.	BB.	SO.
Blue	6⅔	4	2	2	5	4
Odom (W)	⅓	0	0	0	0	0
Fingers (S)	2	1	0	0	1	0

Bases on balls—Off Sutton 1 (Jackson), off Blue 5 (Lopes 2, Cey, Yeager, Marshall), off Fingers 1 (Wynn).

Strikeouts—By Sutton 3 (Blue 2, Jackson), by Marshall 4 (Bando, Fosse, Green, Tenace), by Blue 4 (Yeager 2, Sutton, Ferguson).

aDoubled for Sutton in sixth. bPopped out for Russell in ninth. cGrounded out for Yeager in ninth. Runs batted in—Bando, Fosse, Wynn, Garvey, Rudi. Two-base hit—Paciorek. Home runs—Fosse, Rudi. Stolen bases—North, Campaneris. Caught stealing—Lopes, C. Washington. Sacrifice hit—Buckner. Sacrifice flies—Bando, Wynn. Double play—Campaneris, Green and Rudi. Left on bases—Los Angeles 6, Oakland 3. Umpires—Olsen (N.L.), Luciano (A.L.), Gorman (N.L.), Kunkel (A.L.), Harvey (N.L.), Denkinger (A.L.). Time—2:23. Attendance—49,347.

COMPOSITE BATTING AVERAGES
Oakland Athletics

Player-Position	G.	AB.	R.	H.	2B.	3B.	HR.	RBI.	BA.
Holt, ph-1b	4	3	0	2	0	0	0	2	.667
C.W'ton,rf-ph-cf-lf	5	7	1	4	0	0	0	0	.571
Holtzman, p	2	4	2	2	1	0	1	1	.500
Campaneris, ss	5	17	1	6	2	0	0	2	.353
Rudi, lf-1b	5	18	1	6	0	0	1	4	.333
Jackson, rf	5	14	3	4	1	0	1	1	.286
Tenace, 1b	5	9	0	2	0	0	0	0	.222
Fosse, c	5	14	1	2	0	0	1	1	.143
Bando, 3b	5	16	3	1	0	0	0	0	.063
North, cf	5	17	3	1	0	0	0	0	.059
Alou, ph	1	1	0	0	0	0	0	0	.000
Mangual, ph	1	1	0	0	0	0	0	0	.000
Fingers, p	4	2	0	0	0	0	0	0	.000
Hunter, p	2	2	0	0	0	0	0	0	.000

1975 WORLD SERIES

Player-Position	G.	AB.	R.	H.	2B.	3B.	HR.	RBI.	BA.
Blue, p	2	4	0	0	0	0	0	0	.000
Green, 2b	5	13	1	0	0	0	0	1	.000
H. Washington, pr	3	0	0	0	0	0	0	0	.000
Haney, c	2	0	0	0	0	0	0	0	.000
Maxvill, 2b-pr	2	0	0	0	0	0	0	0	.000
Odom, p	2	0	0	0	0	0	0	0	.000
Totals	5	142	16	30	4	0	4	14	.211

Los Angeles Dodgers

Player-Position	G.	AB.	R.	H.	2B.	3B.	HR.	RBI.	BA.
Messersmith, p	2	4	0	2	0	0	0	0	.500
Paciorek, pr-ph	3	2	1	1	0	0	0	0	.500
Garvey, 1b	5	21	2	8	0	0	0	1	.381
Yeager, c	4	11	0	4	1	0	0	1	.364
Crawford, ph-rf	3	6	1	2	0	0	1	1	.333
Buckner, lf	5	20	1	5	1	0	1	1	.250
Russell, ss	5	18	0	4	0	1	0	2	.222
Wynn, cf	5	16	1	3	1	0	1	2	.188
Cey, 3b	5	17	1	3	0	0	0	0	.176
Ferguson, rf-c	5	16	2	2	0	0	1	2	.125
Lopes, 2b	5	18	2	2	0	0	0	0	.111
Downing, p	1	1	0	0	0	0	0	0	.000
Lacy, ph	1	1	0	0	0	0	0	0	.000
Sutton, p	2	3	0	0	0	0	0	0	.000
Joshua, ph	4	4	0	0	0	0	0	0	.000
Marshall, p	5	0	0	0	0	0	0	0	.000
Auerbach, pr	1	0	0	0	0	0	0	0	.000
Brewer, p	1	0	0	0	0	0	0	0	.000
Hough, p	1	0	0	0	0	0	0	0	.000
Totals	5	158	11	36	4	1	4	10	.228

COMPOSITE PITCHING AVERAGES
Oakland Athletics

Pitcher	G.	IP.	H.	R.	E.	SO.	BB.	W.	L.	ERA.
Odom	2	1⅓	0	0	0	2	1	1	0	0.00
Hunter	2	7⅔	5	1	1	5	2	1	0	1.17
Holtzman	2	12	13	3	2	10	4	1	0	1.50
Fingers	4	9⅓	8	2	2	6	2	1	0	1.93
Blue	2	13⅔	10	5	5	9	7	0	1	3.29
Totals	5	44	36	11	10	32	16	4	1	2.05

Saves—Fingers 2, Hunter.

Los Angeles Dodgers

Pitcher	G.	IP.	H.	R.	E.	SO.	BB.	W.	L.	ERA.
Hough	1	2	0	0	0	4	1	0	0	0.00
Brewer	1	⅓	0	0	0	1	0	0	0	0.00
Marshall	5	9	6	1	1	10	1	0	1	1.00
Downing	1	3⅔	4	3	1	3	4	0	1	2.45
Sutton	2	13	9	4	4	12	3	1	0	2.77
Messersmith	2	14	11	8	7	12	7	0	2	4.50
Totals	5	42	30	16	13	42	16	1	4	2.79

Save—Marshall.

SERIES OF 1975

	W.	L.	Pct.
Cincinnati N. L.	4	3	.571
Boston A. L.	3	4	.429

The 1975 World Series must go down in memory as one of the most exciting ever.

For the first time in four years, the Oakland A's were not involved. The A's won the American League's West Division championship for the fifth time in a row but were eliminated in the Championship Series by the Boston Red Sox in three straight games.

The Cincinnati Reds ran away with the National League West, knocked off the Pittsburgh Pirates in easy fashion in three straight games to win the senior circuit flag and were heavy favorites to win the Series. Their admirers rated them one of the great teams of recent years.

The first game was played at Boston's venerable Fenway Park and turned into a personal triumph for Luis Tiant. The veteran Cuban righthander shut out the Reds on five hits. Lefty Don Gullett held Boston scoreless until the seventh inning when a six-run explosion sent him to the showers and locked up the contest for the home team. Tiant himself, who batted only once all year under the American League designated hitter rule, started the winning rally with a single. He later scored the run that broke the deadlock on Carl Yastrzemski's single. Rico Petrocelli drove in two runs during the inning, also with a single.

The second game was played with rain falling through much of the contest. In fact, there was a 27-minute rain delay after the Reds batted in the seventh inning. But the millions watching on Sunday television were not to be denied.

The Sox, with southpaw Bill Lee on the mound, carried a 2-1 lead into the top of the ninth. But Johnny Bench doubled to right to begin the inning. Lee was excused and replaced by Dick Drago. Drago almost closed out the game. He got the next two batters out but Dave Concepcion then hit a grounder up the middle that scored Bench. Concepcion then stole second and scored on Ken Griffey's double. The Reds' speed on the bases was to be a thorn in the side of the Red Sox throughout the Series.

The third game, played at Cincinnati's Riverfront Stadium after a day off for travel, produced a record-tying six home runs, but a 10th-inning bunt was the key play of the game and gave vent to one of the more controversial happenings in World Series history.

The Red Sox, down at one point, 5-1, fought back and eventually tied the game, 5-5, in the top of the ninth, scoring two runs on Dwight Evans' one-out home run.

Cesar Geronimo opened the bottom of the 10th with a single to right. Ed Armbrister, sent up as a pinch-hitter for relief pitcher Rawly Eastwick, attempted to sacrifice the runner to second and laid down a bunt. The ball bounced just a few feet in front of the plate and catcher Carlton Fisk went to field it. There was a collision between Armbrister and Fisk before Fisk picked up the ball and threw wildly into center field trying to get Geronimo advancing from first to second. Armbrister and Geronimo wound up at second and third, respectively.

The Red Sox claimed interference on the play and argued strenuously. Plate umpire Larry Barnett, an American League arbiter, stuck by his decision. Television replays definitely showed the collision and there was no dearth of commentary and opinions voiced on the air and in the press for several days after the game. Rules were quoted to prove interference or lack of interference. But the decision, of course, stood.

When the game furor had subsided, Pete Rose was given an intentional walk to load the bases. After pinch-hitter Merv Rettenmund struck out, Joe Morgan singled to center to end the game on a winning note for the Reds.

The Red Sox called on Tiant again for the fourth game and again he was equal to the occasion. Although not nearly as sharp as he was in the opener and requiring 163 pitches to do it, Tiant managed to notch a 5-4 verdict and evened the Series at two games apiece.

The Sox got all their runs in the fourth inning on singles by Fisk and Fred Lynn, a wild pitch by Reds' starter Fred Norman, Evans' triple, Rick Burleson's double, Tiant's single, an error and Yastrzemski's single.

The Reds threatened in the late going but Tiant managed to repulse all threats.

Cincinnati first baseman Tony Perez snapped out of a 0-for-15 slump with two home runs and lefty Don Gullett hurled brilliantly to enable the Reds to capture the fifth game. Gullett, who worked 8⅔ innings, had carried a two-hitter into the ninth and at one point retired 16 consecutive batters. Two-out singles by Yastrzemski and Fisk and a double by Lynn gave Boston a ninth-inning run. But Rawly Eastwick came on for the Reds and struck out Petrocelli for the final out.

The teams did not play again for four more days. One of those days was a travel day but the other three were caused by rainstorms which swept the New England coast. When the teams finally resumed, what resulted was one of the really exciting sporting events of modern times.

Lynn got the Sox off in front by blasting a three-run homer off Reds' starter Gary Nolan in the first inning. Tiant, trying for his third Series victory, sailed through the first four frames but started to become unglued in the fifth. In that stanza, a walk to Armbrister, Rose's single, a triple by Griffey that Lynn crashed into the center field wall attempting to catch, and Bench's single tied the score.

The Reds went ahead, 5-3, in the seventh when George Foster doubled off the center-field wall to score Griffey and Morgan who had hit singles. They added another tally an inning later on Geronimo's homer.

The Sox tied the game in the eighth when pinch-hitter Bernie Carbo hit a two-out, three-run homer.

It looked like the Boston club would win in the ninth when Doyle opened with a walk and took third on Yastrzemski's single. After an intentional walk to Fisk, Lynn hit a fly just barely foul to Foster in shallow left field, an estimated 180 feet from the plate. Doyle, against coaching instructions, tried to score after the catch and was thrown out.

A sensational catch by Evans of Morgan's bid for a homer stopped a Cincinnati bid in the top of the 11th.

In the bottom of the 12th, Fisk, first man up for Boston, hit a long blast that caromed off the left-field foul pole for a home run to end the game and set up a climactic seventh game.

The opposing pitchers for the finale were the two lefties, Gullett and Lee. Gullett was plagued by control problems and the Sox appeared to be closing in on a great upset when they got three runs in the third inning, two of the tallies being forced home by bases-loaded walks.

The Reds got two back in the sixth. With one out and Rose on first as the result of a single, Bench hit a grounder to Burleson at shortstop for what might have been a double play. But Rose slid hard into second and Doyle threw the ball past first, Bench reaching second. Perez then hit a home run.

The Reds' base-running speed enabled them to tie the score in their next turn at bat. Griffey walked, stole second and scored on Rose's single.

The last run of the game and the Series and the one that won it all came in the Reds' ninth. Griffey walked, was sacrificed to second and advanced to third on an infield out. Rose was intentionally passed and that left it up to Morgan. He responded with a single to center, scoring Griffey.

Boston went out in order in the ninth and the Series was over.

The box scores:

Saturday, October 11—At Boston

Cincinnati (N.L.)	AB.	R.	H.	O.	A.	E.
Rose, 3b	4	0	0	0	0	0
Morgan, 2b	4	0	2	2	2	0
Bench, c	4	0	0	6	1	0
Perez, 1b	4	0	0	9	0	0
Foster, lf	4	0	2	1	0	0
C'cepcion, ss	4	0	0	2	3	0
Griffey, rf	3	0	1	2	0	0
Geronimo, cf	1	0	0	2	1	0
Gullett, p	3	0	0	0	0	0
Carroll, p	0	0	0	0	0	0
McEnaney, p	0	0	0	0	0	0
Totals	31	0	5	24	7	0

Boston (A.L.)	AB.	R.	H.	O.	A.	E.
Evans, rf	4	1	1	4	0	0
Doyle, 2b	3	1	2	3	3	0
Yastrz'ski, lf	4	1	1	3	0	0
Fisk, c	3	1	0	4	1	0
Lynn, cf	4	0	2	3	0	0
Petrocelli, 3b	3	1	2	1	3	0
Burleson, ss	3	0	3	1	1	0
Cooper, 1b	3	0	0	8	0	0
Tiant, p	3	1	1	0	0	0
Totals	30	6	12	27	8	0

Cincinnati................... 0 0 0 0 0 0 0 0 0—0
Boston .... 0 0 0 0 0 0 6 0 *—6

Cincinnati	IP.	H.	R.	ER.	BB.	SO.
Gullett (L)	6*	10	4	4	4	3
Carroll	0†	0	1	1	1	0
McEnaney	2	2	1	1	1	1

Boston	IP.	H.	R.	ER.	BB.	SO.
Tiant (W)	9	5	0	0	2	3

*Pitched to four batters in seventh.
†Pitched to one batter in seventh.

Bases on balls—Off Gullett 4 (Yastrzemski, Petrocelli, Tiant, Burleson), off Carroll 1 (Fisk), off McEnaney 1 (Doyle), off Tiant 2 (Geronimo 2).

Strikeouts—By Gullett 3 (Cooper 2, Tiant), by McEnaney 1 (Lynn), by Tiant 3 (Perez 2, Concepcion).

Runs batted in—Yastrzemski, Fisk, Petrocelli 2, Burleson, Cooper. Two-base hits—Morgan, Petrocelli, Griffey. Sacrifice hits—Doyle, Evans. Sacrifice fly—Cooper. Caught stealing—Burleson, Foster. Double plays—Geronimo and Bench; Perez unassisted. Balk—Tiant. Left on bases—Cincinnati 6, Boston 9. Umpires—Frantz (A.L.) plate, Colosi (N.L.) first base, Barnett (A.L.) second base, Stello (N.L.) third base, Maloney (A.L.) left field, Davidson (N.L.) right field. Time—2:27. Attendance—35,205.

Sunday, October 12—At Boston

Cincinnati (N.L.)	AB.	R.	H.	O.	A.	E.
Rose, 3b	4	0	2	1	1	0
Morgan, 2b	3	1	0	0	4	0
Bench, c	4	1	2	9	3	0
Perez, 1b	3	0	0	8	0	0
Foster, lf	4	0	1	2	0	0
Concepc'n, ss	4	1	1	2	4	1
Griffey, rf	4	0	1	2	0	0
Geronimo, cf	3	0	0	3	0	0
Billingham, p	2	0	0	0	2	0
Borbon, p	0	0	0	0	0	0
McEnaney, p	0	0	0	0	0	0
aRettenmund	1	0	0	0	0	0
Eastwick, p	1	0	0	0	0	0
Totals	33	3	7	27	14	1

Boston (A.L.)	AB.	R.	H.	O.	A.	E.
Cooper, 1b	5	0	1	10	1	0
Doyle, 2b	4	0	1	2	5	0
Yastrz'ski, lf	3	2	1	1	0	0
Fisk, c	3	0	1	5	1	0
Lynn, cf	4	0	0	5	0	0
Petrocelli, 3b	4	0	2	0	0	0
Evans, rf	2	0	0	2	0	0
Burleson, ss	4	0	1	2	4	0
Lee, p	3	0	0	0	0	0
Drago, p	0	0	0	0	0	0
bCarbo	1	0	0	0	0	0
Totals	33	2	7	27	11	0

Cincinnati .... 0 0 0   1 0 0   0 0 2—3
Boston .... 1 0 0   0 0 1   0 0 0—2

Cincinnati	IP.	H.	R.	ER.	BB.	SO.
Billingham	5⅔	6	2	1	2	5
Borbon	⅓	0	0	0	0	0
McEnaney	1	0	0	0	0	2
Eastwick (W)	2	1	0	0	1	1

Boston	IP.	H.	R.	ER.	BB.	SO.
Lee	8*	5	2	2	2	5
Drago (L)	1	2	1	1	1	0

*Pitched to one batter in ninth.

Bases on balls—Off Billingham 2 (Yastrzemski, Evans), off Eastwick 1 (Fisk), off Lee 2 (Morgan, Perez), off Drago 1 (Geronimo).

Strikeouts—By Billingham 5 (Petrocelli, Lee, Fisk, Evans, Burleson), by McEnaney 2 (Lee, Doyle), by Eastwick 1 (Evans), by Lee 5 (Rose, Perez, Foster, Geronimo, Griffey).

aFouled out for McEnaney in eighth. bLined out for Drago in ninth. Runs batted in—Perez, Concepcion, Griffey, Fisk, Petrocelli. Two-base hits—Cooper, Bench, Griffey. Stolen base—Concepcion. Caught stealing—Evans, Morgan. Double play—Billingham, Concepcion, Bench, Rose and Bench. Hit by pitcher—By Billingham (Evans). Left on bases—Cincinnati 6, Boston 8. Umpires—Colosi (N.L.) plate, Barnett (A.L.) first base, Stello (N.L.) second base, Maloney (A.L.) third base, Davidson (N.L.) left field, Frantz (A.L.) right field. Time—2:38. Attendance—35,205.

Tuesday, October 14—At Cincinnati

Boston (A.L.)	AB.	R.	H.	O.	A.	E.
Cooper, 1b	5	0	0	14	0	0
Doyle, 2b	5	0	1	0	6	0
Yastrz'ski, lf	4	1	0	1	0	0
Fisk, c	3	1	1	5	0	2
Lynn, cf	3	0	1	6	0	0
Petrocelli, 3b	4	1	2	1	5	0
Evans, rf	4	1	2	1	0	0
Burleson, ss	4	0	2	0	1	0
Wise, p	2	0	0	0	0	0
Burton, p	0	0	0	0	0	0
Cleveland, p	0	0	0	0	0	0
aCarbo	1	1	1	0	0	0
Willoughby, p	0	0	0	0	0	0
Moret, p	0	0	0	0	0	0
Totals	35	5	10	28	12	2

Cincinnati (N.L.)	AB.	R.	H.	O.	A.	E.
Rose, 3b	4	1	1	2	1	0
Griffey, rf	3	0	0	1	0	0
cRettenmund	1	0	0	0	0	0
Morgan, 2b	4	0	1	4	5	0
Perez, 1b	3	1	0	13	1	0
Bench, c	4	1	1	2	1	0
Foster, lf	3	0	0	3	0	0
C'cepcion, ss	4	1	1	2	5	0
Geronimo, cf	4	2	2	3	0	0
Nolan, p	1	0	0	0	0	0
Darcy, p	1	0	0	0	0	0
Carroll, p	0	0	0	0	0	0
McEnaney, p	1	0	1	0	0	0
Eastwick, p	0	0	0	0	0	0
bArmbrister	1	0	0	0	0	0
Totals	34	6	7	30	14	0

Boston .... 0 1 0   0 0 1   1 0 2   0—5
Cincinnati .... 0 0 0   2 3 0   0 0 0   1—6

One out when winning run scored.

Boston	IP.	H.	R.	ER.	BB.	SO.
Wise	4⅓	4	5	5	2	1
Burton	⅓	0	0	0	1	0
Cleveland	1⅓	0	0	0	0	2
Willou'by (L)	3†	2	1	0	0	1
Moret	⅓	1	0	0	1	1

Cincinnati	IP.	H.	R.	ER.	BB.	SO.
Nolan	4	3	1	1	1	0
Darcy	2*	2	1	1	2	0
Carroll	⅔	1	1	1	0	0
McEnaney	1⅔	1	1	1	0	2
Eastwick (W)	1⅔	3	1	1	0	0

*Pitched to one batter in seventh.
†Pitched to two batters in tenth.

Bases on balls—Off Wise 2 (Foster, Perez), off Burton 1 (Griffey), off Moret 1 (Rose), off Nolan 1 (Fisk), off Darcy 2 (Yastrzemski, Fisk).

Strikeouts—By Wise 1 (Darcy), by Cleveland 2 (Perez, Bench), by Willoughby 1 (Perez), by Moret 1 (Rettenmund), by McEnaney 2 (Yastrzemski, Lynn).

aHomered for Cleveland in seventh. bSafe on error for Eastwick in tenth. cCalled out on strikes for Griffey in tenth. Runs batted in—Fisk, Lynn, Carbo, Evans 2, Bench 2, Concepcion, Geronimo, Morgan 2. Three-base hit—Rose. Home runs—Fisk, Bench, Concepcion, Geronimo, Carbo, Evans. Stolen bases—Foster, Perez, Griffey. Sacrifice hit—Willoughby. Sacrifice flies—Morgan, Lynn. Double plays—Morgan, Concepcion and Perez; Petrocelli and Cooper; Morgan and Perez.

1975 WORLD SERIES

Wild pitch—Darcy. Left on bases—Boston 5, Cincinnati 5. Umpires—Barnett (A.L.) plate, Stello (N.L.) first base, Maloney (A.L.) second base, Davidson (N.L.) third base, Frantz (A.L.) left field, Colosi (N.L.) right field. Time—3:03. Attendance—55,392.

Wednesday, October 15—At Cincinnati

Boston (A.L.)	AB.	R.	H.	O.	A.	E.
Beniquez, lf	4	0	1	4	0	0
Miller, lf	1	0	0	1	0	0
Doyle, 2b	5	0	1	2	3	1
Yastr'ski, 1b	4	0	2	8	0	0
Fisk, c	5	1	1	4	0	0
Lynn, cf	4	1	1	4	1	0
Petrocelli, 3b	4	0	1	1	2	0
Evans, rf	4	1	2	3	0	0
Burleson, ss	4	1	1	0	2	0
Tiant, p	3	1	1	0	2	0
Totals	38	5	11	27	10	1

Cincinnati (N.L.)	AB.	R.	H.	O.	A.	E.
Rose, 3b	3	1	1	1	3	0
Griffey, rf	5	0	1	0	0	0
Morgan, 2b	3	1	0	2	7	0
Perez, 1b	4	0	0	12	1	1
Bench, c	4	0	1	4	0	0
Foster, lf	4	1	2	0	0	0
C'cepcion, ss	4	1	1	3	4	0
Geronimo, cf	4	0	3	4	0	0
Norman, p	1	0	0	0	0	0
Borbon, p	0	0	0	0	0	0
aCrowley	1	0	0	0	0	0
Carroll, p	0	0	0	1	0	0
bChaney	1	0	0	0	0	0
Eastwick, p	0	0	0	0	0	0
cArmbrister	0	0	0	0	0	0
Totals	34	4	9	27	15	1

Boston .... 0 0 0 5 0 0 0 0 0—5
Cincinnati .... 2 0 0 2 0 0 0 0 0—4

Boston	IP.	H.	R.	ER.	BB.	SO.
Tiant (W)	9	9	4	4	4	4

Cincinnati	IP.	H.	R.	ER.	BB.	SO.
Norman (L)	3⅓	7	4	4	1	2
Borbon	⅔	2	1	0	0	0
Carroll	2	2	0	0	0	2
Eastwick	3	0	0	0	1	0

Bases on balls—Off Tiant 4 (Morgan 2, Rose 2), off Norman 1 (Tiant), off Eastwick 1 (Yastrzemski). Strikeouts—By Tiant 4 (Perez, Crowley, Chaney, Bench), by Norman 2 (Fisk, Lynn), by Carroll 2 (Petrocelli, Tiant).

aStruck out for Borbon in fourth. bStruck out for Carroll in sixth. cSacrificed for Eastwick in ninth. Runs batted in—Evans 2, Burleson, Beniquez, Yastrzemski, Griffey, Bench, Concepcion, Geronimo. Two-base hits—Griffey, Bench, Burleson, Concepcion. Three-base hits—Evans, Geronimo. Sacrifice hit—Armbrister. Double play—Morgan, Concepcion and Perez. Wild pitch—Norman. Left on bases—Boston 8, Cincinnati 8. Umpires—Stello (N.L.) plate, Maloney (A.L.) first base, Davidson (N.L.) second base, Frantz (A.L.) third base, Colosi (N.L.) left field, Barnett (A.L.) right field. Time—2:52. Attendance—55,667.

Thursday, October 16—At Cincinnati

Boston (A.L.)	AB.	R.	H.	O.	A.	E.
Beniquez, lf	3	0	0	2	1	0
Doyle, 2b	4	1	1	1	1	0
Yastrz'ski, 1b	3	1	1	6	0	0
Fisk, c	4	0	1	6	0	0
Lynn, cf	4	0	1	2	0	0
Petrocelli, 3b	4	0	0	2	1	0
Evans, rf	3	0	1	3	0	0
Burleson, ss	3	0	0	1	2	0
Cleveland, p	2	0	0	0	0	0
Willoughby, p	0	0	0	1	0	0
aGriffin	1	0	0	0	0	0
Pole, p	0	0	0	0	0	0
Segui, p	0	0	0	0	0	0
Totals	31	2	5	24	5	0

Cincinnati (N.L.)	AB.	R.	H.	O.	A.	E.
Rose, 3b	3	0	2	1	0	0
Griffey, rf	4	0	1	2	0	0
Morgan, 2b	3	1	1	3	2	0
Bench, c	3	2	1	8	1	0
Perez, 1b	3	2	2	5	0	0
Foster, lf	4	0	0	2	0	0
C'cepcion, ss	2	0	0	0	0	0
Geronimo, cf	4	0	0	6	0	0
Gullett, p	3	1	1	0	0	0
Eastwick, p	0	0	0	0	0	0
Totals	29	6	8	27	3	0

Boston .... 1 0 0 0 0 0 0 0 1—2
Cincinnati .... 0 0 0 1 1 3 0 1 *—6

Boston	IP.	H.	R.	ER.	BB.	SO.
Cleveland (L)	5*	7	5	5	2	3
Willoughby	2	1	0	0	0	1
Pole	0†	0	1	1	2	0
Segui	1	0	0	0	0	0

Cincinnati	IP.	H.	R.	ER.	BB.	SO.
Gullett (W)	8⅔	5	2	2	1	7
Eastwick (S)	⅓	0	0	0	0	1

*Pitched to three batters in sixth.
†Pitched to two batters in eighth.

Bases on balls—Off Cleveland 2 (Rose, Morgan), off Pole 2 (Bench, Perez), off Gullett 1 (Beniquez). Strikeouts—By Cleveland 3 (Griffey, Perez, Gullett), by Willoughby 1 (Gullett), by Gullett 7 (Fisk 2, Petrocelli, Cleveland 2, Lynn, Beniquez), by Eastwick 1 (Petrocelli).

aLined out for Willoughby in eighth. Runs batted in—Yastrzemski, Lynn, Perez 4, Rose, Concepcion. Two-base hits—Rose, Lynn. Three-base hit—Doyle. Home runs—Perez 2. Stolen bases—Morgan, Concepcion. Sacrifice flies—Yastrzemski, Concepcion. Double plays—Beniquez and Fisk; Burleson and Yastrzemski. Hit by pitcher—By Willoughby (Concepcion). Left on bases—Boston 4, Cincinnati 5. Umpires—Maloney (A.L.) plate, Davidson (N.L.) first base, Frantz (A.L.) second base, Colosi (N.L.) third base, Barnett (A.L.) left field, Stello (N.L.) right field. Time—2:23. Attendance—56,393.

Tuesday, October 21—At Boston

Cincinnati (N.L.)	AB.	R.	H.	O.	A.	E.
Rose, 3b	5	1	2	0	2	0
Griffey, rf	5	2	2	0	0	0
Morgan, 2b	6	1	1	4	4	0
Bench, c	6	0	1	8	0	0
Perez, 1b	6	0	2	11	2	0
Foster, lf	6	0	2	4	1	0
C'cepcion, ss	6	0	1	3	4	0
Geronimo, cf	6	1	2	2	0	0
Nolan, p	0	0	0	1	0	0
aChaney	1	0	0	0	0	0
Norman, p	0	0	0	0	0	0
Billingham, p	0	0	0	0	0	0
bArmbrister	0	1	0	0	0	0
Carroll, p	0	0	0	0	0	0
cCrowley	1	0	1	0	0	0
Borbon, p	1	0	0	0	0	0

1975 WORLD SERIES

	AB.	R.	H.	O.	A.	E.
Eastwick, p	0	0	0	0	0	0
McEnaney, p	0	0	0	0	0	0
eDriessen	1	0	0	0	0	0
Darcy, p	0	0	0	0	1	0
Totals	50	6	14	33	14	0

Boston (A.L.)	AB.	R.	H.	O.	A.	E.
Cooper, 1b	5	0	0	8	0	0
Drago, p	0	0	0	0	0	0
fMiller	1	0	0	0	0	0
Wise, p	0	0	0	0	0	0
Doyle, 2b	5	0	1	0	2	0
Yas'mski, lf-1b	6	1	3	7	1	0
Fisk, c	4	2	2	9	1	0
Lynn, cf	4	2	2	2	0	0
Petrocelli, 3b	4	1	0	1	1	0
Evans, rf	5	0	1	5	1	0
Burleson, ss	3	0	0	3	2	1
Tiant, p	2	0	0	0	2	0
Moret, p	0	0	0	0	1	0
dCarbo, lf	2	1	1	1	0	0
Totals	41	7	10	36	11	1

Cincinnati .... 0 0 0 0 3 0 2 1 0 0 0 0—6
Boston .... 3 0 0 0 0 0 0 3 0 0 0 1—7
None out when winning run scored.

Cincinnati	IP.	H.	R.	ER.	BB.	SO.
Nolan	2	3	3	3	0	2
Norman	⅔	1	0	0	2	0
Billingham	1⅓	1	0	0	1	1
Carroll	1	0	0	0	0	0
Borbon	2†	1	2	2	2	1
Eastwick	1‡	2	1	1	1	2
McEnaney	1	0	0	0	1	0
Darcy (L)	2h	1	1	1	0	1

Boston	IP.	H.	R.	ER.	BB.	SO.
Tiant	7*	11	6	6	2	5
Moret	1	0	0	0	0	0
Drago	3	1	0	0	1	1
Wise (W)	1	2	0	0	0	1

*Pitched to one batter in eighth.
†Pitched to two batters in eighth.
‡Pitched to two batters in ninth.
§Pitched to one batter in twelfth.

Bases on balls—Off Norman 2 (Fisk, Lynn), off Billingham 1 (Burleson), off Borbon 2 (Burleson, Petrocelli), off Eastwick 1 (Doyle), off McEnaney 1 (Fisk), off Tiant 2 (Griffey, Armbrister).
Strikeouts—By Nolan 2 (Evans, Tiant), by Billingham 1 (Petrocelli), by Eastwick 2 (Evans, Cooper), by Darcy 1 (Carbo), by Borbon 1 (Tiant), by Tiant 5 (Bench 2, Perez 2, Geronimo), by Drago 1 (Geronimo), by Wise 1 (Geronimo).
aFlied out for Nolan in third. bWalked for Billingham in fifth. cSingled for Carroll in sixth. dHomered for Moret in eighth. eFlied out for McEnaney in tenth. fFlied out for Drago in eleventh. Runs batted in—Griffey 2, Bench, Foster 2, Geronimo, Lynn 3, Carbo 3, Fisk. Two-base hits—Doyle, Evans, Foster. Three-base hit—Griffey. Home runs—Lynn, Geronimo, Carbo, Fisk. Stolen base—Concepcion. Sacrifice hit—Tiant. Double plays—Foster and Bench; Evans, Yastrzemski and Burleson. Hit by pitcher—By Drago (Rose). Left on bases—Cincinnati 11, Boston 9. Umpires—Davidson (N.L.) plate, Frantz (A.L.) first base, Colosi (N.L.) second base, Barnett (A.L.) third base, Stello (N.L.) left field, Maloney (A.L.) right field. Time—4:01. Attendance—35,205.

Wednesday, October 22—At Boston

Cincinnati (N.L.)	AB.	R.	H.	O.	A.	E.
Rose, 3b	4	0	2	2	2	0
Morgan, 2b	4	0	2	2	4	0
Bench, c	4	1	0	7	0	0
Perez, 1b	5	1	1	8	1	0
Foster, lf	4	0	1	1	0	0
Concepcion, ss	4	0	1	0	2	0
Griffey, rf	2	2	1	3	0	0
Geronimo, cf	3	0	0	3	0	0
Gullett, p	1	0	1	0	0	0
aRettenmund	1	0	0	0	0	0
Billingham, p	0	0	0	0	0	0
bArmbrister	0	0	0	0	0	0
Carroll, p	0	0	0	1	0	0
dDriessen	1	0	0	0	0	0
McEnaney, p	0	0	0	0	0	0
Totals	33	4	9	27	9	0

Boston (A.L.)	AB.	R.	H.	O.	A.	E.
Carbo, lf	3	1	1	0	1	0
Miller, lf	0	0	0	0	0	0
eBeniquez	1	0	0	0	0	0
Doyle, 2b	4	1	1	5	3	2
fMontgomery	1	0	0	0	0	0
Yastrz'ski, 1b	5	1	1	9	0	0
Fisk, c	3	0	0	4	0	0
Lynn, cf	2	0	0	1	0	0
Petrocelli, 3b	3	0	1	1	3	0
Evans, rf	2	0	0	5	0	0
Burleson, ss	3	0	0	2	7	0
Lee, p	3	0	1	0	1	0
Moret, p	0	0	0	0	0	0
Willoughby, p	0	0	0	0	0	0
cCooper	1	0	0	0	0	0
Burton, p	0	0	0	0	0	0
Cleveland, p	0	0	0	0	0	0
Totals	31	3	5	27	15	2

Cincinnati .... 0 0 0 0 0 2 1 0 1—4
Boston .... 0 0 3 0 0 0 0 0 0—3

Cincinnati	IP.	H.	R.	ER.	BB.	SO.
Gullett	4	4	3	3	5	5
Billingham	2	1	0	0	2	1
Carroll (W)	2	0	0	0	1	1
McEnaney (S)	1	0	0	0	0	0

Boston	IP.	H.	R.	ER.	BB.	SO.
Lee	6⅓	7	3	3	1	2
Moret	⅓	1	0	0	2	0
Willoughby	1⅓	0	0	0	0	0
Burton (L)	⅔	1	1	1	2	0
Cleveland	⅓	0	0	0	1	0

Bases on balls—Off Gullett 5 (Lynn, Carbo, Fisk, Petrocelli, Evans), off Billingham 2 (Lynn, Burleson), off Carroll 1 (Evans), off Lee 1 (Griffey), off Moret 2 (Armbrister, Morgan), off Burton 2 (Griffey, Rose), off Cleveland 1 (Bench).
Strikeouts—By Gullett 5 (Fisk, Petrocelli, Lee, Lynn, Burleson), by Billingham 1 (Fisk), by Carroll 1 (Fisk), by Lee 2 (Morgan, Geronimo).
aHit into double play for Gullett in fifth. bWalked for Billingham in seventh. cFouled out for Willoughby in eighth. dGrounded out for Carroll in ninth. eFlied out for Miller in ninth. fGrounded out for Doyle in ninth. Runs batted in—Perez 2, Rose, Morgan, Yastrzemski, Petrocelli, Evans. Two-base hit—Carbo. Home run—Perez. Stolen bases—Morgan, Griffey. Sacrifice hit—Geronimo. Double plays—Doyle, Burleson and Yastrzemski; Burleson, Doyle and Yastrzemski; Rose, Morgan and Perez. Wild pitch—Gullett. Left on bases—Cincinnati 9, Boston 9. Umpires—Frantz (A.L.) plate, Colosi (N.L.) first base, Barnett (A.L.) second base, Stello (N.L.) third base, Maloney (A.L.) left field, Davidson (N.L.) right field. Time—2:52. Attendance—35,205.

1976 WORLD SERIES

SERIES OF 1976

	W.	L.	Pct.
Cincinnati N. L.	4	0	1.000
New York A. L.	0	4	.000

COMPOSITE BATTING AVERAGES
Cincinnati Reds

Player-Position	G.	AB.	R.	H.	2B.	3B.	HR.	RBI.	BA.
McEnaney, p	5	1	0	1	0	0	0	0	1.000
Crowley, ph	2	2	0	1	0	0	0	0	.500
Rose, 3b	7	27	3	10	1	1	0	2	.370
Gullett, p	3	7	1	2	0	0	0	0	.286
Geronimo, cf	7	25	3	7	0	1	2	3	.280
Foster, lf	7	29	1	8	1	0	0	2	.276
Griffey, rf	7	26	4	7	3	1	0	4	.269
Morgan, 2b	7	27	4	7	1	0	0	3	.259
Bench, c	7	29	5	6	2	0	1	4	.207
Concepcion, ss	7	28	3	5	1	0	1	4	.179
Perez, 1b	7	28	4	5	0	0	3	7	.179
Armbrister, ph	4	1	1	0	0	0	0	0	.000
Eastwick, p	5	1	0	0	0	0	0	0	.000
Borbon, p	3	1	0	0	0	0	0	0	.000
Darcy, p	2	1	0	0	0	0	0	0	.000
Nolan, p	2	1	0	0	0	0	0	0	.000
Norman, p	2	1	0	0	0	0	0	0	.000
Billingham, p	3	2	0	0	0	0	0	0	.000
Chaney, ph	2	2	0	0	0	0	0	0	.000
Driessen, ph	2	2	0	0	0	0	0	0	.000
Rettenmund, ph	3	3	0	0	0	0	0	0	.000
Carroll, p	5	0	0	0	0	0	0	0	.000
Totals	7	244	29	59	9	3	7	29	.242

Boston Red Sox

Player-Position	G.	AB.	R.	H.	2B.	3B.	HR.	RBI.	BA.
Carbo, ph-lf	4	7	3	3	1	0	2	4	.429
Yastrzemski, lf-1b	7	29	7	9	0	0	0	4	.310
Petrocelli, 3b	7	26	3	8	1	0	0	4	.308
Burleson, ss	7	24	1	7	1	0	0	2	.292
Evans, rf	7	24	3	7	1	1	1	5	.292
Lynn, cf	7	25	3	7	0	0	1	5	.280
Doyle, 2b	7	30	3	8	1	1	0	0	.267
Tiant, p	3	8	2	2	0	0	0	0	.250
Fisk, c	7	25	5	6	0	0	2	4	.240
Lee, p	2	6	0	1	0	0	0	0	.167
Beniquez, lf-ph	3	8	1	1	0	0	0	1	.125
Cooper, 1b-ph	5	19	0	1	1	0	0	0	.053
Griffin, ph	1	1	0	0	0	0	0	0	.000
Montgomery, ph	1	1	0	0	0	0	0	0	.000
Cleveland, p	3	2	0	0	0	0	0	0	.000
Miller, lf-ph	3	2	0	0	0	0	0	0	.000
Wise, p	2	2	0	0	0	0	0	0	.000
Moret, p	3	0	0	0	0	0	0	0	.000
Willoughby, p	3	0	0	0	0	0	0	0	.000
Burton, p	2	0	0	0	0	0	0	0	.000
Drago, p	2	0	0	0	0	0	0	0	.000
Pole, p	1	0	0	0	0	0	0	0	.000
Segui, p	1	0	0	0	0	0	0	0	.000
Totals	7	239	30	60	7	2	6	30	.251

COMPOSITE PITCHING AVERAGES
Cincinnati Reds

Pitcher	G.	IP.	H.	R.	E.	SO.	BB.	W.	L.	ERA.
Billingham	3	9	8	2	1	7	5	0	0	1.00
Eastwick	5	8	6	2	2	4	3	2	0	2.25
McEnaney	5	6⅔	3	2	2	5	2	0	0	2.70
Carroll	5	5⅔	4	2	2	3	2	1	0	3.18
Gullett	3	18⅔	19	9	9	15	10	1	1	4.34
Darcy	2	4	3	2	2	1	2	0	1	4.50
Nolan	2	6	6	4	4	2	1	0	0	6.00
Borbon	3	3	3	3	2	1	2	0	0	6.00
Norman	2	4	8	4	4	2	3	0	1	9.00
Totals	7	65	60	30	28	40	30	4	3	3.88

Saves—Eastwick, McEnaney.

Boston Red Sox

Pitcher	G.	IP.	H.	R.	E.	SO.	BB.	W.	L.	ERA.
Willoughby	3	6⅓	3	1	0	2	0	0	1	0.00
Moret	3	1⅔	2	0	0	1	3	0	0	0.00
Segui	1	1	0	0	0	0	0	0	0	0.00
Drago	2	4	3	1	1	1	0	0	1	2.25
Lee	2	14⅓	12	5	5	7	3	0	0	3.14
Tiant	3	25	25	10	10	12	8	2	0	3.60
Cleveland	3	6⅔	7	5	5	3	2	1	0	6.75
Wise	2	5⅓	6	5	5	2	2	1	0	8.44
Burton	2	1	1	1	1	3	0	0	1	9.00
Pole	1	0	0	1	1	0	2	0	0	......
Totals	7	65⅓	59	29	28	30	25	3	4	3.86

Shutout—Tiant.

The Cincinnati Reds became the first National League team to win two consecutive World Series since the New York Giants of 1921 and 1922 when they swept by the New York Yankees in four straight games.

The Reds, easy winners of the National League West Division, got to the Series by blowing out the N.L. East champs, the Philadelphia Phillies, three games in a row in the playoffs. Thus the Reds became the first team to capture seven straight post-season games since the inauguration of the pennant playoffs in 1969.

The Yankees, leaders in the American League East, won the A.L. pennant by downing the West Division winners, the Kansas City Royals, in a five-game set.

The New Yorkers were making their first appearance in the Classic since 1964 and their subsequent showing bore no resemblance at all to the great Yankee teams of the past that took World Series victories as a matter of course.

The 1976 World Series was the first in which the designated hitter was used. As a concession to the American League, Commissioner Bowie Kuhn ordered that the DH be used in the Series in alternating years. As a concession to television, Kuhn ordered that the first Sunday game be played at night. Both decisions provoked considerable criticism from fans and the press.

Kuhn also made and then rescinded another decision regarding the use by the Yankees of walkie-talkies to help them position their outfielders. The Yankees had been doing it during the season and Kuhn said they could do it in the World Series. But after the first inning of the opening game, he withdrew his approval, claiming the original okay had been to use one man in the stands but that the Yankees had violated the agreement by using three men roaming the upper deck. Later, when the Yankees went back to the one-man in-the-stands operation, permission was again granted. Overall, it was an inconsequential thing with no bearing on the play. But one got the impression watching the Yankee outfielders that they could use all the help they could get.

Cincinnati had its star southpaw, Don Gullett, primed for the Saturday opener—the only game played by daylight—and he was opposed by a surprise starter, right-hander Doyle Alexander. The Yankees had used much of their pitching strength in the playoffs and could not open with their big ace, Catfish Hunter, as they would liked to have done.

The Reds' second baseman, Joe Morgan, set the tone of the Series when he rapped an Alexander fast ball over the fence for a home run in the first inning. The Yankees tied the score in the second on a double by designated hitter Lou Piniella, who moved to third on an infield out and scored on a sacrifice fly by Graig Nettles. But it was the only scoring the Yankees were to manage during the afternoon.

The Reds went ahead for good in the third frame on a triple by shortstop Dave Concepcion and a sacrifice fly by Pete Rose. The score climbed to 3-1 in the sixth on a walk to Rose, a forceout by Ken Griffey, his steal of second and a single by Tony Perez.

Alexander went to the showers in the seventh without retiring a batter. George Foster singled and scored on Johnny Bench's triple. Sparky Lyle replaced Alexander and uncorked a wild pitch, permitting Bench to score.

Gullett kept the Yankees under control while in the game but he was forced to leave the contest in the eighth inning when he suffered the dislocation of a tendon in an ankle. Later it was revealed that the ankle would have to be placed in a cast and the lefty was through for the Series. As events turned out, he wasn't needed anymore. Righthander Pedro Borbon relieved Gullett and retired all five batters he faced.

Hunter was on the mound in the second game and he was opposed by lefty Fred Norman. It was a cold Sunday night and that seemed to bother Hunter. In the second inning the Reds jumped off to a 3-0 lead. Danny Driessen, the first designated hitter ever to be used by the National League, doubled to center and scored on Foster's single. After Foster was thrown out on an attempted steal, Bench doubled to left-center. Cesar Geronimo drew a walk and Concepcion delivered a run-producing single. Rose then walked to load the bases and Geronimo scored on Griffey's sacrifice fly.

But the Yankees came back. They got a run in the fourth on singles by Thurman Munson, Chris Chambliss and Nettles and knocked out Norman in the seventh on a single by Willie Randolph, an RBI double by Fred Stanley and a single by Roy White. Jack Billingham replaced Norman and the tying run came home while a forceout was made at second base.

Hunter had settled down after his early troubles and assumed full command of the game. It looked like extra innings were in order when he retired the first two Reds in the bottom of the ninth. But a throwing error by shortstop Stanley enabled Griffey to reach second base. Morgan was given an intentional base on balls so that Hunter could have the presumed advantage of pitching to the righthanded-hitting Perez. But the Cincinnati first sacker ruined the strategy by lining the first pitch to left field for a single. Griffey scored and the Reds took a 2-0 advantage in the Series.

After a day off for travel, the scene for the third game shifted to refurbished Yankee Stadium. Driessen, the DH for the Reds, had a single, double, homer and walk and scored two runs. Carlos May, the Yankee DH, was 0 for 4.

Dock Ellis, a former National Leaguer, started on the hill for the Yankees and lasted less than four innings. In the second frame, Driessen singled, stole second and rode home on Foster's double. A single by Bench, a forceout, another steal and a single by Concepcion added two more. Driessen hit his homer in the fourth.

The Yankees picked up a run in their half of the fourth on singles by Chambliss and Oscar Gamble wrapped around a walk. They got another in the seventh when Jim Mason, who had replaced Stanley at shortstop in the fifth inning, hit a home run. After Mason's circuit clout, a walk to Mickey Rivers and a two-out single by Munson drove Cincinnati starter Pat Zachry off the mound. But reliever Will McEnaney then slammed the door.

The Cincinnati team got two more runs in the eighth on singles by Rose, Griffey and Foster, with a double by Morgan thrown in for good measure.

A day of rain held off the Reds' clinching of the championship but they finished off the job when play resumed on Thursday night. After the Yankees opened the scoring in their first turn at bat on a single by Munson and a double by Chambliss, the Reds took command in the fourth inning. Morgan walked, stole second and scored on Foster's single. Bench then blasted a homer high off the screen on the left-field foul pole and the Reds took a 3-1 lead.

The Yanks crept within a run in the fifth when Rivers was safe on a bloop single, stole second and scored on Munson's single. Reds' starter Gary Nolan nursed the slender margin into the seventh. When Munson singled with two out, Cincinnati skipper Sparky Anderson brought in McEnaney to face the Bombers' cleanup hitter, Chambliss. Once again the lefthander was equal to the task, getting Chambliss on a ground ball to Morgan and pitching hitless ball the rest of the way to earn his second save.

The Reds put the icing on the cake in their final turn at bat. Perez drew a pass and moved to second on a wild pitch. With Driessen at the plate, action was suspended for several minutes while National League umpire Bruce Froemming ejected Yankee Manager Billy Martin for throwing a baseball onto the field. Martin and A.L. ump Bill Deegan, working behind the plate, had been verbally jousting throughout the game. When play resumed and Driessen drew a walk, starter Ed Figueroa was replaced by Dick Tidrow. Perez advanced to third on Foster's fly to deep center. Bench then came to the plate and hit a line shot into the left-field seats for a three-run homer. Geronimo and Concepcion then belted successive doubles to complete the scoring and Sparky Lyle came on to finally put out the fire.

The Yankees went down 1-2-3 in the ninth and the Series was over.

Bench, who batted .533 and had two homers, a triple and a double and six runs batted in, was voted the No. 1 star of the Series. His counterpart, Munson, batted .529 and finished up with six straight hits, tying a Series record. He was a heroic figure in a losing cause.

The Reds made great use of their overall speed, stealing seven bases, while the Yankees could manage but one.

The box scores:

Saturday, October 16—At Cincinnati

New York (A.L.)	AB.	R.	H.	O.	A.	E.
Rivers, cf	4	0	0	3	0	0
White, lf	4	0	1	4	0	0
Munson, c	4	0	1	5	1	0
Piniella, dh	3	1	1	0	0	0
bMay, dh	1	0	0	0	0	0
Chambliss, 1b	3	0	1	4	0	1
Nettles, 3b	3	0	0	3	0	0
Maddox, rf	2	0	1	0	0	0
cGamble	1	0	0	0	0	0
Randolph, 2b	2	0	0	3	2	0
Stanley, ss	1	0	0	2	3	0
aVelez	1	0	0	0	0	0
Mason, ss	0	0	0	0	1	0
Alexander, p	0	0	0	0	1	0
Lyle, p	0	0	0	0	0	0
Totals	29	1	5	24	8	1

Cincinnati (N.L.)	AB.	R.	H.	O.	A.	E.
Rose, 3b	2	0	0	2	2	0
Griffey, rf	4	1	0	2	0	0
Morgan, 2b	4	1	1	3	4	0
Perez, 1b	4	0	3	11	0	0
Driessen, dh	4	0	0	0	0	0
Foster, lf	3	1	2	0	0	0
Bench, c	3	1	2	5	1	0
Geronimo, cf	3	0	1	2	0	1
Concepcion, ss	3	1	1	2	3	0
Gullett, p	0	0	0	0	1	0
Borbon, p	0	0	0	0	1	0
Totals	30	5	10	27	12	1

New York .... 0 1 0 0 0 0 0 0 0—1
Cincinnati .... 1 0 1 0 0 1 2 0 *—5

New York	IP.	H.	R.	ER.	BB.	SO.
Alexander (L)	6*	9	5	5	2	1
Lyle	2	1	0	0	0	3

Cincinnati	IP.	H.	R.	ER.	BB.	SO.
Gullett (W)	7⅓	5	1	1	3	4
Borbon	1⅔	0	0	0	0	0

*Pitched to two batters in seventh.

Bases on balls—Off Gullett 3 (Stanley, Maddox, Randolph), off Alexander 2 (Foster, Rose). Strikeouts—By Gullett 4 (Rivers, Munson, Stanley, Velez), by Alexander 1 (Morgan), by Lyle 3 (Concepcion, Griffey, Perez). aStruck out for Stanley in seventh. bFlied out for Piniella in eighth. cFouled out for Maddox in ninth. Runs batted in—Nettles, Morgan, Rose, Perez, Bench. Two-base hits—Piniella, Perez, Geronimo. Three-base hits—Concepcion, Maddox, Bench. Home run—Morgan. Stolen base—Griffey. Caught stealing—Perez, Rivers. Sacrifice flies—Nettles, Rose. Double plays—Alexander, Randolph and Chambliss; Randolph, Stanley and Chambliss; Morgan, Concepcion and Perez; Morgan and Perez. Wild pitch—Lyle. Hit by pitcher—By Gullett (Chambliss). Left on bases—New York 6, Cincinnati 4. Umpires—Weyer (N.L.) plate, DiMuro (A.L.) first base, B. Williams (N.L.) second base, Deegan (A.L.) third base, Froemming (N.L.) left field, Phillips (A.L.) right field. Time—2:10. Attendance—54,826.

Sunday, October 17—At Cincinnati

New York (A.L.)	AB.	R.	H.	O.	A.	E.
Rivers, cf	5	0	0	6	0	0
White, lf	3	0	1	6	0	0
Munson, c	4	1	1	7	1	0
Piniella, rf	4	0	2	1	0	0
Chambliss, 1b	4	0	2	2	0	0
Nettles, 3b	4	0	1	2	1	0
Maddox, dh	3	0	0	0	0	0
aMay, dh	1	0	0	0	0	0
Randolph, 2b	4	1	1	2	0	0
Stanley, ss	3	1	1	0	0	1
Hunter, p	0	0	0	0	1	0
Totals	35	3	9	26	3	1

Cincinnati (N.L.)	AB.	R.	H.	O.	A.	E.
Rose, 3b	4	0	0	0	0	0
Griffey, rf	4	1	0	1	0	0
Morgan, 2b	4	0	2	6	3	0
Perez, 1b	5	0	2	8	1	0
Driessen, dh	4	1	2	0	0	0
Foster, lf	4	0	2	2	0	0
Bench, c	4	1	2	3	0	0
Geronimo, cf	2	1	0	4	0	0
Concepcion, ss	4	0	1	2	3	0
Norman, p	0	0	0	0	1	0
Billingham, p	0	0	0	1	0	0
Totals	35	4	10	27	8	0

New York .... 0 0 0 1 0 0 2 0 0—3
Cincinnati .... 0 3 0 0 0 0 0 0 1—4

Two out when winning run scored.

New York	IP.	H.	R.	ER.	BB.	SO.
Hunter (L)	8⅔	10	4	3	4	5

Cincinnati	IP.	H.	R.	ER.	BB.	SO.
Norman	6⅓	9	3	3	2	2
Bill'gham (W)	2⅔	0	0	0	0	1

Bases on balls—Off Norman 2 (Stanley, White), off Hunter 4 (Geronimo 2, Rose, Morgan).

Strikeouts—By Norman 2 (Maddox 2), by Billingham 1 (Randolph), by Hunter 5 (Foster 2, Concepcion, Bench, Rose).

aGrounded out for Maddox in eighth. Runs batted in—Nettles, Stanley, Munson, Foster, Concepcion, Griffey, Perez. Two-base hits—Driessen, Bench, Stanley. Three-base hit—Morgan. Stolen bases—Morgan, Concepcion. Caught stealing—Foster. Sacrifice fly—Griffey. Double play—Concepcion, Morgan and Perez. Left on bases—New York 7, Cincinnati 10. Umpires—DiMuro (A.L.) plate, B. Williams (N.L.) first base, Deegan (A.L.) second base, Froemming (N.L.) third base, Phillips (A.L.) left field, Weyer (N.L.) right field. Time—2:33. Attendance—54,816.

Tuesday, October 19—At New York

Cincinnati (N.L.)	AB.	R.	H.	O.	A.	E.
Rose, 3b	5	1	2	1	1	0
Griffey, rf	4	0	1	0	0	0
Morgan, 2b	4	1	1	2	0	1

	AB.	R.	H.	O.	A.	E.
Perez, 1b	4	0	0	7	2	0
Driessen, dh	3	2	3	0	0	0
Foster, lf	4	1	2	4	0	0
Bench, c	4	0	2	8	0	0
Geronimo, cf	4	1	1	3	0	0
Concepcion, ss	4	0	1	1	2	0
Zachry, p	0	0	0	0	2	1
McEnaney, p	0	0	0	1	0	0
Totals	36	6	13	27	7	2

New York (A.L.)	AB.	R.	H.	O.	A.	E.
Rivers, cf	4	0	2	1	0	0
White, lf	3	0	0	1	0	0
Munson, c	5	0	3	6	2	0
Chambliss, 1b	5	1	1	11	1	0
May, dh	4	0	0	0	0	0
Nettles, 3b	2	0	0	1	4	0
Gamble, rf	3	0	1	2	0	0
bPiniella, rf	1	0	0	0	0	0
Randolph, 2b	4	0	0	4	4	0
Stanley, ss	1	0	0	1	2	0
aHendricks	1	0	0	0	0	0
Mason, ss	1	1	1	0	1	0
cVelez	1	0	0	0	0	0
Ellis, p	0	0	0	0	0	0
Jackson, p	0	0	0	0	3	0
Tidrow, p	0	0	0	0	0	0
Totals	35	2	8	27	17	0

Cincinnati......... 0 3 0 1 0 0 0 2 0—6
New York......... 0 0 0 1 0 0 1 0 0—2

Cincinnati	IP.	H.	R.	ER.	BB.	SO.
Zachry (W)	6⅔	6	2	2	5	6
McEnaney (S)	2⅓	2	0	0	0	1

New York	IP.	H.	R.	ER.	BB.	SO.
Ellis (L)	3⅓	7	4	4	0	1
Jackson	3⅔*	4	2	2	0	3
Tidrow	2	2	0	0	1	1

*Pitched to three batters in eighth.

Bases on balls—Off Tidrow 1 (Driessen), off Zachry 5 (Nettles 2, White 2, Rivers). Strikeouts—By Ellis 1 (Perez), by Jackson 3 (Concepcion, Morgan, Geronimo), by Tidrow 1 (Rose), by Zachry 6 (Chambliss 2, Rivers, May, Nettles, Randolph), by McEnaney 1 (Velez). aFlied out for Stanley in fourth. bGrounded out for Gamble in eighth. cStruck out for Mason in ninth. Runs batted in—Foster 2, Geronimo, Concepcion, Driessen, Morgan, Gamble, Mason. Two-base hits—Foster, Driessen, Morgan. Home runs—Driessen, Mason. Stolen bases—Driessen, Geronimo. Caught stealing—Bench. Double plays—Stanley, Randolph and Chambliss; Nettles and Chambliss; Nettles, Randolph and Chambliss; Perez and Concepcion. Left on bases—Cincinnati 4, New York 11. Umpires—B. Williams (N.L.) plate, Deegan (A.L.) first base, Froemming (N.L.) second base, Phillips (A.L.) third base, Weyer (N.L.) left field, DiMuro (A.L.) right field. Time—2:40. Attendance—56,667.

Thursday, October 21—At New York

Cincinnati (N.L.)	AB.	R.	H.	O.	A.	E.
Rose, 3b	5	0	1	3	0	0
Griffey, rf	5	0	0	2	0	0
Morgan, 2b	3	1	1	2	3	1
Perez, 1b	3	1	0	6	1	0
Driessen, dh	3	1	0	0	0	0
Foster, lf	3	1	1	8	0	0
Bench, c	4	2	2	2	1	0
Geronimo, cf	4	1	2	3	0	0
Concepcion, ss	3	0	2	1	3	1
Nolan, p	0	0	0	0	1	0
McEnaney, p	0	0	0	0	0	0
Totals	33	7	9	27	9	2

New York (A.L.)	AB.	R.	H.	O.	A.	E.
Rivers, cf	5	1	1	4	0	0
White, lf	5	0	0	2	0	0
Munson, c	4	1	4	3	3	0
Chambliss, 1b	4	0	1	9	2	0
May, dh	3	0	0	0	0	0
bPiniella, dh	1	0	0	0	0	0
Nettles, 3b	3	0	2	2	3	0
Gamble, rf	4	0	0	1	0	0
Randolph, 2b	4	0	0	4	2	0
Stanley, ss	1	0	0	1	2	0
aHendricks	1	0	0	0	0	0
Mason, ss	0	0	0	1	0	0
cVelez	1	0	0	0	0	0
Figueroa, p	0	0	0	0	1	0
Tidrow, p	0	0	0	0	0	0
Lyle, p	0	0	0	0	0	0
Totals	36	2	8	27	13	0

Cincinnati......... 0 0 0 3 0 0 0 0 4—7
New York......... 1 0 0 0 1 0 0 0 0—2

Cincinnati	IP.	H.	R.	ER.	BB.	SO.
Nolan (W)	6⅔	8	2	2	1	1
McEnaney (S)	2⅓	0	0	0	1	1

New York	IP.	H.	R.	ER.	BB.	SO.
Figueroa (L)	8*	6	5	5	5	2
Tidrow	⅓	3	2	2	0	0
Lyle	⅔	0	0	0	0	0

*Pitched to two batters in ninth.

Bases on balls—Off Figueroa 5 (Foster, Concepcion, Morgan, Perez, Driessen), off Nolan 1 (Stanley), off McEnaney 1 (Nettles). Strikeouts—By Figueroa 2 (Foster, Geronimo), by Nolan 1 (Randolph), by McEnaney 1 (Velez). aFouled out for Stanley in sixth. bFlied out for May in eighth. cStruck out for Mason in ninth. Runs batted in—Foster, Bench 5, Concepcion, Chambliss, Munson. Two-base hits—Rose, Chambliss, Geronimo, Concepcion. Home runs—Bench 2. Stolen bases—Geronimo, Morgan, Rivers. Caught stealing—Foster, Nettles, Concepcion. Double play—Stanley, Nettles, Chambliss and Randolph. Wild pitch—Figueroa. Left on bases—Cincinnati 4, New York 9. Umpires—Deegan (A.L.) plate, Froemming (N.L.) second base, Phillips (A.L.) third base, DiMuro (A.L.) left field, B. Williams (N.L.) right field. Time—2:36. Attendance—56,700.

COMPOSITE BATTING AVERAGES
Cincinnati Reds

Player-Position	G.	AB.	R.	H.	2B.	3B.	HR.	RBI.	BA.
Bench, c	4	15	4	8	1	1	2	6	.533
Foster, lf	4	14	3	6	1	0	0	4	.429
Concepcion, ss	4	14	1	5	1	1	0	3	.357
Driessen, dh	4	14	4	5	2	0	1	1	.357
Morgan, 2b	4	15	3	5	1	1	1	2	.333
Perez, 1b	4	16	1	5	1	0	0	2	.313
Geronimo, cf	4	13	3	4	2	0	0	1	.308
Rose, 3b	4	16	1	3	0	0	0	1	.188
Griffey, rf	4	17	2	1	0	0	0	1	.059
McEnaney, p	2	0	0	0	0	0	0	0	.000
Borbon, p	1	0	0	0	0	0	0	0	.000
Billingham, p	1	0	0	0	0	0	0	0	.000
Gullett, p	1	0	0	0	0	0	0	0	.000
Nolan, p	1	0	0	0	0	0	0	0	.000
Norman, p	1	0	0	0	0	0	0	0	.000
Zachry, p	1	0	0	0	0	0	0	0	.000
Totals	4	134	22	42	10	3	4	21	.313

New York Yankees

Player-Position	G.	AB.	R.	H.	2B.	3B.	HR.	RBI.	BA.
Mason, ss	3	1	1	1	0	0	1	1	1.000
Munson, c	4	17	2	9	0	0	0	2	.529
Piniella, dh-rf-ph	4	9	1	3	1	0	0	0	.333
Chambliss, 1b	4	16	1	5	0	0	0	1	.313
Nettles, 3b	4	12	0	3	0	0	0	2	.250
Maddox, rf-dh	2	5	0	1	0	0	0	0	.200

Player-Position	G.	AB.	R.	H.	2B.	3B.	HR.	RBI.	BA.
Rivers, cf	4	18	1	3	0	0	0	0	.167
Stanley, ss	4	6	1	1	0	0	0	1	.167
White, lf	4	15	0	2	0	0	0	0	.133
Gamble, ph-rf	3	8	0	1	0	0	0	1	.125
Randolph, 2b	4	14	1	1	0	0	0	0	.071
Hendricks, ph	2	2	0	0	0	0	0	0	.000
Velez, ph	3	3	0	0	0	0	0	0	.000
May, ph-dh	4	9	0	0	0	0	0	0	.000
Tidrow, p	2	0	0	0	0	0	0	0	.000
Lyle, p	2	0	0	0	0	0	0	0	.000
Alexander, p	1	0	0	0	0	0	0	0	.000
Ellis, p	1	0	0	0	0	0	0	0	.000
Figueroa, p	1	0	0	0	0	0	0	0	.000
Hunter, p	1	0	0	0	0	0	0	0	.000
Jackson, p	1	0	0	0	0	0	0	0	.000
Totals	4	135	8	30	3	1	1	8	.222

COMPOSITE PITCHING AVERAGES

Cincinnati Reds

Pitcher	G.	IP.	H.	R.	E.	SO.	BB.	W.	L.	ERA.
McEnaney	2	4⅔	2	0	0	1	2	0	0	0.00
Billingham	1	2⅔	0	0	0	0	1	1	0	0.00
Borbon	1	1⅔	0	0	0	0	0	0	0	0.00
Gullett	1	7⅓	5	1	1	3	4	1	0	1.23
Nolan	1	6⅔	8	2	2	1	1	1	0	2.70
Zachry	1	6⅔	6	2	2	5	6	1	0	2.70
Norman	1	6⅓	9	3	3	2	2	0	0	4.26
Totals	4	36	30	8	8	12	16	4	0	2.00

Saves—McEnaney 2.

New York Yankees

Pitcher	G.	IP.	H.	R.	E.	SO.	BB.	W.	L.	ERA.
Lyle	2	2⅔	1	0	0	0	3	0	0	0.00
Hunter	1	8⅔	10	4	3	4	5	0	1	3.12
Jackson	1	3⅔	4	2	2	0	3	0	0	4.91
Figueroa	1	8	6	5	5	5	2	0	1	5.63
Alexander	1	6	9	5	5	2	1	0	1	7.50
Tidrow	2	2⅓	5	2	2	1	1	0	0	7.71
Ellis	1	3⅓	7	4	4	0	1	0	1	10.80
Totals	4	34⅔	42	22	21	12	16	0	4	5.45

SERIES OF 1977

	W.	L.	Pct.
New York A. L.	4	2	.667
Los Angeles N. L.	2	4	.333

The New York Yankees captured their record 21st World Series when they defeated the Los Angeles Dodgers, four games to two, in a match that produced one of the greatest individual slugging performances in Series history.

For a long time during the season, it seemed that the Yankees would never even reach the World Series. They trailed the Boston Red Sox by a good margin in August in the American League East Division and then, after taking a September lead, managed only with extreme difficulty to hang on.

In the Championship Series against West Division winner Kansas City, the New Yorkers appeared beaten, down by a run in the ninth inning of the fifth game. But they rallied for three tallies and so qualified for baseball's supreme test.

The Dodgers sprinted to a long early lead in the National League West Division and had little trouble staying well ahead of the defending world champion Cincinnati Reds.

In the National League Championship Series they beat the Philadelphia Phillies, losing the first game and then winning three straight.

The opening game of the World Series produced a surprise in that New York Manager Billy Martin nominated Don Gullett as his starting pitcher, opposed by the Dodgers' veteran ace, righthander Don Sutton.

Gullett, a high-priced acquisition of the Yankees as a result of baseball's new free-agency system, had complained of a sore shoulder in the last month of the regular season and lasted a mere two innings in his lone start in the playoffs.

But after a shaky first inning in which the Dodgers scored two runs, the southpaw was in command the remainder of the game and nursed a 3-2 lead into the ninth inning.

But Dusty Baker led off with a single and with one out Steve Yeager walked. Sparky Lyle replaced Gullett with the game on the line. Pinch-hitter Lee Lacy connected for a single to tie the game, but Lyle retired the side without further damage.

After threatening in the 10th and 11th innings, the New York team won the game in the 12th frame. Willie Randolph doubled off Dodger reliever Rick Rhoden and Thurman Munson was intentionally walked. Paul Blair, who had entered the game only as a defensive replacement for Reggie Jackson in right field, failed in two attempts to sacrifice the runners along. He then grounded a single to left, scoring Randolph and giving the Yankees the victory.

Martin tried another gamble in the second game but this time he wasn't successful. He chose for his starting pitcher Jim (Catfish) Hunter, who hadn't worked since September 10 because of a sore arm. Hunter had nothing on the ball. Home runs by Ron Cey, Yeager and Reggie Smith produced five Los Angeles runs in less than three full innings and the contest, for all practical purposes, was over. Righthander Burt Hooton was the Los Angeles hurler and he gave up just one run and five hits while striking out eight. The final score was 6-1.

There was a day off for travel while the Series moved to Los Angeles. But it was not a day without news. Much unfavorable comment filled the newspapers on the rowdy behavior of Yankee fans during the second game when their team was being beaten and many people wished the Series would not have to return to New York.

Reggie Jackson took the day off to criticize Martin for starting Hunter and Munson threatened not to play in Los Angeles unless he was given better tickets for his family and friends.

Regardless, the Series did resume in L.A. and the opposing pitchers were righthander Mike Torrez for the American Leaguers and star lefty Tommy John for the home team.

The Yankees jumped on John for three runs and four hits in their first turn at bat for a lead that held up only until the third inning. In that frame Dusty Baker hit a homer with two men on to tie the score.

But throwing the gopher ball to Baker was the only real mistake Torrez was to make. He shut the Dodgers out the rest of the evening and the Yankees managed to get single runs in the fourth and fifth innings to win the game, 5-3.

The next day it was Dodger Manager Tommy Lasorda's turn to gamble on his pitching selection. He went with Doug Rau, a sore-armed lefty who had done little of consequence the final part of the season.

The Yankees welcomed Rau with open arms. They knocked him out of the box in the second inning before he had retired a batter and plated three runs.

That was all young New York lefthander Ron Guidry needed. The Dodgers managed only four hits off him. One of them was a homer by Davey Lopes with a mate aboard in the third stanza. But Jackson got one of those runs back in the sixth with a homer and the game ended at 4-2.

Martin tried Gullett to put the clincher on the Series the next day but it was not to be. The Dodgers pasted the lefty for eight hits and seven runs in less than five full innings and, behind Sutton, romped to a 10-4 victory.

Jackson hit a home run for the Yankees in his last trip to the plate and it was a portent of things to come when the Series resumed in New York after a day of travel.

Torrez and Hooton, each a complete-game winner in his previous start, were the opposing moundsmen.

Steve Garvey's triple drove in two Dodger runs in the first inning but Chris Chambliss' homer after a walk to Jackson tied the score in the second.

Smith put L.A. in front with a solo homer in the third but that was it for the National League champions.

Jackson hit a two-run homer for the Yankees in the fourth to give them a lead they were not to relinquish.

In the fifth inning, he came to bat with a man on and hit another home run.

That made the score 7-3 and it was obvious the Yankees were home free.

But there was another great thrill in store for the cheering New York crowd. Jackson came to bat in the eighth inning and received a tremendous ovation from the fans. He responded by hitting the first pitch thrown by knuckle-baller Charlie Hough far into the center-field bleachers, a smash of more than 450 feet.

It was the third time in Series history a player had hit three homers in one game (Babe Ruth did it twice, in 1926 and 1928) and gave Jackson five homers for the Series, a record.

All of his homers came on the first pitch.

As he had homered in his last at-bat in the fifth game and walked his first time up in the sixth contest, he had hit four home runs in four successive official times at bat.

The Dodgers got a meaningless run in the ninth to make the final score 8-4.

And so the Yankees, at one time baseball's perennial champions, had regained the crown they had last held in 1962.

The box scores:

Tuesday, October 11—At New York

Los Ang. (N.L.)	AB.	R.	H.	O.	A.	E.
Lopes, 2b	5	1	0	4	2	0
Russell, ss	6	1	1	4	3	0
Smith, rf	4	0	1	2	1	0
Cey, 3b	3	0	0	3	2	0
Garvey, 1b	4	0	1	8	3	0
Baker, lf	4	1	1	2	0	0
Burke, cf	3	0	1	2	0	0
aMota	1	0	0	0	0	0
Monday, cf	1	0	0	0	0	0
Yeager, c	3	0	0	4	1	0
cLandestoy	0	0	0	0	0	0
Grote, c	1	0	0	3	0	0
Sutton, p	2	0	0	1	1	0
Rautzhan, p	0	0	0	0	1	0
Sosa, p	0	0	0	0	0	0
bLacy	1	0	1	0	0	0
Garman, p	0	0	0	0	0	0
dDavalillo	1	0	0	0	0	0
Rhoden, p	0	0	0	0	0	0
Totals	39	3	6	33	17	0

New York (A.L.)	AB.	R.	H.	O.	A.	E.
Rivers, cf	6	0	0	8	1	0
Randolph, 2b	5	3	2	2	4	0
Munson, c	4	1	2	9	1	0
Jackson, rf	2	0	1	1	0	0
Blair, rf	2	0	1	1	0	0
Chambliss, 1b	5	0	1	11	1	0
Nettles, 3b	4	0	0	0	4	0
Piniella, lf	5	0	2	3	0	0
Dent, ss	5	0	2	0	3	0
Gullett, p	1	0	0	1	1	0
Lyle, p	2	0	0	0	0	0
Totals	41	4	11	36	15	0

Los Angeles..........2 0 0 0 0 0 0 0 1 0 0 0—3
New York............1 0 0 0 0 1 0 1 0 0 0 1—4
None out when winning run scored.

Los Angeles	IP.	H.	R.	ER.	BB.	SO.
Sutton	7*	8	3	3	1	4
Rautzhan	⅓	0	0	0	2	0
Sosa	⅔	0	0	0	0	1
Garman	3	1	0	0	1	3
Rhoden (L)	0†	2	1	1	1	0

New York	IP.	H.	R.	ER.	BB.	SO.
Gullett	8⅓	5	3	3	6	6
Lyle (W)	3⅔	1	0	0	0	2

*Pitched to two batters in eighth.
†Pitched to three batters in twelfth.

Bases on balls—Off Gullett 6 (Lopes, Smith, Garvey, Cey, Sutton, Yeager), off Sutton 1 (Randolph), off Rautzhan 2 (Jackson, Nettles), off Garman 1 (Munson), off Rhoden 1 (Munson).

Strikeouts—By Gullett 6 (Burke, Sutton, Lopes 2, Smith, Cey), by Lyle 2 (Garvey, Monday), by Sutton 4 (Gullett, Randolph, Munson, Piniella), by Sosa 1 (Piniella), by Garman 3 (Lyle 2, Rivers).

1977 WORLD SERIES

aFlied out for Burke in ninth. bSingled for Sosa in ninth. cRan for Yeager in ninth. dGrounded out for Garman in twelfth. Runs batted in—Russell, Cey, Lacy, Chambliss, Randolph, Munson, Blair. Two-base hits—Munson, Randolph. Three-base hit—Russell. Home run—Randolph. Caught stealing—Smith. Sacrifice hits—Gullett 2. Sacrifice fly—Cey. Hit by pitcher—By Gullett (Baker), by Sutton (Jackson). Left on bases—Los Angeles 8, New York 12. Umpires—Chylak (A.L.) plate, Sudol (N.L.) first base, McCoy (A.L.) second base, Dale (N.L.) third base, Evans (A.L.) left field, McSherry (N.L.) right field. Time—3:24. Attendance—56,668.

Wednesday, October 12—At New York

Los Ang. (N.L.)	AB.	R.	H.	O.	A.	E.
Lopes, 2b	4	0	0	2	1	0
Russell, ss	4	1	1	0	4	0
Smith, rf	3	2	2	2	0	0
Cey, 3b	4	1	1	1	0	0
Garvey, 1b	4	1	2	6	1	0
Baker, lf	4	0	0	2	0	0
Monday, cf	3	0	1	0	0	0
Burke, cf	1	0	0	5	0	0
Yeager, c	4	1	2	9	0	0
Hooton, p	3	0	0	0	0	0
Totals	34	6	9	27	7	0

New York (A.L.)	AB.	R.	H.	O.	A.	E.
Rivers, cf	4	0	0	4	0	0
Randolph, 2b	4	1	1	2	2	0
Munson, c	4	0	1	3	3	0
Jackson, rf	4	0	0	0	0	0
Chambliss, 1b	4	0	1	11	2	0
Nettles, 3b	2	0	1	0	6	0
Piniella, lf	3	0	1	4	0	0
Dent, ss	2	0	1	0	1	0
bJohnson	1	0	0	0	0	0
Stanley, ss	0	0	0	1	0	0
Hunter, p	0	0	0	1	0	0
Tidrow, p	1	0	0	0	0	0
aZeber	1	0	0	0	0	0
Clay, p	0	0	0	1	0	0
cWhite	1	0	0	0	0	0
Lyle, p	0	0	0	0	0	0
Totals	31	1	5	27	15	0

Los Angeles .... 2 1 2 0 0 0 0 0 1—6
New York .... 0 0 0 1 0 0 0 0 0—1

Los Ang.	IP.	H.	R.	ER.	BB.	SO.
Hooton (W)	9	5	1	1	1	8

New York	IP.	H.	R.	ER.	BB.	SO.
Hunter (L)	2⅓	5	5	5	0	0
Tidrow	2⅔	3	0	0	0	1
Clay	3	0	0	0	1	0
Lyle	1	1	1	1	0	0

Bases on balls—Off Clay 1 (Smith), off Hooton 1 (Nettles). Strikeouts—By Tidrow 1 (Hooton), by Hooton 8 (Randolph, Munson, Jackson 2, Chambliss, Dent, Tidrow, Zeber).

aStruck out for Tidrow in fifth. bFlied out for Dent in seventh. cFlied out for Clay in eighth. Runs batted in—Cey 2, Yeager, Smith 2, Garvey. Two-base hit—Smith. Home runs—Cey, Yeager, Smith, Garvey. Caught stealing—Garvey, Monday. Double play—Garvey, Russell and Garvey. Left on bases—Los Angeles 2, New York 4. Umpires—Sudol (N.L.) plate, McCoy (A.L.) first base, Dale (N.L.) second base, Evans (A.L.) third base, McSherry (N.L.) left field, Chylak (A.L.) right field. Time—2:27. Attendance—56,691.

Friday, October 14—At Los Angeles

New York (A.L.)	AB.	R.	H.	O.	A.	E.
Rivers, cf	5	1	3	4	0	0
Randolph, 2b	4	0	0	1	2	0
Munson, c	5	1	1	9	0	0
Jackson, rf	3	2	1	0	0	0
Blair, rf	1	0	0	0	0	0
Piniella, lf	3	0	2	2	0	0
Chambliss, 1b	4	0	1	8	1	0
Nettles, 3b	4	1	1	1	4	0
Dent, ss	3	0	1	1	2	0
Torrez, p	3	0	0	1	1	0
Totals	35	5	10	27	10	0

Los Ang. (N.L.)	AB.	R.	H.	O.	A.	E.
Lopes, 2b	4	0	0	1	4	0
Russell, ss	4	0	0	2	4	0
Smith, rf	3	1	1	2	0	0
Cey, 3b	3	0	0	1	1	0
Garvey, 1b	4	1	2	9	0	0
Baker, lf	4	1	2	1	0	1
Monday, cf	4	0	0	2	0	0
Yeager, c	4	0	2	9	1	0
John, p	2	0	0	0	0	0
aDavalillo	1	0	0	0	0	0
Hough, p	0	0	0	0	0	0
bMota	1	0	0	0	0	0
Totals	34	3	7	27	11	1

New York .... 3 0 0 1 1 0 0 0 0—5
Los Angeles .... 0 0 3 0 0 0 0 0 0—3

New York	IP.	H.	R.	ER.	BB.	SO.
Torrez (W)	9	7	3	3	3	9

Los Angeles	IP.	H.	R.	ER.	BB.	SO.
John (L)	6	9	5	4	3	7
Hough	3	1	0	0	0	2

Bases on balls—Off John 3 (Randolph, Jackson, Dent), off Torrez 3 (Lopes, Cey, Smith). Strikeouts—By John 7 (Chambliss, Torrez 2, Munson 2, Jackson, Nettles), by Hough 2 (Jackson, Munson, Yeager), by Torrez 9 (Russell, Monday 2, John 2, Smith, Baker, Mota, Lopes).

aHit into force play for John in sixth. bStruck out for Hough in ninth. Runs batted in—Munson, Jackson, Piniella, Rivers, Chambliss, Baker 3. Two-base hits—Rivers 2, Munson, Yeager. Home run—Baker. Stolen bases—Lopes, Rivers. Sacrifice hit—Torrez. Double play—Garvey, Russell and Garvey. Hit by pitcher—By John (Piniella). Left on bases—New York 8, Los Angeles 7. Umpires—McCoy (A.L.) plate, Dale (N.L.) first base, Evans (A.L.) second base, McSherry (N.L.) third base, Chylak (A.L.) left field, Sudol (N.L.) right field. Time—2:31. Attendance—55,992.

Saturday, October 15—At Los Angeles

New York (A.L.)	AB.	R.	H.	O.	A.	E.
Rivers, cf	4	0	1	3	0	0
Randolph, 2b	4	0	3	3	2	0
Munson, c	4	0	1	8	1	0
Jackson, rf	4	2	2	2	0	0
Blair, rf	0	0	0	0	0	0
Piniella, lf	4	1	1	2	0	0
Chambliss, 1b	3	1	1	8	0	0
Nettles, 3b	3	0	0	1	3	0
Dent, ss	3	0	1	0	2	0
Guidry, p	2	0	0	0	0	0
Totals	31	4	7	27	8	0

Los Ang. (N.L.)	AB.	R.	H.	O.	A.	E.
Lopes, 2b	2	1	1	3	6	0
Russell, ss	4	0	0	1	5	0
Smith, cf	4	0	0	1	0	0
Cey, 3b	4	0	2	0	0	0
Garvey, 1b	4	0	0	14	1	0

	AB.	R.	H.	O.	A.	E.
Baker, lf	4	0	0	2	0	0
Lacy, rf	2	0	0	1	0	0
Yeager, c	3	0	0	4	2	0
Rau, p	0	0	0	0	0	0
Rhoden, p	2	1	1	1	1	0
aMota	1	0	0	0	0	0
Garman, p	0	0	0	0	0	0
Totals	30	2	4	27	15	0

New York .... 0 3 0   0 0 1   0 0 0—4
Los Angeles ..... 0 0 2   0 0 0   0 0 0—2

New York	IP.	H.	R.	ER.	BB.	SO.
Guidry (W)	9	4	2	2	3	7

Los Angeles	IP.	H.	R.	ER.	BB.	SO.
Rau (L)	1*	4	3	3	0	0
Rhoden	7	2	1	1	0	5
Garman	1	0	0	0	0	0

*Pitched to three batters in second.

Bases on balls—Off Guidry 3 (Lopes 2, Lacy). Strikeouts—By Rhoden 5 (Rivers, Munson 2, Piniella, Guidry), by Guidry 7 (Russell 2, Cey, Lacy, Smith, Garvey 2).

aFlied out for Rhoden in eighth. Runs batted in—Piniella, Nettles, Dent, Jackson, Lopes 2. Two-base hits—Jackson, Chambliss, Rhoden, Cey. Home runs—Lopes, Jackson. Stolen base—Lopes. Caught stealing—Lopes. Sacrifice hit—Guidry. Double plays—Russell, Lopes and Garvey; Lopes, Russell and Garvey. Left on bases—New York 1, Los Angeles 4. Umpires—Dale (N.L.) plate, Evans (A.L.) first base, McSherry (N.L.) second base, Chylak (A.L.) third base, Sudol (N.L.) left field, McCoy (A.L.) right field. Time—2:07. Attendance—55,995.

New York	IP.	H.	R.	ER.	BB.	SO.
Gullett (L)	4⅓	8	7	6	1	4
Clay	⅔	2	1	1	0	0
Tidrow	1	2	2	2	0	0
Hunter	2	1	0	0	0	1

Los Angeles	IP.	H.	R.	ER.	BB.	SO.
Sutton (W)	9	9	4	4	0	2

Bases on balls—Off Gullett 1 (Smith). Strikeouts—By Sutton 2 (Gullett, Zeber), by Gullett 4 (Cey, Garvey, Sutton 2), by Hunter 1 (Sutton).

aStruck out for Clay in sixth. bPopped out for Tidrow in seventh. cFlied out for Yeager in seventh. dFlied out for Hunter in ninth. Runs batted in—Nettles, Dent, Munson, Jackson, Russell, Baker 2, Yeager 4, Lacy, Smith 2. Two-base hits—Garvey, Randolph, Nettles. Three-base hit—Lopes. Home runs—Yeager, Smith, Munson, Jackson. Sacrifice fly—Yeager. Left on bases—New York 5, Los Angeles 5. Umpires—Evans (A.L.) plate, McSherry (N.L.) first base, Chylak (A.L.) second base, Sudol (A.L.) third base, McCoy (A.L.) left field, Dale (N.L.) right field. Time—2:29. Attendance—55,955.

Sunday, October 16—At Los Angeles

New York (A.L.)	AB.	R.	H.	O.	A.	E.
Rivers, cf	4	0	0	4	0	0
Randolph, 2b	4	0	1	3	1	0
Munson, c	4	1	2	5	0	0
Johnson, c	0	0	0	0	0	0
Jackson, rf	4	2	2	1	0	0
Chambliss, 1b	4	1	2	8	0	0
Nettles, 3b	4	0	2	0	3	1
Piniella, lf	4	0	0	3	0	1
Dent, ss	4	0	0	0	3	0
Gullett, p	1	0	0	0	1	0
Clay, p	0	0	0	0	0	0
aZeber	1	0	0	0	0	0
Tidrow, p	0	0	0	0	1	0
bWhite	1	0	0	0	0	0
Hunter, p	0	0	0	0	0	0
dBlair	1	0	0	0	0	0
Totals	36	4	9	24	9	2

Los Ang. (N.L.)	AB.	R.	H.	O.	A.	E.
Lopes, 2b	5	1	2	2	5	0
Russell, ss	5	1	2	1	1	0
Smith, cf-rf	4	2	1	6	0	0
Cey, 3b	4	0	0	0	2	0
Garvey, 1b	4	2	2	9	0	0
Baker, lf	4	2	3	2	0	0
Lacy, rf	3	1	2	1	0	0
Burke, cf	1	0	0	3	0	0
Yeager, c	2	1	1	2	0	0
cOates, c	1	0	0	1	0	0
Sutton, p	4	0	0	0	0	0
Totals	37	10	13	27	8	0

New York .... 0 0 0   0 0 0   2 2 0— 4
Los Angeles ..... 1 0 0   4 3 2   0 0 *—10

Tuesday, October 18—At New York

Los Ang. (N.L.)	AB.	R.	H.	O.	A.	E.
Lopes, 2b	4	0	1	0	4	0
Russell, ss	3	0	0	1	4	0
Smith, rf	4	2	1	1	0	0
Cey, 3b	3	1	1	0	1	0
Garvey, 1b	4	1	2	13	0	0
Baker, lf	4	0	1	2	0	0
Monday, cf	4	0	1	3	0	0
Yeager, c	3	0	1	4	2	0
bDavalillo	1	0	1	0	0	0
Hooton, p	2	0	0	0	0	0
Sosa, p	0	0	0	0	0	0
Rau, p	0	0	0	0	0	0
aGoodson	1	0	0	0	0	0
Hough, p	0	0	0	0	0	0
cLacy	1	0	0	0	0	0
Totals	34	4	9	24	11	0

New York (A.L.)	AB.	R.	H.	O.	A.	E.
Rivers, cf	4	0	2	1	0	0
Randolph, 2b	4	1	0	2	3	0
Munson, c	4	1	1	6	0	0
Jackson, rf	3	4	3	5	0	0
Chambliss, 1b	4	2	2	9	1	0
Nettles, 3b	4	0	0	0	0	0
Piniella, lf	3	0	0	2	1	0
Dent, ss	2	0	0	1	4	1
Torrez, p	3	0	0	1	2	0
Totals	31	8	8	27	11	1

Los Angeles ..... 2 0 1   0 0 0   0 0 1—4
New York .... 0 2 0   3 2 0   0 1 *—8

Los Angeles	IP.	H.	R.	ER.	BB.	SO.
Hooton (L)	3*	4	4	4	1	1
Sosa	1⅔	3	3	3	1	0
Rau	1⅓	0	0	0	0	1
Hough	2	2	1	1	0	3

New York	IP.	H.	R.	ER.	BB.	SO.
Torrez (W)	9	9	4	4	2	6

*Pitched to three batters in fourth.

Bases on balls—Off Torrez 2 (Cey, Russell), off Hooton 1 (Jackson), off Sosa 1 (Dent).

Strikeouts—By Torrez 6 (Baker, Yeager, Hooton, Cey 2, Goodson), by Hooton 1 (Torrez), by Rau 1 (Nettles), by Hough 3 (Torrez, Munson, Nettles).

1978 WORLD SERIES

aStruck out for Rau in seventh. bBunted safely for Yeager in ninth. cPopped out for Hough in ninth. Runs batted in—Garvey 2, Smith, Davalillo, Chambliss 2, Jackson 5, Piniella. Two-base hit—Chambliss. Three-base hit—Garvey. Home runs—Chambliss, Smith, Jackson 3. Sacrifice fly—Piniella. Double plays—Dent, Randolph and Chambliss; Chambliss, Dent and Chambliss. Passed ball—Munson. Left on bases—Los Angeles 5, New York 2. Umpires—McSherry (N.L.) plate, Chylak (A.L.) first base, Sudol (N.L.) second base, McCoy (A.L.) third base, Dale (N.L.) left field, Evans (A.L.) right field. Time—2:18. Attendance—56,407.

COMPOSITE BATTING AVERAGES
New York Yankees

Player-Position	G.	AB.	R.	H.	2B.	3B.	HR.	RBI.	BA.
Jackson, rf	6	20	10	9	1	0	5	8	.450
Munson, c	6	25	4	8	2	0	1	3	.320
Chambliss, 1b	6	24	4	7	2	0	1	4	.292
Piniella, lf	6	22	1	6	0	0	0	3	.273
Dent, ss	6	19	0	5	0	0	0	2	.263
Blair, rf-ph	4	4	0	1	0	0	0	1	.250
Rivers, cf	6	27	1	6	2	0	0	1	.222
Nettles, 3b	6	21	1	4	1	0	0	0	.190
Randolph, 2b	6	25	5	4	2	0	1	1	.160
Johnson, ph-c	2	1	0	0	0	0	0	0	.000
Tidrow, p	2	1	0	0	0	0	0	0	.000
Guidry, p	1	2	0	0	0	0	0	0	.000
Gullett, p	2	2	0	0	0	0	0	0	.000
Lyle, p	2	2	0	0	0	0	0	0	.000
White, ph	2	2	0	0	0	0	0	0	.000
Zeber, ph	2	2	0	0	0	0	0	0	.000
Torrez, p	2	6	0	0	0	0	0	0	.000
Clay, p	2	0	0	0	0	0	0	0	.000
Hunter, p	2	0	0	0	0	0	0	0	.000
Stanley, ss	1	0	0	0	0	0	0	0	.000
Totals	6	205	26	50	10	0	8	25	.244

Los Angeles Dodgers

Player-Position	G.	AB.	R.	H.	2B.	3B.	HR.	RBI.	BA.
Rhoden, p	2	2	1	1	1	0	0	0	.500
Lacy, ph-rf	4	7	1	3	0	0	0	2	.429
Garvey, 1b	6	24	5	9	1	1	1	3	.375
Davalillo, ph	3	3	0	1	0	0	0	1	.333
Yeager, c	6	19	2	6	1	0	2	5	.316
Baker, lf	6	24	4	7	0	0	1	5	.292
Smith, rf-cf	6	22	7	6	1	0	3	5	.273
Burke, cf	3	5	0	1	0	0	0	0	.200
Cey, 3b	6	21	2	4	1	0	1	3	.190
Lopes, 2b	6	24	3	4	0	1	1	2	.167
Monday, cf	4	12	0	2	0	0	0	0	.167
Russell, ss	6	26	3	4	0	1	0	2	.154
Goodson, ph	1	1	0	0	0	0	0	0	.000
Grote, c	1	1	0	0	0	0	0	0	.000
Oates, ph-c	1	1	0	0	0	0	0	0	.000
John, p	1	2	0	0	0	0	0	0	.000
Mota, ph	3	3	0	0	0	0	0	0	.000
Hooton, p	2	5	0	0	0	0	0	0	.000
Sutton, p	2	6	0	0	0	0	0	0	.000
Garman, p	2	0	0	0	0	0	0	0	.000
Hough, p	2	0	0	0	0	0	0	0	.000
Rau, p	2	0	0	0	0	0	0	0	.000
Sosa, p	2	0	0	0	0	0	0	0	.000
Landestoy, pr	1	0	0	0	0	0	0	0	.000
Rautzhan, p	1	0	0	0	0	0	0	0	.000
Totals	6	208	28	48	5	3	9	28	.231

COMPOSITE PITCHING AVERAGES
New York Yankees

Pitcher	G.	IP.	H.	R.	E.	SO.	BB.	W.	L.	ERA.
Lyle	2	4⅔	2	1	1	0	2	1	0	1.93
Guidry	1	9	4	2	2	3	7	1	0	2.00
Clay	2	3⅔	2	1	1	1	0	0	0	2.45
Torrez	2	18	16	7	5	5	15	2	0	2.50
Tidrow	2	3⅔	5	2	2	0	1	0	0	4.91
Gullett	2	12⅔	13	10	9	7	10	0	1	6.39
Hunter	2	4⅓	6	5	5	0	1	0	1	10.38
Totals	6	56	48	28	25	16	36	4	2	4.02

Los Angeles Dodgers

Pitcher	G.	IP.	H.	R.	E.	SO.	BB.	W.	L.	ERA.
Garman	2	4	2	0	0	1	3	0	0	0.00
Rautzhan	1	⅓	0	0	0	2	0	0	0	0.00
Hough	2	5	3	1	1	0	5	0	0	1.80
Rhoden	2	7	4	2	2	1	5	0	1	2.57
Hooton	2	12	8	5	5	2	9	1	1	3.75
Sutton	2	16	17	7	7	1	6	1	0	3.94
John	1	6	9	5	4	3	7	0	1	6.00
Rau	3	2½	4	3	3	0	1	0	1	11.57
Sosa	2	2½	3	3	3	1	1	0	0	11.57
Totals	6	55	50	26	25	11	37	2	4	4.09

SERIES OF 1978

	W.	L.	Pct.
New York A. L.	4	2	.667
Los Angeles N. L.	2	4	.333

The cast and the final result were essentially the same as in 1977 but the paths the New York Yankees and Los Angeles Dodgers took to the 75th World Series were altogether different. When it was all over, the Yankees had won their 22nd Series, defeating the Dodgers four games to two and became the first team in World Series history to lose the first two games and come back to win it in six games.

In late July it didn't look like either the Yankees or the Dodgers would be meeting for a return engagement in the Series. On July 19, the Yankees were a full 14 games behind the Boston Red Sox with a record of 48-42. The Sox were setting the baseball world on fire with a 62-28 mark. After winning five games in a row, New York Manager Billy Martin resigned on July 24 and was replaced by Bob Lemon. Still nine games back on August 13, the Yankees won 35 of their last 47 games and pulled ahead of Boston on September 11. They weren't caught until the final day of the season, setting up a climactic one-game playoff for the A.L. East Championship in Fenway Park.

New York won a spell-binding game on the strength of Bucky Dent's three-run homer and went into the Championship Series against Kansas City for the third consecutive year. The Royals were optimistic; New York had been forced to use its extraordinary pitcher, Ron Guidry, in the playoff and he would not be available until at least the fourth game. But the Yankees took a 2-1 lead into that fourth game and Guidry, with relief help from Rich Gossage, outdueled Royal pitcher Dennis Leonard, and New York had earned its 32nd trip to the World Series.

Los Angeles, like the Yankees, struggled throughout the early stages of the season but caught fire at almost the same time as the Yankees and won their second straight division title, streaking past the San Francisco Giants and Cincinnati Reds. The Dodgers finished at 95-67 and met the Philadelphia Phillies in the Championship Series.

Like Kansas City, the Phillies were making their third straight appearance in post-season play. But also like the Royals, they would come up empty again. Los Angeles won the first two games and appeared to be breezing, but the Phillies rallied for a third-game victory. However, Los Angeles captured the series in the bottom of the tenth inning of the fourth game after a rare error by Philadelphia center fielder Garry Maddox. And the Series was underway.

Los Angeles came out with its bats smoking and held a 7-0 lead after only five innings. Dusty Baker and Davey Lopes greeted Yankee starter Ed Figueroa with home runs in the second inning to stake the Dodgers to a 3-0 lead. Lopes' two-run shot removed Figueroa from the game with Ken Clay taking over. Two innings later, Lopes reached Clay for a three-run home run and the rout was on. Meanwhile, Dodger starter Tommy John was holding the Yankees to two hits through the first six innings until Reggie Jackson solved him for a leadoff homer in the seventh. It was Jackson's sixth round-tripper in four consecutive Series games, breaking Lou Gehrig's record of five. But with relief help from Terry Forster, John and the Dodgers held off New York, 11-5.

Game Two featured one of the most exciting showdowns in Series history. The Yankees took an early 2-0 lead on a Reggie Jackson double, scoring Roy White and Thurman Munson. The Dodgers came back with a run in the fourth as Ron Cey scored Reggie Smith with a single and two innings later, Cey blasted a three-run homer off Catfish Hunter and the Dodgers led 4-2. But New York wasn't through. White led off the seventh with a single, bringing Forster into the game to replace Dodger starter Burt Hooton. Paul Blair greeted him with a ground-rule double and, after Munson struck out, Jackson bounced out to second, scoring White. That set the stage for the pulsating ninth.

Bucky Dent led off with a single and advanced to second when White grounded out to the pitcher. But after Blair walked, Dodger Manager Tommy Lasorda summoned his young, fire-balling righthander, Bob Welch, to face Munson and Jackson. Welch got Munson to line out to right and in strode Jackson with the game on the line. The count went to 1-2 and Jackson fouled off two pitches. Ball two was issued and Jackson fouled off another. Then came ball three. Full count, two out, two runners would be moving with the pitch. Welch won the duel as Jackson struck out with a mighty swing and the Dodgers were bouyed, going to New York with a 2-0 Series lead.

But in New York, on a brisk Friday evening, Yankee third baseman Graig Nettles was center stage, stealing the spotlight from Guidry, who needed every one of Nettles' remarkable plays. Roy White got the Yankees off and winging with a first-inning homer off Don Sutton and Nettles started the second inning with a single and eventually scored on a groundout. Los Angeles got within a run in the third when North walked, stole second, moved to third on a groundout and scored on Bill Russell's infield single. And that would be as close as they got.

With Guidry walking seven, the Dodgers repeatedly threatened. But there was Nettles, time after time robbing Los Angeles of extra base hits and ending rallies. In fact, he stopped the Dodgers in the fifth and sixth innings, making a spectacular play with the bases loaded in each frame, and forcing a runner at second. In the game, which the Yankees eventually won 5-1, the Dodgers left 11 runners on the bases with Nettles saving at least five runs. There is no doubt that with Game 3 this 75th World Series turned toward the Yankees, thanks to the flawless glove-work of Nettles.

But the Dodgers would argue that the Series turned in the sixth inning of the fourth game, when Jackson was involved in the most controversial play of the entire event. Los Angeles led 3-0 entering the bottom of the sixth on the strength of a Smith three-run homer off Ed Figueroa. With one out in the New York sixth, White singled. Munson walked and Jackson followed with a run-scoring single off John. With Lou Piniella batting, confusion set in. Piniella sent a sinking liner to the left of Dodger shortstop Russell. The ball hit off Russell's glove, falling to the ground. Munson, who had hastily retreated to second when it appeared the ball would be caught, took off for third. Russell ignored Munson, choosing to step on second to force Jackson and throw to first for an inning-ending double play. But Jackson, no more than a few strides from first, froze in the basepath. When Russell made the throw, Jackson turned toward first baseman Garvey and his right hip swiveled toward the ball. It struck Jackson in the right leg and bounced crazily into short right field as Munson scored with the Yankees' second run. The Dodgers argued, to no avail, that Jackson had intentionally interfered with the ball and that Piniella should be ruled out. The umpires stood by their call and the run counted.

New York tied the game in the bottom of the eighth when Munson doubled home Blair who had singled and advanced to second on Roy White's sacrifice. That set the stage for extra innings. Gossage retired the Dodgers in order in the top of the tenth. A walk to White in the bottom of the tenth proved to be Welch's undoing. After White's walk, Munson popped out for the second out, but Jackson, beaten by Welch in Game Two, singled to right, with White stopping at second. Piniella then lined a solid single to right-center, scoring White, and the Yankees had evened the Series at two games apiece.

Game Five was a combination of timely

Yankee hitting, untimely Dodger fielding and the surprising pitching of Jim Beattie. Los Angeles jumped off to a 2-0 lead but the Yankees stormed back for four in the third and three in the fourth and a 7-2 lead. Before it was over, New York would amass 18 hits, 16 of which were singles, while the Dodgers would commit three errors and fail to come up with other balls that were ruled hits. After the first three innings, Beattie held the Dodgers scoreless the rest of the way for his first major league complete game as the Yankees eased to a 12-2 win. Los Angeles registered just four hits over the final six innings of play and the Dodgers were only too happy to depart New York for the friendly confines of Dodger Stadium. But the Yankees would not be generous visitors this time.

Lopes greeted Hunter with a home run in the bottom of the first and the Dodgers were off to an early 1-0 lead. But the bottom of the Yankees batting order did the destruction on Sutton in the second. Nettles led off with a single and Jim Spencer walked. Brian Doyle, in the World Series only due to an injury to regular second baseman Willie Randolph, surprised left fielder Dusty Baker with a double over his head, tying the game. It was Doyle's first extra base hit of his major league career. Dent followed with a single up the middle and the Yankees led 3-1. Hunter was in trouble in the third but Doyle saved him. Joe Ferguson doubled to lead off the inning and advanced to third on a sacrifice by Vic Davalillo. Lopes singled in Ferguson and Russell walked. But Doyle speared Smith's hard hit grounder to his right and turned it into an inning-ending double play.

Sutton sailed along until the top of the sixth when Doyle and Dent turned the trick once again. Piniella led off the inning with a single and advanced to second on a wild pitch. After Nettles flew out and Spencer struck out, Doyle lined a single up the middle scoring Piniella and advanced to second on the throw to the plate. Dent then greeted reliever Bob Welch by blooping a single into short left field, scoring Doyle and giving the Yankees a 5-2 lead. The next inning, Jackson settled things for good with Welch. With White on first, Jackson blasted a home run to deep right field, sealing the Yankees' victory.

Hunter cruised along and at one time retired 10 straight Dodgers. He was relieved by Gossage in the eighth after yielding a double to Ferguson. After Davalillo reached first on an infield hit, Gossage struck out Lopes and induced Russell to hit into a double play, fittingly started by Nettles. Gossage retired the Dodgers in order in the ninth, giving the Yankees their second straight World Series triumph over the Dodgers.

The box scores:

Tuesday, October 10—At Los Angeles

New York (A.L.)	AB.	R.	H.	O.	A.	E.
Rivers, cf	4	0	0	4	0	0
Blair, cf	1	0	0	1	0	0
White, lf	4	0	1	2	0	0
Munson, c	4	1	0	4	1	0
Jackson, dh	4	1	3	0	0	0
Piniella, rf	4	2	1	2	0	0
Nettles, 3b	4	0	1	0	2	0
Chambliss, 1b	4	1	1	5	0	0
Stanley, 2b	2	0	1	4	1	0
bJohnson	1	0	0	0	0	0
Doyle, 2b	0	0	0	1	0	0
Dent, ss	4	0	1	1	3	1
Figueroa, p	0	0	0	0	0	0
Clay, p	0	0	0	0	0	0
Lindblad, p	0	0	0	0	0	0
Tidrow, p	0	0	0	0	0	0
Totals	36	5	9	24	7	1

Los Ang. (N.L.)	AB.	R.	H.	O.	A.	E.
Lopes, 2b	5	2	2	1	2	1
Russell, ss	5	1	3	3	5	1
Smith, rf	5	0	1	1	0	0
Garvey, 1b	5	1	2	14	0	0
Cey, 3b	4	1	1	0	4	0
Baker, lf	4	2	3	1	0	0
Monday, cf	2	2	1	0	0	0
aNorth, cf	1	1	1	0	0	0
Lacy, dh	3	0	1	0	0	0
Yeager, c	4	1	0	7	0	0
John, p	0	0	0	0	4	0
Forster, p	0	0	0	0	0	0
Totals	38	11	15	27	15	2

New York.......... 0 0 0 0 0 0 3 2 0— 5
Los Angeles...... 0 3 0 3 1 0 3 1 *—11

New York	IP.	H.	R.	ER.	BB.	SO.
Figueroa (L)	1⅔	5	3	3	1	0
Clay	2⅓†	4	4	3	2	2
Lindblad	2⅓	4	3	3	0	1
Tidrow	1⅔	2	1	1	0	1

Los Angeles	IP.	H.	R.	ER.	BB.	SO.
John (W)	7⅔	8	5	3	2	4
Forster	1⅓	1	0	0	0	3

†Pitched to two batters in fifth.

Bases on balls—Off John 2 (White, Stanley), off Figueroa 1 (Lacy), off Clay 2 (Cey, Monday). Strikeouts—By John 4 (White 2, Munson, Nettles), by Forster 3 (Johnson, Blair, White), by Clay 2 (Smith, Garvey), by Lindblad 1 (Monday), by Tidrow 1 (Garvey).

aDoubled for Monday in seventh. bStruck out for Stanley in eighth. Runs batted in—Jackson, Piniella, Nettles, Dent 2, Lopes 5, Smith, Baker, North 2, Lacy. Two-base hits—Monday, Stanley, North, Russell. Home runs—Baker, Lopes 2, Jackson. Caught stealing—Smith. Wild pitch—Clay. Double plays—Lopes, Russell and Garvey; Dent, Stanley and Chambliss; Munson and Doyle. Left on bases—New York 6, Los Angeles 6. Umpires—Vargo (N.L.) plate, Haller (A.L.) first base, Kibler (N.L.) second base, Springstead (A.L.) third base, Pulli (N.L.) left field, Brinkman (A.L.) right field. Time—2:48. Attendance—55,997.

Wednesday, Oct. 11—At Los Angeles

New York (A.L.)	AB.	R.	H.	O.	A.	E.
White, lf	5	2	2	1	0	0
Thomasson, cf	3	0	1	2	0	0
aBlair, cf	1	0	1	2	0	0
Munson, c	4	1	1	3	1	0
Jackson, dh	4	0	1	0	0	0

1978 WORLD SERIES

	AB.	R.	H.	O.	A.	E.
Nettles, 3b	4	0	0	3	3	0
Piniella, rf	4	0	2	2	0	0
Spencer, 1b	4	0	1	8	1	0
Doyle, 2b	3	0	1	2	1	0
bJohnson	1	0	0	0	0	0
Stanley, 2b	0	0	0	0	0	0
Dent, ss	4	0	1	0	1	0
Hunter, p	0	0	0	1	0	0
Gossage, p	0	0	0	0	0	0
Totals	37	3	11	24	7	0

Los Ang. (N.L.)	AB.	R.	H.	O.	A.	E.
Lopes, 2b	4	1	1	3	4	0
Russell, ss	4	0	1	2	1	0
Smith, rf	4	2	1	3	0	0
Garvey, 1b	3	0	1	6	1	0
Cey, 3b	3	1	2	1	1	0
Baker, lf	3	0	0	2	0	0
Monday, cf	3	0	0	1	0	0
North, cf	0	0	0	0	0	0
Lacy, dh	3	0	0	0	0	0
Yeager, c	3	0	1	8	1	0
Hooton, p	0	0	0	1	0	0
Forster, p	0	0	0	0	1	0
Welch, p	0	0	0	0	0	0
Totals	30	4	7	27	9	0

New York .... 0 0 2 0 0 0 1 0 0—3
Los Angeles .... 0 0 0 1 0 3 0 0 *—4

New York	IP.	H.	R.	ER.	BB.	SO.
Hunter (L)	6	7	4	4	0	2
Gossage	2	0	0	0	0	0

Los Angeles	IP.	H.	R.	ER.	BB.	SO.
Hooton (W)	6j	8	3	3	1	5
Forster	2⅓	3	0	0	1	3
Welch (S)	⅔	0	0	0	0	1

jPitched to one batter in seventh.

Bases on balls—Off Hooton 1 (Munson), off Forster 1 (Blair).
Strikeouts—By Hooton 5 (Jackson, Nettles 2, Munson, Dent), by Forster 3 (Munson, Nettles, Spencer), by Welch 1 (Jackson), by Hunter 2 (Monday, Yeager).
aDoubled for Thomasson in seventh. bHit into double play for Doyle in eighth. Runs batted in—Jackson 3, Cey 4. Two-base hits—Munson, Jackson, Blair. Home run—Cey. Stolen base—White. Caught stealing—Thomasson. Hit by pitcher—By Hooton (Jackson). Wild pitch—Hooton. Double plays—Nettles and Spencer; Cey, Lopes and Garvey. Left on bases—New York 10, Los Angeles 2. Umpires—Haller (A.L.) plate, Kibler (N.L.) first base, Springstead (A.L.) second base, Pulli (N.L.) third base, Brinkman (A.L.) left field, Vargo (N.L.) right field. Time—2:37. Attendance—55,982.

Friday, October 13—At New York

Los Ang. (N.L.)	AB.	R.	H.	O.	A.	E.
Lopes, 2b	5	0	1	3	2	0
Russell, ss	4	0	2	2	3	0
Smith, rf	4	0	1	2	0	0
Garvey, 1b	4	0	1	4	2	0
Cey, 3b	3	0	0	0	1	0
Baker, lf	3	0	2	5	0	0
Lacy, dh	4	0	1	0	0	0
North, cf	3	1	0	5	0	0
Yeager, c	1	0	0	2	1	0
aMota	0	0	0	0	0	0
Grote, c	0	0	0	0	0	0
Ferguson, c	1	0	0	0	0	0
Sutton, p	0	0	0	0	0	0
Rautzhan, p	0	0	0	0	0	0
Hough, p	0	0	0	1	0	0
Totals	32	1	8	24	9	0

New York (A.L.)	AB.	R.	H.	O.	A.	E.
Rivers, cf	4	0	3	2	0	0
bBlair, cf	0	0	0	0	0	0
White, lf	3	2	1	2	0	0
Munson, c	4	1	1	4	1	0
Jackson, dh	3	0	1	0	0	0
Piniella, rf	4	0	1	1	0	0
Nettles, 3b	4	1	1	2	5	0
Chambliss, 1b	3	0	1	8	0	0
Doyle, 2b	4	0	0	7	2	0
Dent, ss	4	1	1	0	5	1
Guidry, p	0	0	0	1	1	0
Totals	33	5	10	27	14	1

Los Angeles .... 0 0 1 0 0 0 0 0 0—1
New York .... 1 1 0 0 0 0 3 0 *—5

Los Angeles	IP.	H.	R.	ER.	BB.	SO.
Sutton (L)	6⅓	9	5	5	3	2
Rautzhan	⅔	1	0	0	0	0
Hough	1	0	0	0	0	0

New York	IP.	H.	R.	ER.	BB.	SO.
Guidry (W)	9	8	1	1	7	4

Bases on balls—Off Guidry 7 (Smith, Baker, North, Cey, Yeager, Mota, Russell), off Sutton 3 (Jackson, Chambliss, White).
Strikeouts—By Guidry 4 (Cey, Lacy, Ferguson, Smith), by Sutton 2 (Munson 2).
aWalked for Yeager in sixth. bRan for Rivers in seventh. Runs batted in—Russell, White, Munson, Jackson, Piniella, Dent. Two-base hit—Garvey. Home run—White. Stolen bases—North, Piniella. Caught stealing—Russell, Rivers. Double plays—Nettles, Doyle and Chambliss; Dent, Doyle and Chambliss. Left on bases—Los Angeles 11, New York 7. Umpires—Kibler (N.L.) plate, Springstead (A.L.) first base, Pulli (N.L.) second base, Brinkman (A.L.) third base, Vargo (N.L.) left field, Haller (A.L.) right field. Time—2:27. Attendance—56,447.

Saturday, October 14—At New York

Los Ang. (N.L.)	AB.	R.	H.	O.	A.	E.
Lopes, 2b	4	1	0	0	4	0
Russell, ss	5	0	2	3	4	1
Smith, rf	4	1	1	1	1	0
Garvey, 1b	4	0	0	15	0	0
Cey, 3b	4	0	1	0	4	0
Baker, lf	4	0	0	0	0	0
Monday, dh	2	0	1	0	0	0
North, cf	4	0	0	2	0	0
Yeager, c	3	1	1	5	0	0
aDavalillo	1	0	0	0	0	0
Grote, c	0	0	0	3	0	0
John, p	0	0	0	0	0	0
Forster, p	0	0	0	0	0	0
Welch, p	0	0	0	0	0	0
Totals	35	3	6	29	13	1

New York (A.L.)	AB.	R.	H.	O.	A.	E.
Blair, cf	4	1	2	2	0	0
cRivers	1	0	0	0	0	0
White, lf	3	2	1	4	0	0
Munson, c	3	1	2	8	0	0
Jackson, dh	4	0	2	0	0	0
Piniella, rf	5	0	1	5	1	0
Nettles, 3b	4	0	0	2	1	0
Chambliss, 1b	4	0	0	4	1	0
Stanley, 2b	3	0	0	1	1	0
bSpencer	1	0	0	0	0	0
Doyle, 2b	0	0	0	0	0	0
Dent, ss	4	0	1	4	2	0
Figueroa, p	0	0	0	0	0	0
Tidrow, p	0	0	0	0	0	0
Gossage, p	0	0	0	0	0	0
Totals	36	4	9	30	6	0

1978 WORLD SERIES

```
Los Angeles ............ 0 0 0   0 3 0   0 0 0   0—3
New York .............. 0 0 0   0 0 2   0 1 0   1—4
```
Two out when winning run scored.

Los Angeles	IP.	H.	R.	ER.	BB.	SO.
John	7†	6	3	2	2	2
Forster	⅓	1	0	0	0	0
Welch (L)	2⅓	2	1	1	1	3

New York	IP.	H.	R.	ER.	BB.	SO.
Figueroa	5	4	3	3	4	2
Tidrow	3	2	0	0	0	4
Gossage (W)	2	0	0	0	1	2

†Pitched to one batter in eighth.

Bases on balls—Off Figueroa 4 (Smith, Monday, Garvey, Lopes), off Gossage 1 (Monday), off John 2 (Munson 2), off Welch 1 (White). Strikeouts—By Figueroa 2 (Smith, Russell), by Tidrow 4 (Cey, Baker 2, Yeager), by Gossage 2 (Smith, Garvey), by John 2 (Jackson, Blair), by Welch 3 (Nettles, Chambliss, Spencer).

aFlied out for Yeager in ninth. bStruck out for Stanley in ninth. cFouled out for Blair in tenth. Runs batted in—Smith 3, Munson, Jackson, Piniella. Two-base hits—Yeager, Munson. Home run —Smith. Stolen bases—Garvey, Munson. Sacrifice hit—White. Hit by pitcher—By Forster (Jackson). Double play—Piniella, Chambliss and Dent. Left on bases—Los Angeles 7, New York 8. Umpires—Springstead (A.L.) plate, Pulli (N.L.) first base, Brinkman (A.L.) second base, Vargo (N.L.) third base, Haller (A.L.) left field, Kibler (N.L.) right field. Time—3:17. Attendance—56,445.

Sunday, October 15—At New York

Los Ang. (N.L.)	AB.	R.	H.	O.	A.	E.
Lopes, 2b	4	2	2	3	5	0
Russell, ss	5	0	2	1	4	1
Smith, rf	4	0	1	2	0	1
Garvey, 1b	4	0	1	10	0	1
Cey, 3b	3	0	1	0	0	0
Baker, lf	4	0	0	2	0	0
Monday, cf	3	0	0	2	0	0
Lacy, dh	4	0	0	0	0	0
Yeager, c	2	0	1	1	0	0
aOates, c	1	0	1	3	1	0
Hooton, p	0	0	0	0	0	0
Rautzhan, p	0	0	0	0	0	0
Hough, p	0	0	0	0	0	0
Totals	34	2	9	24	10	3

New York (A.L.)	AB.	R.	H.	O.	A.	E.
Rivers, cf	5	2	3	0	0	0
bBlair, cf	1	1	0	0	0	0
White, lf	5	2	2	2	0	0
Johnstone, rf	0	0	0	1	0	0
Munson, c	5	1	3	8	1	0
Heath, c	0	0	0	0	0	0
Jackson, dh	3	0	1	0	0	0
Piniella, rf	4	0	1	4	0	0
Thomasson, lf	1	0	0	0	0	0
Nettles, 3b	5	0	1	1	2	0
Spencer, 1b	4	2	1	6	0	0
Doyle, 2b	5	2	3	5	1	0
Dent, ss	4	2	3	0	2	0
Beattie, p	0	0	0	0	1	0
Totals	42	12	18	27	7	0

```
Los Angeles ............ 1 0 1   0 0 0   0 0 0— 2
New York .............. 0 0 4   3 0 0   4 1 *—12
```

Los Angeles	IP.	H.	R.	ER.	BB.	SO.
Hooton (L)	2⅓	5	4	3	2	1
Rautzhan	1⅓	3	3	3	0	0
Hough	4⅓	10	5	2	2	5

New York	IP.	H.	R.	ER.	BB.	SO.
Beattie (W)	9	9	2	2	4	8

Bases on balls—Off Beattie 4 (Monday, Cey, Oates, Lopes), off Hooton 2 (Jackson, Dent), off Hough 2 (Jackson, Spencer).
Strikeouts—By Beattie 8 (Cey, Lacy 2, Smith, Garvey 2, Russell, Baker), by Hooton 1 (Jackson), by Hough 5 (Dent, Rivers, Thomasson, Nettles, Blair).

aWalked for Yeager in seventh. bRan for Rivers in seventh. Runs batted in—Russell, Smith, Rivers, White 3, Munson 5, Piniella, Dent. Two-base hits—Russell, Munson, Dent. Stolen bases—Lopes, Rivers, White, Russell. Caught stealing—Monday. Wild pitch—Hough. Passed ball—Yeager, Oates. Double plays— Russell, Lopes and Garvey; Lopes, Russell and Garvey; Nettles, Doyle and Spencer. Left on bases—Los Angeles 9, New York 10. Umpires—Pulli (N.L.) plate, Brinkman (A.L.) first base, Vargo (N.L.) second base, Haller (A.L.) third base, Kibler (N.L.) left field, Springstead (A.L.) right field. Time—2:56. Attendance—56,448.

Tuesday, October 17—At Los Angeles

New York (A.L.)	AB.	R.	H.	O.	A.	E.
Rivers, cf	4	0	0	1	0	0
Blair, cf	1	0	0	0	0	0
White, lf	4	1	1	4	0	0
Thomasson, lf	0	0	0	1	0	0
Munson, c	5	0	1	6	1	0
Jackson, dh	5	1	1	0	0	0
Piniella, rf	4	1	1	0	0	0
Johnstone, rf	0	0	0	0	0	0
Nettles, 3b	4	1	1	0	5	0
Spencer, 1b	3	1	0	9	1	0
Doyle, 2b	4	2	3	2	3	0
Dent, ss	4	0	3	3	3	0
Hunter, p	0	0	0	1	0	0
Gossage, p	0	0	0	0	0	0
Totals	38	7	11	27	13	0

Los Ang. (N.L.)	AB.	R.	H.	O.	A.	E.
Lopes, 2b	4	1	2	0	2	0
Russell, ss	3	0	1	0	3	0
Smith, rf	4	0	0	2	0	0
Garvey, 1b	4	0	0	9	0	0
Cey, 3b	4	0	1	1	2	0
Baker, lf	3	0	0	2	0	0
Monday, cf	3	0	0	2	0	0
Ferguson, c	3	1	2	11	0	1
Davalillo, dh	2	0	1	0	0	0
Sutton, p	0	0	0	0	0	0
Welch, p	0	0	0	0	0	0
Rau, p	0	0	0	0	1	0
Totals	30	2	7	27	8	1

```
New York ............... 0 3 0   0 0 2   2 0 0—7
Los Angeles ............ 1 0 1   0 0 0   0 0 0—2
```

New York	IP.	H.	R.	ER.	BB.	SO.
Hunter (W)	7j	6	2	2	1	3
Gossage	2	1	0	0	0	2

Los Angeles	IP.	H.	R.	ER.	BB.	SO.
Sutton (L)	5⅔	8	5	5	1	6
Welch	1⅓	2	2	2	1	2
Rau	2	1	0	0	0	3

jPitched to one batter in eighth.

Bases on balls—Off Sutton 1 (Spencer), off Welch 1 (White), off Hunter 1 (Russell).
Strikeouts—By Sutton 6 (Munson, Jackson 2, Spencer 2, White), by Welch 2 (Rivers, Munson), by Rau 3 (Blair, White, Jackson), by Hunter 3 (Smith, Garvey, Monday), by Gossage 2 (Lopes, Garvey).

Runs batted in—Jackson 2, Doyle 2, Dent 3, Lopes 2. Two-base hits—Doyle, Ferguson 2. Home runs—Lopes, Jackson. Stolen base—Lopes. Caught stealing—Russell. Sacrifice hit—Davalillo. Wild pitch—Sutton. Double plays—Doyle, Dent and Spencer; Nettles, Doyle and Spencer. Left on bases—New York 6, Los Angeles 3. Umpires—Brinkman (A.L.) plate, Vargo (N.L.) first base, Haller (A.L.) second base, Kibler (N.L.) third base, Springstead (A.L.) left field, Pulli (N.L.) right field. Time—2:34. Attendance—55,985.

Pitcher	G.	IP.	H.	R.	E.	SO.	BB.	W.	L.	ERA.
Welch	3	4⅓	4	3	3	2	6	0	1	6.23
Hooton	2	8⅓	13	7	6	3	6	1	1	6.48
Sutton	2	12	17	10	10	4	8	0	2	7.50
Hough	2	5⅓	10	5	5	2	5	0	0	8.44
Rautzhan	2	2	4	3	3	0	0	0	0	13.50
Totals	6	52⅔	68	36	32	16	40	2	4	5.46

SERIES OF 1979

	W.	L.	Pct.
Pittsburgh N. L.	4	3	.571
Baltimore A. L.	3	4	.429

COMPOSITE BATTING AVERAGES
New York Yankees

Player-Position	G.	AB.	R.	H.	2B.	3B.	HR.	RBI.	BA.
Doyle, 2b	6	16	4	7	1	0	0	2	.438
Dent, ss	6	24	3	10	1	0	0	7	.417
Jackson, dh	6	23	2	9	1	0	2	8	.391
Blair, cf-ph-pr	6	8	2	3	1	0	0	0	.375
White, lf	6	24	9	8	0	0	1	4	.333
Rivers, cf-ph	5	18	2	6	0	0	0	1	.333
Munson, c	6	25	5	8	3	0	0	7	.320
Piniella, rf	6	25	3	7	0	0	0	4	.280
Thomasson, cf-lf	3	4	0	1	0	0	0	0	.250
Stanley, 2b	3	5	1	1	0	0	0	0	.200
Chambliss, 1b	3	11	1	2	0	0	0	0	.182
Spencer, 1b-ph	4	12	3	2	0	0	0	0	.167
Nettles, 3b	6	25	2	4	0	0	0	1	.160
Johnson, ph	2	2	0	0	0	0	0	0	.000
Beattie, p	1	0	0	0	0	0	0	0	.000
Clay, p	1	0	0	0	0	0	0	0	.000
Figueroa, p	2	0	0	0	0	0	0	0	.000
Gossage, p	3	0	0	0	0	0	0	0	.000
Guidry, p	1	0	0	0	0	0	0	0	.000
Heath, c	1	0	0	0	0	0	0	0	.000
Hunter, p	2	0	0	0	0	0	0	0	.000
Johnstone, rf	2	0	0	0	0	0	0	0	.000
Lindblad, p	1	0	0	0	0	0	0	0	.000
Tidrow, p	2	0	0	0	0	0	0	0	.000
Totals	6	222	36	68	8	0	3	34	.306

Los Angeles Dodgers

Player-Position	G.	AB.	R.	H.	2B.	3B.	HR.	RBI.	BA.
Oates, ph-c	1	1	0	1	0	0	0	0	1.000
Ferguson, c	2	4	1	2	2	0	0	2	.500
Russell, ss	6	26	1	11	2	0	0	2	.423
Davalillo, ph-dh	2	3	0	1	0	0	0	0	.333
Lopes, 2b	6	26	7	8	0	0	3	7	.308
Cey, 3b	6	21	2	6	0	0	1	4	.286
Baker, lf	6	21	2	5	0	0	1	1	.238
Yeager, c	5	13	2	3	1	0	0	0	.231
Garvey, 1b	6	24	1	5	1	0	0	0	.208
Smith, rf	6	25	3	5	0	0	1	5	.200
Monday, cf-dh	5	13	2	2	1	0	0	0	.154
Lacy, dh	4	14	0	2	0	0	1	1	.143
North, ph-cf	4	8	2	1	1	0	0	2	.125
Forster, p	3	0	0	0	0	0	0	0	.000
Grote, c	2	0	0	0	0	0	0	0	.000
Hooton, p	2	0	0	0	0	0	0	0	.000
Hough, p	2	0	0	0	0	0	0	0	.000
John, p	2	0	0	0	0	0	0	0	.000
Mota, ph	1	0	0	0	0	0	0	0	.000
Rau, p	1	0	0	0	0	0	0	0	.000
Rautzhan, p	2	0	0	0	0	0	0	0	.000
Sutton, p	2	0	0	0	0	0	0	0	.000
Welch, p	3	0	0	0	0	0	0	0	.000
Totals	6	199	23	52	8	0	6	22	.261

COMPOSITE PITCHING AVERAGES
New York Yankees

Pitcher	G.	IP.	H.	R.	E.	SO.	BB.	W.	L.	ERA.
Gossage	3	6	1	0	0	1	4	1	0	0.00
Guidry	1	9	8	1	1	4	7	4	1	0	1.00
Tidrow	2	4⅔	4	1	1	0	5	0	0	1.93
Beattie	1	9	9	2	2	4	8	1	0	2.00
Hunter	2	13	13	6	6	1	5	1	1	4.15
Figueroa	2	6⅔	9	6	6	5	2	0	1	8.10
Clay	1	2⅓	4	4	3	2	2	0	0	11.57
Lindblad	1	2⅓	4	3	3	0	1	0	0	11.57
Totals	6	53	52	23	20	31	4	2	3.74

Los Angeles Dodgers

Pitcher	G.	IP.	H.	R.	E.	SO.	BB.	W.	L.	ERA.
Forster	3	4	5	0	0	1	6	0	0	0.00
Rau	1	2	1	0	0	3	0	0	0	0.00
John	2	14⅔	14	8	5	4	6	1	0	3.07

Led by their seemingly ageless captain, Willie Stargell, the Pittsburgh Pirates became only the fourth team to win a seven-game World Series after trailing three games to one. The 38-year-old first baseman destroyed the Baltimore Orioles with three home runs among his seven extra-base hits and posted a seven-game Series record 25 total bases. It was the bat and heart of Stargell that had carried the Bucs to the National League flag, and fittingly, when the World Series was over, "Pops," as his teammates affectionately called him, had again led the way.

During the season Stargell had contributed a .281 batting average, 32 home runs and 82 RBIs to the Pirates. In addition, he provided a lot of inspiration to the Bucs, a ballclub which had to come from behind frequently during the season, before overtaking the Montreal Expos and winning the East Division championship by two games. Stargell was also voted the N.L. Championship Series MVP, as the Pirates roared past Cincinnati in a three-game sweep.

The Pirates had a well-rounded club, which finished second in the N.L. in batting, home runs and stolen bases. They also possessed a balanced pitching staff which managed to win 98 games during the regular season, despite being the only pennant-winning team in history to not have a 15-game winner.

The Orioles had coasted to the American League East Division title, finishing eight games ahead of the Milwaukee Brewers, before taking three of four games against California in the A.L. Championship Series playoff. Led by their feisty manager, Earl Weaver, the Orioles were very similar to the Pirates in that they had a well-balanced club that rallied in the late innings to win many of their games.

The Series opened in Baltimore, where rain and cold weather caused the first game to be postponed until the following night. Once the Series started, the Orioles wasted no time as they scored five runs in the first inning, thanks to a costly error by Pirate second baseman Phil Garner. With the bases loaded, John Lowenstein, whose pinch-homer won the first game of the A.L. Championship Series, grounded the ball to Garner, who threw wildly past shortstop

Tim Foli on an attempted forceout. Al Bumbry and Mark Belanger scored on the play, while Eddie Murray went to third. A few moments later, Murray scored on Pirate starter Bruce Kison's wild pitch, making the score 3-0. Doug DeCinces then pulled a home run into the left field stands, scoring Lowenstein and giving the Birds an early five-run bulge.

The Pirates managed to come back with a run in the fourth, two in the sixth and one in the eighth, the last on a Stargell home run, but Oriole starter Mike Flanagan managed to hold on for the complete game victory, despite surrendering eleven hits, including four by right fielder Dave Parker.

In the second game, Manny Sanguillen, one of the three Pirates left from the club which defeated Baltimore in the 1971 World Series, was the late-inning hero for Pittsburgh. With two out in the top of the ninth inning and Ed Ott on second, Sanguillen was sent in to pinch-hit against Oriole reliever Don Stanhouse. With two strikes on him, the 35-year-old Panamanian sliced a low pitch to right field, where Ken Singleton grabbed the ball on the bounce and fired toward the plate. First baseman Murray intercepted the throw en route to the plate, and relayed the ball to catcher Rick Dempsey a split second too late to tag the sliding Ott. Ott's run proved to be the margin of victory as the Pirates took the game, 3-2.

Murray's act of cutting off and relaying the ball to the plate was criticized by many, but it was generally felt that Singleton had made a poor throw, which would have had trouble getting to the catcher on time had Murray let the ball go through on the cutoff. This was the second controversial play of the game. The first had occurred in the previous half-inning. With Murray on second, DeCinces on first and nobody out, Lowenstein was the batter. To many observers, the situation dictated that Lowenstein should hit the ball to the right side, in order to move the runners to second and third. Lowenstein, however, hit the ball to shortstop where Foli picked it up and threw to second to retire DeCinces. Murray was trapped between second and third on the play, and was tagged out for a double play. Pirate pitcher Don Robinson retired the next batter and the Bucs were out of trouble.

As the Series shifted to Pittsburgh, the Orioles rebounded in Game Three, led by the bat of shortstop Kiko Garcia. In a game delayed 67 minutes by rain, Garcia collected four hits, including a bases-loaded triple, to highlight a five-run, fourth-inning outburst, as the Orioles coasted, 8-4.

In Game Four, the Pirates were seemingly in control, leading 6-3, until the eighth inning when the Orioles again showed their late-inning magic. In that eighth frame, following singles by Garcia and Singleton and a walk to DeCinces, Lowenstein was sent in to bat for left fielder Gary Roenicke and drilled a Kent Tekulve pitch down the right field line for a double, driving in two runs. After Tekulve walked pinch-batter Billy Smith intentionally, Terry Crowley was sent up to pinch-hit. He worked the count to 3-and-2 before doubling into the right field corner, driving in two more runs.

Pitcher Tim Stoddard was allowed to bat for himself and he bounced a single over a drawn-in infield, driving in the fifth run of the inning. Stoddard's plate appearance represented his first at-bat in the major leagues. Al Bumbry drove in the sixth and final run with a forceout, but the damage had been done.

Stoddard retired the Pirates in the eighth and ninth innings and the Orioles vaulted to a three-games-to-one advantage. It looked like Baltimore would clinch the title, with ace hurlers Flanagan and Jim Palmer set for the next two games.

But the Bucs defeated Flanagan in Game Five, 7-1. Baltimore assumed a 1-0 lead in the fifth and Flanagan was breezing with a four-hitter through the first five innings. But suddenly, the Pirates' bats erupted and they scored two in the sixth and seventh innings and added three more in the eighth, forcing the Series back to Baltimore. Bill Madlock provided the punch for the Bucs, collecting four singles.

Back in Baltimore for Game Six, the Orioles were hoping Palmer would end the Series. The Pirates had 14-game winner John Candelaria pitching and the teams were deadlocked at 0-0 through the first six innings. The Pirates finally managed to put three singles and a sacrifice fly together for a 2-0 lead in the seventh. They added two more in the eighth and went on to win, 4-0.

That brought it down to the decisive seventh game. Rich Dauer started off the scoring in the third inning with a home run into the left field seats. But the relentless Bucs took the lead in the sixth on a two-run homer by Stargell. Going into the ninth, the Orioles trailed by only one, but then everything went wrong for the Birds. Stoddard came in to pitch and he surrendered a leadoff double to Garner. The hit was Garner's 12th of the Series in 24 at-bats, which tied him with Pepper Martin (1931) and Johnny Lindell (1947) for the highest batting average (.500) in a seven-game Series. After the next batter grounded out, Weaver started his merry-go-round of relief pitchers, as each of the next four Pirate batters faced a different hurler. It took a record five Oriole pitchers to complete the inning in which the Pirates scored their final two runs of the season.

Tekulve was again on the mound trying to save the game as he had done 31 times during the regular season. After striking out Roenicke and Dauer, Tekulve retired pinch-hitter Pat Kelly on a fly to center and the Pirates had won their fifth World Championship—all five coming in seven-game Series.

The star of the World Series was Stargell, who batted .400. But there were other outstanding performances for both teams—Garner's .500 batting average, Tekulve's three saves and the Orioles' Garcia batting .400. In addition, five Pirates—Garner, Stargell, Moreno, Parker and Foli—collected ten or more hits. The box scores:

Wednesday, October 10—At Baltimore

Pittsburgh (N.L.)	AB.	R.	H.	O.	A.	E.
Moreno, cf	5	0	0	4	0	0
Foli, ss	5	1	1	1	3	1
Parker, rf	5	1	4	3	0	0
B. Robinson, lf	5	1	1	2	0	0
Stargell, 1b	5	1	1	7	0	1
Madlock, 3b	3	0	0	0	1	0
Nicosia, c	4	0	0	4	1	0
Garner, 2b	4	0	3	3	2	1
Kison, p	0	0	0	0	1	0
Rooker, p	1	0	0	0	2	0
aSanguillen	1	0	0	0	0	0
Romo, p	0	0	0	0	0	0
bLacy	1	0	0	0	0	0
D. Robinson, p	0	0	0	0	0	0
cStennett	1	0	1	0	0	0
Jackson, p	0	0	0	0	0	0
Totals	40	4	11	24	10	3

Baltimore (A.L.)	AB.	R.	H.	O.	A.	E.
Bumbry, cf	4	1	1	3	0	0
Belanger, ss	3	1	0	1	4	1
Singleton, rf	3	0	1	2	0	0
Murray, 1b	2	1	1	12	1	0
Lowenstein, lf	4	1	1	1	0	0
Roenicke, lf	0	0	0	0	0	0
DeCinces, 3b	3	1	1	0	4	2
Smith, 2b	2	0	1	1	3	0
dDauer, 2b	1	0	1	0	1	0
Dempsey, c	4	0	0	7	0	0
Flanagan, p	4	0	0	0	2	0
Totals	30	5	6	27	15	3

Pittsburgh........ 0 0 0 1 0 2 0 1 0—4
Baltimore........ 5 0 0 0 0 0 0 0 *—5

Pittsburgh	IP.	H.	R.	ER.	BB.	SO.
Kison (L)	⅓	3	5	4	2	0
Rooker	3⅔	2	0	0	1	2
Romo	1	0	0	0	2	0
D. Robinson	2	0	0	0	1	1
Jackson	1	1	0	0	0	1

Baltimore	IP.	H.	R.	ER.	BB.	SO.
Flanagan (W)	9	11	4	2	1	7

Bases on balls—Off Kison 2 (Belanger, Murray), off Rooker 1 (DeCinces), off Romo 2 (Murray, Smith), off D. Robinson 1 (Singleton), off Flanagan 1 (Madlock).

Strikeouts—By Rooker 2 (Belanger, Lowenstein), by D. Robinson 1 (Flanagan), by Jackson 1 (Flanagan), by Flanagan 7 (B. Robinson, Stargell 2, Garner, Moreno 2, Nicosia).

aGrounded out for Rooker in fifth. bReached first base on error for Romo in sixth. cSingled for D. Robinson in eighth. dSingled for Smith in eighth. Runs batted in—Lowenstein, DeCinces 2, Stargell 2, Garner 2. Two-base hits—Parker, Garner. Home runs—DeCinces, Stargell. Stolen base—Murray. Caught stealing—Parker. Sacrifice hit—Bumbry. Wild pitch—Kison. Double play—Madlock, Garner and Stargell. Left on bases—Pittsburgh 10, Baltimore 8. Umpires—Neudecker (A.L.) plate, Engel (N.L.) first base, Goetz (A.L.) second base, Tata (N.L.) third base, McKean (A.L.) left field, Runge (N.L.) right field. Time—3:18. Attendance—53,735.

Thursday, October 11—At Baltimore

Pittsburgh (N.L.)	AB.	R.	H.	O.	A.	E.
Moreno, cf	5	0	1	1	0	0
Foli, ss	4	0	1	0	5	1
Parker, rf	4	0	1	1	1	0
Stargell, 1b	4	1	1	12	0	0
Milner, lf	3	1	1	3	0	0
dB. Robinson	1	0	1	0	0	0
eAlexander, lf	0	0	0	0	0	0
Madlock, 3b	4	0	2	0	4	0
Ott, c	3	1	1	6	0	0
Garner, 2b	2	0	1	4	6	0
Blyleven, p	2	0	0	0	0	0
aEasler	0	0	0	0	0	0
D. Robinson, p	0	0	0	0	1	0
fSanguillen	1	0	1	0	0	0
Tekulve, p	0	0	0	0	0	0
Totals	33	3	11	27	17	2

Baltimore (A.L.)	AB.	R.	H.	O.	A.	E.
Bumbry, cf	5	0	0	5	0	0
Belanger, ss	3	0	0	1	2	0
cCrowley	0	0	0	0	0	0
T. Martinez, p	0	0	0	0	0	0
Stanhouse, p	0	0	0	0	0	0
Singleton, rf	4	1	1	1	0	0
Murray, 1b	3	1	3	10	2	0
DeCinces, 3b	4	0	0	0	6	1
Lowenstein, lf	3	0	1	1	0	0
Smith, 2b	4	0	0	3	0	0
Dempsey, c	3	0	1	4	2	0
Palmer, p	2	0	0	1	1	0
bKelly	0	0	0	0	0	0
Garcia, ss	1	0	0	1	0	0
Totals	32	2	6	27	13	1

Pittsburgh........ 0 2 0 0 0 0 0 0 1—3
Baltimore........ 0 1 0 0 0 1 0 0 0—2

Pittsburgh	IP.	H.	R.	ER.	BB.	SO.
Blyleven	6	5	2	2	2	1
D. Rob'son (W)	2	1	0	0	3	2
Tekulve (S)	1	0	0	0	0	2

Baltimore	IP.	H.	R.	ER.	BB.	SO.
Palmer	7	8	2	2	2	3
T. Martinez	1†	1	0	0	0	1
Stanhouse (L)	1	2	1	1	1	0

†Pitched to one batter in ninth.

Bases on balls—Off Blyleven 2 (Lowenstein, Murray), off D. Robinson 3 (Dempsey, Kelly, Crowley), off Palmer 2 (Garner, Easler), off Stanhouse 1 (Garner).

Strikeouts—By Blyleven 1 (Palmer), by D. Robinson 2 (Bumbry, Singleton), by Tekulve 2 (Dempsey, Garcia), by Palmer 3 (Moreno 2, Ott), by T. Martinez 1 (Stargell).

aWalked for Blyleven in seventh. bWalked for Palmer in seventh. cWalked for Belanger in seventh. dSingled for Milner in ninth. eRan for B. Robinson in ninth. fSingled for D. Robinson in ninth. Runs batted in—Madlock, Ott, Murray 2, Sanguillen. Two-base hit—Murray. Home run—Murray. Caught stealing—Madlock, Alexander. Sacrifice fly—Ott. Wild pitch—Palmer. Double plays—Murray and Palmer; Madlock, Garner and Stargell; Murray, Belanger and Smith; Parker and Ott; Foli, Garner, Madlock and Garner. Left on bases—Pittsburgh 7, Baltimore 8.

1979 WORLD SERIES

Umpires—Engel (N.L.) plate, Goetz (A.L.) first base, Tata (N.L.) second base, McKean (A.L.) third base, Runge (N.L.) left field, Neudecker (A.L.) right field. Time—3:13. Attendance—53,739.

Friday, October 12—At Pittsburgh

Baltimore (A.L.)	AB.	R.	H.	O.	A.	E.
Garcia, ss	4	2	4	0	4	0
Ayala, lf	2	1	2	0	0	0
aBumbry, cf	2	1	1	2	0	0
Singleton, rf	5	0	2	4	0	0
Murray, 1b	4	0	0	7	1	0
DeCinces, 3b	5	0	0	0	1	0
Roenicke, cf-lf	5	0	1	5	1	0
Dauer, 2b	5	1	1	2	3	0
Dempsey, c	5	2	2	7	0	0
McGregor, p	3	1	0	0	0	0
Totals	40	8	13	27	10	0

Pittsburgh (N.L.)	AB.	R.	H.	O.	A.	E.
Moreno, cf	4	1	2	2	1	0
Foli, ss	4	0	0	0	6	1
Parker, rf	3	0	0	2	0	0
B. Robinson, lf	4	0	1	4	1	0
Stargell, 1b	4	2	2	8	1	1
Madlock, 3b	4	0	1	0	0	0
Nicosia, c	4	1	1	8	0	0
Garner, 2b	4	0	1	2	1	0
Candelaria, p	1	0	1	0	0	0
Romo, p	1	0	0	0	1	0
Jackson, p	0	0	0	0	0	0
bLacy	1	0	0	0	0	0
Tekulve, p	0	0	0	1	0	0
Totals	34	4	9	27	11	2

Baltimore .... 0 0 2   5 0 0   1 0 0—8
Pittsburgh .... 1 2 0   0 0 1   0 0 0—4

Baltimore	IP.	H.	R.	ER.	BB.	SO.
McGregor (W)	9	9	4	4	0	6

Pittsburgh	IP.	H.	R.	ER.	BB.	SO.
Candelaria (L)	3†	8	6	5	2	2
Romo	3⅔	5	2	2	1	4
Jackson	⅓	0	0	0	0	0
Tekulve	2	0	0	0	0	1

†Pitched to four batters in fourth.

Bases on balls—Off Candelaria 2 (Garcia, Murray), off Romo 1 (McGregor).
Strikeouts—By McGregor 6 (B. Robinson 2, Madlock, Parker, Stargell, Moreno), by Candelaria 2 (Singleton, DeCinces), by Romo 4 (Roenicke, Dauer, Dempsey, McGregor), by Tekulve 1 (Roenicke).
aHit by pitcher for Ayala in fourth. bLined out for Jackson in seventh. Runs batted in—Garcia 4, Ayala 2, Singleton, DeCinces, Parker, Madlock, Garner 2. Two-base hits—Garcia, Moreno 2, Garner, Dauer, Stargell, Dempsey. Three-base hit—Garcia. Home run—Ayala. Sacrifice fly—Parker. Wild pitch—Romo. Hit by pitcher—By Romo (Bumbry). Balk—McGregor. Left on bases—Baltimore 9, Pittsburgh 4. Umpires—Goetz (A.L.) plate, Tata (N.L.) first base, McKean (A.L.) second base, Runge (N.L.) third base, Neudecker (A.L.) left field, Engel (N.L.) right field. Time—2:51. Attendance—50,848.

Saturday, October 13—At Pittsburgh

Baltimore (A.L.)	AB.	R.	H.	O.	A.	E.
Bumbry, cf	5	1	1	1	1	0
Garcia, ss	5	2	2	6	5	0
Belanger, ss	0	0	0	0	0	0
Singleton, rf	5	0	3	0	0	0
Murray, 1b	5	1	0	8	1	0
DeCinces, 3b	1	1	0	2	0	0
Roenicke, lf	3	0	0	2	0	0
cLowenstein, lf	2	1	1	1	0	0
Dauer, 2b	3	0	1	1	2	0
dSmith, 2b	0	1	0	0	0	0
Skaggs, c	3	1	1	2	2	0
eCrowley	1	0	1	0	0	0
fDempsey, c	0	1	0	3	0	0
D. Martinez, p	0	0	0	0	1	0
Stewart, p	1	0	0	1	2	0
aMay	1	0	0	0	0	0
Stone, p	0	0	0	0	0	0
bKelly	1	0	1	0	0	0
Stoddard, p	1	0	1	0	2	0
Totals	37	9	12	27	16	0

Pittsburgh (N.L.)	AB.	R.	H.	O.	A.	E.
Moreno, cf	5	0	2	2	0	0
Foli, ss	4	2	3	1	5	0
Parker, rf	5	0	2	1	0	0
Stargell, 1b	5	1	3	8	0	0
Milner, lf	3	1	2	2	0	0
D. Robinson, p	0	0	0	0	0	0
Tekulve, p	0	0	0	0	0	0
gEasler	1	0	0	0	0	0
Madlock, 3b	3	1	2	0	1	1
Ott, c	5	0	1	8	0	0
Garner, 2b	4	1	2	5	7	0
Bibby, p	3	0	0	0	0	0
Jackson, p	0	0	0	0	0	0
B. Robinson, lf	1	0	0	0	0	0
Totals	39	6	17	27	13	1

Baltimore .... 0 0 3   0 0 0   0 6 0—9
Pittsburgh .... 0 4 0   0 1 1   0 0 0—6

Baltimore	IP.	H.	R.	ER.	BB.	SO.
D. Martinez	1⅓	6	4	4	0	0
Stewart	2⅔	4	0	0	1	0
Stone	2	4	2	2	2	2
Stoddard (W)	3	3	0	0	1	3

Pittsburgh	IP.	H.	R.	ER.	BB.	SO.
Bibby	6⅓	7	3	2	2	7
Jackson	⅔	0	0	0	0	0
D. Robinson	⅓	2	3	3	1	0
Tekulve (L)	1⅔	3	3	3	2	1

Bases on balls—Off Stewart 1 (Milner), off Stone 2 (Foli, Madlock), off Stoddard 1 (Madlock), off Bibby 2 (DeCinces 2), off D. Robinson 1 (DeCinces), off Tekulve 2 (Smith, DeCinces).
Strikeouts—By Stone 2 (Bibby, Stargell), by Stoddard 3 (B. Robinson, Parker, Ott), by Bibby 7 (Garcia, Singleton, Murray 2, Roenicke, Stewart, May), by Tekulve 1 (Garcia).
aStruck out for Stewart in fifth. bSingled for Stone in seventh. cDoubled for Roenicke in eighth. dIntentionally walked for Dauer in eighth. eDoubled for Skaggs in eighth. fRan for Crowley in eighth. gFlied out for Tekulve in ninth. Runs batted in—Bumbry, Garcia 2, Singleton, Lowenstein 2, Crowley 2, Stoddard, Moreno, Parker, Stargell, Milner, Ott 2. Two-base hits—Madlock, Ott, Garcia, Singleton, Stargell, Milner, Parker, Lowenstein, Crowley. Home run—Stargell. Stolen base—DeCinces. Caught stealing—Madlock. Double plays—D. Martinez, Garcia and Murray; Dauer, Garcia and Murray; Foli, Garner and Stargell 2; Garner, Foli and Stargell. Left on bases—Baltimore 6, Pittsburgh 10. Umpires—Tata (N.L.) plate, McKean (A.L.) first base, Runge (N.L.) second base, Neudecker (A.L.) third base, Engel (N.L.) left field, Goetz (A.L.) right field. Time—3:48. Attendance—50,883.

Sunday, October 14—At Pittsburgh

Baltimore (A.L.)	AB.	R.	H.	O.	A.	E.
Garcia, ss	4	0	0	2	1	0
Ayala, lf	1	0	0	2	0	0
bBumbry, cf	1	0	0	1	0	0
Singleton, rf	4	0	0	0	0	0
Murray, 1b	4	0	0	7	1	0
Roenicke, cf-lf	4	1	1	2	0	0
DeCinces, 3b	4	0	2	1	4	0
Dauer, 2b	3	0	0	2	1	0
dLowenstein	1	0	1	0	0	0
Dempsey, c	3	0	2	7	0	0
eCrowley	1	0	0	0	0	0
Flanagan, p	1	0	0	0	2	0
cKelly	1	0	0	0	0	0
Stoddard, p	0	0	0	0	1	1
T. Martinez, p	0	0	0	0	0	0
Stanhouse, p	0	0	0	0	0	1
Totals	32	1	6	24	10	2

Pittsburgh (N.L.)	AB.	R.	H.	O.	A.	E.
Moreno, cf	4	1	0	3	0	0
Foli, ss	4	2	2	3	7	0
Parker, rf	4	1	2	1	0	0
B. Robinson, lf	4	0	1	2	0	0
Stargell, 1b	3	1	1	10	0	0
Madlock, 3b	4	1	4	0	1	0
Nicosia, c	4	0	0	5	0	0
Garner, 2b	4	1	2	2	3	1
Rooker, p	1	0	0	1	0	0
aLacy,	1	0	1	0	0	0
Blyleven, p	1	0	0	0	1	0
Totals	34	7	13	27	12	1

Baltimore .... 0 0 0   0 1 0   0 0 0—1
Pittsburgh .... 0 0 0   0 0 2   2 3 *—7

Baltimore	IP.	H.	R.	ER.	BB.	SO.
Flanagan (L)	6	6	2	2	1	6
Stoddard	⅔	2	2	2	0	0
T. Martinez	⅓†	2	1	1	0	0
Stanhouse	1	3	2	2	2	0

Pittsburgh	IP.	H.	R.	ER.	BB.	SO.
Rooker	5	3	1	1	2	2
Blyleven (W)	4	3	0	0	1	3

†Pitched to one batter in eighth.

Bases on balls—Off Flanagan 1 (Foli), off Stanhouse 2 (Moreno, Parker), off Rooker 2 (Ayala, Flanagan), off Blyleven 1 (Bumbry). Strikeouts—By Flanagan 6 (Moreno 2, Parker 2, Rooker, Nicosia), by Rooker 2 (DeCinces, Singleton), by Blyleven 3 (Roenicke, DeCinces, Kelly). aHad infield single for Rooker in fifth. bFlied out for Ayala in sixth. cStruck out for Flanagan in seventh. dSingled for Dauer in ninth. eFlied out for Dempsey in ninth. Runs batted in—Foli 3, Parker, Stargell, Madlock, Garner. Two-base hits—B. Robinson, Roenicke, Dempsey, Parker. Three-base hit—Foli. Sacrifice hits—B. Robinson, Blyleven. Sacrifice fly—Stargell. Double plays—Garner, Foli and Stargell; Blyleven, Garner, Foli and Stargell. Left on bases—Baltimore 7, Pittsburgh 9. Umpires—McKean (A.L.) plate, Runge (N.L.) first base, Neudecker (A.L.) second base, Engel (N.L.) third base, Goetz (A.L.) left field, Tata (N.L.) right field. Time—2:54. Attendance—50,920.

Tuesday, October 16—At Baltimore

Pittsburgh (N.L.)	AB.	R.	H.	O.	A.	E.
Moreno, cf	5	1	3	4	0	0
Foli, ss	5	1	2	0	5	0
Parker, rf	4	0	1	3	0	0
Stargell, 1b	4	0	0	8	0	0
Milner, lf	3	0	0	0	0	0
Tekulve, p	1	0	0	0	0	0
Madlock, 3b	3	0	0	1	2	0
Ott, c	4	1	2	6	0	0
Garner, 2b	3	1	2	4	2	0
Candelaria, p	2	0	0	0	1	0
aLacy	1	0	0	0	0	0
B. Robinson, lf	0	0	0	1	0	0
Totals	35	4	10	27	10	0

Baltimore (A.L.)	AB.	R.	H.	O.	A.	E.
Garcia, ss	3	0	1	1	2	0
eKelly	1	0	0	0	0	0
Belanger, ss	0	0	0	0	0	0
Ayala, lf	3	0	0	2	0	0
fCrowley	1	0	0	0	0	0
Stoddard, p	0	0	0	0	1	0
Singleton, rf	4	0	3	1	0	0
Murray, 1b	4	0	0	5	1	0
DeCinces, 3b	4	0	0	1	3	0
Roenicke, cf	2	0	0	4	0	0
bBumbry, cf	1	0	0	2	0	1
Dauer, 2b	2	0	1	1	1	0
cSmith, 2b	1	0	1	0	0	0
Dempsey, c	3	0	1	7	0	0
Palmer, p	2	0	0	1	0	0
dLowenstein, lf	1	0	0	1	0	0
Totals	32	0	7	27	7	1

Pittsburgh .... 0 0 0   0 0 0   2 2 0—4
Baltimore .... 0 0 0   0 0 0   0 0 0—0

Pittsburgh	IP.	H.	R.	ER.	BB.	SO.
Candelaria (W)	6	6	0	0	0	2
Tekulve (S)	3	1	0	0	0	4

Baltimore	IP.	H.	R.	ER.	BB.	SO.
Palmer (L)	8	10	4	4	3	5
Stoddard	1	0	0	0	0	0

Bases on balls—Off Palmer 3 (Milner, Madlock, Parker). Strikeouts—by Palmer 5 (Candelaria 2, Parker, Stargell, Lacy), by Candelaria 2 (Palmer 2), by Tekulve 4 (Dempsey, Lowenstein, Singleton, DeCinces). aStruck out for Candelaria in seventh. bFlied out for Roenicke in seventh. cSingled for Dauer in seventh. dStruck out for Palmer in eighth. eFlied out for Garcia in eighth. fGrounded out for Ayala in eighth. Runs batted in—Moreno, Parker, Stargell, B. Robinson. Two-base hits—Foli, Garner. Sacrifice flies—Stargell, B. Robinson. Hit by pitcher—By Palmer (Garner). Double plays—Madlock and Stargell; Foli, Garner and Stargell. Left on bases—Pittsburgh 10, Baltimore 5. Umpires—Runge (N.L.) plate, Neudecker (A.L.) first base, Engel (N.L.) second base, Goetz (A.L.) third base, Tata (N.L.) left field, McKean (A.L.) right field. Time—2:30. Attendance—53,739.

Wednesday, October 17—At Baltimore

Pittsburgh (N.L.)	AB.	R.	H.	O.	A.	E.
Moreno, cf	5	1	3	4	0	0
Foli, ss	4	0	0	3	1	0
Parker, rf	4	0	0	2	0	0
B. Robinson, lf	4	1	1	2	0	0
Stargell, 1b	5	1	4	6	1	0
Madlock, 3b	3	0	0	2	1	0
Nicosia, c	4	0	0	6	1	0
Garner, 2b	3	1	1	1	2	0
Bibby, p	1	0	0	1	0	0
aSanguillen	1	0	0	0	0	0
D. Robinson, p	0	0	0	0	0	0
Jackson, p	1	0	0	0	0	0
Tekulve, p	1	0	0	0	0	0
Totals	36	4	10	27	6	0

1980 WORLD SERIES

Baltimore (A.L.)	AB.	R.	H.	O.	A.	E.
Bumbry, cf	3	0	0	0	0	0
Garcia, ss	3	0	1	0	5	1
eAyala	0	0	0	0	0	0
fCrowley	1	0	0	0	0	0
Stoddard, p	0	0	0	0	1	0
Flanagan, p	0	0	0	0	0	0
Stanhouse, p	0	0	0	0	0	0
T. Martinez, p	0	0	0	0	0	0
D. Martinez, p	0	0	0	0	0	0
Singleton, rf	3	0	0	1	0	0
Murray, 1b	4	0	0	11	0	0
Lowenstein, lf	2	0	0	2	0	1
bRoenicke, lf	2	0	0	1	0	0
DeCinces, 3b	4	0	2	3	3	0
Dempsey, c	3	0	0	3	0	0
gKelly	1	0	0	0	0	0
Dauer, 2b	3	1	1	4	2	0
McGregor, p	1	0	0	1	2	0
cMay	0	0	0	0	0	0
dBelanger, ss	0	0	0	1	1	0
Totals	30	1	4	27	14	2

Pittsburgh .... 0 0 0   0 0 2   0 0 2—4
Baltimore .... 0 0 1   0 0 0   0 0 0—1

Pittsburgh	IP.	H.	R.	ER.	BB.	SO.
Bibby	4	3	1	1	0	3
D. Robinson	⅔	1	0	0	1	0
Jackson (W)	2⅔	0	0	0	2	1
Tekulve (S)	1⅔	0	0	0	1	2

Baltimore	IP.	H.	R.	ER.	BB.	SO.
McGregor (L)	8	7	2	2	2	2
Stoddard	⅓	1	1	1	0	0
Flanagan	0†	1	1	1	0	0
Stanhouse	0†	1	0	0	0	0
T. Martinez	0†	0	0	0	0	0
D. Martinez	⅔	0	0	0	0	0

†Pitched to one batter in ninth.

Bases on balls—Off D. Robinson 1 (McGregor), off Jackson 2 (May, Bumbry), off Tekulve 1 (Singleton), off McGregor 2 (Garner, Madlock).

Strikeouts—By Bibby 3 (Murray 2, Lowenstein), by Jackson 1 (Roenicke), by Tekulve 2 (Roenicke, DeCinces), by McGregor 2 (Parker 2).

aGrounded out for Bibby in fifth. bStruck out for Lowenstein in seventh. cWalked for McGregor in eighth. dRan for May in eighth. eAnnounced as pinch-hitter for Garcia in eighth. fGrounded out for Ayala in eighth. gFlied out for Dempsey in ninth. Runs batted in—Moreno, B. Robinson, Stargell 2, Dauer. Two-base hits—Stargell 2, Garner. Home runs—Dauer, Stargell. Caught stealing—Garcia. Sacrifice hit—Foli. Hit by pitcher—By T. Martinez (Parker), by D. Martinez (B. Robinson). Double play—Belanger and Murray. Left on bases—Pittsburgh 10, Baltimore 6. Umpires—Neudecker (A.L.) plate, Engel (N.L.) first base, Goetz (A.L.) second base, Tata (N.L.) third base, McKean (A.L.) left field, Runge (N.L.) right field. Time—2:54. Attendance—53,733.

COMPOSITE BATTING AVERAGES
Pittsburgh Pirates

Player-Position	G.	AB.	R.	H.	2B.	3B.	HR.	RBI.	BA.
Stennett, ph	1	1	0	1	0	0	0	0	1.000
Garner, 2b	7	24	4	12	4	0	0	5	.500
Stargell, 1b	7	30	7	12	4	0	3	7	.400
Madlock, 3b	7	24	2	9	1	0	0	3	.375
Parker, rf	7	29	2	10	3	0	0	4	.345
Moreno, cf	7	33	4	11	0	0	0	3	.333
Foli, ss	7	30	6	10	1	1	0	3	.333
Ott, c	3	12	2	4	1	0	0	3	.333
Milner, lf	3	9	2	3	1	0	0	1	.333
Candelaria, p	2	3	0	1	0	0	0	0	.333
Sanguillen, ph	3	3	0	1	0	0	0	1	.333
B. Robinson, lf-ph	7	19	2	5	1	0	0	2	.263
Lacy, ph	4	4	0	1	0	0	0	0	.250
Nicosia, c	4	16	1	1	0	0	0	0	.063
Alexander, pr-lf	1	0	0	0	0	0	0	0	.000
Kison, p	1	0	0	0	0	0	0	0	.000
D. Robinson, p	4	0	0	0	0	0	0	0	.000
Easler, ph	2	1	0	0	0	0	0	0	.000
Jackson, p	4	1	0	0	0	0	0	0	.000
Romo, p	2	1	0	0	0	0	0	0	.000
Rooker, p	2	2	0	0	0	0	0	0	.000
Tekulve, p	5	2	0	0	0	0	0	0	.000
Blyleven, p	2	3	0	0	0	0	0	0	.000
Bibby, p	2	4	0	0	0	0	0	0	.000
Totals	7	251	32	81	18	1	3	32	.323

Baltimore Orioles

Player-Position	G.	AB.	R.	H.	2B.	3B.	HR.	RBI.	BA.
Stoddard, p	4	1	0	1	0	0	0	1	1.000
Garcia, ss	6	20	4	8	2	1	0	6	.400
Singleton, rf	7	28	1	10	1	0	0	2	.357
Ayala, lf-ph	4	6	1	2	0	0	1	2	.333
Skaggs, c	1	3	1	1	0	0	0	0	.333
Dauer, ph-2b	6	17	2	5	1	0	1	1	.294
Dempsey, c-pr	7	21	3	6	2	0	0	0	.286
Smith, 2b-ph	4	7	1	2	0	0	0	0	.286
Crowley, ph	5	4	0	1	1	0	0	2	.250
Kelly, ph	5	4	0	1	0	0	0	0	.250
Lowenstein, lf-ph	6	13	2	3	1	0	0	3	.231
DeCinces, 3b	7	25	2	5	0	0	1	3	.200
Murray, 1b	7	26	3	4	1	0	1	2	.154
Bumbry, cf-ph	7	21	3	3	0	0	0	1	.143
Roenicke, lf-cf-ph	6	16	1	2	1	0	0	0	.125
D. Martinez, p	2	0	0	0	0	0	0	0	.000
T. Martinez, p	3	0	0	0	0	0	0	0	.000
Stanhouse, p	3	0	0	0	0	0	0	0	.000
Stone, p	1	0	0	0	0	0	0	0	.000
May, ph	2	1	0	0	0	0	0	0	.000
Stewart, p	1	1	0	0	0	0	0	0	.000
McGregor, p	2	4	1	0	0	0	0	0	.000
Palmer, p	2	4	0	0	0	0	0	0	.000
Flanagan, p	3	5	0	0	0	0	0	0	.000
Belanger, ss-pr	5	6	1	0	0	0	0	0	.000
Totals	7	233	26	54	10	1	4	23	.232

COMPOSITE PITCHING AVERAGES
Pittsburgh Pirates

Pitcher	G.	IP.	H.	R.	E.	SO.	BB.	W.	L.	ERA.
Jackson	4	4⅔	1	0	0	2	2	1	0	0.00
Rooker	2	8⅔	5	1	1	3	4	0	0	1.04
Blyleven	2	10	8	2	2	3	4	1	0	1.80
Bibby	2	10⅓	10	4	3	2	10	0	0	2.61
Tekulve	5	9⅓	4	3	3	10	0	0	1	2.89
Romo	2	4⅔	5	2	2	3	4	0	0	3.86
Candelaria	2	9	14	6	5	7	4	1	1	5.00
D. Robinson	4	5	4	3	3	6	3	1	0	5.40
Kison	1	⅓	4	4	4	0	0	0	1	108.00
Totals	7	62	54	26	22	26	41	4	3	3.19

(NOTE: Pittsburgh individual earned runs do not add up to team total because of rule 10.18(i) applied in Game 3.)

Baltimore Orioles

Pitcher	G.	IP.	H.	R.	E.	SO.	BB.	W.	L.	ERA.
Stewart	1	2⅔	4	0	0	1	0	0	0	0.00
Flanagan	3	15	18	7	5	2	13	1	1	3.00
McGregor	2	17	16	6	6	2	8	1	1	3.18
Palmer	2	15	18	6	6	5	8	0	1	3.60
Stoddard	4	5	6	3	3	1	3	1	0	5.40
T. Martinez	3	1⅓	1	1	1	0	1	0	0	6.75
Stone	1	2	4	2	2	2	0	0	0	9.00
Stanhouse	3	2	6	3	3	3	0	0	1	13.50
D. Martinez	2	2	6	4	4	0	0	0	0	18.00
Totals	7	62	81	32	30	16	35	3	4	4.35

SERIES OF 1980

	W.	L.	Pct.
Philadelphia N. L.	4	2	.667
Kansas City A. L.	2	4	.333

The Philadelphia Phillies finally ended a long post-season drought when they overtook the Kansas City Royals to win the 1980 World Series in six games.

For the Phillies, it marked the first World Championship in their 97-year National League history, putting an end to the jinx which caused the team to fail in three previous Championship Series and two earlier World Series. Philadelphia had won two pennants—in 1915 and 1950—but had managed to win only one out of nine World Series games. In addition, the Phillies had been frustrated in three straight Championship Series—1976 through 1978—when they had won the East Division title, only to lose each playoff series. But 1980 was to be a different story for the come-from-behind gang from Philly.

The World Series was played between two frustrated clubs; the Phillies, for reasons mentioned earlier, and the Kansas City Royals, an exciting young club which had been defeated by the New York Yankees in three consecutive playoff series before sweeping the Yanks in three games in 1980.

Although not a spectacular team during the regular season, the Phillies were never more than 6½ games out of first place. Under the direction of Manager Dallas Green, the Phillies kept pace, led by the superb pitching of Steve Carlton and the slugging of third baseman Mike Schmidt. Carlton, a two-time Cy Young Award winner prior to 1980, compiled another excellent season, leading the N.L. with 24 victories (against only nine defeats) and 286 strikeouts on his way to becoming the major leagues' all-time lefthanded strikeout leader. Schmidt had an equally fine season, batting .286, with a major league-leading 48 homers and an N.L. high of 121 RBIs. His 48th homer won the division title for the Phillies in the 11th inning of a 6-4 win against Montreal—the Phillies' closest rival throughout the season.

The Phillies earned their nickname, the come-from-behind gang, as they won a bitterly-fought five-game Championship Series against the Houston Astros. The Series proved to be probably the most exciting in the 12-year history of the playoffs, as each of the last four games was won in extra innings. Throughout the Series the lead see-sawed between the teams. The last game epitomized the Phillies' season, as they fought back from a 5-2 deficit by scoring five in the eighth. After the Astros tied the game in the bottom of the ninth, the Phillies again came back with a run in the 10th inning to win the Series.

The American League champion Royals had a much easier time in winning their first league title. At one point in the season, the Royals enjoyed a 20-game lead over their second-place rivals. Except for an eight-game losing streak in September, the Royals would have finished with an even larger bulge than the 14-game margin they enjoyed over second-place Oakland. Following the regular season, Kansas City swept past the Yankees in a three-game Championship Series.

The Royals owned the greatest single performer in baseball in 1980, George Brett, who was the talk of the baseball world during the summer. After sitting out a month with an ankle injury, Brett came back and went on a batting tear—climbing to the .400 mark, where he hovered until finally dropping to .390. Brett not only finished with the highest single-season batting average since Ted Williams hit .406 in 1941, but he hit 24 home runs and drove in 118 runs. In addition, it was Brett's three-run homer off Rich Gossage in the final playoff game that vaulted the Royals into the World Series.

There were others on the Royals who had excellent seasons; Willie Wilson, who batted .326 with 230 hits and 79 stolen bases; Hal McRae, who finished another solid season with a .297 batting mark and 83 RBIs; Willie Aikens, who chipped in 20 homers and 98 RBIs. The Royals were a team with hitting and speed; their .286 team batting average was the highest in the major leagues since 1950, while their 185 stolen bases led the American League.

The Series commenced in Philadelphia, where Phillies hurler Bob Walk pitched seven innings in defeating Kansas City, 7-6. Walk, who was the first rookie to start a Series opener since Joe Black of the Brooklyn Dodgers in 1952, was helped by Tug McGraw, who pitched the final two rounds. The Phillies, who at one time in the game were down 4-0, rallied behind the bat of Bake McBride, who went 3-for-4 with a three-run homer in a five-run third inning. Aikens, who was celebrating his 26th birthday, blasted a pair of two-run homers for the losing Royals.

Philadelphia took the second game, 6-4, thanks to more late-inning heroics. Down 4-2 when they came to bat in the bottom of the eighth, the Phillies scored four times on a walk to Bob Boone, a pinch-double by Del Unser, a single by McBride, a double by Schmidt and a single by Keith Moreland. Carlton pitched the first eight innings and picked up the win. Ron Reed hurled the ninth, picking up a save. Brett, who had a perfect evening, going 2-for-2 with a walk, had to leave the game in the sixth inning. It was later revealed that the Royals' third base star was suffering from hemorrhoids. Down by two games and without their top hitter, it looked like the Royals were doomed for the remainder of the Series.

Back in Kansas City for the next three games, the Royals showed what they were made of—but not before another scare from the Phillies. It looked like Game Three would end in another Phillies' comeback victory. As had happened in the first two games, the Royals took early leads, only to be tied by Philadelphia.

Brett, hours after leaving the hospital,

started the scoring with a homer in the first. The Phillies came back with a run in the second. Each team scored another run before Amos Otis put the Royals ahead with a homer in the seventh. But again the Phillies fought back and tied the game on Pete Rose's run-scoring single in the eighth. The tide shifted back to the Royals in the tenth. U.L. Washington started off the inning with a hit, but was caught stealing. Wilson followed with a walk and was successful stealing second. After White struck out, McGraw walked Brett intentionally to get to Aikens. But Aikens, who had struck out in his two previous times at bat, singled into left-center to win the game, 4-3.

In Game Four the Royals wasted no time in building a lead and this time they managed to keep ahead of the Phillies, winning 5-3. Four of the Royals' runs were scored in the first inning. Facing the Phillies' Larry Christenson, Wilson led off with a single and went to third on a wild pickoff attempt by the hurler. Frank White flied out, but Brett tripled in the first run of the game. Aikens then slugged a home run to right field, making the score 3-0. McRae followed with a hit to center and took second when Garry Maddox came in slowly to retrieve the ball. Otis promptly doubled to finish the scoring.

After the Phillies scored once in the second, Aikens hit his second homer of the game in the bottom half of the inning. The blast made Aikens the first player in World Series history to connect for a pair of two-homer games in one Series. The Phillies scored single runs in the seventh and eighth innings, but the Royals held on for the victory to tie the Series at two games apiece.

The come-from-behind gang gained service on foreign soil in Game Five, as they rallied for two runs in the ninth to win, 4-3. The Phillies had a 2-0 lead until Kansas City retaliated with one run in the fifth and two in the sixth. In the ninth, Schmidt triggered the comeback with a single and scored on Unser's second pinch-double of the Series. Unser was sacrificed to third and, one out later, Manny Trillo hit a shot that reliever Dan Quisenberry couldn't handle. Brett grabbed the ball and threw to first, but the throw was too late to catch Trillo, as Unser scored the decisive tally.

The teams returned to Philadelphia for Game Six, where this time the Phillies didn't have to depend on a comeback to win. In the third inning they broke out on top, 2-0, on a walk to Boone, a throwing error by White, and singles by Rose and Schmidt. The Phils added single runs in the fifth and sixth before the Royals finally broke through with a run in the eighth.

With only three outs to go before winning the championship, the Phillies had to hold off one more Kansas City threat. McGraw, relieving for Carlton, started the inning by striking out Otis, but Aikens walked and Onix Concepcion came in to pinch-run. John Wathan and Jose Cardenal singled to load the bases. White then sent a pop foul in front of the Phillies' dugout, where Boone and Rose converged on the ball.

Boone waved Rose away and was ready to make the catch, but the ball popped out of his mitt. Fortunately for the Phillies, Rose was standing nearby and he reached over to grab the ball before it hit the ground. With one out to go, Wilson stood at the plate. McGraw wasted little time in disposing of the batter. Like he had done 11 times previously during the Series, Wilson struck out to end years of Phillies frustration.

Mike Schmidt, who hit two homers, drove in seven runs and batted .381 for the winners, was selected the MVP of the Series.

The box scores:

Tuesday, Oct. 14—At Philadelphia

Kan. City (A.L.)	AB.	R.	H.	O.	A.	E.
Wilson, lf	5	0	0	2	1	0
McRae, dh	3	1	1	0	0	0
G. Brett, 3b	4	1	1	0	2	0
Aikens, 1b	4	2	2	13	0	0
Porter, c	2	1	0	5	1	0
Otis, cf	4	1	3	1	0	0
Hurdle, rf	3	0	1	1	0	0
aWathan, rf	1	0	0	1	0	0
White, 2b	4	0	1	0	5	0
Washington, ss	4	0	0	1	6	0
Leonard, p	0	0	0	0	0	1
Martin, p	0	0	0	0	0	0
Quisenberry, p	0	0	0	0	0	0
Totals	34	6	9	24	15	1

Phila'phia (N.L.)	AB.	R.	H.	O.	A.	E.
Smith, lf	4	0	2	3	1	0
Gross, lf	1	0	0	1	0	0
Rose, 1b	3	1	0	7	2	0
Schmidt, 3b	2	2	1	2	3	0
McBride, rf	4	1	3	3	0	0
Luzinski, dh	3	0	0	0	0	0
Maddox, cf	3	0	0	2	0	0
Trillo, 2b	4	1	1	1	2	0
Bowa, ss	4	1	1	0	3	0
Boone, c	4	1	3	6	0	0
Walk, p	0	0	0	2	0	0
McGraw, p	0	0	0	0	0	0
Totals	32	7	11	27	11	0

Kansas City	0 2 2	0 0 0	0 2 0	—6
Philadelphia	0 0 5	1 1 0	0 0 *	—7

Kansas City	IP.	H.	R.	ER.	BB.	SO.
Leonard (L)	3⅔	6	6	6	1	3
Martin	4	5	1	1	1	1
Quisenberry	⅓	0	0	0	0	0

Philadelphia	IP.	H.	R.	ER.	BB.	SO.
Walk (W)	7†	8	6	3	3	3
McGraw (S)	2	1	0	0	0	2

†Pitched to two batters in eighth.

Bases on balls—Off Leonard 1 (Schmidt), off Martin 1 (Schmidt), off Walk 3 (McRae, Porter 2).

Strikeouts—By Leonard 3 (Schmidt, Luzinski, Maddox), by Martin 1 (Luzinski), by Walk 3 (Wilson, G. Brett, Aikens), by McGraw 2 (Washington, Wilson).

Game-winning RBI—McBride.

aGrounded into double play for Hurdle in eighth. Runs batted in—Aikens 4, Otis 2, McBride 3, Maddox, Boone 2. Two-base hits—Boone 2, G. Brett. Home runs—Otis, Aikens 2, McBride. Stolen bases—Bowa, White. Caught stealing—Smith. Sacrifice fly—Maddox. Hit by pitcher—By Leonard (Rose), by Martin (Luzinski). Wild pitch—Walk. Double play—Bowa, Trillo and Rose. Left on bases—Kansas City 4, Philadelphia 6. Umpires—Wendelstedt (N.L.) plate, Kunkel (A.L.) first base, Pryor (N.L.) second base, Denkinger (A.L.) third base, Rennert (N.L.) left field, Bremigan (A.L.) right field. Time—3:01. Attendance—65,791.

Wednesday, Oct. 15—At Philadelphia

Kan. City (A.L.)	AB.	R.	H.	O.	A.	E.
Wilson, lf	4	1	1	1	0	0
Washington, ss	4	0	1	0	3	0
G. Brett, 3b	2	0	2	2	2	0
Chalk, 3b	0	1	0	0	1	0
cPorter	1	0	0	0	0	0
McRae, dh	4	1	3	0	0	0
Otis, cf	5	1	2	5	0	0
Wathan, c	3	0	0	2	0	0
Aikens, 1b	3	0	1	6	0	0
LaCock, 1b	0	0	0	2	0	0
Cardenal, rf	4	0	0	3	0	0
White, 2b	4	0	1	3	3	0
Gura, p	0	0	0	0	0	0
Quisenberry, p	0	0	0	0	0	0
Totals	34	4	11	24	9	0

Phila'phia (N.L.)	AB.	R.	H.	O.	A.	E.
Smith, lf	3	0	0	0	0	0
aUnser, cf	1	1	1	0	0	0
Rose, 1b	4	0	0	7	1	0
McBride, rf	3	1	1	2	0	0
Schmidt, 3b	4	1	2	1	1	0
Moreland, dh	4	1	2	0	0	0
Maddox, cf	3	1	1	1	0	0
bGross, lf	1	0	0	0	0	0
Trillo, 2b	2	0	0	6	3	1
Bowa, ss	3	0	1	0	6	0
Boone, c	1	1	0	10	1	0
Carlton, p	0	0	0	0	1	0
Reed, p	0	0	0	0	0	0
Totals	29	6	8	27	14	1

Kansas City	0 0 0	0 0 1	3 0 0—4
Philadelphia	0 0 0	0 2 0	0 4 *—6

Kansas City	IP.	H.	R.	ER.	BB.	SO.
Gura	6	4	2	2	2	2
Quisenb'ry (L)	2	4	4	4	1	0

Philadelphia	IP.	H.	R.	ER.	BB.	SO.
Carlton (W)	8	10	4	3	6	10
Reed (S)	1	1	0	0	0	2

Bases on balls—Off Gura 2 (Boone, McBride), off Quisenberry 1 (Boone), off Carlton 6 (Aikens, G. Brett, Wathan, Wilson, Chalk, McRae). Strikeouts—By Gura 2 (Maddox, Smith), by Carlton 10 (Wilson 3, Cardenal 2, White, Washington 2, McRae, Aikens), by Reed 2 (Porter, Wathan).

Game-winning RBI—Schmidt.

aDoubled in one run for Smith in eighth. bGrounded into double play for Maddox in eighth. cCalled out on strikes for Chalk in ninth. Runs batted in—Otis 2, Wathan, Unser, McBride, Schmidt, Moreland, Trillo, Bowa. Two-base hits—Maddox, Otis, Unser, Schmidt. Stolen bases—Wilson, Chalk. Sacrifice hit—Washington. Sacrifice flies—Trillo, Wathan. Wild pitch—Carlton. Double plays—Bowa, Trillo and Rose 3; Washington, White and Aikens; Maddox, Rose and Schmidt; Washington, White and LaCock. Left on bases—Kansas City 11, Philadelphia 3. Umpires—Kunkel (A.L.) plate, Pryor (N.L.) first base, Denkinger (A.L.) second base, Rennert (N.L.) third base, Bremigan (A.L.) left field, Wendelstedt (N.L.) right field. Time—3:01. Attendance—65,775.

Friday, Oct. 17—At Kansas City

Phila'phia (N.L.)	AB.	R.	H.	O.	A.	E.
Smith, lf	4	0	2	0	0	0
bGross, lf	0	0	0	0	0	0
Rose, 1b	4	0	1	11	0	0
Schmidt, 3b	5	1	1	3	3	0
McBride, rf	5	0	2	1	0	0
Moreland, dh	5	0	1	0	0	0
Maddox, cf	4	0	1	3	0	0
Trillo, 2b	5	1	2	2	6	0
Bowa, ss	5	1	3	1	3	0
Boone, c	4	0	1	8	1	0
Ruthven, p	0	0	0	0	0	0
McGraw, p	0	0	0	0	0	0
Totals	41	3	14	29	13	0

Kan. City (A.L.)	AB.	R.	H.	O.	A.	E.
Wilson, lf	4	1	0	3	0	0
White, 2b	5	0	0	4	2	0
G. Brett, 3b	4	1	2	0	3	0
Aikens, 1b	5	1	2	7	1	0
McRae, dh	4	0	2	0	0	0
Otis, cf	4	1	2	9	0	0
Hurdle, rf	4	0	2	1	0	0
aConcepcion	0	0	0	0	0	0
Cardenal, rf	0	0	0	0	0	0
Porter, c	4	0	0	4	0	0
Washington, ss	4	0	1	1	2	0
Gale, p	0	0	0	0	1	0
Martin, p	0	0	0	0	0	0
Quisenberry, p	0	0	0	1	1	0
Totals	38	4	11	30	10	0

Philadelphia	0 1 0	0 1 0	0 1 0	0—3
Kansas City	1 0 0	1 0 0	1 0 0	1—4

Two out when winning run scored.

Philadelphia	IP.	H.	R.	ER.	BB.	SO.
Ruthven	9	9	3	3	0	7
McGraw (L)	⅔	2	1	1	2	1

Kansas City	IP.	H.	R.	ER.	BB.	SO.
Gale	4⅓	7	2	2	3	3
Martin	3⅓	5	1	1	1	1
Quisenb'ry (W)	2⅓	2	0	0	2	0

Bases on balls—Off McGraw 2 (Wilson, G. Brett), off Gale 3 (Schmidt, Boone, Rose), off Martin 1 (Smith), off Quisenberry 2 (Maddox, Rose).

Strikeouts—By Ruthven 7 (Wilson 2, White 2, Aikens 2, Porter), by McGraw 1 (White), by Gale 3 (Rose, Moreland, McBride), by Martin 1 (Rose).

Game-winning RBI—Aikens.

aRan for Hurdle in ninth. bSacrificed for Smith in tenth. Runs batted in—Smith, Rose, Schmidt, G. Brett, Aikens, McRae, Otis. Two-base hits—Trillo, G. Brett. Three-base hit—Aikens. Home Runs—G. Brett, Schmidt, Otis. Stolen bases—Hurdle, Bowa, Wilson. Caught stealing—Washington. Sacrifice hit—Gross. Double plays—White, Washington and Aikens; Bowa, Trillo and Rose; White unassisted. Left on bases—Philadelphia 15, Kansas City 7. Umpires—Pryor (N.L.) plate, Denkinger (A.L.) first base, Rennert (N.L.) second base, Bremigan (A.L.) third base, Wendelstedt (N.L.) left field, Kunkel (A.L.) right field. Time—3:19. Attendance—42,380.

1980 WORLD SERIES

Saturday, Oct. 18—At Kansas City

Phila'phia (N.L.)	AB.	R.	H.	O.	A.	E.
Smith, dh	4	0	0	0	0	0
Rose, 1b	4	1	2	8	2	0
McBride, rf	3	0	1	3	0	0
Schmidt, 3b	3	0	1	2	0	0
Unser, lf	4	0	1	1	0	0
Maddox, cf	4	0	1	2	0	0
Trillo, 2b	4	2	1	0	6	0
Bowa, ss	4	0	2	1	1	0
Boone, c	3	0	1	6	0	0
Christenson, p	0	0	0	0	0	1
Noles, p	0	0	0	1	0	0
Saucier, p	0	0	0	0	0	0
Brusstar, p	0	0	0	0	0	0
Totals	33	3	10	24	9	1

Kan. City (A.L.)	AB.	R.	H.	O.	A.	E.
Wilson, lf	4	1	1	4	0	0
White, 2b	5	0	0	2	4	1
G. Brett, 3b	5	1	1	0	7	0
Aikens, 1b	3	2	2	13	0	0
McRae, dh	4	1	2	0	0	0
Otis, cf	4	0	2	1	0	0
Hurdle, rf	2	0	1	3	0	0
Porter, c	3	0	0	2	1	0
Washington, ss	4	0	1	2	3	1
Leonard, p	0	0	0	0	0	0
Quisenberry, p	0	0	0	0	0	0
Totals	34	5	10	27	15	2

Philadelphia .... 0 1 0   0 0 0   1 1 0—3
Kansas City .... 4 1 0   0 0 0   0 0 *—5

Philadelphia	IP.	H.	R.	ER.	BB.	SO.
Christenson (L)	⅓	5	4	4	0	0
Noles	4⅔	5	1	1	2	6
Saucier	⅔	0	0	0	2	0
Brusstar	2⅓	0	0	0	1	0

Kansas City	IP.	H.	R.	ER.	BB.	SO.
Leonard (W)	7†	9	3	2	1	2
Quisenberry (S)	2	1	0	0	0	0

†Pitched to one batter in eighth.

Bases on balls—Off Noles 2 (Hurdle 2), off Saucier 2 (Wilson, Aikens), off Brusstar 1 (Porter), off Leonard 1 (McBride).
Strikeouts—By Noles 6 (Porter 2, Wilson, G. Brett, Aikens, McRae), by Leonard 2 (Schmidt, Unser).
Game-winning RBI—G. Brett.
Runs batted in—Schmidt, Bowa, Boone, G. Brett, Aikens 3, Otis. Two-base hits—McRae, Otis, Hurdle, McBride, Trillo, Rose. Three-base hit—G. Brett. Home runs—Aikens 2. Stolen base—Bowa. Caught stealing—McBride. Sacrifice flies—Boone, Schmidt. Wild pitches—Leonard, Saucier. Double play—G. Brett, White and Aikens. Left on bases—Philadelphia 6, Kansas City 10. Umpires—Denkinger (A.L.) plate, Rennert (N.L.) first base, Bremigan (A.L.) second base, Wendelstedt (N.L.) third base, Kunkel (A.L.) left field, Pryor (N.L.) right field. Time—2:37. Attendance—42,363.

Sunday, Oct. 19—At Kansas City

Phila'phia (N.L.)	AB.	R.	H.	O.	A.	E.
Rose, 1b	4	0	0	7	1	0
McBride, rf	4	1	0	2	1	0
Schmidt, 3b	4	2	2	1	1	0
Luzinski, lf	2	0	0	1	0	0
aSmith, ph	0	0	0	0	0	0
cUnser, lf	1	1	1	0	0	0
Moreland, dh	3	0	1	0	0	0
Maddox, cf	4	0	0	2	0	0
Trillo, 2b	4	0	1	3	5	0
Bowa, ss	4	0	1	0	2	0
Boone, c	3	0	1	10	0	0
Bystrom, p	0	0	0	1	1	0
Reed, p	0	0	0	0	0	0
McGraw, p	0	0	0	0	1	0
Totals	33	4	7	27	12	0

Kan. City (A.L.)	AB.	R.	H.	O.	A.	E.
Wilson, lf	5	0	2	2	0	0
White, 2b	3	0	0	2	6	0
G. Brett, 3b	5	0	1	1	2	1
Aikens, 1b	3	0	1	10	1	1
dConcepcion	0	0	0	0	0	0
McRae, dh	5	0	1	0	0	0
Otis, cf	3	1	2	3	0	0
Hurdle, rf	3	1	1	3	0	0
bCardenal, rf	2	0	0	0	0	0
Porter, c	4	0	2	2	0	0
Washington, ss	3	1	2	2	2	0
Gura, p	0	0	0	2	4	0
Quisenberry, p	0	0	0	0	0	0
Totals	36	3	12	27	15	2

Philadelphia .... 0 0 0   2 0 0   0 0 2—4
Kansas City .... 0 0 0   0 1 2   0 0 0—3

Philadelphia	IP.	H.	R.	ER.	BB.	SO.
Bystrom	5†	10	3	3	1	4
Reed	1	1	0	0	0	0
McGraw (W)	3	1	0	0	4	5

Kansas City	IP.	H.	R.	ER.	BB.	SO.
Gura	6⅓	4	2	1	1	2
Quisenb'ry (L)	2⅔	3	2	2	0	0

†Pitched to three batters in sixth.

Bases on balls—Off Bystrom 1 (Aikens), off McGraw 4 (Otis 2, White, Aikens), off Gura 1 (Luzinski).
Strikeouts—By Bystrom 4 (Wilson, Aikens, Otis, Hurdle), by McGraw 5 (G. Brett 2, Aikens, Washington, Cardenal), by Gura 2 (Luzinski, Maddox).
Game-winning RBI—Trillo.
aRan for Luzinski in seventh. bFlied out for Hurdle in seventh. cDoubled in one run for Smith in ninth. dRan for Aikens in ninth. Runs batted in—Schmidt 2, Unser, Trillo, G. Brett, Otis, Washington. Two-base hits—Wilson, McRae, Unser. Home runs—Schmidt, Otis. Stolen base—G. Brett. Sacrifice hits—White, Moreland. Sacrifice fly—Washington. Double plays—White, Aikens and Gura; Gura and Aikens. Left on bases—Philadelphia 4, Kansas City 13. Umpires—Rennert (N.L.) plate, Bremigan (A.L.) first base, Wendelstedt (N.L.) second base, Kunkel (A.L.) third base, Pryor (N.L.) left field, Denkinger (A.L.) right field. Time—2:51. Attendance—42,369.

Tuesday, Oct. 21—At Philadelphia

Kan. City (A.L.)	AB.	R.	H.	O.	A.	E.
Wilson, lf	4	0	0	3	0	0
Washington, ss	3	0	1	2	4	0
G. Brett, 3b	4	0	2	1	1	0
McRae, dh	4	0	0	0	0	0
Otis, cf	3	0	0	2	0	0
Aikens, 1b	2	0	0	6	0	1
aConcepcion	0	0	0	0	0	0
Wathan, c	3	1	2	4	1	0
Cardenal, rf	4	0	2	4	0	0
White, 2b	4	0	0	2	1	1
Gale, p	0	0	0	0	0	0
Martin, p	0	0	0	0	0	0
Splittorff, p	0	0	0	0	1	0
Pattin, p	0	0	0	0	0	0
Quisenberry, p	0	0	0	0	0	0
Totals	31	1	7	24	8	2

1981 WORLD SERIES

Phila'phia (N.L.)	AB.	R.	H.	O.	A.	E.
Smith, lf	4	2	1	1	0	0
Gross, lf	0	0	0	0	0	0
Rose, 1b	4	0	3	9	0	0
Schmidt, 3b	3	0	1	0	0	0
McBride, rf	4	0	0	2	0	0
Luzinski, dh	4	0	0	0	0	0
Maddox, cf	4	0	2	1	0	0
Trillo, 2b	4	0	0	2	3	0
Bowa, ss	4	1	1	3	3	0
Boone, c	2	1	1	9	1	0
Carlton, p	0	0	0	0	2	0
McGraw, p	0	0	0	0	0	0
Totals	33	4	9	27	9	0

Kansas City Royals

Player-Position	G.	AB.	R.	H.	2B.	3B.	HR.	RBI.	BA.
Otis, cf	6	23	4	11	2	0	3	7	.478
Hurdle, rf	4	12	1	5	1	0	0	0	.417
Aikens, 1b	6	20	5	8	0	1	4	8	.400
G. Brett, 3b	6	24	3	9	2	1	1	3	.375
McRae, dh	6	24	3	9	3	0	0	1	.375
Wathan, ph-rf-c	3	7	1	2	0	0	0	1	.286
Washington, ss	6	22	1	6	0	0	0	2	.273
Cardenal, ph-rf	4	10	0	2	0	0	0	0	.200
Wilson, lf	6	26	3	4	1	0	0	0	.154
Porter, ph-c	5	14	1	2	0	0	0	0	.143
White, 2b	6	25	0	2	0	0	0	0	.080
Chalk, 3b	1	0	1	0	0	0	0	0	.000
Concepcion, pr	3	0	0	0	0	0	0	0	.000
Gale, p	2	0	0	0	0	0	0	0	.000
Gura, p	2	0	0	0	0	0	0	0	.000
LaCock, 1b	1	0	0	0	0	0	0	0	.000
Leonard, p	2	0	0	0	0	0	0	0	.000
Martin, p	3	0	0	0	0	0	0	0	.000
Pattin, p	1	0	0	0	0	0	0	0	.000
Quisenberry, p	6	0	0	0	0	0	0	0	.000
Splittorff, p	1	0	0	0	0	0	0	0	.000
Totals	6	207	23	60	9	2	8	22	.290

Kansas City .... 0 0 0   0 0 0   0 1 0—1
Philadelphia .... 0 0 2   0 1 1   0 0 *—4

Kansas City	IP.	H.	R.	ER.	BB.	SO.
Gale (L)	2	4	2	1	1	1
Martin	2⅓	1	1	1	1	0
Splittorff	1⅔†	4	1	1	0	0
Pattin	1	0	0	0	0	2
Quisenberry	1	0	0	0	0	0

Philadelphia	IP.	H.	R.	ER.	BB.	SO.
Carlton (W)	7§	4	1	1	3	7
McGraw (S)	2	3	0	0	2	2

†Pitched to one batter in seventh.
§Pitched to two batters in eighth.

Bases on balls—Off Gale 1 (Boone), off Martin 1 (Schmidt), off Carlton 3 (Otis, Aikens, Wathan), off McGraw 2 (Wilson, Aikens).
Strikeouts—By Gale 1 (Luzinski), by Pattin 2 (Schmidt, Luzinski), by Carlton 7 (Wilson 2, Washington, 2, White, Otis, Aikens), by McGraw 2 (Otis, Wilson).
Game-winning RBI—Schmidt.
aRan for Aikens in ninth. Runs batted in—Washington, Schmidt 2, McBride, Boone. Two-base hits—Maddox, Smith, Bowa. Caught stealing—Rose. Sacrifice fly—Washington. Double plays—Bowa, Trillo and Rose; Bowa and Rose; Splittorff, Washington and Aikens. Left on bases—Kansas City 9, Philadelphia 7. Umpires—Bremigan (A.L.) plate, Wendelstedt (N.L.) first base, Kunkel (A.L.) second base, Pryor (N.L.) third base, Denkinger (A.L.) left field, Rennert (N.L.) right field. Time—3:00. Attendance—65,838.

COMPOSITE BATTING AVERAGES
Philadelphia Phillies

Player-Position	G.	AB.	R.	H.	2B.	3B.	HR.	RBI.	BA.
Unser, ph-cf-lf	3	6	2	3	2	0	0	2	.500
Boone, c	6	17	3	7	2	0	0	4	.412
Schmidt, 3b	6	21	6	8	1	0	2	7	.381
Bowa, ss	6	24	3	9	1	0	0	2	.375
Moreland, dh	3	12	1	4	0	0	0	1	.333
McBride, rf	6	23	3	7	1	0	1	5	.304
Smith, pr-lf-dh	6	19	2	5	1	0	0	1	.263
Rose, 1b	6	23	2	6	1	0	0	1	.261
Maddox, cf	6	22	1	5	2	0	0	1	.227
Trillo, 2b	6	23	4	5	2	0	0	2	.217
Brusstar, p	1	0	0	0	0	0	0	0	.000
Bystrom, p	1	0	0	0	0	0	0	0	.000
Carlton, p	2	0	0	0	0	0	0	0	.000
Christenson, p	1	0	0	0	0	0	0	0	.000
McGraw, p	4	0	0	0	0	0	0	0	.000
Noles, p	1	0	0	0	0	0	0	0	.000
Reed, p	2	0	0	0	0	0	0	0	.000
Ruthven, p	1	0	0	0	0	0	0	0	.000
Saucier, p	1	0	0	0	0	0	0	0	.000
Walk, p	1	0	0	0	0	0	0	0	.000
Gross, ph-lf	4	2	0	0	0	0	0	0	.000
Luzinski, dh-lf	3	9	0	0	0	0	0	0	.000
Totals	6	201	27	59	13	0	3	26	.294

COMPOSITE PITCHING AVERAGES
Philadelphia Phillies

Pitcher	G.	IP.	H.	R.	E.	SO.	BB.	W.	L.	ERA.
Brusstar	1	2⅓	0	0	0	1	0	0	0	0.00
Reed	2	2	2	0	0	0	2	0	0	0.00
Saucier	1	⅔	0	0	0	2	0	0	0	0.00
McGraw	4	7⅔	7	1	1	8	10	1	1	1.17
Noles	1	4⅔	5	1	1	2	6	0	0	1.93
Carlton	2	15	14	5	4	9	17	2	0	2.40
Ruthven	1	9	9	3	3	0	7	0	0	3.00
Bystrom	1	5	10	3	3	1	4	0	0	5.40
Walk	1	7	8	6	6	3	3	1	0	7.71
Christenson	1	⅓	5	4	4	0	0	0	1	108.00
Totals	6	53⅔	60	23	22	26	49	4	2	3.69

Kansas City Royals

Pitcher	G.	IP.	H.	R.	E.	SO.	BB.	W.	L.	ERA.
Pattin	1	1	0	0	0	2	0	0	0	0.00
Gura	2	12⅓	8	4	3	3	4	0	0	2.19
Martin	3	9⅔	11	3	3	3	2	0	0	2.79
Gale	2	6⅓	11	4	3	4	4	0	1	4.26
Quisenberry	6	10⅓	10	6	6	3	0	1	2	5.23
Splittorff	1	1⅔	4	1	1	0	0	0	0	5.40
Leonard	2	10⅔	15	9	8	2	5	1	1	6.75
Totals	6	52	59	27	24	15	17	2	4	4.15

SERIES OF 1981

	W.	L.	Pct.
Los Angeles N. L.	4	2	.667
New York A. L.	2	4	.333

The end was near October 28 for the New York Yankees in the 1981 Series. And the waning moments fairly reeked with symbolism.

With one out in the ninth inning of Game 6 and the Yankees trailing the Los Angeles Dodgers, 9-2, Dave Winfield lofted a routine fly ball to Pedro Guerrero in right field.

The putout gave Winfield a final Series batting average of .045, a 1-for-22 effort. Winfield was finishing the first year of a $21 million, 10-year contract.

Now, all that stood between the Yankees and defeat was Reggie Jackson, the Mr. October of Series past. Jackson, who had missed the first three games with a leg injury and committed a costly error in Game 4, bounced a ground ball to Davey Lopes, the Dodgers second baseman. Lopes booted it for his record sixth error of the Series.

Then it was Bob Watson's turn. One week earlier, Watson seemed well on his way to Series most valuable player honors, just as the Yankees, winners of the first two games, seemed on their way to a world championship.

Watson poked a lazy fly ball to center fielder Ken Landreaux. The Dodgers were champions of the world and the Yankees faced the prospect of a long, cold winter.

The Dodgers, who had not won a World Series since 1965, followed an October-long script that read: "Nothing comes easy."

Their four-game Series winning streak, after the early two-game deficit, mirrored their previous post-season method. They won the first-ever National League West Division Series (a concession to the strike-forced split-season format) by taking three straight from the Houston Astros after losing the first two games. They captured the N.L. Championship Series after falling behind two games to one to the Montreal Expos. The Dodgers beat the Expos in the ninth inning of the fifth game on a dramatic Rick Monday home run.

The Yankees, on the other hand, were extended to five games before beating the Milwaukee Brewers in their A.L. East Division series and then hardly worked up a sweat in sweeping the Oakland A's (3-1, 13-3 and 4-0) in the Championship Series.

Buoyed by the one-two relief punch of Ron Davis and Rich Gossage, the Yankees entered the Series with a 61-4 record in games in which they took a lead into the seventh inning. But, ironically, it was the ineffectiveness of that duo, particularly Davis, that would prove the Yankees' undoing.

The Series opened in Yankee Stadium on October 20 and the Yankees, despite the absence of Jackson, went after the Dodgers with a vengeance.

By the end of the first inning, the Yankees owned a 3-0 lead, thanks to Watson's three-run homer off Jerry Reuss. By the end of seven, the lead was 5-1. Yankee starter Ron Guidry had sailed through seven innings, allowing only three singles and a solo home run by Steve Yeager.

But only because of the late-inning glove work of third baseman Graig Nettles did the Yankees prevail. Davis relieved Guidry in the eighth and quickly surrendered walks to Derrel Thomas and Lopes. Gossage took over and was greeted by Jay Johnstone's run-scoring single and Dusty Baker's sacrifice fly. The Yanks held on, however, when Nettles made a diving, back-handed stab of Steve Garvey's line drive down the third-base line that seemed ticketed for a double. New York won, 5-3.

Game 2 matched veteran pitchers Burt Hooton of the Dodgers and Tommy John of the Yankees. It was a touch of deja vu for John, who left the Dodgers for the green free-agent pastures of New York prior to the 1979 season. And his old teammates were no match on this occasion.

John allowed the Dodgers only three hits in seven innings, most of his outs coming on ground balls off his sinker, and Gossage mopped up the final two innings in the 3-0 Yankee victory. Shortstop Larry Milbourne provided the first run with a two-out, fifth-inning double and the others came in the eighth on Watson's single and Willie Randolph's sacrifice fly.

When the scene shifted to Los Angeles for Game 3 on October 23, Dodgers Manager Tom Lasorda rested his team's hopes on the strong left arm of rookie pitching sensation Fernando Valenzuela. The 20-year-old Mexican had scored key victories in both the West Division and Championship Series against Houston and Montreal.

It looked like smooth sailing for the youngster when Ron Cey staked him to a lead with a three-run, first-inning homer off Yankee starter Dave Righetti.

But Valenzuela struggled, surrendering home runs to Watson and catcher Rick Cerone, and trailed, 4-3, entering the bottom of the third. But Lasorda stuck with his young lefty and when the Dodgers regained the lead in the fifth on a scatch single, a walk, a double and a double-play grounder, Valenzuela repaid the confidence. He had thrown 100 pitches to that point, but dispatched the Yankees on 45 the rest of the way, making the 5-4 lead stand up.

The loss went to reliever George Frazier, who later would enter the record book as one of two pitchers in Series history to lose three games. The other was Claude Williams of the Chicago White Sox in the eight-game 1919 Series. That Chicago team, of course, was better known as the Black Sox and Williams was involved in the scheme to dump the Series to Cincinnati.

Game 4 was the pivotal game and who should step into the spotlight but Jackson. Mr. October lived up to his billing offensively, collecting a homer, two singles and two walks in five trips to the plate, but ended up wearing the goat horns after committing a costly error in the sixth.

Dodgers starter Bob Welch failed to retire a batter in the first and by the time the Dodgers came to bat in the bottom of the third, they trailed, 4-0. They scored twice and added a run in the fifth to cut the deficit to one, but the Yankees retaliated with a pair of sixth-inning runs to restore their margin to three.

Davis, who had been called out of the bullpen in the fifth inning, again was not up to protecting the lead. A two-run pinch homer by Johnstone cut it to one and the tying run was set up when Jackson lost Lopes' easy fly in the sun, the ball bouncing off his chest for a two-base error. Bill Russell's single off Davis tied the game.

The momentum now belonged to the Dodgers. They put the game away in the seventh off Frazier with a pair of infield hits, a bloop double and a sacrifice fly, and went on to win, 8-7.

Reuss, the victim of the Yankees and Bob Watson in Game 1, returned with a vengeance on October 25. He allowed only five hits and three walks in outdueling Guidry, 2-1, giving the Dodgers a 3-2 Series lead.

The Yankees had staked their starter to a 1-0 lead in the second inning on Jackson's double and Lou Piniella's RBI single. Guidry made that stand until the seventh when, with one out, Guerrero and Yeager slugged back-to-back homers. Reuss prevailed the rest of the way and the Dodgers returned to Yankee Stadium October 28 looking for the knockout punch.

They got it behind the three-hit, five-RBI performance of Guerrero, who shared Series MVP honors with Cey and Yeager. The Dodger outfielder hit a two-run triple in the fifth off Frazier, a two-run single in the sixth off Rick Reuschel and a solo homer in the eighth off Rudy May.

The controversy of the night surrounded Yankee Manager Bob Lemon and his decision to remove starter John from the game in favor of a pinch-hitter in the fourth with the score tied 1-1. The strategy failed and, with John out of the way, the Dodgers exploded for seven runs in the next two innings.

Los Angeles .... 0 0 0   0 1 0   0 2 0—3
New York .... 3 0 1   1 0 0   0 0 *—5

Los Angeles	IP.	H.	R.	ER.	BB.	SO.
Reuss (L)	2⅔	5	4	4	0	2
Castillo	1	0	1	1	5	0
Goltz	⅓	0	0	0	0	0
Niedenfuer	3	1	0	0	0	0
Stewart	1	0	0	0	1	0

New York	IP.	H.	R.	ER.	BB.	SO.
Guidry (W)	7	4	1	1	2	6
Davis	0†	0	2	2	2	0
Gossage (S)	2	1	0	0	0	2

†Pitched to two batters in eighth.

Bases on balls—Off Castillo 5 (Watson, Cerone, Randolph, Mumphrey, Winfield), off Stewart 1 (Nettles), off Guidry 2 (Baker, Guerrero), off Davis 2 (Thomas, Lopes).
Strikeouts—By Reuss 2 (Winfield, Guidry), by Guidry 6 (Monday 2, Guerrero, Yeager, Reuss, Garvey), by Gossage 2 (Guerrero, Monday).
Game-winning RBI—Watson.
aFlied out for Goltz in fifth. bWalked for Niedenfuer in eighth. cSingled in one run for Russell in eighth. dGrounded out for Yeager in ninth. Runs batted in—Johnstone, Baker, Yeager, Winfield, Piniella, Watson 3. Two-base hit—Piniella. Home runs—Yeager, Watson. Stolen bases—Mumphrey, Piniella. Sacrifice hit—Guidry. Sacrifice fly—Baker. Passed ball—Cerone. Double play—Thomas and Garvey. Left on bases—Los Angeles 5, New York 6. Umpires—Barnett (A.L.) plate, Colosi (N.L.) first, Cooney (A.L.) second, Harvey (N.L.) third, Garcia (A.L.) left, Stello (N.L.) right. Time—2:32. Attendance—56,470.

Tuesday, October 20—At New York

Los Ang. (N.L.)	AB.	R.	H.	O.	A.	E.
Lopes, 2b	3	1	0	3	1	0
Russell, ss	3	0	0	2	1	0
cJohnstone	1	0	1	0	0	0
Stewart, p	0	0	0	0	0	0
Baker, lf	2	0	1	3	0	0
Garvey, 1b	4	0	1	5	0	0
Cey, 3b	4	0	1	0	1	0
Guerrero, cf	3	0	0	3	0	0
Monday, rf	4	0	0	4	0	0
Yeager, c	3	1	1	3	0	0
dLandreaux	1	0	0	0	0	0
Reuss, p	1	0	0	0	1	0
Castillo, p	0	0	0	0	2	0
Goltz, p	0	0	0	0	0	0
aSax, ph	1	0	0	0	0	0
Niedenfuer, p	0	0	0	0	0	0
bThomas, ss	0	1	0	1	1	0
Totals	30	3	5	24	7	0

New York (A.L.)	AB.	R.	H.	O.	A.	E.
Randolph, 2b	3	0	0	3	3	0
Mumphrey, cf	3	2	2	3	0	0
Winfield, lf	3	0	0	0	1	0
Piniella, rf	4	1	2	4	0	0
Watson, 1b	3	1	2	8	0	0
Nettles, 3b	3	0	0	1	3	0
Cerone, c	3	0	0	8	0	0
Milbourne, ss	4	1	0	0	2	0
Guidry, p	2	0	0	0	0	0
Davis, p	0	0	0	0	0	0
Gossage, p	0	0	0	0	0	0
Totals	28	5	6	27	9	0

Wednesday, October 21—At New York

Los Ang. (N.L.)	AB.	R.	H.	O.	A.	E.
Lopes, 2b	3	0	0	7	3	1
eMonday	1	0	0	0	0	0
Howe, p	0	0	0	0	0	0
Stewart, p	0	0	0	0	0	1
Russell, ss	4	0	1	0	5	0
Baker, lf	4	0	0	0	0	0
Garvey, 1b	3	0	2	6	0	0
Cey, 3b	4	0	0	0	3	0
Guerrero, rf	4	0	0	4	0	0
Landreaux, cf	3	0	0	4	0	0
Yeager, c	2	0	0	1	0	0
bJohnstone	1	0	0	0	0	0
Scioscia, c	0	0	0	1	0	0
Hooton, p	2	0	0	1	0	0
Forster, p	0	0	0	0	1	0
cSmith	1	0	1	0	0	0
dSax, 2b	0	0	0	0	0	0
Totals	32	0	4	24	12	2

New York (A.L.)	AB.	R.	H.	O.	A.	E.
Mumphrey, cf	2	0	0	1	0	0
Milbourne, ss	4	0	1	1	3	1
Winfield, lf	4	0	0	1	0	0
Gamble, rf	2	0	0	2	0	0
fPiniella	1	0	1	0	0	0
gBrown, rf	0	1	0	0	0	0
Nettles, 3b	4	1	2	1	5	0
Watson, 1b	4	0	2	13	0	0
Cerone, c	2	0	0	7	0	0
Randolph, 2b	2	1	0	1	3	0
John, p	1	0	0	0	2	0
aMurcer	0	0	0	0	0	0
Gossage, p	1	0	0	0	0	0
Totals	27	3	6	27	13	1

Los Angeles .... 0 0 0   0 0 0   0 0 0—0
New York .... 0 0 0   0 1 0   0 2 *—3

1981 WORLD SERIES

Los Angeles	IP.	H.	R.	ER.	BB.	SO.
Hooton (L)	6†	3	1	0	4	1
Forster	1	0	0	0	1	0
Howe	⅓	2	2	2	0	0
Stewart	⅔	1	0	0	1	1

New York	IP.	H.	R.	ER.	BB.	SO.
John (W)	7	3	0	0	0	4
Gossage (S)	2	1	0	0	1	3

†Pitched to two batters in seventh.

Bases on balls—Off Hooton 4 (Mumphrey, Gamble, Cerone, Randolph), off Forster 1 (Mumphrey), off Stewart 1 (Cerone), off Gossage 1 (Garvey).
Strikeouts—By Hooton 1 (Nettles), by Stewart 1 (Gossage), by John 4 (Hooton 2, Baker, Landreaux), by Gossage 3 (Monday, Cey, Guerrero).
Game-winning RBI—Milbourne.
aSacrificed for John in seventh. bFlied out for Yeager in eighth. cSingled for Forster in eighth. dRan for Smith in eighth. eStruck out for Lopes in eighth. fSingled for Gamble in eighth. gRan for Piniella in eighth and scored. Runs batted in—Milbourne, Watson, Randolph. Two-base hit—Milbourne. Sacrifice hits—John, Murcer. Sacrifice fly—Randolph. Double play—Russell, Lopes and Garvey. Left on bases—Los Angeles 6, New York 9. Umpires—Colosi (N.L.) plate, Cooney (A.L.) first, Harvey (N.L.) second, Garcia (A.L.) third, Stello (N.L.) left, Barnett (A.L.) right. Time—2:29. Attendance—56,505.

Friday, October 23—At Los Angeles

New York (A.L.)	AB.	R.	H.	O.	A.	E.
Randolph, 2b	2	0	0	5	3	0
Mumphrey, cf	5	0	0	0	0	0
Winfield, lf	3	0	0	2	0	0
Piniella, rf	5	1	1	0	0	0
Watson, 1b	4	1	2	9	0	0
Cerone, c	4	2	2	5	1	0
Rodriguez, 3b	4	0	2	1	3	0
Milbourne, ss	2	0	2	2	4	0
Righetti, p	1	0	0	0	0	0
Frazier, p	1	0	0	0	0	0
May, p	0	0	0	0	0	0
cMurcer	1	0	0	0	0	0
Davis, p	0	0	0	0	0	0
Totals	32	4	9	24	11	0

Los Ang. (N.L.)	AB.	R.	H.	O.	A.	E.
Lopes, 2b	4	1	2	7	3	1
Russell, ss	5	1	2	0	3	0
Baker, lf	4	0	0	2	0	0
Garvey, 1b	4	1	2	7	1	0
Cey, 3b	2	2	2	2	3	0
Guerrero, cf-rf	3	0	1	1	0	0
Monday, rf	2	0	1	2	0	0
bThomas, cf	1	0	0	0	0	0
Yeager, c	1	0	0	2	0	0
aScioscia, c	3	0	1	4	1	0
Valenzuela, p	3	0	0	0	1	0
Totals	32	5	11	27	12	1

New York	0	2	2	0	0	0	0	0—4
Los Angeles	3	0	0	0	2	0	0	*—5

New York	IP.	H.	R.	ER.	BB.	SO.
Righetti	2†	5	3	3	2	1
Frazier (L)	2‡	3	2	2	2	1
May	3	2	0	0	0	2
Davis	1	1	0	0	0	1

Los Angeles	IP.	H.	R.	ER.	BB.	SO.
Valenzuela (W)	9	9	4	4	7	6

†Pitched to two batters in third.
‡Pitched to four batters in fifth.

Bases on balls—Off Righetti 2 (Valenzuela, Cey), off Frazier 2 (Cey, Monday), off Valenzuela 7 (Randolph 3, Winfield 2, Milbourne 2).
Strikeouts—By Righetti 1 (Garvey), by Frazier 1 (Guerrero), by May 2 (Baker, Guerrero), by Davis 1 (Lopes), by Valenzuela 6 (Winfield, Righetti, Cerone, Frazier, Mumphrey, Piniella).
Game-winning RBI—None.
aGrounded out for Yeager in third. bHit into double play for Monday in seventh. cBunted into double play for May in eighth. Runs batted in—Watson, Cerone, Milbourne, Cey 3, Guerrero. Two-base hits—Lopes, Cerone, Watson, Guerrero. Home runs—Cey, Watson, Cerone. Caught stealing—Randolph. Sacrifice hits—Righetti, Lopes. Hit by pitcher—By Righetti (Guerrero). Double plays—Randolph and Watson; Milbourne, Randolph and Watson; Russell, Lopes and Garvey; Cey and Lopes. Left on bases—New York 9, Los Angeles 9. Umpires—Cooney (A.L.) plate, Garcia (A.L.) first, Garcia (A.L.) second, Stello (N.L.) third, Barnett (A.L.) left, Colosi (N.L.) right. Time—3:04. Attendance—56,236.

Saturday, October 24—At Los Angeles

New York (A.L.)	AB.	R.	H.	O.	A.	E.
Randolph, 2b	5	3	2	2	0	0
Milbourne, ss	4	1	1	1	3	0
Winfield, cf-lf-cf	4	0	0	4	0	0
Jackson, rf	3	2	3	2	0	1
Gamble, lf	4	1	2	2	0	0
cBrown, cf	0	0	0	1	0	0
fPiniella, lf	1	0	0	0	0	0
Watson, 1b	3	0	1	5	0	0
Cerone, c	5	0	2	7	0	0
hRobertson	0	0	0	0	0	0
Rodriguez, 3b	4	0	2	0	3	0
gFoote	1	0	0	0	0	0
Reuschel, p	2	0	0	0	0	0
May, p	1	0	0	0	1	0
Davis, p	0	0	0	0	0	0
Frazier, p	1	0	0	0	0	0
John, p	0	0	0	0	0	0
iMurcer	1	0	0	0	0	0
Totals	39	7	13	24	7	1

Los Ang. (N.L.)	AB.	R.	H.	O.	A.	E.
Lopes, 2b	5	2	2	5	2	0
Russell, ss	5	0	1	2	5	1
Garvey, 1b	5	1	3	5	1	0
Cey, 3b	5	0	2	1	1	0
Baker, lf	5	1	1	4	0	0
Monday, rf	3	1	1	2	0	0
Thomas, cf	1	0	0	3	0	0
Guerrero, cf-rf	3	0	2	2	1	0
Scioscia, c	1	1	0	2	0	0
eYeager, c	0	0	0	1	0	0
Welch, p	0	0	0	0	0	0
Goltz, p	0	0	0	0	0	0
aLandreaux	1	1	1	0	0	0
Forster, p	0	0	0	0	0	0
bSmith	1	0	0	0	0	0
Niedenfuer, p	0	0	0	0	0	0
dJohnstone	1	1	1	0	0	0
Howe, p	0	0	0	0	1	1
Totals	36	8	14	27	11	2

New York	2	1	1	0	0	2	0	1 0—7
Los Angeles	0	0	2	0	1	3	2	0 *—8

New York	IP.	H.	R.	ER.	BB.	SO.
Reuschel	3‡	6	2	2	1	2
May	1⅓	2	1	1	0	1
Davis	1	2	3	2	1	2
Frazier (L)	⅔§	2	2	2	1	0
John	2	2	0	0	0	2

Los Angeles	IP.	H.	R.	ER.	BB.	SO.
Welch	0†	3	2	2	1	0
Goltz	3	4	2	2	1	2
Forster	1	1	0	0	2	0
Niedenfuer	2	2	2	0	1	0
Howe (W)	3	3	1	1	0	1

†Pitched to four batters in first.
‡Pitched to two batters in fourth.
§Pitched to three batters in seventh.

Bases on balls—Off Reuschel 1 (Monday), off Davis 1 (Scioscia), off Frazier 1 (Guerrero), off Welch 1 (Winfield), off Goltz 1 (Watson), off Forster 2 (Randolph, Jackson), off Niedenfuer 1 (Jackson).
Strikeouts—By Reuschel 2 (Russell, Baker), by May 1 (Smith), by Davis 2 (Baker, Monday), by John 2 (Garvey, Thomas), by Goltz 2 (Rodriguez, Reuschel), by Howe 1 (Foote).
Game-winning RBI—Yeager.
aDoubled for Goltz in third. bStruck out for Forster in fourth. cRan for Gamble in sixth. dHit two-run homer for Niedenfuer in sixth. eHit sacrifice fly for Scioscia in seventh. fGrounded out for Brown in eighth. gStruck out for Rodriguez in ninth. hRan for Cerone in ninth. iReached first base safely on error in ninth. Runs batted in—Randolph, Milbourne, Jackson, Gamble, Watson 2, Cerone, Lopes 2, Russell, Cey 2, Yeager, Johnstone 2. Two-base hits—Milbourne, Landreaux, Garvey, Monday. Three-base hit—Randolph. Home runs—Randolph, Johnstone, Jackson. Stolen bases—Lopes 2, Winfield. Sacrifice hits—Milbourne, Scioscia, Howe. Sacrifice fly—Watson, Yeager. Double plays—None. Left on bases—New York 12, Los Angeles 10. Umpires—Harvey (N.L) plate, Garcia (A.L.) first, Stello (N.L.) second, Barnett (A.L.) third, Colosi (N.L.) left, Cooney (A.L.) right. Time—3:32. Attendance—56,242.

Sunday, October 25—At Los Angeles

New York (A.L.)	AB.	R.	H.	O.	A.	E.
Randolph, 2b	3	0	0	0	0	0
Milbourne, ss	4	0	1	1	1	0
Winfield, cf-lf	4	0	1	4	0	0
Jackson, rf	4	1	0	0	0	0
Gossage, p	0	0	0	0	0	0
Watson, 1b	3	0	0	6	0	0
Piniella, lf-rf	4	0	2	3	0	0
bBrown	0	0	0	0	0	0
Cerone, c	4	0	0	8	1	0
Rodriguez, 3b	3	0	0	2	3	0
Guidry, p	3	0	0	0	0	0
Mumphrey, cf	0	0	0	0	0	0
Totals	32	1	5	24	5	0

Los Ang. (N.L.)	AB.	R.	H.	O.	A.	E.
Lopes, 2b	3	0	0	3	3	3
Russell, ss	4	0	0	0	7	0
Garvey, 1b	4	0	1	12	1	0
Cey, 3b	2	0	0	0	2	0
aLandreaux, cf	0	0	0	1	0	0
Baker, lf	4	0	0	2	0	0
Guerrero, rf	3	1	1	1	0	0
Yeager, c	3	1	2	7	0	0
Thomas, cf-3b	3	0	0	0	0	0
Reuss, p	2	0	0	1	2	0
Totals	28	2	4	27	15	3

New York			0 1 0	0 0 0	0 0 0—1	
Los Angeles			0 0 0	0 0 0	2 0 *—2	

New York	IP.	H.	R.	ER.	BB.	SO.
Guidry (L)	7	4	2	2	2	9
Gossage	1	0	0	0	1	0

Los Angeles	IP.	H.	R.	ER.	BB.	SO.
Reuss (W)	9	5	1	1	3	6

Bases on balls—Off Guidry 2 (Cey, Reuss), off Gossage 1 (Lopes), off Reuss 3 (Randolph, Watson, Rodriguez).
Strikeouts—By Guidry 9 (Lopes, Reuss, Garvey 2, Cey, Baker 2, Guerrero, Thomas), by Reuss 6 (Winfield 2, Guidry 2, Jackson, Rodriguez).
Game-winning RBI—Yeager.
aRan for Cey in eighth. bRan for Piniella in ninth. Runs batted in—Piniella, Guerrero, Yeager. Two-base hits—Jackson, Yeager. Home runs—Guerrero, Yeager. Stolen bases—Lopes, Landreaux. Hit by pitcher—By Gossage (Cey). Double plays—Russell, Lopes and Garvey; Lopes and Garvey. Left on bases—New York 7, Los Angeles 6. Umpires—Garcia (A.L.) plate, Stello (N.L.) first, Barnett (A.L.) second, Colosi (N.L.) third, Cooney (A.L.) left, Harvey (N.L.) right. Time—2:19. Attendance—56,115.

Wednesday, October 28—At New York

Los Ang. (N.L.)	AB.	R.	H.	O.	A.	E.
Lopes, 2b	4	2	1	1	2	1
Russell, ss	4	0	2	0	5	0
Garvey, 1b	4	1	1	9	0	0
Cey, 3b	3	1	2	1	1	0
bThomas, 3b	2	1	0	0	0	0
Baker, lf	5	2	2	2	0	0
Guerrero, cf-rf	5	1	3	6	0	0
Monday, rf	3	0	1	1	0	0
Landreaux, cf	1	0	1	0	0	0
Yeager, c	5	0	1	6	0	0
Hooton, p	2	1	0	0	0	0
Howe, p	2	0	0	0	0	0
Totals	40	9	13	27	8	1

New York (A.L.)	AB.	R.	H.	O.	A.	E.
Randolph, 2b	3	1	2	2	2	0
Mumphrey, cf	5	0	1	2	0	0
Winfield, lf	4	0	0	2	0	0
Jackson, rf	5	0	0	3	0	0
Watson, 1b	5	0	0	10	0	0
Nettles, 3b	3	0	2	1	2	1
cRodriguez, 3b	1	1	1	0	0	0
Cerone, c	3	0	0	7	2	0
Milbourne, ss	2	0	0	0	3	1
John, p	1	0	0	0	1	0
aMurcer	1	0	0	0	0	0
Frazier, p	0	0	0	0	0	0
Davis, p	0	0	0	0	0	0
Reuschel, p	0	0	0	0	0	0
dGamble	0	0	0	0	0	0
ePiniella	1	0	1	0	0	0
May, p	0	0	0	0	0	0
fBrown	1	0	0	0	0	0
LaRoche, p	0	0	0	0	0	0
Totals	35	2	7	27	10	2

Los Angeles			0 0 0	1 3 4	0 1 0—9	
New York			0 0 1	0 0 1	0 0 0—2	

Los Angeles	IP.	H.	R.	ER.	BB.	SO.
Hooton (W)	5⅓	5	2	2	5	2
Howe (S)	3⅔	2	0	0	1	3

New York	IP.	H.	R.	ER.	BB.	SO.
John	4	6	1	1	0	2
Frazier (L)	1	4	3	3	0	1
Davis	⅓	1	3	2	2	1
Reuschel	⅔	1	1	0	2	0
May	2	1	1	1	1	2
LaRoche	1	0	0	0	0	2

Bases on balls—Off Hooton 5 (Randolph, Winfield, Milbourne 2, Cerone), off Howe 1 (Randolph), off Davis 2 (Hooton, Lopes), off Reuschel 2 (Garvey, Monday), off May 1 (Lopes).

Strikeouts—By Hooton 2 (Jackson, Cerone), by Howe 3 (Jackson, Brown, Mumphrey), by John 2 (Cey, Hooton), by Frazier 1 (Monday), by Davis 1 (Yeager), by May 2 (Howe, Landreaux), by LaRoche 2 (Howe, Lopes).

Game-winning RBI—Cey.

aFlied out for John in fourth. bDrove in one run on forceout for Cey in sixth. cRan for Nettles in sixth and scored. dAnnounced for Reuschel in sixth. eSingled in one run for Gamble in sixth. fStruck out for May in eighth. Runs batted in—Russell, Thomas, Cey, Guerrero 5, Yeager, Randolph, Piniella. Two-base hits—Nettles, Randolph. Three-base hit—Guerrero. Home runs—Randolph, Guerrero. Stolen bases—Randolph, Lopes, Russell. Caught stealing—Russell. Sacrifice hit—Russell. Double plays—None. Left on bases—Los Angeles 10, New York 12. Umpires—Stello (N.L.) plate, Barnett (A.L.) first, Colosi (N.L.) second, Cooney (A.L.) third, Harvey (N.L.) left, Garcia (A.L.) right. Time—3:09. Attendance—56,513.

COMPOSITE PITCHING AVERAGES
Los Angeles Dodgers

Pitcher	G.	IP.	H.	R.	E.	SO.	BB.	W.	L.	ERA.
Niedenfuer	2	5	3	2	0	1	0	0	0	0.00
Forster	2	2	1	0	0	3	0	0	0	0.00
Stewart	2	1⅔	1	0	0	2	1	0	0	0.00
Hooton	2	11½	8	3	2	9	3	1	1	1.59
Reuss	2	11⅔	10	5	5	3	8	1	1	3.86
Howe	3	7	7	3	3	1	4	1	0	3.86
Valenzuela	1	9	9	4	4	7	6	1	0	4.00
Goltz	2	3⅓	4	2	2	1	2	0	0	5.40
Castillo	1	1	0	1	1	5	0	0	0	9.00
Welch	1	0*	3	2	2	1	0	0	0	.....
Totals	6	52	46	22	19	33	24	4	2	3.29

*Pitched to four batters in first inning of fourth game.

New York Yankees

Pitcher	G.	IP.	H.	R.	E.	SO.	BB.	W.	L.	ERA.
Gossage	3	5	2	0	0	2	5	0	0	0.00
LaRoche	1	1	0	0	0	2	0	0	0	0.00
John	3	13	11	1	1	9	8	1	0	0.69
Guidry	2	14	8	3	3	4	15	1	1	1.93
May	3	6⅓	5	2	2	1	5	0	0	2.84
Reuschel	2	3⅔	7	3	2	3	2	0	0	4.91
Righetti	1	2	5	3	3	2	1	0	0	13.50
Frazier	3	3⅔	9	7	7	3	2	0	3	17.18
Davis	4	2⅓	4	8	6	5	4	0	0	23.14
Totals	6	51	51	27	24	20	44	2	4	4.24

COMPOSITE BATTING AVERAGES
Los Angeles Dodgers

Player-Position	G.	AB.	R.	H.	2B.	3B.	HR.	RBI.	BA.
Johnstone, ph	3	3	1	2	0	0	1	3	.667
Smith, ph	2	2	0	1	0	0	0	0	.500
Garvey, 1b	6	24	3	10	1	0	0	0	.417
Cey, 3b	6	20	3	7	0	0	1	6	.350
Guerrero, rf-cf	6	21	2	7	1	1	2	7	.333
Yeager, ph-c	6	14	2	4	1	0	2	4	.286
Scioscia, c-ph	3	4	1	1	0	0	0	0	.250
Russell, ss	6	25	1	6	0	0	0	2	.240
Monday, rf-ph	5	13	1	3	1	0	0	0	.231
Lopes, 2b	6	22	6	5	1	0	0	2	.227
L'ndreaux, ph-cf-pr	5	6	1	1	1	0	0	0	.167
Baker, lf	6	24	3	4	0	0	0	1	.167
Forster, p	2	0	0	0	0	0	0	0	.000
Goltz, p	2	0	0	0	0	0	0	0	.000
Niedenfuer, p	2	0	0	0	0	0	0	0	.000
Stewart, p	2	0	0	0	0	0	0	0	.000
Castillo, p	1	0	0	0	0	0	0	0	.000
Welch, p	1	0	0	0	0	0	0	0	.000
Sax, ph-pr-2b	2	1	0	0	0	0	0	0	.000
Howe, p	3	2	0	0	0	0	0	0	.000
Reuss, p	2	3	0	0	0	0	0	0	.000
Valenzuela, p	1	3	0	0	0	0	0	0	.000
Hooton, p	2	4	1	0	0	0	0	0	.000
Th'mas, ph-ss-cf-3b	5	7	2	0	0	0	0	1	.000
Totals	6	198	27	51	6	1	6	26	.258

New York Yankees

Player-Position	G.	AB.	R.	H.	2B.	3B.	HR.	RBI.	BA.
Piniella, rf-ph-lf	6	16	2	7	1	0	0	3	.438
Rodriguez, 3b-pr	4	12	1	5	0	0	0	0	.417
Nettles, 3b	3	10	1	4	1	0	0	0	.400
Jackson, rf	3	12	3	4	1	0	1	1	.333
Gamble, rf-lf-ph	3	6	1	2	0	0	0	1	.333
Watson, 1b	6	22	2	7	1	0	2	7	.318
Milbourne, ss	6	20	2	5	2	0	0	3	.250
Randolph, 2b	6	18	5	4	1	1	2	3	.222
Mumphrey, cf	5	15	2	3	0	0	0	0	.200
Cerone, c	6	21	2	4	1	0	1	3	.190
Winfield, lf-cf	6	22	0	1	0	0	0	1	.045
Davis, p	4	0	0	0	0	0	0	0	.000
LaRoche, p	1	0	0	0	0	0	0	0	.000
Robertson, pr	1	0	0	0	0	0	0	0	.000
Brown, pr-rf-cf-ph	4	1	1	0	0	0	0	0	.000
Foote, ph	1	1	0	0	0	0	0	0	.000
Gossage, p	3	1	0	0	0	0	0	0	.000
May, p	3	1	0	0	0	0	0	0	.000
Righetti, p	1	1	0	0	0	0	0	0	.000
Frazier, p	3	2	0	0	0	0	0	0	.000
John, p	3	2	0	0	0	0	0	0	.000
Reuschel, p	2	2	0	0	0	0	0	0	.000
Murcer, ph	4	3	0	0	0	0	0	0	.000
Guidry, p	2	5	0	0	0	0	0	0	.000
Totals	6	193	22	46	8	1	6	22	.238

SERIES OF 1982

	W.	L.	Pct.
St. Louis N.L.	4	3	.571
Milwaukee A.L.	3	4	.429

The St. Louis Cardinals, who have won more World Series titles than any other National League club, made their first appearance in the Classic since 1968 and captured their first world championship since 1967 by edging the Milwaukee Brewers in seven games.

It was a Series full of irony, not the least of which resulted from a big trade the teams had made during the 1980 winter meetings. In that deal, Cardinal General Manager-Manager Whitey Herzog traded popular catcher Ted Simmons, relief pitcher Rollie Fingers and righthanded pitcher Pete Vuckovich to the Brewers for pitchers Dave LaPoint and Lary Sorensen and outfielders Sixto Lezcano and David Green. Sorensen and Lezcano were playing for other teams by the 1982 Series, but the others played pivotal roles in the outcome. Perhaps the most pivotal role of all was played by Fingers, who didn't throw a pitch because of an arm injury.

The teams took different routes to the World Series.

The Brewers, who had to beat Baltimore on the final day of the regular season to win the American League Eastern Division, rallied from a two games to none deficit to defeat the California Angels in the A.L. Championship Series. They triumphed in the fifth game, 4-3, when first baseman Cecil Cooper singled home two runs in the bottom of the seventh inning.

The Cardinals, however, breezed past Western Division champion Atlanta in a clean sweep. The Cardinal pitching staff allowed only four earned runs in 27 innings to a powerful Brave lineup that featured N.L. Most Valuable Player Dale Murphy.

When the 79th World Series opened in St. Louis on October 12, the matchup was being billed as Beauty (the Cardinals, featuring speed and defense) versus the Beast (the Brewers, featuring raw power). The Brewers had hit 216 home runs and scored 891 runs during the 1982 season. The Cardinals had managed only 67 home runs, but made up for their lack of power with 200 stolen bases and a starting infield that committed only 44 errors.

But it took only one-half inning to alert baseball fans that this World Series would not go according to script. When Gold Glove first baseman Keith Hernandez let Ben Oglivie's grounder go under his glove for an error, the Brewers scored two unearned runs and the pattern of ironies was set.

The Brewers proceeded to knock out 17 hits against Bob Forsch and three relievers to trounce the Cards, 10-0. Paul Molitor became the first player in Series history to get five hits in one game. Robin Yount had four. Ironically, only one of the Brewers' hits went over the boards, and that was a fifth-inning blast by Simmons. Lefty Mike Caldwell went the distance, giving up only three hits, to get the win.

Game 2 didn't start out any better for the Cardinals. Milwaukee led 3-0 after 2½ innings and the hometown fans were getting restless. The Brewers' lead was 4-2 when the Cardinals made their move in the sixth inning.

Darrell Porter, the former Kansas City catcher who was signed as a free agent by Herzog in 1980 to replace Simmons, had struggled through an off-season, incurring the wrath of the St. Louis faithful. But Porter quickly went from goat to hero when he rapped a game-tying, sixth-inning double against Brewer starter Don Sutton, added a single in the Cards' game-winning rally in the eighth against relievers Bob McClure and Pete Ladd and threw out Molitor, the potential tying run, trying to steal in the ninth. The winning run in the Cardinals' 5-4 victory scored when Ladd walked pinch-hitter Steve Braun with the bases loaded, the first of several situations in which Fingers could have made a difference. Relief ace Bruce Sutter got the win for the Cardinals.

When the Series shifted to Milwaukee, Cardinal rookie Willie McGee took center stage. McGee, who only one year before had finished up his baseball season with the New York Yankees' Nashville Class AA affiliate, was traded to St. Louis during the 1981 World Series. But in Game 3 of the '82 Classic, the first-year player's heroics had his manager gushing. "Nobody ever played a better World Series game than Willie McGee did tonight," said Herzog.

What McGee did to deserve such plaudits was belt two home runs off Milwaukee starter and loser Vuckovich and make two excellent catches to rob Molitor and Gorman Thomas of extra-base hits. McGee had hit only four homers during the regular season.

The homers and catches made a 6-2 winner out of Joaquin Andujar, who pitched 6⅓ shutout innings before a line drive off the bat of Simmons struck him just below the kneecap on his right leg and forced him from the game. Sutter pitched 2⅓ innings to pick up the save.

Game 4 was all Cardinals—until the fateful seventh inning that seemingly turned the tide of the Series in Milwaukee's favor. The Cards led 4-0 after only 1½ innings and this time it was the partisan Brewer crowd's turn to get nervous. Things weren't any better as the Brewers came to bat in the seventh, trailing 5-1.

But suddenly the roof caved in on the Cardinals. Pitcher LaPoint, once a promising prospect in the Brewer organization, opened the door by dropping a perfect throw from Hernandez after the first baseman had fielded a grounder hit by Oglivie. What should have been a two-out, nobody-on-base situation was a one-out, one-on problem. Inspired by the LaPoint error, the Brewers got five hits and two walks from their next eight batters to take a 7-5 lead. Don Money, Jim Gantner, Yount and Cooper all got hits to tie the score at 5-5, but the biggest blow came from Thomas, who ripped a Jeff Lahti pitch into left field to drive in two runs. Lahti was the third of three Cardinal relievers who failed to get the Brewers out after the LaPoint miscue. Herzog was criticized by most observers for not using his bullpen ace, Sutter, who had a win and a save in his only two Series appearances to date. Jim Slaton got the win in relief for Milwaukee, Doug Bair the loss in relief for St. Louis.

The Brewers built upon their new-found momentum in Game 5 and continued to confound the so-called baseball experts in the process. Defense was the key factor in a 6-4 victory that put the Brewers one win away from their first world championship.

Yount stole a hit away from Lonnie Smith in the third; Gantner dove to keep a single by George Hendrick from going past the infield for an RBI in the same inning; Molitor leaped high to snare Ozzie Smith's bouncer in the fourth to start a double play; Charlie Moore made a diving catch off Lonnie Smith's drive to prevent a possible inside-the-park homer in the fifth, and Cooper threw out Porter while on his knees after fielding a hot smash by the Cardinals' catcher in the seventh.

Yount also had another great day at the plate. The American League MVP had four hits—and became the first player in history to collect two four-hit World Series games. The Milwaukee club managed 11 hits to support Caldwell, the Game 1 winner who gave up 14 hits in 8⅓ innings before yielding to McClure.

"Caldwell is the only pitcher I know who looks the same to me whether he's throwing a three-hitter (Game 1) or a 14-hitter," said Simmons. Caldwell beat Forsch for the second time in the Series and McClure picked up his second save in as many days.

Down three games to two after losing two of the three contests in Milwaukee, the Cardinals at least had the satisfaction of knowing that their fate would be determined on their own turf.

Game 6 was decided early but ran late. The Cards got two runs in the second inning, three in the fourth, two in the fifth, and six in the sixth to grab an astounding 13-0 lead over their American League visitors. Only a single Milwaukee run in the ninth kept it from being the worst blowout in World Series history (The Yankees beat the Pittsburgh Pirates, 12-0, in 1960). Brewer starter Sutton gave up seven runs in 4⅓ innings and took the loss.

Hernandez and Dane Iorg struck the biggest blows for St. Louis. Hernandez, who didn't get his first Series hit until his 16th at-bat in Game 5, slugged a two-run homer in the fifth and a two-run single in the sixth.

Iorg had two doubles and a triple as the St. Louis designated hitter (at one point he had a perfect 1.000 slugging average as DH) to back up John Stuper's four-hit pitching.

Hernandez had plenty of time to cherish his home run—the game was interrupted by rain for about 2½ hours before he singled in the next inning. In fact, it took longer—2:39—to wait out all the rain delays than it did to play the game itself—2:21.

"We're going to play this game until it is completed," said Commissioner Bowie Kuhn, "even if we have to wait a great many hours." The game didn't end until the early-morning hours of the following day.

The Cardinals capped their comeback less than 24 hours later when they beat the Brewers, 6-3, in the deciding game.

Herzog elected to go with Andujar when the self-proclaimed "one tough Dominican" showed no ill effects from his leg injury in Game 3. Kuenn went with Vuckovich, the former Cardinal who was victimized by McGee in Game 3.

The Cards grabbed an early lead with a run in the fourth, but the Brewers answered that when Oglivie hit Andujar's first pitch in the top of the fifth for a home run. The Brewers took a 3-1 lead in the next inning when a Gantner double, an Andujar throwing error, Molitor's bunt single, Cooper's sacrifice fly and Yount's Series-leading 12th hit made many of the 53,723 fans wonder if this might not be the American League's turn to win the World Series. The Cards got nine runners on base in the first four innings, but only one of them came around to score.

But the Brewers' two-run sixth seemed to inspire the Cardinals. Led by the Smiths, Lonnie and Ozzie, St. Louis scored three times in the bottom half of the inning to regain the lead. The biggest blow came from Hernandez, who singled against Milwaukee reliever McClure with the bases loaded to drive home two runs. Ozzie Smith had singled, Lonnie Smith had doubled and pinch-hitter Gene Tenace had walked to set the stage for Hernandez' heroics. Ironically, Hernandez, the hero, and McClure, the losing pitcher, were boyhood teammates when they played in California as little leaguers.

The Cardinals added two insurance runs for reliever Sutter in the eighth on run-scoring singles by Porter and Braun. Porter, who was voted the MVP award in the National League Championship Series victory over Atlanta, made a clean sweep by winning the same award at the conclusion of the World Series.

Porter, like the rest of his Cardinal teammates, probably spent much of Game 7 thinking about what winning-pitcher Andujar kept repeating over and over before the game began:

"There's no way I let these guys beat me. I die first."

The box scores:

Tuesday, October 12—At St. Louis

Milw'kee (A.L.)	AB.	R.	H.	O.	A.	E.
Molitor, 3b	6	1	5	0	2	0
Yount, ss	6	1	4	1	1	0
Cooper, 1b	4	1	0	14	3	0
Simmons, c	5	1	2	3	0	0
Oglivie, lf	4	1	0	0	0	0
Thomas, cf	4	0	1	2	0	0
Howell, dh	2	0	0	0	0	0
aMoney, dh	2	1	1	0	0	0
Moore, rf	5	2	2	4	0	0
Gantner, 2b	4	2	2	0	7	0
Caldwell, p	0	0	0	3	1	0
Totals	42	10	17	27	14	0

St. Louis (N.L.)	AB.	R.	H.	O.	A.	E.
Herr, 2b	3	0	0	2	5	0
L. Smith, lf	4	0	0	2	0	0
Hernandez, 1b	4	0	0	14	1	1
Hendrick, rf	4	0	0	1	0	0
Tenace, dh	3	0	0	0	0	0
Porter, c	3	0	2	3	0	0
Green, cf	3	0	0	2	0	0
Oberkfell, 3b	3	0	1	0	4	0
O. Smith, ss	3	0	0	3	3	0
Forsch, p	0	0	0	0	0	0
Kaat, p	0	0	0	0	0	0
LaPoint, p	0	0	0	0	0	0
Lahti, p	0	0	0	0	0	0
Totals	30	0	3	27	13	1

Milwaukee .... 2 0 0   1 1 2   0 0 4—10
St. Louis .... 0 0 0   0 0 0   0 0 0— 0

Milwaukee	IP.	H.	R.	ER.	BB.	SO.
Caldwell (W)	9	3	0	0	1	3

St. Louis	IP.	H.	R.	ER.	BB.	SO.
Forsch (L)	5⅔	10	6	4	1	1
Kaat	1⅓	1	0	0	1	1
LaPoint	1⅔	3	2	2	1	0
Lahti	⅓	3	2	2	0	1

Bases on balls—Off Caldwell 1 (Herr), off Forsch 1 (Cooper), off Kaat 1 (Thomas), off LaPoint 1 (Oglivie).

Strikeouts—By Caldwell 3 (L. Smith 2, Tenace), by Forsch 1 (Simmons), by Kaat 1 (Cooper), by Lahti 1 (Yount).

Game-winning RBI—None.

aFlied out for Howell in seventh. Runs batted in—Molitor 2, Yount 2, Simmons, Thomas, Money, Gantner 2. Two-base hits—Moore, Yount, Porter. Three-base hit—Gantner. Home run—Simmons. Sacrifice hit—Gantner. Hit by pitcher—By Forsch (Howell). Double play—Hernandez, O. Smith and Hernandez. Left on bases—Milwaukee 10, St. Louis 4. Umpires—Weyer (N.L.) plate, Haller (A.L.) first, Kibler (N.L.) second, Phillips (A.L.) third, Davidson (N.L.) left, Evans (A.L.) right. Time—2:30. Attendance—53,723.

Wednesday, October 13—At St. Louis

Milw'kee (A.L.)	AB.	R.	H.	O.	A.	E.
Molitor, 3b	5	1	2	0	1	0
Yount, ss	4	1	1	4	3	0
Cooper, 1b	5	0	3	9	2	0
Simmons, c	3	1	1	5	0	0
Oglivie, lf	4	0	1	2	0	1
Thomas, cf	3	0	0	1	0	0
Howell, dh	4	1	0	0	0	0
Moore, rf	4	0	2	3	0	0
Gantner, 2b	3	0	0	0	3	0
Sutton, p	0	0	0	0	0	0
McClure, p	0	0	0	0	0	0
Ladd, p	0	0	0	0	0	0
Totals	35	4	10	24	9	1
St. Louis (N.L.)	AB.	R.	H.	O.	A.	E.
Herr, 2b	3	1	1	2	1	0
Oberkfell, 3b	3	1	2	0	3	0
bTenace	1	0	0	0	0	0
Ramsey, 3b	0	0	0	0	0	0
Hernandez, 1b	3	0	0	7	2	0
Hendrick, rf	3	2	0	0	0	0
Porter, c	4	0	2	8	1	0
L. Smith, lf	3	0	0	1	0	0
Iorg, dh	2	0	1	0	0	0
aGreen, dh	1	0	0	0	0	0
cBraun, dh	0	0	0	0	0	0
McGee, cf	4	1	0	4	0	0
O. Smith, ss	4	0	2	5	3	0
Stuper, p	0	0	0	0	0	0
Kaat, p	0	0	0	0	0	0
Bair, p	0	0	0	0	0	0
Sutter, p	0	0	0	0	0	0
Totals	31	5	8	27	10	0

Milwaukee .... 0 1 2 0 1 0 0 0 0—4
St. Louis .... 0 0 2 0 0 2 0 1 *—5

Milwaukee	IP.	H.	R.	ER.	BB.	SO.
Sutton	6	5	4	4	1	3
McClure (L)	1⅓	2	1	1	2	2
Ladd	⅔	1	0	0	0	2
St. Louis	IP.	H.	R.	ER.	BB.	SO.
Stuper	4*	6	4	4	3	3
Kaat	⅔	0	0	0	0	0
Bair	2	1	0	0	0	3
Sutter (W)	2⅓	2	0	0	1	1

*Pitched to one batter in fifth.

Bases on balls—Off Sutton 1 (Hendrick), off McClure 2 (Herr, Hernandez), off Ladd 2 (L. Smith, Braun), off Stuper 3 (Yount, Thomas, Gantner), off Sutter 1 (Simmons).

Strikeouts—By Sutton 3 (Hendrick, Herr, L. Smith), by McClure 2 (Green, McGee), by Stuper 3 (Oglivie, Howell, Molitor), by Bair 3 (Thomas, Howell, Molitor), by Sutter 1 (Howell).

Game-winning RBI—Braun.

aStruck out for Iorg in seventh. bFlied out for Oberkfell in seventh. cWalked with bases loaded for Green in eighth. Runs batted in—Yount, Cooper, Simmons, Moore, Herr, Oberkfell, Porter 2, Braun. Two-base hits—Moore, Herr, Yount, Porter, Cooper. Home run—Simmons. Stolen bases—Molitor, McGee, Oberkfell, O. Smith. Caught stealing—Molitor. Wild pitches—Stuper 2. Double play—Hernandez, O. Smith and Hernandez. Left on bases—Milwaukee 8, St. Louis 7. Umpires—Haller (A.L.) plate, Kibler (N.L.) first, Phillips (A.L.) second, Davidson (N.L.) third, Evans (A.L.) left, Weyer (N.L.) right. Time—2:54. Attendance—53,723.

Friday, October 15—At Milwaukee

St. Louis (N.L.)	AB.	R.	H.	O.	A.	E.
Herr, 2b	5	0	0	1	3	0
Oberkfell, 3b	4	0	0	1	1	0
Hernandez, 1b	4	0	0	8	0	1
xHendrick, rf	2	1	1	3	0	0
Porter, c	4	0	0	6	0	0
L. Smith, lf	4	2	2	1	0	0
Green, lf	0	0	0	0	0	0
Iorg, dh	4	1	1	0	0	0
McGee, cf	3	2	2	6	0	0
O. Smith, ss	3	0	0	1	3	0
Andujar, p	0	0	0	0	1	0
Kaat, p	0	0	0	0	0	0
Bair, p	0	0	0	0	0	0
Sutter, p	0	0	0	0	0	0
Totals	33	6	6	27	8	1
Milw'kee (A.L.)	AB.	R.	H.	O.	A.	E.
Molitor, 3b	4	0	0	1	0	0
Yount, ss	3	1	0	5	5	0
Cooper, 1b	4	1	1	14	0	1
Simmons, c	4	0	1	1	1	1
Oglivie, lf	4	0	0	4	0	0
Thomas, cf	4	0	1	2	0	0
Howell, dh	2	0	0	0	0	0
aMoney, dh	1	0	0	0	0	0
Moore, rf	3	0	0	0	0	0
Gantner, 2b	3	0	2	0	6	1
Vuckovich, p	0	0	0	0	2	0
McClure, p	0	0	0	0	0	0
Totals	32	2	5	27	14	3

St. Louis .... 0 0 0 0 3 0 2 0 1—6
Milwaukee .... 0 0 0 0 0 0 0 2 0—2

St. Louis	IP.	H.	R.	ER.	BB.	SO.
Andujar (W)	6⅓	3	0	0	1	3
Kaat	⅓	1	0	0	0	1
Bair	0*	0	0	0	1	0
Sutter (S)	2⅓	1	2	2	1	1
Milwaukee	IP.	H.	R.	ER.	BB.	SO.
Vuckovich (L)	8⅔	6	6	4	3	1
McClure	⅓	0	0	0	0	0

*Pitched to one batter in seventh.

Bases on balls—Off Andujar 1 (Moore), off Bair 1 (Money), off Sutter 1 (Yount), off Vuckovich 3 (Hendrick, McGee, O. Smith).

Strikeouts—By Andujar 3 (Thomas, Molitor, Oglivie), by Kaat 1 (Oglivie), by Sutter 1 (Money), by Vuckovich 1 (Porter).

Game-winning RBI—McGee.

xAwarded first base on catcher's interference. aWalked for Howell in seventh. Runs batted in—McGee 4, O. Smith, Cooper 2. Two-base hits—Gantner, L. Smith, Iorg. Three-base hit—L. Smith. Home runs—McGee 2, Cooper. Caught stealing—Hendrick. Double play—Herr, O. Smith and Hernandez. Left on bases—St. Louis 4, Mil-

1982 WORLD SERIES

waukee 6. Umpires—Kibler (N.L.) plate, Phillips (A.L.) first, Davidson (N.L.) second, Evans (A.L.) third, Weyer (N.L.) left, Haller (A.L.) right. Time—2:53. Attendance—56,556.

Saturday, October 16—At Milwaukee

St. Louis (N.L.)	AB.	R.	H.	O.	A.	E.
Herr, 2b	4	0	0	1	1	0
Oberkfell, 3b	2	2	1	0	2	0
bTenace	1	0	0	0	0	0
Hernandez, 1b	4	0	0	8	1	0
Hendrick, rf	4	0	1	1	0	0
Porter, c	3	0	1	5	0	0
L. Smith, lf	4	1	1	2	0	0
Iorg, dh	4	0	2	0	0	0
aGreen, dh	0	0	0	0	0	0
McGee, cf	4	1	1	4	0	0
O. Smith, ss	3	1	1	3	1	0
LaPoint, p	0	0	0	0	2	1
Bair, p	0	0	0	0	0	0
Kaat, p	0	0	0	0	0	0
Lahti, p	0	0	0	0	1	0
Totals	33	5	8	24	8	1
Milw'kee (A.L.)	AB.	R.	H.	O.	A.	E.
Molitor, 3b	4	1	0	1	0	0
Yount, ss	4	1	2	3	3	1
Cooper, 1b	4	1	2	10	0	0
Simmons, c	2	0	0	6	0	0
Thomas, cf	4	0	1	4	0	0
Oglivie, lf	3	1	1	1	0	0
Money, dh	4	2	2	0	0	0
Moore, rf	4	0	1	0	0	0
Gantner, 2b	4	1	1	1	5	1
Haas, p	0	0	0	1	2	0
Slaton, p	0	0	0	0	0	0
McClure, p	0	0	0	0	0	0
Totals	33	7	10	27	10	2

St. Louis .... 1 3 0   0 0 1   0 0 0—5
Milwaukee .... 0 0 0   0 1 0   6 0 *—7

St. Louis	IP.	H.	R.	ER.	BB.	SO.
LaPoint	6⅔	7	4	1	1	3
Bair (L)	0*	1	2	2	1	0
Kaat	0*	1	1	1	1	0
Lahti	1⅓	1	0	0	1	0
Milwaukee	IP.	H.	R.	ER.	BB.	SO.
Haas	5⅓	7	5	4	2	3
Slaton (W)	2	1	0	0	2	1
McClure (S)	1⅔	0	0	0	0	2

*Pitched to two batters in seventh.

Bases on balls—Off LaPoint 1 (Simmons), off Bair 1 (Molitor), off Kaat 1 (Simmons), off Lahti 1 (Oglivie), off Haas 2 (O. Smith, Oberkfell), off Slaton 2 (Oberkfell, Porter).

Strikeouts—By LaPoint 3 (Simmons, Money, Molitor), by Haas 3 (Herr, Hernandez, Porter), by Slaton 1 (L. Smith), by McClure 2 (Herr, Tenace).

Game-winning RBI—Thomas.

aRan for Iorg in eighth. bStruck out for Oberkfell in ninth. Runs batted in—Herr 2, Hendrick, Iorg, Yount 2, Cooper, Thomas 2, Gantner. Two-base hits—Oberkfell, Money, L. Smith, Iorg, Gantner. Three-base hit—Oglivie. Stolen bases—McGee, Oberkfell. Sacrifice fly—Herr. Wild pitches—Haas, Kaat. Double plays—Herr and Hernandez; O. Smith and Hernandez; Gantner, Yount and Cooper; Gantner and Cooper. Left on bases—St. Louis 6, Milwaukee 6. Umpires—Phillips (A.L.) plate, Davidson (N.L.) first, Evans (A.L.) second, Weyer (N.L.) third, Haller (A.L.) left, Kibler (N.L.) right. Time—3:04. Attendance—56,560.

Sunday, October 17—At Milwaukee

St. Louis (N.L.)	AB.	R.	H.	O.	A.	E.
L. Smith, dh	5	0	2	0	0	0
Green, lf	5	2	2	2	0	0
Hernandez, 1b	4	1	3	5	1	0
Hendrick, rf	5	0	3	1	0	0
Porter, c	5	0	1	5	1	0
bRamsey	0	0	0	0	0	0
McGee, cf	5	0	1	4	0	0
Oberkfell, 3b	4	0	3	0	2	0
aTenace	1	0	0	0	0	0
Herr, 2b	4	0	0	3	2	1
O. Smith, ss	3	1	0	3	2	0
Forsch, p	0	0	0	1	0	1
Sutter, p	0	0	0	0	0	0
Totals	41	4	15	24	8	2
Milw'kee (A.L.)	AB.	R.	H.	O.	A.	E.
Molitor, 3b	4	1	1	2	5	0
Yount, ss	4	2	4	3	3	0
Cooper, 1b	4	0	1	8	2	0
Simmons, c	3	0	0	4	1	0
Oglivie, lf	4	1	2	1	0	0
Thomas, cf	4	0	0	3	0	0
Money, dh	3	1	0	0	0	0
Moore, rf	4	1	2	1	0	0
Gantner, 2b	4	0	1	4	4	1
Caldwell, p	0	0	0	1	1	0
McClure, p	0	0	0	0	0	0
Totals	34	6	11	27	16	1

St. Louis .... 0 0 1   0 0 0   1 0 2—4
Milwaukee .... 1 0 1   0 1 0   1 2 *—6

St. Louis	IP.	H.	R.	ER.	BB.	SO.
Forsch (L)	7	8	4	3	2	3
Sutter	1	3	2	2	1	2
Milwaukee	IP.	H.	R.	ER.	BB.	SO.
Caldwell (W)	8⅓	14	4	4	2	3
McClure (S)	⅔	1	0	0	0	1

Bases on balls—Off Forsch 2 (Molitor, Simmons), off Sutter 1 (Money), off Caldwell 2 (Hernandez, O. Smith).

Strikeouts—By Forsch 3 (Thomas, Money, Oglivie), by Sutter 2 (Simmons, Thomas), by Caldwell 3 (Green, Porter, McGee), by McClure 1 (McGee).

Game-winning RBI—Cooper.

aFlied out for Oberkfell in ninth. bRan for Porter in ninth. Runs batted in—Hernandez 2, Hendrick 2, Molitor, Yount, Cooper, Simmons, Moore, Gantner. Two-base hits—Hernandez 2, Yount, Moore, Green. Three-base hit—Green. Home run—Yount. Stolen base—L. Smith. Caught stealing—L. Smith, Oglivie. Double plays—Porter and Herr; Oberkfell, Herr and Hernandez; Molitor and Cooper. Left on bases—St. Louis 12, Milwaukee 7. Umpires—Davidson (N.L.) plate, Evans (A.L.) first, Weyer (N.L.) second, Haller (A.L.) third, Kibler (N.L.) left, Phillips (A.L.) right. Time—3:02. Attendance—56,562.

Tuesday, October 19—At St. Louis

Milw'kee (A.L.)	AB.	R.	H.	O.	A.	E.
Molitor, 3b	4	0	1	0	0	0
Yount, ss	4	0	0	0	3	2
Cooper, 1b	4	0	0	8	2	0
Simmons, c	2	0	0	4	0	0
Yost, c	0	0	0	1	0	0
Oglivie, lf	4	0	1	5	0	0
Thomas, cf	3	0	0	0	0	0
aEdwards, cf	0	0	0	0	0	0
Money, dh	3	0	0	0	0	0
Moore, rf	3	0	1	2	0	0
Gantner, 2b	3	1	1	3	2	2

1982 WORLD SERIES

	AB	R	H	O	A	E
Sutton, p	0	0	0	1	2	0
Slaton, p	0	0	0	0	0	0
Medich, p	0	0	0	0	0	0
Bernard, p	0	0	0	0	0	0
Totals	30	1	4	24	9	4
St. Louis (N.L.)	AB	R	H	O	A	E
L. Smith, lf	3	1	1	1	0	0
Green, lf	1	1	0	0	0	0
Oberkfell, 3b	5	1	0	1	4	1
Hernandez, 1b	5	2	2	8	0	0
Hendrick, rf	5	2	2	3	0	0
Porter, c	4	1	1	2	0	0
Brummer, c	0	0	0	0	0	0
Iorg, dh	4	3	3	0	0	0
McGee, cf	4	1	1	5	0	0
Herr, 2b	3	1	2	1	2	0
O. Smith, ss	4	0	0	5	3	0
Stuper, p	0	0	0	1	1	0
Totals	38	13	12	27	10	1

Milwaukee .... 0 0 0   0 0 0   0 0 1— 1
St. Louis .... 0 2 0   3 2 6   0 0 *—13

Milwaukee	IP	H	R	ER	BB	SO
Sutton (L)	4⅓	7	7	5	0	2
Slaton	⅔	0	0	0	0	0
Medich	2	5	6	4	1	0
Bernard	1	0	0	0	0	1
St. Louis	IP	H	R	ER	BB	SO
Stuper (W)	9	4	1	1	2	2

Bases on balls—Off Medich 1 (Green), off Stuper 2 (Simmons, Yost).

Strikeouts—By Sutton 2 (L. Smith, Hendrick), by Bernard 1 (Green), by Stuper 2 (Gantner, Thomas).

Game-winning RBI—None.

aRan for Thomas in eighth. Runs batted in—Hernandez 4, Hendrick, Porter 2, McGee, Herr 2. Two-base hits—Iorg 2, Herr, Gantner. Three-base hit—Iorg. Home runs—Porter, Hernandez. Stolen base—L. Smith. Caught stealing—L. Smith. Sacrifice hit—Herr. Wild pitches—Medich 2, Stuper. Balk—Sutton. Double plays—Oberkfell, Herr and Hernandez; Herr, O. Smith and Hernandez. Left on bases—Milwaukee 4, St. Louis 3. Umpires—Evans (A.L.) plate, Weyer (N.L.) first, Haller (A.L.) second, Kibler (N.L.) third, Phillips (A.L.) left, Davidson (N.L.) right. Time—2:21. Attendance—53,723.

Wednesday, October 20—At St. Louis

Milw'kee (A.L.)	AB	R	H	O	A	E
Molitor, 3b	4	1	2	0	1	0
Yount, ss	4	0	1	4	1	0
Cooper, 1b	3	0	1	8	1	0
Simmons, c	4	0	0	5	0	0
Oglivie, lf	4	1	1	0	0	0
Thomas, cf	4	0	0	3	0	0
Howell, dh	3	0	0	0	0	0
Moore, rf	3	0	1	3	0	0
Gantner, 2b	3	1	1	1	6	0
Vuckovich, p	0	0	0	0	0	0
McClure, p	0	0	0	0	0	0
Haas, p	0	0	0	0	0	0
Caldwell, p	0	0	0	0	0	0
Totals	32	3	7	24	9	0
St. Louis (N.L.)	AB	R	H	O	A	E
L. Smith, lf	5	2	3	4	0	0
Oberkfell, 3b	3	0	0	1	5	0
aTenace	0	0	0	0	0	0
bRamsey, 3b	1	1	0	0	0	0
Hernandez, 1b	3	1	2	12	2	0
Hendrick, rf	5	0	2	1	0	0
Porter, c	5	0	1	4	0	0
Iorg, dh	3	0	2	0	0	0
cGreen, dh	0	0	0	0	0	0
dBraun, dh	2	0	1	0	0	0
McGee, cf	5	1	1	1	0	0
Herr, 2b	3	0	1	1	5	0
O. Smith, ss	4	1	2	2	2	0
Andujar, p	0	0	0	1	1	1
Sutter, p	0	0	0	0	1	0
Totals	39	6	15	27	17	1

Milwaukee .... 0 0 0   0 1 2   0 0 0—3
St. Louis .... 0 0 0   1 0 3   0 2 *—6

Milwaukee	IP	H	R	ER	BB	SO
Vuckovich	5⅓	10	3	3	2	3
McClure (L)	⅓	2	1	1	1	0
Haas	2	1	2	2	1	1
Caldwell	⅓	2	0	0	0	0
St. Louis	IP	H	R	ER	BB	SO
Andujar (W)	7	7	3	2	0	1
Sutter (S)	2	0	0	0	0	2

Bases on balls—Off Vuckovich 2 (Herr, Hernandez), off McClure 1 (Tenace), off Haas 1 (Hernandez).

Strikeouts—By Vuckovich 3 (Oberkfell, Porter, Hernandez), by Haas 1 (Ramsey), by Andujar 1 (Thomas), by Sutter 2 (Yount, Thomas).

Game-winning RBI—Hendrick.

aWalked for Oberkfell in sixth. bRan for Tenace and scored in sixth. cAnnounced as pinch-hitter for Iorg in sixth. dGrounded out for Green in sixth. Runs batted in—Cooper, Oglivie, L. Smith, Hernandez, Herr, Porter, Braun. Two-base hits—Gantner, L. Smith 2. Home run—Oglivie. Sacrifice fly—Cooper. Double plays—None. Left on bases—Milwaukee 3, St. Louis 13. Umpires—Weyer (N.L.) plate, Haller (A.L.) first, Kibler (N.L.) second, Phillips (A.L.) third, Davidson (N.L.) left, Evans (A.L.) right. Time—2:50. Attendance—53,723.

COMPOSITE BATTING AVERAGES
St. Louis Cardinals

Player-Position	G.	AB.	R.	H.	2B.	3B.	HR.	RBI.	BA.
Iorg, dh	5	17	4	9	4	1	0	1	.529
Braun, ph-dh	2	2	0	1	0	0	0	2	.500
Hendrick, rf	7	28	5	9	0	0	0	5	.321
L. Smith, lf-dh	7	28	6	9	4	1	0	1	.321
Oberkfell, 3b	7	24	4	7	1	0	0	1	.292
Porter, c	7	28	1	8	2	0	1	5	.286
Hernandez, 1b	7	27	4	7	2	0	1	8	.259
McGee, cf	6	25	6	6	0	0	2	5	.240
O. Smith, ss	7	24	3	5	0	0	0	1	.208
Green, cf-ph-dh-lf-pr	7	10	3	2	1	0	0	0	.200
Herr, 2b	7	25	2	4	2	0	0	5	.160
Andujar, p	2	2	0	0	0	0	0	0	.000
Bair, p	3	0	0	0	0	0	0	0	.000
Brummer, c	1	0	0	0	0	0	0	0	.000
Forsch, p	2	0	0	0	0	0	0	0	.000
Kaat, p	4	0	0	0	0	0	0	0	.000
Lahti, p	2	0	0	0	0	0	0	0	.000
LaPoint, p	2	0	0	0	0	0	0	0	.000
Ramsey, 3b-pr	3	1	1	0	0	0	0	0	.000
Stuper, p	2	0	0	0	0	0	0	0	.000
Sutter, p	4	0	0	0	0	0	0	0	.000
Tenace, dh-ph	5	6	0	0	0	0	0	0	.000
Totals	7	245	39	67	16	3	4	34	.273

Milwaukee Brewers

Player-Position	G.	AB.	R.	H.	2B.	3B.	HR.	RBI.	BA.
Yount, ss	7	29	6	12	3	0	1	6	.414
Molitor, 3b	7	31	5	11	0	0	0	3	.355
Moore, rf	7	26	3	9	3	0	0	2	.346
Gantner, 2b	7	24	5	8	4	1	0	4	.333
Cooper, 1b	7	28	3	8	1	0	1	6	.286
Money, ph-dh	5	13	4	3	1	0	0	1	.231
Oglivie, lf	7	27	4	6	0	1	1	1	.222
Simmons, c	7	23	2	4	0	0	2	3	.174
Thomas, cf	7	26	0	3	0	0	0	3	.115

Player-Position	G.	AB.	R.	H.	2B.	3B.	HR.	RBI.	BA.
Bernard, p	1	0	0	0	0	0	0	0	.000
Caldwell, p	3	0	0	0	0	0	0	0	.000
Edwards, pr-cf	1	0	0	0	0	0	0	0	.000
Haas, p	2	0	0	0	0	0	0	0	.000
Howell, dh	4	11	1	0	0	0	0	0	.000
Ladd, p	1	0	0	0	0	0	0	0	.000
McClure, p	5	0	0	0	0	0	0	0	.000
Medich, p	1	0	0	0	0	0	0	0	.000
Slaton, p	2	0	0	0	0	0	0	0	.000
Sutton, p	2	0	0	0	0	0	0	0	.000
Vuckovich, p	2	0	0	0	0	0	0	0	.000
Yost, c	1	0	0	0	0	0	0	0	.000
Totals		238	33	64	12	2	5	29	.269

COMPOSITE PITCHING AVERAGES
St. Louis Cardinals

Pitcher	G.	IP.	H.	R.	E.	SO.	BB.	W.	L.	ERA.
Andujar	2	13⅓	10	3	2	1	4	2	0	1.35
LaPoint	2	8⅓	10	6	3	2	3	0	0	3.24
Stuper	2	13	10	5	5	5	1	0	0	3.46
Kaat	4	2⅓	4	1	1	2	2	0	0	3.86
Sutter	4	7⅔	6	4	4	3	6	1	0	4.70
Forsch	2	12⅔	18	10	7	3	4	0	2	4.97
Bair	3	2	2	2	2	2	3	0	1	9.00
Lahti	2	1⅔	4	2	2	1	1	0	0	10.80
Totals	7	61	64	33	*23	19	28	4	3	3.39

(NOTE: St. Louis' individual earned runs do not add up to team total because of rule 10.18(i) applied in Game 4.)

Milwaukee Brewers

Pitcher	G.	IP.	H.	R.	E.	SO.	BB.	W.	L.	ERA.
Slaton	2	2⅔	1	0	0	2	1	1	0	0.00
Bernard	1	1	0	0	0	1	0	0	0	0.00
Ladd	1	⅔	1	0	0	2	0	0	0	0.00
Caldwell	3	17⅔	19	4	4	3	6	2	0	2.04
McClure	5	4⅓	5	2	2	3	5	0	2	4.15
Vuckovich	2	14	16	9	7	5	4	0	1	4.50
Haas	2	7⅓	8	7	6	3	4	0	0	7.36
Sutton	2	10⅓	12	11	9	1	5	0	1	7.84
Medich	1	2	5	6	4	1	0	0	0	18.00
Totals	7	60	67	39	32	20	26	3	4	4.80

SERIES OF 1983

	W.	L.	Pct.
Baltimore A.L.	4	1	.800
Philadelphia N.L.	1	4	.200

The Baltimore Orioles, who had blown a three-games-to-one lead over the Pittsburgh Pirates in the 1979 World Series, atoned for that collapse in their next opportunity by spotting the Philadelphia Phillies a one-game lead and then sweeping the next four games to win their first world championship since 1970.

Both the Orioles and the Phillies made it to the 1983 Classic by winning their respective league Championship Series in four games. The Western Division champion Chicago White Sox won the first game of the American League playoffs behind the strong pitching of Cy Young Award winner LaMarr Hoyt, but the Orioles came back and scored 18 runs in the last three games. Baltimore pitchers, meanwhile, held the White Sox to one run in the final 31 innings of the playoff series.

Gary Matthews, who had been platooned in the outfield much of the regular season, hit three home runs to lead the Phillies over the Los Angeles Dodgers in the National League playoffs. Philadelphia dropped only the second game of the series en route to its second National League pennant in four years.

The 80th World Series was marked by some strange twists. It saw the Phillies' Pete Rose benched in Game 3—a surprising move that caused some strife in the Philadelphia camp—for the first time ever in a postseason game for which he was eligible. It saw the Orioles' skipper, Joe Altobelli, out-manage Philadelphia's Paul Owens in a year when the designated hitter was not used, a situation that seemingly would be advantageous to the National League representative. It saw a box load of strong bats on both teams go limp. And it saw a strange cast of characters—Mike Boddicker, Jim Palmer, Benny Ayala and Rick Dempsey, to name just a few—emerge as heroes.

When some of the losers in Game 1 decided that the President of the United States was to blame for their team's defeat, you knew right away that this Series was going to provide some surprises.

One surprise was that the first game, as scheduled, was played at all. Rain fell in Baltimore, often hard, almost the entire game, but the powers that be decided the show must go on.

Both starters, Cy Young Award winner John Denny of the Phillies and Scott McGregor of the Orioles, performed almost flawlessly. Neither team drew a walk, the first time that had happened in a Series contest in 16 years.

Their only mistakes were costly. The two pitchers allowed three solo homers, and that determined the final 2-1 score. Denny hung a breaking pitch that right fielder Jim Dwyer belted over the fence for a 1-0 Baltimore lead in the first, and McGregor gave up a sixth-inning home run to 40-year-old Joe Morgan that tied the game.

Mistake No. 3 was surrounded by controversy. McGregor went out to the mound to start his warmups before the top of the eighth inning but had to wait five minutes before delivering his first pitch.

Why the delay? Because ABC-TV's Howard Cosell spent three minutes interviewing first-game guest President Reagan, and the inevitable two minutes of high-priced commercial messages followed.

McGregor, normally a mild-mannered soul, screamed his displeasure at TV hirelings. But, afterward, he didn't blame the long wait for what happened next (although his teammates did).

McGregor's first pitch of the eighth was to Garry Maddox, who made contact. The ball didn't come down until it was beyond the left-field wall.

And that hit, coupled with 1⅓ innings of perfect relief from the Phils' Al Holland, was enough to give Denny the victory.

Boddicker, a rookie, and Philadelphia's Charles Hudson were the starters for Game 2 in Baltimore. Boddicker's arsenal of pitches, which included a fastball, a three-speed curveball (slow, slower and slowest) and a "foshball" (a change-up that dips

World Series MVP Rick Dempsey raises his cap and the rest of the Baltimore Orioles celebrate after dispatching the Philadelphia Phillies in Game 5 of the 1983 classic.

rapidly), had produced a 14-strikeout shutout in Game 2 of the A.L. Championship Series. But in Game 2 of the World Series, it provided him only with a 1-0 deficit against the Phillies at the halfway mark (as Morgan beat out a hit in the fourth inning, stole second, took third on an error and scored on Joe Lefebvre's sacrifice fly).

"I wasn't worried," Boddicker said later. "I figured our hitting slump would end soon."

"Soon" proved to be the fifth inning, when John Lowenstein homered to tie the score. Then the bottom of the Oriole batting order came through. Rich Dauer followed with a single to left, Todd Cruz beat out a bunt, Dempsey doubled Dauer across for a 2-1 Oriole lead and Boddicker hit a sacrifice fly to score Cruz for a 3-1 margin.

Baltimore added an insurance run in the seventh. Contributing to that rally was Dan Ford, who had been beaned in the fifth by Phillies reliever Willie Hernandez. Ford was hardly gun-shy in his next plate appearance, though. He fouled off three inside pitches before punching a single to right. Boddicker, meanwhile, was on his way to a three-hit, complete-game victory—and the only run against him was unearned. Hudson took the loss.

The matter of managerial strategy first arose in the sixth inning of Game 3 in Philadelphia. That was when Owens paid a courtesy visit to 300-game winner Steve Carlton—in the on-deck circle, of all places.

The Phillies had taken a 2-0 lead on bases-empty homers by Matthews (second inning) and Morgan (third inning) off Baltimore starter Mike Flanagan. Jim Palmer, the three-time Cy Young Award recipient who had pitched two games for the Class A Hagerstown (Md.) Suns as part of a summer rehabilitation program, relieved Flanagan in the fifth, and the Orioles proceeded to halve their deficit in the top of the sixth on a home run by Ford.

Now, in the bottom of the sixth, with two men on base and two out, it was Carlton's turn to hit against Palmer.

"I knew Lefty was getting tired," Owens said, "but I really hoped he could pitch seven innings; I didn't want to have to use the big man in my bullpen (Holland) for more than two innings if I could help it."

So, with thoughts of using a pinch-hitter, Owens trudged out to the on-deck circle, where Carlton was taking some practice swings. "I asked Lefty if he was strong enough to pitch another inning," Owens said. "He assured me he was."

So, Carlton was permitted to hit. Palmer struck him out on a 3-and-2 change-up, and the Phils were finished, offensively, for the evening.

Carlton came within one pitch of making good on his vow to his manager. He retired Dauer and Cruz to start the seventh and worked to a full count on Dempsey. One more pitch, one more out, and the veteran lefthander's job would be over.

The out never came. Dempsey doubled to the left-field wall, and pinch-hitter Ayala singled on another 3-and-2 pitch. The score was tied.

Holland replaced Carlton (the eventual loser), only to be greeted by John Shelby's single. Ford followed with a hard shot toward Phils shortstop Ivan DeJesus, and DeJesus, his vision partially obscured by Ayala, couldn't come up with it. The ball trickled out of his glove and into short left field as Ayala raced home with the winning (unearned) run.

With three innings of relief help from Sammy Stewart and Tippy Martinez, Palmer earned his first Series victory in 12 years.

Despite the Carlton and Palmer roles, the evening's loudest story was the benching of Rose—in favor of veteran Tony Perez.

"I wasn't satisfied with our offense," Owens said. Rose, who had been 1 for 8 in the first two games, responded by telling a national television audience that he was "hurt and embarrassed" by his failure to start. Though it may have inspired Rose to go 4 for 7 in the last two games, the benching (along with Rose's TV tantrum) caused disruption in Philly minds that only hurt.

In Game 4, Altobelli proved that American League managers are not necessarily lost when they lose their DH and that they can be crafty in their use of pinch-hitters. Altobelli, who had been shifting platoons when the opposition changed pitching arms all year, notched another spot for the Orioles in the Series record book when he sent four consecutive pinch-hitters to the plate in the sixth inning with Baltimore trailing, 3-2.

Baltimore had runners on second and third with one out. Switch-hitting Ken Singleton, Altobelli's best bat on the bench, was ready and willing in this key situation, but Altobelli, knowing that whoever he sent to the plate probably would be walked intentionally to load the bases, opted for reserve catcher Joe Nolan. He was walked.

Now it became Singleton's turn (to hit for Dempsey). Owens could have brought in lefthanded reliever Hernandez but, because Singleton could hit from either side, decided to stick with Denny, his righthanded starter. Denny walked Singleton on four pitches to force home the tying run and leave the bases loaded.

Altobelli then sent the switch-hitting Shelby to bat for Orioles starter Storm Davis. Hernandez came in for Denny with the hope of retiring Shelby, who would have to bat righthanded, on an inning-ending double play.

But Shelby kept the ball off the ground, launching it toward the left-field fence. Only a great, climbing-the-wall catch by Matthews turned the clout into a game-winning sacrifice fly instead of a game-winning three-run double.

Ford, batting for Al Bumbry, then was employed as the inning's fourth pinch-hitter (tying a Series record). And righthander Ron Reed then relieved Hernandez, as expected, and retired Ford. But by then the damage was done, and the Orioles went on to win, 5-4, with Davis and Denny earning the decisions.

Game 5 was all Baltimore as Eddie Murray, who had been 2 for 16 thus far in the Series, finally awoke from his slumber.

Murray was not the only sleeping giant in the Series. Cal Ripken, the American League's Most Valuable Player, finished the Series with only three hits in 18 at-bats and one run batted in. Even worse, Phils superstar Mike Schmidt went 1 for 20 with no RBIs.

But when Murray came alive, he did so with a vengeance. The powerful first baseman sandwiched two home runs (a bases-empty shot in the second and a two-run blast in the fourth) around a solo shot by Dempsey in the third, all three drives coming off starter (and loser) Hudson. The Phillies, handcuffed by McGregor's brilliant pitching, were finished. The Orioles weren't through yet, though.

The final run of the game came on a rally that started with a leadoff double in the fifth (which finally chased Hudson) by Dempsey, who later was named the World Series Most Valuable Player. A wild pitch and Bumbry's sacrifice fly scored Dempsey. But it turned out to be the day's final run only because of the ultimate Philly futility.

McGregor's shutout seemed doomed in the last of the eighth when Morgan tripled to right and tagged up to score on Rose's fly ball to left. Morgan, however, took two steps, spun his wheels and pitched forward on his face.

That is known as your textbook "symbolic ending."

The box scores:

Tuesday, October 11—At Baltimore

Phila'phia (N.L.)	AB.	R.	H.	O.	A.	E.
Morgan, 2b	4	1	2	1	5	0
Rose, 1b	4	0	1	11	0	0
Schmidt, 3b	4	0	0	1	0	0
Lezcano, rf	3	0	0	0	0	0
dHayes, rf	1	0	0	0	0	0
Matthews, lf	3	0	1	4	0	0
Maddox, cf	3	1	1	3	0	0
Diaz, c	3	0	0	7	0	0
DeJesus, ss	3	0	0	1	5	0
Denny, p	3	0	0	0	0	0
Holland, p	0	0	0	0	0	0
Totals	31	2	5	27	11	0

Baltimore (A.L.)	AB.	R.	H.	O.	A.	E.
Bumbry, cf	4	0	1	4	0	0
Stewart, p	0	0	0	0	0	0
T. Martinez, p	0	0	0	0	0	0
Dwyer, rf	3	1	1	2	0	0
cFord, rf	1	0	0	0	0	0
Ripken, ss	4	0	1	1	4	0
Murray, 1b	4	0	1	8	0	0
Lowenstein, lf	3	0	1	2	0	0
eRoenicke	1	0	0	0	0	0
Dauer, 2b	3	0	0	3	1	0
Cruz, 3b	3	0	0	0	3	1
Dempsey, c	2	0	0	6	1	0
aShelby, cf	1	0	0	0	0	0
McGregor, p	2	0	0	0	0	0
bNolan, c	1	0	0	1	0	0
Totals	32	1	5	27	9	1

Philadelphia	0 0 0	0 0 1	0 1 0—2
Baltimore	1 0 0	0 0 0	0 0 0—1

Philadelphia	IP.	H.	R.	ER.	BB.	SO.
Denny (W)	7⅔	5	1	1	0	5
Holland (S)	1⅓	0	0	0	0	1

Baltimore	IP.	H.	R.	ER.	BB.	SO.
McGregor (L)	8	4	2	2	0	6
Stewart	⅔	1	0	0	0	1
T. Martinez	⅓	0	0	0	0	0

Base on balls—None. Strikeouts—By Denny 5 (Lowenstein, Dauer, Cruz, Ripken, Shelby), by Holland 1 (Murray), by McGregor 6 (Rose, Maddox, DeJesus, Lezcano, Denny, Schmidt), by Stewart 1 (Schmidt).

Game-winning RBI—Maddox.

aStruck out for Dempsey in eighth. bGrounded out for McGregor in eighth. cFlied out for Dwyer in eighth. dGrounded out for Lezcano in ninth. eFlied out for Lowenstein in ninth. Runs batted in—Morgan, Maddox, Dwyer. Two-base hit—Bumbry. Home runs—Dwyer, Morgan, Maddox. Caught stealing—Morgan. Double play—Ripken, Dauer and Murray. Left on bases—Philadelphia 2, Baltimore 4. Umpires—Springstead (A.L.) plate, Vargo (N.L.) first, Clark (A.L.) second, Pulli (N.L.) third, Palermo (A.L.) left, Rennert (N.L.) right. Time—2:22. Attendance—52,204.

Wednesday, October 12—At Baltimore

Phila'phia (N.L.)	AB.	R.	H.	O.	A.	E.
Morgan, 2b	4	1	1	1	1	0
Rose, 1b	4	0	0	7	1	0
Schmidt, 3b	4	0	0	0	3	0
Lefebvre, rf	2	0	0	1	0	0
Matthews, lf	3	0	1	2	0	0
G. Gross, cf	3	0	0	5	0	0
Diaz, c	3	0	1	5	1	0
cSamuel	0	0	0	0	0	0
Virgil, c	0	0	0	1	0	0
DeJesus, ss	3	0	0	1	1	0
Hudson, p	1	0	0	0	0	0
Hernandez, p	0	0	0	0	0	0
bHayes	1	0	0	0	0	0
Andersen, p	0	0	0	1	0	0
dPerez	1	0	0	0	0	0
Reed, p	0	0	0	0	0	0
Totals	29	1	3	24	7	0

Baltimore (A.L.)	AB.	R.	H.	O.	A.	E.
Bumbry, cf	2	0	0	2	0	0
aShelby, cf	2	1	1	1	0	0
Ford, rf	3	0	1	1	0	0
Ripken, ss	3	0	1	1	6	0
Murray, 1b	4	0	0	13	1	1
Lowenstein, lf	4	1	3	0	0	0
eLandrum, lf	0	0	0	0	0	0
Dauer, 2b	4	1	1	2	2	0
Cruz, 3b	4	1	1	0	3	0
Dempsey, c	3	0	1	6	1	0
Boddicker, p	3	0	0	1	2	0
Totals	32	4	9	27	15	1

Philadelphia	0 0 0	1 0 0	0 0 0—1
Baltimore	0 0 0	0 3 0	1 0 x—4

Philadelphia	IP.	H.	R.	ER.	BB.	SO.
Hudson (L)	4⅓	5	3	3	0	3
Hernandez	⅔	0	0	0	1	1
Andersen	2	3	1	1	0	1
Reed	1	1	0	0	1	1

Baltimore	IP.	H.	R.	ER.	BB.	SO.
Boddicker (W)	9	3	1	0	0	6

Bases on balls—Off Hernandez 1 (Ripken), off Reed 1 (Dempsey).

Strikeouts—By Hudson 3 (Boddicker, Bumbry, Ford), by Hernandez 1 (Shelby), by Andersen 1 (Dempsey), by Reed 1 (Dauer), by Boddicker 6 (Morgan, Rose, Schmidt, Lefebvre, Diaz, Hayes).

1983 WORLD SERIES

Game-winning RBI—Dempsey.

aCalled out on strikes for Bumbry in fifth. bStruck out for Hernandez in sixth. cRan for Diaz in eighth. dGrounded into double play for Andersen in eighth. eRan for Lowenstein in eighth. Runs batted in—Lefebvre, Ripken, Lowenstein, Dempsey, Boddicker. Two-base hits—Lowenstein, Dempsey. Home run—Lowenstein. Stolen bases—Morgan, Landrum. Sacrifice flies—Lefebvre, Boddicker. Hit by pitcher—By Hernandez (Ford). Double play—Dauer, Ripken and Murray. Left on bases—Philadelphia 2, Baltimore 8. Umpires—Vargo (N.L.) plate, Clark (A.L.) first, Pulli (N.L.) second, Palermo (A.L.) third, Rennert (N.L.) left, Springstead (A.L.) right. Time—2:27. Attendance—52,132.

Friday, October 14—At Philadelphia

Baltimore (A.L.)	AB.	R.	H.	O.	A.	E.
Shelby, cf	4	0	2	5	0	0
Ford, rf	3	1	1	1	1	0
Ripken, ss	3	0	0	1	3	0
Murray, 1b	4	0	0	10	0	0
Roenicke, lf	4	0	0	1	1	0
Dauer, 2b	4	0	0	4	2	0
Cruz, 3b	3	0	0	0	4	1
Dempsey, c	4	1	2	5	2	0
Flanagan, p	1	0	0	0	0	0
aSingleton	1	0	0	0	0	0
Palmer, p	0	0	0	0	0	0
bAyala	1	1	1	0	0	0
Stewart, p	1	0	0	0	0	0
T. Martinez, p	0	0	0	0	0	0
Totals	33	3	6	27	13	1

Phila'phia (N.L.)	AB.	R.	H.	O.	A.	E.
Morgan, 2b	3	1	1	5	2	0
Lezcano, rf	4	0	1	1	0	0
Hayes, rf	0	0	0	1	0	0
Schmidt, 3b	4	0	0	0	4	1
Matthews, lf	3	1	1	0	0	0
Perez, 1b	4	0	1	8	0	0
Maddox, cf	4	0	0	1	0	0
Diaz, c	3	0	2	11	0	0
cLefebvre	0	0	0	0	0	0
dRose	1	0	0	0	0	0
DeJesus, ss	3	0	2	0	5	1
Carlton, p	3	0	0	0	0	0
Holland, p	0	0	0	0	0	0
eVirgil	1	0	0	0	0	0
Totals	33	2	8	27	11	2

Baltimore	0	0	0	0	0 1	2 0	0—3
Philadelphia	0	1	1	0	0 0	0 0	0—2

Baltimore	IP.	H.	R.	ER.	BB.	SO.
Flanagan	4	6	2	2	1	1
Palmer (W)	2	2	0	0	1	1
Stewart	2	0	0	0	1	3
T. Martinez (S)	1	0	0	0	0	0

Philadelphia	IP.	H.	R.	ER.	BB.	SO.
Carlton (L)	6⅔	5	3	2	3	7
Holland	2⅓	1	0	0	0	4

Bases on balls—Off Flanagan 1 (Matthews), off Palmer 1 (DeJesus), off Stewart 1 (Morgan), off Carlton 3 (Cruz, Ford, Ripken).

Strikeouts—By Flanagan 1 (Maddox), by Palmer 1 (Carlton), by Stewart 3 (Lezcano, Schmidt, Matthews), by Carlton 7 (Shelby 2, Ripken, Murray 2, Flanagan, Singleton), by Holland 4 (Roenicke, Dauer, Dempsey, Stewart).

Game-winning RBI—None.

aCalled out on strikes for Flanagan in fifth. bSingled home one run for Palmer in seventh. cAnnounced as pinch-hitter for Diaz in ninth. dGrounded out for Lefebvre in ninth. eGrounded out for Holland in ninth. Runs batted in—Ford, Ayala, Morgan, Matthews. Two-bases hits—Dempsey 2. Home runs—Matthews, Morgan, Ford. Caught stealing—Morgan. Wild pitches—Palmer, Carlton. Double plays—DeJesus, Morgan and Perez; Schmidt, Morgan and Perez. Left on bases—Baltimore 6, Philadelphia 7. Umpires—Clark (A.L.) plate, Pulli (N.L.) first, Palermo (A.L.) second, Rennert (N.L.) third, Springstead (A.L.) left, Vargo (N.L.) right. Time—2:35. Attendance—65,792.

Saturday, October 15—At Philadelphia

Baltimore (A.L.)	AB.	R.	H.	O.	A.	E.
Bumbry, cf	3	0	0	3	0	0
eFord	1	0	0	0	0	0
Stewart, p	1	0	0	0	0	0
T. Martinez, p	0	0	0	0	0	0
Dwyer, rf	5	2	2	0	0	0
Landrum, rf	0	0	0	0	0	0
Ripken, ss	5	1	1	0	1	0
Murray, 1b	4	0	1	9	0	0
Lowenstein, lf	4	1	1	2	0	1
Dauer, 2b-3b	4	1	3	3	2	0
Cruz, 3b	2	0	1	0	1	0
aNolan, c	1	0	0	2	0	0
Dempsey, c	1	0	0	3	0	0
bSingleton	0	0	0	0	0	0
cSakata, 2b	1	0	0	2	2	0
Davis, p	2	0	0	0	1	0
dShelby, cf	1	0	1	3	0	0
Totals	35	5	10	27	7	1

Phila'phia (N.L.)	AB.	R.	H.	O.	A.	E.
Morgan, 2b	5	0	0	1	1	0
Rose, 1b	3	1	2	5	3	0
Schmidt, 3b	4	0	1	0	0	0
Lefebvre, rf	3	0	1	2	0	0
gPerez	1	0	1	0	0	0
hSamuel	0	0	0	0	0	0
Lezcano, rf	0	0	0	1	0	0
Matthews, lf	3	0	1	3	0	0
G. Gross, cf	3	0	0	3	0	0
iMaddox	1	0	0	0	0	0
Diaz, c	4	1	2	7	0	0
jDernier	0	1	0	0	0	0
DeJesus, ss	4	0	2	1	0	0
Denny, p	2	1	1	3	1	0
Hernandez, p	0	0	0	0	0	0
Reed, p	0	0	0	0	0	0
fHayes	1	0	0	0	0	0
Andersen, p	0	0	0	0	1	0
kVirgil	1	0	1	0	0	0
Totals	35	4	10	27	7	0

Baltimore	0	0	0	2	0 2	1 0	0—5
Philadelphia	0	0	0	1	2 0	0 0	1—4

Baltimore	IP.	H.	R.	ER.	BB.	SO.
Davis (W)	5	6	3	3	1	3
Stewart	2⅔	1	0	0	1	2
T. Martinez (S)	1⅔	3	1	1	0	0

Philadelphia	IP.	H.	R.	ER.	BB.	SO.
Denny (L)	5⅓	7	4	4	3	4
Hernandez	⅓	0	0	0	0	0
Reed	1⅓	2	1	1	3	3
Andersen	2	1	0	0	0	0

Bases on balls—Off Davis 1 (Matthews), off Stewart 1 (Rose), off Denny 3 (Dempsey, Nolan, Singleton), off Reed 1 (Murray).

Strikeouts—By Davis 3 (Morgan, Rose, Schmidt), by Stewart 2 (Diaz, DeJesus), by Denny 4 (Davis 2, Lowenstein, Cruz), by Reed 3 (Ford, Ripken, Lowenstein).

Game-winning RBI—Shelby.

aWalked intentionally for Cruz in sixth.

bWalked, forcing in one run, for Dempsey in sixth. cRan for Singleton in sixth. dHit sacrifice fly for Davis in sixth. eStruck out for Bumbry in sixth. fGrounded out for Reed in seventh. gSingled for Lefebvre in eighth. hRan for Perez in eighth. iGrounded out for G. Gross in ninth. jRan for Diaz in ninth and scored. kSingled home one run for Andersen in ninth. Runs batted in—Dauer 3, Singleton, Shelby, Rose, Lefebvre, Denny, Virgil. Two-base hits—Lefebvre, Diaz, Rose, Dauer, Dwyer. Sacrifice fly—Shelby. Wild pitch—Davis. Balk—Stewart. Double plays—Dauer and Murray; Ripken, Sakata and Murray; Andersen, DeJesus and Morgan. Left on bases—Baltimore 8, Philadelphia 6. Umpires—Pulli (N.L.) plate, Palermo (A.L.) first, Rennert (N.L.) second, Springstead (A.L.) third, Vargo (N.L.) left, Clark (A.L.) right. Time—2:50. Attendance—66,947.

Sunday, October 16—At Philadelphia

Baltimore (A.L.)	AB.	R.	H.	O.	A.	E.
Bumbry, cf	2	0	0	3	0	0
cShelby, cf	1	0	0	1	0	0
Ford, rf	4	0	0	3	0	0
Landrum, rf	0	0	0	1	0	0
Ripken, ss	3	1	0	3	0	0
Murray, 1b	4	2	3	6	0	0
Lowenstein, lf	2	0	0	0	0	0
bRoenicke, lf	2	0	0	1	0	0
Dauer, 2b	4	0	0	2	1	0
Cruz, 3b	4	0	0	0	6	0
Dempsey, c	3	2	2	7	0	0
McGregor, p	3	0	0	0	0	0
Totals	32	5	5	27	7	0

Phila'phia (N.L.)	AB.	R.	H.	O.	A.	E.
Morgan, 2b	3	0	1	0	1	0
Rose, rf	4	0	2	3	0	0
Schmidt, 3b	4	0	0	1	2	0
Matthews, lf	4	0	0	6	0	0
Perez, 1b	4	0	0	5	1	0
Maddox, cf	4	0	2	3	0	0
Diaz, c	2	0	0	7	0	1
DeJesus, ss	3	0	0	1	2	0
Hudson, p	1	0	0	0	0	0
Bystrom, p	0	0	0	0	0	0
aSamuel	1	0	0	0	0	0
Hernandez, p	0	0	0	1	0	0
dLezcano	1	0	0	0	0	0
Reed, p	0	0	0	0	0	0
Totals	31	0	5	27	6	1

Baltimore .... 0 1 1   2 1 0   0 0 0—5
Philadelphia .... 0 0 0   0 0 0   0 0 0—0

Baltimore	IP.	H.	R.	ER.	BB.	SO.
McGregor (W)	9	5	0	0	2	6

Philadelphia	IP.	H.	R.	ER.	BB.	SO.
Hudson (L)	4*	4	5	5	1	3
Bystrom	1	0	0	0	0	1
Hernandez	3	0	0	0	1	3
Reed	1	1	0	0	0	0

*Pitched to one batter in fifth.

Bases on balls—Off McGregor 2 (Morgan, Diaz), off Hudson 1 (Ripken).

Strikeouts—By McGregor 6 (Morgan, Perez 2, Hudson, Matthews, Schmidt), by Hudson 3 (Ford 2, Cruz), by Bystrom 1 (Ripken), by Hernandez 3 (Murray, Roenicke, Ford).

Game-winning RBI—Murray.

aFlied out for Bystrom in fifth. bStruck out for Lowenstein in sixth. cFlied out for Bumbry in eighth. dGrounded out for Hernandez in eighth. Runs batted in—Bumbry, Murray 3, Dempsey. Two-base hits—Dempsey, Maddox. Three-base hit—Morgan. Home runs—Murray 2, Dempsey. Sacrifice fly—Bumbry. Wild pitch—Bystrom. Double play—Cruz, Dauer and Murray. Left on bases—Baltimore 2, Philadelphia 6. Umpires—Palermo (A.L.) plate, Rennert (N.L.) first, Springstead (A.L.) second, Vargo (N.L.) third, Clark (A.L.) left, Pulli (N.L.) right. Time—2:21. Attendance—67,064.

COMPOSITE BATTING AVERAGES
Baltimore Orioles

Player-Position	G.	AB.	R.	H.	2B.	3B.	HR.	RBI.	BA.
Ayala, ph	1	1	1	1	0	0	0	1	1.000
Shelby, ph-cf	5	9	1	4	0	0	0	1	.444
Dempsey, c	5	13	3	5	4	0	1	2	.385
Lowenstein, lf	4	13	2	5	1	0	1	1	.385
Dwyer, rf	2	8	3	3	1	0	1	1	.375
Murray, 1b	5	20	2	5	0	0	2	3	.250
Dauer, 2b-3b	5	19	2	4	1	0	0	3	.211
Ripken, ss	5	18	2	3	0	0	0	1	.167
Ford, ph-rf	5	12	1	2	0	0	1	1	.167
Cruz, 3b	5	16	1	2	0	0	0	0	.125
Bumbry, cf	4	11	0	1	1	0	0	1	.091
Landrum, pr-lf-rf	3	0	0	0	0	0	0	0	.000
T. Martinez, p	3	0	0	0	0	0	0	0	.000
Palmer, p	1	0	0	0	0	0	0	0	.000
Flanagan, p	1	1	0	0	0	0	0	0	.000
Sakata, pr-2b	2	1	0	0	0	0	0	0	.000
Singleton, ph	2	2	0	0	0	0	0	1	.000
Davis, p	1	2	0	0	0	0	0	0	.000
Nolan, ph-c	2	2	0	0	0	0	0	0	.000
Stewart, p	3	2	0	0	0	0	0	0	.000
Boddicker, p	1	3	0	0	0	0	0	1	.000
McGregor, p	2	5	0	0	0	0	0	0	.000
Roenicke, ph-lf	3	7	0	0	0	0	0	0	.000
Totals	5	164	18	35	8	0	6	17	.213

Philadelphia Phillies

Player-Position	G.	AB.	R.	H.	2B.	3B.	HR.	RBI.	BA.
Virgil, ph-c	3	2	0	1	0	0	0	1	.500
Diaz, c	5	15	1	5	1	0	0	0	.333
Rose, ph-1b-rf	5	16	1	5	1	0	0	1	.313
Morgan, 2b	5	19	3	5	0	1	2	2	.263
Matthews, lf	5	16	1	4	0	0	1	1	.250
Maddox, ph-cf	4	12	1	3	1	0	1	1	.250
Perez, ph-1b	4	10	0	2	0	0	0	0	.200
Denny, p	2	5	1	1	0	0	0	1	.200
Lefebvre, ph-rf	3	5	0	1	1	0	0	2	.200
DeJesus, ss	5	16	0	2	0	0	0	0	.125
Lezcano, ph-rf	4	8	0	1	0	0	0	0	.125
Schmidt, 3b	5	20	0	1	0	0	0	0	.050
Andersen, p	2	0	0	0	0	0	0	0	.000
Bystrom, p	1	0	0	0	0	0	0	0	.000
Dernier, pr	1	0	1	0	0	0	0	0	.000
Hernandez, p	3	0	0	0	0	0	0	0	.000
Holland, p	2	0	0	0	0	0	0	0	.000
Reed, p	3	0	0	0	0	0	0	0	.000
Samuel, pr-ph	3	1	0	0	0	0	0	0	.000
Hudson, p	2	2	0	0	0	0	0	0	.000
Carlton, p	1	3	0	0	0	0	0	0	.000
Hayes, ph-rf	4	3	0	0	0	0	0	0	.000
G. Gross, cf	2	6	0	0	0	0	0	0	.000
Totals	5	159	9	31	4	1	4	9	.195

COMPOSITE PITCHING AVERAGES
Baltimore Orioles

Pitcher	G.	IP.	H.	R.	E.	SO.	BB.	W.	L.	ERA.
Boddicker	1	9	3	1	0	6	0	1	0	0.00
Stewart	3	5	2	0	0	2	6	0	0	0.00
Palmer	1	2	2	0	0	1	1	1	0	0.00
McGregor	2	17	9	2	2	12	1	1	1	1.06
T. Martinez	3	3	3	1	1	0	0	0	0	3.00
Flanagan	1	4	6	2	2	1	1	0	0	4.50
Davis	1	5	6	3	3	1	3	1	0	5.40
Totals	5	45	31	9	8	7	29	4	1	1.60

Philadelphia Phillies

Pitcher	G.	IP.	H.	R.	E.	SO.	BB.	W.	L.	ERA.
Hernandez	3	4	0	0	0	1	4	0	0	0.00
Holland	2	3⅔	1	0	0	0	5	0	0	0.00
Bystrom	1	1	0	0	0	1	0	0	0	0.00
Andersen	2	4	4	1	1	0	1	0	0	2.25
Carlton	1	6⅔	7	2	2	3	7	0	1	2.70
Reed	2	3⅓	4	1	1	2	4	0	0	2.70
Denny	2	13	12	5	5	3	9	1	1	3.46
Hudson	2	8⅓	9	8	8	1	6	0	2	8.64
Totals	5	44	35	18	17	10	37	1	4	3.48

WORLD SERIES RESULTS

Year—Winner   Loser
1903—Boston A.L., 5 games; Pittsburgh N.L., 3 games.
1904—No Series.
1905—New York N.L., 4 games; Philadelphia A.L., 1 game.
1906—Chicago A.L., 4 games; Chicago N.L., 2 games.
1907—Chicago N.L., 4 games; Detroit A.L., 0 games; 1 tie.
1908—Chicago N.L., 4 games; Detroit A.L., 1 game.
1909—Pittsburgh N.L., 4 games; Detroit A.L., 3 games.
1910—Philadelphia A.L., 4 games; Chicago N.L., 1 game.
1911—Philadelphia A.L., 4 games; New York N.L., 2 games.
1912—Boston A.L., 4 games; New York N.L., 3 games; 1 tie.
1913—Philadelphia A.L., 4 games; New York N.L., 1 game.
1914—Boston N.L., 4 games; Philadelphia A.L., 0 games.
1915—Boston A.L., 4 games; Philadelphia N.L., 1 game.
1916—Boston A.L., 4 games; Brooklyn N.L., 1 game.
1917—Chicago A.L., 4 games; New York N.L., 2 games.
1918—Boston A.L., 4 games; Chicago N.L., 2 games.
1919—Cincinnati N.L., 5 games; Chicago A.L., 3 games.
1920—Cleveland A.L., 5 games; Brooklyn N.L., 2 games.
1921—New York N.L., 5 games; New York A.L., 3 games.
1922—New York N.L., 4 games; New York A.L., 0 games; 1 tie.
1923—New York A.L., 4 games; New York N.L., 2 games.
1924—Washington A.L., 4 games; New York N.L., 3 games.
1925—Pittsburgh N.L., 4 games; Washington A.L., 3 games.
1926—St. Louis N.L., 4 games; New York A.L., 3 games.
1927—New York A.L., 4 games; Pittsburgh N.L., 0 games.
1928—New York A.L., 4 games; St. Louis N.L., 0 games.
1929—Philadelphia A.L., 4 games; Chicago N.L., 1 game.
1930—Philadelphia A.L., 4 games; St. Louis N.L., 2 games.
1931—St. Louis N.L., 4 games; Philadelphia A.L., 3 games.
1932—New York A.L., 4 games; Chicago N.L., 0 games.
1933—New York N.L., 4 games; Washington A.L., 1 game.
1934—St. Louis N.L., 4 games; Detroit A.L., 3 games.
1935—Detroit A.L., 4 games; Chicago N.L., 2 games.
1936—New York A.L., 4 games; New York N.L., 2 games.
1937—New York A.L., 4 games; New York N.L., 1 game.
1938—New York A.L., 4 games; Chicago N.L., 0 games.
1939—New York A.L., 4 games; Cincinnati N.L., 0 games.
1940—Cincinnati N.L., 4 games; Detroit A.L., 3 games.
1941—New York A.L., 4 games; Brooklyn N.L., 1 game.
1942—St. Louis N.L., 4 games; New York A.L., 1 game.
1943—New York A.L., 4 games; St. Louis N.L., 1 game.
1944—St. Louis N.L., 4 games; St. Louis A.L., 2 games.
1945—Detroit A.L., 4 games; Chicago N.L., 3 games.
1946—St. Louis N.L., 4 games; Boston A.L., 3 games.
1947—New York A.L., 4 games; Brooklyn N.L., 3 games.
1948—Cleveland A.L., 4 games; Boston N.L., 2 games.
1949—New York A.L., 4 games; Brooklyn N.L., 1 game.
1950—New York A.L., 4 games; Philadelphia N.L., 0 games.
1951—New York A.L., 4 games; New York N.L., 2 games.
1952—New York A.L., 4 games; Brooklyn N.L., 3 games.
1953—New York A.L., 4 games; Brooklyn N.L., 2 games.
1954—New York N.L., 4 games; Cleveland A.L., 0 games.
1955—Brooklyn N.L., 4 games; New York A.L., 3 games.
1956—New York A.L., 4 games; Brooklyn N.L., 3 games.
1957—Milwaukee N.L., 4 games; New York A.L., 3 games.
1958—New York A.L., 4 games; Milwaukee N.L., 3 games.
1959—Los Angeles N.L., 4 games; Chicago A.L., 2 games.
1960—Pittsburgh N.L., 4 games; New York A.L., 3 games.
1961—New York A.L., 4 games; Cincinnati N.L., 1 game.
1962—New York A.L., 4 games; San Francisco N.L., 3 games.
1963—Los Angeles N.L., 4 games; New York A.L., 0 games.
1964—St. Louis N.L., 4 games; New York A.L., 3 games.
1965—Los Angeles N.L., 4 games; Minnesota A.L., 3 games.
1966—Baltimore A.L., 4 games; Los Angeles N.L., 0 games.
1967—St. Louis N.L., 4 games; Boston A.L., 3 games.
1968—Detroit A.L., 4 games; St. Louis N.L., 3 games.
1969—New York N.L., 4 games; Baltimore A.L., 1 game.
1970—Baltimore A.L., 4 games; Cincinnati N.L., 1 game.
1971—Pittsburgh N.L., 4 games; Baltimore A.L., 3 games.
1972—Oakland A.L., 4 games; Cincinnati N.L., 3 games.
1973—Oakland A.L., 4 games; New York N.L., 3 games.
1974—Oakland A.L., 4 games; Los Angeles N.L., 1 game.
1975—Cincinnati N.L., 4 games; Boston A.L., 3 games.
1976—Cincinnati N.L., 4 games; New York A.L., 0 games.
1977—New York A.L., 4 games; Los Angeles N.L., 2 games.
1978—New York A.L., 4 games; Los Angeles N.L., 2 games.
1979—Pittsburgh N.L., 4 games; Baltimore A.L., 3 games.
1980—Philadelphia N.L., 4 games; Kansas City A.L., 2 games.
1981—Los Angeles N.L., 4 games; New York A.L., 2 games.
1982—St. Louis N.L., 4 games; Milwaukee A.L., 3 games.
1983—Baltimore A.L., 4 games; Philadelphia N.L., 1 game.
1984—Detroit A.L., 4 games; San Diego N.L., 1 game.

WORLD SERIES ELIGIBLES, 1903 THROUGH 1984

Note—This list includes all players who were eligible for a World Series. When an asterisk (*) precedes a player's name, it means he never appeared in a Series game, while an asterisk (*) before a year indicates the player was eligible for that particular Series but did not play.

A

Aaron, Henry L.—Milwaukee NL 1957-58.
Abbaticchio, Edward J.—Pittsburgh NL 1909.
*Abbott, W. Glenn—Oakland AL *1974.
Abstein, William H.—Pittsburgh NL 1909.
Adair, K. Jerry—Boston AL 1967.
Adams, Charles B.—Pittsburgh NL 1909-25.
Adams, Earl J.—St. Louis NL 1930-31.
*Adams, Elvin C.—St. Louis NL *1946.
*Adams, John B.—Philadelphia NL *1915.
Adams, Spencer D.—Washington AL 1925; New York AL 1926.
Adcock, Joseph W.—Milwaukee NL 1957-58.
Agee, Tommie L.—New York NL 1969.
Agnew, Samuel—Boston AL *1916-18.
Aikens, Willie M.—Kansas City AL 1980.
*Albosta, Edward J.—Brooklyn NL *1941.
*Alcala, Santo—Cincinnati NL *1976.
Aldridge, Victor E.—Pittsburgh NL 1925-27.
Alexander, Doyle L.—New York AL 1976.
Alexander, Grover C.—Philadelphia NL 1915; St. Louis NL 1926-28.
Alexander, Matthew—Pittsburgh NL 1979.
*Allen, Artemus W.—Cincinnati NL *1919.
Allen, John T.—New York AL 1932; Brooklyn NL 1941.
Alley, L. Eugene—Pittsburgh NL 1971.
Allison, W. Robert—Minnesota AL 1965.
*Alomar, Santos—New York AL *1976.
Alou, Felipe R.—San Francisco NL 1962.
Alou, Jesus M.—Oakland AL 1973-74.
Alou, Mateo R.—San Francisco NL 1962; Oakland AL 1972.
Altrock, Nicholas—Chicago AL 1906.
*Amalfitano, J. Joseph—New York NL *1954.
Ames, Leon—New York NL 1905-11-12.
Amoros, Edmundo—Brooklyn NL 1952-55-56.
Andersen, Larry E.—Philadelphia NL 1983.
Anderson, J. Fred—New York NL 1917.
Andrews, Ivy P.—New York AL 1937-*38.
Andrews, Michael J.—Boston AL 1967; Oakland AL 1973.
Andujar, Joaquin—St. Louis NL 1982.
Antonelli, John A.—New York NL 1954.
*Antonello, William J.—Brooklyn NL *1953.
Aparicio, Luis E.—Chicago AL 1959; Baltimore AL 1966.
*Appleton, Edward S.—Brooklyn NL *1916.
Archer, P. James—Detroit AL 1907; Chicago NL 1910.
*Arias, Rodolfo—Chicago AL *1959.
Armbrister, Edison R.—Cincinnati NL 1975-*76.
Arnovich, Morris—Cincinnati NL 1940.
Arroyo, Luis E.—New York AL 1960-61-*62.
*Asbell, James M.—Chicago NL *1938.
Ashburn, Richie—Philadelphia NL 1950.
Atkins, Frank M.—Philadelphia AL *1910.
Auerbach, Frederick S.—Los Angeles NL 1974.
Auker, Elden L.—Detroit AL 1934-35.
Averill, H. Earl—Detroit AL 1940.
Avila, Roberto—Cleveland AL 1954.
*Aviles, Ramon A. A.—Philadelphia NL *1980.
Ayala, Benigno—Baltimore AL 1979-83.

B

*Babe, Loren B.—New York AL *1952.
Bagby, James C., Jr.—Boston AL 1946.
Bagby, James C., Sr.—Cleveland AL 1920.
Bailey, L. Edgar—San Francisco NL 1962.
*Bailey, Robert S.—Cincinnati NL *1976.
Bair, C. Douglas—St. Louis NL 1982; Detroit AL 1984.
*Baird, Albert W.—New York NL *1917.
*Baker, Douglas L.—Detroit AL *1984.
Baker, Eugene W.—Pittsburgh NL 1960.
Baker, Floyd W.—St. Louis AL 1944.
Baker, J. Frank—Philadelphia AL 1910-11-13-14; New York AL 1921-22.
Baker, Johnnie B.—Los Angeles NL 1977-78-81.
*Baker, Thomas C.—New York NL *1937.
Baker, William P.—Cincinnati NL 1940.
Baldwin, Howard E.—New York NL 1924.
Ball, Neal—Boston AL 1912.
Ballou, N. Winford—Washington AL 1925.
Bancroft, David J.—Philadelphia NL 1915; New York NL 1921-22-23.
Bando, Salvatore L.—Oakland AL 1972-73-74.
Bankhead, Daniel R.—Brooklyn NL 1947.
Banta, John K.—Brooklyn NL 1949.
Barber, S. Turner—Chicago NL 1918.
Barbieri, James P.—Los Angeles NL 1966.
Barnes, Jesse L.—New York NL 1921-22.
Barnes, Virgil J.—New York NL *1922-23-24.
Barney, Rex—Brooklyn NL 1947-49.
Barnhart, Clyde L.—Pittsburgh NL 1925-27.
Barrett, Charles H.—St. Louis NL *1946; Boston NL 1948.
Barry, John J.—Philadelphia AL 1910-11-13-14; Boston AL 1915-*16.
Bartell, Richard W.—New York NL 1936-37; Detroit AL 1940.
*Barton, Harry L.—Philadelphia AL *1905.
Battey, Earl J.—Chicago AL *1959; Minnesota AL 1965.
Bauer, Henry A.—New York AL 1949-50-51-52-53-55-56-57-58.
*Baumgartner, Stanwood F.—Philadelphia NL *1915.
*Beall, Walter E.—New York AL *1926.
Beauchamp, James E.—New York NL 1973.
Bearden, H. Eugene—Cleveland AL 1948.
Beattie, James L.—New York AL 1978.
Beaumont, Clarence H.—Pittsburgh NL 1903; Chicago NL 1910.
Beazley, John A.—St. Louis NL 1942-46.
*Beck, Clyde E.—Chicago NL *1929.
Becker, Beals—New York NL 1911-12; Philadelphia NL 1915.
Becker, Heinz R.—Chicago NL 1945.
*Beckendorf, Henry W.—Detroit AL *1909.
Bedient, Hugh C.—Boston AL 1912.
Beggs, Joseph A.—Cincinnati NL 1940.
*Behney, Melvin B.—Cincinnati NL *1970.
Behrman, Henry B.—Brooklyn NL 1947.
Belanger, Mark H.—Baltimore AL 1969-70-71-79.
Belardi, Wayne—Brooklyn NL 1953.
Bell, David R.—Cincinnati NL 1961.
Bell, Gary—Boston AL 1967.
Bell, Herman S.—St. Louis NL 1926-30; New York NL 1933.
Bell, Lester R.—St. Louis NL 1926.
Bench, Johnny L.—Cincinnati NL 1970-72-75-76.
Bender, Charles A.—Philadelphia AL 1905-10-11-13-14.
Bengough, Bernard O.—New York AL *1923-*26-27-28.
Beniquez, Juan J.—Boston AL 1975.
Bentley, John N.—New York NL 1923-24.
Benton, J. Alton—Detroit AL *1940-45.
Benton, John C.—New York NL 1917.
*Benz, Joseph L.—Chicago AL *1917.
*Berardino, John—Cleveland AL *1948.
*Berenguer, Juan B.—Detroit AL *1984.
*Berg, Morris—Washington AL *1933.
Bergamo, August S.—St. Louis NL 1944.
Berger, Walter A.—New York NL 1937; Cincinnati NL 1939.
Bergman, David B.—Detroit AL 1984.
Bernard, Dwight V.—Milwaukee AL 1982.
Berra, Lawrence P.—New York AL 1947-49-50-51-52-53-55-56-57-58-60-61-62-63.

*Bertaina, Frank L.—Baltimore AL *1966.
Bessent, F. Donald—Brooklyn NL 1955-56.
Bevacqua, Kurt A.—San Diego NL 1984.
Bevens, Floyd C.—New York AL 1947.
Bibby, James B.—Pittsburgh NL 1979.
Bickford, Vernon E. —Boston NL 1948.
Bigbee, Carson L.—Pittsburgh NL 1925.
Billingham, John E.—Cincinnati NL 1972-75-76.
Bishop, Max F.—Philadelphia AL 1929-30-31.
*Bithorn, Hiram G.—Chicago NL *1945.
Black, Joseph—Brooklyn NL 1952-53.
Blackwell, Ewell—New York AL 1952.
*Blackwell, Timothy P.—Boston AL *1975.
Blades, F. Raymond—St. Louis NL *1926-28-30-31.
Blair, Clarence V.—Chicago NL 1929.
Blair, Paul L.—Baltimore AL 1966-69-70-71; New York AL 1977-78.
Blake, J. Frederick—Chicago NL 1929.
Blanchard, John E.—New York AL 1960-61-62-63-64.
Blasingame, Donald L.—Cincinnati NL 1961.
Blass, Stephen R.—Pittsburgh NL 1971.
Blefary, Curtis L.—Baltimore AL 1966.
Block, Seymour—Chicago NL 1945.
Bloodworth, James H.—Philadelphia NL 1950.
Blue, Vida R.—Oakland AL 1972-73-74.
Bluege, Oswald L.—Washington AL 1924-25-33.
*Blume, Clinton W.—New York NL *1922.
Blyleven, Rikalbert—Pittsburgh NL 1979.
Bochy, Bruce D.—San Diego NL 1984.
Boddicker, Michael J.—Baltimore AL 1983.
*Boken, Robert A.—Washington AL *1933.
*Boles, Carl T.—San Francisco NL *1962.
Boley, John P.—Philadelphia AL 1929-30-31.
Bolin, Bobby D.—San Francisco NL 1962.
Bollweg, Donald R.—New York AL 1953.
Bolton, W. Clifton—Washington AL 1933.
Bongiovanni, Anthony T.—Cincinnati NL 1939.
Bonham, Ernest E.—New York AL 1941-42-43.
Booker, Gregory S.—San Diego NL 1984.
Boone, Raymond O.—Cleveland AL 1948.
Boone, Robert R.—Philadelphia NL 1980.
Borbon, Pedro R.—Cincinnati NL 1972-75-76.
Bordagaray, Stanley G.—Cincinnati NL 1939; New York AL 1941.
Borom, Edward J.—Detroit AL 1945.
Borowy, Henry L.—New York AL 1942-43; Chicago NL 1945.
Boswell, David W.—Minnesota AL 1965.
Boswell, Kenneth G.—New York NL 1969-73.
Bottomley, James L.—St. Louis NL 1926-28-30-31.
Boudreau, Louis—Cleveland AL 1948.
Bourque, Patrick D.—Oakland AL 1973.
Bouton, James A.—New York AL *1962-63-64.
Bowa, Lawrence R.—Philadelphia NL 1980.
*Bowens, Samuel E.—Baltimore AL *1966.
Bowman, Ernest F.—San Francisco NL 1962.
*Bowerman, Frank E.—New York NL *1905.
Boyer, Cletis L.—New York AL 1960-61-62-63-64.
Boyer, Kenton L.—St. Louis NL 1964.
*Brabender, Eugene M.—Baltimore AL *1966.
*Bradley, Hugh F.—Boston AL *1912.
Bragan, Robert R.—Brooklyn NL 1947.
Branca, Ralph T.—Brooklyn NL 1947-49-*52.
*Branch, Norman D.—New York AL *1941.
*Brandon, Chester M.—Pittsburgh NL *1909.
Bransfield, William E.—Pittsburgh NL 1903.
Braun, Stephen R.—St. Louis NL 1982.
Bravo, Angel A.—Cincinnati NL 1970.
*Braxton, E. Garland—New York AL *1926.
Brazle, Alpha E.—St. Louis NL 1943-46.
Brecheen, Harry D.—St. Louis NL 1943-44-46.
*Breckinridge, William R.—Philadelphia AL *1929.
*Breeding, Marvin E.—Los Angeles NL *1963.
Brennan, J. Donald—New York NL 1937.
Bresnahan, Roger P.—New York NL 1905.
*Bressler, Raymond B.—Philadelphia AL *1914; Cincinnati NL *1919.
Bressoud, Edward F.—St. Louis NL 1967.
Brett, George H.—Kansas City AL 1980.
Brett, Kenneth A.—Boston AL 1967; Kansas City AL *1980.
Breuer, Marvin H.—New York AL 1941-42-*43.
Brewer, James T.—Los Angeles, NL 1965-66-74.
Brickell, Frederick B.—Pittsburgh NL 1927.
*Brideweser, James E.—New York AL *1952.
*Bridges, Everett L.—Brooklyn NL *1952.
Bridges, Marshall—New York AL 1962-*63.
Bridges, Thomas J.—Detroit AL 1934-35-40-45.
Bright, Harry J.—New York AL 1963.
Briles, Nelson K.—St. Louis NL 1967-68; Pittsburgh NL 1971.
*Broaca, John J.—New York AL *1936.
Brock, Louis C.—St. Louis NL 1964-67-68.
Brookens, Thomas D.—Detroit AL 1984.
Brosnan, James P.—Cincinnati NL 1961.
*Brouhard, Mark S.—Milwaukee AL *1982.
*Brown, Carroll W.—Philadelphia AL *1913.
*Brown, Edward W.—New York NL *1921.
Brown, James R.—St. Louis NL 1942.
Brown, Mace S.—Boston AL 1946.
Brown, Mordecai P.—Chicago NL 1906-07-08-10.
Brown, Robert W.—New York AL 1947-49-50-51.
Brown, Rogers L.—New York AL 1981; San Diego NL 1984.
Brown, Thomas M.—Brooklyn NL *1947-49.
*Brown, Walter G.—New York AL *1932-*36.
Brown, W. Gates—Detroit AL 1968.
Browne, George E.—New York NL 1905.
Brummer, Glenn E.—St. Louis NL 1982.
Brusstar, Warren S.—Philadelphia NL 1980.
Bruton, William H.—Milwaukee NL 1958.
Bryant, Claiborne H.—Chicago NL 1938.
Buchek, Gerald P.—St. Louis NL 1964.
Buckner, William J.—Los Angeles NL 1974.
Buford, Donald A.—Baltimore AL 1969-70-71.
Buhl, Robert R.—Milwaukee NL 1957-*58.
Bumbry, Alonza B.—Baltimore AL 1979-83.
Bunker, Wallace E.—Baltimore AL 1966.
Burdette, S. Lewis—Milwaukee NL 1957-58.
Burgess, Forrest H.—Pittsburgh NL 1960.
Burke, Glenn L.—Los Angeles NL 1977.
*Burke, Robert J.—Washington AL *1933.
*Burkhart, W. Kenneth—St. Louis NL *1946.
Burleson, Richard P.—Boston AL 1975.
Burns, Edward J.—Philadelphia NL 1915.
Burns, George H.—Cleveland AL 1920; Philadelphia AL 1929.
Burns, George J.—New York NL *1912-13-17-21.
Burton, James S.—Boston AL 1975.
Bush, Guy T.—Chicago NL 1929-32.
Bush, Leslie A.—Philadelphia AL 1913-14; Boston AL 1918; New York AL 1922-23.
Bush, Owen J.—Detroit AL 1909.
*Buxton, Ralph X.—New York AL *1949.
Byerly, Eldred W.—St. Louis NL 1944.
Byrd, Samuel D.—New York AL 1932.
Byrne, Robert M.—Pittsburgh NL 1909; Philadelphia NL 1915; Chicago AL *1917.
Byrne, Thomas J.—New York AL *1943-49-*50-55-56-57.
Byrnes, Milton J.—St. Louis AL 1944.
Bystrom, Martin E.—Philadelphia NL 1980-83.

C

Caballero, Ralph J.—Philadelphia NL 1950.
Cadore, Leon J.—Brooklyn NL 1920.
Cady, Forrest L.—Boston AL 1912-15-16.
Caldwell, R. Michael—Milwaukee AL 1982.
Caldwell, Raymond B.—Cleveland AL 1920.
*Calmus, Richard L.—Los Angeles NL *1963.
Camilli, Adolph L.—Brooklyn NL 1941.
*Camilli, Douglas J.—Los Angeles NL *1963.
Camnitz, S. Howard—Pittsburgh NL 1909.
Campanella, Roy—Brooklyn NL 1949-52-53-55-56.
Campaneris, Dagoberto B.—Oakland AL 1972-73-74.
Campbell, Bruce D.—Detroit AL 1940.

Campbell, Paul M.—Boston AL 1946.
Candelaria, John R.—Pittsburgh NL 1979.
*Candini, Milo C.—Philadelphia NL *1950.
*Capra, Lee W.—New York NL *1973.
Carbo, Bernardo—Cincinnati NL 1970; Boston AL 1975.
Cardenal, Jose D.—Kansas City AL 1980.
Cardenas, Leonardo A.—Cincinnati NL 1961.
Carey, Andrew A.—New York AL *1953-55-56-57-58.
Carey, Max G.—Pittsburgh NL 1925.
Cardwell, Donald E.—New York NL 1969.
*Carisch, Frederick B.—Pittsburgh NL *1903.
Carleton, James O.—St. Louis NL 1934; Chicago NL 1935-38.
Carlson, Harold G.—Chicago NL 1929.
Carlton, Steven N.—St. Louis NL 1967-68; Philadelphia NL 1980-83.
*Carlyle, Roy E.—New York AL *1926.
Carrigan, William F.—Boston AL 1912-15-16.
Carroll, Clay P.—Cincinnati NL 1970-72-75.
Carroll, Thomas E.—New York AL 1955-*56.
*Carter, Paul W.—Chicago NL *1918.
Casey, Hugh T.—Chicago NL *1935; Brooklyn NL 1941-47.
Cash, David—Pittsburgh NL 1971.
Cash, Norman D.—Chicago AL 1959; Detroit AL 1968.
Caster, George J.—St. Louis AL *1944; Detroit AL 1945.
Castillo, Martin H.—Detroit AL 1984.
Castillo, Robert E.—Los Angeles NL 1981.
Castleman, Clydell—New York NL 1936-*37.
*Castleman, Foster E.—New York NL *1954.
Cather, Theodore P.—Boston NL 1914.
*Causey, Cecil A.—New York NL *1921.
Cavarretta, Philip J.—Chicago NL 1935-38-45.
Cepeda, Orlando M.—San Francisco NL 1962; St. Louis NL 1967-68.
Cerone, Richard A.—New York AL 1981.
Cerv, Robert H.—New York AL 1955-56-60.
Cey, Ronald C.—Los Angeles NL 1974-77-78-81.
Chacon, Elio—Cincinnati NL 1961.
Chalk, David L.—Kansas City AL 1980.
Chalmers, George W.—Philadelphia NL 1915.
Chambliss, C. Christopher—New York AL 1976-77-78.
Chance, Frank L.—Chicago NL 1906-07-08-10.
Chandler, Spurgeon F.—New York AL *1937-*38-*39-41-42-43-47.
Chaney, Darrel L.—Cincinnati NL 1970-72-75.
*Chapman, Edwin V.—Washington AL *1933.
Chapman, W. Benjamin—New York AL 1932.
Charles, Edwin D.—New York NL 1969.
Chartak, Michael G.—St. Louis AL 1944.
Cheney, Lawrence R.—Brooklyn NL 1916.
Cheney, Thomas E.—Pittsburgh NL 1960.
Chiozza, Louis P.—New York NL 1937.
Chipman, Robert H.—Chicago NL 1945.
Christenson, Larry R.—Philadelphia NL 1980.
Christman, Marquette J.—St. Louis AL 1944.
Christopher, Joseph O.—Pittsburgh NL 1960.
Christopher, Russell O.—Cleveland AL 1948.
*Church, Emory N.—Philadelphia NL *1950.
Churn, Clarence N.—Los Angeles NL 1959.
*Cicotte, Alva W.—New York AL *1957.
Cicotte, Edward V.—Chicago AL 1917-19.
Cimoli, Gino N.—Brooklyn NL 1956; Pittsburgh NL 1960.
Clark, Alfred A.—New York AL 1947; Cleveland AL 1948.
*Clark, Robert W.—Cleveland AL *1920.
*Clark, W. Watson—New York NL *1933.
Clarke, Frederick C.—Pittsburgh NL 1903-09.
*Clarke, Thomas A.—Chicago NL *1918.
*Clarke, William J.—New York NL *1905.
Clary, Ellis—St. Louis AL 1944.
Clay, Kenneth E.—New York AL 1977-78.
Clemente, Roberto W.—Pittsburgh NL 1960-71.
Clendenon, Donn A.—New York NL 1969.
Cleveland, Reginald L.—Boston AL 1975.

*Clevenger, Truman E.—New York AL *1961-*62.
Clifton, Herman E.—Detroit AL *1934-35.
Cline, Tyrone A.—Cincinnati NL 1970.
Clines, Eugene—Pittsburgh NL 1971.
Cloninger, Tony L.—Cincinnati NL 1970.
*Clough, Edgar G.—St. Louis NL *1926.
Coakley, Andrew J.—Philadelphia AL 1905.
Coates, James A.—New York AL 1960-61-62.
Cobb, Tyrus R.—Detroit AL 1907-08-09.
*Cochrane, George L.—Boston AL *1918.
Cochrane, Gordon S.—Philadelphia AL 1929-30-31; Detroit AL 1934-35.
*Cocreham, Eugene—Boston NL *1914.
*Coffey, John F.—Boston AL *1918.
Coffman, S. Richard—New York NL 1936-37.
Cole, Leonard L.—Chicago NL 1910.
Coleman, Gerald F.—New York AL 1949-50-51-*53-55-56-57.
Coleman, Gordon C.—Cincinnati NL 1961.
Coleman, W. Gary—New York AL 1955-*56.
Collins, Edward T.—Philadelphia AL 1910-11-13-14; Chicago AL 1917-19; Philadelphia AL *1929-*30.
Collins, H. Warren—New York AL 1921.
Collins, James A.—St. Louis NL 1931-34; Chicago NL 1938.
Collins, James J.—Boston AL 1903.
Collins, John F.—Chicago AL 1917-19.
Collins, Joseph E.—New York AL 1950-51-52-53-55-56-57.
Collins, Raymond W.—Boston AL 1912-*15.
Collins, T. Patrick—New York NL 1926-27-28.
Combs, Earle B.—New York AL 1926-27-28-32.
Comer, H. Wayne—Detroit AL 1968.
Conaster, Clinton A.—Boston NL 1948.
Concepcion, David I.—Cincinnati NL 1970-72-75-76.
Concepcion, Onix—Kansas City AL 1980.
Conigliaro, William M.—Oakland AL 1973.
Conley, D. Eugene—Milwaukee NL 1957-*58.
Coombs, John W.—Philadelphia AL 1910-11-*13-*14; Brooklyn NL 1916.
Connolly, Joseph A.—Boston NL 1914.
Cooper, Cecil C.—Boston AL 1975; Milwaukee AL 1982.
Cooper, Claude—New York NL 1913.
Cooper, Morton C.—St. Louis NL 1942-43-44.
Cooper, W. Walker—St. Louis NL 1942-43-44.
Corrales, Patrick—Cincinnati NL 1970.
Corwin, Elmer N.—New York NL 1951-*54.
Coscarart, Peter J.—Brooklyn NL 1941.
*Cottrell, Ensign S.—Boston NL *1914.
Coughlin, William P.—Detroit AL 1907-08.
Coveleski, Stanley—Cleveland AL 1920; Washington AL 1925.
Covington, J. Wesley—Milwaukee NL 1957-58; Los Angeles NL 1966.
Cox, William R.—Brooklyn NL 1949-52-53.
Craft, Harry F.—Cincinnati NL 1939-40.
Craig, Roger L.—Brooklyn NL 1955-56; Los Angeles NL 1959; St. Louis NL 1964.
Cramer, Roger M.—Philadelphia AL 1931; Detroit AL 1945.
Crandall, Delmar W.—Milwaukee NL 1957-58.
Crandall, Otis J.—New York NL 1911-12-13.
Cravath, Clifford C.—Philadelphia NL 1915.
Crawford, Clifford R.—St. Louis NL 1934.
Crawford, Samuel E.—Detroit AL 1907-08-09.
Crawford, Willie M.—Los Angeles NL 1965-74.
Crespi, Frank A.—St. Louis NL 1942.
Criger, Louis—Boston AL 1903.
Critz, Hugh M.—New York NL 1933.
*Cronin, James J.—Philadelphia AL *1929.
Cronin, Joseph E.—Pittsburgh NL *1927; Washington AL 1933.
Crosetti, Frank J.—New York AL 1932-36-37-38-39-*41-42-43.
*Cross, Joffre J.—St. Louis NL *1946.
Cross, Lafayette N.—Philadelphia AL 1905.
Cross, Montford M.—Philadelphia AL 1905.

Croucher, Frank D.—Detroit AL 1940.
Crowder, Alvin F.—Washington AL 1933; Detroit AL 1934-35.
Crowley, Terrence M.—Baltimore AL 1970-79; Cincinnati NL 1975.
*Crutcher, Richard L.—Boston NL *1914.
Cruz, Todd R.—Baltimore AL 1983.
Cuellar, Miguel—St. Louis NL *1964; Baltimore AL 1969-70-71.
Culberson, D. Leon—Boston AL 1946.
*Cullen, Timothy L.—Oakland AL *1972.
Cullenbine, Roy J.—New York AL 1942; Detroit AL 1945.
*Culloton, Bernard A.—Pittsburgh NL *1925.
Cunningham, William A.—New York NL *1921-22-23.
Cutshaw, George W.—Brooklyn NL 1916.
Cuyler, Hazen S.—Pittsburgh NL 1925-*27; Chicago NL 1929-32.
Cvengros, L. Michael—Pittsburgh NL 1927; Chicago NL *1929.

D

Dahlen, William F.—New York NL 1905.
Dahlgren, Ellsworth T.—New York AL *1938-39.
Daley, Buddy L.—New York AL 1961-62.
Dalrymple, Clayton—Baltimore AL 1969-*71.
*Daly, Thomas F.—Philadelphia AL *1913.
Danforth, David C.—Philadelphia AL *1911; Chicago AL 1917.
Danning, Harry—New York NL *1933-36-37.
Darcy, Patrick L.—Cincinnati NL 1975.
Dark, Alvin R.—Boston NL 1948; New York NL 1951-54.
Daubert, Jacob E.—Brooklyn NL 1916; Cincinnati NL 1919.
Dauer, Richard F.—Baltimore AL 1979-83.
*DaVanon, Frank G.—Baltimore AL *1971.
Davalillo, Victor J.—Pittsburgh NL 1971; Oakland AL 1973; Los Angeles NL 1977-78.
Davenport, James H.—San Francisco NL 1962.
*Davies, Lloyd G.—Philadelphia AL *1914.
Davis, Curtis B.—Brooklyn NL 1941.
*Davis, George A.—Boston NL *1914.
Davis, George E.—Baltimore AL 1983.
Davis, George S.—Chicago AL 1906.
Davis, George W.—New York NL 1933-36.
Davis, H. Thomas—Los Angeles NL 1963-66.
Davis, Harry H.—Philadelphia AL 1905-10-11-*13-*14.
Davis, Ronald E.—St. Louis NL 1968.
Davis, Ronald G.—New York AL 1981.
Davis, Virgil L.—St. Louis NL 1934.
Davis, William H.—Los Angeles NL 1963-65-66.
Dawson, Ralph F.—Pittsburgh NL 1927.
Deal, Charles A.—Boston NL 1914; Chicago NL 1918.
Dean, Jay H.—St. Louis NL 1934; Chicago NL 1938.
Dean, Paul D.—St. Louis NL 1934.
Dean, Wayland O.—New York NL 1924.
DeCinces, Douglas V.—Baltimore AL 1979.
DeJesus, Ivan—Philadelphia NL 1983.
Delahanty, James C.—Detroit AL 1909.
DeLancey, William P.—St. Louis NL 1934.
Dell, Weiser G.—Brooklyn NL 1916.
DeMaestri, Joseph P.—New York AL 1960-*61.
Demaree, Albert W.—New York NL 1913; Philadelphia NL *1915; New York NL *1917.
Demaree, J. Frank—Chicago NL 1932-35-38; St. Louis NL 1943.
DeMerit, John S.—Milwaukee NL 1957.
Demeter, Donald L.—Los Angeles NL 1959.
Dempsey, J. Rikard—Baltimore AL 1979-83.
Denny, John A.—Philadelphia NL 1983.
Dent, Russell E.—New York AL 1977-78.
Dente, Samuel J.—Cleveland AL 1954.
Dernier, Robert E.—Philadelphia NL 1983.
*Derrick, Claude L.—Philadelphia AL *1910-*11.
Derringer, Paul—St. Louis NL 1931; Cincinnati NL 1939-40; Chicago NL 1945.

*Devens, Charles—New York AL *1932.
Devlin, Arthur—New York NL 1905-*11.
Devore, Joshua D.—New York NL 1911-12; Boston NL 1914.
Devormer, Albert E.—New York NL 1921-*22.
Diaz, Baudilio J.—Philadelphia NL 1983.
Dickey, William M.—New York AL *1928-32-36-37-38-39-41-42-43.
Dickson, Murry M.—St. Louis NL *1942-43-46; New York AL 1958.
*DiLauro, John—New York NL *1969.
DiMaggio, Dominic P.—Boston AL 1946.
DiMaggio, Joseph P.—New York AL 1936-37-38-39-41-42-47-49-50-51.
Dinneen, William H.—Boston AL 1903.
Ditmar, Arthur J.—New York AL 1957-58-60.
Dobson, Joseph G.—Boston AL 1946.
Dobson, Patrick E.—Detroit AL 1968; Baltimore AL 1971.
Doby, Lawrence E.—Cleveland AL 1948-54.
Doerr, Robert P.—Boston AL 1946.
*Doheny, Edward R.—Pittsburgh NL *1903.
Doljack, J. Frank—Detroit AL 1934.
Donahue, John A.—Chicago AL 1906.
Donald, R. Atley—New York AL *1939-41-42-*43.
Donlin, Michael J.—New York NL 1905.
Donnelly, Sylvester U.—St. Louis NL 1944; Philadelphia NL *1950.
*Donohue, Patrick W.—Philadelphia AL *1910.
Donovan, Richard E.—Chicago AL 1959.
Donovan, William E.—Detroit AL 1907-08-09.
Dougherty, Patrick H.—Boston AL 1903; Chicago AL 1906.
Douglas, Philip B.—Chicago NL 1918; New York NL 1921.
Douthit, Taylor L.—St. Louis NL 1926-28-30.
Downing, Alphonso E.—New York AL *1961-63-64; Los Angeles NL 1974.
Downs, Jerome W.—Detroit AL *1907-08.
Doyle, Brian R.—New York AL 1978.
Doyle, Lawrence J.—New York NL 1911-12-13.
Doyle, R. Dennis—Boston AL 1975.
Drabowsky, Myron W.—Baltimore AL 1966-70.
Drago, Richard A.—Boston AL 1975.
*Drake, Thomas K.—Brooklyn NL *1941.
Dravecky, David F.—San Diego NL 1984.
Dreisewerd, Clement J.—Boston AL 1946.
*Dressen, Charles W.—New York NL *1933.
Drews, Karl A.—New York AL 1947.
Driessen, Daniel D.—Cincinnati NL 1975-76.
*Drucke, Louis F.—New York NL *1911.
Drysdale, Donald S.—Brooklyn NL 1956; Los Angeles NL 1959-63-65-66.
Dukes, Thomas E.—Baltimore AL 1971.
Dubuc, Jean A.—Boston AL 1918.
*Duffalo, James F.—San Francisco NL *1962.
Dugan, Joseph A.—New York AL 1922-23-26-27-28.
Dugey, Oscar J.—Boston NL *1914; Philadelphia NL 1915.
Duncan, David E.—Oakland AL 1972.
Duncan, Louis B.—Cincinnati NL 1919.
*Dundon, Augustus J.—Chicago AL *1906.
*Durbin, Blaine A.—Chicago NL *1907-*08.
Duren, Rinold G.—New York AL 1958-60.
Durocher, Leo E.—New York AL 1928; St. Louis NL 1934; Brooklyn NL *1941.
Durst, Cedric M.—New York AL 1927-28.
Dusak, Ervin F.—St. Louis NL 1946.
Dwyer, James E.—Baltimore AL 1983.
Dyer, Donald R.—New York NL 1969-*73.
*Dygert, James H.—Philadelphia AL *1905-*10.
Dykes, James J.—Philadelphia AL 1929-30-31.

E

Earnshaw, George L.—Philadelphia AL 1929-30-31.
Easler, Michael A.—Pittsburgh NL 1979.
Eastwick, Rawlins J.—Cincinnati NL 1975-*76.
Eaton, Zebulon V.—Detroit AL 1945.
Edwards, C. Bruce—Brooklyn NL 1947-49.

Edwards, John A.—Cincinnati NL 1961; St. Louis NL 1968.
Edwards, Marshall L.—Milwaukee AL 1982
Ehmke, Howard J.—Philadelphia AL 1929.
Eller, Horace O.—Cincinnati NL 1919.
*Elliott, Claude J.—New York NL *1905.
*Elliott, Harold H.—Brooklyn NL *1920.
Elliott, Robert I.—Boston NL 1948.
Ellis, Dock P.—Pittsburgh NL 1971; New York AL 1976.
*Ellison, George R.—Cleveland AL *1920.
*Endicott, William F.—St. Louis NL *1946.
Engle, Arthur C.—Boston AL 1912.
English, Elwood G.—Chicago NL 1929-32-*35.
Ennis, Delmer—Philadelphia NL 1950.
*Ens, Jewel W.—Pittsburgh NL *1925.
Epstein, Michael P.—Oakland AL 1972.
Erickson, Paul W.—Chicago NL 1945.
Erskine, Carl D.—Brooklyn NL 1949-52-53-55-56.
Esposito, Samuel—Chicago AL 1959.
Essegian, Charles A.—Los Angeles NL 1959.
Etchebarren, Andrew A.—Baltimore AL 1966-69-70-71.
Etten, Nicholas R.—New York AL 1943.
Evans, Darrell W.—Detroit AL 1984.
Evans, Dwight W.—Boston AL 1975.
Evans, Joseph P.—Cleveland AL 1920.
Evers, John J.—Chicago NL 1906-07-08-*10; Boston NL 1914.

F

Faber, Urban C.—Chicago AL 1917-*19.
Face, ElRoy L.—Pittsburgh NL 1960.
Fairly, Ronald R.—Los Angeles NL 1959-63-65-66.
Fallon, George D.—St. Louis NL *1943-44.
Farrell, Charles A.—Boston AL 1903.
*Farrell, Edward S.—New York AL *1932.
Felsch, Oscar—Chicago AL 1917-19.
Feller, Robert W.—Cleveland AL 1948-*54.
Ferguson, Alexander—New York AL *1921; Washington A— 1925.
Ferguson, Joseph V.—Los Angeles NL 1974-78.
*Fernandez, Humberto P.—Brooklyn NL *1956.
Ferrara, Alfred J.—Los Angeles NL *1963-66.
*Ferrell, Wesley C.—New York AL *1938.
Ferrick, Thomas J.—New York AL 1950.
Ferris, Albert S.—Boston AL 1903.
Ferriss, David M.—Boston AL 1946.
Fewster, Wilson L.—New York AL 1921.
*Fiene, Louis H.—Chicago AL *1906.
Figueroa, Eduardo—New York AL 1976-*77-78.
Fingers, Roland G.—Oakland AL 1972-73-74; Milwaukee AL *1982.
*Fischer, Charles W.—Detroit AL *1934.
*Fisher, Eddie G.—Baltimore AL *1966.
Fisher, George A.—Washington AL *1924; St. Louis NL 1930.
Fisher, Raymond L.—Cincinnati NL 1919.
Fisk, Carlton E.—Boston AL 1975.
Fitzsimmons, Frederick L.—New York NL 1933-36; Brooklyn NL 1941—
Flack, Max O.—Chicago NL 1918.
Flanagan, Michael K.—Baltimore AL 1979-83.
Flannery, Timothy E.—San Diego NL 1984.
Fletcher, Arthur—New York NL 1911-12-13-17.
Flood, Curtis C.—St. Louis NL 1964-67-68.
Flowers, D'Arcy R.—St. Louis NL 1926-31.
*Floyd, Robert N.—Baltimore AL *1969.
*Flynn, R. Douglas—Cincinnati NL *1975-*76.
Foli, Timothy J.—Pittsburgh NL 1979.
Foote, Barry C.—New York AL 1981.
Ford, Darnell G.—Baltimore AL 1983.
Ford, Edward C.—New York AL 1950-53-55-56-57-58-60-61-62-63-64.
Forsch, Robert H.—St. Louis NL 1982.
Forster, Terry J.—Los Angeles NL 1978-81.
Fosse, Raymond E.—Oakland AL 1973-74.
Foster, George—Boston AL 1915-16.
Foster, George A.—Cincinnati NL 1972-75-76.
Fox, Ervin—Detroit AL 1934-35-40.

Fox, Nelson J.—Chicago AL 1959.
*Foxen, William A.—Chicago NL *1910.
Foxx, James E.—Philadelphia AL 1929-30-31.
Foy, Joseph A.—Boston AL 1967.
*Frankhouse, Frederick M.—St. Louis NL *1928.
Franks, Herman B.—Brooklyn NL 1941.
*Fraser, Charles C.—Chicago NL *1907-*08.
Frazier, George A.—New York AL 1981.
Freehan, William A.—Detroit AL 1968.
Freeman, John B.—Boston AL 1903.
Freese, Gene L.—Cincinnati NL 1961.
French, Lawrence H.—Chicago NL 1935-38; Brooklyn NL 1941.
French, Walter E.—Philadelphia AL 1929.
Frey, Linus R.—Cincinnati NL 1939-40; New York AL 1947.
Friend, Robert B.—Pittsburgh NL 1960.
Frisch, Frank F.—New York NL 1921-22-23-24; St. Louis NL 1928-30-31-34.
*Frock, Samuel W.—Pittsburgh NL *1909.
*Fromme, Arthur L.—New York NL *1913.
Fullis, Charles P.—St. Louis NL 1934.
Furillo, Carl A.—Brooklyn NL 1947-49-52-53-55-56; Los Angeles NL 1959.

G

Gabler, Frank H.—New York NL 1936.
Gagliano, Philip J.—St. Louis NL 1967-68.
Gainor, Delos C.—Boston AL 1915-16.
Galan, August J.—Chicago NL 1935-38; Brooklyn NL 1941.
Gale, Richard B.—Kansas City AL 1980.
Galehouse, Dennis W.—St. Louis AL 1944.
Gamble, Lee J.—Cincinnati NL 1939.
Gamble, Oscar C.—New York AL 1976-81.
Gandil, Charles A.—Chicago AL 1917-19.
Gantner, James E.—Milwaukee AL 1982.
Garagiola, Joseph H.—St. Louis NL 1946.
*Garbark, Robert M.—Chicago NL *1938.
Garbey, Barbaro G.—Detroit AL 1984.
Garcia, Alfonso R.—Baltimore AL 1979; Philadelphia NL *1983.
Garcia, E. Mike—Cleveland AL 1954.
Gardner, W. Lawrence—Boston AL 1912-15-16; Cleveland AL 1920.
Gardner, William F.—New York NL *1954; New York AL 1961.
*Garibaldi, Bob R.—San Francisco NL *1962.
Garman, Michael D.—Los Angeles NL 1977.
Garms, Debs—St. Louis NL 1943-44.
Garner, Philip M.—Pittsburgh NL 1979.
Garrett, R. Wayne—New York NL 1969-73.
Garvey, Steven P.—Los Angeles NL 1974-77-78-81; San Diego NL 1984.
Gaspar, Rodney E.—New York NL 1969.
*Gaston, Alexander N.—New York NL *1921-*22-*23.
Gazella, Michael—New York AL *1923-26-*27-*28.
Gearin, Dennis J.—New York NL 1923.
Gehrig, H. Louis—New York AL 1926-27-28-32-36-37-38-*39.
Gehringer, Charles L.—Detroit AL 1934-35-40.
Gelbert, Charles M.—St. Louis NL 1930-31.
Gentry, Gary E.—New York NL 1969.
*Gerner, Edwin F.—Cincinnati NL *1919.
Gernert, Richard E.—Cincinnati NL 1961.
Geronimo, Cesar F.—Cincinnati NL 1972-75-76.
Gessler, Harry H.—Chicago NL 1906.
Getz, Gustave—Brooklyn NL 1916.
*Giard, Joseph O.—New York AL *1927.
Gibbon, Joseph C.—Pittsburgh NL 1960.
Gibson, George—Pittsburgh NL 1909; New York NL *1917.
Gibson, J. Russell—Boston AL 1967.
Gibson, Kirk H.—Detroit AL 1984.
*Gibson, Norwood R.—Boston AL *1903.
Gibson, Robert—St. Louis NL 1964-67-68.
*Giel, Paul R.—New York NL *1954.
Gilbert, Lawrence W.—Boston NL 1914.
Gilbert, William O.—New York NL 1905.

Gillespie, Paul A.—Chicago NL 1945.
Gilliam, James—Brooklyn NL 1953-55-56; Los Angeles NL 1959-63-65-66.
Gionfriddo, Albert F.—Brooklyn NL 1947.
Giusti, David J.—Pittsburgh NL 1971.
*Glenn, Joseph C.—New York AL *1936-*37-*38.
Glynn, William V.—Cleveland AL 1954.
Goliat, Mike M.—Philadelphia NL 1950.
Goltz, David A.—Los Angeles NL 1981.
Gomez, Ruben—New York NL 1954.
Gomez, Vernon L.—New York AL 1932-36-37-38-39-*41-*42.
*Gonzalez, Julio C.—St. Louis NL *1982.
Gonzalez, Miguel A.—New York NL *1921; Chicago NL 1929; St. Louis NL*1931.
Gonzalez, Pedro—New York AL 1964.
Gooch, John B.—Pittsburgh NL 1925-27.
Goodman, Ival R.—Cincinnati NL 1939-40.
Goodman, William D.—Chicago AL 1959.
Goodson, James E.—Los Angeles NL 1977.
Gordon, Joseph L.—New York AL 1938-39-41-42-43; Cleveland AL 1948.
Gorman, Thomas A.—New York AL 1952-53.
Gorsica, John J.—Detroit AL 1940.
Goslin, Leon A.—Washington AL 1924-25-33; Detroit AL 1934-35.
Gossage, Richard M.—New York AL 1978-81; San Diego NL 1984.
Gowdy, Henry M.—Boston NL 1914; New York NL 1923-24.
*Grabowski, Albert F.—St. Louis NL *1930.
Grabowski, John P.—New York AL 1927-*28.
*Grampp, Henry E.—Chicago NL *1929.
Graney, John G.—Cleveland AL 1920.
Granger, Wayne A.—St. Louis NL 1968; Cincinnati NL 1970.
Grant, Edward L.—New York NL 1913.
Grant, James T.—Minnesota AL 1965.
Grantham, George F.—Pittsburgh NL 1925-27.
Grasso, Newton M.—Cleveland AL 1954.
Grba, Eli—New York AL 1960.
Green, David A.—St. Louis NL 1982.
Green, Fred A.—Pittsburgh NL 1960.
Green, Richard L.—Oakland AL 1972-73-74.
Greenberg, Henry B.—Detroit AL 1934-35-40-45.
Gregg, Harold D.—Brooklyn NL 1947.
*Gregg, Sylveanus A.—Boston AL *1915-*16.
*Grich, Robert—Baltimore AL *1970.
Griffey, G. Kenneth—Cincinnati NL 1975-76.
Griffin, Douglas L.—Boston AL 1975.
Griffith, Thomas H.—Brooklyn NL 1920.
Grim, Robert A.—New York AL 1955-*56-57.
Grimes, Burleigh A.—Brooklyn NL 1920; St. Louis NL 1930-31; Chicago NL 1932.
*Grimes, Oscar R., Jr.—New York AL *1943.
Grimm, Charles J.—Chicago NL 1929-32-*35.
Grimsley, Ross A.—Cincinnati NL 1972.
Grissom, Leo T.—Cincinnati NL 1939.
Grissom, Marvin E.—New York NL 1954.
Groat, Richard M.—Pittsburgh NL 1960; St. Louis NL 1964.
*Grodzicki, John—St. Louis NL *1946.
Groh, Henry K.—New York NL *1912; Cincinnati NL 1919; New York NL 1922-23-24; Pittsburgh NL 1927.
Gromek, Stephen J.—Cleveland AL 1948.
Gross, Gregory E.—Philadelphia NL 1980-83.
*Gross, Kevin F.—Philadelphia NL *1983.
Grote, Gerald W.—New York NL 1969-73; Los Angeles NL 1977-78.
Grove, Robert M.—Philadelphia AL 1929-30-31.
Grubb, John M.—Detroit AL 1984.
Gudat, Marvin J.—Chicago NL 1932.
Guerrero, Pedro—Los Angeles NL 1981.
Guidry, Ronald A.—New York AL *76-77-78-81.
*Guise, Witt O.—Cincinnati NL *1940.
Gullett, Donald E.—Cincinnati NL 1970-72-75-76; New York AL 1977.
Gumbert, Harry E.—New York NL 1936-37; St. Louis NL 1942-*43.
*Gumpert, Randall P.—New York AL *1947.

Gura, Lawrence C.—Kansas City AL 1980.
Gutteridge, Donald J.—St. Louis AL 1944; Boston AL 1946.
Gwynn, Anthony K.—San Diego NL 1984.

H

Haas, Bryan—Milwaukee AL 1982.
Haas, George W.—Pittsburgh NL *1925; Philadelphia AL 1929-30-31.
Hack, Stanley C.—Chicago NL 1932-35-38-45.
Haddix, Harvey—Pittsburgh NL 1960.
Hadley, Irving D.—New York AL 1936-37-*38-39.
Hafey, Charles J.—St. Louis NL 1926-28-30-31.
Hague, Joe C.—Cincinnati NL 1972.
Hahn, Donald A.—New York NL 1973.
Hahn, Edgar—Chicago AL 1906.
*Haid, Harold A.—St. Louis NL *1928.
Haines, Henry L.—New York AL 1923.
Haines, Jesse J.—St. Louis NL 1926-28-30-*31-34.
*Hale, Robert H.—New York AL *1961.
*Hale, Samuel D.—Philadelphia AL *1929.
Hall, Charles L.—Boston AL 1912.
Hall, Jimmie R.—Minnesota AL 1965.
Hall, Richard W.—Baltimore AL *1966-69-70-71.
Hall, Tom E.—Cincinnati NL 1972.
Hallahan, William A.—St. Louis NL 1926-30-31-34.
Haller, Thomas F.—San Francisco NL 1962.
Hamilton, David E.—Oakland AL 1972-*74.
Hamilton, Steve A.—New York AL 1963-64.
*Hamlin, Luke D.—Detroit AL *1934; Brooklyn NL *1941.
Hamner, Granville W.—Philadelphia NL 1950.
Hanebrink, Harry A.—Milwaukee NL 1958.
Haney, W. Larry—Baltimore AL *1966; Oakland AL 1974.
*Hanyzewski, Edward M.—Chicago NL *1945.
*Hardin, James W.—Baltimore AL *1969-*70.
*Hargrave, William M.—Washington AL *1924.
*Harper, Charles W.—Chicago NL *1906.
Harper, George W.—St. Louis NL 1928.
Harper, Harry C.—New York AL 1921.
Harrelson, Derrel M.—New York NL 1969-73.
Harrelson, Kenneth S.—Boston AL 1967.
Harris, David S.—Washington AL 1933.
Harris, Greg A.—San Diego NL 1984.
Harris, Joseph—Washington AL 1925; Pittsburgh NL 1927.
Harris, Maurice C.—Boston AL 1946.
Harris, Stanley R.—Washington AL 1924-25.
*Hart, James H.—Chicago AL *1906.
*Hartley, Grover C.—New York NL *1911-*12-*13.
Hartnett, Charles L.—Chicago NL 1929-32-35-38.
Hartsel, T. Frederick—Philadelphia AL 1905-10-*11.
Hartung, Clinton C.—New York NL 1951.
*Hasbrouck, Robert L.—Chicago AL *1917.
*Haslin, Michael J.—New York NL *1937.
Hassett, John A.—New York AL 1942.
Hatten, Joseph H.—Brooklyn NL 1947-49.
Hawkins, M. Andrew—San Diego NL 1984.
*Hawks, Nelson L.—New York AL *1921.
Hayes, Von F.—Philadelphia NL 1983.
Hayworth, Myron C.—St. Louis AL 1944.
Hayworth, Raymond H.—Detroit AL *1934-*35.
Hazle, Robert S.—Milwaukee NL 1957.
*Healy, Francis X.—St. Louis NL *1934.
*Healy, Francis X.—New York AL *1976-*77.
Hearn, James T.—New York NL 1951-*54.
Heath, Michael T.—New York AL 1978.
Heathcote, Clifton E.—Chicago NL 1929.
Hebner, Richard J.—Pittsburgh NL 1971.
*Heffner, Donald H.—New York AL *1936-*37.
Hegan, James E.—Cleveland AL 1948-54.
Hegan, J. Michael—New York AL 1964; Oakland AL 1972.
*Heimach, Fred A.—New York AL *1928.
Heintzelman, Kenneth A.—Philadelphia NL 1950.
*Heise, Robert L.—Boston AL *1975.
*Held, Woodson G.—Baltimore AL *1966.

Helms, Tommy V.—Cincinnati NL 1970.
Hemsley, Ralston B.—Chicago NL 1932; New York AL *1942-*43.
Hendrick, George A.—Oakland AL 1972; St. Louis NL 1982.
Hendrick, Harvey L.—New York AL 1923.
Hendricks, Elrod J.—Baltimore AL 1969-70-71; New York AL 1976.
Hendrix, Claude R.—Chicago NL 1918.
*Henley, Weldon—Philadelphia AL *1905.
Henrich, Thomas D.—New York AL *1937-38-*39-41-47-49.
Henriksen, Olaf—Boston AL 1912-15-16.
Henry, William R.—Cincinnati NL 1961.
Henshaw, Roy J.—Chicago NL 1935.
Herman, William J.—Chicago NL 1932-35-38; Brooklyn NL 1941.
Hermanski, Eugene V.—Brooklyn NL 1947-49.
Hernandez, Guillermo—Philadelphia NL 1983; Detroit AL 1984.
Hernandez, Jacinto—Pittsburgh NL 1971.
Hernandez, Keith—St. Louis NL 1982.
Herndon, Larry D.—Detroit AL 1984.
Herr, Thomas M.—St. Louis NL 1982.
*Herrmann, LeRoy G.—Chicago NL *1932.
Hershberger, Willard M.—Cincinnati NL 1939.
Herzog, Charles L.—New York NL 1911-12-13-17.
*Hess, Otto C.—Boston NL *1914.
Heving, John A.—Philadelphia AL 1931.
Higbe, W. Kirby—Brooklyn NL 1941.
Higgins, Michael F.—Philadelphia AL *1930; Detroit AL 1940; Boston AL 1946.
High, Andrew A.—St. Louis NL 1928-30-31.
Hildebrand, Oral C.—New York AL 1939.
Hill, Carmen P.—New York NL *1922; Pittsburgh NL 1927.
Hiller, Charles J.—San Francisco NL 1962.
Hiller, John F.—Detroit AL 1968.
Hoag, Myril O.—New York AL 1932-37-38.
Hoak, Donald A.—Brooklyn NL 1955; Pittsburgh NL 1960.
Hoblitzel, Richard C.—Boston AL 1915-16.
Hodges, Gilbert R.—Brooklyn NL 1947-49-52-53-55-56; Los Angeles NL1959.
Hodges, Ronald W.—New York NL 1973.
Hoerner, Joseph W.—St. Louis NL 1967-68.
Hoffman, Daniel J.—Philadelphia AL 1905.
Hofman, Arthur F.—Chicago NL 1906-*07-08-10.
*Hofman, Robert G.—New York NL *1954.
Hofmann, Fred—New York AL *1922-23.
Hogsett, Elon C.—Detroit AL 1934-35.
Hogue, Robert C.—Boston NL *1948; New York AL 1951.
Holke, Walter H.—New York NL 1917.
Holland, Alfred W.—Philadelphia NL 1983.
Hollingsworth, Albert W.—St. Louis AL 1944.
*Hollmig, Stanley E.—Philadelphia NL *1950.
Hollocher, Charles J.—Chicago NL 1918.
Holm, Roscoe A.—St. Louis NL 1926-28.
Holmes, Thomas F.—Boston NL 1948; Brooklyn NL 1952.
Holt, James W.—Oakland AL 1974.
Holtzman, Kenneth D.—Oakland AL 1972-73-74; New York AL *1976-*77.
*Hook, James W.—Cincinnati NL *1961.
Hooper, Harry B.—Boston AL 1912-15-16-18.
*Hooper, Robert N.—Cleveland AL *1954.
Hooton, Burt C.—Los Angeles NL 1977-78-81.
Hoover, Robert J.—Detroit AL 1945.
*Hopkins, Gail E.—Los Angeles NL *1974.
Hopp, John L.—St. Louis NL 1942-43-44; New York AL 1950-51.
Horlen, Joel E.—Oakland AL 1972.
Hornsby, Rogers—St. Louis NL 1926; Chicago NL 1929.
Horton, William W.—Detroit AL 1968.
Hostetler, Charles C.—Detroit AL 1945.
*Houck, Byron W.—Philadelphia AL *1913.
Hough, Charles O.—Los Angeles NL 1974-77-78.
Houk, Ralph G.—New York AL 1947-*50-*51-52.
*Houser, Benjamin F.—Philadelphia AL *1910.

Houtteman, Arthur J.—Detroit AL *1945; Cleveland AL 1954.
Howard, Elston G.—New York AL 1955-56-57-58-60-61-62-63-64; Boston AL 1967.
Howard, Frank O.—Los Angeles NL 1963.
Howard, George E.—Chicago NL 1907-08.
Howe, Steven R.—Los Angeles NL 1981.
*Howell, Homer E.—Brooklyn NL *1955-*56.
Howell, Roy L.—Milwaukee AL 1982.
Hoyt, Waite C.—New York AL 1921-22-23-26-27-28; Philadelphia AL 1931.
Hubbell, Carl O.—New York NL 1933-36-37.
*Hudlin, G. Willis—St. Louis AL *1944.
Hudson, Charles L.—Philadelphia NL 1983.
Hughes, James R.—Brooklyn NL 1953.
Hughes, Richard H.—St. Louis NL 1967-68.
Hughes, Roy J.—Chicago NL 1945.
Hughes, Thomas J.—Boston AL 1903.
Hughson, Cecil C.—Boston AL 1946.
Humphreys, Robert W.—St. Louis NL 1964.
Hunt, Kenneth R.—Cincinnati NL 1961.
*Hunter, G. William—New York AL *1956.
Hunter, James A.—Oakland AL 1972-73-74; New York AL 1976-77-78.
*Huntzinger, Walter H.—New York NL *1924.
Hurdle, Clinton M.—Kansas City AL 1980.
Hutchings, John R.—Cincinnati NL 1940.
Hutchinson, Frederick C.M Detroit AL 1940.
Hyatt, R. Hamilton—Pittsburgh NL 1909.

I

Iorg, Dane C.—St. Louis NL 1982.
Irvin, Monford M.—New York NL 1951-54.
Isbell, W. Frank—Chicago AL 1906.

J

*Jackson, Alvin N.—St. Louis NL *1967.
Jackson, Grant D.—Baltimore AL 1971; New York AL 1976; Pittsburgh NL 1979.
Jackson, Joseph J.—Chicago AL 1917-19.
Jackson, Ransom J.—Brooklyn NL 1956.
Jackson, Reginald M.—Oakland AL 1973-74; New York AL 1977-78-81.
Jackson, Travis C.—New York NL 1923-24-33-36.
Jakucki, S. Jack—St. Louis AL 1944.
*James, R. Byrne—New York NL *1933.
James, Charles W.—St. Louis NL 1964.
James, William H.—Chicago AL 1919.
James, William L.—Boston NL 1914.
Jamieson, Charles D.—Cleveland AL 1920.
Jansen, Lawrence J.—New York NL 1951.
Janvrin, Harold C.—Boston AL 1915-16.
Jaster, Larry E.—St. Louis NL 1967-68.
Javier, M. Julian—St. Louis NL 1964-67-68; Cincinnati NL 1972.
Jay, Joseph R.—Cincinnati NL 1961.
*Jeanes, Ernest L.—Washington AL *1925.
*Jenkins, Joseph D.—Chicago AL *1917-*19.
Jensen, Jack E.—New York AL 1950.
John, Thomas, E.—Los Angeles NL 1977-78; New York AL 1981.
*Johnson, Alexander—St. Louis NL *1967.
Johnson, Clifford—New York AL 1977-78.
Johnson, Darrell D.—New York AL *1957-*58.; Cincinnati NL 1961.
Johnson, David A.—Baltimore AL 1966-69-70-71.
Johnson, Deron R.—Oakland AL 1973.
*Johnson, Donald R.—New York AL *1947.
Johnson, Donald S.—Chicago NL 1945.
Johnson, Earl D.—Boston AL 1946.
Johnson, Ernest R.—New York AL 1923.
Johnson, Ernest T.—Milwaukee NL 1957-*58.
*Johnson, Henry W.—Cincinnati NL *1939.
Johnson, Howard M.—Detroit AL 1984.
Johnson, Kenneth C.—Philadelphia NL 1950.
Johnson, Kenneth T.—Cincinnati NL 1961.
Johnson, Louis B.—Los Angeles NL 1965-66.
Johnson, Robert D.—Pittsburgh NL 1971.
*Johnson, Robert W.—Baltimore AL *1966.
Johnson, Roy C.—New York AL 1936.

Johnson, Sylvester W.—St. Louis NL *1926-28-30-31.
Johnson, Walter P.—Washington AL 1924-25.
Johnson, William R.—New York AL 1943-47-49-50.
Johnston, James H.—Brooklyn NL 1916-20.
Johnston, Wheeler R.—Cleveland AL 1920.
Johnstone, John W.—New York AL 1978; Los Angeles NL 1981.
*Jolly, David—Milwaukee NL *1957.
Jones, Cleon J.—New York NL 1969-73.
Jones, David J.—Detroit AL 1907-08-09.
Jones, Fielder A.—Chicago AL 1906.
Jones, J. Dalton—Boston AL 1967.
Jones, Ruppert S.—Detroit AL 1984.
Jones, Samuel P.—Boston AL *1916-18; New York AL 1922-23-26.
Jones, Sheldon L.—New York NL 1951.
Jones, Sherman J.—Cincinnati NL 1961.
Jones, Thomas—Detroit AL 1909.
Jones, Vernal L.—St. Louis NL 1946; Milwaukee NL 1957.
Jones, Willie E.—Philadelphia NL 1950.
Jonnard, Claude A.—New York NL *1922-23-24.
Joost, Edwin D.—Cincinnati NL *1939-40.
*Jorgens, Arndt, L.—New York AL *1932-*36-*37-*38-*39.
Jorgensen, John D.—Brooklyn NL 1947-49.
Joshua, Von E.—Los Angeles NL 1974.
*Jourdan, Theodore C.—Chicago AL *1917.
Judge, Joseph I.—Washington AL 1924-25.
Judnich, Walter F.—Cleveland AL 1948.
Jurges, William F.—Chicago NL 1932-35-38.
Jurisich, Alvin J.—St. Louis NL 1944.

K

Kaat, James L.—Minnesota AL 1965; St. Louis NL 1982.
Kaline, Albert W.—Detroit AL 1968.
Kane, John F.—Chicago NL 1910.
Kasko, Edward M.—Cincinnati NL 1961.
*Katt, Raymond F.—New York NL *1954.
Kauff, Benjamin M.—New York NL 1917.
*Kaufmann, Anthony C.—St. Louis NL *1931.
*Keely, Robert W.—St. Louis NL *1944.
Keen, H. Victor—St. Louis NL 1926.
*Kekich, Michael D.—Los Angeles NL *1965.
Keller, Charles E.—New York AL 1939-41-42-43-*47-*49.
Kellert, Frank W.—Brooklyn NL 1955.
Kelly, George L.—New York NL 1921-22-23-24.
Kelly, H. Patrick—Baltimore AL 1979.
Keltner, Kenneth F.—Cleveland AL 1948.
Kennedy, John E.—Los Angeles NL 1965-66.
Kennedy, Montia C.—New York NL 1951.
Kennedy, Robert D.—Cleveland AL 1948.
Kennedy, Terrence E.—San Diego NL 1984.
Kennedy, William V.—Pittsburgh NL 1903.
Kerr, John F.—Washington AL 1933.
Kerr, Richard H.—Chicago AL 1919.
Kilduff, Peter J.—Brooklyn NL 1920.
Killebrew, Harmon C.—Minnesota AL 1965.
*Killefer, Wade H.—Detroit AL *1908.
Killefer, William L.—Philadelphia NL 1915; Chicago NL 1918.
Killian, Edward H.—Detroit AL 1907-08-*09.
*Kimball, Newell W.—Brooklyn NL *1941.
*Kindall, Gerald D.—Minnesota AL *1965.
*King, Clyde E.—Brooklyn NL *1947-*52.
King, Lee—New York NL 1922.
*Kinney, Walter W.—Boston AL *1918.
*Kirby, Clayton L.—Cincinnati NL *1975.
Kison, Bruce E.—Pittsburgh NL 1971-79.
Klein, Charles H.—Chicago NL 1935.
Klein, Louis F.—St. Louis NL 1943.
Klieman, Edward F.—Cleveland AL 1948.
Kling, John G.—Chicago NL 1906-07-08-10.
Klinger, Robert H.—Boston AL 1946.
Klippstein, John C.—Los Angeles NL 1959; Minnesota AL 1965.
Kluszewski, Theodore B.—Chicago AL 1959.
*Klutts, Gene E.—New York AL *1977.
*Kluttz, Clyde F.—St. Louis NL *1946.
*Knabe, F. Otto—Chicago NL *1918.
*Knickerbocker, William H.—New York AL *1938-*39.
*Knight, John W.—Philadelphia AL *1905.
Knowles, Darold D.—Oakland AL 1973-*74.
Koenig, Mark A.—New York AL 1926-27-28; Chicago NL 1932; New York NL 1936.
Konetchy, Edward J.—Brooklyn NL 1920.
Konikowski, Alexander J.—New York NL 1951-*54.
Konstanty, C. James—Philadelphia NL 1950.
*Koonce, Calvin L.—New York NL *1969.
Koosman, Jerry M.—New York NL 1969-73.
*Kopf, Walter H.—New York NL *1921.
Kopf, William L.—Philaldephia AL *1914; Cincinnati NL 1919.
Koslo, George B.—New York NL 1951.
Koufax, Sanford—Brooklyn NL *1955-*56; Los Angeles NL 1959-63-65-66.
Kowalik, Fabian L.—Chicago NL 1935.
*Kraly, Steve C.—New York AL *1953.
Kramer, John H.—St. Louis AL 1944.
Kranepool Edward E.—New York NL 1969-73.
*Krause, Harry W.—Philadelphia AL *1910-*11.
*Krausse, Lewis B.—Philadelphia AL *1931.
Kreevich, Michael A.—St. Louis AL 1944.
Kremer, Remy—Pittsburgh NL 1925-27.
Krist, Howard W.—St. Louis NL *1942-43-*46.
*Kroh, Floyd H.—Chicago NL *1908.
Krueger, Ernest G.—Brooklyn NL 1920.
*Krug, Martin J.—Boston AL *1912.
*Kruger, Lloyd D.—Pittsburgh NL *1903.
Kubek, Anthony C.—New York AL 1957-58-60-61-62-63.
Kubiak, Theodore R.—Oakland AL 1972-73-*74.
Kucks, John C.—New York AL 1955-56-57-58.
Kuenn, Harvey E.—San Francisco NL 1962.
Kuhel, Joseph A.—Washington AL 1933.
*Kunkel, William G.—New York AL *1963.
Kuntz, Russell J.—Detroit AL 1984.
Kurowski, George J.—St. Louis NL 1942-43-44-46.
Kuzava, Robert L.—New York AL 1951-52-53.

L

Laabs, Chester P.—St. Louis AL 1944.
Labine, Clement W.—Brooklyn NL *1952-53-55-56; Los Angeles NL 1959; Pittsburgh NL 1960.
Lacy, Leondaus—Los Angeles NL 1974-77-78; Pittsburgh NL 1979.
LaChance, George—Boston AL 1903.
LaCock, Ralph P.—Kansas City AL 1980.
Ladd, Peter L.—Milwaukee AL 1982.
Lahti, Jeffrey A.—St. Louis NL 1982.
Lamabe, John A.—St. Louis NL 1967.
Lamar, William H.—Brooklyn NL 1920.
Landestoy, Rafael S.—Los Angeles NL 1977.
Landis, James H.—Chicago AL 1959.
Landreaux, Kenneth F.—Los Angeles NL 1981.
*Landrum, Joseph B.—Brooklyn NL *1952.
Landrum, Terry L.—Baltimore AL 1983.
Lanier, H. Max—St. Louis NL 1942-43-44.
LaPoint, David J.—St. Louis NL 1982.
Lapp, John W.—Philadelphia AL 1910-11-13-14.
Larker, Norman H.—Los Angeles NL 1959.
LaRoche, David E.—New York AL 1981.
Larsen, Don J.—New York AL 1955-56-57-58; San Francisco NL 1962.
*Lary, Lynford H.—New York AL *1932.
*Lasher, Frederick W.—Detroit AL 1968.
*Latman, A. Barry—Chicago AL *1959.
Lavagetto, Harry A.—Brooklyn NL 1941-47.
*Lavan, John L.—Philadelphia AL *1913.
Law, Vernon S.—Pittsburgh NL 1960.
*Lawson, Alfred V.—Detroit AL *1935.
*Lazor, John P.—Boston AL *1946.
Lazzeri, Anthony M.—New York AL 1926-27-28-32-36-37; Chicago NL 1938.
Leach, Thomas W.—Pittsburgh NL 1903-09.

*LeBourveau, DeWitt W.—Philadelphia AL *1929.
Lee, William C.—Chicago NL 1935-38.
Lee, William F.—Boston AL 1975.
Leever, Samuel W.—Pittsburgh NL 1903-*09.
Lefebvre, James K.—Los Angeles NL 1965-66.
Lefebvre, Joseph H.—Philadelphia NL 1983.
Lefferts, Craig L.—San Diego NL 1984.
Lehman, Kenneth—Brooklyn NL 1952-*56.
Leiber, Henry E.—New York NL 1936-37.
Leibold, Harry L.—Chicago AL 1917-19; Washington AL 1924-25.
Leifield, Albert P.—Pittsburgh NL 1909.
*Leja, Frank J.—New York AL *1955.
LeJohn, Donald E.—Los Angeles NL 1965.
Lemon, Chester E.—Detroit AL 1984.
Lemon, Robert G.—Cleveland AL 1948-54.
Leonard, Dennis P.—Kansas City AL 1980.
Leonard, Hubert B.—Boston AL 1915-16.
Leonhard, David P.—Baltimore AL 1969-*70-71.
Leslie, Samuel A.—New York NL 1936-37.
Lewis, Allan S.—Oakland AL 1972-73.
Lewis, George E.—Boston AL 1912-15-16.
Lezcano, Sixto—Philadelphia NL 1983.
Liddle, Donald E.—New York NL 1954.
Lindblad, Paul A.—Oakland AL 1973-*74; New York AL 1978.
Lindell, John H.—New York AL *1942-43-47-49.
Lindsey, James K.—St. Louis NL 1930-31.
Lindstrom, Frederick C.—New York NL 1924; Chicago NL 1935.
Linz, Philip F.—New York AL *1962-63-64.
Litwhiler, Daniel W.—St. Louis NL 1943-44.
*Livingston, Patrick J.—Philadelphia AL *1910-*11.
Livingston, Thompson O.—Chicago NL 1945.
*Lobert, John B.—New York NL *1917.
Locker, Robert A.—Oakland AL 1972.
Lockman, Carroll W.—New York NL 1951-54.
Loes, William—Brooklyn NL 1952-53-55.
Logan, John—Milwaukee NL 1957-58.
Lohrke, Jack W.—New York NL 1951.
Lolich, Michael S.—Detroit AL 1968.
Lollar, J. Sherman—New York AL 1947; Chicago AL 1959.
Lollar, W. Timothy—San Diego NL 1984.
Lombardi, Ernesto N.—Cincinnati NL 1939-40.
Lombardi, Victor A.—Brooklyn NL 1947.
Lonborg, James R.—Boston AL 1967.
Long, R. Dale—New York AL 1960-62.
Lopat, Edmund W.—New York AL 1949-50-51-52-53.
Lopata, Stanley E.—Philadelphia NL 1950.
Lopes, David E.—Los Angeles NL 1974-77-78-81.
Lopez, Aurelio A.—Detroit AL 1984.
Lopez, Hector H.—New York AL 1960-61-62-63-64.
Lopez, Marcelino—Baltimore AL *1969-70.
Lord, Briscoe R.—Philadelphia AL 1905-10-11.
*Lowe, Robert L.—Detroit AL *1907.
Lowdermilk, Grover C.—Chicago AL 1919.
Lowenstein, John L.—Baltimore AL 1979-83.
Lowrey, Harry L.—Chicago NL 1945.
Lown, Omar J.—Chicago AL 1959.
Luderus, Frederick W.—Philadelphia NL 1915.
*Lum, Michael K.—Cincinnati NL *1976.
Lumpe, Jerry D.—New York AL 1957-58.
*Lundgren, Carl L.—Chicago NL *1906-*07-*08.
Lunte, Harry A.—Cleveland AL 1920.
Luque, Adolfo—Cincinnati NL 1919; New York NL 1933.
Luzinski, Gregory M.—Philadelphia NL 1980.
Lyle, Albert W.—New York AL 1976-77-*78.
Lynch, Gerald T.—Cincinnati NL 1961.
Lynn, Byrd—Chicago AL 1917-19.
Lynn, Fredric M.—Boston AL 1975.
*Lyons, Albert H.—Boston NL *1948.

M

Maas, Duane F.—New York AL 1958-60.
*MacFayden, Daniel K.—New York AL *1932.

Maddox, Elliott—New York AL 1976.
Maddox, Garry L.—Philadelphia NL 1980-83.
Maddox, Nicholas—Pittsburgh NL 1909.
*Madjeski, Edward W.—New York NL *1937.
Madlock, Bill—Pittsburgh NL 1979.
Magee, Sherwood R.—Cincinnati NL 1919.
Maglie, Salvatore A.—New York NL 1951-54; Brooklyn NL 1956.
Maguire, Frederick E.—New York NL 1923.
Mahaffey, Lee Roy—Philadelphia AL *1930-31.
Maier, Robert P.—Detroit AL 1945.
Mails, J. Walter—Brooklyn NL *1916; Cleveland AL 1920.
Majeski, Henry—Cleveland AL 1954.
*Makosky, Frank—New York AL *1937.
Malone, Perce L.—Chicago NL 1929-32; New York AL 1936-*37.
Maloney, James W.—Cincinnati NL 1961.
Mamaux, Albert L.—Brooklyn NL 1920.
Mancuso, August R.—St. Louis NL 1930-31; New York NL 1933-36-37.
Mancuso, Frank O.—St. Louis AL 1944.
Mangual, Angel L.—Oakland AL 1972-73-74.
Mann, Leslie—Boston NL 1914; Chicago NL 1918.
Mantilla, Felix—Milwaukee NL 1957-58.
Mantle, Mickey C.—New York AL 1951-52-53-55-56-57-58-60-61-62-63-64.
Manush, Henry E.—Washington AL 1933.
Mapes, Clifford F.—New York AL 1949-50.
Maranville, Walter J.—Boston AL 1914; St. Louis NL 1928.
Marberry, Frederick—Washington AL 1924-25; Detroit AL 1934.
Marichal, Juan A.—San Francisco NL 1962.
Marion, Martin W.—St. Louis NL 1942-43-44-46.
Maris, Roger E.—New York AL 1960-61-62-63-64; St. Louis NL 1967-68.
Marquard, Richard—New York NL 1911-12-13; Brooklyn NL 1916-20.
Marquez, Gonzalo—Oakland AL 1972.
*Marshall, Clarence W.—New York AL *1949.
*Marshall, Joseph H.—Pittsburgh NL *1903.
Marshall, Michael G.—Los Angeles NL 1974.
*Marshall, William R.—Chicago NL *1908.
Martin, Alfred M.—New York AL *1950-51-52-53-55-56.
Martin, D. Renie—Kansas City AL 1980.
*Martin, Elwood G.—Chicago NL *1918.
*Martin, Harold W.—Philadelphia AL *1911.
Martin, John L.—St. Louis NL 1928-31-34-*44.
*Martin, John R.—St. Louis NL *1982.
Martin, Joseph C.—New York NL 1969.
*Martin, William G.—Boston NL *1914.
Martina, Joseph J.—Washington AL 1924.
Martinez, Carmelo—San Diego NL 1984.
Martinez, Felix A.—Baltimore AL 1979-83.
Martinez, J. Dennis—Baltimore AL 1979-*83.
Martinez, Teodoro N.—New York NL 1973; Los Angeles NL *1978.
Marty, Joseph A.—Chicago NL 1938.
Masi, Philip S.—Boston NL 1948.
Mason, James P.—New York AL 1976.
Matchick, J. Thomas—Detroit AL 1968.
Mathews, Edwin L.—Milwaukee NL 1957-58; Detroit AL 1968.
Mathewson, Christopher—New York NL 1905-11-12-13.
Matlack, Jonathan T.—New York NL 1973.
Matthews, Gary N.—Philadelphia NL 1983.
*Maun, Ernest G.—New York NL *1924.
Maxvill, C. Dallan—St. Louis NL 1964-67-68; Oakland AL *1972-74.
May, Carlos—New York AL 1976.
May, David L.—Baltimore AL 1969.
May, Frank S.—Chicago NL 1932.
May, Lee A.—Cincinnati NL 1970; Baltimore AL 1979.
May, Milton S.—Pittsburgh NL 1971.
May, Rudolph—New York AL 1981.
Mayer, J. Erskine—Philadelphia NL 1915; Chicago AL 1919.

*Mayer, Walter A.—Boston AL *1918.
Mayo, Edward J.—New York NL 1936; Detroit AL 1945.
Mayo, John L.—Philadelphia NL 1950.
Mays, Carl W.—Boston AL *1915-16-18; New York AL 1921-22-*23.
Mays, Willie H.—New York NL (Giants) 1951-54; San Francisco NL 1962; NewYork NL (Mets) 1973.
Mazeroski, William S.—Pittsburgh NL 1960-71.
McAnany, James—Chicago AL 1959.
*McAndrew, James C.—New York NL*1969-*73.
McAuliffe, Richard J.—Detroit AL 1968.
*McAvoy, James E.—Philadelphia AL *1914.
McBride, Arnold R.—Philadelphia NL 1980.
*McBride, Kenneth F.—Chicago AL *1959.
McBride, Thomas R.—Boston AL 1946.
McCabe, William F.—Chicago NL 1918; Brooklyn NL 1920.
McCall, John W.—New York NL *1954.
McCarthy, John J.—New York NL 1937.
McCarty, G. Lewis—New York NL 1917.
McCarver, J. Timothy—St. Louis NL 1964-67-68.
*McClellan, Harvey M.—Chicago AL *1919.
McClure, Robert C.—Milwaukee AL 1982.
McColl, Alexander B.—Washington AL 1933.
McCormick, Frank A.—Cincinnati NL 1939-40; Boston NL 1948.
McCormick, Harry E.—New York NL 1912-13.
*McCormick, Michael—San Francisco NL *1962.
McCormick, Myron W.—Cincinnati NL 1940; Boston NL 1948; Brooklyn NL 1949.
McCosky, W. Barney—Detroit AL 1940.
McCovey, Willie L.—San Francisco NL 1962.
McCullough, Clyde E.—Chicago NL 1945.
McDermott, Maurice J.—New York AL 1956.
*McDevitt, Daniel E.—Los Angeles NL *1959.
*McDonald, Henry M.—Philadelphia AL *1931.
McDonald, James L.—New York AL *1952-53.
McDougald, Gilbert J.—New York AL 1951-52-53-55-56-57-58-60.
McEnaney, William H.—Cincinnati NL 1975-76.
McFarland, Edward W.—Chicago AL 1906.
*McGah, Edward J.—Boston AL *1946.
McGann, Dennis L.—New York NL 1905.
McGee, Willie D.—St. Louis NL 1982.
McGinnity, Joseph J.—New York NL 1905.
McGlothlin, James M.—Cincinnati NL 1970-72.
McGraw, Frank E.—New York NL *1969-73; Philadelphia NL 1980.
McGregor, Scott H.—Baltimore AL 1979-83.
McHale, John J.—Detroit AL 1945.
McInnis, John P.—Philadelphia AL *1910-11-13-14; Boston AL 1918; Pittsburgh NL 1925.
McIntire, Harry M.—Chicago NL 1910.
McIntyre, Matthew W.—Detroit AL *1907-08-09.
McKain, Archibald R.—Detroit AL 1940.
McLain, Dennis D.—Detroit AL 1968.
McLean, John B.—New York NL 1913.
McMahon, Donald J.—Milwaukee NL 1957-58; Detroit AL 1968.
McMillan, Norman A.—New York AL 1922; Chicago NL 1929.
*McMullen, Kenneth L.—Los Angeles NL *1963-*74.
McMullin, Frederick W.—Chicago AL 1917-19.
McNair, D. Eric—Philadelphia AL 1930-31.
McNally, David A.—Baltimore AL 1966-69-70-71.
McNally, Michael J.—Boston AL *1915-16; New York AL 1921-22-*23.
McNeely, G. Earl—Washington AL 1924-25.
*McQuaid, Herbert G.—New York AL *1926.
*McQuillan, George W.—Philadelphia NL *1915.
McQuillan, Hugh A.—New York NL 1922-23-24.
McQuinn, George H.—St. Louis AL 1944; New York AL 1947.
McRae, Harold A.—Cincinnati NL 1970-72; Kansas City AL 1980.
Meadows, H. Lee—Pittsburgh NL 1925-27.
Medich, George F.—Milwaukee AL 1982.
Medwick, Joseph M.—St. Louis NL 1934; Brooklyn NL 1941.
Melton, Clifford, G.—New York NL 1937.
Menke, Denis J.—Cincinnati NL 1972.
Merkle, Frederick C.—New York NL 1911-12-13; Brooklyn NL 1916; Chicago NL 1918.
Merritt, James J.—Minnesota AL 1965; Cincinnati NL 1970.
Mertes, Samuel B.—New York NL 1905.
Merullo, Leonard R.—Chicago NL 1945.
Messersmith, John A. (Andy)—Los Angeles NL 1974.
*Metcalf, Thomas J.—New York AL *1963.
Metheny, Arthur B.—New York AL 1943.
Metkovich, George M.—Boston AL 1946.
Meusel, Emil F.—New York NL 1921-22-23-24.
Meusel, Robert W.—New York AL 1921-22-23-26-27-28.
*Meyer, Lambert D.—Detroit AL *1940.
Meyer, Russell C.—Philadelphia NL 1950; Brooklyn NL 1953-55.
Meyers, John T.—New York NL 1911-12-13; Brooklyn NL 1916.
Mierkowicz, Edward F.—Detroit AL 1945.
Mikkelsen, Peter J.—New York AL 1964.
Miksis, Edward T.—Brooklyn NL 1947-49.
Milbourne, Lawrence W.—New York AL 1981.
Miljus, John K.—Brooklyn NL *1920; Pittsburgh NL 1927.
Millan, Felix B. M.—New York NL 1973.
Miller, Edmund J.—Philadelphia AL 1929-30-31.
Miller, Elmer—New York AL 1921.
*Miller, James E.—Detroit *1945.
Miller, John B.—Pittsburgh NL 1909.
*Miller, John E.—Baltimore AL *1966.
Miller, Lawrence H.—Boston AL 1918.
Miller, Otto L.—Brooklyn, NL 1916-20.
Miller, Ralph J.—Washington AL 1924.
Miller, Richard A.—Boston AL 1975.
Miller, Robert J.—Philadelphia NL 1950.
Miller, Robert L.—Los Angeles NL *1963-65-66; Pittsburgh NL 1971.
Miller, Stuart L.—San Francisco NL 1962; Baltimore AL *1966.
*Miller, William F.—New York AL *1952-*53.
Milliken, Robert—Brooklyn NL 1953.
Milner, John D.—New York NL 1973; Pittsburgh NL 1979.
Mincher, Donald R.—Minnesota AL 1965; Oakland AL 1972.
Minner, Paul E.—Brooklyn NL 1949.
*Miranda, Guillermo P.—New York AL *1953.
*Mitchell, A. Roy—Cincinnati *1919.
Mitchell, Clarence E.—Brooklyn NL 1920; St. Louis NL 1928.
*Mitchell, John F.—New York AL *1921.
Mitchell, L. Dale—Cleveland AL 1948-54; Brooklyn NL 1956.
Mize, John R.—New York AL 1949-50-51-52-53.
Mizell, Wilmer D.—Pittsburgh NL 1960.
Moeller, Joseph D.—Los Angeles NL 1966.
Mogridge, George A.—Washington AL 1924.
*Mohart, George B.—Brooklyn NL *1920.
Molitor, Paul L.—Milwaukee AL 1982.
Monday, Robert J.—Los Angeles NL 1977-78-81.
Money, Donald—Milwaukee AL 1982.
Monroe, Zackie C.—New York AL 1958.
Montgomery, Robert E.—Boston AL 1975.
Moon, Wallace W.—Los Angeles NL 1959-*63-65.
Mooney, James I.—St. Louis NL 1934.
*Moore, Archie F.—New York AL *1964.
Moore, Charles W.—Milwaukee AL 1982.
Moore, Eugene, Jr.—St. Louis AL 1944.
*Moore, Eugene, Sr.—Pittsburgh NL *1909.
Moore, G. Edward—Pittsburgh NL 1925.
Moore, James W.—Philadelphia AL 1930-31.
Moore, John F.—Chicago NL *1929-32.
Moore, Joseph G.—New York NL 1933-36-37.
Moore, Lloyd A.—Cincinnati NL 1939-40; St. Louis NL *1942.
Moore, Raymond L.—Brooklyn NL *1952; Chicago AL 1959.

Moore, Terry B.—St. Louis NL 1942-46.
Moore, W. Wilcey—New York AL 1927-32.
Moose, Robert R.—Pittsburgh NL 1971.
Moran, J. Herbert—Boston NL 1914.
Moran, Patrick J.—Chicago NL 1906-07-*08.
*Morehart, Raymond—New York AL *1927.
Morehead, David M.—Boston AL 1967.
Moreland, B. Keith—Philadelphia NL 1980.
Moreno, Omar R.—Pittsburgh NL 1979.
Moret, Rogelio—Boston AL 1975.
*Morgan, Harry R.—Philadelphia AL *1910-*11.
Morgan, Joe L.—Cincinnati NL 1972-75-76; Philadelphia NL 1983.
Morgan, Robert, M.—Brooklyn NL 1952-53.
Morgan, Thomas S.—New York AL 1951-55-56.
Moriarty, George J.—Detroit AL 1909.
Morris, John S.—Detroit AL 1984.
Morrison, John D.—Pittsburgh NL 1925.
*Morton, Guy—Cleveland AL *1920.
Moses, Wallace—Boston AL 1946.
Mossi, Donald L.—Cleveland AL 1954.
Mota, Manuel R.—Los Angeles NL *1974-77-78.
Motton, Curtell H.—Baltimore AL 1969-*70-*71.
Mowrey, Harry H.—Brooklyn NL 1916.
Mueller, Donald F.—New York NL *1951-54.
Mueller, Leslie C.—Detroit AL 1945.
Mullin, George E.—Detroit AL 1907-08-09.
*Mulliniks, S. Rance—Kansas City AL *1980.
Mumphrey, Jerry W.—New York NL 1981.
Muncrief, Robert C.—St. Louis AL 1944; Cleveland AL 1948.
Munger, George D.—St. Louis NL *1943-46.
Munson, Thurman L.—New York AL 1976-77-78.
*Mura, Stephen A.—St. Louis NL *1982.
Murcer, Bobby R.—New York AL 1981.
Murphy, Daniel F.—Philadelphia AL 1905-10-11-*13.
Murphy, J. Edward—Philadelphia AL 1913-14; Chicago AL *1917-19.
Murphy, John J.—New York AL 1936-37-38-39-41-*42-43.
Murray, Eddie C.—Baltimore AL 1979-83.
*Murray, George K.—New York AL *1922.
Murray, John J.—New York AL 1911-12-13-*17.
Musial, Stanley F.—St. Louis NL 1942-43-44-46.
Myer, Charles S.—Washington AL 1925-33.
Myers, Henry H.—Brooklyn NL 1916-20.
Myers, William H.—Cincinnati NL 1939-40.

N

Naragon, Harold—Cleveland AL 1954.
Narleski, Raymond E.—Cleveland AL 1954.
Narron, Samuel—St. Louis NL 1942-43.
Neal, Charles L.—Brooklyn NL 1956; Los Angeles NL 1959.
Neale, Alfred E.—Cincinnati NL 1919.
Needham, Thomas J.—Chicago NL 1910.
Nehf, Arthur N.—New York NL 1921-22-23-24; Chicago NL 1929.
Neis, Bernard E.—Brooklyn NL 1920.
Nelson, Glenn R.—Brooklyn NL 1952; Pittsburgh NL 1960.
Nelson, Melvin—Minnesota AL *1965; St. Louis NL 1968.
Nettles, Graig—New York AL 1976-77-78-81; San Diego NL 1984.
Newcombe, Donald—Brooklyn NL 1949-55-56.
Newhouser, Harold—Detroit AL *1940-45; Cleveland AL 1954.
Newsom, Louis N.—Detroit AL 1940; New York AL 1947.
Niarhos, Constantine—New York AL 1949.
Nicholson, William B.—Chicago NL 1945.
Nicosia, Steven R.—Pittsburgh NL 1979.
Niedenfuer, Thomas E.—Los Angeles NL 1981.
Niehoff, J. Albert—Philadelphia NL 1915.
Nieman, Robert C.—San Francisco NL 1962.
*Niggeling, John A.—Cincinnati NL *1939.
Noble, Rafael—New York NL 1951.
Nolan, Gary L.—Cincinnati NL 1970-72-75-76.
Nolan, Joseph W.—Baltimore AL 1983.

Noles, Dickie R.—Philadelphia NL 1980.
Noren, Irving A.—New York AL 1952-53-55.
Norman, Fredie H.—Cincinnati NL 1975-76.
North, William A.—Oakland AL 1974; Los Angeles NL 1978.
Northrup, James T.—Detroit AL 1968.
Nossek, Joseph R.—Minnesota AL 1965.
Nunamaker, Leslie G.—Boston AL *1912; Cleveland AL 1920.
*Nunn, Howard R.—Cincinnati NL *1961.

O

Oates, Johnny L.—Los Angeles NL 1977-78.
Oberkfell, Kenneth R.—St. Louis NL 1982.
O'Brien, John J.—Boston AL 1903.
O'Brien, Thomas J.—Boston AL 1912.
O'Connell, James J.—New York NL 1923-*24.
O'Connor, Patrick F.—Pittsburgh NL 1909.
O'Dea, J. Kenneth—Chicago NL 1935-38; St. Louis NL 1942-43-44.
O'Dell, William O.—San Francisco NL 1962.
Odom, Johnny L.—Oakland AL 1972-73-74.
O'Doul, Francis J.—New York AL *1922; New York NL 1933.
O'Farrell, Robert A.—Chicago NL 1918; St. Louis NL 1926.
Ogden, Warren H.—Washington AL 1924.
Oglivie, Benjamin—Milwaukee AL 1982.
O'Leary, Charles T.—Detroit AL 1907-08-09.
Oldham, John C.—Pittsburgh NL 1925.
Oldis, Robert C.—Pittsburgh NL 1960.
Oldring, Reuben N.—Philadelphia AL *1910-11-13-14.
Oliva, Pedro—Minnesota AL 1965.
Oliver, Albert—Pittsburgh NL 1971.
Oliver, Nathaniel—Los Angeles NL 1966.
Olmo, Luis R.—Brooklyn NL 1949.
Olson, Ivan M.—Brooklyn NL 1916-20.
O'Mara, Oliver E.—Brooklyn NL 1916.
O'Neill, Stephen F.—Cleveland AL 1920.
O'Neill, William J.—Chicago AL 1906.
*Onslow, John J.—New York NL *1917.
*Orr, William J.—Philadelphia AL *1913.
Orsatti, Ernest R.—St. Louis NL 1928-30-31-34.
Orsino, John—San Francisco NL 1962.
Osinski, Daniel—Boston AL 1967.
Osteen, Claude W.—Los Angeles NL 1965-66.
Ostrowski, Joseph P.—New York AL *1950-51-*52.
Otis, Amos J.—Kansas City AL 1980.
O'Toole, James J.—Cincinnati NL 1961.
Ott, Melvin T.—New York NL 1933-36-37.
Ott, N. Edward—Pittsburgh NL 1979.
Outlaw, James P.—Detroit AL 1945.
Overall, Orval—Chicago NL 1906-07-08-10.
Overmire, Frank—Detroit AL 1945; New York AL *1951.
Owen, Arnold M.—Brooklyn NL 1941.
Owen, Frank M.—Chicago AL 1906.
Owen, Marvin J.—Detroit AL 1934-35.
Oyler, Raymond F.—Detroit AL 1968.

P

Paciorek, Thomas M.—Los Angeles NL 1974.
Pafko, Andrew—Chicago NL 1945; Brooklyn NL 1952; Milwaukee NL 1957-58.
Pagan, Jose A.—San Francisco NL 1962; Pittsburgh NL 1971.
Page, Joseph F.—New York AL 1947-49-*50.
Page, Vance L.—Chicago NL 1938.
Paige, Leroy—Cleveland AL 1948.
Palica, Ervin M.—Brooklyn NL 1949-*53.
Palmer, James A.—Baltimore AL 1966-69-70-71-79-83.
*Palmisano, Joseph A.—Philadelphia AL *1931.
*Pape, Lawrence A.—Boston AL *1912.
Parent, Frederick A.—Boston AL 1903.
Parker, David G.—Pittsburgh NL 1979.
Parker, Harry W.—New York NL 1973.
Parker, M. Wesley—Los Angeles NL 1965-66.
*Parmelee, LeRoy E.—New York NL *1933.

Parrish, Lance M.—Detroit AL 1984.
Partee, Roy R.—Boston AL 1946.
Paschal, Benjamin E.—New York AL 1926-*27-28.
Pascual, Camilo—Minnesota, AL 1965.
Paskert, George H.—Philadelphia NL 1915; Chicago NL 1918.
Passeau, Claude W.—Chicago NL 1945.
Patterson, Daryl A.—Detroit AL 1968.
*Patterson, Roy C.—Chicago AL *1906.
Pattin, Martin W.—Kansas City AL 1980.
*Paulette, E. Eugene—New York NL *1911.
Payne, Frederick T.—Detroit AL 1907.
Pearson, Marcellus M.—New York AL 1936-37-38-39.
Peck, Harold A.—Cleveland AL 1948.
Peckinpaugh, Roger T.—New York AL 1921; Washington AL 1924-25.
*Peek, Stephen G.—New York AL *1941.
Peel, Homer H.—New York NL 1933.
*Pellagrini, Edward C.—Boston AL *1946.
*Pena, Alejandro—Los Angeles NL 1981.
*Penner, Kenneth W.—Chicago NL *1929.
Pennock, Herbert J.—Philadelphia AL *1913-14; New York AL 1923-26-27-*28-32.
Pepitone, Joseph A.—New York AL 1963-64.
Perez, Atanasio R.—Cincinnati NL 1970-72-75-76; Philadelphia NL 1983.
*Perkins, Charles S.—Philadelphia AL *1930.
*Perkins, Ralph F.—Philadelphia AL *1929-*30.
Perranoski, Ronald P.—Los Angeles NL 1963-65-66.
Perritt, William D.—New York NL 1917.
Perry, James E.—Minnesota AL 1965.
*Pertica, William A.—Boston AL *1918.
Pesky, John M.—Boston AL 1946.
*Peterson, James N.—Philadelphia AL *1931.
Petrocelli, Americo P.—Boston AL 1967-75.
Petry, Daniel J.—Detroit AL 1984.
Pfeffer, Edward J.—Brooklyn NL 1916-20.
*Pfeffer, Francis X.—Chicago NL *1910.
Pfiester, John T.—Pittsburgh NL *1903; Chicago NL 1906-07-08-10.
Phelps, Edward J.—Pittsburgh NL 1903.
Philley, David E.—Cleveland AL 1954.
Phillippe, Charles L.—Pittsburgh NL 1903-09.
Phillips, John D.—New York AL 1947.
Phillips, John M.—Chicago AL 1959.
*Phillips, W. Taylor—Milwaukee *1957.
Phoebus, Thomas H.—Baltimore AL *1969-70.
*Picciolo, Robert M.—Milwaukee AL *1982.
Pick, Charles T.—Chicago NL 1918.
Pierce, W. William—Detroit AL *1945; Chicago AL 1959; San Francisco NL 1962.
Piercy, William B.—New York AL 1921.
Pignatano, Joseph B.—Los Angeles NL 1959.
*Pillette, Duane X.—New York AL *1949.
Pina, Horacio—Oakland AL 1973.
Piniella, Louis V.—New York AL 1976-77-78-81.
Pinson, Vada E.—Cincinnati NL 1961.
Pipgras, George W.—New York AL *1923-27-28-32.
Pipp, Walter C.—New York AL 1921-22-23.
Pizarro, Juan—Milwaukee NL 1957-58.
Plank, Edward S.—Philadelphia AL 1905-*10-11-13-14.
Pleis, William—Minnesota AL 1965.
*Plummer, William F.—Cincinnati *1972-*75-*76.
Podres, John J.—Brooklyn NL 1953-55; Los Angeles NL 1959-63-*65.
Pole, Richard H.—Boston AL 1975.
Pollet, Howard J.—St. Louis NL 1942-46.
Pope, David—Cleveland AL 1954.
Porter, Darrell R.—Kansas City AL 1980; St. Louis NL 1982.
Post, Walter C.—Cincinnati NL 1961.
Potter, Nelson T.—St. Louis AL 1944; Boston NL 1948.
Powell, A. Jacob—New York AL 1936-37-38-*39.
Powell, John W.—Baltimore AL 1966-69-70-71.

*Powell, William B.—Pittsburgh NL *1909.
Powers, Michael R.—Philadelphia AL 1905.
Price, Jimmy W.—Detroit AL 1968.
Priddy, Gerald E.—New York AL *1941-42.
Prim, Raymond L.—Chicago NL 1945.
Puccinelli, George C.—St. Louis NL 1930.
*Purdin, John N.—Los Angeles NL *1965.
Purkey, Robert T.—Cincinnati NL 1961.

Q

Quilici, Frank R.—Minnesota AL 1965.
Quinn, John P.—New York AL 1921; Philadelphia AL 1929-30.
*Quirk, James P.—Kansas City AL *1980.
Quisenberry, Daniel R.—Kansas City AL 1980.

R

Rackley, Marvin E.—Brooklyn NL 1949.
*Ramirez, Mario—San Diego NL *1984.
Ramsey, Michael J.—St. Louis NL 1982.
Randolph, William L.—New York AL 1976-77-81.
Rariden, William A.—New York NL 1917; Cincinnati NL 1919.
Raschi, Victor J.—New York AL 1947-49-50-51-52-53.
Rath, Maurice C.—Cincinnati NL 1919.
Rau, Douglas J.—Los Angeles NL *1974-77-78.
Rautzhan, Clarence G.—Los Angeles NL 1977-78.
Rawlings, John W.—New York NL 1921-*22; Pittsburgh NL *1925.
Reed, Howard D.—Los Angeles NL 1965.
Reed, John B.—New York AL 1961-*62-*63.
Reed, Ronald L.—Philadelphia NL 1980-83.
Reese, Harold H.—Brooklyn NL 1941-47-49-52-53-55-56.
Regalado, Rudolph—Cleveland AL 1954.
Regan, Philip R.—Los Angeles NL 1966.
*Reiber, Frank B.—Detroit AL *1935.
Reinhart, Arthur C.—St. Louis NL 1926-*28.
Reiser, Harold P.—Brooklyn NL 1941-47.
Reniff, Harold E.—New York AL *1961-63-64.
*Renna, William B.—New York AL *1953.
Repulski, Eldon J.—Los Angeles NL 1959.
Rettenmund, Mervin W.—Baltimore AL 1969-70-71; Cincinnati NL 1975.
Reulbach, Edward M.—Chicago NL 1906-07-08-10.
Reuschel, Rick E.—New York AL 1981.
Reuss, Jerry—Los Angeles NL 1981.
*Revering, David A.—New York AL *1981.
Reynolds, Allie P.—New York AL 1947-49-50-51-52-53.
Reynolds, Carl N.—Chicago NL 1938.
Rhem, Charles F.—St. Louis NL 1926-28-30-31.
Rhoden, Richard A.—Los Angeles NL 1977-*78.
Rhodes, James L.—New York NL 1954.
Rhyne, Harold J.—Pittsburgh NL 1927.
Rice, Delbert W.—St. Louis NL 1946; Milwaukee NL 1957-*58.
Rice, Edgar C.—Washington AL 1924-25-33.
*Rice, Leonard O.—Chicago NL *1945.
Richards, Paul R.—New York NL *1933; Detroit AL 1945.
Richardson, Gordon C.—St. Louis NL 1964.
Richardson, Robert C.—New York AL 1957-58-60-61-62-63-64.
Richert, Peter G.—Los Angeles NL *1963; Baltimore AL 1969-70-71.
Richie, Lewis A.—Chicago NL 1910.
Rickert, Marvin L.—Boston NL 1948.
Ricketts, David W.—St. Louis NL 1967-68.
Riddle, Elmer R.—Cincinnati NL 1940.
Riggs, Lewis S.—Cincinnati NL *1939-40; Brooklyn NL 1941.
Righetti, David A.—New York AL 1981.
Rigney, William J.—New York NL 1951.
Ring, James J.—Cincinnati NL 1919.
Ripken, Calvin E.—Baltimore AL 1983.
Ripple, James A.—New York NL 1936-37; Cincinnati NL 1940.
Risberg, Charles A.—Chicago AL 1917-19.

Ritchey, Claude C.—Pittsburgh NL 1903.
Rivera, Manuel J.—Chicago AL 1959.
Rivers, John M.—New York AL 1976-77-78.
Rixey, Eppa—Philadelphia NL 1915.
Rizzuto, Philip F.—New York AL 1941-42-47-49-50-51-52-53-55.
*Roach, Melvin E.—Milwaukee *1957.
*Roberts, David A.—Pittsburgh NL *1979.
Roberts, Robin E.—Philadelphia NL 1950.
Robertson, Andre L.—New York AL 1981.
Robertson, Davis A.—New York NL 1917-*22.
Robertson, Eugene E.—New York AL 1928.
Robertson, Robert E.—Pittsburgh NL 1971.
Robinson, Aaron A.—New York AL 1947.
Robinson, Brooks C.—Baltimore AL 1966-69-70-71.
Robinson, Don A.—Pittsburgh NL 1979.
Robinson, Frank—Cincinnati NL 1961; Baltimore AL 1966-69-70-71.
*Robinson, Humberto V.—Milwaukee *1958.
Robinson, Jack R.—Brooklyn NL 1947-49-52-53-55-56.
Robinson, W. Edward—Cleveland AL 1948; New York AL 1955.
Robinson, William H.—Pittsburgh NL 1979.
Rodriguez, Aurelio—New York AL 1981.
Roe, Elwin C.—Brooklyn NL 1949-52-53.
Roebuck, Edward J.—Brooklyn NL 1955-56.
Roenicke, Gary S.—Baltimore AL 1979-83.
Roenicke, Ronald J.—San Diego NL 1984.
*Roettger, Oscar F. L.—New York AL *1923.
Roettger, Walter H.—St. Louis NL *1928-31.
Rogell, William G.—Detroit AL 1934-35.
Rogers, Thomas A.—New York AL 1921.
Rohe, George A.—Chicago AL 1906.
*Rojek, Stanley A.—Brooklyn NL *1947.
Rolfe, Robert A.—New York AL 1936-37-38-39-41-42.
Rollins, Richard J.—Minnesota AL 1965.
Romano, John A.—Chicago AL 1959.
*Romero, Edgardo—Milwaukee AL *1982.
Rommel, Edwin A.—Philadelphia AL 1929-*30-31.
Romo, Enrique—Pittsburgh NL 1979.
Rooker, James P.—Pittsburgh NL 1979.
Root, Charles H.—Chicago NL 1929-32-35-38.
Rosar, Warren V.—New York AL *1939-41-42.
Rose, Peter E.—Cincinnati NL 1970-72-75-76; Philadelphia NL 1980-83.
Roseboro, John—Los Angeles NL 1959-63-65-66.
Rosen, Albert L.—Cleveland AL 1948-54.
Rossman, Claude R.—Detroit AL 1907-08.
*Roth, Robert F.—New York AL *1921.
Rothrock, John H.—St. Louis NL 1934.
Roush, Edd J.—Cincinnati NL 1919.
*Rowe, Kenneth D.—Los Angeles NL *1963.
Rowe, Lynwood T.—Detroit AL 1934-35-40.
*Rozema, David S.—Detroit AL *1984.
*Roznovsky, Victor J.—Baltimore AL *1966.
Rucker, George N.—Brooklyn NL 1916.
Rudolph, Richard—Boston NL 1914.
Rudi, Joseph O.—Oakland AL 1972-73-74.
Ruel, Herold D.—Washington AL 1924-25.
Ruether, Walter H.—Cincinnati NL 1919; Washington AL 1925; New York AL 1926-*27.
Ruffing, Charles H.—New York AL 1932-36-37-38-39-41-42.
Rush, Robert R.—Milwaukee NL 1958.
Russell, Allan E.—Washington AL 1924-*25.
Russell, Ewell A.—Chicago AL 1917.
Russell, Glen D.—Boston AL 1946.
Russell, Jack E.—Washington AL 1933; Chicago NL 1938.
Russell, William E.—Los Angeles NL 1974-77-78-81.
Russo, Marius U.—New York AL *1939-41-*42-43.
Ruth, George H.—Boston AL 1915-16-18; New York AL 1921-22-23-26-27-28-32.
Rutherford, John W.—Brooklyn NL 1952.
Ruthven, Richard D.—Philadelphia NL 1980.

Ryan, Cornelius J.—Boston NL 1948.
Ryan, John C.—New York NL 1933-37.
Ryan, L. Nolan—New York NL 1969.
Ryan, Michael J.—Boston AL 1967.
Ryan, Wilfred D.—New York NL *1921-22-23-24; New York AL *1928.
Ryba, Dominic J.—Boston AL 1946.

S

Sadecki, Raymond M.—St. Louis NL 1964; New York NL 1973.
Sain, John F.—Boston NL 1948; New York AL 1951-52-53.
Sakata, Lenn H.—Baltimore AL 1983.
Salazar, Luis E.—San Diego NL 1984.
Salkeld, William F.—Boston NL 1948.
Sallee, Harry F.—New York NL 1917; Cincinnati NL 1919; New York NL *1921.
Salmon, Ruthford E.—Baltimore AL 1969-70-*71.
*Saltzgaver, Otto H.—New York AL *1936-*37.
*Salveson, John T.—New York NL *1933.
Samuel, Juan M.—Philadelphia NL 1983.
Sanders, Raymond F.—St. Louis NL 1942-43-44; Boston NL 1948.
Sands, Charles D.—Pittsburgh NL 1971.
*Sanford, J. Frederick—New York AL *1949-*50.
Sanford, John S.—San Francisco NL 1962.
Sanguillen, Manuel de J.—Pittsburgh NL 1971-79.
Santiago, Jose R.—Boston AL 1967.
*Sarmiento, Manuel E.—Cincinnati NL *1976.
Saucier, Kevin A.—Philadelphia NL 1980.
Sauer, Edward—Chicago NL 1945.
Sawatski, Carl E.—Milwaukee NL 1957.
Sax, Steven L.—Los Angeles NL 1981.
Scarborough, Ray W.—New York AL 1952.
*Scarsella, Leslie G.—Cincinnati NL *1939.
Schaefer, Herman A.—Detroit AL 1907-08.
Schalk, Raymond W.—Chicago AL 1917-1919.
Schallock, Arthur L.—New York AL *1951-53.
Schang, Walter H.—Philadelphia AL 1913-14; Boston AL 1918; New York AL 1921-22-23; Philadelphia AL *1930.
Schenz, Henry L.—New York NL 1951.
Scherrer, William J.—Detroit AL 1984.
Schmandt, Raymond H.—Brooklyn NL 1920.
Schmidt, Charles—Detroit AL 1907-08-09.
Schmidt, Charles J.—Boston NL 1914.
Schmidt, Frederick A.—St. Louis NL 1944-*46.
Schmidt, Michael J.—Philadelphia NL 1980-83.
Schoendienst, Albert F.—St. Louis NL 1946; Milwaukee NL 1957-58.
Schofield, J. Richard—Pittsburgh NL 1960; St. Louis NL 1968.
Schreckengost, Ossee F.—Philadelphia AL 1905.
*Schreiber, Henry W.—Cincinnati NL *1919.
*Schuble, Henry G.—Detroit AL *1934-*35.
Schulte, Frank—Chicago NL 1906-07-08-10.
Schulte, Frederick W.—Washington AL 1933.
*Schulte, John C.—Chicago NL *1929.
Schultz, George W.—St. Louis NL 1964.
Schumacher, Harold H.—New York NL 1933-36-37.
Schupp, Ferdinand M.—New York NL 1917.
Schuster, William C.—Chicago NL 1945.
Scioscia, Michael L.—Los Angeles NL 1981.
Scott, George—Boston AL 1967.
*Scott, James—Chicago AL *1917.
Scott, John W.—New York AL 1922-23.
Scott, L. Everett—Boston AL 1915-16-18; New York AL 1922-23; Washington AL 1925.
*Sears, Kenneth E.—New York AL *1943.
*Seats, Thomas E.—Detroit AL *1940.
Seaver, G. Thomas—New York NL 1969-73.
Sebring, James D.—Pittsburgh NL 1903.
Secory, Frank E.—Chicago NL 1945.
*See, Charles H.—Cincinnati NL *1919.
Seeds, Robert I.—New York AL 1936.
Segui, Diego P.—Boston AL 1975.
Selkirk, George A.—New York AL 1936-37-38-39-41-42.
Seminick, Andrew W.—Philadelphia NL 1950.

WORLD SERIES RECORDS

*Sessi, Walter A.—St. Louis NL *1946.
*Sevcik, John J.—Minnesota AL *1965.
Severeid, Henry L.—Washington AL 1925; New York AL 1926.
Sewell, J. Luther—Washington AL 1933.
Sewell, Joseph W.—Cleveland AL 1920; New York AL 1932.
Seybold, Ralph O.—Philadelphia AL 1905.
Shafer, Arthur J.—New York NL 1912-13.
Shamsky, Arthur L.—New York NL 1969.
Shannon, T. Michael—St. Louis NL 1964-67-68.
Shantz, Robert C.—New York AL 1957-*58-60.
Shaw, Robert J.—Chicago AL 1959.
Shawkey, J. Robert—Philadelphia AL *1913-14; New York AL 1921-22-23-26-*27.
Shea, Francis J.—New York AL 1947-*51.
*Shea, Patrick H.—New York NL *1921.
Shean, David W.—Boston AL 1918.
Sheckard, S. James T.—Chicago NL 1906-07-08-10.
Sheehan, John T.—Brooklyn NL 1920.
*Sheehan, Thomas C.—Pittsburgh NL *1925.
Shelby, John T.—Baltimore AL 1983.
Sheldon, Roland F.—New York AL *1961-*62-64.
*Shelley, Hubert L.—Detroit AL *1935.
Sherdel, William H.—St. Louis NL 1926-28.
Sherry, Lawrence—Los Angeles NL 1959-*63.
*Shinners, Ralph P.—New York NL *1923.
Shirley, A. Newman—St. Louis AL 1944.
Shirley, Ernest R.—Washington AL 1924.
Shocker, Urban J.—New York AL 1926-*27.
*Shoffner, Milburn J.—Cincinnati NL *1939-*40.
Shopay, Thomas M.—Baltimore AL 1971.
Shore, Ernest G.—Boston AL 1915-16.
Shores, William D.—Philadelphia AL *1929-30.
Shorten, Charles H.—Boston AL 1916.
*Shoun, Clyde M.—Chicago NL *1935; Boston NL *1948.
Show, Eric V.—San Diego NL 1984.
Shuba, George T.—Brooklyn NL 1952-53-55.
Siebern, Norman L.—New York AL 1956-58; Boston AL 1967.
Siever, Edward T.—Detroit AL 1907.
*Signer, Walter D.—Chicago NL *1945.
Silvera, Charles A.—New York AL 1949-*50-*51-*52-*53-*55-*56.
Silvestri, Kenneth J.—New York AL *1941; Philadelphia NL 1950.
Simmons, Aloysius H.—Philadelphia AL 1929-30-31; Cincinnati NL 1939.
Simmons, Curtis T.—St. Louis NL 1964.
Simmons, Ted L.—Milwaukee AL 1982.
*Simon, Michael E.—Pittsburgh NL *1909.
Simpson, Harry L.—New York AL 1957.
*Simpson, Wayne K.—Cincinnati NL *1972.
Singleton, Kenneth W.—Baltimore AL 1979-83.
Sisler, Richard A.—St. Louis NL 1946; Philadelphia NL 1950.
Sisti, Sebastian D.—Boston NL 1948.
Skaggs, David L.—Baltimore AL 1979.
*Skinner, E. Camp—New York AL *1922.
Skinner, Robert R.—Pittsburgh NL 1960; St. Louis NL 1964.
Skowron, William J.—New York AL 1955-56-57-58-60-61-62; Los Angeles NL 1963.
Slagle, James J.—Chicago NL *1906-07-*08.
Slaton, James M.—Milwaukee AL 1982.
Slaughter, Enos B.—St. Louis NL 1942-46; New York AL 1956-57-58.
Smith, Alfred J.—New York NL 1936-37.
Smith, Alphonse E.—Cleveland AL 1954; Chicago AL 1959.
Smith, Billy E.—Baltimore AL 1979.
Smith, C. Reginald—Boston AL 1967; Los Angeles NL 1977-78-81.
Smith, Clay J.—Detroit AL 1940.
Smith, Earl S.—New York NL 1921-22; Pittsburgh NL 1925-27; St. Louis NL 1928.
Smith, Elmer J.—Cleveland AL 1920; New York AL 1922-*23.
*Smith, Frank E.—Chicago AL *1906.
Smith, Harold W.—Pittsburgh NL 1960.
Smith, Harry T.—Pittsburgh NL 1903.
*Smith, J. Carlisle—Boston NL *1914.
Smith, James L.—New York NL *1917; Cincinnati NL 1919.
Smith, Lonnie—Philadelphia NL 1980; St. Louis NL 1982.
Smith, Osborne E.—St. Louis NL 1982.
Smith, Robert E.—Chicago NL 1932.
Smith, Sherrod M.—Brooklyn NL 1916-20.
Snider, Edwin D.—Brooklyn NL 1949-52-53-55-56; Los Angeles NL 1959.
Snodgrass, Frederick C.—New York NL 1911-12-13.
Snyder, Frank J.—New York NL 1921-22-23-24.
Snyder, Russell H.—Baltimore AL 1966.
*Solomon, Eddie—Los Angeles NL *1974.
*Sorrell, Victor G.—Detroit AL *1934-*35.
Sosa, Elias—Los Angeles NL 1977.
*Sothoron, Allan S.—St. Louis NL *1926.
Southworth, William H.—New York NL 1924; St. Louis NL 1926.
Spahn, Warren E.—Boston NL 1948; Milwaukee NL 1957-58.
Sparma, Joseph B.—Detroit AL 1968.
Speaker, Tristram—Boston AL 1912-15; Cleveland AL 1920.
Speece, Byron F.—Washington AL 1924.
*Speer, George N.—Detroit AL *1909.
Spencer, George E.—New York NL 1951.
*Spencer, Glenn E.—New York NL *1933.
Spencer, James L.—New York AL 1978.
Spencer, Roy H.—Pittsburgh NL *1925-27; New York NL *1936.
Spiezio, Edward W.—St. Louis NL *1964-67-68.
Splittorff, Paul W.—Kansas City AL 1980.
Spooner, Karl B.—Brooklyn NL 1955.
*Sprague, Edward N.—Cincinnati NL *1972.
Stafford, William C.—New York AL 1960-61-62-*63-*64.
Stahl, Charles S.—Boston AL 1903.
Stahl, J. Garland—Boston AL *1903-12.
Stainback, George T.—Chicago NL *1935; Detroit AL *1940; New York AL 1942-43.
Staley, Gerald L.—Chicago AL 1959.
*Stanceu, Charles—New York AL *1941.
Stanage, Oscar H.—Detroit AL 1909.
Stange, A. Lee—Boston AL 1967.
Stanhouse, Donald J.—Baltimore AL 1979.
Stanky, Edward R.—Brooklyn NL 1947; Boston NL 1948; New York NL 1951.
Stanley, Frederick B.—New York AL 1976-77-78.
Stanley, Mitchell J.—Detroit AL 1968.
Stargell, Wilver D.—Pittsburgh NL 1971-79.
*Starr, Raymond F.—Chicago NL *1945.
Staub, Daniel J.—New York NL 1973.
Steinfeldt, Harry M.—Chicago NL 1906-07-08-10.
Stengel, Charles D.—Brooklyn NL 1916; New York NL *1921-22-23.
Stennett, Renaldo A.—Pittsburgh NL 1979.
Stephens, Vernon D.—St. Louis AL 1944.
Stephenson, J. Riggs—Chicago NL 1929-32.
Stephenson, Jerry J.—Boston AL 1967.
Stephenson, Walter M.—Chicago NL 1935.
Stewart, David N.—Los Angeles NL 1981.
Stewart, James F.—Cincinnati NL 1970.
Stewart, Samuel L.—Baltimore AL 1979-83.
Stewart, Walter C.—Washington AL 1933.
*Stigman, Richard L.—Minnesota AL *1965.
Stirnweiss, George H.—New York AL 1943-47-49.
Stock, Milton J.—Philadelphia NL 1915.
Stoddard, Timothy P.—Baltimore AL 1979-*83.
Stone, George H.—New York NL 1973.
Stone, Steven M.—Baltimore AL 1979.
Stottlemyre, Melvin L.—New York AL 1964.
*Stout, Allyn M.—St. Louis NL *1931.
*Strand, Paul E.—Boston NL *1914.
Strang, Samuel N.—New York NL 1905.
Strickland, George B.—Cleveland AL 1954.
Strunk, Amos A.—Philadelphia AL 1910-11-13-14; Boston AL 1918.

Stuart, Richard L.—Pittsburgh NL 1960; Los Angeles NL 1966.
Stuper, John A.—St. Louis NL 1982.
Sturdivant, Thomas V.—New York AL 1955-56-57-*58.
*Sturgeon, Robert H.—Boston NL *1948.
Sturm, John P.—New York AL 1941.
*Suggs, George F.—Detroit AL *1908.
*Sullivan, John J.—Chicago AL *1919.
*Sullivan, Joseph—Detroit AL *1935.
Sullivan, William J., Sr.—Chicago AL 1906.
Sullivan, William J., Jr.—Detroit AL 1940.
Summa, Homer W.—Philadelphia AL 1929-*30.
Summers, John J.—Detroit AL 1984.
Summers, Oren E.—Detroit AL 1908-09.
Sundra, Stephen R.—New York AL *1938-39.
Sutter, H. Bruce—St. Louis NL 1982.
Sutton, Donald H.—Los Angeles NL *1966-74-77-78; Milwaukee AL 1982.
Swift, Robert V.—Detroit AL 1945.
Swoboda, Ronald A.—New York NL 1969.

T

Tannehill, Lee F.—Chicago AL 1906.
Tartabull, Jose—Boston AL 1967.
Tate, H. Bennett—Washington AL 1924-*25.
Taylor, James H.—Brooklyn NL 1947.
Taylor, James W.—Brooklyn NL *1920; Chicago NL 1929-*32.
*Taylor, John W.—Chicago NL *1906.
*Taylor, Luther H.—New York NL *1905.
Taylor, Ronald W.—St. Louis NL 1964; New York NL 1969.
Taylor, Thomas L.—Washington AL 1924.
*Taylor, William M.—New York NL *1954.
Tebbetts, George R.—Detroit AL 1940.
Tekulve, Kenton C.—Pittsburgh NL 1979.
Templeton, Garry L.—San Diego NL 1984.
Tenace, F. Gene—Oakland AL 1972-73-74; St. Louis NL 1982.
Terry, Ralph W.—New York AL 1960-61-62-63-64.
Terry, William H.—New York NL 1924-33-36.
Tesreau, Charles M.—New York NL 1912-13-17.
Thevenow, Thomas J.—St. Louis NL 1926-28.
Theodore, George B.—New York NL 1973.
Thomas, Alphonse T.—Washington AL 1933.
Thomas, Chester D.—Boston AL *1912-15-16; Cleveland AL 1920.
Thomas, Derrel—Los Angeles NL 1981.
Thomas, Frederick H.—Boston AL 1918.
Thomas, George E.—Boston AL 1967.
Thomas, J. Gorman—Milwaukee AL 1982.
Thomas, Ira F.—Detroit AL 1908; Philadelphia AL 1910-11-*13-*14.
Thomas, Myles L.—New York AL 1926-*27-*28.
Thomasson, Gary L.—New York AL 1978.
Thompson, Donald N.—Brooklyn NL 1953.
Thompson, Eugene E.—Cincinnati NL 1939-40.
Thompson, Henry—New York NL 1951-54.
Thompson, John G.—Pittsburgh NL 1903.
*Thompson, James A.—Philadelphia AL *1914.
*Thompson, John S.—Philadelphia NL *1950.
*Thompson, L. Fresco—Pittsburgh NL *1925.
Thomson, Robert B.—New York NL 1951.
Thorpe, James F.—New York NL *1913-17.
Throneberry, Marvin E.—New York AL 1958.
Thurmond, Mark A.—San Diego NL 1984.
Tiant, Luis C.—Boston AL 1975.
Tidrow, Richard W.—New York AL 1976-77-78.
*Tincup, A. Ben—Philadelphia NL *1915.
Tinker, Joseph B.—Chicago NL 1906-07-08-10.
Tinning, Lyle F.—Chicago NL 1932.
Tipton, Joseph J.—Cleveland AL 1948.
Tobin, James A.—Detroit AL 1945.
Todt, Philip J.—Philadelphia AL 1931.
Tolan, Robert—St. Louis NL 1967-68; Cincinnati NL 1970-72.
Tolson, Charles J.—Chicago NL 1929.
Toney, Frederick A.—New York NL 1921.
Toporcer, George—St. Louis NL 1926.

*Torborg, Jeffrey A.—Los Angeles NL *1965-*1966.
Torgeson, C. Earl—Boston NL 1948; Chicago AL 1959.
Torre, Frank J.—Milwaukee NL 1957-58.
Torrez, Michael A.—New York AL 1977.
Towne, Jay K.—Chicago AL 1906.
Tracewski, Richard J.—Los Angeles NL 1963-65; Detroit AL 1968.
*Trail, Chester B.—New York AL *1964.
Trammell, Alan S.—Detroit AL 1984.
Traynor, Harold J.—Pittsburgh NL 1925-27.
Tresh, Thomas M.—New York AL 1962-63-64.
*Triandos, C. Gus—New York AL *1953.
Trillo, J. Manuel—Philadelphia NL 1980.
*Triplett, H. Coaker—St. Louis NL *1942.
Trout, Paul H.—Detroit AL 1940-45.
Trowbridge, Robert—Milwaukee NL 1957-*58.
Trucks, Virgil O.—Detroit AL 1945; New York AL *1958.
Tucker, Thurman L.—Cleveland AL 1948.
Turley, Robert L.—New York AL 1955-56-57-58-60-*61-*62.
Turner, James R.—Cincinnati NL 1940; New York AL 1942-*43.
Turner, Thomas R.—St. Louis AL 1944.
*Twitty, Jeffrey D.—Kansas City AL *1980.
Tyler, George A.—Boston NL 1914; Chicago NL 1918.

U

*Uecker, Robert G.—St. Louis NL *1964.
Uhlaender, Theodore O.—Cincinnati NL 1972.
Uhle, George E.—Cleveland AL 1920.
Unser, Delbert B.—Philadelphia NL 1980.

V

Valdespino, Hilario—Minnesota AL 1965.
Valenzuela, Fernando—Los Angeles NL 1981.
Vance, Arthur C.—St. Louis NL 1934.
Vandenberg, Harold H.—Chicago NL 1945.
Vander Meer, John S.—Cincinnati NL *1939-40.
Vaughan, J. Floyd—Brooklyn NL 1947.
Vaughn, James L.—Chicago NL 1918.
Veach, Robert H.—Washington AL 1925.
Veale, Robert A.—Pittsburgh NL 1971.
Veil, Frederick W.—Pittsburgh NL 1903.
Velez, Otoniel—New York AL 1976.
Verban, Emil M.—St. Louis NL 1944.
*Vergez, John L.—New York NL *1933.
Versalles, Zoilo—Minnesota AL 1965.
*Vick, Henry A.—St. Louis NL *1926.
Virdon, William C.—Pittsburgh NL 1960.
Virgil, Osvaldo J.—Philadelphia NL 1983.
Voiselle, William S.—Boston NL 1948.
Vuckovich, Peter D.—Milwaukee AL 1982.
*Vukovich, George S.—Philadelphia NL *1980.
*Vukovich, John C.—Philadelphia NL *1980.

W

*Waddell, George E.—Philadelphia AL *1905.
Wade, Benjamin S.—Brooklyn NL *1952-53.
*Wagner, Charles T.—Boston AL *1946.
Wagner, Charles F.—Boston AL 1912-*15-*16-*18.
Wagner, Harold E.—Boston AL 1946.
Wagner, John P.—Pittsburgh NL 1903-09.
Waitkus, Edward S.—Philadelphia NL 1950.
Walberg, George E.—Philadelphia AL 1929-30-31.
Walk, Robert V.—Philadelphia NL 1980.
Walker, Albert B.—Brooklyn NL *1952-*53-*55-56.
Walker, Clarence W.—Boston AL 1916.
Walker, Fred—Brooklyn NL 1941-47.
Walker, Gerald H.—Detroit AL 1934-35.
Walker, Harry W.—St. Louis NL 1942-43-46.
Walker, Harvey W.—Detroit AL 1945.
Walker, James Luke—Pittsburgh NL 1971.
*Walker, James R.—Chicago NL *1918.
Walker, William H.—St. Louis NL 1934.
*Walls, R. Lee—Los Angeles NL *1963.

Walsh, Edward A.—Chicago AL 1906.
Walsh, James C.—Philadelphia AL *1913-14; Boston AL 1916.
*Walsh, Thomas J.—Chicago NL *1906-*07.
Walters, William H.—Cincinnati NL 1939-40.
Wambsganss, William A.—Cleveland AL 1920.
Waner, Lloyd J.—Pittsburgh NL 1927.
Waner, Paul G.—Pittsburgh NL 1927.
Ward, Aaron L.—New York AL 1921-22-23-*26.
*Ward, Charles W.—Brooklyn NL *1920.
*Warden, Jonathan E.—Detroit AL *1968.
Warneke, Lonnie—Chicago NL 1932-35-*45.
Warwick, Carl W.—St. Louis NL 1964.
Wasdell, James C.—Brooklyn NL 1941.
Washburn, Ray C.—St. Louis NL *1964-67-68; Cincinnati NL 1970.
Washington, Claudell—Oakland AL 1974.
Washington, Herbert—Oakland AL 1974.
Washington, U. L.—Kansas City AL 1980.
Waslewski, Gary L.—Boston AL 1967.
Wathan, John D.—Kansas City AL 1980.
Watkins, George A.—St. Louis NL 1930-31.
Watson, John R.—New York NL 1923-24.
Watson, Robert J.—New York AL 1981.
Watt, Edward D.—Baltimore AL *1966-69-70-71.
Weatherly, C. Roy—New York AL 1943.
*Weaver, Arthur C.—Pittsburgh NL *1903.
Weaver, George D.—Chicago AL 1917-19.
Weaver, Montgomery M.—Washington AL 1933.
*Weaver, Orville F.—Chicago NL *1910.
Webb, James L.—Detroit AL 1945.
Weis, Albert J.—New York NL 1969.
*Weiser, Harry—Philadelphia NL *1915.
Welch, Robert L.—Los Angeles NL 1978-81.
*Wells, Edwin L.—New York AL *1932.
Wensloff, Charles W.—New York AL *1943-47.
*Wera, Julian V.—New York AL *1927.
Werber, William M.—Cincinnati NL 1939-40.
Wert, Donald R.—Detroit AL 1968.
Wertz, Victor W.—Cleveland AL 1954.
Westlake, Waldon T.—Cleveland AL 1954.
Westrum, Wesley N.—New York NL 1951-54.
*Whaling, Albert—Boston NL *1914.
Wheat, Zachary D.—Brooklyn NL 1916-20.
Whitaker, Louis R.—Detroit AL 1984.
White, Ernest D.—St. Louis NL 1942-43; Boston NL *1948.
White, Frank—Kansas City AL 1980.
White, G. Harris—Chicago AL 1906.
White, Joyner C.—Detroit AL 1934-35.
White, Roy H.—New York AL 1976-77-78.
White, William D.—St. Louis NL 1964.
Whitehead, Burgess U.—St. Louis NL 1934; New York NL 1936-37.
Whitehill, Earl O.—Washington AL 1933.
Whiteman, George—Boston AL 1918.
Whitman, Richard C.—Brooklyn NL 1949; Philadelphia NL 1950.
Whitson, Eddie L.—San Diego NL 1984.
Whitted, George B.—Boston NL 1914; Philadelphia NL 1915.
Wicker, Kemp C.—New York AL *1936-37.
*Wiesler, Robert G.—New York AL *1955.
Wiggins, Alan A.—San Diego NL 1984.
Wilcox, Milton E.—Cincinnati NL 1970; Detroit AL 1984.
*Wilhelm, Irving K.—Pittsburgh NL *1903.
Wilhelm, J. Hoyt—New York NL 1954.
Wilhoit, Joseph W.—New York NL 1917.
Wilkinson, Roy H.—Chicago AL 1919.
Wilks, Theodore—St. Louis NL 1944-46.
Willett, Robert E.—Detroit AL *1907-*08-09.
Willey, Carlton F.—Milwaukee NL 1958.
*Willhite, J. Nicholas—Los Angeles NL *1965.
Williams, Claude P.—Chicago AL 1917-19.
Williams, David C.—New York NL 1951-54.
Williams, Dewey E.—Chicago NL 1945.
Williams, E. Dibrell—Philadelphia AL *1930-31.
Williams, Richard H.—Brooklyn NL *1952-53.
Williams, Stanley W.—Los Angeles NL 1959; New York AL 1963-*64.
Williams, Theodore S.—Boston AL 1946.

*Williamson, N. Howard—St. Louis NL *1928.
Willis, Ronald E.—St. Louis NL 1967-68.
Willis, Victor G.—Pittsburgh NL 1909.
Willoughby, James A.—Boston AL 1975.
Wills, Maurice M.—Los Angeles NL 1959-63-65-66.
Wilson, Arthur E.—New York NL 1911-12-13.
Wilson, George W.—New York AL 1956.
Wilson, James—St. Louis NL 1928-30-31; Cincinnati NL 1940.
Wilson, J. Owen—Pittsburgh NL 1909.
Wilson, Lewis R.—New York NL 1924; Chicago NL 1929.
Wilson, R. Earl—Detroit AL 1968.
*Wilson, Walter W.—Detroit AL *1945.
Wilson, Willie J.—Kansas City AL 1980.
Wiltse, George L.—New York NL *1905-11-*12-13.
Winfield, David M.—New York AL 1981.
Wingo, Ivy B.—Cincinnati NL 1919.
Winter, George L.—Boston AL *1903; Detroit AL 1908.
Wise, Kendall C.—Milwaukee NL 1958.
Wise, Richard C.—Boston AL 1975.
Witt, George A.—Pittsburgh NL 1960.
Witt, Lawton W.—New York AL 1922-23.
*Wolfgang, Meldon J.—Chicago AL *1917.
Wood, Joseph—Boston AL 1912-*15; Cleveland AL 1920.
Woodeshick, Harold J.—St. Louis NL 1967.
Woodling, Eugene R.—New York AL 1949-50-51-52-53.
Woodward, William F.—Cincinnati NL 1970.
Works, Ralph T.—Detroit AL 1909.
Worthington, Allan F.—New York NL *1954; Minnesota AL 1965.
Wortman, William L.—Chicago NL 1918.
Wright, F. Glenn—Pittsburgh NL 1925-27.
Wyatt, John T.—Boston AL 1967.
Wyatt, J. Whitlow—Brooklyn NL 1941.
Wyckoff, J. Weldon—Philadelphia AL *1913-14; Boston AL *1916.
Wynn, Early—Cleveland AL 1954; Chicago AL 1959.
Wynn, James S.—Los Angeles NL 1974.
Wyse, Henry W.—Chicago NL 1945.

Y

Yastrzemski, Carl M.—Boston AL 1967-75.
Yde, Emil O.—Pittsburgh NL 1925-27.
Yeager, Stephen W.—Los Angeles NL 1974-77-78-81.
*Yerkes, C. Carroll—Philadelphia AL *1929.
Yerkes, Stephen D.—Boston AL 1912.
York, Rudolph P.—Detroit AL 1940-45; Boston AL 1946.
Yost, Edgar F.—Milwaukee AL 1982.
Young, Denton T.—Boston AL 1903.
*Youngblood, Joel R.—Cincinnati NL *1976.
Youngs, Ross—New York NL 1921-22-23-24.
Yount, Robin R.—Milwaukee AL 1982.
Yvars, Salvatore A.—New York NL 1951.

Z

Zachary, Jonathan T.—Washington AL 1924-25; New York AL 1928.
Zachry, Patrick P.—Cincinnati NL 1976.
*Zahn, Geoffrey C.—Los Angeles NL *1974.
*Zahniser, Paul V.—Washington AL *1924.
Zarilla, Allen L.—St. Louis AL 1944.
Zeber, George W.—New York AL 1977.
Zeider, Rolla H.—Chicago NL 1918.
Zimmer, Donald W.—Brooklyn NL 1955; Los Angeles NL 1959.
Zimmerman, Gerald R.—Cincinnati NL 1961; Minnesota AL 1965.
Zimmerman, Henry—Chicago NL 1907-*08-10; New York NL 1917.
*Zoldak, Samuel W.—St. Louis AL *1944; Cleveland AL *1948.
Zuber, William H.—New York AL *1943; Boston AL 1946.

WORLD SERIES MANAGERS (69)

Alston, Walter E.—Brooklyn NL 1955-56; Los Angeles NL 1959-63-65-66-74.
Altobelli, Joseph S.—Baltimore AL 1983.
Anderson, George L.—Cincinnati NL 1970-72-75-76; Detroit AL 1984.
Baker, Delmer D.—Detroit AL 1940.
Barrow, Edward G.—Boston AL 1918.
Bauer, Henry A.—Baltimore AL 1966.
Berra, Lawrence P.—New York AL 1964; New York NL 1973.
Boudreau, Louis—Cleveland AL 1948.
Bush, Owen J.—Pittsburgh NL 1927.
Carrigan, William F.—Boston AL 1915-16.
Chance, Frank L.—Chicago NL 1906-07-08-10.
Clarke, Fred C.—Pittsburgh NL 1903-09.
Cochrane, Gordon S.—Detroit AL 1934-35.
Collins, James J.—Boston AL 1903.
Cronin, Joseph E.—Washington AL 1933; Boston AL 1946.
Dark, Alvin R.—San Francisco NL 1962; Oakland AL 1974.
Dressen, Charles W.—Brooklyn NL 1952-53.
Durocher, Leo E.—Brooklyn NL 1941; New York NL 1951-54.
Dyer, Edwin H.—St. Louis NL 1946.
Frey, James G.—Kansas City AL 1980.
Frisch, Frank F.—St. Louis NL 1934.
Gleason, William—Chicago AL 1919.
Green, G. Dallas—Philadelphia NL 1980.
Grimm, Charles J.—Chicago NL 1932-35-45.
Haney, Fred G.—Milwaukee NL 1957-58.
Harris, Stanley R.—Washington AL 1924-25; New York AL 1947.
Hartnett, Charles L.—Chicago NL 1938.
Herzog, Dorrel N.—St. Louis NL 1982.
Hodges, Gilbert R.—New York NL 1969.
Hornsby, Rogers—St. Louis NL 1926.
Houk, Ralph G.—New York AL 1961-62-63.
Huggins, Miller J.—New York AL 1921-22-23-26-27-28.
Hutchinson, Frederick C.—Cincinnati NL 1961.
Jennings, Hugh A.—Detroit AL 1907-08-09.
Johnson, Darrell D.—Boston AL 1975.
Jones, Fielder A.—Chicago AL 1906.
Keane, John J.—St. Louis NL 1964.
Kuenn, Harvey E.—Milwaukee AL 1982.
Lasorda, Thomas C.—Los Angeles NL 1977-78-81.
Lemon, Robert G.—New York AL 1978-81.
Lopez, Alfonso R.—Cleveland AL 1954; Chicago AL 1959.
Mack, Connie—Philadelphia AL 1905-10-11-13-14-29-30-31.
Martin, Alfred M.—New York AL 1976-77.
McCarthy, Joseph V.—Chicago NL 1929; New York AL 1932-36-37-38-39-41-42-43.
McGraw, John J.—New York NL 1905-11-12-13-17-21-22-23-24.
McKechnie, William B.—Pittsburgh NL 1925; St. Louis NL 1928; Cincinnati NL 1939-40.
Mele, Sabath A.—Minnesota AL 1965.
Mitchell, Fred F.—Chicago NL 1918.
Moran, Patrick J.—Philadelphia NL 1915; Cincinnati NL 1919.
Murtaugh, Daniel E.—Pittsburgh NL 1960-71.
O'Neill, Stephen F.—Detroit AL 1945.
Owens, Paul F.—Philadelphia NL 1983.
Robinson, Wilbert—Brooklyn NL 1916-20.
Rowland, Clarence H.—Chicago AL 1917.
Sawyer, Edwin M.—Philadelphia NL 1950.
Schoendienst, Albert F.—St. Louis NL 1967-68.
Sewell, J. Luther—St. Louis AL 1944.
Shotton, Burton E.—Brooklyn NL 1947-49.
Smith, E. Mayo—Detroit AL 1968.
Southworth, William H.—St. Louis NL 1942-43-44; Boston NL 1948.
Speaker, Tris E.—Cleveland AL 1920.
Stahl, J. Garland—Boston AL 1912.
Stallings, George T.—Boston NL 1914.
Stengel, Charles D.—New York AL 1949-50-51-52-53-55-56-57-58-60.
Street, Charles E.—St. Louis NL 1930-31.
Tanner, Charles W.—Pittsburgh NL 1979.
Terry, William H.—New York NL 1933-36-37.
Weaver, Earl S.—Baltimore AL 1969-70-71-79.
Williams, Richard H.—Boston AL 1967; Oakland AL 1972-73; San Diego NL 1984.

WORLD SERIES RECORDS
WINNING, LOSING CLUBS

WINNING CLUBS

New York, A.L. .... 22—1923-27-28-32-36-37-38-39-41-43-47-49-50-51-52-53-56-58-61-62-77-78
St. Louis, N.L. .... 9—1926-31-34-42-44-46-64-67-82
Boston, A.L. .... 5—1903-12-15-16-18
⌈Philadelphia, A.L. .... 5—1910-11-13-29-30
 Kansas City, A.L. .... 0—
⌊Oakland, A.L. .... 3—1972-73-74
New York, N.L. .... 5—1905-21-22-33-54
Pittsburgh, N.L. .... 5—1909-25-60-71-79
⌈Los Angeles, N.L. .... 4—1959-63-65-81
⌊Brooklyn, N.L. .... 1—1955
Cincinnati, N.L. .... 4—1919-40-75-76
Detroit, A.L. .... 4—1935-45-68-84
⌈Baltimore A.L. .... 3—1966-70-83
⌊St. Louis, A.L. .... 0—
Chicago, N.L. .... 2—1907-08
Chicago A.L. .... 2—1906-17
Cleveland, A.L. .... 2—1920-48
⌈Milwaukee, N.L. .... 1—1957
⌊Boston, N.L. .... 1—1914
Washington A.L. .... 1—1924
New York, N.L. (Mets) .... 1—1969
Philadelphia, N.L. .... 1—1980

American League Has Won 47, National 34

LOSING CLUBS

New York, A.L. .... 11—1921-22-26-42-55-57-60-63-64-76-81
⌈New York, N.L. .... 9—1911-12-13-17-23-24-36-37-51
⌊San Francisco, N.L. .... 1—1962
⌈Brooklyn, N.L. .... 8—1916-20-41-47-49-52-53-56
⌊Los Angeles, N.L. .... 4—1966-74-77-78
Chicago, N.L. .... 8—1906-10-18-29-32-35-38-45
Detroit, A.L. .... 5—1907-08-09-34-40
St. Louis, N.L. .... 4—1928-30-43-68
Cincinnati, N.L. .... 4—1939-61-70-72
⌈St. Louis, A.L. .... 1—1944
⌊Baltimore, A.L. .... 3—1969-71-79
⌈Philadelphia, A.L. .... 3—1905-14-31
⌊Kansas City, A.L. .... 0—
⌈Washington, A.L. .... 2—1925-33
⌊Minnesota, A.L. .... 1—1965
Boston, A.L. .... 3—1946-67-75
Philadelphia, N.L. .... 3—1915-50-83
Pittsburgh, N.L. .... 2—1903-27
Chicago, A.L. .... 2—1919-59
⌈Milwaukee, N.L. .... 1—1958
⌊Boston, N.L. .... 1—1948
Cleveland, A.L. .... 1—1954
New York, N.L. (Mets) .... 1—1973
Kansas City, A.L. .... 1—1980
Milwaukee, A.L. .... 1—1982
San Diego, N.L. .... 1—1984

SERIES WON

4-game Series—6—New York A.L., 1927, 1928, 1932, 1938, 1939, 1950.
              1—Boston N.L., 1914.
              1—New York N.L., 1954.
              1—Los Angeles N.L., 1963.
              1—Baltimore A.L., 1966.
              1—Cincinnati N.L., 1976.

WORLD SERIES RECORDS

5-game Series— 5—New York A.L., 1937, 1941, 1943, 1949, 1961.
3—Philadelphia A.L., 1910, 1913, 1929.
3—New York N.L., 1905, 1922 (1 tie), 1933.
2—Chicago N.L., 1907 (1 tie), 1908.
2—Boston A.L., 1915, 1916.
2—Baltimore A.L., 1970, 1983.
1—St. Louis N.L., 1942.
1—New York N.L. (Mets), 1969.
1—Oakland A.L., 1974.
1—Detroit A.L., 1984.

6-game Series— 6—New York A.L., 1923, 1936, 1951, 1953, 1977, 1978.
2—Philadelphia A.L., 1911, 1930.
2—Chicago A.L., 1906, 1917.
2—Los Angeles N.L., 1959, 1981.
1—Boston A.L., 1918.
1—Detroit A.L., 1935.
1—St. Louis N.L., 1944.
1—Cleveland A.L., 1948.
1—Philadelphia N.L., 1980.

7-game Series— 7—St. Louis N.L., 1926, 1931, 1934, 1946, 1964, 1967, 1982.
5—New York A.L., 1947, 1952, 1956, 1958, 1962.
5—Pittsburgh N.L., 1909, 1925, 1960, 1971, 1979.
2—Detroit A.L., 1945, 1968.
2—Oakland A.L., 1972, 1973.
2—Cincinnati N.L., 1940, 1975.
⎡1—Los Angeles N.L., 1965.
⎣1—Brooklyn N.L., 1955.
1—Cleveland A.L., 1920.
1—Washington A.L., 1924.
1—Milwaukee N.L., 1957.

8-game Series— 2—Boston A.L., 1903, 1912 (1 tie).
1—Cincinnati N.L., 1919.
1—New York N.L., 1921.

SERIES LOST

4-game Series— 2—Chicago N.L., 1932, 1938.
2—New York A.L., 1963, 1976.
1—Philadelphia A.L., 1914.
1—Pittsburgh N.L., 1927.
1—St. Louis N.L., 1928.
1—Cincinnati N.L., 1939.
1—Philadelphia N.L., 1950.
1—Cleveland A.L., 1954.
1—Los Angeles N.L., 1966.

5-game Series— 3—Brooklyn N.L., 1916, 1941, 1949.
2—Detroit A.L., 1907 (1 tie), 1908.
2—Chicago N.L., 1910, 1929.
2—New York N.L. 1913, 1937.
2—New York A.L., 1922 (1 tie), 1942.
2—Cincinnati N.L., 1961, 1970.
2—Philadelphia N.L., 1915, 1983.
1—Philadelphia A.L., 1905.
1—Washington A.L., 1933.
1—St. Louis N.L., 1943.
1—Baltimore A.L., 1969.
1—Los Angeles N.L., 1974.
1—San Diego N.L., 1984.

6-game Series— 5—New York N.L., 1911, 1917, 1923, 1936, 1951.
3—Chicago N.L., 1906, 1918, 1935.
⎡1—Brooklyn N.L., 1953.
⎣2—Los Angeles N.L., 1977, 1978.
1—St. Louis N.L., 1930.
1—St. Louis A.L., 1944.
1—Boston N.L., 1948.
1—Chicago A.L., 1959.
1—Kansas City A.L., 1980.
1—New York A.L., 1981.

7-game Series—5—New York A.L., 1926, 1955, 1957, 1960, 1964.
                4—Brooklyn N.L., 1920, 1947, 1952, 1956.
                3—Detroit A.L., 1909, 1934, 1940.
                3—Boston A.L., 1946, 1967, 1975.
                2—Baltimore A.L., 1971, 1979.
                ⎡1—New York N.L., 1924.
                ⎣1—San Francisco N.L., 1962.
                ⎡1—Minnesota A.L., 1965.
                ⎣1—Washington A.L., 1925.
                1—Philadelphia A.L., 1931.
                1—Chicago N.L., 1945.
                1—Milwaukee N.L., 1958.
                1—St. Louis N.L., 1968.
                1—Cincinnati N.L., 1972.
                1—New York N.L., (Mets) 1973.
                1—Milwaukee A.L., 1982.

8-game Series—1—Pittsburgh N.L., 1903.
                1—New York N.L., 1912 (1 tie).
                1—Chicago A.L., 1919.
                1—New York A.L., 1921.

WORLD SERIES STANDINGS
Series Won and Lost

American League

	W.	L.	Pct.
New York	22	11	.667
Cleveland	2	1	.667
⎡Oakland	3	0	1.000
⎣Philadelphia	5	3	.625
Boston	5	3	.625
Chicago	2	2	.500
⎡Baltimore	3	3	.500
⎣St. Louis	0	1	.000
Detroit	4	5	.444
⎡Washington	1	2	.333
⎣Minnesota	0	1	.000
Kansas City	0	1	.000
Milwaukee	0	1	.000
Totals	47	34	.580

National League

	W.	L.	Pct.
St. Louis	9	4	.692
Pittsburgh	5	2	.714
⎡Boston	1	1	.500
⎣Milwaukee	1	1	.500
New York Mets	1	1	.500
Cincinnati	4	4	.500
⎡New York	5	9	.357
⎣San Francisco	0	1	.000
⎡Los Angeles	4	4	.500
⎣Brooklyn	1	8	.111
Philadelphia	1	3	.250
Chicago	2	8	.200
San Diego	0	1	.000
Totals	34	47	.420

Games Won and Lost

American League

	W.	L.	Tie	Pct.
New York	109	77	1	.586
⎡Baltimore	19	14		.576
⎣St. Louis	2	4		.333
⎡Philadelphia	24	19		.558
⎣Oakland	12	7		.632
Boston	30	22	1	.577
Cleveland	9	8		.529
Chicago	13	13		.500
Detroit	26	29	1	.473
Milwaukee	3	4		.429
⎡Minnesota	3	4		.429
⎣Washington	8	11		.421
Kansas City	2	4		.333
Totals	260	216	3	.546

National League

	W.	L.	Tie	Pct.
New York Mets	7	5		.583
⎡Los Angeles	21	23		.477
⎣Brooklyn	20	36		.357
⎡Boston	6	4		.600
⎣Milwaukee	7	7		.500
St. Louis	42	40		.512
⎡New York	39	41	2	.488
⎣San Francisco	3	4		.429
Pittsburgh	23	24		.489
Cincinnati	22	25		.468
Chicago	19	33	1	.365
Philadelphia	6	14		.300
San Diego	1	4		.200
Totals	216	260	3	.454

CITY-BY-CITY BREAKDOWN
Series Games Played Home and Away

American League

	Ser.	G.	Ho.	Abr.
New York	33	187	91	96
Philadelphia	8	43	20	23
Oakland	3	19	10	9
Detroit	9	56	28	28
Boston	8	53	28	25
Chicago	4	26	13	13
Washington	3	19	10	9
Minnesota	1	7	4	3
Cleveland	3	17	9	8
St. Louis	1	6	3	3
Baltimore	6	33	17	16
Milwaukee	1	7	3	4
Kansas City	1	6	3	3
Totals	81	479	239	240

National League

	Ser.	G.	Ho.	Abr.
New York	14	82	41	41
San Francisco	1	7	4	3
Brooklyn	9	56	28	28
Los Angeles	8	44	21	23
St. Louis	13	82	41	41
Chicago	10	53	27	26
Cincinnati	8	47	24	23
Pittsburgh	7	47	23	24
Milwaukee	2	14	7	7
Boston	2	10	5	5
Philadelphia	4	20	11	9
New York Mets	2	12	6	6
San Diego	1	5	2	3
Totals	81	479	240	239

Series Games Played in Each City

New York	138
St. Louis	44
Chicago	40
Boston	33
Philadelphia	31
Brooklyn	28
Detroit	28
Cincinnati	24
Pittsburgh	23
Los Angeles	21
Baltimore	17
Washington	10
Oakland	10
Milwaukee	10
Cleveland	9
San Francisco	4
Minn. (Bloomington)	4
Kansas City	3
San Diego	2

WORLD SERIES TIE GAMES

October 8, 1907—at Chicago, 12 innings, Chicago N.L. 3, Detroit A.L. 3.
October 9, 1912—at Boston, 11 innings, Boston A.L. 6, New York N.L. 6.
October 5, 1922—at New York, 10 innings, New York A.L. 3, New York N.L. 3.

WORLD SERIES SHUTOUT GAMES (92)

October   2, 1903—Dinneen, Boston A.L. 3, Pittsburgh N.L. 0, 3 hits.
October 13, 1903—Dinneen, Boston A.L. 3, Pittsburgh N.L. 0, 4 hits.
October   9, 1905—Mathewson, New York N.L. 3, Philadelphia A.L. 0, 4 hits.
October 10, 1905—Bender, Philadelphia A.L. 3, New York N.L. 0, 4 hits.
October 12, 1905—Mathewson, New York N.L. 9, Philadelphia A.L. 0, 4 hits.
October 13, 1905—McGinnity, New York N.L. 1, Philadelphia A.L. 0, 5 hits.
October 14, 1905—Mathewson, New York N.L. 2, Philadelphia A.L. 0, 6 hits.
October 11, 1906—Walsh, Chicago A.L. 3, Chicago N.L. 0, 2 hits.
October 12, 1906—Brown, Chicago N.L. 1, Chicago A.L. 0, 2 hits.
October 12, 1907—Brown, Chicago N.L. 2, Detroit A.L. 0, 7 hits.
October 13, 1908—Brown, Chicago N.L. 3, Detroit A.L. 0, 4 hits.
October 14, 1908—Overall, Chicago N.L. 2, Detroit A.L. 0, 3 hits.
October 12, 1909—Mullin, Detroit A.L. 5, Pittsburgh N.L. 0, 5 hits.
October 16, 1909—Adams, Pittsburgh N.L. 8, Detroit A.L. 0, 6 hits.
October   8, 1913—Mathewson, New York N.L. 3, Philadelphia A.L. 0, 8 hits (ten innings).
October 10, 1914—James, Boston N.L. 1, Philadelphia A.L. 0, 2 hits.
October 10, 1917—Benton, New York N.L. 2, Chicago A.L. 0, 5 hits.
October 11, 1917—Schupp, New York N.L. 5, Chicago A.L. 0, 7 hits.
Sept.   5, 1918—Ruth, Boston A.L. 1, Chicago N.L. 0, 6 hits.
Sept.   10, 1918—Vaughn, Chicago N.L. 3, Boston A.L. 0, 5 hits.
October   3, 1919—Kerr, Chicago A.L. 3, Cincinnati N.L. 0, 3 hits.
October   4, 1919—Ring, Cincinnati N.L. 2, Chicago A.L. 0, 3 hits.
October   6, 1919—Eller, Cincinnati N.L. 5, Chicago A.L. 0, 3 hits.
October   6, 1920—Grimes, Brooklyn N.L. 3, Cleveland A.L. 0, 7 hits.
October 11, 1920—Mails, Cleveland A.L. 1, Brooklyn N.L. 0, 3 hits.
October 12, 1920—Coveleski, Cleveland A.L. 3, Brooklyn N.L. 0, 5 hits.
October   5, 1921—Mays, New York A.L. 3, New York N.L. 0, 5 hits.
October   6, 1921—Hoyt, New York A.L. 3, New York N.L. 0, 2 hits.
October 13, 1921—Nehf, New York N.L. 1, New York A.L. 0, 4 hits.
October   6, 1922—Scott, New York N.L. 3, New York A.L. 0, 4 hits.
October 12, 1923—Nehf, New York N.L. 1, New York A.L. 0, 6 hits.
October 11, 1925—Johnson, Washington A.L. 4, Pittsburgh N.L. 0, 6 hits.
October   5, 1926—Haines, St. Louis N.L. 4, New York A.L. 0, 5 hits.
October   4, 1930—Hallahan, St. Louis N.L. 5, Philadelphia A.L. 0, 7 hits.
October   6, 1930—Earnshaw, Grove, Philadelphia A.L. 2, St. Louis N.L. 0, 3 hits.

October 2, 1931—Hallahan, St. Louis N.L. 2, Philadelphia A.L. 0, 3 hits.
October 6, 1931—Earnshaw, Philadelphia A.L. 3, St. Louis N.L. 0, 2 hits.
October 5, 1933—Whitehill, Washington A.L. 4, New York N.L. 0, 5 hits.
October 9, 1934—J. Dean, St. Louis N.L. 11, Detroit A.L. 0, 6 hits.
October 2, 1935—Warneke, Chicago N.L. 3, Detroit A.L. 0, 4 hits.
October 5, 1939—Pearson, New York A.L. 4, Cincinnati N.L. 0, 2 hits.
October 6, 1940—Newsom, Detroit A.L. 8, Cincinnati N.L. 0, 3 hits.
October 7, 1940—Walters, Cincinnati N.L. 4, Detroit A.L. 0, 5 hits.
October 3, 1942—White, St. Louis N.L. 2, New York A.L. 0, 6 hits.
October 11, 1943—Chandler, New York A.L. 2, St. Louis N.L. 0, 10 hits.
October 8, 1944—Cooper, St. Louis N.L. 2, St. Louis A.L. 0, 7 hits.
October 3, 1945—Borowy, Chicago N.L. 9, Detroit A.L. 0, 6 hits.
October 5, 1945—Passeau, Chicago N.L. 3, Detroit A.L. 0, 1 hit.
October 7, 1946—Brecheen, St. Louis N.L. 3, Boston A.L. 0, 4 hits.
October 9, 1946—Ferriss, Boston A.L. 4, St. Louis N.L. 0, 6 hits.
October 6, 1948—Sain, Boston N.L. 1, Cleveland A.L. 0, 4 hits.
October 8, 1948—Bearden, Cleveland A.L. 2, Boston N.L. 0, 5 hits.
October 5, 1949—Reynolds, New York A.L. 1, Brooklyn N.L. 0, 2 hits.
October 6, 1949—Roe, Brooklyn N.L. 1, New York A.L. 0, 6 hits.
October 4, 1950—Raschi, New York A.L. 1, Philadelphia N.L. 0, 2 hits.
October 4, 1952—Reynolds, New York A.L. 2, Brooklyn N.L. 0, 4 hits.
October 4, 1955—Podres, Brooklyn N.L. 2, New York A.L. 0, 8 hits.
October 8, 1956—Larsen, New York A.L. 2, Brooklyn N.L. 0, 0 hits.
October 9, 1956—Labine, Brooklyn N.L. 1, New York A.L. 0, 7 hits (ten innings).
October 10, 1956—Kucks, New York A.L. 9, Brooklyn N.L. 0, 3 hits.
October 7, 1957—Burdette, Milwaukee N.L. 1, New York A.L. 0, 7 hits.
October 10, 1957—Burdette, Milwaukee N.L. 5, New York A.L. 0, 7 hits.
October 4, 1958—Larsen, Duren, New York A.L. 4, Milwaukee N.L. 0, 6 hits.
October 5, 1958—Spahn, Milwaukee N.L. 3, New York A.L. 0, 2 hits.
October 6, 1958—Turley, New York A.L. 7, Milwaukee N.L. 0, 5 hits.
October 1, 1959—Wynn, Staley, Chicago A.L. 11, Los Angeles N.L. 0, 8 hits.
October 6, 1959—Shaw, Pierce, Donovan, Chicago A.L. 1, Los Angeles N.L. 0, 9 hits.
October 8, 1960—Ford, New York A.L. 10, Pittsburgh N.L. 0, 4 hits.
October 12, 1960—Ford, New York A.L. 12, Pittsburgh N.L. 0, 7 hits.
October 4, 1961—Ford, New York A.L. 2, Cincinnati N.L. 0, 2 hits.
October 8, 1961—Ford, Coates, New York A.L. 7, Cincinnati N.L. 0, 5 hits.
October 5, 1962—Sanford, San Francisco N.L. 2, New York A.L. 0, 3 hits.
October 16, 1962—Terry, New York A.L. 1, San Francisco N.L. 0, 4 hits.
October 5, 1963—Drysdale, Los Angeles N.L. 1, New York A.L. 0, 3 hits.
October 9, 1965—Osteen, Los Angeles N.L. 4, Minnesota A.L. 0, 5 hits.
October 11, 1965—Koufax, Los Angeles N.L. 7, Minnesota A.L. 0, 4 hits.
October 14, 1965—Koufax, Los Angeles N.L. 2, Minnesota A.L. 0, 3 hits.
October 6, 1966—Palmer, Baltimore A.L. 6, Los Angeles N.L. 0, 4 hits.
October 8, 1966—Bunker, Baltimore A.L. 1, Los Angeles N.L. 0, 6 hits.
October 9, 1966—McNally, Baltimore A.L. 1, Los Angeles N.L. 0, 4 hits.
October 5, 1967—Lonborg, Boston A.L. 5, St. Louis N.L. 0, 1 hit.
October 8, 1967—Gibson, St. Louis N.L. 6, Boston A.L. 0, 5 hits.
October 2, 1968—Gibson, St. Louis N.L. 4, Detroit A.L. 0, 5 hits.
October 14, 1969—Gentry, Ryan, New York N.L. 5, Baltimore A.L. 0, 4 hits.
October 14, 1971—Briles, Pittsburgh N.L. 4, Baltimore A.L. 0, 2 hits.
October 18, 1972—Billingham, Carroll, Cincinnati N.L. 1, Oakland A.L. 0, 3 hits.
October 18, 1973—Koosman, McGraw, New York N.L. 2, Oakland A.L. 0, 3 hits.
October 11, 1975—Tiant, Boston A.L. 6, Cincinnati N.L. 0, 5 hits.
October 16, 1979—Candelaria, Tekulve, Pittsburgh N.L. 4, Baltimore A.L. 0, 7 hits.
October 21, 1981—John, Gossage, New York A.L. 3, Los Angeles N.L. 0, 4 hits.
October 12, 1982—Caldwell, Milwaukee A.L. 10, St. Louis N.L. 0, 3 hits.
October 16, 1983—McGregor, Baltimore A.L. 5, Philadelphia N.L. 0, 5 hits.

.400 HITTERS PLAYING IN ALL GAMES OF SERIES
(10 or more at-bats)

Player and Club	Year	G.	AB.	R.	H.	2B.	3B.	HR.	TB.	B.A.
Ruth, George H., New York A.L.	1928	4	16	9	10	3	0	3	22	.625
Gowdy, Henry M., Boston N.L.	1914	4	11	3	6	3	1	1	14	.545
Gehrig, H. Louis, New York A.L.	1928	4	11	5	6	1	0	4	19	.545
Bench, Johnny L., Cincinnati N.L.	1976	4	15	4	8	1	1	2	17	.533
Gehrig, H. Louis, New York A.L.	1932	4	17	9	9	1	0	3	19	.529
Munson, Thurman L., New York A.L.	1976	4	17	2	9	0	0	0	9	.529
McLean, John B., New York N.L.	1913	5	12	0	6	0	0	0	6	.500
Robertson, Davis A., New York N.L.	1917	6	22	3	11	1	1	0	14	.500
Koenig, Mark A., New York A.L.	1927	4	18	5	9	2	0	0	11	.500
Martin, John L., St. Louis N.L.	1931	7	24	5	12	4	0	1	19	.500
Gordon, Joseph L., New York A.L.	1941	5	14	2	7	1	1	1	13	.500
Martin, Alfred M., New York A.L.	1953	6	24	5	12	1	2	2	23	.500
Wertz, Victor W., Cleveland A.L.	1954	4	16	2	8	2	1	1	15	.500
Garner, Philip M., Pittsburgh N.L.	1979	7	24	4	12	4	0	0	16	.500
McCarver, J. Timothy, St. Louis N.L.	1964	7	23	4	11	1	1	1	17	.478

.400 HITTERS PLAYING IN ALL GAMES OF SERIES—Cont.
(10 or more at-bats)

Player	Year	G	AB	R	H	2B	3B	HR	RBI	BA
Otis, Amos J., Kansas City A.L.	1980	6	23	4	11	2	0	3	22	.478
Groh, Henry K., New York N.L.	1922	5	19	4	9	0	1	0	11	.474
Blair, Paul L., Baltimore A.L.	1970	5	19	5	9	1	0	0	10	.474
Steinfeldt, Harry M., Chicago N.L.	1907	5	17	2	8	1	1	0	11	.471
Frisch, Frank F., New York N.L.	1922	5	17	3	8	1	0	0	9	.471
Wilson, Lewis R., Chicago N.L.	1929	5	17	2	8	0	1	0	10	.471
Hack, Stanley C., Chicago N.L.	1938	4	17	3	8	1	0	0	9	.471
Brock, Louis C., St. Louis N.L.	1968	7	28	6	13	3	1	2	24	.464
Cavarretta, Philip J., Chicago N.L.	1938	4	13	1	6	1	0	0	7	.462
Carey, Max, Pittsburgh N.L.	1925	7	24	6	11	4	0	0	15	.458
Irvin, Monford, New York N.L.	1951	6	24	3	11	0	1	0	13	.458
Powell, Alvin J., New York A.L.	1936	6	22	8	10	1	0	1	14	.455
Weis, Albert J., New York, N.L.	1969	5	11	1	5	0	0	1	8	.455
Baker, J. Frank, Philadelphia A.L.	1913	5	20	2	9	0	0	1	12	.450
Jackson, Reginald M., New York A.L.	1977	6	20	10	9	1	0	5	25	.450
Trammell, Alan S., Detroit A.L.	1984	5	20	5	9	1	0	2	16	.450
Lewis, George E., Boston A.L.	1915	5	18	1	8	1	0	1	12	.444
Stephenson, J. Riggs, Chicago, N.L.	1932	4	18	2	8	1	0	0	9	.444
Harris, Joseph, Washington A.L.	1925	7	25	5	11	2	0	3	22	.440
Keller, Charles E., New York A.L.	1939	4	16	8	7	1	1	3	19	.438
Evers, John J., Boston N.L.	1914	4	16	2	7	0	0	0	7	.438
Luderus, Fred W., Philadelphia N.L.	1915	5	16	1	7	2	0	1	12	.438
Dickey, William M., New York A.L.	1932	4	16	2	7	0	0	0	7	.438
McQuinn, George H., St. Louis A.L.	1944	6	16	2	7	2	0	1	12	.438
Doyle, Brian R., New York A.L.	1978	6	16	4	7	1	0	0	8	.438
Piniella, Louis V., New York A.L.	1981	6	16	2	7	1	0	0	8	.438
Perez, Atanasio R., Cincinnati N.L.	1972	7	23	3	10	2	0	0	12	.435
Woodling, Eugene, New York A.L.	1950	4	14	2	6	0	0	0	6	.429
Hamner, Granville W., Phila. N.L.	1950	4	14	1	6	2	1	0	10	.429
Berra, Lawrence P., New York A.L.	1953	6	21	3	9	1	0	1	13	.429
Collins, Edward T., Philadelphia A.L.	1910	5	21	5	9	4	0	0	13	.429
Robinson, Brooks C., Baltimore A.L.	1970	5	21	5	9	2	0	2	17	.429
Cavarretta, Philip J., Chicago N.L.	1945	7	26	7	11	2	0	1	16	.423
Staub, Daniel J., New York N.L.	1973	7	26	1	11	2	0	1	16	.423
Russell, William E., Los Angeles N.L.	1978	6	26	1	11	2	0	0	13	.423
Chance, Frank L., Chicago N.L.	1908	5	19	4	8	0	0	0	8	.421
Collins, Edward T., Philadelphia A.L.	1913	5	19	5	8	0	2	0	12	.421
Dykes, James J., Philadelphia A.L.	1929	5	19	2	8	1	0	0	9	.421
Ward, Aaron L., New York A.L.	1923	6	24	4	10	0	0	1	13	.417
Stengel, Charles D., New York N.L.	1923	6	12	3	5	0	0	2	11	.417
Thevenow, Thomas, St. Louis N.L.	1926	7	24	5	10	1	0	1	14	.417
Dark, Alvin R., New York N.L.	1951	6	24	5	10	3	0	1	16	.417
Berra, Lawrence P., New York A.L.	1955	7	24	5	10	1	0	1	14	.417
Dent, Russell E., New York A.L.	1978	6	24	3	10	1	0	0	11	.417
Garvey, Steven P., Los Angeles N.L.	1981	6	24	3	10	1	0	0	11	.417
Brock, Louis C., St. Louis N.L.	1967	7	29	8	12	2	1	1	19	.414
Clemente, Roberto W., Pittsburgh N.L.	1971	7	29	3	12	2	1	2	22	.414
Yount, Robin R., Milwaukee A.L.	1982	7	29	6	12	3	0	1	18	.414
Verban, Emil M., St. Louis N.L.	1944	6	17	1	7	0	0	0	7	.412
Walker, Harry W., St. Louis N.L.	1946	7	17	3	7	2	0	0	9	.412
Dark, Alvin R., New York N.L.	1954	4	17	2	7	0	0	0	7	.412
Bruton, William H., Milwaukee N.L.	1958	7	17	2	7	0	0	1	10	.412
Boone, Robert R., Philadelphia N.L.	1980	6	17	3	7	2	0	0	9	.412
Bevacqua, Kurt A., San Diego N.L.	1984	5	17	4	7	2	0	2	15	.412
Baker, J. Frank, Philadelphia A.L.	1910	5	22	6	9	3	0	0	12	.409
Collins, Edward T., Chicago A.L.	1917	6	22	4	9	1	0	0	11	.409
Richardson, Robert C., New York A.L.	1964	7	32	3	13	2	0	0	15	.406
Rossman, Claude, Detroit A.L.	1907	5	20	1	8	0	1	0	10	.400
Herzog, Charles L., New York N.L.	1912	8	30	6	12	4	1	0	18	.400
Frisch, Frank F., New York N.L.	1923	6	25	2	10	0	1	0	12	.400
Ruth, George H., New York A.L.	1927	4	15	4	6	0	0	2	12	.400
Waner, Lloyd J., Pittsburgh N.L.	1927	4	15	5	6	1	1	0	9	.400
Cochrane, Gordon S., Phila. A.L.	1929	5	15	5	6	1	0	0	7	.400
Rolfe, Robert A., New York A.L.	1936	6	25	5	10	0	0	0	10	.400
Lazzeri, Anthony M., New York A.L.	1937	5	15	3	6	0	1	1	11	.400
Gordon, Joseph L., New York A.L.	1938	4	15	3	6	2	0	1	11	.400
Dickey, William M., New York A.L.	1938	4	15	2	6	0	1	0	9	.400
McCormick, Frank A., Cinn. N.L.	1939	4	15	1	6	1	0	0	7	.400
Mantle, Mickey C., New York A.L.	1960	7	25	8	10	1	0	3	20	.400
Davis H. Thomas, Los Angeles N.L.	1963	4	15	0	6	0	2	0	10	.400
Yastrzemski, Carl M., Boston A.L.	1967	7	25	4	10	2	0	3	21	.400
Stargell, Wilver D., Pittsburgh N.L.	1979	7	30	7	12	4	0	3	25	.400
Aikens, Willie M., Kansas City A.L.	1980	6	20	5	8	0	1	4	22	.400

LEADING BATSMEN, WORLD SERIES

PLAYING IN ALL GAMES, EACH SERIES

Capitalized name denotes leader (or tied) for Series, both clubs

NATIONAL LEAGUE

Year — Player and Club	G.	AB.	R.	H.	2B.	3B.	HR.	TB.	B.A.
1903—JAMES D. SEBRING, Pittsburgh	8	30	3	11	0	1	1	16	.367
1904—No Series.									
1905—MICHAEL J. DONLIN, New York	5	19	4	6	1	0	0	7	.316
1906—Arthur F. Hofman, Chicago	6	23	3	7	1	0	0	8	.304
1907—HARRY M. STEINFELDT, Chicago	5	17	2	8	1	1	0	11	.471
1908—FRANK L. CHANCE, Chicago	5	19	4	8	0	0	0	8	.421
1909—John P. Wagner, Pittsburgh	7	24	4	8	2	1	0	12	.333
1910—Frank M. Schulte, Chicago	5	17	3	6	3	0	0	9	.353
Frank L. Chance, Chicago	5	17	1	6	1	1	0	9	.353
1911—Lawrence J. Doyle, New York	6	23	3	7	3	1	0	12	.304
1912—CHARLES L. HERZOG, New York	8	30	6	12	4	1	0	18	.400
1913—JOHN B. McLEAN, New York	5	12	1	6	0	0	0	6	.500
1914—HENRY M. GOWDY, Boston	4	11	3	6	3	1	1	14	.545
1915—Fred W. Luderus, Philadelphia	5	16	1	7	2	0	1	12	.438
1916—Ivan M. Olson, Brooklyn	5	16	1	4	0	1	0	6	.250
1917—DAVIS A. ROBERTSON, New York	6	22	3	11	1	1	0	14	.500
1918—CHARLES PICK, Chicago	6	18	2	7	1	0	0	8	.389
1919—A. Earle Neale, Cincinnati	8	28	3	10	1	1	0	13	.357
1920—ZACHARIAH D. WHEAT, Brooklyn	7	27	2	9	2	0	0	11	.333
1921—EMIL F. MEUSEL, New York	8	29	4	10	2	1	1	17	.345
1922—HENRY K. GROH, New York	5	19	4	9	0	1	0	11	.474
1923—CHARLES D. STENGEL, New York	6	12	3	5	0	0	2	11	.417
1924—Frank F. Frisch, New York	7	30	1	10	4	1	0	16	.333
Fred C. Lindstrom, New York	7	30	1	10	2	0	0	12	.333
1925—MAX G. CAREY, Pittsburgh	7	24	6	11	4	0	0	15	.458
1926—THOMAS J. THEVENOW, St. Louis	7	24	5	10	1	0	1	14	.417
1927—Lloyd J. Waner, Pittsburgh	4	15	5	6	1	1	0	9	.400
1928—Walter J. Maranville, St. Louis	4	13	2	4	1	0	0	5	.308
1929—Lewis R. Wilson, Chicago	5	17	2	8	0	1	0	10	.471
1930—Charles M. Gelbert, St. Louis	6	17	2	6	0	1	0	8	.353
1931—JOHN L. MARTIN, St. Louis	7	24	5	12	4	0	1	19	.500
1932—J. Riggs Stephenson, Chicago	4	18	2	8	1	0	0	9	.444
1933—MELVIN T. OTT, New York	5	18	3	7	0	0	2	13	.389
1934—JOSEPH M. MEDWICK, St. Louis	7	29	4	11	0	1	1	16	.379
1935—William Herman, Chicago	6	24	3	8	2	1	1	15	.333
1936—Richard Bartell, New York	6	21	5	8	3	0	1	14	.381
1937—Joseph G. Moore, New York	5	23	1	9	1	0	0	10	.391
1938—STANLEY C. HACK, Chicago	4	17	3	8	1	0	0	9	.471
1939—Frank A. McCormick, Cincinnati	4	15	1	6	1	0	0	7	.400
1940—WILLIAM M. WERBER, Cincinnati	7	27	5	10	4	0	0	14	.370
1941—Joseph M. Medwick, Brooklyn	5	17	1	4	1	0	0	5	.235
1942—James R. Brown, St. Louis	5	20	2	6	0	0	0	6	.300
1943—MARTIN W. MARION, St. Louis	5	14	1	5	2	0	1	10	.357
1944—Emil Verban, St. Louis	6	17	1	7	0	0	0	7	.412
1945—PHILIP J. CAVARRETTA, Chicago	7	26	7	11	2	0	1	16	.423
1946—HARRY W. WALKER, St. Louis	7	17	3	7	2	0	0	9	.412
1947—Harold H. Reese, Brooklyn	7	23	5	7	1	0	0	8	.304
1948—ROBERT I. ELLIOTT, Boston	6	21	4	7	0	0	2	13	.333
1949—HAROLD H. REESE, Brooklyn	5	19	2	6	1	0	1	10	.316
1950—GRANVILLE W. HAMNER, Philadelphia	4	14	1	6	2	1	0	10	.429
1951—MONFORD IRVIN, New York	6	24	3	11	0	1	0	13	.458
1952—Edwin D. Snider, Brooklyn	7	29	5	10	2	0	4	24	.345
Harold H. Reese, Brooklyn	7	29	4	10	0	0	1	13	.345
1953—Gilbert R. Hodges, Brooklyn	6	22	3	8	0	0	1	11	.364
1954—Alvin R. Dark, New York	4	17	2	7	0	0	0	7	.412
1955—Edwin D. Snider, Brooklyn	7	25	5	8	1	0	4	21	.320
1956—Edwin D. Snider, Brooklyn	7	23	5	7	1	0	1	11	.304
Gilbert R. Hodges, Brooklyn	7	23	5	7	2	0	1	12	.304
1957—HENRY AARON, Milwaukee	7	28	5	11	0	1	3	22	.393
1958—WILLIAM BRUTON, Milwaukee	7	17	2	7	0	0	1	10	.412
1959—GILBERT R. HODGES, Los Angeles	6	23	2	9	0	1	1	14	.391
1960—William S. Mazeroski, Pittsburgh	7	25	4	8	2	0	2	16	.320
1961—Walter C. Post, Cincinnati	5	18	3	6	1	0	1	10	.333
1962—JOSE A. PAGAN, San Francisco	7	19	2	7	0	0	1	10	.368
1963—H. THOMAS DAVIS, Los Angeles	4	15	0	6	0	2	0	10	.400
1964—J. TIMOTHY McCARVER, St. Louis	7	23	4	11	1	1	1	17	.478
1965—RONALD R. FAIRLY, Los Angeles	7	29	7	11	3	0	2	20	.379
1966—Louis B. Johnson, Los Angeles	4	15	1	4	1	0	0	5	.267
1967—LOUIS C. BROCK, St. Louis	7	29	8	12	2	1	1	19	.414
1968—LOUIS C. BROCK, St. Louis	7	28	6	13	3	1	2	24	.464
1969—ALBERT J. WEIS, New York	5	11	1	5	0	0	1	8	.455

WORLD SERIES RECORDS

Year	Player and Club	G.	AB.	R.	H.	2B.	3B.	HR.	TB.	B.A.
1970	Lee A. May, Cincinnati	5	18	6	7	2	0	2	15	.389
1971	ROBERTO W. CLEMENTE, Pittsburgh	7	29	3	12	2	1	2	22	.414
1972	ATANASIO R. PEREZ, Cincinnati	7	23	3	10	2	0	0	12	.435
1973	DANIEL J. STAUB, New York	7	26	1	11	2	0	1	16	.423
1974	STEVEN P. GARVEY, Los Angeles	5	21	2	8	0	0	0	8	.381
1975	PETER E. ROSE, Cincinnati	7	27	3	10	1	0	0	13	.370
1976	JOHNNY L. BENCH, Cincinnati	4	15	4	8	1	1	2	17	.533
1977	Steven P. Garvey, Los Angeles	6	24	5	9	1	1	1	15	.375
1978	William E. Russell, Los Angeles	6	26	1	11	2	0	0	13	.423
1979	PHILIP M. GARNER, Pittsburgh	7	24	4	12	4	0	0	16	.500
1980	Robert R. Boone, Philadelphia	6	17	3	7	2	0	0	9	.412
1981	Steven P. Garvey, Los Angeles	6	24	3	10	1	0	0	11	.417
1982	George A. Hendrick, St. Louis	7	28	5	9	0	0	0	9	.321
	Lonnie Smith, St. Louis	7	28	6	9	4	1	0	15	.321
1983	Baudilio J. Diaz, Philadelphia	5	15	1	5	1	0	0	6	.333
1984	Kurt A. Bevacqua, San Diego	5	17	4	7	2	0	2	15	.412

AMERICAN LEAGUE

Year	Player and Club	G.	AB.	R.	H.	2B.	3B.	HR.	TB.	B.A.
1903	Charles S. Stahl, Boston	8	33	6	10	1	3	0	17	.303
1904	No Series									
1905	T. Frederick Hartsel, Philadelphia	5	17	1	5	1	0	0	6	.294
1906	GEORGE ROHE, Chicago	6	21	2	7	1	2	0	12	.333
	JOHN A. DONAHUE, Chicago	6	18	0	6	2	1	0	10	.333
1907	Claude Rossman, Detroit	5	20	1	8	0	1	0	10	.400
1908	Tyrus R. Cobb, Detroit	5	19	3	7	1	0	0	8	.368
1909	JAMES C. DELAHANTY, Detroit	7	26	2	9	4	0	0	13	.346
1910	EDWARD T. COLLINS, Philadelphia	5	21	5	9	4	0	0	13	.429
1911	J. FRANKLIN BAKER, Philadelphia	6	24	7	9	2	0	2	17	.375
1912	Tris Speaker, Boston	8	30	4	9	1	2	0	14	.300
1913	J. Franklin Baker, Philadelphia	5	20	2	9	0	0	1	12	.450
1914	J. Franklin Baker, Philadelphia	4	16	0	4	2	0	0	6	.250
1915	GEORGE E. LEWIS, Boston	5	18	1	8	1	0	1	12	.444
1916	GEORGE E. LEWIS, Boston	5	17	3	6	2	1	0	10	.353
1917	Edward T. Collins, Chicago	6	22	4	9	1	0	0	10	.409
1918	John P. McInnis, Boston	6	20	2	5	0	0	0	5	.250
	George Whiteman, Boston	6	20	2	5	0	1	0	7	.250
1919	JOSEPH J. JACKSON, Chicago	8	32	5	12	3	0	1	18	.375
1920	STEPHEN F. O'NEILL, Cleveland	7	21	1	7	3	0	0	10	.333
1921	Walter H. Schang, New York	8	21	1	6	1	1	0	9	.296
1922	Robert W. Meusel, New York	5	20	2	6	1	0	0	7	.300
1923	AARON L. WARD, New York	6	24	4	10	0	0	1	13	.417
1924	JOSEPH I. JUDGE, Washington	7	26	4	10	1	0	0	11	.385
1925	Joseph Harris, Washington	7	25	5	11	2	0	3	22	.440
1926	Earle B. Combs, New York	7	28	3	10	2	0	0	12	.357
1927	MARK A. KOENIG, New York	4	18	5	9	2	0	0	11	.500
1928	GEORGE H. RUTH, New York	4	16	9	10	3	0	3	22	.625
1929	James Dykes, Philadelphia	5	19	2	8	1	0	0	9	.421
1930	ALOYSIUS H. SIMMONS, Philadelphia	6	22	4	8	2	0	2	16	.364
1931	James E. Foxx, Philadelphia	7	23	3	8	0	0	1	11	.348
1932	H. LOUIS GEHRIG, New York	4	17	9	9	1	0	3	19	.529
1933	Fred W. Schulte, Washington	5	21	1	7	1	0	1	21	.333
1934	CHARLES L. GEHRINGER, Detroit	7	29	5	11	1	0	1	15	.379
1935	ERVIN FOX, Detroit	6	26	1	10	3	1	0	15	.385
1936	ALVIN J. POWELL, New York	6	22	8	10	1	0	1	14	.455
1937	ANTHONY M. LAZZERI, New York	5	15	3	6	0	1	1	11	.400
1938	William B. Dickey, New York	4	15	2	6	0	0	1	9	.400
	Joseph L. Gordon, New York	4	15	3	6	2	0	1	11	.400
1939	CHARLES E. KELLER, New York	4	16	8	7	1	1	3	19	.438
1940	Bruce D. Campbell, Detroit	7	25	4	9	1	0	1	13	.360
1941	JOSEPH L. GORDON, New York	5	14	2	7	1	1	1	13	.500
1942	PHILIP F. RIZZUTO, New York	5	21	2	8	0	0	1	11	.381
1943	William Johnson, New York	5	20	3	6	1	1	0	9	.300
1944	GEORGE H. McQUINN, St. Louis	6	16	2	7	2	0	1	12	.438
1945	Roger M. Cramer, Detroit	7	29	7	11	0	0	0	11	.379
1946	Rudolph P. York, Boston	7	23	6	6	1	1	2	15	.261
1947	THOMAS D. HENRICH, New York	7	31	2	10	2	0	1	15	.323
1948	Lawrence E. Doby, Cleveland	6	22	1	7	1	0	1	11	.318
1949	Thomas D. Henrich, New York	5	19	4	5	0	0	1	8	.263
1950	EUGENE R. WOODLING, New York	4	14	2	6	0	0	0	6	.429
1951	Philip F. Rizzuto, New York	6	25	5	8	0	0	1	11	.320
1952	EUGENE R. WOODLING, New York	7	23	4	8	1	1	1	14	.348
1953	ALFRED M. MARTIN, New York	6	24	5	12	1	2	2	23	.500
1954	VICTOR W. WERTZ, Cleveland	4	16	2	8	2	1	1	15	.500
1955	LAWRENCE P. BERRA, New York	7	24	5	10	1	0	1	14	.417
1956	LAWRENCE P. BERRA, New York	7	25	5	9	2	0	3	20	.360
1957	Gerald F. Coleman, New York	7	22	2	8	2	0	0	10	.364
1958	Henry A. Bauer, New York	7	31	6	10	0	0	4	22	.323

Year	Player and Club	G.	AB.	R.	H.	2B.	3B.	HR.	TB.	B.A.
1959	THEODORE B. KLUSZEWSKI, Chicago	6	23	5	9	1	0	3	19	.391
1960	MICKEY C. MANTLE, New York	7	25	8	10	1	0	3	20	.400
1961	ROBERT C. RICHARDSON, New York	5	23	2	9	1	0	0	10	.391
1962	Thomas M. Tresh, New York	7	28	5	9	2	0	1	13	.321
1963	Elston G. Howard, New York	4	15	0	5	0	0	0	5	.333
1964	Robert C. Richardson, New York	7	32	3	13	2	0	0	15	.406
1965	Zoilo Versalles, Minnesota	7	28	3	8	1	1	1	14	.286
	Harmon C. Killebrew, Minnesota	7	21	2	6	0	0	1	9	.286
1966	JOHN W. POWELL, Baltimore	4	14	1	5	1	0	0	6	.357
1967	Carl M. Yastrzemski, Boston	7	25	4	10	2	0	3	21	.400
1968	Norman D. Cash, Detroit	7	26	5	10	0	0	1	13	.385
1969	John W. Powell, Baltimore	5	19	0	5	0	0	0	5	.263
1970	PAUL L. BLAIR, Baltimore	5	19	5	9	1	0	0	10	.474
1971	Brooks C. Robinson, Baltimore	7	22	2	7	0	0	0	7	.318
1972	F. Gene Tenace, Oakland	7	23	5	8	1	0	4	21	.348
1973	Joseph O. Rudi, Oakland	7	27	3	9	2	0	0	11	.333
1974	Dagoberto B. Campaneris, Oakland	5	17	1	6	2	0	0	8	.353
1975	Carl M. Yastrzemski, Boston	7	29	7	9	0	0	0	9	.310
1976	Thurman L. Munson, New York	4	17	2	9	0	0	0	9	.529
1977	REGINALD M. JACKSON, New York	6	20	10	9	1	0	5	25	.450
1978	BRIAN R. DOYLE, New York	6	16	4	7	1	0	0	8	.438
1979	Kenneth W. Singleton, Baltimore	7	28	1	10	1	0	0	11	.357
1980	AMOS J. OTIS, Kansas City	6	23	4	11	2	0	3	22	.478
1981	LOUIS V. PINIELLA, New York	6	16	2	7	1	0	0	8	.438
1982	ROBIN R. YOUNT, Milwaukee	7	29	6	12	3	0	1	18	.414
1983	JOHN T. SHELBY, Baltimore	5	9	1	4	0	0	0	4	.444
1984	ALAN S. TRAMMELL, Detroit	5	20	5	9	1	0	2	16	.450

WORLD SERIES EXTRA-INNING GAMES (40)

October 8, 1907—at Chicago, 12 innings, Chicago N.L. 3, Detroit A.L. 3, tie.
October 22, 1910—at Chicago, 10 innings, Chicago N.L. 4, Philadelphia A.L. 3.
October 17, 1911—at New York, 11 innings, Philadelphia A.L. 3, New York N.L. 2.
October 25, 1911—at New York, 10 innings, New York N.L. 4, Philadelphia A.L. 3.
October 9, 1912—at Boston, 11 innings, Boston A.L. 6, New York N.L. 6, tie.
October 16, 1912—at Boston, 10 innings, Boston A.L. 3, New York N.L. 2.
October 8, 1913—at Philadelphia, 10 innings, New York N.L. 3, Philadelphia A.L. 0.
October 12, 1914—at Boston, 12 innings, Boston N.L. 5, Philadelphia A.L. 4.
October 9, 1916—at Boston, 14 innings, Boston A.L. 2, Brooklyn N.L. 1.
October 7, 1919—at Cincinnati, 10 innings, Chicago A.L. 5, Cincinnati N.L. 4.
October 5, 1922—at New York (A.L.), 10 innings, New York N.L. 3, New York A.L. 3, tie.
October 4, 1924—at Washington, 12 innings, New York N.L. 4, Washington A.L. 3.
October 10, 1924—at Washington, 12 innings, Washington A.L. 4, New York N.L.3.
October 7, 1926—at St. Louis, 10 innings, New York A.L. 3, St. Louis N.L. 2.
October 6, 1933—at Washington, 11 innings, New York N.L. 2, Wahington A.L. 1.
October 7, 1933—at Washington, 10 innings, New York N.L. 4, Washington A.L. 3.
October 4, 1934—at Detroit, 12 innings, Detroit A.L. 3, St. Louis N.L. 2.
October 4, 1935—at Chicago, 11 innings, Detroit A.L. 6, Chicago N.L. 5.
October 5, 1936—at New York (A.L.), 10 innings, New York N.L. 5, New York A.L. 4
October 8, 1939—at Cincinnati, 10 innings, New York A.L. 7, Cincinnati N.L. 4.
October 5, 1944—at St. Louis (N.L.), 11 innings, St. Louis N.L. 3, St. Louis A.L. 2.
October 8, 1945—at Chicago, 12 innings, Chicago N.L. 8, Detroit A.L. 7.
October 6, 1946—at St. Louis, 10 innings, Boston A.L. 3, St. Louis N.L. 2.
October 5, 1950—at Philadelphia, 10 innings, New York A.L. 2, Philadelphia N.L. 1.
October 5, 1952—at New York, 11 innings, Brooklyn N.L. 6, New York A.L. 5.
Sept. 29, 1954—at New York, 10 innings, New York N.L. 5, Cleveland A.L. 2.
October 9, 1956—at Brooklyn, 10 innings Brooklyn N.L. 1, New York A.L. 0.
October 6, 1957—at Milwaukee, 10 innings, Milwaukee N.L. 7, New York A.L. 5.
October 1, 1958—at Milwaukee, 10 innings, Milwaukee N.L. 4, New York A.L. 3.
October 8, 1958—at Milwaukee, 10 innings, New York A.L. 4, Milwaukee N.L. 3.
October 12, 1964—at New York, 10 innings, St. Louis N.L. 5, New York A.L. 2.
October 15, 1969—at New York, 10 innings, New York N.L. 2, Baltimore A.L. 1.
October 16, 1971—at Baltimore, 10 innings, Baltimore A.L. 3, Pittsburgh N.L. 2.
October 14, 1973—at Oakland, 12 innings, New York N.L. 10, Oakland A.L. 7.
October 16, 1973—at New York, 11 innings, Oakland A.L. 3, New York N.L. 2, night game.
October 14, 1975—at Cincinnati, 10 innings, Cincinnati N.L. 6, Boston A.L. 5, night game.
October 21, 1975—at Boston, 12 innings, Boston A.L. 7, Cincinnati N.L. 6, night game.
October 11, 1977—at New York, 12 innings, New York A.L. 4, Los Angeles N.L. 3, night game.
October 14, 1978—at New York, 10 innings, New York A.L. 4, Los Angeles N.L. 3.
October 17, 1980—at Kansas City, 10 innings, Kansas City A.L. 4, Philadelphia N.L. 3, night game.

CLUB BATTING

Year	Club	G.	AB.	R.	H.	TB.	2B.	3B.	HR.	Sac.	SB.	BB.	SO.	RBI.	B.A.
1903—	Pittsburgh N.L.	8	270	24	64	92	7	9	1	3	7	14	45	23	.237
	Boston A.L.	8	282	39	71	113	4	16	2	6	5	13	27	35	.252
1904—	No Series.														
1905—	New York N.L.	5	153	15	32	39	7	0	0	5	11	15	26	13	.209
	Philadelphia A.L.	5	155	3	25	30	5	0	0	3	2	5	25	2	.161
1906—	Chicago N.L.	6	184	18	36	45	9	0	0	13	8	18	27	11	.196
	Chicago A.L.	6	187	22	37	53	10	3	0	6	6	18	35	19	.198
1907—	Chicago N.L.	5	167	19	43	51	6	1	0	9	18	12	25	16	.257
	Detroit A.L.	5	173	6	36	41	1	2	0	3	7	9	21	6	.208
1908—	Chicago N.L.	5	164	24	48	59	4	2	1	9	13	13	26	21	.293
	Detroit A.L.	5	158	15	32	37	5	0	0	5	5	12	26	14	.203
1909—	Pittsburgh N.L.	7	223	34	49	70	12	1	2	12	18	20	34	26	.220
	Detroit A.L.	7	234	28	55	77	16	0	2	4	6	20	22	25	.235
1910—	Chicago N.L.	5	158	15	35	48	11	1	0	7	3	18	31	13	.222
	Philadelphia A.L.	5	177	35	56	80	19	1	1	7	7	17	24	29	.316
1911—	New York N.L.	6	189	13	33	46	11	1	0	6	4	14	44	10	.175
	Philadelphia A.L.	6	205	27	50	74	15	0	3	9	4	4	31	21	.244
1912—	New York N.L.	8	274	31	74	99	14	4	1	7	12	22	39	25	.270
	Boston A.L.	8	273	25	60	89	14	6	1	8	6	19	36	21	.220
1913—	New York N.L.	5	164	15	33	41	3	1	1	2	5	8	19	15	.201
	Philadelphia A.L.	5	174	23	46	64	4	4	2	7	5	7	16	21	.264
1914—	Boston N.L.	4	135	16	33	46	6	2	1	3	9	15	18	14	.244
	Philadelphia A.L.	4	128	6	22	31	9	0	0	3	2	13	28	5	.172
1915—	Philadelphia N.L.	5	148	10	27	36	4	1	1	5	2	10	25	9	.182
	Boston A.L.	5	159	12	42	57	2	2	3	7	1	11	25	11	.264
1916—	Brooklyn N.L.	5	170	13	34	49	2	5	1	6	1	14	19	11	.200
	Boston A.L.	5	164	21	39	64	7	6	2	12	1	18	25	18	.238
1917—	New York N.L.	6	199	17	51	70	5	4	2	3	4	6	27	16	.256
	Chicago A.L.	6	197	21	54	63	6	0	1	3	6	11	28	18	.274
1918—	Chicago N.L.	6	176	10	37	44	5	1	0	4	3	18	14	10	.210
	Boston A.L.	6	217	9	32	40	2	3	0	8	3	16	21	6	.186
1919—	Cincinnati N.L.	8	251	35	64	88	10	7	0	13	7	25	22	34	.255
	Chicago A.L.	8	263	20	59	78	10	3	1	7	5	15	30	17	.224
1920—	Brooklyn N.L.	7	215	8	44	51	5	1	0	5	1	10	20	8	.205
	Cleveland A.L.	7	217	21	53	72	9	2	2	3	2	21	21	18	.244
1921—	New York N.L.	8	264	29	71	98	13	4	2	6	7	22	38	28	.269
	New York A.L.	8	241	22	50	65	7	1	2	9	6	27	44	20	.207
1922—	New York N.L.	5	162	18	50	57	2	1	1	5	1	12	15	18	.309
	New York A.L.	5	158	11	32	46	6	1	2	6	2	8	20	11	.203
1923—	New York N.L.	6	201	17	47	70	2	3	5	0	1	12	18	17	.234
	New York A.L.	6	205	30	60	91	8	4	5	6	1	20	22	29	.293
1924—	New York N.L.	7	253	27	66	91	9	2	4	7	3	25	40	22	.261
	Washington A.L.	7	248	26	61	95	9	0	5	6	5	29	34	23	.246
1925—	Pittsburgh N.L.	7	230	25	61	89	12	2	4	8	7	17	32	25	.265
	Washington A.L.	7	225	26	59	91	8	0	8	10	2	17	31	25	.262
1926—	St. Louis N.L.	7	239	31	65	91	12	1	4	12	2	11	30	30	.272
	New York A.L.	7	223	21	54	78	10	1	4	10	1	31	31	19	.242
1927—	Pittsburgh N.L.	4	130	10	29	37	6	1	0	6	0	4	7	10	.223
	New York A.L.	4	136	23	38	54	6	2	2	6	2	13	25	19	.279
1928—	St. Louis N.L.	4	131	10	27	37	5	1	1	2	3	11	29	9	.206
	New York A.L.	4	134	27	37	71	7	0	9	5	4	13	12	25	.276
1929—	Chicago N.L.	5	173	17	43	56	6	2	1	2	1	13	50	15	.249
	Philadelphia A.L.	5	171	26	48	71	5	0	6	7	0	13	27	26	.281
1930—	St. Louis N.L.	6	190	12	38	56	10	1	2	4	1	11	33	11	.200
	Philadelphia A.L.	6	178	21	35	67	10	2	6	7	0	24	32	21	.197
1931—	St. Louis N.L.	7	229	19	54	71	11	0	2	4	8	9	41	17	.236
	Philadelphia A.L.	7	227	22	50	64	5	0	3	4	0	28	46	20	.220
1932—	Chicago N.L.	4	146	19	37	58	8	2	3	1	2	11	24	16	.253
	New York A.L.	4	144	37	45	75	6	0	8	1	0	23	26	36	.313
1933—	New York N.L.	5	176	16	47	61	5	0	3	6	0	11	21	16	.267
	Washington A.L.	5	173	11	37	47	4	0	2	3	1	13	25	11	.214
1934—	St. Louis N.L.	7	262	34	73	103	14	5	2	4	2	11	31	32	.279
	Detroit A.L.	7	250	23	56	76	12	1	2	6	4	25	43	20	.224
1935—	Chicago N.L.	6	202	18	48	73	6	2	5	7	1	11	29	17	.238
	Detroit A.L.	6	206	21	51	67	11	1	3	1	1	25	27	18	.248
1936—	New York N.L.	6	203	23	50	71	9	0	4	7	0	21	33	20	.246
	New York A.L.	6	215	43	65	96	8	1	7	3	6	26	35	41	.302
1937—	New York N.L.	5	169	12	40	49	6	0	1	0	1	11	21	12	.237
	New York A.L.	5	169	28	42	68	6	4	4	2	0	21	21	25	.249
1938—	Chicago N.L.	4	136	9	33	45	4	1	2	1	0	6	26	8	.243
	New York A.L.	4	135	22	37	60	6	1	5	1	3	11	16	21	.274
1939—	Cincinnati N.L.	4	133	8	27	32	3	1	0	2	1	6	22	8	.203
	New York A.L.	4	131	20	27	54	4	1	7	2	0	9	20	18	.206

WORLD SERIES RECORDS

Year	Club	G.	AB.	R.	H.	TB.	2B.	3B.	HR.	Sac.	SB.	BB.	SO.	RBI.	B.A.
1940—	Cincinnati N.L.	7	232	22	58	78	14	0	2	4	1	15	30	21	.250
	Detroit A.L.	7	228	28	56	83	9	3	4	3	0	30	30	24	.246
1941—	Brooklyn N.L.	5	159	11	29	43	7	2	1	0	0	14	21	11	.182
	New York A.L.	5	166	17	41	54	5	1	2	0	2	23	18	16	.247
1942—	St. Louis N.L.	5	163	23	39	53	4	2	2	7	0	17	19	23	.239
	New York A.L.	5	178	18	44	59	6	0	3	1	3	8	22	14	.247
1943—	St. Louis N.L.	5	165	9	37	48	5	0	2	5	1	11	26	8	.224
	New York A.L.	5	159	17	35	50	5	2	2	4	2	12	30	14	.220
1944—	St. Louis N.L.	6	204	16	49	69	9	1	3	7	0	19	43	15	.240
	St. Louis A.L.	6	197	12	36	50	9	1	1	1	0	23	49	9	.183
1945—	Chicago N.L.	7	247	29	65	90	16	3	1	10	2	19	48	27	.263
	Detroit A.L.	7	242	32	54	70	10	0	2	3	3	33	22	32	.223
1946—	St. Louis N.L.	7	232	28	60	86	19	2	1	8	3	19	30	27	.259
	Boston A.L.	7	233	20	56	77	7	1	4	3	2	22	28	18	.240
1947—	Brooklyn N.L.	7	226	29	52	70	13	1	1	3	7	30	32	26	.230
	New York A.L.	7	238	38	67	100	11	5	4	3	2	38	37	36	.282
1948—	Boston N.L.	6	187	17	43	61	6	0	4	7	1	16	19	16	.230
	Cleveland A.L.	6	191	17	38	57	7	0	4	3	2	12	26	16	.199
1949—	Brooklyn N.L.	5	162	14	34	55	7	1	4	2	1	15	38	14	.210
	New York A.L.	5	164	21	37	57	10	2	2	3	2	18	27	20	.226
1950—	Philadelphia N.L.	4	128	5	26	34	6	1	0	6	1	7	24	3	.203
	New York A.L.	4	135	11	30	41	3	1	2	2	1	13	12	10	.222
1951—	New York N.L.	6	194	18	46	61	7	1	2	2	2	25	22	15	.237
	New York A.L.	6	199	29	49	75	7	2	5	0	0	26	23	25	.246
1952—	Brooklyn N.L.	7	233	20	50	75	7	0	6	6	5	24	49	18	.215
	New York A.L.	7	232	26	50	89	5	2	10	2	1	31	32	24	.216
1953—	Brooklyn N.L.	6	213	27	64	103	13	1	8	2	2	15	30	26	.300
	New York A.L.	6	201	33	56	97	6	4	9	4	2	25	43	32	.279
1954—	New York N.L.	4	130	21	33	42	3	0	2	8	1	17	24	20	.254
	Cleveland A.L.	4	137	9	26	42	5	1	3	3	0	16	23	9	.190
1955—	Brooklyn N.L.	7	223	31	58	95	8	1	9	8	2	33	38	30	.260
	New York A.L.	7	222	26	55	87	4	2	8	1	3	22	39	25	.248
1956—	Brooklyn N.L.	7	215	25	42	61	8	1	3	5	1	32	47	24	.195
	New York A.L.	7	229	33	58	100	6	0	12	6	2	21	43	33	.253
1957—	Milwaukee N.L.	7	225	23	47	79	6	1	8	6	1	22	40	22	.209
	New York A.L.	7	230	25	57	87	7	1	7	4	1	22	34	25	.248
1958—	Milwaukee N.L.	7	240	25	60	81	10	1	3	7	1	27	56	24	.250
	New York A.L.	7	233	29	49	86	5	1	0	4	1	21	42	29	.210
1959—	Los Angeles N.L.	6	203	21	53	79	3	1	7	4	5	12	27	19	.261
	Chicago A.L.	6	199	23	52	74	10	0	4	4	2	20	33	19	.261
1960—	Pittsburgh N.L.	7	234	27	60	83	11	0	4	3	2	12	26	26	.256
	New York A.L.	7	269	55	91	142	13	4	10	3	0	18	40	54	.338
1961—	Cincinnati N.L.	5	170	13	35	52	8	0	3	0	0	8	27	11	.206
	New York A.L.	5	165	27	42	73	8	1	7	4	1	24	25	26	.255
1962—	San Francisco N.L.	7	226	21	51	80	10	2	5	4	1	12	39	19	.226
	New York A.L.	7	222	20	44	61	6	1	3	2	4	21	39	17	.199
1963—	Los Angeles N.L.	4	117	12	25	41	3	2	3	3	2	12	25	12	.214
	New York A.L.	4	129	4	22	31	3	0	2	1	0	5	37	4	.171
1964—	St. Louis N.L.	7	240	32	61	90	8	3	5	6	3	18	30	29	.254
	New York A.L.	7	239	33	60	101	21	0	10	3	2	25	54	34	.251
1965—	Los Angeles N.L.	7	234	24	64	91	10	1	5	6	9	13	31	21	.274
	Minnesota A.L.	7	215	20	42	71	7	2	6	2	2	19	54	19	.195
1966—	Los Angeles N.L.	4	120	2	17	23	3	0	1	1	1	13	28	2	.142
	Baltimore A.L.	4	120	13	24	41	3	1	4	2	0	11	17	10	.200
1967—	St. Louis N.L.	7	229	25	51	81	11	2	5	2	7	17	30	24	.223
	Boston A.L.	7	222	21	48	80	6	1	8	6	1	17	49	19	.216
1968—	St. Louis N.L.	7	239	27	61	95	7	3	7	1	11	21	40	27	.255
	Detroit A.L.	7	231	34	56	90	4	3	8	3	0	27	59	33	.242
1969—	New York N.L.	5	159	15	35	61	8	0	6	3	1	15	35	13	.220
	Baltimore A.L.	5	157	9	23	33	1	0	3	1	1	15	28	9	.146
1970—	Cincinnati N.L.	5	164	20	35	58	6	1	5	3	1	15	23	20	.213
	Baltimore A.L.	5	171	33	50	87	7	0	10	2	0	20	33	32	.292
1971—	Pittsburgh N.L.	7	238	23	56	84	9	2	5	4	5	26	47	21	.235
	Baltimore A.L.	7	219	24	45	65	3	1	5	5	1	20	35	22	.205
1972—	Cincinnati N.L.	7	220	21	46	75	8	1	3	8	12	27	46	21	.209
	Oakland A.L.	7	220	16	46	65	4	0	5	6	1	21	37	16	.209
1973—	New York N.L.	7	261	24	66	89	7	2	4	4	0	26	36	16	.253
	Oakland A.L.	7	241	21	51	75	12	3	2	3	3	28	62	20	.212
1974—	Los Angeles N.L.	5	158	11	36	54	4	1	4	4	3	16	32	10	.228
	Oakland A.L.	5	142	16	30	46	4	0	4	8	3	16	42	14	.211
1975—	Cincinnati N.L.	7	244	29	59	95	9	3	7	4	9	25	30	29	.242
	Boston A.L.	7	239	30	60	89	7	2	6	7	0	30	40	30	.251
1976—	Cincinnati N.L.	4	134	22	42	70	10	3	4	2	7	12	16	21	.313
	New York A.L.	4	135	8	30	38	3	1	1	1	1	12	16	8	.222
1977—	Los Angeles N.L.	6	208	28	48	86	5	3	9	2	2	16	36	28	.231
	New York A.L.	6	205	26	50	84	10	0	8	5	1	11	37	25	.244

WORLD SERIES RECORDS

Year	Club	G.	AB.	R.	H.	TB.	2B.	3B.	HR.	Sac.	SB.	BB.	SO.	RBI.	B.A.
1978—	Los Angeles N.L.	6	199	23	52	78	8	0	6	1	5	20	31	22	.261
	New York A.L.	6	222	36	68	85	8	0	3	1	5	16	40	34	.306
1979—	Pittsburgh N.L.	7	251	32	81	110	18	1	3	8	0	16	35	32	.323
	Baltimore A.L.	7	233	26	54	78	10	1	4	1	2	26	41	23	.232
1980—	Philadelphia N.L.	6	201	27	59	81	13	0	3	6	3	15	17	26	.294
	Kansas City A.L.	6	207	23	60	97	9	2	8	5	6	26	49	22	.290
1981—	Los Angeles N.L.	6	198	27	51	77	6	1	6	6	6	20	44	26	.258
	New York A.L.	6	193	22	46	74	8	1	6	7	4	33	24	22	.238
1982—	St. Louis N.L.	7	245	39	67	101	16	3	4	2	7	20	26	34	.273
	Milwaukee A.L.	7	238	33	64	95	12	2	5	2	1	19	28	29	.269
1983—	Philadelphia N.L.	5	159	9	31	49	4	1	4	1	1	7	29	9	.195
	Baltimore A.L.	5	164	18	35	61	8	0	6	3	1	10	37	17	.213
1984—	San Diego N.L.	5	166	15	44	60	7	0	3	4	2	11	26	14	.265
	Detroit A.L.	5	158	23	40	65	4	0	7	4	7	24	27	23	.253

MISCELLANEOUS
Club Fielding, Left on Bases, Players, Pitchers, Etc.

Year	Club	G.	PO.	A.	E.	DP.	PB.	F.A.	LOB.	Pl.	Pi.	PH.	PR.
1903—	Pittsburgh N.L.	8	210	96	18	5	0	.944	51	14	5	1	0
	Boston A.L.	8	213	102	14	6	2	.957	55	13	3	4	0
1904—	No Series.												
1905—	New York N.L.	5	135	78	6	2	0	.973	31	12	3	1	0
	Philadelphia A.L.	5	129	56	9	2	0	.954	26	13	3	1	0
1906—	Chicago N.L.	6	159	84	7	4	3	.972	37	14	4	4	0
	Chicago A.L.	6	162	99	14	2	1	.949	33	16	4	2	1
1907—	Chicago N.L.	5	144	65	10	6	1	.954	35	15	4	2	0
	Detroit A.L.	5	138	70	9	2	0	.959	36	14	4	1	1
1908—	Chicago N.L.	5	135	74	5	4	1	.977	30	13	4	1	0
	Detroit A.L.	5	131	63	10	5	1	.951	27	16	5	4	1
1909—	Pittsburgh N.L.	7	182	88	15	3	0	.947	44	17	6	3	0
	Detroit A.L.	7	183	87	19	4	1	.934	50	16	5	5	0
1910—	Chicago N.L.	5	132	77	12	3	0	.946	31	18	7	6	1
	Philadelphia A.L.	5	136	59	11	6	0	.947	36	12	2	0	0
1911—	New York N.L.	6	162	79	16	2	1	.938	31	15	5	4	0
	Philadelphia A.L.	6	167	72	11	2	0	.956	29	14	3	0	1
1912—	New York N.L.	8	221	108	17	4	0	.951	53	17	5	5	3
	Boston A.L.	8	222	101	14	5	0	.958	55	17	5	5	1
1913—	New York N.L.	5	135	67	7	1	1	.967	24	20	5	6	5
	Philadelphia A.L.	5	138	54	5	6	0	.975	30	12	3	0	0
1914—	Boston N.L.	4	117	62	4	4	0	.978	27	15	3	3	1
	Philadelphia A.L.	4	111	66	3	4	1	.983	21	16	6	1	0
1915—	Philadelphia N.L.	5	131	54	3	3	0	.984	23	16	4	2	2
	Boston A.L.	5	132	58	4	2	0	.979	35	17	3	3	1
1916—	Brooklyn N.L.	5	142	70	13	2	2	.942	32	20	7	6	1
	Boston A.L.	5	147	90	6	5	1	.975	31	20	5	3	1
1917—	New York N.L.	6	153	72	11	3	1	.953	37	17	6	3	0
	Chicago A.L.	6	156	82	12	7	1	.952	37	16	5	5	0
1918—	Chicago N.L.	6	156	76	5	7	2	.979	31	17	4	8	2
	Boston A.L.	6	159	88	1	4	0	.996	32	15	4	5	0
1919—	Cincinnati N.L.	8	216	96	12	7	0	.963	46	17	6	3	1
	Chicago A.L.	8	213	116	12	9	1	.965	52	19	7	6	0
1920—	Brooklyn N.L.	7	177	91	6	5	2	.978	39	21	7	7	3
	Cleveland A.L.	7	182	89	12	8	0	.958	43	20	5	12	1
1921—	New York N.L.	8	212	102	5	5	2	.984	54	13	4	2	0
	New York A.L.	8	210	106	6	8	0	.981	43	19	8	3	2
1922—	New York N.L.	5	138	70	6	4	0	.972	32	16	5	3	1
	New York A.L.	5	129	62	1	7	1	.995	25	17	5	4	0
1923—	New York N.L.	6	159	80	6	8	0	.976	35	22	8	9	3
	New York A.L.	6	162	77	3	6	0	.988	43	17	5	4	2
1924—	New York N.L.	7	200	94	6	4	0	.980	59	21	9	7	3
	Washington A.L.	7	201	99	12	10	1	.962	57	21	8	8	2
1925—	Pittsburgh N.L.	7	182	89	7	4	0	.980	54	18	7	5	2
	Washington A.L.	7	180	75	9	8	1	.966	46	21	6	7	4
1926—	St. Louis N.L.	7	189	99	5	6	0	.983	43	19	8	6	0
	New York A.L.	7	189	82	7	3	1	.975	55	19	7	7	2
1927—	Pittsburgh N.L.	4	104	46	6	2	0	.962	23	21	7	5	1
	New York A.L.	4	108	44	3	4	0	.981	29	15	4	1	0
1928—	St. Louis N.L.	4	102	36	5	3	0	.965	27	20	6	6	1
	New York A.L.	4	108	28	6	3	0	.958	24	16	3	4	0
1929—	Chicago N.L.	5	131	44	7	4	0	.962	36	19	6	8	0
	Philadelphia A.L.	5	135	40	4	2	6	.978	35	17	6	3	0
1930—	St. Louis N.L.	6	153	55	5	4	1	.977	37	21	7	7	0
	Philadelphia A.L.	6	156	41	3	2	0	.985	36	15	5	3	0

WORLD SERIES RECORDS

Year	Club	G.	PO.	A.	E.	DP.	PB.	F.A.	LOB.	Pl.	Pi.	PH.	PR.
1931—	St. Louis N.L.	7	186	73	4	7	0	.985	40	21	6	6	1
	Philadelphia A.L.	7	183	69	2	4	0	.992	52	20	6	8	1
1932—	Chicago N.L.	4	102	40	6	7	0	.959	31	22	8	6	1
	New York A.L.	4	108	41	8	1	0	.949	33	16	6	6	1
1933—	New York N.L.	5	141	67	4	5	0	.981	39	15	5	2	0
	Washington A.L.	5	138	65	4	4	0	.981	37	10	7	5	1
1934—	St. Louis N.L.	7	196	73	15	2	0	.947	49	20	8	5	2
	Detroit A.L.	7	195	70	12	6	0	.957	64	17	6	4	0
1935—	Chicago N.L.	6	164	74	6	5	0	.975	33	18	7	5	0
	Detroit A.L.	6	165	72	9	7	1	.963	51	15	5	2	0
1936—	New York N.L.	6	159	62	7	7	0	.969	46	22	8	10	2
	New York A.L.	6	162	57	6	2	0	.973	43	16	6	2	2
1937—	New York N.L.	5	129	46	9	5	0	.951	36	20	7	7	0
	New York A.L.	5	132	47	0	2	0	1.000	36	17	7	1	0
1938—	Chicago N.L.	4	102	35	3	3	0	.979	26	20	8	8	0
	New York A.L.	4	108	39	6	4	0	.961	24	14	4	1	0
1939—	Cincinnati N.L.	4	106	34	4	1	0	.972	23	18	5	3	2
	New York A.L.	4	111	50	2	5	0	.988	16	15	7	0	0
1940—	Cincinnati N.L.	7	183	67	8	9	1	.969	49	23	9	9	1
	Detroit A.L.	7	180	80	4	4	0	.985	50	20	8	6	0
1941—	Brooklyn N.L.	5	132	60	4	5	0	.980	27	20	7	6	0
	New York A.L.	5	135	55	2	7	0	.990	42	18	7	2	1
1942—	St. Louis N.L.	5	135	45	10	3	0	.947	32	18	6	4	1
	New York A.L.	5	132	45	5	2	0	.973	34	20	7	4	2
1943—	St. Louis N.L.	5	129	53	10	4	0	.948	37	20	6	6	1
	New York A.L.	5	135	63	5	3	0	.975	29	16	5	2	0
1944—	St. Louis N.L.	6	165	59	1	3	1	.996	51	20	8	7	0
	St. Louis A.L.	6	163	60	10	4	0	.957	44	22	7	13	1
1945—	Chicago N.L.	7	195	78	6	5	1	.978	50	25	8	14	3
	Detroit A.L.	7	197	85	5	4	2	.983	53	26	9	11	1
1946—	St. Louis N.L.	7	186	68	4	7	1	.984	50	19	7	5	0
	Boston A.L.	7	183	76	10	5	0	.963	53	26	11	10	3
1947—	Brooklyn N.L.	7	180	71	8	8	2	.969	46	24	8	19	5
	New York A.L.	7	185	70	4	4	2	.985	63	24	9	11	0
1948—	Boston N.L.	6	156	54	6	3	0	.972	34	20	6	8	4
	Cleveland A.L.	6	159	72	3	9	0	.987	34	23	8	3	0
1949—	Brooklyn N.L.	5	132	40	5	1	0	.972	31	25	9	11	0
	New York A.L.	5	135	44	3	5	0	.984	32	20	5	4	2
1950—	Philadelphia N.L.	4	107	35	4	1	0	.973	26	20	5	6	4
	New York A.L.	4	111	41	2	4	0	.987	33	18	5	2	2
1951—	New York N.L.	6	156	65	10	4	0	.957	45	24	9	10	2
	New York A.L.	6	159	67	4	10	1	.982	41	21	8	5	2
1952—	Brooklyn N.L.	7	192	71	4	4	0	.985	52	19	6	8	1
	New York A.L.	7	192	66	10	7	1	.963	48	19	8	6	1
1953—	Brooklyn N.L.	6	154	62	7	3	0	.969	49	23	10	8	0
	New York A.L.	6	156	60	1	5	0	.995	47	20	9	7	0
1954—	New York N.L.	4	111	40	7	2	0	.955	28	15	6	3	0
	Cleveland A.L.	4	106	40	4	2	0	.973	37	24	7	16	2
1955—	Brooklyn N.L.	7	180	84	6	12	0	.978	55	22	10	6	1
	New York A.L.	7	180	72	2	7	0	.992	41	24	9	12	3
1956—	Brooklyn N.L.	7	183	69	2	8	0	.992	42	21	8	9	0
	New York A.L.	7	185	66	6	7	0	.977	40	22	8	6	0
1957—	Milwaukee N.L.	7	186	93	3	10	1	.989	46	23	8	9	2
	New York A.L.	7	187	72	6	5	0	.977	45	23	9	10	2
1958—	Milwaukee N.L.	7	189	78	7	5	0	.974	58	19	6	8	5
	New York A.L.	7	191	65	3	5	1	.988	40	22	9	9	0
1959—	Los Angeles N.L.	6	159	69	4	7	0	.983	42	24	9	13	4
	Chicago A.L.	6	156	62	4	2	1	.982	43	21	7	9	2
1960—	Pittsburgh N.L.	7	186	67	4	7	3	.984	42	25	10	9	2
	New York A.L.	7	183	93	8	9	0	.972	51	25	10	11	3
1961—	Cincinnati N.L.	5	132	42	4	7	1	.978	33	24	9	15	1
	New York A.L.	5	135	50	5	1	1	.974	34	18	6	4	1
1962—	San Francisco N.L.	7	183	67	8	9	1	.969	39	21	7	7	1
	New York A.L.	7	183	67	5	5	0	.980	43	18	6	4	0
1963—	Los Angeles N.L.	4	108	31	3	1	0	.979	17	13	4	1	0
	New York A.L.	4	102	49	1	7	0	.993	24	20	7	7	0
1964—	St. Louis N.L.	7	189	64	4	6	0	.984	47	21	8	12	3
	New York A.L.	7	186	82	9	6	3	.968	47	21	9	8	1
1965—	Los Angeles N.L.	7	180	72	6	7	0	.977	52	20	7	7	1
	Minnesota A.L.	7	180	58	5	3	0	.979	36	21	9	7	0
1966—	Los Angeles N.L.	4	102	44	6	4	0	.961	24	23	8	8	1
	Baltimore A.L.	4	108	33	0	4	0	1.000	18	13	4	0	0
1967—	St. Louis N.L.	7	183	66	4	3	0	.984	40	23	10	8	0
	Boston A.L.	7	183	66	4	4	1	.984	43	25	10	13	1
1968—	St. Louis N.L.	7	186	48	2	7	0	.992	49	25	10	8	1
	Detroit A.L.	7	186	72	11	4	0	.959	44	24	9	8	1

WORLD SERIES RECORDS

Year	Club	G.	PO.	A.	E.	DP.	PB.	F.A.	LOB.	Pl.	Pi.	PH.	PR.
1969—	New York N.L.	5	135	42	2	0	0	.989	34	21	6	4	1
	Baltimore A.L.	5	129	51	4	4	0	.978	29	21	7	5	3
1970—	Cincinnati N.L.	5	129	50	3	4	0	.984	28	24	9	13	0
	Baltimore A.L.	5	135	43	5	3	0	.973	31	21	9	3	0
1971—	Pittsburgh N.L.	7	185	70	3	7	1	.988	63	25	10	8	1
	Baltimore A.L.	7	183	69	9	2	0	.966	39	21	10	6	1
1972—	Cincinnati N.L.	7	187	89	5	5	0	.982	49	22	8	16	2
	Oakland A.L.	7	186	65	9	4	0	.965	45	23	8	13	8
1973—	New York N.L.	7	195	72	10	3	1	.964	72	22	7	15	3
	Oakland A.L.	7	198	79	9	8	1	.969	58	24	8	20	4
1974—	Los Angeles N.L.	5	126	50	6	5	0	.967	36	19	6	9	2
	Oakland A.L.	5	132	51	5	6	0	.973	26	20	5	6	4
1975—	Cincinnati N.L.	7	195	76	2	8	0	.993	50	22	9	8	0
	Boston A.L.	7	196	72	6	6	0	.978	52	23	10	13	0
1976—	Cincinnati N.L.	4	108	36	5	4	0	.966	22	16	7	0	0
	New York A.L.	4	104	41	2	6	0	.986	33	21	7	9	0
1977—	Los Angeles N.L.	6	165	69	1	4	0	.996	31	25	9	10	1
	New York A.L.	6	168	68	3	2	1	.987	32	20	7	6	0
1978—	Los Angeles N.L.	6	158	64	7	4	0	.969	38	23	8	4	0
	New York A.L.	6	159	54	2	9	1	.991	47	24	8	5	2
1979—	Pittsburgh N.L.	7	186	79	9	11	0	.967	60	24	9	11	1
	Baltimore A.L.	7	186	85	9	5	0	.968	49	25	9	23	2
1980—	Philadelphia N.L.	6	161	68	2	8	0	.991	41	22	10	4	1
	Kansas City A.L.	6	156	72	7	8	0	.970	54	21	7	3	3
1981—	Los Angeles N.L.	6	156	65	9	6	0	.961	46	24	10	14	2
	New York A.L.	6	153	55	4	2	1	.981	55	24	9	10	5
1982—	St. Louis N.L.	7	183	74	7	9	0	.973	49	22	8	8	3
	Milwaukee A.L.	7	180	81	11	3	0	.960	44	21	9	2	1
1983—	Philadelphia N.L.	5	132	42	3	3	0	.983	23	23	8	12	3
	Baltimore A.L.	5	135	51	4	5	0	.979	28	23	7	13	2
1984—	San Diego N.L.	5	126	40	4	5	0	.976	34	24	10	4	3
	Detroit A.L.	5	132	52	4	2	0	.979	39	22	7	10	1

WORLD SERIES HOME RUNS
AMERICAN LEAGUE (347)

1903—2—Boston, Patrick H. Dougherty (2).
1904—No Series.
1905—0—Philadelphia.
1906—0—Chicago.
1907—0—Detroit.
1908—0—Detroit.
1909—2—Detroit, David J. Jones (1), Samuel Crawford (1).
1910—1—Philadelphia, Daniel F. Murphy (1).
1911—3—Philadelphia, J. Franklin Baker (2), Reuben N. Oldring (1).
1912—1—Boston, William L. Gardner (1).
1913—2—Philadelphia, J. Franklin Baker (1), Walter H. Schang (1).
1914—0—Philadelphia.
1915—3—Boston, Harry B. Hooper (2), George E. Lewis (1).
1916—2—Boston, William L. Gardner (2).
1917—1—Chicago, Oscar C. Felsch (1).
1918—0—Boston.
1919—1—Chicago, Joseph J. Jackson (1).
1920—2—Cleveland, Elmer J. Smith (1), James C. Bagby (1).
1921—2—New York, George H. Ruth (1), Wilson L. Fewster (1).
1922—2—New York, Aaron L. Ward (2).
1923—5—New York, George H. Ruth (3), Aaron L. Ward (1), Joseph A. Dugan (1).
1924—5—Washington, Leon A. Goslin (3), Stanley R. Harris (2).
1925—8—Washington, Joseph Harris (3), Leon A. Goslin (3), Joseph I. Judge (1), Roger T. Peckinpaugh (1).
1926—4—New York, George H. Ruth (4).
1927—2—New York, George H. Ruth (2).
1928—9—New York, H. Louis Gehrig (4), George H. Ruth (3), Robert W. Meusel (1), Cedric N. Durst (1).
1929—6—Philadelphia, James E. Foxx (2), Aloysius H. Simmons (2), George W. Haas (2).
1930—6—Philadelphia, Gordon S. Cochrane (2), Aloysius H. Simmons (2), James E. Foxx (1), James J. Dykes (1).
1931—3—Philadelphia, Aloysius H. Simmons (2), James E. Foxx (1).
1932—8—New York, H. Louis Gehrig (3), George H. Ruth (2), Anthony M. Lazzeri (2), Earle B. Combs (1).
1933—2—Washington, Leon A. Goslin (1), Fred W. Schulte (1).
1934—2—Detroit, Henry B. Greenberg (1), Charles L. Gehringer (1).
1935—1—Detroit, Henry B. Greenberg (1).

WORLD SERIES RECORDS

1936—7—New York, H. Louis Gehrig (2), George A. Selkirk (2), Anthony M. Lazzeri (1), William M. Dickey (1), Alvin J. Powell (1).
1937—4—New York, Anthony M. Lazzeri (1), H. Louis Gehrig (1), Myril O. Hoag (1), Joseph P. DiMaggio (1).
1938—5—New York, Frank P. Crosetti (1), Joseph P. DiMaggio (1), Joseph L. Gordon (1), William M. Dickey (1), Thomas D. Henrich (1).
1939—7—New York, Charles E. Keller (3), William M. Dickey (2), Ellsworth T. Dahlgren (1), Joseph P. DiMaggio (1).
1940—4—Detroit, Bruce D. Campbell (1), Rudolph P. York (1), Michael F. Higgins (1), Henry B. Greenberg (1).
1941—2—New York, Joseph L. Gordon (1), Thomas D. Henrich (1).
1942—3—New York, Charles E. Keller (2), Philip F. Rizzuto (1).
1943—2—New York, Joseph L. Gordon (1), William M. Dickey (1).
1944—1—St. Louis, George H. McQuinn (1).
1945—2—Detroit, Henry B. Greenberg (2).
1946—4—Boston, Rudolph P. York (2), Robert P. Doerr (1), D. Leon Culberson (1).
1947—4—New York, Joseph P. DiMaggio (2), Thomas D. Henrich (1), Lawrence P. Berra (1).
1948—4—Cleveland, Lawrence E. Doby (1), L. Dale Mitchell (1), James E. Hegan (1), Joseph L. Gordon (1).
1949—2—New York, Thomas D. Henrich (1), Joseph P. DiMaggio (1).
1950—2—New York, Joseph P. DiMaggio (1), Lawrence P. Berra (1).
1951—5—New York, Joseph E. Collins (1), Eugene R. Woodling (1), Joseph P. DiMaggio (1), Gilbert J. McDougald (1), Philip F. Rizzuto (1).
1952—10—New York, John R. Mize (3), Mickey C. Mantle (2), Lawrence P. Berra (2), Gilbert J. McDougald (1), Alfred M. Martin (1), Eugene R. Woodling (1).
1953—9—New York, Mickey C. Mantle (2), Gilbert J. McDougald (2), Alfred M. Martin (2), Lawrence P. Berra (1), Joseph E. Collins (1), Eugene R. Woodling (1).
1954—3—Cleveland, Alphonse E. Smith (1), Victor W. Wertz (1), Henry Majeski (1).
1955—8—New York, Joseph E. Collins (2), Lawrence P. Berra (1), Robert H. Cerv (1), Elston G. Howard (1), Mickey C. Mantle (1), Gilbert J. McDougald (1), William J. Skowron (1).
1956—12—New York, Mickey C. Mantle (3), Lawrence P. Berra (3), Alfred M. Martin (2), Enos B. Slaughter (1), Henry A. Bauer (1), Elston G. Howard (1), William J. Skowron (1).
1957—7—New York, Henry A. Bauer (2), Anthony C. Kubek (2), Mickey C. Mantle (1), Lawrence P. Berra (1), Elston G. Howard (1).
1958—10—New York, Henry A. Bauer (4), Gilbert J. McDougald (2), Mickey C. Mantle (2), William J. Skowron (2).
1959—4—Chicago, Theodore B. Kluszewski (3), J. Sherman Lollar (1).
1960—10—New York, Mickey C. Mantle (3), Roger E. Maris (2), William J. Skowron (2), Lawrence P. Berra (1), Elston G. Howard (1), Robert C. Richardson (1).
1961—7—New York, John E. Blanchard (2), Lawrence P. Berra (1), Elston G. Howard (1), Hector Lopez (1), Roger E. Maris (1), William J. Skowron (1).
1962—3—New York, Thomas M. Tresh (1), Roger E. Maris (1), Cletis L. Boyer (1).
1963—2—New York, Thomas M. Tresh (1), Mickey C. Mantle (1).
1964—10—New York, Mickey C. Mantle (3), Philip F. Linz (1), Thomas M. Tresh (2), Roger E. Maris (1), Joseph A. Pepitone (1), Cletis L. Boyer (1).
1965—6—Minnesota, Zoilo Versalles (1), Pedro Oliva (1), Harmon C. Killebrew (1), Donald R. Mincher (1), W. Robert Allison (1), James T. Grant (1).
1966—4—Baltimore, Frank Robinson (2), Brooks C. Robinson (1), Paul L. Blair (1).
1967—8—Boston, Carl Yastrzemski (3), C. Reginald Smith (2), Americo P. Petrocelli (2), Jose R. Santiago (1).
1968—8—Detroit, Albert W. Kaline (2), James T. Northrup (2), Norman D. Cash (1), William W. Horton (1), Michael S. Lolich (1), Richard J. McAuliffe (1).
1969—3—Baltimore, Donald A. Buford (1), David A. McNally (1), Frank Robinson (1).
1970—10—Baltimore, John W. Powell (2), Frank Robinson (2), Brooks C. Robinson (2), Donald A. Buford (1), Elrod J. Hendricks (1), David A. McNally (1), Mervin W. Rettenmund (1).
1971—5—Baltimore, Donald A. Buford (2), Frank Robinson (2), Mervin W. Rettenmund (1).
1972—5—Oakland, F. Gene Tenace (4), Joseph O. Rudi (1).
1973—2—Oakland, Dagoberto B. Campaneris (1), Reginald M. Jackson (1).
1974—4—Oakland, Raymond E. Fosse (1), Kenneth D. Holtzman (1), Reginald M. Jackson (1), Joseph O. Rudi (1).
1975—6—Boston, Bernardo Carbo (2), Carlton E. Fisk (2), Dwight M. Evans (1), Fredric M. Lynn (1).
1976—1—New York, James P. Mason (1).
1977—8—New York, Reginald M. Jackson (5), C. Christopher Chambliss (1), Thurman L. Munson (1), William L. Randolph (1).
1978—3—New York, Reginald M. Jackson (2), Roy H. White (1).
1979—4—Baltimore, Douglas V. DeCinces (1), Eddie C. Murray (1), Benigno Ayala (1), Richard F. Dauer (1).
1980—8—Kansas City, Willie M. Aikens (4), Amos J. Otis (3), George H. Brett (1).
1981—6—New York, William L. Randolph (2), Robert J. Watson (2), Richard A. Cerone (1), Reginald M. Jackson (1).
1982—5—Milwaukee, Ted L. Simmons (2), Cecil C. Cooper (1), Benjamin A. Oglivie (1), Robin R. Yount (1).
1983—6—Baltimore, Eddie C. Murray (2), James E. Dwyer (1), John L. Lowenstein (1), Darnell G. Ford (1), J. Rikard Dempsey (1).
1984—7—Detroit, Kirk H. Gibson (2), Alan S. Trammell (2), Martin H. Castillo (1), Larry D. Herndon (1), Lance M. Parrish (1).

WORLD SERIES RECORDS
NATIONAL LEAGUE (240)

1903—1—Pittsburgh, James D. Sebring (1).
1904—No Series.
1905—0—New York.
1906—0—Chicago.
1907—0—Chicago.
1908—1—Chicago, Joseph B. Tinker (1).
1909—2—Pittsburgh, Fred C. Clarke (2).
1910—0—Chicago.
1911—0—New York.
1912—1—New York, Lawrence J. Doyle (1).
1913—1—New York, Fred C. Merkle (1).
1914—1—Boston, Henry M. Gowdy (1).
1915—1—Philadelphia, Fred W. Luderus (1).
1916—1—Brooklyn, Henry H. Myers (1).
1917—2—New York, Benjamin M. Kauff (2).
1918—0—Chicago.
1919—0—Cincinnati.
1920—0—Brooklyn.
1921—2—New York, Frank Snyder (1), Emil F. Meusel (1).
1922—1—New York, Emil F. Meusel (1).
1923—5—New York, Charles D. Stengel (2), Emil F. Meusel (1), Ross Youngs (1), Frank Snyder (1).
1924—4—New York, George L. Kelly (1), William H. Terry (1), Wilfred D. Ryan (1), John N. Bentley (1).
1925—4—Pittsburgh, Harold J. Traynor (1), F. Glenn Wright (1), Hazen S. Cuyler (1), G. Edward Moore (1).
1926—4—St. Louis, William H. Southworth (1), Thomas J. Thevenow (1), Jesse J. Haines (1), Lester R. Bell (1).
1927—0—Pittsburgh.
1928—1—St. Louis, James L. Bottomley (1).
1929—1—Chicago, Charles J. Grimm. (1).
1930—2—St. Louis, George A. Watkins (1), Taylor L. Douthit (1).
1931—2—St. Louis, John L. Martin (1), George A. Watkins (1).
1932—3—Chicago, Hazen S. Cuyler (1), Charles L. Hartnett (1), J. Frank Demaree (1).
1933—3—New York, Melvin T. Ott (2), William H. Terry (1).
1934—2—St. Louis, Joseph M. Medwick (1), William DeLancey (1).
1935—5—Chicago, J. Frank Demaree (2), Charles L. Hartnett (1), Charles H. Klein (1), William Herman (1).
1936—4—New York, Richard Bartell (1), James A. Ripple (1), Melvin T. Ott (1), Joseph G. Moore (1).
1937—1—New York, Melvin T. Ott. (1).
1938—2—Chicago, Joseph A. Marty (1), James K. O'Dea (1).
1939—0—Cincinnati.
1940—2—Cincinnati, James A. Ripple (1), William H. Walters (1).
1941—1—Brooklyn, Harold P. Reiser (1).
1942—2—St. Louis, Enos B. Slaughter (1), George J. Kurowski (1).
1943—2—St. Louis, Martin W. Marion (1), Raymond F. Sanders (1).
1944—3—St. Louis, Stanley F. Musial (1), Raymond F. Sanders (1), Daniel W. Litwhiler (1).
1945—1—Chicago, Philip J. Cavarretta (1).
1946—1—St. Louis, Enos B. Slaughter (1).
1947—1—Brooklyn, Fred E. Walker (1).
1948—4—Boston, Robert I. Elliott (2), Marvin A. Rickert (1), William F. Salkeld (1).
1949—4—Brooklyn, Harold H. Reese (1), Luis R. Olmo (1), Roy Campanella (1), Gilbert R. Hodges (1).
1950—0—Philadelphia.
1951—2—New York, Alvin R. Dark (1), Carroll W. Lockman (1).
1952—6—Brooklyn, Edwin D. Snider (4), Jack R. Robinson (1), Harold H. Reese (1).
1953—8—Brooklyn, James Gilliam (2), Roy Campanella (1), William R. Cox (1), Carl A. Furillo (1), Gilbert R. Hodges (1), George T. Shuba (1), Edwin D. Snider (1).
1954—2—New York, James L. Rhodes (2).
1955—9—Brooklyn, Edwin D. Snider (4), Roy Campanella (2), Edmundo Amoros (1), Carl A. Furillo (1), Gilbert R. Hodges (1).
1956—3—Brooklyn, Edwin D. Snider (1), Jack R. Robinson (1), Gilbert R. Hodges (1).
1957—8—Milwaukee, Henry L. Aaron (3), Frank J. Torre (2), Edwin L. Mathews (1), John Logan (1), Delmar W. Crandall (1).
1958—3—Milwaukee, Delmar W. Crandall (1), William H. Bruton (1), S. Lewis Burdette (1).
1959—7—Los Angeles, Charles L. Neal (2), Charles A. Essegian (2), Wallace W. Moon (1), Edwin D. Snider (1), Gilbert R. Hodges (1).
1960—4—Pittsburgh, William S. Mazeroski (2), Glenn R. Nelson (1), Harold W. Smith (1).
1961—3—Cincinnati, Gordon C. Coleman (1), Walter C. Post (1), Frank Robinson (1).
1962—5—San Francisco, Charles J. Hiller (1), Willie L. McCovey (1), Thomas F. Haller (1), L. Edgar Bailey (1), Jose A. Pagan (1).
1963—3—Los Angeles, John Roseboro (1), William J. Skowron (1), Frank O. Howard (1).
1964—5—St. Louis, Kenton L. Boyer (2), Louis C. Brock (1), T. Michael Shannon (1), J. Timothy McCarver (1).
1965—5—Los Angeles, Ronald R. Fairly (2), Louis B. Johnson (2), M. Wesley Parker (1).
1966—1—Los Angeles, James K. Lefebvre (1).
1967—5—St. Louis, Louis C. Brock (1), Robert Gibson (1), M. Julian Javier (1), Roger E. Maris (1), T. Michael Shannon (1).

1968—7—St. Louis, Louis C. Brock (2), Orlando Cepeda (2), Robert Gibson (1), J. Timothy McCarver (1), T. Michael Shannon (1).
1969—6—New York, Donald A. Clendenon (3), Tommie L. Agee (1), Edward E. Kranepool (1), Albert J. Weis (1).
1970—5—Cincinnati, Lee A. May (2), Johnny L. Bench (1), Peter E. Rose (1), Robert Tolan (1).
1971—5—Pittsburgh, Robert E. Robertson (2), Roberto W. Clemente (2), Richard J. Hebner (1).
1972—3—Cincinnati, Johnny L. Bench (1), Denis J. Menke (1), Peter E. Rose (1).
1973—4—New York, R. Wayne Garrett (2), Cleon J. Jones (1), Daniel J. Staub (1).
1974—4—Los Angeles, William J. Buckner (1), Willie M. Crawford (1), Joseph V. Ferguson (1), James S. Wynn (1).
1975—7—Cincinnati, Atanasio R. Perez (3), Cesar F. Geronimo (2), Johnny L. Bench (1), David I. Concepcion (1).
1976—4—Cincinnati, Johnny L. Bench (2), Daniel Driessen (1), Joe L. Morgan (1).
1977—9—Los Angeles, C. Reginald Smith (3), Stephen W. Yeager (2), Johnnie B. Baker (1), Ronald C. Cey (1), Steven P. Garvey (1), David E. Lopes (1).
1978—6—Los Angeles, David E. Lopes (3), Johnnie B. Baker (1), Ronald C. Cey (1), C. Reginald Smith (1).
1979—3—Pittsburgh, Wilver D. Stargell (3).
1980—3—Philadelphia, Michael J. Schmidt (2), Arnold R. McBride (1).
1981—6—Los Angeles, Pedro Guerrero (2), Stephen W. Yeager (2), Ronald C. Cey (1), John W. Johnstone (1).
1982—4—St. Louis, Willie D. McGee (2), Keith Hernandez (1), Darrell R. Porter (1).
1983—4—Philadelphia, Joe L. Morgan (2), Garry L. Maddox (1), Gary N. Matthews (1).
1984—3—San Diego, Kurt A. Bevacqua (2), Terrence E. Kennedy (1).

WORLD SERIES ATTENDANCE

Year	Games	Attendance	Year	Games	Attendance	Year	Games	Attendance
1903	8	100,429	1931	7	231,567	1958	7	393,909
1905	5	91,723	1932	4	191,998	1959	6	420,784
1906	6	99,845	1933	5	163,076	1960	7	349,813
1907	5	78,068	1934	7	281,510	1961	5	223,247
1908	5	62,232	1935	6	286,672	1962	7	376,864
1909	7	145,295	1936	6	302,924	1963	4	247,279
1910	5	124,222	1937	5	238,142	1964	7	321,807
1911	6	179,851	1938	4	200,833	1965	7	364,326
1912	8	252,037	1939	4	183,849	1966	4	220,791
1913	5	151,000	1940	7	281,927	1967	7	304,085
1914	4	111,009	1941	5	235,773	1968	7	379,670
1915	5	143,351	1942	5	277,101	1969	5	272,378
1916	5	162,859	1943	5	277,312	1970	5	253,183
1917	6	186,654	1944	6	206,708	1971	7	351,091
1918	6	128,483	1945	7	333,457	1972	7	363,149
1919	8	236,928	1946	7	250,071	1973	7	358,289
1920	7	178,737	1947	7	389,763	1974	5	260,004
1921	8	269,976	1948	6	358,362	1975	7	308,272
1922	5	185,947	1949	5	236,716	1976	4	223,009
1923	6	301,430	1950	4	196,009	1977	6	337,708
1924	7	283,665	1951	6	341,977	1978	6	337,304
1925	7	282,848	1952	7	340,706	1979	7	367,597
1926	7	328,051	1953	6	307,350	1980	6	324,516
1927	4	201,705	1954	4	251,507	1981	6	338,081
1928	4	199,072	1955	7	362,310	1982	7	384,570
1929	5	190,490	1956	7	345,903	1983	5	304,139
1930	6	212,619	1957	7	394,712	1984	5	271,820

All-Time World Series Records
1903 Through 1984

INDIVIDUAL BATTING, BASE-RUNNING—GAME, INNING

Most At-Bats, Game, Nine Innings (22 times)
  6—Dougherty, Patrick H., Boston A.L., October 7, 1903.
   Collins, James J., Boston, A.L., October 7, 1903.
   Sheckard, James T., Chicago N.L., October 10, 1908.
   Groh, Henry K., Cincinnati N.L., October 9, 1919.
   Burns, George J., New York N.L., October 7, 1921.
   Koenig, Mark A., New York A.L., October 6, 1926.
   Crosetti, Frank P., New York A.L., October 2, 1932.
   Dickey, William M., New York A.L., October 2, 1932.
   Sewell, Joseph W., New York A.L., October 2, 1932.
   Rolfe, Robert A., New York A.L., October 6, 1936.
   DiMaggio, Joseph P., New York A.L., October 6, 1936.
   Brown, James R., St. Louis N.L., October 4, 1942.
   Schoendienst, Albert F., St. Louis N.L., October 10, 1946.
   Slaughter, Enos, St. Louis N.L., October 10, 1946.
   Reese, Harold H., Brooklyn N.L., October 5, 1956.
   Kubek, Anthony C., New York A.L., October 6, 1960.
   Skowron, William J., New York A.L., October 6, 1960.
   Boyer, Cletis L., New York A.L., October 12, 1960.
   Richardson, Robert C., New York A.L., October 9, 1961.
   Kubek, Anthony C., New York A.L., October 9, 1961.
   Molitor, Paul L., Milwaukee A.L., October 12, 1982.
   Yount, Robin R., Milwaukee A.L., October 12, 1982.

Most At-Bats, Extra-Inning Game
  7—Hahn, Donald A., New York N.L., October 14, 1973, 12 innings.

Most Times Faced Pitcher, Game, No Official At-Bats
  5—Clarke, Fred C., Pittsburgh N.L., October 16, 1909, 4 bases on balls, one sacrifice hit.

Most At-Bats, Inning
  2—Held by many players. Last player—Garbey, Barbaro G., Detroit A.L., October 12, 1984, second inning.

Most Times Faced Pitcher, Inning
  2—Held by many players. Last player—Garbey, Barbaro G., Detroit A.L., October 12, 1984, second inning.

Most At-Bats, Inning, Pinch-Hitter
  2—Burns, George H., Philadelphia A.L., October 12, 1929, seventh inning. (Flied out to shortstop and struck out.)

Most Times Faced Pitcher Twice, Inning, Series
  2—Musial, Stanley F., St. Louis N.L., September 30, ninth inning; October 4, 1942, fourth inning.

Most Times Faced Pitcher Twice, Inning, Total Series
  3—DiMaggio, Joseph P., New York A.L., October 6, 1936, ninth inning; October 6, 1937, sixth inning; September 30, 1947, fifth inning.

Most Runs, Game
  4—Ruth, George H., New York A.L., October 6, 1926.
   Combs, Earle B., New York A.L., October 2, 1932.
   Crosetti, Frank P., New York A.L., October 2, 1936.
   Slaughter, Enos B., St. Louis N.L., October 10, 1946.
   Jackson, Reginald M., New York A.L., October 18, 1977.

Most Runs, Inning
  2—Frisch, Frank F., New York N.L., October 7, 1921, seventh inning.
   Simmons, Aloysius H., Philadelphia A.L., October 12, 1929, seventh inning.
   Foxx, James E., Philadelphia A.L., October 12, 1929, seventh inning.
   McAuliffe, Richard J., Detroit A.L., October 9, 1968, third inning.
   Stanley, Mitchell J., Detroit A.L., October 9, 1968, third inning.
   Kaline, Albert W., Detroit A.L., October 9, 1968, third inning.

Most Runs Batted In, Game
  6—Richardson, Robert C., New York A.L., October 8, 1960.

Most Runs Batted In, Inning (12 times)
  4—Smith, Elmer J., Cleveland A.L., October 10, 1920, first inning.
   Lazzeri, Anthony M., New York A.L., October 2, 1936, third inning.
   McDougald, Gilbert J., New York A.L., October 9, 1951, third inning.

Mantle, Mickey C., New York A.L., October 4, 1953, third inning.
Berra, Lawrence P., New York A.L., October 5, 1956, second inning.
Skowron, William J. New York A.L., October 10, 1956, seventh inning.
Richardson, Robert C., New York A.L., October 8, 1960, first inning.
Hiller, Charles J., San Francisco, N.L., October 8, 1962, seventh inning.
Boyer, Kenton L., St. Louis N.L., October 11, 1964, sixth inning.
Pepitone, Joseph A., New York A.L., October 14, 1964, eighth inning.
Northrup, James T., Detroit A.L., October 9, 1968, third inning.
McNally, David A., Baltimore A.L., October 13, 1970, sixth inning.

Batting in All Club's Runs, Game (Most)

4—Bauer, Henry A., New York A.L., October 4, 1958; won, 4-0.
Boyer, Kenton L., St. Louis N.L., October 11, 1964; won 4-3.
Cey, Ronald C., Los Angeles N.L., October 11, 1978; won 4-3.
Trammell, Alan S., Detroit A.L., October 13, 1984; won 4-2.

Most Times Reached First Base Safely, Nine-Inning Game (Batting 1.000)

5—Ruth, George H., New York A.L., October 6, 1926, three home runs, two bases on balls.
Ruth, George H., New York A.L., October 10, 1926, one home run, four bases on balls.
Brock, Louis C., St. Louis N.L., October 4, 1967, four singles, one base on balls.
Robinson, Brooks C., Baltimore A.L., October 11, 1971, three singles, two bases on balls.
Staub, Daniel J., New York N.L., October 17, 1973, three singles, one home run, one base on balls.
Garcia, Alfonso R., Baltimore A.L., October 12, 1979, two singles, one double, one triple, one base on balls.
Jackson, Reginald M., New York A.L., October 24, 1981, two singles, one home run, two bases on balls.

Most Hits, Game

5—Molitor, Paul L., Milwaukee A.L., October 12, 1982.

Getting All Club's Hits, Game (Most)

3—Meusel, Emil F., New York N.L., October 14, 1923, one single, one double, one triple.

Most At-Bats, Game, Nine Innings, No Hits

5—Held by many players.

Most At-Bats, Extra-Inning Game, No Hits

6—Jackson, Travis C., New York N.L., October 10, 1924, 12 innings.
Critz, Hugh M., New York N.L., October 6, 1933, 11 innings.
Millan, Felix B., New York N.L., October 14, 1973, 12 innings.
Rivers, John M., New York A.L., October 11, 1977, 12 innings.

Most Hits, Two Consecutive Games, One Series

7—Isbell, Frank, Chicago A.L., October 13 (4), October 14 (3), 1906.
Lindstrom, Fred C., New York N.L., October 7 (3), October 8 (4), 1924.
Irvin, Monford M., New York N.L., October 4 (4), October 5 (3), 1951.
Munson, Thurman L., New York A.L., October 19 (3), October 21 (4), 1976.
Molitor, Paul L., Milwaukee A.L., October 12 (5), October 13 (2), 1982.

Most Hits, Inning (16 times)

2—Youngs, Ross, New York N.L., October 7, 1921, seventh inning.
Simmons, Aloysius H., Philadelphia A.L., October 12, 1929, seventh inning.
Foxx, James E., Philadelphia A.L., October 12, 1929, seventh inning.
Dykes, James, Philadelphia A.L., October 12, 1929, seventh inning.
Moore, Joseph G., New York N.L., October 4, 1933, sixth inning.
Dean, Jerome H., St. Louis N.L., October 9, 1934, third inning.
DiMaggio, Joseph P., New York A.L., October 6, 1936, ninth inning.
Leiber, Henry, New York N.L., October 9, 1937, second inning.
Musial Stanley F., St. Louis N.L., October 4, 1942, fourth inning.
Howard, Elston G., New York A.L., October 6, 1960, sixth inning.
Richardson, Robert C., New York A.L., October 6, 1960, sixth inning.
Cerv, Robert H., New York A.L., October 8, 1960, first inning.
Quilici, Frank R., Minnesota A.L., October 6, 1965, third inning.
Kaline, Albert W., Detroit A.L., October 9, 1968, third inning.
Cash, Norman D., Detroit A.L., October 9, 1968, third inning.
Rettenmund, Mervin W., Baltimore A.L., October 11, 1971, fifth inning.

Most One-Base Hits, Game

5—Molitor, Paul L., Milwaukee A.L., October 12, 1982.

Most One-Base Hits, Inning (8 times)

2—Foxx, James E., Philadelphia A.L., October 12, 1929, seventh inning.
Moore, Joseph G., New York N.L., October 4, 1933, sixth inning.
DiMaggio, Joseph P., New York A.L., October 6, 1936, ninth inning.
Leiber, Henry, New York N.L., October 9, 1937, second inning.
Cerv, Robert H., New York A.L., October 8, 1960, first inning.
Kaline, Albert W., Detroit A.L., October 9, 1968, third inning.
Cash, Norman D., Detroit A.L., October 9, 1968, third inning.
Rettenmund, Mervin W., Baltimore A.L., October 11, 1971, fifth inning.

WORLD SERIES RECORDS

Most Two-Base Hits, Game
    4—Isbell, Frank, Chicago A.L., October 13, 1906.

Most Two-Base Hits, Game, Batting in Three Runs
    1—Frisch, Frank F., St. Louis N.L., October 9, 1934, third inning.
       Richards, Paul R., Detroit A.L., October 10, 1945, first inning.
       Brock, Louis C., St. Louis N.L., October 6, 1968, eighth inning.

Most Two-Base Hits, Inning
    1—Held by many players.

Most Three-Base Hits, Game (5 times)
    2—Leach, Thomas W., Pittsburgh N.L., October 1, 1903.
       Dougherty, Patrick H., Boston A.L., October 7, 1903.
       Ruether, Walter H., Cincinnati N.L., October 1, 1919.
       Richardson, Robert C., New York A.L., October 12, 1960.
       Davis, H. Thomas, Los Angeles N.L., October 3, 1963.

Most Three-Base Hits, Game, Batting in Three Runs (7 times)
    1—Rohe, George, Chicago A.L., October 11, 1906, sixth inning.
       Youngs, Ross, New York N.L., October 7, 1921, seventh inning.
       Johnson, William R., New York A.L., October 7, 1943, eighth inning.
       Brown, Robert W., New York A.L., October 8, 1949, fifth inning.
       Bauer, Henry A., New York A.L., October 10, 1951, sixth inning.
       Martin, Alfred M., New York A.L., September 30, 1953, first inning.
       Garcia, Alfonso R., Baltimore A.L., October 12, 1979, fourth inning.

Most Three-Base Hits, Inning
    1—Held by many players.

Most Home Runs, Game (3 home runs, 3 times; 2 home runs, 31 times)
    3—Ruth, George H., New York A.L., October 6, 1926, and October 9, 1928, (two consecutive in each game).
       Jackson, Reginald M., New York A.L., October 18, 1977 (consecutive, each on first pitch).
    2—Dougherty, Patrick H., Boston A.L., October 2, 1903.
       Hooper, Harry B., Boston A.L., October 13, 1915.
       Kauff, Benjamin M., New York N.L., October 11, 1917.
       Ruth, George H., New York A.L., October 11, 1923, (consecutive).
       Gehrig, H. Louis, New York A.L., October 7, 1928, (consecutive).
       Gehrig, H. Louis, New York A.L., October 1, 1932, (consecutive).
       Ruth, George H., New York A.L., October 1, 1932.
       Lazzeri, Anthony M., New York A.L., October 2, 1932.
       Keller, Charles E., New York A.L., October 7, 1939.
       Elliott, Robert I., Boston N.L., October 10, 1948, (consecutive).
       Snider, Edwin D., Brooklyn N.L., October 6, 1952, (consecutive).
       Collins, Joseph E., New York A.L., September 28, 1955, (consecutive).
       Snider, Edwin D., Brooklyn N.L., October 2, 1955, (consecutive).
       Berra, Lawrence P., New York A.L., October 10, 1956, (consecutive).
       Kubek, Anthony C., New York A.L., October 5, 1957.
       Mantle, Mickey C., New York A.L., October 2, 1958.
       Kluszewski, Theodore B., Chicago A.L., October 1, 1959, (consecutive).
       Neal, Charles L., Los Angeles N.L., October 2, 1959, (consecutive).
       Mantle, Mickey C., New York A.L., October 6, 1960.
       Yastrzemski, Carl M., Boston A.L., October 5, 1967.
       Petrocelli, Americo, Boston A.L., October 11, 1967, (consecutive).
       Tenace, F. Gene, Oakland A.L., October 14, 1972, (consecutive).
       Perez, Atanasio R., Cincinnati N.L., October 16, 1975, night game, (consecutive).
       Bench, Johnny L., Cincinnati N.L., October 21, 1976, night game.
       Lopes, David E., Los Angeles N.L., October 10, 1978; night game, (consecutive).
       Aikens, Willie M., Kansas City A.L., October 14, 1980; night game.
       Aikens, Willie M., Kansas City A.L., October 18, 1980.
       McGee, Willie D., St. Louis N.L., October 15, 1982; night game, (consecutive).
       Murray, Eddie C., Baltimore A.L., October 16, 1983, (consecutive).
       Trammell, Alan S., Detroit A.L., Octobert 13, 1984, (consecutive).
       Gibson, Kirk H., Detroit A.L., October 14, 1984.

Most Home Runs, Game, by Rookie
    2—Keller, Charles E., New York A.L., October 7, 1939.
       Kubek, Anthony C., New York A.L., October 5, 1957.
       McGee, Willie D., St. Louis N.L., October 15, 1982.

Hitting Home Runs in First Two World Series At-Bats
    Tenace, F. Gene, Oakland A.L., October 14, 1972, second and fifth inning.

Hitting Home Run in First World Series At-Bat (18 times)
    Harris, Joseph, Washington A.L., vs. Pittsburgh N.L., October 7, 1925, second inning.
    Watkins, George A., St. Louis N.L., vs. Philadelphia A.L., October 2, 1930, second inning.
    Ott, Melvin T., New York N.L., vs. Washington A.L., October 3, 1933, first inning.

WORLD SERIES RECORDS

Selkirk, George A., New York A.L., vs. New York N.L., September 30, 1936, third inning.
Rhodes, James L., New York N.L., vs. Cleveland A.L., September 29, 1954, tenth inning.
Howard, Elston G., New York A.L., vs. Brooklyn N.L., September 28, 1955, second inning.
Maris, Roger E., New York A.L., vs. Pittsburgh N.L., October 5, 1960, first inning.
Mincher, Donald R., Minnesota A.L., vs. Los Angeles N.L., October 6. 1965, second inning.
Robinson, Brooks C., Baltimore A.L., vs. Los Angeles N.L., October 5, 1966, first inning.
Santiago, Jose R., Boston A.L., vs. St. Louis N.L., October 4, 1967, third inning.
Lolich, Michael S., Detroit A.L., vs. St. Louis N.L., October 3, 1968, third inning.
Buford, Donald A., Baltimore A.L., vs. New York N.L., October 11, 1969, first inning.
Tenace, F. Gene, Oakland A.L., vs. Cincinnati N.L., October 14, 1972, second inning.
Mason, James P., New York A.L., vs. Cincinnati N.L., October 19, 1976, seventh inning.
DeCinces, Douglas V., Baltimore A.L. vs. Pittsburgh N.L., October 10, 1979, first inning.
Otis, Amos J., Kansas City A.L. vs. Philadelphia N.L., October 14, 1980, second inning.
Watson, Robert J., New York A.L. vs. Los Angeles N.L., October 20, 1981, first inning.
Dwyer, James E., Baltimore A.L. vs. Philadelphia N.L., October 11, 1983, first inning.

Most Times Home Run Winning 1-0 Game

1—Stengel, Charles D., New York N.L., October 12, 1923, seventh inning.
Henrich, Thomas D., New York A.L., October 5, 1949, ninth inning.
Blair, Paul L., Baltimore A.L., October 8, 1966, fifth inning.
Robinson, Frank, Baltimore A.L., October 9, 1966, fourth inning.

Most Times Home Runs, Game, Leadoff Batter Start of Game (13 times)

1—Dougherty, Patrick H., Boston A.L., October 2, 1903 (game 2).
Jones, David J., Detroit A.L., October 13, 1909 (game 5).
Rizzuto, Philip F., New York A.L., October 5, 1942 (game 5).
Mitchell, L. Dale, Cleveland A.L., October 10, 1948 (game 5).
Woodling, Eugene R., New York A.L., October 4, 1953 (game 5).
Smith, Alphonse E., Cleveland A.L., September 30, 1954 (game 2).
Bruton, William H., Milwaukee N.L., October 2, 1958 (game 2).
Brock, Louis C., St. Louis N.L., October 6, 1968 (game 4).
Buford, Donald A., Baltimore A.L., October 11, 1969 (game 1).
Agee, Tommie L., New York N.L., October 14, 1969 (game 3).
Rose, Peter E., Cincinnati N.L., October 20, 1972 (game 5).
Garrett, R. Wayne, New York N.L., October 16, 1973 (game 3).
Lopes, David E., Los Angeles N.L., October 17, 1978 (game 6).

Most Home Runs, By Pitcher, Game (14 times)

1—Bagby, James C., Cleveland A.L., October 10, 1920, 2 on base.
Ryan, Wilfred P., New York N.L., October 6, 1924, 0 on base.
Bentley, John N., New York N.L., October 8, 1924, 1 on base.
Haines, Jesse J., St. Louis N.L., October 5, 1926, 1 on base.
Walters, William H., Cincinnati N.L., October 7, 1940, 0 on base.
Burdette, S. Lewis, Milwaukee N.L., October 2, 1958, 2 on base.
Grant, James T., Minnesota A.L., October 13, 1965, 2 on base.
Santiago, Jose R., Boston A.L., October 4, 1967, 0 on base.
Gibson, Robert, St. Louis N.L., October 12, 1967, 0 on base.
Lolich, Michael S., Detroit A.L., October 3, 1968, 0 on base.
Gibson, Robert, St. Louis N.L., October 6, 1968, 0 on base.
McNally, David A., Baltimore A.L., October 16, 1969, 1 on base.
McNally, David A., Baltimore A.L., October 13, 1970, 3 on base.
Holtzman, Kenneth D., Oakland A.L., October 16, 1974, 0 on base.

Most Home Runs, Inning or Game, Pinch-Hitter (13 times)

1—Berra, Lawrence, New York A.L., October 2, 1947, seventh inning, none on base.
Mize, John R., New York A.L., October 3, 1952, ninth inning, none on base.
Shuba, George T., Brooklyn N.L., September 30, 1953, sixth inning, one on base.
Rhodes, James L., New York N.L., September 29, 1954, tenth inning, two on base.
Majeski, Henry, Cleveland A.L., October 2, 1954, fifth inning, two on base.
Cerv, Robert H., New York A.L., October 2, 1955, seventh inning, none on base.
Essegian, Charles A., Los Angeles N.L., October 2, 1959, seventh inning, none on base.
Essegian, Charles A., Los Angeles N.L., October 8, 1959, ninth inning, none on base.
Howard, Elston G., New York A.L., October 5, 1960, ninth inning, one on base.
Blanchard, John E., New York A.L., October 7, 1961, eighth inning, none on base.
Carbo, Bernardo, Boston A.L., October 14, 1975, night game, seventh inning, none on base.
Carbo, Bernardo, Boston A.L., October 21, 1975, night game, eighth inning, two on base.
Johnstone, John W., Los Angeles N.L., October 24, 1981, night game, sixth inning, one on base.

Most Home Runs With Bases Filled, Game (12 times)

1—Smith, Elmer J., Cleveland A.L., October 10, 1920, first inning.
Lazzeri, Anthony M., New York A.L., October 2, 1936, third inning.
McDougald, Gilbert J., New York A.L., October 9, 1951, third inning.
Mantle, Mickey C., New York A.L., October 4, 1953, third inning.
Berra, Lawrence P., New York A.L., October 5, 1956, second inning.
Skowron, William J., New York A.L., October 10, 1956, seventh inning.
Richardson, Robert C., New York A.L., October 8, 1960, first inning.
Hiller, Charles J., San Francisco N.L., October 8, 1962, seventh inning.
Boyer, Kenton L., St. Louis N.L., October 11, 1964, sixth inning.

Pepitone, Joseph A., New York A.L., October 14, 1964, eighth inning.
Northrup, James T., Detroit A.L., October 9, 1968, third inning.
McNally, David A., Baltimore A.L., October 13, 1970, sixth inning.

Most Home Runs, Inning

1—Held by many players.

Most Home Runs, Two Consecutive Innings

2—Ruth, George H., New York A.L., October 11, 1923, fourth and fifth innings, none on base.
Ruth, George H., New York A.L., October 9, 1928, seventh and eighth innings, none on base.
Kluszewski, Theodore B., Chicago A.L., October 1, 1959, third and fourth innings, two on base, each home run.
Jackson, Reginald M., New York A.L., October 18, 1977, fourth and fifth innings, none on base.
Aikens, Willie M., Kansas City A.L., October 18, 1980, first and second innings.

Most Long Hits, Game

4—Isbell, Frank, Chicago A.L., October 13, 1906, four doubles.

Most Long Hits, Two Consecutive Games, One Series

5—Brock, Louis C., St. Louis N.L., October 6 (3), double, triple, home run—October 7 (2), 2 doubles, 1968.

Most Long Hits, Inning

2—Youngs, Ross, New York N.L., October 7, 1921, seventh inning, double and triple.

Most Total Bases, Game

12—Ruth, George H., New York A.L., October 6, 1926, three home runs.
Ruth, George H., New York A.L., October 9, 1928, three home runs.
Jackson, Reginald M., New York A.L., October 18, 1977, three home runs.

Most Total Bases, Inning

5—Youngs, Ross, New York N.L., October 7, 1921, seventh inning, double and triple.
Simmons, Aloysius H., Philadelphia A.L., October 12, 1929, seventh inning, home run and single.

Most Sacrifices, Game

3—Tinker, Joseph B., Chicago N.L., October 12, 1906 (all sacrifice hits).
Westrum, Wesley N., New York N.L., October 2, 1954 (one sacrifice hit and two sacrifice flies).

Most Sacrifice Hits, Inning

1—Held by many players.

Most Sacrifice Flies, Game

2—Westrum, Wesley N., New York N.L., October 2, 1954.

Most Sacrifice Flies, Inning

1—Held by many players.

Most Runs Batted in on Sacrifice Fly

2—Herr, Thomas M., St. Louis N.L., October 16, 1982; second inning.

Most Bases on Balls, Game

4—Clarke, Fred C., Pittsburgh N.L., October 16, 1909.
Hoblitzel, Richard C., Boston A.L., October 9, 1916 (14 innings).
Youngs, Ross, New York N.L., October 10, 1924 (12 innings).
Ruth, George H., New York A.L., October 10, 1926.
Robinson, Jack R., Brooklyn N.L., October 5, 1952 (11 innings).
DeCinces, Douglas V., Baltimore A.L., October 13, 1979.

Most Bases on Balls with Bases Filled, Game

2—Palmer, James A., Baltimore A.L., October 11, 1971, consecutive, fourth and fifth innings.

Most Bases on Balls, Inning

2—Gomez, Vernon L., New York A.L., October 6, 1937, sixth inning.
McAuliffe, Richard J., Detroit A.L., October 9, 1968, third inning.

Most Consecutive Bases on Balls, One Series

5—Gehrig, H. Louis, New York A.L., October 7 (2), October 9 (3), 1928.

Most Bases on Balls, Two Consecutive Games

6—Sheckard, James T., Chicago N.L., October 18 (3), October 20 (3), 1910.

Most Strikeouts, Game (All Consecutive)

5—Pipgras, George W., New York A.L., October 1, 1932.
4—Devore, Joshua, New York N.L., October 16, 1911.
James, William L., Boston N.L., October 10, 1914.
Mogridge, George, Washington A.L., October 7, 1924.
Rowe, Lynwood T., Detroit A.L., October 4, 1934.
Bonham, Ernest E., New York A.L., October 6, 1941.
Collins, Joseph E., New York A.L., October 2, 1953.
Mantle, Mickey C., New York A.L., October 2, 1953.
Stottlemyre, Melvin L., New York A.L., October 8, 1964 (not consecutive).

WORLD SERIES RECORDS

Most Consecutive Strikeouts, One Series
   5—Devore, Joshua, New York N.L., October 16 (4), October 17 (1), 1911.
      Mogridge, George, Washington A.L., October 7 (4), October 10 (1), 1924.
      Pipgras, George W., New York A.L., October 1, 1932.
      Mantle, Mickey C., New York A.L., October 2 (4), October 3 (1), 1953.
      Shannon, T. Michael, St. Louis, N.L., October 12 (2), October 14 (3), 1964.

Most Strikeouts, Inning
   1—Held by many players

Most Stolen Bases, Game
   3—Wagner, John P., Pittsburgh N.L., October 11, 1909.
      Davis, William H., Los Angeles N.L., October 11, 1965.
      Brock, Louis C., St. Louis N.L., October 12, 1967.
      Brock, Louis C., St. Louis N.L., October 5, 1968.

Most Times Stealing Home, Game (12 times)
   1—Dahlen, William F., New York N.L., October 12, 1905, fifth inning. (Front end of double steal.)
      Davis, George S., Chicago A.L., October 13, 1906, third inning. (Front end of double steal.)
      Slagle, James F., Chicago N.L., October 11, 1907, seventh inning.
      Cobb, Tyrus R., Detroit A.L., October 9, 1909, third inning.
      Herzog, Charles L., New York N.L., October 14, 1912, first inning. (Front end of double steal.)
      Schmidt, Charles J., Boston N.L., October 9, 1914, eighth inning. (Front end of double steal.)
      McNally, Michael J., New York A.L., October 5, 1921, fifth inning.
      Meusel, Robert W., New York A.L., October 6, 1921, eighth inning.
      Meusel, Robert W., New York A.L., October 7, 1928, sixth inning. (Front end of double steal.)
      Irvin, Monford, New York N.L., October 4, 1951, first inning.
      Robinson, Jack R., Brooklyn N.L., September 28, 1955, eighth inning.
      McCarver, J. Timothy, St. Louis N.L., October 15, 1964, fourth inning. (Front end of double steal.)

Most Stolen Bases, Inning (7 times)
   2—Slagle, James F., Chicago N.L., October 8, 1907, tenth inning.
      Browne, George E., New York N.L., October 12, 1905, ninth inning.
      Cobb, Tyrus R., Detroit A.L., October 12, 1908, ninth inning.
      Collins, Edward T., Chicago A.L., October 7, 1917, sixth inning.
      Ruth, George H., New York A.L., October 6, 1921, fifth inning.
      Brock, Louis C., St. Louis N.L., October 12, 1967, fifth inning.
      Lopes, David E., Los Angeles N.L., October 15, 1974, first inning.

Most Times Caught Stealing, Game (6 times)
   2—Schulte, Frank, Chicago N.L., October 17, 1910.
      Schulte, Frank, Chicago N.L., October 23, 1910.
      Luderus, Fred W., Philadelphia N.L., October 8, 1915.
      Johnston, James H., Brooklyn N.L., October 9, 1916.
      Livingston, Thompson O., Chicago N.L., October 3, 1945.
      Martin, Alfred M., New York A.L., September 28, 1955.

Most Times Caught Stealing, Inning
   1—Held by many players.

Most Caught Off Base, Game
   2—Flack, Max O., Chicago N.L., September 9, 1918, first base in first inning, second base in third inning.

Most Hit by Pitch, Game
   2—Carey, Max, Pittsburgh N.L., October 7, 1925.
      Berra, Lawrence P., New York A.L., October 2, 1953.
      Robinson, Frank, Cincinnati N.L., October 8, 1961.

Most Hit by Pitch, Inning
   1—Held by many players.

Most Grounded Into Double Play, Game
   3—Mays, Willie H., New York N.L., October 8, 1951.

Most First on Error, Game
   3—Clarke, Fred C., Pittsburgh N.L., October 10, 1903.

Most Times Awarded First Base On Catcher's Interference, Game
   1—Peckinpaugh, Roger T., Washington A.L., October 15, 1925, first inning.
      Metheny, Arthur B., New York A.L., October 6, 1943, sixth inning.
      Boyer, Kenton L., St. Louis N.L., October 12, 1964, first inning.
      Rose, Peter E., Cincinnati N.L., October 10, 1970, fifth inning.
      Hendrick, George A., St. Louis N.L., October 15, 1982, ninth inning.

INDIVIDUAL BATTING, BASE-RUNNING—SERIES RECORDS

Most Series Played
   14—Berra, Lawrence P., New York A.L., 1947, 1949, 1950, 1951, 1952, 1953, 1955, 1956, 1957, 1958, 1960, 1961, 1962, 1963 (75 games, 65 consecutive).

Most Series Eligible, But Did Not Play
   6—Silvera, Charles A., New York A.L., 1950, 1951, 1952, 1953, 1955, 1956 (37 games), played one game, 1949.
   5—Jorgens, Arndt L., New York A.L., 1932, 1936, 1937, 1938, 1939 (23 games).

Most Consecutive Series Played (17 times)
   5—Bauer, Henry A., New York A.L., 1949 through 1953.
      Berra, Lawrence P., New York A.L., 1949 through 1953.
      Lopat, Edmund W., New York A.L., 1949 through 1953.
      Mize, John R., New York A.L., 1949 through 1953.
      Raschi, Victor J., New York A.L., 1949 through 1953.
      Reynolds, Allie P., New York A.L., 1949 through 1953.
      Rizzuto, Philip R., New York A.L., 1949 through 1953.
      Woodling, Eugene R., New York A.L., 1949 through 1953.
      Blanchard, John E., New York A.L., 1960 through 1964.
      Boyer, Cletis L., New York A.L., 1960 through 1964.
      Terry, Ralph W., New York A.L., 1960 through 1964.
      Ford, Edward C., New York A.L., 1960 through 1964.
      Howard, Elston G., New York A.L., 1960 through 1964.
      Lopez, Hector H., New York A.L., 1960 through 1964.
      Mantle, Mickey C., New York A.L., 1960 through 1964.
      Maris, Roger E., New York A.L., 1960 through 1964.
      Richardson, Robert C., New York A.L., 1960 through 1964.

Most Series Played, One Club
   14—Berra, Lawrence P., New York A.L., 1947, 1949, 1950, 1951, 1952, 1953, 1955, 1956, 1957, 1958, 1960, 1961, 1962, 1963 (75 games, 65 consecutive).

Most Series Playing in All Games
   10—DiMaggio, Joseph P., New York A.L., 1936, 1937, 1938, 1939, 1941, 1942, 1947, 1949, 1950, 1951 (51 games).

Most Times Member Winning Club, As Active Player Only
   10—Berra, Lawrence P., New York A.L., 1947, 1949, 1950, 1951, 1952, 1953, 1956, 1958, 1961, 1962.

Most Times on Winning Club—Playing One or More Games Each Series
   10—Berra, Lawrence P., New York A.L., 1947, 1949, 1950, 1951, 1952, 1953, 1956, 1958, 1961, 1962.

Most Times on Losing Club
   6—Reese, Harold H., Brooklyn N.L., 1941, 1947, 1949, 1952, 1953, 1956.
     Howard, Elston G., New York A.L., 1955, 1957, 1960, 1963, 1964. Boston A.L., 1967.

Most Series Played, First Four Years in Major Leagues
   4—DiMaggio, Joseph P., New York A.L., 1936 through 1939.
     Howard, Elston G., New York A.L., 1955 through 1958.
     Kucks, John C., New York A.L., 1955 through 1958.

Most Games, Total Series
   75—Berra, Lawrence P., New York A.L., 1947, 1949, 1950, 1951, 1952, 1953, 1955, 1956, 1957, 1958, 1960, 1961, 1962, 1963 (14 Series, 65 consecutive games).

Most Games, Total Series, One Club
   75—Berra, Lawrence P., New York A.L., 1947, 1949, 1950, 1951, 1952, 1953, 1955, 1956, 1957, 1958, 1960, 1961, 1962, 1963 (14 Series, 65 consecutive games).

Most Consecutive Games Played
   30—Richardson, Robert C., New York A.L., October 5, 1960 through October 15, 1964.

Most Series Batting .300 or Over
   6—Ruth, George H., New York A.L., 1921, 1923, 1926, 1927, 1928, 1932.

Highest Batting Average, Total Series (20 or More Games)
   .391—Brock, Louis C., St. Louis N.L., 1964, 1967, 1968 (3 Series, 21 games, 87 at-bats, 34 hits).
   .363—Baker, J. Franklin, Philadelphia A.L., 1910, 1911, 1913, 1914; New York A.L., 1921, 1922 (6 Series, 25 games, 91 at-bats, 33 hits).
   .361—Gehrig, H. Louis, New York A.L., 1926, 1927, 1928, 1932, 1936, 1937, 1938 (7 Series, 34 games, 119 at-bats, 43 hits).

Highest Batting Average, Series
   4-game Series—.625—Ruth, George H., New York A.L., 1928.
   5-game Series—.500—McLean, John B., New York N.L., 1913.
                   Gordon, Joseph L., New York A.L., 1941.
   6-game Series—.500—Robertson, Davis A., New York N.L., 1917.
                   Martin, Alfred M., New York A.L., 1953.

7-game Series—.500—Martin, John L., St. Louis N.L., 1931.
                       Lindell, John H., New York A.L., 1947 (played only six games due to broken rib).
                       Garner, Philip M., Pittsburgh N.L., 1979.
8-game Series—.400—Herzog, Charles L., New York N.L., 1912.

Most Series Leading Club in Batting Average
   3—Baker, J. Franklin, Philadelphia A.L., 1911, 1913, 1914.
      Reese, Harold H., Brooklyn, N.L., 1947, 1949, 1952 (tied).
      Snider, Edwin D., Brooklyn N.L., 1952 (tied), 1955, 1956 (tied).
      Hodges, Gilbert R., Brooklyn N.L., Los Angeles N.L., 1953, 1956 (tied), 1959.
      Garvey, Steven P., Los Angeles N.L., 1974, 1977, 1981.

Highest Slugging Average, Total Series (20 or More Games)
   .755—Jackson, Reginald M., Oakland A.L., 1973, 1974; New York A.L., 1977, 1978, 1981; 5 Series, 30 games, 98 at-bats, 35 hits, 7 doubles, 1 triple, 10 home runs, 74 total bases.

Highest Slugging Average, Series
   4-game Series—1.727—Gehrig, H. Louis, New York A.L., 1928.
   5-game Series— .929—Gordon, Joseph L., New York A.L., 1941.
                     (Clendenon, Donn A., New York N.L., 1969, had slugging average of 1.071 but played only four games.)
   6-game Series—1.250—Jackson, Reginald M., New York A.L., 1977.
   7-game Series— .913—Tenace, F. Gene, Oakland A.L., 1972.
   8-game Series— .600—Herzog, Charles L., New York N.L., 1912.

Most At-Bats, Total Series
   259—Berra, Lawrence P., New York A.L., 1947, 1949, 1950, 1951, 1952, 1953, 1955, 1956, 1957, 1958, 1960, 1961, 1962, 1963 (14 Series, 75 games).

Most At-Bats, Series
   4-game Series—19—Koenig, Mark A., New York A.L., 1928.
   5-game Series—23—Janvrin, Harold C., Boston A.L., 1916.
                  Moore, Joseph G., New York N.L., 1937.
                  Richardson, Robert C., New York A.L., 1961.
   6-game Series—28—Moore, Joseph G., New York N.L., 1936.
   7-game Series—33—Harris, Stanley R., Washington A.L., 1924.
                  Rice, Edgar C., Washington A.L., 1925.
                  Moreno, Omar R., Pittsburgh N.L., 1979.
   8-game Series—36—Collins, James J., Boston A.L., 1903.

Most Runs, Total Series
   42—Mantle, Mickey C., New York A.L., 1951, 1952, 1953, 1955, 1956, 1957, 1958, 1960, 1961, 1962, 1963, 1964 (12 Series, 65 games).

Most Series, One or More Runs, Total Series
   12—Berra, Lawrence P., New York A.L., 1947, 1949, 1950, 1951, 1952, 1953, 1955, 1956, 1957, 1958, 1960, 1961.

Most Runs, Series
   4-game Series— 9—Ruth, George H., New York A.L., 1928.
                   Gehrig, H. Louis, New York A.L., 1932.
   5-game Series— 6—Baker, J. Franklin, Philadelphia A.L., 1910.
                   Murphy, Daniel F., Philadelphia A.L., 1910.
                   Hooper, Harry B., Boston A.L., 1916.
                   Simmons, Aloysius H., Philadelphia A.L., 1929.
                   May, Lee A., Cincinnati N.L., 1970.
                   Powell, John W., Baltimore A.L., 1970.
                   Whitaker, Louis R., Detroit A.L., 1984.
   6-game Series—10—Jackson, Reginald M., New York A.L., 1977.
   7-game Series— 8—Leach, Thomas W., Pittsburgh N.L., 1909.
                   Martin, John L., St. Louis N.L., 1934.
                   Johnson, William R., New York A.L., 1947.
                   Mantle, Mickey C., New York A.L., 1960.
                   Richardson, Robert C., New York A.L., 1960.
                   Mantle, Mickey C., New York A.L., 1964.
                   Brock, Louis C., St. Louis N.L., 1967.
   8-game Series— 8—Parent, Fred N., Boston A.L., 1903.

Fewest Runs, Series
   0—Owen, Marvin J., Detroit A.L., 7 games, 1934, 29 at-bats.
     Campanella, Roy, Brooklyn N.L., 7 games, 1952, 28 at-bats.
     Myers, Henry H., Brooklyn N.L., 7 games, 1920, 26 at-bats.
     Thomas, J. Gorman, Milwaukee A.L., 7 games, 1982, 26 at-bats.
     White, Frank, Kansas City A.L., 6 games, 1980, 25 at-bats.
     Also many other players with fewer at-bats.

Most Consecutive Games, One or More Runs, Total Series
   9—Ruth, George H., New York A.L., 1927, last 2 games; 1928, 4 games; 1932, first 3 games.

WORLD SERIES RECORDS

Most Runs Batted In, Total Series
    40—Mantle, Mickey C., New York A.L., 1951, 1952, 1953, 1955, 1956, 1957, 1958, 1960, 1961, 1962, 1963, 1964 (12 Series, 65 games).

Most Series, One or More Runs Batted In, Total Series
    11—Berra, Lawrence P., New York A.L., 1947, 1949, 1950, 1952, 1953, 1955, 1956, 1957, 1958, 1960, 1961.

Most Consecutive Games, One or More Runs Batted In, Total Series
    8—Gehrig, H. Louis, New York A.L., 1928 (4), 1932 (4), 17 runs batted in.
       Jackson, Reginald M., New York A.L., 1977 (4), 1978 (4), 14 runs batted in.

Most Runs Batted In, Series
    4-game Series— 9—Gehrig, H. Louis, New York A.L., 1928.
    5-game Series— 8—Murphy, Daniel F., Philadelphia A.L., 1910.
                            May, Lee A., Cincinnati N.L., 1970.
    6-game Series—10—Kluszewski, Theodore B., Chicago A.L., 1959.
    7-game Series—12—Richardson, Robert C., New York A.L., 1960.
    8-game Series— 8—Leach, Thoms W., Pittsburgh N.L., 1903.
                            Duncan, Louis B., Cincinnati N.L., 1919.

Most Runs Batted In, Series, Pinch-Hitter
    6—Rhodes, James L., New York N.L., 3 games, 1954.

Fewest Runs Batted In, Series
    0—Clarke, Frederick C., Pittsburgh N.L., 8 games, 1903 (34 at-bats).
       Weaver, George D., Chicago A.L., 8 games, 1919 (34 at-bats).
       Wagner, Charles F., Boston A.L., 8 games, 1912 (30 at-bats).
       Pesky, John M., Boston A.L., 7 games, 1946 (30 at-bats).
       Schoendienst, Albert F., Milwaukee N.L., 7 games, 1958 (30 at-bats).
       Grote, Gerald W., New York N.L., 7 games, 1973 (30 at-bats).
       Doyle, Robert D., Boston A.L., 7 games, 1975 (30 at-bats).
       Also many other players with fewer at-bats.

Most Hits, Series
    4-game Series—10—Ruth, George H., New York A.L., 1928.
    5-game Series— 9—Baker, J. Franklin, Philadelphia A.L., 1910.
                            Collins, Edward T., Philadelphia A.L., 1910.
                            Baker, J. Franklin, Philadelphia A.L., 1913.
                            Groh, Henry K., New York N.L., 1922.
                            Moore, Joseph G., New York N.L., 1937.
                            Richardson, Robert C., New York A.L., 1961.
                            Blair, Paul L., Baltimore A.L., 1970.
                            Robinson, Brooks C., Baltimore A.L., 1970.
                            Trammell, Alan S., Detroit A.L., 1984.
    6-game Series—12—Martin, Alfred M., New York A.L., 1953.
    7-game Series—13—Richardson, Robert C., New York A.L., 1964.
                            Brock, Louis C., St. Louis N.L., 1968.
    8-game Series—12—Herzog, Charles L., New York N.L., 1912.
                            Jackson, Joseph J., Chicago A.L., 1919.

Most Hits, Two Consecutive Series
    25—Brock, Louis C., St. Louis N.L., 1967 (12), 1968 (13).

Most Consecutive Hits, One Series
    6—Goslin, Leon A., Washington A.L., October 6 (1), October 7 (4), October 8 (1), 1924.
       Munson, Thurman L., New York A.L., October 19 (2), October 21 (4), 1976.

Most Consecutive Hits, Two Consecutive Series
    7—Munson, Thurman L., New York A.L., October 19 (2), October 21 (4), 1976, October 11, 1977 (1). All one-base hits.

Most Series, One or More Hits, Total Series
    12—Berra, Lawrence P., New York A.L., 1947, 1949, 1950, 1951, 1952, 1953, 1955, 1956, 1957, 1958, 1960, 1961.
        Mantle, Mickey C., New York A.L., 1951, 1952, 1953, 1955, 1956, 1957, 1958, 1960, 1961, 1962, 1963, 1964.

Most Games, Four or More Hits, Series
    2—Yount, Robin R., Milwaukee A.L., October 12 (4), 16 (4), 1982.

Most Hits, Total Series
    71—Berra, Lawrence P., New York A.L., 1947, 1949, 1950, 1951, 1952, 1953, 1955, 1956, 1957, 1958, 1960, 1961, 1962, 1963 (14 Series, 75 games).

Most Hits, Total Series, One Club
    71—Berra, Lawrence P., New York A.L., 1947, 1949, 1950, 1951, 1952, 1953, 1955, 1956, 1957, 1958, 1960, 1961, 1962, 1963 (14 Series, 75 games).

WORLD SERIES RECORDS

Most Hits, Series, Pinch-Hitter
   3—Brown, Robert W., New York A.L., 4 games, 1947 (consecutive; one base on balls, one single, two doubles, three runs batted in).
      Rhodes, James L., New York N.L., 3 games, 1954 (consecutive; one home run, two singles, six runs batted in).
      Warwick, Carl W., St. Louis N.L., 5 games, 1964 (consecutive; two singles, walk, single, one run batted in).
      Marquez, Gonzalo, Oakland A.L., 5 games, 1972 (consecutive in second, third, fourth games, three singles, one run batted in).
      Boswell, Kenneth G., New York N.L., 3 games, 1973 (consecutive; three singles).

Most Hits, Total Series, Pinch-Hitter
   3—O'Dea, James K., Chicago N.L., 1935 (1), 1938 (0); St. Louis N.L., 1942 (1), 1943 (0), 1944 (1), 5 Series, 8 games.
      Brown, Robert W., New York A.L., 1947 (3), 1949 (0), 1950 (0), 1951 (0), 4 Series, 7 games.
      Mize, John R., New York A.L., 1949 (2), 1950 (0), 1951 (0), 1952 (1), 1953 (0), 5 Series, 8 games.
      Rhodes, James L., New York N.L., 1954 (3), 3 games.
      Furillo, Carl A., Brooklyn N.L., 1947 (2), 1949 (0); Los Angeles N.L., 1959 (1), 3 Series, 7 games.
      Cerv, Robert H., New York A.L., 1955 (1), 1956 (1), 1960 (1), 3 Series 3 games.
      Blanchard, John E., New York A.L., 1960 (1), 1961 (1), 1962 (0), 1964 (1), 4 Series, 10 games.
      Warwick, Carl W., St. Louis N.L., 1964 (3), 1 Series, 5 games.
      Marquez, Gonzalo, Oakland A.L., 1972 (3), 1 Series, 5 games.
      Boswell, Kenneth G., New York N.L., 1973 (3), 1 Series, 3 games.

One or More Hits Each Game, Series
   Held by many players in Series of all lengths.

Most Consecutive Games, One or More Hits, Total Series
   17—Bauer, Henry A., New York A.L., 1956, 7 games; 1957, 7 games; 1958, first 3 games.

Fewest Hits, Series
   0—Maxvill, C. Dallan, St. Louis N.L., 7 games, 1968 (22 at-bats).
      Sheckard, James T., Chicago N.L., 6 games, 1906 (21 at-bats).
      Sullivan, William J., Chicago A.L., 6 games, 1906 (21 at-bats).
      Murray, John J., New York N.L., 6 games, 1911 (21 at-bats).
      Hodges, Gilbert R., Brooklyn N.L., 7 games, 1952 (21 at-bats).
      Also many other players with fewer times at bat.

Most At-Bats, Total Series, Without a Hit
   22—Earnshaw, George L., Philadelphia A.L., 1929 (5), 1930 (9), 1931 (8).

Most Consecutive Hitless Times at Bat, Total Series
   31—Owen, Marvin J., Detroit A.L., 1934 (last 12 times at bat), 1935 (first 19 times at bat).

Most One-Base Hits, Total Series
   49—Berra, Lawrence P., New York A.L., 1947, 1949, 1950, 1951, 1952, 1953, 1955, 1956, 1957, 1958, 1960, 1961, 1962, 1963 (14 Series, 75 games).

Most One-Base Hits, Series
   4-game Series— 9—Munson, Thurman L., New York A.L., 1976.
   5-game Series— 8—Chance, Frank L., Chicago N.L., 1908.
                      Baker, J. Franklin, Philadelphia A.L., 1913.
                      Groh, Henry K., New York N.L., 1922.
                      Moore, Joseph G., New York N.L., 1937.
                      Richardson, Robert C., New York A.L., 1961.
                      Blair, Paul L., Baltimore A.L., 1970.
                      Garvey, Steven P., Los Angeles N.L., 1974.
   6-game Series—10—Rolfe, Robert A., New York A.L., 1936.
                      Irvin, Monford, New York N.L., 1951.
   7-game Series—12—Rice, Edgar C., Washington A.L., 1925.
   8-game Series— 9—Sebring, James D., Pittsburgh N.L., 1903.
                      Meyers, John T., New York N.L., 1912.

Most Two-Base Hits, Total Series
   10—Frisch, Frank F., New York N.L. (5), 1921, 1922, 1923, 1924; St. Louis N.L. (5), 1928, 1930, 1931, 1934; 8 Series, 50 games.
      Berra, Lawrence P., New York A.L., 1947, 1949, 1950, 1951, 1952, 1953, 1955, 1956, 1957, 1958, 1960, 1961, 1962, 1963; 14 Series, 75 games.

Most Two-Base Hits, Series
   4-game Series—3—Gowdy, Henry M., Boston N.L., 1914.
                 Ruth, George H., New York A.L., 1928.
   5-game Series—4—Collins, Edward T., Philadelphia A.L., 1910.
                 Dempsey, J. Rikard, Baltimore A.L., 1983.
   6-game Series—5—Hafey, Charles J., St. Louis N.L., 1930.
   7-game Series—6—Fox, Ervin, Detroit A.L., 1934.
   8-game Series—4—Murray, John J., New York N.L., 1912.
                 Herzog, Charles L., New York N.L., 1912.
                 Weaver, George L., Chicago A.L., 1919.
                 Burns, George J., New York N.L., 1921.

Most Three-Base Hits, Total Series
    4—Leach, Thomas W., Pittsburgh N.L. (4), 1903, 1909; 2 Series, 15 games.
       Speaker, Tris, Boston A.L. (3), 1912, 1915; Cleveland A.L. (1), 1920; 3 Series, 20 games.
       Johnson, William R., New York A.L., 1943 (1), 1947 (3), 1949 (0), 1950 (0); 4 Series, 18 games.

Fewest Three-Base Hits, Total Series (Most Games)
    0—Berra, Lawrence P., New York A.L., 14 Series, 75 games, 259 at-bats.
       DiMaggio, Joseph P., New York A.L., 10 Series, 51 games, 199 at-bats.
       Rizzuto, Philip F., New York A.L., 9 Series, 52 games, 183 at-bats.

Most Three-Base Hits, Series
    4-game Series—2—Gehrig, H. Louis, New York A.L., 1927.
                     Davis, H. Thomas, Los Angeles N.L., 1963.
    5-game Series—2—Collins, Edward T., Philadelphia A.L., 1913.
                     Brown, Robert W., New York A.L., 1949.
    6-game Series—2—Rohe, George, Chicago A.L., 1906.
                     Meusel, Robert W., New York A.L., 1923.
                     Martin, Alfred M., New York A.L., 1953.
    7-game Series—3—Johnson, William R., New York A.L., 1947.
    8-game Series—4—Leach, Thomas W., Pittsburgh N.L., 1903.

Most Home Runs, Total Series
    18—Mantle, Mickey C., New York A.L., 1951, 1952, 1953, 1955, 1956, 1957, 1958, 1960, 1961, 1962, 1963, 1964; 12 Series, 65 games.

Most Home Runs, Pitcher, Total Series, as Batter
    2—Gibson, Robert, St. Louis N.L., 1964 (0), 1967 (1), 1968 (1), 3 Series, 9 games.
       McNally, David A., Baltimore A.L., 1966 (0), 1969 (1), 1970 (1), 1971 (0), 4 Series, 9 games.

Fewest Home Runs, Total Series (Most Games)
    0—Frisch, Frank F., New York N.L., St. Louis N.L., 8 Series, 50 games, 197 at-bats.

Most Home Runs, Series
    4-game Series—4—Gehrig, H. Louis, New York A.L., 1928.
    5-game Series—3—Clendenon, Donn A., New York N.L., 1969.
    6-game Series—5—Jackson, Reginald M., New York, 1977.
    7-game Series—4—Ruth, George H., New York A.L., 1926.
                     Snider, Edwin D., Brooklyn N.L., 1952.
                     Snider, Edwin D., Brooklyn N.L., 1955.
                     Bauer, Henry A., New York A.L., 1958.
                     Tenace, F. Gene, Oakland A.L., 1972.
    8-game Series—2—Dougherty, Patrick H., Boston A.L., 1903.

Most Home Runs, Series, Pinch-Hitter
    2—Essegian, Charles A., Los Angeles N.L., 4 games, 1959.
       Carbo, Bernardo, Boston A.L., 3 games, 1975.

Most Home Runs, Series, by Rookie
    3—Keller, Charles E., New York A.L., 1939.

Most Series, One or More Home Runs, Total Series
    9—Berra, Lawrence P., New York A.L., 1947 (1), 1950 (1), 1952 (2), 1953 (1), 1955 (1), 1956 (3), 1957 (1), 1960 (1), 1961 (1).
       Mantle, Mickey C., New York A.L., 1952 (2), 1953 (2), 1955 (1), 1956 (3), 1957 (1), 1958 (2), 1960 (3), 1963 (1), 1964 (3).

Four or More Home Runs, Total Series

Player	Series	HR.
Mantle, Mickey C.	12	18
Ruth, George H.	10	15
Berra, Lawrence P.	14	12
Snider, Edwin D.	6	11
Gehrig, H. Louis	7	10
Jackson, Reginald M.	5	10
Robinson, Frank	5	8
DiMaggio, Joseph P.	10	8
Skowron, William J.	8	8
Goslin, Leon A.	5	7
McDougald, Gilbert J.	8	7
Bauer, Henry A.	9	7
Maris, Roger E.	7	6
Simmons, Aloysius H.	4	6
Smith, C. Reginald	4	6
Keller, Charles E.	4	5
Greenberg, Henry	4	5
Bench, Johnny L.	4	5
Martin, Alfred M.	5	5
Hodges, Gilbert R.	7	5
Dickey, William M.	8	5
Howard, Elston G.	9	5
Lazzeri, Anthony M.	7	4
Foxx, James E.	3	4
Ott, Melvin T.	3	4
Henrich, Thomas D.	4	4
Gordon, Joseph L.	6	4
Campanella, Roy	5	4
Collins, Joseph	7	4
Tresh, Thomas M.	3	4
Buford, Donald A.	3	4
Brock, Louis C.	3	4
Tenace, F. Gene	3	4
Lopes, David E.	4	4
Aikens, Willie M.	1	4
Yeager, Stephen W.	4	4

Home Runs, Both Leagues
  Skowron, William J., A.L. (7), N.L. (1).
  Robinson, Frank, N.L. (1), A.L. (7).
  Maris, Roger E., A.L. (5), N.L. (1).
  Smith, C. Reginald, A.L. (2), N.L. (4).
  Slaughter, Enos B., N.L. (2), A.L. (1).

Most Home Runs, Four Consecutive Games, Total Series, Hitting Homer in Each Game
  6—Jackson, Reginald M., New York A.L., 1977 (5), last three games; 1978 (1), first game.
  5—Gehrig, H. Louis, New York A.L., 1928 (4), last three games; 1932 (1), first game.

Most Home Runs, Three Consecutive Games, One Series, Hitting Homer Each Game
  5—Jackson, Reginald M., New York A.L., October 15 (1), 16 (1), 18 (3), 1977.
  4—Gehrig, H. Louis, New York A.L., October 5, 7 (2), 9, 1928.

Most Home Runs, Two Consecutive Games, One Series, Hitting Homer Each Game
  4—Jackson, Reginald M., New York A.L., October 16 (1), 18 (3), 1977.

Most Consecutive Home Runs, Two Consecutive Games, Series
  4—Jackson, Reginald M., New York A.L., October 16 (1), 18 (3), one base on balls included.

Most Series, Two or More Home Runs, Game
  4—Ruth, George H., New York A.L., 1923, 1926, 1928, 1932 (two home runs in one game twice, three home runs in one game twice).

Most Series, Two or More Home Runs
  6—Mantle, Mickey C., New York A.L., 1952 (2), 1953 (2), 1956 (3), 1956 (3), 1958 (2), 1960 (3), 1964 (3).
  5—Ruth, George H., New York A.L., 1923 (3), 1926 (4), 1927 (2), 1928 (3), 1932 (2).

Most Series, Three or More Home Runs
  3—Ruth, George H., New York A.L., 1923 (3), 1926 (4), 1928 (3).
    Mantle, Mickey C., New York A.L., 1956 (3), 1960 (3), 1964 (3).

Most Series, Four or More Home Runs
  2—Snider, Edwin D., Brooklyn N.L., 1952, 1955.

Most Home Runs, Two Consecutive Series (Two Consecutive Years)
  7—Jackson, Reginald M., New York A.L., 1977 (5), 1978 (2).

Most Home Runs, Three Consecutive Series (Three Consecutive Years)
  9—Ruth, George H., New York A.L., 1926 (4), 1927 (2), 1928 (3).

Most Total Bases, Total Series
  123—Mantle, Mickey C., New York A.L., 1951, 1952, 1953, 1955, 1956, 1957, 1958, 1960, 1961, 1962, 1963, 1964; 12 Series, 65 games.

Most Total Bases
  4-game Series—22—Ruth, George H., New York A.L., 1928.
  5-game Series—17—Robinson, Brooks C., Baltimore A.L., 1970.
  6-game Series—25—Jackson, Reginald M., New York A.L., 1977.
  7-game Series—25—Stargell, Wilver D., Pittsburgh N.L., 1979.
  8-game Series—18—Herzog, Charles L., New York N.L., 1912.
         Jackson, Joseph J., Chicago A.L., 1919.

Most Total Bases, Series, Pinch-Hitter
  8—Essegian, Charles A., Los Angeles N.L., 4 games, 1959; two home runs.
    Carbo, Bernardo, Boston A.L., 3 games, 1975; two home runs.

Most Long Hits, Total Series
  26—Mantle, Mickey C., New York A.L., 1951, 1952, 1953, 1955, 1956, 1957, 1958, 1960, 1961, 1962, 1963, 1964; 12 Series, 65 games.

Most Long Hits, Series
  4-game Series—6—Ruth, George H., New York A.L., 1928.
  5-game Series—5—Dempsey, J. Rikard, Baltimore A.L., 1983.
  6-game Series—6—Jackson, Reginald M., New York A.L., 1977; one double, five home runs.
  7-game Series—7—Stargell, Wilver D., Pittsburgh N.L., 1979.
  8-game Series—5—Murray, John J., New York N.L., 1912.
         Herzog, Charles L., New York N.L., 1912.
         Weaver, George D., Chicago A.L., 1919.
         Burns, George J., New York N.L., 1921.

Most Extra Bases on Long Hits, Total Series
  64—Mantle, Mickey C., New York A.L., 1951, 1952, 1953, 1955, 1956, 1957, 1958, 1960, 1961, 1962, 1963, 1964; 12 Series, 65 games.

Most Extra Bases on Long Hits, Series
4-game Series—13—Gehrig, H. Louis, New York A.L., 1928; one double, four home runs.
5-game Series—10—Clendenon, Donn A., New York N.L., 1969; one double, three home runs.
6-game Series—16—Jackson, Reginald M., New York A.L., 1977; one double, five home runs.
7-game Series—14—Snider, Edwin D., Brooklyn N.L., 1952; two doubles, four home runs.
8-game Series—10—Dougherty, Patrick H., Boston A.L., 1903; two triples, two home runs.

Most Bases on Balls, Series
4-game Series— 7—Thompson, Henry, New Yrok N.L., 1954.
5-game Series— 7—Sheckard, James T., Chicago N.L., 1910.
                Cochrane, Gordon S., Philadelphia A.L., 1929.
                Gordon, Joseph L., New York A.L., 1941.
6-game Series— 9—Randolph, William L., New York A.L., 1981.
7-game Series—11—Ruth, George H., New York A.L., 1926.
                Tenace, F. Gene, Oakland A.L., 1973.
8-game Series— 7—Devore, Joshua, New York N.L., 1912.
                Youngs, Ross M., New York N.L., 1921.

Most Bases on Balls, Total Series
43—Mantle, Mickey C., New York A.L., 1951, 1952, 1953, 1955, 1956, 1957, 1958, 1960, 1961, 1962, 1963, 1964; 12 Series, 65 games.

Most Series, One or More Bases on Balls, Total Series
13—Berra, Lawrence P., New York A.L., 1947, 1949, 1950, 1951, 1952, 1953, 1955, 1956, 1957, 1958, 1960, 1961, 1962.

Most Bases on Balls, Series, Pinch-Hitter
3—Tate, H. Bennett, Washington A.L., 3 games, 1924.

Fewest Bases on Balls, Series
0—Weaver, George D., Chicago A.L., 8 games, 1919; 34 at-bats (also many other players with fewer at-bats).

Fewest Bases on Balls and Strikeouts, Series
0—Southworth, William H., St. Louis N.L., 7 games, 1926; 29 at-bats (also many other players with fewer at-bats).

Most Strikeouts, Total Series
54—Mantle, Mickey C., New York A.L., 1951, 1952, 1953, 1955, 1956, 1957, 1958, 1960, 1961, 1962, 1963, 1964; 12 Series, 65 games.

Most Strikeouts, Series
4-game Series— 7—Meusel, Robert W., New York A.L., 1927.
5-game Series— 9—Martinez, Carmelo, San Diego N.L., 1984.
6-game Series—12—Wilson, Willie J., Kansas City A.L., 1980.
7-game Series—11—Mathews, Edwin L., Milwaukee N.L., 1958.
                Garrett, R. Wayne, New York N.L., 1973.
8-game Series—10—Kelly, George L., New York N.L., 1921.

Most Series, One or More Strikeouts, Total Series
12—Mantle, Mickey C., New York A.L., 1951, 1952, 1953, 1955, 1956, 1957, 1958, 1960, 1961, 1963, 1964.

Most Strikeouts, Series, Pinch-Hitter
3—Hartnett, Charles L., Chicago N.L., 3 games, 1929.
Hemsley, Ralston B., Chicago N.L., 3 games, 1932.
Velez, Otoniel, New York A.L., 3 games, 1976.

Fewest Strikeouts, Series
0—Foli, Timothy J., Pittsburgh N.L., 7 games, 1979 (30 at-bats).
Southworth, William H., St. Louis N.L., 7 games, 1926 (29 at-bats).
Roush, Edd J., Cincinnati N.L., 8 games, 1919 (28 at-bats).
Gehringer, Charles L., Detroit A.L., 7 games, 1940 (28 at-bats).
Gilliam, James, Los Angeles N.L., 7 games, 1965 (28 at-bats).
Berra, Lawrence P., New York A.L., 7 games, 1958 (27 at-bats).
Moore, Charles W., Milwaukee A.L., 7 games, 1982 (26 at-bats).
Frisch Frank F., New York N.L., 6 games, 1923 (25 at-bats).
Robinson, Jack R., Brooklyn N.L., 6 games, 1953 (25 at-bats).
Berra, Lawrence P., New York A.L., 7 games, 1957 (25 at-bats).
Also many other players with fewer at-bats.

Most Sacrifices, Total Series
8—Collins, Edward T., Philadelphia A.L. (6), 1910, 1911, 1913, 1914; Chicago A.L. (2), 1917, 1919; 6 Series, 34 games.

Most Sacrifices, Series
4-game Series—3—Westrum, Wesley N., New York N.L., 1954 (one sacrifice hit and two sacrifice flies).
5-game Series—4—Lewis, George E., Boston A.L., 1916.

WORLD SERIES RECORDS

6-game Series—3—Sheckard, James T., Chicago N.L., 1906.
Steinfeldt, Harry E., Chicago N.L., 1906.
Tinker, Joseph B., Chicago N.L., 1906.
Barry, John J., Philadelphia A.L., 1911.
Lee, William C., Chicago N.L., 1935.
7-game Series—5—Clarke, Fred C., Pittsburgh N.L., 1909.
8-game Series—5—Daubert, Jacob E., Cincinnati N.L., 1919.

Most Sacrifice Flies, Total Series

3—Robinson, Brooks C., Baltimore A.L., 1966 (0), 1969 (1), 1970 (0), 1971 (2); 4 Series, 21 games.
Concepcion, David I., Cincinnati N.L., 1970 (1), 1972 (1), 1975 (1); 3 Series, 16 games.

Most Stolen Bases, Total Series

14—Collins, Edward T., Philadelphia A.L. (10), 1910, 1911, 1913, 1914; Chicago A.L. (4), 1917, 1919; 6 Series, 34 games.
Brock, Louis C., St. Louis N.L., 1964 (0), 1967 (7), 1968 (7); 3 Series, 21 games.

Most Stolen Bases, Series

4-game Series—2—Deal, Charles A., Boston N.L., 1914.
Maranville, Walter J. V., Boston N.L., 1914.
Geronimo, Cesar F., Cincinnati N.L., 1976.
Morgan, Joe L., Cincinnati N.L., 1976.
5-game Series—6—Slagle, James F., Chicago N.L., 1907.
6-game Series—4—Lopes, David E., Los Angeles N.L., 1981.
7-game Series—7—Brock, Louis C., St. Louis N.L., 1967.
Brock, Louis C., St. Louis N.L., 1968.
8-game Series—4—Devore, Joshua, New York N.L., 1912.

Most Caught Stealing, Total Series

9—Schulte, Frank, Chicago N.L., 1906, 1907, 1908, 1910; 4 Series, 21 games, 3 stolen bases.

Most Caught Stealing, Series

4-game Series—2—Aparicio, Luis, Baltimore A.L., 1966, 0 stolen bases.
Foster, George A., Cincinnati N.L., 1976, 0 stolen bases.
5-game Series—5—Schulte, Frank, Chicago N.L., 1910, 0 stolen bases.
6-game Series—3—Devore, Joshua D., New York N.L., 1911, 0 stolen bases.
7-game Series—3—Brock, Louis C., St. Louis N.L., 1968, 7 stolen bases.
8-game Series—4—Neale, Alfred E., Cincinnati N.L., 1919, 1 stolen base.

Most Games, Series, Pinch-Hitter

5—McCormick, Harry, New York N.L., 1912.
Paschal, Benjamin, New York A.L., 1926.
Secory, Frank, Chicago N.L., 1945.
Lavagetto, Harry A., Brooklyn N.L., 1947.
Warwick, Carl W., St. Louis N.L., 1964.
Shopay, Thomas M., Baltimore A.L., 1971.
Marquez, Gonzalo, Oakland A.L., 1972.
Mangual, Angel L., Oakland A.L., 1973.
Crowley, Terrence M., Baltimore A.L., 1979.
Kelly, H. Patrick, Baltimore A.L., 1979.

Most Games, Total Series, Pinch-Hitter

10—Blanchard, John E., New York A.L., 1960 (3), 1961 (2), 1962 (1), 1964 (4).

Most Hit by Pitch, Series

3—Carey, Max, Pittsburgh N.L., 7 games, 1925.

Most Hit by Pitch, Total Series

3—Chance, Frank L., Chicago N.L., 1906 (2), 1907 (1).
Wagner, John P., Pittsburgh N.L., 1903 (1), 1909 (2).
Snodgrass, Frederick C., New York N.L., 1911 (2), 1912 (1).
Carey, Max, Pittsburgh N.L., 1925 (3).
Berra, Lawrence P., New York A.L., 1953 (2), 1955 (1).
Howard, Elston G., New York A.L., 1960 (1), 1962 (1), 1964 (1).
Robinson, Frank, Cincinnati N.L., 1961 (2), Baltimore A.L., 1971 (1).
Campaneris, Dagoberto B., Oakland A.L., 1973 (2), 1974 (1).
Jackson, Reginald M., New York A.L., 1977 (1), 1978 (2).

Most Grounded Into Double Play, Total Series

7—DiMaggio, Joseph P., New York A.L., 1936, 1937, 1938, 1939, 1941, 1942, 1947, 1949, 1950, 1951; 10 Series, 51 games.

Most Grounded Into Double Play, Series

5—Noren, Irving A., New York A.L., 1955 (16 times at bat in 5 games of 7-game Series).

Most Clubs, Total Series

3—Schang, Walter H.; Merkle, Fred C.; Grimes, Burleigh A.; Bush, Leslie A.; Derringer, Paul; McInnis, John P.; Koenig, Mark A.; Groh, Henry K.; Reuther, Walter H.; Smith, Earl S.; McCormick, Myron W.; Stanky, Edward R.; Pafko, Andrew; Davalillo, Victor J.; Jackson, Grant D.

Most Years Between First and Second Series, Infielder
  14—Maranville, Walter J., Boston N.L., 1914; St. Louis N.L., 1928.

Most Years Between First and Second Series, Pitcher
  17—Kaat, James L., Minnesota A.L., 1965; St. Louis N.L., 1982.

Most Years Between First and Last Series, Outfielder
  22—Mays, Willie H., New York N.L., 1951 (Giants); New York N.L., 1973 (Mets).

Most Years Between First and Last Series, Pitcher
  18—Pennock, Herbert J., Philadelphia A.L., 1914; New York A.L., 1932.

Most Years Played in Major Leagues Before Playing in World Series
  18—Johnson, Walter P., Washington A.L., 1907; first World Series game on October 4, 1924, at Washington.

Youngest World Series Player
  Lindstrom, Frederick C., New York N.L., 18 years, 10 months, 13 days, first World Series game on October 4, 1924, at Washington. Born November 21, 1905.

Oldest World Series Player (Except Pitcher)
  Rose, Peter E., Philadelphia N.L., 42 years, 6 months, 2 days, last World Series game on October 16, 1983, at Philadelphia. Born April 14, 1941.

Most Games, Series, Pinch-Runner
  6—Lewis, Allan S., Oakland A.L., 1972, 2 runs.

Most Games, Total Series, Pinch-Runner
  9—Lewis, Allan S., Oakland A.L., 1972, 1973; 2 Series, 3 runs.

Most Positions Played, Series
  3—Snodgrass, Frederick C., New York N.L., 1912, center field, right field, left field, 8-game Series, 8 games.
  Kelly, George L., New York N.L., 1924, center field, second base, first base, 7-game Series, 7 games.
  Kubek, Anthony C., New York A.L., 1957, left field, third base, center field, 7-game Series, 7 games.
  Pafko, Andrew, Milwaukee N.L., 1958, center field, left field, right field, 7-game Series, 4 games.
  Moon, Wallace W., Los Angeles N.L., 1959, left field, center field, right field, 6-game Series, 6 games.
  Berra, Lawrence P., New York A.L., 1960, catcher, left field, right field, 7-game Series, 7 games.
  McCovey, Willie L., San Francisco N.L., 1962, first base, right field, left field, 7-game Series, 4 games.
  Rettenmund, Mervin W., Baltimore A.L., 1971, center field, left field, right field, 7-game Series, 7 games.
  Washington, Claudell, Oakland A.L., 1974, right field, center field, left field, 5-game Series, 5 games.
  Thomas, Derrel O., Los Angeles N.L., 1981, shortstop, center field, third base.

Most Positions Played, Total Series
  4—Ruth, George H., Boston A.L., 1915, 1916, 1918, New York A.L., 1921, 1922, 1923, 1926, 1927, 1928, 1932, 41 games, pitcher, left field, right field, first base.
  Robinson, Jack R., Brooklyn N.L., 1947, 1949, 1952, 1953, 1955, 1956, 38 games, first base, second base, left field, third base.
  Howard, Elston G., New York A.L., 1955, 1956, 1957, 1958, 1960, 1961, 1962, 1963, 1964, Boston A.L., 1967, 54 games, left field, right field, first base, catcher.
  Kubek, Anthony C., New York A.L., 1957, 1958, 1960, 1961, 1962, 1963, 37 games, left field, third base, center field, shortstop.
  Rose, Peter E., Cincinnati N.L., 1970, 1972, 1975, 1976, Philadelphia N.L., 1980, 1983, 34 games, right field, left field, third base, first base.

CLUB BATTING, BASE-RUNNING—GAME, INNING

Most At-Bats, Game, Nine Innings, One Club
  45—New York A.L., vs. Chicago N.L., October 2, 1932.
  New York A.L., vs. New York N.L., October 6, 1936.
  New York A.L., vs. Pittsburgh N.L., October 6, 1960.

Most At-Bats, Extra-Inning Game, One Club
  54—New York N.L., vs Oakland A.L., October 14, 1973, 12 innings.

Most At-Bats, Game, Nine Innings, Both Clubs
  84—New York A.L., 45; Chicago N.L., 39, October 2, 1932.
  New York A.L., 45; Pittsburgh N.L., 39, October 6, 1960.

Most At-Bats, Extra-Inning Game, Both Clubs
  101—New York N.L., 54, Oakland A.L., 47, October 14, 1973, 12 innings.

WORLD SERIES RECORDS

Most At-Bats, Inning, One Club
  13—Philadelphia A.L., vs. Chicago N.L., October 12, 1929, seventh inning.

Most At-Bats, Inning, Both Clubs
  17—Philadelphia A.L., 13, Chicago N.L., 4, October 12, 1929, seventh inning.

Most Men Facing Pitcher, Inning, One Club
  15—Philadelphia A.L., vs. Chicago N.L., October 12, 1929, seventh inning.
  Detroit A.L., vs. St. Louis N.L., October 9, 1968, third inning.

Most Men Facing Pitcher, Inning, Both Clubs
  20—Philadelphia A.L., 15, Chicago N.L., 5, October 12, 1929, seventh inning.

Fewest Official At-Bats, Game, Nine Innings, One Club
  25—Philadelphia A.L., vs. Boston N.L., October 10, 1914.

Fewest Official At-Bats, Game, Nine Innings, Both Clubs
  54—Chicago N.L., 27, Chicago A.L., 27, October 12, 1906.
  53—Cleveland A.L., 28, Brooklyn N.L., 25, October 7, 1920 (Brooklyn N.L. batted 8 innings).
  New York N.L., 27, New York A.L., 26, October 6, 1921 (New York A.L., batted 8 innings).
  Brooklyn N.L., 27, New York A.L., 26, October 8, 1956 (New York A.L. batted 8 innings).
  New York A.L., 29, Los Angeles N.L., 24, October 5, 1963 (Los Angeles N.L. batted 8 innings).

Most Runs, Game, One Club
  18—New York A.L., vs. New York N.L., October 2, 1936 (Won 18-4).

Largest Score, Shutout Game
  New York A.L., 12, Pittsburgh N.L., 0, October 12, 1960.

Most Earned Runs, Game, One Club
  17—New York A.L., vs. New York N.L., October 2, 1936 (Won 18-4).

Most Runs, Game, Both Clubs.
  22—New York A.L., 18, New York N.L., 4, October 2, 1936.

Most Runs, Inning, One Club
  10—Philadelphia A.L., vs. Chicago N.L., October 12, 1929, seventh inning.
  Detroit A.L., vs. St. Louis N.L., October 9, 1968, third inning.

Most Runs, Inning, Both Clubs
  11—Philadelphia A.L., Chicago N.L., 1, October 12, 1929, seventh inning.
  Brooklyn N.L., 6, New York A.L., 5, October 5, 1956, second inning.

Most Runs, Two Consecutive Innings, One Club
  12—Detroit A.L., vs. St. Louis N.L., October 9, 1968, 2 in second inning, 10 in third inning.

Most Runs, First Inning, One Club
  7—Milwaukee N.L., vs. New York A.L., October 2, 1958.

Most Runs, Second Inning, One Club
  6—New York A.L., vs. New York N.L., October 13, 1923.
  New York N.L., vs. New York A.L., October 9, 1937.
  Brooklyn N.L., vs. New York A.L., October 2, 1947.
  Brooklyn N.L., vs. New York A.L., October 5, 1956.

Most Runs, Third Inning, One Club
  10—Detroit A.L., vs. St. Louis N.L., October 9, 1968.

Most Runs, Fourth Inning, One Club
  6—St. Louis N.L., vs. New York A.L., October 4, 1942.
  Los Angeles N.L., vs. Chicago A.L., October 8, 1959.

Most Runs, Fifth Inning, One Club
  6—Baltimore A.L., vs. Pittsburgh N.L., October 11, 1971.

Most Runs, Sixth Inning, One Club
  7—New York A.L., vs. New York N.L., October 6, 1937.
  New York A.L., vs. Pittsburgh N.L., October 6, 1960.

Most Runs, Seventh Inning, One Club
  10—Philadelphia A.L., vs. Chicago N.L., October 12, 1929.

Most Runs, Eighth Inning, One Club
  6—Chicago N.L., vs. Detroit A.L., October 11, 1908.
  Baltimore A.L., vs. Pittsburgh N.L., October 13, 1979.

Most Runs, Ninth Inning, One Club
  7—New York A.L., vs. New York N.L., October 6, 1936.

Most Runs, Ninth Inning, One Club, With None on Base, Two Out
  4—New York A.L., vs. Brooklyn N.L., October 5, 1941.

WORLD SERIES RECORDS

Most Runs, Tenth Inning, One Club
   3—New York N.L., vs. Philadelphia A.L., October 8, 1913.
     New York A.L., vs. Cincinnati N.L., October 8, 1939.
     New York N.L., vs. Cleveland A.L., September 29, 1954.
     Milwaukee N.L., vs. New York A.L., October 6, 1957.
     St. Louis N.L., vs. New York A.L., October 12, 1964.

Most Runs, Eleventh Inning, One Club
   2—Philadelphia A.L., vs. New York N.L., October 17, 1911.

Most Runs, Twelfth Inning, One Club
   4—New York N.L., vs. Oakland A.L., October 14, 1973.

Most Runs, Extra Inning, One Club
   4—New York N.L., vs. Oakland A.L., October 14, 1973, twelfth inning.

Most Innings Scored, Game, One Club
   6—New York A.L., vs. St. Louis N.L., October 6, 1926.
     New York A.L., vs. Brooklyn N.L., October 1, 1947.
     New York A.L., vs. Pittsburgh N.L., October 6, 1960.

Most Innings Scored, Game, Both Clubs
   9—New York A.L., 6, St. Louis N.L., 3, October 6, 1926.
     New York A.L., 5, New York N.L., 4, October 6, 1936.
     New York A.L., 6, Brooklyn N.L., 3, October 1, 1947.
     New York A.L., 5, Brooklyn N.L., 4, October 4, 1953.
     Brooklyn N.L., 5, New York A.L., 4, October 5, 1956.
     Oakland A.L., 5, New York N.L., 4, October 14, 1973, 12 innings.
     New York A.L., 5, Los Angeles N.L., 4, October 24, 1981.

Most Runs, Game, Pinch-Hitters, One Club
   3—New York A.L., vs. Brooklyn N.L., October 2, 1947.

Most Runs Batted In, Game, One Club
   18—New York A.L., vs. New York N.L., October 2, 1936.

Most Runs Batted In, Game, Both Clubs
   21—New York A.L., 18, New York N.L., 3, October 2, 1936.
      Brooklyn N.L., 13, New York A.L., 8, October 5, 1956.

Fewest Runs Batted In, Game, One Club
   0—Held by many clubs.

Most Runs Batted In, Inning, One Club
   10—Philadelphia A.L., vs. Chicago N.L., October 12, 1929, seventh inning.
      Detroit A.L., vs. St. Louis N.L., October 9, 1968, third inning.

Most Runs Batted In, Inning, Both Clubs
   11—Philadelphia A.L., 10, Chicago N.L., 1, October 12, 1929, seventh inning.
      Brooklyn N.L., 6, New York A.L., 5, October 5, 1956, second inning.

Fewest Runs Batted In, Game, Both Clubs
   0—New York N.L., 0, Philadelphia A.L., 0, October 13, 1905.
     New York N.L., 0, New York A.L., 0, October 13, 1921.
     Chicago A.L., 0, Los Angeles N.L., 0, October 6, 1959.
     New York A.L., 0, San Francisco N.L., 0, October 16, 1962.

Most Hits, Game, One Club
   20—New York N.L., vs. New York A.L., October 7, 1921; St. Louis N.L., vs. Boston A.L., October 10, 1946.

Most Hits, Game, Losing Club
   17—Pittsburgh N.L., vs. Baltimore A.L., October 13, 1979.

Most Hits, Game, Both Clubs
   32—New York A.L., 19, Pittsburgh N.L., 13, October 6, 1960.

Fewest Hits, Game, One Club
   0—Brooklyn N.L., vs. New York A.L., October 8, 1956.

Fewest Hits, Game, Both Clubs
   5—New York A.L., 3, New York N.L., 2, October 6, 1921.
     New York A.L., 5, Brooklyn N.L., 0, October 8, 1956.

Most Consecutive Hitless Innings, No Player Reaching Base, One Club, Series
   10⅓—Brooklyn N.L., vs. New York A.L., October 7, 1956 (last two batters); October 8, 1956 (9 innings—all 27 batters); October 9, 1956 (first two batters).

Most Hits, Inning, One Club
   10—Philadelphia A.L., vs. Chicago N.L., October 12, 1929, seventh inning.

WORLD SERIES RECORDS

Most Hits, Inning, Both Clubs
  12—Philadelphia A.L., 10, Chicago N.L., 2, October 12, 1929, seventh inning.

Most Consecutive Hits, Inning, One Club
  8—New York N.L., vs. New York A.L., October 7, 1921, seventh inning. (Base on balls and sacrifice fly during streak.)

Most Consecutive Hits, Inning, One Club (Consecutive Plate Appearances)
  6—Chicago N.L., vs. Detroit A.L., October 10, 1908, ninth inning, six singles.

Most Hits, Inning, Pinch-Hitters, One Club
  3—Oakland A.L., vs. Cincinnati N.L., October 19, 1972, ninth inning, three singles.

Most Hits, Game, Pinch-Hitters, One Club
  3—Oakland A.L., vs. Cincinnati N.L., October 19, 1972, three singles in ninth inning.
     Baltimore A.L., vs. Pittsburgh N.L., October 13, 1979, single in seventh inning, two doubles in eighth inning.

Most One-Base Hits, Game, One Club
  16—New York A.L., vs. Los Angeles N.L., October 15, 1978.

Most One-Base Hits, Game, Both Clubs
  24—New York A.L., 16, Los Angeles N.L., 8, October 15, 1978.

Most One-Base Hits, Inning, One Club
  7—Philadelphia A.L., vs. Chicago N.L., October 12, 1929, seventh inning.
     New York N.L., vs. Washington A.L., October 4, 1933, sixth inning.
     Brooklyn N.L., vs. New York A.L., October 8, 1949, sixth inning.

Most One-Base Hits, Inning, Both Clubs
  8—Philadelphia A.L., 7, Chicago N.L., 1, October 12, 1929, seventh inning.
     New York N.L., 7, Washington A.L., 1, October 4, 1933, sixth inning.
     Brooklyn N.L., 7, New York A.L., 1, October 8, 1949, sixth inning.

Fewest One-Base Hits, Game, One Club
  0—Philadelphia A.L., vs. St. Louis N.L., October 1, 1930, 8 innings.
     Philadelphia A.L., vs. St. Louis N.L., October 8, 1930, 8 innings.
     Brooklyn N.L., vs. New York A.L., October 3, 1947, 8⅔ innings.
     New York A.L., vs. Brooklyn N.L., October 4, 1952, 8 innings.
     Brooklyn N.L., vs. New York A.L., October 8, 1956, 9 innings.
     St. Louis N.L., vs. Boston A.L., October 5, 1967, 9 innings.

Fewest One-Base Hits, Game, Both Clubs
  2—St. Louis N.L., 2, Philadelphia A.L., 0, October 8, 1930.
  3—Chicago A.L., 2, Chicago N.L., 1, October 11, 1906.

Most Two-Base Hits, Game, One Club
  8—Chicago A.L., vs. Chicago N.L., October 13, 1906.
     Pittsburgh N.L., vs. Washington A.L., October 15, 1925.

Most Two-Base Hits, Game, Both Clubs
  11—Chicago A.L., 8, Chicago N.L., 3, October 13, 1906.

Most Two-Base Hits, Inning, One Club
  3—Chicago A.L. vs. Chicago N.L., October 13, 1906, fourth inning.
     Philadelphia A.L., vs. Chicago N.L., October 18, 1910, seventh inning.
     Philadelphia A.L., vs. New York N.L., October 24, 1911, fourth inning, consecutive.
     Pittsburgh N.L., vs. Washington A.L., October 15, 1925, eighth inning.
     St. Louis N.L., vs. Detroit A.L., October 9, 1934, third inning.
     Brooklyn N.L., vs. New York A.L., October 2, 1947, second inning.
     Brooklyn N.L., vs. New York A.L., October 5, 1947, third inning, consecutive.
     New York A.L., vs. Brooklyn N.L., October 8, 1949, fourth inning.
     Chicago A.L., vs. Los Angeles N.L., October 1, 1959, third inning.

Most Three-Base Hits, Game, Nine Innings, One Club
  5—Boston A.L., vs. Pittsburgh N.L., October 7, 1903, October 10, 1903.

Most Three-Base Hits, Game, Nine Innings, Both Clubs
  7—Boston A.L., 5, Pittsburgh N.L., 2, October 10, 1903.

Most Three-Base Hits, Game, Eleven Innings, Both Clubs
  5—New York N.L., 3, Boston A.L., 2, October 9, 1912.

Most Three-Base Hits, Inning, One Club
  2—Boston A.L., vs. Pittsburgh N.L., October 7, 1903, eighth inning.
     Boston A.L., vs. Pittsburgh N.L., October 10, 1903, first inning, also fourth inning.
     Boston A.L., vs. New York N.L., October 12, 1912, third inning.
     Philadelphia A.L., vs. New York N.L., October 7, 1913, fourth inning.
     Boston A.L., vs. Chicago N.L., September 6, 1918, ninth inning.
     New York A.L., vs. Brooklyn N.L., October 1, 1947, third inning.
     New York A.L., vs. Brooklyn N.L., September 30, 1953, first inning.
     Detroit A.L., vs. St. Louis N.L., October 7, 1968, fourth inning.

Most Home Runs, Game, One Club
    5—New York A.L., vs. St. Louis N.L., October 9, 1928.

Most Home Runs, Game, Both Clubs
    6—New York A.L., 4, Chicago N.L., 2, October 1, 1932.
    New York A.L., 4. Brooklyn N.L., 2, October 4, 1953.
    Cincinnati N.L., 3, Boston A.L., 3, October 14, 1975, night game, ten innings.

Most Times Hitting Two Home Runs in Inning, Game, One Club
    2—New York A.L., vs. St. Louis N.L., October 9, 1928, seventh and eighth innings.

Most Home Runs, Inning, One Club (Two Home Runs, 26 times)
    3—Boston A.L., vs. St. Louis N.L., October 11, 1967, fourth inning, Yastrzemski, Smith, Petrocelli, two consecutive.
    2—New York N.L., vs. New York A.L., October 11, 1921, second inning.
    Washington A.L., vs. Pittsburgh N.L., October 11, 1925, third inning.
    New York A.L., vs. St. Louis N.L., October 9, 1928, seventh inning.
    New York A.L., vs. St. Louis N.L., October 9, 1928, eighth inning.
    Philadelphia A.L., vs. Chicago N.L., October 12, 1929, seventh inning.
    New York A.L., vs. Chicago N.L., October 1, 1932, fifth inning.
    New York A.L., vs. Chicago N.L., October 2, 1932, ninth inning.
    New York A.L., vs. Cincinnati N.L., October 7, 1939, fifth inning.
    New York A.L., vs. Cincinnati N.L., October 8, 1939, seventh inning.
    Detroit A.L., vs. Cincinnati N.L., October 4, 1940, seventh inning.
    Brooklyn N.L., vs. New York A.L., October 7, 1949, ninth inning.
    Brooklyn N.L., vs. New York A.L., September 30, 1953, sixth inning.
    Brooklyn N.L., vs. New York A.L., October 1, 1955, fourth inning.
    Milwaukee N.L., vs. New York A.L., October 6, 1957, fourth inning.
    Milwaukee N.L., vs. New York A.L., October 2, 1958, first inning.
    New York A.L., vs. Milwaukee N.L., October 2, 1958, ninth inning.
    Los Angeles N.L. vs. Chicago A.L., October 2, 1959, seventh inning.
    New York A.L., vs. St. Louis N.L., October 14, 1964, sixth inning.
    New York A.L., vs. St. Louis N.L., October 15, 1964, ninth inning.
    Baltimore A.L., vs. Los Angeles N.L., October 5, 1966, first inning.
    Baltimore A.L., vs. New York N.L., October 16, 1969, third inning.
    Oakland A.L., vs. New York N.L., October 21, 1973, third inning.
    Cincinnati N.L., vs. Boston A.L., October 14, 1975, fifth inning.
    New York A.L., vs. Los Angeles N.L., October 16, 1977, eighth inning.
    Los Angeles N.L., vs. New York A.L., October 10, 1978, second inning.
    Los Angeles N.L., vs. New York A.L., October 25, 1981, seventh inning.

Most Home Runs, Inning, Both Clubs
    3—New York N.L., 2, New York A.L., 1, October 11, 1921, second inning.
    Boston A.L., 3, St. Louis N.L. 0, October 11, 1967, fourth inning.

Most Consecutive Home Runs, Inning, One Club (9 times)
    2—Washington A.L., vs. Pittsburgh N.L., October 11, 1925, third inning.
    New York A.L., vs. St. Louis N.L., October 9, 1928, seventh inning.
    New York A.L., vs. Chicago N.L., October 1, 1932, fifth inning.
    New York A.L., vs. St. Louis N.L., October 14, 1964, sixth inning.
    Baltimore A.L., vs. Los Angeles N.L., October 5, 1966, first inning.
    Boston A.L., vs. St. Louis N.L., October 11, 1967, fourth inning.
    Cincinnati N.L., vs. Boston A.L., October 14, 1975, fifth inning.
    New York A.L., vs. Los Angeles N.L., October 16, 1977, eighth inning.
    Los Angeles N.L., vs. New York A.L., October 25, 1981, seventh inning.

Most Consecutive Games, Series, One or More Home Runs
    7—Washington A.L., vs. Pittsburgh N.L., October 7 to 15, inclusive, 1925, eight home runs.
    New York A.L., vs. Brooklyn N.L., October 1 to 7, inclusive, 1952, 10 home runs.

Most Consecutive Games, Total Series, One or More Home Runs
    9—New York A.L., last 2 games vs. Chicago N.L. in 1932 (7 home runs), all 6 games vs. New York N.L. in 1936 (7 home runs) and first game vs. New York N.L. in 1937 (1 home run); total 15 home runs.
    New York A.L., all 7 games vs. Brooklyn N.L. in 1952 (10 home runs) and first 2 games vs. Brooklyn N.L. in 1953 (4 home runs); total 14 home runs.

Most Total Bases, Game, One Club
    32—New York A.L., vs. St. Louis N.L., October 9, 1928.
    New York A.L., vs. Chicago N.L., October 2, 1932.

Most Total Bases, Game, Both Clubs
    47—New York A.L., 27, Brooklyn N.L., 20, October 4, 1953.

Fewest Total Bases, Game, One Club
    0—Brooklyn N.L., vs. New York A.L., October 8, 1956.

Fewest Total Bases, Game, Both Clubs
    5—New York A.L., 3, New York N.L., 2, October 6, 1921.

WORLD SERIES RECORDS

Most Total Bases, Inning, One Club
17—Philadelphia A.L., vs. Chicago N.L., October 12, 1929, seventh inning.

Most Total Bases, Inning, Both Clubs
21—Philadelphia A.L., 17, Chicago N.L., 4, October 12, 1929, seventh inning.

Most Long Hits, Game, One Club
9—Pittsburgh N.L., vs. Washington A.L., October 15, 1925; 8 doubles, one triple.

Most Long Hits, Game, Both Clubs
11—Chicago A.L., 8 (8 doubles), Chicago N.L., 3 (3 doubles), October 13, 1906.
Pittsburgh N.L., 9 (8 doubles, one triple), Washington A.L., 2 (one double, one home run), October 15, 1925.
New York A.L., 7 (4 doubles, 1 triple, 2 home runs), Cincinnati N.L., 4 (2 doubles, 2 home runs), October 9, 1961.

Longest Extra-Inning Game, Without a Long Hit, One Club
12 innings—Chicago N.L., vs. Detroit A.L., October 8, 1907.
Detroit A.L., vs. Chicago N.L., October 8, 1907.

Longest Extra-Inning Game, Without a Long Hit, Both Clubs
12 innings—Chicago N.L., 0, Detroit N.L., 0, October 8, 1907.

Most Bases on Balls, Game, One Club
11—Brooklyn N.L., vs. New York A.L., October 5, 1956.
New York A.L., vs. Milwaukee N.L., October 5, 1957.
Detroit A.L., vs. San Diego N.L., October 12, 1984.

Most Bases on Balls, Game, Both Clubs
19—New York A.L. 11, Milwaukee N.L. 8, October 5, 1957.

Longest Game No Bases on Balls, One Club
12 innings—St. Louis N.L. vs. Detroit A.L., October 4, 1934.

Fewest Bases on Balls, Game, Both Clubs
0—Philadelphia A.L., 0, New York N.L., 0, October 16, 1911.
New York N.L., 0, Chicago A.L., 0, October 10, 1917.
New York N.L., 0, New York A.L., 0, October 9, 1921.
Boston A.L., 0, St. Louis N.L., 0, October 7, 1967.
Philadelphia N.L., 0, Baltimore A.L., 0, October 11, 1983.

Most Bases on Balls, Inning, One Club
5—New York A.L., vs. St. Louis N.L., October 6, 1926, fifth inning.

Most Bases on Balls, Inning, Both Clubs
6—New York A.L., 3, New York N.L., 3, October 7, 1921, third inning.
New York A.L., 5, St. Louis N.L., 1, October 6, 1926, fifth inning.

Most Bases on Balls, Inning, Pinch-Hitters, One Club
2—New York A.L., vs. New York N.L., October 15, 1923, eighth inning.
Baltimore A.L. vs. Philadelphia N.L., October 15, 1983, sixth inning.

Most Strikeouts, Game, Nine Innings, One Club
17—Detroit A.L., vs. St. Louis N.L., October 2, 1968.

Most Strikeouts, Game, Nine Innings, Both Clubs
25—New York A.L., 15, Los Angeles N.L., 10, October 2, 1963.

Most Strikeouts, Extra-Inning Game, Both Clubs
25—Oakland A.L., 15, New York N.L., 10, October 14, 1973, 12 innings.

Fewest Strikeouts, Game, One Club
0—Chicago N.L., vs. Boston A.L., September 6, 1918, (did not bat in ninth inning).
Chicago N.L., vs. Boston A.L., September 9, 1918.
New York A.L., vs. New York N.L., October 6, 1921 (did not bat in ninth inning).
New York A.L., vs. Philadelphia N.L., October 4, 1950.
Brooklyn, N.L., vs. New York A.L., October 3, 1952.
Pittsburgh N.L., vs. New York A.L., October 6, 1960.
Pittsburgh N.L., vs. New York A.L., October 13, 1960.
New York A.L., vs. Pittsburgh N.L., October 13, 1960.

Fewest Strikeouts, Game, Both Clubs
0—Pittsburgh N.L., 0, New York A.L., 0, October 13, 1960.

Most Consecutive Strikeouts, Game, One Club
6—Chicago A.L., vs. Cincinnati N.L., October 6, 1919; 3 in second inning; 3 in third inning.
Los Angeles N.L., vs. Baltimore A.L., October 5, 1966; 3 in fourth inning; 3 in fifth inning.

Most Strikeouts, Inning, One Club
4—Detroit A.L., vs. Chicago N.L., October 14, 1908, first inning.

Most Strikeouts, Inning, Both Clubs
    6—Cincinnati N.L., 3, Oakland A.L., 3, October 18, 1972, fifth inning.

Most Strikeouts, Game, Pinch-Hitters, One Club
    4—St. Louis A.L., vs. St. Louis N.L., October 8, 1944, and October 9, 1944, both consecutive.

Most Strikeouts, Inning, Pinch-Hitters, One Club
    3—St. Louis A.L., vs. St. Louis N.L., October 8, 1944, ninth inning.

Most Consecutive Strikeouts, Two Successive Games, Pinch-Hitters, One Club
    8—St. Louis A.L., vs. St. Louis N.L., October 8, 1944 (4), October 9, 1944 (4).

Most Sacrifices, Game, One Club
    5—Chicago N.L., vs. Chicago A.L., October 12, 1906 (all sacrifice hits).
       Chicago N.L., vs. Detroit A.L., October 10, 1908 (all sacrifice hits).
       Pittsburgh N.L., vs. Detroit A.L., October 16, 1909 (4 sacrifice hits and one sacrifice fly).
       New York N.L., vs. Cleveland A.L., October 2, 1954 (3 sacrifice hits and two sacrifice flies).

Most Sacrifices, Game, Both Clubs
    7—Chicago N.L., 5, Detroit A.L., 2, October 10, 1908 (all sacrifice hits).

Most Sacrifices, Inning, One Club
    3—Brooklyn N.L., vs. New York A.L., October 4, 1955, sixth inning (2 sacrifice hits, one sacrifice fly).

Most Sacrifice Flies, Game, One Club
    2—Made in many games.

Most Sacrifice Flies, Game, Both Clubs
    2—Made in many games.

Most Sacrifice Flies, Inning, One Club
    2—Baltimore A.L., vs. Pittsburgh N.L., October 13, 1971, first inning.

Most Stolen Bases, Nine-Inning Game, One Club
    5—New York N.L., vs. Philadelphia A.L., October 12, 1905.
       Chicago N.L., vs. Chicago A.L., October 10, 1906.
       Chicago N.L., vs. Detroit A.L., October 9, 1907.

Most Stolen Bases, Extra-Inning Game, One Club
    7—Chicago N.L., vs. Detroit A.L., October 8, 1907, 10 innings.

Most Stolen Bases, Nine-Inning Game, Both Clubs
    6—New York N.L. 5, Philadelphia A.L. 1, October 12, 1905.
       Pittsburgh N.L., 4, Detroit A.L., 2, October 13, 1909.
       New York N.L., 3, Philadelphia A.L., 3, October 9, 1913.

Most Stolen Bases, Extra-Inning Game, Both Clubs
    11—Chicago N.L., 7, Detroit A.L., 4, October 8, 1907, 12 innings.

Longest Extra-Inning Game No Stolen Bases, One Club
    14 innings—Boston A.L., vs. Brooklyn N.L., October 9, 1916.
                   Brooklyn N.L., vs. Boston A.L., October 9, 1916.

Longest Extra-Inning Game No Stolen Bases, Both Clubs
    14 innings—Boston A.L., vs. Brooklyn N.L., October 9, 1916.

Most Stolen Bases, Inning, One Club
    3—Pittsburgh N.L., vs. Boston A.L., October 1, 1903, first inning.
       New York N.L., vs. Philadelphia A.L., October 12, 1905, ninth inning.
       Chicago N.L., vs. Detroit A.L., October 8, 1907, tenth inning.
       Chicago N.L., vs. Detroit A.L., October 11, 1908, eighth inning.
       New York N.L., vs. Boston A.L., October 14, 1912, first inning.
       Chicago A.L., vs. New York N.L., October 7, 1917, sixth inning.

Most Caught Stealing, Inning, One Club
    2—Made in many innings.

Most Caught Stealing, Nine-Inning Game, One Club
    3—Made in many games. Last time—Chicago A.L., vs. Los Angeles, N.L., October 4, 1959.

Most Caught Stealing, Extra-Inning Game, One Club
    5—New York N.L., vs. Philadelphia A.L., October 17, 1911, 11 innings, 0 stolen bases.

Most Caught Stealing, Nine-Inning Game, Both Clubs
    5—Philadelphia A.L., 3, Chicago N.L., 2, October 17, 1910.

Most Left on Base, Nine-Inning Game, One Club
    14—Chicago N.L., vs. Philadelphia A.L., October 18, 1910.
        Milwaukee N.L., vs. New York A.L., October 5, 1957.
        Pittsburgh N.L., vs. Baltimore A.L., October 11, 1971.
        Detroit A.L., vs. San Diego N.L., October 12, 1984.

WORLD SERIES RECORDS

Most Left on Base, Ten-Inning Game, One Club
   15—Philadelphia N.L., vs. Kansas City A.L., October 17, 1980.

Most Left on Base, Twelve-Inning Game, One Club
   15—New York N.L., vs. Oakland A.L., October 14, 1973.

Most Left on Base, Two Consecutive Nine-Inning Games, One Club
   26—Cleveland A.L., vs. New York N.L., September 29 (13), September 30 (13), 1954.

Most Left on Base, Eight-Inning Game, One Club
   13—Detroit A.L., vs. Cincinnati N.L., October 6, 1940.
   St. Louis N.L., vs. Milwaukee A.L., October 20, 1982.

Most Left on Base, Nine-Inning Shutout Defeat, One Club
   11—Philadelphia A.L., vs. St. Louis N.L., October 4, 1930, (Lost 5-0).
   St. Louis N.L., vs. New York A.L., October 11, 1943, (Lost 2-0).
   Los Angeles N.L., vs. Chicago A.L., October 6, 1959, (Lost 1-0).
   Baltimore A.L., vs. New York N.L., October 14, 1969, (Lost 5-0).

Most Left on Base Twelve-Inning Game, Both Clubs
   27—New York N.L., 15, Oakland A.L., 12, October 14, 1973.

Most Left on Base, Nine-Inning Game, Both Clubs
   24—Detroit A.L., 14, San Diego N.L., 10, October 12, 1984.

Fewest Left on Base, Game, One Club
   0—Brooklyn N.L., vs. New York A.L., October 8, 1956, 9 innings.
   Los Angeles N.L., vs. New York A.L., October 6, 1963, 8 innings.

Fewest Left on Base, Game, Both Clubs
   3—New York A.L., 3, Brooklyn N.L., 0, October 8, 1956.

Most Hit by Pitch, Inning, One Club
   2—Pittsburgh N.L., vs. Detroit A.L., October 11, 1909, second inning, consecutive.
   Detroit A.L., vs. St. Louis N.L., October 9, 1968, eighth inning.
   Pittsburgh N.L., vs. Baltimore A.L., October 17, 1979, ninth inning, consecutive.

Most Hit by Pitch, Game, One Club
   3—Detroit A.L., vs. St. Louis N.L., October 9, 1968.
   Baltimore A.L., vs. Pittsburgh N.L., October 13, 1971.

Most Hit by Pitch, Game, Both Clubs
   3—Philadelphia N.L., 2, Boston A.L., 1, October 13, 1915.
   Cincinnati N.L., 2, Chicago A.L., 1, October 9, 1919.
   Pittsburgh N.L., 2, Washington A.L., 1, October 7, 1925.
   Detroit A.L., 3, St. Louis N.L., 0, October 9, 1968.
   Baltimore A.L., 3, Pittsburgh N.L., 0, October 13, 1971.
   New York N.L., 2, Oakland A.L., 1, October 14, 1973.

Most Players, One or More Hits, Game, One Club
   11—New York A.L., vs. St. Louis N.L., October 9, 1928.
   New York A.L., vs. Pittsburgh N.L., October 6, 1960.

Most Players, One or More Hits, Game, Both Clubs
   19—New York A.L., 11, Pittsburgh N.L., 8, October 6, 1960.

Most Players, One or More Hits and Runs, Game, One Club
   9—New York A.L., vs. New York N.L., October 2, 1936.
   New York A.L., vs. Pittsburgh N.L., October 6, 1960.

Most Players, One or More Runs, Game, One Club
   9—St. Louis N.L., vs. Detroit A.L., October 9, 1934.
   New York A.L., vs. New York N.L., October 2, 1936.
   Milwaukee N.L., vs. New York A.L., October 2, 1958.
   New York A.L., vs. Pittsburgh N.L., October 6, 1960.
   Pittsburgh N.L., vs. New York A.L., October 13, 1960.

Most Players, One or More Runs, Game, Both Clubs
   15—Pittsburgh N.L., 9, New York A.L., 6, October 13, 1960.

Most First on Error, Game, One Club
   5—Chicago N.L., vs. Chicago A.L., October 13, 1906.

Most First on Error, Game, Both Clubs
   6—Pittsburgh N.L., 4, Boston A.L., 2, October 10, 1903.
   New York N.L., 4, Philadelphia A.L., 2, October 26, 1911.
   Chicago N.L., 4, Philadelphia A.L., 2, October 18, 1910.

CLUB BATTING, BASE-RUNNING—SERIES RECORDS

Highest Batting Average, Series, One Club
 4-game Series—.313—New York A.L., vs. Chicago N.L., 1932.
                    Cincinnati N.L., vs. New York A.L., 1976.
 5-game Series—.316—Philadelphia A.L., vs. Chicago N.L., 1910.
 6-game Series—.306—New York A.L., vs. Los Angeles N.L., 1978.
 7-game Series—.338—New York A.L., vs. Pittsburgh N.L., 1960.
 8-game Series—.270—New York N.L., vs. Boston A.L., 1912.

Highest Batting Average, Series, Both Clubs
 4-game Series—.283—New York A.L., .313, Chicago N.L., .253, 1932.
 5-game Series—.272—Philadelphia A.L., .316, Chicago N.L., .222, 1910.
 6-game Series—.292—Philadelphia N.L., .294, Kansas City A.L., .290, 1980.
 7-game Series—.300—New York A.L., .338, Pittsburgh N.L., .256, 1960.
 8-game Series—.245—New York N.L., .270, Boston A.L., .220, 1912.

Highest Batting Average, Series, World Series Loser
 4-game Series—.253—Chicago N.L., vs. New York A.L., 1932.
 5-game Series—.265—San Diego N.L., vs. Detroit A.L., 1984.
 6-game Series—.300—Brooklyn N.L., vs. New York A.L., 1953.
 7-game Series—.338—New York A.L., vs. Pittsburgh N.L., 1960.
 8-game Series—.270—New York N.L., vs. Boston A.L., 1912.

Lowest Batting Average, Series, One Club
 4-game Series—.142—Los Angeles N.L., vs. Baltimore A.L., 1966.
 5-game Series—.146—Baltimore A.L., vs. New York N.L., 1969.
 6-game Series—.175—New York N.L., vs. Philadelphia A.L., 1911.
 7-game Series—.195—Brooklyn N.L., vs. New York A.L., 1956.
                    Minnesota A.L., vs. Los Angeles N.L., 1965.
 8-game Series—.207—New York A.L., vs. New York N.L., 1921.

Lowest Batting Average, Series, Both Clubs
 4-game Series—.171—Los Angeles N.L., .142, Baltimore A.L., .200, 1966.
 5-game Series—.184—Baltimore A.L., .146, New York N.L., .220, 1969.
 6-game Series—.197—Chicago A.L., .198, Chicago N.L., .196, 1906.
 7-game Series—.209—Oakland A.L., .209, Cincinnati N.L., .209, 1972.
 8-game Series—.239—Cincinnati N.L., .255, Chicago A.L., .224, 1919.

Lowest Batting Average, Series, World Series Winner
 4-game Series—.200—Baltimore A.L., vs. Los Angeles N.L., 1966.
 5-game Series—.209—New York N.L., vs. Philadelphia A.L., 1905.
 6-game Series—.186—Boston A.L., vs. Chicago N.L., 1918.
 7-game Series—.199—New York A.L., vs. San Francisco N.L., 1962.
 8-game Series—.220—Boston A.L., vs. New York N.L., 1912.

Highest Slugging Average, Series, One Club
 4-game Series—.530—New York A.L., vs. St. Louis N.L., 1928.
 5-game Series—.509—Baltimore A.L., vs. Cincinnati N.L., 1970.
 6-game Series—.484—Brooklyn N.L., vs. New York A.L., 1953.
 7-game Series—.528—New York A.L., vs. Pittsburgh N.L., 1960.
 8-game Series—.401—Boston A.L., vs. Pittsburgh N.L., 1903.

Highest Slugging Average, Series, Both Clubs
 4-game Series—.459—New York A.L., .521, Chicago N.L., .397, 1932.
 5-game Series—.433—Baltimore A.L., .509, Cincinnati N.L., .354, 1970.
 6-game Series—.436—Kansas City A.L., .469, Philadelphia N.L., .403, 1980.
 7-game Series—.447—New York A.L., .528, Pittsburgh N.L., .355, 1960.
 8-game Series—.344—New York N.L., .361, Boston A.L., .326, 1912.

Lowest Slugging Average, Series, One Club
 4-game Series—.192—Los Angeles N.L., vs. Baltimore A.L., 1966.
 5-game Series—.194—Philadelphia A.L., vs. New York N.L., 1905.
 6-game Series—.233—Boston A.L., vs. Chicago N.L., 1918.
 7-game Series—.237—Brooklyn N.L., vs. Cleveland A.L., 1920.
 8-game Series—.270—New York A.L., vs. New York N.L., 1921.

Lowest Slugging Average, Series, Both Clubs
 4-game Series—.267—Baltimore A.L., .342, Los Angeles N.L., .192, 1966.
 5-game Series—.224—New York N.L., .255, Philadelphia A.L., .194, 1905.
 6-game Series—.241—Chicago N.L., .250, Boston A.L., .233, 1918.
 7-game Series—.285—Cleveland A.L., .332, Brooklyn N.L., .237, 1920.
 8-game Series—.323—New York N.L., .371, New York A.L., .270, 1921.

Most At-Bats, Total Series, One Club
 6,255—New York A.L., 33 Series, 187 games.

Most At-Bats, Series, One Club
 4-game Series—146—Chicago N.L., vs. New York A.L., 1932.

WORLD SERIES RECORDS

    5-game Series—178—New York A.L., vs. St. Louis N.L., 1942.
    6-game Series—222—New York A.L., vs. Los Angeles, N.L., 1978.
    7-game Series—269—New York A.L., vs. Pittsburgh N.L., 1960.
    8-game Series—282—Boston A.L., vs. Pittsburgh N.L., 1903.

Most At-Bats, Series, Both Clubs

    4-game Series—290—Chicago N.L., 146, New York A.L., 144, 1932.
    5-game Series—349—New York N.L., 176, Washington A.L., 173, 1933.
    6-game Series—421—New York A.L., 222, Los Angeles N.L., 199, 1978.
    7-game Series—512—St. Louis N.L., 262, Detroit A.L., 250, 1934.
    8-game Series—552—Boston A.L., 282, Pittsburgh N.L., 270, 1903.

Fewest At-Bats, Series, One Club

    4-game Series—117—Los Angeles N.L., vs. New York A.L., 1963.
    5-game Series—142—Oakland A.L., vs. Los Angeles N.L., 1974.
    6-game Series—172—Boston A.L., vs. Chicago N.L., 1918.
    7-game Series—215—Brooklyn N.L., vs. Cleveland A.L., 1920.
                      Brooklyn N.L., vs. New York A.L., 1956.
                        Minnesota A.L., vs. Los Angeles N.L., 1965.
    8-game Series—241—New York A.L., vs. New York N.L., 1921.

Fewest At-Bats, Series, Both Clubs

    4-game Series—240—Baltimore A.L., 120, Los Angeles N.L., 120, 1966.
    5-game Series—300—Los Angeles N.L., 158, Oakland A.L., 142, 1974.
    6-game Series—348—Chicago N.L., 176, Boston A.L., 172, 1918.
    7-game Series—432—Cleveland A.L., 217, Brooklyn N.L., 215, 1920.
    8-game Series—505—New York N.L., 264, New York A.L., 241, 1921.

Most Runs, Total Series, One Club

    838—New York A.L., 33 Series, 187 games.

Most Runs, Series, One Club

    4-game Series—37—New York A.L., vs. Chicago N.L., 1932.
    5-game Series—35—Philadelphia A.L., vs. Chicago N.L., 1910.
    6-game Series—43—New York A.L., vs. New York N.L., 1936.
    7-game Series—55—New York A.L., vs. Pittsburgh N.L., 1960.
    8-game Series—39—Boston A.L., vs. Pittsburgh N.L., 1903.

Most Runs, Series, Both Clubs

    4-game Series—56—New York A.L., 37, Chicago N.L., 19, 1932.
    5-game Series—53—Baltimore A.L., 33, Cincinnati N.L., 20, 1970.
    6-game Series—66—New York A.L., 43, New York N.L., 23, 1936.
    7-game Series—82—New York A.L., 55, Pittsburgh N.L., 27, 1960.
    8-game Series—63—Boston A.L., 39, Pittsburgh N.L., 24, 1903.

Most Runs, Series, World Series Loser

    4-game Series—19—Chicago N.L., vs. New York A.L., 1932.
    5-game Series—20—Cincinnati N.L., vs. Baltimore A.L., 1970.
    6-game Series—28—Los Angeles N.L., vs. New York A.L., 1977.
    7-game Series—55—New York A.L., vs. Pittsburgh N.L., 1960.
    8-game Series—31—New York N.L., vs. Boston A.L., 1912.

Most Runs Allowed, Total Series, One Club

    651—New York A.L., 33 Series, 187 games.

Fewest Runs, Series, One Club

    4-game Series— 2—Los Angeles N.L., vs. Baltimore A.L., 1966.
    5-game Series— 3—Philadelphia A.L., vs. New York N.L., 1905.
    6-game Series— 9—Boston A.L., vs. Chicago N.L., 1918.
    7-game Series— 8—Brooklyn A.L., vs. Cleveland A.L., 1920.
    8-game Series—20—Chicago A.L., vs. Cincinnati N.L., 1919.

Fewest Runs, Series, Both Clubs

    4-game Series—15—Baltimore A.L., 13, Los Angeles N.L., 2, 1966.
    5-game Series—18—New York N.L., 15, Philadelphia A.L., 3, 1905.
    6-game Series—19—Chicago N.L., 10, Boston A.L., 9, 1918.
    7-game Series—29—Cleveland A.L., 21, Brooklyn N.L., 8, 1920.
    8-game Series—51—New York N.L., 29, New York A.L., 22, 1921.

Most Runs Batted In, Total Series, One Club

    791—New York, A.L., 33 Series, 187 games.

Most Runs Batted In, Series, One Club

    4-game Series—36—New York A.L., vs. Chicago N.L., 1932.
    5-game Series—32—Baltimore A.L., vs. Cincinnati N.L., 1970.
    6-game Series—41—New York A.L., vs. New York N.L., 1936.
    7-game Series—54—New York A.L., vs. Pittsburgh N.L., 1960.
    8-game Series—35—Boston A.L., vs. Pittsburgh N.L., 1903.

Most Runs Batted In, Series, Both Clubs
  4-game Series—52—New York A.L., 36, Chicago N.L., 16, 1932.
  5-game Series—52—Baltimore A.L., 32, Cincinnati N.L., 20, 1970.
  6-game Series—61—New York A.L., 41, New York N.L., 20, 1936.
  7-game Series—80—New York A.L., 54, Pittsburgh N.L., 26, 1960.
  8-game Series—58—Boston A.L., 35, Pittsburgh N.L., 23, 1903.

Fewest Runs Batted In, Series, One Club
  4-game Series— 2—Los Angeles N.L. vs. Baltimore A.L., 1966.
  5-game Series— 2—Philadelphia A.L., vs. New York N.L., 1905.
  6-game Series— 6—Boston A.L., vs. Chicago N.L., 1918.
  7-game Series— 8—Brooklyn N.L., vs. Cleveland A.L., 1920.
  8-game Series—17—Chicago A.L., vs. Cincinnati N.L., 1919.

Fewest Runs Batted In, Series, Both Clubs
  4-game Series—12—Los Angeles N.L., 2, Baltimore A.L., 10, 1966.
  5-game Series—15—Philadelphia A.L., 2, New York N.L., 13, 1905.
  6-game Series—16—Boston A.L., 6, Chicago N.L., 10, 1918.
  7-game Series—26—Brooklyn N.L., 8, Cleveland A.L., 18, 1920.
  8-game Series—46—Boston A.L., 21, New York N.L., 25, 1912.

Most Hits, Total Series, One Club
  1,568—New York A.L., 33 Series, 187 games.

Most Hits, Series, One Club
  4-game Series—45—New York A.L., vs. Chicago N.L., 1932.
  5-game Series—56—Philadelphia A.L., vs. Chicago N.L., 1910.
  6-game Series—68—New York A.L., vs. Los Angeles N.L., 1978.
  7-game Series—91—New York A.L., vs. Pittsburgh N.L., 1960.
  8-game Series—74—New York N.L., vs. Boston A.L., 1912.

Most Hits, Series, Both Clubs
  4-game Series— 82—New York A.L., 45, Chicago N.L., 37, 1932.
  5-game Series— 91—Philadelphia A.L., 56, Chicago N.L., 35, 1910.
  6-game Series—120—Brooklyn N.L., 64, New York A.L., 56, 1953.
                    New York A.L., 68, Los Angeles N.L., 52, 1978.
  7-game Series—151—New York A.L., 91, Pittsburgh N.L., 60, 1960.
  8-game Series—135—Boston A.L., 71, Pittsburgh N.L., 64, 1903.

Fewest Hits, Series, One Club
  4-game Series—17—Los Angeles N.L., vs. Baltimore A.L., 1966.
  5-game Series—23—Baltimore A.L., vs. New York N.L., 1969.
  6-game Series—32—Boston A.L., vs. Chicago N.L., 1918.
  7-game Series—42—Brooklyn N.L., vs. New York N.L., 1956.
                    Minnesota A.L., vs. Los Angeles N.L., 1965.
  8-game Series—50—New York A.L., vs. New York N.L., 1921.

Fewest Hits, Series, Both Clubs
  4-game Series— 41—Baltimore A.L., 24, Los Angeles N.L., 17, 1966.
  5-game Series— 57—New York N.L., 32, Philadelphia A.L., 25, 1905.
  6-game Series— 69—Chicago N.L., 37, Boston A.L., 32, 1918.
  7-game Series— 92—Oakland A.L., 46, Cincinnati N.L., 46, 1972.
  8-game Series—121—New York N.L., 71, New York A.L., 50, 1921.

Most Hits, Series, Pinch-Hitters, One Club
  6—New York A.L., vs. Brooklyn N.L., 1947 (seven games).
    New York A.L., vs. Pittsburgh N.L., 1960 (seven games).
    Oakland A.L., vs. Cincinnati N.L., 1972 (seven games).
    Baltimore A.L., vs. Pittsburgh N.L., 1979 (seven games).

Most Hits, Series, Pinch-Hitters, Both Clubs
  11—New York A.L., 6, Brooklyn N.L., 5, 1947 (seven games).

Most Players One or More Hits, Each Game, Series, One Club
  4—New York A.L., vs. Los Angeles N.L., 1978 (six games).

Most One-Base Hits, Total Series, One Club
  1,116—New York A.L., 33 Series, 187 games.

Most One-Base Hits, Series, One Club
  4-game Series—31—New York A.L., vs. Chicago N.L., 1932.
  5-game Series—46—New York N.L., vs. New York A.L., 1922.
  6-game Series—57—New York A.L., vs. Los Angeles, N.L., 1978.
  7-game Series—64—New York A.L., vs. Pittsburgh N.L., 1960.
  8-game Series—55—New York N.L., vs. Boston A.L., 1912.

Most One-Base Hits, Series, Both Clubs
  4-game Series— 55—New York A.L., 31, Chicago N.L., 24, 1932.
  5-game Series— 70—New York N.L., 39, Washington A.L., 31, 1933.

6-game Series— 95—New York A.L., 57, Los Angeles N.L., 38, 1978.
7-game Series—109—New York A.L., 64, Pittsburgh N.L., 45, 1960.
8-game Series— 96—Boston A.L. 49, Pittsburgh N.L., 47, 1903.

Fewest One-Base Hits, Series, One Club
4-game Series—13—Philadelphia A.L., vs. Boston N.L., 1914.
                  Los Angeles N.L., vs. Baltimore A.L., 1966.
5-game Series—19—Brooklyn N.L., vs. New York A.L., 1941.
                  Baltimore A.L., vs. New York N.L., 1969.
6-game Series—17—Philadelphia A.L., vs. St. Louis N.L., 1930.
7-game Series—27—Minnesota A.L., vs. Los Angeles N.L., 1965.
8-game Series—39—Boston A.L., vs. New York N.L., 1912.

Fewest One-Base Hits, Series, Both Clubs
4-game Series—29—Baltimore A.L., 16, Los Angeles N.L., 13, 1966.
5-game Series—40—New York N.L., 21, Baltimore A.L., 19, 1969.
6-game Series—42—St. Louis N.L., 25, Philadelphia A.L., 17, 1930.
7-game Series—66—St. Louis N.L., 33, Boston A.L., 33, 1967.
8-game Series—92—Cincinnati N.L., 47, Chicago A.L., 45, 1919.
                  New York N.L., 52, New York A.L., 40, 1921.

Most Two-Base Hits, Total Series, One Club
224—New York A.L., 33 Series, 187 games.

Most Two-Base Hits, Series, One Club
4-game Series— 9—Philadelphia A.L., vs. Boston N.L., 1914.
5-game Series—19—Philadelphia A.L., vs. Chicago N.L., 1910.
6-game Series—15—Philadelphia A.L., vs. New York N.L., 1911.
7-game Series—19—St. Louis N.L., vs. Boston A.L., 1946.
8-game Series—14—Boston A.L., vs. New York N.L., 1912.
                  New York N.L., vs. Boston A.L., 1912.

Most Two-Base Hits, Series, Both Clubs
4-game Series—15—Philadelphia A.L., 9, Boston N.L., 6, 1914.
5-game Series—30—Philadelphia A.L., 19, Chicago N.L., 11, 1910.
6-game Series—26—Philadelphia A.L., 15, New York N.L., 11, 1911.
7-game Series—29—Detroit A.L., 16, Pittsburgh N.L., 13, 1909.
8-game Series—28—Boston A.L., 14, New York N.L., 14, 1912.

Fewest Two-Base Hits, Series, One Club
4-game Series—3—Cincinnati N.L., vs. New York A.L., 1939.
                 New York A.L., vs. Philadelphia N.L., 1950.
                 New York N.L., vs. Cleveland A.L., 1954.
                 Los Angeles N.L., vs. New York A.L., 1963.
                 New York A.L., vs. Los Angeles N.L., 1963.
                 Baltimore A.L., vs. Los Angeles N.L., 1966.
                 Los Angeles N.L., vs. Baltimore A.L., 1966.
                 New York A.L., vs. Cincinnati N.L., 1976.
5-game Series—1—Detroit A.L., vs. Chicago N.L., 1907
                 Baltimore A.L., vs. New York N.L., 1969.
6-game Series—2—Boston A.L., vs. Chicago N.L., 1918.
                 New York N.L., vs. New York A.L., 1923.
7-game Series—3—Baltimore A.L., vs. Pittsburgh N.L., 1971.
8-game Series—4—Boston A.L., vs. Pittsburgh N.L., 1903.

Fewest Two-Base Hits, Series, Both Clubs
4-game Series— 6—Los Angeles N.L., 3, New York A.L., 3, 1963.
                  Baltimore A.L., 3, Los Angeles N.L., 3, 1966.
5-game Series— 6—Philadelphia N.L., 4, Boston A.L., 2, 1915.
6-game Series— 7—Chicago N.L., 5, Boston A.L., 2, 1918.
7-game Series—11—St. Louis N.L., 7, Detroit A.L., 4, 1968.
8-game Series—11—Pittsburgh N.L., 7, Boston A.L., 4, 1903.

Most Three-Base Hits, Total Series, One Club
47—New York A.L., 33 Series, 187 games.

Most Three-Base Hits, Series, One Club
4-game Series— 3—Cincinnati N.L., vs. New York A.L., 1976.
5-game Series— 6—Boston A.L., vs. Brooklyn N.L., 1916.
6-game Series— 4—New York N.L., vs. Chicago A.L., 1917.
                  New York A.L., vs. New York N.L., 1923.
                  New York A.L., vs. Brooklyn N.L., 1953.
7-game Series— 5—St. Louis N.L., vs. Detroit A.L., 1934.
                  New York A.L., vs. Brooklyn N.L., 1947.
8-game Series—16—Boston A.L., vs. Pittsburgh N.L., 1903.

Most Three-Base Hits, Series, Both Clubs
4-game Series— 4—Cincinnati N.L., 3, New York A.L., 1, 1976.
5-game Series—11—Boston A.L., 6, Brooklyn N.L., 5, 1916.

6-game Series— 7—New York A.L., 4, New York N.L., 3, 1923.
7-game Series— 6—St. Louis N.L., 5, Detroit A.L., 1, 1934.
                    New York A.L., 5, Brooklyn N.L., 1, 1947.
                    Detroit A.L., 3, St. Louis N.L., 3, 1968.
8-game Series—25—Boston A.L., 16, Pittsburgh N.L., 9, 1903.

Fewest Three-Base Hits, Series, One Club

4-game Series—0—Held by many clubs.
5-game Series—0—Held by many clubs. Last Clubs—Detroit A.L., 1984; San Diego N.L., 1984.
6-game Series—0—Held by many clubs. Last Club—Philadelphia N.L., 1980.
7-game Series—0—Held by many clubs. Last Club—Oakland A.L., 1972.
8-game Series—1—New York A.L., vs. New York N.L., 1921.

Fewest Three-Base Hits, Series, Both Clubs

4-game Series—1—St. Louis N.L., 1, New York A.L., 0, 1928.
                Cleveland A.L., 1, New York N.L., 0, 1954.
                Baltimore A.L., 1, Los Angeles N.L., 0, 1966.
5-game Series—0—New York N.L., 0, Philadelphia A.L., 0, 1905.
                New York N.L., 0, Washington A.L., 0, 1933.
                New York N.L., 0, Baltimore, A.L., 0, 1969.
                Detroit A.L., 0, San Diego N.L., 0, 1984.
6-game Series—0—Cleveland A.L., 0, Boston N.L., 0, 1948.
                New York A.L., 0, Los Angeles N.L., 0, 1978.
7-game Series—0—St. Louis N.L., 0, Philadelphia A.L., 0, 1931.
8-game Series—5—New York N.L., 4, New York A.L., 1, 1921.

Most Home Runs, Total Series, One Club

181—New York A.L., 33 Series, 187 games.

Most Home Runs, Series, by Pitchers as Batters, One Club

2—New York N.L., vs. Washington A.L., 1924.

Most Home Runs, Series, One Club

4-game Series— 9—New York A.L., vs. St. Louis N.L., 1928.
5-game Series—10—Baltimore A.L., vs. Cincinnati N.L., 1970.
6-game Series— 9—New York A.L., vs. Brooklyn N.L., 1953.
                Los Angeles N.L., vs. New York A.L., 1977.
7-game Series—12—New York A.L., vs. Brooklyn N.L., 1956.
8-game Series— 2—Boston A.L., vs. Pittsburgh N.L., 1903.
                New York A.L., vs. New York N.L., 1921.
                New York N.L., vs. New York A.L., 1921.

Most Home Runs, Series, Both Clubs

4-game Series—11—New York A.L., 8, Chicago N.L., 3, 1932.
5-game Series—15—Baltimore A.L., 10, Cincinnati N.L., 5, 1970.
6-game Series—17—New York A.L., 9, Brooklyn N.L., 8, 1953.
                Los Angeles N.L., 9, New York A.L., 8, 1977.
7-game Series—17—Brooklyn N.L., 9, New York A.L., 8, 1955.
8-game Series— 4—New York N.L., 2, New York A.L., 2, 1921.

Most Home Runs, Series, by Pitchers as Batters, Both Clubs

2—New York N.L., 2, Washington A.L., 0, 1924.
   Boston A.L., 1, St. Louis N.L., 1, 1967.
   Detroit A.L., 1, St. Louis N.L., 1, 1968.

Fewest Home Runs, Series, One Club

4-game Series—0—Held by many clubs.
5-game Series—0—Held by many clubs.
6-game Series—0—Chicago N.L., vs. Chicago A.L., 1906.
                Chicago A.L., vs. Chicago N.L., 1906.
                New York N.L., vs. Philadelphia A.L., 1911.
                Boston A.L., vs. Chicago N.L., 1918.
                Chicago N.L., vs. Boston A.L., 1918.
7-game Series—0—Brooklyn N.L., vs. Cleveland A.L., 1920.
8-game Series—0—Cincinnati N.L., vs. Chicago A.L., 1919.

Fewest Home Runs, Series, Both Clubs

4-game Series—1—Boston N.L., 1, Philadelphia A.L., 0, 1914.
5-game Series—0—New York N.L., 0, Philadelphia A.L., 0, 1905.
                Chicago N.L., 0, Detroit A.L., 0, 1907.
6-game Series—0—Chicago A.L., 0, Chicago N.L., 0, 1906.
                Boston A.L., 0, Chicago N.L., 0, 1918.
7-game Series—2—Cleveland A.L., 2, Brooklyn N.L., 0, 1920.
8-game Series—1—Chicago A.L., 1, Cincinnati N.L., 0, 1919.

Most Times Two Home Runs, Inning, Series, One Club

2—New York A.L., 1928, 1932, 1939, 1964.

Most Times Two Home Runs, Inning, Total Series, One Club

10—New York A.L., 1928 (2), 1932 (2), 1939 (2), 1958 (1), 1964 (2), 1977 (1).

Most Home Runs With Bases Filled, Total Series, One Club
    7—New York A.L., 33 Series, 187 games.

Most Home Runs With Bases Filled, Series, One Club
    2—New York A.L., vs. Brooklyn N.L., 1956.

Most Home Runs With Bases Filled, Series, Both Clubs
    2—New York A.L., 2, Brooklyn N.L., 0, 1956.
       St. Louis N.L., 1, New York A.L., 1, 1964.

Most Home Runs, Pinch-Hitters, Total Series, One Club
    5—New York A.L., 33 Series, 187 games.

Most Home Runs, Pinch-Hitters, Series, One Club
    2—Los Angeles N.L., vs. Chicago A.L., 1959.
       Boston A.L., vs. Cincinnati N.L., 1975.

Most Home Runs, Pinch-Hitters, Series, Both Clubs
    2—New York N.L., 1, Cleveland A.L., 1 1954.
       Los Angeles N.L., 2, Chicago A.L., 0, 1959.
       Boston A.L., 2, Cincinnati N.L., 0, 1975.

Most Total Bases, Total Series, One Club
    2,429—New York A.L., 33 Series, 187 games.

Most Total Bases, Series, One Club
    4-game Series— 75—New York A.L., vs. Chicago N.L., 1932.
    5-game Series— 87—Baltimore A.L., vs. Cincinnati N.L., 1970.
    6-game Series—103—Brooklyn N.L., vs. New York A.L., 1953.
    7-game Series—142—New York A.L., vs. Pittsburgh N.L., 1960.
    8-game Series—113—Boston A.L., vs. Pittsburgh N.L., 1903.

Most Total Bases, Series, Both Clubs
    4-game Series—133—New York A.L., 75, Chicago N.L., 58, 1932.
    5-game Series—145—Baltimore A.L., 87, Cincinnati N.L., 58, 1970.
    6-game Series—200—Brooklyn N.L., 103, New York A.L., 97, 1953.
    7-game Series—225—New York A.L., 142, Pittsburgh N.L., 83, 1960.
    8-game Series—205—Boston A.L., 113, Pittsburgh N.L., 92, 1903.

Fewest Total Bases, Series, One Club
    4-game Series—23—Los Angeles N.L., vs. Baltimore A.L., 1966.
    5-game Series—30—Philadelphia A.L., vs. New York N.L., 1905.
    6-game Series—40—Boston A.L., vs. Chicago N.L., 1918.
    7-game Series—51—Brooklyn N.L., vs. Cleveland A.L., 1920.
    8-game Series—65—New York A.L., vs. New York N.L., 1921.

Fewest Total Bases, Series, Both Clubs
    4-game Series— 64—Baltimore A.L., 41, Los Angeles N.L., 23, 1966.
    5-game Series— 69—New York N.L., 39, Philadelphia A.L., 30, 1905.
    6-game Series— 84—Chicago N.L., 44, Boston A.L., 40, 1918.
    7-game Series—123—Cleveland A.L., 72, Brooklyn N.L., 51, 1920.
    8-game Series—163—New York N.L., 98, New York A.L., 65, 1921.

Most Long Hits, Total Series, One Club
    452—New York A.L., 33 Series, 187 games.
        (224 doubles, 47 triples, 181 homers).

Most Long Hits, Series, One Club
    4-game Series—17—Cincinnati N.L., vs. New york A.L., 1976.
    5-game Series—21—Philadelphia A.L., vs. Chicago N.L., 1910.
    6-game Series—22—Brooklyn N.L., vs. New York A.L., 1953.
    7-game Series—27—New York A.L., vs. Pittsburgh N.L., 1960.
    8-game Series—22—Boston A.L., vs. Pittsburgh N.L., 1903.

Most Long Hits, Series, Both Clubs
    4-game Series—27—New York A.L., 14, Chicago N.L., 13, 1932.
    5-game Series—33—Philadelphia A.L., 21, Chicago N.L., 12, 1910.
    6-game Series—41—Brooklyn N.L., 22, New York A.L., 19, 1953.
    7-game Series—42—New York A.L., 27, Pittsburgh N.L., 15, 1960.
                    St. Louis N.L., 23, Milwaukee A.L., 19, 1982.
    8-game Series—40—Boston A.L., 21, New York N.L., 19, 1912.

Fewest Long Hits, Series, One Club
    4-game Series— 4—Cincinnati N.L., vs. New York A.L., 1939.
                      Los Angeles N.L., vs. Baltimore A.L., 1966.
    5-game Series— 3—Detroit A.L., vs. Chicago N.L., 1907.
    6-game Series— 5—Boston A.L., vs. Chicago N.L., 1918.
    7-game Series— 6—Brooklyn N.L., vs. Cleveland A.L., 1920.
    8-game Series—10—New York A.L., vs. New York N.L., 1921.

Fewest Long Hits, Series, Both Clubs
    4-game Series—12—Baltimore A.L., 8, Los Angeles N.L., 4, 1966.
    5-game Series—10—Chicago N.L., 7, Detroit A.L., 3, 1907.
    6-game Series—11—Chicago N.L., 6, Boston A.L., 5, 1918.
    7-game Series—19—Cleveland A.L., 13, Brooklyn N.L., 6, 1920.
    8-game Series—29—New York N.L., 19, New York A.L., 10, 1921.

Most Extra Bases on Long Hits, Total Series, One Club
    861—New York A.L., 33 Series, 187 games.
        (224 on doubles, 94 on triples, 543 on homers).

Most Extra Bases on Long Hits, Series, One Club
    4-game Series—34—New York A.L., vs. St. Louis N.L., 1928.
    5-game Series—37—Baltimore A.L., vs. Cincinnati N.L., 1970.
    6-game Series—41—New York A.L., vs. Brooklyn N.L., 1953.
    7-game Series—51—New York A.L., vs. Pittsburgh N.L., 1960.
    8-game Series—42—Boston A.L., vs. Pittsburgh N.L., 1903.

Most Extra Bases on Long Hits, Series, Both Clubs
    4-game Series—51—New York A.L., 30, Chicago N.L., 21, 1932.
    5-game Series—60—Baltimore A.L., 37, Cincinnati N.L., 23, 1970.
    6-game Series—80—New York A.L., 41, Brooklyn N.L., 39, 1953.
    7-game Series—74—New York A.L., 51, Pittsburgh N.L., 23, 1960.
    8-game Series—70—Boston A.L., 42, Pittsburgh N.L., 28, 1903.

Fewest Extra Bases on Long Hits, Series, One Club
    4-game Series— 5—Cincinnati N.L., vs. New York A.L., 1939.
    5-game Series— 5—Philadelphia A.L., vs. New York N.L., 1905.
                   Detroit A.L., vs. Chicago N.L., 1907.
                   Detroit A.L., vs. Chicago N.L., 1908.
    6-game Series— 7—Chicago N.L., vs. Boston A.L., 1918.
    7-game Series— 7—Brooklyn N.L., vs. Cleveland A.L., 1920.
    8-game Series—15—New York A.L., vs. New York N.L., 1921.

Fewest Extra Bases on Long Hits, Series, Both Clubs
    4-game Series—19—New York A.L., 11, Philadelphia N.L., 8, 1950.
    5-game Series—12—New York N.L., 7, Philadelphia A.L., 5, 1905.
    6-game Series—15—Boston A.L., 8, Chicago N.L., 7, 1918.
    7-game Series—26—Cleveland A.L., 19, Brooklyn N.L., 7, 1920.
    8-game Series—42—New York N.L., 27, New York A.L., 15, 1921.

Most Bases on Balls, Total Series, One Club
    645—New York A.L., 33 Series, 187 games.

Most Bases on Balls, Series, One Club
    4-game Series—23—New York A.L., vs. Chicago N.L., 1932.
    5-game Series—24—New York A.L., vs. Cincinnati N.L., 1961.
    6-game Series—33—New York A.L., vs. Los Angeles N.L., 1981.
    7-game Series—38—New York A.L., vs. Brooklyn N.L., 1947.
    8-game Series—27—New York A.L., vs. New York N.L., 1921.

Most Bases on Balls, Series, Both Clubs
    4-game Series—34—New York A.L., 23, Chicago N.L., 11, 1932.
    5-game Series—37—New York A.L., 23, Brooklyn N.L., 14, 1941.
    6-game Series—53—New York A.L., 33, Los Angeles N.L., 20, 1981.
    7-game Series—68—New York A.L., 38, Brooklyn N.L., 30, 1947.
    8-game Series—49—New York A.L., 27, New York N.L., 22, 1921.

Fewest Bases on Balls, Series, One Club
    4-game Series— 4—Pittsburgh N.L., vs. New York A.L., 1927.
    5-game Series— 5—Philadelphia A.L., vs. New York N.L., 1905.
    6-game Series— 4—Philadelphia A.L., vs. New York N.L., 1911.
    7-game Series— 9—St. Louis N.L., vs. Philadelphia A.L., 1931.
    8-game Series—13—Boston A.L., vs. Pittsburgh N.L., 1903.

Fewest Bases on Balls, Series, Both Clubs
    4-game Series—15—New York A.L., 9, Cincinnati N.L., 6, 1939.
    5-game Series—15—New York N.L., 8, Philadelphia A.L., 7, 1913.
    6-game Series—17—Chicago A.L., 11, New York N.L., 6, 1917.
    7-game Series—30—New York A.L., 18, Pittsburgh N.L., 12, 1960.
    8-game Series—27—Pittsburgh N.L., 14, Boston A.L., 13, 1903.

Most Strikeouts, Total Series, One Club
    986—New York A.L., 33 Series, 187 games.

Most Strikeouts, Series, One Club
    4-game Series—37—New York A.L., vs. Los Angeles N.L., 1963.
    5-game Series—50—Chicago N.L., vs. Philadelphia A.L., 1929.
    6-game Series—49—St. Louis A.L., vs. St. Louis N.L., 1944.
                    Kansas City A.L., vs. Philadelphia N.L., 1980.

WORLD SERIES RECORDS

7-game Series—62—Oakland A.L., vs. New York N.L., 1973.
8-game Series—45—Pittsburgh N.L., vs. Boston A.L., 1903.

Most Strikeouts, Series, Both Clubs
4-game Series—62—New York A.L., 37, Los Angeles N.L., 25, 1963.
5-game Series—77—Chicago N.L., 50, Philadelphia A.L., 27, 1929.
6-game Series—92—St. Louis A.L., 49, St. Louis N.L., 43, 1944.
7-game Series—99—Detroit A.L., 59, St. Louis N.L., 40, 1968.
8-game Series—82—New York A.L., 44, New York N.L., 38, 1921.

Fewest Strikeouts, Series, One Club
4-game Series— 7—Pittsburgh N.L., vs. New York A.L., 1927.
5-game Series—15—New York N.L., vs. New York A.L., 1922.
6-game Series—14—Chicago N.L., vs. Boston A.L., 1918.
7-game Series—20—Brooklyn N.L., vs. Cleveland A.L., 1920.
8-game Series—22—Cincinnati N.L., vs. Chicago N.L., 1919.

Fewest Strikeouts, Series, Both Clubs
4-game Series—32—New York A.L., 25, Pittsburgh N.L., 7, 1927.
             Cincinnati N.L., 16, New York A.L., 16, 1976.
5-game Series—35—New York N.L., 19, Philadelphia A.L., 16, 1913.
             New York A.L., 20, New York N.L., 15, 1922.
6-game Series—35—Boston A.L., 21, Chicago N.L., 14, 1918.
7-game Series—41—Cleveland A.L., 21, Brooklyn N.L., 20, 1920.
8-game Series—52—Chicago A.L., 30, Cincinnati N.L., 22, 1919.

Most Sacrifices, Total Series, One Club
108—New York A.L., 33 Series, 187 games.

Most Sacrifices, Series, One Club
4-game Series— 8—New York N.L., vs. Cleveland A.L., 1954.
5-game Series—12—Boston A.L., vs. Brooklyn N.L., 1916.
6-game Series—14—Chicago N.L., vs. Chicago A.L., 1906.
7-game Series—12—Pittsburgh N.L., vs. Detroit A.L., 1909.
             St. Louis N.L., vs. New York A.L., 1926.
8-game Series—13—Cincinnati N.L., vs. Chicago A.L., 1919.

Most Sacrifices, Series, Both Clubs
4-game Series—12—New York A.L., 6, Pittsburgh N.L., 6, 1927.
5-game Series—18—Boston A.L., 12, Brooklyn N.L., 6, 1916.
6-game Series—20—Chicago N.L., 14, Chicago A.L., 6, 1906.
7-game Series—22—St. Louis N.L., 12, New York A.L., 10, 1926.
8-game Series—20—Cincinnati N.L., 13, Chicago A.L., 7, 1919.

Fewest Sacrifices, Series, One Club
4-game Series—0—Cincinnati N.L., vs. New York A.L., 1976.
             New York A.L., vs. Cincinnati N.L., 1976.
5-game Series—0—New York N.L., vs. New York A.L., 1937.
             Brooklyn N.L., vs. New York A.L., 1941.
             New York A.L., vs. Brooklyn N.L., 1941.
             Cincinnati N.L., vs. New York A.L., 1961.
             Baltimore A.L., vs. Philadelphia N.L., 1983.
             Philadelphia N.L., vs. Baltimore A.L., 1983.
6-game Series—0—New York N.L., vs. New York A.L., 1923.
             New York A.L., vs. New York N.L., 1951.
             Los Angeles N.L., vs. New York A.L., 1977.
7-game Series—1—New York A.L., vs. Brooklyn N.L., 1955.
             St. Louis N.L., vs. Detroit A.L., 1968.
             Baltimore A.L., vs. Pittsburgh N.L., 1979.
             St. Louis N.L., vs. Milwaukee A.L., 1982.
             Milwaukee A.L., vs. St. Louis N.L., 1982.
8-game Series—3—Pittsburgh N.L., vs. Boston A.L., 1903.

Fewest Sacrifices, Series, Both Clubs
4-game Series—0—Cincinnati N.L., 0, New York A.L., 0, 1976.
5-game Series—0—New York A.L., 0, Brooklyn N.L., 0, 1941.
             Baltimore A.L., 0, Philadelphia N.L., 0, 1983.
6-game Series—2—New York N.L., 2, New York A.L., 0, 1951.
             New York A.L., 1, Los Angeles N.L., 1, 1978.
7-game Series—2—St. Louis N.L., 1, Milwaukee A.L., 1, 1982.
8-game Series—9—Boston A.L., 6, Pittsburgh N.L., 3, 1903.

Most Sacrifice Flies, Total Series, Since 1955, One Club
14—New York A.L., 13 Series, 80 games.

Most Sacrifice Flies, Series, One Club
4-game Series—2—New York N.L., vs. Cleveland A.L., 1954.
             Cincinnati N.L., vs. New York A.L., 1976.

5-game Series—3—Baltimore A.L., vs. Philadelphia N.L., 1983.
San Diego N.L., vs. Detroit A.L., 1984.
6-game Series—4—Philadelphia N.L., vs. Kansas City A.L., 1980.
7-game Series—5—Pittsburgh N.L., vs. Baltimore A.L., 1979.

Most Sacrifice Flies, Series, Both Clubs
4-game Series—3—Cincinnati N.L., 2, New York A.L., 1, 1976.
5-game Series—5—San Diego N.L., 3, Detroit A.L., 2, 1984.
6-game Series—7—Philadelphia N.L., 4, Kansas City A.L., 3, 1980.
7-game Series—5—Brooklyn N.L., 3, New York A.L., 2, 1956.
Milwaukee N.L., 3, New York A.L., 2, 1958.
Boston A.L., 3, Cincinnati N.L., 2, 1975.
Pittsburgh N.L., 5, Baltimore A.L., 0, 1979.

Most Stolen Bases, One Club, Total Series
60—New York A.L., 33 Series, 187 games.

Most Stolen Bases, Series, One Club
4-game Series— 9—Boston N.L., vs. Philadelphia A.L., 1914.
5-game Series—18—Chicago N.L., vs. Detroit A.L., 1907.
6-game Series— 8—Chicago N.L., vs. Chicago A.L., 1906.
7-game Series—18—Pittsburgh N.L., vs. Detroit A.L., 1909.
8-game Series—12—New York N.L., vs. Boston A.L., 1912.

Most Stolen Bases, Series, Both Clubs
4-game Series—11—Boston N.L., 9, Philadelphia A.L., 2, 1914.
5-game Series—25—Chicago N.L., 18, Detroit A.L., 7, 1907.
6-game Series—14—Chicago N.L., 8, Chicago A.L., 6, 1906.
7-game Series—24—Pittsburgh N.L., 18, Detroit A.L., 6, 1909.
8-game Series—18—New York N.L., 12, Boston A.L., 6, 1912.

Fewest Stolen Bases, Series, One Club
4-game Series—0—Held by many clubs.
5-game Series—0—Held by many clubs.
6-game Series—0—Held by many clubs.
7-game Series—0—Philadelphia A.L., vs. St. Louis N.L., 1931.
Detroit A.L., vs. Cincinnati N.L., 1940.
New York A.L., vs. Pittsburgh N.L., 1960.
Detroit A.L., vs. St. Louis N.L., 1968.
New York N.L., vs. Oakland A.L., 1973.
Boston A.L., vs. Cincinnati N.L., 1975.
Pittsburgh N.L., vs. Baltimore A.L., 1979.
8-game Series—5—Boston A.L., vs. Pittsburgh N.L., 1903.
Chicago A.L., vs. Cincinnati N.L., 1919.
New York N.L., 1, Cleveland A.L., 0, 1954.

Fewest Stolen Bases, Series, Both Clubs
4-game Series— 1—Cincinnati N.L., 1, New York A.L., 0, 1939.
New York N.L., 1, Cleveland A.L., 0, 1954.
Los Angeles N.L., 1, Baltimore A.L., 0, 1966.
5-game Series— 1—Chicago N.L., 1, Philadelphia A.L., 0, 1929.
Washington A.L., 1, New York N.L., 0, 1933.
New York N.L., 1, New York A.L., 0, 1937.
New York A.L., 1, Cincinnati N.L., 0, 1961.
Cincinnati N.L., 1, Baltimore A.L., 0, 1970.
6-game Series— 0—St. Louis N.L., 0, St. Louis A.L., 0, 1944.
7-game Series— 1—Cincinnati N.L., 1, Detroit A.L., 0, 1940.
8-game Series—12—Pittsburgh N.L., 7, Boston A.L., 5, 1903.
Cincinnati N.L., 7, Chicago A.L., 5, 1919.

Most Caught Stealing, Series, One Club
4-game Series— 5—Boston N.L., vs. Philadelphia A.L., 1914.
Cincinnati N.L., vs. New York, A.L., 1976.
5-game Series— 8—Chicago N.L., vs. Philadelphia A.L., 1910.
6-game Series—13—New York N.L., vs. Philadelphia A.L., 1911.
7-game Series— 7—Cleveland A.L., vs. Brooklyn N.L., 1920.
Washington A.L., vs. Pittsburgh N.L., 1925.
St. Louis N.L., vs. Detroit A.L., 1968.
8-game Series—11—New York N.L., vs. Boston A.L., 1912.

Most Caught Stealing, Series, Both Clubs
4-game Series— 7—Cincinnati N.L., 5, New York A.L., 2, 1976.
New York A.L., 3, Chicago N.L., 3, 1938.
5-game Series—15—Chicago N.L., 8, Philadelphia A.L., 7, 1910.
6-game Series—19—New York N.L., 13, Philadelphia A.L., 6, 1911.
7-game Series—11—Pittsburgh N.L., 6, Detroit A.L., 5, 1909.
8-game Series—16—New York N.L., 11, Boston A.L., 5, 1912.

WORLD SERIES RECORDS

Fewest Caught Stealing, Series, One Club
4-game Series—0—Pittsburgh N.L., 1927. New York A.L., 1928, 1939.
              Philadelphia N.L., 1950. Cleveland A.L., 1954.
5-game Series—0—New York N.L., 1933. New York A.L., 1937, 1942, 1943, 1949.
              Brooklyn N.L., 1949. Cincinnati N.L., 1961.
              Baltimore A.L., 1983.
6-game Series—0—St. Louis N.L., 1930. St. Louis A.L., 1944.
              Boston N.L., 1948. New York A.L., 1977.
7-game Series—0—Philadelphia A.L., 1931. New York A.L., 1956, 1964.
              Milwaukee N.L., 1958. St. Louis N.L., 1964. Pittsburgh N.L., 1972.
8-game Series—2—Boston A.L., 1903.

Fewest Caught Stealing, Series, Both Clubs
4-game Series—1—New York A.L., 1, Pittsburgh N.L. 0, 1927.
              Cincinnati N.L., 1, New York A.L., 0, 1939.
              New York A.L., 1, Philadelphia N.L., 0, 1950.
              New York A.L., 1, Cleveland A.L., 0, 1954.
5-game Series—0—New York A.L., 0, Brooklyn N.L., 0, 1949.
6-game Series—1—St. Louis N.L., 1, St. Louis A.L., 0, 1944.
              Cleveland A.L., 1, Boston N.L., 0, 1948.
7-game Series—0—St. Louis N.L., 0, New York A.L., 0, 1964.
8-game Series—6—Pittsburgh N.L., 4, Boston A.L., 2, 1903.

Most Left on Bases, Total Series, One Club
1,272—New York A.L., 33 Series, 187 games.

Most Left on Bases, Series, One Club
4-game Series—37—Cleveland A.L., vs. New York N.L., 1954.
5-game Series—42—New York A.L., vs. Brooklyn N.L., 1941.
6-game Series—55—New York A.L., vs. Los Angeles N.L., 1981.
7-game Series—72—New York N.L., vs. Oakland A.L., 1973.
8-game Series—55—Boston A.L., vs. Pittsburgh N.L., 1903.
              Boston A.L., vs. New York N.L., 1912.

Most Left on Bases, Series, Both Clubs
4-game Series— 65—Cleveland A.L., 37, New York N.L., 28, 1954.
5-game Series— 76—New York N.L., 39, Washington A.L., 37, 1933.
6-game Series—101—New York A.L., 55, Los Angeles N.L., 46, 1981.
7-game Series—130—New York N.L., 72, Oakland A.L., 58, 1973.
8-game Series—108—Boston A.L., 55, New York N.L., 53, 1912.

Fewest Left on Bases, Series, One Club
4-game Series—16—New York A.L., vs. Cincinnati N.L., 1939.
5-game Series—23—Philadelphia N.L. vs. Baltimore A.L., 1983.
6-game Series—29—Philadelphia A.L., vs. New York N.L., 1911.
7-game Series—36—Minnesota A.L., vs. Los Angeles N.L., 1965.
8-game Series—43—New York A.L., vs. New York N.L., 1921.

Fewest Left on Bases, Series, Both Clubs
4-game Series—39—Cincinnati N.L., 23, New York A.L., 16, 1939.
5-game Series—51—Baltimore A.L., 28, Philadelphia N.L., 23, 1983.
6-game Series—60—New York N.L., 31, Philadelphia A.L., 29, 1911.
7-game Series—82—Cleveland A.L., 43, Brooklyn N.L., 39, 1920.
              Brooklyn N.L., 42, New York A.L., 40, 1956.
              New York A.L., 43, San Francisco N.L., 39, 1962.
8-game Series—97—New York N.L., 54, New York A.L., 43, 1921.

Most Hit by Pitch, Total Series, One Club
39—New York A.L., 33 Series, 187 games.

Most Hit by Pitch, Series, One Club
4-game Series—4—New York A.L., vs. Chicago N.L., 1932.
5-game Series—4—Chicago N.L., vs. Detroit A.L., 1907.
6-game Series—4—New York A.L., vs. Brooklyn N.L., 1953.
7-game Series—6—Pittsburgh N.L., vs. Detroit A.L., 1909.
8-game Series—5—Cincinnati N.L., vs. Chicago A.L., 1919.

Most Hit by Pitch, Series, Both Clubs
4-game Series— 4—New York A.L., 4, Chicago N.L., 0, 1932.
5-game Series— 5—Chicago N.L., 4, Detroit A.L., 1, 1907.
6-game Series— 6—New York A.L., 4, Brooklyn N.L., 2, 1953.
7-game Series—10—Pittsburgh N.L., 6, Detroit A.L., 4, 1909.
8-game Series— 8—Cincinnati N.L., 5, Chicago A.L., 3, 1919.

Fewest Hit by Pitch, Series, One Club
4-game Series—0—Held by many clubs.
5-game Series—0—Held by many clubs.
6-game Series—0—Held by many clubs.
7-game Series—0—Held by many clubs.

8-game Series—1—Held by three clubs: Boston A.L., 1912; New York A.L., 1921; New York N.L., 1921.

Fewest Hit by Pitch, Series, Both Clubs
4-game Series—0—Los Angeles N.L., 0, Baltimore A.L., 0, 1966.
5-game Series—0—Washington A.L., 0, New York N.L., 0, 1933.
       New York A.L., 0, St. Louis N.L., 0, 1942.
       New York A.L., 0, St. Louis N.L., 0, 1943.
6-game Series—0—St. Louis A.L., 0, St. Louis N.L., 0, 1944.
7-game Series—0—Cleveland A.L., 0, Brooklyn N.L., 0, 1920.
       Detroit A.L., 0, Cincinnati N.L., 0, 1940.
       New York A.L., 0, Brooklyn N.L., 0, 1956.
       New York A.L., 0, Milwaukee N.L., 0, 1958.
8-game Series—2—New York A.L., 1, New York N.L., 1, 1921.

FIRST BASEMEN'S FIELDING RECORDS

Most Series Played
8—Skowron, William J., New York A.L., 1955, 1956, 1957, 1958, 1960, 1961, 1962; Los Angeles N.L., 1963 (37 games).

Most Games Played, Total Series
38—Hodges, Gilbert R., Brooklyn N.L., Los Angeles N.L., 1949, 1952, 1953, 1955, 1956, 1959; (6 Series).

Highest Fielding Average, Series, With Most Chances Accepted
4-game Series—1.000—Schmidt, Charles J., Boston N.L., 1914 (55 chances accepted).
5-game Series—1.000—Hoblitzel, Richard C., Boston A.L., 1916 (73 chances accepted).
6-game Series—1.000—McInnis, John P., Boston A.L., 1918 (72 chances accepted).
7-game Series—1.000—Bottomley, James L., St. Louis N.L., 1926 (80 chances accepted).
8-game Series—1.000—Kelly, George L., New York N.L., 1921 (93 chances accepted).
        Pipp, Walter C., New York A.L., 1921 (93 chances accepted).

Most Consecutive Errorless Games, Total Series
31—Skowron, William J., New York A.L., Los Angeles N.L., October 10, 1956 through October 6, 1963.

Most Putouts, Total Series
326—Hodges, Gilbert R., Brooklyn N.L., Los Angeles N.L., 1949, 1952, 1953, 1955, 1956, 1959; 6 Series, 38 games.

Most Putouts, Series
4-game Series—52—Schmidt, Charles J., Boston N.L., 1914.
5-game Series—69—Hoblitzel, Richard C., Boston A.L., 1916.
6-game Series—79—Donahue, John A., Chicago A.L., 1906.
7-game Series—79—Bottomley, James L., St. Louis N.L., 1926.
8-game Series—92—Pipp, Walter C., New York A.L., 1921.

Most Assists, Series
4-game Series— 6—Wertz, Victor W., Cleveland A.L., 1954.
       Pepitone, Joseph A., New York A.L., 1963.
5-game Series— 5—Rossman, Claude, Detroit A.L., 1908.
       Camilli, Adolph, Brooklyn N.L., 1941.
       Sanders, Raymond F., St. Louis N.L., 1943.
       Skowron, William J., New York A.L., 1961.
6-game Series— 9—Merkle, Fred C., Chicago N.L., 1918.
7-game Series—10—Cooper, Cecil C., Milwaukee A.L., 1982.
8-game Series— 7—Kelly, George L., New York N.L., 1921.

Most Assists, Total Series
29—Skowron, William J., New York A.L., 1955, 1956, 1957, 1958, 1960, 1961, 1962; Los Angeles N.L., 1963; 8 Series 37 games.

Most Chances Accepted, Series
4-game Series—55—Schmidt, Charles J., Boston N.L., 1914.
5-game Series—73—Hoblitzel, Richard C., Boston A.L., 1916.
6-game Series—87—Donahue, John A., Chicago A.L., 1906.
7-game Series—81—Cooper, Cecil C., Milwaukee A.L., 1982.
8-game Series—93—Kelly, George L., New York N.L., 1921.
       Pipp, Walter C., New York A.L., 1921.

Most Chances Accepted, Total Series
350—Hodges, Gilbert R., Brooklyn N.L., Los Angeles N.L., 1949, 1952, 1953, 1955, 1956, 1959; 6 Series, 38 games.

Most Errors, Series
4-game Series—1—McInnis, John P., Philadelphia A.L., 1914.
Gehrig, H. Louis, New York A.L., 1932.
Wertz, Victor W. Cleveland A.L., 1954.
Pepitone, Joseph A., New York A.L., 1963.
Chambliss, C. Christopher, New York A.L., 1976.
5-game Series—3—Chance, Frank L., Chicago N.L., 1908.
Davis, Harry H., Philadelphia A.L., 1910.
6-game Series—3—Greenberg, Henry, Detroit A.L., 1935.
7-game Series—5—Abstein, William H., Pittsburgh N.L., 1909.
8-game Series—3—Merkle, Fred C., New York N.L., 1912.

Most Errors, Total Series
8—Merkle, Frederick C., New York N.L., 1911, 1912, 1913 (7); Brooklyn N.L., 1916 (1), Chicago N.L., 1918 (0), 5 Series, 25 games.

Most Double Plays, Series
4-game Series— 7—Pepitone, Joseph A., New York A.L., 1963.
5-game Series— 7—Pipp, Walter C., New York A.L., 1922.
6-game Series— 8—Robinson, W. Edward, Cleveland A.L., 1948.
Rose, Peter E., Philadelphia N.L., 1980.
7-game Series—11—Hodges, Gilbert R., Brooklyn N.L., 1955.
8-game Series— 6—Gandil, Charles A., Chicago A.L., 1919.

Most Double Plays, Total Series
31—Hodges, Gilbert R., Brooklyn N.L., Los Angeles N.L., 1949, 1952, 1953, 1955, 1956, 1959; 6 Series, 38 games.

Most Double Plays, Started, Series
4-game Series—1—Held by many first basemen.
5-game Series—2—May, Lee A., Cincinnati N.L., 1970.
Garvey, Steven P., San Diego N.L., 1984.
6-game Series—1—Held by many first basemen.
7-game Series—3—Hodges, Gilbert R., Brooklyn N.L., 1955.
8-game Series—1—Stahl, J. Garland, Boston A.L., 1912.

Most Putouts, Game, Nine Innings
19—Kelly, George L., New York N.L., October 15, 1923.

Most Putouts, Inning
3—Held by many first basemen.

Fewest Putouts, Game, Nine Innings
1—Cepeda, Orlando M., St. Louis N.L., October 2, 1968.

Most Assists, Game, Nine Innings
4—Owen, Marvin J., Detroit A.L., October 6, 1935.
Mincher, Donald R., Minnesota A.L., October 7, 1965.

Most Assists, Inning
2—Held by many first basemen.

Most Errors, Game, Nine Innings
2—Held by many first basemen.

Most Errors, Inning
2—Greenberg, Henry, Detroit A.L., October 3, 1935, fifth inning.
McCarthy, John J., New York N.L., October 8, 1937, fifth inning.
Torre, Frank J., Milwaukee N.L., October 9, 1958, second inning.

Most Chances Accepted, Game, Nine Innings
19—Konetchy, Edward J., Brooklyn N.L., October 7, 1920; 17 putouts, 2 assists, 0 errors.
Kelly, George L., New York N.L., October 15, 1923; 19 putouts, 0 assists, 0 errors.

Most Chances Accepted, Inning
3—Held by many first basemen.

Fewest Chances Offered, Game, Nine Innings
2—Pipp, Walter C., New York A.L., October 11, 1921; 2 putouts, 0 assists.
Cepeda, Orlando M., St. Louis N.L., October 2, 1968; 1 putout, 1 assist.

Most Double Plays, Game, Nine Innings
4—McInnis, John P., Philadelphia A.L., October 9, 1914.
Collins, Joseph E., New York A.L., October 8, 1951.
Tenace, F. Gene, Oakland A.L., October 17, 1973.
Rose, Peter E., Philadelphia N.L., October 15, 1980.

Most Double Plays Started, Game
2—Murray, Eddie C., Baltimore A.L., October 11, 1979.

Most Unassisted Double Plays, Game

1—Grantham, George F., Pittsburgh N.L., October 7, 1925.
  Judge, Joseph I., Washington A.L., October 13, 1925.
  Foxx, James E., Philadelphia A.L., October 8, 1930.
  Bottomley, James L., St. Louis N.L., October 1, 1931.
  Gehrig, H. Louis, New York A.L., October 10, 1937.
  Collins, James A., Chicago N.L., October 5, 1938.
  Collins, Joseph E., New York A.L., October 7, 1956.
  Coleman, Gordon C., Cincinnati, N.L., October 8, 1961.
  Perez, Atanasio R., Cincinnati N.L., October 11, 1975.
  Garvey, Steven P., San Diego N.L., October 9, 1984.

SECOND BASEMEN'S FIELDING RECORDS

Most Series Played

7—Frisch, Frank F., New York N.L., 1922, 1923, 1924; St. Louis N.L., 1928, 1930, 1931, 1934 (42 games).

Most Games Played, Total Series

42—Frisch, Frank F., New York N.L. (18), 1922, 1923, 1924; St. Louis N.L., (24), 1928, 1930, 1931, 1934; 7 Series.

Highest Fielding Average, Series, With Most Chances Accepted

4-game Series—1.000—Johnson, David A., Baltimore A.L., 1966 (24 chances accepted).
5-game Series—1.000—Gordon, Joseph L., New York A.L., 1943 (43 chances accepted).
6-game Series—1.000—Gehringer, Charles L., Detroit A.L., 1935 (39 chances accepted).
7-game Series—1.000—Doerr, Robert P., Boston A.L., 1946 (49 chances accepted).
8-game Series—1.000—Ritchey, Claude C., Pittsburgh N.L., 1903 (48 chances accepted).

Most Consecutive Errorless Games, Total Series

23—Martin, Alfred M., New York A.L., October 5, 1952 through October 10, 1956.

Most Putouts, Series

4-game Series—13—Goliat, Mike, Philadelphia N.L., 1950.
              Morgan, Joe L., Cincinnati N.L., 1976.
5-game Series—20—Gordon, Joseph L., New York A.L., 1943.
6-game Series—26—Lopes, David E., Los Angeles N.L., 1981.
7-game Series—26—Harris, Stanley R., Washington A.L., 1924.
8-game Series—22—Rath, Maurice C., Cincinnati N.L., 1919.

Most Putouts, Total Series

104—Frisch, Frank F., New York N.L., St. Louis N.L., 1922, 1923, 1924, 1928, 1930, 1931, 1934; 7 Series, 42 games.

Most Assists, Series

4-game Series—18—Lazzeri, Anthony M., New York A.L., 1927.
5-game Series—23—Gordon, Joseph L. New York A.L., 1943.
6-game Series—27—Ward, Aaron L., New York A.L., 1923.
7-game Series—33—Gantner, James E., Milwaukee A.L., 1982.
8-game Series—34—Ward, Aaron L., New York A.L., 1921.

Most Assists, Total Series

135—Frisch, Frank F., New York N.L., St. Louis N.L., 1922, 1923, 1924, 1928, 1930, 1931, 1934; 7 Series, 42 games.

Most Chances Accepted, Series

4-game Series—28—Lazzeri, Anthony M., New York A.L., 1927.
5-game Series—43—Gordon, Joseph L., New York A.L., 1943.
6-game Series—40—Lopes, David E., Los Angeles N.L., 1981.
7-game Series—54—Harris, Stanley R., Washington A.L., 1924.
8-game Series—52—Collins, Edward T., Chicago A.L., 1919.
              Ward, Aaron L., New York A.L., 1921.

Most Chances Accepted, Total Series

239—Frisch, Frank F., New York N.L., St. Louis N.L., 1922, 1923, 1924, 1928, 1930, 1931, 1934; 7 Series, 42 games.

Most Errors, Series

2-game Series—2—Lazzeri, Anthony M., New York A.L., 1928.
              Gordon, Joseph L., New York A.L., 1938.
              Herman, William J., Chicago A.L., 1938.
              Morgan, Joe L., Cincinnati N.L., 1976.
5-game Series—4—Murphy, Daniel F., Philadelphia A.L., 1905.
6-game Series—6—Lopes, David E., Los Angeles N.L., 1981.
7-game Series—5—Gantner, James E., Milwaukee A.L., 1982.
8-game Series—4—Doyle, Lawrence J., New York N.L., 1912.

Most Errors, Total Series
8—Doyle, Lawrence J., New York N.L., 1911, 1912, 1913; 3 Series, 19 games.
Collins, Edward T., Philadelphia A.L., 1910, 1911, 1913, 1914, Chicago A.L., 1917, 1919; 6 Series, 34 games.

Most Double Plays, Series
4-game Series—6—Herman, William J., Chicago N.L., 1932.
5-game Series—6—Green, Richard L., Oakland A.L., 1974.
6-game Series—7—Frisch, Frank F., New York N.L., 1923.
                    Gordon, Joseph L., Cleveland A.L., 1948.
                    Neal, Charles L., Los Angeles N.L., 1959.
7-game Series—9—Garner, Philip M., Pittsburgh N.L., 1979.
8-game Series—7—Collins, Edward T., Chicago A.L., 1919.

Most Double Plays, Total Series
24—Frisch, Frank F., New York N.L., St. Louis N.L., 1922, 1923, 1924, 1928, 1930, 1931, 1934; 7 Series, 42 games.

Most Double Plays Started, Series
4-game Series—5—Herman, William J., Chicago N.L., 1932.
5-game Series—4—Gordon, Joseph L., New York A.L., 1941.
                    Green, Richard L., Oakland A.L., 1974.
6-game Series—2—Held by many second basemen.
7-game Series—4—Frisch, Frank F., St. Louis N.L., 1931.
8-game Series—4—Ritchey, Claude C., Pittsburgh N.L., 1903.

Most Putouts, Game, Nine Innings
8—Harris, Stanley R., Washington A.L., October 8, 1924.
Lopes, David E., Los Angeles N.L., October 16, 1974.

Most Putouts, Game, Eleven Innings
9—Critz, Hugh M., New York N.L., October 6, 1933.

Most Putouts, Inning
3—Doyle, Lawrence J., New York N.L., October 9, 1913, seventh inning.
Wambsganss, William A., Cleveland A.L., October 10, 1920, fifth inning.
Rawlings, John M., New York N.L., October 11, 1921, ninth inning.
Lopes, David E., Los Angeles N.L., October 16, 1974, sixth inning.
Lopes, David E., Los Angeles N.L., October 21, 1981, fourth inning.

Most Assists, Game, Nine Innings
8—Ritchey, Claude C., Pittsburgh, N.L., October 10, 1903.
Schaefer, Herman, Detroit A.L., October 12, 1907.
Janvrin, Harold C., Boston A.L., October 7, 1916.
Collins, Edward T., Chicago A.L., October 15, 1917.
Harris, Stanley R., Washington A.L., October 7, 1924.
Gordon, Joseph L., New York A.L., October 5, 1943.
Doerr, Robert P., Boston A.L., October 9, 1946.

Most Assists, Inning
3—Collins, Edward T., Philadelphia A.L., October 12, 1914, fourth inning.
Kilduff, Peter J., Brooklyn N.L., October 10, 1920, third inning.
Ward, Aaron L., New York A.L., October 12, 1921, sixth inning.
Gordon, Joseph L., New York A.L., October 11, 1943, eighth inning.
Robinson, Jack R., Brooklyn N.L., October 8, 1949, seventh inning.
Garner, Philip M., Pittsburgh N.L., October 13, 1979, ninth inning.

Most Errors, Game, Nine Innings
3—Murphy, Daniel F., Philadelphia A.L., October 12, 1905.
Myer, Charles S., Washington A.L., October 3, 1933.
Lopes, David E., Los Angeles N.L., October 25, 1981.

Most Errors, Inning
2—Murphy, Daniel F., Philadelphia A.L., October 12, 1905, fifth inning.
Andrews, Michael J., Oakland A.L., October 14, 1973, twelfth inning.
Lopes, David E., Los Angeles N.L., October 25, 1981, fourth inning.

Most Chances Accepted, Game, Nine Innings
13—Ritchey, Claude C., Pittsburgh N.L., October 10, 1903; 5 putouts, 8 assists, 0 errors.
Harris, Stanley R., Washington A.L., October 11, 1925; 6 putouts, 7 assists, 0 errors.
Lopes, David E., Los Angeles N.L., October 16, 1974; 8 putouts, 5 assists, 0 errors.

Most Chances Accepted, Game, Eleven Innings.
14—Critz, Hugh M., New York N.L., October 6, 1933; 9 putouts, 5 assists, 0 errors.

Most Chances Accepted, Inning
3—Held by many second basemen.

Fewest Chances Offered, Game, Nine Innings
   0—Pick, Charles, Chicago N.L., September 7, 1918.
      Bishop, Max F., Philadelphia A.L., October 6, 1931.
      Coleman, Gerald F., New York A.L., October 8, 1949.
      Randolph, William L., New York A.L., October 25, 1981.

Unassisted Triple Play
   1—Wambsganss, William A., Cleveland A.L., October 10, 1920.

Most Unassisted Double Plays, Game
   1—Ferris, Hobart, Boston A.L., October 2, 1903.
      Doyle, Lawrence J., New York N.L., October 9, 1913.
      Herzog, Charles L., New York N.L., October 7, 1917.
      White, Frank, Kansas City A.L., October 17, 1980.

Most Double Plays, Game, Nine Innings
   3—Held by many second basemen.

Most Double Plays Started, Game, Nine Innings
   3—Green, Richard L., Oakland A.L., October 15, 1974.

THIRD BASEMEN'S FIELDING RECORDS

Most Series Played
   6—Rolfe, Robert A., New York A.L., 1936, 1937, 1938, 1939, 1941, 1942 (28 games).

Most Games Played, Total Series
   31—McDougald, Gilbert J., New York A.L., 1951, 1952, 1953, 1955, 1960.

Highest Fielding Average, Series, With Most Chances Accepted
   4-game Series—1.000—Baker, J. Frank, Philadelphia A.L., 1914 (25 chances accepted).
   5-game Series—1.000—Groh, Henry K., New York N.L., 1922 (20 chances accepted).
   6-game Series—1.000—Nettles, Graig, New York A.L., 1978 (26 chances accepted).
   7-game Series—1.000—Menke, Denis J., Cincinnati N.L., 1972 (29 chances accepted).
   8-game Series—1.000—Herzog, Charles L., New York N.L., 1912 (27 chances accepted).

Most Consecutive Errorless Games, Total Series
   22—Cey, Ronald C., Los Angeles N.L., October 13, 1974 through October 28, 1981.

Most Putouts, Series
   4-game Series—10—Baker, J. Frank, Philadelphia A.L., 1914.
   5-game Series—10—Steinfeldt, Harry M., Chicago N.L., 1907.
   6-game Series—14—Rolfe, Robert A., New York A.L., 1936.
   7-game Series—13—Kurowski, George J., St. Louis N.L., 1946.
   8-game Series—13—Frisch, Frank F., New York N.L., 1921.

Most Putouts, Total Series
   37—Baker, J. Frank, Philadelphia A.L., New York A.L., 1910, 1911, 1913, 1914, 1921; 5 Series, 22 games.

Most Assists, Series
   4-game Series—15—Baker, J. Frank, Philadelphia A.L., 1914.
   5-game Series—18—Gardner, W. Lawrence, Boston A.L., 1916.
   6-game Series—20—Nettles, Graig, New York A.L., 1977.
   7-game Series—30—Higgins, Michael F., Detroit A.L., 1940.
   8-game Series—24—Frisch, Frank F., New York N.L., 1921.

Most Assists, Total Series
   68—Nettles, Graig, New York A.L., 1976, 1977, 1978, 1981; San Diego N.L., 1984; 5 Series, 24 games.

Most Chances Accepted, Series
   4-game Series—25—Baker, J. Frank, Philadelphia A.L., 1914.
   5-game Series—25—Gardner, W. Lawrence, Boston A.L., 1916.
   6-game Series—27—Thomson, Robert B., New York N.L., 1951.
   7-game Series—34—Higgins, Michael F., Detroit A.L., 1940.
   8-game Series—37—Frisch, Frank F., New York N.L., 1921.

Most Chances Accepted, Total Series
   96—Nettles, Graig, New York A.L., 1976, 1977, 1978, 1981; San Diego N.L., 1984; 5 Series, 24 games.

Most Errors, Series
   4-game Series—2—Rolfe, Robert A., New York A.L., 1938.
   5-game Series—4—Steinfeldt, Harry M., Chicago N.L., 1910.
   6-game Series—3—Rohe, George, Chicago A.L., 1906.
                   Herzog, Charles L., New York N.L., 1911.
                   Jackson, Travis C., New York N.L., 1936.
                   Elliott, Robert I., Boston N.L., 1948.

7-game Series—4—Martin, John L., St. Louis N.L., 1934.
                  McDougald, Gilbert J., New York A.L., 1952.
8-game Series—4—Leach, Thomas W., Pittsburgh N.L., 1903.
                  Gardner, W. Lawrence, Boston A.L., 1912.

Most Errors, Total Series
    8—Gardner, W. Lawrence, Boston A.L., 1912, 1915, 1916 (6), Cleveland A.L., 1920 (2), 4 Series, 25 games.

Most Double Plays, Series
4-game Series—3—Nettles, Graig, New York A.L., 1976.
5-game Series—2—Jackson, Travis C., New York N.L., 1933.
                  Robinson, Brooks C., Baltimore A.L., 1970.
6-game Series—3—Nettles, Graig, New York A.L., 1978.
                  Dugan, Joseph A., New York A.L., 1923.
7-game Series—4—Davenport, James H., San Francisco N.L., 1962.
                  Madlock, Bill, Pittsburgh N.L., 1979.
8-game Series—3—Frisch, Frank F., New York N.L., 1921.

Most Double Plays, Total Series
    7—Nettles, Graig, New York A.L., 1976, 1977, 1978, 1981; San Diego N.L., 1984; 5 Series, 24 games.

Most Double Plays Started, Series
4-game Series—2—Rolfe, Robert A., New York A.L., 1939.
                  Nettles, Graig, New York A.L., 1976.
5-game Series—2—Jackson, Travis C., New York N.L., 1933.
                  Robinson, Brooks C., Baltimore A.L., 1970.
6-game Series—3—Nettles, Graig, New York A.L., 1978.
7-game Series—4—Davenport, James H., San Francisco N.L., 1962.
8-game Series—2—Frisch, Frank F., New York N.L., 1921.

Most Putouts, Game, Nine Innings
    4—Devlin, Arthur, New York N.L., October 13, 1905.
      Coughlin, William P., Detroit A.L., October 10, 1907.
      Byrne, Robert M., Pittsburgh N.L., October 9, 1909.
      Leach, Thomas W., Pittsburgh N.L., October 16, 1909.
      Baker, J. Frank, Philadelphia A.L., October 24, 1911.
      Zimmerman, Henry, New York N.L., October 7, 1917.
      Dykes, James, Philadelphia A.L., October 2, 1930.
      Elliott, Robert I., Boston N.L., October 11, 1948.
      Jones, Willie E., Philadelphia N.L., October 4, 1950.

Most Putouts, Inning
    2—Held by many third basemen.

Most Assists, Game
    9—Higgins, Michael F., Detroit A.L., October 5, 1940.

Most Assists, Inning
    3—Pagan, Jose A., Pittsburgh N.L., October 14, 1971, ninth inning.
      Bando, Salvatore L., Oakland A.L., October 16, 1974, sixth inning.

Most Chances Accepted, Game, Nine Innings
    10—Higgins, Michael F., Detroit A.L., October 5, 1940, 1 putout, 9 assists, 1 error.

Most Chances Accepted, Inning
    4—Mathews, Edwin L., Milwaukee N.L., October 5, 1957, third inning.

Fewest Chances Offered, Game, Nine Innings
    0—Held by many third basemen.

Most Errors, Game, Nine Innings
    3—Martin, John L., St. Louis N.L., October 6, 1934.

Most Errors, Inning
    2—Steinfeldt, Harry M., Chicago N.L., October 18, 1910, third inning.
      DeCinces, Douglas V., Baltimore A.L., October 10, 1979, sixth inning.

Most Double Plays, Game, Nine Innings
    2—Held by many third basemen.

Most Unassisted Double Plays, Game
    Never accomplished.

Most Double Plays Started, Game, Nine Innings.
    2—McMullin, Fred W., Chicago A.L., October 13, 1917.
      Bluege, Oswald L., Washington A.L., October 5, 1924.
      Kurowski, George J., St. Louis N.L., October 13, 1946.
      Boyer, Cletis L., New York A.L., October 12, 1960.
      Jones, J. Dalton, Boston A.L., October 4, 1967.
      Nettles, Graig, New York A.L., October 19, 1976.

WORLD SERIES RECORDS
SHORTSTOPS' FIELDING RECORDS

Most Series Played
 9—Rizzuto, Philip F., New York A.L., 1941, 1942, 1947, 1949, 1950, 1951, 1952, 1953, 1955 (52 games).

Most Games Played, Total Series
 52—Rizzuto, Philip F., New York A.L., 1941, 1942, 1947, 1949, 1950, 1951, 1952, 1953, 1955; 9 Series.

Highest Fielding Average, Series, With Most Chances Accepted
 4-game Series—1.000—Wills, Maurice M., Los Angeles N.L., 1966 (27 chances accepted).
 5-game Series—1.000—Dahlen, William F., New York N.L., 1905 (29 chances accepted).
             Scott, L. Everett, New York A.L., 1922 (29 chances accepted).
             Marion, Martin W., St. Louis N.L., 1942 (29 chances accepted).
             Harrelson, Derrel M., New York N.L., 1969 (29 chances accepted).
 6-game Series—1.000—Scott, L. Everett, Boston A.L., 1918 (36 chances accepted).
 7-game Series—1.000—Gelbert, Charles M., St. Louis N.L., 1931 (42 chances accepted).
 8-game Series— .979—Peckinpaugh, Roger T., New York A.L., 1921 (46 chances accepted).

Most Consecutive Errorless Games, Total Series
 21—Rizzuto, Philip F., New York A.L., October 3, 1942 through October 5, 1951.

Most Putouts, Series
 4-game Series—16—Crosetti, Frank P. J., New York A.L., 1938.
 5-game Series—15—Tinker, Joseph B., Chicago N.L., 1907.
              Rizzuto, Philip F., New York A.L., 1942.
 6-game Series—16—Jurges, William F., Chicago N.L., 1935.
 7-game Series—22—Smith, Osborne E., St. Louis N.L., 1982.
 8-game Series—24—Wagner, Charles, Boston A.L., 1912.

Most Putouts, Total Series
 107—Rizzuto, Philip F., New York A.L., 1941, 1942, 1947, 1949, 1950, 1951, 1952, 1953, 1955; 9 Series, 52 games.

Most Assists, Series
 4-game Series—21—Barry, John J., Philadelphia A.L., 1914.
 5-game Series—25—Scott, L. Everett, Boston A.L., 1916.
 6-game Series—26—Russell, William E., Los Angeles N.L., 1981.
 7-game Series—32—Foli, Timothy J., Pittsburgh N.L., 1979.
 8-game Series—30—Parent, Frederick A., Boston A.L., 1903.

Most Assists, Total Series
 143—Rizzuto, Philip F., New York A.L., 1941, 1942, 1947, 1949, 1950, 1951, 1952, 1953, 1955; 9 Series, 52 games.

Most Chances Accepted, Series
 4-game Series—27—Wills, Maurice M., Los Angeles N.L., 1966.
 5-game Series—38—Tinker, Joseph B., Chicago N.L., 1907.
 6-game Series—37—Rizzuto, Philip F., New York A.L., 1951.
 7-game Series—42—Gelbert, Charles M., St. Louis N.L., 1931.
 8-game Series—51—Risberg, Charles A., Chicago A.L., 1919.

Most Chances Accepted, Total Series
 250—Rizzuto, Philip F., New York A.L., 1941, 1942, 1947, 1949, 1950, 1951, 1952, 1953, 1955; 9 Series, 52 games.

Most Errors, Series
 4-game Series—4—Crosetti, Frank P. J., New York A.L., 1932.
 5-game Series—4—Olson, Ivan M., Brooklyn N.L., 1916.
              English, Elwood G., Chicago N.L., 1929.
 6-game Series—4—Fletcher, Arthur, New York N.L., 1911.
              Weaver, George D., Chicago A.L., 1917.
 7-game Series—8—Peckinpaugh, Roger T., Washington A.L., 1925.
 8-game Series—6—Wagner, John P., Pittsburgh N.L., 1903.

Most Errors, Total Series
 12—Fletcher, Arthur, New York N.L., 1911, 1912, 1913, 1917; 4 Series, 25 games.

Most Double Plays, Series
 4-game Series—5—Jurges, William F., Chicago N.L., 1932.
              Kubek, Anthony C., New York A.L., 1963.
 5-game Series—6—Scott, L. Everett, New York A.L., 1922.
              Rizzuto, Philip F., New York A.L., 1941.
 6-game Series—6—Rizzuto, Philip F., New York A.L., 1951.
 7-game Series—7—Reese, Harold H., Brooklyn N.L., 1955, 1956.
              Foli, Timothy J., Pittsburgh N.L., 1979.
 8-game Series—6—Risberg, Charles A., Chicago A.L., 1919.

WORLD SERIES RECORDS

Most Double Plays, Total Series
    32—Rizzuto, Philip F., New York A.L., 1941, 1942, 1947, 1949, 1950, 1951, 1952, 1953, 1955; 9 Series, 52 games.

Most Double Plays Started, Series
    4-game Series—3—Koenig, Mark A., New York A.L., 1928.
    5-game Series—4—Tinker, Joseph B., Chicago N.L., 1907.
    6-game Series—7—Bowa, Lawrence R., Philadelphia N.L., 1980.
    7-game Series—4—Reese, Harold H., Brooklyn N.L., 1947.
                       McDougald, Gilbert J., New York A.L., 1957.
                       Linz, Philip F., New York A.L., 1964.
                       Wills, Maurice M., Los Angeles N.L., 1965.
                       Foli, Timothy J., Pittsburgh N.L., 1979.
    8-game Series—4—Risberg, Charles A., Chicago A.L., 1919.

Most Putouts, Game, Nine Innings
    7—Weaver, George D., Chicago A.L., October 7, 1917.
      Rizzuto, Philip F., New York A.L., October 5, 1942.

Most Putouts, Inning
    3—Stanley, Mitchell J., Detroit A.L., October 10, 1968, sixth inning.

Most Assists, Extra-Inning Game
    10—Logan, John, Milwaukee N.L., October 6, 1957, ten innings.

Most Assists, Game, Nine Innings
    9—Peckinpaugh, Roger T., New York A.L., October 5, 1921.

Most Assists, Inning
    3—Bancroft, David J., New York N.L., October 8, 1922, third inning.
      Bluege, Oswald L., Washington, October 7, 1924, sixth inning.
      Wright, F. Glenn, Pittsburgh N.L., October 8, 1927, second inning.
      Ryan, John C., New York N.L., October 7, 1933, third inning.
      Rizzuto, Philip F., New York A.L., October 3, 1942, second inning.
      Bowman, Ernest F., San Francisco N.L., October 8, 1962, ninth inning.
      Harrelson, Derrel M., New York N.L., October 14, 1969, fifth inning.
      Belanger, Mark H., Baltimore A.L., October 16, 1971, seventh inning.
      Harrelson, Derrel M., New York, N.L., October 13, 1973, seventh inning.
      Foli, Timothy J., Pittsburgh N.L., October 12, 1979, second inning.

Most Chances Accepted, Game, Nine Innings
    13—Weaver, George D., Chicago A.L., October 7, 1917; 7 putouts, 6 assists, 0 errors.

Most Chances Accepted, Inning
    3—Held by many shortstops.

Fewest Chances Offered, Game, Nine Innings
    0—Boley, John P., Philadelphia A.L., October 8, 1929.
      Rizzuto, Philip F., New York A.L., October 7, 1949.
      Versalles, Zoilo, Minnesota A.L., October 7, 1965.
      Petrocelli, Americio, Boston A.L., October 4, 1967.
      Campaneris, Dagoberto B., Oakland A.L., October 18, 1972.
      Concepcion, David I., Cincinnati N.L., October 16, 1975, night game.

Fewest Chances Offered, Game, Eight Innings
    0—Bancroft, David J., New York N.L., October 12, 1915.
      Reese, Harold H., Brooklyn N.L., October 1, 1947.

Most Errors, Game, Nine Innings
    3—Barry, John J., Philadelphia A.L., October 26, 1911.
      Fletcher, Arthur, New York N.L., October 9, 1912.
      Weaver, George D., Chicago A.L., October 13, 1917.

Most Errors, Inning
    2—Peckinpaugh, Roger T., Washington A.L., October 8, 1925, eighth inning.
      English, Elwood G., Chicago N.L., October 8, 1929, ninth inning.
      Bartell, Richard, New York N.L., October 9, 1937, third inning.
      Reese, Harold H., Brooklyn N.L., October 2, 1941, eighth inning.

Most Double Plays, Game, Nine Innings
    4—Rizzuto, Philip F., New York A.L., October 8, 1951.

Most Double Plays Started, Game, Nine Innings
    3—Rizzuto, Philip F., New York A.L., October 10, 1951.
      Wills, Maurice M., Los Angeles N.L., October 11, 1965.
      Bowa, Lawrence, R., Philadelphia N.L., October 15, 1980.

Most Unassisted Double Plays, Game
    1—Tinker, Joseph B., Chicago N.L., October 10, 1907, and October 11, 1907.
      Gelbert, Charles M., St. Louis N.L., October 2, 1930.
      Kasko, Edward M., Cincinnati N.L., October 7, 1961.

Most Unassisted Double Plays, Series
   2—Tinker, Joseph B., Chicago N.L., October 10, 11, 1907.

OUTFIELDERS' FIELDING RECORDS

Most Series Played
   12—Mantle, Mickey C., New York A.L., 1951, 1952, 1953, 1955, 1956, 1957, 1958, 1960, 1961, 1962, 1963, 1964 (63 games).

Most Games Played, Total Series
   63—Mantle, Mickey C., New York A.L., 1951, 1952, 1953, 1955, 1956, 1957, 1958, 1960, 1962, 1963, 1964; 12 Series.

Highest Fielding Average, Series, With Most Chances Accepted
   4-game Series—1.000—Combs, Earle B., New York A.L., 1927 (16 chances accepted).
   5-game Series—1.000—DiMaggio, Joseph P., New York A.L., 1942 (20 chances accepted).
   6-game Series—1.000—Rivers, John M., New York A.L., 1977 (25 chances accepted).
   7-game Series—1.000—Evans, Dwight M., Boston A.L., 1975 (24 chances accepted).
                         Geronimo, Cesar F., Cincinnati N.L., 1975 (24 chances accepted).
                         Lynn, Fredric M., Boston A.L., 1975 (24 chances accepted).
                         McGee, Willie D., St. Louis N.L., 1982 (24 chances accepted).
   8-game Series—1.000—Murray, John J., New York N.L., 1912 (24 chances accepted).

Most Consecutive Errorless Games, Total Series
   45—DiMaggio, Joseph P., New York A.L., October 6, 1937 through October 10, 1951.

Most Putouts, Series
   4-game Series—16—Combs, Earle B., New York A.L., 1927.
   5-game Series—20—DiMaggio, Joseph P., New York A.L., 1942.
   6-game Series—24—Rivers, John M., New York A.L., 1977.
   7-game Series—24—McCormick, Myron W., Cincinnati N.L., 1940.
                         Pafko, Andrew, Chicago N.L., 1945.
                         McGee, Willie D., St. Louis N.L., 1982.
   8-game Series—30—Roush, Edd J., Cincinnati N.L., 1919.

Most Putouts, Total Series
   150—DiMaggio, Joseph P., New York A.L., 1936, 1937, 1938, 1939, 1941, 1942, 1947, 1949, 1950, 1951; 10 Series, 51 games.

Most Assists, Series
   4-game Series—2—Connally, Joseph A., Boston, N.L., 1914.
   5-game Series—2—Held by many outfielders.
   6-game Series—2—Held by many outfielders.
   7-game Series—4—Rice, Edgar C., Washington A.L., 1924.
   8-game Series—3—Dougherty, Patrick H., Boston A.L., 1903.
                         Hooper, Harry, Boston A.L., 1912.
                         Roush, Edd J., Cincinnati N.L., 1919.

Most Assists, Total Series
   5—Hooper, Harry B., Boston A.L., 1912, 1915, 1916, 1918; 4 Series, 24 games.
       Youngs, Ross M., New York N.L., 1921, 1922, 1923, 1924; 4 Series, 26 games.

Fewest Assists, Total Series (Most Games)
   0—DiMaggio, Joseph P., New York A.L., 1936, 1937, 1938, 1939, 1941, 1942, 1947, 1949, 1950, 1951; 10 Series, 51 games.

Most Chances Accepted, Series
   4-game Series—16—Combs, Earle B., New York A.L., 1927.
   5-game Series—20—DiMaggio, Joseph P., New York A.L., 1942.
   6-game Series—25—Rivers, John M., New York A.L., 1977.
   7-game Series—26—Pafko, Andrew, Chicago N.L., 1945.
   8-game Series—33—Roush, Edd J., Cincinnati N.L., 1919.

Most Chances Accepted, Total Series
   150—DiMaggio, Joseph P., New York A.L., 1936, 1937, 1938, 1939, 1941, 1942, 1947, 1949, 1950, 1951; 10 Series, 51 games.

Most Errors, Series
   4-game Series—3—Davis, William H., Los Angeles N.L., 1966.
   5-game Series—2—Held by many outfielders.
   6-game Series—3—Murray, John J., New York N.L., 1911.
                         Collins, John F., Chicago A.L., 1917.
   7-game Series—2—Wheat, Zachary D., Brooklyn N.L., 1920.
                         Orsatti, Ernest R., St. Louis N.L., 1934.
                         Goslin, Leon A., Detroit A.L., 1934.
                         Mantle, Mickey C., New York A.L., 1964.
                         Northrup, James T., Detroit A.L., 1968.
   8-game Series—2—Held by 4 outfielders (2 in 1912; 2 in 1919).

Most Errors, Total Series
  4—Youngs, Ross, New York N.L., 1921, 1922, 1923, 1924; 4 Series, 26 games.

Most Double Plays, Series
  4-game Series—0—Held by many outfielders.
  5-game Series—2—Murphy, Daniel F., Philadelphia A.L., 1910.
  6-game Series—1—Held by many outfielders.
  7-game Series—2—Howard, Elston G., New York A.L., 1958.
  8-game Series—2—Speaker, Tris, Boston A.L., 1912.
                  Roush, Edd J., Cincinnati N.L., 1919.

Most Double Plays, Total Series
  2—Held by many outfielders.

Most Double Plays Started, Series
  4-game Series—0—Held by many outfielders.
  5-game Series—2—Murphy, Daniel F., Philadelphia A.L., 1910.
  6-game Series—1—Held by many outfielders.
  7-game Series—2—Howard, Elston G., New York A.L., 1958.
  8-game Series—2—Speaker, Tris, Boston A.L., 1912.
                  Roush, Edd J., Cincinnati N.L., 1919.

Most Putouts, Game, Nine Innings
  8—Roush, Edd J., Cincinnati N.L., October 1, 1919.
     Foster, George A., Cincinnati N.L., October 21, 1976.

Most Putouts, Game, Nine Innings, Center Field
  8—Roush, Edd J., Cincinnati N.L., October 1, 1919.

Most Putouts, Extra-Inning Game, Center Field
  9—Otis, Amos J., Kansas City A.L., October 17, 1980, 10 innings.

Most Putouts, Game, Nine Innings, Left Field
  8—Foster, George A., Cincinnati N.L., October 21, 1976.

Most Putouts, Extra-Inning Game, Left Field
  7—Rudi, Joseph O., Oakland A.L., October 16, 1973, 11 innings.

Most Putouts, Game, Nine Innings, Right Field
  7—Murray, John J., New York N.L., October 14, 1912.
     Miller, Edmund J., Philadelphia A.L., October 5, 1930.
     Blades, Raymond F., St. Louis N.L., October 5, 1930.
     Oliva, Pedro, Minnesota A.L., October 6, 1965.
     Kaline, Albert W., Detroit A.L., October 9, 1968.
     Robinson, Frank, Baltimore A.L., October 14, 1969.

Most Assists, Game, Nine Innings
  2—Held by many outfielders.

Most Errors, Game
  3—Davis, William H., Los Angeles N.L., October 6, 1966.

Most Errors, Inning
  3—Davis, William H., Los Angeles N.L., October 6, 1966, fifth inning.

Most Putouts, Inning, Center Field
  3—Donlin, Michael J., New York N.L., October 13, 1905, fourth inning.
     Paskert, George H., Philadelphia N.L., October 11, 1915, fourth inning.
     Orsatti, Ernest R., St. Louis N.L., October 8, 1934, fifth inning.
     DiMaggio, Joseph P., New York A.L., October 2, 1936, ninth inning, and October 7, 1937, sixth inning.
     Maris, Roger E., New York A.L., October 11, 1964, third inning.
     Smith, C. Reginald, Boston A.L., October 11, 1967, seventh inning.
     Agee, Tommie L., New York N.L., October 14, 1969, seventh inning.

Most Putouts, Inning, Left Field
  3—Keller, Charles E., New York A.L., October 1, 1941, third inning.
     Irvin, Monford M., New York N.L., September 29, 1954, ninth inning.
     Davis, H. Thomas, Los Angeles N.L., October 3, 1963, seventh inning.
     Oglivie, Benjamin A., Milwaukee A.L., October 19, 1982, seventh inning.

Most Putouts, Inning, Right Field
  3—Ott, Melvin T., New York N.L., October 4, 1933, seventh inning.
     Hazle, Robert S., Milwaukee N.L., October 10, 1957, fourth inning.
     Swoboda, Ronald A., New York N.L., October 15, 1969, ninth inning.
     Moore, Charles W., Milwaukee A.L., October 12, 1982, eighth inning.

Most Consecutive Putouts, Game
  4—Donlin, Michael J., New York N.L., October 13, 1905 (1 in third inning. 3 in fourth inning, center field).

Paskert, George H., Philadelphia N.L., October 11, 1915 (3 in fourth inning, 1 in fifth inning, center field).
Keller, Charles E., New York A.L., October 1, 1941 (1 in second inning, 3 in third inning, left field).
Irvin, Monford M., New York N.L., September 29, 1954 (1 in eighth inning, 3 in ninth inning, left field; Irvin dropped fly for error after second putout in ninth inning).
Agee, Tommie L., New York N.L., October 14, 1969 (3 in seventh inning, 1 in eighth inning, center field).
Oglivie, Benjamin A., Milwaukee A.L., October 19, 1982 (1 in sixth inning, 3 in seventh inning, left field).

Most Chances Accepted, Game, Nine Innings, Center Field
8—Roush, Edd J., Cincinnati N.L., October 1, 1919 (8 putouts, 0 assists, 0 errors).
Leiber, Henry, New York N.L., October 2, 1926 (7 putouts, 1 assist, 0 errors).

Most Chances Accepted, Game, Ten Innings, Center Field
9—Roush, Edd J., Cincinnati N.L., October 7, 1919 (7 putouts, 2 assists, 0 errors).
Otis, Amos J., Kansas City A.L., October 17, 1980 (9 putouts, 0 assists, 0 errors).

Most Chances Accepted, Game, Nine Innings, Left Field
8—Foster, George A., Cincinnati N.L., October 21, 1976 (8 putouts, 0 assists, 0 errors).

Most Chances Accepted, Extra-Inning Game, Left Field
7—Rudi, Joseph O., Oakland A.L., October 16, 1973, 11 innings.

Most Chances Accepted, Game, Nine Innings, Right Field
7—Murray, John J., New York N.L., October 14, 1912 (7 putouts, 0 assists, 0 errors).
Miller, Edmund J., Philadelphia A.L., October 5, 1930 (7 putouts, 0 assists, 0 errors).
Blades, Raymond F., St. Louis N.L., October 5, 1930 (7 putouts, 0 assists, 0 errors).
Oliva, Pedro, Minnesota A.L., October 6, 1965 (7 putouts, 0 assists, 0 errors).
Kaline, Albert W., Detroit A.L., October 9, 1968 (7 putouts, 0 assists, 0 errors).
Robinson, Frank, Baltimore A.L., October 14, 1969 (7 putouts, 0 assists, 0 errors).

Most Chances Accepted, Inning
3—Held by many outfielders.

Fewest Chances Offered, Longest Extra-Inning Game
0—Cobb, Tyrus R., Detroit A.L., right field, October 8, 1907 (12 innings).
McNeeley, George E., Washington A.L., center field, October 10, 1924 (12 innings).
Medwick, Joseph M., St. Louis N.L., left field, October 4, 1934 (11⅔ innings).
Hahn, Donald A., New York N.L., center field, right field, October 14, 1973 (12 innings).
Jones, Cleon J., New York N.L., left field, October 14, 1973 (12 innings).
Griffey, G. Kenneth, Cincinnati N.L., right field, October 21, 1975, night game. (Boston A.L., won 7-6, none out in 12th inning).

Fewest Chances Offered, Three Consecutive Games
0—Browne, George E., New York N.L., right field, October 12, 1905 (9 innings); October 13, 1905 (9 innings); October 14, 1905 (9 innings).
Carey, Max, Pittsburgh N.L., center field, October 11, 1925 (8 innings); October 12, 1925 (9 innings); October 13, 1925 (9 innings).
Simmons, Aloysius H., Philadelphia A.L., left field, October 11, 1929 (9 innings); October 12, 1929 (9 innings); October 14, 1929 (9 innings).
Wilson, J. Owen, Pittsburgh N.L., right field, October 8, 1909 (9 innings); October 9, 1909 (9 innings); October 11, 1909 (9 innings).

Fewest Chances Offered, Four Consecutive Games
0—Wilson, J. Owen, Pittsburgh N.L., right field, October 8, 1909 (9 innings); October 9, 1909 (9 innings); October 11, 1909 (9 innings); October 12, 1909 (8 innings).

Most Double Plays, Game
2—Roush, Edd J., Cincinnati N.L., October 7, 1919 (fifth and eighth innings of ten-inning game).

Most Double Plays Started, Game
2—Roush, Edd J., Cincinnati N.L., October 7, 1919 (fifth and eighth innings of ten-inning game).

Most Unassisted Double Plays, Game
1—Speaker, Tristram, Boston A.L., October 15, 1912.

CATCHERS' FIELDING RECORDS

Most Series Played
12—Berra, Lawrence P., New York A.L., 1947, 1949, 1950, 1951, 1952, 1953, 1955, 1956, 1957, 1958, 1960, 1962 (63 games).

Most Games Caught, Total Series
63—Berra, Lawrence P., New York A.L., 1947, 1949, 1950, 1951, 1952, 1953, 1955, 1956, 1957, 1958, 1960, 1962 (12 Series).

Highest Fielding Average, Series, With Most Chances Accepted

4-game Series—1.000—Roseboro, John, Los Angeles N.L., 1963; 43 chances accepted.
5-game Series—1.000—Cochrane, Gordon S., Philadelphia A.L., 1929; 61 chances accepted.
6-game Series—1.000—Campanella, Roy, Brooklyn N.L., 1953; 56 chances accepted.
7-game Series—1.000—Grote, Gerald W., New York N.L., 1973; 71 chances accepted.
8-game Series—1.000—Schang, Walter H., New York A.L., 1921; 50 chances accepted.

Most Consecutive Errorless Games, Total Series

30—Berra, Lawrence P., New York A.L., October 4, 1952 through October 9, 1957.

Most Putouts, Series

4-game Series—43—Roseboro, John, Los Angeles N.L., 1963.
5-game Series—59—Cochrane, Gordon S., Philadelphia A.L., 1929.
6-game Series—55—Cooper, W. Walker, St. Louis N.L., 1944.
7-game Series—67—Grote, Gerald W., New York N.L., 1973.
8-game Series—54—Criger, Louis, Boston A.L., 1903.

Most Putouts, Total Series

421—Berra, Lawrence P., New York A.L., 1947, 1949 1950, 1951, 1952, 1953, 1955, 1956, 1957, 1958, 1960, 1962; 12 Series, 63 games.

Most Assists, Series

4-game Series— 7—Munson, Thurman L., New York A.L., 1976.
5-game Series— 9—Schmidt, Charles, Detroit A.L., 1907.
                Kling, John G., Chicago N.L., 1907.
                Burns, Edward, Philadelphia N.L., 1915.
6-game Series—12—Meyers, John T., New York N.L., 1911.
7-game Series—11—Schmidt, Charles, Detroit A.L., 1909.
8-game Series—15—Schalk, Raymond W., Chicago A.L., 1919.

Most Assists, Total Series

36—Berra, Lawrence P., New York A.L., 1947, 1949, 1950, 1951, 1952, 1953, 1955, 1956, 1957, 1958, 1960, 1962; 12 Series, 63 games.

Most Chances Accepted, Series

4-game Series—43—Roseboro, John, Los Angeles N.L., 1963.
5-game Series—61—Cochrane, Gordon S., Philadelphia A.L., 1929.
6-game Series—56—Kling, John G., Chicago N.L., 1906.
                 Campanella, Roy, Brooklyn N.L., 1953.
7-game Series—71—Grote, Gerald W., New York N.L., 1973.
8-game Series—62—Criger, Louis, Boston A.L., 1903.

Most Chances Accepted, Total Series

457—Berra, Lawrence P., New York A.L., 1947, 1949, 1950, 1951, 1952, 1953, 1955, 1956, 1957, 1958, 1960, 1962; 12 Series, 63 games.

Most Errors, Series

4-game Series—2—Wilson, James, St. Louis N.L., 1928.
5-game Series—2—Schmidt, Charles, Detroit A.L., 1907.
               Cooper, W. Walker, St. Louis N.L., 1943.
               Ferguson, Joseph V., Los Angeles N.L., 1974.
6-game Series—2—Schalk, Raymond W., Chicago A.L., 1917.
7-game Series—5—Schmidt, Charles, Detroit A.L., 1909.
8-game Series—3—Criger, Louis, Boston A.L., 1909.

Most Errors, Total Series

7—Schmidt, Charles, Detroit A.L., 1907, 1908, 1909; 3 Series, 13 games.

Most Double Plays, Series

4-game Series—2—Hartnett, Charles L., Chicago N.L., 1932.
5-game Series—2—Burns, Edward J., Philadelphia N.L., 1915.
               Mancuso, August R., New York N.L., 1933.
6-game Series—3—Kling, John G., Chicago N.L., 1906.
7-game Series—3—Schmidt, Charles, Detroit A.L., 1909.
               Bench, Johnny L., Cincinnati N.L., 1975.
8-game Series—3—Schang, Walter H., New York A.L., 1921.

Most Double Plays, Total Series

6—Berra, Lawrence P., New York A.L., 1947, 1949, 1950, 1951, 1952, 1953, 1955, 1956, 1957, 1958, 1960, 1962; 12 Series, 63 games.
  Bench, Johnny L., Cincinnati N.L., 1970 (1), 1972 (2), 1975 (3), 1976 (0); 4 Series, 23 games.

Most Double Plays Started, Series

4-game Series—1—Held by many catchers.
5-game Series—1—Held by many catchers.
6-game Series—1—Held by many catchers.
7-game Series—2—Schmidt, Charles, Detroit A.L., 1909.
               Crandall, Delmar D., N.L., 1957 and 1958.
               Battey, Earl J., Minnesota A.L., 1965.
8-game Series—3—Schang, Walter H., New York A.L., 1921.

Most Passed Balls, Series
3—Kling, John G., Chicago N.L., 1906.
Burgess, Forrest H., Pittsburgh N.L., 1960.
Howard, Elston G., New York A.L., 1964.

Most Passed Balls, Total Series
5—Kling, John G., Chicago N.L., 1906 (3), 1907, 1908.
4—Howard, Elston G., New York A.L., 1961 (1), 1964 (3).

Most Players Caught Stealing, Series
4-game Series— 5—Munson, Thurman L., New York A.L., 1976.
5-game Series— 6—Kling, John G., Chicago N.L., 1910.
Thomas, Ira F., Philadelphia A.L., 1910.
6-game Series— 8—Lapp, John W., Philadelphia A.L., 1911.
7-game Series— 5—Gibson, George, Pittsburgh N.L., 1909.
Miller, Otto L., Brooklyn N.L., 1920.
Battey, Earl J., Minnesota A.L., 1965.
Freehan, William A., Detroit A.L., 1968.
8-game Series—10—Schalk, Raymond W., Chicago A.L., 1919.

Most Players Caught Stealing, Total Series
20—Schang, Philadelphia A.L., 1913, 1914, Boston A.L., 1918, New York A.L., 1921, 1922, 1923. 6 Series, 32 games.

Most Putouts, Game, Nine Innings
18—Roseboro, John, Los Angeles N.L., October 2, 1963 (15 strikeouts).

Fewest Putouts, Game, Nine Innings
1—Schang, Walter H., Philadelphia A.L., October 11, 1913.
Schalk, Raymond W., Chicago A.L., October 7, 1917.
Wingo, Ivy B., Cincinnati N.L., October 1, 1919.
Schang, Walter H., New York A.L., October 11, 1923.
Ruel, Herold D., Washington A.L., October 5, 1924.
Cochrane, Gordon S., Detroit A.L., October 6, 1934.
Hartnett, Charles L., Chicago N.L., October 2, 1935.
Seminick, Andrew W., Philadelphia N.L., October 4, 1950.
Berra, Lawrence P., New York A.L., October 3, 1952 and October 10, 1956.
Lollar, J. Sherman, Chicago A.L., October 6, 1959.
Howard, Elston G., New York A.L., October 6, 1960.
Simmons, Ted L., Milwaukee A.L., October 15, 1982.

Most Putouts, Inning
3—Held by many catchers.

Most Assists, Game, Nine Innings
4—Kling, John G., Chicago N.L., October 9, 1907.
Schmidt, Charles, Detroit A.L., October 11, 1907 and October 14, 1908.
Gibson, George Pittsburgh N.L., October 12, 1909.
Rariden, William A., New York N.L., October 10, 1917.
Agnew, Samuel, Boston A.L., September 6, 1918.
Delancey, William P., St. Louis N.L., October 8, 1934.

Most Assists, Game, 11 Innings
6—Lapp, John W., Philadelphia A.L., October 17, 1911.

Most Assists, Inning
2—Held by many catchers.

Most Chances Accepted, Game, Nine Innings
18—Roseboro, John, Los Angeles N.L., October 2, 1963 (18 putouts, 0 assists, 0 errors, 15 strikeouts).
McCarver, J. Timothy, St. Louis N.L., October 2, 1968 (17 putouts, 1 assist, 0 errors, 17 strikeouts).

Most Chances Accepted, Inning
4—McCarver, J. Timothy, St. Louis N.L., October 9, 1967, ninth inning (3 putouts, 1 assist, 2 strikeouts).

Fewest Chances Offered, Game, Nine Innings
1—Schang, Walter H., Philadelphia A.L., October 11, 1913 (strikeout).
Schang, Walter H., New York A.L., October 11, 1923 (strikeout).
Ruel, Herold D., Washington A.L., October 5, 1924 (strikeout).
Cochrane, Gordon S., Detroit A.L., October 6, 1934 (strikeout).
Hartnett, Charles L., Chicago N.L., October 2, 1935 (strikeout).
Lollar, J. Sherman, Chicago A.L., October 6, 1959 (strikeout).
Howard, Elston G., New York A.L., October 6, 1960.

Fewest Chances Offered, Game, Eight Innings
1—Killefer, Chicago N.L., September 9, 1918 (strikeout).

Most Errors, Game, Nine Innings
  2—Criger, Louis, Boston A.L., October 1, 1903.
    Wilson, James, St. Louis, N.L., October 7, 1928.
    Ferguson, Joseph V., Los Angeles N.L., October 15, 1974.
    Fisk, Carlton E., Boston A.L., October 14, 1975, night game, 9⅓ innings.

Most Errors, Inning
  2—Criger, Louis, Boston A.L., October 1, 1903, first inning.
    Wilson, James, St. Louis N.L., October 7, 1928, sixth inning.

Most Passed Balls, Game, Nine Innings
  2—Kling, John G., Chicago N.L., October 9, 1906.
    Killefer, William, Chicago N.L., September 9, 1918.
    Richards, Paul R., Detroit A.L., October 3, 1945.
    Edwards, Bruce, Brooklyn N.L., October 4, 1947.
    Burgess, Forrest H., Pittsburgh N.L., October 6, 1960.
    Howard, Elston G., New York A.L., October 7, 1964.

Most Passed Balls, Inning
  1—Held by many catchers.

Most Players Caught Stealing, Inning
  2—Lapp, John W., Philadelphia A.L., October 17, 1911, tenth inning.
    Robinson, Aaron A., New York A.L., October 6, 1947, first inning.
    Carrigan, William F., Boston A.L., October 9, 1912, eleventh inning.
    Campanella, Roy, Brooklyn N.L., October 2, 1952, first inning.

Most Players Caught Stealing, Game, Nine Innings
  3—(8 times)—Held by 7 catchers. Last time, Roseboro, John, Los Angeles N.L., October 4, 1959.

Most Players Caught Stealing, Extra-Inning Game
  5—Lapp, John W., Philadelphia A.L., October 17, 1911, 11 innings.

Most Double Plays Started, Game, Nine Innings
  2—Schmidt, Charles, Detroit A.L., October 14, 1909.
    Schang, Walter H., New York A.L., October 11, 1921.

Most Double Plays, Game, Nine Innings
  2—Schmidt, Charles, Detroit A.L., October 14, 1909.
    Schang, Walter H., New York A.L., October 11, 1921.
    Hartnett, Charles L., Chicago N.L., September 29, 1932.
    Rice, Delbert W., Milwaukee N.L., October 9, 1957.

Most Unassisted Double Plays, Game
  Never accomplished.

PITCHERS' FIELDING RECORDS

Most Series Played
  11—Ford, Edward C., New York A.L., 1950, 1953, 1955, 1956, 1957, 1958, 1960, 1961, 1962, 1963, 1964 (22 games).

Most Games, Pitched, Series
  4-game Series—3—French, Lawrence H., Chicago N.L., 1938, 3⅓ innings.
                  Konstanty, C. James, Philadelphia N.L., 1950, 15 innings.
                  Mossi, Donald L., Cleveland A.L., 1954, 4 innings.
                  Reniff, Harold E., New York A.L., 1963, 3 innings.
  5-game Series—5—Marshall, Michael G., Los Angeles N.L., 1974, 9 innings.
  6-game Series—6—Quisenberry, Daniel R., Kansas City A.L., 1980, 10⅓ innings.
  7-game Series—7—Knowles, Darold D., Oakland A.L., 1973, 6⅓ innings.
  8-game Series—5—Phillippe, Charles L., Pittsburgh N.L., 1903, 44 innings.

Most Games Pitched, Total Series
  22—Ford, Edward C., New York N.L., 1950, 1953, 1955, 1956, 1957, 1958, 1960, 1961, 1962, 1963, 1964 (11 Series).

Highest Fielding Average, Series, With Most Chances Accepted
  4-game Series—1.000—Ruffing, Charles H., New York A.L., 1938 (6 chances accepted).
  5-game Series—1.000—Marquard, Richard W., New York N.L., 1913 (8 chances accepted).
                      Shore, Ernest G., Boston A.L., 1916 (8 chances accepted).
                      Smith, Sherrod M., Brooklyn N.L., 1916 (8 chances accepted).
  6-game Series—1.000—Altrock, Nicholas, Chicago A.L., 1906 (17 chances accepted).
                      Vaughn, James L., Chicago N.L., 1918 (17 chances accepted).
  7-game Series—1.000—Mullin, George E., Detroit A.L., 1909 (12 chances accepted).
  8-game Series—1.000—Mathewson, Christopher, New York N.L., 1912 (13 chances accepted).

Most Consecutive Errorless Games, Total Series
  18—Ford, Edward C., New York A.L., October 7, 1950 through October 8, 1962.

WORLD SERIES RECORDS

Most Putouts, Series
 4-game Series—3—Ford, Edward C., New York A.L., 1963.
 5-game Series—5—Morris, John S., Detroit A.L., 1984.
 6-game Series—6—Altrock, Nicholas, Chicago A.L., 1906.
             Vaughn, James L., Chicago N.L., 1918.
 7-game Series—5—Kaat, James L., Minnesota A.L., 1965.
 8-game Series—2—Phillippe, Charles L., Pittsburgh N.L., 1903.
             Douglas, Philip B., New York N.L., 1921.

Most Putouts, Total Series
 11—Ford, Edward C., New York A.L., 1950, 1953, 1955, 1956, 1957, 1958, 1960, 1961, 1962, 1963, 1964
    (11 Series, 22 games).

Most Assists, Series
 4-game Series— 5—Bush, Leslie A., Philadelphia A.L., 1914.
             Tyler, George, Boston N.L., 1914.
             James, William L., Boston N.L., 1914.
             Moore, Wilcey, New York A.L., 1927.
             Pearson, Monte, New York A.L., 1939.
 5-game Series—10—Brown, Mordecai P., Chicago N.L., 1910.
 6-game Series—12—Brown, Mordecai P., Chicago N.L., 1906.
 7-game Series—12—Mullin, George, Detroit A.L., 1909.
 8-game Series—12—Mathewson, Christopher, New York N.L., 1912.

Most Assists, Total Series
 34—Mathewson, Christopher, New York N.L., 1905, 1911, 1912, 1913; 4 Series, 11 games.

Most Chances Accepted, Series
 4-game Series— 6—Tyler, George A., Boston N.L., 1914.
             Ruffing, Charles H., New York A.L., 1938.
 5-game Series—10—Mathewson, Christopher, New York N.L., 1905.
             Brown, Mordecai P., Chicago N.L., 1910.
 6-game Series—17—Altrock Nicholas, Chicago A.L., 1906.
             Vaughn, James L., Chicago N.L., 1918.
 7-game Series—12—Mullin, George, Detroit A.L., 1909.
 8-game Series—13—Mathewson, Christopher, New York N.L., 1912.

Most Chances Accepted, Total Series
 40—Mathewson, Christopher, New York N.L., 1905, 1911, 1912, 1913; 4 Series, 11 games.

Fewest Chances Offered (Most Innings), Series
 0—Grove, Robert M., Philadelphia A.L., 1931; 3 games, 26 innings.

Most Errors, Series
 4-game Series—1—Held by many pitchers.
 5-game Series—2—Coombs, John W., Philadelphia A.L., 1910.
             Lanier, H. Max, St. Louis N.L., 1942.
 6-game Series—2—Potter, Nelson T., St. Louis A.L., 1944.
 7-game Series—2—Phillippe, Charles L., Pittsburgh N.L., 1909.
             Reynolds, Allie P., New York A.L., 1952.
 8-game Series—2—Cicotte, Edward V., Chicago A.L., 1919.

Most Errors, Total Series
 3—Phillippe, Charles, Pittsburgh N.L., 1903, 1909, 2 Series, 7 games.
    Cicotte, Edward, Chicago A.L., 1917, 1919, 2 Series, 6 games.
    Lanier, H. Max, St. Louis N.L., 1942, 1943, 1944, 3 Series, 7 games.

Most Double Plays, Series
 4-game Series—2—Bender, Charles A., Philadelphia A.L., 1914.
 5-game Series—2—Bush, Leslie A., New York A.L., 1922.
 6-game Series—2—Faber, Urban C., Chicago A.L., 1917.
             Reynolds, Allie P., New York A.L., 1951.
             Gura, Lawrence C., Kansas City A.L., 1980.
 7-game Series—2—Johnson, Walter P., Washington A.L., 1924.
             Stafford, William C., New York A.L., 1960.
 8-game Series—1—Wood, Joseph, Boston A.L., 1912.
             Cicotte, Edward V., Chicago A.L., 1919.
             Quinn, John P., New York A.L., 1921.

Most Double Plays, Total Series
 3—Bender, Charles A., Philadelphia A.L., 1905, 1910, 1911, 1913, 1914; 5 Series, 10 games.
    Bush, Leslie A., Philadelphia A.L., Boston A.L., New York A.L., 1913, 1914, 1918, 1922, 1923; 5
      Series, 9 games.
    Reynolds, Allie P., New York A.L., 1947, 1949, 1950, 1951, 1952, 1953; 6 Series, 15 games.

Most Double Plays Started, Series
 4-game Series—2—Bender, Charles A., Philadelphia A.L., 1914.
 5-game Series—2—Bush, Leslie A., New York A.L., 1922.

6-game Series—2—Faber, Urban C., Chicago A.L., 1917.
　　　　　　　　Reynolds, Allie P., New York A.L., 1951.
7-game Series—2—Stafford, William C., New York A.L., 1960.
8-game Series—1—Cicotte, Edward V., Chicago A.L., 1919.
　　　　　　　　Quinn, John P., New York A.L., 1921.

Most Putouts Game, Nine Innings
　5—Kaat, James L., Minnesota A.L., October 7, 1965.

Most Putouts, Inning
　2—Beazley, John A., St. Louis N.L., October 5, 1942 (eighth inning).
　Turley, Robert L., New York A.L., October 9, 1957 (seventh inning).
　Ford, Edward C., New York A.L., October 8, 1960 (ninth inning).
　Purkey, Robert T., Cincinnati N.L., October 7, 1961 (ninth inning).
　Denny, John A., Philadelphia N.L., October 15, 1983 (fifth inning).

Most Assists, Game, Nine Innings
　8—Altrock, Nicholas, Chicago A.L., October 12, 1906.
　Warneke, Lonnie, Chicago N.L., October 2, 1935.

Most Assists, Inning
　3—Plank, Edward S., Philadelphia A.L., October 13, 1905, eighth inning.
　Marquard, Richard W., New York N.L., October 7, 1913, fourth inning.
　Warneke, Lonnie, Chicago N.L., October 2, 1935, third inning.
　Murphy, John J., New York A.L., October 8, 1939, eighth inning.
　Rush, Robert R., Milwaukee N.L., October 4, 1958, third inning.

Most Chances Accepted, Game, Nine Innings
　11—Altrock, Nicholas Chicago A.L., October 12, 1906 (3 putouts, 8 assists, 0 errors).

Fewest Chances Offered, Extra-Inning Game
　0—Pollet, Howard J., St. Louis N.L., October 6, 1946 (ten innings).
　Roberts, Robin E., Philadelphia N.L., October 5, 1950 (ten innings).

Most Chances Accepted, Inning
　3—Held by many pitchers.

Most Errors, Game, Nine Innings
　2—Phillippe, Charles L., Pittsburgh N.L., October 12, 1909.
　Coombs, John W., Philadelphia A.L., October 18, 1910.
　Cicotte, Edward V., Chicago A.L., October 4, 1919.
　Lanier, H. Max, St. Louis N.L., September 30, 1942.
　Potter, Nelson T., St. Louis A.L., October 5, 1944 (starting pitcher, pitched 6 innings).

Most Errors, Inning
　2—Coombs, John W., Philadelphia A.L., October 18, 1910, fifth inning.
　Cicotte, Edward V., Chicago A.L., October 4, 1919, fifth inning.
　Lanier, H. Max, St. Louis N.L., September 30, 1942, ninth inning.
　Potter, Nelson T., St. Louis A.L., October 5, 1944, third inning.

Most Unassisted Double Plays, Game
　Never accomplished.

Most Double Plays Started, Game
　2—Bender, Charles A., Philadelphia A.L., October 9, 1914.
　Bush, Leslie A., New York A.L., October 8, 1922.
　Reynolds, Allie P., New York A.L., October 8, 1951.

CLUB FIELDING—GAME AND INNING

Most Assists, Game, One Club, Nine Innings
　21—Chicago A.L., vs. New York N.L., October 7, 1917.
　Boston A.L., vs. Chicago N.L., September 9, 1918.

Most Assists, Game, Both Clubs, Nine Innings
　38—Chicago A.L., 20, Chicago N.L., 18, October 12, 1906.

Fewest Assists, Game, One Club, Nine Innings.
　2—St. Louis N.L., vs. Detroit A.L., October 2, 1968.

Fewest Assists, Game, Both Clubs, Nine Innings
　8—Philadelphia A.L., 5, St. Louis N.L., 3, October 2, 1930.
　Boston A.L., 5, Cincinnati N.L., 3, October 16, 1975.

Most Assists, Outfield, One Inning, One Club
　2—Boston A.L., vs. St. Louis N.L., October 10, 1946, fifth game.

Most Errors, Game, One Club, Nine Innings
  6—Chicago A.L., vs. Chicago N.L., October 13, 1906.
    Pittsburgh N.L., vs. Detroit A.L., October 12, 1909.
    Chicago A.L., vs. New York N.L., October 13, 1917.
    Los Angeles N.L., vs. Baltimore A.L., October 6, 1966.

Most Errors, Game, Both Clubs, Nine Innings
  9—Chicago A.L., 6, New York N.L., 3, October 13, 1917.

Most Errors, Inning, One Club
  3—Chicago A.L., October 13, 1917, fourth inning.
    New York N.L., October 8, 1937, fifth inning.
    New York N.L., October 9, 1937, third inning.
    Cincinnati N.L., October 8, 1939, tenth inning.
    Los Angeles N.L., October 1, 1959, third inning.
    Los Angeles N.L., October 6, 1966, fifth inning.

Longest Errorless Game, One Club
  12 innings—Detroit A.L., vs. St. Louis N.L., October 4, 1934
      (fielded 12 complete innings).
    New York A.L., vs. Los Angeles N.L., October 11, 1977
      (fielded 12 complete innings).

Longest Errorless Game, Both Clubs
  12 innings—New York A.L., vs. Los Angeles N.L., October 11, 1977
      (Los Angeles only fielded 11 complete innings).
  10 innings—New York A.L., vs. Philadelphia N.L., October 5, 1950.
    Brooklyn N.L., vs. New York A.L., October 9, 1956
      (New York fielded 9⅔ innings).
    New York A.L., vs. Milwaukee N.L., October 6, 1957
      (New York fielded 9⅔ innings).
    Philadelphia N.L., vs. Kansas City A.L., October 17, 1980
      (Philadelphia fielded 9⅔ innings).

Most Putouts, Outfield, Game, One Club, Nine Innings
  15—New York N.L., vs. Boston A.L., October 14, 1912.
    Boston N.L., vs. Cleveland A.L., October 6, 1948.

Most Putouts, Outfield, Game, One Club, Eleven Innings
  16—Brooklyn N.L., vs. New York A.L., October 5, 1952.

Most Putouts, Outfield, Game, Nine Innings, Both Clubs
  23—Pittsburgh N.L., 13, New York A.L., 10, October 6, 1927.

Most Putouts, Outfield, Game, Both Clubs, Eleven Innings
  23—Brooklyn N.L., 16, New York A.L., 7, October 5, 1952.

Most Putouts, Outfield, Inning, One Club
  3—Made in many games.

Most Putouts, Outfield, Inning, Both Clubs
  5—New York N.L., 3, Philadelphia A.L., 2, October 13, 1905, fourth inning.
    Brooklyn N.L., 3, New York A.L., 2, October 5, 1956, sixth inning.
    Milwaukee N.L., 3, New York A.L., 2, October 2, 1957, second inning.
    Milwaukee N.L., 3, New York A.L., 2, October 3, 1957, third inning.
    Milwaukee N.L., 3, New York A.L., 2, October 10, 1957, fourth inning.
    Los Angeles N.L., 3, Chicago A.L., 2, October 2, 1959, fifth inning.
    Minnesota A.L., 3, Los Angeles N.L., 2, October 9, 1965, seventh inning.
    New York N.L., 3, Baltimore A.L., 2, October 14, 1969, seventh inning.
    New York A.L., 3, Los Angeles N.L., 2, October 24, 1981, sixth inning.

Fewest Putouts, Outfield, Game, Nine Innings, One Club
  0—New York N.L., vs. New York A.L., October 5, 1921 (1 assist).
    New York N.L., vs. New York A.L., September 30, 1936.

Fewest Putouts, Outfield, Extra-Inning Game, One Club
  1—New York N.L., vs. Oakland A.L., October 14, 1973, 12 innings.

Fewest Putouts, Outfield, Game, Nine Innings, Both Clubs
  3—New York A.L., 2, Brooklyn N.L., 1, October 10, 1956.

Most Putouts, Catchers, Inning, Both Clubs
  6—Chicago A.L., 3, Cincinnati N.L., 3, October 6, 1919, second inning.
    Cincinnati N.L., 3, Oakland A.L., 3, October 18, 1972, fifth inning.

Fewest Assists, Infield, Game, One Club, Nine Innings
  1—St. Louis N.L., vs. Detroit A.L., October 2, 1968.

Most Double Plays, Game, One Club, Nine Innings
  4—Philadelphia A.L., vs. Boston N.L., October 9, 1914.
   Boston A.L., vs. Brooklyn N.L., October 7, 1916.
   Chicago N.L., vs. New York A.L., September 29, 1932.
   Cleveland A.L., vs. Boston N.L., October 11, 1948.
   New York A.L., vs. New York N.L., October 8, 1951.
   Oakland A.L., vs. New York N.L., October 17, 1973.
   Philadelphia N.L., vs. Kansas City A.L., October 15, 1980.

Most Double Plays, Game, Both Clubs, Nine Innings
  6—New York A.L., 3, Brooklyn N.L., 3, September 29, 1955.
   Philadelphia N.L., 4, Kansas City A.L., 2, October 15, 1980.

Most Errors, Infield, Game, One Club
  5—Chicago A.L., vs. Chicago N.L., October 13, 1906.
   New York N.L., vs. Philadelphia A.L., October 17, 1911 (11 innings).
   Detroit A.L., vs. St. Louis N.L., October 3, 1934.

Most Errors, Infield, Game, Both Clubs
  7—New York N.L., 5, Philadelphia A.L., 2, October 17, 1911 (11 innings).
   Chicago A.L., 4, New York N.L., 3, October 13, 1917.

Most Errors, Outfield, Game, One Club
  4—Los Angeles N.L., vs. Baltimore A.L., October 6, 1966.

Most Errors, Outfield, Game, Both Clubs
  4—Los Angeles N.L., 4, Baltimore A.L., 0, October 6, 1966.

Fewest Chances Offered, Outfield, Game, Nine Innings, One Club
  0—New York N.L., vs. New York A.L., September 30, 1936.

Fewest Chances Offered, Outfield, Extra-Inning Game, One Club
  1—New York N.L. vs. Oakland A.L., October 14, 1973, 12 innings.

Fewest Chances Offered, Outfield, Game, Nine Innings, Both Clubs
  3—New York A.L., 2, Brooklyn N.L., 1, October 10, 1956.

Fewest Chances Offered, Infield, Game, One Club, Excluding First Base
  2—Philadelphia A.L., vs. St. Louis N.L., October 6, 1931.

Most Players, Nine-Inning Game, One Club, One or More Putouts
  11—New York A.L., vs. Milwaukee N.L., October 2, 1957.
   Baltimore A.L., vs. Pittsburgh N.L., October 16, 1979.

Most Players, Nine-Inning Game, Both Clubs, One or More Putouts
  19—New York A.L., 11, Milwaukee N.L., 8, October 2, 1957.
   Baltimore A.L., 10, Pittsburgh N.L., 9, October 11, 1971.

Most Players, Extra-Inning Game, Both Clubs, One or More Putouts
  20—Chicago N.L., 10, Detroit A.L., 10, October 8, 1945, 12 innings.

Most Players, Nine-Inning Game, One Club, One or More Assists
  9—Chicago A.L., vs. New York N.L., October 7, 1917.
   New York A.L., vs. New York N.L., October 6, 1922.
   Chicago N.L., vs. Detroit A.L., October 8, 1945, 12 innings.
   Brooklyn N.L., vs. New York A.L., October 3, 1947.

Most Players, Nine-Inning Game, Both Clubs, One or More Assists
  15—New York A.L., 9, New York N.L., 6, October 6, 1922.
   Chicago N.L., 9, Detroit A.L., 6, October 8, 1945, 12 innings.

Most Players, Extra-Inning Game, Both Clubs, One or More Assists
  16—Los Angeles N.L., 9, New York A.L., 7, October 11, 1977, 12 innings.

CLUB FIELDING—SERIES

Highest Fielding Average, Series, One Club
  4-game Series—1.000—Baltimore A.L., vs. Los Angeles N.L., 1966.
  5-game Series—1.000—New York A.L., vs. New York N.L., 1937.
  6-game Series— .996—Boston A.L., vs. Chicago N.L., 1918.
          St. Louis N.L., vs. St. Louis A.L., 1944.
          Los Angeles N.L., vs. New York A.L., 1977.
  7-game Series— .993—Cincinnati N.L., vs. Boston A.L., 1975.
  8-game Series— .984—New York N.L., vs. New York A.L., 1921.

Highest Fielding Average, Series, Both Clubs
  4-game Series—.986—New York A.L., .993, Los Angeles N.L., .979, 1963.
  5-game Series—.985—New York A.L., .990, Brooklyn N.L., .980, 1941.
  6-game Series—.991—Los Angeles N.L., .996, New York A.L., .987, 1977.

7-game Series—.988—Philadelphia A.L., .992, St. Louis N.L., .985, 1931.
8-game Series—.983—New York N.L., .984, New York A.L., .981, 1921.

Lowest Fielding Average, Series, One Club

4-game Series—.949—New York A.L., vs. Chicago N.L., 1932.
5-game Series—.942—Brooklyn N.L., vs. Boston A.L., 1916.
6-game Series—.938—New York N.L., vs. Philadelphia A.L., 1911.
7-game Series—.934—Detroit A.L., vs. Pittsburgh N.L., 1909.
8-game Series—.944—Pittsburgh N.L., vs. Boston A.L., 1903.

Lowest Fielding Average, Series, Both Clubs

4-game Series—.954—Chicago N.L., .959, New York A.L., .949, 1932.
5-game Series—.946—Philadelphia A.L., .947, Chicago N.L., .946, 1910.
6-game Series—.947—Philadelphia A.L., .956, New York N.L., 938, 1911.
7-game Series—.941—Pittsburgh N.L., .947, Detroit A.L., .934, 1909.
8-game Series—.951—Boston A.L., .957, Pittsburgh N.L., .944, 1903

Most Putouts, Total Series, One Club

4,983—New York A.L., 33 Series, 187 games.

Most Putouts, Series, One Club

4-game Series—117—Boston N.L., vs. Philadelphia A.L., 1914.
5-game Series—147—Boston A.L., vs. Brooklyn N.L., 1916.
6-game Series—168—New York A.L., vs. Los Angeles N.L., 1977.
7-game Series—201—Washington A.L., vs. New York N.L., 1924.
8-game Series—222—Boston A.L., vs. New York N.L., 1912.

Most Putouts, Series, Both Clubs

4-game Series—228—Boston N.L., 117, Philadelphia A.L., 111, 1914.
5-game Series—289—Boston A.L., 147, Brooklyn N.L., 142, 1916.
6-game Series—333—New York A.L., 168, Los Angeles N.L., 165, 1977.
7-game Series—401—Washington A.L., 201, New York N.L., 200, 1924.
8-game Series—443—Boston A.L., 222, New York N.L., 221, 1912.

Fewest Putouts, Series, One Club

4-game Series—102—St. Louis N.L., vs. New York A.L., 1928.
              Chicago N.L., vs. New York A.L., 1932.
              Chicago N.L., vs. New York A.L., 1938.
              New York A.L., vs. Los Angeles N.L., 1963.
              Los Angeles N.L., vs. Baltimore A.L., 1966.
5-game Series—126—Los Angeles N.L., vs. Oakland A.L., 1974.
              San Diego N.L., vs. Detroit A.L., 1984.
6-game Series—153—New York N.L., vs. Chicago A.L., 1917.
              St. Louis N.L., vs. Philadelphia A.L., 1930.
              New York A.L., vs. Los Angeles N.L., 1981.
7-game Series—177—Brooklyn N.L., vs. Cleveland A.L., 1920.
8-game Series—210—Pittsburgh N.L., vs. Boston A.L., 1903.
              New York A.L., vs. New York N.L., 1921.

Fewest Putouts, Series, Both Clubs

4-game Series—210—New York A.L., 108, St. Louis N.L., 102, 1928.
              New York A.L., 108, Chicago N.L., 102, 1932.
              New York A.L., 108, Chicago N.L., 102, 1938.
              Los Angeles N.L., 108, New York A.L., 102, 1963.
              Baltimore A.L., 108, Los Angeles N.L., 102, 1966.
5-game Series—258—Oakland A.L., 132, Los Angeles N.L., 126, 1974.
              Detroit A.L., 132, San Diego N.L., 126, 1984.
6-game Series—309—Chicago A.L., 156, New York N.L., 153, 1917.
              Philadelphia A.L., 156, St. Louis N.L., 153, 1930.
              Los Angeles N.L., vs. New York A.L., 1981.
7-game Series—359—Cleveland A.L., 182, Brooklyn N.L., 177, 1920.
8-game Series—422—New York N.L., 212, New York A.L., 210, 1921.

Most Assists, Total Series, One Club

1,978—New York A.L., 33 Series, 187 games.

Most Assists, Series, One Club

4-game Series— 67—Philadelphia A.L., vs. Boston N.L., 1914.
5-game Series— 90—Boston A.L., vs. Brooklyn N.L., 1916.
6-game Series— 99—Chicago A.L., vs. Chicago N.L., 1906.
7-game Series— 99—Washington A.L., vs. New York N.L., 1924.
              St. Louis N.L., vs. New York A.L., 1926.
8-game Series—116—Chicago A.L., vs. Cincinnati N.L., 1919

Most Assists, Series, Both Clubs

4-game Series—129—Philadelphia A.L., 67, Boston N.L., 62, 1914.
5-game Series—160—Boston A.L., 90, Brooklyn N.L., 70, 1916.
6-game Series—183—Chicago A.L., 99, Chicago N.L., 84, 1906.

WORLD SERIES RECORDS

7-game Series—193—Washington A.L., 99, New York N.L., 94, 1924.
8-game Series—212—Chicago A.L., 116, Cincinnati N.L., 96, 1919.

Fewest Assists, Series, One Club

4-game Series—28—New York A.L., vs. St. Louis N.L., 1928.
5-game Series—40—Philadelphia A.L., vs. Chicago N.L., 1929.
                       Brooklyn N.L., vs. New York A.L., 1949.
                       San Diego N.L., vs. Detroit A.L., 1984.
6-game Series—41—Philadelphia A.L., vs. St. Louis N.L., 1930.
7-game Series—48—St. Louis N.L., vs. Detroit A.L., 1968.
8-game Series—96—Pittsburgh N.L., vs. Boston A.L., 1903.
                       Cincinnati N.L., vs. Chicago A.L., 1919.

Fewest Assists, Series, Both Clubs

4-game Series— 64—St. Louis N.L., 36, New York A.L., 28, 1928.
5-game Series— 84—New York A.L., 44, Brooklyn N.L., 40, 1949.
6-game Series— 96—St. Louis N.L., 55, Philadelphia A.L., 41, 1930.
7-game Series—120—Detroit A.L., 72, St. Louis N.L., 48, 1968.
8-game Series—198—Boston A.L., 102, Pittsburgh N.L., 96, 1903.

Most Errors, Total Series, One Club

140—New York A.L., 33 Series, 187 games.

Most Errors, Series, One Club

4-game Series— 8—New York A.L., vs. Chicago N.L., 1932.
5-game Series—13—Brooklyn N.L., vs. Boston A.L., 1916.
6-game Series—16—New York N.L., vs. Philadelphia A.L., 1911.
7-game Series—19—Detroit A.L., vs. Pittsburgh N.L., 1909.
8-game Series—18—Pittsburgh N.L., vs. Boston A.L., 1903.

Most Errors, Series, Both Clubs

4-game Series—14—New York A.L., 8, Chicago N.L., 6, 1932.
5-game Series—23—Chicago N.L., 12, Philadelphia A.L., 11, 1910.
6-game Series—27—New York N.L., 16, Philadelphia A.L., 11, 1911.
7-game Series—34—Detroit A.L., 19, Pittsburgh N.L., 15, 1909.
8-game Series—32—Pittsburgh N.L., 18, Boston A.L., 14, 1903.

Fewest Errors, Series, One Club

4-game Series—0—Baltimore A.L., vs. Los Angeles N.L., 1966.
5-game Series—0—New York A.L., vs. New York N.L., 1937.
6-game Series—1—Boston A.L., vs. Chicago N.L., 1918.
                 St. Louis N.L., vs. St. Louis A.L., 1944.
                 New York A.L., vs. Brooklyn N.L., 1953.
                 Los Angeles N.L., vs. New York A.L., 1977.
7-game Series—2—Philadelphia A.L., vs. St. Louis N.L., 1931.
                 New York A.L., vs. Brooklyn N.L., 1955.
                 Brooklyn N.L., vs. New York A.L., 1956.
                 St. Louis N.L., vs. Detroit A.L., 1968.
                 Cincinnati N.L., vs. Boston A.L., 1975.
8-game Series—5—New York N.L., vs. New York A.L., 1921.

Fewest Errors, Series, Both Clubs

4-game Series— 4—Los Angeles N.L., 3, vs. New York A.L., 1, 1963.
5-game Series— 6—Brooklyn N.L., 4, New York A.L., 2, 1941.
                      Baltimore A.L., 4, New York N.L., 2, 1969.
6-game Series— 4—New York A.L., 3, Los Angeles N.L., 1, 1977.
7-game Series— 6—St. Louis N.L., 4, Philadelphia A.L., 2, 1931.
8-game Series—11—New York A.L., 6, New York N.L., 5, 1921.

Most Errorless Games, Total Series, One Club

89—New York A.L., 33 Series, 187 games.

Most Errorless Games, Series, One Club

4-game Series—4—Baltimore A.L., vs. Los Angeles N.L., 1966.
5-game Series—5—New York A.L., vs. New York N.L., 1937.
6-game Series—5—Boston A.L., vs. Chicago N.L., 1918.
                 St. Louis N.L., vs. St. Louis A.L., 1944.
                 New York A.L., vs. Brooklyn N.L., 1953.
                 Los Angeles N.L., vs. New York A.L., 1977.
7-game Series—5—Philadelphia A.L., vs. St. Louis N.L., 1931.
                 New York A.L., vs. Brooklyn N.L., 1955.
                 Brooklyn N.L., vs. New York A.L., 1956.
                 St. Louis N.L., vs. Detroit A.L., 1968.
                 Cincinnati N.L., vs. Boston A.L., 1975.
8-game Series—5—New York N.L., vs. New York A.L., 1921.

Fewest Errorless Games, Series, One Club

4-game Series—0—Held by many clubs.
5-game Series—0—Held by many clubs.

6-game Series—0—Held by many clubs.
7-game Series—0—St. Louis N.L., vs. Detroit A.L., 1934.
   New York N.L., vs. Oakland A.L., 1973.
8-game Series—0—New York N.L., vs. Boston A.L., 1912.

Most Consecutive Errorless Games, Total Series, One Club
   7—Philadelphia A.L., vs. St. Louis N.L., October 6, 7, 1930; October 1, 2, 5, 6, 7, 1931.

Most Consecutive Errorless Games, Series, One Club
   5—Philadelphia A.L., vs. St. Louis N.L., October 1, 2, 5, 6, 7, 1931 (first 5 games).
   New York A.L., vs. New York N.L., October 6, 7, 8, 9, 10, 1937 (full Series).
   New York A.L., vs. Brooklyn N.L., September 29, 30, October 1, 2, 3, 1955.

Most Errorless Games, Series, Both Clubs
4-game Series—7—Baltimore A.L., 4, Los Angeles N.L., 3, 1966.
5-game Series—7—New York A.L., 5, New York N.L., 2, 1937.
6-game Series—9—Los Angeles N.L., 5, New York A.L., 4, 1977.
7-game Series—9—Philadelphia A.L., 5, St. Louis N.L., 4, 1931.
8-game Series—8—New York N.L., 5, New York A.L., 3, 1921.

Most Double Plays, Total Series, One Club
   163—New York A.L., 33 Series, 187 games.

Most Double Plays, Series, One Club
4-game Series— 7—Chicago N.L., vs. New York A.L., 1932.
   New York A.L., vs. Los Angeles N.L., 1963.
5-game Series— 7—New York A.L., vs. New York N.L., 1922.
   New York A.L., vs. Brooklyn N.L., 1941.
   Cincinnati N.L., vs. New York A.L., 1961.
6-game Series—10—New York A.L., vs. New York N.L., 1951.
7-game Series—12—Brooklyn N.L., vs. New York A.L., 1955.
8-game Series— 9—Chicago A.L., vs. Cincinnati N.L., 1919.

Most Double Plays, Series, Both Clubs
4-game Series—10—New York A.L., 6, Cincinnati N.L., 4, 1976.
   Boston N.L., 4, Philadelphia A.L., 4, 1914.
   New York A.L., 7, Los Angeles N.L., 1, 1963.
   Baltimore A.L., 4, Los Angeles N.L., 4, 1966.
5-game Series—12—New York A.L., 7, Brooklyn N.L., 5, 1941.
6-game Series—16—Philadelphia N.L., 8, Kansas City A.L., 8, 1980.
7-game Series—19—Brooklyn N.L., 12, New York A.L., 7, 1955.
8-game Series—16—Chicago A.L., 9, Cincinnati N.L., 7, 1919.

Fewest Double Plays, Series, One Club
4-game Series—1—New York A.L., vs. Chicago N.L., 1932.
   Cincinnati N.L., vs. New York A.L., 1939.
   Philadelphia N.L., vs. New York A.L., 1950.
   Los Angeles N.L., vs. New York A.L., 1963.
5-game Series—0—New York N.L., vs. Baltimore A.L., 1969.
6-game Series—2—Chicago A.L., vs. Chicago N.L., 1906.
   New York N.L., vs. Philadelphia A.L., 1911.
   Philadelphia A.L., vs. New York N.L., 1911.
   Philadelphia A.L., vs. St. Louis N.L., 1930.
   New York A.L., vs. New York N.L., 1936.
   Chicago A.L., vs. Los Angeles N.L., 1959.
   New York A.L., vs. Los Angeles N.L., 1977, 1981.
7-game Series—2—St. Louis N.L., vs. Detroit A.L., 1934.
   Baltimore A.L., vs. Pittsburgh N.L., 1971.
8-game Series—4—New York N.L., vs. Boston A.L., 1912.

Fewest Double Plays, Series, Both Clubs
4-game Series—4—New York N.L., 2, Cleveland A.L., 2, 1954.
5-game Series—4—New York N.L., 2, Philadelphia A.L., 2, 1905.
   Baltimore A.L., 4, New York N.L., 0, 1969.
6-game Series—4—Philadelphia A.L., 2, New York N.L., 2, 1911.
7-game Series—7—Detroit A.L., 4, Pittsburgh N.L., 3, 1909.
   Boston A.L., 4, St. Louis N.L., 3, 1967.
8-game Series—9—Boston A.L., 5, New York N.L., 4, 1912.

Most Triple Plays, Series, One Club
   1—Cleveland A.L., vs. Brooklyn N.L., 1920.

Most Passed Balls, Total Series, One Club
   13—New York A.L., 33 series, 187 games.

Most Passed Balls, Series, One Club
   3—Chicago N.L., vs. Chicago A.L., 1906.
   Pittsburgh N.L., vs. New York A.L., 1960.
   New York A.L., vs. St. Louis N.L., 1964.

Most Passed Balls, Series, Both Clubs
  4—Chicago N.L., 3, Chicago A.L., 1, 1906 (6-game Series).
  New York A.L., 2, Brooklyn N.L., 2, 1947 (7-game Series).

Fewest Passed Balls, Series, One Club
  0—Held by many clubs in Series of all lengths.

Fewest Passed Balls, Series, Both Clubs
  0—Held by many clubs in Series of all lengths.

INDIVIDUAL PITCHING RECORDS

Most Series Played
  11—Ford, Edward C., New York A.L., 1950, 1953, 1955, 1956, 1957, 1958, 1960, 1961, 1962, 1963, 1964 (22 games).

Most Games, Pitched, Series
  4-game Series—3—French, Lawrence H., Chicago N.L., 1938, 3⅓ innings.
        Konstanty, C. James, Philadelphia N.L., 1950, 15 innings.
        Mossi, Donald L., Cleveland A.L., 1954, 4 innings.
        Reniff, Harold E., New York A.L., 1963, 3 innings.
  5-game Series—5—Marshall, Michael G., Los Angeles N.L., 1974, 9 innings.
  6-game Series—6—Quisenberry, Daniel R., Kansas City A.L., 1980, 10⅓ innings.
  7-game Series—7—Knowles, Darold D., Oakland A.L., 1973, 6⅓ innings.
  8-game Series—5—Phillippe, Charles L., Pittsburgh N.L., 1903, 44 innings.

Most Games Pitched, Total Series
  22—Ford, Edward C., New York A.L., 1950, 1953, 1955, 1956, 1957, 1958, 1960, 1961, 1962, 1963, 1964 (11 Series).

Most Complete Games Pitched, Total Series
  10—Mathewson, Christopher, New York N.L., 1905, 1911, 1912, 1913.

Most Consecutive Games Pitched, Series
  7—Knowles, Darold D., Oakland A.L., October 13, 14, 16, 17, 18, 20, 21, 1973.

Most Consecutive Games Started, Series
  2—Phillippe, Charles L., Pittsburgh N.L., October 3, 6, 1903.
    Phillippe, Charles L., Pittsburgh N.L., October 10, 13, 1903.
    Coombs, John W., Philadelphia A.L., October 18, 20, 1910.
    Mathewson, Christopher, New York N.L., October 17, 24, 1911.
    Earnshaw, George L., Philadelphia A.L., October 9, 11, 1929.
    Earnshaw, George L., Philadelphia A.L., October 6, 8, 1930.

Most Consecutive Complete Games Pitched, Total Series
  8—Gibson, Robert, St. Louis N.L., 1964 (2), 1967 (3), 1968 (3), (won 7, lost 1).

Most Games Started, Total Series
  22—Ford, Edward C., New York A.L., 1950, 1953, 1955, 1956, 1957, 1958, 1960, 1961, 1962, 1963, 1964 (11 Series).

Most Opening Games Started, Total Series
  8—Ford, Edward C., New York A.L., 1955, 1956, 1957, 1958, 1961, 1962, 1963, 1964 (won 4, lost 3, no decision 1).

Most Opening Games Won, Total Series
  5—Ruffing, Charles H., New York A.L., 1932, 1938, 1939, 1941, 1942, four complete (lost complete game opener in 1936).

Most Games Started, Series
  4-game Series—2—Held by 12 pitchers. Last pitcher—McNally, David A., Baltimore A.L., 1966 (1 complete).
  5-game Series—3—Mathewson, Christopher, New York N.L., 1905 (3 complete).
        Coombs, John W., Philadelphia A.L., 1910 (3 complete).
  6-game Series—3—Held by 9 pitchers. Last pitcher—Wynn, Early, Chicago A.L., 1959 (0 complete).
  7-game Series—3—37 times—19 in A.L., 18 in N.L.—Held by 33 pitchers. Last two pitchers—Tiant, Luis C., Boston A.L., 1975; Gullett, Donald E., Cincinnati N.L., 1975.
  8-game Series—5—Phillippe, Charles L., Pittsburgh N.L., 1903 (5 complete).

Most Series Three Games Started, Total Series
  3—Gibson, Robert, St. Louis N.L., 1964, 1967, 1968.

Most Games, Total Series, Relief Pitcher
  16—Fingers, Roland G., Oakland A.L., 1972 (6), 1973 (6), 1974 (4), 33⅓ innings.

Most Series, One or More Games as Relief Pitcher
  6—Murphy, John J., New York A.L., 1936 (1), 1937 (1), 1938 (1), 1939 (1), 1941 (2), 1943 (2), 8 games as relief pitcher.

Most Games Pitched, Series, Relief Pitcher

4-game Series—3—French, Lawrence H., Chicago N.L., 1938, 3⅓ innings.
                    Mossi, Donald L., Cleveland A.L., 1954, 4 innings.
                    Reniff, Harold E., New York A.L., 1963, 3 innings.
5-game Series—5—Marshall, Michael G., Los Angeles N.L., 1974, 9 innings.
6-game Series—6—Quisenberry, Daniel R., Kansas City A.L., 1980, 10⅓ innings.
7-game Series—7—Knowles, Darold D., Oakland A.L., 1973, 6⅓ innings.
8-game Series—3—Barnes, Jesse L., New York N.L., 1921, 16⅓ innings.

Most Games Finished, Series

4-game Series—3—Reniff, Harold E., New York A.L., 1963, 3 innings.
5-game Series—5—Marshall, Michael G., Los Angeles N.L., 1974, 9 innings.
6-game Series—6—Quisenberry, Daniel R., Kansas City A.L., 1980, 10⅓ innings.
7-game Series—6—Casey, Hugh T., Brooklyn N.L., 1947, 10⅓ innings.
8-game Series—3—Barnes, Jesse L., New York N.L., 1921, 16⅓ innings.

Most Games Won, Total Series

10—Ford, Edward C., New York A.L., 1950, 1953, 1955, 1956, 1957, 1958, 1960, 1961, 1962, 1963, 1964 (won 10, lost 8), 11 Series, 22 games.

Most Games Won, Total Series, No Defeats

6—Gomez, Vernon, New York A.L., 1932, 1936, 1937, 1938.

Most Games Won, Series

4-game Series—2—Rudolph, Richard, Boston N.L., 1914, (complete).
                    James, William L., Boston N.L., 1914, (one complete).
                    Hoyt, Waite C., New York A.L., 1928, (complete).
                    Ruffing, Charles H., New York A.L., 1938, (complete).
                    Koufax, Sanford, Los Angeles N.L., 1963, (complete).
5-game Series—3—Mathewson, Christopher, New York N.L., 1905, (complete).
                    Coombs, John W., Philadelphia A.L., 1910, (complete).
6-game Series—3—Faber, Urban C., Chicago A.L., 1917, (two complete).
7-game Series—3—Adams, Charles B., Pittsburgh N.L., 1909, (complete).
                    Coveleski, Stanley, Cleveland A.L., 1920, (complete).
                    Brecheen, Harry D., St. Louis N.L., 1946, (two complete).
                    Burdette, S. Lewis, Milwaukee N.L., 1957, (complete).
                    Gibson, Robert, St. Louis N.L., 1967, (complete).
                    Lolich, Michael S., Detroit A.L., 1968, (complete).
8-game Series—3—Dinneen, William H., Boston, A.L., 1903, (complete).
                    Phillippe, Charles L., Pittsburgh N.L., 1903, (complete).
                    Wood, Joseph, Boston A.L., 1912, (two complete).

Most Games Won, Series, Losing None

4-game Series—2—Rudolph, Richard, Boston N.L., 1914.
                    James, William L., Boston N.L., 1914.
                    Hoyt, Waite C., New York N.L., 1928.
                    Ruffing, Charles H., New York A.L., 1938.
                    Koufax, Sanford, Los Angeles N.L., 1963.
5-game Series—3—Mathewson, Christopher, New York N.L., 1905.
                    Coombs, John W., Philadelphia A.L., 1910.
6-game Series—2—Held by many pitchers. Last pitcher—Carlton, Steven N., Philadelphia N.L., 1980.
7-game Series—3—Adams, Charles B., Pittsburgh N.L., 1909.
                    Coveleski, Stanley, Cleveland A.L., 1920.
                    Brecheen, Harry D., St. Louis N.L., 1946.
                    Burdette, S. Lewis, Milwaukee N.L., 1957.
                    Gibson, Robert, St. Louis N.L., 1967.
                    Lolich, Michael S., Detroit A.L., 1968.
8-game Series—2—Marquard, Richard W., New York N.L., 1912.
                    Eller, Horace O., Cincinnati N.L., 1919.
                    Kerr, Richard, Chicago A.L., 1919.
                    Barnes, Jesse L., New York N.L., 1921.

Most Games Won, Series, as Relief Pitcher

2—Barnes, Jesse L., New York N.L., 1921 (8-game Series).
  Casey, T. Hugh, Brooklyn N.L., 1947 (7-game Series).
  Sherry, Lawrence, Los Angeles N.L., 1959 (6-game Series).
  Grimsley, Ross A., Cincinnati N.L., 1972 (6-game Series).
  Eastwick, Rawlins J., Cincinnati N.L., 1975 (7-game Series).

Pitchers Winning Four or More Games, Total Series

Pitcher and Club	Years	W.	L.
Ford, Edward C., New York A.L.	1950-3-5-6-7-8-60-1-2-3-4	10	8
Ruffing, Charles H., New York A.L.	1932-36-37-38-39-41-42	7	2
Reynolds, Allie P., New York A.L.	1947-49-50-51-52-53	7	2
Gibson, Robert, St. Louis N.L.	1964-67-68	7	2
Gomez, Vernon, New York A.L.	1932-36-37-38	6	0
Bender, Charles A., Philadelphia A.L.	1905-10-11-13-14	6	4

WORLD SERIES RECORDS

Pitcher and Club	Years	W.	L.
Hoyt, Waite C., New York-Philadelphia A.L.	1921-22-26-27-28-31	6	4
Coombs, John W., Phil. A.L.-Brooklyn N.L.	1910-11-16	5	0
Pennock, Herbert J., New York A.L.	1923-26-27	5	0
Raschi, Victor J., New York A.L.	1949-50-51-52-53	5	3
Hunter, James A., Oakland-New York A.L.	1972-73-74-76-77-78	5	3
Brown, Mordecai P., Chicago N.L.	1906-07-08-10	5	4
Mathewson, Christopher, New York N.L.	1905-11-12-13	5	5
Pearson, Monte M., New York A.L.	1936-37-38-39	4	0
Bridges, Thomas D., Detroit A.L.	1934-35-40	4	1
Brecheen, Harry, St. Louis N.L.	1943-44-46	4	1
Lopat, Edmund W., New York A.L.	1949-51-52-53	4	1
Podres, John J., Brooklyn-Los Ang. N.L.	1953-55-59-63	4	1
Holtzman, Kenneth D., Oakland A.L.	1972-73-74	4	1
Grove, Robert M., Philadelphia A.L.	1930-31	4	2
Hubbell, Carl O., New York N.L.	1933-36-37	4	2
Burdette, S. Lewis, Milwaukee N.L.	1957-58	4	2
Larsen, Don J., N.Y. A.L.-S.F. N.L.	1955-56-57-58-62	4	2
McNally, David A., Baltimore A.L.	1966-69-70-71	4	2
Palmer, James A., Baltimore A.L.	1966-69-70-71-79-83	4	2
Koufax, Sanford, Los Angeles N.L.	1959-63-65-66	4	3
Earnshaw, George L., Philadelphia A.L.	1929-30-31	4	3
Spahn, Warren E., Boston N.L.-Milw. N.L.	1948-57-58	4	3
Turley, Robert L., New York A.L.	1955-56-57-58-60	4	3
Nehf, Arthur N., New York N.L.	1921-22-23-24	4	4

Most Saves, Total Series, Since 1969
    6—Fingers, Roland G., Oakland A.L., 1972 (2), 1973 (2), 1974 (2).

Most Saves, Series, Since 1969
    4-game Series—2—McEnaney, William H., Cincinnati N.L., 1976.
    5-game Series—2—Fingers, Roland G., Oakland A.L., 1974.
                    Martinez, Felix A., Baltimore A.L., 1983.
                    Hernandez, Guillermo, Detroit A.L., 1984.
    6-game Series—2—McGraw, Frank E., Philadelphia N.L., 1980.
                    Gossage, Richard M., New York A.L., 1981.
    7-game Series—3—Tekulve, Kenton C., Pittsburgh N.L., 1979.

Most Games Lost, Total Series, No Victories
    4—Summers, O. Edgar, Detroit A.L., 1908 (2), 1909 (2).
       Sherdel, William H., St. Louis N.L., 1926 (2), 1928 (2).
       Newcombe, Donald, Brooklyn N.L., 1949 (2), 1955 (1), 1956 (1).

Most Consecutive Games Lost, Total Series
    5—Bush, Leslie A., Philadelphia A.L., Boston A.L., New York A.L., 1914 (1), 1918 (1), 1922 (2), 1923 (1).

Most Games Lost, Series
    4-game Series—2—Sherdel, William H., St. Louis N.L., 1928.
                    Lee, William C., Jr., Chicago N.L., 1938.
                    Walters, William H., Cincinnati N.L., 1939.
                    Lemon, Robert G., Cleveland A.L., 1954.
                    Ford, Edward C., New York A.L., 1963.
                    Drysdale, Donald S., Los Angeles N.L., 1966.
    5-game Series—2—Held by many pitchers. Last pitcher—Hudson, Charles L., Philadelphia N.L., 1983.
    6-game Series—3—Frazier, George A., New York A.L., 1981.
    7-game Series—2—Held by many pitchers. Last pitchers—Forsch, Robert H., St. Louis N.L., 1982; McClure, Robert C., Milwaukee A.L., 1982.
    8-game Series—3—Williams, Claude P., Chicago A.L., 1919.

Most Games Lost, Total Series
    8—Ford, Edward C., New York A.L., 1950, 1953, 1955, 1956, 1957, 1958, 1960, 1961, 1962, 1963, 1964 (won 10, lost 8), 11 Series, 22 games.

Most Complete Games, Series
    4-game Series—2—Rudolph, Richard, Boston N.L., 1914.
                    Hoyt, Waite C., New York A.L., 1928.
                    Ruffing, Charles H., New York A.L., 1938.
                    Koufax, Sanford, Los Angeles N.L., 1963.
    5-game Series—3—Mathewson, Christopher, New York N.L., 1905.
                    Coombs, John W., Philadelphia A.L., 1910.
    6-game Series—3—Bender, Charles A., Philadelphia A.L., 1911.
                    Vaughn, James L., Chicago N.L., 1918.
    7-game Series—3—Adams, Charles B., Pittsburgh N.L., 1909.
                    Mullin, George, Detroit A.L., 1909.
                    Coveleski, Stanley, Cleveland A.L., 1920.
                    Johnson, Walter P., Washington A.L., 1925.

Newsom, Louis N., Detroit A.L., 1940.
Burdette, S. Lewis, Milwaukee N.L., 1957.
Gibson, Robert, St. Louis N.L., 1967.
Gibson, Robert, St. Louis N.L., 1968.
Lolich, Michael S., Detroit A.L., 1968.
8-game Series—5—Phillippe, Charles L., Pittsburgh N.L., 1903.

Most Innings Pitched, Total Series
146—Ford, Edward C., New York A.L., 1950, 1953, 1955, 1956, 1957, 1958, 1960, 1961, 1962, 1963, 1964; 11 Series, 22 games.

Most Innings Pitched, Series
4-game Series—18—Rudolph, Richard, Boston N.L., 1914.
Hoyt, Waite C., New York A.L., 1928.
Ruffing, Charles H., New York A.L., 1938.
Koufax, Sanford, Los Angeles N.L., 1963.
5-game Series—27—Mathewson, Christopher, New York N.L., 1905.
Coombs, John W., Philadelphia A.L., 1910.
6-game Series—27—Mathewson, Christopher, New York N.L., 1911.
Faber, Urban C., Chicago A.L., 1917.
Vaughn, James L., Chicago N.L., 1918.
7-game Series—32—Mullin, George, Detroit A.L., 1909.
8-game Series—44—Phillippe, Charles L., Pittsburgh N.L., 1903.

Most Innings Pitched, Game
14 —Ruth, George H., Boston A.L., October 9, 1916, complete game, won 2 to 1.
13⅓—Smith, Sherrod M., Brooklyn N.L., October 9, 1916, complete game, lost 2 to 1.

Most Consecutive Games Won, Total Series
7—Gibson, Robert, St. Louis N.L., October 12, 15, 1964; October 4, 8, 12, 1967; October 2, 6, 1968 (7 complete).
6—Gomez, Vernon, New York A.L., September 29, 1932; October 2, 6, 1936; October 6, 10, 1937; October 6, 1938 (four complete, two incomplete).
Ruffing, Charles H., New York A.L., October 7, 1937; October 5, 9, 1938; October 4, 1939; October 4, 1941; September 30, 1942 (five complete, one incomplete).

Most Consecutive Complete Games Won, Total Series
7—Gibson, Robert, St. Louis N.L., October 12, 15, 1964; October 4, 8, 12, 1967; October 2, 6, 1968.
5—Ruffing, Charles H., New York A.L., October 7, 1937; October 5, 9, 1938; October 4, 1939; October 4, 1941.

Most Runs Allowed, Series
4-game Series—11—Alexander, Grover C., St. Louis N.L., 1928.
Lemon, Robert G., Cleveland A.L., 1954.
5-game Series—16—Brown, Mordecai P., Chicago N.L., 1910.
6-game Series—10—Sallee, Harry F., New York N.L., 1917.
Ruffing, Charles H., New York A.L., 1936.
Gullett, Donald E., New York A.L., 1977.
Sutton, Donald H., Los Angeles N.L., 1978.
7-game Series—17—Burdette, S. Lewis, Milwaukee N.L., 1958.
8-game Series—19—Phillippe, Charles L., Pittsburgh N.L., 1903.

Most Runs Allowed, Game, Nine Innings
9—Coakley, Andrew J., Philadelphia A.L., October 12, 1905.
Brown, Mordecai P., Chicago N.L., October 18, 1910.
Johnson, Walter P., Washington A.L., October 15, 1925.

Most Earned Runs Allowed, Game, Nine Innings
7—Brown, Mordecai P., Chicago N.L., October 18, 1910.

Most Runs Allowed, Inning
7—Wiltse, George L., New York N.L., October 26, 1911, seventh inning.
Hubbell, Carl O., New York N.L., October 6, 1937, sixth inning.

Most Earned Runs Allowed, Inning
6—Wiltse, George L., New York N.L., October 26, 1911, seventh inning.

Most Hits Allowed, Series
4-game Series—17—Ruffing, Charles H., New York A.L., 1938.
5-game Series—23—Coombs, John W., Philadelphia A.L., 1910.
Brown, Mordecai P., Chicago N.L., 1910.
6-game Series—25—Mathewson, Christopher, New York N.L., 1911.
7-game Series—30—Johnson, Walter P., Washington A.L., 1924.
8-game Series—38—Phillippe, Charles L., Pittsburgh N.L., 1903.

Most Hits Allowed, Game, Nine Innings
15—Johnson, Walter P., Washington A.L., October 15, 1925.

Most Hits Allowed, Inning
7—Wood, Joseph, Boston A.L., October 15, 1912, first inning.

WORLD SERIES RECORDS

Most Consecutive Hits Allowed, Inning (Consecutive Plate Appearances)
  6—Summers, Oren E., Detroit A.L., October 10, 1908, ninth inning, six singles.

Fewest Hits Allowed, Game, Nine Innings
  0—Larsen, Don J., New York A.L., October 8, 1956 (perfect game).

One and Two-Hit Games, Nine Innings (Pitching Complete Game)
  1—Reulbach, Edward M., Chicago N.L., October 10, 1906 (none out in seventh).
  Passeau, Claude W., Chicago N.L., October 5, 1945 (two out in second).
  Bevens, Floyd, New York A.L., October 3, 1947 (two out in ninth).
  Lonborg, James R., Boston A.L., October 5, 1967 (two out in eighth).
  2—Walsh, Edward A., Chicago A.L., October 11, 1906.
  Brown, Mordecai P., Chicago N.L., October 12, 1906.
  Plank, Edward S., Philadelphia A.L., October 11, 1913.
  James, William L., Boston N.L., October 10, 1914.
  Hoyt, Waite C., New York A.L., October 6, 1921.
  Grimes, Burleigh A., St. Louis N.L., October 5, 1931.
  Earnshaw, George L., Philadelphia A.L., October 6, 1931.
  Pearson, Monte M., New York A.L., October 5, 1939.
  Cooper, Morton C., St. Louis N.L., October 4, 1944.
  Feller, Robert W., Cleveland A.L., October 6, 1948.
  Reynolds, Allie, New York A.L., October 5, 1949.
  Raschi, Victor A. J., New York A.L., October 4, 1950.
  Spahn, Warren E., Milwaukee N.L., October 5, 1958.
  Ford, Edward C., New York A.L., October 4, 1961.
  Briles, Nelson K., Pittsburgh N.L., October 14, 1971.

Fewest Hits Allowed, Two Consecutive Complete Games
  4—Lonborg, James R., Boston A.L., October 5 (1), October 9 (3), 1967.

Fewest Hits Allowed, Three Consecutive Complete Games
  14—Mathewson, Christopher New York N.L., October 5 (4), October 12 (4), October 14 (6), 1905.
  Gibson, Robert, St. Louis N.L., October 4 (6), October 8 (5), October 12 (3), 1967.

Most Consecutive Hitless Innings, Game
  9—Larsen, Don J., New York A.L., October 8, 1956.

Most Consecutive Hitless Innings, Total Series
  11⅓—Larsen, Don J., New York A.L., October 8, 1956 (9 innings), October 5, 1957 (2⅓ innings).

Most Two-Base Hits Allowed, Game
  8—Johnson, Walter P., Washington A.L., October 15, 1925.

Most Three-Base Hits Allowed, Game
  5—Phillippe, Charles L., Pittsburgh N.L., October 10, 1903.

Most Home Runs Allowed, Game
  4—Root, Charles H., Chicago N.L., October 1, 1932.
  Thompson, Eugene E., Jr., Cincinnati N.L., October 7, 1939.
  Hughes, Richard H., St. Louis N.L., October 11, 1967.

Most Home Runs Allowed, Inning
  3—Hughes, Richard H., St. Louis N.L., October 11, 1967, fourth inning.

Most Consecutive Home Runs Allowed, Inning (9 times)
  2—Yde, Emil O., Pittsburgh N.L., October 11, 1925, third inning.
  Sherdel, William H., St. Louis N.L., October 9, 1928, seventh inning.
  Root, Charles H., Chicago N.L., October 1, 1932, fifth inning.
  Simmons, Curtis T., St. Louis N.L., October 14, 1964, sixth inning.
  Drysdale, Donald S., Los Angeles N.L., October 5, 1966, first inning.
  Hughes, Richard H., St. Louis N.L., October 11, 1967, fourth inning.
  Wise, Richard C., Boston A.L., October 14, 1975, fifth inning.
  Sutton, Donald H., Los Angeles N.L., October 16, 1977, eighth inning.
  Guidry, Ronald A., New York A.L., October 25, 1981, seventh inning.

Most Home Runs Allowed, Series
  4-game Series—4—Sherdel, William H., St. Louis N.L., 1928.
  Root, Charles H., Chicago N.L., 1932.
  Thompson, Eugene E., Cincinnati N.L., 1939.
  5-game Series—4—Nolan, Gary L., Cincinnati N.L., 1970.
  Hudson, Charles L., Philadelphia N.L., 1983.
  6-game Series—4—Reynolds, Allie P., New York A.L., 1953.
  7-game Series—5—Burdette, S. Lewis, Milwaukee N.L., 1958.
  Hughes, Richard H., St. Louis N.L., 1967.
  8-game Series—2—Adams, Charles B., Pittsburgh N.L., 1909.
  Harper, Harry C., New York A.L., 1921.

Most Home Runs Allowed, Total Series
  9—Hunter, James A., Oakland A.L., New York A.L., 1972, 1973, 1974, 1976, 1977, 1978; 6 Series, 12 games.

WORLD SERIES RECORDS

Most Long Hits Allowed, Game
   9—Johnson, Walter P., Washington A.L., October 15, 1925.

Most Total Bases Allowed, Game
   25—Johnson, Walter P., Washington A.L., October 15, 1925.

Most Bases on Balls, Series
   4-game Series— 8—Lemon, Robert G., Cleveland A.L., 1954.
   5-game Series—14—Coombs, John W., Philadelphia A.L., 1910.
   6-game Series—11—Tyler, George A., Chicago N.L., 1918.
                      Gomez, Vernon, New York A.L., 1936.
                      Reynolds, Allie P., New York A.L., 1951.
   7-game Series—11—Johnson, Walter P., Washington A.L., 1924.
                      Bevens, Floyd C., New York A.L., 1947.
   8-game Series—13—Nehf, Arthur N., New York N.L., 1921.

Most Bases on Balls, Total Series
   34—Ford, Edward C., New York A.L., 1950, 1953, 1955, 1956, 1957, 1958, 1960, 1961, 1962, 1963, 1964; 11 Series, 22 games.

Most Bases on Balls, Game
   10—Bevens, Floyd C., New York A.L., October 3, 1947.

Most Bases on Balls, Inning
   4—Donovan, William E., Detroit A.L., October 16, 1909, second inning.
      Reinhart, Arthur C., St. Louis N.L., October 6, 1926, fifth inning (3 consecutive).
      Bush, Guy T., Chicago N.L., September 28, 1932, sixth inning (3 consecutive).
      Gullett, Donald E., Cincinnati N.L., October 22, 1975, night game, third inning (two BB with bases full).

Most Consecutive Bases on Balls, Inning
   3—Shawkey, J. Robert, New York A.L., October 7, 1921, fourth inning, (two BB with bases full).
      Reinhart, Arthur C., St. Louis N.L., October 6, 1926, fifth inning, (one BB with bases full).
      Bush, Guy T., Chicago N.L., September 28, 1932, sixth inning.
      Hoerner, Joseph W., St. Louis N.L., October 3, 1968, ninth inning, (two BB with bases full).

Longest Game Without Allowing Base on Balls
   12 innings—Rowe, Lynwood T., Detroit A.L., October 4, 1934.

Most Innings Pitched, Series, Without Allowing Base on Balls
   26—Mays, Carl W., New York A.L., 1921.

Most Strikeouts, Total Series
   94—Ford, Edward C., New York A.L., 1950, 1953, 1955, 1956, 1957, 1958, 1960, 1961, 1962, 1963, 1964; 11 Series, 22 games.

Most Strikeouts, Series
   4-game Series—23—Koufax, Sanford, Los Angeles N.L., 1963.
   5-game Series—18—Mathewson, Christopher, New York N.L., 1905.
   6-game Series—20—Bender, Charles A., Philadelphia A.L., 1911.
   7-game Series—35—Gibson, Robert, St. Louis N.L., 1968.
   8-game Series—28—Dinneen, William H., Boston A.L., 1903.

Most Strikeouts, Inning
   4—Overall, Orval, Chicago N.L., October 14, 1908, first inning.

Most Strikeouts, Game
   17—Gibson, Robert, St. Louis N.L., October 2, 1968.

Most Games, Ten or More Strikeouts, Total Series
   5—Gibson, Robert, St. Louis N.L., 1964 (1), 1967 (2), 1968 (2).

Ten or More Strikeouts in Game by Pitcher in World Series

Date	Pitcher and Club	SO.	Score
Oct. 1, 1903	Phillippe, Pittsburgh N.L., vs. Boston A.L.	10	7-3
Oct. 2, 1903	Dinneen, Boston A.L., vs. Pittsburgh N.L.	11	3-0
Oct. 11, 1906	Walsh, Chicago A.L., vs. Chicago N.L.	12	3-0
Oct. 8, 1907	Donovan, Detroit A.L., vs. Chicago N.L. (12 inn.)	12	3-3
Oct. 14, 1908	Overall, Chicago N.L., vs. Detroit A.L.	10	2-0
Oct. 12, 1909	Mullin, Detroit A.L., vs. Pittsburgh N.L.	10	5-0
Oct. 14, 1911	Bender, Phila. A.L., vs. New York N.L. (8 inn.)	11	1-2
Oct. 8, 1912	Wood, Boston A.L., vs. New York N.L.	11	4-3
Oct. 11, 1921	Barnes, New York N.L., vs. New York A.L.	10	8-5
Oct. 4, 1924	Johnson, Wash. A.L., vs. New York N.L. (12 inn.)	12	3-4
Oct. 7, 1925	Johnson, Washington A.L., vs. Pittsburgh N.L.	10	4-1
Oct. 3, 1926	Alexander, St. Louis N.L., vs. New York A.L.	10	6-2
Oct. 8, 1929	Ehmke, Philadelphia A.L., vs. Chicago N.L.	13	3-1
Oct. 11, 1929	Earnshaw, Philadelphia A.L., vs. Chicago N.L.	10	1-3
Sept. 28, 1932	Ruffing, New York A.L., vs. Chicago N.L.	10	12-6

WORLD SERIES RECORDS

Date	Pitcher and Club	SO.	Score
Oct. 3, 1933	Hubbell, New York N.L., vs. Washington A.L.	10	4-2
Oct. 5, 1936	Schumacher, N.Y. N.L., vs. N.Y. A.L. (10 inn.)	10	5-4
Oct. 6, 1944	Kramer, St. Louis A.L., vs. St. Louis N.L.	10	6-2
Oct. 8, 1944	Galehouse, St. Louis A.L., vs. St. Louis N.L.	10	0-2
Oct. 8, 1944	Cooper, St. Louis N.L., vs. St. Louis A.L.	12	2-0
Oct. 10, 1945	Newhouser, Detroit A.L., vs. Chicago N.L.	10	9-3
Oct. 5, 1949	Newcombe, Brook. N.L., vs. N.Y. A.L. (8 inn.)	11	0-1
Oct. 4, 1952	Reynolds, New York A.L., vs. Brooklyn N.L.	10	2-0
Oct. 2, 1953	Erskine, Brooklyn N.L., vs. New York A.L.	14	3-2
Oct. 3, 1956	Maglie, Brooklyn N.L., vs. New York A.L.	10	6-3
Oct. 9, 1956	Turley, New York A.L., vs. Brooklyn N.Ln.)	11	0-1
Oct. 6, 1958	Turley, New York A.L., vs. Milwaukee N.L.	10	7-0
Oct. 10, 1962	Sanford, San Francisco N.L., vs. New York A.L.	10	3-5
Oct. 2, 1963	Koufax, Los Angeles N.L., vs. New York A.L.	15	5-2
Oct. 12, 1964	Gibson, St. Louis N.L., vs. New York A.L. (10 inn.)	13	5-2
Oct. 10, 1965	Drysdale, Los Angeles N.L., vs. Minnesota A.L.	11	7-2
Oct. 11, 1965	Koufax, Los Angeles N.L., vs. Minnesota A.L.	10	7-0
Oct. 14, 1965	Koufax, Los Angeles N.L., vs. Minnesota A.L.	10	2-0
Oct. 5, 1966	Drabowsky, Baltimore A.L., vs. Los Angeles N.L.	11	5-2
Oct. 4, 1967	Gibson, St. Louis N.L., vs. Boston A.L.	10	2-1
Oct. 12, 1967	Gibson, St. Louis N.L., vs. Boston A.L.	10	7-2
Oct. 2, 1968	Gibson, St. Louis N.L., vs. Detroit A.L.	17	4-0
Oct. 6, 1968	Gibson, St. Louis N.L., vs. Detroit A.L.	10	10-1
Oct. 11, 1971	Palmer, Baltimore A.L., vs. Pittsburgh N.L.	10	11-3
Oct. 18, 1972	Odom, Oakland A.L., vs. Cincinnati N.L. (7 inn.)	11	0-1
Oct. 16, 1973	Seaver, New York N.L., vs. Oakland A.L. (8 inn.)	12	2-3
Oct. 15, 1980	Carlton, Phila. N.L., vs. Kansas City A.L. (8 inn.)	10	6-4

Most Strikeouts, Game, Losing Pitcher, Nine Inning Game
11—Bender, Charles A., Philadelphia A.L., October 14, 1911.
  Newcombe, Donald, Brooklyn N.L., October 5, 1949.
  Odom, Johnny L., Oakland A.L., October 18, 1972, pitched first 7 innings.

Most Strikeouts, Game, Losing Pitcher, 10 Inning Game
11—Turley, Robert L., New York A.L., October 9, 1956.

Most Strikeouts, Game, Losing Pitcher, 12 Inning Game
12—Johnson, Walter P., Washington A.L., October 4, 1924.

Most Strikeouts, Game, Relief Pitcher
11—Drabowsky, Myron W., Baltimore A.L., October 5, 1966, last six and two-thirds innings.

Most Consecutive Strikeouts, Game
6—Eller, Horace O., Cincinnati N.L., October 6, 1919; 3 in second inning, 3 in third inning.
  Drabowsky, Myron W., Baltimore A.L., October 5, 1966; 3 in fourth inning, 3 in fifth inning.

Most Consecutive Strikeouts, Start of Game
5—Cooper, Morton C., St. Louis N.L., October 11, 1943.
  Koufax, Sanford, Los Angeles N.L., October 2, 1963.

Most Innings, One or More Strikeouts, Nine-Inning Game
9—Walsh, Edward A., Chicago A.L., October 11, 1906 (12 strikeouts).
  Gibson, Robert, St. Louis N.L., October 2, 1968 (17 strikeouts).

Retiring Side on Three Pitched Balls
Mathewson, Christopher, New York N.L., October 9, 1912, eleventh inning, and October 16, 1912, fifth inning.
Walberg, George E., Philadelphia A.L., October 14, 1929, seventh inning.
Bonham, Ernest E., New York A.L., October 6, 1941, seventh inning.

Lowest Earned-Run Average, Series, 14 or More Innings
0.00—Mathewson, Christopher, New York N.L., 1905, 27 innings.
  Hoyt, Waite C., New York A.L., 1921, 27 innings.
  Hubbell, Carl O., New York N.L., 1933, 20 innings.
  Ford, Edward C., New York A.L., 1960, 18 innings.
  McGinnity, Joseph J., New York N.L., 1905, 17 innings.
  Mails, J. Walter, Cleveland A.L., 1920, 15⅔ innings.
  Benton, John C., New York N.L., 1917, 14 innings.
  Ford, Edward C., New York A.L., 1961, 14 innings.

Most Complete Shutouts Won, Series
3—Mathewson, Christopher, New York N.L., 1905 (consecutive, October 9, 12, 14).

Most Complete Shutouts Won, Total Series
4—Mathewson, Christopher, New York N.L., 1905 (3), 1913 (1).

Most Complete 1-0 Shutouts Won, Total Series
2—Nehf, Arthur N., New York N.L., October 13, 1921, October 12, 1923.

WORLD SERIES RECORDS

Most Shutouts Lost, Total Series
  3—Plank, Edward S., Philadelphia A.L., 1905 (2), 1914 (1).

Most 1-0 Shutouts Lost, Total Series
  2—Plank, Edward S., Philadelphia A.L., October 13, 1905, October 10, 1914.

Most Consecutive Scoreless Innings, Total Series
  33⅔—Ford, Edward C., New York A.L., October 8, 1960, 9 innings; October 12, 1960, 9 innings; October 4, 1961, 9 innings; October 8, 1961, 5 innings; October 4, 1962, 1⅔ innings.

Most Consecutive Scoreless Innings, Series
  27—Mathewson, Christopher, New York N.L., October 9, 12, 14, 1905.

Most Consecutive Innings, Game, No Player Reaching First Base
  9—Larsen, Don J., New York A.L., October 8, 1956 (perfect game).

Most Consecutive Innings, Series, No Player Reaching First Base
  9—Larsen, Don J., New York A.L., October 8, 1956.

Most Consecutive Innings, Total Series, No Player Reaching First Base
  11⅓—Larsen, Don J., New York A.L., October 8, 1956 (9 innings), October 5, 1957 (2⅓ innings).

Most Wild Pitches, Game
  2—Tesreau, Charles M., New York N.L., October 15, 1912.
  Pfeffer, Edward J., Brooklyn N.L., October 12, 1916.
  Shawkey, Robert J., New York A.L., October 5, 1922.
  Aldridge, Victor, Pittsburgh N.L., October 15, 1925.
  Miljus, John K., Pittsburgh N.L., October 8, 1927.
  Carleton, James O., Chicago N.L., October 9, 1938.
  Bouton, James A., New York A.L., October 5, 1963.
  Stuper, John A., St. Louis N.L., October 13, 1982.
  Medich, George F., Milwaukee A.L., October 19, 1982.
  Morris, John S., Detroit A.L., October 13, 1984.

Most Wild Pitches, Inning
  2—Shawkey, J. Robert, New York A.L., October 5, 1922, fifth inning.
  Aldridge, Victor, Pittsburgh N.L., October 15, 1925, first inning.
  Miljus, John K., Pittsburgh N.L., October 8, 1927, ninth inning.
  Carleton, James O., Chicago N.L., October 9, 1938, eighth inning.
  Medich, George F., Milwaukee A.L., October 19, 1982, sixth inning.

Most Wild Pitches, Series
  3—Tesreau, Charles M., New York N.L., 1912.
  Stuper, John A., St. Louis N.L., October 13, 1982.

Most Wild Pitches, Total Series
  5—Shumaher, Harold H., New York N.L., 1933 (2), 1936 (2), 1937 (1).

Most Hit Batsmen, Series
  3—Donovan, William E., Detroit A.L., 1907.
  Kison, Bruce E., Pittsburgh N.L., 1971.

Most Hit Batsmen, Game
  3—Kison, Bruce E., Pittsburgh N.L., October 13, 1971, 6⅓ innings.

Most Hit Batsmen, Inning
  2—Willett, Robert E., Detroit A.L., October 11, 1909, second inning (consecutive).
  Granger, Wayne A., St. Louis N.L., October 9, 1968, eighth inning.

Most Hit Batsmen, Total Series
  4—Donovan, William E., Detroit A.L., 1907 (3), 1908 (0), 1909 (1).
  Plank, Edward S., Philadelphia A.L., 1905 (1), 1911 (1), 1913 (1), 1914 (1).

Most Balks, Inning, Game, Series or Total Series
  1—Held by 17 pitchers. Last pitcher—Petry, Daniel J., Detroit A.L., October 10, 1984, second inning.

Youngest World Series Pitcher
  19 years, 20 days—Brett, Kenneth A., Boston A.L., October 8, 1967, pitched one inning in relief.

Oldest World Series Pitcher
  46 years, 3 months—Quinn, John P., Philadelphia A.L., October 4, 1930, pitched two innings, finishing game.

Youngest Pitcher to Pitch Complete World Series Game
  20 years, 10 months, 12 days—Bush, Leslie A., Philadelphia A.L., October 9, 1913; Philadelphia A.L. 8, New York N.L. 2.

Oldest Pitcher to Pitch Complete World Series Game
  39 years, 7 months, 13 days—Alexander, Grover C., St. Louis N.L., October 9, 1926, St. Louis N.L., 10, New York A.L., 2.

Oldest Pitcher to Start World Series Game
  45 years, 3 months, 7 days—Quinn, John P., Philadelphia A.L., October 12, 1929, pitched 5 innings.

Oldest Pitcher to Finish World Series Game
  46 years, 3 months—Quinn, John P., Philadelphia A.L., October 4, 1930, pitched 2 innings.

Youngest Pitcher to Win Complete World Series Game
  20 years, 10 months, 12 days—Bush, Leslie A., Philadelphia A.L., October 9, 1913; Philadelphia A.L., 8, New York N.L., 2.

Youngest Pitcher to Win Complete World Series Shutout Game
  20 years, 11 months, 21 days—Palmer, James A., Baltimore A.L., October 6, 1966; Baltimore A.L., 6, Los Angeles N.L., 0.

Oldest Pitcher to Win Complete World Series Shutout Game
  37 years, 11 months, 5 days—Johnson, Walter P., Washington A.L., October 11, 1925; Washington A.L., 4, Pittsburgh N.L., 0.

CLUB PITCHING RECORDS

Most Complete Games, Series, One Club
  4-game Series—4—New York A.L., vs. St. Louis N.L., 1928.
  5-game Series—5—Philadelphia A.L., vs. New York N.L., 1905.
             Philadelphia A.L., vs. Chicago N.L., 1910.
             Philadelphia A.L., vs. New York N.L., 1913.
             Boston A.L., vs. Philadelphia N.L., 1915.
  6-game Series—5—Philadelphia A.L., vs. New York N.L., 1911.
             Boston A.L., vs. Chicago N.L., 1918.
  7-game Series—5—Cleveland A.L., vs. Brooklyn N.L., 1920.
             New York A.L., vs. Brooklyn N.L., 1956.
  8-game Series—7—Boston A.L., vs. Pittsburgh N.L., 1903.

Most Complete Games, Series, Both Clubs
  4-game Series— 5—Boston N.L., 3, Philadelphia A.L., 2, 1914.
  5-game Series— 9—Philadelphia A.L., 5, New York N.L., 4, 1905.
             Boston A.L., 5, Philadelphia N.L., 4, 1915.
  6-game Series— 9—Boston A.L., 5, Chicago N.L., 4, 1918.
  7-game Series— 8—(Series of 1909, 1920, 1925, 1934, 1940, 1956.)
  8-game Series—13—Boston A.L., 7, Pittsburgh N.L., 6, 1903.

Fewest Complete Games, Series, One Club
  4-game Series—0—Pittsburgh N.L., vs. New York A.L., 1927.
             St. Louis N.L., vs. New York A.L., 1928.
             Chicago N.L., vs. New York A.L., 1938.
             New York A.L., vs. Los Angeles N.L., 1963.
             Cincinnati N.L., vs. New York A.L., 1976.
  5-game Series—0—Cincinnati N.L., vs. Baltimore A.L., 1970.
             Oakland A.L., vs. Los Angeles N.L., 1974.
             Los Angeles N.L., vs. Oakland A.L., 1974.
             Philadelphia N.L., vs. Baltimore A.L., 1983.
  6-game Series—0—Chicago A.L., vs. Los Angeles N.L., 1959.
             Los Angeles N.L., vs. Chicago A.L., 1959.
             Los Angeles N.L., vs. New York A.L., 1978.
             Kansas City A.L., vs. Philadelphia N.L., 1980.
             Philadelphia N.L., vs. Kansas City A.L., 1980.
             New York A.L., vs. Los Angeles N.L., 1981.
  7-game Series—0—Brooklyn N.L., vs. New York A.L., 1947.
             Pittsburgh N.L., vs. New York A.L., 1960.
             Oakland A.L., vs. Cincinnati N.L., 1972.
             Cincinnati N.L., vs. Oakland A.L., 1972.
             Oakland A.L., vs. New York N.L., 1973.
             New York N.L., vs. Oakland A.L., 1973.
             Cincinnati N.L., vs. Boston A.L., 1975.
             Pittsburgh N.L., vs. Baltimore A.L., 1979.
  8-game Series—3—Boston A.L., vs. New York N.L., 1912.

Fewest Complete Games, Series, Both Clubs
  4-game Series—1—New York A.L., 1, Cincinnati N.L., 0, 1976.
  5-game Series—0—Oakland A.L., 0, Los Angeles N.L., 0, 1974.
  6-game Series—0—Chicago A.L., 0, Los Angeles N.L., 0, 1959.
             Kansas City A.L., 0, Philadelphia N.L., 0, 1980.
  7-game Series—0—Oakland A.L., 0, Cincinnati N.L., 0, 1972.
             Oakland A.L., 0, New York N.L., 0, 1973.
  8-game Series—9—New York N.L., 6, Boston A.L., 3, 1912.

Most Appearances by Pitchers, Series, One Club
  4-game Series—13—Chicago N.L., vs. New York A.L., 1932.
                          Chicago N.L., vs. New York A.L., 1938.
  5-game Series—18—Cincinnati N.L., vs. Baltimore A.L., 1970.
  6-game Series—22—New York A.L., vs. Los Angeles N.L., 1981.
  7-game Series—30—Cincinnati N.L., vs. Boston A.L., 1975.
  8-game Series—14—Boston A.L., vs. New York N.L., 1912.

Most Appearances by Pitchers, Series, Both Clubs
  4-game Series—21—Cleveland A.L., 12, New York N.L., 9, 1954.
  5-game Series—31—San Diego N.L., 17, Detroit A.L., 14, 1984.
  6-game Series—40—New York A.L., 22, Los Angeles N.L., 18, 1981.
  7-game Series—52—Cincinnati N.L., 30, Boston A.L., 22, 1975.
  8-game Series—25—Chicago A.L., 13, Cincinnati N.L., 12, 1919.

Most Saves, Series, One Club (Since 1969)
  4-game Series—2—Cincinnati N.L., vs. New York A.L., 1976.
  5-game Series—3—Oakland A.L., vs. Los Angeles N.L., 1974.
  6-game Series—3—Philadelphia N.L., vs. Kansas City A.L., 1980.
  7-game Series—4—Oakland A.L., vs. New York N.L., 1973.

Most Saves, Series, Both Clubs (Since 1969)
  4-game Series—2—Cincinnati N.L., 2, New York A.L., 0, 1976.
  5-game Series—4—Oakland A.L., 3, Los Angeles N.L., 1, 1974.
  6-game Series—4—Philadelphia N.L., 3, Kansas City A.L., 1, 1980.
  7-game Series—7—Oakland A.L., 4, New York N.L., 3, 1973.

Fewest Saves, Series, One Club (Since 1969)
  4-game Series—0—New York A.L., vs. Cincinnati N.L., 1976.
  5-game Series—0—Baltimore A.L., vs. New York N.L., 1969.
                        Cincinnati N.L., vs. Baltimore A.L., 1970.
  6-game Series—0—New York A.L., vs. Los Angeles N.L., 1977, 1978.
                        Los Angeles N.L., vs. New York A.L., 1977.
  7-game Series—0—Boston A.L., vs. Cincinnati N.L., 1975.
                        Baltimore A.L., vs. Pittsburgh N.L., 1979.

Fewest Saves, Series, Both Clubs (Since 1969)
  4-game Series—2—Cincinnati N.L., 2, New York A.L., 0, 1976.
  5-game Series—2—New York N.L., 2, Baltimore A.L., 0, 1976.
                        Baltimore A.L., 2, Cincinnati N.L., 0, 1970.
  6-game Series—0—New York A.L., 0, Los Angeles N.L., 0, 1977.
  7-game Series—2—Cincinnati N.L., 2, Boston A.L., 0, 1975.

Most Balks, Series, One Club
  2—Cleveland A.L., vs. Boston N.L., 1948.

Most Balks, Series, Both Clubs
  2—Cleveland A.L., 2, Boston N.L., 0, 1948.

Fewest Balks, Series, Both Clubs
  0—Held by many clubs in Series of all lengths.

Most Wild Pitches, Series, One Club
  5—Pittsburgh N.L., vs. New York A.L., 1960.

Most Wild Pitches, Series, Both Clubs
  8—New York A.L., 4, Brooklyn N.L., 4, 1947.

Fewest Wild Pitches, Series, Both Clubs
  0—Cincinnati N.L., 0, Chicago A.L., 0, 1919 (8-game Series). Also in many shorter Series.

GENERAL RECORDS

Earliest Date for World Series Game, Except 1918
  September 28, 1932, at New York, New York A.L., 12, Chicago N.L., 6.
  September 28, 1955, at New York, New York A.L., 6, Brooklyn N.L., 5.

Earliest Date for World Series Final Game, Except 1918
  October 2, 1932, at Chicago, New York A.L., 13, Chicago N.L., 6 (4-game Series).
  October 2, 1954, at Cleveland, New York N.L., 7, Cleveland A.L., 4 (4-game Series).

Latest Date for World Series Start
  October 20, 1981, at New York, New York A.L., 5, Los Angeles N.L., 3 (6-game Series ended at New York on October 28, 1981).

Latest Date for World Series Finish
  October 28, 1981—Series started October 20, at New York A.L. (6-game Series ended at New York).

WORLD SERIES RECORDS

First World Series Night Game
   October 13, 1971, at Pittsburgh, Pittsburgh N.L., 4, Baltimore A.L., 3.

Largest Attendance, Game
   92,706—At Los Angeles, October 6, 1959, Chicago A.L., 1, Los Angeles N.L., 0, fifth game.

Smallest Attendance, Game
   6,210—At Detroit, Wednesday, October 14, 1908; Chicago N.L., 2, Detroit A.L., 0, fifth game.

Largest Attendance, Series
   4-game Series—251,507—New York N.L., vs. Cleveland A.L., 1954.
   5-game Series—304,139—Baltimore A.L., vs. Philadelphia N.L., 1983.
   6-game Series—420,784—Los Angeles N.L., vs. Chicago A.L., 1959.
   7-game Series—394,712—Milwaukee N.L., vs. New York A.L., 1957.
   8-game Series—269,976—New York N.L., vs. New York A.L., 1921.

Smallest Attendance, Series
   4-game Series—111,009—Boston N.L., vs. Philadelphia A.L., 1914.
   5-game Series— 62,232—Chicago N.L., vs. Detroit A.L., 1908.
   6-game Series— 99,845—Chicago A.L., vs. Chicago N.L., 1906.
   7-game Series—145,295—Pittsburgh N.L., vs. Detroit A.L., 1909.
   8-game Series—100,429—Pittsburgh N.L., vs. Boston A.L., 1903.

Shortest Time Average Per Game, Series
   4-game Series—One hour, 46 minutes—New York A.L., vs. Cincinnati N.L., 1939.
   5-game Series—One hour, 46 minutes—Detroit A.L., vs. Chicago N.L., 1908.
   6-game Series—One hour, 49 minutes—Philadelphia A.L., vs. St. Louis N.L., 1930.
   7-game Series—One hour, 47 minutes—Cleveland A.L., vs. Brooklyn N.L., 1920.
   8-game Series—One hour, 48 minutes—Boston A.L., vs. Pittsburgh N.L., 1903.

Longest Time Average Per Game, Series
   4-game Series—Two hours, 50 minutes—New York N.L., vs. Cleveland A.L., 1954.
   5-game Series—Two hours, 54 minutes—Detroit A.L., vs. San Diego N.L., 1984.
   6-game Series—Two hours, 58 minutes—Kansas City A.L., vs. Philadelphia N.L., 1980.
   7-game Series—Three hours, four minutes—Pittsburgh N.L., vs. Baltimore A.L., 1979.
   8-game Series—Two hours, 14 minutes—Boston A.L., vs. New York N.L., 1912.

Longest Tie Game
   12 innings—Chicago N.L., 3, Detroit A.L., 3, at Chicago, October 8, 1907.

Longest Day Game
   14 innings—Boston A.L., 2, Brooklyn N.L., 1, at Boston, October 9, 1916.

Longest Night Game
   12 innings—Boston A.L., 7, Cincinnati N.L., 6, at Boston, October 21, 1975.
         New York A.L., 4, Los Angeles N.L., 3, at New York, October 11, 1977.

Shortest Game by Time
   1 hour, 25 minutes—Chicago N.L., 2, Detroit A.L., 0, at Detroit, October 14, 1908.

Longest Day Game by Time, Nine Innings
   3 hours, 48 minutes—Baltimore A.L., 9, Pittsburgh N.L., 6, October 13, 1979.

Longest Night Game by Time, Nine Innings
   3 hours, 18 minutes—Baltimore A.L., 5, Pittsburgh N.L., 4, October 10, 1979.
         Detroit A.L., 3, San Diego N.L., 2, October 9, 1984.

Longest Day Game by Time, Extra Innings
   4 hours, 13 minutes—New York N.L., 10, Oakland A.L., 7, at Oakland, October 14, 1973, 12 innings.

Longest Night Game by Time, Extra Innings
   4 hours, 1 minute—Boston A.L., 7, Cincinnati N.L., 6, at Boston, October 21, 1975, 12 innings.

Most Shutouts, Won, Series, One Club
   4—New York N.L., vs. Philadelphia A.L., 1905.

Most Shutouts, Series, Lost, One Club
   4—Philadelphia A.L., vs. New York N.L., 1905.

Most Consecutive Shutouts Won, Series, One Club
   3—New York N.L., vs. Philadelphia A.L., October 12, 13, 14, 1905.
      Baltimore A.L., vs. Los Angeles N.L., October 6, 8, 9, 1966.

Most Consecutive Shutouts Lost, Series, One Club
   3—Philadelphia A.L., vs. New York N.L., October 12, 13, 14, 1905.
      Los Angeles N.L., vs. Baltimore A.L., October 6, 8, 9, 1966.

Most Shutouts, Series, Both Clubs
   5—New York N.L., 4, Philadelphia A.L., 1, 1905.

Largest Score, Shutout Game
  12-0—New York A.L., 12, Pittsburgh N.L., 0, October 12, 1960.

Fewest Shutouts, Series, One Club
  0—Held by many clubs in Series of all lengths.

Fewest Shutouts, Series, Both Clubs
  0—Held by many clubs in Series of all lengths.

Longest Shutout Game
  10 innings—New York N.L., 3, Philadelphia A.L., 0, October 8, 1913.
      Brooklyn N.L., 1, New York A.L., 0, October 9, 1956.

Most 1-0 Games, Series, One Club
  2—Baltimore A.L., vs. Los Angeles N.L., October 8, 9, 1966.

Most 1-0 Games, Series, Both Clubs
  2—New York A.L., 1 (October 5), Brooklyn N.L., 1 (October 6), 1949.
    Baltimore A.L., 2 (October 8-9), Los Angeles N.L., 0, 1966.

Most Shutouts Won, Total Series, One Club
  17—New York A.L.

Most Shutouts Lost, Total Series, One Club
  13—New York A.L.

Most 1-0 Games Won, Total Series, One Club
  3—New York A.L.
    New York N.L.

Most 1-0 Games Lost, Total Series, One Club
  6—New York A.L.

Most Consecutive Innings Shut Out Opponent, Series
  33—Baltimore A.L., vs. Los Angeles N.L., October 5, fourth inning to end of game, October 6, 8, 9, 1966.

Most Consecutive Innings, Shut Out Opponents, Total Series
  39—Baltimore A.L., October 5, 1966, fourth inning through October 11, 1969, first six innings.

Most Consecutive Games, Total Series, Without Being Shut Out
  42—New York A.L., October 6, 1926 through October 1, 1942.

Most Players, Series, One Club
  4-game Series—24—Cleveland A.L., vs. New York N.L., 1954.
  5-game Series—25—Brooklyn N.L., vs. New York A.L., 1949.
  6-game Series—25—Los Angeles N.L., vs. New York A.L., 1977.
  7-game Series—26—Detroit A.L., vs. Chicago N.L., 1945.
      Boston A.L., vs. St. Louis N.L., 1946.
  8-game Series—19—Chicago A.L., vs. Cincinnati N.L., 1919.
      New York A.L., vs. New York N.L., 1921.

Most Players, Series, Both Clubs
  4-game Series—39—Cleveland A.L., 24, New York N.L., 15, 1954.
  5-game Series—46—Baltimore A.L., 23, Philadelphia N.L., 23, 1983.
      San Diego N.L., 24, Detroit A.L., 22, 1984.
  6-game Series—48—New York A.L., 24, Los Angeles N.L., 24, 1981.
  7-game Series—51—Detroit A.L., 26, Chicago N.L., 25, 1945.
  8-game Series—36—Chicago A.L., 19, Cincinnati N.L., 17, 1919.

Fewest Players, Series, One Club
  4-game Series—13—Los Angeles N.L., vs. New York A.L., 1963.
      Baltimore A.L., vs. Los Angeles N.L., 1966.
  5-game Series—12—New York N.L., vs. Philadelphia A.L., 1905.
      Philadelphia A.L., vs. Chicago N.L., 1910.
      Philadelphia A.L., vs. New York N.L., 1913.
  6-game Series—14—Chicago N.L., vs. Chicago A.L., 1906.
      Philadelphia A.L., vs. New York N.L., 1911.
  7-game Series—16—Detroit A.L., vs. Pittsburgh N.L., 1909.
  8-game Series—13—Boston A.L., vs. Pittsburgh N.L., 1903.
      New York N.L., vs. New York A.L., 1921.

Fewest Players, Series, Both Clubs
  4-game Series—31—Philadelphia A.L., 16, Boston N.L., 15, 1914.
  5-game Series—25—Philadelphia A.L., 13, New York N.L., 12, 1905.
  6-game Series—29—New York N.L., 15, Philadelphia A.L., 14, 1911.
  7-game Series—33—Pittsburgh N.L., 17, Detroit A.L., 16, 1909.
  8-game Series—27—Pittsburgh N.L., 14, Boston A.L., 13, 1903.

Most Times, One Club Using Only 9 Players in Game, Series
  5-game Series—5—Philadelphia A.L., vs. Chicago N.L., 1910.
                    Philadelphia A.L., vs. New York N.L., 1913.
  7-game Series—5—New York A.L., vs. Brooklyn N.L., 1956.
  8-game Series—6—Pittsburgh N.L., vs. Boston A.L., 1903.

Most Times, Both Clubs Using Only 9 Players in Game, Series
  7-game Series— 7—New York A.L., 5, Brooklyn N.L., 2, 1956.
  8-game Series—11—Pittsburgh N.L., 6; Boston A.L., 5, 1903.

Most Players, Game, Nine Innings, One Club
  21—New York A.L., vs. Brooklyn N.L., October 5, 1947.
       Cincinnati N.L., vs. New York A.L., October 9, 1961.

Most Players Extra-Inning Game, One Club
  21—Oakland A.L., vs. New York N.L., October 14, 1973, 12 innings.

Most Players, Game, Nine Innings, Both Clubs
  38—New York A.L., 21, Brooklyn N.L., 17, October 5, 1947.

Most Players, Extra-Inning Game, Both Clubs
  38—Chicago N.L., 19, Detroit A.L., 19, October 8, 1945, 12 innings.
       Oakland A.L., 21, New York N.L., 17, October 14, 1973, 12 innings.

Most Times Pinch-Hitter Used, Series, One Club
  4-game Series—16—Cleveland A.L., vs. New York N.L., 1954.
  5-game Series—15—Cincinnati N.L., vs. New York A.L., 1961.
  6-game Series—13—St. Louis A.L., vs. St. Louis N.L., 1944.
                    Los Angeles N.L., vs. Chicago A.L., 1959.
  7-game Series—23—Baltimore A.L., vs. Pittsburgh N.L., 1979.
  8-game Series— 6—Chicago A.L., vs. Cincinnati N.L., 1919.

Most Times Pinch-Hitter Used, Series, Both Clubs
  4-game Series—19—Cleveland A.L., 16, New York N.L., 3, 1954.
  5-game Series—25—Baltimore A.L. 13, Philadelphia N.L., 12, 1983.
  6-game Series—22—Los Angeles N.L., 13, Chicago A.L., 9, 1959.
  7-game Series—35—Oakland A.L., 20, New York N.L., 15, 1973.
  8-game Series—10—New York N.L., 5, Boston A.L., 5, 1912.

Fewest Times Pinch-Hitter Used, Series, One Club
  4-game Series—0—New York A.L., vs. Cincinnati N.L., 1939.
                 Baltimore A.L., vs. Los Angeles N.L., 1966.
                 Cincinnati N.L., vs. New York A.L., 1976.
  5-game Series—0—Philadelphia A.L., vs. Chicago N.L., 1910.
                 Philadelphia A.L., vs. New York N.L., 1913.
  6-game Series—0—Philadelphia A.L., vs. New York N.L., 1911.
  7-game Series—2—Milwaukee A.L., vs. St. Louis N.L., 1982.
  8-game Series—1—Pittsburgh N.L., vs. Boston A.L., 1903.

Fewest Times Pinch-Hitter Used, Series, Both Clubs
  4-game Series—3—Boston N.L., 2, Philadelphia A.L., 1, 1914.
                 Cincinnati N.L., 3, New York A.L., 0, 1939.
  5-game Series—2—New York N.L., 1, Philadelphia A.L., 1, 1905.
  6-game Series—4—New York N.L., 4, Philadelphia A.L., 0, 1911.
  7-game Series—8—Detroit A.L., 5, Pittsburgh N.L., 3, 1909.
  8-game Series—5—Boston A.L., 4, Pittsburgh N.L., 1, 1903.
                 New York A.L., 3, New York N.L., 2, 1921.

Most Pinch-Hitters, Inning, One Club
  4—New York N.L., vs. Oakland A.L., October 13, 1973, ninth inning.
     Baltimore A.L., vs. Philadelphia N.L., October 15, 1983, sixth inning.

Most Pinch-Hitters, Game, One Club
  6—Los Angeles N.L., vs. Chicago A.L., October 6, 1959.

Most Pinch-Hitters, Game, Both Clubs
  8—Oakland A.L., 5, New York N.L., 3, October 14, 1973.
    Baltimore A.L., 4, Philadelphia N.L., 4, October 15, 1983.

Most Times Pinch-Runner Used, Series, One Club
  4-game Series—4—Philadelphia N.L., vs. New York A.L., 1950.
  5-game Series—5—New York N.L., vs. Philadelphia A.L., 1913.
  6-game Series—5—New York A.L., vs. Los Angeles N.L., 1981.
  7-game Series—8—Oakland A.L., vs. Cincinnati N.L., 1972.
  8-game Series—3—New York A.L., vs. Boston A.L., 1912.

Most Times Pinch-Runner Used, Series, Both Clubs
  4-game Series— 6—Philadelphia N.L., 4, New York A.L., 2, 1950.
  5-game Series— 6—Oakland A.L., 4, Los Angeles N.L., 2, 1974.

6-game Series— 7—New York A.L., 5, Los Angeles N.L., 2, 1981.
7-game Series—10—Oakland A.L., 8, Cincinnati N.L., 2, 1972.
8-game Series— 4—New York N.L., 3, Boston A.L., 1, 1912.

Fewest Times Pinch-Runner Used, Series, One Club
0—Held by many clubs in Series of all lengths.

Fewest Times Pinch-Runner Used, Series, Both Clubs
4-game Series—0—New York A.L., 0, Chicago N.L., 0, 1938.
               Los Angeles N.L., 0, New York A.L., 0, 1963.
               Cincinnati N.L., 0, New York A.L., 0, 1976.
5-game Series—0—New York A.L., 0, Philadelphia A.L., 0, 1905.
               Philadelphia A.L., 0, Chicago N.L., 0, 1929.
               New York A.L., 0, New York N.L., 0, 1937.
               Baltimore A.L., 0, Cincinnati N.L., 0, 1970.
6-game Series—0—Chicago A.L., 0, New York N.L., 0, 1917.
               Philadelphia A.L., 0, St. Louis N.L., 0, 1930.
               Detroit A.L., 0, Chicago N.L., 0, 1935.
               New York A.L., 0, Brooklyn N.L., 0, 1953.
7-game Series—0—Pittsburgh N.L., 0, Detroit A.L., 0, 1909.
               New York A.L., 0, Brooklyn N.L., 0, 1956.
               Cincinnati N.L., 0, Boston A.L., 0, 1975.
8-game Series—0—Boston A.L., 0, Pittsburgh N.L., 0, 1903.

Most Pinch-Runners, Game, One Club
2—Made in many games.

Most Pinch-Runners, Inning, One Club
2—New York N.L., vs. New York A.L., October 10, 1923, third inning.
  New York A.L., vs. New York N.L., October 15, 1923, eighth inning.
  Brooklyn N.L., vs. New York A.L., October 3, 1947, ninth inning.
  Boston N.L., vs. Cleveland A.L., October 6, 1948, eighth inning.
  Philadelphia N.L., vs. New York A.L., October 7, 1950, ninth inning.
  Los Angeles N.L., vs. Chicago A.L., October 6, 1959, seventh inning.
  Oakland A.L., vs. Cincinnati N.L., October 19, 1972, ninth inning.

Most Pinch-Runners, Game, Both Clubs
3—St. Louis N.L. 2, New York A.L. 1, October 7, 1964.
  Philadelphia N.L. 2, Baltimore A.L. 1, October 15, 1983.

Most Pinch-Runners, Inning, Both Clubs
2—Made in many games.

Winning Series After Winning First Game
Accomplished 47 times.

Winning Series After Losing First Game
Accomplished 34 times.

Winning Series After Winning One Game and Losing Three
Boston A.L., vs. Pittsburgh N.L., 1903 (best-out-of-nine Series).
Pittsburgh N.L., vs. Washington A.L., 1925 (best-out-of seven Series).
New York A.L., vs. Milwaukee N.L., 1958 (best-out-of-seven Series).
Detroit A.L., vs. St. Louis N.L., 1968 (best-out-of-seven Series).
Pittsburgh N.L., vs. Baltimore A.L., 1979 (best-out-of-seven Series).

Winning Series After Losing First Two Games
New York N.L., vs. New York A.L., 1921 (best-out-of-nine Series).
Brooklyn N.L., vs. New York A.L., 1955 (best-out-of-seven Series).
New York A.L., vs. Brooklyn N.L., 1956 (best-out-of-seven Series).
New York A.L., vs. Milwaukee N.L., 1958 (best-out-of-seven Series).
Los Angeles N.L., vs. Minnesota A.L., 1965 (best-out-of-seven Series).
Pittsburgh N.L., vs. Baltimore A.L., 1971 (best-out-of-seven Series).
New York A.L., vs. Los Angeles N.L., 1978 (best-out-of-six Series).
Los Angeles N.L., vs. New York A.L., 1981 (best-out-of-six Series).

Winning Series After Losing First Three Games
Never accomplished.

Most Series, Manager
10—Stengel, Charles D., New York A.L., 1949, 1950, 1951, 1952, 1953, 1955, 1956, 1957, 1958, 1960 (won 7, lost 3).

Most World Series Winners Managed
7—McCarthy, Joseph V., New York A.L., 1932, 1936, 1937, 1938, 1939, 1941, 1943.
  Stengel, Charles D., New York A.L., 1949, 1950, 1951, 1952, 1953, 1956, 1958.

WORLD SERIES RECORDS

Most Consecutive Years Managed World Series Winners
  5—Stengel, Charles D., New York A.L., 1949, 1950, 1951, 1952, 1953 (his first five years as manager, New York A.L.).

Most Consecutive World Series Winners Managed, Total Series
  6—McCarthy, Joseph V., New York A.L., 1932, 1936, 1937, 1938, 1939, 1941.

Most World Series Losers Managed
  6—McGraw, John J., New York N.L., 1911, 1912, 1913, 1917, 1923, 1924.

Most Consecutive Years Managed World Series Losers
  3—Jennings, Hugh A., Detroit A.L., 1907, 1908, 1909.
  McGraw, John J., New York N.L., 1911, 1912, 1913.

Most Consecutive World Series Losers, Managed, Total Series
  4—McGraw, John J., New York N.L., 1911, 1912, 1913, 1917.

Managers Representing Both Leagues
  McCarthy, Joseph V., Chicago N.L., 1929; New York A.L., 1932, 1936, 1937, 1938, 1939, 1941, 1942, 1943.
  Berra, Lawrence P., New York A.L., 1964; New York N.L., 1973.
  Dark, Alvin R., San Francisco N.L., 1962; Oakland A.L., 1974.
  Anderson, George L., Cincinnati N.L., 1970, 1972, 1975, 1976; Detroit A.L., 1984.
  Williams, Richard H., Boston A.L., 1967; Oakland A.L., 1972, 1973; San Diego N.L., 1984.

Most Different World Series Winners Managed
  2—McKechnie, William B., Pittsburgh N.L., 1925; Cincinnati N.L., 1940.
  Harris, Stanley R., Washington A.L., 1924; New York A.L., 1947.
  Anderson, George L., Cincinnati N.L., 1975, 1976; Detroit A.L., 1984.

Most Different Clubs Managed, League
  3—McKechnie, William B., Pittsburgh N.L., 1925; St. Louis N.L., 1928; Cincinnati N.L., 1939, 1940.

Most Series as Coach
  15—Crosetti, Frank P., New York A.L., 1947, 1949, 1950, 1951, 1952, 1953, 1955, 1956, 1957, 1958, 1960, 1961, 1962, 1963, 1964 (10 World Series winners).

Most Series Eligible as Player and Coach
  23—Crosetti, Frank P., New York A.L., 1932, 1936, 1937, 1938, 1939, 1941, 1942, 1943 (8 Series as player); 1947, 1949, 1950, 1951, 1952, 1953, 1955, 1956, 1957, 1958, 1960, 1961, 1962, 1963, 1964 (15 Series as coach).

Most Series as Official Scorer
  11—Spink, J. G. Taylor, 1910 through 1920.

Youngest Manager, World Series Club
  26 years, 11 months, 21 days—Cronin, Joseph E., Washington A.L., vs. New York N.L., October 3, 1933. (Born October 12, 1906.)

Youngest Manager, World Series Winner
  27 years, 11 months, 2 days—Harris, Stanley R., Washington A.L., vs. New York N.L., October 10, 1924. (Born November 8, 1896.)

Most New York Clubs as Player and Coach
  3—Dressen, Charles W., New York N.L., 1933 (eligible as player—did not play); Brooklyn N.L., 1941 (coach); New York A.L., 1947 (coach); Brooklyn N.L., 1952, 1953 (manager).

Most New York Clubs as Player and Manager
  3—Durocher, Leo E., New York A.L., 1928 (player); Brooklyn N.L., 1941 (manager); New York N.L., 1951, 1954 (manager).
  Stengel, Charles D., Brooklyn, N.L., 1916 (player); New York N.L., 1922, 1923 (player); New York A.L., 1949, 1950, 1951, 1952, 1953, 1955, 1956, 1957, 1958, 1960 (manager).

Most Series Played
  33—New York A.L., 1921, 1922, 1923, 1926, 1927, 1928, 1932, 1936, 1937, 1938, 1939, 1941, 1942, 1943, 1947, 1949, 1950, 1951, 1952, 1953, 1955, 1956, 1957, 1958, 1960, 1961, 1962, 1963, 1964, 1976, 1977, 1978, 1981 (won 22, lost 11).
  17—Brooklyn-Los Angeles N.L., 1916, 1920, 1941, 1947, 1949, 1952, 1953, 1955, 1956, 1959, 1963, 1965, 1966, 1974, 1977, 1978, 1981 (won 5, lost 12).

Most Consecutive Series, Between Same Clubs
  3—New York N.L., vs. New York A.L., 1921, 1922, 1923.

Most Series Won
  22—New York A.L., 1923, 1927, 1928, 1932, 1936, 1937, 1938, 1939, 1941, 1943, 1947, 1949, 1950, 1951, 1952, 1953, 1956, 1958, 1961, 1962, 1977, 1978 (lost 11).

Most Series Umpired
  18—Klem, William J., 1908, 1909, 1911, 1912, 1913, 1914, 1915, 1917, 1918, 1920, 1922, 1924, 1926, 1929, 1931, 1932, 1934, 1940.

Most Consecutive Series Umpired
  5—Klem, William J., 1911, 1912, 1913, 1914, 1915.

Most Games Umpired
  104—Klem, William J. (18 Series).

Most Consecutive Years Winning Series
  5—New York A.L., 1949, 1950, 1951, 1952, 1953.

Most Consecutive Series Won
  8—New York A.L., 1927, 1928, 1932, 1936, 1937, 1938, 1939, 1941.

Most Times Winning Series in Four Consecutive Games
  6—New York A.L., 1927, 1928, 1932, 1938, 1939, 1950.

Most Series Lost
  12—Brooklyn-Los Angeles N.L., 1916, 1920, 1941, 1947, 1949, 1952, 1953, 1956, 1966, 1974, 1977, 1978 (won 5).
  11—New York A.L., 1921, 1922, 1926, 1942, 1955, 1957, 1960, 1963, 1964, 1976, 1981 (won 22).

Most Consecutive Years Losing Series
  3—Detroit A.L., 1907, 1908, 1909.
      New York N.L., 1911, 1912, 1913.

Most Consecutive Series Lost
  7—Chicago N.L., 1910, 1918, 1929, 1932, 1935, 1938, 1945.
      Brooklyn N.L., 1916, 1920, 1941, 1947, 1949, 1952, 1953.

Most Games Played, Total Series, One Club
  187—New York A.L., 33 Series (won 109, lost 77, tied 1).

Most Games Won, Total Series, One Club
  109—New York A.L., 33 Series (won 109, lost 77, tied 1).

Most Games Lost, Total Series, One Club
  77—New York A.L., 33 Series (won 109, lost 77, tied 1).

Most Games Won by One Run, Series, One Club
  4—Boston A.L., vs. Philadelphia N.L., 1915 (Lost 1).
      Boston A.L., vs. Chicago N.L., 1918 (Lost 0).
      Oakland A.L., vs. Cincinnati N.L., 1972 (Lost 2).

Most Extra-Inning Games, Total Series
  13—New York A.L., 33 Series, 187 games; Won 6, lost 6, 1 tie.

Most Extra-Inning Games Won, Total Series
  7—New York N.L., 14 Series, 82 games; Won 7, lost 3, 2 ties.

Most Extra-Inning Games Lost, Total Series
  6—New York A.L., 33 Series, 187 games; Won 6, lost 6, 1 tie.

Most Extra-Inning Games, Series
  4-game Series—1—Boston N.L., vs. Philadelphia A.L., 1914.
                   New York A.L., vs. Cincinnati N.L., 1939.
                   New York A.L., vs. Philadelphia N.L., 1950.
                   New York N.L., vs. Cleveland A.L., 1954.
  5-game Series—2—New York N.L., vs. Washington A.L., 1933.
  6-game Series—2—Philadelphia A.L., vs. New York N.L., 1911.
  7-game Series—2—Washington A.L., vs. New York N.L., 1924.
                   New York A.L., vs. Milwaukee N.L., 1958.
                   Oakland A.L., vs. New York N.L., 1973.
                   Cincinnati N.L., vs. Boston A.L., 1975.
  8-game Series—2—Boston A.L., vs. New York N.L., 1912.

Most Games, Decided by One Run, Total Series
  54—New York A.L., 33 Series (won 26, lost 28).

Most Games Won, Decided by One Run, Total Series
  26—New York A.L., 33 Series (won 26, lost 28).

Most Games, Lost, Decided by One Run, Total Series
  28—New York A.L., 33 Series (won 26, lost 28).

Most Games Decided by One Run, Series, Both Clubs
  4-game Series—3—New York A.L. (Won 3), vs. Philadelphia N.L., 1950.
  5-game Series—4—Boston A.L. (Won 4), vs. Philadelphia N.L., 1915.
                   Oakland A.L. (Won 3), Los Angeles N.L., (Won 1), 1974.
  6-game Series—4—Boston A.L. (Won 4), vs. Chicago N.L., 1918.
  7-game Series—6—Oakland A.L. (Won 4), vs. Cincinnati N.L. (Won 2), 1972.
  8-game Series—4—Boston A.L. (Won 3), vs. New York N.L. (Won 1), 1912.

Most Games Won by One Run, Series, One Club
4-game Series—3—New York A.L., vs. Philadelphia N.L., 1950.
5-game Series—4—Boston A.L., vs. Philadelphia N.L., 1915.
6-game Series—4—Boston A.L., vs. Chicago N.L., 1918.
7-game Series—4—Oakland A.L., vs. Cincinnati N.L., 1972.
8-game Series—3—Boston A.L., vs. New York N.L., 1912.

Most Consecutive Games Won by One Run, Total Series
6—Boston A.L., 1915 (last 4), 1916 (first two).

Most Consecutive Games Lost by One Run, Total Series
7—Philadelphia N.L., 1915 (last 4), 1950 (first 3).

Most Consecutive Series Won, League
7—American League, 1947, 1948, 1949, 1950, 1951, 1952, 1953.

Most Consecutive Series Lost, League
7—National League, 1947, 1948, 1949, 1950, 1951, 1952, 1953.

Most Consecutive Games Won, Total Series
12—New York A.L., 1927 (4), 1928 (4), 1932 (4).

Most Consecutive Games Lost, Total Series
8—New York A.L., 1921 (last 3), 1922 (4), 1923 (first 1).
Philadelphia N.L., 1915 (last 4), 1950 (4).

Most Consecutive Games Won, League
10—American League, 1927 (4), 1928 (4), 1929 (first 2); also 1937 (last 1), 1938 (4), 1939 (4), 1940 (first 1).

Most Consecutive Series Ending in Shutouts
3—1907, 1908, 1909; 1955, 1956, 1957.

Most Consecutive Series, With Shutouts
9—1955 through 1963.

Most Consecutive Series Without Shutouts
3—1910, 1911, 1912.
1927, 1928, 1929.
1936, 1937, 1938.
1976, 1977, 1978.

WORLD SERIES MANAGERS

American League (36)

	Series	Series Won	Series Lost	Games Won	Games Lost	Tie
Altobelli, Joseph S., Baltimore	1	1	0	4	1	0
Anderson, George L., Detroit	1	1	0	4	1	0
Baker, Delmer D., Detroit	1	0	1	3	4	0
Barrow, Edward G., Boston	1	1	0	4	2	0
Bauer, Henry A., Baltimore	1	1	0	4	0	0
Berra, Lawrence P., New York	1	0	1	3	4	0
Boudreau, Louis, Cleveland	1	1	0	4	2	0
Carrigan, William F., Boston	2	2	0	8	2	0
Cochrane, Gordon S., Detroit	2	1	1	7	6	0
Collins, James J., Boston	1	1	0	5	3	0
Cronin, Joseph E., Washington-Boston	2	0	2	4	8	0
Dark, Alvin R., Oakland	1	1	0	4	1	0
Frey, James G., Kansas City	1	0	1	2	4	0
Gleason, William, Chicago	1	0	1	3	5	0
Harris, Stanley R., Washington-New York	3	2	1	11	10	0
Houk, Ralph G., New York	3	2	1	8	8	0
Huggins, Miller J., New York	6	3	3	18	15	1
Jennings, Hugh A., Detroit	3	0	3	4	12	1
Johnson, Darrell D., Boston	1	0	1	3	4	0
Jones, Fielder A., Chicago	1	1	0	4	2	0
Kuenn, Harvey E., Milwaukee	1	0	1	3	4	0
Lemon, Robert G., New York	2	1	1	6	6	0
Lopez, Alfonso R., Cleveland-Chicago	2	0	2	2	8	0
Mack, Connie, Philadelphia	8	5	3	24	19	0
Martin, Alfred M., New York	2	1	1	4	6	0
McCarthy, Joseph V., New York	8	7	1	29	9	0
Mele, Sabath A., Minnesota	1	0	1	3	4	0
O'Neill, Stephen F., Detroit	1	1	0	4	3	0
Rowland, Clarence H., Chicago	1	1	0	4	2	0
Sewell, J. Luther, St. Louis	1	0	1	2	4	0

	Series	Series Won	Series Lost	Games Won	Games Lost	Tie
Smith, E. Mayo, Detroit	1	1	0	4	3	0
Speaker, Tris, Cleveland	1	1	0	5	2	0
Stahl, J. Garland, Boston	1	1	0	4	3	1
Stengel, Charles D., New York	10	7	3	37	26	0
Weaver, Earl S., Baltimore	4	1	3	11	13	0
Williams, Richard H., Boston-Oakland	3	2	1	11	10	0
	81	47	34	260	216	3

Managers Representing Both Leagues (5)

	Series	Series Won	Series Lost	Games Won	Games Lost	Tie
Combined record of McCarthy, Joseph V., Chicago N.L. and New York A.L.	9	7	2	30	13	0
Combined record of Berra, Lawrence P., New York A.L. and New York N.L.	2	0	2	6	8	0
Combined record of Dark, Alvin R., San Fran. N.L. and Oakland A.L.	2	1	1	7	5	0
Combined record of Anderson, George L., Cincinnati N.L. and Detroit A.L.	5	3	2	16	12	0
Combined record of Williams, Richard H., Boston A.L., Oakland A.L. and San Diego N.L.	4	2	2	12	14	0

National League (38)

	Series	Series Won	Series Lost	Games Won	Games Lost	Tie
Alston, Walter E., Brooklyn, Los Angeles	7	4	3	20	20	0
Anderson, George L., Cincinnati	4	2	2	12	11	0
Berra, Lawrence P., New York	1	0	1	3	4	0
Bush, Owen J., Pittsburgh	1	0	1	0	4	0
Chance, Frank L., Chicago	4	2	2	11	9	1
Clarke, Fred C., Pittsburgh	2	1	1	7	8	0
Dark, Alvin R., San Francisco	1	0	1	3	4	0
Dressen, Charles W., Brooklyn	2	0	2	5	8	0
Durocher, Leo E., Brooklyn-New York	3	1	2	7	8	0
Dyer, Edwin H., St. Louis	1	1	0	4	3	0
Frisch, Frank F., St. Louis	1	1	0	4	3	0
Green, G. Dallas, Philadelphia	1	1	0	4	2	0
Grimm, Charles J., Chicago	3	0	3	5	12	0
Haney Fred G., Milwaukee	2	1	1	7	7	0
Hartnett, Charles L., Chicago	1	0	1	0	4	0
Herzog, Dorrell N.E., St. Louis	1	1	0	4	3	0
Hodges, Gilbert R., New York	1	1	0	4	1	0
Hornsby, Rogers, St. Louis	1	1	0	4	3	0
Hutchinson, Frederick C., Cincinnati	1	0	1	1	4	0
Keane, John J., St. Louis	1	1	0	4	3	0
Lasorda, Thomas C., Los Angeles	3	1	2	8	10	0
McCarthy, Joseph V., Chicago	1	0	1	1	4	0
McGraw, John J., New York	9	3	6	26	28	2
McKechnie, William B., Pitt.-St.L.-Cin.	4	2	2	8	14	0
Mitchell, Fred F., Chicago	1	0	1	2	4	0
Moran, Patrick J., Philadelphia-Cincinnati	2	1	1	6	7	0
Murtaugh, Daniel E., Pittsburgh	2	2	0	8	6	0
Owens, Paul F., Philadelphia	1	0	1	1	4	0
Robinson, Wilbert, Brooklyn	2	0	2	3	9	0
Sawyer, Edwin M. Philadelphia	1	0	1	0	4	0
Schoendienst, Albert F., St. Louis	2	1	1	7	7	0
Shotton, Burton E., Brooklyn	2	0	2	4	8	0
Southworth, William H., St. Louis-Boston	4	2	2	11	11	0
Stallings, George T., Boston	1	1	0	4	0	0
Street, Charles E., St. Louis	2	1	1	6	7	0
Tanner, Charles W., Pittsburgh	1	1	0	4	3	0
Terry, William H., New York	3	1	2	7	9	0
Williams, Richard H., San Diego	1	0	1	1	4	0
	81	34	47	216	260	3

Most games—63—Stengel, Charles C., New York A.L.

Most games won—37—Stengel, Charles D., New York A.L.

Most games lost—28—McGraw, John J., New York N.L.

WORLD SERIES UMPIRES (127)

Ashford, Emmett L. .... A. L. — 1970
Ballanfant, E. Lee .... N. L. — 1940-46-51-55
Barlick, Albert J. .... N. L. — 1946-50-51-54-58-62-67
Barnett, Lawrence R. .... A. L. — 1975-81-84
Barr, George .... N. L. — 1937-42-48-49
Basil, Stephen J. .... A. L. — 1937-40
Berry, Charles F. .... A. L. — 1946-50-54-58-62
Boggess, Lynton R. .... N. L. — 1940-52-56-60
Boyer, James M. .... A. L. — 1947
Bremigan, Nicholas G. .... A. L. — 1980
Brennan, William T. .... N. L. — 1911
Brinkman, Joseph N. .... A. L. — 1978
Burkhart, William K. .... N. L. — 1962-64-70
Byron, William J. .... N. L. — 1914
Chill, Ollie P. .... A. L. — 1921
Chylak, Nestor .... A. L. — 1957-60-66-71-77
Clark, Alan M. .... A. L. — 1983
Colosi, Nicholas .... N. L. — 1975-81
Conlan, John B. .... N. L. — 1945-50-54-57-61
Connolly, Thomas H. .... A. L. — 1903-08-10-11-13-16-20-24
Cooney, Terrance J. .... A. L. — 1981
Crawford, Henry C. .... N. L. — 1961-63-69
Dale, Jerry P. .... N. L. — 1977
Dascoli, Frank .... N. L. — 1953-55-59
Davidson, David L. .... N. L. — 1975-82
Deegan, William E. .... A. L. — 1976
Denkinger, Donald A. .... A. L. — 1974-80
DiMuro, Louis J. .... A. L. — 1969-76
Dinneen, William H. .... N. L. — 1911-14-16-20-26-29-32
Dixon, Hal H. .... A. L. — 1959
Donatelli, August J. .... N. L. — 1955-57-61-67-73
Drummond, Calvin T. .... A. L. — 1966
Dunn, Thomas P. .... N. L. — 1944
Egan, John J. .... A. L. — 1913
Engel, Robert A. .... N. L. — 1972-79
Evans, James B. .... A. L. — 1977-82
Evans, William G. .... A. L. — 1909-12-15-17-19-23
Flaherty, John F. .... A. L. — 1955-58-65-70
Frantz, Arthur F. .... A. L. — 1975
Froemming, Bruce N. .... N. L. — 1976-84
Garcia, Richard R. .... A. L. — 1981-84
Geisel, Harry C. .... A. L. — 1930-34-36
Goetz, Lawrence J. .... N. L. — 1941-47-52
Goetz, Russell L. .... A. L. — 1973-79
Gore, Arthur J. .... N. L. — 1951-53
Gorman, Thomas D. .... N. L. — 1956-58-63-68-74
Grieve, William T. .... N. L. — 1941-48-53
Haller, William E. .... A. L. — 1968-72-78-82
Hart, Eugene F. .... N. L. — 1923
Harvey, H. Douglas .... N. L. — 1968-74-81-84
Hildebrand, George A. .... A. L. — 1914-18-22-26
Honochick, G. James .... N. L. — 1952-55-60-62-68-72
Hubbard, Calvin .... A. L. — 1938-42-46-49
Hurley, Edwin .... A. L. — 1949-53-59-65
Jackowski, William .... N. L. — 1958-60-66
Johnstone, James E. .... N. L. — 1906-09
Jorda, Louis D. .... N. L. — 1945-49
Kinnamon, William E. .... A. L. — 1968
Kibler, John W. .... N. L. — 1971-78-82
Klem, William J. .... N. L. — 1908-09-11-12-13-14-15-17-18-20-22-24-26-29-31-32-34-40
Kolls, Louis C. .... A. L. — 1938
Kunkel, William G. .... A. L. — 1974-80
Landes, Stanley .... N. L. — 1960-62-68
Luciano, Ronald M. .... A. L. — 1974
McCormick, William J. .... N. L. — 1922-25
McCoy, Larry S. .... A. L. — 1977
McGowan, William A. .... A. L. — 1928-31-35-39-41-44-47-50
McKean, James G. .... A. L. — 1979
McKinley, William F. .... A. L. — 1950-52-57-64
McSherry, John P. .... N. L. — 1977
Magerkurth, George L. .... N. L. — 1932-36-42-47
Maloney, George P. .... A. L. — 1975
Moran, Charles B. .... N. L. — 1927-29-33-38
Moriarty, George .... A. L. — 1921-25-30-33-35
Nallin, Richard F. .... A. L. — 1919-23-27-31

Napp, Larry A. .... A. L. — 1954-56-63-69
Neudecker, Jerome A .... A. L. — 1973-79
O'Day, Henry .... N. L. — 1903-05-07-08-10-16-18-20-23-26
Odom, James C. .... A. L. — 1971
Olsen, Andrew H. .... N. L. — 1974
O'Loughlin, Francis H. .... A. L. — 1906-09-12-15-17
Ormsby, Emmett T. .... A. L. — 1927-33-37-40
Owens, Clarence B. .... A. L. — 1918-22-25-28-34
Palermo, Stephen M. .... A. L. — 1983
Paparella, Joseph .... A. L. — 1948-51-57-63
Passarella, Arthur .... A. L. — 1945-49-52
Pelekoudas, Chris G. .... N. L. — 1966-72
Pfirman, Charles H. .... N. L. — 1928-33-36
Phillips, David R. .... A. L. — 1976-82
Pinelli, Ralph A. .... N. L. — 1939-41-47-48-52-56
Pipgras, George W. .... A. L. — 1944
Pryor, J. Paul .... N. L. — 1967-73-80
Pulli, Frank V. .... N. L. — 1978-83
Quigley, Ernest C. .... N. L. — 1916-19-21-24-27-35
Reardon, John E. .... N. L. — 1930-34-39-43-49
Reilly, Michael .... A. L. — 1984
Rennert, Laurence H. .... N. L. — 1980-83
Rice, John L. .... A. L. — 1959-63-66-71
Rigler, Charles .... N. L. — 1910-12-13-15-17-19-21-25-28-30
Rommel, Edwin A. .... A. L. — 1943-47
Rue, Joseph .... A. L. — 1943
Runge, Edward P. .... A. L. — 1956-61-67
Runge, Paul E. .... N. L. — 1979-84
Sears, John W. .... N. L. — 1938-44
Secory, Frank E. .... N. L. — 1957-59-64-69
Sheridan, John F. .... A. L. — 1905-07-08-10
Smith, W. Alaric .... A. L. — 1964
Smith, Vincent A. .... N. L. — 1964
Soar, A. Henry .... A. L. — 1953-56-62-64-69
Springstead, Martin J. .... A. L. — 1973-78-83
Stark, Albert D. .... N. L. — 1931-35
Steiner, Melvin J. .... N. L. — 1966-72
Stello, Richard J. .... N. L. — 1975-81
Stevens, John W. .... A. L. — 1951-54-60-67
Stewart, Robert W. .... A. L. — 1961-65-70
Stewart, William J. .... N. L. — 1937-43-48-53
Sudol, Edward L. .... N. L. — 1965-71-77
Summers, William R. .... A. L. — 1936-39-42-45-48-51-55-59
Tata, Terry A. .... N. L. — 1979
Umont, Frank .... A. L. — 1958-61-67-72
Van Graflan, Roy .... A. L. — 1929-32
Vargo, Edward P. .... N. L. — 1965-71-78-83
Venzon, Anthony .... N. L. — 1963-65-70
Warneke, Lonnie .... N. L. — 1954
Wendelstedt, Harry H. .... N. L. — 1973-80
Weyer, Lee H. .... A. L. — 1969-76-82
Williams, William G. .... N. L. — 1970-76

Note—Two umpires used, 1903-1907, inclusive; two sets of two umpires each, 1908-1909 (alternate pair stationed in outfield because of overflow crowds for last five games of 1909 Series); four umpires used, 1910 through 1946, six umpires used, 1947 to date.

MOST PLAYERS USED AT POSITIONS
FIRST BASEMEN

Most First Basemen, Game, One Club
    3—New York A.L., vs. Milwaukee N.L., October 2, 1957.
    New York A.L., vs. Milwaukee N.L., October 5, 1957.

Most First Basemen, Game, Both Clubs
    5—New York A.L., 3, Milwaukee N.L., 2, October 2, 1957.
    New York A.L., 3, Milwaukee N.L., 2, October 5, 1957.

Most First Basemen, Series, One Club
    4-game Series—3—New York A.L., vs. Philadelphia N.L., 1950.
    5-game Series—3—New York N.L., vs. Philadelphia A.L., 1913.
                         Oakland A.L., vs. Los Angeles N.L., 1974.
    6-game Series—2—Held by many clubs.
    7-game Series—4—New York A.L., vs. Milwaukee N.L., 1957.
                         Oakland A.L., vs. New York N.L., 1973.
    8-game Series—1—Held by many clubs.

Most First Basemen, Series, Both Clubs
 4-game Series—4—New York A.L., 3, Philadelphia N.L., 1, 1950.
 5-game Series—4—New York N.L., 3, Philadelphia A.L., 1, 1913.
  Philadelphia N.L., 2, Boston A.L., 2, 1915.
  Oakland A.L., 3, Los Angeles N.L., 1, 1974.
 6-game Series—3—Made in many Series.
 7-game Series—6—New York A.L., 4, Milwaukee N.L., 2, 1957.
 8-game Series—2—Made in many Series.

SECOND BASEMEN

Most Second Basemen, Game, One Club
 3—St. Louis N.L., vs. New York, A.L., October 7, 1964.
  Oakland A.L., vs. New York N.L., October 14, 1973, 12 innings.

Most Second Basemen, Game, Both Clubs
 4—New York A.L., 2, Milwaukee N.L., 2, October 7, 1957.
  St. Louis N.L., 3, New York A.L., 1, October 7, 1964.
  Oakland A.L., 3, New York N.L., 1, October 14, 1973, 12 innings.

Most Second Basemen, Series, One Club
 4-game Series—2—Pittsburgh N.L., vs. New York A.L., 1927.
  New York A.L., vs. St. Louis N.L., 1928.
  Philadelphia N.L., vs. New York A.L., 1950.
 5-game Series—2—Held by many clubs.
 6-game Series—2—Held by many clubs.
 7-game Series—3—St. Louis N.L., vs. New York A.L., 1964.
  Oakland A.L., vs. New York N.L., 1973.
 8-game Series—1—Held by many clubs.

Most Second Basemen, Series, Both Clubs
 4-game Series—3—Pittsburgh N.L., 2, New York A.L., 1, 1927.
  New York A.L., 2, St. Louis N.L., 1, 1928.
  Philadelphia N.L., 2, New York A.L., 1, 1950.
 5-game Series—3—Made in many series.
 6-game Series—4—St. Louis N.L., 2, St. Louis A.L., 2, 1944.
 7-game Series—4—Brooklyn N.L., 2, New York A.L., 2, 1956.
  Milwaukee N.L., 2, New York A.L., 2, 1957.
  St. Louis N.L., 3, New York A.L., 1, 1964.
  Oakland A.L., 3, New York N.L., 1, 1973.
 8-game Series—2—Made in four series.

THIRD BASEMEN

Most Third Basemen, Game, One Club
 2—Made in many games.

Most Third Basemen, Game, Both Clubs
 4—Pittsburgh N.L., 2, Detroit A.L., 2, October 16, 1909.
  New York N.L., 2, Washington A.L., 2, October 6, 1924.
  Los Angeles N.L., 2, New York A.L., 2, October 28, 1981.
  San Diego N.L., 2, Detroit A.L., 2, October 9, 1984.

Most Third Basemen, Series, One Club
 4-game Series—3—Cleveland A.L., vs. New York N.L., 1954.
 5-game Series—3—New York A.L., vs. St. Louis, N.L., 1942.
  Brooklyn N.L., vs. New York A.L., 1949.
  Detroit A.L., vs. San Diego N.L., 1984.
 6-game Series—3—Chicago A.L., vs. Los Angeles N.L., 1959.
 7-game Series—3—Washington A.L., vs. New York N.L., 1924.
  St. Louis N.L., vs. Philadelphia A.L., 1931.
  New York A.L., vs. Milwaukee N.L., 1957.
  New York A.L., vs. Milwaukee N.L., 1958.
  Detroit A.L., vs. St. Louis N.L., 1968.
 8-game Series—2—New York A.L., vs. New York N.L., 1921.

Most Third Basemen, Series, Both Clubs
 4-game Series—4—Cleveland A.L., 3, New York N.L., 1, 1954.
 5-game Series—5—Brooklyn N.L., 3, New York A.L., 2, 1949.
  Detroit A.L., 3, San Diego N.L., 2, 1984.
 6-game Series—4—Chicago N.L., 2, Detroit A.L., 2, 1945.
  Chicago A.L., 2, Los Angeles N.L., 2, 1959.
  Los Angeles N.L., 2, New York A.L., 2, 1981.
 7-game Series—5—Washington A.L., 3, New York N.L., 2, 1924.
 8-game Series—3—New York A.L., 2, New York N.L., 1, 1921.

SHORTSTOPS

Most Shortstops, Game, One Club
   3—New York A.L., vs. Pittsburgh N.L., October 13, 1960.
      Cincinnati N.L., vs. Baltimore A.L., October 14, 1970.

Most Shortstops, Game, Both Clubs
   4—Made in many games.

Most Shortstops, Series, One Club
   4-game Series—2—St. Louis N.L., vs. New York, A.L., 1928.
                      Chicago N.L., vs. New York, A.L., 1932.
                      Cleveland A.L., vs. New York N.L., 1954.
                      New York A.L., vs. Cincinnati N.L., 1976.
   5-game Series—3—Cincinnati N.L., vs. Baltimore A.L., 1970.
   6-game Series—2—Held by many clubs.
   7-game Series—3—Chicago N.L., vs. Detroit A.L., 1945.
                      New York A.L., vs. Pittsburgh N.L., 1960.
   8-game Series—2—New York N.L., vs. Boston A.L., 1912.

Most Shortstops, Series, Both Clubs
   4-game Series—3—St. Louis N.L., 2, New York A.L., 1, 1928.
                      Chicago N.L., 2, New York A.L., 1, 1932.
                      Cleveland A.L., 2, New York N.L., 1, 1954.
                      New York A.L., 2, Cincinnati N.L., 1, 1976.
   5-game Series—4—Cincinnati N.L., 3, Baltimore A.L., 1, 1970.
   6-game Series—3—Made in many series.
   7-game Series—5—Chicago N.L., 3, Detroit A.L., 2, 1945.
                      New York A.L., 3, Pittsburgh N.L., 2, 1960.
   8-game Series—3—New York N.L., 2, Boston A.L., 1, 1912.

LEFT FIELDERS

Most Left Fielders, Game, One Club
   3—New York N.L., vs. Washington A.L., October 10, 1924, 12 innings.
      Brooklyn N.L., vs. New York A.L., October 5, 1947.
      Brooklyn N.L., vs. New York A.L., October 5, 1952, 11 innings.
      Philadelphia N.L., vs. Kansas City A.L., October 19, 1980.
      New York A.L., vs. Los Angeles N.L., October 24, 1981.

Most Left Fielders, Game, Both Clubs
   5—Brooklyn N.L., 3, New York A.L., 2, October 5, 1947.

Most Left Fielders, Series, One Club
   4-game Series—3—New York A.L., vs. Chicago N.L., 1938.
   5-game Series—3—Philadelphia N.L., vs. Boston A.L., 1915.
                      Baltimore A.L., vs. Philadelphia N.L., 1983.
                      San Diego N.L., vs. Detroit A.L., 1984.
   6-game Series—4—Philadelphia N.L., vs. Kansas City A.L., 1980.
   7-game Series—4—Brooklyn N.L., vs. New York A.L., 1947.
                      New York A.L., vs. Pittsburgh N.L., 1960.
                      San Francisco N.L., vs. New York A.L., 1962.
                      Boston A.L., vs. Cincinnati N.L., 1975.
   8-game Series—3—New York N.L., vs. Boston A.L., 1912.

Most Left Fielders, Series, Both Clubs
   4-game Series—5—New York A.L., 3, Chicago N.L., 2, 1938.
   5-game Series—5—San Diego N.L., 3, Detroit A.L., 2, 1984.
   6-game Series—5—Philadelphia N.L., 4, Kansas City A.L., 1, 1980.
   7-game Series—6—Brooklyn N.L., 4, New York A.L., 2, 1947.
                      Pittsburgh N.L., 3, Baltimore A.L., 3, 1979.
   8-game Series—4—New York N.L., 3, Boston A.L., 1, 1912.

CENTER FIELDERS

Most Center Fielders, Game, One Club
   3—New York N.L., vs. New York A.L., October 5, 1922, 10 innings.

Most Center Fielders, Game, Both Clubs
   4—New York N.L., 3, New York A.L., 1, October 5, 1922.
      New York A.L., 2, New York N.L., 2, October 15, 1923, 10 innings.
      New York A.L., 2, Los Angeles N.L., 2, October 11, 1978.
      New York A.L., 2, Los Angeles N.L., 2, October 24, 25, 1981.

Most Center Fielders, Series, One Club
   4-game Series—2—Made by seven clubs.

5-game Series—3—Brooklyn N.L., vs. Boston A.L., 1916.
　　　　　　　　　New York N.L., vs. New York A.L., 1922.
　　　　　　　　　New York A.L., vs. Cincinnati N.L., 1961.
6-game Series—4—Los Angeles N.L., vs. Chicago A.L., 1959.
7-game Series—3—New York N.L., vs. Washington A.L., 1924.
　　　　　　　　　New York A.L., vs. Brooklyn N.L., 1955.
　　　　　　　　　Milwaukee N.L., vs. New York A.L., 1958.
8-game Series—2—New York N.L., vs. Boston A.L., 1912.
　　　　　　　　　Chicago A.L., vs. Cincinnati N.L., 1919.

Most Center Fielders, Series, Both Clubs
4-game Series—4—New York A.L., 2, St. Louis N.L., 2, 1928.
5-game Series—5—New York N.L., 3, New York A.L., 2, 1922.
6-game Series—6—New York A.L., 3, Los Angeles N.L., 3, 1981.
7-game Series—5—New York N.L., 3, Washington A.L., 2, 1924.
　　　　　　　　　New York A.L., 3, Brooklyn N.L., 2, 1955.
8-game Series—3—New York N.L., 2, Boston A.L., 1, 1912.
　　　　　　　　　Chicago A.L., 2, Cincinnati N.L., 1, 1919.

RIGHT FIELDERS

Most Right Fielders, Game, One Club
　3—Held by many clubs.

Most Right Fielders, Game, Both Clubs
　5—Los Angeles N.L., 3, Chicago A.L., 2, October 8, 1959.

Most Right Fielders, Series, One Club
4-game Series—3—Cleveland A.L., vs. New York N.L., 1954.
　　　　　　　　　New York A.L., vs. Los Angeles N.L., 1963.
　　　　　　　　　New York A.L., vs. Cincinnati N.L., 1976.
5-game Series—4—Philadelphia N.L., vs. Baltimore A.L., 1983.
6-game Series—5—Los Angeles N.L., vs. Chicago A.L., 1959.
7-game Series—4—New York A.L., vs. Brooklyn N.L., 1955.
　　　　　　　　　San Francisco N.L., vs. New York A.L., 1962.
　　　　　　　　　Boston A.L., vs. St. Louis N.L., 1967.
8-game Series—3—Chicago A.L., vs. Cincinnati N.L., 1919.

Most Right Fielders, Series, Both Clubs
4-game Series—5—New York A.L., 3, Los Angeles N.L., 2, 1963.
5-game Series—7—Philadelphia N.L., 4, Baltimore A.L., 3, 1983.
6-game Series—9—Los Angeles N.L., 5, Chicago A.L., 4, 1959.
7-game Series—5—Made in many Series.
8-game Series—4—Chicago A.L., 3, Cincinnati N.L., 1, 1919.

CATCHERS

Most Catchers, Game, One Club
　3—Philadelphia N.L., vs. New York A.L., October 5, 1950, 10 innings.
　　Los Angeles N.L., vs. New York A.L., October 13, 1978.

Most Catchers, Game, Both Clubs
　4—Detroit A.L., 2, Chicago N.L., 2, October 8, 1945, 12 innings.
　　Boston A.L., 2, St. Louis N.L., 2, October 15, 1946.
　　Philadelphia N.L., 3, New York A.L., 1, October 5, 1950, 10 innings.
　　Los Angeles N.L., 3, New York A.L., 1, October 13, 1978.
　　Los Angeles N.L., 2, New York A.L., 2, October 15, 1978.

Most Catchers, Series, One Club
4-game Series—3—New York A.L., vs. Pittsburgh N.L., 1927.
　　　　　　　　　Pittsburgh N.L., vs. New York A.L., 1927.
　　　　　　　　　Philadelphia N.L., vs. New York A.L., 1950.
5-game Series—3—Detroit A.L., vs. Chicago N.L., 1908.
　　　　　　　　　Boston A.L., vs. Brooklyn N.L., 1916.
　　　　　　　　　New York A.L., vs. Brooklyn N.L., 1949.
　　　　　　　　　Cincinnati N.L., vs. New York A.L., 1961.
6-game Series—4—Los Angeles N.L., vs. New York A.L., 1978.
7-game Series—3—Held by many clubs.
8-game Series—2—Held by many clubs.

Most Catchers, Series, Both Clubs
4-game Series—6—New York A.L., 3, Pittsburgh N.L., 3, 1927.
5-game Series—5—Boston A.L., 3, Brooklyn N.L., 2, 1916.
6-game Series—6—Los Angeles N.L., 4, New York A.L., 2, 1978.
7-game Series—6—New York A.L., 3, Pittsburgh N.L., 3, 1960.
8-game Series—4—Boston A.L., 2, New York N.L., 2, 1912.
　　　　　　　　　Chicago A.L., 2, Cincinnati N.L., 2, 1919.
　　　　　　　　　New York N.L., 2, New York A.L., 2, 1921.

WORLD SERIES RECORDS
PITCHERS

Most Pitchers, Series, One Club
    4-game Series— 8—Chicago N.L., vs. New York A.L., 1932.
                            Chicago N.L., vs. New York A.L., 1938.
                            Los Angeles N.L., vs. Baltimore A.L., 1966.
    5-game Series—10—San Diego N.L., vs. Detroit A.L., 1984.
    6-game Series—10—Brooklyn N.L., vs. New York A.L., 1953.
                            Philadelphia N.L., vs. Kansas City A.L., 1980.
                            Los Angeles N.L., vs. New York A.L., 1981.
    7-game Series—11—Boston A.L., vs. St. Louis N.L., 1946.
    8-game Series— 8—New York A.L., vs. New York N.L., 1921.

Most Pitchers, Series, Both Clubs
    4-game Series—14—Chicago N.L., 8, New York A.L., 6, 1932.
                            Cincinnati N.L., 7, New York A.L., 7, 1976.
    5-game Series—18—Baltimore A.L., 9, Cincinnati N.L., 9, 1970.
    6-game Series—19—Brooklyn N.L., 10, New York A.L., 9, 1953.
                            Los Angeles N.L., 10, New York A.L., 9, 1981.
    7-game Series—20—Pittsburgh N.L., 10, New York A.L., 10, 1960.
                            St. Louis N.L., 10, Boston A.L., 10, 1967.
                            Pittsburgh N.L., 10, Baltimore A.L., 10, 1971.
    8-game Series—12—New York A.L., 8, New York N.L., 4, 1921.

Fewest Pitchers, Series, One Club
    4-game Series—3—Boston N.L., vs. Philadelphia A.L., 1914.
                        New York A.L., vs. St. Louis N.L., 1928.
    5-game Series—2—Philadelphia A.L., vs. Chicago N.L., 1910.
    6-game Series—3—Philadelphia A.L., vs. New York N.L., 1911.
    7-game Series—5—Detroit A.L., vs. Pittsburgh N.L., 1909.
                        Cleveland A.L., vs. Brooklyn N.L., 1920.
    8-game Series—3—Boston A.L., vs. Pittsburgh N.L., 1903.

Fewest Pitchers, Series, Both Clubs
    4-game Series— 9—Philadelphia A.L., 6, Boston N.L., 3, 1914.
                         St. Louis N.L., 6, New York A.L., 3, 1928.
    5-game Series— 6—Philadelphia A.L., 3, New York N.L., 3, 1905.
    6-game Series— 8—Chicago A.L., 4, Chicago N.L., 4, 1906.
                         New York N.L., 5, Philadelphia A.L., 3, 1911.
                         Boston A.L., 4, Chicago N.L., 4, 1918.
    7-game Series—11—Pittsburgh N.L., 6, Detroit A.L., 5, 1909.
    8-game Series— 8—Pittsburgh N.L., 5, Boston A.L., 3, 1903.

Most Different Starting Pitchers, Series, One Club
      6—Brooklyn N.L., vs. New York A.L., 1947.
         Brooklyn N.L., vs. New York A.L., 1955.
         Pittsburgh N.L., vs. Baltimore A.L., 1971.

Most Different Starting Pitchers, Series, Both Clubs
    11—Brooklyn N.L., 6, New York A.L., 5, 1955.

Most Pitchers, Inning, One Club
    5—Baltimore A.L., vs. Pittsburgh N.L., October 17, 1979, ninth inning.

Most Pitchers, Game, One Club
    8—Cincinnati N.L., vs. New York A.L., October 9, 1961.
    St. Louis N.L., vs. Boston A.L., October 11, 1967.
    Cincinnati N.L., vs. Boston A.L., October 21, 1975, night game, 12 innings.

Most Pitchers, Game, Winning Club
    6—Cincinnati N.L., vs. Oakland A.L., October 20, 1972 (Won 5-4).

Most Pitchers, Game, Losing Club
    8—Cincinnati N.L., vs. New York A.L., October 9, 1961 (Lost 13-5).
    St. Louis N.L., vs. Boston A.L., October 11, 1967 (Lost 8-4).
    Cincinnati N.L., vs. Boston A.L., October 21, 1975, night game, 12 innings (Lost 7-6).

Most Pitchers, Game, Nine-Innings, Both Clubs
    11—St. Louis N.L., 8, Boston A.L., 3, October 11, 1967.

Most Pitchers, Extra-Inning Game, Both Clubs
    12—Cincinnati N.L., 8, Boston A.L., 4, October 21, 1975, night game, 12 innings.